PLUNKETT'S ENGINEERING & RESEARCH INDUSTRY ALMANAC 2025

The only comprehensive guide to the engineering & research industry

Jack W. Plunkett

Published by:
Plunkett Research®, Ltd., Houston, Texas
www.plunkettresearch.com

PLUNKETT'S ENGINEERING & RESEARCH INDUSTRY ALMANAC 2025

Editor and Publisher:
Jack W. Plunkett

Executive Editor and Database Manager:
Martha Burgher Plunkett

Senior Editor and Researchers:
Isaac Snider

Editors, Researchers and Assistants:
Kausthubh Eleti
Trevor Parton
Andre Staubo

Information Technology Manager:
Rebeca Tijiboy

Special Thanks to:
Intellectual Property Owners Association
Pharmaceutical Research and Manufacturers of
America (PhRMA)
U.S. Bureau of the Census
U.S. Bureau of Labor Statistics
U.S. Department of Energy, Office of Science
U.S. National Aeronautics & Space
Administration (NASA)
U.S. National Nanotechnology Initiative
U.S. National Science Foundation
U.S. Office of Management and Budget
U.S. Patent and Trademark Office

Plunkett Research®, Ltd.
P. O. Drawer 541737, Houston, Texas 77254 USA
www.plunkettresearch.com

Plunkett Research®, Ltd.
P. O. Drawer 541737
Houston, Texas 77254-1737
www.plunkettresearch.com

ISBN13 # 978-1-64788-076-7 (eBook Edition # 978-1-64788-568-7)

Limited Warranty and Terms of Use:

PLUNKETT'S ENGINEERING & RESEARCH INDUSTRY ALMANAC 2025

CONTENTS

Continued on next page

INTRODUCTION

PLUNKETT'S ENGINEERING & RESEARCH INDUSTRY ALMANAC is designed as a general source for researchers of all types.

The data and areas of interest covered are intentionally broad, ranging from the various aspects of the engineering and research industry, to emerging technology, to an in-depth look at the major firms (which we call "THE ENGINEERING & RESEARCH 500") within the many segments that make up the engineering and research industry.

This reference book is designed to assist with market research, strategic planning, employment searches, contact or prospect list creation and financial research, and as a data resource for executives and students.

PLUNKETT'S ENGINEERING & RESEARCH INDUSTRY ALMANAC takes a rounded approach for the general reader. This book presents a complete overview of the engineering and research field (see "How To Use This Book"). For example, advances in design automation are discussed, as well as changes in research and development spending and patents.

THE ENGINEERING & RESEARCH 500 is our grouping of the biggest, most successful corporations in all segments of the engineering and research industry. Tens of thousands of pieces of information,

gathered from a wide variety of sources, have been researched and are presented in a unique form that can be easily understood. This section includes thorough indexes to THE ENGINEERING & RESEARCH 500, by geography, industry, sales, brand names, subsidiary names and many other topics. (See Chapter 4.)

Especially helpful is the way in which PLUNKETT'S ENGINEERING & RESEARCH INDUSTRY ALMANAC enables readers who have no business or financial background to readily compare the strategies, financial records and growth plans of engineering and research companies and major industry groups. You'll see the mid-term financial record of each firm, along with the impact of earnings, sales and strategic plans on each company's potential to fuel growth and provide investment and employment opportunities.

No other source provides this book's easy-to-understand comparisons of growth, expenditures, technologies, corporations, research and many other items of great importance. The information within is crucial to people of all types who may be studying this, one of the most exciting industries in the world today.

By scanning the data groups and the unique indexes, you can find the best information to fit your personal research needs. The major companies are profiled and then ranked using several different groups of specific criteria. Which firms are the biggest employers? Which companies earn the most profits? These things and much more are easy to find.

In addition to individual company profiles, an analysis of engineering and research technologies and trends is provided. This book's job is to help you sort through clear summaries of today's technologies and trends in a quick and effective manner.

Whatever your purpose for researching the engineering and research field, you'll find this book to be a valuable guide. Nonetheless, as is true with all resources, this volume has limitations that the reader should be aware of:

- Financial data and other corporate information can change quickly. A book of this type can be no more current than the data that was available as of the time of editing. Consequently, the financial picture, management and ownership of the firm(s) you are studying may have changed since the date of this book. For example, this almanac includes the most up-to-date sales figures and profits available to the editors as of mid-2025. That means that we have typically used corporate financial data as of late 2024.

- Corporate mergers, acquisitions and downsizing are occurring at a very rapid rate. Such events may have created significant change, subsequent to the publishing of this book, within a company you are studying.

- Some of the companies in THE ENGINEERING & RESEARCH 500 are so large in scope and in variety of business endeavors conducted within a parent organization, that we have been unable to completely list all subsidiaries, affiliations, divisions and activities within a firm's corporate structure.

- This volume is intended to be a general guide to a rapidly changing industry. That means that researchers should look to this book for an overview and, when conducting in-depth research, should contact the specific corporations or industry associations in question for the very latest changes and data. Where possible, we have listed contact names, toll-free telephone numbers

and internet site addresses for the companies, government agencies and industry associations involved so that the reader may get further details without unnecessary delay.

- Tables of industry data and statistics used in this book include the latest numbers available at the time of printing, generally through late 2024. In a few cases, the only complete data available was for earlier years.

- We have used exhaustive efforts to locate and fairly present accurate and complete data. However, when using this book or any other source for business and industry information, the reader should use caution and diligence by conducting further research where it seems appropriate. We wish you success in your endeavors, and we trust that your experience with this book will be both satisfactory and productive.

Jack W. Plunkett
Houston, Texas
July 2025

HOW TO USE THIS BOOK

The two primary sections of this book are devoted first to the engineering and research industry as a whole and then to the "Individual Data Listings" for THE ENGINEERING & RESEARCH 500. If time permits, you should begin your research in the front chapters of this book. Also, you will find lengthy indexes in Chapter 4 and in the back of the book.

THE ENGINEERING & RESEARCH INDUSTRY

Chapter 1: Major Trends Affecting the Engineering & Research Industry. This chapter presents an encapsulated view of the major trends that are creating rapid changes in the engineering industry today.

Chapter 2: Engineering & Research Industry Statistics. This chapter contains an extensive set of industry statistics.

Chapter 3: Important Engineering & Research Industry Contacts – Addresses, Telephone Numbers and Internet Sites. This chapter covers contacts for important government agencies and trade groups. Included are numerous important Internet sites.

THE ENGINEERING & RESEARCH 500

Chapter 4: THE ENGINEERING & RESEARCH 500: Who They Are and How They Were Chosen. The companies compared in this book were carefully selected from the engineering and research industry, largely in the United States. Many additional firms are based outside the U.S. For a complete description, see THE ENGINEERING & RESEARCH 500 indexes in this chapter.

Individual Data Listings:

Look at one of the companies in THE ENGINEERING & RESEARCH 500's Individual Data Listings. You'll find the following information fields:

Company Name:

The company profiles are in alphabetical order by company name. If you don't find the company you are seeking, it may be a subsidiary or division of one of the firms covered in this book. Try looking it up in the Index by Subsidiaries, Brand Names and Selected Affiliations in the back of the book.

Industry Code:

Industry Group Code: An NAIC code used to group companies within like segments.

Types of Business:

A listing of the primary types of business specialties conducted by the firm.

Brands/Divisions/Affiliations:

Major brand names, operating divisions or subsidiaries of the firm, as well as major corporate affiliations—such as another firm that owns a significant portion of the company's stock. A complete Index by Subsidiaries, Brand Names and Selected Affiliations is in the back of the book.

Contacts:

The names and titles up to 27 top officers of the company are listed, including human resources contacts.

Growth Plans/ Special Features:

Listed here are observations regarding the firm's strategy, hiring plans, plans for growth and product development, along with general information regarding a company's business and prospects.

Financial Data:

Revenue (2024 or the latest fiscal year available to the editors, plus up to five previous years): This figure represents consolidated worldwide sales from all operations. These numbers may be estimates.

R&D Expense (2024 or the latest fiscal year available to the editors, plus up to five previous years): This figure represents expenses associated with the research and development of a company's goods or services. These numbers may be estimates.

Operating Income (2024 or the latest fiscal year available to the editors, plus up to five previous years): This figure represents the amount of profit realized from annual operations after deducting operating expenses including costs of goods sold, wages and depreciation. These numbers may be estimates.

Operating Margin % (2024 or the latest fiscal year available to the editors, plus up to five previous years): This figure is a ratio derived by dividing operating income by net revenues. It is a measurement of a firm's pricing strategy and operating efficiency. These numbers may be estimates.

SGA Expense (2024 or the latest fiscal year available to the editors, plus up to five previous years): This figure represents the sum of selling, general and administrative expenses of a company, including costs such as warranty, advertising, interest, personnel, utilities, office space rent, etc. These numbers may be estimates.

Net Income (2024 or the latest fiscal year available to the editors, plus up to five previous years): This figure represents consolidated, after-tax net profit from all operations. These numbers may be estimates.

Operating Cash Flow (2024 or the latest fiscal year available to the editors, plus up to five previous years): This figure is a measure of the amount of cash generated by a firm's normal business operations. It is calculated as net income before depreciation and after income taxes, adjusted for working capital. It is a prime indicator of a company's ability to generate enough cash to pay its bills. These numbers may be estimates.

Capital Expenditure (2024 or the latest fiscal year available to the editors, plus up to five previous years): This figure represents funds used for investment in or improvement of physical assets such as offices, equipment or factories and the purchase or creation of new facilities and/or equipment. These numbers may be estimates.

EBITDA (2024 or the latest fiscal year available to the editors, plus up to five previous years): This figure is an acronym for earnings before interest, taxes, depreciation and amortization. It represents a company's financial performance calculated as revenue minus expenses (excluding taxes, depreciation and interest), and is a prime indicator of profitability. These numbers may be estimates.

Return on Assets % (2024 or the latest fiscal year available to the editors, plus up to five previous years): This figure is an indicator of the profitability of a company relative to its total assets. It is calculated by dividing annual net earnings by total assets. These numbers may be estimates.

Return on Equity % (2024 or the latest fiscal year available to the editors, plus up to five previous years): This figure is a measurement of net income as a percentage of shareholders' equity. It is also called the rate of return on the ownership interest. It is a vital indicator of the quality of a company's operations. These numbers may be estimates.

Debt to Equity (2024 or the latest fiscal year available to the editors, plus up to five previous years): A ratio of the company's long-term debt to its shareholders' equity. This is an indicator of the overall financial leverage of the firm. These numbers may be estimates.

Address:

The firm's full headquarters address, the headquarters telephone, plus toll-free and fax numbers where available. Also provided is the internet address.

Stock Ticker, Exchange: When available, the unique stock market symbol used to identify this firm's common stock for trading and tracking purposes is indicated. Where appropriate, this field may contain "private" or "subsidiary" rather than a ticker symbol. If the firm is a publicly-held company headquartered outside of the U.S., its international ticker and exchange are given.

Total Number of Employees: The approximate total number of employees, worldwide, as of the end of 2024 (or the latest data available to the editors).

Parent Company: If the firm is a subsidiary, its parent company is listed.

Salaries/Bonuses:

(The following descriptions generally apply to U.S. employers only.)

Highest Executive Salary: The highest executive salary paid, typically a 2024 amount (or the latest year available to the editors) and typically paid to the Chief Executive Officer.

Highest Executive Bonus: The apparent bonus, if any, paid to the above person.

Second Highest Executive Salary: The next-highest executive salary paid, typically a 2024 amount (or the latest year available to the editors) and typically paid to the President or Chief Operating Officer.

Second Highest Executive Bonus: The apparent bonus, if any, paid to the above person.

Other Thoughts:

Estimated Female Officers or Directors: It is difficult to obtain this information on an exact basis, and employers generally do not disclose the data in a public way. However, we have indicated what our best efforts reveal to be the apparent number of women who either are in the posts of corporate officers or sit on the board of directors. There is a wide variance from company to company.

Hot Spot for Advancement for Women/Minorities: A "Y" in appropriate fields indicates "Yes." These are firms that appear either to have posted a substantial number of women and/or minorities to high posts or that appear to have a good record of going out of their way to recruit, train, promote and retain women or minorities. (See the Index of Hot Spots For Women and Minorities in the back of the book.) This information may change frequently and can be difficult to obtain and verify. Consequently, the reader should use caution and conduct further investigation where appropriate.

Glossary: A short list of engineering and research industry terms.

Chapter 1

MAJOR TRENDS AFFECTING THE ENGINEERING & RESEARCH INDUSTRY

Major Trends Affecting the Engineering & Research Industry:

1) Major Trends Affecting the Engineering & Research Industry
2) Introduction to the Engineering & Research Industry
3) A Short History of U.S. Industrial Research & Development
4) R&D Expands in Chinese Research Parks/Patent Filings Soar
5) Outsourcing and Offshoring of Research, Development and Engineering Grow Along With Globalization
6) Original Design Manufacturing (ODM) Adds Value to Contract Electronics Manufacturing
7) The State of the Biotechnology Industry Today
8) Nations Compete Fiercely in Biotech Development
9) Globalization and Worldwide Collaboration Fuel the Research Efforts of Major Corporations
10) Number of Patent Applications Remains High/Patent Laws Change
11) 3D Printing (Additive Manufacturing), Rapid Prototyping and Computer Aided Design
12) Industrial Robots and Factory Automation Advance Through Artificial Intelligence (AI)
13) Fuel Cell and Hydrogen Power Research Continues/Fuel Cell Cars Enter Market
14) Electric Cars (EVs) and Plug-in Hybrids (PHEVs) Spur Changes at Auto Makers/Hybrid Sales See Sharp Growth
15) Major Technology Research in Batteries/Massive Investments in Battery Factories and Power Storage

16) Supercomputing Hits 1,742 Petaflops
17) Superconductivity Provides Advanced Electricity Distribution Technology
18) Private, Reusable Rockets Launch Commercial Satellites and Serve Both the U.S. Military & NASA
19) Technology Discussion—Synthetic Biology
20) The Future of Transportation and Supply Chains: Massive Investments in Infrastructure & Mobility Services
21) HPTP Thermoplastics, Thermoset and Engineered Plastics Enable Advanced Products/Nanocomposites Offer the Ultimate in Advanced Materials
22) Artificial Intelligence (AI), Deep Learning and Machine Learning Advance into Commercial Applications, Including Health Care and Robotics
23) Artificial Intelligence (AI) Enables Efficiencies and Accelerated Innovation in R&D
24) The Future of Space Commercialization and Private Rocket Launch Services

---

1)   Major Trends Affecting the Engineering & Research Industry

The engineering and research industry is experiencing a remarkable transformation, driven by a confluence of advanced technologies, global collaboration and strategic investments. As of 2025, key trends are reshaping how research is conducted and how innovations reach the market.

1. Global R&D Expansion and Collaboration

Global R&D spending is projected to exceed $2.7 trillion in 2024, with the U.S. leading in absolute investment, though countries like Israel and South Korea surpass the U.S. in R&D spending as a share of GDP. China, in particular, has become a dominant force, investing heavily in research parks, patent development and education, with over $780 billion allocated in 2023 alone. Additionally, countries such as India, Taiwan and Singapore are becoming key players through offshored research partnerships and domestic innovation incentives.

2. Artificial Intelligence (AI): The New Engine of Innovation

AI has rapidly emerged as a cornerstone of both engineering design and scientific discovery. In engineering, AI accelerates virtual prototyping and system testing. In pharmaceuticals and biotech, it expedites the discovery of new compounds and optimizes clinical trial processes. AI also supports predictive maintenance in industries like aerospace and manufacturing, reducing costs and boosting efficiency.

3. The Biotech Boom

The biotech industry is entering a "bioindustrial era," characterized by genetically engineered drugs, CRISPR gene editing and personalized medicine. Advances in synthetic biology, bioenzymes for manufacturing and biofuels from algae illustrate biotechnology's potential to revolutionize not just healthcare, but agriculture and energy. Governments and private firms worldwide are investing heavily in biotech parks and R&D, particularly in China, India and Singapore.

4. Electrification and Sustainable Transportation

Electric vehicles (EVs) and plug-in hybrids (PHEVs) are driving significant changes in the automotive sector. Global EV sales reached 14 million units in 2023, with automakers investing in next-generation battery technologies and infrastructure. However, challenges persist, including battery costs, charging networks and supply chain dependencies, particularly on China. Meanwhile, hydrogen fuel cell research and electric trucks are gaining traction, especially for long-haul and industrial use.

5. Space: The Final (Commercial) Frontier

Space research is undergoing privatization at scale. Companies like SpaceX and Blue Origin are pioneering reusable rocket technologies, drastically cutting launch costs and opening up opportunities in satellite deployment, space tourism and even pharmaceutical manufacturing in microgravity. With geopolitical tensions rising, space is also becoming increasingly strategic for national defense and economic interests.

6. Advanced Materials and Robotics

Engineering breakthroughs are also being driven by new materials such as high-performance thermoplastics and nanocomposites. These materials enable stronger, lighter and more efficient products across industries, from aerospace to consumer electronics. Meanwhile, industrial robotics and automation, powered by AI, are revolutionizing manufacturing, particularly in high-cost labor markets such as the U.S. and China.

2) Introduction to the Engineering & Research Industry

In industrialized nations, R&D investment has risen from an average of about 1.5% of Gross Domestic Product (GDP) in 1980 to about 2.0% today (in terms of current US dollars). Nothing could better illustrate the world's vital need for continual massive investments in R&D than the Coronavirus pandemic that swept across the world. An intense, global effort resulted in the availability of effective vaccines and therapies in record time—a few months compared to what typically would take a few years. The recent boom in artificial intelligence platforms and products also shows how intense focus and investment in one sector can rapidly launch entirely new solutions.

Meanwhile, vast numbers of university students around the globe are enrolled in engineering and scientific disciplines—many of them dreaming about potential rewards if their future research efforts become commercialized. Global research collaboration (between companies and between companies and universities) is booming, as is patenting. In fact, it is difficult for patent authorities in the U.S. and elsewhere to keep up with demand. Globalization, immigration and cross-national collaboration have such a dramatic effect on research and design that nearly one-half of all patents granted in America list at least one non-U.S. citizen as a co-inventor. Major U.S. universities, like the University of Texas and the University of Wisconsin, as well as universities in such nations as China, South Korea and Singapore, are eager to patent their inventions and reap the benefits of commercialized research. Top research universities earn millions of dollars each in yearly royalties on their patents.

Plunkett Research estimated global spending on research and development at $2.7 trillion for 2024, on a PPP or "purchasing power parity" basis. "PPP" means that the amounts are adjusted to account for the difference in the cost of living from nation to nation, relative to the United States. For example, PPP analysis finds that the cost of buying a given standard of living is considerably lower in China or India than it is in the U.S. Thus, $1 spent in China or India has more purchasing power than $1 spent in America.

The U.S. continues to lead the world in terms of total investment in research and development, with forecast investments of $770.5 billion for 2024 in current U.S. Dollars. However, America ranks behind some other industrialized nations in terms of R&D as a percentage of GDP.

Massive research outlays and grants are made by the U.S. federal government. The proposed federal research budget for fiscal 2024 was $209.7 billion (up from $142.2 billion in 2023 and $140.1 estimated for 2022). Substantial federal research dollars are flowing into such areas as advanced batteries, electronic patient health records, cancer research, nanotechnology, robotics, biotechnology, defense and renewable energy. Government research grants feed projects at universities throughout the U.S. and at many types of private corporations.

Many of the 50 U.S. states are also active in funding local research efforts, in the interest of boosting their statewide economies and their universities. This generates significant competition between tech-savvy states for leading-edge research efforts, at both corporate and university facilities.

The federal government of the U.S. not only funds research, but also engineering projects. This was particularly true for 2023-2024 and will likely be for several years thereafter due to the Infrastructure Investment and Jobs Act, signed into law in November 2021, with potential funding of $1.2 trillion over the mid-term. The act makes funds available for such areas as roads, bridges, public transportation, ports, airports, water and energy. While much of the money will go to construction, it will also fund very significant amounts of engineering, and many engineering/design firms will benefit greatly. In fact, the funding provided by this act is so massive that it may create a historic opportunity for some companies.

Meanwhile, U.S. corporations continue to fund massive engineering projects and research budgets of their own. Top research investors among U.S. companies include Amazon, Alphabet (parent company of Google), Merck & Co., Pfizer, Microsoft, IBM, Johnson & Johnson and Intel. Recently, much of this investment if focused on artificial intelligence (AI).

Engineering, science and research and development provide large numbers of well-paying jobs in America and around the world. Officially, the U.S. Bureau of Labor Statistics (BLS) estimates 1.7 million Americans working in architectural and engineering services as of March 2025. Also, as of March 2025, BLS categorizes 937,000 Americans as employed in scientific research and development positions.

Corporations know that they must invest in R&D in order to stay competitive, but in many cases their R&D strategies are evolving. One change is the way in which funding is allocated. Strategies are shifting to include more alliances and joint ventures with other companies; more subsidiary spin-offs based on established technologies; more contracts and cooperative efforts with federal labs and agencies; and higher grants and projects of greater scope in partnership with universities. Companies are looking for ways to leverage their R&D investments in order to get more return on costs while gaining competitive advantage on a global scale.

Historically, corporate America's R&D dollars were spent at labs within the bounds of the U.S., but today, more and more projects are going to company-owned or outsourced labs overseas. Due to relatively low costs and large talent pools (including large numbers of new graduates with engineering and scientific degrees), the nations of Eastern Europe, China and India in particular have been attracting more of the total research dollars invested by major companies. Other global hot beds of research include Israel, Singapore, Taiwan and Korea. However, recent trade friction with China is changing the landscape. In 2024, for example, IBM announced the closure of its 1,000-person research lab in China.

Certain countries have the lion's share of the world's R&D activity. In North America, corporations with the largest R&D budgets are headquartered in the U.S. and Canada; in Europe the UK, France, Germany, Switzerland, The Netherlands, Sweden and Italy are regional leaders; and in the Asia-Pacific the nations of China, India, Taiwan, Japan, South Korea and Singapore lead the way. Korean government leaders are focused on increasing basic research capabilities and basic sciences, particularly at research-oriented universities. Technical education is emphasized in India for a select group of students, particularly at its famous Indian Institute of Technology (IIT) campuses.

Technology-oriented Israel invests a very high 5+ percent of GDP in research and development, and that nation has created one of the world's most successful high-tech industries. Finland, Denmark and Sweden also spend very high ratios of their domestic economies on R&D.

Artificial intelligence (AI) is playing an increasingly important role in both engineering and research and development. In engineering, AI has the potential to accelerate both the design and the virtual testing of structures and systems. In R&D, one of the most promising uses for AI lies in identifying and testing chemical compounds that have potential to become new drug therapies—possibly cutting years and millions of dollars from the process. AI is also being used with great success to rapidly determine new uses for drugs that have already been approved by the FDA.

3) A Short History of U.S. Industrial Research & Development

Organized corporate research efforts began in the chemical dyes industry in Europe in the mid-1800s and soon were launched at a fairly rapid rate in America. In 1876, at the age of 29, Thomas Alva Edison opened a private laboratory in Menlo Park, New Jersey. Edison's efforts led to his record-setting 1,093 U.S. patents, including those for the phonograph and the incandescent light bulb. Edison's creativity and drive eventually enabled the birth of what would become GE, the General Electric Company. By 1900, about 40 corporate research facilities were operating in the U.S. Rapid acceleration was fostered by a growing middle class that created demand for new products and was later fueled by the intense demands for leading-edge armaments, transport and other products created by World War II.

During the war, a man named Vannevar Bush was posted as the director of the Office of Scientific Research and Development within the U.S. Government. Bush's mandate was to spur intense innovation that would give America a technological edge in warfare. The results, over an astonishingly short period of time, ranged from advanced radar to the atomic bomb. Vannevar Bush argued persuasively for a long-term federal commitment to supporting industrial research. By 1962, the federal government was subsidizing nearly 60% of America's corporate research budget, for everything from medical breakthroughs to electronics to defense systems.

Thereafter, corporations rapidly increased their own investments in research and development efforts, resulting in a nationwide research base of unprecedented scope and cost. By 1992, however, corporate restructuring and cost cutting led to a brief period of retrenching and research budget slashing.

In the mid-1990s, companies creating or embracing new technologies were among the most exciting and successful firms in America. As corporations were striving to compete, the floodgates of research dollars were once again cranked open.

A final important thought about the development of industrial R&D: Depending on the nature of their industries, firms enter into research with widely varying expectations. For example, while aircraft maker Boeing invests billions of dollars in R&D yearly, that effort may yield a completely new aircraft model only once every eight or 10 years. In contrast, semiconductor maker Intel, which invests billions of dollars yearly, introduces breakthrough chip designs on a continual basis and invests only a tiny amount of its total budget in truly long-term research. Pharmaceutical makers are accustomed to a research-to-market cycle of as long as 10 years in order to discover, develop and commercially launch a new drug.

4) R&D Expands in Chinese Research Parks/Patent Filings Soar

There are three trends at work in the growth of R&D in China. The first is that R&D spending has been growing significantly for many years. For 2023, gross expenditures on R&D in China were expected to reach $780.7 billion (or 4.39% of GDP), according to the Organisation for Economic Cooperations (OECD). (This number is on a PPP or purchasing power parity basis—an attempt to create a fair comparison to U.S. prices.) China has R&D goals laid out in the *National Medium- and Long-Term Plan for the Development of Science and Technology*. This is a 15-year plan, originally published in 2014, which is updated on a regular basis.

Of importance, the plan outlines ways to assimilate and then improve upon Western innovations. Methods include significant investment in domestic manufacturers along with patent laws that favor Chinese companies. The result has long been pressure on foreign firms to transfer technology into Chinese joint ventures in order to capture sales within China. Over the long term, this has enabled China-based companies to compete head-on with foreign firms by taking advantage of foreign design, research and engineering. These objectives have created significant controversy in other nations. In particular, the Trump administration was a highly vocal critic of Chinese research and development ambitions.

Second, many Chinese companies have seen significant success in the global marketplace. Telecommunications equipment makers such as Huawei Technologies, computer hardware makers such as Lenovo Group (which purchased the IBM laptop brand) and a host of companies like them found increased investments in research to be key to their continued growth. In the case of Huawei, the firm maintains major research facilities around the world, including a $90 million facility in Helsinki. At the same time, Chinese firms are increasing their investments in product design and factory automation in order to create products in very high volume suitable for the rapidly growing number of middle-class Chinese consumers.

Research in China is driven by multiple factors, including relatively low operating costs and salaries, the large base of engineers and scientists coming out of Chinese universities and the desire to have labs in close proximity to Chinese manufacturing centers and business markets. The biggest factor, however, is Chinese government investments in a few key areas, including semiconductors, electric vehicles, batteries, AI and biotech.

China produces hundreds of thousands of electrical engineering graduates on the bachelor's level yearly. Also, China is going out of its way to lure home thousands of Chinese-born scientists and engineers who have been working in the U.S. and elsewhere abroad.

The result is a growing perception of Chinese technical expertise as among the best in the world. While China grew in strength for many years as a low-end manufacturer of items like apparel and toys, it now attracts buyers both at home and in the West for its telecommunications equipment, mobile devices and online services.

Chinese research facilities tend to be located in the same districts as the high-tech manufacturing centers that cater to foreign markets: the southern and eastern coastal regions. For example, on the eastern coast near Beijing, you'll find the Zhongguancun Science Park and the Tianjin High-Tech Industrial Park, as well as the Beijing Frontier International AI Research Institute. Further down the coast, near Shanghai, you'll find the Caohejing and Zhangjiang High-Tech Parks. There are also major research parks near the nation's leading universities, such as the major science park next to the world-class Tsinghua University in Beijing. In addition, the city of Nanjing (located less than 200 miles north of Shanghai) has developed a 134 square-mile research park that is home to dozens of major tech companies and startups.

Chinese technology sectors are quickly expanding well beyond consumer electronics and computer and telecom hardware where China has long had strength. For example, the semiconductor fabrication and chip design industries are developing rapidly there. This is part of the Made in China 2025 initiative, which also focuses on 5G, artificial intelligence (AI) and electric vehicles.

5) Outsourcing and Offshoring of Research, Development and Engineering Grow Along with Globalization

The long-term relationship between Western firms (and governments) and research facilities in India, China and other nations in Asia will continue to evolve. While many Western companies are keenly interested in selling products and services into Asian markets, there has recently been a clear increase in Western governments' interest in retaining control over domestic intellectual property. While there is always the potential for increased global research collaboration, such as offshored research labs, many observers are concerned about the potential permanent loss of Western nations' vital research data and competitive advantage, particularly in the areas of drugs, computer technologies, electronics, aerospace and defense.

Over recent years, a growing global demand for technology products and for many types of engineering, coupled with the communications capabilities of the internet, have launched an R&D boom in many other nations as well. As in China, some of this research is for locally owned manufacturers, but a great deal of it is conducted as offshoring for companies based in other nations. These nations with growing research and development bases have recently included Israel, Singapore, Taiwan and Korea.

For example, consider Taiwan. It invests significant amounts in R&D for a relatively small nation. Taiwan is on the leading edge of technology-based manufacturing, and many of the world's top-ranked corporations by R&D budget are headquartered there. The country has great expertise, both in the laboratory and on the manufacturing floor, in such sectors as networking gear, semiconductors, computer memory and PC components. Taiwan's researchers are so prolific that they account for more than 5,000 U.S. patent filings yearly. Taiwan graduates about 49,000 scientists and engineers from its universities each year—an amazing number for a nation with a total population of a little more than 23 million. Taiwan operates three major science parks containing nearly 800 total manufacturers.

India has a need to greatly increase investments in R&D, particularly as it continues to advance into high technology manufacturing and becomes an alternative site to China for designing and manufacturing advanced electronics. Western drug discovery and manufacturing companies are forging partnerships with Indian firms at a great rate. For example, Eli

Lilly, Amgen and Endo Pharmaceuticals have all entered into agreements with Bangalore-based Jubilant Biosys to develop potential candidates for the next blockbuster drugs. In a surprising shift from the Indian focus on developing low-cost generic versions of Western drugs, Indian firms are now working on developing new drugs with Western partners. At the same time, Western pharma firms are offering to share intellectual property rights on new drugs as well as a portion of the profits. GlaxoSmithKline was the first to begin this practice in its partnership with Ranbaxy Laboratories Limited. In addition to drug development, R&D in India is concerned with the InfoTech sector. Microsoft's research center in Bangalore has dozens of full-time researchers on staff who are credited with the development of a valuable search tool used by Bing, Microsoft's search engine. India produces about 300,000 computer science graduates per year, and about 100 computer science PhDs.

South Korea's R&D spending is substantial as well. Korean government leaders are focused on increasing basic research capabilities and basic sciences, particularly at research-oriented universities.

Since a great deal of research equipment and facilities are underused, a shared system that works along the same lines as Uber and Airbnb was created called Science Exchange. Backed by silicon-valley investor Y Combinator, Science Exchange (www.scienceexchange.com) enables market-based collaboration between users and research facilities such as Harvard Medical School, Johns Hopkins University and the Mayo Clinic. The exchange provides ratings and reviews to help users find the best fit with regard to facilities and expertise, and also requires each party to sign an agreement outlining expectations, logistics and fees at the start.

6) Original Design Manufacturing (ODM) Adds Value to Contract Electronics Manufacturing

One of the hottest growth areas in manufacturing over the past twenty years has been contract electronics manufacturing, that is, the manufacture by third-party firms of electronic goods ranging from smartphones to computer components to complete PCs and laptop computers. Some of the world's largest manufacturers are in this category, such as China's Hon Hai Precision Industry Co., Ltd. This industry is sometimes referred to as "Electronic Contract Manufacturing (ECM)" or "Electronics Manufacturing Services (EMS)". The popularity of consumer electronics and wireless devices worldwide fueled this growth.

This growth in contract manufacturing has been part of a steady, long-term evolution from traditional, in-house manufacturing. For many years, the world of manufacturing has been acquainted with the concept of original equipment manufacturers (OEMs). An OEM is a company that manufactures a component (or sometimes a completed product) for sale to a company that will integrate that component into a final product or assembly. For example, a personal computer made under a brand name by a given company may contain various components, such as hard drives, graphics cards, chips or speakers, manufactured by several different OEM "vendors," but the firm doing the final assembly/manufacturing process is the final manufacturer and the owner of the brand name.

Today, however, engineering and R&D also enter the picture, as many OEMs are evolving into "original design manufacturers" (ODMs): contract manufacturers that offer complete, end-to-end design, engineering and manufacturing services. ODMs, in close collaboration with their clients, design and build components or products, such as consumer electronics, that client companies can then brand and sell as their own. ODMs are the ultimate result of the convergence of several trends at once, including offshoring, globalization, value-added services, contract manufacturing, outsourcing and design collaboration via the internet.

Savvy managers began to see that they could differentiate themselves by becoming more than mere manufacturers. After all, manufacturing services alone can be commoditized—that is, they can become common services offered by a large number of firms at increasingly competitive prices. However, when manufacturers combine the ability to offer complete engineering, design and manufacturing in one turnkey deal, it's a new story. This collaboration with the client on the design and engineering of products also gives the contract manufacturer a chance to build a deeper relationship with the client. Thus, ODM was born.

ODM services can be particularly effective in nations that are noted for having an experienced technical talent pool. An example is Taiwan's expertise in personal computers, where such firms as Quanta Computer, Inc., Compal Electronics, Inc. and Inventec Corporation are known to be world-leading laptop designers and manufacturers for clients that sell under name brands. Other examples include India's expertise in chips and Israel's expertise in optical communications equipment.

ODM has also been highly effective in the automobile and passenger aircraft manufacturing industries. To a rapidly growing extent, carmakers are relying on their suppliers to perform the design, engineering and manufacturing of everything from transmissions to dashboard assemblies. The same holds true in the aircraft business. To a large degree, Boeing and Airbus are conducting final assembly of components manufactured (and in many cases designed and engineered) by their suppliers. The fact that components used in transportation equipment can be heavy and bulky doesn't mean that ODMs in these sectors have to be close to home. In fact, components for Boeing's new 787 are being made as far away as Japan, and automobile components are often manufactured in China for use in U.S. automotive plants.

(It is worth noting here that the phrase OEM has evolved to have a second meaning in addition to its traditional definition. A firm that buys a component and then incorporates it into a final product or buys a completed product and then resells it under the firm's own brand name, is sometimes called an OEM. This confusing usage is most often found in the computer industry, where OEM is sometimes used as a verb. For example, a company executive describing his firm's strategy for the manufacture of a new tablet computer might say "we're going to OEM it.")

7) The State of the Biotechnology Industry Today

Biotechnology can be defined as the use of living organisms (such as bacteria), biological processes or biological systems to create a desired end-result or end-product. Primary markets for biotechnology include: 1) Agriculture, where genetically modified seeds are now in wide use in many nations. These seeds deliver plants that have can much higher crop yields per acre, and often have qualities such as disease-resistance, resistance to herbicides and drought-resistance. 2) The manufacture of enzymes, including enzymes used in food processing (such as the making of certain dairy products) and in converting organic matter into ethanol for fuel. 3) Pharmaceuticals, where biotechnology creates such therapies as antibodies, interleukins and vaccines based on living organisms (as opposed to the chemical compounds that make up traditional drugs) that can target specific cellular conditions, often with dramatic results (such as the drug Keytruda that famously

fought cancer for former U.S. President Jimmy Carter).

Biotechnology is a modern word that describes a very old science. For example, bio-enzymes have always been essential in the production of cheese. The modern difference is that much of the world's cheese production today utilizes a bio-engineered version of an enzyme called microbial chymosin. This chymosin is made by cloning natural genes into useful bacteria. Another example: For thousands of years, mankind has used naturally occurring microbes to convert fruit juices into wine.

The Coronavirus pandemic provided a massive boost to the biotech industry. Around the world, biopharmaceutical firms poured an immense effort into research that might lead to a greater understanding of the virus, how to prevent it and how to cure it. Much of this research effort was fueled by emergency injections of government funding.

Genetically engineered drugs, or "biotech" drugs, represent a rapidly growing portion of the global prescription drugs market, which will be boosted by the fact that generic (bioequivalent) biotech drugs are gaining approval. The U.S. Centers for Medicare & Medicaid Services (CMS) forecast called for prescription drug purchases in the U.S. to total about $463.6 billion during 2024, representing about $1,370 per capita. That projected total is up from only $200 billion in 2005 and a mere $40 billion in 1990.

Estimates of the size of the drugs market vary by source. Plunkett Research forecast the global pharmaceuticals market at $1.8 trillion for 2024. By 2027, American drug purchases alone may top $576.7 billion, according to the CMS, thanks to a rapidly aging U.S. population, increased access to insurance and the continued introduction of expensive new drugs.

China is the second-largest pharmaceuticals market in the world after the U.S. according to IQVIA. Spending on drugs in China during 2023 reached $169 billion and is expected to reach approximately $194 billion by 2027. Also in 2023, U.S. pharmaceutical exports to China reached $9.9 billion according to the United Nations COMTRADE database.

Advanced generations of drugs developed through biotechnology continually enter the marketplace. The results may be very promising for patients, as a technology-driven tipping point of medical care is approaching where drugs that target specific genes and proteins may eventually become widespread. However, it continues to be difficult and expensive to introduce a new drug in the U.S.

According to FDA figures, 50 new molecular entities (NMEs) and new biotech drugs (BLAs) were approved in the U.S. during 2024. These NMEs are novel, new active substances that are categorized differently from "NDAs" or New Drug Applications. NDAs may seek approval for drugs based on combinations of substances that have been approved in the past. Also, a large number of generic drug applications are being approved each year. That is, an application to manufacture a drug that was created as a brand name and has now lost its patent so that competing firms may seek FDA approval to manufacture it.

In R&D, one of the most promising uses for AI lies in identifying and testing chemical compounds that have potential to become new drug therapies— possibly cutting years and millions of dollars from the process. All major drug companies, including Astra Zeneca, are investing in their AI capabilities in the lab.

Dozens of exciting biotech drugs that target specific genes are seeking regulatory approval. Many of these drugs are for the treatment of specific forms of cancer. In a few instances, doctors are making treatment decisions based on a patient's personal genetic makeup. (This strategy is often referred to as personalized medicine.) New breakthroughs in genetically targeted drugs occur regularly. A drug for certain patients who suffer from the skin cancer known as melanoma is a good example. Zelboraf, developed by drug firms Roche Holding and Daiichi Sankyo, will dramatically aid melanoma patients who are shown through genetic tests to have a mutated gene called BRAF. In trials, about 50% of such patients saw their tumors shrink, compared to only 5.5% of patients who received traditional chemotherapy.

New Drug Application Categories

Applications for drug approval by the FDA fall under the following categories:

BLA (Biologics License Application): An application for approval of a drug synthesized from living organisms. That is, they are drugs created using biotechnology. Such drugs are sometimes referred to as biopharmaceuticals.

NME (New Molecular Entity): A new chemical compound that has never before been approved for marketing in any form in the U.S.

NDA (New Drug Application): An application requesting FDA approval, after completion of the all-important Phase III Clinical Trials, to market a new drug for human use in the U.S. The drug may contain active ingredients that were previously approved by the FDA.

Biosimilars (generic biotech drugs): A term used to describe generic versions of drugs that have been created using biotechnology. Because biotech drugs ("biologics") are made from living cells, a generic version of a drug may not be biochemically identical to the original branded version of the drug. Consequently, they are described as "biosimilars" or "follow-on biologics" to set them apart.

Priority Reviews: The FDA places some drug applications that appear to promise "significant improvements" over existing drugs for priority approval, with a goal of returning approval within six months.

Accelerated Approval: A process at the FDA for reducing the clinical trial length for drugs designed for certain serious or life-threatening diseases.

Fast Track Development: An enhanced process for rapid approval of drugs that treat certain life-threatening or extremely serious conditions. Fast Track is independent of Priority Review and Accelerated Approval.

Personal genetic codes are becoming less expensive and more widely attainable. Today, the cost of decoding the most important sections of the human genome for an individual patient has dropped dramatically.

Although total drug expenditures are currently small in developing nations such as India, China and Brazil, they have tremendous potential over the mid-term. This means that major international drug makers will be expanding their presence in these nations. However, it also means that local drug manufacturers have tremendous incentive to invest in domestic research and marketing.

The Coming BioIndustrial Era:

Some of the most exciting developments in the world of technology today are occurring in the biotech sector. These include advances in agricultural biotechnology, the convergence of nanotechnology and information technology with biotech and breakthroughs in synthetic biotechnology.

The rapidly growing worldwide base of biotechnology knowledge has the potential to create a new "bioindustrial era." For example, scientists' ability to capture refinable oils from algae and other organisms (organisms that remove carbon from the atmosphere as they grow) may eventually create a new source of transportation fuel.

The use of enzymes in industrial processes may enable us to bioengineer a long list of highly desirable substances at modest cost. The result could easily be a lower carbon footprint for many industrial processes, less industrial and residential waste to deal with and a significant increase in yields in chemicals, coatings, food and other vital sectors. DuPont's acquisition of global enzyme leader Danisco is a good indicator of the looming era of bioindustrial advancements, as DuPont made a $5.8 billion bet that it can help a vast variety of manufacturers to achieve significant product enhancements and efficiencies.

Source: Plunkett Research, Ltd.

Significant ethical issues face the biotech industry as it moves forward. They include, for example, the ability to determine an individual's likelihood to develop a disease in the future, based on his or her genetic makeup today; the potential to harvest replacement organs and tissues from animals or from cloned human genetic material; and the ability to genetically alter the basic foods that we eat. These are only a handful of the powers of biotechnology that must be dealt with by society. Watch for intense, impassioned discussion of such issues and a raft of governmental regulation as new technologies and therapies emerge.

Another breakthrough in gene therapy is CRISPR (Clustered Regularly Interspaced Short Palindromic Repeats). The technology focuses on the use of a DNA-cutting protein that is guided by an RNA molecule, targeted at a specific gene. This technology enables a scientist to quickly and easily edit or re-engineer specific bits of DNA. A defective gene can be precisely edited within the laboratory and then reintroduced to a patient's body as a form of gene therapy with far more accuracy than previous gene therapies. CRISPR is sometimes referred to as "genetic editing," and it is considered to be a very significant breakthrough. Practical applications may include treatments or even cures for sickle-cell anemia, HIV and cystic fibrosis. Libraries of CRISPRs have been created by researchers at MIT that account for nearly all human genes. CRISPR is also being utilized to modify seeds and plants for agricultural use.

The biggest single issue may be privacy. Who should have access to your personal genetic records? Where should they be stored? How should they be accessed? Can you be denied employment or insurance coverage due to your genetic makeup?

Global Factors Boosting Biotech Today:

1) A rapid aging of the population in nations including the EU, much of Asia and the U.S., such as millions of surviving Baby Boomers who are entering senior years in rising numbers and require a growing level of health care are boosting demand for drugs. A significant portion of that care may be in the form of biotech drugs.

2) Major pharmaceuticals firms are paying top prices to acquire young biotech drug companies that own promising drugs.

3) A very significant market exists for genetically engineered agricultural seeds ("Agribio"), with farmers in dozens of nations planting genetically modified seeds.

4) Aggressive investment is ongoing in biotechnology research in Singapore, China and India, often with government sponsorship—for example, Singapore's massive Biopolis project.

5) Very promising research into synthetic biology is showing good results.

6) Dramatic decreases in the cost of personal genetic studies are a big boost to personalized medicine.

7) Highly advanced biotech technologies known as gene therapies are slowly beginning to prove their ability to cure patients.

8) A focus on the discovery and manufacture of new drugs ("orphan drugs") that impact rare diseases or relatively small portions of the population is increasing.

9) The advent of the genetic engineering process known as CRISPR is enabling scientists to alter cells and repair defective cells. This has profound potential in both human and animal health therapies.

10) CRISPR also has major potential to modify agricultural seeds and plants through gene editing.

11) Artificial Intelligence (AI) is dramatically speeding up and expanding scientists' ability to discover and test new drug compounds and therapies. AI also makes it much easier to identify additional uses for drugs that have already been approved by regulators.

12) GLP-1 drugs such as Ozempic are showing significant capabilities to reduce obesity, and related diabetes and cardiovascular disease. Potential further uses under research include treating cancer, Parkinson's disease and Alzheimer's disease.

Source: Plunkett Research, Ltd.

Internet Research Tip:
For the latest biotech developments check out www.biospace.com, a private sector portal for the biotech community, and www.bio.org, the web site of the highly regarded Biotechnology Industry Organization.

8) Nations Compete Fiercely in Biotech Development

Drug companies and government research agencies in many other countries are enhancing their positions on the biotech playing field, building their own educational and technological infrastructures, and in some case creating vast new biotech research districts or complexes. Not surprisingly, countries such as India, Singapore and China, which have already made deep inroads into other technology-based industries, are investing in major efforts in biotechnology, which is very much an information-based science. Firms that manufacture generics and provide contract research, development and clinical trials services are already common in such nations. In most cases, this was just a beginning, with original drug and technology development a rapidly evolving, symbiotic industry.

India already has hundreds of firms involved in biotechnology and related support services. The nation has tight intellectual property laws in order to provide stronger patent protection to the drug industry. As a result, drug development activity by pharma firms from around the world has increased in Indian locations in recent years, although at least one foreign firm was disappointed when it attempted to enforce its patents in India. The FDA has approved hundreds of industrial plants in India for drug manufacturing and raw material production for use in the U.S. (Many factories have also been approved within China.) Meanwhile, pharmaceutical firms have hired sales representatives within India in the thousands.

The costs of developing a new drug in India can be a small fraction of those in the U.S., although drugs developed in India still are required to go through the lengthy and expensive U.S. FDA approval process before they can be sold to American patients. India

has its own robust biotech parks, including the well-established S. P. Biotech Park covering 300 acres in Hyderabad.

China has made drug research a priority, and Chinese drug research spending has grown rapidly. In addition, China is the world's largest producer of raw materials for drugs. This became controversial during the Coronavirus pandemic, as many members of the U.S. Congress called for much less reliance on China in this regard.

The Made in China 2025 initiative includes efforts to speed up drug approvals and spend more on health care. This is a shift from focusing on cheap generics and the production of basic ingredients necessary to the pharmaceuticals manufacturing industry. China is making strides in new therapies such a cancer drugs based on PD-1 inhibitors, which are cutting edge treatments for advanced cancer. Shanghai-based Junshi Biosciences Co. offers Tuoyi for melanoma for about a third of the cost of a rival drug made by Merck. In 2018, China began accepting clinical trial data from other countries rather than requiring separate tests on Chinese patients, which further speeds the drug approval process.

Meanwhile, leading biotech firms, including Roche, Pfizer and Eli Lilly, took advantage of China's education systems and relatively low operating costs in order to establish R&D centers there. In this manner, offshore research can be complemented by offshore clinical trials.

Taiwan has four biotech research parks. The Taiwanese government has a biotech development action plan which includes a $2 billion venture capital fund, a super-incubator and plans for expansion of the country's existing Development Center for Biotechnology. Meanwhile, Vietnam has plans to open six biotech research labs. Australia also has a rapidly developing biotechnology industry.

South Korea is a world leader in research and development in a wide variety of technical sectors, and it is pushing ahead boldly into biotechnology. Korean government leaders are focused on increasing research capabilities and basic sciences, particularly at research-oriented universities. The combination of government backing and extensive private capital in Korea could make this nation a biotech powerhouse. One area of emphasis there is stem cell research. (In Seoul, the government is also backing Digital Media City, a hub of developers and entrepreneurs in electronic games, media content and communications technology.

Another initiative is the Korea Research Institute of Bioscience and Biotechnology. In addition to fewer restrictions, many countries outside of the U.S. have lower labor costs, even for highly educated professionals such as doctors and scientists.

9) Globalization and Worldwide Collaboration Fuel the Research Efforts of Major Corporations

Globalization is deeply affecting the corporate world at all levels. This can be seen in everything from the inexpensive consumer goods flooding into the U.S. from manufacturers in China to the growing business that American software makers have found overseas. The advent of extremely fast communication systems, such as the internet, global fiber-optic lines, e-mail and instant messaging, as well as overnight international courier services and well-established airline service to nearly anywhere in the world, helps to spur on globalization. Nonetheless, recent global trade tension may slow globalization and lead at least some research to return to domestic facilities in the U.S., EU, U.K. and Japan.

Meanwhile, there are legions of well-educated scientists and engineers in areas such as India and Eastern Europe who can be hired for salaries that are below those of their U.S.-based peers (although rising wages in India are diluting this effect). These factors all combine to make globalized research efforts attractive for many reasons. For example, a major automotive, pharmaceutical, software or hardware company in the U.S. can create a cost-effective, 24/7 research department by handing off research or design work from America to Ireland to India to Japan—it will always be daylight in some part of the world, and collaboration software makes it possible for employees to work together on the same project from anywhere on the planet.

Another concept with regard to collaboration is open innovation, in which ideas from a variety of sources including business partners, suppliers, employees, consumers and media are used by companies to develop new products outside of their normal internal R&D departments. First coined by Henry Chesbrough of the Center for Open Innovation at the Haas School of Business at the University of California, the approach affords greater speed and efficiency than traditional development processes.

10) Number of Patent Applications Remains High/Patent Laws Change

In fiscal year 2024, the U.S. Patent & Trademark Office (PTO) received 663,591 patent applications, up from only 109,359 in 1970. To some extent, patents tend to reflect the health of R&D budgets. The greater the funding, the more patents are filed. At the same time, however, the rapid growth in the number of patent applications reflects today's increased focus on protection of intellectual property by corporations and universities along with the extremely high traffic from biotech firms attempting to patent gene expressions and other biological discoveries.

A patent application leads either to a patent grant or to a denial. The PTO granted 324,043 total patents during calendar year 2024 (which includes utility patents in addition to design, plant and reissue patents). In contrast, there were only 67,964 patents granted in 1970. A patent typically takes 18 to 24 months after application to receive a grant. The term of patent protection is currently defined as beginning on the date the patent is granted and ending 20 years from the earliest filing date of the application.

Patent Categories in the United States:

Utility Patent: may be granted to anyone who invents or discovers any new, useful and non-obvious process, machine, article of manufacture, or composition of matter, or any new and useful improvement thereof.

Design Patent: may be granted to anyone who invents a new, original, and ornamental design for an article of manufacture.

Plant Patent: may be granted to anyone who invents or discovers and asexually reproduces any distinct and new variety of plant.

Internet Research Tip:
For the latest official statistics from the U.S. Patent & Trademark Office, visit the web site of TAF, the patent office's Technology Assessment and Forecast branch. www.uspto.gov/web/offices/ac/ido/oeip/taf

---

Globally, there are roughly 120 different national patent systems, and recent proposals to create a unified global patent system are creating buzz. "Harmonization" is the word used to describe the effort, and it will be difficult to bring about. According to the World Intellectual Property Organization (www.wipo.int), 90% of the millions of applications filed annually worldwide are filed in more than one country, which exponentially multiplies application fees, legal fees and hours spent (fees for multinational applications can surpass $75,000, and legal fees often reach $200,000 or more).

An aborted 1989 attempt to establish an international system was bogged down when the U.S. could not agree with most other participating countries on a simple first-to-file regulation when awarding patents to filers with similar claims. In the U.S., the practice traditionally had been to award a patent to the filer who is proven to be the first to conceive an idea and develop it. Although fair, the system can prove costly as applicants spend time and money in the court systems to establish who was first with an idea.

An international patent system of a sort does exist in the form of the Patent Cooperation Treaty (PCT), overseen by WIPO and signed in 1970. A PCT application establishes a filing date in all contracting nations (of which there are about 150). Filers must then proceed to file the necessary documents with the patent offices of separate contracting nations of the PCT, after an initial centralized processing and evaluation period (which usually is about 18 months). Filers thereby postpone examination and related expenses in national offices during that period. Top filing countries include the U.S., Japan, China and Germany.

Since patent applications have grown exponentially in recent years, examiners have less and less time to spend studying each application and researching past inventions. Some detractors claim that patents awarded in recent years may not have been for original ideas.

Critics of the old U.S. patent system also cite unscrupulous patent-licensing companies called "trolls" that seek licensing fees by sending demand letters to presumed patent infringers, in many cases without basis of proof. Trolls also seek injunctions against large numbers of defendants, hoping to become enough of a nuisance that the supposed infringers will pay license fees just to make the problem go away.

Another critical difference between the U.S. patent system and those elsewhere around the globe was the one-year waiting period, during which American filers may publish or speak at public forums about their ideas without jeopardizing their patent rights. Abroad, filers are required to keep their ideas top secret until a patent is awarded.

Yet another point of argument centers on patent subject matter. Traditionally, in the U.S., just about anything or any idea can be patented. Business practices, for example, are commonly patented, such as Amazon.com's "one-click" technology, as well as genetic discoveries and treatments. The latter is a particularly sticky point for developing nations such as those in Latin America and Africa.

In September 2011, the America Invents Act was signed into law by President Obama to further reform U.S. patent law. The act calls for a "first to file"

system that awards patents based on the date the application is filed as opposed to the date the invention was made. It also creates new procedures, such as the ability to challenge a patent's validity directly with the Patent and Trademark Office (PTO) rather than going to court, to fight bad patents more efficiently. In addition, the act expands the ability of third parties to show prior art, meaning evidence of previous activity relating to the patent in question, to the PTO, thereby avoiding lengthy (and costly) court time. Detractors of the new law are concerned that a "first to file" system favors large, sophisticated filers who have knowledge of patent law over small entities or individuals. Another concern is that no additional funding was awarded to the PTO to handle the backlog of cases before it.

Further legislation was passed by the U.S. House of Representatives in 2013 due to a massive upswing in patent litigation since the passage of the America Invents Act. The Innovation Act is designed to neutralize patent trolls. It requires specificity in patent lawsuits, makes patent ownership more transparent, holds losing plaintiffs responsible for court costs and delays lengthy discovery phases (in which sometimes millions of internal documents such as emails and memos must be produced) to allow the courts to address the meaning of patent claims. The Innovation Act also protects end users such as small businesses by allowing technology vendors to fight lawsuits against trolls instead of their customers.

Among competing tech companies, patents are something like badges of honor. Patents protect ideas and technologies as well as exclude competitors from making strides in particular areas of research.

11) 3-D Printing and Robotics Revolutionize Manufacture of Shoes and Fabrics

With the advent of 3-D printers, advanced software and robots in factories, shoes and clothing can be made more quickly and efficiently than ever before. Nike launched a revolutionary new running shoe called the Flyknit. The 5.6-ounce, high tech shoe is made from synthetic yarn, using a machine that knits together the upper part of the shoe, which is then attached to the sole. This process not only produces a lighter-weight shoe (which running enthusiasts have long awaited) with less manufacturing waste, the Flyknit requires far less labor since it has 35 fewer pieces to assemble than comparable shoes.

The savings may make it possible for Nike to have the Flyknit manufactured in the U.S. While still more expensive than production overseas, the company will spend less on shipping and fulfill orders more quickly to meet demand. Nike also offers Nike By You, a customizable shoe option both in stores and online.

Adidas, the German shoe and athletic apparel manufacturer, has a new facility called Speedfactory in the town of Anspach, Germany with robots and 3-D printers. The plant has a capacity of 500,000 pairs of athletic shoes per year.

Brooks, a shoe manufacturer based in Seattle, Washington, is utilizing HP's FitStation biomechanical measuring system for its new bespoke shoes. The system makes a 3-D scan of customer's feet while in motion, enabling Brooks to make shoes of ideal density for up to 30 zones of the foot.

Carbon, Inc. (www.carbon3d.com) is a 3-D printer manufacturer in California that has made athletic shoe soles for Adidas. Carbon's process employs a technology called digital light synthesis, which uses software to control chemical reactions, resulting in the "growth" of parts based on liquid polymers. The technology produces 12 classes of materials including heat-resistant cyanate ester for use in automotive and aerospace parts and elastomers that are used in shoes. Another company, Betabrand (www.betabrand.com), partners with shoe and accessory manufacturer Li and Fung to combine crowdsourcing with 3-D digital rendering. Website visitors vote on popular styles, with winners becoming available in as little as five days.

SPOTLIGHT: Garment Factory Automation

While many industries are automating, with robots replacing workers in factories, the garment industry has been somewhat protected by the complexity of cutting and sewing. The work has remained in the hands of millions of factory workers around the world. However, Steve Dickerson, a professor at the Georgia Institute of Technology and the founder of a startup called SoftWear Automation, built and patented a robotic sewing machine. The machines, called Sewbots, use high-speed photography that captures up to 1,000 frames per second to track material as it is sewn. Software analyzes the photographs fast enough to make tiny adjustments necessary to switch positions when necessary and even feed fabric into the sewing machine when needed.

A materials-handling system called LOWRY was developed to pick up pieces of fabric and move them to other machines for buttonholes, zippers or related finishing tasks. Tianyuan Garments Co. in eastern China was recently opened a $20 million factory staffed by robots built by SoftWear Automation. As more garment factories automate and are freed from cost of labor issues, look for more companies to relocate production to areas where the bulk of their customers reside.

---

12) Industrial Robots and Factory Automation Advance Through Artificial Intelligence (AI)

The International Organization for Standardization (ISO) 8373 defines industrial robots as being automatically controlled, reprogrammable, featuring a multipurpose manipulator capable of movement in three or more directions, including linear or rotational movement. It may be either fixed or mobile.

The type of joints used industrial robots indicate the classification and potential uses of a robot. The primary types of joints include:

Revolute joints—may include a hinge, a pin or an axle. They have one degree of freedom (DoF). That is, they can move in one direction or one manner.

Prismatic joints—also have one DoF. They move along a fixed axis. That is, they are pistons or similar sliding objects.

Spherical joints—with three DoFs. They can rotate or pivot around a round bearing. Ball joints used in automobiles are spherical joints.

Industrial robots are further classified by their mechanical organization:

- Articulated robots—feature an arm that can closely resemble the movement of a human arm. The arm may have several joints that are revolute joints.
- Cylindrical robots—feature an arm and design that do well in circular workspaces. They may include a combination of revolute and prismatic joints.
- Cartesian robots—feature an arm that has prismatic joints only and tend to be linear in action. This type of robot typically has great strength and lifting capacity. A gantry robot is a related type of cartesian robot.

- Parallel robots (also known as "parallel manipulators")—consist of three or more rotary or prismatic rotation points (axes). They can be used to manipulate large loads. A flight simulator (used to train pilots on the ground in a virtual environment) may be manipulated by a parallel robot.
- SCARA robots (Selective Compliance Arm for Robotic Assembly, or Selective Compliance Articulated Robot Arm)—a robot used to install components and move parts. It can mimic the motions of a human arm.

An additional, informal classification of robots is collaborative robots, or "cobots." This refers to robots that work closely alongside human workers, with the intent of making repetitive tasks easier and faster to complete.

The International Federation of Robotics (IFR) estimated the total worldwide base of operational industrial robots at the end of 2024 at 4.3 million, up from about 3.5 million in 2022. The automotive and electronics industries have been prime drivers of robot sector growth in recent years. The largest markets for sales of robots are China, Korea, Japan, the U.S. and Germany. U.S. investment in factory automation and robotics is expected to be very substantial in coming years. China is investing very heavily in both robots within its factories and the development of its own robotic technologies.

China used its massive population base (1.4 billion), low wages and heavy investment of funds by both government agencies and corporations (domestic and foreign), to become a massive manufacturing engine over several decades. Today, however, China is at a dramatic point of change, with rapidly rising wages, an aging population, a shrinking workforce and very effective competition from lower-cost nations such as Vietnam. Consequently, China is seen as one of the highest growth markets in the world for factory automation. Chinese government policies focus on automating many key manufacturing and technology sectors, including automobiles, electronics, home appliances, logistics and food production. Chinese robotics makers such as Anhui Effort Intelligent Equipment and Siasun Robot & Automation are expected to compete heavily against Western companies like Adept Technology for dominance in the global robotics market. Artificial intelligence and automation are a particular focus of China's long-term plans. Robotics companies plan significant investments in China-based factories and marketing efforts to capture their share of this market.

China's government launched an initiative to make billions of yuan available for manufacturers to upgrade their facilities and technology with robots. The region of Guangdong pledged to invest $150 billion in industrial robotic equipment and the creation of two centers for advanced automation.

Robotics will not only help China with its workforce challenges while restraining total wage costs, it will also assist China in its vital effort to move its manufacturing upmarket into aerospace, medical technology and other sectors requiring very high levels of manufacturing precision and quality.

In the automotive sector, General Motors (GM) is working with Fanuc, a Japanese robotics manufacturer, Cisco Systems and Rockwell Automation to monitor robots and plant working conditions (such as temperature and humidity). Gathered data, stored in a cloud network, is analyzed and workers can service robots before they break or alter conditions to limit costly downtime when robots fail.

The future of the robotics and factory automation industry is extremely bright. China is a perfect example of the types of trends that will drive the industry forward: rising wages, a rapidly growing manufacturing sector, soaring global trade in manufactured goods and demographic challenges. Combined with today's very low penetration of robotics in most of the world's nations, dramatic increases in industrial robotics sales will occur for decades to come. Industries that will rely more and more on robotics and automation include food processing, pharmaceuticals, oil and gas, logistics and warehousing, automobile manufacturing, chemicals and textiles.

New cutting-edge robots allow humans to work alongside them. Thought to be too dangerous until recently, new models such as Baxter, made by Rethink Robotics, "learns" new tasks when a human moves the robot's arms through an operation. Baxter is in use on U.S. conveyor lines helping package items. Auto maker BMW uses heavy assembly robots made by Universal Robots to help humans complete final vehicle door assembly.

The transportation and logistics sector will be heavily influenced by robotics. For example, giant robots are in use at the Port of Los Angeles and the Port of Long Beach in the U.S. to unload container ships and move cargo containers on the docks. The Port of Long Beach has an automated terminal with a capacity of handling 3.3 million 20-foot container units yearly. Industry analysts estimate that robots can improve dock productivity by as much as 30%.

13) Fuel Cell and Hydrogen Power Research Continues/Fuel Cell Cars Enter Market

The fuel cell is nothing new, despite the excitement it is now generating. It has been around since 1839, when Welsh physics professor William Grove created an operating model based on platinum and zinc components. Much later, the U.S. Apollo space program used fuel cells for certain power needs in the Apollo space vehicles that traveled from the Earth to the Moon.

In basic terms, a fuel cell consists of quantities of hydrogen and oxygen separated by a catalyst. Inside the cell, a chemical reaction within the catalyst generates electricity. Byproducts of this reaction include heat and water. Several enhancements to basic fuel cell technology are under research and development at various firms worldwide. These include fuel cell membranes manufactured with advanced nanotechnologies and "solid oxide" technologies that could prove efficient enough to use on aircraft. Another option for fuel cell membranes is those made of hydrocarbon, which cost about one-half as much as membranes using fluorine compounds.

Fuel cells require a steady supply of hydrogen. Therein lies the biggest problem in promoting the widespread use of fuel cells: how to create, transport and store the hydrogen. At present, no one has been able to put a viable plan in place that would create a network of hydrogen fueling stations substantial enough to meet the needs of everyday motorists in the U.S. or anywhere else.

Many current fuel cells burn hydrogen extracted from such sources as gasoline, natural gas or methanol. Each source has its advantages and disadvantages. Unfortunately, burning a hydrocarbon such as oil, natural gas or coal to produce the energy necessary to create hydrogen results in unwanted emissions. Ideally, hydrogen would be created using renewable, non-polluting means, such as solar power or wind power. Also, nuclear or renewable sources could be used to generate electricity that would be used to extract hydrogen molecules from water.

The potential market for fuel cells encompasses diverse uses in fixed applications (such as providing an electric generating plant for a home or a neighborhood), portable systems (such as portable generators for construction sites) or completely mobile uses (powering anything from small hand-held devices to automobiles). The likely advantages of fuel cells as clean, efficient energy sources are enormous. The fuel cell itself is a proven technology—fuel cells are already in use, powering a U.S. Post Office in Alaska, for example. (This project, in Chugach, Alaska, is the result of a joint venture between the local electric association and the U.S. Postal Service to install a one-megawatt fuel cell facility.) Tiny fuel cells are also on the market for use in powering cellular phones and laptop computers.

Oil companies including BP PLC, Royal Dutch Shell PLC and TotalEnergies SE have invested billions of dollars on green hydrogen projects. The Hydrogen Council reported 680 large-scale green hydrogen projects planned globally as of 2022. However, only about 10% of those reached final investment approval.

In July 2020, Hanwha Energy (www.hanwha.com) completed a 114-fuel cell plant in the Daesan Industrial Complex in Seosan, Korea with a capacity of 50-megawatts of electricity. It was the largest industrial hydrogen fuel cell plant in the world at that time. (The Shinincheon Bitdream Hydrogen Fuel Cell Power Plant in Incheon opened in 2021 and has a capacity of 78.96-megawatts.)

In Bridgeport, Connecticut, a 14.9-megawatt fuel-cell complex generates enough electricity to power 15,000 homes (out of a total 51,000 in the city). In April 2015, a 1.4-megawatt cell went online at the University of Bridgeport.

U.S. industrial gas supplier Air Products & Chemicals (www.airproducts.com) built a "green hydrogen" plant in Saudi Arabia. Hydrogen is manufactured utilizing electricity from nearby wind and solar farms. This plant has a capacity of 4-gigawatts. Similar green hydrogen plants are under development elsewhere in the world.

The trucking industry is becoming a new market for hydrogen-fueled transportation. Nikola Corp. (nikolamotor.com) designs and manufactures heavy-duty commercial battery-electric vehicles (BEV) and fuel cell electric vehicles (FCEV). The company was founded in 2015, and is headquartered in Phoenix, Arizona with manufacturing facilities in Arizona and in Germany. In September 2023, Nikola announced the commercial launch of its HYLA brand hydrogen fuel cell electric truck. The fuel-cell truck has a range of up to 500 miles and can be refilled in as little as 20 minutes.

The aviation industry (a massive user of fossil fuels) is also experimenting with hydrogen. Unlike electric batteries, which are too heavy at present to be feasible in long-range aircraft, hydrogen delivers power even more efficiently than jet fuel when calculated by weight. Jet fuel delivers 40 megajoules per kilogram of weight, while hydrogen delivers 140 megajoules per kilogram. Universal Hydrogen (hydrogen.aero) and ZeroAvia (www.zeroavia.com) are using hydrogen fuel cells to power light and regional aircraft.

SPOTLIGHT: Sunhydrogen, Inc.

Sunhydrogen, Inc. (www.sunhydrogen.com) is a pioneer in large scale solar-to-hydrogen plants. It states that it has developed a "low-cost method" to harness solar cells to power hydrolysis—splitting water molecules so that hydrogen and oxygen are separated. Part of the firm's technology is based on nanotechnology. See the YouTube video: www.youtube.com/watch?v=dkIDRZH273A.

Yet another breakthrough is the ability for wind turbines to create the energy needed to produce hydrogen. (A strategy referred to as "green hydrogen.") Siemens Gamesa Renewable Energy is working with its parent company, Siemens Energy, to develop the technology onshore in Denmark. Offshore projects are also under consideration.

A looming issue is that many people still have concerns about the safety of hydrogen. Naturally gaseous at room temperature, storing hydrogen involves using pressurized tanks that can leak and, if punctured, could cause explosions. It is also difficult to store enough hydrogen in a vehicle to take it the 300+ miles that drivers are used to getting on a tank of gasoline. To do so, hydrogen must be compressed to 10,000 pounds per square inch and stored on board in bulky pressure tanks.

14) Electric Cars (EVs) and Plug-in Hybrids (PHEVs) Spur Changes at Auto Makers/Hybrid Sales See Sharp Growth

Automotive manufacturers in the U.S. and around the world are investing very heavily in research, design and factory capacity for new electric vehicles (EVs) of all types. This includes fully electric cars and trucks as well as hybrids. Plug-in hybrids (PHEVs) are similar to standard hybrids (in that they can run on their gasoline-powered engines or battery power), but they enable the owner the option of plugging-in at home overnight to recharge the battery. This will eliminate the need to run the car's gasoline engine, using only battery power as long as the relatively short range isn't exceeded. (Standard hybrids recharge only by running the gasoline-powered side of the car, and by drawing on the drag produced by using the brakes.)

According to Cox Automotive, sales within America of all-electric vehicles rose from 490,456 in 2021 to 807,180 in 2022 and 1.1 million in 2023. EVs accounted for 7.1% of U.S. auto sales in 2023, compared to 5.8% in 2022 and 3.2% in 2021. Worldwide, there were about 14 million electric and plug-in hybrid cars sold in 2023, according to the International Energy Agency (IEA).

In the U.S., the Schumer-Manchin tax bill includes EV subsidies in which certain purchasers qualify for a $7,500 tax credit. The bill eases a previously established cap of 200,000 total all-time EVs sold per manufacturer that could qualify for credits and establishes an income limit of $150,000 per year for an individual, $225,000 for a head of household, or $300,000 for married couples who purchase the cars and want the tax credit. It also sets qualifying price limits of $80,000 for pickups, SUVs and vans and $55,000 for sedans. In addition, credits are being adjusted so that EV batteries must be made of materials mined or processed in the U.S. or in countries with which the U.S. has free trade agreements.

Competition is driving price drops to some extent, as Tesla now has lots of competitors in EVSs, ranging from well established companies like Ford and Volvo to startups like Rivian. Also, new, cheaper battery technology is being developed to make this possible. In 2023, Tesla dropped prices by $5,000 each for two of its popular base models, and also reduced prices for its Model 3 sedan and some Model Y crossovers.

Challenges For EV Makers' Lofty Production Goals

The EV market is facing very significant challenges. EV sales represent a modest market share in most nations. Charging station networks are not well developed, and many potential buyers are concerned they will not be able to recharge when needed, particularly on long trips. Batteries remain costly. EV sales are so small compared to the expenses involved in manufacturing EVs that some manufacturers, including Ford and Rivian, are estimated to have been losing tens of thousands of dollars on each EV sold as of 2024. Tesla is faring better, with its substantial sales base, but its ability to earn a profit has largely hinged on the fees it earns by selling by selling "carbon offset credits" (nearly $2 billion in some years) to other car companies that do not meet emissions standards set by the State of California. Meanwhile, the world's reliance on much of the EV supply chain coming from China, as well as controversy over the environmental challenges in mining and utilizing cobalt, nickel, manganese and other metals in batteries, pose other challenges to this sector. The bottom line is that it remains to be seen whether or not either governments' goals or car manufacturers' goals for EV production and market share can be met over the mid-term.

Electric pickups are garnering the lion's share of EV attention in the U.S. Plug-in versions of the Chevy Silverado and the Ford F-150 have hit the market. Tesla delivered its first futuristic Cybertruck pickups in late 2023 (originally planned for 2021) while Rivian Automotive delivered the first of its R1T pickups in 2022. In 2023, the IEA reported electric truck sales in the U.S. reached 1,200 units, about three times the number sold in 2022 but still less than 0.1% of total truck sales.

As EV sales slow, sales of hybrid vehicles were moving upward. Manufacturers reported hybrid vehicle sales up 43% in the U.S. in the first quarter of 2024 compared to the same period in 2023. More buyers are choosing hybrids over EVs due to their fuel efficiency without the recharging concerns relating to fully-electric vehicles.

SPOTLIGHT: EVs Could Transform Detroit

The shift away from internal combustion engines (ICEs) is changing the face of automotive manufacturing in America and elsewhere. Vehicles that run on batteries require fewer parts than ICEs, making them less labor intensive to produce (needing about 30% fewer manufacturing workhours from start to finish). Yet another facet to the EV industry is the relative ease of production compared to that of internal combustion engines. According to Volkswagen, EV production takes 30% less effort that internal combustion vehicles. Ford concurs, saying that the simplified production of EVs could lead to a 30% reduction in labor hours per vehicle (which is not good news for the United Autoworkers Union). On the other hand, EVs rely on electrical engineers, software developers and other technicians and researchers, which may offset at least some of the job losses. Plants are undergoing major conversions. However, as of mid-2024, American manufacturers were scaling back on EV production and manufacturing plant construction due to sales that were falling far below initial expectations. JD Power forecast EV sales in the U.S. for all of 2024 of 1.2 million units, or only about 9% of all vehicles sold, down from a previous prediction of 12%.

Tesla has a massive network of Tesla-owned charging stations. As of mid-2024, Tesla's Supercharger network (where Tesla owners can get a rapid recharge of batteries) had more than 50,000 stations worldwide, including about 2,260 housing more than 27,000 ports) in the U.S. Tesla recently agreed to open part of its U.S. charging network to certain non-Tesla owners. Another player in this sector, Electrify America, had more than 950 charging stations in operation by early 2024. The U.S. Government is providing massive financial incentives to qualified installations of new charging stations in America, both in homes and at commercial facilities.

SPOTLIGHT: Charging Stations

There are three levels of EV charging stations.
- Level 1 (120 volts), approximately five miles of range per hour of charging, typically at home.
- Level 2 (240 volts), approximately 25 miles of range per hour of charging, again typically at home.
- Level 3 (Fast Charging), approximately 100 to 200+ miles of range per 30 minutes of charging, typically at public charging stations.

China has imposed increasingly strict mandates boosting zero-emission vehicles due to the massive air pollution problem in Chinese cities. Tesla began exporting its China-made Model 3 to several EU countries in late 2020. The nation of India is also boosting sales of its electric vehicles. India, China and the EU are all likely to see very high ratios of electric car sales by 2030.

Internet Research Tip: Electric Cars

For the latest on electric car manufacturers see:
Electric Drive Transportation Association,
www.goelectricdrive.org
Global Electric Motorcars, www.gemcar.com
Tesla Motors, www.teslamotors.com

Electric Vans and Long-Range Trucks: Tesla has developed heavy-duty electric trucks capable of hauling major loads up to 500 miles at a price of about $150,000 and up (considerably higher than the price of traditional diesel-powered truck costs). The first truck was delivered (about 3 years behind schedule) to PepsiCo in December 2022. Other early orders were on-hand from major companies like Walmart and FedEx.

Daimler delivered its first Freightliner eCascadia all-electric semi in August 2019. The problem with electrifying 18-wheeled trucks is the weight of including enough batteries to allow long driving range. Other truck industry firms, including Volvo, Peterbilt and BYD are active in electric truck research or manufacture. A diesel-powered engine weighs about two tons while an electric version with its batteries would weigh between four and nine tons, depending on range. However, long-range heavy electric trucks face massive challenges, including the lack of the specialized, high-capacity charging facilities needed at truck stops.

Improvements in EV technology are enabling the development of larger electric vehicles. Retail giant Amazon is purchasing electric delivery vehicles from Rivian Automotive. Amazon hopes to have 100,000 EVs on the road by 2030.

Electric vans are also being developed. GM created a new company, BrightDrop, in early 2021 to manufacture the vehicles. BrightDrop delivered its first 150 electric vans to FedEx in mid-2022. Startup electric van manufacturer Canoo delivered its first electric vans to NASA in 2023, for use as crew transportation vehicles at the launchpad.

15) Major Technology Research in Batteries/Major Investments in Battery Factories and Power Storage

There remain many obstacles to all-electric vehicles: a shortage of battery charging stations available to the driving public, battery cost and driving range. Another challenge is the increasing demand for lithium, which is a major component of these batteries. Cobalt, nickel and manganese are also used in lithium-ion batteries. There is concern as to whether miners can keep up with demand. Mining of these metals often creates significant environmental problems. Some are produced largely in nations with terrible records of labor abuse and environmental disdain. Meanwhile, governments and auto industry leaders in many nations are concerned about China's dominance in the EV battery supply chain.

For EVs to gain high market share, there are several logistical challenges. EVs in massive numbers would not only require vastly higher numbers of charging stations but could also require a very significant increase in the generation and distribution of electricity required to keep millions of EVs charged.

Batteries can account for as much as 40% of an EV's price. In recent years, great strides have been made in reducing the cost of batteries. This is partly due to economies of scale since manufacturers are now able to produce batteries in greater quantities. In addition, battery technology has progressed in efficiency and performance to the extent that costs fell 90% between 2010 and 2020, according to the director of sustainability at driving service Lyft, Paul Augustine.

Some of the biggest news in advanced batteries for automobiles is being made at Tesla, the U.S.-based maker of all-electric vehicles. Tesla owns a massive battery factory, known as the Gigafactory, near Reno, Nevada. The long-term plan is for a 10 million square foot plant capable of manufacturing enough batteries to power 500,000 new cars per year. Some of Tesla's Gigafactories produce batteries; others build cars based on batteries from other firms. A facility known as Gigafactory 2 in the state of New York manufactures solar panels and solar roof tiles. Gigafactory 3 is an automobile plant in Shanghai, China. Tesla also opened Gigafactory 4 Berlin-Brandenburg (Germany) in March 2022. However, later that year the company shifted some of its manufacturing focus back to the U.S. in order to qualify for recently passed American tax credits that require batteries to made domestically. Gigafactory 5 opened near Austin, Texas in early 2022, with about

10 million square feet of space, making it one of the world's largest buildings.

Toyota is investing billions of dollars to build lithium-ion battery manufacturing plants in several locations around the world. The company plans to have 10 production lines in place by 2025 (a single plant can house several production lines).

South Korea firms plan to dramatically boost their share of the electric vehicle batter market in the U.S. Three companies, LG Energy, SK Innovation and Samsung SDI, are investing billions to expand production in the U.S. In early 2023, LG Energy announced plans to invest $5.6 billion in a lithium-ion battery plant in Arizona. Production is expected to start in 2025.

There is an advanced battery technology called lithium ferrophosphate (LFP) which has a relatively lower risk of catching fire and uses iron instead of cobalt or nickel, making it cheaper to produce. Tesla is using the battery in one version of its Model 3 made in China. Rivian and Ford are also embracing the technology, especially since recent improvements have increased range per charge.

The holy grail of electric car research is the development of advanced battery technology that will enable a car to go 400 to 500 miles between recharges, while maintaining a competitive retail price for the car.

Samsung Electronics is working to incorporate graphene into a lithium-ion battery. This ultra-thin form of carbon could increase a battery's capacity by as much as 45% and significantly reduce recharging time.

Startups including Sila Nanotechnologies (silanano.com), Global Graphene Group, www.theglobalgraphenegroup.com), Enovix (enovix.com)and Enevate (www.enevate.com) produce materials for lithium-silicon batteries which have the potential to increase capacity by as much as 40%. Innolith AG (innolith.com), a Swiss startup, built the world's first rechargeable battery capable of powering a vehicle for more than 600 miles between charges. In mid-2023, the company announced the commercialization of its I-State battery technology platform that cuts EV costs and increases vehicle range. The 20% reduction of lithium, cobalt and nickel afforded by the platform will help alleviate environmental and sourcing concerns, while typically reducing the weight of an EV battery pack by 7% to 8%.

Another startup, Form Energy, Inc. (www.formenergy.com) is building its Form Factory 1 plant in West Virginia with an opening expected in mid- to late 2024. Form Energy's technology focuses on iron-air batteries, which inexpensively use iron pellets. The process exposes iron to water and oxygen to create rust, and then converts the rust back into iron, thereby emitting oxygen to charge or discharge a battery. The goal is to increase battery storage capacity for use in the U.S. electric grid.

A looming shortage of lithium is on the horizon, spurring manufacturers to acquire stakes in lithium mining companies or invest in refiners or recyclers. General Motors, for example, agreed to invest $650 million in Lithium Americas Corp. that would afford the car maker exclusive access to a new mine planned close to the Nevada-Oregon border. Demand for lithium-ion batteries skyrocketed from 59 gigawatt hours in 2015 to 400 gigawatt hours in 2021, with another 50% jump expected to follow in 2022 according to Benchmark Mineral Intelligence.

A new technology called direct lithium extraction uses salty water (brine), found thousands of feet below the Earth's surface, which contains lithium. The brine is pumped to the surface where the lithium is separated. The remaining brine is injected back into the below-ground aquifer and the lithium is crystallized into a battery-grade product. Abundant deep-brine aquifers are found in southeastern U.S. states from Texas to Florida. Companies including Exxon Mobil, Standard Lithium and Tetra Technologies are scouting the area and making plans to build lithium plants. In Exxon Mobil's case, a proposed facility in a small town in Arkansas may have a capacity of 75,000 to 100,000 metric tons on lithium per year, or about 15% of all finished lithium produced worldwide during 2022.

The U.S. May Become the World Leader in Advanced Sodium-Ion Batteries for Storage and for EVs

As of 2025, the world depends largely on China for lithium-ion batteries, the typical battery used in both electric vehicles and many energy storage facilities. Sodium-ion may provide America with an opportunity to significantly advance domestic battery production and break its reliance on Chinese supplies, while building less expensive batteries that are much less likely to suffer fires associated with lithium technology.

Sodium-ion units rely on soda ash (sodium carbonate). America holds as much as 90% of the world's reserves of soda ash. Peak Energy, based in Denver, is a pioneer in sodium-ion batteries. The U.S. Department of Energy provided, in 2024, $50 million to a consortium of universities and laboratories to advance such technology.

Natron Energy (natron.energy) is investing $1.4 billion to build a major sodium-ion battery plant in North Carolina with annual manufacturing capacity of 24 GW of batteries. Natron has an existing sodium-ion plant in Michigan that began commercial operation in April 2024. Natron states that its high-performance batteries outperform lithium-ion batteries in both power density and recharging speed, and that they do not require minerals such as cobalt, copper or nickel.

Top Producers of Lithium-Ion Batteries Include:
Panasonic Corporation, www.panasonic.com
LG Chem. www.lgchem.com
Samsung SDI Co., www.samsungsdi.com
BYD, www.byd.com
CATL, www.catlbattery.com

16) Supercomputing Hits 1,742 Petaflops

The claim to the title of the world's fastest computer is a moving target. By June 2022, China was estimated by trackers of the "Top500" supercomputers list to have grown its base of such computers to 173 machines, up from only 37 in early 2015. This ranked China ahead of the U.S., as America had about 128 units, down considerably from 169 systems as of late 2016. In 2024, the U.S. once again had the highest number of supercomputers, with 173 compared to China's 63 and Germany's 40. Massive, supercomputing systems are very costly, both to develop and to operate. However, the growing use of cloud computing strategies means that more users can take advantage of one system, such as IBM's Watson.

Hi-level IT teams understand the need to work on new, advanced systems in order to avoid falling behind in areas where strong computing matters most, such as simulating complex systems like weather forecasting, and biotechnology projects like protein folding, as well as for the most advanced artificial intelligence projects. Simulation capability is vital for national security (for example, where simulations take the place of underground testing for weapons of mass destruction) and the advancement of basic science.

Speeds multiplied dramatically in recent years. As of November 2024, the El Capitan system at the Lawrence Livermore National Laboratory in California was considered to be ranked at the top, reaching 1,742 petaflops (or 1.742 exaflops). It was followed by the Frontier system at Oak Ridge National Laboratory (ORNL) in Tennessee reaching 1,194 petaflops (or 1.194 exaflops). Third was the Aurora at Argonne National Laboratory, also in the U.S. in Illinois, reaching 585.34 petaflops. Fourth was the Eagle system at the National Renewable Energy Laboratory (NREL) in the U.S., reaching 561.2 petaflops, followed by the HPC6 at Italy's Eni S.p.A reaching 477.9 petaflops. Supercomputer Fugaku at the RIKEN Center for Computational Science in Japan reaching 442.01 petaflops was number six.

Aurora, an HPE Cray exascale system installed in 2023 and only partly functional, is expected to reach a peak performance of 2 exaflops when fully completed. Aurora will utilize AI to attempt to address new areas of research including cancer, nuclear fission, vaccines and other complex technologies and scientific needs. In real-world performance, as of May 2024, Aurora reached 1.012 exaflops. This performance should improve as installation continues.

Government and corporate customers alike will benefit from this race. While aerospace and biotech firms want supercomputing power for breakthrough research, government agencies benefit from supercomputers for a wide variety of needs. Additionally, major manufacturers in such areas as automobiles and health imaging equipment see supercomputers as a tool for improved product engineering and faster time-to-market.

17) Superconductivity Provides Advanced Electricity Distribution Technology

Superconductivity is based on the use of super-cooled cable to distribute electricity over distance, with little of the significant loss of electric power incurred during traditional transmission over copper wires. It is one of the most promising technologies for upgrading the ailing electricity grid.

Superconductivity dates back to 1911, when a Dutch physicist determined that the element mercury, when cooled to minus 452 degrees Fahrenheit, has virtually no electrical resistance. That is, it lost zero electric power when used as a means to distribute electricity from one spot to another. Two decades later, in 1933, a German physicist named Walther Meissner discovered that superconductors have no interior magnetic field. This property enabled superconductivity to be put to commercial use by 1984, when magnetic resonance imaging machines (MRIs) were commercialized for medical imaging.

In 1986, IBM researchers K. Alex Muller and Georg Bednorz paved the path to superconductivity at slightly higher temperatures using a ceramic alloy as a medium. Shortly thereafter, a team led by University of Houston physicist Paul Chu created a ceramic capable of superconductivity at temperatures high enough to encourage true commercialization.

In May 2001, the Danish city of Copenhagen established a first when it implemented a 30-meter-long "high temperature" superconductivity (HTS) cable in its own energy grids. Other small but successful implementations have occurred in the U.S.

Today, the Holy Grail for researchers is a quest for materials that will permit superconductivity at temperatures above the freezing point, even at room temperature. There are two types of super-conductivity: "low-temperature" superconductivity (LTS), which requires temperatures lower than minus 328 degrees Fahrenheit; and "high-temperature" superconductivity (HTS), which operates at any temperature higher than that. The former type requires the use of liquid helium to maintain these excessively cold temperatures, while the latter type can reach the required temperatures with much cheaper liquid nitrogen. Liquid nitrogen is pumped through HTS cable assemblies, chilling thin strands of ceramic material that can carry electricity with no loss of power as it travels through the super-cooled cable. HTS wires are capable of carrying more than 130 times the electrical current of conventional copper wire of the same dimension. Consequently, the weight of such cable assemblies can be one-tenth the weight of old-fashioned copper wire. HTS wiring is improving substantially thanks to the development of second-generation technologies.

While cable for superconductivity is both exotic and expensive, the cost is decreasing as production ramps up, and the advantages can be exceptional. Increasing production to commercial levels at an economic cost, as well as producing lengths suitable for transmission purposes remain among the largest hurdles for the superconductor industry. Applications that are currently being implemented include use in electric transmission bottlenecks and in expensive engine systems such as those found in submarines.

Another major player in HTS components is Sumitomo Electric Industries, the largest cable and wire manufacturer in Japan. The firm has begun commercial production of HTS wire at a facility in Osaka. In addition, Sumitomo has developed electric motors based on HTS coil. The superconducting motors are much smaller and lighter than conventional electric motors, at about 90% less volume and 80% less weight.

Another leading firm, AMSC, formerly American Superconductor, sells technology to wind turbine makers, enabling them to design full 10-megawatt class superconductor wind turbines that will operate with higher efficiency than traditional models. It is also participating in advanced-technology electric transmission projects.

Advanced-generation HTS cable has been developed at American Superconductor, utilizing multiple coatings on top of a 100-millimeter substrate, a significant improvement over its earlier 40-millimeter technology. The goal is to achieve the highest level of alignment of the atoms in the superconductor material resulting in higher electrical current transmission capacity. This will increase manufacturing output while increasing efficiency. This is a convergence of nanotechnology with superconductivity since it deals with materials at the atomic level. The company is well set up to increase production as demand increases.

In 2023, researchers at the University of Rochester reported a breakthrough in superconductivity in which a superconductor made of a hydrogen, nitrogen and lutetium (a rare-earth metal) combination operates at room temperature and at much lower pressure than previous models. The combination, called "reddmatter," is heated by a laser and compressed in a device called a diamond anvil cell (DAC), which enables researchers to test materials under extreme pressures. The breakthrough could theoretically make a commercial superconductor product viable, thereby creating loss-free electrical grids, as well as cost-effective, advanced magnets for use in nuclear fusion reactors.

In 2024, researchers at Terra Quantum (terraquantum.swiss) announced the successful demonstration of a "Type III" superconductor. This new class of superconductor, which utilizes superconducting islands separated by non-superconducting regions, has minimal energy loss under electromagnetic fields. Potential applications include quantum computing and electronics.

Leading Firms in Superconductivity Technology:
Sumitomo Electric Industries, sumitomoelectric.com
AMSC, www.amsc.com
Nexans, www.nexans.com
SuperPower, Inc., www.superpower-inc.com
Terra Quantum, terraquantum.swiss

18) Private, Reusable Rockets Launch Commercial Satellites and Serve Both the U.S. Military & NASA

Satellite launches are benefitting from aerospace technology trends, as satellites are becoming much smaller, lighter and cheaper to make, but also because the rockets that blast them into orbit are evolving as well. There are several companies worldwide involved in the development of reusable rockets, led by SpaceX, Boeing, Sierra Nevada Corp. and Blue Origin, among others. All are engaged in building spacecraft to deliver cargo and astronauts to platforms such as the International Space Station (ISS) as well as launch to satellites.

Blue Origin (www.blueorigin.com), which is backed by Amazon's Jeff Bezos, led the pack with its development of a reusable rocket, first achieved when its New Shepard rocket completed a controlled, upright landing after a brief trip to space in November 2015. In December 2017, the company launched the first flight of its Crew Capsule 2.0 with a test dummy aboard, followed by five successful flights with human crew and passengers. As of October 2024, the company completed its ninth human spaceflight and the 27th flight overall for the New Shepherd program.

Tesla Motors founder Elon Musk started Space Exploration Technologies Corp., which is commonly called SpaceX (www.spacex.com). The firm's reusable rocket, called the Falcon 9, has successfully delivered numerous payloads and returned to Earth. SpaceX also developed the Falcon Heavy, intended to be the world's most powerful rocket, which made its first successful test flight in February 2018. The Falcon Heavy generates more than 5 million pounds of thrust, is 230 feet tall and weighs 3.1 million pounds. In addition, SpaceX's Dragon free-flying spacecraft was the first commercial spacecraft to deliver cargo to the International Space Station and return cargo to Earth in 2012.

The company has utilized its unique technologies and services to dramatically reduce the cost of orbital launches. In May 2020, SpaceX's first crewed mission of its Dragon spacecraft delivered two NASA astronauts to the International Space Station (ISS) using an automated docking system. This was the first time that such a launch was completed by a private, non-government firm. By mid-2024, the Dragon had 46 total launches, 42 visits to the ISS and 25 reflight missions. SpaceX is a contractor to NASA's Artemis space program, which plans to send astronauts to the moon as early as 2025. Boeing is also a major private space rocket contractor, as the prime supplier for NASA's Space Launch System. Boeing's Starliner made its first crewed flight to the ISS on June 5, 2024. However, in March 2025, SpaceX equipment had to rescue two NASA astronauts, Suni Williams and Butch Wilmore, who were significantly delayed in returning from the International Space Station due to problems plaguing the Boeing Starliner, which was originally planned to be their return transportation to Earth.

SpaceX owns two repurposed offshore oil rigs called Deimos and Phobos (names for the two moons of the planet Mars). These are now floating launch and landing sites that serve the Starship reusable rocket and its booster, the Super Heavy. Starship made its fifth successful test flight in October 2024, when an uncrewed Starship capsule orbited the Earth. Meanwhile, the Super Heavy booster successfully landed using cutting edge technology in which it returned to Earth, was slowed to essentially zero speed and was caught in an upright position by mechanical arms extending from its launch tower. This proves reusability of this massive booster rocket, saving vast amounts of money per launch over traditional rockets. Sadly, a June 2025 test flight of the Starship ended in a massive explosion due to a rupture in a high-pressure nitrogen tank on the vehicle's nose cone. Further enhancements and testing will occur on a steady basis.

Ultimately, SpaceX hopes to use its launch and landing sites as part of a global network of hypersonic travel hubs, taking up to 100 people and cargo from point to point around the Earth in minutes rather than hours. In 2020, the firm signed an agreement with the U.S. Pentagon to study the feasibility of this network. SpaceX has also worked with the U.S. Air Force and Army to demonstrate communications links. In addition, the company has worked deals with the military for launching national security satellites and improving weather forecasts.

Meanwhile, The Biden administration earmarked $1.5 billion in funds in 2022 for NASA's moon-lander program, which made an uncrewed launch in early 2025 a precursor for a manned mission on a SpaceX rocket (part of a $2.9 billion contract awarded from NASA in 2021). In May 2023, NASA announced the selection of Blue Origin to develop the Artemis V mission, which will once again carry humans to the moon. A crewed demonstration flight is expected as early as 2029.

Launch cost is measured by a cost-to-Low Earth Orbit (LEO) metric, or the price for one rocket to launch one kilogram of cargo into low Earth orbit. The Saturn V, a rocket used in the 1960s, had a cost-to-LEO of between $20,000 and $25,000, while the

Falcon 9's ratio is between $4,000 and $5,000. Consider also the size differential between rockets. SpaceX's Falcon 9 has a payload of about 20 tons, which has to be filled in order to fly. Rocket Lab's much smaller 330.7-pound payload can more easily be filled, making it much faster and easier to schedule a flight, especially if multiple satellite firms can schedule loads on one flight.

A startup called Relativity Space (www.relativityspace.com) is one of several up-and-coming firms working with 3D printing technology for reusable rockets. The company's printers (which are among the largest in the world), utilize 18-foot robotic arms with lasers capable of building a 7-foot by 14-foot fuel tank in a few days, and an engine in 10 to 12 days. The goal is to create a rocket's entire body in a single piece. On March 22, 2023, the firm's methane powered Terran 1 became the first 3D printed rocket to fly to space. The company is also working on the Terran R with capabilities of missions from Earth to the Moon, Mars and beyond.

Rocket Companies to Watch:

ArianeSpace, (www.arianespace.com)
Blue Origin (www.blueorigin.com)
Firefly Aerospace (www.fireflyspace.com)
Relativity Space (www.relativityspace.com)
Rocket Lab (www.rocketlabusa.com)
SpaceX (www.spacex.com)
Vector Launch (vector-launch.com)

In addition, the governments of India, Russia, China and Japan are already operating, or working to develop, launch industries.

SPOTLIGHT: SpinLaunch

Silicon Valley-based SpinLaunch (www.spinlaunch.com) is an aerospace startup that has raised $80 million in venture capital to build a catapult capable of hurling rockets into space. The proposed technology would power a rocket in a tight radius, moving faster and faster until the system releases the craft with enough force to break free of the Earth's gravity. Investors include Airbus Ventures, Alphabet's GV (formerly Google Ventures) and Kleiner Perkins Caufield & Byers. SpinLaunch had a prototype of a rocket built in its California factory by early 2022, but it will need to build a centrifuge to launch the rocket that will be roughly three times the size of its test facility in New Mexico.

---

19) Technology Discussion—Synthetic Biology

Scientists have followed up on the task of mapping genomes by attempting to directly alter them. This effort has gone past the point of injecting a single gene into a plant cell in order to provide a single trait, as in many agricultural biotech efforts. There are now several projects underway to create entirely new versions of life forms, such as bacteria, with genetic material inserted in the desired combination in the laboratory.

Synthetic biology can be defined as the design and construction of new entities, including enzymes and cells, or the reformatting of existing biological systems. This science capitalizes on previous advances in molecular biology and systems biology, by applying a focus on the design and construction of unique core components that can be integrated into larger systems in order to solve specific problems.

Engineers and scientists from MIT, Harvard and other institutions are working on a concept called BioBricks, which are strands of DNA with connectors at each end. BioBricks comprise a standard for interchangeable parts. They were developed to speed the building of biological systems within living cells. There is now a Registry of Standard Biological Parts.

Researchers at Stanford University and the J. Craig Venter Institute developed the first software simulation of an entire 525-gene organism, a single-cell human bacterium found in genital and respiratory tracts. The breakthrough is a major step towards the development of computerized labs that could conduct thousands of experiments at accelerated rates.

A notable company in synthetic biology is Precigen, Inc. (formerly Intrexon Corporation), a biotech firm based in Blacksburg, Virginia and founded in 1998. Scientists at Precigen have built a library of 70,000 standard DNA components that can be used to construct genes, thereby controlling gene expression. Uses for the technology include manufacturing proteins that might be used to create generic versions of patented biotech drugs, such as the growth hormone Epogen. The components also have potential in the agricultural and industrial sectors. Precigen itself describes synthetic biology as "the engineering of biological systems to enable rational, design-based control of cellular function for a specific purpose." The firm's RheoSwitch Therapeutic System (RTS) enables *in vivo* transcriptional regulation of protein expression under control of an orally administered small-molecule ligand. It also allows for the reprogramming of living cell systems. Other companies active in synthetic biology include Blue

Heron Biotech, ATUM (formerly DNA 2.0 and now owned by Eurofins Geonomics LLC) and Thermo Fisher Scientific (which offers the GeneArt Gene Synthesis system).

20) The Future of Transportation and Supply Chains: Massive Investments in Infrastructure & Mobility Services

Rapidly advancing technologies will relieve some of the pressure and potential congestion caused by ever-growing automobile, truck, ship and airplane traffic. These technologies can be grouped in three broad areas: 1) self-driving cars and trucks, including robotaxis, 2) improved traffic control in the skies and on the roads, and 3) improvements in freight handling and tracking technologies. Many of these advances will be based upon utilizing remote data sensors and the Internet of Things (IoT) to gather data 24/7, analyze that input and make rapid changes or recommendations in order to reduce congestion, improve conditions or project supply chain needs.

Self-driving (autonomous) automobiles and trucks will be of particular benefit on today's highly congested roads and highways. It is relatively easy for self-driving vehicles to understand and respond to road conditions on long stretches of divided highway, with prominent striping, little or no cross-traffic and fewer impediments like stop signs and sharp turns than found on city streets. These vehicles will be able to travel while closely spaced on highways, reducing the need for new highway construction. They will also travel together at consistent speeds, meaning less stop and go driving. Fully self-driving vehicles could eventually become so advanced that they can provide passenger transportation on crowded city streets, with safety records that will far exceed those of human drivers. The term Mobility Services is widely used to describe car-sharing strategies like Uber and other alternative personal transportation systems, including bicycle sharing.

Autonomous vehicles capable of driving themselves could eventually have very profound effects on automobile manufacturing, usage, sales and ownership patterns. At least in dense urban environments, the result is very likely to be a large proportion of individuals who opt to use shared vehicles rather than user-owned cars. Automobile makers are keenly aware that individual car ownership may decline over the long term. These firms are positioning themselves to build and distribute cars best suited for the sharing economy and mobility services market.

While self-driving technology may enable cars to be spaced very close together on roadways, incredibly tight, bumper-to-bumper traffic already exists on busy streets in many of the world's largest cities. Variable pricing ("congestion pricing") for toll roads, toll bridges and tunnels may be one answer, by charging vehicles, self-driving or not, much higher tolls during times of highest congestion. This strategy gives drivers economic incentive to delay trips until hours with lighter traffic. Cities including London, Singapore and Stockholm have been testing variable toll systems in this regard. London instituted congestion pricing in 2003 and initially reduced traffic congestion by as much as 30%.

Starting in January 2025, the Metropolitan Transportation Authority (MTA) in New York City began charging tolls to vehicles entering a Congestion Relief Zone, drawn in the city from 60th Street south to the Battery and known as the Central Business District (CBD). The MTA reports over 700,000 vehicles enter the CBD on a typical weekday. Passenger vehicles and passenger-type vehicles with commercial license plates are charged $9 during peak daylight periods (5 a.m. to 9 p.m. on weekdays) and $2.25 overnight. Trucks and buses are to be charged $14.40 during peak periods ($3.60 overnight). Motorcycles are to be charged one-half the passenger vehicle toll. Passengers taking taxis, green cabs or for-hire vehicles are charged $0.75 per trip and $1.50 per trip for high-volume for-hire services. Payments can be made via E-ZPass tags or Tolls by Mail, enforced by photographs of license plates taken at toll plazas. 80% of those payments go towards improvements to subways and buses (overseen by New York City Transit); 10% for Long Island Railroad; and 10% to Metro-North Railroad. The cities of London and Singapore operate similar strategies.

In addition to the traffic control advantages of self-driving car technology, other advanced technologies will improve traffic efficiency at airports and on congested city streets. Closely spaced traffic sensors in cities will alert ITS (intelligent transportation system) systems within cars and trucks in order to warn of congestion and suggest better routes. Advanced systems will also be able to control traffic lights for better demand-based timing.

At airports, highly advanced technologies will enable air traffic control to safely space aircraft closer together, reduce delays and route airlines so they can travel more directly to destinations with less circling and less fuel burned. Basic routing technologies such as these have already been applied to many railroad systems, greatly improving operating efficiencies.

Meanwhile, advancements in technology will improve the efficiencies of freight handling and tracking. RFID tags are already in widespread use, enabling freight systems to electronically receive vital details about freight containers, such as contents, shipper, date shipped and intended routing. Gathering big data from RFIDs and then analyzing that data with predictive software will enable more efficient warehousing and freight routing. An additional boost is now widely seen from warehouse robotics, efficiently moving the right pallet or parcel to the right place with greater speed and safety. Amazon.com, in its massive warehouses, is a world leader in this area. Automation is rapidly being adopted in ocean shipping ports as well.

While ride dispatch services like Uber and Lyft have dramatically changed the way that consumers get local transport on-demand, such technologies will soon revolutionize freight trucking as well, including the Uber Freight system. As the world speeds towards roughly 10 billion in global population by 2050, and the rapidly expanding global middle class buys more, consumes more, ships more and travels more, the opportunities for technology companies to fulfill these needs will spur innovation and investment on a very major scale worldwide.

Technologies for high-speed long-distance trains as well as light rail will continue to advance. Ultra-fast Maglev trains may eventually be funded in select markets.

While various engineering associations and global think tanks have long pointed out this dire need for engineering and construction, one massive problem is constantly in the way of progress: funding. To begin with, governments are poor planners and savers. While voters are faced with crowded, out-of-date airports, potholes in roads and leaks in water mains, governments rarely have amassed reserves for replacement and expansion of infrastructure. This means that funding most often comes through borrowing via the issuance of bonds.

Another avenue for construction, ownership and funding of infrastructure is through private companies, such as Australia's massive Macquarie Infrastructure Company, which owns and operates such facilities as airport hangars and solar power generation plants. Elsewhere, private company Heathrow Airport Holdings owns and operates London's Heathrow Airport, as well as the airports at Glasgow, Aberdeen and Southampton.

Such projects are often funded through public-private partnerships. Since governments have generally failed to reserve sufficient funds for future infrastructure replacement and maintenance, and there is some practical limit to how much of future needs can be filled by private companies, such partnerships may be increasingly vital to the transportation and utilities sectors.

21) HPTP Thermoplastics, Thermoset and Engineered Plastics Enable Advanced Products/Nanocomposites Offer the Ultimate in Advanced Materials

HPTPs: Engineered plastics are generating novel ways to reduce weight, reduce costs and increase performance of a wide variety of products. Sometimes referred to as HPTP for High Performance Thermoplastics, these advanced plastics generate performance enhancements that may include heat resistance, chemical resistance, compressive strength or stiffness. Such plastics can be very effective replacements for steel, titanium, ceramics or aluminum, particularly in applications like consumer electronics, aircraft, space vehicles or automobiles, where the reduction of overall product weight can be a vital concern. They have the added advantage of being corrosion resistant, which may eventually prove to be very important for new uses in ultradeep offshore oil wells.

Applications vary, and may include final plastics, or the use of thermoplastic resins as a compound in other materials. Today, high volume use of engineering thermoplastic (ETP) resins is found compounded into such basic plastic stocks as nylons, polyesters, polycarbonates (PC), polyphenylene ethers (PPE), polyacetals (POM) and polyphenylene sulfides (PPS).

Thermoplastics can also be compounded or combined with non-plastic materials to achieve even higher performance. Common composites of thermoplastics include high strength glass fibers. This can create a strong, lightweight material for uses such as aircraft seat frames or aircraft window bezels. Some composite manufacturers claim to achieve products that are 40% lighter than aluminum and much stiffer than steel or typical injection-molded plastics.

For example, Houston, Texas-based G.S.F. Plastics offers a wide variety of high-performance thermoplastic compounds. Its GSF 1200 and GSF 2200 materials are available unfilled, or blended with fiberglass, carbon, graphite, and PTFE (Polytetrafluoroethylene). Each additive is used to enhance the exceptional properties of GSF's proprietary PEEK brand of plastics in a particular application. Glass fibers add rigidity. Carbon fibers or graphite allow for improved wear resistance. Also, the combination of PTFE, graphite and glass fibers give finished parts added lubricity, rigidity and enhanced wear.

Nanocomposites: The compounding of thermoplastics with nanoparticles has a great deal of potential for the future. Significant research is now going into thermoplastic nanocomposites. These composites will eventually be engineered to achieve a wide variety of desired levels of strength, smoothness or weight reduction. Additional properties that may be enhanced in this manner include optical, electrical, thermal or magnetic capabilities. Products using nanocomposites may enjoy better dimensional stability and flame retardance. For uses in such areas as automobile bodies or interiors, they may offer scratch resistance and reduced warping.

The carbon-based nano material known as graphene offers some of the greatest potential in such composites. Graphene, compared to more common carbon nanotubes, offers incredible strength, and it is the world's greatest conductor of electricity. Using graphene in a nanocomposite with thermoplastic has potential use as advanced smart materials in applications ranging from down-hole oil well testing and monitoring to advanced engine components. A great deal of basic research has been achieved in this area, and many nanocomposite patents will result, including patents on composites outside of plastics. In 2010, a patent was granted to Princeton University for a functional graphene-rubber nanocomposite. It appears to offer superb mechanical strength and thermal stability, as well as electrical conductivity. In 2011, a patent was granted for a composite of graphene and an elastomer for use in automobile tires. Graphene nanocomposites have the potential to save a great deal of weight over more conventional composites, due to its high strength-to-weight ratio.

NanoMaster is a government-sanctioned EU research project aimed at creating advanced uses for graphene-plastic nanocomposites. Several major EU-based chemicals firms have been active in this consortium. According to the NanoMaster group, the addition of 5% graphene doubles the mechanical properties of TPO (thermoplastic polyolefin) and PP (polypropylene), and a tensile strength increase of 80% was seen when compounding 1% (by weight) of graphene with PMMA (polymethylmethacrylate, a clear acrylic than can be used as a replacement for glass).

Elsewhere, Ovation Polymers of Medina, Ohio, is manufacturing graphene-thermoplastic compounds at commercial scale. Its Extima brand of graphene polymer utilizes a dispersion technology that the company states maximizes the effect of nano-materials for injection molding or extrusion, while retaining the physical, structural and thermal properties of the compound.

Thermoset plastics are different from thermoplastics. Thermosets contain polymers that cross-link together during the curing process. This reduces the risk that products will melt in the presence of heat. This makes thermosets particularly useful in appliances or in electronics that produce excess heat. However, they cannot easily be recycled. Thermoplastics, on the other hand, can be cured without creating any bonding. This means that they can be remolded or recycled readily.

Engineered thermoplastics are primarily processed into molded parts and objects. Usually, the polymers are compounded for injection-molding applications with the addition of fibers (for reinforcement), mineral fillers, or any of a variety of additives such as impact modifiers, lubricants, thermal and ultraviolet (UV) stabilizers, pigments, and other materials. The effect of incorporating additives can be pronounced. For example, a general-purpose PC (polycarbonate) that exhibits a tensile strength of 69 million pascals (MPa), when modified or reinforced with 30% glass fiber, will show a tensile strength of 145 MPa.

22) Artificial Intelligence (AI), Deep Learning and Machine Learning Advance into Commercial Applications, Including Health Care and Robotics

While the ultimate capabilities of AI are being tested and debated, a very wide variety of industries have already put AI to work, and the technology companies that supply these industries continue to invest very heavily in advanced development. Today, AI has synergies with many sectors and with highly advanced technologies such as virtual reality, factory automation, robotics, self-driving cars, speech recognition and predictive analytics.

Among the most compelling opportunities for the development and use of artificial intelligence software may be in health care. Simply put, health care is one of the world's largest and fastest-growing industries, and virtually all of the government and private health initiatives that pay for health care are desperately seeking ways to improve patient care outcomes, cut billing fraud, create operating efficiencies and generally cut costs overall.

Google and U.S. hospital chain HCA Healthcare, Inc. signed a deal in May 2021 to develop algorithms that will analyze data from digital health care records for 32 million patients. The goal is to improve operating efficiency and promote better medical outcomes. This technology may boost patient monitoring and assist medical personnel in making treatment decisions. In 2023, these two companies announced a new collaboration that uses generative AI to improve workflows on such time-consuming tasks as the recording, transcribing and filing of office visit and patient care notes. (This use of GenAI is spreading rapidly throughout the health care industry, as it can save an attending physician hours of work daily.)

The total amount of digital health care data is expanding rapidly, driven by the move to electronic health records and the growing complexity of patient care. One of the first commercial applications of AI to medical equipment to be approved by the FDA was the Acumen Hypotension Prediction Index. This system utilizes machine learning to alert doctors in real time to the probability that a patient's blood pressure might plummet. It is applicable to patients in life-threatening situations, such as those that doctors are attempting to stabilize after surgery or a trauma. Likewise, AI has tremendous promise for enhancing the ability of ambulance and emergency room personnel to instantly diagnose patient conditions and suggest the best possible treatment—even before the patient arrives at the hospital.

In R&D, one of the most promising uses for AI lies in identifying and testing chemical compounds that have potential to become new drug therapies— possibly cutting years and millions of dollars from the process. All major drug companies, including Astra Zeneca, are investing in their AI capabilities in the lab.

Outside of health care, demand is growing for advanced data tools in factories in order to monitor operations and equipment performance. This will increase efficiency and speed as well as reduce waste. According to some analysts, global manufacturers are expected to increase spending on data management and analytics to as much as $20 billion by 2026, up from approximately $5 billion in 2020.

However, a significant portion of the investment in systems that gather and analyze vital, proprietary data needs to focus on cybersecurity. Data gathering via sensors, customer or patient records, webcams and monitors is an invitation for fraudsters to attempt to use such devices and records as ways to hack into

networks for ransomware or data theft. (A large number of major hospital systems have been hacked in recent years and held for ransom.) Connected devices at homes and government or commercial facilities (including everything from webcams to digital door locks to smart thermostats) are extremely susceptible to easy hacking, unless they are properly installed with strong passwords and protected by firewalls or similar authentication systems. These weaknesses have been exploited mercilessly by criminals.

23) Artificial Intelligence (AI) Enables Efficiencies and Accelerated Innovation in R&D

Artificial intelligence (AI) is playing a significant role in driving innovation and advancement across various industries, including research and development (R&D). Several notable trends have emerged in the application of AI in R&D, with companies harnessing its capabilities to enhance productivity, optimize processes and develop groundbreaking solutions. For example, AI-powered predictive maintenance systems enable companies to monitor equipment and predict potential failures or malfunctions. By analyzing real-time sensor data, AI algorithms can identify patterns and indicators of equipment degradation, allowing companies to proactively schedule maintenance and avoid costly downtime. For instance, airlines use AI algorithms to monitor jet engines, predicting maintenance needs and optimizing performance.

AI is also revolutionizing the pharmaceutical industry by expediting drug discovery and development processes. AI algorithms can analyze vast amounts of medical literature, genomic data and clinical trial results to identify potential drug targets and design novel compounds. Companies like Insilico Medicine (insilico.com) and BenevolentAI (www.benevolent.com) are leveraging AI to accelerate the identification and optimization of new drug candidates, improving the efficiency and success rate of the drug development pipeline.

In addition, AI systems are being employed to enhance quality control processes in manufacturing. By analyzing visual data from cameras or sensors, AI algorithms can detect defects, anomalies or deviations in real-time, ensuring product quality and reducing waste. For example, Foxconn (www.foxconn.com), a major electronics manufacturer and a subsidiary of Hon Hai Precision Industry Co., Ltd., utilizes computer vision systems powered by AI to inspect electronic components and identify defects quickly and accurately.

Primary Goals of Using AI in R&D:

1) Productivity: AI enables companies to streamline processes, automate repetitive tasks and enhance overall efficiency. By reducing manual effort, scientists and engineers can focus on more complex and creative aspects of their work, leading to increased productivity.

2) Innovation: AI can significantly speed up the innovation cycle by analyzing vast amounts of data, identifying patterns and generating insights that may be challenging for humans to discover. It enables researchers to explore more possibilities, leading to faster development of new products, processes or solutions.

3) Cost Reduction: AI can help optimize various R&D processes, leading to cost reduction and resource optimization. By identifying inefficiencies, AI algorithms can suggest improvements, optimize workflows and reduce waste.

AI has the potential to assist scientists and engineers in myriad ways. However, many observers believe that it will primarily augment their capabilities rather than replacing humans entirely. AI can handle repetitive and data-intensive tasks, enabling researchers to focus on higher-level decision-making, creative problem-solving and scientific discovery. Human knowledge, input and experience remain crucial in research and development, and AI serves as a powerful tool to augment human capabilities and accelerate progress.

24) The Future of Space Commercialization and Private Rocket Launch Services

1) Privatization and Market Growth

The World Economic Forum estimated the Space economy at $630 billion for 2023 and expected it to grow to $1.8 trillion by 2035. Many massive changes are going on within the space industry and space technology sector. The most important include:

a. Small Sats: Small satellites that can be launched dozens at one time by one rocket. They are relatively inexpensive to manufacture, lightweight and easy to launch, and they can have their software updated by ground stations. These are the satellites that are powering global internet access systems like SpaceX's Starlink.

b. Low Earth Orbit Satellites: Satellites that orbit the Earth at much lower altitudes than earlier generations of satellites. This makes them ideal for internet service and satphone communications, as there is a shorter time lag for signals to and from the Earth.

c. Reusable Rockets: Earlier generations of rockets were use-once only. Today's innovative rockets, pioneered by SpaceX, can be reused multiple times—saving massive amounts of time and money and dramatically lowering the cost to launch a satellite or space vehicle.

d. Private Rocket Launch Services: Launch services provided by private firms such as Elon Musk's SpaceX. Historically, space launches were strictly the provenance of government agencies. Today, private industries are providing these services with advanced rockets at much lower cost. In addition to SpaceX, such firms already providing services, or planning to, include Boeing, Blue Origin, Northrup Grumman Innovation Systems and Sierra Space.

2) Private (non-government) Space Industry Innovation, Research and Development (R&D)

New technologies and services will continue to broadly shape the space industry of the future. The major shift in space technologies is that they have rapidly become dominated by private industry—shifting away from government-managed research efforts, government laboratories, government management of space projects and launches, and government micro-management of space related contracts and the rules and obligations spelled out in those contracts. Much, if not most, of the funding is coming from private investors, including venture capital firms.

The space industry of the future is shaping up as one led by private companies, and many of those private companies have U.S. roots, whether they are rocket manufacturers, launch services or satellite communications services providers. This is a huge change, as space activities in the past all originated through, and were almost entirely funded by, government agencies such NASA.

SpaceX's reusable rockets are a massive game-changer, dramatically reducing the cost of making a space launch. SpaceX has not only been able to become a reliable, low-cost provider of launch services, it has also successfully manufactured rockets capable of carrying larger and larger payloads. At Plunkett Research, we expect the future of space commercialization to be dominated by SpaceX and a few other private firms. Meanwhile, SpaceX has already garnered a majority market share of space launches.

Another example of just how big this privatization trend is: A Houston, Texas-based firm, Intuitive Machines, recently landed the first American vehicle on the moon in over 50 years.

3) Russia Loses Rocket Manufacturing and Launch Business Contracts

The U.S. and EU for many years relied on Russia for the manufacture of certain powerful rocket engines and/or for rocket launch services. The war in Ukraine and geopolitical tensions in general have encouraged Western nations to rapidly develop replacement resources outside of Russia. This has been a rapid, massive boost to SpaceX. Major developed nations such as the U.S. will no longer be willing to rely on non-allied nations for space industry services.

4) Increased Militarization and Politization of Space

Space will increasingly be a hotbed of political tensions and militarization. China has set up a "Rocket Force" as a special branch of its armed forces. This does not bode well for global relations, and it will force the U.S. to focus on and invest in better space-based defense capabilities. Russia is said to have developed a rocket-based weapon that uses a nuclear blast to wipe out large numbers of satellites in one launch, potentially devastating a rival's satellite communications and Earth-observation capabilities in seconds.

India is increasingly active in space as well, while North Korea continues to increase the size and scope of its rocket-based weapons. There is extreme risk that hostile or competing military orbiting bases or moon-based facilities could be developed. Israel has very successfully demonstrated that anti-missile systems, such as its Iron Dome, can provide high levels of protection against incoming missiles. Watch for an acceleration of investment and development of such systems by major nations worldwide.

5) Manufacturing in Space (including Pharmaceuticals)

Innovative, privately launched orbiting labs, lunar landers and satellites can be put to good use by specialty manufacturers. The weightless aspect (and/or extremely low temperatures and near-perfect vacuum) of space creates unique opportunities to conduct advanced manufacturing in this environment, sometimes more effectively than on gravity-bound earth, and sometimes in ways that cannot be accomplished at all on Earth. For Example, Varda Space, well-funded by venture capital firms, seeks to manufacture complex, specialty pharmaceuticals in

space. UK-based Space Forge is a company that is exploring space manufacturing potential.

6) Mining in Space

Asteroids and moons often contain vast quantities of rare and/or precious ores. Researchers at the highly respected Colorado School of Mines are keen on this possibility. Mining in space could potentially reduce environmental impacts on Earth, while providing rare metals for solar panels and electric vehicles. NASA has identified 12,000+ asteroids that are relatively close to the Earth. (In addition to mining, some firms are interested in the potential to tap extremely powerful solar rays in outer space in order to generate electricity on Earth.) Thanks to the availability of venture capital, intense demand for rare metals, and advances in the private space launch and space vehicle sector, mining in space could easily become a significant reality over the long term. Firms investing in this sector include Karman+, TransAstra, AstroFOrrge, Origin Space and Asteroid Mining Corporation. Watch for continued funding of research and development in this sector. At the same time, watch for consolidation of the industry around a few very well-funded companies.

7) Space Tourism

Initial success in space tourism services will likely spawn further interest among affluent consumers and lead to advanced, private space flight vehicles and itineraries over the long term. While personal space flights are extremely expensive, a large number of consumers are clearly willing to pay the fees and take the risks. Leading companies operating or making plans in this sector include Virgin Galactic, SpaceX, Blue Origin and Boeing.

Chapter 2

ENGINEERING & RESEARCH INDUSTRY STATISTICS

Contents:

Engineering & Research Industry Statistics and Market Size Overview

	Quantity	Unit	Year	Source
Total R&D Spending, Worldwide, PPP[1]	2.7	Tril. US$	2024	PRE
Total U.S. R&D Spending	770.5	Bil. US$	2024	PRE
Total Proposed U.S. Federal R&D Budget	209.7	Bil. US$	2024	OMB
Proposed R&D, National defense	90.6	Bil. US$	2024	OMB
Proposed R&D, Health and Human Services	47.6	Bil. US$	2024	OMB
Proposed R&D, Energy	22.2	Bil. US$	2024	OMB
Proposed R&D, NASA	11.8	Bil. US$	2024	OMB
Proposed R&D, National Science Foundation	7.8	Bil. US$	2024	OMB
Proposed R&D, Agriculture	3.4	Bil. US$	2024	OMB
Proposed R&D, Veterans Affairs	1.8	Bil. US$	2024	OMB
Proposed R&D, Commerce	3.9	Bil. US$	2024	OMB
Proposed R&D, Transportation	1.5	Bil. US$	2024	OMB
Proposed R&D, Interior	1.3	Bil. US$	2024	OMB
Proposed R&D, Homeland Security	0.6	Bil. US$	2024	OMB
Proposed R&D, Smithsonian Institution	0.3	Bil. US$	2024	OMB
Proposed R&D, Environmental Protection Agency	0.6	Bil. US$	2024	OMB
Proposed R&D, Education	0.4	Bil. US$	2024	OMB
U.S. Employment in Architecture & Engineering Occupations	1.7	Million	Mar-25	BLS
U.S. Employment in Scientific R&D Occupations	937.0	Thous.	Mar-25	BLS
Proposed Budget for Nanotechnology R&D, U.S. Government	2.2	Bil. US$	2025	NNI
Biopharmaceutical R&D Spending, PhRMA Member Companies, U.S.	71.4	Bil. US$	2023	PhRMA
Biopharmaceutical R&D Spending, PhRMA Member Companies, Worldwide	96.0	Bil. US$	2023	PhRMA
U.S. Patents Issued	365,614		2024	USPTO
Utility[2]	321,020		2024	USPTO
Design	43,383		2024	USPTO
Plant	755		2024	USPTO
Reissue	456		2024	USPTO

BLS = U.S. Bureau of Labor Statistics   OMB = Office of Management and Budget

PRE = Plunkett Research estimate   NNI = U.S. National Nanotechnology Initiative

PhRMA = Pharmaceutical Research and Manufacturers of America   USPTO = U.S. Patent and Trademark Office

[1] PPP = Purchasing Power Parity Basis (an attempt to account for differences in local prices between one country and another, allowing the relative value of comparable goods or services to be compared across different economies).

[2] Includes chemical, electrical, and mechanical applications.

Quarterly Engineering & Research Industry Revenues, U.S.: 2024

(In Millions of US$)

Kind of Business	Revenue				Prelim. Total
Class of Customer	4Q[P]	3Q	2Q	1Q	
Engineering Services (NAICS 54133)	96,297	89,718	89,838	84,462	360,315
Government	29,590	27,546	28,417	25,972	111,525
Business	64,622	60,280	59,127	56,889	240,918
Household consumers & individual users	S	S	S	S	S
Scientific Research & Development Services (NAICS 5417)	78,441	78,157	76,559	74,331	307,488
Government	21,906	24,443	22,234	21,063	89,646
Business	52,689	50,101	50,583	49,461	202,834
Household consumers & individual users	3,846	S	S	S	3,846
Kind of Business	**Percent of Revenue**				**Prelim. Avg.**
Class of Customer	4Q[P]	3Q	2Q	1Q	
Engineering Services (NAICS 54133)	100.0	100.0	100.0	100.0	100.0
Government	30.7	30.7	31.6	30.7	31.0
Business	67.1	67.2	65.8	67.4	66.9
Household consumers & individual users	S	S	S	S	S
Scientific Research & Development Services (NAICS 5417)	100.0	100.0	100.0	100.0	100.0
Government	27.9	31.3	29.0	28.3	29.2
Household consumers & individual users	S	S	S	S	S

Note: Estimates have not been adjusted for seasonal variation or for price changes, and are based on data from the Quarterly Services Survey. Sector totals and subsector totals may include data for kinds of business not shown. Detail percents may not add to 100 percent due to rounding.

P = Preliminary estimate. S = Estimate has sampling variability higher than publication standard.

Source: U.S. Census Bureau

Plunkett Research, ® Ltd.

www.plunkettresearch.com

Engineering & Scientific Research & Development Services: Estimated Sources of Revenue, U.S.: 2018-2022

(In Millions of US$; Latest Year Available)

NAICS	Kind of business	2022	2021	2020	2019	2018
Revenue for Taxable Firms						
54133	Engineering services	305,233	274,912	259,888	264,653	249,085
54138	Testing laboratories	27,518	24,790	24,010	23,115	21,426
54171	R&D in the physical, engineering and life sciences	267,969	250,199	205,809	191,017	164,953
Revenue for Tax-Exempt Firms						
54171	R&D in the physical, engineering and life sciences	50,782	55,011	45,961	47,182	41,175
Sources of Revenue		**2022**	**2021**	**2020**		
Total Revenue: Engineering Services (NAICS 54133)		305,233	274,912	259,888		
Residential engineering projects (excludes apartment building projects)		14,235	11,613	9,739		
Commercial, public, and institutional engineering projects (includes apartment building projects)		34,147	34,690	33,923		
Industrial and manufacturing engineering projects		41,445	38,642	36,017		
Transportation infrastructure engineering projects		S	33,407	33,771		
Municipal utility engineering projects		13,320	11,105	13,688(s)		
Power generation and distribution engineering projects		19,921	18,368	14,874		
Telecommunications and broadcasting engineering projects		7,178	5,774	6,274		
Hazardous and industrial waste engineering projects		S	7,076	6,321		
Other engineering projects		S	37,900	32,628		
Construction services		24,805	26,458	25,092		
Engineering advisory and drafting services		16,658	11,981	13,592		
Surveying and mapping services		3,769(s)	3,072	3,359		
All other operating revenue		S	34,826	30,610		
Total Revenue: Scientific R&D Svcs. (NAICS 5417), Taxable Employer Firms		**221,105**	**198,558**	**162,795**		
Basic and applied research in natural and exact sciences, except biological sciences		34,653	26,468	19,160		
Basic and applied research in engineering and technology		50,082(s)	44,261(s)	36,250		
Basic and applied research in the biological and biomedical sciences		S	44,078	37,788		
Basic and applied research in the social sciences and humanities		2,693	2,054	2,034		
Production services for development		9,632	S	S		
Licensing of right to use intellectual property		S	S	9,251		
Original works of intellectual property		S	S	1,794(s)		
All other operating revenue		71,080	57,907	45,227		
Total Revenue: Scientific R&D Svcs. (NAICS 5417), Tax-Exempt Employer Firms		**56,669**	**60,752**	**50,564**		
Basic and applied research in natural and exact sciences, except biological sciences		6,525	6,940	7,965		
Basic and applied research in engineering and technology		20,266	19,330	15,926		
Basic and applied research in the biological and biomedical sciences		6,639	6,387	5,881		
Basic and applied research in the social sciences and humanities		3,034	2,609	2,201		
Production services for development		1,237	1,015	957		
Licensing of right to use intellectual property		456	607	300		
Original works of intellectual property		9	21	19		
All other operating revenue		4,069	3,607	3,162		
Contributions, gifts, and grants received		12,993	13,415	11,346		
Investment and property income		S	3,395	1,093		
All other non-operating revenue		1,834	3,426	1,714		

NA = Not Available.

S = Estimate does not meet publication standards because of high sampling variability (coefficient of variation is greater than 30%) or poor response quality (total quantity response rate is less than 50%).

Source: U.S. Census Bureau

Plunkett Research, ® Ltd.

www.plunkettresearch.com

Federal R&D Funding by Character of Work and Facilities and Equipment, U.S.: Fiscal Years 2023-2025

(In Millions of US$)

	2023 Actual	2024 Estimated[1]	2025 Proposed	Change, 2024-25	
				Dollar	Percent
Basic Research	47,023	46,105	47,684	1,579	3.0%
Applied Research	49,725	47,930	51,221	3,291	7.0%
Experimental Development	98,017	94,803	96,831	2,028	2.0%
Facilities and Equipment	5,190	5,726	6,213[2]	487	9.0%
Total	199,955	194,564	201,949[2]	7,385	4.0%

Note: Components may not sum to totals because of rounding. FY2025 data include both advance appropriations and new appropriations proposed by the President.

Source: CRS analysis of data from Executive Office of the President, OMB, "Research and Development," in Analytical Perspectives, Budget of the United States Government, Fiscal Year 2025, March 2024, https://www.whitehouse.gov/omb/budget/analytical-perspectives/.

Plunkett Research, ® Ltd.

www.plunkettresearch.com

Federal R&D Budget & Distribution by Agency, U.S.: Fiscal Years 2023-2025

(In Millions of US$)

Funding Category	2023 Actual	2024 Estimated[1]	2025 Proposed	% of Total R&D ('25)
Defense[2]	95,541	90,632	92,757	45.93%
Health and Human Services	48,393	47,591	51,364	25.43%
Energy	20,790	22,237	23,440	11.61%
NASA	11,691	11,797	11,715	5.80%
National Science Foundation	7,988	7,800	8,122	4.02%
Agriculture	3,380	3,379	3,283	1.63%
Commerce	5,141	3,930	3,926	1.94%
Veterans Affairs	1,684	1,799	1,709	0.85%
Transportation	1,411	1,462	1,513	0.75%
Interior	1,296	1,258	1,330	0.66%
Homeland Security	634	634	544	0.27%
Environmental Protection Agency	568	568	614	0.30%
Education	389	446	441	0.22%
Smithsonian Institution	347	347	390	0.19%
Other	702	684	601	0.30%
Artificial Intelligence (AI) Mandatory Proposal[3]	0	0	200	0.10%
Total	**199,955**	**194,564**	**201,949**	100.00%

Notes: This table shows funding levels for Departments or Independent agencies with major levels of R&D activities.
[1] The FY 2024 Estimate column applies the main 2025 Budget volume approach of using annualized appropriations provided by the 2024 Continuing Resolution.
[2] DOD's contribution to the overall Federal R&D budget includes DOD Research, Development, Test, and Evaluation Budget Activities 6.1 through 6.6 (Basic Research; Applied Research; Advanced Technology Development; Advanced Component Development and Prototypes; 4 System Development and Demonstration; and Management Support).
[3] According to the Analytical Perspectives report, the FY2025 budget request incudes "$200 million in mandatory R&D funding that will bolster efforts to harness the capacity of AI to accelerate scientific research across a variety of disciplines at multiple agencies."
Source: U.S. EOP, OMB, Analytical Perspectives, Budget of the United States Government, Fiscal Year 2024
Plunkett Research, ® Ltd.
www.plunkettresearch.com

Federal R&D & R&D Plant Funding for National Defense, U.S.: Fiscal Years 2023-2025

(In Millions of US$)

Funding Category and Agency	2023 Actual	2024 Estimated	2025 Proposed
Defense[1]	95,541	90,632	92,757
Military Construction	9,770	12,640	15,919
Defense Health Program	5,760	5,840	6,140

[1] DOD's contribution to the overall Federal R&D budget includes DOD Research, Development, Test, and Evaluation Budget Activities 6.1 through 6.6
(Basic Research; Applied Research; Advanced Technology Development; Advanced Component Development and Prototypes; System Development
and Demonstration; and Management Support)

Source: EOP, OMB, Analytical Perspectives, Budget of the United States Government, Fiscal Year 2025

Plunkett Research, ® Ltd.

www.plunkettresearch.com

Federal R&D & R&D Plant Funding for Health and Human Services, U.S.: Fiscal Years 2023-2025

(In Millions of US$; Latest Year Available)

	2023 Actual	2024 Prelim.	2025 Proposed	Change, 2023-25	
				Dollar	Percent
Total	47,753	47,188	49,588	2,400	5.1
National Cancer Institute	7,317	7,104	9,287	2183.0	30.7
National Institute of Allergy and Infectious Diseases	6,561	6,562	6,581	19.0	0.3
National Institute on Aging	4,412	4,407	4,425	18.0	0.4
National Heart, Lung, and Blood Institute	3,985	3,982	3,997	15.0	0.4
National Institute of Neurological Disorders and Stroke	2,809	2,674	2,833	159.0	5.9
National Institute of Diabetes and Digestive and Kidney Diseases	2,444	2,551	2,570	19.0	0.7
National Institute of Mental Health	2,341	2,198	2,548	350.0	15.9
Office of the Director	3,062	2,886	3,044	158.0	5.5
National Institute of General Medical Sciences	1,827	1,827	1,230	-597.0	-32.7
National Institute of Child Health and Human Development	1,747	1,749	1,766	17.0	1.0
National Institute on Drug Abuse	1,663	1,662	1,668	6.0	0.4
National Center for Advancing Translational Sciences	923	923	926	3.0	0.3
National Eye Institute	896	896	898	2.0	0.2
National Institute of Environmental Health Sciences	997	997	1,000	3.0	0.3
National Institute of Arthritis and Musculoskeletal and Skin Diseases	687	685	689	4.0	0.6
National Human Genome Research Institute	660	663	663	0.0	0.0
National Institute on Alcohol Abuse and Alcoholism	596	595	598	3.0	0.5
National Institute on Deafness and Other Communication Disorders	534	534	535	1.0	0.2
National Institute of Dental and Craniofacial Research	520	520	521	1.0	0.2
National Library of Medicine	495	497	526	29.0	5.8
National Institute on Minority Health and Health Disparities	525	524	527	3.0	0.6
National Institute of Biomedical Imaging and Bioengineering	440	440	442	2.0	0.5
National Institute of Nursing Research	197	197	198	1.0	0.5
National Center for Complementary and Integrative Health	170	170	171	1.0	0.6
John E. Fogarty International Center	95	95	95	0.0	0.0
Advanced Research Projects Agency-Health[b]	1,500	1,500	1,500	0	0.0
Buildings and facilities	350	350	350	0.0	0.0

Notes: Detail may not add to total because of rounding. Percent change is calculated on unrounded data. Institute totals exclude non-R&D components of institute budgets. NA - Not Available/Applicable

Source: EOP, OMB, Analytical Perspectives, Budget of the United States Government, Fiscal Year 2025

Plunkett Research, ® Ltd.

www.plunkettresearch.com

Federal R&D & R&D Plant Funding for Space Flight, Research & Supporting Activities, U.S.: Fiscal Years 2023-2025

(In Millions of US$; Latest Year Available)

	2023 Actual	2024 Prelim.[1]	2025 Proposed
National Aeronautics and Space Administration	25,384	25,384	25,384
Science	7,792	7,795	7,566
Aeronautics	935	935	966
STEM Engagement	144	144	144
Safety, Security and Mission Services	3,137	3,130	3,044
Deep Space Exploration Systems	7,448	7,469	7,618
Construction and Environmental Compliance and Restoration	422	414	424
Space Technology	1,193	1,200	1,182

Notes: Detail may not add to total because of rounding.

[1]The FY 2024 Estimate column applies the main FY 2023 President's Budget volume approach of using FY 2024 enacted appropriations

Source: EOP, OMB, Analytical Perspectives, Budget of the United States Government, Fiscal Year 2025

Plunkett Research, ® Ltd.

www.plunkettresearch.com

NASA Budget Appropriations & Projections: 2023-2029

(In Millions of US$)

Budget Authority	FY 2023	FY 2024	FY 2025	FY 2026	FY 2027	FY 2028	FY 2029
NASA Total	**25,383.7**	**25,383.7**	**25,383.7**	**25,891.3**	**26,409.1**	**26,937.3**	**27,476.1**
Deep Space Exploration Systems	7,447.6	7,468.9	7,618.2	7,803.7	7,959.8	8,119.0	8,281.4
Space Operations	4,266.7	4,250.0	4,389.7	4,497.6	4,587.6	4,679.4	4,773.0
International Space Station	1,286.2	NA	1,269.6	1,267.8	1,262.8	1,259.4	1,259.4
Space Transportation	1,759.6	NA	1,862.1	1,876.2	1,840.9	1,895.7	1,804.1
Space and Flight Support(SFS)	983.4	NA	1,088.4	1,051.3	1,048.7	1,059.0	1,080.2
Commercial LEO Development	224.3	NA	169.6	302.3	435.2	465.2	629.3
Science	7,791.5	7,795.0	7,565.7	7,717.0	7,871.3	8,028.7	8,189.3
Earth Science	2,175.0	NA	2,378.7	2,396.3	2,446.1	2,489.7	2,543.4
Planetary Science	3,216.5	NA	2,731.5	2,850.5	2,911.6	2,976.8	3,042.5
Astrophysics	1,510.0	NA	1,578.1	1,587.0	1,613.6	1,647.1	1,673.4
Heliophysics	805.0	NA	786.7	791.9	807.0	820.3	833.4
Biological and Physical Sciences	85.0	NA	90.8	91.3	93.0	94.8	96.6
Aeronautics	935.0	935.0	965.8	985.1	1,004.8	1,024.9	1,045.4
STEM Engagement	143.5	143.5	143.5	146.4	149.3	152.3	155.3
Safety, Security, and Mission Services	3,136.5	3,129.5	3,044.4	3,105.3	3,167.4	3,230.7	3,295.3
Mission Services & Capabilities	2,067.4	NA	2,058.1	2,099.2	2,141.3	2,184.1	2,227.6
Engineering, Safety, & Operations	1,069.1	NA	986.3	1,006.1	1,026.1	1,046.6	1,067.7
Construction and Environmental Compliance and Restoration	422.4	414.3	424.1	379.3	386.9	394.6	402.5
Construction of Facilities	346.2	NA	344.7	298.3	304.3	310.4	316.6
Environmental Compliance and Restoration	76.2	NA	79.4	81.0	82.6	84.2	85.9
Inspector General	47.6	47.6	50.5	51.5	52.5	53.6	54.7

Source: U.S. National Aeronautics & Space Administration (NASA)

Plunkett Research, ® Ltd.

www.plunkettresearch.com

Federal R&D & R&D Funding for Basic Research, U.S.:
Fiscal Years 2023-2025

(In Millions of US$; Latest Year Available)

Funding Category and Agency	2023 Actual	2024 Estimate[1]	2025 Proposed	Change, 2024-25	
				Dollar	Percent
All functions conducting R&D	**$47,021**	**$46,103**	**$47,568**	**$1,465**	**$3.2**
National defense	$3,013	$2,679	$2,666	-$13	-$0.5
Health	$23,097	$22,748	$23,586	$838	$3.7
Space flight, research, and supporting activities	$5,115	$5,417	$5,302	-$115	-$2.1
General science and basic research	$12,875	$12,275	$12,994	$719	$5.9
Energy	$24	$23	$23	$0	$0.0
Natural resources and environment	$222	$220	$216	-$4	-$1.8
Agriculture	$1,271	$1,265	$1,272	$7	$0.6
Transportation	$0	$0	$0	$0	-
Veterans benefits and services	$683	$756	$718	-$38	-$5.0
Commerce and housing credit	$316	$316	$355	$39	$12.3
Education, training, employment, and social services	$343	$342	$379	$37	$10.8
Administration of justice	$60	$60	$55	-$5	-$8.3
International affairs	$2	$2	$2	$0	$0.0

Notes: This table shows funding levels for Departments or Independent Agencies with more than $200 million in R&D activities in 2025. Detail may not add to total because of rounding.

[1]The preliminary data available from the agencies for FY 2024 at the time of this report reflect the annualized continuing resolution funding levels that existed through early-March 2024 and not those of the finalized appropriations enacted shortly thereafter.

Source: The White House

Plunkett Research, ® Ltd.

www.plunkettresearch.com

Federal R&D & R&D Plant Funding for Agriculture, U.S.:
Fiscal Years 2023-2025

(In Millions of US$; Latest Year Available)

Funding Category and Agency	2023 Actual	2024 Estimate[1]	2025 Proposed	Change, 2024-25	
				Dollar	Percent
Agricultural Research Service	1,895	1,893	1,801	-92	-4.86%
Animal & Plant Health Inspection Service	48	49	49	0	0.00%
Economic Research Service	93	93	98	5	5.38%
National Agricultural Statistics Service	11	11	11	0	0.00%
National Institute of Food and Agriculture	925	921	913	-8	-0.87%

Notes: This table shows funding levels for Departments or Independent Agencies with major levels of funding. Detail may not add to total because of rounding.

[1] The preliminary data available from the agencies for FY 2024 at the time of this report reflect the annualized continuing resolution funding levels that existed through early-March 2024 and not those of the finalized appropriations enacted shortly thereafter.

Source: National Center for Science and Engineering Statistics, Survey of Federal Funds for Research and Development

Plunkett Research, ® Ltd.

www.plunkettresearch.com

Federal R&D & R&D Plant Funding for Transportation, U.S.:
Fiscal Years 2023-2025

(In Millions of US$; Latest Year Available)

Funding Category & Agency	2023 Actual	2024 Prelim.[1]	2025 Proposed	Change, 2024-25	
				Dollar	Percent
Total	1,689	1,686	1,964	278	16.5
Air transportation	1,151	1,141	1,304	163	14.3
Federal Aviation Administration (DOT)	533	479	545	66	13.8
National Aeronautics and Space Administration (Aeronautics research)	595	632	723	91	14.4
Transportation Security Administration (DHS)	23	30	36	6	20.0
Ground transportation (DOT)	522	509	614	105	20.6
Federal Highway Administration	380	376	420	44	11.7
Federal Motor Carrier Safety Administration	9	9	9	0	0.0
Federal Railroad Administration	45	42	54	12	28.6
Federal Transit Administration	33	30	60	30	100.0
National Highway Traffic Safety Administration	55	52	71	19	36.5
Water transportation	0	11	8	-3	-27.3
Coast Guard (DHS)	0	11	8	-3	-27.3
Other transportation (DOT)[3]	16	25	38	13	52.0

DHS = Department of Homeland Security; DOT = Department of Transportation.
Note: Detail may not add to total because of rounding. Percent change is calculated on unrounded data.

[1]The preliminary data available from the agencies for FY 2024 at the time of this report reflect the annualized continuing resolution funding levels that existed through early-March 2024 and not those of the finalized appropriations enacted shortly thereafter.

Source: Agencies' submissions to the Office of Management and Budget (OMB) per MAX Schedule C, agencies' budget justification documents, supplemental data obtained from agencies' budget offices, and Executive Office of the President, OMB, Budget of the United States Government, Fiscal Year 2025.

Plunkett Research,® Ltd.

www.plunkettresearch.com

Federal R&D & R&D Plant Funding for Energy, U.S.: Fiscal Years 2023-2025

(In Millions of US$; Latest Year Available)

	2023 Actual	2024 Estimated[1]	2025 proposed
Department of Energy	6,259	8,483	8,583
Energy efficiency and renewable energy	2,012	4,354	4,354
Fossil energy and carbon management	1,846	1,862	1,846
Nuclear energy	1,442	1,308	1,454
Electricity delivery	167	167	190
Cybersecurity, Energy Security, and Emergency Response	103	103	108
Advanced Research Projects Agency-Energy (ARPA-E)	470	470	450
Bonneville Power Administration Fund	2	2	2
Nuclear Regulatory Commission	90	71	59
Tennessee Valley Authority	111	121	98

*Energy Total also includes DOE Science R&D and National Security sector totals. Excluding Bonneville Power Administration Fund, Nuclear Regulatory Commission, and Tennessee Valley Authority.

[1] The preliminary data available from the agencies for FY 2024 at the time of this report reflect the annualized continuing resolution funding levels that existed through early-March 2024 and not those of the finalized appropriations enacted shortly thereafter.

Source: EOP, OMB, Analytical Perspectives, Budget of the United States Government

Plunkett Research, Ltd.

www.plunkettresearch.com

U.S. Department of Energy
Funding for Science & Energy Programs: 2023-2025

(In Thousands of US$)

Area of Scientific Research	FY 2023 Enacted	FY 2024 Annualized CR	FY 2025 Request
Energy Efficiency and Renewable Energy	3,460,000	3,460,000	3,118,000
Sustainable transportation	905,000	905,000	951,790
Vehicle technologies	455,000	455,000	501,790
Bioenergy technologies	280,000	280,000	280,000
Hydrogen and fuel cell technologies	170,000	170,000	170,000
Renewable power	747,000	747,000	833,191
Solar energy technologies	318,000	318,000	318,000
Wind energy technologies	132,000	132,000	199,000
Water power technologies	179,000	179,000	160,000
Geothermal technologies	118,000	118,000	156,191
Electricity	350,000	350,000	293,000
Total Grid Controls and Communications	135,000	135,000	134,000
Transmission Reliability and Resilience	34,000	34,000	39,000
Energy Delivery Grid Operations Technology	31,000	31,000	31,000
Resilient Distribution Systems	55,000	55,000	49,000
Cyber Resilient and Secure Utility Communications Networks (SecureNet)	15,000	15,000	15,000
Total, Grid Hardware, Components, and Systems	132,500	132,500	139,300
Energy Storage	95,000	95,000	94,800
Transformer Resilience and Advanced Components	27,500	27,500	32,500
Applied Grid Transformation Solutions	10,000	10,000	12,000
Nuclear Energy	1,623,000	1,623,000	1,440,660
Fossil Energy and Carbon Management	890,000	890,000	900,000
Uranium Enrichment Decontamination and Decommissioning (UED&D)	879,052	879,052	854,182
Energy Information Administration	135,000	135,000	141,653
Non-Defense Environmental Cleanup	358,583	358,583	314,636
Science	8,100,000	8,100,000	8,583,000
Advanced Research Projects Agency - Energy.	470,000	470,000	450,000
Nuclear Waste Fund Oversight	10,205	10,205	12,040
Departmental Administration	283,000	283,000	334,671
Indian Energy Policy and Programs	75,000	75,000	95,000
Inspector General	86,000	86,000	149,000

Source: U.S. Department of Energy, Office of Science
Plunkett Research, ® Ltd.
www.plunkettresearch.com

U.S. National Nanotechnology Initiative (NNI) Budget:
Fiscal Years 2023-2025

(In Millions of US$)

Government Agency	FY 2023 Actual	FY 2024 Estimated *	FY 2025 Proposed
Consumer Product Safety Commission (CPSC)	0.4	0.1	0.1
DHS Countering Weapons of Mass Destruction Office (CWMD)	0.4	0.5	0.0
Department of Commerce, National Institute of Standards and Technology (DOC/NIST)	53.3	53.2	53.6
Department of Defense (DOD)	269.7	354.7	335.6
Department of Energy (DOE)**	441.2	442.7	457.8
Department of Justice, National Institute of Justice (DOJ/NIJ)	2.2	1.8	1.3
Department of Transportation, Federal Highway Administration (DOT/FHWA)	0.6	0.3	0.3
Environmental Protection Agency (EPA)	4.2	4.3	2.8
Health and Human Services (HHS)	876.4	866.2	926.3
Biomedical Advanced Research and Development Authority (BARDA)	2.1	2.1	2.1
Food and Drug Administration (FDA)	10.4	11.9	10.6
National Institutes of Health (NIH)	854.7	842.6	903.9
National Institute for Occupational Safety and Health (NIOSH)	9.2	9.6	9.6
National Aeronautics & Space Administration (NASA)	14.3	11.5	5.3
National Science Foundation (NSF)	477.7	362.6	430.8
U.S. Department of Agriculture (USDA)	21.4	20.6	21.6
Agricultural Research Services (ARS)	5.0	5.0	5.0
Forest Services (FS)	4.4	4.6	4.6
National Institute of Food and Agriculture (NIFA)	12.0	11.0	12.0
Total Nanotechnology	**2,161.7**	**2,118.3**	**2,235.2**

Notes: Totals may not add, due to rounding.

* 2024 numbers are based on appropriated levels.

** Funding levels for DOE include the combined budgets of the Office of Science, the Office of Energy Efficiency and Renewable Energy, the Office of Fossil Energy, and the Office of Nuclear Energy.

*** Funding levels for DOE include the combined budgets of the Office of Science, Office of Energy Efficiency and Renewable Energy, Office of Nuclear Energy, Office of Fossil Energy and Carbon Management, and the Advanced Research Projects Agency-Energy.

Source: U.S. National Nanotechnology Initiative (NNI)

Plunkett Research, ® Ltd.

www.plunkettresearch.com

NSF Budget by Appropriation (Dollars in Millions), Fiscal Years: 2023-2025

(In Millions of US$)

Account	FY 2023	FY 2024	FY 2025	Change over FY 2023 Enacted	
	Actual	Request	Request	Amount	Percent
Research and Related Activities	$7,631.02	$9,017.90	$8,045.32	$414.30	0.054
STEM Education	$1,229.28	$1,496.18	$1,300.00	$70.72	0.058
Major Research Equipment and Facilities Construction	$187.23	$304.67	$300.00	$112.77	0.602
Agency Operations and Award Management	$463.00	$503.87	$504.00	$41.00	0.089
Office of Inspector General	$23.39	$26.81	$28.46	$5.07	0.217
National Science Board	$5.09	$5.25	$5.22	$0.13	0.026
Total (NSF)	**$9,539.01**	**$11,354.68**	**$10,183.00**	**$643.99**	**0.068**

Note: Totals may not add due to rounding. * indicates <$500,000.

Source: U.S. National Science Foundation

Plunkett Research, ® Ltd.

www.plunkettresearch.com

Research Funding for Biological Sciences, U.S. National Science Foundation: Fiscal Years 2023-2025

(In Millions of US$)

Biological Sciences:	FY 2023	FY 2024	FY 2025	Change over 2023 Base Total	
Subactivity Area	**Actual[1]**	**Request**	**Request**	**Amount**	**Percent**
Biological Infrastructure (DBI)	$205.47	$157.02	$230.37	$24.90	12.10%
Environmental Biology (DEB)	167.35	214.96	162.87	-4.48	-2.70%
Emerging Frontiers (EF)	132.64	188.55	140.48	7.84	5.90%
Integrative Organismal Systems (IOS)	194.58	227.92	187.99	-6.59	-3.40%
Molecular & Cellular Biosciences (MCB)	144.87	183.96	141.22	-3.65	-2.50%
Total Biological Sciences Activity	**$844.91**	**$972.41**	**$862.93**	**$18.02**	**2.10%**

Note: Totals may not add due to rounding.

[1] Excludes $43.53 million in American Rescue Plan supplemental funding.

Source: U.S. National Science Foundation

Plunkett Research, ® Ltd.

www.plunkettresearch.com

Research Funding for Engineering, U.S. National Science Foundation: Fiscal Years 2023-2025

(In Millions of US$)

Engineering: Subactivity Area	FY 2023 Actual [1]	FY 2024 Request	FY 2025 Request	Change over FY 2023 Actual	
				Amount	Percent
Chemical, Bioengineering, Environmental & Transport Systems (CBET)	200.50	214.99	201.84	1.34	0.7%
Civil, Mechanical & Manufacturing Innovation (CMMI)	235.84	252.87	237.15	1.31	0.6%
Electrical, Communications & Cyber Systems (ECCS)	121.32	130.09	121.99	0.67	0.6%
Engineering Education & Centers (EEC)	132.12	156.23	132.85	0.73	0.6%
Emerging Frontiers and Multidisciplinary Activities (EFMA)	107.79	215.82	114.31	6.52	6.0%
Total, Engineering Activity	**797.57**	**970.00**	**808.14**	**10.57**	**1.3%**

Note: Totals may not add due to rounding.

NA - No data is available

[1]For comparability with FY 2025, the FY 2023 levels do not include this organization's share of Mission Support Services that were funded through the R&RA and EDU directorates and offices.

Source: U.S. National Science Foundation

Plunkett Research, ® Ltd.

www.plunkettresearch.com

Top 30 U.S. Patent Recipient Organizations: 2024

(By Utility Patents Granted; Latest Year Available)

Rank	Patents	Organization
1	9,304	Samsung Electronics Co., Ltd.
2	5,156	Lg Corporation
3	4,010	TSMC
4	3,489	Qualcomm
5	3,285	Huawei Technologies Co., Ltd.
6	3,115	Apple Inc.
7	2,774	IBM
8	2,698	Alphabet Inc.
9	2,654	Canon K.K.
10	2,428	Toyota Jidosha K.K.
11	2,424	Sony Corporation
12	2,047	Rtx Corporation
13	2,018	Intel Corporation
14	1,993	Boe Technology Group Co., Ltd
15	1,888	Dell Technologies
16	1,869	Micron Technology Inc.
17	1,836	Hyundai Motor Company
18	1,781	Microsoft Corporation
19	1,769	Panasonic Corporation
20	1,688	Amazon.Com, Inc
21	1,590	Johnson & Johnson
22	1,530	Telefonaktiebolaget Lm Ericsson
23	1,425	Hitachi, Ltd.
24	1,347	Nippon Telegraph & Telephone
25	1,281	Fujifilm Holdings Corp
26	1,187	Nec Corporation
27	1,182	Medtronic Plc
28	1,165	Sk Group
29	1,139	Murata Manufacturing Co., Ltd
30	1,132	Capital One Financia

Source: Intellectual Property Owners Association (IPO)

Plunkett Research, ® Ltd.

www.plunkettresearch.com

The U.S. Drug Discovery & Approval Process

		Investigational New Drug (IND) Application Submitted ↓		New Drug Application FDA Review → → →		FDA Approves 1 New Drug ↓	
Years							
2	4	6	8	10	12	14	16

Drug Discovery 5,000-10,000 Compounds → Pre-Clinical Trials Begin 250 Compounds

Phase I Trials Begin 20-100 Volunteers

Phase II Trials Begin 100-500 Volunteers 5 Compounds → Phase III Trials Begin 1,000-5,000 Volunteers

Phase IV Large Scale Manufacturing Post-Marketing Surveillance

Note: The actual length of the development process varies. On average, it takes 10-15 years and an estimated $2.6 billion to create a successful new medicine (in 2013 dollars). Less than 12% of the candidate medicines that make it into phase I clinical trials will be approved by the FDA.

Source: Pharmaceutical Research and Manufacturers Association (PhRMA)

Employment in Engineering Occupations
by Business Type, U.S.: 2021 - 2025

NAICS[1]	Industry Sector	2021	2022	2023	2024	Mar-25
Number of Employed Workers *(Annual Estimates in Thousands of Employed Workers)*						
5413	Architectural and engineering services	1,536.5	1,603.6	1,660.2	1,703.5	1,716.0
54133,4	Engineering and drafting services	1,044.4	1,093.1	1,145.0	1,189.3	1,204.0
54138	Testing laboratories	175.6	180.0	178.8	179.5	178.6
5417	Scientific research and development services	826.9	892.9	929.0	936.8	937.0
54171	Physical, engineering and life sciences R&D	764.7	827.9	861.2	866.7	865.7
541713	Research and development in nanotechnology	23.8	24.7	26.0	23.7	21.9
541714	Research and development in biotechnology, except nanobiotechnology	252.0	283.0	292.3	294.9	299.9
541715	Research and development in the physical, engineering, and life sciences, except nanotechnology and biotechnology	488.9	520.2	542.8	548.2	543.9

Engineering Employment & Wage Estimates: May 2024 *(Wage & Salary in US$; Latest Year Available)*	Employ-ment[2]	Median Hourly Wage	Mean Hourly Wage	Mean Annual Salary[3]	Mean Wage RSE[4] (%)
Aerospace Engineers	68,440	$64.82	$67.88	$141,180	2.3%
Agricultural Engineers	1,680	$40.69	$40.50	$84,240	33.6%
Bioengineers and Biomedical Engineers	21,860	$51.42	$55.30	$115,020	4.%
Chemical Engineers	20,330	$58.59	$61.75	$128,430	3.7%
Civil Engineers	355,410	$47.88	$51.47	$107,050	1.1%
Computer Hardware Engineers	75,710	$74.53	$75.37	$156,770	2.8%
Electrical Engineers	188,790	$53.80	$58.16	$120,980	1.4%
Electronics Engineers, Except Computer	93,940	$61.34	$63.70	$132,500	1.7%
Environmental Engineers	37,950	$50.08	$53.16	$110,570	3.2%
Health and Safety Engineers, Except Mining Safety Engineers and Inspectors	23,220	$52.72	$54.70	$113,770	3.5%
Industrial Engineers	350,230	$48.63	$51.87	$107,900	0.6%
Marine Engineers and Naval Architects	8,440	$50.80	$56.10	$116,680	5.2%
Materials Engineers	22,770	$52.07	$55.95	$116,380	2.4%
Mechanical Engineers	286,760	$49.19	$52.92	$110,080	1.%
Mining and Geological Engineers, Including Mining Safety Engineers	6,770	$48.57	$52.37	$108,940	7.%
Nuclear Engineers	14,740	$61.31	$64.89	$134,980	3.7%
Petroleum Engineers	18,970	$67.92	$73.83	$153,560	5.8%
Engineers, All Other	150,750	$56.61	$58.52	$121,720	1.2%
Architectural and Civil Drafters	109,550	$30.90	$33.11	$68,860	2.%
Electrical and Electronics Drafters	20,020	$35.44	$37.48	$77,960	3.6%
Mechanical Drafters	39,900	$32.94	$35.59	$74,040	3.4%
Drafters, All Other	16,010	$29.81	$31.99	$66,530	3.6%
Aerospace Engineering and Operations Technicians	9,060	$38.38	$41.50	$86,330	4.3%
Civil Engineering Technologists and Technicians	62,130	$30.86	$32.91	$68,450	2.2%
Electro-Mechanical and Mechatronic Technologists and Technicians	14,680	$34.02	$36.40	$75,710	3.%
Environmental Engineering Technologists and Technicians	12,500	$28.31	$30.32	$63,070	6.4%
Industrial Engineering Technologists and Technicians	73,410	$31.15	$33.55	$69,780	1.1%
Mechanical Engineering Technologists and Technicians	37,450	$33.04	$34.83	$72,450	2.4%
Engineering Technologists and Technicians, Except Drafters	64,410	$37.21	$38.34	$79,740	2.3%
Surveying and Mapping Technicians	56,720	$24.97	$27.35	$56,890	2.6%

[1] For a full description of the NAICS codes used in this table, see www.census.gov/eos/www/naics/.
[2] Estimates for detailed occupations do not sum to the totals because the totals include occupations not shown separately. Estimates do not include self-employed workers.
[3] Annual wages have been calculated by multiplying the hourly mean wage by a "year-round, full-time" hours figure of 2,080 hours; for those occupations where there is not an hourly mean wage published, the annual wage has been directly calculated from the reported survey data.
[4] The relative standard error (RSE) is a measure of the reliability of a survey statistic. The smaller the relative standard error, the more precise the estimate.
P = Preliminary Estimate.
Source: U.S. Bureau of Labor Statistics
Plunkett Research, ® Ltd.
www.plunkettresearch.com

Employment in Life & Physical Science Occupations by Business Type, U.S.: May 2024

(Wage & Salary in US$; Latest Year Available)

	Employ-ment[1]	Median Hourly Wage	Mean Hourly Wage	Mean Annual Salary[2]	Mean Wage RSE[3] (%)
Life, Physical, and Social Science Occupations	**1,446,770**	**$37.97**	**$43.12**	**$89,690**	**0.4**
Life Scientists	374,670	$43.51	$49.03	$101,980	0.8
Agricultural and Food Scientists	33,440	$37.87	$42.59	$88,590	3.5
Animal Scientists	2,470	$38.04	$50.47	$104,970	10.2
Food Scientists and Technologists	14,370	$41.02	$44.32	$92,190	5.9
Soil and Plant Scientists	16,600	$34.33	$39.92	$83,040	4.9
Biological Scientists	130,910	$44.88	$48.43	$100,730	1.5
Biochemists and Biophysicists	34,520	$49.83	$55.56	$115,570	3.6
Microbiologists	19,760	$41.98	$45.77	$95,200	4.0
Zoologists and Wildlife Biologists	16,920	$35.03	$37.46	$77,920	2.3
Biological Scientists, All Other	59,710	$44.87	$48.29	$100,440	1.9
Conservation Scientists	25,590	$32.67	$35.73	$74,310	2.2
Foresters	9,650	$33.97	$35.90	$74,670	4.3
Medical Scientists	167,760	$47.97	$53.57	$111,430	1.3
Epidemiologists	11,460	$40.38	$45.27	$94,160	2.6
Medical Scientists, Except Epidemiologists	156,300	$48.36	$54.18	$112,690	1.3
Life Scientists, All Other	7,320	$42.21	$49.01	$101,940	5.2
Physical Scientists	259,000	$44.59	$50.03	$104,070	1.1
Astronomers	1,560	$63.54	$64.63	$134,430	8.4
Physicists	21,340	$79.95	$79.81	$166,000	2.2
Atmospheric and Space Scientists	8,780	$46.85	$49.99	$103,980	2.7
Chemists	83,250	$40.46	$46.13	$95,940	2.5
Materials Scientists	8,330	$50.08	$53.56	$111,410	5.9
Environmental Scientists and Specialists, Including Health	84,930	$38.49	$42.62	$88,640	1.5
Geoscientists, Except Hydrologists and Geographers	22,510	$47.71	$53.52	$111,310	3.6
Hydrologists	5,720	$44.26	$47.18	$98,130	3.9
Physical Scientists, All Other	22,580	$56.71	$59.17	$123,070	2.4
Life, Physical, and Social Science Technicians	373,260	$26.83	$29.42	$61,200	0.8
Agricultural and Food Science Technicians	28,550	$23.31	$25.01	$52,030	3.0
Biological Technicians	76,190	$25.00	$27.89	$58,020	1.7
Chemical Technicians	55,640	$27.78	$29.47	$61,300	2.1
Environmental Science and Protection Technicians, Including Health	39,390	$23.79	$27.29	$56,770	2.5
Geological Technicians, Except Hydrologic Technicians	9,710	$23.27	$27.99	$58,220	8.6
Hydrologic Technicians	2,940	$28.16	$30.97	$64,410	7.9
Nuclear Technicians	5,990	$50.11	$48.43	$100,730	2.6
Forest and Conservation Technicians	31,080	$26.11	$27.24	$56,660	1.3
Miscellaneous Life, Physical, and Social Science Technicians	90,840	$29.60	$32.17	$66,910	1.5
Forensic Science Technicians	19,450	$32.42	$36.18	$75,260	1.8
Life, Physical, and Social Science Technicians, All Other	71,400	$28.91	$31.08	$64,640	1.9

[1] Estimates for detailed occupations do not sum to the totals because the totals include occupations not shown separately. Estimates do not include self-employed workers.

[2] Annual wages have been calculated by multiplying the hourly mean wage by a "year-round, full-time" hours figure of 2,080 hours; for those occupations where there is not an hourly mean wage published, the annual wage has been directly calculated from the reported survey data.

[3] The relative standard error (RSE) is a measure of the reliability of a survey statistic. The smaller the relative standard error, the more precise the estimate.

Source: U.S. Bureau of Labor Statistics
Plunkett Research, ® Ltd.
www.plunkettresearch.com

Chapter 3

IMPORTANT ENGINEERING & RESEARCH INDUSTRY CONTACTS

Addresses, Telephone Numbers and Internet Sites

Contents:

1) Advertising/Marketing Associations
2) Aerospace & Defense Industry Associations
3) Aerospace Resources
4) Artificial Intelligence Associations
5) Automotive Industry Associations
6) Automotive Industry Resources
7) Automotive Parts, Repair & Supplies Associations
8) Automotive Safety
9) Biotechnology & Biological Industry Associations
10) Biotechnology Resources
11) Brazilian Government Agencies-Scientific
12) Business Model Resources
13) Business Representation Associations
14) Canadian Government Agencies-Communications
15) Canadian Government Agencies-Defense
16) Canadian Government Agencies-General
17) Canadian Government Agencies-Scientific
18) Careers-Computers/Technology
19) Careers-First Time Jobs/New Grads
20) Careers-General Job Listings
21) Careers-Job Reference Tools
22) Careers-Science
23) Chemicals Industry Associations
24) Chinese Government Agencies-Science & Technology
25) Computer & Electronics Industry Associations
26) Computer & Electronics Industry Resources
27) Computer-Aided Engineering Resources
28) Construction Industry Resources & Associations
29) Corporate Information Resources
30) Drone Associations
31) Economic Data & Research
32) Energy Associations-Natural Gas
33) Energy Associations-Oil Field Services/Drilling
34) Energy Associations-Petroleum, Exploration, Production, etc.
35) Engineering Industry Resources
36) Engineering, Research & Scientific Associations
37) Environmental Organizations
38) Environmental Resources
39) Food Industry Associations, General
40) Geoengineering
41) Health Care Business & Professional Associations
42) Industry Research/Market Research
43) Internet Industry Associations
44) Internet Industry Resources
45) Manufacturing Associations-Machinery & Technology
46) Maritime Associations
47) MBA Resources
48) Metals & Steel Industry Associations
49) Nanotechnology Associations
50) Nanotechnology Resources
51) Nuclear Energy Associations
52) Patent Organizations

53) Patent Resources
54) Plastics Industry Associations
55) Research & Development, Laboratories
56) RFID Industry Associations
57) Road & Highway Construction Industry Associations
58) Robotics & Automation Industry Associations
59) Satellite-Related Professional Organizations
60) Science & Technology Resources
61) Science Parks
62) Software Industry Associations
63) Software Industry Resources
64) Supercomputing
65) Sustainable Transportation
66) Technology Transfer Associations
67) Telecommunications Industry Associations
68) Telecommunications Resources
69) Temporary Staffing Firms
70) Trade Associations-General
71) Trade Associations-Global
72) Transportation Industry Resources
73) U.S. Government Agencies
74) Wireless & Cellular Industry Associations

1)   Advertising/Marketing Associations

American Marketing Association (AMA)
130 E. Randolph St., Fl. 22
Chicago, IL 60601 USA
Phone: 312-542-9000
Fax: 312-542-9001
Toll Free: 800-262-1150
Web Address: www.ama.org
The American Marketing Association (AMA) is a massive association for marketing professionals in both business and education and serves all levels of marketing practitioners,

educators and students, across all industries.

2)   Aerospace & Defense Industry Associations

Aerospace Industries Association
1000 Wilson Blvd., Ste. 1700
Arlington, VA 22209-3928 USA
Phone: 703-358-1000
E-mail Address: aia@aia-aerospace.org
Web Address: www.aia-aerospace.org
The Aerospace Industries Association represents the nation's leading manufacturers and suppliers of civil, military, and business aircraft, helicopters, unmanned aerial vehicles, space systems, aircraft engines, missiles, materiel, and related components, equipment, services, and information technology.

Aerospace Industries Association of Canada (AIAC)
255 Albert St., Ste. 703
Ottawa, ON K1P 6A9 Canada
Phone: 613-232-4297
E-mail Address: info@aiac.ca
Web Address: www.aiac.ca
The Aerospace Industries Association of Canada (AIAC) is the national trade organization of Canada's aerospace manufacturing and service sector.

American Institute of Aeronautics and Astronautics (AIAA)
12700 Sunrise Valley Dr., Ste. 200
Reston, VA 20191-5807 USA
Toll Free: 800-639-2422
E-mail Address: custserv@aiaa.org
Web Address: www.aiaa.org
The American Institute of Aeronautics and Astronautics (AIAA) is a nonprofit society aimed at advancing the arts, sciences and technology of aeronautics and astronautics. The institute represents the U.S. in the International Astronautical Federation and the International Council on the Aeronautical Sciences.

China National Space Administration
8, Fucheng Rd.
Haidian District
Beijing, 100048 China

E-mail Address: webmaster@cnsa.gov.cn
Web Address: www.cnsa.gov.cn
The China National Space Administration is the governmental agency representing China in the space science, technology and the aerospace industry.

Council of Defense & Space Industry Associations (CODSIA)
4401 Wilson Blvd., Ste. 1110
Arlington, VA 22203 USA
E-mail Address: codsia@codsia.org
Web Address: www.codsia.org
The Council of Defense and Space Industry Associations (CODSIA) provides a central channel of communications for improving industry-wide consideration of the many policies, regulations, implementation problems, procedures and questions involved in federal procurement actions.

Defense MicroElectronics Activity (DMEA)
4234 54th St.
McClellan, CA 95652-2100 USA
Phone: 916-231-1555
Fax: 916-231-2855
Web Address: www.dmea.osd.mil
Defense MicroElectronics Activity (DMEA) was established by the Department of Defense to provide a broad spectrum of microelectronics services.

German Aerospace Industries Association (BDLI)
Bundesverband der Deutschen Luft- und Raumfahrtindustrie eV (BDLI)
ATRIUM Friedrichstrasse 60
Berlin, D-10117 Germany
Phone: 49-30-2061-40-0
Fax: 49-30-2061-40-90
E-mail Address: contact@bdli.de
Web Address: www.bdli.de
The German Aerospace Industries Association (BDLI) represents the German aviation and aerospace industry at the national and international levels.

National Defense Industrial Association (NDIA)
2101 Wilson Blvd., Ste. 700
Arlington, VA 22201 USA
Phone: 703-522-1820
Fax: 703-522-1885
E-mail Address: trice@ndia.org
Web Address: www.ndia.org
The National Defense Industrial Association (NDIA), an association with more than 47,000 individuals as well as 1,375 corporate members, is dedicated to discussing defense industry concerns and promoting national security.

Washington Space Business Roundtable (WSBR)
c/o Giuffrida Associates
515 2nd St. NE
Washington, DC 20002 USA
Phone: 202-547-6340
E-mail Address:
asummers@thegateam.com
Web Address: www.wsbr.org
Washington Space Business Roundtable (WSBR) is a non-profit, membership-based group that acts as a leadership forum for the promotion of commercial space business and education in Washington D.C. and the surrounding area.

3) Aerospace Resources

Defense Science Technology Lab (DSTL)
Porton Down
Salisbury, Wiltshire SP4 0JQ UK
Phone: 44-1980-950000
E-mail Address:
centralenquiries@dstl.gov.uk
Web Address:
www.gov.uk/government/organisation s/defence-science-and-technology-laboratory
Defense Science Technology Lab (DSTL) supplies scientific research and advice to the Ministry of Defense (MOD) and other government departments.

Space Foundation
4425 Arrowswest Dr.
Colorado Springs, CO 80907 USA
Phone: 719-576-8000
Toll Free: 800-691-4000
E-mail Address:
custserv@SpaceFoundation.org
Web Address:
www.spacefoundation.org
Space Foundation represents the global space community. The Space Foundation is a nonprofit organization supporting space activities, professionals and education.

4) Artificial Intelligence Associations

Allen Institute for Artificial Intelligence (AI2)
2157 N. Northlake Way, Ste. 110
Seattle, WA 98103 USA
Phone: 206-548-5600
E-mail Address: ai2-info@allenai.org
Web Address: allenai.org
AI2 was founded in 2014 with the singular focus of conducting high-impact research and engineering in the field of artificial intelligence, all for the common good. AI2 was the creation of late Paul Allen, Microsoft co-founder. Situated on the shores of Lake Union, AI2 employs over 40 of the world's best scientific talent in the field of AI, attracting individuals of varied interests and backgrounds from across the globe.

Neural Information Processing System Foundation, Inc. (NIPS)
1269 Law St.
San Diego, CA 92109 USA
Toll Free: 858-208-3810
E-mail Address: meperry@salk.edu
Web Address: https://nips.cc
NIPS is a leading organization gathering leaders from academia and the corporate world together for a highly regarded annual conference on artificial intelligence (AI), machine learning and related topics.

OpenAI
3180 18th St.
San Francisco, CA 94110 USA
E-mail Address: info@openai.com
Web Address: www.openai.com
Near the end of 2015, a group of well-known Silicon Valley investors, including Elon Musk and Peter Thiel, announced a long-term commitment to raise funds of as much a $1 billion for a new organization to be known as OpenAI, www.openai.com. OpenAI is a nonprofit research organization focused on long-term, fundamental AI projects. In 2023, the organization created a for-profit partnership to commercialize its ChatGPT tool. Microsoft provided multi-billion funding for and owns an interest in this for-profit unit.

5) Automotive Industry Associations

Alliance for Automotive Innovation
1050 K St. NW, Ste. 650
Washington, DC 20001 USA
Phone: 202-326-5500
E-mail Address:
info@autosinnovate.org
Web Address: www.autosinnovate.org
The Alliance for Automotive Innovation is a Washington, D.C.-based trade association and lobby group whose members include international automobile and light duty truck manufacturers that build and sell products in the U.S. From the manufacturers producing most vehicles sold in the U.S. to autonomous vehicle innovators to equipment suppliers, battery producers and semiconductor makers, Alliance for Automotive Innovation represents the full auto industry, a sector supporting 10 million American jobs and five percent of the economy. Active in Washington, D.C. and all 50 states, the association is committed to a cleaner, safer and smarter personal transportation future.

Canadian Transportation Equipment Association (CTEA)
116 Albert St., Ste. 200-300
Ottawa, ON K1P 5G3 Canada
Phone: 226-620-0779
E-mail Address: admin@ctea.ca
Web Address: www.ctea.ca
The Canadian Transportation Equipment Association (CTEA) standardizes the commercial vehicle equipment manufacturing industry in Canada.

**Canadian Vehicle Manufacturers'
Association (CVMA)**
116 Albert St., Ste. 300
Ottawa, ON K1P 5G3 Canada
Phone: 416-364-9333
E-mail Address: info@cvma.ca
Web Address: www.cvma.ca
The Canadian Vehicle Manufacturers'
Association (CVMA) is the industry
organization representing
manufacturers of light and heavy-duty
motor vehicles in Canada. Association
members collaborate to solve industry
objectives in the way of consumer
protection, the environment and
vehicle safety.

**United States Council for
Automotive Research Inc.
(USCAR)**
3000 Town Center Dr., Ste. 35
Southfield, MI 48075 USA
Phone: 248-223-9000
Web Address: www.uscar.org
The United States Council for
Automotive Research (USCAR) was
founded in 1992. Its goal is to further
strengthen the technology base of the
U.S. auto industry through
cooperative research and
development. Its main focus is to
create, support and direct U.S.
cooperative research and development
to advance automotive technologies.
USCAR is composed of a number of
specialized groups that focus on
specific research areas. USCAR is
governed by the three-member
USCAR Council, whose membership
includes the R&D vice presidents
from each of the U.S. automakers.

**6)   Automotive Industry
Resources**

Automotive Center
5750 New King Dr., Ste. 120
Troy, MI 48098 USA
Phone: 248-244-8920
Web Address:
www.automotiveplastics.com
The Automotive Center, sponsored by
the American Chemistry Council's
Plastics Division, strives to provide
the automobile designer, stylist or
engineer with up-to-the-minute
research and information on plastics
applications in cars.

**7)   Automotive Parts, Repair
& Supplies Associations**

**Motor & Equipment
Manufacturers Association
(MEMA)**
79 TW Alexander Dr.
4501 Research Commons, Ste. 200
Research Triangle Park,
NC 27709 USA
Phone: 919-549-4800
Fax: 919-406-1465
E-mail Address: info@mema.org
Web Address: www.mema.org
The Motor & Equipment
Manufacturers Association (MEMA)
exclusively represents and serves
manufacturers of motor vehicle
components, tools and equipment,
automotive chemicals and related
products used in the production,
repair and maintenance of all classes
of motor vehicles.

**Truck and Engine Manufacturers
Association (EMA)**
333 West Wacker Dr., Ste. 810
Chicago, IL 60606 USA
Phone: 312-929-1970
Fax: 312-929-1970
E-mail Address: ema@emamail.org
Web Address:
www.truckandenginemanufacturers.or
g
The Truck and Engine Manufacturers
Association (EMA) is the voice of the
engine manufacturing and on-
highway medium- and heavy-duty
truck industries on domestic and
international public policy, as well as
regulatory and technical issues.

8)   Automotive Safety

**American Traffic Safety Services
Institute (The) (ATSSA)**
15 Riverside Pkwy., Ste. 100
Fredericksburg, VA 22406-1077 USA
Phone: 540-368-1701
Fax: 540-368-1717
Toll Free: 800-272-8772
E-mail Address:
communications@atssa.com
Web Address: www.atssa.com
The American Traffic Safety Services
Institute (ATSSA) is an international
trade association whose members
provide pavement markings, signage,

work zone traffic control devices and
other safety features on our nation's
roadways.

**9)   Biotechnology &
Biological Industry
Associations**

**Biomedical Engineering Society
(BMES)**
8201 Corporate Dr., Ste. 1125
Landover, MD 20785-2224 USA
Phone: 301-459-1999
Fax: 301-459-2444
Toll Free: 877-871-2637
Web Address: www.bmes.org
The Biomedical Engineering Society
(BMES) supports and advances the
use of engineering and technology for
human health and well being. It
promotes the development of
professionals in the biomedical
engineering and bioengineering
industry.

**Biomedical Engineering Society of
India**
c/o Department of Biomedical
Engineering
Manipal Insatiate of Technology
Manipal, Karnataka 576 104 India
Phone: 91-820-2924-214
E-mail Address:
gm.bairy@manipal.edu
Web Address: www.bmesi.org.in
The Biomedical Engineering Society
of India is an all India association
which seeks to advance
interdisciplinary cooperation among
scientists, engineers, and medical
doctors for the growth of teaching,
research and practices of biomedical
engineering.

**Biotechnology Industry
Organization (BIO)**
1201 Maryland Ave. SW, Ste. 900
Washington, DC 20024 USA
Phone: 202-962-9200
Fax: 202-488-6301
E-mail Address: info@bio.org
Web Address: www.bio.org
The Biotechnology Industry
Organization (BIO) represents
members involved in the research and
development of health care,
agricultural, industrial and
environmental biotechnology

products. BIO has both small and large member organizations.

Society for Industrial Microbiology and Biotechnology (SIMB)
3929 Blenheim Blvd., Ste. 92A
Fairfax, VA 22030-2421 USA
Phone: 703-691-3357
Fax: 703-691-7991
E-mail Address: info@simbhq.org
Web Address: www.simbhq.org
The Society for Industrial Microbiology and Biotechnology (SIMB) is a nonprofit professional association that works for the advancement of microbiological sciences as they apply to industrial products, biotechnology, materials and processes.

10) Biotechnology Resources

Bioengineering Industry Links
210 S. 33rd St., Rm. 240 Skirkanich Hall
UPenn, Dept. of Bioengineering, School of Eng. & Applied Science
Philadelphia, PA 19104-6321 USA
Phone: 215-898-8501
E-mail Address: be@seas.upenn.edu
Web Address:
be.seas.upenn.edu/areas-of-focus/
Bioengineering Industry Links is a web site provided by the University of Pennsylvania's Department of Bioengineering. This site features links to companies involved in cell and tissue engineering.

Centre for Cellular and Molecular Biology (CCMB)
Habsiguda, Uppal Rd.
Hyderabad, Telangana 500007 India
Phone: 91-40-2716-0222-31
Fax: 91-040-2716-0591
Web Address: www.ccmb.res.in
Centre for Cellular and Molecular Biology (CCMB) is one of the constituent Indian national laboratories of the Council of Scientific and Industrial Research (CSIR), a multidisciplinary research and development organization of the Government of India. CCMB's research is focused on seven areas: Biomedicine and Biotechnology; Genetics, Evolution and Genomics; Cell Biology and Development;

Molecular and Structural Biology; Biochemistry and Biophysics; Infectious Diseases; and Computational Biology and Bioinformatics.

Institute for Cellular and Molecular Biology (ICMB)
100 E. 24th St., NHB 4500
Austin, TX 78712 USA
Phone: 512-471-1156
Fax: 512-471-2149
E-mail Address:
icmb@austin.utexas.edu
Web Address: www.icmb.utexas.edu
The Institute for Cellular and Molecular Biology (ICMB) web site offers a comprehensive dictionary of biotech terms, plus extensive research data regarding biotechnology. ICMB is located in The Louise and James Robert Moffett Molecular Biology Building at the University of Texas at Austin.

11) Brazilian Government Agencies-Scientific

National Council for Scientific & Technological Development
SHIS QI 1 Conjunto B - Blocos A, B, C & D
Edificio Santos Dumont
Brasilia, DF 71605-001 Brazil
Toll Free: 800-61-96-97
Web Address: www.cnpq.br
The National Council for Scientific & Technological Development (Conselho Nacional de Desenvolvimento Cientifico e Tecnologico, or CNPq) is a Brazilian government agency affiliated with the country's Ministry of Science and Technology. CNPq works to promote scientific and technological research in Brazil through grants and other support services. The organization also seeks to encourage the development of Brazilian scientists and researchers through the awarding of scholarships and fellowships to students in the sciences.

12) Business Model Resources

Fraunhofer Institute for Industrial Engineering & Organization
Nobelstrasse 12
Stuttgart, 70569 Germany
Phone: 49-711-970-01
E-mail Address:
presse@iao.fraunhofer.de
Web Address:
www.iao.fraunhofer.de/lang-en/
The Fraunhofer Institute for Industrial Engineering & Organization assists companies and institutions in introducing new business models and efficient processes in Germany. Clients range from major corporations and SMEs to public sector bodies and institutions.

13) Business Representation Associations

U.S.-China Business Council (USCBC)
1818 N. St. NW, Ste. 200
Washington, DC 20036 USA
Phone: 202-429-0340
E-mail Address: info@uschina.org
Web Address: www.uschina.org
The U.S.-China Business Council (USCBC) is a private, nonpartisan, nonprofit association of more than 270 American companies that do business with China. Its membership includes some of the largest and most iconic American brands, in addition to professional services firms and small- and medium-sized enterprises. The USCBC is headquartered in Washington, DC, and maintains offices in Beijing and Shanghai.

14) Canadian Government Agencies-Communications

Canadian Radio-Television and Telecommunications Commission (CRTC)
Les Terrasses de la Chaudiere, Central Bldg.
1 Promenade du Portage
Gatineau, QC J8X 4B1 Canada
Phone: 819-997-0313
Fax: 819-994-0218

Toll Free: 877-249-2782
Web Address: www.crtc.gc.ca
The Canadian Radio-Television and Telecommunications Commission (CRTC) is the government agency responsible for the regulation of the Canadian broadcasting and telecommunications industries.

15) Canadian Government Agencies-Defense

Defense Research & Development Canada (DRDC)
101 Colonel By Dr., National Defense HQ.
Major-Gen. George R. Pearkes Bldg.
Ottawa, ON K1A 0K2 Canada
Phone: 613-995-2534
Fax: 613-992-4739
Toll Free: 888-995-2534
E-mail Address: mlo-blm@forces.gc.ca
Web Address: www.drdc-rddc.gc.ca
The Defense Research & Development Canada (DRDC) is a branch of the Canadian Department of National Defense responsible for the technological and scientific R&D for the Canadian defense forces.

16) Canadian Government Agencies-General

Canadian Intellectual Property Office (CIPO)
Place du Portage, 50 Victoria St.
Rm. C-229
Gatineau, QC K1A 0C9 Canada
Phone: 819-934-0544
Fax: 819-953-2476
Toll Free: 866-997-1936
Web Address: www.cipo.ic.gc.ca
The Canadian Intellectual Property Office (CIPO) is the agency responsible for the administration and processing of intellectual property in Canada, including patents, trademarks, copyrights, industrial designs and integrated circuit topographies.

Infrastructure Canada
180 Kent St., Ste. 1100
Ottawa, ON K1P 0B6 Canada
Phone: 613-948-1148
Toll Free: 877-250-7154

E-mail Address: info@infc.gc.ca
Web Address:
www.infrastructure.gc.ca
Infrastructure Canada works with Transport Canada and sixteen crown corporations to coordinate federal projects that focus on cities and communities, as well as supports infrastructure improvement nationwide.

17) Canadian Government Agencies-Scientific

National Research Council of Canada's Herzberg Institute of Astronomy and Astrophysics (NRC-HIA)
5071 W. Saanich Rd.
Victoria, BC V9E 2E7 Canada
Phone: 250-363-0001
E-mail Address:
HerzbergAstroInfo@nrc-cnrc.gc.ca
Web Address:
https://nrc.canada.ca/en/research-development/research-collaboration/research-centres/herzberg-astronomy-astrophysics-research-centre
The National Research Council of Canada's Herzberg Institute of Astronomy and Astrophysic (NRC-Herzberg) operates Canada's national observatories, national astronomy data center and develops advanced astronomical instruments through industrial partnerships. In addition, it operates three research programs, Astronomy Technology Program (ATP), Optical Astronomy Program (OAP) and Radio Astronomy Program (RAP).

National Science Library
1200 Montreal Rd.
Ottawa, ON K1A 0R6 Canada
Phone: 613-993-9101
Fax: 613-991-909
Toll Free: 877-672-2672
E-mail Address: info@nrc-cnrc.gc.ca
Web Address: science-libraries.canada.ca/eng/national-science-library/
The National Science Library, a division of National Research Council Canada is one of the largest information source service organizations in the world, with

particular emphasis on the scientific and technical sectors.

18) Careers-Computers/ Technology

ComputerJobs.com, Inc.
675 Alpha Dr., Ste. E
Highland Heights, OH 44143 USA
Toll Free: 800-850-0045
Web Address:
www.computerjobs.com
ComputerJobs.com, Inc. is an employment web site that offers users links to computer-related job opportunities organized by skill and market.

Dice.com
6465 S. Greenwood Plaza Blvd.
Ste. 400
Centennial, CO 80111 USA
Phone: 515-280-1144
Fax: 515-280-1452
Toll Free: 888-321-3423
E-mail Address:
techsupport@dice.com
Web Address: www.dice.com
Dice.com provides free employment services for IT jobs. The site includes advanced job searches by geographic location and category, availability announcements and resume postings, as well as employer profiles, a recruiter's page and career links. It is maintained by Dice Holdings, Inc., a publicly traded company.

Institute for Electrical and Electronics Engineers (IEEE) Job Site
445 Hoes Ln.
Piscataway, NJ 08855-1331 USA
Phone: 732-981-0060
Toll Free: 800-678-4333
E-mail Address:
candidatejobsite@ieee.org
Web Address: careers.ieee.org
The Institute for Electrical and Electronics Engineers (IEEE) Job Site provides a host of employment services for technical professionals, employers and recruiters. The site offers job listings by geographic area, a resume bank and links to employment services.

Pencom Systems, Inc.
152 Remsen St.
Brooklyn, NY 11201 USA
Phone: 718-923-1111
Fax: 718-923-6065
E-mail Address: tom@pencom.com
Web Address: www.pencom.com
Pencom Systems, Inc., an open system recruiting company, hosts a career web site geared toward high-technology and scientific professionals, featuring an interactive salary survey, career advisor, job listings and technology resources. Its focus is the financial services industry within the New York City area.

19) Careers-First Time Jobs/New Grads

CollegeGrad.com, Inc.
950 Tower Ln., Fl. 6
Foster City, CA 94404 USA
E-mail Address: info@quinstreet.com
Web Address: www.collegegrad.com
CollegeGrad.com, Inc. offers in-depth resources for college students and recent grads seeking entry-level jobs.

National Association of Colleges and Employers (NACE)
62 Highland Ave.
Bethlehem, PA 18017-9085 USA
Phone: 610-868-1421
E-mail Address: customerservice@naceweb.org
Web Address: www.naceweb.org
The National Association of Colleges and Employers (NACE) is a premier U.S. organization representing college placement offices and corporate recruiters who focus on hiring new grads.

20) Careers-General Job Listings

CareerBuilder, Inc.
200 N La Salle Dr., Ste. 1100
Chicago, IL 60601 USA
Phone: 773-527-3600
Fax: 773-353-2452
Toll Free: 800-891-8880
Web Address: www.careerbuilder.com
CareerBuilder, Inc. focuses on the needs of companies and also provides a database of job openings. The site has over 1 million jobs posted by 300,000 employers and receives an average of 23 million unique visitors monthly. The company also operates online career centers for 140 newspapers and 9,000 online partners. Resumes are sent directly to the company, and applicants can set up a special e-mail account for job-seeking purposes. CareerBuilder is primarily a joint venture between three newspaper giants: The McClatchy Company, Gannett Co., Inc. and Tribune Company.

CareerOneStop
Toll Free: 877-872-5627
E-mail Address: info@careeronestop.org
Web Address: www.careeronestop.org
CareerOneStop is operated by the employment commissions of various state agencies. It contains job listings in both the private and government sectors, as well as a wide variety of useful career resources and workforce information. CareerOneStop is sponsored by the U.S. Department of Labor.

LaborMarketInfo (LMI)
Employment Development Dept.
P.O. Box 826880, MIC 57
Sacramento, CA 94280-0001 USA
Phone: 916-262-2162
Fax: 916-262-2352
Web Address: www.labormarketinfo.edd.ca.gov
LaborMarketInfo (LMI) provides job seekers and employers a wide range of resources, namely the ability to find, access and use labor market information and services. It provides statistics for employment demographics on both a local and regional level, as well as career searching tools for California residents. The web site is sponsored by California's Employment Development Office.

Recruiters Online Network
E-mail Address: rossi.tony@comcast.net
Web Address: www.recruitersonline.com
The Recruiters Online Network provides job postings from thousands of recruiters, Careers Online Magazine, a resume database, as well as other career resources.

USAJOBS
USAJOBS Program Office
1900 E St. NW, Ste. 6500
Washington, DC 20415-0001 USA
Phone: 818-934-6600
Web Address: www.usajobs.gov
USAJOBS, a program of the U.S. Office of Personnel Management, is the official job site for the U.S. Federal Government. It provides a comprehensive list of U.S. government jobs, allowing users to search for employment by location; agency; type of work; or by senior executive positions. It also has special employment sections for individuals with disabilities, veterans and recent college graduates; an information center, offering resume and interview tips and other information; and allows users to create a profile and post a resume.

21) Careers-Job Reference Tools

Vault.com, Inc.
132 W. 31st St., Fl. 16
New York, NY 10001 USA
Fax: 212-366-6117
Toll Free: 800-535-2074
E-mail Address: customerservice@vault.com
Web Address: www.vault.com
Vault.com, Inc. is a comprehensive career web site for employers and employees, with job postings and valuable information on a wide variety of industries. Its features and content are largely geared toward MBA degree holders.

22) Careers-Science

New Scientist Jobs
25 Bedford St.
London, WC2E 9ES UK
Phone: 617-283-3213
E-mail Address: nssales@newscientist.com
Web Address: jobs.newscientist.com
New Scientist Jobs is a web site produced by the publishers of New Scientist Magazine that connects

jobseekers and employers in the bioscience fields. The site includes a job search engine and a free-of-charge e-mail job alert service.

Science Careers
Phone: 201-210-5012
E-mail Address: advertise@sciencecareers.org
Web Address: jobs.sciencecareers.org
Science Careers is a web site that contains many useful categories of links, including employment newsgroups, scientific journals, hob postings and placement agencies. It also links to sites containing information regarding internship and fellowship opportunities for high school students, undergrads, graduates, doctoral and post-doctoral students.

23) Chemicals Industry Associations

American Chemical Society (ACS)
1155 16th St. NW
Washington, DC 20036 USA
Phone: 202-872-4600
Toll Free: 800-333-9511
E-mail Address: service@acs.org
Web Address: www.acs.org
The American Chemical Society (ACS) is a nonprofit organization aimed at promoting the understanding of chemistry and chemical sciences. It represents a wide range of disciplines including chemistry, chemical engineering and other technical fields.

Brazilian Chemical Industry Association
Av. Chedid Jafet, 222, Bloco C, Fl. 4
Vila Olimpia
Sao Paulo, SP 04551-065 Brazil
Phone: 55-11-2148-4700
Fax: 55-11-2148-4760
Web Address: www.abiquim.org.br
The Brazilian Chemical Industry Association (Associacao Brasileira da Industria Quimica, ABIQUIM) represents Brazilian manufacturers of chemical products and assists with a variety of issues related to the industry, including product quality; environmental and safety issues; human resource development; product advocacy; tariff negotiations; and

trade agreements. ABIQUIM runs a 24-hour hotline for chemical transportation safety issues, and is also involved with plastics recycling efforts.

Council for Chemical Research (CCR)
120 Wall St., Fl. 23
New York, NY 10005-4020 USA
Phone: 856-439-0500
Fax: 856-439-0525
E-mail Address: info@ccrhq.org
Web Address: www.ccrhq.org
The Council for Chemical Research (CCR) represents industry, academia and government members involved in the chemical sciences and engineering.

24) Chinese Government Agencies-Science & Technology

China Ministry of Science and Technology (MOST)
15B Fuxing Rd.
Beijing, 100862 China
Web Address: www.most.gov.cn
The China Ministry of Science and Technology (MOST) is the PRC's official body for science and technology related activities. It drafts laws, policies and regulations regarding science and technology; oversees budgeting and accounting for funds; and supervises research institutes operating in China, among other duties.

25) Computer & Electronics Industry Associations

Business Technology Association (BTA)
12411 Wornall Rd., Ste. 200
Kansas City, MO 64145 USA
Phone: 816-941-3100
Fax: 816-941-4843
Toll Free: 800-505-2821
E-mail Address: info@bta.org
Web Address: www.bta.org
The Business Technology Association (BTA) is an organization for resellers and dealers of business technology products. Its site offers buying groups, message boards, legal advice,

news on industry trends and live chats.

Canadian Advanced Technology Alliances (CATAAlliance)
207 Bank St., Ste. 416
Ottawa, ON K2P 2N2 Canada
Phone: 613-236-6550
E-mail Address: info@cata.ca
Web Address: www.cata.ca
The Canadian Advanced Technology Alliances (CATAAlliance) is one of Canada's leading trade organizations for the research, development and technology sectors.

Computer & Communications Industry Association (CCIA)
25 Massachusetts Ave., Ste. 300C
Washington, DC 20001 USA
Phone: 202-783-0070
Fax: 202-783-0534
Web Address: www.ccianet.org
The Computer & Communications Industry Association (CCIA) is a non-profit membership organization for companies and senior executives representing the computer, Internet, information technology (IT) and telecommunications industries.

Electronics Technicians Association international (ETA International)
5 Depot St.
Greencastle, IN 46135 USA
Phone: 765-653-8262
Fax: 765-653-4287
Toll Free: 800-288-3824
E-mail Address: eta@eta-i.org
Web Address: www.eta-i.org
The Electronics Technicians Association International (ETA International) is a nonprofit professional association for electronics technicians worldwide. The organization provides recognized professional credentials for electronics technicians.

Global Semiconductor Alliance (GSA)
12400 Coit Rd., Ste. 650
Dallas, TX 75251 USA
Phone: 972-866-7579
Fax: 972-239-2292
Toll Free: 888-322-5195
E-mail Address: contact@gsaglobal.org

Web Address: www.gsaglobal.org
The Global Semiconductor Alliance (GSA) serves the entire supply chain of the global semiconductor industry, including intellectual property (IP), electronic design automation (EDA)/design, wafer manufacturing, test and packaging activities.

Indian Electrical & Electronics Manufacturers Association (IEEMA)
501 Kakad Chambers
132 Dr. Annie Besant Rd., Worli
Mumbai, 400018 India
Phone: 91-22-2493-0532
Fax: 91-22-2493-2705
E-mail Address: mumbai@ieema.org
Web Address: www.ieema.org
The Indian Electrical & Electronics Manufacturers Association (IEEMA) represents all sectors of the electrical and allied products businesses of the Indian electrical industry.

Institute for Interconnecting and Packaging Electronic Circuits (IPC)
3000 Lakeside Dr., Ste. 105 N
Bannockburn, IL 60015 USA
Phone: 847-615-7100
Fax: 847-615-7105
E-mail Address: answers@ipc.org
Web Address: www.ipc.org
The Institute for Interconnecting and Packaging Electronic Circuits (IPC) is a trade association for companies in the global printed circuit board and electronics manufacturing services industries.

International Disk Drive Equipment and Materials Association (IDEMA)
1226 Lincoln Ave., Ste. 100
San Jose, CA 95125 USA
Phone: 530-434-6933
Fax: 408-294-0087
E-mail Address: info@idema.org
Web Address: www.idema.org
The International Disk Drive Equipment and Materials Association (IDEMA) is a not-for-profit trade association that represents its members on issues concerning the hard drive industry worldwide.

International Microelectronics Assembly and Packaging Society (IMAPS)
P.O. Box 110127
Research Triangle Park, NC 27709-5127 USA
Phone: 919-293-5000
Fax: 919-287-2339
E-mail Address: info@imaps.org
Web Address: www.imaps.org
The International Microelectronics Assembly and Packaging Society (IMAPS) is dedicated to the advancement and growth of the use of microelectronics and electronic packaging through professional education, workshops and conferences.

Korea Association of Information and Telecommunications (KAIT)
NO. 1678-2, 2nd Fl. Dong-Ah Villat 2 Town
Seocho-dong, Seocho-gu
Seoul, 137-070 Korea
Phone: 82-2-580-0582
E-mail Address: webmaster@kait.or.kr
Web Address: www.kait.or.kr/eng
The Korea Association of Information and Telecommunications (KAIT) was created to develop and promote the InfoTech, computer, consumer electronics, wireless, software and telecommunications sectors in Korea.

Korea Electronics Association (KEA)
World Cup buk-ro 54-gil, Mapo-gu
Fl. 11
Seoul, 03924 Korea
Phone: 82-2-6388-6000
Fax: 82-02-6388-6009
Web Address: www.gokea.org
The Korea Electronics Association (KEA) was established by Korea's Ministry of Commerce to promote the growth and development of the nation's electronics industry.

Korea Semiconductor Industry Association (KSIA)
182, Pangyoyeok-ro, Bundang-gu, Seongnam-si
Fl. 9-12, KSIA Bldg.
Gyeonggi-do, Korea
Phone: 82-2-576-3472
Fax: 82-2-570-5269

E-mail Address: admin@ksia.or.kr
Web Address: www.ksia.or.kr
The Korean Semiconductor Industry Association (KSIA) represents the interests of Korean semiconductor manufacturers.

North America Chinese Clean-tech & Semiconductor Association (NACSA)
809-B Cuesta Dr., Ste. 208
Mountain View, CA 94040 USA
Web Address: www.nacsa.com
The North America Chinese Clean-tech & Semiconductor Association (NACSA), founded in Silicon Valley in 1996, is dedicated to the advancement of Chinese professionals in high-tech and related industries, including chip design, chip manufacture, system manufacture, equipment manufacture and software.

Semiconductor Equipment and Materials International (SEMI)
673 S. Milpitas Blvd.
Milpitas, CA 95035 USA
Phone: 408-943-6900
Fax: 408-428-9600
E-mail Address: semihq@semi.org
Web Address: www.semi.org
Semiconductor Equipment and Materials International (SEMI) is a trade association serving the global semiconductor equipment, materials and flat-panel display industries.

Semiconductor Industry Association (SIA)
1101 K St. NW, Ste. 450
Washington, DC 20005 USA
Phone: 202-446-1700
Fax: 202-216-9745
Toll Free: 866-756-0715
Web Address: www.semiconductors.org
The Semiconductor Industry Association (SIA) is a trade association representing the semiconductor industry in the U.S. Through its coalition of more than 60 companies, SIA members represent roughly 80% of semiconductor production in the U.S. The coalition aims to advance the competitiveness of the chip industry and shape public policy on issues particular to the industry.

Storage Network Industry Association (SNIA)
5201 Great America Pkwy., Ste. 320
Santa Clara, CA 95054 USA
Phone: 719-694-1380
Fax: 719-694-1385
E-mail Address: emerald@snia.org
Web Address: www.snia.org
The Storage Network Industry Association (SNIA) is a trade associated dedicated to viability of storage networks within the IT industry. SNIA sponsors technical work groups, produces the Storage Networking Conference series and maintains a Technology Center in Colorado Springs, Colorado.

Surface Mount Technology Association (SMTA)
6600 City West Pkwy., Ste. 300
Eden Prairie, MN 55424 USA
Phone: 952-920-7682
Fax: 952-926-1819
E-mail Address: smta@smta.org
Web Address: www.smta.org
The Surface Mount Technology Association (SMTA) is an international network of professionals whose careers encompass electronic assembly technologies, microsystems, emerging technologies and associated business operations.

26) Computer & Electronics Industry Resources

Cisco Cloud Index
170 W. Tasman Dr.
San Jose, CA 95134 USA
Toll Free: 800-553-6387
Web Address:
www.cisco.com/go/cloudindex
The Cisco Cloud Index covers three areas focused on data center and cloud traffic trends and next-generation service or application adoption. They include: Data center and cloud traffic forecast; Workload transition, which provides projections for workloads moving from traditional IT to cloud-based architectures; and Cloud readiness, which provides regional statistics on broadband adoption as a precursor for cloud services.

EETimes
Web Address: www.eetimes.com
The EETimes is an online magazine devoted to electronic engineers in the semiconductor, systems and software design fields.

Information Technology and Innovation Foundation (ITIF)
700 K St. NW
Ste. 600
Washington, DC 20001 USA
Phone: 202-449-1351
E-mail Address: mail@itif.org
Web Address: www.itif.org
Information Technology and Innovation Foundation (ITIF) is a non-partisan research and educational institute (a think tank) with a mission to formulate and promote public policies to advance technological innovation and productivity internationally, in Washington, and in the States. Recognizing the vital role of technology in ensuring American prosperity, ITIF focuses on innovation, productivity, and digital economy issues.

27) Computer-Aided Engineering Resources

Center for Design Research (CDR) at Stanford University
Center for Design Research
Bldg. 560, 424 Panama Mall
Stanford, CA 94305-2232 USA
Phone: 650-723-9233
Fax: 650-725-8475
E-mail Address:
gosiaw@stanford.edu
Web Address:
centerfordesignresearch.stanford.edu
The web site of the Center for Design Research (CDR) at Stanford University provides information on the center's staff, laboratories and projects on design process and design tool development for engineering.

28) Construction Industry Resources & Associations

Precast/Prestressed Concrete Institute
8770 W. Bryn Mawr Ave., Ste. 1150
Chicago, IL 60631 USA
Phone: 312-786-0300
E-mail Address: info@pci.org
Web Address: www.pci.org
The Precast/Prestressed Concrete Institute (PCI) is an organization dedicated to the precast and prestressed concrete industry and includes a staff of technical and marketing specialists.

29) Corporate Information Resources

Business Journals (The)
120 W. Morehead St., Ste. 400
Charlotte, NC 28202 USA
Toll Free: 866-853-3661
E-mail Address:
gmurchison@bizjournals.com
Web Address: www.bizjournals.com
Bizjournals.com is the online media division of American City Business Journals, the publisher of dozens of leading city business journals nationwide. It provides access to research into the latest news regarding companies both small and large. The organization maintains 42 websites and 64 print publications and sponsors over 700 annual industry events.

Business Wire
101 California St., Fl. 20
San Francisco, CA 94111 USA
Phone: 415-986-4422
Fax: 415-788-5335
Toll Free: 800-227-0845
E-mail Address:
info@businesswire.com
Web Address: www.businesswire.com
Business Wire offers news releases, industry- and company-specific news, top headlines, conference calls, IPOs on the Internet, media services and access to tradeshownews.com and BW Connect On-line through its informative and continuously updated web site.

Edgar Online, Inc.
35 W. Wacker Dr.
Chicago, IL 60601 USA
Phone: 301-287-0300
Fax: 301-287-0390
Toll Free: 800-823-5304
Web Address: www.edgar-online.com
Edgar Online, Inc. is an SEC gateway and search tool for viewing corporate documents, such as annual reports on Form 10-K, filed with the U.S. Securities and Exchange Commission.

PR Newswire Association LLC
200 Vesey St., Fl. 19
New York, NY 10281 USA
Fax: 800-793-9313
Toll Free: 800-776-8090
E-mail Address: mediainquiries@cision.com
Web Address: www.prnewswire.com
PR Newswire Association LLC provides comprehensive communications services for public relations and investor relations professionals, ranging from information distribution and market intelligence to the creation of online multimedia content and investor relations web sites. Users can also view recent corporate press releases from companies across the globe. The Association is owned by United Business Media plc.

Silicon Investor
E-mail Address: si.admin@siliconinvestor.com
Web Address: www.siliconinvestor.com
Silicon Investor is focused on providing information about technology companies. Its web site serves as a financial discussion forum and offers quotes, profiles and charts.

30) Drone Associations

Unmanned Systems Technology (UST)
Office 1 Ste. C, Mulberry Ct.
Christchurch, BH23 1PS UK
Phone: 44-01202-485884
E-mail Address: hello@ust.team

Web Address: www.unmannedsystemstechnology.com
Unmanned Systems Technology (UST) is a dedicated directory of component, service and platform suppliers within the unmanned systems industry. All categories of unmanned systems are included: Air vehicles (UAV/UAS/RPAS), Ground Vehicles and Robotic Systems (UGVs), Surface and Subsea vehicles (USV, UUV) and Space vehicles.

31) Economic Data & Research

Centre for European Economic Research (The, ZEW)
L 7, 1
Mannheim, 68161 Germany
Phone: 49-621-1235-01
Fax: 49-621-1235-224
E-mail Address: empfang@zew.de
Web Address: www.zew.de/en
Zentrum fur Europaische Wirtschaftsforschung, The Centre for European Economic Research (ZEW), distinguishes itself in the analysis of internationally comparative data in a European context and in the creation of databases that serve as a basis for scientific research. The institute maintains a special library relevant to economic research and provides external parties with selected data for the purpose of scientific research. ZEW also offers public events and seminars concentrating on banking, business and other economic-political topics.

Economic and Social Research Council (ESRC)
Polaris House
North Star Ave.
Swindon, SN2 1UJ UK
Phone: 44-01793 413000
E-mail Address: esrcenquiries@esrc.ac.uk
Web Address: www.esrc.ac.uk
The Economic and Social Research Council (ESRC) funds research and training in social and economic issues. It is an independent organization, established by Royal Charter. Current research areas

include the global economy; social diversity; environment and energy; human behavior; and health and well-being.

Eurostat
5 Rue Alphonse Weicker
Joseph Bech Bldg.
Luxembourg, L-2721 Luxembourg
Phone: 00 800 6789 1011
E-mail Address: https://ec.europa.eu/eurostat/web/main/home
Web Address: ec.europa.eu/eurostat
Eurostat is the European Union's service that publishes a wide variety of comprehensive statistics on European industries, population, trade, agriculture, technology, environment and other vital business topics.

Federal Statistical Office of Germany
Gustav-Stresemann-Ring 11
Wiesbaden, D-65189 Germany
Phone: 49-611-75-2405
Fax: 49-611-72-4000
Web Address: www.destatis.de
Federal Statistical Office of Germany publishes a wide variety of nation and regional economic data of interest to anyone who is studying Germany, one of the world's leading economies. Data available includes population, consumer prices, labor markets, health care, industries and output.

India Brand Equity Foundation (IBEF)
Fl. 20, Jawahar Vyapar Bhawan
Tolstoy Marg
New Delhi, 110001 India
Phone: 91-11-43845500
Fax: 91-11-23701235
E-mail Address: info.brandindia@ibef.org
Web Address: www.ibef.org
India Brand Equity Foundation (IBEF) is a public-private partnership between the Ministry of Commerce and Industry, the Government of India and the Confederation of Indian Industry. The foundation's primary objective is to build positive economic perceptions of India globally. It aims to effectively present the India business perspective and

leverage business partnerships in a globalizing marketplace.

National Bureau of Statistics (China)
57, Yuetan Nanjie, Sanlihe
Xicheng District
Beijing, 100826 China
Fax: 86-10-6878-2000
E-mail Address: info@gj.stats.cn
Web Address:
www.stats.gov.cn/english
The National Bureau of Statistics (China) provides statistics and economic data regarding China's economy and society.

Organization for Economic Co-operation and Development (OECD)
2 rue Andre Pascal
Cedex 16
Paris, 75775 France
Phone: 33-1-45-24-82-00
Fax: 33-1-45-24-85-00
E-mail Address:
webmaster@oecd.org
Web Address: www.oecd.org
The Organization for Economic Co-operation and Development (OECD) publishes detailed economic, government, population, social and trade statistics on a country-by-country basis for over 30 nations representing the world's largest economies. Sectors covered range from industry, labor, technology and patents, to health care, environment and globalization.

Statistics Bureau, Director-General for Policy Planning (Japan)
19-1 Wakamatsu-cho
Shinjuku-ku
Tokyo, 162-8668 Japan
Phone: 81-3-5273-2020
E-mail Address:
toukeisoudan@soumu.go.jp
Web Address: www.stat.go.jp/english
The Statistics Bureau, Director-General for Policy Planning (Japan) and Statistical Research and Training Institute, a part of the Japanese Ministry of Internal Affairs and Communications, plays the central role of producing and disseminating basic official statistics and coordinating statistical work under

the Statistics Act and other legislation.

Statistics Canada
150 Tunney's Pasture Driveway
Ottawa, ON K1A 0T6 Canada
Phone: 514-283-8300
Fax: 514-283-9350
Toll Free: 800-263-1136
E-mail Address: STATCAN.infostats-infostats.STATCAN@canada.ca
Web Address: www.statcan.gc.ca
Statistics Canada provides a complete portal to Canadian economic data and statistics. Its conducts Canada's official census every five years, as well as hundreds of surveys covering numerous aspects of Canadian life.

32) Energy Associations-Natural Gas

Gas Technology Institute (GTI)
1700 S. Mount Prospect Rd.
Des Plaines, IL 60018 USA
Phone: 847-768-0500
Fax: 847-768-0501
E-mail Address:
publicrelations@gti.org
Web Address: www.git.energy
The Gas Technology Institute (GTI) is a not-for-profit research and development organization, and works to develop and deploy technologies related to affordable energy production, sustainable energy development and the efficient use of energy resources. Its network of partners, investors and clients includes state and federal government agencies; natural gas utilities and pipeline companies; industrial companies; electric utilities; independent power producers; technology developers; and national laboratories. In addition to its Illinois headquarters (which houses 28 specialized laboratories working on various advanced energy technologies), GTI also maintains smaller offices and facilities in locations including Houston, Texas; Sacramento, California; and Washington D.C.

33) Energy Associations-Oil Field Services/Drilling

EnerGeo Alliance
1225 N. Loop W., Ste. 220
Houston, TX 77008 USA
Phone: 713-957-8080
Fax: 713-957-0008
Toll Free: 866-558-1756
E-mail Address:
info@energeoalliance.org
Web Address: energeoalliance.org
The EnerGeo Alliance is a global trade alliance for the energy geoscience industry. EnerGeo represents geoscience companies, innovators and energy developers that use earth science to discover, develop and deliver energy.

Energy Workforce & Technology Council
2500 Citywest Blvd., Ste. 1110
Houston, TX 77042 USA
Phone: 713-932-0168
E-mail Address:
info@energyworkforce.org
Web Address: energyworkforce.org
The Energy Workforce & Technology Council, formerly the Petroleum Equipment Suppliers Association (PESA), is an organization of equipment manufacturers, well site service providers and supply companies serving the drilling and production segments of the petroleum industry.

34) Energy Associations-Petroleum, Exploration, Production, etc.

International Association of Drilling Contractors (IADC)
3657 Briarpark Dr., Ste. 200
Houston, TX 77042 USA
Phone: 713-292-1945
Fax: 713-292-1946
E-mail Address: info@iadc.org
Web Address: www.iadc.org
The International Association of Drilling Contractors (IADC) represents the worldwide oil and gas drilling industry and promotes commitment to safety, preservation of the environment and advances in drilling technology.

UK Offshore Energies Association Limited, The (OEUK)
1st Fl. Paternoster House
65 St. Paul's Churchyard
London, EC4M 8AB UK
Phone: 44-20-7802-2400
E-mail Address: Info@oeuk.org.uk
Web Address: oeuk.org.uk
The UK Offshore Energies Association Limited (OEUK) is the representative organization for the U.K. offshore oil and gas industry.

35) Engineering Industry Resources

Cornell Engineering Library (The)
Engineering Library Cornell University
Carpenter Hall, Fl. 1
Ithaca, NY 14853 USA
Phone: 607-254-6261
E-mail Address: engrref@cornell.edu
Web Address: engineering.library.cornell.edu
Cornell University's Engineering Library web site has a number of resources concerning engineering research, as well as links to other engineering industry information sources.

Engineering News-Record (ENR)
2401 W. Big Beaver Rd., Ste. 700
Troy, MI 48084-3333 USA
Phone: 248-362-3700
Fax: 248-362-0317
E-mail Address: enr@enr.com
Web Address: www.enr.com
Engineering News-Record (ENR) provides the news, analysis, commentary and data that engineering and construction industry professionals need to do their jobs more effectively. ENR publishes a weekly magazine with more than 70,000 paid subscribers, a website with over 90,000 unique visitors a month and a series of in-person events. Those who read ENR include contractors, project owners, engineers, architects, government regulators and industry suppliers. As such, the engineering information portal connects these diverse sectors of the industry with coverage about issues such as business management, design, construction methods, technology, safety, law, legislation, environment and labor.

36) Engineering, Research & Scientific Associations

Agency For Science, Technology And Research (A*STAR)
1 Fusionopolis Way
20-10 Connexis N. Twr.
Singapore, 138632 Singapore
Phone: 65-6826-6111
Fax: 65-6777-1711
E-mail Address: contact@a-star.edu.sg
Web Address: www.a-star.edu.sg
The Agency For Science, Technology And Research (A*STAR) of Singapore comprises the Biomedical Research Council (BMRC), the Science and Engineering Research Council (SERC), A*STAR Joint Council (A*JC), the A*STAR Graduate Academy (A*GA) and the Corporate Group. Both Councils fund the A*STAR public research institutes which conducts research in specific niche areas in science, engineering and biomedical science.

Alfred P. Sloan Foundation
630 Fifth Ave., Ste. 2550
New York, NY 10111 USA
Phone: 212-649-1649
Fax: 212-757-5117
E-mail Address: frontdesk@sloan.org
Web Address: www.sloan.org
The Alfred P. Sloan Foundation funds science and technology, economic performance, education, national issues and civics programs through research fellowships and grants.

American Association for the Advancement of Science (AAAS)
1200 New York Ave. NW
Washington, DC 20005 USA
Phone: 202-326-6400
Web Address: www.aaas.org
The American Association for the Advancement of Science (AAAS) is the world's largest scientific society and the publisher of Science magazine. It is an international nonprofit organization dedicated to advancing science around the globe.

American Association of Petroleum Geologists (AAPG)
1444 S. Boulder Ave.
Tulsa, OK 74119 USA
Phone: 918-584-2555
Fax: 918-560-2665
Toll Free: 800-364-2274
E-mail Address: Members@aapg.org
Web Address: www.aapg.org
The American Association of Petroleum Geologists (AAPG) is an international geological organization that supports educational and scientific programs and projects related to geosciences.

American Institute of Chemical Engineers (AIChE)
120 Wall St., Fl. 23
New York, NY 10005-4020 USA
Phone: 203-702-7660
Fax: 203-775-5177
Toll Free: 800-242-4363
Web Address: www.aiche.org
The American Institute of Chemical Engineers (AIChE) provides leadership in advancing the chemical engineering profession. The organization, which is comprised of more than 50,000 members from over 100 countries, provides informational resources to chemical engineers.

American Institute of Mining, Metallurgical and Petroleum Engineers (AIME)
12999 E. Adam Aircraft Cir.
Englewood, CO 80112 USA
Phone: 303-948-4255
Fax: 888-702-0049
E-mail Address: aime@aimehq.org
Web Address: www.aimehq.org
The American Institute of Mining, Metallurgical and Petroleum Engineers (AIME) is a trade association devoted to the science of the production and use of minerals, metals, energy sources and materials.

American Institute of Physics (AIP)
1 Physics Ellipse
College Park, MD 20740-3843 USA
Phone: 301-209-3100
E-mail Address: mmoloney@aip.org
Web Address: www.aip.org
The American Institute of Physics (AIP) is a nonprofit organization aimed at the advancement and

diffusion of knowledge of the science of physics and its application to human welfare. It serves individual scientists, students and the general public alike. Besides its Maryland headquarters, the AIP maintains a publishing center in New York and an international office in Beijing.

American National Standards Institute (ANSI)
1899 L St. NW, Fl. 11
Washington, DC 20036 USA
Phone: 202-293-8020
Fax: 202-293-9287
E-mail Address: info@ansi.org
Web Address: www.ansi.org
The American National Standards Institute (ANSI) is a private, nonprofit organization that administers and coordinates the U.S. voluntary standardization and conformity assessment system. Its mission is to enhance both the global competitiveness of U.S. business and the quality of life by promoting and facilitating voluntary consensus standards and conformity assessment systems and safeguarding their integrity.

American Nuclear Society (ANS)
555 N. Kensington Ave.
La Grange Park, IL 60526 USA
Phone: 708-352-6611
Fax: 708-579-8314
Toll Free: 800-323-3044
Web Address: www.ans.org
The American Nuclear Society (ANS) is a nonprofit organization unifying professional activities within the nuclear science and technology fields. ANS seeks to promote awareness and understanding of the application of nuclear science and technology.

American Physical Society (APS)
One Physics Ellipse
College Park, MD 20740-3844 USA
Phone: 301-209-3200
Fax: 301-209-0865
Web Address: www.aps.org
The American Physical Society (APS) develops and implements effective programs in physics education and outreach. APS publishes a number of research journals dedicated to physics research, including Physical Review,

Physical Review Letters and Reviews of Modern Physics.

American Society for Engineering Education (ASEE)
1818 North St. NW, Ste. 600
Washington, DC 20036-2479 USA
Phone: 202-331-3500
Fax: 202-265-8504
E-mail Address: board@asee.org
Web Address: www.asee.org
The American Society for Engineering Education (ASEE) is nonprofit organization dedicated to promoting and improving engineering and technology education.

American Society for Healthcare Engineering (ASHE)
155 N. Wacker Dr., Ste. 400
Chicago, IL 60606 USA
Phone: 312-422-3800
Fax: 312-422-4571
E-mail Address: ashe@aha.org
Web Address: www.ashe.org
The American Society for Healthcare Engineering (ASHE) is the advocate and resource for continuous improvement in the health care engineering and facilities management professions. It is devoted to professionals who design, build, maintain and operate hospitals and other healthcare facilities.

American Society for Nondestructive Testing (ASNT)
1201 Dublin Rd., Ste. G04
Columbus, OH 43215-1045 USA
Phone: 614-274-6003
Toll Free: 800-222-2768
E-mail Address: customersupport@asnt.org
Web Address: www.asnt.org
The American Society for Nondestructive Testing (ASNT) is the world's largest technical society for nondestructive testing professionals. It promotes the discipline of nondestructive testing as a profession and facilitates nondestructive testing research and technology applications.

American Society of Agricultural and Biological Engineers (ASABE)
2950 Niles Rd.
St. Joseph, MI 49085 USA
Phone: 269-429-0300

Fax: 269-429-3852
E-mail Address: hq@asabe.org
Web Address: www.asabe.org
The American Society of Agricultural and Biological Engineers (ASABE) is a nonprofit professional and technical organization interested in engineering knowledge and technology for food and agriculture and associated industries.

American Society of Civil Engineers (ASCE)
1801 Alexander Bell Dr.
Reston, VA 20191-4400 USA
Phone: 703-295-6300
Toll Free: 800-548-2723
Web Address: www.asce.org
The American Society of Civil Engineers (ASCE) is a leading professional organization serving civil engineers. It ensures safer buildings, water systems and other civil engineering works by developing technical codes and standards.

American Society of Heating, Refrigerating and Air-Conditioning Engineers
180 Technology Parkway NW
Peachtree Corners, GA 30092 USA
Phone: 404-636-8400
Fax: 404-321-5478
Toll Free: 800-527-4723
E-mail Address: ashrae@ashrae.org
Web Address: www.ashrae.org
ASHRAE is a global society advancing human well-being through sustainable technology for the built environment. The Society and its members focus on building systems, energy efficiency, indoor air quality, refrigeration and sustainability within the industry. Through research, standards writing, publishing and continuing education, ASHRAE shapes tomorrow's built environment today

American Society of Mechanical Engineers (ASME)
Two Park Ave.
New York, NY 10016-5990 USA
Phone: 646-616-3100
Toll Free: 800-843-2763
E-mail Address: CustomerCare@asme.org
Web Address: www.asme.org

The American Society of Mechanical Engineers (ASME) offers quality programs and activities in mechanical engineering. It also facilitates the development and application of technology in areas of interest to the mechanical engineering profession.

American Society of Mechanical Engineers (ASME), Textile Engineering Division
Two Park Ave.
New York, NY 10016-5990 USA
Phone: 646-616-3100
Toll Free: 800-843-2763
E-mail Address: CustomerCare@asme.org
Web Address: www.asme.org
The textile engineering division of the American Society of Mechanical Engineers (ASME) promotes product and process technology improvement in the retail fiber industry.

American Society of Naval Engineers (ASNE)
423 Powhatan St., Ste. 1
Alexandria, VA 22314 USA
Phone: 703-836-6727
E-mail Address: asnehq@navalengineers.org
Web Address: www.navalengineers.org
The American Society of Naval Engineers (ASNE) is a nonprofit professional organization dedicated to advancing the knowledge and practice of naval engineering in public and private operations.

American Society of Safety Engineers (ASSE)
520 N. Northwest Hwy
Park Ridge, IL 60068 USA
Phone: 847-699-2929
E-mail Address: customerservice@asse.org
Web Address: www.asse.org
The American Society of Safety Engineers (ASSE) is the world's oldest and largest professional safety organization. It manages, supervises and consults on safety, health and environmental issues in industry, insurance, government and education.

American Vacuum Society (AVS)
125 Maiden Ln., Fl. 15, Ste. 15B
New York, NY 10038 USA
Phone: 212-248-0200
Fax: 212-248-0245
E-mail Address: ricky@avs.org
Web Address: www.avs.org
The American Vacuum Society (AVS) is a nonprofit organization that promotes communication, dissemination of knowledge, recommended practices, research and education in the use of vacuum and other controlled environments to develop new materials, process technology and devices. AVS facilitates communication between academia, government laboratories and industry.

ASM International
9639 Kinsman Rd.
Materials Park, OH 44073-0002 USA
Phone: 440-338-5151
Fax: 440-338-4634
E-mail Address: memberservicecenter@asminternatio nal.org
Web Address: www.asminternational.org
ASM International is a worldwide network of materials engineers, aimed at advancing industry, technology and applications of metals and materials. It provides materials information, education and training, as well as networking opportunities for professionals within the materials industry.

Association for Consultancy and Engineering (ACE)
3 Hanbury Dr.
Leytonstone House
London, E11 1GA UK
Phone: 44-20-7222-6557
E-mail Address: membership@acenet.co.uk
Web Address: www.acenet.co.uk
The Association for Consultancy and Engineering (ACE) represents the business interests of the consultancy and engineering industry in the U.K.

Association for Electrical, Electronic & Information Technologies (VDE)
Stresemannallee 15

Frankfurt, 60596 Germany
Phone: 49-69-6308-0
Fax: 49-69-6308-9865
E-mail Address: service@vde.com
Web Address: www.vde.com
The Association for Electrical, Electronic & Information Technologies (VDE) is a German organization with roughly 36,000 members, representing one of the largest technical associations in Europe.

Association for Facilities Engineering (AFE)
1101 Pennsylvania Ave. NW
Ste. 300
Washington, DC 20004 USA
Toll Free: 888 432-1264
E-mail Address: admin@afe.org
Web Address: www.afe.org
The Association for Facilities Engineering (AFE) provides education, certification, technical information and other relevant resources for plant and facility engineering, operations and maintenance professionals worldwide.

Association of Consulting Chemists and Chemical Engineers (ACC&CE)
c/o J. Stephen Duerr, Ph.D., P.E., CPC, ACC&CE Treasurer
514 Corrigan Way
Cary, NC 27519 USA
Phone: 908-500-9333
E-mail Address: accce@chemconsult.org
Web Address: www.chemconsult.org
The Association of Consulting Chemists and Chemical Engineers (ACC&CE) was established to advance the practices of consulting chemists and chemical engineers.

Association of Consulting Engineers of Hong Kong
7/F., Pearl Oriental Tower
225 Nathan Road, Kowloon
Hong Kong, Hong Kong
Phone: 852-9327-0676
Fax: 852-3922-9797
E-mail Address: info@acehk.org.hk
Web Address: www.acehk.org.hk
The Association of Consulting Engineers of Hong Kong promotes the professional consulting engineers,

their business interests and rights, as well as sets standards of professional conduct and ethics for the consulting engineering profession.

Association of Consulting Engineers Singapore (ACES)
18 Sin Ming Ln.
#06-01, Midview City
Singapore, 573960 Singapore
Phone: 65-6659-5023
Fax: 65-6659-2093
E-mail Address: secretariat@aces.org.sg
Web Address: www.aces.org.sg
The Association of Consulting Engineers Singapore (ACES) is a nonprofit association representing the independent consulting engineering profession in Singapore.

Association of Federal Communications Consulting Engineers (AFCCE)
P.O. Box 19333
Washington, DC 20036 USA
Web Address: www.afcce.org
The Association of Federal Communications Consulting Engineers (AFCCE) is a professional organization of individuals who regularly assist clients on technical issues before the Federal Communications Commission (FCC).

Association of German Engineers (The, VDI)
VDI Verein Deutscher Ingenieure e.V.
VDI-Platz 1
Dusseldorf, 40468 Germany
Phone: 49-211-6214-0
Fax: 49-211-6214-575
E-mail Address: vdi@vdi.de
Web Address: www.vdi.de
The Association of German Engineers (VDI) promotes innovation and technology in Germany and represents one of the largest technical-scientific associations in Europe.

Association of German Machinery and Equipment Engineering (VDMA)
Lyoner Strasse 18
Frankfurt am Main,
Hesse 60528 Germany
Phone: 49-69-6603-0
Fax: 49-69-6603-1511
E-mail Address: info@vdma.org
Web Address: www.vdma.org
The Association of German Machinery and Equipment Engineering (VDMA) represents the machinery and plant manufacturing industry and the associated information technology and system engineering sector. The website includes product database, and member company lists as well as publications and links.

Association of Official Analytical Chemists (AOAC)
2275 Research Blvd., Ste. 300
Rockville, MD 20850-3250 USA
Phone: 301-924-7626
Toll Free: 800-379-2622
E-mail Address: customerservice@aoac.org
Web Address: www.aoac.org
The Association of Official Analytical Chemists (AOAC) is a nonprofit scientific association committed to worldwide standards in analytical results. It develops analytical methods with focus on public health and safety in areas, including fertilizers, veterinary drugs, feeds, foods and beverages, soil and water, infant formula, pharmaceuticals and dietary supplements.

Association of Professional Engineers of Nova Scotia (APENS)
1355 Barrington St.
Halifax, NS B3J 1Y9 Canada
Phone: 902-429-2250
Fax: 902-423-9769
Toll Free: 888-802-7367
E-mail Address: info@engineersnovascotia.ca
Web Address: www.engineersnovascotia.ca
The Association of Professional Engineers of Nova Scotia (APENS) is the licensing and regulatory body for the more than 5,000 professional engineers and engineers-in-training practicing in Nova Scotia.

ASTM International
100 Barr Harbor Dr.
P.O. Box C700
West Conshohocken, PA 19428-2959 USA
Phone: 610-832-9585
Toll Free: 877-909-2786
E-mail Address: news@astm.org
Web Address: www.astm.org
ASTM International, formerly the American Society for Testing & Materials, provides and develops voluntary consensus standards and related technical information that promote public health and safety. It also contributes to the reliability of materials for industries worldwide.

Audio Engineering Society, Inc. (AES)
551 Fifth Ave., Ste. 1225
New York, NY 10176 USA
Phone: 212-661-8528
Web Address: www.aes.org
The Audio Engineering Society (AES) provides information on educational and career opportunities in audio technology and engineering.

Brazilian Association of Chemical Engineering (ABEQ)
Av. Lineu Prestes, 580, Conjunto das Quimicas
BL.21 inferior, Cidade Universitaria
Sao Paulo, SP 05508-000 Brazil
Phone: 55-11-3091-2246
E-mail Address: abeq@abeq.org.br
Web Address: www.abeq.org.br
The Brazilian Association of Chemical Engineering is a non-profit organization that works to promote the development of chemical engineering throughout the country. Among other activities, it sponsors a variety of industry networking meetings and publishes a quarterly scientific journal and a technical magazine, as well as distributing annual scholarships to undergraduate and graduate students in the sciences.

Brazilian Association of Mechanical Sciences and Engineering
Praca Tiradentes
Fl. 9/10, Centro
Rio de Janeiro, RJ 20060-070 Brazil
Phone: 55-21-2221-0438
E-mail Address: abcm@abcm.org.br
Web Address: www.abcm.org.br
The Brazilian Association of Mechanical Sciences and Engineering (Associacao Brasileira de Engenharia e Ciencias Mecanicas, or ABCM),

founded in 1975, is a non-profit group that links engineers, universities, scientific institutions and businesses to develop the field of mechanical engineering in Brazil. ABCM publishes several technical journals and also sponsors a number of regular conferences for both students and professionals.

Broadcast Engineering Society (India)
912 Surya Kiran Bldg.
19, K.G. Marg
New Delhi, Delhi 110 001 India
Phone: 91-11-23316709
Fax: 91-11-23316710
E-mail Address: bes@besindia.com
Web Address: www.besindia.com
The Broadcast Engineering Society (India) aims to promote the interests of the broadcast engineering profession at the national and international levels.

Canadian Council of Professional Engineers (CCPE)
55 Metcalfe St., Ste. 300
Ottawa, Ontario K1P 6L5 Canada
Phone: 613-232-2474
Toll Free: 877-408-9273
E-mail Address: info@engineerscanada.ca
Web Address: www.engineerscanada.ca
The Canadian Council of Professional Engineers (CCPE), operating as Engineers Canada, is a national organization in Canada consisting of 12 provincial and territorial associations and organizations that license more than 160,000 professional engineers.

Center for Innovative Technology (CIT)
2214 Rock Hill Rd., Ste. 600
Herndon, VA 20170-4228 USA
Phone: 703-689-3000
Fax: 703-689-3041
E-mail Address: info@cit.org
Web Address: www.cit.org
The Center for Innovative Technology is a nonprofit organization designed to enhance research and development capabilities by creating partnerships between innovative technology start-up companies and advanced technology consumers.

Chemical Industry and Engineering Society of China (CIESC)
Fl. 7, Block B, 33 Anding Rd.
Chaoyang District
Beijing, 100029 China
Phone: 86-10-6444-1885
Fax: 86-10-6441-1194
E-mail Address: ciesc@ciesc.cn
Web Address: www.ciesc.cn
The Chemical Industry and Engineering Society of China (CIESC) aims to advance chemical engineering professionals and the chemical industry through academic and educational development. CIESC is affiliated with the China Association for Science and Technology.

China Academy of Building Research (CABR)
30, Bei San Huan Dong Lu
Beijing, 100013 China
Phone: 010-84272233
Fax: 010-84281369
E-mail Address: office@cabr.com.cn
Web Address: www.cabr.com.cn
CABR is responsible for the development and management of the major engineering construction and product standards of China and is also the largest comprehensive research and development institute in the building industry in China. Some related institutes include Institute of Earthquake Engineering, Institute of Building Fire Research, Institute of Building Environment and Energy Efficiency (Building Physics), Institute of Foundation Engineering as well as many others.

China Association for Science and Technology (CAST)
3 Fuxing Rd.
Beijing, 100863 China
Phone: 8610-6857-1898
Fax: 8610-6857-1897
E-mail Address: cast-liasion@cast.org.cn
Web Address: english.cast.org.cn
The China Association for Science and Technology (CAST) is the largest national non-governmental organization of scientific and technological workers in China. The association has nearly 207 member organizations in the fields of engineering, science and technology.

China Engineering Cost Association (CECA)
No. 22 No.22 Baiwanzhuang St.
Bldg. 2 Fl. 7
Beijing, 100037 China
Phone: 86-10-68331163
Web Address:
www.ccea.pro/english/mission.shtml
The China Engineering Cost Association aims to improve and promote the profession of engineering cost engineers and engineering project managers. The association provides examinations for engineering cost engineers, establishes standards in the industry and collects price information on materials and equipment. The association intercommunicates with many engineering cost organizations and specialists from Great Britain, Hong Kong, Korea, Japan, New Zealand, and Australia.

Chinese Academy of Sciences (CAS)
52 Sanlihe Rd.
Beijing, 100864 China
Phone: 86-10-6859-7521
Fax: 86-10-6851-1095
E-mail Address: cas_en@cas.cn
Web Address: english.cas.ac.cn
The Chinese Academy of Sciences (CAS) is an academic institution and research center active within the fields of natural and technological sciences. It brings together the operations of 124 science institutions, including five universities and supporting entities and over 104 research institutes throughout China.

Chinese Ceramic Society (CCS)
11 Sanlihe Rd.
Haidian District
Beijing, 100831 China
Phone: 86-10-57811248
E-mail Address:
guisuanyanxuehui@ceramsoc.com
Web Address: www.ceramsoc.com
The Chinese Ceramic Society (CCS) is an academic, nonprofit organization

for professionals engaged in the science and technology of inorganic nonmetallic materials.

Chinese Hydraulic Engineering Society (CHES)
16-2 BaiGuang Rd.
Beijing, 100053 China
Phone: 86-10-6320-4863
E-mail Address: ches1931@163.com
Web Address: www.ches.org.cn
The Chinese Hydraulic Engineering Society (CHES) aims to promote hydraulic engineering professionals and the water resources sciences and technologies. CHES has 31 regional societies in China.

CIEMAT
Avenida Complutense 40
Madrid, 28040 Spain
Phone: 91-346-60-00
Fax: 91-346-64-80
E-mail Address: contacto@ciemat.es
Web Address: www.ciemat.es
The CIEMAT, a unit of Spain's Ministry of Education and Science, is a public research agency. Its areas of focus include solar energy, biomass energy, wind energy, environment, basic research, fusion by magnetic confinement, nuclear safety, and technology transfer. Primary operations include PSA, the Solar Platform of Almeria, where concentrating solar power (CSP) is researched; CEDER, the Centre for the Development of Renewable Energy Sources; and CETA-CIEMAT, a center for information technology research.

Community Research and Development Information Service (CORDIS)
Office for Official Publications of the European Union Communities
2 rue Mercier
Luxembourg, L-2985 Luxembourg
Phone: 352-2929-42210
E-mail Address:
cordis@publications.europa.eu
Web Address: cordis.europa.eu
The Community Research and Development Information Service (CORDIS) provides information about research and development sponsored and supported by the

European Union. It is managed by the Office for Official Publications of the European Union Communities (Publications Office).

DECHEMA (Society for Chemical Engineering and Biotechnology)
Theodor-Heuss-Allee 25
Frankfurt am Main, 60486 Germany
Phone: 49-69-75-64-0
Fax: 49-69-75-64-201
E-mail Address: info@dechema.de
Web Address: dechema.de
The DECHEMA (Society for Chemical Engineering and Biotechnology) is a nonprofit scientific and technical society based in Germany. It was founded in 1926 to promote research and technical advances in the areas of chemical engineering, biotechnology and environmental protection.

Earthquake Engineering Research Institute (EERI)
499 14th St., Ste. 220
Oakland, CA 94612-1934 USA
Phone: 510-451-0905
Fax: 510-451-5411
E-mail Address: eeri@eeri.org
Web Address: www.eeri.org
The Earthquake Engineering Research Institute (EERI) is a national nonprofit technical organization of engineers, geoscientists, architects, planners, public officials and social scientists aimed at reducing earthquake risk by advancing the science and practice of earthquake engineering.

Engineer's Club (The) (TEC)
1737 Silverwood Dr.
San Jose, CA 95124 USA
Phone: 408-316-0488
E-mail Address:
INFO@engineers.com
Web Address: www.engineers.com
The Engineer's Club (TEC) provides a variety of resources for engineers and technical professionals.

European Association of Geoscientists & Engineers (EAGE)
Kosterijland 48
Bunnik, 3981 AJ The Netherlands
Phone: 31-88-995-5055
Fax: 31-30-634-3524

E-mail Address: eage@eage.org
Web Address: www.eage.org
EAGE is a professional association for geoscientists and engineers. It is a European-based organization with a worldwide membership providing a global network of commercial and academic professionals to all members. The association is truly multi-disciplinary and international in form and pursuits.

European Industrial Research Management Association
rue de al Loi, 81 A
Brussels, 1040 Belgium
Phone: 33-2-233-11-80
E-mail Address: info@eirma.org
Web Address: www.eirma.org
EIRMA is a not-for-profit organization which focuses on the effective global management and organization of business R&D and innovation within a European perspective. EIRMA engages over 100 major companies which are based in over 20 countries and operate in a wide range of sectors.

Federal Ministry of Education and Research - Germany
Heinemannstr. 2
Bonn, 53175 Germany
Phone: 49-228-9957-0
E-mail Address:
information@bmbf.bund.de
Web Address:
www.bmbf.de/en/nanotechnologie.php
The German Federal Ministry of Education and Research, Bundesministerium fur Bildung und Forschung (BMBF), is funding research and development in the field of future-oriented new technologies in Germany. The BMBF focuses its research efforts on high technology, life sciences and nanotechnologies, among other fields.

Federation of Technology Industries (FHI)
Leusderend 12
Leusden, 3832 RC The Netherlands
Phone: 31-33-465-7507
Fax: 31-33-461-6638
E-mail Address: info@fhi.nl
Web Address: federatie.fhi.nl

The Federation of Technology Industries (FHI) is the Dutch trade organization representing the industrial electronics, automation, laboratory technology and medical technology sectors in the Netherlands.

German Association of High-Tech Industries (SPECTARIS)
Werderscher Markt 15
Berlin, 10117 Germany
Phone: 49-30-4140-210
Fax: 49-30-4140-2133
E-mail Address: info@spectaris.de
Web Address: www.spectaris.de
The German Association of High-Tech Industries (SPECTARIS) is the trade association for technology and research in the consumer optics, photonics, biotech, laboratory technology and medical technology sectors.

Hong Kong Institution of Engineers (HKIE)
9/F Island Beverley
No. 1 Great George St.
Causeway Bay Hong, Hong Kong Hong Kong
Phone: 852-2895-4446
Fax: 852-2577-7791
E-mail Address: hkie-sec@hkie.org.hk
Web Address: www.hkie.org.hk
The Hong Kong Institution of Engineers (HKIE) promotes engineering professionals and maintains the standards of the profession.

IEEE Broadcast Technological Society (IEEE BTS)
445 Hoes Ln.
Piscataway, NJ 08854 USA
Phone: 732-562-6061
Fax: 732-235-1627
E-mail Address: a.temple@ieee.org
Web Address: bts.ieee.org
The IEEE Broadcast Technological Society (IEEE BTS) is the arm of the Institute of Electrical & Electronics Engineers (IEEE) devoted to devices, equipment, techniques and systems related to broadcast technology.

IEEE Communications Society (ComSoc)
3 Park Ave., Fl. 17
New York, NY 10016 USA
Phone: 212-705-8900
Fax: 212-705-8999
Web Address: www.comsoc.org
The IEEE Communications Society (ComSoc) is composed of industry professionals with a common interest in advancing communications technologies.

IEEE Oceanic Engineering Society (OES)
3 Park Ave., Fl. 17
New York, NY 10016-5997 USA
Phone: 212-419-7900
Fax: 212-752-4929
Toll Free: 800-678-4333
E-mail Address: president@ieeeoes.org
Web Address: ieeeoes.org
The IEEE Oceanic Engineering Society (OES) is the division of the IEEE that deals with electrical engineering at sea, including unmanned submarines and offshore oil platforms.

Illuminating Engineering Society (IES)
120 Wall St., Fl. 17
New York, NY 10005-4001 USA
Phone: 212-248-5000
E-mail Address: ies@ies.org
Web Address: www.ies.org
A recognized authority on lighting in North America, the Illuminating Engineering Society (IES) establishes scientific lighting recommendations. Members include engineers, architects, designers, educators, students, manufacturers and scientists.

Indian Institute of Technology - Roorkee
Roorkee, Uttarakhand 247 667 India
Phone: 91-1332-285311
E-mail Address: registar@iitr.ernet.in
Web Address: www.iitr.ac.in
Indian Institute of Technology - Roorkee is among the foremost institutes in higher technological education and engineering in India for basic and applied research.

Industrial Research Institute (IRI)
P.O. Box 13968
Arlington, VA 22219 USA
Phone: 703-647-2580
Fax: 703-647-2581
E-mail Address: information@iriweb.org
Web Address: www.iriweb.org
The Innovation Research Interchange (IRI) is a nonprofit organization of over 200 leading industrial companies, representing industries such as aerospace, automotive, chemical, computers and electronics, which carry out industrial research efforts in the U.S. manufacturing sector. IRI helps members improve research and development capabilities.

Institute of Bioengineering and Bioimaging, Singapore
31 Biopolis Way
The Nanos 07-01
Singapore, 138669 Singapore
Phone: 65-6824-7000
Fax: 65-6478-9083
E-mail Address: enquiry@ibb.a-star.edu.sg
Web Address: www.a-star.edu.sg/ibb
The Institute of Bioengineering & Bioimaging strives to develop new technologies and engineering solutions addressing health, medical and sustainability challenges and to promote the advancement of disease prevention, diagnosis and therapy.

Institute of Biological Engineering (IBE)
446 E. High St., Ste. 10
Lexington, KY 40507 USA
Phone: 859-977-7450
Fax: 859-271-0607
E-mail Address: info@ibe.org
Web Address: www.ibe.org
The Institute of Biological Engineering (IBE) is a professional organization encouraging inquiry and interest in biological engineering and professional development for its members.

Institute of Electrical and Electronics Engineers (IEEE)
3 Park Ave., Fl. 17
New York, NY 10016-5997 USA
Phone: 212-419-7900

Fax: 212-752-4929
Toll Free: 800-678-4333
E-mail Address: society-info@ieee.org
Web Address: www.ieee.org
The Institute of Electrical and Electronics Engineers (IEEE) is a nonprofit, technical professional association of more than 430,000 individual members in approximately 160 countries. The IEEE sets global technical standards and acts as an authority in technical areas ranging from computer engineering, biomedical technology and telecommunications to electric power, aerospace and consumer electronics.

Institute of Industrial & Systems Engineers (IISE)
3577 Parkway Ln., Ste. 200
Norcross, GA 30092 USA
Phone: 770-449-0460
Toll Free: 800-494-0460
E-mail Address: cs@iise.org
Web Address: www.iise.org/Home/
Institute of Industrial & Systems Engineers (IISE) is an international, non-profit association dedicated to the education, development, training and research in the field of industrial engineering.

Institute of Marine Engineering, Science and Technology (IMarEST)
1 Birdcage Walk
London, SW1H 9JJ UK
Phone: 44-20-7382-2600
E-mail Address: info@imarest.org
Web Address: www.imarest.org
The Institute of Marine Engineering, Science and Technology (IMarEST) works to promote the development of marine engineering, science and technology.

Institute of Physics and Engineering in Medicine (IPEM)
230 Tadcaster Rd.
Fairmount House
York, YO24 1ES UK
Phone: 44-1904-610-821
Fax: 44-1904-612-279
E-mail Address: office@ipem.ac.uk
Web Address: www.ipem.ac.uk
The Institute of Physics and Engineering in Medicine (IPEM) is an organization of scientists applying

physics and engineering in medical and biological applications.

Institute of Structural Engineers (IStructE)
47-58 Bastwick St.
London, EC1V 3PS UK
Phone: 44-20-7235-4535
E-mail Address: pr@istructe.org
Web Address: www.istructe.org.uk
The Institute of Structural Engineers (IStructE) is a professional organization, headquartered in the U.K., that sets and maintains standards for professional structural engineers. It has 27,000 members in 105 countries worldwide.

Institution of Engineering and Technology (The) (IET)
Michael Faraday House
Six Hills Way
Stevenage, Herts SG1 2AY UK
Phone: 44-1438-313-311
Fax: 44-1438-765-526
E-mail Address: postmaster@theiet.org
Web Address: www.theiet.org
The Institution of Engineering and Technology (IET) is an innovative international organization for electronics, electrical, manufacturing and IT professionals.

Institution of Engineers, Singapore
70 Bukit Tinggi Rd.
Singapore, 289758 Singapore
Phone: 65-6469-5000
E-mail Address: ies@iesnet.org.sg
Web Address: www.ies.org.sg
The Institution of Engineers, Singapore is the national society of engineers and its mission is the advancement of engineering in Singapore, and to advance and to promote the science, art and the profession of engineering.

Institution of Engineers, The (India)
8 Gokhale Rd.
Kolkata, 700 020 India
Phone: 91-33-40106-248
E-mail Address: iei_fb@ieindia.org
Web Address: www.ieindia.org
The Institution of Engineers (India) is one of the largest multi-disciplinary engineering professional societies in

India and was established to promote and advance the science, practice and business of engineering.

Institution of Mechanical Engineers-UK
1 Birdcage Walk
Westminster
London, SW1H 9JJ UK
Phone: 44-20-7222-7899
E-mail Address: enquiries@imeche.org
Web Address: www.imeche.org
The Institution of Mechanical Engineers represents the mechanical engineering profession in UK. The UK has the sixth largest manufacturing industry in the world and this association recognizes engineering professionals in this field. In addition, its other major themes are the energy, environment and transport industries as well as hosting educational opportunities for engineers.

International Commission of Agricultural and Biosystems Engineering (CIGR)
Rogers Hall 109
University of Florida
Gainesville, FL 32611 Japan
E-mail Address: secretarygeneral@cigr.org
Web Address: www.cigr.org
International Commission of Agricultural and Biosystems Engineering (CIGR) encourages and facilitates interregional exchange and the development of sciences and technologies in the field of agricultural engineering.

International Electrotechnical Commission (IEC)
3, rue de Varembe
P.O. Box 131
Geneva 20, CH-1211 Switzerland
Phone: 41-22-919-02-11
Fax: 41-22-919-03-00
E-mail Address: info@iec.ch
Web Address: www.iec.ch
The International Electrotechnical Commission (IEC), based in Switzerland, promotes international cooperation on all questions of standardization and related matters in electrical and electronic engineering.

International Federation of Automotive Engineering Societies (FISITA)
29 M11 Business Link
Parsonage Lane
Stansted, Essex CM24 8GF UK
Phone: 44-0-1279-833-470
E-mail Address: info@fisita.com
Web Address: www.fisita.com
The Federation Internationale des Societes d'Ingenieurs des Techniques de l'Automobile (FISITA) was founded in Paris in 1948 with the purpose of bringing engineers from around the world together in a spirit of cooperation to share ideas and advance the technological development of the automobile. FISITA is the umbrella organization for the national automotive societies in 37 countries around the world. Its network of member societies represents more than 200,000 automotive engineers around the globe.

International Federation of Consulting Engineers (FIDIC)
World Trade Center II, Geneva
Airport Box 311
29 Route de Pre-Bois, Cointrin
Geneva 15, CH-1215 Switzerland
Phone: 41-22-568-0500
E-mail Address: fidic@fidic.org
Web Address: fidic.org
The International Federation of Consulting Engineers (FIDIC) represents globally its national member associations and the consulting engineering industry and profession. Its web site also promotes best practices in areas such as international contracts, risk management, and sustainable development.

International Society of Automation (ISA), The
3252 S. Miami Blvd., Ste. 102
Durham, NC 27703 USA
Phone: 919-549-8411
Fax: 919-549-8288
E-mail Address: info@isa.org
Web Address: www.isa.org
The International Society of Automation (ISA), formerly known as the International Society for Measurement and Control is a

nonprofit organization that serves the professional development and credential needs of control system engineers, instrument technicians and others within the field of automation and control.

International Society of Pharmaceutical Engineers (ISPE)
6110 Executive Blvd., Ste. 600
North Bethesda, MD 20852 USA
Phone: 301-364-9201
Fax: 240-204-6024
E-mail Address: ASK@ispe.org
Web Address: www.ispe.org
The International Society of Pharmaceutical Engineers (ISPE) is a worldwide nonprofit society dedicated to educating and advancing pharmaceutical manufacturing professionals and the biopharmaceutical industry.

International Standards Organization (ISO)
Chemin de Blandonnet 8
1214 Vernier
Geneva, CP 401 Switzerland
Phone: 41-22-749-01-11
Fax: 41-22-733-34-30
E-mail Address: central@iso.org
Web Address: www.iso.org
The International Standards Organization (ISO) is a global consortium of national standards institutes from 162 countries. The established International Standards are designed to make products and services more efficient, safe and clean.

International Union of Pure and Applied Physics (IUPAP)
c/o OBERSON ABELS SA
Rue De-Candolle 20
Geneve, 1205 Switzerland
Phone: 39-040-630397
E-mail Address: communication@iupap.org
Web Address: www.iupap.org
The International Union of Pure and Applied Physics (IUPAP) was established in 1922 as a global group. The aims of the Union are to stimulate and promote international cooperation in physics; sponsor international meetings; publish

papers; and foster research and education.

Japan Science and Technology Agency (JST)
Kawaguchi Ctr. Bldg.
4-1-8 Honcho, Kawaguchi-shi
Saitama, 332-0012 Japan
Phone: 81-48-226-5601
Fax: 81-48-226-5651
Web Address: www.jst.go.jp/EN
The Japan Science and Technology Agency (JST) acts as a core organization for implementation of the nation's science and technology policies by conducting research and development, with particular emphasis on new technological needs.

Marine Technology Society (MTS)
One Thomas Cir., Ste. 700
Washington, DC 20005 USA
Phone: 202-717-8705
E-mail Address: mtsoffice@mtsociety.org
Web Address: www.mtsociety.org
The Marine Technology Society (MTS) is an organization devoted to the advancement, information exchange and application of marine technology.

Materials Research Society (MRS)
506 Keystone Dr.
Warrendale, PA 15086-7573 USA
Phone: 724-779-3003
Fax: 724-779-8313
Web Address: www.mrs.org
The Materials Research Society (MRS) is dedicated to basic and applied research on materials of technological importance. MRS emphasizes an interdisciplinary approach to materials science and engineering. It is responsible for the publication of the Journal of Materials Science, a peer-reviewed journal focused on printing advanced research in materials science.

Minerals, Metals & Materials Society (The) (TMS)
5700 Corporate Dr., Ste. 750
Pittsburgh, PA 15237 USA
Phone: 724-776-9000
Fax: 724-776-3770
Toll Free: 800-759-4867
E-mail Address: tmsgeneral@tms.org

Web Address: www.tms.org
The Minerals Metals & Materials Society (TMS) is an organization of professionals and students involved in metallurgy and material engineering, promoting the exchange of information, education and technology.

National Academies of Sciences, Engineering and Medicine
500 5th St. NW
Washington, DC 20001 USA
Phone: 202-334-2000
E-mail Address: contact@nas.edu
Web Address: www.nationalacademies.org
The National Academies of Sciences, Engineering and Medicine are private, nonprofit institutions that provide science, technology and health policy advice under a congressional charter. Its membership consists of world's most distinguished scientists, physicians and researchers; and activities include consensus studies, journals and periodicals, education and outreach and acknowledging exemplary professional achievement.

National Academy of Engineering (NAE)
500 5th St. NW
Washington, DC 20001 USA
Phone: 202-334-3200
Fax: 202-334-2290
E-mail Address: lerickson@nae.edu
Web Address: www.nae.edu
The National Academy of Engineering (NAE) is a nonprofit institution that conducts independent studies to examine important topics in engineering and technology. It is the portal for all engineering activities at the National Academies, which include the National Academy of Sciences, the Institute of Medicine and the National Research Council.

National Academy of Science (NAS)
500 5th St. NW
Washington, DC 20001 USA
Phone: 202-334-2000
E-mail Address: worldwidefeedback@nas.edu
Web Address: www.nasonline.org
The National Academy of Science (NAS) is a private, nonprofit, self-perpetuating society of scholars engaged in scientific and engineering research. Three organizations comprise the NAS: The National Academy of Engineering, the National Academy of Sciences and the National Academy of Medicine.

National Society of Professional Engineers (NSPE)
1420 King St.
Alexandria, VA 22314-2794 USA
Toll Free: 888-285-6773
E-mail Address: memserv@nspe.org
Web Address: www.nspe.org
The National Society of Professional Engineers (NSPE) represents individual engineering professionals and licensed engineers across all disciplines. NSPE serves approximately 45,000 members and has more than 500 chapters.

Netherlands Organization for Applied Scientific Research (TNO)
Motion Building
Radarweg 60
Amsterdam, 1043 NT The Netherlands
Phone: 31-88-866-0866
E-mail Address: info@tno.nl
Web Address: www.tno.nl
The Netherlands Organization for Applied Scientific Research (TNO) is a contract research organization that provides a link between fundamental research and practical application.

Optical Society of America (OSA)
2010 Massachusetts Ave. NW
Washington, DC 20036-1023 USA
Phone: 202-223-8130
Fax: 202-223-1096
E-mail Address: info@osa.org
Web Address: www.osa.org
The Optical Society of America (OSA) is an interdisciplinary society offering synergy between all components of the optics industry, from basic research to commercial applications such as fiber-optic networks. It has a membership group of over 16,000 individuals from over 100 countries. Members include scientists, engineers, educators, technicians and business leaders.

Professional Engineers Board, Singapore (PEB)
52 Jurong Gateway Rd., #07-03
Singapore, 608550 Singapore
Phone: 65-6334-2310
Fax: 65-6334-2347
E-mail Address: registrar@peb.gov.sg
Web Address: www.peb.gov.sg
The Professional Engineers Board, Singapore (PEB) is a statutory board in the Ministry of National Development. PEB was established since 1971 under the Professional Engineers Act in order to keep and maintain a register of professional engineers, a register of practitioners and a register of licensed corporations.

Royal Society (The)
6-9 Carlton House Ter.
London, SW1Y 5AG UK
Phone: 44-20-7451-2500
E-mail Address: science.policy@royalsociety.org
Web Address: royalsociety.org
The Royal Society, originally founded in 1660, is the UK's leading scientific organization and the oldest scientific community in continuous existence. It operates as a national academy of science, supporting scientists, engineers, technologists and researchers. Its web site contains a wealth of data about the research and development initiatives of its fellows and foreign members.

Royal Society of Chemistry (RSC)
Thomas Graham House
290 Science Park, Milton Rd.
Cambridge, CB4 0WF UK
Phone: 44-1223-420066
Fax: 44-1223-423623
Web Address: www.rsc.org
The Royal Society of Chemistry (RSC) is U.K.'s professional body for advancing the chemical sciences. The organization has 50,000 members.

Society of Automotive Engineers (SAE)
400 Commonwealth Dr.
Warrendale, PA 15096 USA
Phone: 724-776-4841
Fax: 724-776-0790
Toll Free: 877-606-7323

E-mail Address:
automotive_hq@sae.org
Web Address: www.sae.org
The Society of Automotive Engineers
(SAE) is a resource for technical
information and expertise used in
designing, building, maintaining and
operating self-propelled vehicles for
use on land, sea, air or space.

**Society of Broadcast Engineers,
Inc. (SBE)**
9102 N. Meridian St., Ste. 150
Indianapolis, IN 46260 USA
Phone: 317-846-9000
E-mail Address: jporay@sbe.org
Web Address: www.sbe.org
The Society of Broadcast Engineers
(SBE) exists to increase knowledge of
broadcast engineering and promote its
interests, as well as to continue the
education of professionals in the
industry.

**Society of Cable
Telecommunications Engineers
(SCTE)**
140 Philips Rd.
Exton, PA 19341-1318 USA
Phone: 610-363-6888
Fax: 610-884-7237
Toll Free: 800-542-5040
E-mail Address: info@scte.org
Web Address: www.scte.org
The Society of Cable
Telecommunications Engineers
(SCTE) is a nonprofit professional
association dedicated to advancing
the careers and serving the industry of
telecommunications professionals by
providing technical training,
certification and information
resources.

**Society of Consulting Marine
Engineers and Ship Surveyors
(SCMS)**
Unit 5, Prospect House
7 Ocean Way
Southampton, SO14 3TJ UK
Phone: 44-23-8001-6494
E-mail Address: sec@scmshq.org
Web Address: www.scmshq.org
The Society of Consulting Marine
Engineers and Ship Surveyors
(SCMS) is a professional organization
for marine engineers in the U.K.

**Society of Exploration
Geophysicists (SEG)**
8801 S. Yale, Ste. 500
Tulsa, OK 74137-3575 USA
Phone: 918-497-5581
Fax: 918-497-5558
Toll Free: 877-778-5463
E-mail Address: members@seg.org
Web Address: www.seg.org
The Society of Exploration
Geophysicists (SEG) promotes the
science of geophysics. The website
provides access to their foundation,
online publications and employment
and education services.

**Society of Hispanic Professional
Engineers (SHPE)**
13181 Crossroads Pkwy. N., Ste. 450
City of Industry, CA 91746 USA
Phone: 323-725-3970
E-mail Address:
shpenational@shpe.org
Web Address: shpe.org
The Society of Hispanic Professional
Engineers (SHPE) is a national
nonprofit organization that promotes
Hispanics in science, engineering and
math.

**Society of Manufacturing
Engineers (SME)**
1000 Town Ctr., Ste. 1910
Southfield, MI 48075 USA
Phone: 313-425-3000
Toll Free: 800-733-4763
E-mail Address: service@sme.org
Web Address: www.sme.org
The Society of Manufacturing
Engineers (SME) is a leading
professional organization serving
engineers in the manufacturing
industries.

**Society of Motion Picture and
Television Engineers (SMPTE)**
455 Hamilton Ave., Ste. 601
White Plains, NY 10601 USA
Phone: 914-761-1100
Fax: 914-206-4216
E-mail Address:
marketing@smpte.org
Web Address: www.smpte.org
The Society of Motion Picture and
Television Engineers (SMPTE) is the
leading technical society for the
motion imaging industry. The firm
publishes recommended practice and

engineering guidelines, as well as the
SMPTE Journal.

**Society of Naval Architects and
Marine Engineers (SNAME)**
99 Canal Ctr. Plz., Ste. 310
Alexandria, VA 22314 USA
Phone: 703-997-6701
E-mail Address: sname@sname.org
Web Address: www.sname.org
The Society of Naval Architects and
Marine Engineers (SNAME) is an
internationally recognized nonprofit,
professional society of members
serving the maritime and offshore
industries and their suppliers.

**Society of Petroleum Engineers
(SPE)**
222 Palisades Creek Dr.
Richardson, TX 75080 USA
Phone: 972-952-9393
Fax: 214-545-5201
Toll Free: 800-456-6863
E-mail Address: spedal@spe.org
Web Address: www.spe.org
The Society of Petroleum Engineers
(SPE) helps connect engineers in the
oil and gas industry with ideas,
answers, resources and technological
information.

Society of Plastics Engineers (SPE)
83 Wooster Heights Rd., Ste. 125
Danbury, CT 06810 USA
Phone: 203-740-5400
E-mail Address: spe@4spe.org
Web Address: www.4spe.org
The Society of Plastics Engineers
(SPE) is a recognized medium of
communication among scientists and
engineers engaged in the
development, conversion and
applications of plastics.

Society of Women Engineers (SWE)
130 East Randolph St., Ste. 3500
Chicago, IL 60601 USA
Phone: 312-596-5223
Toll Free: 877-793-4636
E-mail Address: hq@swe.org
Web Address: swe.org
The Society of Women Engineers
(SWE) is a nonprofit educational and
service organization of female
engineers.

SPIE

1000 20th St.
Bellingham, WA 98225-6705 USA
Phone: 360-676-3290
Fax: 360-647-1445
Toll Free: 888-504-8171
E-mail Address:
customerservice@spie.org
Web Address: www.spie.org
SPIE is a nonprofit technical society
aimed at the advancement and
dissemination of knowledge in optics,
photonics and imaging.

**United Engineering Foundation
(UEF)**
c/o Glenmede
1650 Market St. Ste. 1200
Philadelphia, PA 19103 USA
E-mail Address:
director@unitedengineeringfnd.org
Web Address: www.uefoundation.org
The United Engineering Foundation
(UEF) is a nonprofit organization
chartered for the advancement of
engineering arts and sciences in all
branches.

**World Federation of Engineering
Organizations**
Maison de l'UNESCO
1, rue Miollis
Paris, 75015 France
Phone: 33-1-45-68-48-47
Fax: 33-1-45-68-48-65
E-mail Address: secretariat@wfeo.net
Web Address: www.wfeo.org
World Federation of Engineering
Organizations (WFEO) is an
international non-governmental
organization that represents major
engineering professional societies in
over 90 nations. It has several
standing committees including
engineering and the environment,
technology, communications, capacity
building, education, energy and
women in engineering.

37) Environmental Organizations

**Center for Environmental Systems
Research (CESR)**
University of Kassel
Wilhelmshoher Allee 47, Raum 1130
Kassel, 34109 Germany
Phone: 49-561-804-6110
Fax: 49-561-804-6112

E-mail Address: info@cesr.de
Web Address: www.uni-
kassel.de/forschung/en/cesr/start
The Center for Environmental
Systems Research (CESR) is part of
the University of Kassel. It operates
four research groups: Global and
Regional Dynamics, covering water
and land use changes; Socio-
Environmental Systems; Integrated
Water Management; and Sustainable
Energy and Material Flow
Management. The CESR publishes
many important papers and boosts
education and research.

38) Environmental Resources

**Environment and Climate Change
Canada (ECCC)**
200 Sacre-Coeur Blvd
Fontaine Building, Fl. 12
Gatineau, QC K1A 0H3 Canada
Phone: 819-997-2800
Fax: 819-994-1412
Toll Free: 800 668-6767
E-mail Address: enviroinfo@ec.gc.ca
Web Address: www.ec.gc.ca
Environment and Climate Change
Canada is the Canadian government's
natural environment preservation
department.

39) Food Industry Associations, General

**Institute of Food Technologies
(IFT)**
525 W. Van Buren, Ste. 1000
Chicago, IL 60607 USA
Phone: 312-782-8424
Toll Free: 800-438-3663
E-mail Address: info@ift.org
Web Address: www.ift.org
The Institute of Food Technologies
(IFT) is devoted to the advancement
of the science and technology of food
through the exchange of knowledge.
The site also provides information
and resources for job seekers in the
food industry. Members work in food
science, food technology and related
professions in industry, academia and
government.

40) Geoengineering

**International Society for Soil
Mechanics and Geotechnical
Engineering (ISSMGE)**
Geotechnical Engineering Research
Ctr.
City University, Northampton Square
London, EC1V 0HB UK
Phone: 44-20-7040-8154
E-mail Address:
secretariat@issmge.org
Web Address: www.issmge.org
The International Society for Soil
Mechanics and Geotechnical
Engineering (ISSMGE) is a
professional body representing the
interests and activities of engineers,
academics and contractors all over the
world that actively participate in
geotechnical engineering. Its
activities include conferences and
publications.

41) Health Care Business & Professional Associations

**Advanced Medical Technology
Association (AdvaMed)**
701 Pennsylvania Ave. NW, Ste. 800
Washington, DC 20004-2654 USA
Phone: 202-783-8700
Fax: 202-783-8750
E-mail Address: info@advamed.org
Web Address: www.advamed.org
The Advanced Medical Technology
Association (AdvaMed) strives to be
the advocate for a legal, regulatory
and economic climate that advances
global health care by assuring
worldwide access to the benefits of
medical technology.

**Cryogenic Society of America, Inc.
(CSA)**
218 Lake St.
Oak Park, IL 60302-2609 USA
Phone: 708-383-6220
Fax: 708-383-9337
E-mail Address:
csa@cryogenicsociety.org
Web Address:
www.cryogenicsociety.org
The Cryogenic Society of America,
Inc. (CSA) is a nonprofit organization
that brings together those in all

disciplines concerned with the applications of cryogenics, which refers to the art and science of achieving extremely low-temperatures. With membership spanning over 47 countries, the organization works to promote information sharing, increase awareness and conduct research in low temperature processes and techniques.

42) Industry Research/ Market Research

Forrester Research
60 Acorn Park Dr.
Cambridge, MA 02140 USA
Phone: 617-613-5730
Toll Free: 866-367-7378
E-mail Address: press@forrester.com
Web Address: www.forrester.com
Forrester Research is a publicly traded company that identifies and analyzes emerging trends in technology and their impact on business. Among the firm's specialties are the financial services, retail, health care, entertainment, automotive and information technology industries.

Gartner, Inc.
56 Top Gallant Rd.
Stamford, CT 06902 USA
Phone: 203-964-0096
E-mail Address: info@gartner.com
Web Address: www.gartner.com
Gartner, Inc. is a publicly traded IT company that provides competitive intelligence and strategic consulting and advisory services to numerous clients worldwide.

MarketResearch.com
6116 Executive Blvd., Ste. 550
Rockville, MD 20852 USA
Phone: 240-747-3093
Fax: 240-747-3004
Toll Free: 800-298-5699
E-mail Address:
customerservice@marketresearch.com
Web Address:
www.marketresearch.com
MarketResearch.com is a leading broker for professional market research and industry analysis. Users

are able to search the company's database of research publications including data on global industries, companies, products and trends.

Plunkett Research, Ltd.
P.O. Drawer 541737
Houston, TX 77254-1737 USA
Phone: 713-932-0000
Fax: 713-932-7080
E-mail Address:
customersupport@plunkettresearch.com
Web Address:
www.plunkettresearch.com
Plunkett Research, Ltd. is a leading provider of market research, industry trends analysis and business statistics. Since 1985, it has served clients worldwide, including corporations, universities, libraries, consultants and government agencies. At the firm's web site, visitors can view product information and pricing and access a large amount of basic market information on industries such as financial services, InfoTech, ecommerce, health care and biotech.

43) Internet Industry Associations

Cooperative Association for Internet Data Analysis (CAIDA)
9500 Gilman Dr.
Mail Stop 0505
La Jolla, CA 92093-0505 USA
Phone: 858-534-5000
E-mail Address: info@caida.org
Web Address: www.caida.org
The Cooperative Association for Internet Data Analysis (CAIDA), representing organizations from the government, commercial and research sectors, works to promote an atmosphere of greater cohesion in the engineering and maintenance of the Internet. CAIDA is located at the San Diego Supercomputer Center (SDSC) on the campus of the University of California, San Diego (UCSD).

Internet Society (ISOC)
11710 Plaza America Dr., Ste. 400
Reston, VA 20190 USA
Phone: 703-439-2120
Fax: 703-326-9881
E-mail Address: isoc@isoc.org

Web Address: www.isoc.org
The Internet Society (ISOC) is a nonprofit organization that provides leadership in public policy issues that influence the future of the Internet. The organization is the home of groups that maintain infrastructure standards for the Internet, such as the Internet Engineering Task Force (IETF) and the Internet Architecture Board (IAB).

Internet Systems Consortium, Inc. (ISC)
P.O. Box 360
Newmarket, NH 03857 USA
Phone: 650-423-1300
Fax: 650-423-1355
E-mail Address: info@isc.org
Web Address: www.isc.org
The Internet Systems Consortium, Inc. (ISC) is a nonprofit organization with extensive expertise in the development, management, maintenance and implementation of Internet technologies.

W3C (World Wide Web Consortium)
32 Vassar St., Bldg. 32-G515
Cambridge, MA 02139 USA
Phone: 617-253-2613
Fax: 617-258-5999
E-mail Address: susan@w3.org
Web Address: www.w3.org
The World Wide Web Consortium (W3C) develops technologies and standards to enhance the performance and utility of the World Wide Web. The W3C is hosted by three different organizations: the European Research Consortium for Informatics and Mathematics (ERICM) handles inquiries about the W3C in the EMEA region; Keio University handles W3C's Japanese and Korean correspondence; and the Computer Science & Artificial Intelligence Lab (CSAIL) at MIT handles all other countries, include Australia and the U.S.

44) Internet Industry Resources

American Registry for Internet Numbers (ARIN)
P.O. Box 232290

Centreville, VA 20120 USA
Phone: 703-227-9840
Fax: 703-263-0417
E-mail Address: info@arin.net
Web Address: www.arin.net
The American Registry for Internet
Numbers (ARIN) is a nonprofit
organization that administers and
registers Internet protocol (IP)
numbers. The organization also
develops policies and offers
educational outreach services.

**Berkman Center for Internet &
Society**
23 Everett St., Fl. 2
Cambridge, MA 02138 USA
Phone: 617-495-7547
Fax: 617-495-7641
E-mail Address:
cyber@law.harvard.edu
Web Address: cyber.law.harvard.edu
The Berkman Center for Internet &
Society, housed at Harvard
University's law school, focuses on
the exploration of the development
and inner-workings of laws pertaining
to the Internet. The center offers
Internet courses, conferences,
advising and advocacy.

**Congressional Internet Caucus
Advisory Committee (CICA)**
1440 G St. NW
Washington, DC 20005 USA
Phone: 202-638-4370
E-mail Address:
tlordan@netcaucus.org
Web Address: www.netcaucus.org
The Congressional Internet Caucus
Advisory Committee (ICAC) works
to educate the public, as well as a
bipartisan group from the U.S. House
and Senate about Internet-related
policy issues.

**Internet Assigned Numbers
Authority (IANA)**
12025 Waterfront Dr., Ste. 300
Los Angeles, CA 90094 USA
Phone: 424-254-5300
Fax: 424-254-5033
E-mail Address: iana@iana.org
Web Address: www.iana.org
The Internet Assigned Numbers
Authority (IANA) serves as the
central coordinator for the assignment
of parameter values for Internet

protocols. IANA is operated by the
Internet Corporation for Assigned
Names and Numbers (ICANN).

45) Manufacturing Associations-Machinery & Technology

**Association for Manufacturing
Technology (AMT)**
Jones Branch Dr., Ste. 900
McLean, VA 22102-3316 USA
Phone: 703-893-2900
Fax: 703-893-1151
Toll Free: 800-524-0475
E-mail Address: amt@amtonline.org
Web Address: www.amtonline.org
The Association for Manufacturing
Technology (AMT) actively supports
and promotes American
manufacturers of machine tools and
manufacturing technology.

**German Machine Tool Builders'
Association (VDW)**
Lyoner Strasse 18
Frankfurt am Main, 60528 Germany
Phone: 49 69 756081 0
E-mail Address: vdw@vdw.de
Web Address: www.vdw.de
German Machine Tool Builders'
Association (VDW) represents the
industry nationally and
internationally. The organization
offers information, news and updates
from fields, such as economics and
statistics, technology, research, law
and taxation to its members.

**Indian Machine Tool
Manufacturers Association
(IMTMA)**
Tumkur Rd., Madavara Post, 10th
Mile
Bangalore Int'l Exhibition Ctr.
Bangalore, 562123 India
Phone: 91-80-6624-6600
Fax: 91-80-6624-6661
E-mail Address: imtma@imtma.in
Web Address: www.imtma.in
Indian Machine Tool Manufacturers
Association (IMTMA) has a
membership of over 492
organizations of all sizes spread
across the country. Membership of
IMTMA specializes in the complete
range of metalworking machine tools
and manufacturing solutions,

accessories for machines, as well as
the varied range of cutting tools and
tooling systems.

**National Center for Manufacturing
Sciences (NCMS)**
3025 Boardwalk Dr.
Ann Arbor, MI 48108-3230 USA
Fax: 734-995-1150
Toll Free: 800-222-6267
E-mail Address: contact@ncms.org
Web Address: www.ncms.org
The National Center for
Manufacturing Sciences (NCMS) is a
non-profit membership organization
dedicated to advancing the global
competitiveness of North American
manufacturing industry.

**National Tooling and Machining
Association (NTMA)**
1357 Rockside Rd.
Cleveland, OH 44134 USA
Fax: 216-264-2840
Toll Free: 800-248-6862
E-mail Address: info@ntma.org
Web Address: www.ntma.org
The National Tooling and Machining
Association (NTMA) helps members
of the U.S. precision custom
manufacturing industries achieve
business success in a global economy
through advocacy, advice,
networking, information, programs
and services.

**Singapore Institute of
Manufacturing Technology
(SIMTech)**
1 Fusionopolis Way
#20-10 Connexis North Tower
Singapore, 138632 Singapore
Phone: 65-6826-6111
E-mail Address: contact@a-
star.edu.sg
Web Address: www.a-
star.edu.sg/simtech
The Singapore Institute of
Manufacturing Technology
(SIMTech) has completed more than
880 projects with more than 410
companies, big and small, in the
electronics, semiconductor, precision
engineering, aerospace, automotive,
marine, logistics and other sectors.

46) Maritime Associations

German Shipbuilding and Ocean Industries Association
Verband fur Schiffbau und Meerestechnik e.V.
Steinhoft 11 (Slomanhaus)
Hamburg, 20459 Germany
Phone: 49-040-2801-52-0
Fax: 49-040-2801-52-30
E-mail Address: info@vsm.de
Web Address: www.vsm.de
The VSM represents the political and commercial interests of the German maritime industry; shipyards building; oceangoing and inland waterway vessels; and marine equipment suppliers.

47) MBA Resources

MBA Depot
Web Address: www.mbadepot.com
MBA Depot is an online community and information portal for MBAs, potential MBA program applicants and business professionals.

48) Metals & Steel Industry Associations

Chinese Society for Metals
9th Fl., Bldg. 8
No. 9 Qixiang Rd., Haidian Dist.
Beijing, 100081 Phone: 86-10-6521-1205
Fax: 86-10-6512-4122
E-mail Address: csmoffice@csm.org.cn
Web Address: www.csm.org.cn
The Chinese Society for Metals is a non-profit organization that focuses on advancing science and technology in the metallurgical industry, materials science and engineering and the professionals in these fields.

Society for Mining, Metallurgy and Exploration (SME)
12999 E. Adam Aircraft Cir.
Englewood, CO 80112 USA
Phone: 720-738-4085
Toll Free: 800-958-1550
E-mail Address: cs@smenet.org
Web Address: www.smenet.org
The Society for Mining, Metallurgy and Exploration (SME) advances the worldwide mining and minerals community through information exchange and professional development.

49) Nanotechnology Associations

International Association of Nanotechnology (IANT)
NASA Ames Research Center
P.O. Box 151
Moffett Field, CA 94035 USA
Phone: 408-280-6222
Fax: 877-636-6266
E-mail Address: info@ianano.org
Web Address: www.ianano.org
The International Association of Nanotechnology is a non-profit organization that promotes research collaboration in nanoscience worldwide for the benefit of society. The IANT sponsors panel discussions, regional meetings and an international congress to discuss the development of nanotechnology.

50) Nanotechnology Resources

Center for Directed Assembly of Nanostructures
110 8th St., 1st Fl. MRC
Rensselaer Polytechnic Institute
Troy, NY 12180-3590 USA
Phone: 518-276-8846
Fax: 518-276-6540
E-mail Address: nanocenter@rpi.edu
Web Address: www.rpi.edu/dept/nsec
The Center for Directed Assembly of Nanostructures focuses on learning to produce nanomaterials in controlled ways, incorporating them into polymer and ceramic composites and assembling them into complex structures. It is part of the Rensselaer Polytechnic Institute and was one of the first six National Science Foundation Nanoscale Science and Engineering Centers (NSF NSEC) established in 2001.

National Institute of Advanced Industrial Science and Technology-Nanomaterials Research Institute
1-1-1 Higashi
AIST Tusukubs Central 5
Tsukuba, Ibaraki 305-8565 Japan
E-mail Address: nmri-info-ml@aist.go.jp
Web Address:
https://unit.aist.go.jp/nmri/index_en.html
The National Institute of Advanced Industrial Science and Technology-Nanomaterials Research Institute is Japan's foremost nanomaterials research institute.

National Nanotechnology Initiative (NNI)
2415 Eisenhower Ave.
Alexandria, VA 22314 USA
Phone: 202-517-1050
E-mail Address: info@nnco.nano.gov
Web Address: www.nano.gov
The National Nanotechnology Initiative (NNI) is a federal R&D program established to coordinate multiagency efforts in nanoscale science, engineering and technology. 20 departments and independent agencies participate in the NNI. Other federal organizations contribute with studies, applications of the results from those agencies performing R&D and other collaborations. The NNI is part of the National Nanotechnology Coordination Office within the Nanoscale Science Engineering and Technology (NSET) subcommittee of the National Science and Technology Council (NSTC).

51) Nuclear Energy Associations

China Atomic Energy Authority
A 8 Fucheng Lu
Haidian district
Beijing, 100048 China
E-mail Address: webmaster@caea.gov.cn
Web Address: www.caea.gov.cn
The China Atomic Energy Authority is involved in developing policies and regulations and the development programming, planning and industrial standards for peaceful uses of nuclear energy.

Fusion Industry Association (FIA)
800 Maine Ave. SW, Ste. 223
Washington, DC 20024 USA

Web Address:
www.fusionindustryassociation.org
The Fusion Industry Association
(FIA) is working to transform the
energy system with commercially
viable fusion power, founded as an
initiative in 2018.

52) Patent Organizations

European Patent Office
Bob-van-Benthem-Platz 1
Munich, 80469 Germany
Phone: 49 89 2399-0
Toll Free: 08-800-80-20-20-20
E-mail Address: press@epo.org
Web Address: www.epo.org
The European Patent Office (EPO)
provides a uniform application
procedure for individual inventors
and companies seeking patent
protection in up to 38 European
countries. It is the executive arm of
the European Patent Organization and
is supervised by the Administrative
Council.

**World Intellectual Property
Organization (WIPO)**
34 chemin des Colombettes
Geneva, CH-1211 Switzerland
Phone: 41-22-338-9111
Fax: 41-22-733-5428
Web Address: www.wipo.int
The World Intellectual Property
Organization (WIPO) has a United
Nations mandate to assist
organizations and companies in filing
patents and other intellectual property
data on a global basis. At its web site,
users can download free copies of its
WIPO magazine and search its
international patent applications.

53) Patent Resources

Patent Board (The)
E-mail Address:
support@CONTRIB.com
Web Address: www.patentboard.com
The Patent Board is an online
platform, which offers tools and
metrics for patent analysis and
intellectual property investing. Its
services include technology landscape
analysis, portfolio assessment and
merger and acquisition due diligence.

The Patent Board platform is owned
by Global Ventures, LLC.

54) Plastics Industry Associations

**China Plastics Processing Industry
Association (CPPIA)**
Rm. 918, Gaohe Lanfeng Bldg.
No. 98, East Third Ring S. Rd.,
Chaoyang Dist.
Beijing, 100122 China
Phone: 86-10-6528-1529
Fax: 86-10-6527-8590
E-mail Address: cppiabgs@163.com
Web Address: www.cppia.com.cn
The China Plastics Processing
Industry Association (CPPIA)
promotes the industry which includes
plastic pipe, injection molded
products and other engineering
plastics.

55) Research & Development, Laboratories

**Advanced Technology Laboratory
(ARL)**
10000 Burnet Rd.
University of Texas at Austin
Austin, TX 78758 USA
Phone: 512-835-3200
Fax: 512-835-3259
Web Address: www.arlut.utexas.edu
Advanced Technology Laboratory
(ARL) at the University of Texas at
Austin provides research programs
dedicated to improving the military
capability of the United States in
applications of acoustics,
electromagnetic and information
technology.

**Argonne National Laboratory,
Nuclear Engineering Division
(ANL)**
9700 S. Cass Ave.
Argonne, IL 60439-4814 USA
E-mail Address: neinfo@anl.gov
Web Address: www.ne.anl.gov
The Argonne National Laboratory-
Nuclear Engineering Division (ANL)
is engaged in research and
development in the area of applied
nuclear technologies such as
nonproliferation, environmental

remediation, fusion power and new
initiatives.

Battelle Memorial Institute
505 King Ave.
Columbus, OH 43201-2693 USA
Phone: 614-424-6424
Toll Free: 800-201-2011
E-mail Address:
solutions@battelle.org
Web Address: www.battelle.org
Battelle Memorial Institute serves
commercial and governmental
customers in developing new
technologies and products. The
institute adds technology to systems
and processes for manufacturers;
pharmaceutical and agrochemical
industries; trade associations; and
government agencies supporting
energy, the environment, health,
national security and transportation.

**Brookhaven National Laboratory
(BNL)**
P.O. Box 5000
Upton, NY 11973-5000 USA
Phone: 631-344-8000
E-mail Address: privacy@bnl.gov
Web Address: www.bnl.gov
Brookhaven National Laboratory
(BNL) is a research facility funded by
the Office of Science within the
Department of Energy. BNL conducts
research in the physical, biomedical
and environmental sciences, as well
as in energy technologies and national
security.

**CERN (European Organization for
Nuclear Research, LHC)**
1 Esplanade des Particules
Meyrin
Geneva, CH-1217 Switzerland
Phone: 41-22-76-784-84
E-mail Address:
cern.reception@cern.ch
Web Address: home.web.cern.ch
CERN, the European Organization for
Nuclear Research, is one of the
world's largest centers for scientific
research. Its business is fundamental
physics, finding out what the universe
is made of and how it works. CERN
is the operator of the Large Hadron
Collider (LHC), a particle accelerator
used by physicists to study the
smallest known particles.

Commonwealth Scientific and Industrial Research Organization (CSRIO)
CSIRO Enquiries
Private Bag 10
Clayton South,
Victoria 3169 Australia
Phone: 61-3-9545-2176
Toll Free: 1300-363-400
Web Address: www.csiro.au
The Commonwealth Scientific and Industrial Research Organization (CSRIO) is Australia's national science agency and a leading international research agency. CSRIO performs research in Australia over a broad range of areas including agriculture, minerals and energy, manufacturing, communications, construction, health and the environment.

Computational Neurobiology Laboratory
CNL-S c/o The Salk Institute
10010 N. Torrey Pines Rd.
La Jolla, CA 92037 USA
Phone: 858-453-4100
Fax: 858-587-0417
Web Address: www.cnl.salk.edu
The Computational Neurobiology Laboratory at The Salk Institute strives to understand the computational resources of the brain from the biophysical to the systems levels.

Council of Scientific & Industrial Research (CSIR)
2 Rafi Marg
Anusandhan Bhawan
New Delhi, 110001 India
Phone: 91-11-2373-7889
Fax: 91-11-2371-0618
E-mail Address: itweb@csir.res.in
Web Address: www.csir.res.in
The Council of Scientific & Industrial Research (CSIR) is a government-funded organization that promotes research and development initiatives in India. It operates in the fields of energy, biotechnology, space, science and technology.

Daresbury Laboratory
Sci Tech Daresbury
Keckwick Ln.
Warrington, Cheshire WA4 4AD UK
Phone: 44-1925-603-000
E-mail Address: info@sci-techdaresbury.com
Web Address: www.sci-techdaresbury.com/science-facilities/daresbury-laboratory/
Daresbury Laboratory, operated by the Science & Technology Facilities Council (STFC), is a strong resource in computational science and engineering. The STFC was formed in April 2007 from the merger of the Council for the Central Laboratory of the Research Councils (CCLRC) and the Particle Physics and Astronomy Council (PPARRC).

Electronics and Telecommunications Research Institute (ETRI)
218 Gajeongno
Yuseong-gu
Daejeon, 34129 Korea
Phone: 82-42-860-6114
E-mail Address: k21human@etri.re.kr
Web Address: www.etri.re.kr
Established in 1976, the Electronics and Telecommunications Research Institute (ETRI) is a nonprofit government-funded research organization that promotes technological excellence. The research institute has successfully developed information technologies such as TDX-Exchange, High Density Semiconductor Microchips, Mini-Super Computer (TiCOM), and Digital Mobile Telecommunication System (CDMA). ETRI's focus is on information technologies, robotics, telecommunications, digital broadcasting and future technology strategies.

Fraunhofer-Gesellschaft (FhG) (The)
Fraunhofer-Gesellschaft zur Forderung der angewandten Forschung e.V.
Postfach 20 07 33
Munich, 80007 Germany
Phone: 49-89-1205-0
Fax: 49-89-1205-7531
Web Address: www.fraunhofer.de
The Fraunhofer-Gesellschaft (FhG) institute focuses on research in health, security, energy, communication, the environment and mobility. FhG includes over 80 research units in Germany. Over 70% of its projects are derived from industry contracts.

Hanford Nuclear Site
2420 Stevens Center Pl., H520
Richland, WA 99352 USA
Phone: 509-376-7411
E-mail Address: Webmaster@rl.gov
Web Address: www.hanford.gov
The Hanford Nuclear Site is designed to solve critical problems related to the environment, energy production and use, U.S. economic competitiveness and national security.

Helmholtz Association
Anna-Louisa-Karsch-Strasse 2
Berlin, 10178 Germany
Phone: 49-30-206329-0
E-mail Address: info@helmholtz.de
Web Address: www.helmholtz.de/en
The Helmholtz Association is a community of 18 scientific-technical and biological-medical research centers. Helmholtz Centers perform top-class research in strategic programs in several core fields: energy, earth and environment, health, key technologies, structure of matter, aeronautics, space and transport.

Idaho National Laboratory (INL)
1955 N. Fremont Ave.
Idaho Falls, ID 83415 USA
Toll Free: 866-495-7440
Web Address: www.inl.gov
Idaho National Laboratory (INL) is a multidisciplinary, multiprogram laboratory that specializes in developing nuclear energy with research concerning the environment, energy, science and national defense.

Industrial Technology Research Institute (ITRI)
195, Sec. 4, Chung Hsing Rd
Chutung, 31040 Taiwan
Phone: 886-3-582-0100
Fax: 886-3-582-0045
Web Address: www.itri.org.tw
The Industrial Technology Research Institute (ITRI) is a nonprofit R&D organization founded in 1973 by the Ministry of Economic Affairs (MOEA) of Taiwan. It engages in applied research and technical service for Taiwan's industrial development.

ITRI focuses on six areas of development: Information and Communications; Electronics and Optoelectronics; Material, Chemical and Nanotechnology; Medical devices and biomedical; Mechanical Systems; and Green Energy and Environment.

Institute for Telecommunication Sciences (ITS)
325 Broadway
Boulder, CO 80305-3337 USA
Phone: 303-497-3571
E-mail Address: info@its.bldrdoc.gov
Web Address: www.its.bldrdoc.gov
The Institute for Telecommunication Sciences (ITS) is the research and engineering branch of the National Telecommunications and Information Administration (NTIA), a division of the U.S. Department of Commerce (DOC). Its research activities are focused on advanced telecommunications and information infrastructure development.

Leibniz Association of German Research Institutes (WGL)
Chaussee Strasse 111
Berlin, D-10115 Germany
Phone: 49-030/20-60-49-0
Fax: 49-030/20-60-49-55
E-mail Address: info@leibniz-gemeinschaft.de
Web Address: www.leibniz-gemeinschaft.de
The Leibniz Association of German Research Institutes (WGL) is a research organization that comprises over 89 institutes. WGL works on international interdisciplinary research and acts as a bridge between traditional research and customer oriented applications. The association focuses on scientific excellence and social relevance.

Los Alamos National Laboratory (LANL)
P.O. Box 1663
Los Alamos, NM 87545 USA
Phone: 505-667-5061
E-mail Address: community@lanl.gov
Web Address: www.lanl.gov
The Los Alamos National Laboratory (LANL), a national energy lab in New Mexico, was originally built as a

work site for the team that designed the first atomic bomb during World War II. Currently, it provides a continual stream of research in physics and energy matters. Much of that research is put to use in the commercial sector.

MITRE Corporation
202 Burlington Rd.
Bedford, MA 01730-1420 USA
Phone: 781-271-2000
E-mail Address: media@mitre.org
Web Address: www.mitre.org
MITRE Corporation is a nonprofit engineering institution offering expertise in communications, information, space, environmental and aviation systems. It operates three federally funded research and development centers for the U.S. government.

National Renewable Energy Laboratory (NREL)
15013 Denver W. Pkwy.
Golden, CO 80401 USA
Phone: 303-275-3000
Web Address: www.nrel.gov
The National Renewable Energy Laboratory (NREL) reduces nuclear danger, transfers applied environmental technology to government and non-government entities and forms economic and industrial alliances.

National Research Council Canada (NRC)
1200 Montreal Rd., Bldg. M-58
Ottawa, ON K1A 0R6 Canada
Phone: 613-993-9101
Fax: 613-952-9907
Toll Free: 877-672-2672
E-mail Address: info@nrc-cnrc.gc.ca
Web Address: www.nrc-cnrc.gc.ca
National Research Council Canada (NRC) is comprised of 12 government organization, research institutes and programs that carry out multidisciplinary research. It maintains partnerships with industries and sectors key to Canada's economic development.

Oak Ridge National Laboratory (ORNL)
1 Bethel Valley Rd.

P.O. Box 2008
Oak Ridge, TN 37831 USA
Phone: 865-576-7658
Web Address: www.ornl.gov
The Oak Ridge National Laboratory (ORNL) is a multi-program science and technology laboratory managed for the U.S. Department of Energy by U.T.-Battelle, LLC. It conducts basic and applied research and development to create scientific knowledge and technological solutions.

Pacific Northwest National Laboratory (PNNL)
902 Battelle Blvd.
Richland, WA 99352 USA
Phone: 509-375-2121
Toll Free: 888-375-7665
E-mail Address:
greg.koller@pnnl.gov
Web Address: www.pnnl.gov
The Pacific Northwest National Laboratory (PNNL) is a Department of Energy facility that conducts research in 10 areas of focus: Chemical and Molecular Sciences; Biological Systems Science; Climate Change Science; Subsurface Science; Chemical Engineering; Applied Materials Science and Engineering; Applied Nuclear Science and Technology; Advanced Computer Science, Visualization and Data; Systems Engineering and Integration; and Large-Scale User Facilities and Advanced Instrumentation.

Program on Vehicle and Mobility Innovation (PVMI)
Steinberg Hall-Dietrich Hall 3400
3620 Locust Walk
Philadelphia, PA 19104-6371 USA
Phone: 215-746-4831
E-mail Address:
mackinstitute@wharton.upenn.edu
Web Address:
pvmi.wharton.upenn.edu
The Program on Vehicle and Mobility Innovation (PVMI), formerly the International Motor Vehicle Program (IMVP), is a research project, funded by leading global car makers as well as government agencies, focused on enhancing automotive design and manufacturing methods. In 2013, the IMVP changed its name to the PVMI and was integrated into the Mack

Institute for Innovation Management at the Wharton School, University Pennsylvania.

Sandia National Laboratories
1515 Eubank SE
Albuquerque, NM 87125 USA
Phone: 505-844-8066
Web Address: www.sandia.gov
Sandia National Laboratories is a national security laboratory operated for the U.S. Department of Energy by the Sandia Corporation. It designs all nuclear components for the nation's nuclear weapons and performs a wide variety of energy research and development projects.

Savannah River Site (SRS)
U.S. Dept. of Energy, P.O. Box A
Savannah River Operations Office
Aiken, SC 29802 USA
Phone: 803-952-7697
E-mail Address:
will.callicott@srs.gov
Web Address: www.srs.gov
The Savannah River Site (SRS) is a nuclear fuel storage and production site that works to protect the people and the environment of the U.S. through safe, secure, cost-effective management of the country's nuclear weapons stockpile and nuclear materials. While the site is owned by the U.S. Department of Energy, it is operated by the subsidiaries of Washington Savannah River Company, LLC (WSRC), itself a wholly owned subsidiary of Washington Group International.

Sloan Automotive Laboratory
60 Vassar St., Bldg. 31-153
Cambridge, MA 02139-4307 USA
Phone: 617-253-4529
Fax: 617-253-9453
E-mail Address: jsabio@mit.edu
Web Address: web.mit.edu/sloan-auto-lab
The Sloan Automotive Laboratory at MIT was founded in 1929 by Professor C.F. Taylor, with a grant from Alfred P. Sloan, Jr., CEO of General Motors, as a major laboratory for automotive research in the US and the world. The goals of the Laboratory are to provide the fundamental knowledge base for

automotive engineering and to educate students to become technological leaders in the automotive industry.

SRI International
1100 Wilson Blvd., Ste. 2800
Arlington, VA 22209 USA
Phone: 650-859-2000
Web Address: www.sri.com
SRI International is a nonprofit research organization that offers contract research services to government agencies, as well as commercial enterprises and other private sector institutions. It is organized around broad divisions including biosciences, global partnerships, education, products and solutions division, advanced technology and systems and information and computing sciences division.

56) RFID Industry Associations

EPCglobal Inc.
300 Princeton S. Corporate Ctr.
Ewing Township, NJ 08628 USA
Phone: 937-435-3870
E-mail Address: info@gs1us.org
Web Address: www.gs1.org/epcglobal
EPCglobal Inc. is a global standards organization for the Electronic Product Code (EPC), which supports the use of RFID. It was initially developed by the Auto-ID Center, an academic research project at the Massachusetts Institute of Technology (MIT). Today, offices and affiliates of EPCglobal are based in nearly every nation of the world. The nonprofit organization is a joint venture between GS1, formerly known as EAN International, and GS1 US, formerly known as the Uniform Code Council.

57) Road & Highway Construction Industry Associations

American Road & Transportation Builders Association (ARTBA)
250 E St. SW, Ste. 900
Washington, DC 20024 USA
Phone: 202-289-4434
Fax: 202-289-4435
E-mail Address: chalpern@artba.org
Web Address: www.artba.org
ARTBA is a leading association that represents the interests of firms involved in designing, building and maintaining American roads and highways. Its membership totals about 6,500 firms and organizations. It publishes a significant amount of economic research and market intelligence regarding this industry.

58) Robotics & Automation Industry Associations

International Federation of Robotics (IFR)
Lyoner St. 18
Frankfurt am Main, 60528 Germany
Phone: 49-69-6603-1502
Fax: 49-69-6603-2502
E-mail Address: secretariat@ifr.org
Web Address: www.ifr.org
The International Federation of Robotics (IFR) promotes the robotics industry worldwide, including the fields of industrial robots for manufacturing and other purposes, service robots and robotics research. Among other things, it is focused on research, development, use and international co-operation in the entire field of robotics, and it seeks to act as a focal point for organizations and governmental representatives in activities related to robotics.

Laboratory Robotics Interest Group (LRIG)
E-mail Address:
andy.zaayenga@lrig.org
Web Address: www.lrig.org
Laboratory Robotics Interest Group (LRIG) is a membership group focused on the application of robotics in the laboratory. The organization currently has over 12,000 members,

with individual chapters across the U.S. and in Europe.

Singapore Industrial Automation Association (SIAA)
9, Town Hall Rd., Ste. 02-23
Singapore, 609431 Singapore
Phone: 65-6749-1822
Fax: 65-6841-3986
E-mail Address: secretariat@siaa.org
Web Address: www.siaa.org
The Singapore Industrial Automation Association (SIAA) is a non-profit organization which promotes the application of industrial automation with reference to business, technology & information services.

59) Satellite-Related Professional Organizations

Geospatial Information and Technology Association (GITA)
2851 S. Parker Rd., Ste. 1210
Aurora, CO 80014 USA
Phone: 720-250-9584
Fax: 303-200-7099
E-mail Address: admin@gita.org
Web Address: www.gita.org
The Geospatial Information and Technology Association (GITA) is an educational association for geospatial information and technology professionals.

Society of Satellite Professionals International (SSPI)
250 Park Ave., Fl. 7
The New York Information Technology Ctr.
New York, NY 10177 USA
Phone: 212-809-5199
Fax: 212-825-0075
E-mail Address: vkrisman@sspi.org
Web Address: www.sspi.org
The Society of Satellite Professionals International (SSPI) is a nonprofit member-benefit society that serves satellite professionals worldwide.

60) Science & Technology Resources

Technology Review
1 Main St., Fl. 13
Cambridge, MA 02142 USA

Phone: 617-475-8000
Fax: 617-475-8000
Web Address: www.technologyreview.com
Technology Review, an MIT enterprise, publishes tech industry news, covers innovation and writes in-depth articles about research, development and cutting-edge technologies.

61) Science Parks

International Association of Science Parks (IASP)
Calle Maria Curie 35, Campanillas
Malaga, 29590 Spain
Phone: 34-95-202-83-03
Fax: 34-95-202-04-64
E-mail Address: iasp@iasp.ws
Web Address: www.iasp.ws
The International Association of Science Parks (IASP) is a worldwide network of science and technology parks. It enjoys Special Consultative status with the Economic and Social Council of the United Nations. Its 394 members represent science parks in 75 nations. It is also a founding member of the World Alliance for Innovation (WAINOVA). Its world headquarters are located in Spain, with an additional office in the Tsinghua University Science Park, Beijing, China.

62) Software Industry Associations

National Association of Software and Service Companies of India (NASSCOM)
Plot No. 7-10 NASSCOM Campus
Sector 126
Noida, 201303 India
Phone: 91-120-4990111
Fax: 91-120-4990119
E-mail Address: north@nasscom.in
Web Address: www.nasscom.im
The National Association of Software and Service Companies (NASSCOM) is the trade body and chamber of commerce for the IT and business process outsourcing (BPO) industry in India. The association's 1,400 members consist of corporations located around the world involved in software development, software

services, software products, IT-enabled/BPO services and e-commerce.

63) Software Industry Resources

Software Engineering Institute (SEI)-Carnegie Mellon
4500 5th Ave.
Pittsburgh, PA 15213-2612 USA
Phone: 412-268-5800
Fax: 412-268-5758
Toll Free: 888-201-4479
E-mail Address: info@sei.cmu.edu
Web Address: www.sei.cmu.edu
The Software Engineering Institute (SEI) is a federally funded research and development center at Carnegie Mellon University, sponsored by the U.S. Department of Defense through the Office of the Under Secretary of Defense for Acquisition, Technology, and Logistics [OUSD (AT&L)]. The SEI's core purpose is to help users make measured improvements in their software engineering capabilities.

64) Supercomputing

Top 500 Supercomputer Sites
Prometeus GmbH
Fliederstr. 2
Waibstadt-Daisbach, D-74915 Germany
Phone: 49-7261-913-160
E-mail Address: info@top500.org
Web Address: www.top500.org
The Top 500 project was started in 1993 to provide a reliable basis for tracking and detecting trends in high-performance computing. Twice a year, a list of the sites operating the 500 most powerful computer systems is assembled and released. The Linpack benchmark is used as a performance measure for ranking the computer systems. The list contains a variety of information including system specifications and major application areas. The Top 500 web site is promoted by Prometeus GmbH.

65) Sustainable Transportation

Transportation Sustainability Research Center (TSRC)
University of California Richmond Field Station
1301 S. 46th St., Building 190
Richmond, CA 94804 USA
Phone: 510-642-9168
E-mail Address:
sshaheen@berkeley.edu
Web Address: tsrc.berkeley.edu/
The Transportation Sustainability Research Center (TSRC) was formed in 2006 to combine the research forces of six campus groups at UC Berkeley: the University of California Transportation Center, the University of California Energy Institute, the Institute of Transportation Studies, the Energy and Resources Group, the Center for Global Metropolitan Studies, and the Berkeley Institute of the Environment. Research efforts are primarily concentrated in six main areas: advanced vehicles and fuels; energy and infrastructure; goods movement; innovative mobility; Mobility for special populations; and transportation and energy systems analysis.

66) Technology Transfer Associations

Association of University Technology Managers (AUTM)
111 W. Jackson Blvd., Ste. 1412
Chicago, IL 60604 USA
Phone: 847-686-2244
Fax: 847-686-2253
E-mail Address: info@autm.net
Web Address: www.autm.net
The Association of University Technology Managers (AUTM) is a nonprofit professional association whose members belong to over 300 research institutions, universities, teaching hospitals, government agencies and corporations. The association's mission is to advance the field of technology transfer and enhance members' ability to bring academic and nonprofit research to people around the world.

Federal Laboratory Consortium for Technology Transfer
111 W. Jackson Blvd., Ste. 1412
Chicago, IL 60604 USA
Phone: 847-686-2298
E-mail Address: info@federallabs.org
Web Address: www.federallabs.org
In keeping with the aims of the Federal Technology Transfer Act of 1986 and other related legislation, the Federal Laboratory Consortium (FLC) works to facilitate the sharing of research results and technology developments between federal laboratories and the mainstream U.S. economy. FLC affiliates include federal laboratories, large and small businesses, academic and research institutions, state and local governments and various federal agencies. The group has regional support offices and local contacts throughout the U.S.

Licensing Executives Society (USA and Canada), Inc.
11130 Sunrise Valley Dr., Ste. 350
Reston, VA 20191 USA
Phone: 703-234-4058
Fax: 703-435-4390
E-mail Address: info@les.org
Web Address: www.lesusacanada.org
Licensing Executives Society (USA and Canada), Inc., established in 1965, is a professional association composed of about 3,000 members who work in fields related to the development, use, transfer, manufacture and marketing of intellectual property. Members include executives, lawyers, licensing consultants, engineers, academic researchers, scientists and government officials. The society is part of the larger Licensing Executives Society International, Inc. (same headquarters address), with a worldwide membership.

State Science and Technology Institute (SSTI)
5015 Pine Creek Dr.
Westerville, OH 43081 USA
Phone: 614-901-1690
E-mail Address: contactus@ssti.org
Web Address: www.ssti.org
The State Science and Technology Institute (SSTI) is a national nonprofit group that serves as a resource for technology-based economic development. In addition to the information on its web site, the Institute publishes a free weekly digest of news and issues related to technology-based economic development efforts, as well as a members-only publication listing application information, eligibility criteria and submission deadlines for a variety of funding opportunities, federal and otherwise.

67) Telecommunications Industry Associations

Alliance for Telecommunications Industry Solutions (ATIS)
1200 G St. NW, Ste. 500
Washington, DC 20005 USA
Phone: 202-628-6380
E-mail Address: mwolfe@atis.org
Web Address: www.atis.org
The Alliance for Telecommunications Industry Solutions (ATIS) is a U.S.-based body committed to rapidly developing and promoting technical and operations standards for the communications and related information technologies industry worldwide.

China Communications Standards Association (CCSA)
52 Garden Rd., Haidian District
Beijing, 100083 China
Phone: 86-10-6230-2730
Fax: 86-10-6230-1849
Web Address:
www.ccsa.org.cn/english
The China Communications Standards Association (CCSA) is a nonprofit organization that works to standardize the field of communications technology across China. Its membership includes operators, telecom equipment manufacturers and universities and academies from across China.

European Telecommunications Standards Institute (ETSI)
ETSI Secretariat
650, route des Lucioles
Sophia-Antipolis Cedex,
06921 France
Phone: 33-4-92-94-42-00

Fax: 33-4-93-65-47-16
E-mail Address: info@etsi.org
Web Address: www.etsi.org
The European Telecommunications
Standards Institute (ETSI) is a nonprofit organization whose mission is
to produce telecommunications
standards to be implemented
throughout Europe.

**International Telecommunications
Union (ITU)**
Place des Nations
Geneva 20, 1211 Switzerland
Phone: 41-22-730-5111
Fax: 41-22-733-7256
E-mail Address: itumail@itu.int
Web Address: www.itu.int
The International
Telecommunications Union (ITU) is
an international organization for the
standardization of the radio and
telecommunications industry. It is an
agency of the United Nations (UN).

68) Telecommunications Resources

**Infocomm Development Authority
of Singapore (IMDA)**
10 Pasir Panjang Rd.
#10-01 Mapletree Business City
Singapore, 117438 Singapore
Phone: 65-6211-0888
Fax: 65-6211-2222
E-mail Address: info@imda.gov.sg
Web Address: www.imda.gov.sg
The goal of the Infocomm Media
Development Authority of Singapore
(IMDA) is to actively seek
opportunities to grow infocomm
industry in both the domestic and
international markets.

**International Communications
Project (The)**
Unit 2, Marine Action
Birdhill Industrial Estate
Birdhill, Co Tipperary Ireland
Phone: 353-86-108-3932
Fax: 353-61-749-801
E-mail Address:
robert.alcock@intercomms.net
Web Address: www.intercomms.net
The International Communications
Project (InterComms) is an
authoritative policy, strategy and
reference publication for the

international telecommunications
industry.

69) Temporary Staffing Firms

Allegis Group
7301 Parkway Dr.
Hanover, MD 21076 USA
Toll Free: 800-927-8090
Web Address: www.allegisgroup.com
The Allegis Group provides technical,
professional and industrial recruiting
and staffing services. Allegis
specializes in information technology
staffing services. The firm operates in
the United Kingdom, Germany and
The Netherlands as Aerotek and
TEKsystems, and in India as Allegis
Group India. Aerotek provides
staffing solutions for aviation,
engineering, automotive and scientific
personnel markets.

CDI Corporation
1735 Market St., Ste. 200
Philadelphia, PA 190103 USA
Phone: 215-636-1240
E-mail Address:
engineeringsolutions@cdicorp.com
Web Address: www.cdicorp.com
CDI Corporation specializes in
engineering and information
technology staffing services.
Company segments include CDI IT
Solutions, specializing in information
technology; CDI Engineering
Solutions, specializing in engineering
outsourcing services; AndersElite
Limited, operating in the United
Kingdom and Australia; and
MRINetwork, specializing in
executive recruitment.

70) Trade Associations-General

**Associated Chambers of Commerce
and Industry of India
(ASSOCHAM)**
5, Sardar Patel Marg
Chanakyapuri
New Delhi, 110 021 India
Phone: 91-11-4655-0555
Fax: 91-11-2301-7008
E-mail Address: assocham@nic.in
Web Address: www.assocham.org

The Associated Chambers of
Commerce and Industry of India
(ASSOCHAM) has a membership of
more than 300 chambers and trade
associations and serves members
from all over India. It works with
domestic and international
government agencies to advocate for
India's industry and trade activities.

**Brazilian Trade & Investment
Promotion Agency (Apex-Brasil)**
SAUN, Quadra 05, Lote C, Torre B,
#12-18 Edificio Apex-Brasil
Brasilia, DF 70040-020 Brazil
Phone: 55-61-2027-0202
Web Address: www.apexbrasil.com.br
Apex-Brasil works to promote
exports of Brazilian products and
services, supporting some 70 industry
sectors such as agribusiness,
technology, civil engineering,
entertainment, apparel and industrial
equipment.

BUSINESSEUROPE
168 Ave. de Cortenbergh 168
Brussels, 1000 Belgium
Phone: 32-2-237-65-11
Fax: 32-2-231-14-45
E-mail Address:
main@businesseurope.eu
Web Address:
www.businesseurope.eu
BUSINESSEUROPE is a major
European trade federation that
operates in a manner similar to a
chamber of commerce. Its members
are the central national business
federations of the 34 countries
throughout Europe from which they
come. Companies cannot become
direct members of
BUSINESSEUROPE, though there is
a support group which offers the
opportunity for firms to encourage
BUSINESSEUROPE objectives in
various ways.

**Coalition of Service Industries
(CSI)**
1707 L St. NW, Ste. 1000
Washington, DC 20036 USA
Phone: 202-289-7460
E-mail Address: admin@uscsi.org
Web Address: uscsi.or
The Coalition of Service Industries
(CSI) is a business organization

dedicated to the reduction of barriers to U.S. service exports and to the development of constructive domestic service policies. It also publishes statistical information relating to the service industry on both state and national levels.

United States Council for International Business (USCIB)
1212 Ave. of the Americas
New York, NY 10036 USA
Phone: 212-354-4480
Fax: 212-575-0327
E-mail Address: news@uscib.org
Web Address: www.uscib.org
The United States Council for International Business (USCIB) promotes an open system of world trade and investment through its global network. Standard USCIB members include corporations, law firms, consulting firms and industry associations. Limited membership options are available for chambers of commerce and sole legal practitioners.

71) Trade Associations-Global

World Trade Organization (WTO)
Centre William Rappard
Rue de Lausanne 154
Geneva 21, CH-1211 Switzerland
Phone: 41-22-739-51-11
Fax: 41-22-731-42-06
E-mail Address: enquiries@wto.og
Web Address: www.wto.org
The World Trade Organization (WTO) is a global organization dealing with the rules of trade between nations. To become a member, nations must agree to abide by certain guidelines. Membership increases a nation's ability to import and export efficiently.

72) Transportation Industry Resources

Institute of Transportation Studies
University of California
109 McLaughlin Hall, MC1720
Berkeley, CA 94720 USA
Phone: 510-642-3585
E-mail Address: its@its.berkeley.edu

Web Address: its.berkeley.edu/
The UC Berkeley Institute of Transportation Studies is one of the world's leading centers for transportation research, education, and scholarship. Areas of research focus include: transportation planning, logistics, infrastructure management, safety, transportation economics and public transportation.

73) U.S. Government Agencies

Bureau of Economic Analysis (BEA)
4600 Silver Hill Rd.
Washington, DC 20233 USA
Phone: 301-278-9004
E-mail Address:
customerservice@bea.gov
Web Address: www.bea.gov
The Bureau of Economic Analysis (BEA), is an agency of the U.S. Department of Commerce, is the nation's economic accountant, preparing estimates that illuminate key national, international and regional aspects of the U.S. economy.

Bureau of Labor Statistics (BLS)
2 Massachusetts Ave. NE
Washington, DC 20212-0001 USA
Phone: 202-691-5200
Fax: 202-691-7890
Toll Free: 800-877-8339
E-mail Address:
blsdata_staff@bls.gov
Web Address: stats.bls.gov
The Bureau of Labor Statistics (BLS) is the principal fact-finding agency for the Federal Government in the field of labor economics and statistics. It is an independent national statistical agency that collects, processes, analyzes and disseminates statistical data to the American public, U.S. Congress, other federal agencies, state and local governments, business and labor. The BLS also serves as a statistical resource to the Department of Labor.

Federal Communications Commission (FCC)
445 12th St. SW
Washington, DC 20554 USA
Fax: 866-418-0232

Toll Free: 888-225-5322
E-mail Address: PRA@fcc.gov
Web Address: www.fcc.gov
The Federal Communications Commission (FCC) is an independent U.S. government agency established by the Communications Act of 1934 responsible for regulating interstate and international communications by radio, television, wire, satellite and cable.

Federal Communications Commission (FCC)-Wireless Telecommunications Bureau
445 12th St. SW
Washington, DC 20554 USA
Phone: 202-418-0600
Fax: 202-418-0787
Toll Free: 888-225-5322
E-mail Address: PRA@fcc.gov
Web Address: www.fcc.gov/wireless-telecommunications#block-menu-block-4
The Federal Communications Commission (FCC)-Wireless Telecommunications Bureau handles nearly all FCC domestic wireless telecommunications programs and policies, including cellular and smartphones, pagers and two-way radios. The bureau also regulates the use of radio spectrum for businesses, aircraft/ship operators and individuals.

National Aeronautics and Space Administration (NASA)
Mary W. Jackson NASA Headquarters
00 E. Street SW, Ste. 5R30
Washington, DC 20546 USA
Phone: 202-358-0001
Fax: 202-358-4338
E-mail Address: ig-reports-request@hq.nasa.gov
Web Address: www.nasa.gov
The National Aeronautics and Space Administration (NASA) is the U.S. space agency, handling all space-related research and development. The agency's work is organized into four principal areas: Aeronautics, Exploration Systems, Science and Space Operations.

National Institute of Standards and Technology (NIST)

100 Bureau Dr.
Gaithersburg, MD 20899-1070 USA
Phone: 301-975-6478
Toll Free: 800-877-8339
E-mail Address: inquiries@nist.gov
Web Address: www.nist.gov
The National Institute of Standards
and Technology (NIST) is an agency
of the U.S. Department of Commerce
that works with various industries to
develop and apply technology,
measurements and standards.

National Science Foundation (NSF)
2415 Eisenhower Ave.
Alexandria, VA 22314 USA
Phone: 703-292-5111
Toll Free: 800-877-8339
E-mail Address: info@nsf.gov
Web Address: www.nsf.gov
The National Science Foundation
(NSF) is an independent U.S.
government agency responsible for
promoting science and engineering.
The foundation provides colleges and
universities with grants and funding
for research into numerous scientific
fields.

U.S. Census Bureau
4600 Silver Hill Rd.
Washington, DC 20233-8800 USA
Phone: 301-763-4636
Toll Free: 800-923-8282
E-mail Address: pio@census.gov
Web Address: www.census.gov
The U.S. Census Bureau is the
official collector of data about the
people and economy of the U.S.
Founded in 1790, it provides official
social, demographic and economic
information. In addition to the
Population & Housing Census, which
it conducts every 10 years, the U.S.
Census Bureau conducts numerous
other surveys annually.

**U.S. Department of Commerce
(DOC)**
1401 Constitution Ave. NW
Washington, DC 20230 USA
Phone: 202-482-2000
E-mail Address:
publicaffairs@doc.gov
Web Address: www.commerce.gov
The U.S. Department of Commerce
(DOC) regulates trade and provides

valuable economic analysis of the
economy.

U.S. Department of Labor (DOL)
200 Constitution Ave. NW
Washington, DC 20210 USA
Phone: 202-693-4676
Toll Free: 866-487-2365
E-mail Address: m-
DOLPublicAffairs@dol.gov
Web Address: www.dol.gov
The U.S. Department of Labor (DOL)
is the government agency responsible
for labor regulations. The Department
of Labor's goal is to foster, promote,
and develop the welfare of the wage
earners, job seekers, and retirees of
the United States; improve working
conditions; advance opportunities for
profitable employment; and assure
work-related benefits and rights.

**U.S. Nuclear Regulatory
Commission (NRC)**
11555 Rockville Pike
Rockville, MD 20852 USA
Phone: 301-415-7000
Fax: 301-415-3716
Toll Free: 800-368-5642
E-mail Address:
OPA.Resource@nrc.gov
Web Address: www.nrc.gov
The U.S. Nuclear Regulatory
Commission (NRC) is an independent
agency established by Congress to
ensure adequate protection of public
health and safety, common defense
and security and the environment in
use of nuclear materials in the United
States.

**U.S. Patent and Trademark Office
(PTO)**
600 Dulany St.
Madison Bldg.
Alexandria, VA 22314 USA
Phone: 571-272-1000
Toll Free: 800-786-9199
E-mail Address: usptoinfo@uspto.gov
Web Address: www.uspto.gov
The U.S. Patent and Trademark
Office (PTO) administers patent and
trademark laws for the U.S. and
enables registration of patents and
trademarks.

**U.S. Securities and Exchange
Commission (SEC)**
100 F St. NE
Washington, DC 20549 USA
Phone: 202-942-8088
Fax: 202-772-9295
Toll Free: 800-732-0330
E-mail Address: help@sec.gov
Web Address: www.sec.gov
The U.S. Securities and Exchange
Commission (SEC) is a nonpartisan,
quasi-judicial regulatory agency
responsible for administering federal
securities laws. These laws are
designed to protect investors in
securities markets and ensure that
they have access to disclosure of all
material information concerning
publicly traded securities. Visitors to
the web site can access the EDGAR
database of corporate financial and
business information.

**74) Wireless & Cellular
        Industry Associations**

CDMA Development Group (CDG)
P.O. Box 22249
San Diego, CA 92129-2249 USA
Phone: 714-987-2362
Fax: 714-545-4601
Toll Free: 888-800-2362
E-mail Address: info@mobilitydg.org
Web Address: www.cdg.org
The CDMA Development Group
(CDG) is composed of the world's
leading code division multiple access
(CDMA) service providers and
manufacturers that have joined
together to lead the adoption and
evolution of CDMA wireless systems
around the world.

Connectivity Standards Alliance
508 Second St., Ste. 206
Davis, CA 95616 USA
Phone: 530-564-4565
Fax: 530-564-4721
E-mail Address:
zigbee_media@mail.zigbee.org
Web Address: www.csa-iot.org
The Connectivity Standards Alliance,
formerly the ZigBee Alliance, is an
association of companies working
together to enable reliable, cost-
effective, low-power, wirelessly
networked monitoring and control

products based on an open global standard.

Global System for Mobile Communication Association (GSMA)

The Wallbrook Bldg.
Fl. 2, 25 Wallbrook
London, EC4N 8AF UK
Phone: 44-207-356-0600
Fax: 44-20-7356-0601
E-mail Address: info@gsma.com
Web Address: www.gsmworld.com
The Global System for Mobile Communications Association (GSMA) is a global trade association representing nearly 800 GSM mobile phone operators from 219 countries.

Wireless Communications Association International (WCAI)

1333 H St. NW, Ste. 700 W
Washington, DC 20005-4754 USA
Phone: 202-452-7823
Web Address:
www.wcainternational.com/
The Wireless Communications Association International (WCAI) is a nonprofit trade association representing the wireless broadband industry.

Chapter 4

THE ENGINEERING & RESEARCH 500: WHO THEY ARE AND HOW THEY WERE CHOSEN

Includes Indexes by Company Name, Industry & Location

The companies chosen to be listed in PLUNKETT'S ENGINEERING & RESEARCH INDUSTRY ALMANAC comprise a unique list. THE ENGINEERING & RESEARCH 500 were chosen specifically for their dominance in the many facets of the engineering and research industry in which they operate. Complete information about each firm can be found in the "Individual Profiles," beginning at the end of this chapter. These profiles are in alphabetical order by company name.

THE ENGINEERING & RESEARCH 500 companies are from all parts of the United States, Asia, Canada, Europe and beyond. Essentially, THE ENGINEERING & RESEARCH 500 includes companies that are deeply involved in the technologies, services and trends that keep the entire industry forging ahead.

Simply stated, THE ENGINEERING & RESEARCH 500 contains the largest, most successful, fastest growing firms in engineering, research and related industries in the world. To be included in our list, the firms had to meet the following criteria:

1) Generally, these are corporations based in the U.S., however, many firms are located in other nations.

2) Prominence, or a significant presence, in engineering, research, engineering services, equipment and supporting fields. (See the following Industry Codes section for a complete list of types of businesses that are covered).

3) The companies in THE ENGINEERING & RESEARCH 500 do not have to be exclusively in the engineering and research field.

4) Financial data and vital statistics must have been available to the editors of this book, either directly from the company being written about or from outside sources deemed reliable and accurate by the editors. A small number of companies that we would like to have included are not listed because of a lack of sufficient, objective data.

INDEX OF COMPANIES WITHIN INDUSTRY GROUPS

The industry codes shown below are based on the 2012 NAIC code system (NAIC is used by many analysts as a replacement for older SIC codes because NAIC is more specific to today's industry sectors, see www.census.gov/NAICS). Companies are given a primary NAIC code, reflecting the main line of business of each firm.

Industry Group/Company	Industry Code	2024 Sales	2024 Profits
Agricultural Equipment or Machinery (Farm Implement) Manufacturing			
Deere & Company (John Deere)	333111	50,517,999,616	7,100,000,256
Agricultural Seeds, Pesticides, Herbicides and Other Agricultural Chemical Manufacturing			
Syngenta Group Co Ltd	325320	34,000,000,000	
Aircraft Components, Parts, Assemblies, Interiors and Systems Manufacturing (Aerospace)			
Spirit AeroSystems Holdings Inc	336413	6,316,599,808	-2,139,800,064
Aircraft Engine and Engine Parts Manufacturing			
Honeywell International Inc	336412	38,498,000,896	5,704,999,936
Rolls-Royce Holdings plc	336412	25,457,186,381	3,394,022,144
RTX Corp (Raytheon Technologies)	336412	80,738,000,896	4,774,000,128
Safran SA	336412	31,459,704,624	-757,094,208
Aircraft Manufacturing (Aerospace), including Passenger Airliners and Military Aircraft			
Airbus SE	336411	78,581,160,329	4,803,632,128
Boeing Company (The)	336411	66,517,000,192	-11,816,999,936
Bombardier Inc	336411	8,664,999,936	370,000,000
Dassault Aviation SA	336411	7,082,529,134	1,048,608,384
Embraer SA	336411	6,394,699,776	352,500,000
General Dynamics Corporation	336411	47,715,999,744	3,782,000,128
Gulfstream Aerospace Corporation	336411	9,450,000,000	
Lockheed Martin Corporation	336411	71,042,998,272	5,336,000,000
Northrop Grumman Corporation	336411	41,032,998,912	4,174,000,128
Saab AB	336411	6,649,803,545	435,072,864
Singapore Technologies Engineering Limited	336411	8,732,021,033	543,836,416
Textron Inc	336411	13,701,999,616	824,000,000
Aircraft, Missile and Space Vehicle (including Rockets), Drones, Satellites Manufacturing			
BAE Systems plc	336410	35,423,845,066	2,633,362,688
Airport Related Services, Baggage Handling			
Ferrovial SE	488119	10,382,519,657	3,676,504,064
Appliances, incl Kitchen (Refrigerators, Stoves, etc.), Laundry & Appliance Manufacturing			
Whirlpool Corporation	335220	16,606,999,552	-323,000,000
ATV, Snowmobile, Golf Cart, Go-cart and Race Car Equipment Manufacturing			
Kawasaki Heavy Industries Ltd	336999	12,838,704,829	176,180,224
Automation, Robots (Robotics, AI), Process, Flow Meter, Environmental Monitoring, Control Manufacturing			
Emerson Electric Co	334513	17,492,000,768	1,968,000,000
Rockwell Automation Inc	334513	8,264,200,192	952,499,968
Siemens AG	334513	86,186,153,791	9,422,247,936

Industry Group/Company	Industry Code	2024 Sales	2024 Profits
Automobile (Car) and Truck Parts (Air Bags, Air-Conditioners, Mufflers & Radiators) Manufacturing			
Toyoda Gosei Co Ltd	336390	7,436,177,793	357,220,224
Automobile (Car) and Truck Parts, Components & Systems Manufacturing, Engines, Electronics			
Aisin Corporation	336300	34,084,679,585	630,470,720
Autoliv Inc	336300	10,389,999,616	646,000,000
Cummins Inc	336300	34,101,999,616	3,945,999,872
Dana Incorporated	336300	10,284,000,256	-57,000,000
Denso Corporation	336300	49,602,425,567	2,171,556,608
Eaton Corp plc	336300	24,878,000,128	3,793,999,872
Forvia SE	336300	30,617,706,966	-210,215,664
Georg Fischer AG	336300	4,735,976,189	260,405,680
GKN Aerospace	336300	4,477,883,025	
Lear Corporation	336300	23,306,000,384	506,600,000
Magna International Inc	336300	42,836,000,768	1,009,000,000
Marelli Corporation	336300	14,242,999,680	
Rheinmetall AG	336300	11,068,104,511	813,847,872
Robert Bosch GmbH	336300	103,725,726,000	
Tenneco Inc	336300	20,481,987,750	
Valeo SA	336300	24,395,006,573	183,881,952
Visteon Corporation	336300	3,865,999,872	274,000,000
Wanxiang Group Corporation	336300	26,250,000,000	
Automobile (Car) and Truck Transmission and Power Train Parts Manufacturing			
ZF Friedrichshafen AG (ZF)	336350	54,032,393,100	
Automobile (Car) Manufacturing (incl. Autonomous or Self-Driving)			
Aston Martin Lagonda Global Holdings PLC	336111	2,132,404,622	-435,528,064
Audi AG	336111	80,961,099,450	
Bayerische Motoren Werke AG (BMW Group)	336111	161,611,813,367	8,274,687,488
BYD Company Limited	336111	107,875,453,922	5,588,009,472
China FAW Group Co Ltd (First Automotive Works)	336111		
Daihatsu Motor Co Ltd	336111	17,668,236,600	
Dongfeng Motor Corporation	336111	16,460,377,500	
Ferrari SpA	336111	7,578,510,682	1,727,442,688
Ford Motor Company	336111	184,992,006,144	5,879,000,064
General Motors Company (GM)	336111	187,442,003,968	6,008,000,000
GM Korea	336111	10,255,714,350	
Group Lotus plc	336111	127,050,000	
Honda Motor Co Ltd	336111	141,827,290,269	7,686,573,056
Hyundai Motor Company	336111	126,797,171,543	9,064,306,688
Isuzu Motors Limited	336111	23,512,053,558	1,224,951,424
Jaguar Land Rover Limited	336111	29,579,726,400	
Kia Corporation	336111	77,749,856,161	7,071,706,112
Mazda Motor Corporation	336111	33,516,123,372	1,441,932,928
Mercedes-Benz Group AG	336111	165,259,940,645	11,585,697,792
Mitsubishi Motors Corp	336111	19,366,767,658	1,074,069,760
Nissan Motor Co Ltd	336111	88,070,792,136	2,962,017,536

Industry Group/Company	Industry Code	2024 Sales	2024 Profits
Opel Automobile GmbH	336111	9,828,000,000	
Porsche Automobil Holding SE	336111	-22,544,835,003	-22,720,772,096
Renault SA	336111	63,827,470,597	853,575,488
SAIC Motor Corporation Limited	336111		
SAIC-GM-Wuling Automobile Company	336111		
Stellantis North America	336111	100,238,103,000	
Stellantis NV	336111	178,068,100,114	6,212,258,816
Subaru Corporation	336111	32,650,287,410	2,673,451,776
Suzuki Motor Corp	336111	37,310,852,629	1,858,629,632
Tata Motors Limited	336111		
Tesla Inc	336111	97,690,001,408	7,129,999,872
Toyota Motor Corporation	336111	313,075,014,987	34,330,275,840
Volkswagen AG (VW)	336111	368,507,366,243	12,884,222,976
Volvo Car AB	336111	41,748,010,076	1,606,462,976
Basic Inorganic Chemicals Manufacturing, Including Acids, Carbides and Alkalis			
Arkema	325180	10,833,143,585	401,816,128
Solvay SA	325180	5,822,928,351	253,121,456
Battery Manufacturing (Primary), Incl. Auto (Car, EV), Lithium Batteries			
Contemporary Amperex Technology Co Limited (CATL)	335912		
Boilers and Condensers (Including Nuclear Reactors) and Heat Exchangers Manufacturing			
Babcock & Wilcox Enterprises Inc	332410	717,332,992	-59,915,000
Orano SA	332410		
Westinghouse Electric Company LLC	332410	4,695,600,000	
Chemicals Manufacturing, Incl Basic, Specialty, Petrochemicals, Pharmaceuticals, Soaps, Paints			
Sumitomo Chemical Co Ltd	325000	16,987,594,208	-2,164,940,544
Chemicals, Specialty Manufacturing, Including Fragrances, Silicones, Biodiesel & Enzymes			
BASF SE	325199	74,074,914,077	1,473,325,824
Dow Inc	325199	42,964,000,768	1,116,000,000
Commercial and Institutional Building Construction			
Kumho Engineering & Construction Co Ltd	236220		
Suffolk Construction Company	236220		
Computer and Data Systems Design, Consulting and Integration Services			
Accenture plc	541512	64,896,462,848	7,264,786,944
Capgemini Engineering	541512	7,604,748,060	
CGI Inc	541512	10,682,110,364	1,232,051,072
Leidos Holdings Inc	541512	16,661,999,616	1,254,000,000
NTT Data Corp	541512	30,320,654,518	929,387,712
Science Applications International Corporation (SAIC)	541512	7,443,999,744	477,000,000
Tata Consultancy Services Limited (TCS)	541512		
Unisys Corporation	541512	2,008,400,000	-193,400,000
Wipro Limited	541512	10,496,365,724	1,291,600,640
Computer Disks (Discs) and Storage Drives, including Magnetic and Optical Media Manufacturing			
NetApp Inc	334112	6,268,000,256	986,000,000

Industry Group/Company	Industry Code	2024 Sales	2024 Profits
Nidec Corp	334112	16,302,430,867	870,501,248
Seagate Technology Public Limited Company	334112	6,551,000,064	335,000,000
Western Digital Corporation	334112	13,002,999,808	-798,000,000
Computer Manufacturing, Including Servers, PCs, Laptops, and Tablets			
Acer Inc	334111	8,851,662,324	185,249,456
ASUSTeK Computer Inc	334111	19,633,706,362	1,049,891,520
Casio Computer Co Ltd	334111	1,866,342,745	82,678,424
Dell Technologies Inc	334111	88,424,996,864	3,388,000,000
Fujitsu Limited	334111	26,076,500,434	1,766,717,568
Hewlett Packard Enterprise Company	334111	30,126,999,552	2,579,000,064
Hitachi Limited	334111	67,541,771,417	4,095,362,816
HP Inc	334111	53,559,001,088	2,775,000,064
Lenovo Group Limited	334111	56,863,784,960	1,010,505,984
NEC Corp	334111	24,140,948,027	1,038,052,032
Nintendo Co Ltd	334111	11,606,950,119	3,406,012,416
QuTech	334111		
Computer Monitors & Terminals (ATMs, Point of Sale, POS) Manufacturing			
Diebold Nixdorf Incorporated	334118	3,751,099,904	-16,500,000
NCR Voyix Corp	334118	2,825,999,872	958,000,000
Seiko Epson Corp	334118	9,122,452,251	365,287,424
TPV Technology Co Ltd	334118		
Xerox Corporation	334118	6,221,000,192	-1,320,999,936
Computer Software: Accounting, Banking & Financial			
Intuit Inc	511210Q	16,284,999,680	2,963,000,064
Computer Software: Business Management & Enterprise Resource Planning (ERP)			
BMC Software Inc	511210H	2,110,000,000	
Microsoft Corporation	511210H	245,122,007,040	88,135,999,488
Oracle Corporation	511210H	52,961,001,472	10,467,000,320
SAP SE	511210H	38,792,281,540	3,545,970,432
SAS Institute Inc	511210H	3,532,140,000	
Computer Software: Educational & Training			
Wolfram Research Inc	511210P		
Computer Software: Electronic Games, Apps & Entertainment			
Activision Blizzard	511210G	9,547,200,000	
Electronic Arts Inc (EA)	511210G	7,561,999,872	1,272,999,936
Konami Group Corp	511210G	2,501,485,860	410,795,616
Reality Labs	511210G		
Take-Two Interactive Software Inc	511210G	5,349,600,256	-3,744,199,936
Computer Software: Multimedia, Advertising, Graphics & Publishing			
Adobe Inc	511210F	21,504,999,424	5,560,000,000
Computer Software: Network Management, System Testing, & Storage			
Citrix Systems Inc	511210B	3,511,040,000	

Industry Group/Company	Industry Code	2024 Sales	2024 Profits
Computer Software: Product Lifecycle, Engineering, Design & CAD			
Autodesk Inc	511210N	5,496,999,936	906,000,000
Cadence Design Systems Inc	511210N	4,641,264,128	1,055,484,032
Dassault Systemes SA	511210N	7,052,894,736	1,362,315,520
PTC Inc	511210N	2,298,471,936	376,332,992
Siemens Digital Industries Software Inc	511210N		
Siemens EDA	511210N	1,947,429,225	
Synopsys Inc	511210N	6,127,435,776	2,263,379,968
Computer Software: Sales & Customer Relationship Management			
Amdocs Limited	511210K	5,004,988,928	493,196,992
Computer Software: Security, Signon, ID (Identity) & Anti-Virus			
Gen Digital Inc	511210E	3,800,000,000	607,000,000
McAfee Corp	511210E	2,194,400,000	
VeriSign Inc	511210E	1,557,400,064	785,699,968
Connectors for Electronics and Similar Components Manufacturing			
Belden Inc	334417	2,460,978,944	198,432,992
Luxshare Precision Industry Co Ltd	334417		
Molex LLC	334417	5,156,840,000	
Construction Equipment and Machinery Manufacturing			
Caterpillar Inc	333120	64,809,000,960	10,791,999,488
Terex Corporation	333120	5,127,000,064	335,000,000
Construction of Railways, Marine Facilities and Subways			
China Railway Construction Company Limited (CRCC)	237990		
Construction of Telecommunications Lines and Systems & Electric Power Lines & Systems			
Bouygues SA	237130	64,417,708,382	1,200,908,032
Doosan Enerbility Co Ltd	237130		
Construction of Water & Sewer Lines and Systems			
Layne-A Granite Company	237110	543,074,700	
Consulting Services, Environmental			
OYO Corporation	541620	514,336,306	27,839,490
Contract Electronics Manufacturing Services (CEM) and Printed Circuits Assembly			
Benchmark Electronics Inc	334418	2,656,104,960	63,327,000
Celestica Inc	334418	9,646,000,128	428,000,000
Compal Electronics Inc	334418	30,441,209,104	335,844,096
Flex Ltd	334418	26,414,999,552	1,006,000,000
Hon Hai Precision Industry Company Ltd	334418	229,403,230,402	5,106,851,328
HTC Corporation	334418		
Jabil Inc	334418	28,882,999,296	1,388,000,000
Plexus Corp	334418	3,960,826,880	111,815,000
Rohm Co Ltd	334418	3,247,570,294	374,652,896
Sanmina Corporation	334418	7,568,328,192	222,536,000
Electric Power Generation, Fossil Fuel			
Sembcorp Industries Ltd	221112	4,969,410,400	782,931,904

Industry Group/Company	Industry Code	2024 Sales	2024 Profits
Electrical Appliance Manufacturing, Small			
Dyson Singapore Pte Ltd	335210	9,490,438,650	
Electricity Control Panels, Circuit Breakers, Switches Equipment (Switchgear) Manufacturing			
ABB Ltd	335313	32,849,999,872	3,935,000,064
Alps Alpine Co Ltd	335313	6,693,210,460	-206,984,176
Broadcom Inc	335313	51,574,001,664	5,895,000,064
LITE-ON Technology Corporation	335313		
Engineering Services, Incl Civil, Mechanical, Electronic, Computer & Environmental			
AF Gruppen ASA	541330	2,958,821,951	69,315,264
AFRY AB	541330	2,833,032,698	128,195,760
Amey Ltd	541330	1,902,852,000	
Arcadis NV	541330	5,669,693,318	275,822,944
Artelia	541330	1,139,121,900	
ARUP Group Limited	541330	2,805,853,050	
Associated Consulting Engineers	541330		
AtkinsRealis Group Inc	541330	7,036,908,344	206,616,208
Atomic Energy of Canada Limited (AECL)	541330		
Aurecon Group Brand (Pty) Ltd	541330	1,255,800,000	
Austin Engineering Limited	541330	201,914,459	16,812,454
Beca Group Limited	541330	430,500,000	
Bilfinger Tebodin BV	541330	108,150,000	
BIOS-BIOENERGYSYSTEME GmbH	541330	53,976,000	
Black & Veatch Holding Company	541330	4,515,000,000	
Burns & McDonnell Inc	541330	7,770,000,000	
Buro Happold Limited	541330	386,970,150	
CannonDesign	541330	180,600,000	
Carso Infraestructura y Construccion SAB de CV	541330		
CHA Consulting Inc	541330	336,000,000	
China Chengda Engineering Co Ltd	541330		
China Energy Engineering Corporation Limited	541330		
China National Machinery Industry Corporation	541330		
China Petroleum Pipeline Engineering Co Ltd	541330		
Chiyoda Corporation	541330	3,512,781,355	-109,906,976
COWI A/S	541330	1,221,462,900	
CRB	541330		
Dar Al-Handasah Consultants (Shair and Partners)	541330		
DLZ Corporation	541330	198,450,000	
DNV AS	541330	3,257,703,750	
Dorsch Holding GmbH	541330		
Downer EDI Limited	541330	7,070,615,768	44,541,848
ECC (Environmental Chemical Corp)	541330	13,650,000,000	
Enviri Corporation	541330	2,342,644,992	-127,973,000
Estudios y Proyectos Tecnicos Industriales SA (Eptisa)	541330	124,950,000	
Gannett Fleming Inc	541330	778,596,000	
Geosyntec Consultants Inc	541330		
Ghafari Associates LLC	541330		
GHD Group Pty Ltd	541330	1,860,701,850	

Industry Group/Company	Industry Code	2024 Sales	2024 Profits
Golder Associates Corporation	541330	1,155,000,000	
Gulf Interstate Engineering Company	541330		
Hatch Ltd	541330		
HDR Inc	541330	3,255,000,000	
HKS Inc	541330	423,150,000	
HNTB Corporation	541330	756,756,000	
HOK Group Inc	541330	521,976,000	
IDOM	541330	336,000,000	
ILF Consulting Engineers Austria GmbH	541330		
Integrated Design & Engineering Holdings Co Ltd	541330		
Introba Inc	541330		
IPS - Integrated Project Services LLC	541330		
JGC Holdings Corp	541330	5,780,304,051	-54,359,904
Jutal Offshore Oil Services Ltd	541330	288,604,731	25,690,408
Keller Group PLC	541330	4,020,994,271	191,578,496
KEO International Consultants WLL	541330		
KEPCO Engineering & Construction Company Inc	541330		
Khatib & Alami	541330		
Kimley-Horn and Associates Inc	541330	1,638,000,000	
Kleinfelder Group Inc (The)	541330		
Langan Engineering and Environmental Services Inc	541330		
Leo A Daly Company	541330	218,400,000	
Mason & Hanger	541330		
McDermott International Ltd	541330	8,873,592,000	
Michael Baker International LLC	541330	1,791,972,000	
Middough Inc	541330		
Mott MacDonald Limited	541330	3,167,935,050	
NORR Group Inc	541330		
NV5 Global Inc	541330	941,265,024	27,979,000
Oriental Consultants Global Co Ltd	541330	241,500,000	
Page Southerland Page Inc	541330	178,500,000	
Parsons Corporation	541330	6,750,576,128	235,052,992
Pininfarina SpA	541330		
PM Group	541330	563,784,900	
Power Construction Corporation of China Ltd (PowerChina)	541330		
POWER Engineers Incorporated	541330		
Primoris Services Corp	541330	6,366,837,760	180,888,000
Ramboll Group A/S	541330	2,644,789,350	
Regulus Group LLC	541330		
Ricardo plc	541330	639,088,613	942,410
RIZZO International Inc	541330		
Royal HaskoningDHV	541330	853,242,955	
Sargent & Lundy LLC	541330		
Seatrium Limited	541330	7,148,378,499	121,457,440
Sener Ingenieria y Sistemas SA	541330	689,052,000	
SEPCO Electric Power Construction Corporation	541330		
Shanghai Construction Group Co Ltd	541330		
Sheladia Associates Inc	541330		
SK Ecoplant	541330	6,977,250,000	

Industry Group/Company	Industry Code	2024 Sales	2024 Profits
Skidmore Owings & Merrill LLP	541330	367,500,000	
SMEC Holdings Pty Ltd	541330	533,988,000	
SSOE Group	541330	175,350,000	
Stanley Consultants Inc	541330		
Stellar Group Inc (The)	541330	786,145,500	
STV Incorporated	541330	611,520,000	
Taisei Corp	541330	12,253,700,919	279,588,992
Tecnica y Proyectos SA (TYPSA)	541330	330,750,000	
Thinkpath Inc	541330		
Thornton Tomasetti Inc	541330		
Tractebel Engineering GmbH	541330	757,870,050	
TRC Companies Inc	541330	829,920,000	
Trevi-Finanziaria Industriale SpA (Trevi Group)	541330		
UniversalPegasus International Inc	541330		
VEPICA USA Inc	541330	122,850,000	
Versar Inc	541330		
VSE Corporation	541330	1,080,131,968	15,324,000
Waldemar S Nelson and Company Inc	541330		
WL Meinhardt Group Pty Ltd	541330		
WSP Global Inc	541330	11,767,085,962	495,960,384
WSP New Zealand Ltd	541330	294,000,000	
Facilities Support Services			
Abertis Infraestructuras SA	561210	7,262,952,900	
Fibers, Artificial and Synthetic and Filaments Manufacturing			
Eastman Chemical Company	325220	9,381,999,616	905,000,000
Fluid Power Pump and Motor Manufacturing			
IMI plc	333996	2,975,322,841	334,555,552
Fuel Cells Manufacturing			
FuelCell Energy Inc	335999A	112,132,000	-126,009,000
Gasket, Packing and Sealing Device Manufacturing			
Smiths Group plc	339991	4,216,611,619	336,575,008
Generators, and Wind, Steam and Gas Turbine Equipment Manufacturing			
Alstom SA	333611	19,998,864,149	-350,737,792
ENERCON GmbH	333611	5,540,000,000	
GE Vernova Inc	333611	34,935,001,088	1,552,000,000
Siemens Gamesa Renewable Energy SA	333611	10,313,439,150	
Vestas Wind Systems A/S	333611	19,631,100,534	566,401,792
Heavy Construction, Civil, Land Subdivision, Infrastructure, Utilities, Highways & Bridges			
Balfour Beatty plc	237000	11,085,434,076	239,641,408
Baran Group Ltd	237000	194,715,885	11,923,744
Bechtel Group Inc	237000	17,115,000,000	
Bilfinger SE	237000	5,717,934,063	203,745,744
CDM Smith Inc	237000	1,664,754,000	
Daelim Co Ltd	237000		
Fluor Corporation	237000	16,314,999,808	2,144,999,936
Fomento de Construcciones y Contratas SA (FCC)	237000	10,296,726,821	487,928,480

Industry Group/Company	Industry Code	2024 Sales	2024 Profits
GS Engineering & Construction Corporation	237000		
HOCHTIEF AG	237000	37,799,399,051	880,391,616
Hyundai Engineering & Construction Company Ltd	237000		
Jacobs Solutions Inc	237000	11,500,941,312	806,092,992
KBR Inc	237000	7,742,000,128	375,000,000
Larsen & Toubro Limited (L&T)	237000	25,622,890,369	1,527,102,592
PCL Construction Group Inc	237000	8,736,000,000	
Webuild SpA	237000	12,516,721,630	220,745,728
Heavy Duty Truck (including Buses) Manufacturing			
Daimler Trucks North America LLC	336120	27,223,046,424	
PACCAR Inc	336120	33,663,799,296	4,161,999,872
Volvo AB	336120	54,951,652,613	5,256,026,624
Highway, Street, Tunnel & Bridge Construction (Infrastructure)			
ACC Companies	237310		
Acciona SA	237310	21,782,065,422	479,001,120
ACS Actividades de Construccion y Servicios SA	237310	47,256,663,224	939,364,416
AECOM	237310	16,105,497,600	402,265,984
Aecon Group Inc	237310	3,088,092,838	-43,324,840
Empresas ICA SAB de CV	237310	1,207,500,000	
Granite Construction Incorporated	237310	4,007,574,016	126,346,000
Kiewit Corporation	237310	17,955,000,000	
Sino-Thai Engineering & Construction PCL	237310		
Tutor Perini Corporation	237310	122,336,002,048	10,947,999,744
VINCI SA	237310	82,597,044,248	5,519,863,808
Home Entertainment Equipment Manufacturing, Stereo, TV, Radio Entertainment Sys, AV			
Koninklijke Philips NV (Royal Philips)	334310	20,455,163,663	-796,821,824
Panasonic Corporation	334310	58,986,533,173	3,082,435,584
Pioneer Corporation	334310	2,106,359,840	
Samsung Electronics Co Ltd	334310	217,710,030,352	24,328,398,848
Sharp Corp	334310	16,119,974,706	-1,041,238,592
Sony Group Corporation	334310	90,396,892,526	6,738,219,008
HVAC (Cooling, Heating, Ventilation, Air Conditioning) & Refrigeration Equipment Manufacturing			
Trane Technologies plc	333400	19,838,199,808	2,567,899,904
Industrial Gas (i.e., Helium, Nitrogen, Oxygen, Neon) Manufacturing			
Air Products and Chemicals Inc	325120	12,100,599,808	3,828,199,936
Industrial Machinery Manufacturing, Misc & Other			
Illinois Tool Works Inc	333249	15,898,000,384	3,488,000,000
Internet Search Engines, Online Publishing, Sharing, Streaming Entertainment, Social Media			
Alphabet Inc (Google)	519130	350,018,011,136	100,118,003,712
Meta Platforms Inc (Facebook)	519130	164,500,996,096	62,359,998,464
Iron and Steel Forging			
Vatana Phaisal Engineering Co Ltd	332111		
Iron and Steel Mills and Ferroalloy Manufacturing			
Tata Group	331110	137,550,000,000	

Industry Group/Company	Industry Code	2024 Sales	2024 Profits
LCD (Liquid-Crystal Display), Radio Frequency (RF, RFID) and Microwave Equipment Manufacturing			
AUO Corporation	334419	9,372,130,206	-102,473,648
Innolux Corporation	334419		
LG Display Co Ltd	334419	19,258,849,968	-1,854,300,288
Machine Shops and Machined Products Manufacturing (Including Screws and Bolts)			
Mayville Engineering Company Inc	332700	581,603,968	25,968,000
Machine Tool & Laser Manufacturing (for Bending, Buffing, Boring, Pressing, Grinding, Forming)			
ATS Corp	333517	2,207,498,915	141,010,992
Desktop Metal Inc	333517	199,182,900	
Machinery & Engines Manufacturing, Incl Construction, Agricultural, Mining, Industrial, HVAC			
GE Aerospace	333000	38,701,998,080	6,556,000,256
Medical Equipment and Supplies Manufacturing			
3M Company	339100	24,575,000,576	4,172,999,936
Bausch & Lomb Corp	339100	4,791,000,064	-317,000,000
Baxter International Inc	339100	10,636,000,256	-649,000,000
Becton Dickinson and Company	339100	20,177,999,872	1,704,999,936
Boston Scientific Corporation	339100	16,746,999,808	1,854,000,000
EssilorLuxottica SA	339100	30,088,534,915	2,677,639,168
Hill-Rom Holdings Inc	339100	3,209,388,000	
Stryker Corporation	339100	22,595,000,320	2,992,999,936
Medical Imaging Equipment Manufacturing, MRI, Ultrasound, Pacemakers, EKG, PET			
Beckman Coulter Inc	334510	7,226,557,800	
Demant AS	334510	3,411,217,558	363,199,808
GE HealthCare Technologies Inc	334510	19,672,000,512	1,992,999,936
Medtronic plc	334510	32,363,999,232	3,676,000,000
Siemens Healthineers AG	334510	25,383,655,909	2,204,313,344
Missile (Aerospace Defense) and Space Vehicle Manufacturing			
SpaceX (Space Exploration Technologies Corporation)	336414	9,135,000,000	
Oil and Gas (Petroleum) Exploration & Production			
BP plc	211100	189,184,999,424	381,000,000
Chevron Corporation	211100	193,414,004,736	17,660,999,680
ConocoPhillips Company	211100	54,745,001,984	9,244,999,680
Eni SpA	211100	100,791,150,819	2,978,433,536
Equinor ASA	211100	102,501,998,592	8,805,999,616
Exxon Mobil Corporation (ExxonMobil)	211100	339,247,005,696	33,679,998,976
Petrobras (Petroleo Brasileiro SA)	211100	91,416,002,560	7,528,000,000
PetroChina Company Limited	211100	407,843,317,528	22,859,917,312
Petroleos Mexicanos (Pemex)	211100		
PJSC Lukoil Oil Company	211100		
Saudi Aramco (Saudi Arabian Oil Company)	211100	479,398,426,000	106,246,000,000
Shell plc	211100	284,312,010,752	16,094,000,128
TotalEnergies SE	211100	195,610,001,408	15,758,000,128
Oil and Gas Field Services			
Baker Hughes Company	213112	27,829,000,192	2,979,000,064

Industry Group/Company	Industry Code	2024 Sales	2024 Profits
Halliburton Company	213112	22,944,000,000	2,500,999,936
SLB	213112	36,288,999,424	4,461,000,192
Oil and Natural Gas Field Drilling & Production Machinery and Equipment Manufacturing			
TechnipFMC plc	333132	9,083,299,840	842,899,968
Ophthalmic Goods Manufacturing			
Hoya Corp	339115	5,502,832,517	1,259,205,760
Outsourced Computer Facilities Management and Operations Services			
International Business Machines Corporation (IBM)	541513	62,753,001,472	6,023,000,064
Paints and Coatings Manufacturing			
Akzo Nobel NV	325510	12,157,775,341	615,209,984
Altana AG	325510	3,177,490,050	
Clariant International Ltd	325510	5,052,356,921	296,911,136
Paper Bag and Coated and Treated Paper Manufacturing			
Nitto Denko Corp	322220	6,353,367,343	712,850,624
Petrochemicals (Oil) Manufacturing			
ALFA SAB de CV	325110	8,407,991,975	-10,919,336
Evonik Industries AG	325110	17,204,313,517	251,986,384
ExxonMobil Product Solutions Company	325110	302,005,000,000	9,662,000,000
LyondellBasell Industries NV	325110	40,301,998,080	1,360,000,000
Mitsui Chemicals Inc	325110	12,147,619,406	347,118,880
Resonac Holdings Corp	325110	9,660,372,521	510,295,744
Sasol Limited	325110	15,302,221,266	-2,462,441,216
Pharmaceuticals, Biopharmaceuticals, Generics and Drug Manufacturing			
Abbott Laboratories	325412	41,949,999,104	13,402,000,384
AbbVie Inc	325412	56,334,000,128	4,278,000,128
Allergan plc	325412	17,848,740,000	
Amgen Inc	325412	33,423,998,976	4,089,999,872
Astellas Pharma Inc	325412	11,133,518,476	118,335,192
AstraZeneca plc	325412	54,072,999,936	7,034,999,808
Bayer AG	325412	52,901,248,783	-2,896,708,352
Bayer Corporation	325412	16,903,736,850	
Bayer HealthCare Pharmaceuticals Inc	325412	4,999,341,900	
Biogen Inc	325412	9,675,899,904	1,632,199,936
Bristol-Myers Squibb Company	325412	48,299,999,232	-8,947,999,744
Eisai Co Ltd	325412	5,149,618,308	294,411,264
Eli Lilly and Company	325412	45,042,700,288	10,590,000,128
Genentech Inc	325412	26,550,888,000	
Gilead Sciences Inc	325412	28,753,999,872	480,000,000
GSK PLC	325412	42,241,507,607	3,466,722,560
Johnson & Johnson	325412	88,820,998,144	14,065,999,872
Merck & Co Inc	325412	64,168,001,536	17,116,999,680
Merck KGaA	325412	24,013,620,621	3,152,099,840
Merck Serono SA	325412	9,235,636,200	
Novartis AG	325412	51,721,998,336	11,941,000,192
Novo Nordisk AS	325412	44,186,976,078	15,366,076,416
Pfizer Inc	325412	63,627,001,856	8,031,000,064

Industry Group/Company	Industry Code	2024 Sales	2024 Profits
Roche Holding AG	325412	75,925,289,970	10,071,859,200
Sanofi SA	325412	50,267,878,774	6,311,010,304
Takeda Pharmaceutical Company Limited	325412	29,601,236,286	1,000,187,520
UCB SA	325412	6,982,973,901	1,208,853,632
Photographic and Photocopying Equipment Manufacturing			
Agfa-Gevaert NV	333316	1,291,713,963	-104,426,784
Canon Inc	333316	31,309,505,615	1,110,976,128
FUJIFILM Holdings Corporation	333316	20,556,206,968	1,690,565,248
Nikon Corp	333316	4,979,484,953	226,117,744
Ricoh Company Ltd	333316	16,307,879,764	306,692,576
Plastics Material and Resin Manufacturing			
Celanese Corporation	325211	10,279,999,488	-1,522,000,000
Huntsman Corporation	325211	6,035,999,744	-189,000,000
Kaneka Corp	325211	5,292,293,788	161,205,232
Lanxess AG	325211	7,225,879,835	-200,908,064
Shin-Etsu Chemical Co Ltd	325211	16,765,740,009	3,611,080,448
Union Carbide Corporation	325211	5,678,400,000	
Power Tools (Power-Driven Handtools) Manufacturing			
Stanley Black & Decker Inc	333991	15,365,699,584	294,300,000
Power, Distribution and Specialty Transformer Manufacturing			
Mitsubishi Electric Corporation	335311	36,503,152,797	1,978,262,912
Schneider Electric SA	335311	43,306,468,732	4,845,629,952
Pressed and Blown Glass and Glassware (except Glass Packaging Containers) Manufacturing			
Corning Incorporated	327212	13,118,000,128	506,000,000
Printing Ink Manufacturing			
DIC Corporation	325910	7,436,316,564	147,965,840
Radar, Navigation, Sonar, Guidance, Flight Systems & Marine Instrument Manufacturing			
Teledyne FLIR LLC	334511	1,830,192,000	
Teledyne Technologies Inc	334511	5,670,000,128	819,200,000
Thales SA	334511	23,355,959,235	1,611,237,248
Real Estate Rental, Leasing, Development and Management, including REITs			
China State Construction Engineering Corp (CSCEC)	531100		
Research and Development (R&D) in Engineering, Materials, Aerospace, Health, Pharma and Medical			
Amazon Lab126 Inc	541710		
BASF New Business GmbH	541710		
Curia Inc	541710	992,736,150	
Fujitsu Research and Development	541710		
GE Global Research	541710		
Hewlett Packard Laboratories (HP Labs)	541710		
Hitachi High Technologies America Inc	541710		
IBM Research	541710		
Intellectual Ventures Management LLC	541710		
IQVIA Holdings Inc	541710	15,404,999,680	1,372,999,936
NEC Laboratories America Inc	541710		

Industry Group/Company	Industry Code	2024 Sales	2024 Profits
Nokia Bell Labs	541710		
Palo Alto Research Center Inc (PARC)	541710		
PPD Inc	541710	5,395,790,400	
Siemens USA	541710	24,548,448,750	
SRI International	541710		
Toshiba Corporate R&D Center	541710		
X Development LLC	541710		
Reservations, Car Rentals, Car Sharing, Ticket Offices, Time Share and Vacation Club Rentals			
Waymo LLC	561599		
Road Transportation, Support Activities for			
Globalvia Inversiones SAU	488490		
Security Guard, Patrol, Armored Car, Security System & Locksmith Services			
Johnson Controls International plc	561600	22,951,999,488	1,704,999,936
Semiconductor & Solar Cell Manufacturing, Chips, Transistors, Integrated Circuits (IC), AI Chips			
Advanced Micro Devices Inc (AMD)	334413	25,784,999,936	1,640,999,936
Analog Devices Inc	334413	9,427,156,992	1,635,272,960
ASE Technology Holding Co Ltd	334413	19,912,031,632	1,082,835,072
Infineon Technologies AG	334413	16,975,028,177	1,476,730,880
Intel Corporation	334413	53,100,998,656	-18,755,999,744
Micron Technology Inc	334413	25,110,999,040	778,000,000
NVIDIA Corporation	334413	60,921,999,360	29,760,000,000
Qualcomm Incorporated	334413	38,961,999,872	10,142,000,128
STMicroelectronics NV	334413	13,269,000,192	1,556,999,936
Taiwan Semiconductor Manufacturing Co Ltd (TSMC)	334413	96,793,117,416	38,739,222,528
Texas Instruments Incorporated	334413	15,640,999,936	4,799,000,064
Toshiba Corporation	334413	23,000,000,000	
United Microelectronics Corporation	334413	7,768,797,834	1,631,305,600
Semiconductor & Wafer Machinery (Etching, Lithography, Manufacturing Equip. & Systems)			
Applied Materials Inc	333242	27,175,999,488	7,176,999,936
Ship Building and Repairing			
Hanwha Ocean Co Ltd	336611		
Spices, Flavors and Fragrances Manufacturing			
Tate & Lyle plc	311942	2,217,356,196	253,104,400
Surgical Appliance and Supplies (Medical Devices) Manufacturing			
Smith & Nephew plc	339113	5,809,999,872	412,000,000
Telecom, Telephone & Computer & PC Network Equip Manufacturing, Routers, Switches, LAN			
Avaya Holdings Corp	334210	3,291,600,000	
Cisco Systems Inc	334210	53,802,999,808	10,320,000,000
Huawei Technologies Co Ltd	334210		
Juniper Networks Inc	334210	5,073,600,000	287,900,000
Tellabs Inc	334210	1,821,352,000	
VTech Holdings Limited	334210	2,145,699,968	166,600,000
ZTE Corporation	334210	16,838,395,917	1,169,508,992

Industry Group/Company	Industry Code	2024 Sales	2024 Profits
Test Equipment for Electrical Devices, Electronics and Semiconductors Manufacturing			
Agilent Technologies Inc	334515	6,510,000,128	1,288,999,936
Testing Laboratories, Safety and Compliance Services			
Intertek Group plc	541380	4,568,265,352	465,012,032
Transportation Equipment Manufacturing, Automobiles (Cars), Components, Trucks, Aircraft			
ITT Inc	336000	3,630,700,032	518,300,000
Mitsubishi Corporation	336000	135,848,383,103	6,692,821,504
Utilities Construction, Incl Pipelines, Water & Sewer, Telecommunications & Electric Power			
Matrix Service Company	237100	728,212,992	-24,976,000
Vaccines, Skin Replacement Products and Biologicals Manufacturing			
CSL Limited	325414	14,689,999,872	2,641,999,872
Novonesis AS	325414	4,351,305,231	347,105,568
Wireless, Cellular, Cellphone (incl. Handsets), GPS, Radio, Broadcast & Comm. Equip. Manufacturing			
Apple Inc	334220	391,034,994,688	93,736,001,536
L3Harris Technologies Inc	334220	21,325,000,704	1,502,000,000
LG Electronics Inc	334220	63,480,063,277	265,933,664
LM Ericsson Telephone Company (Ericsson)	334220	25,856,117,587	2,086,180
Nokia Corporation	334220	21,816,118,943	1,449,489,152
Sony Corporation	334220	19,603,678,500	

ALPHABETICAL INDEX

Clariant International Ltd
Compal Electronics Inc
ConocoPhillips Company
Contemporary Amperex Technology Co Limited (CATL)
Corning Incorporated
COWI A/S
CRB
CSL Limited
Cummins Inc
Curia Inc
Daelim Co Ltd
Daihatsu Motor Co Ltd
Daimler Trucks North America LLC
Dana Incorporated
Dar Al-Handasah Consultants (Shair and Partners)
Dassault Aviation SA
Dassault Systemes SA
Deere & Company (John Deere)
Dell Technologies Inc
Demant AS
Denso Corporation
Desktop Metal Inc
DIC Corporation
Diebold Nixdorf Incorporated
DLZ Corporation
DNV AS
Dongfeng Motor Corporation
Doosan Enerbility Co Ltd
Dorsch Holding GmbH
Dow Inc
Downer EDI Limited
Dyson Singapore Pte Ltd
Eastman Chemical Company
Eaton Corp plc
ECC (Environmental Chemical Corp)
Eisai Co Ltd
Electronic Arts Inc (EA)
Eli Lilly and Company
Embraer SA
Emerson Electric Co
Empresas ICA SAB de CV
ENERCON GmbH
Eni SpA
Enviri Corporation
Equinor ASA
EssilorLuxottica SA
Estudios y Proyectos Tecnicos Industriales SA (Eptisa)
Evonik Industries AG
Exxon Mobil Corporation (ExxonMobil)
ExxonMobil Product Solutions Company
Ferrari SpA
Ferrovial SE
Flex Ltd
Fluor Corporation
Fomento de Construcciones y Contratas SA (FCC)
Ford Motor Company
Forvia SE
FuelCell Energy Inc

FUJIFILM Holdings Corporation
Fujitsu Limited
Fujitsu Research and Development
Gannett Fleming Inc
GE Aerospace
GE Global Research
GE HealthCare Technologies Inc
GE Vernova Inc
Gen Digital Inc
Genentech Inc
General Dynamics Corporation
General Motors Company (GM)
Georg Fischer AG
Geosyntec Consultants Inc
Ghafari Associates LLC
GHD Group Pty Ltd
Gilead Sciences Inc
GKN Aerospace
Globalvia Inversiones SAU
GM Korea
Golder Associates Corporation
Granite Construction Incorporated
Group Lotus plc
GS Engineering & Construction Corporation
GSK PLC
Gulf Interstate Engineering Company
Gulfstream Aerospace Corporation
Halliburton Company
Hanwha Ocean Co Ltd
Hatch Ltd
HDR Inc
Hewlett Packard Enterprise Company
Hewlett Packard Laboratories (HP Labs)
Hill-Rom Holdings Inc
Hitachi High Technologies America Inc
Hitachi Limited
HKS Inc
HNTB Corporation
HOCHTIEF AG
HOK Group Inc
Hon Hai Precision Industry Company Ltd
Honda Motor Co Ltd
Honeywell International Inc
Hoya Corp
HP Inc
HTC Corporation
Huawei Technologies Co Ltd
Huntsman Corporation
Hyundai Engineering & Construction Company Ltd
Hyundai Motor Company
IBM Research
IDOM
ILF Consulting Engineers Austria GmbH
Illinois Tool Works Inc
IMI plc
Infineon Technologies AG
Innolux Corporation
Integrated Design & Engineering Holdings Co Ltd

Intel Corporation
Intellectual Ventures Management LLC
International Business Machines Corporation (IBM)
Intertek Group plc
Introba Inc
Intuit Inc
IPS - Integrated Project Services LLC
IQVIA Holdings Inc
Isuzu Motors Limited
ITT Inc
Jabil Inc
Jacobs Solutions Inc
Jaguar Land Rover Limited
JGC Holdings Corp
Johnson & Johnson
Johnson Controls International plc
Juniper Networks Inc
Jutal Offshore Oil Services Ltd
Kaneka Corp
Kawasaki Heavy Industries Ltd
KBR Inc
Keller Group PLC
KEO International Consultants WLL
KEPCO Engineering & Construction Company Inc
Khatib & Alami
Kia Corporation
Kiewit Corporation
Kimley-Horn and Associates Inc
Kleinfelder Group Inc (The)
Konami Group Corp
Koninklijke Philips NV (Royal Philips)
Kumho Engineering & Construction Co Ltd
L3Harris Technologies Inc
Langan Engineering and Environmental Services Inc
Lanxess AG
Larsen & Toubro Limited (L&T)
Layne-A Granite Company
Lear Corporation
Leidos Holdings Inc
Lenovo Group Limited
Leo A Daly Company
LG Display Co Ltd
LG Electronics Inc
LITE-ON Technology Corporation
LM Ericsson Telephone Company (Ericsson)
Lockheed Martin Corporation
Luxshare Precision Industry Co Ltd
LyondellBasell Industries NV
Magna International Inc
Marelli Corporation
Mason & Hanger
Matrix Service Company
Mayville Engineering Company Inc
Mazda Motor Corporation
McAfee Corp
McDermott International Ltd
Medtronic plc
Mercedes-Benz Group AG

Merck & Co Inc
Merck KGaA
Merck Serono SA
Meta Platforms Inc (Facebook)
Michael Baker International LLC
Micron Technology Inc
Microsoft Corporation
Middough Inc
Mitsubishi Corporation
Mitsubishi Electric Corporation
Mitsubishi Motors Corp
Mitsui Chemicals Inc
Molex LLC
Mott MacDonald Limited
NCR Voyix Corp
NEC Corp
NEC Laboratories America Inc
NetApp Inc
Nidec Corp
Nikon Corp
Nintendo Co Ltd
Nissan Motor Co Ltd
Nitto Denko Corp
Nokia Bell Labs
Nokia Corporation
NORR Group Inc
Northrop Grumman Corporation
Novartis AG
Novo Nordisk AS
Novonesis AS
NTT Data Corp
NV5 Global Inc
NVIDIA Corporation
Opel Automobile GmbH
Oracle Corporation
Orano SA
Oriental Consultants Global Co Ltd
OYO Corporation
PACCAR Inc
Page Southerland Page Inc
Palo Alto Research Center Inc (PARC)
Panasonic Corporation
Parsons Corporation
PCL Construction Group Inc
Petrobras (Petroleo Brasileiro SA)
PetroChina Company Limited
Petroleos Mexicanos (Pemex)
Pfizer Inc
Pininfarina SpA
Pioneer Corporation
PJSC Lukoil Oil Company
Plexus Corp
PM Group
Porsche Automobil Holding SE
Power Construction Corporation of China Ltd
(PowerChina)
POWER Engineers Incorporated
PPD Inc

Primoris Services Corp
PTC Inc
Qualcomm Incorporated
QuTech
Ramboll Group A/S
Reality Labs
Regulus Group LLC
Renault SA
Resonac Holdings Corp
Rheinmetall AG
Ricardo plc
Ricoh Company Ltd
RIZZO International Inc
Robert Bosch GmbH
Roche Holding AG
Rockwell Automation Inc
Rohm Co Ltd
Rolls-Royce Holdings plc
Royal HaskoningDHV
RTX Corp (Raytheon Technologies)
Saab AB
Safran SA
SAIC Motor Corporation Limited
SAIC-GM-Wuling Automobile Company
Samsung Electronics Co Ltd
Sanmina Corporation
Sanofi SA
SAP SE
Sargent & Lundy LLC
SAS Institute Inc
Sasol Limited
Saudi Aramco (Saudi Arabian Oil Company)
Schneider Electric SA
Science Applications International Corporation (SAIC)
Seagate Technology Public Limited Company
Seatrium Limited
Seiko Epson Corp
Sembcorp Industries Ltd
Sener Ingenieria y Sistemas SA
SEPCO Electric Power Construction Corporation
Shanghai Construction Group Co Ltd
Sharp Corp
Sheladia Associates Inc
Shell plc
Shin-Etsu Chemical Co Ltd
Siemens AG
Siemens Digital Industries Software Inc
Siemens EDA
Siemens Gamesa Renewable Energy SA
Siemens Healthineers AG
Siemens USA
Singapore Technologies Engineering Limited
Sino-Thai Engineering & Construction PCL
SK Ecoplant
Skidmore Owings & Merrill LLP
SLB
SMEC Holdings Pty Ltd
Smith & Nephew plc

Smiths Group plc
Solvay SA
Sony Corporation
Sony Group Corporation
SpaceX (Space Exploration Technologies Corporation)
Spirit AeroSystems Holdings Inc
SRI International
SSOE Group
Stanley Black & Decker Inc
Stanley Consultants Inc
Stellantis North America
Stellantis NV
Stellar Group Inc (The)
STMicroelectronics NV
Stryker Corporation
STV Incorporated
Subaru Corporation
Suffolk Construction Company
Sumitomo Chemical Co Ltd
Suzuki Motor Corp
Syngenta Group Co Ltd
Synopsys Inc
Taisei Corp
Taiwan Semiconductor Manufacturing Co Ltd (TSMC)
Takeda Pharmaceutical Company Limited
Take-Two Interactive Software Inc
Tata Consultancy Services Limited (TCS)
Tata Group
Tata Motors Limited
Tate & Lyle plc
TechnipFMC plc
Tecnica y Proyectos SA (TYPSA)
Teledyne FLIR LLC
Teledyne Technologies Inc
Tellabs Inc
Tenneco Inc
Terex Corporation
Tesla Inc
Texas Instruments Incorporated
Textron Inc
Thales SA
Thinkpath Inc
Thornton Tomasetti Inc
Toshiba Corporate R&D Center
Toshiba Corporation
TotalEnergies SE
Toyoda Gosei Co Ltd
Toyota Motor Corporation
TPV Technology Co Ltd
Tractebel Engineering GmbH
Trane Technologies plc
TRC Companies Inc
Trevi-Finanziaria Industriale SpA (Trevi Group)
Tutor Perini Corporation
UCB SA
Union Carbide Corporation
Unisys Corporation
United Microelectronics Corporation

UniversalPegasus International Inc
Valeo SA
Vatana Phaisal Engineering Co Ltd
VEPICA USA Inc
VeriSign Inc
Versar Inc
Vestas Wind Systems A/S
VINCI SA
Visteon Corporation
Volkswagen AG (VW)
Volvo AB
Volvo Car AB
VSE Corporation
VTech Holdings Limited
Waldemar S Nelson and Company Inc
Wanxiang Group Corporation
Waymo LLC
Webuild SpA
Western Digital Corporation
Westinghouse Electric Company LLC
Whirlpool Corporation
Wipro Limited
WL Meinhardt Group Pty Ltd
Wolfram Research Inc
WSP Global Inc
WSP New Zealand Ltd
X Development LLC
Xerox Corporation
ZF Friedrichshafen AG (ZF)
ZTE Corporation

INDEX OF U.S. HEADQUARTERS LOCATION BY STATE

To help you locate members of the firms geographically, the city and state of the headquarters of each company are in the following index.

ARIZONA
Gen Digital Inc; Tempe

CALIFORNIA
Activision Blizzard; Santa Monica
Adobe Inc; San Jose
Advanced Micro Devices Inc (AMD); Santa Clara
AECOM; Los Angeles
Agilent Technologies Inc; Santa Clara
Allergan plc; Irvine
Alphabet Inc (Google); Mountain View
Amazon Lab126 Inc; Sunnyvale
Amgen Inc; Thousand Oaks
Apple Inc; Cupertino
Applied Materials Inc; Santa Clara
Autodesk Inc; San Rafael
Beckman Coulter Inc; Brea
Broadcom Inc; San Jose
Cadence Design Systems Inc; San Jose
Chevron Corporation; San Ramon
Cisco Systems Inc; San Jose
ECC (Environmental Chemical Corp); Burlingame
Electronic Arts Inc (EA); Redwood City
Genentech Inc; San Francisco
Gilead Sciences Inc; Foster City
Granite Construction Incorporated; Watsonville
Hewlett Packard Laboratories (HP Labs); Palo Alto
HP Inc; Palo Alto
Intel Corporation; Santa Clara
Intuit Inc; Mountain View
Juniper Networks Inc; Sunnyvale
Kleinfelder Group Inc (The); San Diego
McAfee Corp; San Jose
Meta Platforms Inc (Facebook); Menlo Park
NetApp Inc; Sunnyvale
NVIDIA Corporation; Santa Clara
Palo Alto Research Center Inc (PARC); Palo Alto
Qualcomm Incorporated; San Diego
Reality Labs; Menlo Park
Sanmina Corporation; San Jose
SpaceX (Space Exploration Technologies Corporation); Hawthorne
SRI International; Menlo Park
Synopsys Inc; Mountain View
Teledyne Technologies Inc; Thousand Oaks
Tesla Inc; Palo Alto
Tutor Perini Corporation; Sylmar
Waymo LLC; Mountain View
Western Digital Corporation; San Jose
X Development LLC; Mountain View

COLORADO
ACC Companies; Littleton

CONNECTICUT
FuelCell Energy Inc; Danbury
Stanley Black & Decker Inc; New Britain
Terex Corporation; Norwalk
TRC Companies Inc; Windsor
Xerox Corporation; Norwalk

DISTRICT OF COLUMBIA
Siemens USA; Washington

FLORIDA
Citrix Systems Inc; Fort Lauderdale
Geosyntec Consultants Inc; Boca Raton
Jabil Inc; St. Petersburg
L3Harris Technologies Inc; Melbourne
NV5 Global Inc; Hollywood
Stellar Group Inc (The); Jacksonville

GEORGIA
Gulfstream Aerospace Corporation; Savannah
Introba Inc; Atlanta
NCR Voyix Corp; Atlanta

IDAHO
Micron Technology Inc; Boise
POWER Engineers Incorporated; Hailey

ILLINOIS
Abbott Laboratories; Abbott Park
AbbVie Inc; North Chicago
Baxter International Inc; Deerfield
Boeing Company (The); Chicago
Caterpillar Inc; Deerfield
Deere & Company (John Deere); Moline
GE HealthCare Technologies Inc; Chicago
Hill-Rom Holdings Inc; Chicago
Hitachi High Technologies America Inc; Schaumburg
Illinois Tool Works Inc; Glenview
Molex LLC; Lisle
Sargent & Lundy LLC; Chicago
Skidmore Owings & Merrill LLP; Chicago
Wolfram Research Inc; Champaign

INDIANA
Cummins Inc; Columbus
Eli Lilly and Company; Indianapolis

IOWA
Stanley Consultants Inc; Muscatine

KANSAS
Black & Veatch Holding Company; Overland Park
Layne-A Granite Company; Kansas City
Spirit AeroSystems Holdings Inc; Wichita

KENTUCKY
Mason & Hanger; Lexington

LOUISIANA
Waldemar S Nelson and Company Inc; New Orleans

MARYLAND
Lockheed Martin Corporation; Bethesda
Sheladia Associates Inc; Rockville

MASSACHUSETTS
Analog Devices Inc; Wilmington
Biogen Inc; Cambridge
Boston Scientific Corporation; Marlborough
CDM Smith Inc; Boston
Desktop Metal Inc; Burlington
GE Aerospace; Boston
GE Vernova Inc; Cambridge
PTC Inc; Boston
RTX Corp (Raytheon Technologies); Waltham
Suffolk Construction Company; Boston

MICHIGAN
Dow Inc; Midland
Ford Motor Company; Dearborn
General Motors Company (GM); Detroit
Ghafari Associates LLC; Dearborn
Lear Corporation; Southfield
Stellantis North America; Auburn Hills
Stryker Corporation; Kalamazoo
Tenneco Inc; Southfield
Visteon Corporation; Van Buren Township
Whirlpool Corporation; Benton Harbor

MINNESOTA
3M Company; St. Paul

MISSOURI
Amdocs Limited; Chesterfield
Belden Inc; St. Louis
Burns & McDonnell Inc; Kansas City
CRB; Kansas City
Emerson Electric Co; St. Louis
HNTB Corporation; Kansas City
HOK Group Inc; St. Louis

NEBRASKA
HDR Inc; Omaha
Kiewit Corporation; Omaha
Leo A Daly Company; Omaha

NEW JERSEY
Avaya Holdings Corp; Morristown
Bayer Corporation; Whippany
Bayer HealthCare Pharmaceuticals Inc; Whippany
Becton Dickinson and Company; Franklin Lakes
Johnson & Johnson; New Brunswick

Langan Engineering and Environmental Services Inc; Parsippany
Merck & Co Inc; Kenilworth
NEC Laboratories America Inc; Princeton
Nokia Bell Labs; Murray Hill

NEW YORK
Bristol-Myers Squibb Company; New York
CannonDesign; New York
CHA Consulting Inc; Albany
Corning Incorporated; Corning
Curia Inc; Albany
GE Global Research; Niskayuna
IBM Research; Yorktown Heights
International Business Machines Corporation (IBM); Armonk
ITT Inc; White Plains
Pfizer Inc; New York
Take-Two Interactive Software Inc; New York
Thornton Tomasetti Inc; New York

NORTH CAROLINA
Honeywell International Inc; Charlotte
IQVIA Holdings Inc; Durham
Kimley-Horn and Associates Inc; Raleigh
PPD Inc; Wilmington
SAS Institute Inc; Cary

OHIO
Babcock & Wilcox Enterprises Inc; Akron
Dana Incorporated; Maumee
Diebold Nixdorf Incorporated; North Canton
DLZ Corporation; Columbus
Middough Inc; Cleveland
SSOE Group; Toledo
Thinkpath Inc; Miamisburg

OKLAHOMA
Matrix Service Company; Tulsa

OREGON
Daimler Trucks North America LLC; Portland
Siemens EDA; Wilsonville
Teledyne FLIR LLC; Wilsonville

PENNSYLVANIA
Air Products and Chemicals Inc; Allentown
Enviri Corporation; Camp Hill
Gannett Fleming Inc; Camp Hill
IPS - Integrated Project Services LLC; Blue Bell
Michael Baker International LLC; Pittsburgh
RIZZO International Inc; Pittsburgh
STV Incorporated; Douglassville
Unisys Corporation; Blue Bell
Westinghouse Electric Company LLC; Cranberry Township

RHODE ISLAND
Textron Inc; Providence

TENNESSEE
Eastman Chemical Company; Kingsport

TEXAS
Baker Hughes Company; Houston
Benchmark Electronics Inc; Angleton
BMC Software Inc; Houston
Celanese Corporation; Irving
ConocoPhillips Company; Houston
Dell Technologies Inc; Round Rock
Exxon Mobil Corporation (ExxonMobil); Irving
ExxonMobil Product Solutions Company; Spring
Fluor Corporation; Irving
Gulf Interstate Engineering Company; Houston
Halliburton Company; Houston
Hewlett Packard Enterprise Company; Houston
HKS Inc; Dallas
Huntsman Corporation; The Woodlands
Jacobs Solutions Inc; Dallas
KBR Inc; Houston
McDermott International Ltd; Houston
Oracle Corporation; Austin
Page Southerland Page Inc; Houston
Primoris Services Corp; Dallas
Siemens Digital Industries Software Inc; Plano
SLB; Houston
Tellabs Inc; Carrollton
Texas Instruments Incorporated; Dallas
Union Carbide Corporation; North Seadrift
UniversalPegasus International Inc; Houston
VEPICA USA Inc; Katy

VIRGINIA
Bechtel Group Inc; Reston
General Dynamics Corporation; Renton
Leidos Holdings Inc; Reston
Northrop Grumman Corporation; Falls Church
Parsons Corporation; Centreville
Regulus Group LLC; Woodstock
Science Applications International Corporation (SAIC); Reston
VeriSign Inc; Reston
Versar Inc; Washington DC
VSE Corporation; Alexandria

WASHINGTON
Intellectual Ventures Management LLC; Bellevue
Microsoft Corporation; Redmond
PACCAR Inc; Bellevue

WISCONSIN
Mayville Engineering Company Inc; Mayville
Plexus Corp; Neenah
Rockwell Automation Inc; Milwaukee

INDEX OF NON-U.S. HEADQUARTERS LOCATION BY COUNTRY

AUSTRALIA
Aurecon Group Brand (Pty) Ltd; Docklands
Austin Engineering Limited; Kewdale, Western Australia
CSL Limited; Parkville
Downer EDI Limited; North Ryde
GHD Group Pty Ltd; Sydney
SMEC Holdings Pty Ltd; North Sydney

AUSTRIA
BIOS-BIOENERGYSYSTEME GmbH; Graz
ILF Consulting Engineers Austria GmbH; Rum/Innsbruck

BELGIUM
Agfa-Gevaert NV; Mortsel
Solvay SA; Brussels
UCB SA; Brussels

BRAZIL
Embraer SA; Sao Paulo
Petrobras (Petroleo Brasileiro SA); Rio de Janeiro

CANADA
Aecon Group Inc; Toronto
AtkinsRealis Group Inc; Montreal
Atomic Energy of Canada Limited (AECL); Chalk River
ATS Corp; Cambridge
Bausch & Lomb Corp; Vaughan
Bombardier Inc; Montreal
Celestica Inc; Toronto
CGI Inc; Montreal
Golder Associates Corporation; Mississauga
Hatch Ltd; Mississauga
Magna International Inc; Aurora
NORR Group Inc; Toronto
PCL Construction Group Inc; Edmonton
WSP Global Inc; Montreal

CHINA
BYD Company Limited; Shenzhen
China Chengda Engineering Co Ltd; Chengdu
China Energy Engineering Corporation Limited; Beijing
China FAW Group Co Ltd (First Automotive Works); Changchun
China National Machinery Industry Corporation; Beijing
China Petroleum Pipeline Engineering Co Ltd; Langfang
China Railway Construction Company Limited (CRCC); Beijing
China State Construction Engineering Corp (CSCEC); Beijing
Contemporary Amperex Technology Co Limited (CATL); Ningde
Dongfeng Motor Corporation; Wuhan
Huawei Technologies Co Ltd; Shenzhen
Jutal Offshore Oil Services Ltd; Shenzhen
Luxshare Precision Industry Co Ltd; Dongguan
PetroChina Company Limited; Beijing
Power Construction Corporation of China Ltd (PowerChina); Beijing
SAIC Motor Corporation Limited; Shanghai
SAIC-GM-Wuling Automobile Company; Liuzhou
SEPCO Electric Power Construction Corporation; Jinan City
Shanghai Construction Group Co Ltd; Shanghai
TPV Technology Co Ltd; Nanjing
Wanxiang Group Corporation; Hangzhou
ZTE Corporation; Shenzhen

DENMARK
COWI A/S; Kongens Lyngby
Demant AS; Smorum
Novo Nordisk AS; Bagsvaerd
Novonesis AS; Bagsvaerd
Ramboll Group A/S; Copenhagen
Vestas Wind Systems A/S; Aarhus

FINLAND
Nokia Corporation; Espoo

FRANCE
Alstom SA; Paris
Arkema; Colombes
Artelia; Auvergne
Bouygues SA; Paris
Capgemini Engineering; Neuilly-sur-Seine
Dassault Aviation SA; Paris
Dassault Systemes SA; Velizy-Villacoublay
EssilorLuxottica SA; Paris
Forvia SE; Nanterre
Orano SA; Issy-les-Moulineaux
Renault SA; Billancourt
Safran SA; Paris
Sanofi SA; Paris
Schneider Electric SA; Rueil Malmaison
Thales SA; Neuilly-sur-Seine
TotalEnergies SE; Courbevoie
Valeo SA; Paris
VINCI SA; Nanterre Cedex

GERMANY
Altana AG; Wesel
Audi AG; Ingolstadt
BASF New Business GmbH; Ludwigshafen
BASF SE; Ludwigshafen am Rhein
Bayer AG; Leverkusen
Bayerische Motoren Werke AG (BMW Group); Munich
Bilfinger SE; Mannheim
Dorsch Holding GmbH; Frankfurt am Main
ENERCON GmbH; Aurich
Evonik Industries AG; Essen
HOCHTIEF AG; Essen
Infineon Technologies AG; Neubiberg

Lanxess AG; Cologne
Mercedes-Benz Group AG; Stuttgart
Merck KGaA; Darmstadt
Merck Serono SA; Darmstadt
Opel Automobile GmbH; Russelsheim
Porsche Automobil Holding SE; Stuttgart
Rheinmetall AG; Dusseldorf
Robert Bosch GmbH; Gerlingen-Schillerhohe
SAP SE; Walldorf
Siemens AG; Munich
Siemens Healthineers AG; Erlangen
Tractebel Engineering GmbH; Bad Vilbel
Volkswagen AG (VW); Wolfsburg
ZF Friedrichshafen AG (ZF); Friedrichshafen

HONG KONG
Lenovo Group Limited; Hong Kong
VTech Holdings Limited; Hong Kong

INDIA
Larsen & Toubro Limited (L&T); Mumbai
Tata Consultancy Services Limited (TCS); Mumbai
Tata Group; Mumbai
Tata Motors Limited; Mumbai
Wipro Limited; Bengaluru

IRELAND
Accenture plc; Dublin
Eaton Corp plc; Dublin
Johnson Controls International plc; Cork
Medtronic plc; Dublin
PM Group; Dublin
Seagate Technology Public Limited Company; Dublin
Trane Technologies plc; Dublin

ISRAEL
Baran Group Ltd; Beit-Dagan

ITALY
Eni SpA; Rome
Ferrari SpA; Maranello
Pininfarina SpA; Cambiano
Trevi-Finanziaria Industriale SpA (Trevi Group); Cesena
Webuild SpA; Milan

JAPAN
Aisin Corporation; Kariya
Alps Alpine Co Ltd; Tokyo
Astellas Pharma Inc; Tokyo
Canon Inc; Tokyo
Casio Computer Co Ltd; Tokyo
Chiyoda Corporation; Yokohama
Daihatsu Motor Co Ltd; Osaka
Denso Corporation; Kariya
DIC Corporation; Tokyo
Eisai Co Ltd; Tokyo
FUJIFILM Holdings Corporation; Tokyo

Fujitsu Limited; Tokyo
Hitachi Limited; Tokyo
Honda Motor Co Ltd; Tokyo
Hoya Corp; Tokyo
Integrated Design & Engineering Holdings Co Ltd; Tokyo
Isuzu Motors Limited; Tokyo
JGC Holdings Corp; Yokohama-shi, Kanagawa
Kaneka Corp; Osaka
Kawasaki Heavy Industries Ltd; Kobe
Konami Group Corp; Tokyo
Marelli Corporation; Saitama
Mazda Motor Corporation; Hiroshima
Mitsubishi Corporation; Tokyo
Mitsubishi Electric Corporation; Tokyo
Mitsubishi Motors Corp; Tokyo
Mitsui Chemicals Inc; Tokyo
NEC Corp; Tokyo
Nidec Corp; Kyoto
Nikon Corp; Tokyo
Nintendo Co Ltd; Kyoto
Nissan Motor Co Ltd; Kanagawa
Nitto Denko Corp; Osaka
NTT Data Corp; Tokyo
Oriental Consultants Global Co Ltd; Tokyo
OYO Corporation; Tokyo
Panasonic Corporation; Osaka
Pioneer Corporation; Tokyo
Resonac Holdings Corp; Tokyo
Ricoh Company Ltd; Tokyo
Rohm Co Ltd; Kyoto
Seiko Epson Corp; Nagano
Sharp Corp; Sakai City, Osaka
Shin-Etsu Chemical Co Ltd; Tokyo
Sony Corporation; Tokyo
Sony Group Corporation; Tokyo
Subaru Corporation; Tokyo
Sumitomo Chemical Co Ltd; Tokyo
Suzuki Motor Corp; Hamamatsu
Taisei Corp; Tokyo
Takeda Pharmaceutical Company Limited; Osaka
Toshiba Corporate R&D Center; Kawasaki-shi
Toshiba Corporation; Tokyo
Toyoda Gosei Co Ltd; Kiyosu
Toyota Motor Corporation; Toyota

JORDAN
Associated Consulting Engineers; Amman

KOREA
Daelim Co Ltd; Seoul
Doosan Enerbility Co Ltd; Changwon
GM Korea; Incheon
GS Engineering & Construction Corporation; Seoul
Hanwha Ocean Co Ltd; Gyeongsangnam-do
Hyundai Engineering & Construction Company Ltd; Seoul
Hyundai Motor Company; Seoul
KEPCO Engineering & Construction Company Inc;
Gyeongshangbuk-do

Kia Corporation; Seoul
Kumho Engineering & Construction Co Ltd; Jongno-gu, Seoul
LG Display Co Ltd; Seoul
LG Electronics Inc; Seoul
Samsung Electronics Co Ltd; Suwon-si
SK Ecoplant; Seoul

KUWAIT
KEO International Consultants WLL; Safat

LEBANON
Dar Al-Handasah Consultants (Shair and Partners); Beirut
Khatib & Alami; Beirut

MEXICO
ALFA SAB de CV; San Pedro Garza Garcia
Carso Infraestructura y Construccion SAB de CV; Mexico City
Empresas ICA SAB de CV; Mexico City
Petroleos Mexicanos (Pemex); Mexico City

NEW ZEALAND
Beca Group Limited; Auckland
WSP New Zealand Ltd; Wellington

NORWAY
AF Gruppen ASA; Oslo
DNV AS; Hovik
Equinor ASA; Stavanger

RUSSIA
PJSC Lukoil Oil Company; Moscow

SAUDI ARABIA
Saudi Aramco (Saudi Arabian Oil Company); Dhahran

SINGAPORE
Dyson Singapore Pte Ltd; Singapore
Flex Ltd; Singapore
Seatrium Limited; Singapore
Sembcorp Industries Ltd; Singapore
Singapore Technologies Engineering Limited; Singapore
WL Meinhardt Group Pty Ltd; Singapore

SOUTH AFRICA
Sasol Limited; Sandton

SPAIN
Abertis Infraestructuras SA; Barcelona
Acciona SA; Madrid
ACS Actividades de Construccion y Servicios SA; Madrid
Estudios y Proyectos Tecnicos Industriales SA (Eptisa); Madrid
Fomento de Construcciones y Contratas SA (FCC); Madrid
Globalvia Inversiones SAU; Madrid

IDOM; Bilbao
Sener Ingenieria y Sistemas SA; Getxo (Biscay)
Siemens Gamesa Renewable Energy SA; Zamudio
Tecnica y Proyectos SA (TYPSA); Madrid

SWEDEN
AFRY AB; Stockholm
Autoliv Inc; Stockholm
LM Ericsson Telephone Company (Ericsson); Stockholm
Saab AB; Stockholm
Volvo AB; Gothenburg
Volvo Car AB; Goteborg

SWITZERLAND
ABB Ltd; Zurich
Clariant International Ltd; Pratteln
Georg Fischer AG; Schaffhausen
Novartis AG; Basel
Roche Holding AG; Basel
STMicroelectronics NV; Geneva
Syngenta Group Co Ltd; Basel

TAIWAN
Acer Inc; Xizhi, New Taipei City
ASE Technology Holding Co Ltd; Kaohsiung
ASUSTeK Computer Inc; Taipei
AUO Corporation; Hsinchu
Compal Electronics Inc; Taipei
Hon Hai Precision Industry Company Ltd; Tu-Chen City, Taipei
HTC Corporation; Taoyuan
Innolux Corporation; Taipei City
LITE-ON Technology Corporation; Taipei
Taiwan Semiconductor Manufacturing Co Ltd (TSMC); Hsinchu
United Microelectronics Corporation; Hsinchu City

THAILAND
Sino-Thai Engineering & Construction PCL; Bangkok
Vatana Phaisal Engineering Co Ltd; Smutprakarn

THE NETHERLANDS
Airbus SE; Leiden
Akzo Nobel NV; Amsterdam
Arcadis NV; Amsterdam
Bilfinger Tebodin BV; Den Haag
Ferrovial SE; Amsterdam
Koninklijke Philips NV (Royal Philips); Amsterdam
LyondellBasell Industries NV; Rotterdam
QuTech; Delft
Royal HaskoningDHV; Amersfoort
Shell plc; The Hague
Stellantis NV; Lijnden

UNITED KINGDOM
Amey Ltd; London
ARUP Group Limited; London

Aston Martin Lagonda Global Holdings PLC; Warwick
AstraZeneca plc; London
BAE Systems plc; London
Balfour Beatty plc; London
BP plc; London
Buro Happold Limited; Bath
Fujitsu Research and Development; Slough
GKN Aerospace; Worcestershire
Group Lotus plc; Norwich
GSK PLC; Middlesex
IMI plc; Birmingham
Intertek Group plc; London
Jaguar Land Rover Limited; Coventry
Keller Group PLC; London
Mott MacDonald Limited; Croydon
Ricardo plc; West Sussex
Rolls-Royce Holdings plc; London
Smith & Nephew plc; Watford, Herfordshire
Smiths Group plc; London
Tate & Lyle plc; London
TechnipFMC plc; London

Individual Profiles
On Each Of
THE ENGINEERING & RESEARCH 500

3M Company

NAIC Code: 339100

TYPES OF BUSINESS:

Health Care Products
Specialty Materials & Textiles
Industrial Products
Safety, Security & Protection Products
Display & Graphics Products
Consumer & Office Products
Electronics & Communications Products
Fuel Cell Technology

BRANDS/DIVISIONS/AFFILIATES:

Scotch
Post-it
Nexcare
Filtrete
Command
Futuro
Littmann
Ace

CONTACTS: *Note: Officers with more than one job title may be intentionally listed here more than once.*

Bryan Hanson, CEO, Divisional
William Brown, CEO
Anurag Maheshwari, CFO
Michael Roman, Chairman of the Board
Theresa Reinseth, Chief Accounting Officer
Mark Murphy, Chief Information Officer
John Banovetz, Chief Technology Officer
Torie Clarke, Executive VP
Kevin Rhodes, Executive VP
Zoe Dickson, Executive VP
Beatriz Karina Chavez Rodriguez, President, Divisional
Peter Gibbons, President, Divisional
Christian Goralski, President, Divisional

GROWTH PLANS/SPECIAL FEATURES:

3M, a multinational conglomerate founded in 1902, sells tens of thousands of products ranging from sponges to respirators. The firm is well known for its extensive research and development capabilities, and it is a pioneer in inventing new use cases for its proprietary technologies. 3M is organized across three business segments: safety and industrial (representing around 44% of revenue), transportation and electronics (36%), and consumer (20%). The firm recently spun off its healthcare business, now known as Solventum. Nearly half of 3M's revenue comes from outside the Americas.

3M offers its employees medical and dental insurance, tuition reimbursement, flexible spending accounts, disability coverage, a 401(k), adoption assistance and more.

FINANCIAL DATA: *Note: Data for latest year may not have been available at press time.*

In U.S. $	2024	2023	2022	2021	2020	2019
Revenue	24,575,000,576	24,610,000,896	26,161,000,448	35,355,000,832	32,184,000,512	32,135,999,488
R&D Expense	1,085,000,000	1,154,000,000	1,160,000,000	1,994,000,000	1,878,000,000	1,911,000,000
Operating Income	4,822,000,000	-10,725,000,000	1,916,000,000	7,369,000,000	6,772,000,000	6,060,000,000
Operating Margin %	.20%	-.44%	.07%	.21%	.21%	.19%
SGA Expense	4,221,000,000	19,198,000,000	7,232,000,000	7,197,000,000	6,929,000,000	7,029,000,000
Net Income	4,173,000,000	-6,995,000,000	5,777,000,000	5,921,000,000	5,449,000,000	4,517,000,000
Operating Cash Flow	1,819,000,000	6,680,000,000	5,591,000,000	7,454,000,000	8,113,000,000	7,070,000,000
Capital Expenditure	1,181,000,000	1,615,000,000	1,749,000,000	1,603,000,000	1,501,000,000	1,699,000,000
EBITDA	7,373,000,000	-8,343,000,000	6,497,000,000	9,607,000,000	9,235,000,000	7,684,000,000
Return on Assets %	.09%	-.14%	.12%	.13%	.12%	.11%
Return on Equity %	.96%	-.72%	.39%	.42%	.48%	.45%
Debt to Equity	3.01%	2.83%	1.00%	1.11%	1.453	1.812

CONTACT INFORMATION:

Phone: 651 733-1110   Fax: 651 733-9973
Toll-Free: 800-364-3577
Address: 3M Center, St. Paul, MN 55144-1000 United States

STOCK TICKER/OTHER:

Stock Ticker: MMM   Exchange: NYS
Employees: 85,000   Fiscal Year Ends: 12/31
Parent Company:

SALARIES/BONUSES:

Top Exec. Salary: $1,200,000   Bonus: $3,000,000
Second Exec. Salary: Bonus: $3,150,000
$350,000

OTHER THOUGHTS:

Estimated Female Officers or Directors: 7
Hot Spot for Advancement for Women/Minorities: Y

ABB Ltd

NAIC Code: 335313

TYPES OF BUSINESS:

Diversified Engineering Services
Power Transmission & Distribution Systems
Control & Automation Technology Products
Industrial Robotics
Energy Trading Software
Artificial Intelligence

BRANDS/DIVISIONS/AFFILIATES:

GROWTH PLANS/SPECIAL FEATURES:

ABB is a supplier of electrical equipment and automation products. Founded in the late 19th century, the company was created out of the merger of two old industrial companies: ASEA and BBC. Its products include electrical equipment, industrial robots, and equipment used for industrial automation that are sold via approximately 19 business divisions. ABB is the number one or two supplier in two thirds of its product segments.

CONTACTS: Note: Officers with more than one job title may be intentionally listed here more than once.

Peter Voser, Chairman of the Board
Jacob Wallenberg, Director

FINANCIAL DATA: Note: Data for latest year may not have been available at press time.

In U.S. $	2024	2023	2022	2021	2020	2019
Revenue	32,849,999,872	32,234,999,808	29,446,000,640	28,945,000,448	26,133,999,616	27,978,000,384
R&D Expense	1,469,000,000	1,317,000,000	1,166,000,000	1,219,000,000	1,127,000,000	1,198,000,000
Operating Income	5,097,000,000	4,354,000,000	3,412,000,000	3,086,000,000	1,856,000,000	2,261,000,000
Operating Margin %	.16%	.14%	.12%	.11%	.07%	.08%
SGA Expense	5,708,000,000	5,543,000,000	5,132,000,000	5,162,000,000	4,895,000,000	5,447,000,000
Net Income	3,935,000,000	3,745,000,000	2,475,000,000	4,546,000,000	5,146,000,000	1,439,000,000
Operating Cash Flow	4,675,000,000	4,290,000,000	1,287,000,000	3,330,000,000	1,693,000,000	2,325,000,000
Capital Expenditure	845,000,000	770,000,000	762,000,000	820,000,000	694,000,000	762,000,000
EBITDA	6,134,000,000	5,833,000,000	4,338,000,000	6,828,000,000	1,996,000,000	3,038,000,000
Return on Assets %	.10%	.09%	.06%	.11%	.12%	.03%
Return on Equity %	.28%	.29%	.17%	.29%	.35%	.10%
Debt to Equity	.50%	.44%	.45%	.31%	0.354	0.554

CONTACT INFORMATION:

Phone: 41-43-317-7111   Fax: 41-43-317-4420
Toll-Free:
Address: Affolternstrasse 44, Zurich, CH-8050 Switzerland

STOCK TICKER/OTHER:

Stock Ticker: ABLZF   Exchange: PINX
Employees: 107,900   Fiscal Year Ends: 12/31
Parent Company:

SALARIES/BONUSES:

Top Exec. Salary: $2,154,845   Bonus: $2,606,491
Second Exec. Salary: Bonus: $1,627,341
$1,131,681

OTHER THOUGHTS:

Estimated Female Officers or Directors: 2
Hot Spot for Advancement for Women/Minorities: Y

Abbott Laboratories

www.abbott.com

NAIC Code: 325412

TYPES OF BUSINESS:

Nutritional Products Manufacturing
Immunoassays
Diagnostics
Consumer Health Products
Medical & Surgical Devices
Generic Pharmaceutical Products
LASIK Devices

BRANDS/DIVISIONS/AFFILIATES:

BinaxNOW

GROWTH PLANS/SPECIAL FEATURES:

Abbott manufactures and markets cardiovascular and diabetes devices, adult and pediatric nutritional products, diagnostic equipment and testing kits, and branded generic drugs. Products include pacemakers, implantable cardioverter defibrillators, neuromodulation devices, coronary stents, catheters, infant formula, nutritional liquids for adults, continuous glucose monitors, and immunoassays and point-of-care diagnostic equipment. Abbott derives approximately 60% of sales outside the United States.

Abbott offers its employees comprehensive benefits.

CONTACTS: Note: Officers with more than one job title may be intentionally listed here more than once.

Robert Ford, CEO
Philip Boudreau, CFO
John Mccoy, Chief Accounting Officer
Mary Moreland, Executive VP, Divisional
Louis Morrone, Executive VP, Divisional
Andrea Wainer, Executive VP, Divisional
Lisa Earnhardt, Executive VP
Daniel Salvadori, Executive VP
Hubert Allen, Executive VP

FINANCIAL DATA: Note: Data for latest year may not have been available at press time.

In U.S. $	2024	2023	2022	2021	2020	2019
Revenue	41,949,999,104	40,108,998,656	43,653,001,216	43,074,998,272	34,608,001,024	31,904,000,000
R&D Expense	2,844,000,000	2,741,000,000	2,888,000,000	2,742,000,000	2,420,000,000	2,440,000,000
Operating Income	6,825,000,000	6,478,000,000	8,362,000,000	8,425,000,000	5,357,000,000	4,532,000,000
Operating Margin %	.16%	.16%	.19%	.20%	.15%	.14%
SGA Expense	11,697,000,000	10,949,000,000	11,248,000,000	11,324,000,000	9,696,000,000	9,765,000,000
Net Income	13,402,000,000	5,723,000,000	6,933,000,000	7,071,000,000	4,495,000,000	3,687,000,000
Operating Cash Flow	8,558,000,000	7,261,000,000	9,581,000,000	10,533,000,000	7,901,000,000	6,136,000,000
Capital Expenditure	2,207,000,000	2,202,000,000	1,777,000,000	1,885,000,000	2,177,000,000	1,638,000,000
EBITDA	10,790,000,000	10,544,000,000	12,131,000,000	12,282,000,000	8,841,000,000	7,761,000,000
Return on Assets %	.17%	.08%	.09%	.10%	.06%	.05%
Return on Equity %	.31%	.15%	.19%	.21%	.14%	.12%
Debt to Equity	.28%	.38%	.42%	.51%	0.593	0.56

CONTACT INFORMATION:

Phone: 847 937-6100   Fax: 847 937-1511
Toll-Free:
Address: 100 Abbott Park Rd., Abbott Park, IL 60064-6400 United States

STOCK TICKER/OTHER:

Stock Ticker: ABT   Exchange: NYS
Employees: 114,000   Fiscal Year Ends: 12/31
Parent Company:

SALARIES/BONUSES:

Top Exec. Salary: $1,500,000   Bonus: $
Second Exec. Salary: Bonus: $
$911,154

OTHER THOUGHTS:

Estimated Female Officers or Directors: 5
Hot Spot for Advancement for Women/Minorities: Y

AbbVie Inc

www.abbvie.com

NAIC Code: 325412

TYPES OF BUSINESS:

Pharmaceuticals Manufacturing
Biopharmaceutical Production
Biopharmaceutical Development

GROWTH PLANS/SPECIAL FEATURES:

AbbVie is a pharmaceutical firm with a strong exposure to immunology (with Humira, Skyrizi, and Rinvoq) and oncology (with Imbruvica and Venclexta). The company was spun off from Abbott in early 2013. The 2020 acquisition of Allergan added several new products and drugs in aesthetics (including Botox).

Depending on the country, AbbVie offers healthcare and retirement benefits, life and disability insurance and a variety of incentives and employee assistance programs.

BRANDS/DIVISIONS/AFFILIATES:

HUMIRA
IMBRUVICA
MAVYRET
Botox
Lumigan
Lo Loestrin

CONTACTS: *Note: Officers with more than one job title may be intentionally listed here more than once.*

Robert Michael, CEO
Roopal Thakkar, Other Executive Officer
Scott Reents, CFO
Richard Gonzalez, Chairman of the Board
Kevin Buckbee, Chief Accounting Officer
Thomas Hudson, Chief Scientific Officer
Nicholas Donoghoe, Chief Strategy Officer
David Purdue, Controller
Perry Siatis, Executive VP
Jeffrey Stewart, Executive VP
Timothy Richmond, Executive VP
Azita Saleki-Gerhardt, Executive VP

FINANCIAL DATA: *Note: Data for latest year may not have been available at press time.*

In U.S. $	2024	2023	2022	2021	2020	2019
Revenue	56,334,000,128	54,317,998,080	58,054,000,640	56,197,001,216	45,803,999,232	33,265,999,872
R&D Expense	12,791,000,000	7,675,000,000	6,510,000,000	8,046,000,000	7,755,000,000	6,792,000,000
Operating Income	11,894,000,000	13,535,000,000	18,814,000,000	17,924,000,000	11,363,000,000	12,983,000,000
Operating Margin %	.21%	.25%	.32%	.32%	.25%	.39%
SGA Expense	14,752,000,000	12,872,000,000	15,260,000,000	12,349,000,000	11,299,000,000	6,942,000,000
Net Income	4,278,000,000	4,863,000,000	11,836,000,000	11,542,000,000	4,616,000,000	7,882,000,000
Operating Cash Flow	18,806,000,000	22,839,000,000	24,943,000,000	22,777,000,000	17,588,000,000	13,324,000,000
Capital Expenditure	974,000,000	777,000,000	695,000,000	787,000,000	798,000,000	552,000,000
EBITDA	14,910,000,000	17,172,000,000	24,174,000,000	23,933,000,000	12,323,000,000	12,227,000,000
Return on Assets %	.03%	.04%	.08%	.08%	.04%	.11%
Return on Equity %	.62%	.35%	.72%	.81%	1.86%	
Debt to Equity	18.15%	5.04%	3.43%	4.17%	5.931	

CONTACT INFORMATION:

Phone: 847-932-7900   Fax:
Toll-Free: 800-255-5162
Address: 1 N. Waukegan Rd., North Chicago, IL 60064 United States

STOCK TICKER/OTHER:

Stock Ticker: ABBV   Exchange: NYS
Employees: 50,000   Fiscal Year Ends: 12/31
Parent Company:

SALARIES/BONUSES:

Top Exec. Salary: $1,607,404   Bonus: $
Second Exec. Salary: Bonus: $
$1,603,846

OTHER THOUGHTS:

Estimated Female Officers or Directors:
Hot Spot for Advancement for Women/Minorities:

Abertis Infraestructuras SA

NAIC Code: 561210

www.abertis.com

TYPES OF BUSINESS:

Transport & Communications
Toll Road Management
Toll Road Operations
Infrastructure Technology
Smart Engineering
Electric Vehicle Charging Services

BRANDS/DIVISIONS/AFFILIATES:

Atlantia SpA
Actividades de Construccion Y Servicios SA
A4holding
Abertis Mobility Services
Autopistas
Metropistas
Viaschile
BIP&GO

CONTACTS: *Note: Officers with more than one job title may be intentionally listed here more than once.*

Francisco Jose Aljaro Navarro, CEO
Juan Santamaria Cases, Pres.
Jose Maria Coronas Guinart, Sec.

GROWTH PLANS/SPECIAL FEATURES:

Abertis Infraestructuras SA is an international group of toll-road operators, managing high-quality, high-capacity roads worldwide. Abertis has approximately 5,000 road miles (8,000 km) under management, operating in 15 countries such as Spain, Chile, Brazil, France, Italy, Mexico, the U.S., Puerto Rico and Argentina. The company has equity stakes in more than 124 miles (200 km) in the Francia and the U.K. More than 78% of revenue is derived outside of Spain, with primary countries including France, Brazil and Chile. Abertis invests in technology and smart engineering to ensure the safe and continual operation of the toll roads. Subsidiaries of the firm include A4holding, Abertis Mobility Services, Arteris, Autopistas, Elizabeth River Crossings, emovis, Isadak, Metropistas, RCO, Red Viacorta, Sanef, Viaschile, Bip&Drive.es and BIP&GO. Abertis Infraestructuras is a joint venture between Atlantia SpA of Italy and Actividades de Construccion Y Servicios, S.A. (ACS) of Spain. The Abertis Foundation is a non-profit that has partnered up with UNICEF which is committed to promoting sustainable mobility and Road Safety in Brazil, India and Mexico. The firm is owned by Mundys, aCS and Hochtief. In August 2024, Abertis was awarded the Ruta 5 Santiago-Los Vilos concession in Chile through its ViasChile1 subsidiary, which will invest $1.1 billion over the next seven years to improve and expand the 139 mile motorway that connects Santiago with the coastal city of Los Vilos.

FINANCIAL DATA: *Note: Data for latest year may not have been available at press time.*

In U.S. $	2024	2023	2022	2021	2020	2019
Revenue	7,262,952,900	6,917,098,000	5,534,807,124	5,265,627,010	4,978,870,000	6,617,870,000
R&D Expense						
Operating Income						
Operating Margin %						
SGA Expense						
Net Income		696,690,000	217,850,000	302,510,575	-632,283,000	361,721,000
Operating Cash Flow						
Capital Expenditure						
EBITDA						
Return on Assets %						
Return on Equity %						
Debt to Equity						

CONTACT INFORMATION:

Phone: 34 932305000   Fax: 34 932305001
Toll-Free:
Address: Avinguda de Pedralbes, 17, Barcelona, 08040 Spain

STOCK TICKER/OTHER:

Stock Ticker: Subsidiary   Exchange:
Employees: 13,000   Fiscal Year Ends: 12/31
Parent Company: Atlantia SpA

SALARIES/BONUSES:

Top Exec. Salary: $ Bonus: $
Second Exec. Salary: $ Bonus: $

OTHER THOUGHTS:

Estimated Female Officers or Directors:
Hot Spot for Advancement for Women/Minorities:

ACC Companies

www.accbuilt.com

NAIC Code: 237310

TYPES OF BUSINESS:

Heavy Construction & Civil Engineering
Civil Construction Services
Heavy Equipment Fleet
Road and Highway Reconstruction
Golf Course Development
Athletic Fields
Environmental Restoration
Site Development

BRANDS/DIVISIONS/AFFILIATES:

MasTec Inc
ACC Mountain West

GROWTH PLANS/SPECIAL FEATURES:

ACC Companies stands for American Civil Constructors, which solve challenges that accompany complex construction projects via equipment and technology for clients throughout the U.S. The firm's ACC Mountain West (ACCMW) is a full-service civil contractor engaged in infrastructure projects, delivering region-specific expertise and specialized service across technology and construction strategies. ACCMW utilizes an extensive fleet of modern and sophisticated heavy equipment; and provides commercial and industrial landscape construction services, with specialties in golf courses, athletic fields and environmental restoration. Featured project by ACC span state highway improvements, creek draining improvements, highway reconstruction, lawn parks, regional parks, country clubs, university sports fields and site development services. ACC is a subsidiary of MasTec, Inc.

CONTACTS: Note: Officers with more than one job title may be intentionally listed here more than once.

Randy Maher, COO
Jody Randall, Chief Admin. Officer
Nicole R. Smith, Controller
Norm Watkins, Dir.-Safety
Mark Krumm, Pres., Arizona Area
Robert Terril, Pres., Nevada Area
Shane Haycock, VP-Nevada Area

FINANCIAL DATA: Note: Data for latest year may not have been available at press time.

In U.S. $	2024	2023	2022	2021	2020	2019
Revenue						
R&D Expense						
Operating Income						
Operating Margin %						
SGA Expense						
Net Income						
Operating Cash Flow						
Capital Expenditure						
EBITDA						
Return on Assets %						
Return on Equity %						
Debt to Equity						

CONTACT INFORMATION:

Phone: 303 795-2582   Fax: 303 347-1844
Toll-Free:
Address: 4901 S. Windermere St., Littleton, CO 80120 United States

STOCK TICKER/OTHER:

Stock Ticker: Subsidiary   Exchange:
Employees: 600   Fiscal Year Ends: 12/31
Parent Company: MasTec Inc

SALARIES/BONUSES:

Top Exec. Salary: $ Bonus: $
Second Exec. Salary: $ Bonus: $

OTHER THOUGHTS:

Estimated Female Officers or Directors: 1
Hot Spot for Advancement for Women/Minorities:

Accenture plc

NAIC Code: 541512

www.accenture.com

TYPES OF BUSINESS:

IT Consulting
Technology
Artificial Intelligence
Data
Analytics
Supply Chain Management
Cloud
Automation

BRANDS/DIVISIONS/AFFILIATES:

Zestgroup

GROWTH PLANS/SPECIAL FEATURES:

Accenture is a leading global IT services firm that provides consulting, strategy, and technology and operational services. These services run the gamut from aiding enterprises with digital transformation to procurement services to software system integration. The company provides its IT offerings to a variety of sectors, including communications, media and technology, financial services, health and public services, consumer products, and resources. Accenture employs just under 500,000 people throughout 200 cities in 51 countries.

CONTACTS: *Note: Officers with more than one job title may be intentionally listed here more than once.*

Manish Sharma, CEO, Geographical
Mauro Macchi, CEO, Geographical
Atsushi Egawa, CEO, Geographical
Ryoji Sekido, CEO, Geographical
Julie Sweet, CEO
Angie Park, CFO
Jean-Marc Ollagnier, Chairman of the Board, Geographical
Melissa Burgum, Chief Accounting Officer
John Walsh, COO
Joel Unruch, General Counsel
Angela Beatty, Other Executive Officer

FINANCIAL DATA: *Note: Data for latest year may not have been available at press time.*

In U.S. $	2024	2023	2022	2021	2020	2019
Revenue	64,896,462,848	64,111,742,976	61,594,304,512	50,533,388,288	44,327,038,976	43,215,011,840
R&D Expense						
Operating Income	9,595,847,000	8,809,889,000	9,367,181,000	7,621,529,000	6,513,644,000	6,305,074,000
Operating Margin %	.15%	.14%	.15%	.15%	.15%	.15%
SGA Expense	11,128,030,000	10,858,570,000	10,334,360,000	8,742,599,000	7,462,514,000	7,009,614,000
Net Income	7,264,787,000	6,871,557,000	6,877,169,000	5,906,809,000	5,107,839,000	4,779,112,000
Operating Cash Flow	9,131,027,000	9,524,268,000	9,541,129,000	8,975,148,000	8,215,152,000	6,626,953,000
Capital Expenditure	516,509,000	528,172,000	717,998,000	580,132,000	599,132,000	599,009,000
EBITDA	11,188,330,000	10,587,610,000	10,554,220,000	9,711,850,000	8,580,526,000	7,167,520,000
Return on Assets %	.14%	.14%	.15%	.15%	.15%	.18%
Return on Equity %	.27%	.29%	.33%	.32%	.33%	.39%
Debt to Equity	.09%	.09%	.12%	.14%	0.16	0.001

CONTACT INFORMATION:

Phone: 353 1-646-2000   Fax:
Toll-Free:
Address: 1 Grand Canal Sq., Dublin, 2 Ireland

STOCK TICKER/OTHER:

Stock Ticker: ACN   Exchange: NYS
Employees: 774,000   Fiscal Year Ends: 08/31
Parent Company:

SALARIES/BONUSES:

Top Exec. Salary: $1,550,000   Bonus: $
Second Exec. Salary: Bonus: $
$1,238,787

OTHER THOUGHTS:

Estimated Female Officers or Directors: 6
Hot Spot for Advancement for Women/Minorities: Y

Acciona SA

NAIC Code: 237310

www.acciona.es

TYPES OF BUSINESS:

Heavy Construction
Energy Solutions
Infrastructure Transport Solutions
Water Solutions
Social Solutions
Efficient Cities
Sustainable Real Estate
Asset Management

BRANDS/DIVISIONS/AFFILIATES:

Bestinver Gestion
Bestinver Securities

GROWTH PLANS/SPECIAL FEATURES:

Acciona SA is an engineering and construction firm providing sustainable solutions for infrastructure and renewable energy projects across the world. It works in various phases, from design and construction to operations and maintenance. The company operates two business divisions energy and infrastructure. The infrastructure division encompasses construction, water treatment, industrial, and service business lines. Projects may be granted under concessions from governments or acquired independently when Acciona identifies an opportunity. Energy developments focus on renewable technologies and primarily revolve around wind, solar, hydro, and biomass. The company has a presence on five continents and utilizes an organizational structure to ensure availability.

CONTACTS: Note: Officers with more than one job title may be intentionally listed here more than once.

Jose Manuel Domecq, CEO
Juan Franco, Director

FINANCIAL DATA: Note: Data for latest year may not have been available at press time.

In U.S. $	2024	2023	2022	2021	2020	2019
Revenue	21,782,065,422	19,320,090,463	12,707,150,761	9,198,637,921	7,357,516,721	8,161,848,962
R&D Expense						
Operating Income	1,156,640,000	1,249,716,000	1,315,551,000	758,229,300	414,626,600	786,356,500
Operating Margin %	.05%	.06%	.10%	.08%	.06%	.10%
SGA Expense	8,904,654,000	8,517,594,000	5,272,418,000	4,000,000,000	2,854,471,000	3,138,045,000
Net Income	479,001,100	614,074,900	500,567,600	376,844,500	439,332,600	399,180,500
Operating Cash Flow	2,541,430,000	1,923,950,000	1,870,602,000	651,532,400	1,098,210,000	893,635,600
Capital Expenditure	3,099,887,000	3,284,904,000	2,491,487,000	1,076,050,000	1,028,079,000	1,494,159,000
EBITDA	2,908,059,000	2,753,689,000	2,240,636,000	1,730,987,000	1,509,565,000	1,633,648,000
Return on Assets %		.02%	.02%	.02%	.02%	.02%
Return on Equity %		.11%	.10%	.09%	.11%	.10%
Debt to Equity	1.99%	1.81%	1.26%	1.13%	1.583	1.735

CONTACT INFORMATION:

Phone: 34 916632850   Fax: 34 916632851
Toll-Free:
Address: Ave. De Europa, 18, Parque Empresarial La Moreleja, Madrid, 28108 Spain

STOCK TICKER/OTHER:

Stock Ticker: ACXIF   Exchange: PINX
Employees: 39,699   Fiscal Year Ends: 12/31
Parent Company:

SALARIES/BONUSES:

Top Exec. Salary: $ Bonus: $
Second Exec. Salary: $ Bonus: $

OTHER THOUGHTS:

Estimated Female Officers or Directors: 2
Hot Spot for Advancement for Women/Minorities:

Sales, profits and employees may be estimates. Financial information, benefits and other data can change quickly and may vary from those stated here.

Acer Inc

NAIC Code: 334111

TYPES OF BUSINESS:

Computer Manufacturing
Information Technology
Communication Technology
Software
Hardware
Gaming Solutions
Education Solutions
Connectivity and Display Solutions

BRANDS/DIVISIONS/AFFILIATES:

GROWTH PLANS/SPECIAL FEATURES:

Acer Inc is a hardware and electronics company specializing in electronics technology. Its products are sold under three brands: Acer, Gateway, and Packard Bell. It includes desktop PCs, clamshell laptops, 2-in-1 laptops, convertible laptops, Chromebooks, tablets, servers, storage devices, virtual reality devices, displays, smartphones, and peripherals. A large majority of the firm's revenue is derived from personal computers and the rest from peripherals and other products. The firm generates revenue in the Americas, Mainland China, Taiwan, and other countries across the world.

CONTACTS: Note: Officers with more than one job title may be intentionally listed here more than once.

Jason Chen, CEO

FINANCIAL DATA: Note: Data for latest year may not have been available at press time.

In U.S. $	2024	2023	2022	2021	2020	2019
Revenue	8,851,662,324	8,069,966,570	9,210,880,786	10,668,365,312	9,267,356,328	7,835,106,406
R&D Expense	75,787,700	70,844,660	81,895,620	88,494,750	79,681,930	86,006,150
Operating Income	163,165,000	141,308,600	231,680,000	473,642,600	298,837,500	102,930,000
Operating Margin %	.02%	.02%	.03%	.04%	.03%	.01%
SGA Expense	701,338,200	653,449,600	685,774,200	685,382,300	636,409,000	639,706,700
Net Income	185,249,500	164,936,900	167,336,200	364,438,100	201,634,900	88,039,760
Operating Cash Flow	-50,926,930	424,170,300	198,462,800	217,303,700	919,354,600	-46,165,780
Capital Expenditure	162,337,300	33,433,820	29,137,210	30,972,380	18,253,360	17,690,820
EBITDA	394,863,600	329,692,200	326,339,500	578,140,400	358,242,000	181,044,400
Return on Assets %	.03%	.02%	.02%	.05%	.04%	.02%
Return on Equity %	.07%	.07%	.08%	.18%	.10%	.05%
Debt to Equity	.23%	.17%	.18%	.18%	0.079	0.125

CONTACT INFORMATION:

Phone: 886 2 2719 5000   Fax:
Toll-Free:
Address: Fl. 1, 88 Sec., 1 Xintai 5th Rd., Xizhi, New Taipei City, 221 Taiwan

STOCK TICKER/OTHER:

Stock Ticker: ACEYY
Employees: 1,599
Parent Company:

Exchange: PINX
Fiscal Year Ends: 12/31

SALARIES/BONUSES:

Top Exec. Salary: $269,020   Bonus: $
Second Exec. Salary: $269,020   Bonus: $

OTHER THOUGHTS:

Estimated Female Officers or Directors:
Hot Spot for Advancement for Women/Minorities:

Sales, profits and employees may be estimates. Financial information, benefits and other data can change quickly and may vary from those stated here.

ACS Actividades de Construccion Y Servicios SA

www.grupoacs.com
NAIC Code: 237310

TYPES OF BUSINESS:

Heavy Construction
Engineering Services
Civic Construction & Infrastructure
Industrial Services
Facility Maintenance
Passenger Transportation
Transportation Concessions
Water Treatment & Desalination Plants

BRANDS/DIVISIONS/AFFILIATES:

Dragados SA
Hochtief AG
Iridium Concesiones de Infraestructuras
Cimic Group
Turner Construction Company

GROWTH PLANS/SPECIAL FEATURES:

ACS Actividades de Construccion Y Servicios SA completes construction and service activities for infrastructure and energy projects. In addition to infrastructure-related developments, the company constructs buildings and projects related to the mining sector. It has four operating segments: construction (majority of total revenue), Concessions, Services (which offers comprehensive maintenance services for buildings, public places and organizations) and corporate. Its services revolve around industrial engineering and operating energy, industrial, and mobility infrastructures. Additional sales are generated from aftermarket services and contracts to perform upkeep on existing structures. Approximately half of total revenue derives from the Americas.

CONTACTS: Note: Officers with more than one job title may be intentionally listed here more than once.

Juan Cases, CEO
Florentino Rodriguez, Chairman of the Board
Jose Luis Perez, Director
Pedro Jose Jimenez, Director

FINANCIAL DATA: Note: Data for latest year may not have been available at press time.

In U.S. $	2024	2023	2022	2021	2020	2019
Revenue	47,256,663,224	40,564,994,078	38,155,769,648	31,596,660,265	33,262,993,035	44,323,350,713
R&D Expense						
Operating Income	936,076,000	951,847,900	315,283,700	616,534,600	-288,045,400	1,790,252,000
Operating Margin %	.02%	.02%	.01%	.02%	-.01%	.04%
SGA Expense						
Net Income	939,364,400	885,497,200	758,487,000	3,456,769,000	651,538,000	1,091,972,000
Operating Cash Flow	3,170,118,000	1,705,263,000	1,978,817,000	230,580,000	1,295,900,000	2,149,742,000
Capital Expenditure	750,114,600	562,465,400	323,694,700	438,373,400	994,847,900	1,322,118,000
EBITDA	2,900,957,000	2,538,988,000	2,399,039,000	914,470,000	2,298,344,000	3,818,527,000
Return on Assets %	.02%	.02%	.02%	.08%	.01%	.03%
Return on Equity %	.16%	.14%	.11%	.62%	.14%	.22%
Debt to Equity	2.36%	1.65%	1.69%	1.43%	2.488	1.687

CONTACT INFORMATION:

Phone: 34 913439200   Fax: 34 913439456
Toll-Free:
Address: Avenida Pio XII n 102, Madrid, 28036 Spain

STOCK TICKER/OTHER:

Stock Ticker: ACSAF   Exchange: PINX
Employees: 128,721   Fiscal Year Ends: 12/31
Parent Company:

SALARIES/BONUSES:

Top Exec. Salary: $ Bonus: $
Second Exec. Salary: $ Bonus: $

OTHER THOUGHTS:

Estimated Female Officers or Directors:
Hot Spot for Advancement for Women/Minorities:

Activision Blizzard

NAIC Code: 511210G

www.activisionblizzard.com

TYPES OF BUSINESS:

Electronic Games, Apps & Entertainment
League-Based, Live Gaming Competition
Apps
TV Distribution of Gaming Events
Merchandising
Licensing Game Content for Movies
Licensing Content to Comic Books

BRANDS/DIVISIONS/AFFILIATES:

Microsoft Corp
World of Warcraft
Call of Duty
Diablo
Hearthstone
Overwatch
Candy Crush
Activision

GROWTH PLANS/SPECIAL FEATURES:

Activision Blizzard was formed in 2008 by the merger of Activision, one of the largest console video game publishers; and Blizzard, one of largest PC video game publishers. The combined firm remains one of the world's largest video game publishers. Activision's impressive franchise portfolio includes World of Warcraft, Call of Duty, Diablo, Candy Crush, Overwatch and Hearthstone. The firm's operating units consists of Activision, a leading worldwide developer, publisher and distributor of interactive entertainment for gaming consoles, handheld platforms and PC; Blizzard Entertainment, a premier developer and publisher of entertainment software; and King, a mobile game developer behind the world-famous Candy Crush. The company is owned by Microsoft Corp.

CONTACTS: *Note: Officers with more than one job title may be intentionally listed here more than once.*

Johanna Faries, CEO
Armin Zerza, CFO
Daniel Alegre, COO
Julie Hodges, Other Executive Officer

FINANCIAL DATA: *Note: Data for latest year may not have been available at press time.*

In U.S. $	2024	2023	2022	2021	2020	2019
Revenue	9,547,200,000	9,180,000,000	7,528,000,000	8,803,000,320	8,086,000,128	6,488,999,936
R&D Expense						
Operating Income						
Operating Margin %						
SGA Expense						
Net Income			1,512,999,936	2,699,000,064	2,196,999,936	1,503,000,064
Operating Cash Flow						
Capital Expenditure						
EBITDA						
Return on Assets %						
Return on Equity %						
Debt to Equity						

CONTACT INFORMATION:

Phone: 310 255-2000   Fax: 310 255-2100
Toll-Free:
Address: 3100 Ocean Park Blvd., Santa Monica, CA 90405 United States

STOCK TICKER/OTHER:

Stock Ticker: Subsidiary   Exchange:
Employees: 13,000   Fiscal Year Ends: 12/31
Parent Company: Microsoft Corp

SALARIES/BONUSES:

Top Exec. Salary: $ Bonus: $
Second Exec. Salary: $ Bonus: $

OTHER THOUGHTS:

Estimated Female Officers or Directors:
Hot Spot for Advancement for Women/Minorities:

Adobe Inc

NAIC Code: 511210F

www.adobe.com

TYPES OF BUSINESS:

Computer Software, Multimedia, Graphics & Publishing
Document Management Software
Photo Editing & Management Software
Graphic Design Software
Digital Media Solutions
Marketing Solutions
Workflow Solutions
Cloud Solutions

BRANDS/DIVISIONS/AFFILIATES:

Adobe Experience Cloud
Adobe LiveCycle
Adobe Connect
Frame.io

GROWTH PLANS/SPECIAL FEATURES:

Adobe provides content creation, document management, and digital marketing and advertising software and services to creative professionals and marketers for creating, managing, delivering, measuring, optimizing, and engaging with compelling content multiple operating systems, devices, and media. The company operates with three segments: digital media content creation, digital experience for marketing solutions, and publishing for legacy products (less than 5% of revenue).

Adobe offers its employees comprehensive benefits.

CONTACTS: Note: Officers with more than one job title may be intentionally listed here more than once.

Shantanu Narayen, CEO
Daniel Durn, CFO
Jillian Forusz, Chief Accounting Officer
Lara Balazs, Chief Marketing Officer
Scott Belsky, Chief Strategy Officer
Gloria Chen, Executive VP, Divisional
David Wadhwani, President, Divisional
Anil Chakravarthy, President, Divisional

FINANCIAL DATA: Note: Data for latest year may not have been available at press time.

In U.S. $	2024	2023	2022	2021	2020	2019
Revenue	21,504,999,424	19,409,000,448	17,606,000,640	15,784,999,936	12,867,999,744	11,171,000,320
R&D Expense	3,944,000,000	3,473,000,000	2,987,000,000	2,540,000,000	2,188,000,000	1,930,000,000
Operating Income	7,741,000,000	6,650,000,000	6,098,000,000	5,802,000,000	4,237,000,000	3,268,000,000
Operating Margin %	.36%	.34%	.35%	.37%	.33%	.29%
SGA Expense	7,293,000,000	6,764,000,000	6,187,000,000	5,406,000,000	4,559,000,000	4,125,000,000
Net Income	5,560,000,000	5,428,000,000	4,756,000,000	4,822,000,000	5,260,000,000	2,951,000,000
Operating Cash Flow	8,056,000,000	7,302,000,000	7,838,000,000	7,230,000,000	5,727,000,000	4,422,000,000
Capital Expenditure	183,000,000	360,000,000	442,000,000	348,000,000	419,000,000	395,000,000
EBITDA	7,957,000,000	7,784,000,000	6,976,000,000	6,606,000,000	5,049,000,000	4,119,000,000
Return on Assets %	.19%	.19%	.17%	.19%	.23%	.15%
Return on Equity %	.36%	.36%	.33%	.34%	.44%	.30%
Debt to Equity	.32%	.24%	.29%	.31%	0.348	0.094

CONTACT INFORMATION:

Phone: 408 536-6000   Fax: 408 536-6799
Toll-Free: 800-833-6687
Address: 345 Park Ave., San Jose, CA 95110-2704 United States

STOCK TICKER/OTHER:

Stock Ticker: ADBE   Exchange: NAS
Employees: 30,709   Fiscal Year Ends: 11/30
Parent Company:

SALARIES/BONUSES:

Top Exec. Salary: $1,500,000   Bonus: $
Second Exec. Salary: Bonus: $
$900,000

OTHER THOUGHTS:

Estimated Female Officers or Directors: 5
Hot Spot for Advancement for Women/Minorities: Y

Advanced Micro Devices Inc (AMD)

NAIC Code: 334413

www.amd.com

TYPES OF BUSINESS:

Microprocessors
Semiconductors
Chipsets
Wafer Manufacturing
Multimedia Graphics

BRANDS/DIVISIONS/AFFILIATES:

AMD
ATI
Athlon
EPYC
Radeon
Ryzen
Threadripper

GROWTH PLANS/SPECIAL FEATURES:

Advanced Micro Devices designs a variety of digital semiconductors for markets such as PCs, gaming consoles, data centers, industrial, and automotive applications. AMD's traditional strength was in central processing units and graphics processing units used in PCs and data centers. Additionally, the firm supplies the chips found in prominent game consoles such as the Sony PlayStation and Microsoft Xbox. In 2022, the firm acquired field-programmable gate array leader Xilinx to diversify its business and augment its opportunities in key end markets such as data center and automotive.

CONTACTS: *Note: Officers with more than one job title may be intentionally listed here more than once.*

Lisa Su, CEO
Jean Hu, CFO
Philip Carter, Chief Accounting Officer
Mark Papermaster, Chief Technology Officer
Darren Grasby, Executive VP, Divisional
Forrest Norrod, Executive VP
Philip Guido, Executive VP
Ava Hahn, General Counsel
Jack Huynh, General Manager, Divisional

FINANCIAL DATA: *Note: Data for latest year may not have been available at press time.*

In U.S. $	2024	2023	2022	2021	2020	2019
Revenue	25,784,999,936	22,680,000,512	23,601,000,448	16,433,999,872	9,763,000,320	6,730,999,808
R&D Expense	6,456,000,000	5,872,000,000	5,005,000,000	2,845,000,000	1,983,000,000	1,547,000,000
Operating Income	2,086,000,000	401,000,000	1,264,000,000	3,648,000,000	1,369,000,000	631,000,000
Operating Margin %	.08%	.02%	.05%	.22%	.14%	.09%
SGA Expense	2,783,000,000	2,352,000,000	2,336,000,000	1,448,000,000	995,000,000	750,000,000
Net Income	1,641,000,000	854,000,000	1,320,000,000	3,162,000,000	2,490,000,000	341,000,000
Operating Cash Flow	3,041,000,000	1,667,000,000	3,565,000,000	3,521,000,000	1,071,000,000	493,000,000
Capital Expenditure	636,000,000	546,000,000	450,000,000	301,000,000	294,000,000	217,000,000
EBITDA	5,258,000,000	4,149,000,000	5,534,000,000	4,166,000,000	1,676,000,000	724,000,000
Return on Assets %	.02%	.01%	.03%	.30%	.33%	.06%
Return on Equity %	.03%	.02%	.04%	.47%	.57%	.17%
Debt to Equity	.04%	.04%	.05%	.05%	0.091	0.242

CONTACT INFORMATION:

Phone: 408 749-4000   Fax:
Toll-Free:
Address: 2485 Augustine Dr., Santa Clara, CA 95054 United States

STOCK TICKER/OTHER:

Stock Ticker: AMD
Employees: 26,000
Parent Company:

Exchange: NAS
Fiscal Year Ends: 12/31

SALARIES/BONUSES:

Top Exec. Salary: $558,750   Bonus: $2,000,000
Second Exec. Salary: $1,230,000   Bonus: $

OTHER THOUGHTS:

Estimated Female Officers or Directors: 3
Hot Spot for Advancement for Women/Minorities: Y

Sales, profits and employees may be estimates. Financial information, benefits and other data can change quickly and may vary from those stated here.

AECOM

NAIC Code: 237310

www.aecom.com

TYPES OF BUSINESS:

Engineering & Design Services
Transportation Projects
Environmental Projects
Building Projects
Consulting
Water Projects
Energy Projects

BRANDS/DIVISIONS/AFFILIATES:

GROWTH PLANS/SPECIAL FEATURES:

Aecom is one of the largest global providers of design, engineering, construction, and management services. It serves a broad spectrum of end markets including infrastructure, water, transportation, and energy. Based in Los Angeles, Aecom has a presence in over 150 countries and employs 51,000. The company generated $16.1 billion in sales in fiscal 2024.

CONTACTS: *Note: Officers with more than one job title may be intentionally listed here more than once.*

W. Rudd, CEO
Gaurav Kapoor, CFO
Douglas Stotlar, Chairman of the Board
David Gan, Chief Legal Officer
Lara Poloni, President

FINANCIAL DATA: *Note: Data for latest year may not have been available at press time.*

In U.S. $	2024	2023	2022	2021	2020	2019
Revenue	16,105,497,600	14,378,461,184	13,148,181,504	13,340,852,224	13,239,975,936	13,642,455,040
R&D Expense						
Operating Income	924,236,000	791,890,000	700,665,000	643,349,000	521,025,000	463,532,000
Operating Margin %	.06%	.06%	.05%	.05%	.04%	.03%
SGA Expense	160,105,000	153,575,000	147,309,000	155,072,000	188,535,000	148,123,000
Net Income	402,266,000	55,332,000	310,611,000	173,185,000	-186,370,000	-261,050,000
Operating Cash Flow	827,490,000	695,980,000	713,636,000	704,670,000	329,622,000	777,616,000
Capital Expenditure	119,597,000	105,600,000	137,017,000	136,262,000	114,591,000	100,664,000
EBITDA	1,082,384,000	548,467,000	831,842,000	823,556,000	629,893,000	671,837,000
Return on Assets %	.03%	.00%	.03%	.01%	- .01%	- .02%
Return on Equity %	.18%	.02%	.12%	.06%	- .05%	- .07%
Debt to Equity	1.36%	1.20%	1.11%	1.05%	0.846	0.872

CONTACT INFORMATION:

Phone: 213 593-8100   Fax: 213 593-8730
Toll-Free:
Address: 300 S. Grand Ave., Ste. 900, Los Angeles, CA 90071 United States

STOCK TICKER/OTHER:

Stock Ticker: ACM   Exchange: NYS
Employees: 51,000   Fiscal Year Ends: 09/30
Parent Company:

SALARIES/BONUSES:

Top Exec. Salary: $1,312,269   Bonus: $
Second Exec. Salary: $829,320   Bonus: $

OTHER THOUGHTS:

Estimated Female Officers or Directors: 6
Hot Spot for Advancement for Women/Minorities: Y

Aecon Group Inc

NAIC Code: 237310

www.aecon.com

TYPES OF BUSINESS:

Highway, Street, Tunnel & Bridge Construction (Infrastructure)
Infrastructure Development
Civil Infrastructure
Urban Transportation
Nuclear Power Infrastructure
Conventional Industrial Infrastructure
Private Finance Solutions
Operations Management

BRANDS/DIVISIONS/AFFILIATES:

Groupe Aecon Quebec Ltee

GROWTH PLANS/SPECIAL FEATURES:

Aecon Group Inc is a Canada-based company that operates in two segments: Construction and Concessions. The Construction segment includes various aspects of the construction of public and private infrastructure projects, mainly in the transportation sector. Its concessions segment is engaged in the development, financing, construction, and operation of infrastructure projects. The company generates the maximum revenue from the Construction segment.

Aecon Group offers medical and dental insurance, an employee stock purchase program, a pension plan and tuition reimbursement.

CONTACTS: Note: Officers with more than one job title may be intentionally listed here more than once.

Jean-Louis Servranckx, CEO
John Beck, Chairman of the Board
Thomas Clochard, Executive VP, Divisional
Eric MacDonald, Executive VP, Divisional
Steven Nackan, Executive VP
Ernie Chan, Other Corporate Officer
Martina Doyle, Other Corporate Officer
Alistair MacCallum, Senior VP, Divisional
Gordana Terkalas, Senior VP, Divisional

FINANCIAL DATA: Note: Data for latest year may not have been available at press time.

In U.S. $	2024	2023	2022	2021	2020	2019
Revenue	3,088,092,838	3,380,043,501	3,418,334,495	2,894,913,562	2,652,025,495	2,518,682,465
R&D Expense						
Operating Income	-86,287,210	-946,211	47,576,240	69,996,360	92,545,300	65,538,240
Operating Margin %	- .03%	.00%	.01%	.02%	.03%	.03%
SGA Expense	155,213,600	129,441,000	142,979,100	132,674,100	132,773,800	133,513,400
Net Income	-43,324,840	117,832,400	22,112,960	36,161,290	64,073,070	53,026,420
Operating Cash Flow	5,530,970	37,173,010	-82,728,720	-22,861,920	198,673,800	142,622,400
Capital Expenditure	38,771,380	17,466,340	30,069,140	30,290,410	101,374,200	149,441,700
EBITDA	26,307,590	228,350,700	141,353,800	151,238,100	176,572,500	148,087,900
Return on Assets %	- .02%	.05%	.01%	.02%	.03%	.02%
Return on Equity %	- .06%	.16%	.03%	.06%	.10%	.09%
Debt to Equity	.28%	.21%	.58%	.76%	0.768	0.788

CONTACT INFORMATION:

Phone: 416 293-7004   Fax: 416 293-0271
Toll-Free: 877-232-2677
Address: 20 Carlson Court, Ste. 800, Toronto, ON M9W 7K6 Canada

STOCK TICKER/OTHER:

Stock Ticker: ARE   Exchange: TSE
Employees: 9,074   Fiscal Year Ends: 12/31
Parent Company:

SALARIES/BONUSES:

Top Exec. Salary: $ Bonus: $
Second Exec. Salary: $ Bonus: $

OTHER THOUGHTS:

Estimated Female Officers or Directors: 2
Hot Spot for Advancement for Women/Minorities:

AF Gruppen ASA

NAIC Code: 541330

www.afgruppen.no

TYPES OF BUSINESS:
Civil Engineering Services

BRANDS/DIVISIONS/AFFILIATES:

GROWTH PLANS/SPECIAL FEATURES:
AF Gruppen ASA A is one of Norway's contracting and industrial groups. The company provides services in areas of civil engineering and services geared toward environmental, building, and energy markets. The company conducts projects related to roads, railways, ports, power, and energy development. For buildings and property development, its services span the entire value chain, and resources are utilized for planning and execution. The majority of revenue comes from traditional building activities, including new projects and rehabilitation ventures. Environmental services revolve around demolition, removal, and environmental clean-up of buildings and industrial plants.

CONTACTS: Note: Officers with more than one job title may be intentionally listed here more than once.
Amund Toftum, CEO
Anny Oen, CFO
Morten Grongstad, Chairman of the Board

FINANCIAL DATA: Note: Data for latest year may not have been available at press time.

In U.S. $	2024	2023	2022	2021	2020	2019
Revenue	2,958,821,951	2,952,262,424	3,032,053,257	2,716,903,839	2,637,896,179	2,202,424,007
R&D Expense						
Operating Income	96,336,470	61,483,030	112,784,200	135,106,000	112,098,800	102,308,500
Operating Margin %	.03%	.02%	.04%	.05%	.04%	.05%
SGA Expense	36,224,080	32,601,670	26,335,880	22,713,480	23,692,510	23,398,800
Net Income	69,315,260	39,356,970	93,790,990	99,763,070	95,063,730	83,609,090
Operating Cash Flow	217,050,800	151,945,300	142,938,300	138,532,600	116,406,600	147,637,600
Capital Expenditure	24,965,240	52,378,060	28,489,750	20,265,900	21,440,740	31,720,540
EBITDA	185,819,700	134,714,400	192,966,700	213,820,000	203,050,700	188,169,400
Return on Assets %	.05%	.03%	.07%	.08%	.08%	.08%
Return on Equity %	.29%	.16%	.37%	.39%	.41%	.43%
Debt to Equity	.31%	.33%	.26%	.24%	0.304	0.397

CONTACT INFORMATION:
Phone: 47 22891100   Fax: 47 22891101
Toll-Free:
Address: Innspurten 15, Postboks 6272 Etterstad, Oslo, 0603 Norway

STOCK TICKER/OTHER:
Stock Ticker: AGRUF
Employees: 5,413
Parent Company:

Exchange: PINX
Fiscal Year Ends: 12/31

SALARIES/BONUSES:
Top Exec. Salary: $ Bonus: $
Second Exec. Salary: $ Bonus: $

OTHER THOUGHTS:
Estimated Female Officers or Directors:
Hot Spot for Advancement for Women/Minorities:

Sales, profits and employees may be estimates. Financial information, benefits and other data can change quickly and may vary from those stated here.

AFRY AB

NAIC Code: 541330

afry.com/en

TYPES OF BUSINESS:
Engineering Services
Engineering
Design
Advisory Services

BRANDS/DIVISIONS/AFFILIATES:
AFRY
Efterklang
Light Bureau
Gottlieb Paludan Architects
Sandell Sandbers
inUse
Koncept
Advansia

CONTACTS: *Note: Officers with more than one job title may be intentionally listed here more than once.*
Jonas Gustavsson, CEO
Bo Sandstrom, CFO
Tom Erixon, Chairman of the Board

GROWTH PLANS/SPECIAL FEATURES:
Afry AB is an engineering and consulting firm with projects in energy, industrial, and infrastructure markets. It develops solutions for public and private clients and can serve all regions of the world. The business divisions are Industrial & Digital Solutions, Infrastructure, Process Industries, Energy, and Management Consulting. It constructs plants and provides market analysis for power generation, manufacturing facilities, and refining chemicals. It also offers engineering, design, and advisory services across three main sectors: infrastructure, industry, and energy. It generates the majority of its revenue from the Infrastructure segment.

FINANCIAL DATA: *Note: Data for latest year may not have been available at press time.*

In U.S. $	2024	2023	2022	2021	2020	2019
Revenue	2,833,032,698	2,814,048,498	2,456,685,745	2,097,028,234	1,980,932,315	2,064,483,770
R&D Expense						
Operating Income	199,856,100	184,418,300	157,089,400	155,211,800	139,878,400	120,268,300
Operating Margin %	.07%	.07%	.06%	.07%	.07%	.06%
SGA Expense					138,313,700	167,728,900
Net Income	128,195,800	114,739,900	101,597,000	117,764,900	97,320,300	85,637,700
Operating Cash Flow	207,992,200	187,130,400	108,690,000	156,254,900	209,035,200	207,887,800
Capital Expenditure	13,873,100	18,358,390	15,750,660	11,891,230	8,449,030	21,174,730
EBITDA	304,478,000	289,040,300	237,198,700	247,421,000	230,001,400	217,171,400
Return on Assets %	.04%	.04%	.04%	.05%	.04%	.04%
Return on Equity %	.10%	.09%	.08%	.11%	.10%	.11%
Debt to Equity	.46%	.49%	.49%	.56%	0.536	0.743

CONTACT INFORMATION:
Phone: 46-10-505-00-00   Fax: 46-10-505-00-10
Toll-Free:
Address: Frosundaleden 2, Stockholm, SE-169 99 Sweden

STOCK TICKER/OTHER:
Stock Ticker: AFXXF
Employees: 18,984
Parent Company:

Exchange: PINX
Fiscal Year Ends: 12/31

SALARIES/BONUSES:
Top Exec. Salary: $ Bonus: $
Second Exec. Salary: $ Bonus: $

OTHER THOUGHTS:
Estimated Female Officers or Directors:
Hot Spot for Advancement for Women/Minorities:

Agfa-Gevaert NV

www.agfa.com

NAIC Code: 333316

TYPES OF BUSINESS:

Imaging Equipment
Commercial Printing Equipment & Products
Image Publishing Software
Consumer Photographic Products
Medical Imaging Systems
X-Ray Films
Inkjet Printers
Network Collaboration Software

BRANDS/DIVISIONS/AFFILIATES:

ORBIS

GROWTH PLANS/SPECIAL FEATURES:

Agfa-Gevaert NV develops, produces, and distributes a range of analog and digital imaging systems and information technology solutions, for the printing sector, healthcare sector, and specific industrial applications. The company's operating segment includes CONOPS; Digital Print and Chemicals; Radiology Solutions and Healthcare IT. It generates maximum revenue from the Digital Print and Chemicals segment. The company operates in Europe, NAFTA, Latin America and Asia/Oceania/Africa.

CONTACTS:
Note: Officers with more than one job title may be intentionally listed here more than once.

Pascal Juery, CEO
Frank Aranzana, Chairman of the Board

FINANCIAL DATA:
Note: Data for latest year may not have been available at press time.

In U.S. $	2024	2023	2022	2021	2020	2019
Revenue	1,291,713,963	1,305,334,848	1,299,659,407	1,997,729,855	1,939,841,019	2,241,770,790
R&D Expense	79,455,170	82,860,380	93,076,050	107,832,000	107,832,000	116,912,600
Operating Income	-52,213,390	-11,350,740	-43,132,800	22,701,480	27,241,770	70,374,580
Operating Margin %	-.04%	-.01%	-.03%	.01%	.01%	.03%
SGA Expense	334,846,800	351,872,900	396,140,700	438,138,500	416,572,100	485,811,600
Net Income	-104,426,800	-115,777,500	-250,851,300	-19,296,250	695,800,300	-60,158,910
Operating Cash Flow	-4,540,295	-34,052,210	-113,507,400	-131,668,600	-173,666,300	139,614,100
Capital Expenditure	51,078,320	38,592,510	37,457,440	29,511,920	37,457,440	43,132,800
EBITDA	-20,431,330	24,971,620	-85,130,540	87,400,680	15,891,030	72,644,720
Return on Assets %	-.07%	-.07%	-.11%	-.01%	.27%	-.02%
Return on Equity %	-.26%	-.22%	-.38%	-.03%	1.88%	-.32%
Debt to Equity	.44%	.17%	.08%	.07%	0.095	2.699

CONTACT INFORMATION:

Phone: 32 34442111   Fax: 32 34447094
Toll-Free:
Address: Septestraat 27, Mortsel, B-2640 Belgium

STOCK TICKER/OTHER:

Stock Ticker: AFGVY   Exchange: PINX
Employees: 5,026   Fiscal Year Ends: 12/31
Parent Company:

SALARIES/BONUSES:

Top Exec. Salary: $ Bonus: $
Second Exec. Salary: $ Bonus: $

OTHER THOUGHTS:

Estimated Female Officers or Directors:
Hot Spot for Advancement for Women/Minorities:

Sales, profits and employees may be estimates. Financial information, benefits and other data can change quickly and may vary from those stated here.

Agilent Technologies Inc

www.agilent.com

NAIC Code: 334515

TYPES OF BUSINESS:

Test Equipment
Communications Test Equipment
Integrated Circuits Test Equipment
Bioanalysis Equipment
Laboratory Automation and Robotics
Bioinstrumentation
Software Products
Informatics Products

BRANDS/DIVISIONS/AFFILIATES:

Agilent CrossLab
Agilent Technologies Research Laboratories
Resolution Bioscience

GROWTH PLANS/SPECIAL FEATURES:

Originally spun out of Hewlett-Packard in 1999, Agilent has evolved into a leading life science and diagnostic firm. Today, Agilent's measurement technologies serve a broad base of customers with its three operating segments: life science and applied tools, cross lab consisting of consumables and services related to life science and applied tools, and diagnostics and genomics. Over half of its sales are generated from the biopharmaceutical, chemical, and advanced materials end markets, which we view as the stickiest end markets, but it also supports clinical lab, environmental, forensics, food, academic, and government-related organizations. The company is geographically diverse, with operations in the US and China representing the largest country concentrations.

Agilent offers its employees health and financial benefits as well as on-site amenities and services.

CONTACTS: *Note: Officers with more than one job title may be intentionally listed here more than once.*

Padraig McDonnell, CEO
Robert McMahon, CFO
Boon Koh, Chairman of the Board
Rodney Gonsalves, Chief Accounting Officer
Bret DiMarco, Chief Legal Officer
Jonah Kirkwood, Other Executive Officer
Angelica Reimann, President, Divisional
Mike Zhang, President, Divisional
Simon May, President, Divisional
Henrik Ancher-Jensen, President, Divisional

FINANCIAL DATA: *Note: Data for latest year may not have been available at press time.*

In U.S. $	2024	2023	2022	2021	2020	2019
Revenue	6,510,000,128	6,832,999,936	6,848,000,000	6,319,000,064	5,338,999,808	5,162,999,808
R&D Expense	479,000,000	481,000,000	467,000,000	441,000,000	495,000,000	404,000,000
Operating Income	1,488,000,000	1,350,000,000	1,618,000,000	1,347,000,000	846,000,000	941,000,000
Operating Margin %	.23%	.20%	.24%	.21%	.16%	.18%
SGA Expense	1,568,000,000	1,634,000,000	1,637,000,000	1,619,000,000	1,496,000,000	1,460,000,000
Net Income	1,289,000,000	1,240,000,000	1,254,000,000	1,210,000,000	719,000,000	1,071,000,000
Operating Cash Flow	1,751,000,000	1,772,000,000	1,312,000,000	1,485,000,000	921,000,000	1,021,000,000
Capital Expenditure	378,000,000	298,000,000	291,000,000	188,000,000	119,000,000	156,000,000
EBITDA	1,874,000,000	1,705,000,000	1,905,000,000	1,762,000,000	1,228,000,000	1,231,000,000
Return on Assets %	.11%	.12%	.12%	.12%	.08%	.12%
Return on Equity %	.22%	.22%	.23%	.24%	.15%	.23%
Debt to Equity	.57%	.47%	.52%	.51%	0.469	0.377

CONTACT INFORMATION:

Phone: 408 345-8886   Fax:
Toll-Free: 800-227-9770
Address: 5301 Stevens Creek Blvd., Santa Clara, CA 95051 United States

STOCK TICKER/OTHER:

Stock Ticker: A
Employees: 17,900
Parent Company:

Exchange: NYS
Fiscal Year Ends: 10/31

SALARIES/BONUSES:

Top Exec. Salary: $1,209,769   Bonus: $
Second Exec. Salary: $869,962   Bonus: $

OTHER THOUGHTS:

Estimated Female Officers or Directors: 6
Hot Spot for Advancement for Women/Minorities: Y

Sales, profits and employees may be estimates. Financial information, benefits and other data can change quickly and may vary from those stated here.

Air Products and Chemicals Inc

www.airproducts.com

NAIC Code: 325120

TYPES OF BUSINESS:

Industrial Gases & Chemicals
Respiratory Therapy & Home Medical Equipment
Specialty Resins
Hydrogen Refinery
Natural Gas Liquefaction
Semiconductor Materials
Gasification Technology

BRANDS/DIVISIONS/AFFILIATES:

GROWTH PLANS/SPECIAL FEATURES:

Since its founding in 1940, Air Products has become one of the leading industrial gas suppliers globally, with operations in 50 countries and 19,000 employees. The company is the largest supplier of hydrogen and helium in the world. It has a unique portfolio serving customers in a number of industries, including chemicals, energy, healthcare, metals, and electronics. Air Products generated $12.1 billion in revenue in fiscal 2024.

CONTACTS: Note: Officers with more than one job title may be intentionally listed here more than once.

Seifollah Ghasemi, CEO
Melissa Schaeffer, CFO
William Pellicciotti, Chief Accounting Officer
Brian Galovich, Chief Information Officer
Sean Major, Executive VP
Victoria Brifo, Executive VP
Wolfgang Brand, President, Divisional
Wilbur Mok, President, Divisional
Kurt Lefevere, President, Geographical
Ivo Bols, President, Geographical
Francesco Maione, President, Geographical
Ahmed Hababou, President, Geographical
Walter Nelson, Senior VP, Divisional

FINANCIAL DATA: Note: Data for latest year may not have been available at press time.

In U.S. $	2024	2023	2022	2021	2020	2019
Revenue	12,100,599,808	12,600,000,512	12,698,600,448	10,323,000,320	8,856,299,520	8,918,899,712
R&D Expense	100,200,000	105,600,000	102,900,000	93,500,000	83,900,000	72,900,000
Operating Income	2,947,500,000	2,739,200,000	2,412,500,000	2,267,800,000	2,237,600,000	2,169,800,000
Operating Margin %	.24%	.22%	.19%	.22%	.25%	.24%
SGA Expense	942,400,000	957,000,000	900,600,000	828,400,000	742,100,000	750,000,000
Net Income	3,828,200,000	2,300,200,000	2,256,100,000	2,099,100,000	1,886,700,000	1,760,000,000
Operating Cash Flow	3,646,700,000	3,206,300,000	3,230,200,000	3,341,900,000	3,264,700,000	2,969,900,000
Capital Expenditure	6,796,700,000	4,626,400,000	2,926,500,000	2,464,200,000	2,509,000,000	1,989,700,000
EBITDA	6,491,100,000	4,418,200,000	4,220,900,000	3,970,500,000	3,718,100,000	3,509,300,000
Return on Assets %	.11%	.08%	.08%	.08%	.09%	.09%
Return on Equity %	.24%	.17%	.17%	.16%	.16%	.16%
Debt to Equity	.83%	.70%	.58%	.57%	0.643	0.292

CONTACT INFORMATION:

Phone: 610 481-4911   Fax: 610 481-5900
Toll-Free:
Address: 7201 Hamilton Blvd., Allentown, PA 18195 United States

STOCK TICKER/OTHER:

Stock Ticker: APD   Exchange: NYS
Employees: 23,000   Fiscal Year Ends: 09/30
Parent Company:

SALARIES/BONUSES:

Top Exec. Salary: $1,350,000   Bonus: $
Second Exec. Salary: Bonus: $
$838,462

OTHER THOUGHTS:

Estimated Female Officers or Directors: 4
Hot Spot for Advancement for Women/Minorities: Y

Sales, profits and employees may be estimates. Financial information, benefits and other data can change quickly and may vary from those stated here.

Airbus SE

NAIC Code: 336411

TYPES OF BUSINESS:

Aircraft Manufacturing
Helicopter Manufacturing
Transport Aircraft
Military Aircraft
Defense Communications Systems
Satellites
Space Systems
Maintenance Services

BRANDS/DIVISIONS/AFFILIATES:

Hforce
Hcare
SmartForce
ArianeGroup

GROWTH PLANS/SPECIAL FEATURES:

Airbus is a global aerospace and defense firm that designs, develops, and manufactures commercial and military aircraft, as well as space launch vehicles and satellites. The company operates three divisions: commercial, defense and space, and helicopters. Commercial offers multiple configurations of aircraft ranging from the narrow-body (120-200 seats) A220 and A320 series to the much larger A330 and A350 wide-body models. The defense and space segment supplies governments with military hardware, including transport aircraft, aerial tankers, and the Eurofighter Typhoon multirole jet. The helicopter division manufactures turbine helicopters for the civil and public markets.

CONTACTS: Note: Officers with more than one job title may be intentionally listed here more than once.

Guillaume Faury, CEO
Rene Obermann, Chairman of the Board

FINANCIAL DATA: Note: Data for latest year may not have been available at press time.

In U.S. $	2024	2023	2022	2021	2020	2019
Revenue	78,581,160,329	74,286,037,074	66,700,342,700	59,192,960,499	56,653,803,139	79,997,725,434
R&D Expense	3,688,990,000	3,696,935,000	3,494,892,000	3,116,912,000	3,244,041,000	3,811,578,000
Operating Income	5,452,894,000	4,842,225,000	5,961,407,000	5,485,812,000	753,689,000	1,160,045,000
Operating Margin %	.07%	.07%	.09%	.09%	.01%	.01%
SGA Expense	2,975,028,000	2,861,521,000	2,542,565,000	2,329,171,000	2,429,058,000	6,952,327,000
Net Income	4,803,632,000	4,300,794,000	4,820,658,000	4,782,066,000	-1,286,039,000	-1,545,970,000
Operating Cash Flow	8,401,816,000	7,099,887,000	7,137,344,000	5,265,607,000	-6,152,100,000	4,259,932,000
Capital Expenditure	4,164,586,000	3,463,110,000	2,796,822,000	2,188,422,000	1,996,595,000	2,656,073,000
EBITDA	10,417,710,000	8,816,118,000	9,311,010,000	8,745,743,000	2,425,652,000	4,967,083,000
Return on Assets %	.03%	.03%	.04%	.04%	-.01%	-.01%
Return on Equity %	.23%	.25%	.38%	.53%	-.18%	-.17%
Debt to Equity	.53%	.58%	.82%	1.38%	2.185	1.371

CONTACT INFORMATION:

Phone: 31 715245600   Fax: 31 715232807
Toll-Free:
Address: Mendelweg 30, Leiden, ZH 2333 CS Netherlands

STOCK TICKER/OTHER:

Stock Ticker: EADSF   Exchange: PINX
Employees: 147,893   Fiscal Year Ends: 12/31
Parent Company:

SALARIES/BONUSES:

Top Exec. Salary: $ Bonus: $
Second Exec. Salary: $ Bonus: $

OTHER THOUGHTS:

Estimated Female Officers or Directors: 1
Hot Spot for Advancement for Women/Minorities:

Aisin Corporation

www.aisin.com

NAIC Code: 336300

TYPES OF BUSINESS:

Automobile Parts Manufacturing
Sewing & Embroidery Machines
Air Conditioners
Hospital & Biotechnology Equipment
Lasers & Laser Imaging Technology

BRANDS/DIVISIONS/AFFILIATES:

Aisin Corporation
Aisin Holdings of America Inc
IRMA Europe SAS
Zheijiang Aisin Hongda Auto Parts Co Ltd
Aisin Asia Pte Ltd
ENE-FARM
COREMO
TAOC

GROWTH PLANS/SPECIAL FEATURES:

Aisin Corp is a manufacturer and seller of automotive parts, lifestyle and energy-related products, and wellness products. The majority of revenue is generated selling automotive parts and related services, automatic transmissions, car navigation systems, and lifestyle products such as sewing machines and beds, and heat-pumps. Other operations include cast-iron parts for engines and brakes. Aisin Seiki has operations across the world, supplying a wide range of car manufacturers around the globe.

CONTACTS: Note: Officers with more than one job title may be intentionally listed here more than once.

Shintaro Ito, Chief Administrative Officer
Yoshihisa Yamamoto, Chief Strategy Officer
Masahiro Nishikawa, Director
Moritaka Yoshida, Director

FINANCIAL DATA: Note: Data for latest year may not have been available at press time.

In U.S. $	2024	2023	2022	2021	2020	2019
Revenue	34,084,679,585	30,566,668,408	27,196,849,401	24,477,917,006	26,274,542,553	28,069,357,260
R&D Expense						
Operating Income	995,529,000	402,277,200	1,263,614,000	1,008,977,000	389,676,500	1,427,118,000
Operating Margin %	.03%	.01%	.05%	.04%	.01%	.05%
SGA Expense	2,899,924,000	2,354,728,000	2,030,575,000	1,879,728,000	2,086,796,000	2,128,513,000
Net Income	630,470,700	261,524,600	985,427,600	733,393,500	167,043,900	764,530,700
Operating Cash Flow	3,469,453,000	1,652,111,000	1,342,287,000	2,383,463,000	2,274,035,000	2,464,190,000
Capital Expenditure	1,697,195,000	1,658,359,000	1,624,792,000	1,494,883,000	2,260,573,000	2,711,768,000
EBITDA	3,018,016,000	2,551,354,000	3,397,730,000	3,007,075,000	2,332,665,000	3,160,504,000
Return on Assets %	.02%	.01%	.03%	.03%	.01%	.03%
Return on Equity %	.05%	.02%	.09%	.08%	.02%	.08%
Debt to Equity	.32%	.42%	.46%	.56%	0.692	0.392

CONTACT INFORMATION:

Phone: 81-566-24-8441   Fax:
Toll-Free:
Address: 2-1, Asahi-machi, Kariya, Kariya, 448-8650 Japan

STOCK TICKER/OTHER:

Stock Ticker: ASEKY
Employees: 148,359
Parent Company:

Exchange: PINX
Fiscal Year Ends: 03/31

SALARIES/BONUSES:

Top Exec. Salary: $ Bonus: $
Second Exec. Salary: $ Bonus: $

OTHER THOUGHTS:

Estimated Female Officers or Directors:
Hot Spot for Advancement for Women/Minorities:

Akzo Nobel NV

NAIC Code: 325510

www.akzonobel.com

TYPES OF BUSINESS:

Paint and Coating Manufacturing

GROWTH PLANS/SPECIAL FEATURES:

Netherlands-based AkzoNobel is the world's third-largest paint and coatings producer. Europe is the largest market, with around 47% of sales generated in Europe, the Middle East, and Africa. Cumulatively, the Asia-Pacific and Latin American divisions have grown quickly to more than 40% of sales. Construction-related end markets are the most important, but meaningful revenue is also generated from the industrial, consumer goods, and transportation markets.

BRANDS/DIVISIONS/AFFILIATES:

Alba
Coral
Dulux
Interpon
Flexa
Relest
Trimetal
Zweihorn

CONTACTS: *Note: Officers with more than one job title may be intentionally listed here more than once.*

Nils Andersen, Chairman of Supervisory Board
Ben Noteboom, Chairman of the Board
Byron Grote, Deputy Chairman

FINANCIAL DATA: *Note: Data for latest year may not have been available at press time.*

In U.S. $	2024	2023	2022	2021	2020	2019
Revenue	12,157,775,341	12,108,967,386	12,311,010,374	10,881,952,702	9,682,179,207	10,528,944,683
R&D Expense	335,981,800	306,469,900	292,849,000	261,067,000	270,147,600	297,389,300
Operating Income	1,040,863,000	1,167,991,000	803,632,300	1,269,012,000	1,093,076,000	954,597,100
Operating Margin %	.09%	.10%	.07%	.12%	.11%	.09%
SGA Expense	1,774,120,000	1,745,743,000	1,737,798,000	1,526,674,000	1,413,167,000	1,701,476,000
Net Income	615,210,000	501,702,600	399,546,000	940,976,200	715,096,500	611,804,700
Operating Cash Flow	763,904,600	1,278,093,000	298,524,400	686,719,600	1,384,790,000	37,457,440
Capital Expenditure	347,332,600	324,631,100	331,441,500	326,901,200	292,849,000	242,905,800
EBITDA	1,587,968,000	1,514,188,000	1,221,339,000	1,736,663,000	1,562,996,000	1,429,058,000
Return on Assets %	.04%	.03%	.02%	.06%	.05%	.03%
Return on Equity %	.12%	.10%	.07%	.15%	.10%	.06%
Debt to Equity	.80%	.73%	.77%	.37%	0.482	0.322

CONTACT INFORMATION:

Phone: 31 26-366-4433   Fax:
Toll-Free:
Address: Christian Neefestraat 2, Amsterdam, NH 1077 WW Netherlands

STOCK TICKER/OTHER:

Stock Ticker: AKZOF
Employees: 35,200
Parent Company:

Exchange: PINX
Fiscal Year Ends: 12/31

SALARIES/BONUSES:

Top Exec. Salary: $ Bonus: $
Second Exec. Salary: $ Bonus: $

OTHER THOUGHTS:

Estimated Female Officers or Directors:
Hot Spot for Advancement for Women/Minorities:

ALFA SAB de CV

NAIC Code: 325110

www.alfa.com.mx

TYPES OF BUSINESS:

Petrochemicals
Synthetic Fibers
Frozen Food
Telecommunications Services
Oil & Natural Gas Exploration & Production
Production Plants
Meats and Cheeses

GROWTH PLANS/SPECIAL FEATURES:

Alfa SAB de CV is a Mexican company controlling principal businesses: Alpek and Sigma. It operates in two primary segments, that are: Alpek segment operates in the petrochemical and synthetic fibers industry, and its revenues are derived from sales of its products: polyester, plastics, and chemicals; Sigma segment operates in the refrigerated food sector, and its revenues are derived from sales of its main products: deli meats, dairy, and other processed foods; Other segments, include all other companies operating in business services and others that are non-reportable segments.

BRANDS/DIVISIONS/AFFILIATES:

Sigma
Newpek
Alpek
Axtel

CONTACTS: Note: Officers with more than one job title may be intentionally listed here more than once.

Armando Sada, Chairman of the Board
Alvaro Garza, Director

FINANCIAL DATA: Note: Data for latest year may not have been available at press time.

In U.S. $	2024	2023	2022	2021	2020	2019
Revenue	8,407,991,975	7,888,550,528	7,808,252,883	15,287,173,442	12,962,488,577	13,412,293,107
R&D Expense						
Operating Income	662,010,500	561,161,200	407,517,900	1,420,904,000	806,897,700	688,845,300
Operating Margin %	.08%	.07%	.05%	.09%	.06%	.05%
SGA Expense	1,975,833,000	1,779,903,000	1,606,018,000	1,864,683,000	1,832,028,000	2,031,563,000
Net Income	-10,919,340	-630,952,300	603,808,400	211,484,900	202,368,300	299,097,100
Operating Cash Flow	1,395,203,000	1,208,956,000	1,377,742,000	1,358,633,000	1,511,967,000	1,574,445,000
Capital Expenditure	247,281,800	210,763,800	266,133,100	513,208,800	287,508,200	513,311,800
EBITDA	639,399,200	517,123,300	576,870,600	1,664,529,000	1,253,457,000	1,591,081,000
Return on Assets %	.00%	-.05%	.04%	.02%	.01%	.02%
Return on Equity %	-.01%	-.38%	.29%	.11%	.07%	.08%
Debt to Equity	1.79%	4.03%	2.48%	3.10%	3.135	1.903

CONTACT INFORMATION:

Phone: 81-8748-1111   Fax: 81-8748-2552
Toll-Free:
Address: Ave. Gomez Morin 1111, Sur Colonia Carrizalejo, San Pedro Garza Garcia, NL 666254 Mexico

STOCK TICKER/OTHER:

Stock Ticker: ALFFF   Exchange: PINX
Employees: 54,060   Fiscal Year Ends: 12/31
Parent Company:

SALARIES/BONUSES:

Top Exec. Salary: $ Bonus: $
Second Exec. Salary: $ Bonus: $

OTHER THOUGHTS:

Estimated Female Officers or Directors:
Hot Spot for Advancement for Women/Minorities:

Sales, profits and employees may be estimates. Financial information, benefits and other data can change quickly and may vary from those stated here.

Allergan plc

NAIC Code: 325412

TYPES OF BUSINESS:

Pharmaceutical Development
Aesthetics Products
Dermatological Products
Product Development
Product Manufacturing
Facial Injectables
Body Contouring
Fat Transplanting

BRANDS/DIVISIONS/AFFILIATES:

AbbVie Inc
BOTOX
JUVEDERM
KYBELLA
CoolSculpting
Natrelle
KELLER FUNNEL
DiamondGlow

CONTACTS: Note: Officers with more than one job title may be intentionally listed here more than once.

Brenton Saunders, CEO
William Meury, Executive VP, Divisional
Charles Mayr, Other Executive Officer
Patrick Eagan, Other Executive Officer
Karen Ling, Other Executive Officer
Robert Bailey, Other Executive Officer

GROWTH PLANS/SPECIAL FEATURES:

Allergan plc, a subsidiary of AbbVie, Inc., is a developer, manufacturer and marketer of aesthetic products and technologies. Allergan's portfolio includes facial injectables, body contouring, plastics, skin care and more. The firm's research and development team drives innovation in aesthetics to provide science-based, personalized product offerings. Brands of Allergan include BOTOX cosmetic treatment, JUVEDERM fillers, KYBELLA injections, CoolSculpting fat-freezing technology, CoolTone body contouring treatment, Natrelle breast implants, KELLER FUNNEL 2 plastic surgery device for delivering breast implants, REVOLVE fat processing and transplanting, SkinMedica skin rejuvenation care, LATISSE eyelash growth treatment and DiamondGlow skin resurfacing treatment. Other brand lines include the AlloDerm, Strattice and Artia regenerative and reconstructive tissue portfolio. The Alle Rewards Program is the company's loyalty program, earing points for savings on Allergan products.

FINANCIAL DATA: Note: Data for latest year may not have been available at press time.

In U.S. $	2024	2023	2022	2021	2020	2019
Revenue	17,848,740,000	16,998,800,000	18,200,000,000	17,903,727,920	16,732,456,000	16,088,900,000
R&D Expense						
Operating Income						
Operating Margin %						
SGA Expense						
Net Income						
Operating Cash Flow						
Capital Expenditure						
EBITDA						
Return on Assets %						
Return on Equity %						
Debt to Equity						

CONTACT INFORMATION:

Phone: 714 246 6748   Fax:
Toll-Free:
Address: 2525 Dupont Dr., Irvine, CA 92612 United States

STOCK TICKER/OTHER:

Stock Ticker: Subsidiary   Exchange:
Employees: 17,400   Fiscal Year Ends: 12/31
Parent Company: AbbVie Inc

SALARIES/BONUSES:

Top Exec. Salary: $ Bonus: $
Second Exec. Salary: $ Bonus: $

OTHER THOUGHTS:

Estimated Female Officers or Directors: 2
Hot Spot for Advancement for Women/Minorities: Y

Alphabet Inc (Google)

NAIC Code: 519130

abc.xyz/investor

TYPES OF BUSINESS:

Search Engine-Internet
Paid Search Listing Advertising Services
Online Software and Productivity Tools
Online Video and Photo Services
Travel Booking
Web Analytical Tools
Venture Capital
Online Ad Exchanges

BRANDS/DIVISIONS/AFFILIATES:

Google LLC
Android
YouTube
GooglePlay
Gmail
Google Ad Manager
AdSense
AdMob

GROWTH PLANS/SPECIAL FEATURES:

Alphabet is a holding company that wholly owns internet giant Google. The California-based company derives slightly less than 90% of its revenue from Google services, the vast majority of which is advertising sales. Alongside online ads, Google services houses sales stemming from Google's subscription services (YouTube TV, YouTube Music among others), platforms (sales and in-app purchases on Play Store), and devices (Chromebooks, Pixel smartphones, and smart home products such as Chromecast). Google's cloud computing platform, or GCP, accounts for roughly 10% of Alphabet's revenue with the firm's investments in up-and-coming technologies such as self-driving cars (Waymo), health (Verily), and internet access (Google Fiber) making up the rest.

CONTACTS: *Note: Officers with more than one job title may be intentionally listed here more than once.*

Sundar Pichai, CEO
Anat Ashkenazi, CFO
John Hennessy, Chairman of the Board
Amie OToole, Chief Accounting Officer
Ruth Porat, Chief Investment Officer
Kent Walker, Chief Legal Officer
Sergey Brin, Co-Founder
Larry Page, Co-Founder
Prabhakar Raghavan, Other Corporate Officer
Philipp Schindler, Other Executive Officer

FINANCIAL DATA: *Note: Data for latest year may not have been available at press time.*

In U.S. $	2024	2023	2022	2021	2020	2019
Revenue	350,018,011,136	307,393,986,560	282,836,008,960	257,637,007,360	182,527,000,576	161,856,995,328
R&D Expense	49,326,000,000	45,427,000,000	39,500,000,000	31,562,000,000	27,573,000,000	26,018,000,000
Operating Income	112,390,000,000	84,293,000,000	74,842,000,000	78,714,000,000	41,224,000,000	35,928,000,000
Operating Margin %	.32%	.27%	.26%	.31%	.23%	.22%
SGA Expense	41,996,000,000	44,342,000,000	42,291,000,000	36,422,000,000	28,998,000,000	28,015,000,000
Net Income	100,118,000,000	73,795,000,000	59,972,000,000	76,033,000,000	40,269,000,000	34,343,000,000
Operating Cash Flow	125,299,000,000	101,746,000,000	91,495,000,000	91,652,000,000	65,124,000,000	54,520,000,000
Capital Expenditure	52,535,000,000	32,251,000,000	31,485,000,000	24,640,000,000	22,281,000,000	23,548,000,000
EBITDA	135,394,000,000	97,971,000,000	85,160,000,000	103,521,000,000	61,914,000,000	51,506,000,000
Return on Assets %	.23%	.19%	.17%	.22%	.14%	.14%
Return on Equity %	.33%	.27%	.24%	.32%	.19%	.18%
Debt to Equity	.07%	.09%	.11%	.10%	0.113	0.073

CONTACT INFORMATION:

Phone: 650 253-0000   Fax: 650 253-0001
Toll-Free:
Address: 1600 Amphitheatre Pkwy., Mountain View, CA 94043 United States

STOCK TICKER/OTHER:

Stock Ticker: GOOGL
Employees: 182,502
Parent Company:

Exchange: NAS
Fiscal Year Ends: 12/31

SALARIES/BONUSES:

Top Exec. Salary: $423,077   Bonus: $9,900,000
Second Exec. Salary: $2,015,385   Bonus: $

OTHER THOUGHTS:

Estimated Female Officers or Directors: 3
Hot Spot for Advancement for Women/Minorities: Y

Alps Alpine Co Ltd

NAIC Code: 335313

www.alps.com

TYPES OF BUSINESS:

Electronic Components Manufacturing
Electronic Components
Automotive Infotainment
Internet of Things
Consumer Electronics
Logistics

BRANDS/DIVISIONS/AFFILIATES:

GROWTH PLANS/SPECIAL FEATURES:

Alps Alpine Co Ltd operates in two major business segments: electronic components, automotive infotainment, logistics and others.. The electronic components segment develops, manufactures, and sells a broad range of electronic components in both consumer and automotive markets. The automotive infotainment segment develops, produces, and markets audio, information, and communication equipment. The company generates the majority of revenue from the electronic components segment and the automotive infotainment segment. It has a business presence worldwide, with the United States, Japan, China, and Germany its four largest markets.

CONTACTS: *Note: Officers with more than one job title may be intentionally listed here more than once.*

Hideo Izumi, CEO
Satoshi Kodaira, CFO
Junji Kobayashi, Director
Hiroshi Yamagami, Director

FINANCIAL DATA: *Note: Data for latest year may not have been available at press time.*

In U.S. $	2024	2023	2022	2021	2020	2019
Revenue	6,693,210,460	6,478,159,192	5,573,826,971	4,984,816,920	5,627,395,509	5,910,386,009
R&D Expense						
Operating Income	136,850,900	233,240,800	244,432,100	91,016,380	186,031,700	344,640,400
Operating Margin %	.02%	.04%	.04%	.02%	.03%	.06%
SGA Expense						
Net Income	-206,984,200	79,630,660	159,400,200	-26,638,430	-27,832,550	153,526,800
Operating Cash Flow	619,085,000	107,005,000	238,156,100	296,001,100	605,456,800	504,519,600
Capital Expenditure	389,065,600	363,482,400	334,601,500	263,565,700	282,213,300	422,757,600
EBITDA	195,098,600	519,848,700	590,752,600	327,013,300	436,844,000	601,735,600
Return on Assets %	-.04%	.02%	.03%	-.01%	-.01%	.03%
Return on Equity %	-.08%	.03%	.06%	-.01%	-.01%	.07%
Debt to Equity	.20%	.11%	.14%	.19%	0.134	0.193

CONTACT INFORMATION:

Phone: 81 33726-1211   Fax: 81-33728-1741
Toll-Free:
Address: 1-7, Yukigaya-otsukamachi, Tokyo, 145-8501 Japan

STOCK TICKER/OTHER:

Stock Ticker: APELF   Exchange: PINX
Employees: 47,738   Fiscal Year Ends: 03/31
Parent Company:

SALARIES/BONUSES:

Top Exec. Salary: $ Bonus: $
Second Exec. Salary: $ Bonus: $

OTHER THOUGHTS:

Estimated Female Officers or Directors:
Hot Spot for Advancement for Women/Minorities:

Alstom SA

NAIC Code: 333611

www.alstom.com

TYPES OF BUSINESS:

Equipment-Electric Power Distribution
High-Speed Trains
Monorails
Trams
Integrated Systems
Signaling Products and Solutions
Digital Mobility Solutions
Manufacture

BRANDS/DIVISIONS/AFFILIATES:

Shunter
Bombardier Transportation
Helion Hydrogen Power
Flertex

GROWTH PLANS/SPECIAL FEATURES:

Alstom develops and markets systems, equipment, and services for the railway transport sector, including rolling stock, maintenance and modernization services, signaling, and infrastructure, which are offered separately, bundled, or as fully integrated solutions. The company is one of the key international players in the industry with a strong position in European markets.

CONTACTS: Note: Officers with more than one job title may be intentionally listed here more than once.

Henri Poupart-Lafarge, CEO

FINANCIAL DATA: Note: Data for latest year may not have been available at press time.

In U.S. $	2024	2023	2022	2021	2020	2019
Revenue	19,998,864,149	18,736,662,685	17,560,725,958	9,971,623,675	9,308,740,005	
R&D Expense	691,259,900	658,342,800	685,584,600	360,953,500	342,792,300	
Operating Income	562,996,600	329,171,400	141,884,200	492,622,000	644,721,900	
Operating Margin %	.03%	.02%	.01%	.05%	.07%	
SGA Expense	1,257,662,000	1,244,041,000	1,130,534,000	718,501,700	670,828,600	
Net Income	-350,737,800	-149,829,700	-659,477,900	280,363,200	530,079,500	
Operating Cash Flow	-93,076,050	687,854,700	-654,937,600	-516,458,600	540,295,100	
Capital Expenditure	550,510,800	489,216,800	485,811,600	300,794,600	311,010,200	
EBITDA	900,113,500	898,978,400	855,845,600	762,769,600	942,111,200	
Return on Assets %	-.01%	.00%	-.02%	.01%	.04%	
Return on Equity %	-.03%	-.01%	-.06%	.04%	.13%	
Debt to Equity	.36%	.35%	.36%	.25%	0.378	

CONTACT INFORMATION:

Phone: 33 14149200   Fax: 33 14149248
Toll-Free:
Address: 48, rue Albert Dhalenne, Paris, 93400 France

STOCK TICKER/OTHER:

Stock Ticker: AOMFF   Exchange: PINX
Employees: 84,748   Fiscal Year Ends: 03/31
Parent Company:

SALARIES/BONUSES:

Top Exec. Salary: $ Bonus: $
Second Exec. Salary: $ Bonus: $

OTHER THOUGHTS:

Estimated Female Officers or Directors: 4
Hot Spot for Advancement for Women/Minorities: Y

Altana AG

NAIC Code: 325510

TYPES OF BUSINESS:

Specialty Chemical Manufacturing
Imaging Products
Electrical Insulation
Coatings
Inks
Product Development
Product Manufacturing

BRANDS/DIVISIONS/AFFILIATES:

BYK
ECKART
ELANTAS
ACTEGA
BYK-Chemie
BYK-Gardner

CONTACTS: Note: Officers with more than one job title may be intentionally listed here more than once.

Carina Meier-Hedde, Chief Human Resources Officer
Petra Severit, CTO
Roland Peter, Pres., Coatings & Sealants
Christoph Schlunken, Pres., Additives & Instruments Div.
Wolfgang Schutt, Pres., Effect Pigments Div.
Guido Forstbach, Pres., Electrical Insulation
Martin Babilas, Chmn.

GROWTH PLANS/SPECIAL FEATURES:

Altana AG is an international chemicals company that develops, manufactures and markets products for a range of targeted, highly specialized applications. The company serves customers in the coatings, paint, plastics, printing, cosmetics, electrical and electronics industries. Altana has over 65 production facilities and 69 service and research labs in 28 different countries. Approximately 7% of sales are invested in R&D every year. The firm operates through four divisions: BYK additives and instruments, ECKART effect pigments, ELANTAS electrical insulation and ACTEGA coatings and sealants. BYK offers a range of chemical additives, produced by subsidiary BYK-Chemie, that help to improve and regulate the quality and processability of coatings and plastics. This division also offers testing and measuring equipment, produced by subsidiary BYK-Gardner, allowing manufacturers to predetermine the color, gloss and other physical properties of paints and plastics products. Major markets for this division are in neighboring European countries, the U.S. and far East. ECKART develops and produces metallic effect and pearlescent pigments as well as gold-bronze and zinc pigments, used to produce certain optical effects in paints, inks, cosmetics and coatings. ELANTAS specializes in producing liquid insulation materials used in electrical and electronics applications, including electric motors, household appliances, cars, generators, transformers, capacitors, televisions, computers, windmills, circuit boards and sensors. ACTEGA develops and produces specialty coatings, sealants, adhesives and printing inks used primarily by the graphic arts and packaging industries.

FINANCIAL DATA: Note: Data for latest year may not have been available at press time.

In U.S. $	2024	2023	2022	2021	2020	2019
Revenue	3,177,490,050	3,026,181,000	3,277,381,421	2,892,848,165	2,675,303,238	2,771,149,500
R&D Expense						
Operating Income						
Operating Margin %						
SGA Expense						
Net Income		121,400,000	1,051,101,252	1,023,791,819	92,298,551	212,794,550
Operating Cash Flow						
Capital Expenditure						
EBITDA						
Return on Assets %						
Return on Equity %						
Debt to Equity						

CONTACT INFORMATION:

Phone: 49-281-670-8   Fax: 49-281-670-10999
Toll-Free:
Address: Abelstrasse 43, Wesel, 46483 Germany

STOCK TICKER/OTHER:

Stock Ticker: Private   Exchange:
Employees: 7,000   Fiscal Year Ends: 12/31
Parent Company:

SALARIES/BONUSES:

Top Exec. Salary: $ Bonus: $
Second Exec. Salary: $ Bonus: $

OTHER THOUGHTS:

Estimated Female Officers or Directors: 3
Hot Spot for Advancement for Women/Minorities: Y

Amazon Lab126 Inc

www.lab126.com

NAIC Code: 541710

TYPES OF BUSINESS:

Research and Development in the Physical, Engineering and Life Sciences (except Biotechnology)
Innovative Consumer Electronic Products
Product Engineering
Product Development
Product Design
Research
Consumer Electronic Devices
Cloud-based Solutions and Services

BRANDS/DIVISIONS/AFFILIATES:

Amazon.com Inc
Kindle
Kindle Touch
Kindle Voyage
Kindle Oasis
Amazon Dash
Amazon Fire TV
Amazon Echo

CONTACTS: Note: Officers with more than one job title may be intentionally listed here more than once.

Marcel S., Sr. Hardware Engineer
Mike W., Sr. Mgr. - Oper.

GROWTH PLANS/SPECIAL FEATURES:

Amazon Lab126, Inc., a subsidiary of Amazon.com, Inc., operates as a lab focused on research, innovation and development of consumer electronic products. The Lab126 name originated from the arrow in the Amazon logo, which draws a line from A to Z; the 1 stands for A and the 26 stands for Z. Since the launch of Amazon's first eReader, the Kindle, in 2007, the firm has expanded its product range and added Kindle Keyboard, Kindle Touch, Kindle Paperwhite eReaders, Kindle Fire tablets, Kindle Voyage and Kindle Oasis to its portfolio. In addition, the company also offers Amazon Fire TV, a streaming media player which can be connected to a HDTV and supports services such as Hulu, Netflix, Pandora, YouTube and Spotify; and Amazon Echo, which is an audio streaming device offering immersive, omni-directional audio and powered by Alexa app (a cloud-based service). Through the app, the device interacts with a user's voice, which it can recognize across the room and can play music, answer questions, read audiobooks, news, report traffic and weather and controls lights and other switches. The device is compatible with WeMo, Wink, Samsung and other smart home devices. The Amazon Dash is a handheld, push-button consumer goods ordering device. The customer can either scan the barcode of the product or voice request it into their Amazon shopping cart. Additionally, the one-click button allows shoppers to reorder their favorite, frequently used products. Lab126 is headquartered in Sunnyvale, California.

FINANCIAL DATA: Note: Data for latest year may not have been available at press time.

In U.S. $	2024	2023	2022	2021	2020	2019
Revenue						
R&D Expense						
Operating Income						
Operating Margin %						
SGA Expense						
Net Income						
Operating Cash Flow						
Capital Expenditure						
EBITDA						
Return on Assets %						
Return on Equity %						
Debt to Equity						

CONTACT INFORMATION:

Phone: 650-456-1100   Fax:
Toll-Free:
Address: 1100 Enterprise Way, Sunnyvale, CA 94043 United States

STOCK TICKER/OTHER:

Stock Ticker: Subsidiary   Exchange:
Employees: 4,000   Fiscal Year Ends: 12/31
Parent Company: Amazon.com Inc

SALARIES/BONUSES:

Top Exec. Salary: $ Bonus: $
Second Exec. Salary: $ Bonus: $

OTHER THOUGHTS:

Estimated Female Officers or Directors:
Hot Spot for Advancement for Women/Minorities:

Sales, profits and employees may be estimates. Financial information, benefits and other data can change quickly and may vary from those stated here.

Amdocs Limited

www.amdocs.com

NAIC Code: 511210K

TYPES OF BUSINESS:

Software-Customer Services & Business Operations
Customer Relationship Management Software
Billing Management Software
Directory Publishing Systems
Technical & Support Services
Managed Services

BRANDS/DIVISIONS/AFFILIATES:

amdocsOne

GROWTH PLANS/SPECIAL FEATURES:

Amdocs Ltd is a provider of software and services to communications, cable and satellite, entertainment, and media industry service providers. The Company and its subsidiaries operate in one operating segment, providing software products and services for the communications, entertainment and media industry service being designed, develop, market, support, implement, and operate its open and modular cloud offering. The company offers business support systems, operational support systems, and managed services. Geographically, it derives a majority of revenue from North America and also has a presence in Europe and the Rest of the world.

CONTACTS: *Note: Officers with more than one job title may be intentionally listed here more than once.*

Shuky Sheffer, CEO
Tamar Dagim, CFO
Eli Gelman, Chairman of the Board
Matthew Smith, Other Corporate Officer
Rajat Raheja, President, Subsidiary

FINANCIAL DATA: *Note: Data for latest year may not have been available at press time.*

In U.S. $	2024	2023	2022	2021	2020	2019
Revenue	5,004,988,928	4,887,549,952	4,576,696,832	4,288,640,000	4,169,039,104	4,086,669,056
R&D Expense	360,798,000	374,855,000	354,706,000	312,941,000	282,042,000	273,936,000
Operating Income	759,696,000	724,891,000	664,797,000	598,693,000	594,758,000	569,746,000
Operating Margin %	.15%	.15%	.15%	.14%	.14%	.14%
SGA Expense	572,845,000	570,707,000	528,572,000	487,255,000	458,539,000	492,457,000
Net Income	493,197,000	540,709,000	549,501,000	688,374,000	497,840,000	479,446,000
Operating Cash Flow	724,428,000	822,630,000	756,719,000	925,807,000	658,136,000	656,377,000
Capital Expenditure	105,495,000	124,362,000	227,219,000	210,438,000	205,510,000	128,086,000
EBITDA	819,029,000	855,155,000	889,852,000	1,044,411,000	792,158,000	777,570,000
Return on Assets %	.08%	.08%	.08%	.11%	.08%	.09%
Return on Equity %	.14%	.15%	.15%	.19%	.14%	.14%
Debt to Equity	.22%	.22%	.22%	.23%	0.241	

CONTACT INFORMATION:

Phone: 314 212-7000   Fax: 314-212-7500
Toll-Free:
Address: 1390 Timberlake Manor Pkwy., Chesterfield, MO 63017 United States

STOCK TICKER/OTHER:

Stock Ticker: DOX   Exchange: NAS
Employees: 29,058   Fiscal Year Ends: 09/30
Parent Company:

SALARIES/BONUSES:

Top Exec. Salary: $ Bonus: $
Second Exec. Salary: $ Bonus: $

OTHER THOUGHTS:

Estimated Female Officers or Directors: 1
Hot Spot for Advancement for Women/Minorities: Y

Amey Ltd

www.amey.co.uk

NAIC Code: 541330

TYPES OF BUSINESS:

Engineering Services
Infrastructure Services
Engineering
Road and Rail Infrastructure
Asset Maintenance
Facilities Maintenance
Engineering and Facilities Design
Consulting Services

BRANDS/DIVISIONS/AFFILIATES:

One Equity Partners
Buckthorn Partners LLP

CONTACTS: Note: Officers with more than one job title may be intentionally listed here more than once.

Andy Milner, CEO
John Faulkner, COO
Andrew Nelson, CFO
Kelvin Dryden, CCO
Michael Burgess, Chief People Officer
Wayne Robertson, Head-Legal
John Faulkner, Dir.-Strategy & Development
Valerie Hughes-D'Aeth, Dir.-Communications
Andy Milner, Managing Dir.-Consulting, Rail & Strategic Highway
Gillian Duggan, Managing Dir.-Built Environment
Dan Holland, Managing Dir.-Utilities & Defense
Nick Gregg, Managing Dir.-Gov't
Colin Moynihan, Chmn.

GROWTH PLANS/SPECIAL FEATURES:

Amey Ltd., owned by One Equity Partners and Buckthorn Partners LLP, is a leading infrastructure services and engineering company that provides critical services to the U.K. The firm designs, maintains and transforms the nation's strategic assets, such as road and rail infrastructure, and facilities for the defense, justice, education and health sectors. Amey's consulting division provides data-driven insights across the firm's specialties and is one of the U.K.'s leading engineering consultancies. Essential services are delivered through Amey across England, Wales, Scotland and Northern Ireland, looking after 130+ schools and colleges, 18,000 military properties and 60 prisons. As a defense contractor, Amey ensures that the U.K. Armed Forces have suitable workplaces, vehicles, equipment and housing. The company maintains NHS Estates for Birmingham and Solihull Mental Health Trust, and a variety of workplaces for public sector organizations in regard to national highways, the hydrographic office and local authorities. Its energy specialists utilize data analysis and technologies to generate savings on client energy costs and carbon emissions.

FINANCIAL DATA: Note: Data for latest year may not have been available at press time.

In U.S. $	2024	2023	2022	2021	2020	2019
Revenue	1,902,852,000	1,812,240,000	1,742,538,000	1,786,780,890		3,095,452,500
R&D Expense						
Operating Income						
Operating Margin %						
SGA Expense						
Net Income						
Operating Cash Flow						
Capital Expenditure						
EBITDA						
Return on Assets %						
Return on Equity %						
Debt to Equity						

CONTACT INFORMATION:

Phone: 44 1865-713-100   Fax: 44-1865-713-357
Toll-Free:
Address: Chancery Exchange, 10 Furnival St., London, EC4A 1AB
United Kingdom

STOCK TICKER/OTHER:

Stock Ticker: Private   Exchange:
Employees: 11,000   Fiscal Year Ends: 12/31
Parent Company: One Equity Partners

SALARIES/BONUSES:

Top Exec. Salary: $ Bonus: $
Second Exec. Salary: $ Bonus: $

OTHER THOUGHTS:

Estimated Female Officers or Directors: 2
Hot Spot for Advancement for Women/Minorities:

Amgen Inc

NAIC Code: 325412

www.amgen.com

TYPES OF BUSINESS:

Drugs-Diversified
Oncology Drugs
Nephrology Drugs
Inflammation Drugs
Neurology Drugs

BRANDS/DIVISIONS/AFFILIATES:

ENBREL
Prolia
Neulasta
Otezla
XGEVA
Aranesp
KYPROLIS
Repatha

CONTACTS: Note: Officers with more than one job title may be intentionally listed here more than once.

Robert Bradway, CEO
Derek Miller, Sr. VP, Divisional
Peter Griffith, CFO
Matthew Busch, Chief Accounting Officer
Nancy Grygiel, Chief Compliance Officer
James Bradner, Chief Scientific Officer
David Reese, Chief Technology Officer
Murdo Gordon, Executive VP, Divisional
Esteban Santos, Executive VP, Divisional
Jonathan Graham, Executive VP
Rachna Khosla, Senior VP, Divisional

GROWTH PLANS/SPECIAL FEATURES:

Amgen is a leader in biotechnology-based human therapeutics. Flagship drugs include red blood cell boosters Epogen and Aranesp, immune system boosters Neupogen and Neulasta, and Enbrel and Otezla for inflammatory diseases. Amgen introduced its first cancer therapeutic, Vectibix, in 2006 and markets bone-strengthening drugs Prolia/Xgeva (approved 2010) and Evenity (2019). The acquisition of Onyx Pharmaceuticals bolstered the firm's therapeutic oncology portfolio with Kyprolis. Recent launches include Repatha (cholesterol-lowering), Aimovig (migraine), Lumakras (lung cancer), and Tezspire (asthma). The 2023 Horizon acquisition brought several rare-disease drugs, including thyroid eye disease drug Tepezza. Amgen also has a growing biosimilar portfolio.

Amgen offers its employees health, disability and life insurance; paid time off; home and auto insurance; tuition reimbursement; childcare services; telecommuting options; and recreation/fitness classes.

FINANCIAL DATA: Note: Data for latest year may not have been available at press time.

In U.S. $	2024	2023	2022	2021	2020	2019
Revenue	33,423,998,976	28,189,999,104	26,322,999,296	25,979,000,832	25,423,998,976	23,362,000,896
R&D Expense	5,964,000,000	4,784,000,000	4,434,000,000	4,819,000,000	4,207,000,000	4,116,000,000
Operating Income	7,258,000,000	7,897,000,000	9,566,000,000	9,144,001,000	9,139,000,000	9,674,000,000
Operating Margin %	.22%	.28%	.36%	.35%	.36%	.41%
SGA Expense	7,096,000,000	6,179,000,000	5,414,000,000	5,368,000,000	5,730,000,000	5,150,000,000
Net Income	4,090,000,000	6,717,000,000	6,552,000,000	5,893,000,000	7,264,000,000	7,842,000,000
Operating Cash Flow	11,490,000,000	8,471,000,000	9,721,000,000	9,261,000,000	10,497,000,000	9,150,000,000
Capital Expenditure	1,096,000,000	1,112,000,000	936,000,000	880,000,000	608,000,000	618,000,000
EBITDA	13,356,000,000	14,801,000,000	12,169,000,000	11,296,000,000	12,996,000,000	12,633,000,000
Return on Assets %	.04%	.08%	.10%	.09%	.12%	.12%
Return on Equity %	.68%	1.36%	1.26%	.73%	.76%	.71%
Debt to Equity	9.62%	10.14%	10.20%	4.96%	3.496	2.786

CONTACT INFORMATION:

Phone: 805 447-1000   Fax: 805 447-1010
Toll-Free: 800-772-6436
Address: 1 Amgen Center Dr., Thousand Oaks, CA 91320 United States

STOCK TICKER/OTHER:

Stock Ticker: AMGN   Exchange: NAS
Employees: 26,700   Fiscal Year Ends: 12/31
Parent Company:

SALARIES/BONUSES:

Top Exec. Salary: $1,214,331   Bonus: $1,021,429
Second Exec. Salary: Bonus: $
$1,869,242

OTHER THOUGHTS:

Estimated Female Officers or Directors: 4
Hot Spot for Advancement for Women/Minorities: Y

Analog Devices Inc

www.analog.com

NAIC Code: 334413

TYPES OF BUSINESS:

Integrated Circuits-Analog & Digital
MEMS Products
DSP Products
Accelerometers & Gyroscopes

BRANDS/DIVISIONS/AFFILIATES:

GROWTH PLANS/SPECIAL FEATURES:

Analog Devices is a leading analog, mixed-signal, and digital-signal processing chipmaker. The firm has a significant market share lead in converter chips, which are used to translate analog signals to digital and vice versa. The company serves tens of thousands of customers; more than half of its chip sales are to industrial and automotive end markets. ADI's chips are also incorporated into wireless infrastructure equipment.

ADI offers its employees medical, dental and vision coverage; life insurance; and various employee assistance programs.

CONTACTS: Note: Officers with more than one job title may be intentionally listed here more than once.

Vincent Roche, CEO
Richard Puccio, CFO
Michael Sondel, Chief Accounting Officer
Janene asgeirsson, Chief Legal Officer
Alan Lee, Chief Technology Officer
Joseph Hassett, COO, Subsidiary
Ray Stata, Director
Vivek Jain, Executive VP, Divisional
Anelise Sacks, Executive VP
Mariya Trickett, Other Executive Officer
Martin Cotter, Senior VP, Divisional

FINANCIAL DATA: Note: Data for latest year may not have been available at press time.

In U.S. $	2024	2023	2022	2021	2020	2019
Revenue	9,427,156,992	12,305,539,072	12,013,953,024	7,318,285,824	5,603,056,128	5,991,065,088
R&D Expense	1,487,863,000	1,660,194,000	1,700,518,000	1,296,126,000	1,050,519,000	1,130,348,000
Operating Income	2,070,056,000	3,983,822,000	3,553,209,000	1,776,657,000	1,550,581,000	1,806,267,000
Operating Margin %	.22%	.32%	.30%	.24%	.28%	.30%
SGA Expense	1,068,640,000	1,273,584,000	1,266,175,000	915,418,000	659,923,000	648,094,000
Net Income	1,635,273,000	3,314,579,000	2,748,561,000	1,390,422,000	1,220,761,000	1,363,011,000
Operating Cash Flow	3,852,529,000	4,817,634,000	4,475,402,000	2,735,069,000	2,008,487,000	2,253,100,000
Capital Expenditure	730,463,000	1,261,463,000	699,308,000	343,676,000	165,692,000	275,372,000
EBITDA	4,203,883,000	6,165,747,000	5,596,656,000	2,588,173,000	2,315,845,000	2,526,054,000
Return on Assets %	.03%	.07%	.05%	.04%	.06%	.07%
Return on Equity %	.05%	.09%	.07%	.06%	.10%	.12%
Debt to Equity	.19%	.17%	.18%	.16%	0.429	0.443

CONTACT INFORMATION:

Phone: 781 935-5565   Fax:
Toll-Free: 800-262-5643
Address: One Analog Way, Wilmington, MA 01887 United States

STOCK TICKER/OTHER:

Stock Ticker: ADI   Exchange: NAS
Employees: 24,000   Fiscal Year Ends: 10/31
Parent Company:

SALARIES/BONUSES:

Top Exec. Salary: $1,137,692   Bonus: $
Second Exec. Salary: $711,058   Bonus: $

OTHER THOUGHTS:

Estimated Female Officers or Directors: 3
Hot Spot for Advancement for Women/Minorities: Y

Sales, profits and employees may be estimates. Financial information, benefits and other data can change quickly and may vary from those stated here.

Apple Inc

NAIC Code: 334220

TYPES OF BUSINESS:

Electronics Design and Manufacturing
Software
Computers and Tablets
Retail Stores
Smartphones
Online Music Store
Apps Store
Home Entertainment Software & Systems

BRANDS/DIVISIONS/AFFILIATES:

iPhone
iPad
Apple Watch
Apple TV
iOS
watchOS
HomePod
AirPods

GROWTH PLANS/SPECIAL FEATURES:

Apple is among the largest companies in the world, with a broad portfolio of hardware and software products targeted at consumers and businesses. Apple's iPhone makes up a majority of the firm sales, and Apple's other products like Mac, iPad, and Watch are designed around the iPhone as the focal point of an expansive software ecosystem. Apple has progressively worked to add new applications, like streaming video, subscription bundles, and augmented reality. The firm designs its own software and semiconductors while working with subcontractors like Foxconn and TSMC to build its products and chips. Slightly less than half of Apple's sales come directly through its flagship stores, with a majority of sales coming indirectly through partnerships and distribution.

Apple offers employees comprehensive health benefits, retirement plans and various employee assistance programs.

CONTACTS:
Note: Officers with more than one job title may be intentionally listed here more than once.

Timothy Cook, CEO
Kevan Parekh, CFO
Arthur Levinson, Chairman of the Board
Chris Kondo, Chief Accounting Officer
Jeffery Williams, COO
Katherine Adams, General Counsel
Deirdre OBrien, Senior VP, Divisional

FINANCIAL DATA:
Note: Data for latest year may not have been available at press time.

In U.S. $	2024	2023	2022	2021	2020	2019
Revenue	391,034,994,688	383,285,002,240	394,328,014,848	365,817,004,032	274,515,001,344	260,174,004,224
R&D Expense	31,370,000,000	29,915,000,000	26,251,000,000	21,914,000,000	18,752,000,000	16,217,000,000
Operating Income	123,216,000,000	114,301,000,000	119,437,000,000	108,949,000,000	66,288,000,000	63,930,000,000
Operating Margin %	.32%	.30%	.30%	.30%	.24%	.25%
SGA Expense	26,097,000,000	24,932,000,000	25,094,000,000	21,973,000,000	19,916,000,000	18,245,000,000
Net Income	93,736,000,000	96,995,000,000	99,803,000,000	94,680,000,000	57,411,000,000	55,256,000,000
Operating Cash Flow	118,254,000,000	110,543,000,000	122,151,000,000	104,038,000,000	80,674,000,000	69,391,000,000
Capital Expenditure	9,447,000,000	10,959,000,000	10,708,000,000	11,085,000,000	7,309,000,000	10,495,000,000
EBITDA	134,661,000,000	125,820,000,000	130,541,000,000	123,136,000,000	81,020,000,000	81,860,000,000
Return on Assets %	.26%	.28%	.28%	.28%	.17%	.16%
Return on Equity %	1.57%	1.72%	1.75%	1.47%	.74%	.56%
Debt to Equity	1.51%	1.53%	2.17%	1.89%	1.638	1.015

CONTACT INFORMATION:

Phone: 408 996-1010   Fax: 408 974-2483
Toll-Free: 800-692-7753
Address: One Apple Park Way, Cupertino, CA 95014 United States

STOCK TICKER/OTHER:

Stock Ticker: AAPL   Exchange: NAS
Employees: 164,000   Fiscal Year Ends: 09/30
Parent Company:

SALARIES/BONUSES:

Top Exec. Salary: $3,000,000   Bonus: $
Second Exec. Salary: $1,000,000   Bonus: $

OTHER THOUGHTS:

Estimated Female Officers or Directors:
Hot Spot for Advancement for Women/Minorities:

Applied Materials Inc

www.appliedmaterials.com

NAIC Code: 333242

TYPES OF BUSINESS:

Semiconductor Manufacturing Equipment
LCD Display Technology Equipment
Automation Software
Energy Generation & Conversion Technologies

BRANDS/DIVISIONS/AFFILIATES:

GROWTH PLANS/SPECIAL FEATURES:

Applied Materials is the largest semiconductor wafer fabrication equipment, or WFE, manufacturer in the world. Applied Materials has a broad portfolio spanning nearly every corner of the WFE ecosystem. Specifically, Applied Materials holds a market share leadership position in deposition, which entails the layering of new materials on semiconductor wafers. It is more exposed to general-purpose logic chips made at integrated device manufacturers and foundries. It counts the largest chipmakers in the world as customers, including TSMC, Intel, and Samsung.

Applied Materials offers comprehensive benefits, retirement options and employee assistance programs.

CONTACTS: Note: Officers with more than one job title may be intentionally listed here more than once.

Gary Dickerson, CEO
Brice Hill, CFO
James Morgan, Chairman Emeritus
Thomas Iannotti, Chairman of the Board
Adam Sanders, Chief Accounting Officer
Teri Little, Chief Legal Officer
Omkaram Nalamasu, Chief Technology Officer
Prabu Raja, President, Divisional
Timothy Deane, Vice President, Divisional

FINANCIAL DATA: Note: Data for latest year may not have been available at press time.

In U.S. $	2024	2023	2022	2021	2020	2019
Revenue	27,175,999,488	26,517,000,192	25,784,999,936	23,062,999,040	17,201,999,872	14,608,000,000
R&D Expense	3,233,000,000	3,102,000,000	2,771,000,000	2,485,000,000	2,234,000,000	2,054,000,000
Operating Income	7,867,000,000	7,654,000,000	7,784,000,000	7,200,000,000	4,365,000,000	3,350,000,000
Operating Margin %	.29%	.29%	.30%	.31%	.25%	.23%
SGA Expense	1,797,000,000	1,628,000,000	1,438,000,000	1,229,000,000	1,093,000,000	982,000,000
Net Income	7,177,000,000	6,856,000,000	6,525,000,000	5,888,000,000	3,619,000,000	2,706,000,000
Operating Cash Flow	8,677,000,000	8,700,000,000	5,399,000,000	5,442,000,000	3,804,000,000	3,247,000,000
Capital Expenditure	1,190,000,000	1,106,000,000	787,000,000	668,000,000	422,000,000	441,000,000
EBITDA	8,791,000,000	8,469,000,000	8,271,000,000	7,401,000,000	4,782,000,000	3,869,000,000
Return on Assets %	.22%	.24%	.25%	.24%	.17%	.15%
Return on Equity %	.41%	.48%	.53%	.52%	.39%	.36%
Debt to Equity	.30%	.35%	.47%	.46%	0.533	0.574

CONTACT INFORMATION:

Phone: 408 727-5555   Fax: 408 727-9943
Toll-Free:
Address: 3050 Bowers Ave., Santa Clara, CA 95052-8039 United States

STOCK TICKER/OTHER:

Stock Ticker: AMAT   Exchange: NAS
Employees: 35,700   Fiscal Year Ends: 10/31
Parent Company:

SALARIES/BONUSES:

Top Exec. Salary: $1,030,000   Bonus: $
Second Exec. Salary: $792,308   Bonus: $

OTHER THOUGHTS:

Estimated Female Officers or Directors: 2
Hot Spot for Advancement for Women/Minorities: Y

Arcadis NV
NAIC Code: 541330

www.arcadis.com

TYPES OF BUSINESS:
Engineering Services
Consulting Services
Project Management
Environmental Services
Infrastructure Construction Management
Power Generation Facilities
Industrial & Residential Development

BRANDS/DIVISIONS/AFFILIATES:

GROWTH PLANS/SPECIAL FEATURES:

Arcadis NV designs, engineers, and provides solutions for various construction and environmental projects. It constructs advanced buildings, plants, and transportation networks, and delivers management services for each project. Planning and cost management solutions help customers meet economic objectives and address potential operational or regulatory liabilities. Arcadis operates four business lines: infrastructure, water, environment, and buildings. It designs drinking water supply systems and treatment technologies for waste water. The segments of the company are Places, Mobility, Resilience and Intelligence. The company delivers services all over the world, with no single customer or country constituting a majority of total sales.

Arcadis offers U.S. employees medical, dental and vision coverage; 401(k); and various employee assistance programs.

CONTACTS: Note: Officers with more than one job title may be intentionally listed here more than once.
Michiel Lap, Chairman of the Board
Michael Putnam, Director

FINANCIAL DATA: Note: Data for latest year may not have been available at press time.

In U.S. $	2024	2023	2022	2021	2020	2019
Revenue	5,669,693,318	5,678,773,908	4,573,138,384	3,834,830,896	3,749,384,721	3,942,531,346
R&D Expense						
Operating Income	454,029,500	337,116,900	276,094,200	262,326,900	234,262,200	109,269,000
Operating Margin %	.08%	.06%	.06%	.07%	.06%	.03%
SGA Expense	111,237,200	91,940,980	99,701,470	74,670,830	58,070,380	68,492,620
Net Income	275,822,900	181,611,800	149,284,900	190,559,600	21,425,650	13,963,680
Operating Cash Flow	397,275,800	350,737,800	322,388,200	373,963,700	486,959,100	247,173,700
Capital Expenditure	51,078,320	46,538,020	45,559,590	39,481,270	28,607,260	55,006,810
EBITDA	618,615,200	526,674,200	391,489,200	401,778,700	273,004,500	261,222,500
Return on Assets %	.06%	.04%	.04%	.06%	.01%	.00%
Return on Equity %	.21%	.16%	.13%	.18%	.02%	.01%
Debt to Equity	.78%	1.02%	1.15%	.37%	0.703	0.733

CONTACT INFORMATION:
Phone: 31 202011011   Fax: 31 202011002
Toll-Free:
Address: Gustav Mahlerplein 97-103, Amsterdam, 1082 MS Netherlands

STOCK TICKER/OTHER:
Stock Ticker: ARCVF   Exchange: PINX
Employees: 35,999   Fiscal Year Ends: 12/31
Parent Company:

SALARIES/BONUSES:
Top Exec. Salary: $ Bonus: $
Second Exec. Salary: $ Bonus: $

OTHER THOUGHTS:
Estimated Female Officers or Directors: 4
Hot Spot for Advancement for Women/Minorities: Y

Sales, profits and employees may be estimates. Financial information, benefits and other data can change quickly and may vary from those stated here.

Arkema

NAIC Code: 325180

TYPES OF BUSINESS:

Chemicals, Manufacturing
Vinyl Products
Industrial Chemicals
Performance Products
Plexiglas
Agrochemicals
Nanomaterials

BRANDS/DIVISIONS/AFFILIATES:

GROWTH PLANS/SPECIAL FEATURES:

Arkema SA is a French chemical company formerly known for its large presence in the acrylics market. However, the company has now developed a strong portfolio of speciality materials. Arkema is organized into four segments. Adhesive solutions, advanced materials, and coatings solutions contain the more specialized material businesses. The intermediates segment houses the remaining commodity chemical businesses. Geographically, sales are split fairly equally among Europe, the US, and Asia.

CONTACTS: *Note: Officers with more than one job title may be intentionally listed here more than once.*

Thierry Le Henaff, CEO

FINANCIAL DATA: *Note: Data for latest year may not have been available at press time.*

In U.S. $	2024	2023	2022	2021	2020	2019
Revenue	10,833,143,585	10,799,092,388	13,110,102,316	10,804,766,813	8,948,921,980	9,918,274,553
R&D Expense	315,550,500	312,145,300	306,469,900	275,822,900	273,552,800	282,633,400
Operating Income	841,089,700	920,544,800	1,636,776,000	1,266,742,000	637,911,500	997,729,900
Operating Margin %	.08%	.09%	.12%	.12%	.07%	.10%
SGA Expense	1,044,268,000	992,054,500	985,244,000	889,897,900	845,630,000	877,412,000
Net Income	401,816,100	474,460,800	1,095,346,000	1,485,811,000	376,844,500	616,345,100
Operating Cash Flow	1,272,418,000	1,443,814,000	1,698,070,000	1,038,593,000	1,265,607,000	1,475,596,000
Capital Expenditure	863,791,200	769,580,000	828,603,800	866,061,300	686,719,600	750,283,800
EBITDA	1,482,406,000	1,492,622,000	2,237,231,000	2,885,358,000	1,497,162,000	1,585,698,000
Return on Assets %	.02%	.03%	.07%	.11%	.03%	.05%
Return on Equity %	.05%	.06%	.14%	.23%	.06%	.10%
Debt to Equity	.49%	.52%	.35%	.43%	0.513	0.451

CONTACT INFORMATION:

Phone: 33 149008080   Fax: 33 149008396
Toll-Free:
Address: 420, rue d'Estienne d'Orves, Colombes, 92700 France

STOCK TICKER/OTHER:

Stock Ticker: ARKAF   Exchange: PINX
Employees: 21,125   Fiscal Year Ends: 12/31
Parent Company:

SALARIES/BONUSES:

Top Exec. Salary: $ Bonus: $
Second Exec. Salary: $ Bonus: $

OTHER THOUGHTS:

Estimated Female Officers or Directors:
Hot Spot for Advancement for Women/Minorities:

Sales, profits and employees may be estimates. Financial information, benefits and other data can change quickly and may vary from those stated here.

Artelia

NAIC Code: 541330

TYPES OF BUSINESS:

Engineering Services
Engineering
Project Management
Master Planning and Feasibility
Construction and Design
Asset and Facility Management
Digital and Innovative Technology Solutions
Research and Development

BRANDS/DIVISIONS/AFFILIATES:

CONTACTS: *Note: Officers with more than one job title may be intentionally listed here more than once.*

Benoit Clocheret, Chmn.

GROWTH PLANS/SPECIAL FEATURES:

Artelia is a multi-disciplinary engineering and project management company, partnering on the entire lifecycle of client projects. The firm's engineering services range from technical expertise to complex project delivery via consulting, master planning and feasibility, design and engineering, construction and project management, asset and facility management and turn-key solutions. Types of challenges Artelia addresses includes climate change resilience, energy transition, sustainable use of resources, advanced industrial facilities, multi-modal mobility, urban cities and regenerating built environments. The company offers digital and innovative solutions and engages in research and development across its engineering platform. Sectors served by Artelia span airports, energy, environment, facility and asset management, healthcare, hospitality, maritime, nuclear facilities, oil and gas, structures and civil works. Artelia has a presence in more than 40 countries and is among the Top 15 consulting engineering companies in Europe. On top of this, Artelia operates in more than 40 countries each year, completing projects as needed. Subsidiaries of the company include ANG, a U.K.-based consultancy; Hydraulic Laboratory, which is an Artelia identity dedicated to the physical modeling of civil engineering structures; PCSI, an expert fire safety consultancy; and many more.

FINANCIAL DATA: *Note: Data for latest year may not have been available at press time.*

In U.S. $	2024	2023	2022	2021	2020	2019
Revenue	1,139,121,900	1,084,878,000	903,696,710	843,638,000	685,073,565	691,993,500
R&D Expense						
Operating Income						
Operating Margin %						
SGA Expense						
Net Income						
Operating Cash Flow						
Capital Expenditure						
EBITDA						
Return on Assets %						
Return on Equity %						
Debt to Equity						

CONTACT INFORMATION:

Phone: 33-1-55-84-10-10   Fax: 33-1-55-84-11-11
Toll-Free:
Address: 16, rue Simone Veil, Auvergne, 93400 France

STOCK TICKER/OTHER:

Stock Ticker: Private   Exchange:
Employees: 8,900   Fiscal Year Ends: 12/31
Parent Company:

SALARIES/BONUSES:

Top Exec. Salary: $ Bonus: $
Second Exec. Salary: $ Bonus: $

OTHER THOUGHTS:

Estimated Female Officers or Directors:
Hot Spot for Advancement for Women/Minorities:

ARUP Group Limited

www.arup.com

NAIC Code: 541330

TYPES OF BUSINESS:

Engineering Consulting Services
Engineering
Consultancy
Structural Design and Planning
Infrastructure
Building
Architecture
Technical Services

BRANDS/DIVISIONS/AFFILIATES:

CONTACTS: Note: Officers with more than one job title may be intentionally listed here more than once.

Jerome Frost, CEO
Rob Boardman, CFO

GROWTH PLANS/SPECIAL FEATURES:

ARUP Group Ltd., which consists of 18,000 designers, advisors and experts working throughout 140 countries, provides design, planning, engineering, consultancy and technical services to a broad international market. The firm was famously involved in the structural design process of the Sydney Opera House. Its services are grouped into several categories including advisory, buildings, climate and sustainability, digital, infrastructure, planning and technical consulting. Markets served by ARUP include travel, commercial and residential property, highways, advanced manufacturing, data centers and technology, hotels and leisure, retail, arts and culture, education, international development, scientific research facilities, aviation, energy, maritime, sport, cities, healthcare, rail, water and more. The firm established its own University in 2009, Arup University, that works to raise standards across the company and its industries by expanding knowledge, strengthening capabilities and accelerating progress towards a sustainable future.

FINANCIAL DATA: Note: Data for latest year may not have been available at press time.

In U.S. $	2024	2023	2022	2021	2020	2019
Revenue	2,805,853,050	2,672,241,000	2,364,873,000	2,360,566,054	2,242,190,000	2,242,840,000
R&D Expense						
Operating Income						
Operating Margin %						
SGA Expense						
Net Income		32,853,000	2,364,873	49,215,692	45,852,600	171,318,000
Operating Cash Flow						
Capital Expenditure						
EBITDA						
Return on Assets %						
Return on Equity %						
Debt to Equity						

CONTACT INFORMATION:

Phone: 44-20-7636-1531   Fax: 44-20-7580-3924
Toll-Free:
Address: 13 Fitzroy St., London, W1T 4BJ United Kingdom

STOCK TICKER/OTHER:

Stock Ticker: Private   Exchange:
Employees: 18,837   Fiscal Year Ends: 03/31
Parent Company:

SALARIES/BONUSES:

Top Exec. Salary: $ Bonus: $
Second Exec. Salary: $ Bonus: $

OTHER THOUGHTS:

Estimated Female Officers or Directors:
Hot Spot for Advancement for Women/Minorities:

ASE Technology Holding Co Ltd

www.aseglobal.com

NAIC Code: 334413

TYPES OF BUSINESS:

Semiconductor Manufacturing
Semiconductor Packaging Services
Design & Testing Services

BRANDS/DIVISIONS/AFFILIATES:

Advanced Semiconductor Engineering Inc
Siliconware Precision Industries Co Ltd
Universal Scientific Industrial Co Ltd

GROWTH PLANS/SPECIAL FEATURES:

ASE Technology Holding Co Ltd is a semiconductor assembly and testing firm. The company operates in segments: Packaging, Testing, and Electronic Manufacturing Services. Of these, Packaging segment contribute the maximum revenue. The packaging segment involves packaging bare semiconductors into completed semiconductors with improved electrical and thermal characteristics. The Testing Segment includes front-end engineering testing, wafer probing, and final testing services. In the EMS segment, the company designs manufactures, and sells electronic components and telecommunication equipment motherboards. The company is based in Taiwan but garners over half its sales from firms in the United States.

CONTACTS: *Note: Officers with more than one job title may be intentionally listed here more than once.*

Kenneth Hsiang, CEO, Subsidiary
Chi-Pin Chang, General Manager, Subsidiary
Nicolas Denis, CEO, Subsidiary
Tien Wu, CEO, Subsidiary
Jason Chang, CEO
Joseph Tung, CFO
Chi-Wen Tsai, Chairman of the Board, Subsidiary
Jeffrey Chen, Chairman, Subsidiary
Chen-Yen Wei, Chairman, Subsidiary
Du-Tsuen Uang, Chief Administrative Officer
Yen-Chun Chang, COO, Subsidiary
Raymond Lo, Director
Rutherford Chang, Director
Tien-Szu Chen, Director
Richard Chang, Director
Chun-Che Lee, General Manager, Subsidiary
Chih-Hsiao Chung, General Manager, Subsidiary
Ta-I Lin, General Manager, Subsidiary

FINANCIAL DATA: *Note: Data for latest year may not have been available at press time.*

In U.S. $	2024	2023	2022	2021	2020	2019
Revenue	19,912,031,632	19,460,720,427	22,435,711,180	19,062,174,229	15,951,398,240	13,817,878,377
R&D Expense	964,160,000	852,766,000	814,992,600	704,087,700	645,522,700	615,187,500
Operating Income	1,351,326,000	1,400,656,000	2,727,075,000	2,139,045,000	1,222,639,000	806,346,500
Operating Margin %	.07%	.07%	.12%	.11%	.08%	.06%
SGA Expense	967,662,500	867,166,700	1,016,137,000	909,330,300	796,126,300	748,747,800
Net Income	1,082,835,000	1,185,804,000	2,056,770,000	2,011,577,000	901,965,800	570,550,100
Operating Cash Flow	3,036,177,000	3,826,562,000	3,712,159,000	2,733,392,000	2,510,222,000	2,418,007,000
Capital Expenditure	2,731,681,000	1,825,621,000	2,464,894,000	2,439,026,000	2,112,850,000	1,956,701,000
EBITDA	3,621,712,000	3,576,771,000	4,722,248,000	4,598,922,000	3,025,386,000	2,606,298,000
Return on Assets %	.05%	.05%	.09%	.10%	.05%	.03%
Return on Equity %	.11%	.12%	.22%	.26%	.13%	.09%
Debt to Equity	.46%	.37%	.49%	.65%	0.725	0.89

CONTACT INFORMATION:

Phone: 886 287805489   Fax: 886 227576121
Toll-Free:
Address: 26 Chin Third Rd., Nantze Export Processing Zone, Kaohsiung, 811 Taiwan

STOCK TICKER/OTHER:

Stock Ticker: ASX   Exchange: NYS
Employees: 91,384   Fiscal Year Ends: 12/31
Parent Company:

SALARIES/BONUSES:

Top Exec. Salary: $ Bonus: $
Second Exec. Salary: $ Bonus: $

OTHER THOUGHTS:

Estimated Female Officers or Directors:
Hot Spot for Advancement for Women/Minorities: Y

Associated Consulting Engineers
www.ace-jor.com

NAIC Code: 541330

TYPES OF BUSINESS:
Engineering Consulting Services
Architecture Services
Engineering
Consulting

BRANDS/DIVISIONS/AFFILIATES:

GROWTH PLANS/SPECIAL FEATURES:

Associated Consulting Engineers (ACE) provides architectural and engineering consulting services across a broad spectrum of professional practices, as well as to both public and private customers. ACE's consulting division serves the following fields: building projects, roads and infrastructure, traffic engineering, high-rise buildings, topographical surveys and bridge projects. These services cover all aspects, including inception, conceptual design, detailed design, implementation, commissioning, operation, maintenance and hand over upon completion. Its engineering division serves the following industries: automation and instrumentation, electrical, environmental, geotechnical, mechanical, structural and other ancillary engineering services. These services also cover all aspects from inception to hand over upon completion.

CONTACTS: *Note: Officers with more than one job title may be intentionally listed here more than once.*
Khaled Kheshman, Chmn.

FINANCIAL DATA: *Note: Data for latest year may not have been available at press time.*

In U.S. $	2024	2023	2022	2021	2020	2019
Revenue						
R&D Expense						
Operating Income						
Operating Margin %						
SGA Expense						
Net Income						
Operating Cash Flow						
Capital Expenditure						
EBITDA						
Return on Assets %						
Return on Equity %						
Debt to Equity						

CONTACT INFORMATION:
Phone: 962 6 566 0742   Fax: 962 6 568 6426
Toll-Free:
Address: 926307 Amman, Amman, 11190 Jordan

STOCK TICKER/OTHER:
Stock Ticker: Private   Exchange:
Employees: Fiscal Year Ends:
Parent Company:

SALARIES/BONUSES:
Top Exec. Salary: $ Bonus: $
Second Exec. Salary: $ Bonus: $

OTHER THOUGHTS:
Estimated Female Officers or Directors:
Hot Spot for Advancement for Women/Minorities:

Astellas Pharma Inc

www.astellas.com

NAIC Code: 325412

TYPES OF BUSINESS:

Drugs, Manufacturing
Biologics
Technology
Disease Prevention
Diagnostic Solutions
Data and Analytics
Product Pipeline

BRANDS/DIVISIONS/AFFILIATES:

GROWTH PLANS/SPECIAL FEATURES:

Astellas Pharma Inc is a specialty global pharmaceutical company. The company focuses on accelerating the discovery, development and commercialization of ground-breaking innovations that could redefine expectations of care for difficult-to-treat diseases. The group is committed to driving innovation in immuno-oncology, gene therapy, mitochondria, blindness and regeneration, and targeted protein degradation. The company operates its business in approximately 70 countries around the world. Its core products include anticancer agents like XTANDI, XOSPATA, and PADCEV; VEOZAH for the treatment of vasomotor symptoms due to menopause; Betanis / Myrbetriq / BETMIGA for the treatment of overactive bladder (OAB); and Prograf, an immunosuppressant for organ transplantation.

CONTACTS: *Note: Officers with more than one job title may be intentionally listed here more than once.*

Naoki Okamura, CEO
Kenji Yasukawa, Chairman of the Board
Katsuyoshi Sugita, Chief Compliance Officer

FINANCIAL DATA: *Note: Data for latest year may not have been available at press time.*

In U.S. $	2024	2023	2022	2021	2020	2019
Revenue	11,133,518,476	10,543,036,549	8,998,632,704	8,674,868,292	9,031,123,164	9,069,341,882
R&D Expense	2,042,398,000	1,917,023,000	1,707,928,000	1,558,519,000	1,556,693,000	1,448,778,000
Operating Income	131,539,900	913,336,600	909,212,700	941,217,700	1,705,443,000	1,704,658,000
Operating Margin %	.01%	.09%	.10%	.11%	.19%	.19%
SGA Expense	5,138,226,000	4,375,674,000	3,810,331,000	3,501,222,000	3,466,364,000	3,403,659,000
Net Income	118,335,200	685,323,600	861,469,100	837,191,100	1,356,644,000	1,543,078,000
Operating Cash Flow	1,197,411,000	2,275,528,000	1,787,309,000	2,130,262,000	1,541,225,000	1,795,543,000
Capital Expenditure	572,736,800	614,697,300	530,741,500	537,635,400	540,738,700	361,899,500
EBITDA	1,352,499,000	1,713,954,000	1,676,750,000	1,529,513,000	2,185,157,000	2,178,055,000
Return on Assets %	.01%	.04%	.05%	.05%	.09%	.12%
Return on Equity %	.01%	.07%	.09%	.09%	.15%	.18%
Debt to Equity	.28%	.03%				

CONTACT INFORMATION:

Phone: 81-3-3244-3000   Fax:
Toll-Free:
Address: 2-5-1, Nihonbashi-Honcho, Tokyo, 103-8411 Japan

STOCK TICKER/OTHER:

Stock Ticker: ALPMY   Exchange: PINX
Employees: 16,243   Fiscal Year Ends: 03/31
Parent Company:

SALARIES/BONUSES:

Top Exec. Salary: $ Bonus: $
Second Exec. Salary: $ Bonus: $

OTHER THOUGHTS:

Estimated Female Officers or Directors:
Hot Spot for Advancement for Women/Minorities:

Aston Martin Lagonda Global Holdings PLC

www.astonmartinlagonda.com

NAIC Code: 336111

TYPES OF BUSINESS:

Automobile Manufacturing
Sports Cars
Antique Vehicle Maintenance & Restoration
Clothing & Fashion Accessories
Automobile Racing
SUV

BRANDS/DIVISIONS/AFFILIATES:

DBX
DB11
DBS
Vantage
Heritage

GROWTH PLANS/SPECIAL FEATURES:

Aston Martin Lagonda Global Holdings PLC is a luxury automotive manufacturer. It designs, engineers, and produces sports cars in Warwickshire, United Kingdom, and sells those models through a network of dealers. It is also involved in the servicing of sports cars, all the activities are carried out under the brand name of Aston Martin. The Group has only one operating segment, the automotive segment. The automotive segment includes all activities relating to the design, development, manufacture, and marketing of vehicles including consulting services, as well as the sale of parts, servicing, and automotive brand activities. Geographically, it derives key revenue from the Americas, followed by the United Kingdom, the Rest of Europe, Middle East and Africa, and the Asia Pacific region.

CONTACTS: Note: Officers with more than one job title may be intentionally listed here more than once.

Adrian Hallmark, CEO
Douglas Lafferty, CFO
Lawrence Strulovitch, Chairman of the Board
Elizabeth Miles, Secretary

FINANCIAL DATA: Note: Data for latest year may not have been available at press time.

In U.S. $	2024	2023	2022	2021	2020	2019
Revenue	2,132,404,622	2,198,238,650	1,859,913,501	1,474,602,353	823,666,344	1,320,047,113
R&D Expense						
Operating Income	-111,339,000	-103,799,700	-158,728,800	-100,030,100	-302,782,900	12,251,330
Operating Margin %	-.05%	-.05%	-.09%	-.07%	-.37%	.01%
SGA Expense	419,507,100	450,472,000	765,506,200	562,753,400	452,356,800	442,528,800
Net Income	-435,528,100	-307,091,000	-711,654,200	-257,951,100	-564,503,600	-170,172,300
Operating Cash Flow	166,806,600	196,425,200	171,114,700	240,853,100	-267,375,200	26,118,220
Capital Expenditure	539,327,800	535,019,600	386,253,500	248,661,600	350,980,400	417,622,300
EBITDA	310,052,900	416,814,500	-9,424,100	215,004,100	-131,668,100	164,517,900
Return on Assets %	-.10%	-.07%	-.18%	-.07%	-.17%	-.06%
Return on Equity %	-.39%	-.28%	-.82%	-.28%	-.76%	-.34%
Debt to Equity	1.99%	1.18%	1.70%	1.97%	1.352	2.968

CONTACT INFORMATION:

Phone: 44-1926-644644   Fax: 44-1926-644733
Toll-Free: 866-278-6661
Address: Banbury Rd., Warwick, CV35 0DB United Kingdom

STOCK TICKER/OTHER:

Stock Ticker: AMGDF   Exchange: PINX
Employees: 2,832   Fiscal Year Ends: 12/31
Parent Company:

SALARIES/BONUSES:

Top Exec. Salary: $44,428   Bonus: $807,780
Second Exec. Salary: $770,084   Bonus: $57,891

OTHER THOUGHTS:

Estimated Female Officers or Directors:
Hot Spot for Advancement for Women/Minorities:

AstraZeneca plc

NAIC Code: 325412

www.astrazeneca.com

TYPES OF BUSINESS:

Pharmaceuticals, Biopharmaceuticals, Generics and Drug Manufacturing
Pharmaceutical Research & Development

GROWTH PLANS/SPECIAL FEATURES:

A merger between Astra of Sweden and Zeneca Group of the United Kingdom formed AstraZeneca in 1999. The firm sells branded drugs across a number of major therapeutic areas, including oncology (about 40% of total revenue), cardiovascular, renal, and metabolic (25%), rare disease (17%), and respiratory and immunology (15%). The majority of sales comes from international markets, with the United States representing close to one third of its sales.

BRANDS/DIVISIONS/AFFILIATES:

Atacand
Crestor
Lokelma
Arimidex
Faslodex
Accolate
Bricanyl
Symbicort pMDI

CONTACTS:
Note: Officers with more than one job title may be intentionally listed here more than once.

Pascal Soriot, CEO
Aradhana Sarin, CFO
Michel Demare, Chairman of the Board
Adrian Kemp, Secretary

FINANCIAL DATA:
Note: Data for latest year may not have been available at press time.

In U.S. $	2024	2023	2022	2021	2020	2019
Revenue	54,072,999,936	45,810,999,296	44,351,000,576	37,417,000,960	26,616,999,936	24,384,000,000
R&D Expense	13,583,000,000	10,935,000,000	9,762,000,000	9,735,999,000	5,991,000,000	6,059,000,000
Operating Income	10,251,000,000	8,722,000,000	4,512,000,000	-139,000,000	3,916,000,000	1,738,000,000
Operating Margin %	.19%	.19%	.10%	.00%	.15%	.07%
SGA Expense	20,224,000,000	18,222,000,000	17,984,000,000	15,590,000,000	11,896,000,000	11,985,000,000
Net Income	7,035,000,000	5,955,000,000	3,288,000,000	112,000,000	3,196,000,000	1,335,000,000
Operating Cash Flow	11,861,000,000	10,345,000,000	9,808,000,000	5,963,000,000	4,799,000,000	2,969,000,000
Capital Expenditure	4,586,000,000	3,778,000,000	2,571,000,000	2,200,000,000	2,606,000,000	2,460,000,000
EBITDA	15,438,000,000	13,422,000,000	9,085,000,000	5,113,000,000	8,084,000,000	6,712,000,000
Return on Assets %			.03%	.00%	.05%	.02%
Return on Equity %			.09%	.00%	.22%	.10%
Debt to Equity	.68%	.59%	.64%	.74%	1.152	1.235

CONTACT INFORMATION:

Phone: 44 2037495000   Fax: 44 1223352858
Toll-Free:
Address: 15 Stanhope Gate, London, W1K 1LN United Kingdom

STOCK TICKER/OTHER:

Stock Ticker: AZN   Exchange: NAS
Employees: 89,900   Fiscal Year Ends: 12/31
Parent Company:

SALARIES/BONUSES:

Top Exec. Salary: $2,000,602   Bonus: $4,710,704
Second Exec. Salary: Bonus: $2,011,372
$1,280,331

OTHER THOUGHTS:

Estimated Female Officers or Directors: 3
Hot Spot for Advancement for Women/Minorities: Y

ASUSTeK Computer Inc

www.asus.com/tw

NAIC Code: 334111

TYPES OF BUSINESS:

Electronic Computer Manufacturing
Computer Components & Accessories
Networking Devices
Wireless Communication Products
Smartphones
Personal Computers
Computer Monitors
Computers for Video Game Players

BRANDS/DIVISIONS/AFFILIATES:

Asustor Inc
ASUS Cloud Corporation
ASUS
ProArt

GROWTH PLANS/SPECIAL FEATURES:

Asustek Computer Inc is a computer hardware and electronics company producing and selling 3C products including PCs, mainboards other boards and cards, tablet PCs, smartphones, and other handheld devices, etc. The company operates in Taiwan, China, Singapore, Europe, the United States, and other countries. Its segment includes BC Brand and Others.

CONTACTS: Note: Officers with more than one job title may be intentionally listed here more than once.

Jonney Shih, Chairman of the Board
Ted Hsu, Chief Strategy Officer
S. Y. Hsu, Co-CEO
Samson Hu, Co-CEO
Joe Hsieh, COO

FINANCIAL DATA: Note: Data for latest year may not have been available at press time.

In U.S. $	2024	2023	2022	2021	2020	2019
Revenue	19,633,706,362	16,129,838,202	17,965,084,008	17,899,763,889	13,804,442,204	11,749,398,095
R&D Expense	736,953,200	723,661,900	689,742,200	671,820,400	564,343,400	472,210,700
Operating Income	1,159,021,000	393,127,500	434,034,600	1,649,925,000	835,148,400	388,492,200
Operating Margin %	.06%	.02%	.02%	.09%	.06%	.03%
SGA Expense	1,564,346,000	1,304,257,000	1,355,684,000	1,367,504,000	1,049,365,000	928,077,800
Net Income	1,049,892,000	532,682,900	491,297,800	1,489,860,000	888,157,100	405,944,600
Operating Cash Flow	268,556,400	1,741,927,000	-525,763,000	1,093,276,000	-70,014,940	1,181,435,000
Capital Expenditure	85,694,540	67,963,580	58,457,600	72,842,650	100,855,300	257,022,600
EBITDA	1,532,466,000	854,725,800	836,024,600	2,101,788,000	1,227,016,000	737,232,500
Return on Assets %	.06%	.03%	.03%	.10%	.07%	.03%
Return on Equity %	.12%	.07%	.07%	.21%	.14%	.07%
Debt to Equity	.01%	.00%	.00%	.00%	0.003	0.004

CONTACT INFORMATION:

Phone: 886 228943447   Fax:
Toll-Free:
Address: Li-De Rd., No. 15, Peitou, Taipei, 112 Taiwan

STOCK TICKER/OTHER:

Stock Ticker: ASUUY   Exchange: PINX
Employees: 7,603   Fiscal Year Ends: 12/31
Parent Company:

SALARIES/BONUSES:

Top Exec. Salary: $ Bonus: $
Second Exec. Salary: $ Bonus: $

OTHER THOUGHTS:

Estimated Female Officers or Directors:
Hot Spot for Advancement for Women/Minorities:

Sales, profits and employees may be estimates. Financial information, benefits and other data can change quickly and may vary from those stated here.

AtkinsRealis Group Inc

NAIC Code: 541330

www.snclavalin.com

TYPES OF BUSINESS:

Engineering Services
Consulting
Project Management
Professional Services
Engineering
Design
Infrastructure

BRANDS/DIVISIONS/AFFILIATES:

GROWTH PLANS/SPECIAL FEATURES:

Based in Montreal, AtkinsRealis is a fully integrated professional services and project management firm that offers a wide range of services, including financing, consulting, engineering and construction, procurement, and operations and maintenance. The firm serves clients in the infrastructure, nuclear, and engineering design and project management industries. Additionally, it owns infrastructure projects through its capital segment. AtkinsRealis generated approximately CAD 9.5 billion in sales in 2024.

CONTACTS: *Note: Officers with more than one job title may be intentionally listed here more than once.*

Ian Edwards, CEO
Jeffrey Bell, CFO
William Young, Chairman of the Board
Nigel White, Chief Risk Officer
Philip Hoare, COO
Andree-Claude Berube, Executive VP
James Cullens, Other Executive Officer
Joseph St. Julian, President, Divisional
Steve Morriss, President, Divisional
Christine Healy, President, Geographical
Richard Robinson, President, Geographical
Stephanie Vaillancourt, President, Geographical

FINANCIAL DATA: *Note: Data for latest year may not have been available at press time.*

In U.S. $	2024	2023	2022	2021	2020	2019
Revenue	7,036,908,344	6,284,524,408	5,494,599,646	5,365,202,545	5,100,444,264	5,553,411,259
R&D Expense						
Operating Income	414,721,600	368,743,000	149,119,300	185,424,700	-129,088,000	253,568,600
Operating Margin %	.06%	.06%	.03%	.03%	- .03%	.05%
SGA Expense	141,561,200	128,260,400	90,232,180	105,592,100	128,053,700	53,820,510
Net Income	206,616,200	209,045,800	7,096,586	485,161,200	-702,705,400	238,895,800
Operating Cash Flow	382,694,500	48,011,500	-178,586,500	97,676,680	88,423,460	-258,587,200
Capital Expenditure	116,405,100	75,381,020	79,938,130	77,364,430	55,186,690	89,121,470
EBITDA	559,697,200	547,348,400	248,368,800	323,547,500	38,739,350	2,424,331,000
Return on Assets %	.03%	.03%	.00%	.07%	- .09%	.03%
Return on Equity %	.08%	.09%	.00%	.24%	- .31%	.09%
Debt to Equity	.56%	.56%	.65%	.66%	0.858	0.577

CONTACT INFORMATION:

Phone: 514 393-1000   Fax: 514 866-0795
Toll-Free:
Address: 455 Rene-Levesque Boulevard West, Montreal, QC H2Z 1Z3 Canada

STOCK TICKER/OTHER:

Stock Ticker: ATRL
Employees: 37,246
Parent Company:

Exchange: TSE
Fiscal Year Ends: 12/31

SALARIES/BONUSES:

Top Exec. Salary: $ Bonus: $
Second Exec. Salary: $ Bonus: $

OTHER THOUGHTS:

Estimated Female Officers or Directors: 3
Hot Spot for Advancement for Women/Minorities: Y

Sales, profits and employees may be estimates. Financial information, benefits and other data can change quickly and may vary from those stated here.

Atomic Energy of Canada Limited (AECL)

www.aecl.ca

NAIC Code: 541330

TYPES OF BUSINESS:

Nuclear Reactor Design
Nuclear Waste Management
Research & Laboratories

BRANDS/DIVISIONS/AFFILIATES:

CONTACTS:
Note: Officers with more than one job title may be intentionally listed here more than once.

Fred Dermarkar, CEO
Thomas Assimes, CFO
William Kupferschmidt, VP-R&D
Yvonne Penning, General Counsel
Randy Lesco, VP-Oper.
Joan Miller, VP-Waste Mgmt. & Decommissioning
Jon Lundy, Chief Legal Officer
Richard V. Cote, VP-Isotopes Strategy
James Burpee, Chmn.

GROWTH PLANS/SPECIAL FEATURES:

Atomic Energy of Canada, Ltd. (AECL) is a global nuclear technology and engineering company owned by the Canadian government. AECL has project sites all over Canada with laboratories, disposal facilities, reactors and office spaces. AECL is responsible for enabling nuclear science and technology and to fulfill the Government of Canada's radioactive waste and decommissioning activities. Nuclear science and technology are utilized to sustain and develop the country's capabilities in a cost-effective manner. AECL delivers its services through a long-term contract with Canadian Nuclear Laboratories (CNL) for the management and operation of its nuclear sites. The firm also works with CNL to provide technical services and research and development products for third parties on a commercial basis. AECL's radioactive waste and decommissioning division manages various types of radioactive waste at its sites, including high-level waste (used fuel), intermediate-level waste and low-level waste. AECL receives federal funding to deliver its services and reports to Parliament through the Minister of Natural Resources.

FINANCIAL DATA:
Note: Data for latest year may not have been available at press time.

In U.S. $	2024	2023	2022	2021	2020	2019
Revenue		917,976,000	1,169,000,000	824,109,962	810,370,000	721,537,000
R&D Expense						
Operating Income						
Operating Margin %						
SGA Expense						
Net Income		636,137,000	-6,340,000	5,196,241	-249,781,000	118,230,000
Operating Cash Flow						
Capital Expenditure						
EBITDA						
Return on Assets %						
Return on Equity %						
Debt to Equity						

CONTACT INFORMATION:

Phone: 613-584-3311   Fax: 613-584-8272
Toll-Free: 888-220-2465
Address: 286 Plant Rd., Station 508A, Chalk River, ON K0J 1J0 Canada

STOCK TICKER/OTHER:

Stock Ticker: Government-Owned   Exchange:
Employees: 49   Fiscal Year Ends: 03/31
Parent Company: Canadian Federal Crown corp.

SALARIES/BONUSES:

Top Exec. Salary: $ Bonus: $
Second Exec. Salary: $ Bonus: $

OTHER THOUGHTS:

Estimated Female Officers or Directors: 2
Hot Spot for Advancement for Women/Minorities: Y

Sales, profits and employees may be estimates. Financial information, benefits and other data can change quickly and may vary from those stated here.

ATS Corp

NAIC Code: 333517

TYPES OF BUSINESS:

Machine Tool Manufacturing
Testing Equipment
Manufacturing Consulting
Photovoltaic Cells Manufacturing
Photovoltaic Cells Installation & Design
Photovoltaic Cells Research & Development

BRANDS/DIVISIONS/AFFILIATES:

GROWTH PLANS/SPECIAL FEATURES:

ATS Corp is a Canada-based company that provides automation systems. The company designs and builds customized automated manufacturing and testing systems for customers, and provides pre- and post-automation services. The company's products comprise conveyor systems, automated electrified monorails, tray handlers, laser systems, and other hardware and software products. The company also provides pre-automation solutions, including strategic direction and planning services, as well as aftermarket support. The company's clients come from the life sciences, food and beverage transportation, consumer products and electronics, and energy sectors. The company generates the majority of its sales from the North American and European markets.

CONTACTS: Note: Officers with more than one job title may be intentionally listed here more than once.

Andrew Hider, CEO
Ryan McLeod, CFO
David McAusland, Chairman of the Board
Jeff Adamson, Chief Information Officer
Stewart Mccuaig, General Counsel
Heinrich Sielemann, Managing Director, Subsidiary
Prakash Mahesh, Other Corporate Officer
Angella Alexander, Other Executive Officer
Christian Debus, President, Divisional
Jeremy Patten, President, Divisional
Miroslav Kafedzhiev, President, Divisional
Simon Roberts, Senior VP, Divisional
Steve Emery, Vice President, Divisional
Joe Tassone, Vice President, Divisional
Cameron Moyer, Vice President, Divisional

FINANCIAL DATA: Note: Data for latest year may not have been available at press time.

In U.S. $	2024	2023	2022	2021	2020	2019
Revenue	2,207,498,915	1,875,961,700	1,588,701,358	1,040,870,428	1,040,639,005	
R&D Expense						
Operating Income	246,146,700	181,946,300	140,155,800	97,506,360	88,970,810	
Operating Margin %	.11%	.10%	.09%	.09%	.09%	
SGA Expense	314,173,500	286,609,600	247,892,800	182,177,000	174,610,900	
Net Income	141,011,000	92,752,740	88,871,820	46,649,680	38,502,070	
Operating Cash Flow	15,124,830	93,019,860	157,335,300	134,768,900	14,809,670	
Capital Expenditure	64,384,600	58,443,840	38,769,920	22,979,840	41,172,570	
EBITDA	333,753,500	254,704,800	220,205,200	139,855,900	123,065,700	
Return on Assets %	.05%	.04%	.05%	.03%	.03%	
Return on Equity %	.14%	.12%	.13%	.07%	.06%	
Debt to Equity	.75%	1.09%	1.10%	.55%	0.743	

CONTACT INFORMATION:

Phone: 519 653-4483   Fax: 519 653-6520
Toll-Free:
Address: 730 Fountain Street North, Cambridge, ON N3H 4R7 Canada

STOCK TICKER/OTHER:

Stock Ticker: ATS   Exchange: NYS
Employees: 7,000   Fiscal Year Ends: 03/31
Parent Company:

SALARIES/BONUSES:

Top Exec. Salary: $1,269,600   Bonus: $
Second Exec. Salary: Bonus: $
$657,700

OTHER THOUGHTS:

Estimated Female Officers or Directors: 2
Hot Spot for Advancement for Women/Minorities: Y

Sales, profits and employees may be estimates. Financial information, benefits and other data can change quickly and may vary from those stated here.

Audi AG

NAIC Code: 336111

TYPES OF BUSINESS:

Automobile Manufacturing
Luxury & Sports Cars
Automobile Customization & Accessories
Engine Manufacturing
Automotive Electronics

BRANDS/DIVISIONS/AFFILIATES:

Volkswagen AG
Audi Sport GmbH
Automobili Lamborghini SpA
Ducati Motor Holding SpA
Q3
A1
e-tron
R8

CONTACTS: Note: Officers with more than one job title may be intentionally listed here more than once.

Jurgen Rittersberger, CFO
Hildegard Wortmann, CMO
Xavier Ros, Chief People Officer
Oliver Hoffmann, CTO
Frank Dreves, Dir.-Prod.
Bernd Martens, Dir.-Procurement
Gernot Dollner, Chmn.
Ulf Berkenhagen, Dir.-Purchasing

GROWTH PLANS/SPECIAL FEATURES:

Audi AG, a wholly owned subsidiary of Volkswagen AG, is a Germany-based designer and manufacturer of high-end luxury cars. The firm participates in companies like sports car manufacturer Lamborghini, motorcycle manufacturer Ducati, and vehicle upgrade and technology firm Audi Sport GmbH. Audi AG's current (2023) serial models include the e-tron, e-tron GT, Q3, Q4, Q5, Q7, Q8, A3, A4, A5, A6, A7, A8, TT and R8. These models come in a range of body styles, including electrified, sport utility vehicle (SUV), sedans and wagons, sportbacks, coupes, convertibles and sport. Audi's vehicles comprise alternative drive systems, digital services such as connected navigation, infotainment, emergency calling/servicing, vehicle control and more. The firm was one of the first to utilize artificial intelligence (AI) in production. Audi is present in more than 100 markets worldwide and procures at 21 locations in 12 countries via Audi AG, Audi Sport GmbH, Automobili Lamborghini SpA and Ducati Motor Holding SpA. Services offered by the firm include Audi Interaction GmbH, Audi Business Innovation, A4nXT, Passion to the last bolt: Audi Sport GmbH, Audi Denkwerkstatt, Audi Innovation Research, heycar and Audi Consulting. Audi AG is headquartered in Ingolstadt, Germany.

FINANCIAL DATA: Note: Data for latest year may not have been available at press time.

In U.S. $	2024	2023	2022	2021	2020	2019
Revenue	80,961,099,450	77,105,809,000	76,920,606,000	60,130,440,000	55,700,000,000	65,414,262,784
R&D Expense						
Operating Income						
Operating Margin %						
SGA Expense						
Net Income		6,908,786,000	9,459,492,000	6,228,200,000	4,500,000,000	4,523,238,912
Operating Cash Flow						
Capital Expenditure						
EBITDA						
Return on Assets %						
Return on Equity %						
Debt to Equity						

CONTACT INFORMATION:

Phone: 49-800-2834444   Fax:
Toll-Free:
Address: Grosskunden-Platz, Ingolstadt, D-85045 Germany

STOCK TICKER/OTHER:

Stock Ticker: Subsidiary   Exchange:
Employees: 87,000   Fiscal Year Ends: 12/31
Parent Company: Volkswagen AG

SALARIES/BONUSES:

Top Exec. Salary: $ Bonus: $
Second Exec. Salary: $ Bonus: $

OTHER THOUGHTS:

Estimated Female Officers or Directors:
Hot Spot for Advancement for Women/Minorities:

AUO Corporation

NAIC Code: 334419

www.auo.com

TYPES OF BUSINESS:

LCD (Liquid Crystal Display) Unit Screens Manufacturing
Information Technology Displays
Television Displays
Consumer Product Displays
Solar Module Design, Production & Installation
Silicon Wafer Production

BRANDS/DIVISIONS/AFFILIATES:

MSetek Co Ltd
AUO SunPower Sdn Bhd
AUO Crystal Corp
AUO Green Energy America Corp
AUO Green Energy Europe BV
AUO Crystal (Malaysia) Sdn Bhd
BenQ Solar

GROWTH PLANS/SPECIAL FEATURES:

AUO Corp is a Taiwan-based company that manufactures & distributes thin-film-transistor liquid-crystal-display (TFT-LCD) panels to original equipment manufacturers. The display segment generally is engaged in the research, development, design, manufacturing, & sale of flat panel displays. The energy segment mainly is engaged in the design, manufacturing, and sale of ingots, solar wafers, and solar modules, as well as providing technical engineering services and maintenance services for solar system projects AU Optronics has manufacturing facilities in Taiwan, Japan, and Malaysia. It operates in two segments - The display segment & energy segment, the majority is derived from the Display segment. Geographically, the majority is from the PRC (including Hong Kong).

AUO offers its employees onsite wellness and fitness centers; profit sharing; onsite cafeteria, convenience store, bakery and coffee shop discounts; and subsidized travel and entertainment discounts.

CONTACTS:
Note: Officers with more than one job title may be intentionally listed here more than once.

Frank Ko, CEO
Shuang-Lang Peng, Chairman of the Board

FINANCIAL DATA:
Note: Data for latest year may not have been available at press time.

In U.S. $	2024	2023	2022	2021	2020	2019
Revenue	9,372,130,206	8,292,570,240	8,253,383,319	12,396,667,463	9,061,446,783	8,989,087,495
R&D Expense	536,028,300	442,493,800	430,331,800	437,083,600	343,993,000	328,057,900
Operating Income	-283,123,400	-734,466,400	-801,631,900	2,109,411,000	69,662,300	-684,500,900
Operating Margin %	- .03%	- .09%	- .10%	.17%	.01%	- .08%
SGA Expense	556,940,500	446,155,200	423,721,600	489,013,000	347,676,400	371,691,000
Net Income	-102,473,600	-608,764,400	-705,684,400	2,051,054,000	112,913,000	-641,604,500
Operating Cash Flow	774,050,200	334,210,500	901,978,400	3,502,148,000	861,044,700	693,286,000
Capital Expenditure	900,397,500	895,812,100	1,202,366,000	569,628,400	521,723,100	988,173,200
EBITDA	1,230,940,000	453,092,300	450,408,800	3,420,807,000	1,375,462,000	657,626,000
Return on Assets %	- .01%	- .05%	- .05%	.15%	.01%	- .05%
Return on Equity %	- .02%	- .11%	- .10%	.30%	.02%	- .10%
Debt to Equity	.72%	.69%	.44%	.20%	0.599	0.639

CONTACT INFORMATION:

Phone: 886 35008800   Fax: 886 35643370
Toll-Free:
Address: 1 Li-Hsin Rd. 2, Hsin-chu Science Park, Hsinchu, 30078 Taiwan

STOCK TICKER/OTHER:

Stock Ticker: AUOTY   Exchange: PINX
Employees: 54,645   Fiscal Year Ends: 12/31
Parent Company:

SALARIES/BONUSES:

Top Exec. Salary: $2,314   Bonus: $5,258
Second Exec. Salary: $ Bonus: $

OTHER THOUGHTS:

Estimated Female Officers or Directors:
Hot Spot for Advancement for Women/Minorities:

Aurecon Group Brand (Pty) Ltd

www.aurecongroup.com

NAIC Code: 541330

TYPES OF BUSINESS:

Engineering Services
Civil Structure Design
Consulting
Buildings
Engineering

BRANDS/DIVISIONS/AFFILIATES:

GROWTH PLANS/SPECIAL FEATURES:

Aurecon Group Brand (Pte) Ltd. is an engineering, design and advisory company. The firm is comprised of 25+ areas of expertise, including asset management and performance, bridges and civil structures, bulk transport, digital engineering and advisory, environment and planning, future energy, geospatial systems, ports, infrastructure advisory, integrated transport and mobility, power generation, power transmission and distribution, mass transit, water infrastructure engineering and advisory and many more. Markets served by Aurecon include aviation, construction, data and telecommunications, defense and national security, education and research, energy, government, health, manufacturing, property, resources and chemicals, sports and entertainment, transport and water. Based in Australia, Aurecon Group has global locations in New Zealand, Asia and the Middle East.

CONTACTS: Note: Officers with more than one job title may be intentionally listed here more than once.

Louise Adams, CEO
Andrew Muller, CFO
Liam Hayes, Chief People Officer
Giam Swiegers, Chmn.

FINANCIAL DATA: Note: Data for latest year may not have been available at press time.

In U.S. $	2024	2023	2022	2021	2020	2019
Revenue	1,255,800,000	1,196,000,000	1,150,000,000	1,091,376,000	1,029,600,000	1,040,000,000
R&D Expense						
Operating Income						
Operating Margin %						
SGA Expense						
Net Income						
Operating Cash Flow						
Capital Expenditure						
EBITDA						
Return on Assets %						
Return on Equity %						
Debt to Equity						

CONTACT INFORMATION:

Phone: 61-3-9975-3000   Fax: 61-3-9975-3444
Toll-Free:
Address: 850 Collins St., Level 8, Docklands, VIC 3008 Australia

STOCK TICKER/OTHER:

Stock Ticker: Private   Exchange:
Employees: 6,500   Fiscal Year Ends:
Parent Company:

SALARIES/BONUSES:

Top Exec. Salary: $ Bonus: $
Second Exec. Salary: $ Bonus: $

OTHER THOUGHTS:

Estimated Female Officers or Directors:
Hot Spot for Advancement for Women/Minorities:

Austin Engineering Limited

www.austineng.com.au

NAIC Code: 541330

TYPES OF BUSINESS:

Engineering Services
Manufacturing
Engineering Services and Solutions
Dump Truck Bodies
Water Tanks
Mining Equipment
Repair and Maintenance Services
Heavy Equipment Lifting Services

BRANDS/DIVISIONS/AFFILIATES:

GROWTH PLANS/SPECIAL FEATURES:

Austin Engineering Ltd is an Australia-based engineering company. It designs and manufactures customized off-highway truck bodies, buckets, water tanks, tire handlers, and other ancillary products. It is a complete service provider through the product's life cycle, offering on and off-site repair and maintenance. Its geographical segments include Asia-Pacific, North America, and South America. The company generates maximum revenue from the Asia-Pacific segment which is engaged in mining equipment, other products, and repair and maintenance services located in Australia and Indonesia.

CONTACTS: Note: Officers with more than one job title may be intentionally listed here more than once.

David Singleton, CEO
Jim Walker, Chmn.

FINANCIAL DATA: Note: Data for latest year may not have been available at press time.

In U.S. $	2024	2023	2022	2021	2020	2019
Revenue	201,914,459	166,498,853	130,806,720	130,559,833	147,993,031	151,613,753
R&D Expense						
Operating Income	22,227,090	7,649,467	16,407,650	7,851,871	7,474,136	7,084,153
Operating Margin %	.11%	.05%	.13%	.06%	.05%	.05%
SGA Expense	53,089,240	46,880,460	36,893,030	44,214,390	48,520,960	59,789,220
Net Income	16,812,450	1,836,465	10,833,790	-348,084	3,342,250	-2,958,713
Operating Cash Flow						
Capital Expenditure	3,538,209	7,104,135	2,698,940	3,832,146	2,862,668	5,042,705
EBITDA	30,773,840	13,087,960	20,919,200	7,791,279	12,839,140	9,127,534
Return on Assets %	.09%	.01%	.09%	.00%	.03%	-.02%
Return on Equity %	.21%	.03%	.17%	-.01%	.05%	-.05%
Debt to Equity	.06%	.15%	.10%	.13%	0.146	0.045

CONTACT INFORMATION:

Phone: 61 8 9334 0666   Fax:
Toll-Free:
Address: 100 Chisholm Crescent, Kewdale, Western Australia, 6105 Australia

STOCK TICKER/OTHER:

Stock Ticker: AUSTF
Employees: 1,446
Parent Company:

Exchange: PINX
Fiscal Year Ends: 06/30

SALARIES/BONUSES:

Top Exec. Salary: $ Bonus: $
Second Exec. Salary: $ Bonus: $

OTHER THOUGHTS:

Estimated Female Officers or Directors:
Hot Spot for Advancement for Women/Minorities:

Autodesk Inc

www.autodesk.com

NAIC Code: 511210N

TYPES OF BUSINESS:

Computer Software-Design & Drafting
Computer Assisted Design Software
Mapping & Infrastructure Management Technology
Film & Media Production Software

GROWTH PLANS/SPECIAL FEATURES:

Founded in 1982, Autodesk is an application software company that serves industries in architecture, engineering, and construction; product design and manufacturing; and media and entertainment. Autodesk software enables design, modeling, and rendering needs of these industries. The company has over 4 million paid subscribers across 180 countries.

BRANDS/DIVISIONS/AFFILIATES:

AutoCAD
AutoCAD Civil 3D
BIM Collaborative Pro
Fusion 360
Inventor
Maya
Revit
ShotGrid

CONTACTS:
Note: Officers with more than one job title may be intentionally listed here more than once.

Andrew Anagnost, CEO
Janesh Moorjani, CFO
Stacy Smith, Chairman of the Board
Stephen Hope, Chief Accounting Officer
Ruth Keene, Chief Legal Officer
Deborah Clifford, Chief Strategy Officer
Steven Blum, COO
Rebecca Pearce, Executive VP

FINANCIAL DATA: *Note: Data for latest year may not have been available at press time.*

In U.S. $	2024	2023	2022	2021	2020	2019
Revenue	5,496,999,936	5,005,000,192	4,385,999,872	3,790,000,128	3,274,299,904	
R&D Expense	1,373,000,000	1,219,000,000	1,115,000,000	932,000,000	851,100,000	
Operating Income	1,128,000,000	989,000,000	618,000,000	629,000,000	343,500,000	
Operating Margin %	.21%	.20%	.14%	.17%	.10%	
SGA Expense	2,443,000,000	2,277,000,000	2,195,000,000	1,854,000,000	1,715,900,000	
Net Income	906,000,000	823,000,000	497,000,000	1,208,000,000	214,500,000	
Operating Cash Flow	1,313,000,000	2,071,000,000	1,531,000,000	1,437,000,000	1,415,100,000	
Capital Expenditure	61,000,000	46,000,000	67,000,000	96,000,000	53,200,000	
EBITDA	1,267,000,000	1,167,000,000	766,000,000	722,000,000	476,100,000	
Return on Assets %	.09%	.09%	.06%	.18%	.04%	
Return on Equity %	.60%	.83%	.55%	2.92%		
Debt to Equity	1.38%	2.25%	3.09%	2.11%		

CONTACT INFORMATION:

Phone: 415 507-5000   Fax: 415 507-5100
Toll-Free:
Address: 111 McInnis Pkwy., San Rafael, CA 94903 United States

STOCK TICKER/OTHER:

Stock Ticker: ADSK   Exchange: NAS
Employees: 14,100   Fiscal Year Ends: 01/31
Parent Company:

SALARIES/BONUSES:

Top Exec. Salary: $2,386,525   Bonus: $
Second Exec. Salary: $1,047,969   Bonus: $

OTHER THOUGHTS:

Estimated Female Officers or Directors: 4
Hot Spot for Advancement for Women/Minorities: Y

Sales, profits and employees may be estimates. Financial information, benefits and other data can change quickly and may vary from those stated here.

Autoliv Inc

NAIC Code: 336300

www.autoliv.com

TYPES OF BUSINESS:

Automotive Safety Products Manufacturing
Seat Belts
Airbags
Seat Components
Steering Wheels
Child Seats
Safety Electronics
Anti-Whiplash Systems

BRANDS/DIVISIONS/AFFILIATES:

GROWTH PLANS/SPECIAL FEATURES:

Autoliv Inc is the world-wide leader in passive safety components and systems for the auto industry. Products include seat belts, frontal air bags, side-impact air bags, air bag inflators, and steering wheels. The Renault-Nissan-Mitsubishi alliance is the company's largest customer at 10% of 2023 revenue, with Stellantis accounting for 10% and Volkswagen 9%. At 34% of 2023 revenue, the Americas was Autoliv's largest geographic region, followed by Europe at 27%, China at 20%, and rest of world at 19%.

CONTACTS: *Note: Officers with more than one job title may be intentionally listed here more than once.*

Mikael Bratt, CEO
Fredrik Westin, CFO
Jan Carlson, Chairman of the Board
Fabien Dumont, Chief Technology Officer
Mikael Hagstrom, Controller
Jonas Per Jademyr, Executive VP, Divisional
Petra Albuschus, Executive VP, Divisional
Christian Swahn, Executive VP, Divisional
Anthony Nellis, Executive VP, Divisional
Magnus Jarlegren, President, Geographical
Colin Naughton, President, Geographical
Kevin Fox, President, Geographical
Sng Yih, President, Geographical

FINANCIAL DATA: *Note: Data for latest year may not have been available at press time.*

In U.S. $	2024	2023	2022	2021	2020	2019
Revenue	10,389,999,616	10,474,999,808	8,842,000,384	8,230,000,128	7,447,000,064	8,547,999,744
R&D Expense	398,000,000	425,000,000	390,000,000	391,000,000	376,000,000	406,000,000
Operating Income	980,000,000	690,000,000	659,000,000	675,000,000	382,000,000	724,000,000
Operating Margin %	.09%	.07%	.07%	.08%	.05%	.08%
SGA Expense	530,000,000	500,000,000	440,000,000	432,000,000	389,000,000	399,000,000
Net Income	646,000,000	488,000,000	423,000,000	435,000,000	187,000,000	462,000,000
Operating Cash Flow	1,059,000,000	982,000,000	713,000,000	754,000,000	849,000,000	641,000,000
Capital Expenditure	579,000,000	573,000,000	585,000,000	458,000,000	344,000,000	483,000,000
EBITDA	1,370,000,000	1,083,000,000	1,026,000,000	1,068,000,000	735,000,000	1,069,000,000
Return on Assets %	.08%	.06%	.06%	.06%	.03%	.07%
Return on Equity %	.27%	.19%	.16%	.17%	.08%	.23%
Debt to Equity	.72%	.57%	.45%	.67%	0.919	0.875

CONTACT INFORMATION:

Phone: 46-8-587-20-600   Fax:
Toll-Free:
Address: Klarabergsviadukten 70, Section B7, Stockholm, SE-107 24 Sweden

STOCK TICKER/OTHER:

Stock Ticker: ALV   Exchange: NYS
Employees: 70,300   Fiscal Year Ends: 12/31
Parent Company:

SALARIES/BONUSES:

Top Exec. Salary: $1,217,983   Bonus: $
Second Exec. Salary: Bonus: $
$720,142

OTHER THOUGHTS:

Estimated Female Officers or Directors: 1
Hot Spot for Advancement for Women/Minorities:

Avaya Holdings Corp

www.avaya.com

NAIC Code: 334210

TYPES OF BUSINESS:

Telecommunications Systems
Telecommunications Software
Consulting Services
Networking Systems & Software
Network Maintenance, Management & Security Services
Systems Planning & Integration
Unified Communications Systems

BRANDS/DIVISIONS/AFFILIATES:

Avaya Experience Platform
AXP On-Prem
AXP Private Cloud
AXP Public Cloud
Avaya Aura
Avaya Cloud Office
Avaya IP Office

CONTACTS: Note: Officers with more than one job title may be intentionally listed here more than once.

Patrick Dennis, CEO
Amy O'Keefe, CFO
Pete Lavache, CMO
John Hoffman, Chief People Officer
Soren Abildgaard, CTO
Stephen Spears, Executive VP

GROWTH PLANS/SPECIAL FEATURES:

Avaya Holdings Corp. provides digital communications products, solutions and services for businesses. The firm offers contact center products including the Avaya Experience Platform, which is a comprehensive enterprise customer experience platform designed for the age of artificial intelligence (AI). Other contact center products offered include AXP On-Prem, a full-featured contact center solution with real-time reporting; AXP Private Cloud, a secure, dedicated cloud contact center on Microsoft Azure; and AXP Public Cloud, offering a scalable and advanced enterprise customer experience solution. Avaya also offers products for integrated communications that include Avaya Aura, Avaya Cloud Office and Avaya IP Office. Avaya's solutions address business outcomes by improving customer experience through self-service, assisted service and seamless digital access solutions; increase employee engagement by connecting employees and workforce engagement; and drive business growth through the reduction of costs and streamlining customer support. Its solutions primarily serve the industries of healthcare, education, financial services, media, entertainment and government. The firm partners with big name tech partners, such as Microsoft, Verint, Zoom and Ring Central, to name a few.

FINANCIAL DATA: Note: Data for latest year may not have been available at press time.

In U.S. $	2024	2023	2022	2021	2020	2019
Revenue	3,291,600,000	3,120,000,000	3,000,000,000	2,972,999,936	2,872,999,936	2,887,000,064
R&D Expense						
Operating Income						
Operating Margin %						
SGA Expense						
Net Income				-13,000,000	-680,000,000	-671,000,000
Operating Cash Flow						
Capital Expenditure						
EBITDA						
Return on Assets %						
Return on Equity %						
Debt to Equity						

CONTACT INFORMATION:

Phone: 908 953-6000   Fax:
Toll-Free: 866-462-8292
Address: 350 Mt. Kemble Ave., Morristown, NJ 07960 United States

STOCK TICKER/OTHER:

Stock Ticker: Private   Exchange:
Employees: 8,266   Fiscal Year Ends: 09/30
Parent Company:

SALARIES/BONUSES:

Top Exec. Salary: $ Bonus: $
Second Exec. Salary: $ Bonus: $

OTHER THOUGHTS:

Estimated Female Officers or Directors: 2
Hot Spot for Advancement for Women/Minorities:

Sales, profits and employees may be estimates. Financial information, benefits and other data can change quickly and may vary from those stated here.

Babcock & Wilcox Enterprises Inc

www.babcock.com

NAIC Code: 332410

TYPES OF BUSINESS:

Power Generation Systems
Steam Generators
Environmental Equipment
Engineering & Construction Services
Power Plants
Emissions Reduction Equipment
Waste-to-Energy & Biomass Energy Systems

BRANDS/DIVISIONS/AFFILIATES:

Fosler Construction Company Inc
VODA A/S

GROWTH PLANS/SPECIAL FEATURES:

Babcock & Wilcox Enterprises Inc is a power generation equipment supplier and servicing company that operates in three segments: B&W Renewable, B&W Environmental, and B&W Thermal. B&W Thermal, focuses on steam generation products and solutions for plants in the power generation, oil, and gas, and industrial sectors, generates the majority of the company's revenue. B&W Renewable focuses on sustainable power and heat generation while B&W Environmental focuses on emissions control. The company's customer base spans the industrial, electrical utility, and municipal industries located predominantly in the United States, Canada, Denmark, the United Kingdom, and other regions. Business in the U.S. contributes the vast majority of its revenue.

CONTACTS: Note: Officers with more than one job title may be intentionally listed here more than once.

Kenneth Young, CEO
Cameron Frymyer, CFO
Jimmy Morgan, COO
Christopher Riker, COO
John Dziewisz, Executive VP

FINANCIAL DATA: Note: Data for latest year may not have been available at press time.

In U.S. $	2024	2023	2022	2021	2020	2019
Revenue	717,332,992	727,315,008	609,436,992	710,873,024	566,316,992	859,110,976
R&D Expense	5,794,000	7,197,000	2,557,000	1,595,000	4,379,000	2,861,000
Operating Income	29,755,000	19,358,000	-10,119,000	8,606,000	6,849,000	-21,615,000
Operating Margin %	.04%	.03%	-.02%	.01%	.01%	-.03%
SGA Expense	141,476,000	150,147,000	152,697,000	164,847,000	154,624,000	179,012,000
Net Income	-59,915,000	-197,208,000	-22,861,000	30,894,000	-10,318,000	-121,974,000
Operating Cash Flow	-118,735,000	-42,270,000	-30,637,000	-111,196,000	-40,806,000	-176,317,000
Capital Expenditure	11,205,000	9,800,000	13,238,000	6,679,000	8,230,000	3,804,000
EBITDA	2,065,000	-2,409,000	58,674,000	79,150,000	56,212,000	-56,451,000
Return on Assets %	-.10%	-.25%	-.04%	.03%	-.02%	-.18%
Return on Equity %			-2.48%			
Debt to Equity				11.61%		

CONTACT INFORMATION:

Phone: 330 753-4511   Fax:
Toll-Free:
Address: 1200 E. Market St., Ste. 650, Akron, OH 44305 United States

STOCK TICKER/OTHER:

Stock Ticker: BW   Exchange: NYS
Employees: 2,250   Fiscal Year Ends: 12/31
Parent Company:

SALARIES/BONUSES:

Top Exec. Salary: $766,666   Bonus: $1,972,222
Second Exec. Salary: Bonus: $383,334
$525,000

OTHER THOUGHTS:

Estimated Female Officers or Directors: 3
Hot Spot for Advancement for Women/Minorities: Y

BAE Systems plc

NAIC Code: 336410

www.baesystems.com/en-uk/home

TYPES OF BUSINESS:
Defense and Aerospace Systems
Military Vehicles
Military Aircraft
Naval Vessels & Submarines
Satellite Manufacturing
Electronic Systems
Advanced Materials & Technologies
Security & Surveillance Technology

BRANDS/DIVISIONS/AFFILIATES:
BAE Systems Applied Intelligence
BAE Systems Australia
BAE Systems US
BAE Systems Saudi Arabia

GROWTH PLANS/SPECIAL FEATURES:
BAE Systems is a British global defense, security, and aerospace company and the largest defense contractor in Europe; it is one of six prime contractors to the US Department of Defense. For reporting purposes, the company has five operating segments: electronics systems is the group's US- and UK-based electronic warfare systems; the cyber, security, and intelligence segment supplies intelligence and security solutions to the US government; platforms and services manufactures combat vehicles and munitions and performs ship repair services to the US Defense Department; the air segment includes BAE's share of US and European air programs as well as its businesses in Saudi Arabia and Australia; and the maritime segment comprises UK land- and marine-based activities.

CONTACTS:
Note: Officers with more than one job title may be intentionally listed here more than once.

Thomas Arseneault, CEO, Subsidiary
Charles Woodburn, CEO
Bradley Greve, CFO
Cressida Hogg, Chairman of the Board
Anthony Clarke, Secretary

FINANCIAL DATA:
Note: Data for latest year may not have been available at press time.

In U.S. $	2024	2023	2022	2021	2020	2019
Revenue	35,423,845,066	31,069,912,398	28,619,646,043	26,281,121,640	25,952,626,162	24,644,020,833
R&D Expense						
Operating Income	3,286,318,000	3,105,914,000	2,842,039,000	2,556,624,000	2,365,449,000	2,331,792,000
Operating Margin %	.09%	.10%	.10%	.10%	.09%	.09%
SGA Expense						
Net Income	2,633,363,000	2,500,079,000	2,141,963,000	2,366,796,000	1,748,844,000	1,987,139,000
Operating Cash Flow	5,284,228,000	5,062,088,000	3,822,146,000	3,294,396,000	1,569,786,000	2,150,041,000
Capital Expenditure	1,565,747,000	1,288,409,000	932,985,900	823,935,600	642,185,100	632,761,000
EBITDA	5,347,504,000	4,640,696,000	4,118,332,000	4,207,187,000	3,477,493,000	3,547,501,000
Return on Assets %	.06%	.06%	.05%	.06%	.05%	.06%
Return on Equity %	.18%	.17%	.17%	.29%	.26%	.27%
Debt to Equity	.81%	.54%	.59%	.76%	1.287	0.765

CONTACT INFORMATION:
Phone: 44 1252373232   Fax: 44 1252383991
Toll-Free:
Address: Stirling Square, 6 Carlton Gardens, London, SW1Y 5AD United Kingdom

STOCK TICKER/OTHER:
Stock Ticker: BAESF
Employees: 99,800
Parent Company:

Exchange: PINX
Fiscal Year Ends: 12/31

SALARIES/BONUSES:
Top Exec. Salary: $1,661,334   Bonus: $
Second Exec. Salary: $1,204,939   Bonus: $

OTHER THOUGHTS:
Estimated Female Officers or Directors: 4
Hot Spot for Advancement for Women/Minorities: Y

Sales, profits and employees may be estimates. Financial information, benefits and other data can change quickly and may vary from those stated here.

Baker Hughes Company

www.bakerhughes.com

NAIC Code: 213112

TYPES OF BUSINESS:

Oil Field Services
Energy Technology Products and Solutions
Technology Development
Energy Transition
Subsea Connection Solutions
Energy Artificial Intelligence
Emissions Management Solutions
Industrial Technology

BRANDS/DIVISIONS/AFFILIATES:

General Electric Company
Baker Hughes Holdings LLC
Ekona Power Inc

GROWTH PLANS/SPECIAL FEATURES:

Following a 2022 reorganization, Baker Hughes operates across two segments: oilfield services and equipment, and industrial and energy technology. The firm's oilfield services and equipment segment, or OFSE, is one of the Big Three oilfield service players, along with SLB and Halliburton, and mostly supplies to hydrocarbon developers and producers, including national oil companies, major integrated firms, and independents. Markets outside of North America buy roughly three quarters of the firm's OFSE. Baker Hughes' industrial and energy technology segment manufactures and sells turbines, compressors, pumps, valves, and related testing and monitoring services across various energy and industrial applications.

CONTACTS: Note: Officers with more than one job title may be intentionally listed here more than once.

Lorenzo Simonelli, CEO
Nancy Buese, CFO
Rebecca Charlton, Chief Accounting Officer
Maria Magno, Chief Legal Officer
Maria Borras, Executive VP, Divisional
Ganesh Ramaswamy, Executive VP, Divisional
James Apostolides, Senior VP, Divisional

FINANCIAL DATA: Note: Data for latest year may not have been available at press time.

In U.S. $	2024	2023	2022	2021	2020	2019
Revenue	27,829,000,192	25,506,000,896	21,155,999,744	20,501,999,616	20,704,999,424	23,837,999,104
R&D Expense						
Operating Income	3,382,000,000	2,640,000,000	1,890,000,000	1,579,000,000	795,000,000	1,600,000,000
Operating Margin %	.12%	.10%	.09%	.08%	.04%	.07%
SGA Expense	2,458,000,000	2,611,000,000	2,510,000,000	2,470,000,000	2,404,000,000	2,832,000,000
Net Income	2,979,000,000	1,943,000,000	-601,000,000	-219,000,000	-9,940,000,000	128,000,000
Operating Cash Flow	3,332,000,000	3,062,000,000	1,888,000,000	2,374,000,000	1,304,000,000	2,126,000,000
Capital Expenditure	1,278,000,000	1,224,000,000	989,000,000	856,000,000	974,000,000	1,240,000,000
EBITDA	4,599,000,000	3,958,000,000	1,335,000,000	1,832,000,000	-13,621,000,000	2,408,000,000
Return on Assets %	.08%	.05%	- .02%	- .01%	- .22%	.00%
Return on Equity %	.18%	.13%	- .04%	- .02%	- .57%	.01%
Debt to Equity	.35%	.38%	.42%	.45%	0.523	0.287

CONTACT INFORMATION:

Phone: 713 439-8600   Fax: 713 739-8699
Toll-Free:
Address: 17021 Aldine Westfiled Rd., Houston, TX 77073-5101 United States

STOCK TICKER/OTHER:

Stock Ticker: BKR
Employees: 58,000
Parent Company:

Exchange: NAS
Fiscal Year Ends: 12/31

SALARIES/BONUSES:

Top Exec. Salary: $1,645,000   Bonus: $
Second Exec. Salary: $969,231   Bonus: $

OTHER THOUGHTS:

Estimated Female Officers or Directors:
Hot Spot for Advancement for Women/Minorities: Y

Balfour Beatty plc

NAIC Code: 237000

www.balfourbeatty.com

TYPES OF BUSINESS:

Heavy Construction
Engineering Services
Railway Services
Property Management
Utility & Roadway Infrastructure Management
Financial Services

BRANDS/DIVISIONS/AFFILIATES:

Gammon Construction

GROWTH PLANS/SPECIAL FEATURES:

Balfour Beatty PLC finances builds, and maintains infrastructure projects. It finances, develops, builds, maintains, and operates the increasingly complex and critical infrastructure that supports national economies and delivers projects at the heart of local communities. It operates three business segments: Construction services (majority of total revenue), Support services, and Infrastructure investments. It will invest directly in infrastructure assets also invests in real estate-type assets, in particular private residential and student accommodation assets. The majority of sales are derived from the United Kingdom and the United States.

CONTACTS: *Note: Officers with more than one job title may be intentionally listed here more than once.*

Leo Quinn, CEO
Philip Harrison, CFO
Charles Allen of Kensington, Chairman of the Board
Tracey Wood, Secretary

FINANCIAL DATA: *Note: Data for latest year may not have been available at press time.*

In U.S. $	2024	2023	2022	2021	2020	2019
Revenue	11,085,434,076	10,760,975,861	10,270,923,004	9,673,165,456	9,854,916,043	9,845,491,857
R&D Expense						
Operating Income	95,587,300	180,404,200	228,871,000	18,848,200	12,116,700	149,439,300
Operating Margin %	.01%	.02%	.02%	.00%	.00%	.02%
SGA Expense						
Net Income	239,641,400	265,221,100	387,734,400	188,482,000	40,389,000	175,019,000
Operating Cash Flow	356,769,500	383,695,500	226,178,400	475,243,900	368,886,200	284,069,300
Capital Expenditure	37,696,400	129,244,800	43,081,600	49,813,100	88,855,800	110,396,600
EBITDA	503,516,200	525,057,000	581,601,600	316,380,500	236,948,800	352,730,600
Return on Assets %	.03%	.04%	.06%	.03%	.01%	.03%
Return on Equity %	.15%	.15%	.21%	.10%	.02%	.10%
Debt to Equity	.77%	.68%	.35%	.39%	0.449	0.444

CONTACT INFORMATION:

Phone: 44 2072166800   Fax: 44 2072166950
Toll-Free:
Address: 5 Churchill Place, London, E14 5HU United Kingdom

STOCK TICKER/OTHER:

Stock Ticker: BAFBF   Exchange: PINX
Employees: 26,000   Fiscal Year Ends: 12/31
Parent Company:

SALARIES/BONUSES:

Top Exec. Salary: $1,182,455   Bonus: $817,405
Second Exec. Salary: Bonus: $479,117
$685,502

OTHER THOUGHTS:

Estimated Female Officers or Directors: 2
Hot Spot for Advancement for Women/Minorities:

Sales, profits and employees may be estimates. Financial information, benefits and other data can change quickly and may vary from those stated here.

Baran Group Ltd

www.barangroup.com

NAIC Code: 237000

TYPES OF BUSINESS:

Civil Engineering and Heavy Construction
Engineering Solutions
Construction Solutions
Telecommunication Solutions
Technology Solutions
Feasibility Studies
Permitting
Infrastructure Projects

BRANDS/DIVISIONS/AFFILIATES:

GROWTH PLANS/SPECIAL FEATURES:

Baran Group Ltd is a provider of Engineering, Technology, Telecommunication and Construction solutions. The company offers creative, innovative and proven integrated sustainable engineering solutions to complex and challenging projects, customized to clients' requirements. Its engineering solutions include feasibility studies, engineering and detailed design solutions, preparation for obtaining regulatory permits, construction and site management, project management and control including Engineering, Procurement and Construction Management services and turnkey projects. The company operates in sectors such as general building, transportation, telecommunication and more.

CONTACTS: *Note: Officers with more than one job title may be intentionally listed here more than once.*

Izek Frank, CEO
Mor Cohen, CFO
Ornit Barak, VP-Human Resources
Haim Assael, General Counsel
Arik Shaked, Mgr.-Bus. Dev.
Dan Shenbach, CEO-Baran Israel
Issac Friedman, Gen. Mgr.-Infrastructure & Construction Div.
Meir Dor, Chmn.
Steven Senter, CEO-Baran Intl

FINANCIAL DATA: *Note: Data for latest year may not have been available at press time.*

In U.S. $	2024	2023	2022	2021	2020	2019
Revenue	194,715,885	193,600,985	110,040,929	81,980,147	83,544,421	106,918,070
R&D Expense					-180,887	
Operating Income	15,623,390	11,641,040	4,372,286	1,829,631	5,382,807	3,755,109
Operating Margin %	.08%	.06%	.04%	.02%	.06%	.04%
SGA Expense	3,346,692	3,587,874	2,549,765	2,016,490	2,706,762	3,253,973
Net Income	11,923,740	12,172,040	4,028,999	4,331,899	2,821,665	991,749
Operating Cash Flow	10,396,440	6,649,583	19,409,500	7,565,394	3,958,749	-3,184,007
Capital Expenditure	6,235,478	4,680,874	9,492,294	265,073	328,782	395,050
EBITDA	21,973,770	19,106,890	11,719,250	7,616,304	8,829,327	7,609,478
Return on Assets %	.06%	.06%	.03%	.04%	.03%	.01%
Return on Equity %	.18%	.23%	.10%	.12%	.10%	.04%
Debt to Equity	.28%	.29%	.44%	.54%	0.629	0.63

CONTACT INFORMATION:

Phone: 972 39775000   Fax: 972 39775001
Toll-Free:
Address: 5 Menachem Begin Avenue, Beit-Dagan, 50200 Israel

STOCK TICKER/OTHER:

Stock Ticker: BRANF   Exchange: PINX
Employees: 754   Fiscal Year Ends: 12/31
Parent Company:

SALARIES/BONUSES:

Top Exec. Salary: $ Bonus: $
Second Exec. Salary: $ Bonus: $

OTHER THOUGHTS:

Estimated Female Officers or Directors:
Hot Spot for Advancement for Women/Minorities:

BASF New Business GmbH

www.basf.com/global/en

NAIC Code: 541710

TYPES OF BUSINESS:

Chemistry & Materials Research
Epower Management Solutions
3D Printing Solutions
Additive Manufacturing Solutions
Functional Feed Additives
Animal Health Additives

BRANDS/DIVISIONS/AFFILIATES:

BASF SE

GROWTH PLANS/SPECIAL FEATURES:

BASF New Business GmbH is a subsidiary of BASF SE that focuses on new chemistry-based materials, technologies and system solutions. The firm has 234 production sites in 93 countries, with 112,000 employees worldwide. Industry solutions include agriculture, automotive/transportation, chemicals, construction, electronics/electric, energy/resources, furniture/wood, home care/industrial/institutional cleaning solutions, nutrition, packaging/print, paints/coatings, personal care/hygiene, pharmaceuticals, plastics/rubber, pulp/paper and textile/leather/footwear. BASF is present in 93 countries around the world.

CONTACTS:
Note: Officers with more than one job title may be intentionally listed here more than once.

Wolfgang Hormuth, Dir.-Strategy & Scouting
Joachim Rosch, VP-Foresight
Carla Siedel, VP-E-Power Mgmt.
Dejana Drew, Dir.-Medical Industry
Felix Gorth, Dir.-Organic Electronics
Markus Kamieth, Chmn.-Corp.

FINANCIAL DATA:
Note: Data for latest year may not have been available at press time.

In U.S. $	2024	2023	2022	2021	2020	2019
Revenue						
R&D Expense						
Operating Income						
Operating Margin %						
SGA Expense						
Net Income						
Operating Cash Flow						
Capital Expenditure						
EBITDA						
Return on Assets %						
Return on Equity %						
Debt to Equity						

CONTACT INFORMATION:

Phone: 49-621-60-76811   Fax: 49-621-60-76818
Toll-Free:
Address: Benckiserplatz 1 BE01, Ludwigshafen, 67059 Germany

STOCK TICKER/OTHER:

Stock Ticker: Subsidiary   Exchange:
Employees: 80   Fiscal Year Ends: 12/31
Parent Company: BASF SE

SALARIES/BONUSES:

Top Exec. Salary: $ Bonus: $
Second Exec. Salary: $ Bonus: $

OTHER THOUGHTS:

Estimated Female Officers or Directors: 2
Hot Spot for Advancement for Women/Minorities:

BASF SE

www.basf.com

NAIC Code: 325199

TYPES OF BUSINESS:

Chemicals Manufacturing
Agricultural Products
Oil & Gas Production
Plastics
Coatings
Nanotechnology Research
Nutritional Products
Agricultural Biotechnology

BRANDS/DIVISIONS/AFFILIATES:

GROWTH PLANS/SPECIAL FEATURES:

Founded in 1865 and based in Germany, BASF is the world's largest chemical company, with products spanning the full chemical spectrum of commodity to specialty. In addition, the company is a strong player in agricultural crop protection chemicals and emissions control catalysts for cars and trucks. Given its sheer size, BASF has a top-three market position in approximately 70% of its businesses. The company is undergoing a transformation where it will divest the surface technologies and agricultural solutions businesses over the next several years. These two segments combine to generate nearly 35% of total revenue.

CONTACTS: *Note: Officers with more than one job title may be intentionally listed here more than once.*

Kurt Bock, Chairman of the Board
Sinischa Horvat, Co-Vice Chairman of the Board
Stefan Asenkerschbaumer, Co-Vice Chairman of the Board

FINANCIAL DATA: *Note: Data for latest year may not have been available at press time.*

In U.S. $	2024	2023	2022	2021	2020	2019
Revenue	74,074,914,077	78,208,856,710	99,122,586,404	89,214,525,117	67,138,479,872	67,328,034,942
R&D Expense	2,339,387,000	2,417,707,000	2,608,399,000	2,515,323,000	2,367,764,000	2,449,489,000
Operating Income	3,787,741,000	3,698,070,000	8,355,278,000	8,934,166,000	4,120,318,000	4,889,897,000
Operating Margin %	.05%	.05%	.08%	.10%	.06%	.07%
SGA Expense	11,632,240,000	11,684,450,000	12,636,780,000	11,148,690,000	9,903,519,000	10,467,650,000
Net Income	1,473,326,000	255,391,600	-711,691,300	6,269,012,000	-1,203,178,000	9,558,456,000
Operating Cash Flow	7,884,222,000	9,206,583,000	8,750,284,000	8,223,610,000	6,144,155,000	8,483,542,000
Capital Expenditure	7,035,187,000	6,123,723,000	4,965,948,000	4,009,081,000	3,551,646,000	4,340,522,000
EBITDA	8,820,658,000	8,322,361,000	6,936,436,000	13,316,680,000	6,659,478,000	9,493,757,000
Return on Assets %	.02%	.00%	-.01%	.07%	-.01%	.10%
Return on Equity %	.04%	.01%	-.02%	.15%	-.03%	.22%
Debt to Equity	.57%	.52%	.41%	.36%	0.501	0.388

CONTACT INFORMATION:

Phone: 49 621600   Fax: 49 6216042525
Toll-Free: 800-526-1072
Address: Carl-Bosch-Strasse 38, Ludwigshafen am Rhein, 67056 Germany

STOCK TICKER/OTHER:

Stock Ticker: BFFAF   Exchange: PINX
Employees: 111,991   Fiscal Year Ends: 12/31
Parent Company:

SALARIES/BONUSES:

Top Exec. Salary: $2,154,080   Bonus: $4,885,723
Second Exec. Salary: $1,432,463   Bonus: $3,249,968

OTHER THOUGHTS:

Estimated Female Officers or Directors: 2
Hot Spot for Advancement for Women/Minorities: Y

Bausch & Lomb Corp

www.bausch.com

NAIC Code: 339100

TYPES OF BUSINESS:

Supplies-Eye Care
Contact Lens Products
Ophthalmic Pharmaceuticals
Surgical Products
Product Development
Product Manufacture

BRANDS/DIVISIONS/AFFILIATES:

Bausch Health Companies Inc
Biotrue
Bausch + Lomb
PureVision
ReNu
Alaway
Alrex
PreserVision

CONTACTS: Note: Officers with more than one job title may be intentionally listed here more than once.

Brenton Saunders, CEO
Sam Eldessouky, CFO
Frederick Munsch, Chief Accounting Officer
A. Robert Bailey, Chief Legal Officer
Yehia Hashad, Chief Medical Officer
Andrew Stewart, President, Divisional
Luc Bonnefoy, President, Divisional

GROWTH PLANS/SPECIAL FEATURES:

Bausch & Lomb is one of the largest vision care companies in the US. The firm was previously a subsidiary under parent company Bausch Health and it was spun off to become a public company in 2022. It operates in three segments: vision care, surgical, and ophthalmic pharmaceuticals. Vision care is composed of contact lenses, a market that B&L controls 10%, and ocular health products, which includes Biotrue and Lumify. Surgical includes a suite of intraocular lenses, equipment for cataract and vitreoretinal surgeries, as well as surgical instruments. Ophthalmic pharmaceuticals has a diverse lineup of products, including Xipere, Vyzulta, and Lotemax that treat different complications. With over 100 products, B&L has the largest portfolio of eye care prescriptions in the space.

B&L offers its employees medical and dental coverage, a 401(k) account plan, a vacation buy/sell program, flexible spending accounts and education reimbursement.

FINANCIAL DATA: Note: Data for latest year may not have been available at press time.

In U.S. $	2024	2023	2022	2021	2020	2019
Revenue	4,791,000,064	4,145,999,872	3,768,000,000	3,764,999,936	3,412,000,000	3,777,999,872
R&D Expense	343,000,000	324,000,000	307,000,000	271,000,000	253,000,000	258,000,000
Operating Income	206,000,000	204,000,000	220,000,000	346,000,000	298,000,000	463,000,000
Operating Margin %	.04%	.05%	.06%	.09%	.09%	.12%
SGA Expense	2,082,000,000	1,736,000,000	1,478,000,000	1,389,000,000	1,253,000,000	1,382,000,000
Net Income	-317,000,000	-260,000,000	6,000,000	182,000,000	-18,000,000	298,000,000
Operating Cash Flow	232,000,000	-17,000,000	345,000,000	873,000,000	522,000,000	799,000,000
Capital Expenditure	291,000,000	181,000,000	175,000,000	193,000,000	259,000,000	180,000,000
EBITDA	601,000,000	499,000,000	598,000,000	733,000,000	732,000,000	932,000,000
Return on Assets %	-.02%	-.02%	.00%	.02%	.00%	.03%
Return on Equity %	-.05%	-.04%	.00%	.02%	.00%	.03%
Debt to Equity	.73%	.66%	.34%			

CONTACT INFORMATION:

Phone: 905 695-7700   Fax:
Toll-Free:
Address: 520 Applewood Crescent, Vaughan, ON L4K 4B4 Canada

STOCK TICKER/OTHER:

Stock Ticker: BLCO   Exchange: NYS
Employees: 13,300   Fiscal Year Ends: 12/31
Parent Company: Bausch Health Companies Inc

SALARIES/BONUSES:

Top Exec. Salary: $1,600,000   Bonus: $
Second Exec. Salary: $767,423   Bonus: $

OTHER THOUGHTS:

Estimated Female Officers or Directors: 1
Hot Spot for Advancement for Women/Minorities: Y

Baxter International Inc

NAIC Code: 339100   **www.baxter.com**

TYPES OF BUSINESS:

Medical Equipment Manufacturing
Healthcare Product Manufacturing
Critical Care Products
Hospital Care Products
Nutritional Care Products
Renal Care Products
Surgical Care Products

BRANDS/DIVISIONS/AFFILIATES:

Amia
Sharesource
Spectrum IQ Infusion System
Numeta G13E
Theranova
HDx
Floseal
Hill-Rom Holdings Inc

CONTACTS: *Note: Officers with more than one job title may be intentionally listed here more than once.*

Jose Almeida, CEO
Joel Grade, CFO
David Rosenbloom, Executive VP
James Borzi, Executive VP
Jeanne Mason, Executive VP
Christopher Toth, Executive VP
Reazur Rasul, Executive VP
Heather Knight, Executive VP
Alok Sonig, Executive VP

GROWTH PLANS/SPECIAL FEATURES:

Baxter offers a variety of medical supplies and equipment to providers. From its legacy operations, Baxter sells injectable therapies for use in care settings, including IV pumps, administrative sets, and solutions; nutritional products; and surgical sealants and hemostatic agents. Baxter expanded its portfolio of hospital-focused offerings by acquiring Hillrom in late 2021, which added basic equipment like hospital beds, operating room equipment, and patient monitoring tools to the portfolio. Baxter also sold its kidney care tools in early 2025.

FINANCIAL DATA: *Note: Data for latest year may not have been available at press time.*

In U.S. $	2024	2023	2022	2021	2020	2019
Revenue	10,636,000,256	10,360,000,512	10,056,999,936	12,145,999,872	11,672,999,936	11,361,999,872
R&D Expense	590,000,000	518,000,000	450,000,000	531,000,000	521,000,000	595,000,000
Operating Income	439,000,000	707,000,000	-33,000,000	1,344,000,000	1,597,000,000	1,772,000,000
Operating Margin %	.04%	.07%	.00%	.11%	.14%	.16%
SGA Expense	2,967,000,000	2,953,000,000	3,097,000,000	2,845,000,000	2,469,000,000	2,535,000,000
Net Income	-649,000,000	2,656,000,000	-2,433,000,000	1,284,000,000	1,102,000,000	1,001,000,000
Operating Cash Flow	1,019,000,000	1,726,000,000	1,211,000,000	2,222,000,000	1,868,000,000	2,104,000,000
Capital Expenditure	460,000,000	436,000,000	635,000,000	691,000,000	709,000,000	696,000,000
EBITDA	1,116,000,000	1,734,000,000	-1,763,000,000	2,190,000,000	2,268,000,000	1,870,000,000
Return on Assets %	-.02%	.09%	-.08%	.05%	.06%	.06%
Return on Equity %	-.08%	.37%	-.33%	.14%	.13%	.13%
Debt to Equity	1.52%	1.35%	2.69%	1.95%	0.724	0.675

CONTACT INFORMATION:

Phone: 847 948-2000   Fax: 847 948-2964
Toll-Free: 800-422-9837
Address: 1 Baxter Pkwy., Deerfield, IL 60015 United States

STOCK TICKER/OTHER:

Stock Ticker: BAX   Exchange: NYS
Employees: 60,000   Fiscal Year Ends: 12/31
Parent Company:

SALARIES/BONUSES:

Top Exec. Salary: $810,000   Bonus: $500,000
Second Exec. Salary: Bonus: $
$1,300,000

OTHER THOUGHTS:

Estimated Female Officers or Directors: 6
Hot Spot for Advancement for Women/Minorities: Y

Bayer AG

www.bayer.com

NAIC Code: 325412

TYPES OF BUSINESS:

Chemicals Manufacturing
Pharmaceuticals
Animal Health Products
Health Care Products
Crop Science
Plant Biotechnology
Over-the-Counter Drugs
Personal Care Products

BRANDS/DIVISIONS/AFFILIATES:

Capital Group International Inc
Aspirin
Aleve
Bepanthen
Canesten
Talcid
Elevit
Claritin

GROWTH PLANS/SPECIAL FEATURES:

Bayer is a German healthcare and agriculture conglomerate. Healthcare provides close to half of the company's sales and includes pharmaceutical drugs as well as vitamins and other consumer healthcare products. The firm's crop science business sells seeds, pesticides, herbicides, and fungicides, which was expanded through its 2018 acquisition of Monsanto.

CONTACTS: Note: Officers with more than one job title may be intentionally listed here more than once.

Norbert Winkeljohann, Chairman of the Board
Heike Hausfeld, Director

FINANCIAL DATA: Note: Data for latest year may not have been available at press time.

In U.S. $	2024	2023	2022	2021	2020	2019
Revenue	52,901,248,783	54,071,509,924	57,592,507,776	50,035,187,849	46,992,055,115	49,426,790,046
R&D Expense	7,047,673,000	6,096,481,000	7,459,705,000	6,143,019,000	8,088,536,000	6,017,027,000
Operating Income	3,776,391,000	9,121,453,000	8,323,496,000	7,842,225,000	-810,442,700	5,349,603,000
Operating Margin %	.07%	.17%	.14%	.16%	-.02%	.11%
SGA Expense	18,090,810,000	16,952,330,000	19,207,720,000	17,395,010,000	18,084,000,000	18,269,010,000
Net Income	-2,896,708,000	-3,338,252,000	4,710,556,000	1,135,074,000	-11,912,600,000	4,643,587,000
Operating Cash Flow	8,363,224,000	5,808,173,000	8,051,079,000	5,776,390,000	5,565,267,000	9,315,550,000
Capital Expenditure	3,153,235,000	3,122,588,000	3,347,333,000	2,963,678,000	2,744,608,000	3,007,945,000
EBITDA	9,996,595,000	11,856,980,000	14,790,010,000	7,320,091,000	-2,718,502,000	11,427,920,000
Return on Assets %	-.02%	-.02%	.03%	.01%	-.09%	.03%
Return on Equity %	-.08%	-.08%	.12%	.03%	-.27%	.09%
Debt to Equity	1.11%	1.16%	.87%	1.10%	1.088	0.781

CONTACT INFORMATION:

Phone: 49 214301   Fax: 49 2143066328
Toll-Free: 800-269-2377
Address: Kaiser-Wilhelm-Allee 1, Leverkusen, NW 51368 Germany

STOCK TICKER/OTHER:

Stock Ticker: BAYZF
Employees: 99,723
Parent Company:

Exchange: PINX
Fiscal Year Ends: 12/31

SALARIES/BONUSES:

Top Exec. Salary: $1,363,000   Bonus: $1,828,000
Second Exec. Salary: $899,000   Bonus: $1,051,000

OTHER THOUGHTS:

Estimated Female Officers or Directors: 1
Hot Spot for Advancement for Women/Minorities:

Bayer Corporation

NAIC Code: 325412

TYPES OF BUSINESS:

Chemicals Manufacturing
Pharmaceuticals
Product Development
Medicines
Pain Relievers
Dietary Supplements
Crop Seeds and Traits
Crop Protection Products

BRANDS/DIVISIONS/AFFILIATES:

Bayer AG
Afrin
Aleve
Alka-Seltzer
Bayer
Claritin
Midol
One A Day

CONTACTS: *Note: Officers with more than one job title may be intentionally listed here more than once.*

Lars Benecke, General Counsel
Stefan Scholz, VP-Corp. Auditing
Philip Blake, Head-Bayer Representative, U.S.
Mark Torsten Minuth, VP-Mergers & Acquisitions
Tracy Spagnol, VP
Bill Anderson, Chmn.-Corp.

GROWTH PLANS/SPECIAL FEATURES:

Bayer Corporation., the U.S. subsidiary of chemical and pharmaceutical giant Bayer AG, operates through three divisions: pharmaceuticals, consumer health and agriculture. The pharmaceuticals division discovers and develops medicines, with focus areas including women's healthcare, oncology, hemophilia, cardiovascular, renal, pulmonary hypertension and radiology. The consumer health unit manufactures pain relievers, allergy medications and dietary supplements, with brands including Afrin, Aleve, Alka-Seltzer, Bayer (aspirin), Claritin, Midol, MiraLAX and One A Day. The agriculture division develops, produces and offers a wide range of seeds and traits, crop protection products (fungicides, herbicides, insecticides) and related digital tools (data, software and infrastructure) and services for customers. Bayer works with brands to perfect corn, soy, cotton, sorghum, vegetables, alfalfa, canola, wheat and more; and works on behalf of U.S. farmers to develop new innovations in biotechnology, from gene editing to advanced plant breeding.

Bayer offers its employees life, disability, medical, dental and vision coverage; prescription drug reimbursement; a 401(k); and adoption assistance.

FINANCIAL DATA: *Note: Data for latest year may not have been available at press time.*

In U.S. $	2024	2023	2022	2021	2020	2019
Revenue	16,903,736,850	16,098,797,000	16,743,581,000	15,170,763,000	15,825,872,000	15,180,822,000
R&D Expense						
Operating Income						
Operating Margin %						
SGA Expense						
Net Income						
Operating Cash Flow						
Capital Expenditure						
EBITDA						
Return on Assets %						
Return on Equity %						
Debt to Equity						

CONTACT INFORMATION:

Phone: 862-404-3000   Fax: 781-356-0165
Toll-Free:
Address: 100 Bayer Blvd., Whippany, NJ 07981-0915 United States

STOCK TICKER/OTHER:

Stock Ticker: Subsidiary   Exchange:
Employees: 19,500   Fiscal Year Ends: 12/31
Parent Company: Bayer AG

SALARIES/BONUSES:

Top Exec. Salary: $ Bonus: $
Second Exec. Salary: $ Bonus: $

OTHER THOUGHTS:

Estimated Female Officers or Directors: 1
Hot Spot for Advancement for Women/Minorities:

Sales, profits and employees may be estimates. Financial information, benefits and other data can change quickly and may vary from those stated here.

Bayer HealthCare Pharmaceuticals Inc

www.bayer.com/en/pharma/pharmaceuticals

NAIC Code: 325412

TYPES OF BUSINESS:

Pharmaceuticals Discovery, Development & Manufacturing
Pharmaceuticals
Cardiology Treatments
Oncology Treatments
Hematology Treatments
Chronic Kidney Treatments
Eye and Aging Solutions
Hormonal and Reproductive Solutions

BRANDS/DIVISIONS/AFFILIATES:

Bayer AG

CONTACTS: Note: Officers with more than one job title may be intentionally listed here more than once.

Stefan Oelrich, Mngr.-Pharmaceuticals
Olivier Mauroy Bressier, CFO
Anne-Grethe Mortensen, CMO
Michael Devoy, Head-Medical Affairs & Pharmacovigilance
Jeanne Kehren, CIO
Oliver Renner, Head-Global Corp. Comm.

GROWTH PLANS/SPECIAL FEATURES:

Bayer HealthCare Pharmaceuticals, Inc. (Bayer Pharmaceuticals) is the pharmaceutical division and subsidiary of Bayer AG. The firm utilizes advanced technologies, collaboration and pipeline development for the manufacture and marketing of its prescription drugs and therapeutic products. Bayer Pharmaceuticals engages in seven main disease groups: cardiology, including thrombosis, heart attack, heart disease diagnosis, heart failure, high blood pressure, and stroke/atrial fibrillation; hematology; oncology, including gastrointestinal stromal tumor, breast cancer, kidney cancer, liver cancer, prostate cancer, TRK fusion cancer and thyroid cancer; chronic kidney disease; eye conditions, including age-related macular degeneration and diabetic macular edema; healthy aging, such as managing the costs associated with longer term care, and how to handle declining health at the local and global levels; and women's healthcare, including contraception, endometriosis, heavy menstrual bleeding, menopause, uterine fibroids and acne therapy. Innovation and technology categories by Bayer Pharmaceuticals span AAV therapeutics, stem cells, pharmacogenetics, biomarkers, precision medicine, and finding solutions for undruggable situations. Currently (May 2024), Bayer and Google Cloud are developing AI-powered healthcare applications for radiologists.

Bayer offers its employees health/wellbeing and other benefits, which vary per location.

FINANCIAL DATA: Note: Data for latest year may not have been available at press time.

In U.S. $	2024	2023	2022	2021	2020	2019
Revenue	4,999,341,900	4,761,278,000	4,578,151,400	4,705,122,000	4,734,865,200	4,524,240,000
R&D Expense						
Operating Income						
Operating Margin %						
SGA Expense						
Net Income						
Operating Cash Flow						
Capital Expenditure						
EBITDA						
Return on Assets %						
Return on Equity %						
Debt to Equity						

CONTACT INFORMATION:

Phone: 862-404-3000   Fax:
Toll-Free:
Address: 100 Bayer Blvd., Whippany, NJ 07981 United States

STOCK TICKER/OTHER:

Stock Ticker: Subsidiary
Employees: 7,900
Parent Company: Bayer AG

Exchange:
Fiscal Year Ends: 12/31

SALARIES/BONUSES:

Top Exec. Salary: $ Bonus: $
Second Exec. Salary: $ Bonus: $

OTHER THOUGHTS:

Estimated Female Officers or Directors:
Hot Spot for Advancement for Women/Minorities:

Sales, profits and employees may be estimates. Financial information, benefits and other data can change quickly and may vary from those stated here.

Bayerische Motoren Werke AG (BMW Group) www.bmwgroup.com

NAIC Code: 336111

TYPES OF BUSINESS:
Automobile Manufacturing
Financial Services
Motorcycles
Software
Consulting Services
Fleet Management
IT Solutions
Engines

BRANDS/DIVISIONS/AFFILIATES:
MINI
Rolls-Royce Motor Cars
BMW Motoren
Bavaria Wirtschaftsagentur GmbH
BMW Technik
X1
i4
C 650 GT

GROWTH PLANS/SPECIAL FEATURES:
BMW is a premium passenger car and motorcycle original equipment manufacturer, home to the brands BMW, Mini Cooper, Rolls-Royce, and BMW Motorrad. BMW sold 2.8 million vehicles in 2023 (2.6 million being passenger cars). In terms of sales volumes, Asia and Europe are BMW's largest regions, contributing 39% and 38%, respectively. BMW's core competence is in the "affordable" luxury channel, with limited exposure to high-end priced vehicles.

CONTACTS: Note: Officers with more than one job title may be intentionally listed here more than once.
Norbert Reithofer, Chairman of the Board
Martin Kimmich, Deputy Chairman
Kurt Bock, Deputy Chairman
Stefan Quandt, Deputy Chairman
Stefan Schmid, Deputy Chairman
Gerhard Kurz, Director

FINANCIAL DATA: Note: Data for latest year may not have been available at press time.

In U.S. $	2024	2023	2022	2021	2020	2019
Revenue	161,611,813,367	176,501,707,885	161,872,878,739	126,264,467,750	112,360,951,403	118,286,036,249
R&D Expense						
Operating Income	12,933,030,000	20,971,620,000	16,128,260,000	15,271,280,000	5,402,951,000	8,612,940,000
Operating Margin %	.08%	.12%	.10%	.12%	.05%	.07%
SGA Expense	12,821,790,000	12,514,190,000	12,049,940,000	10,480,140,000	9,982,974,000	10,632,240,000
Net Income	8,274,687,000	12,814,980,000	20,364,360,000	14,054,480,000	4,284,904,000	5,578,887,000
Operating Cash Flow	8,587,969,000	19,911,460,000	26,700,340,000	18,063,560,000	15,040,860,000	4,156,640,000
Capital Expenditure	13,853,580,000	12,350,740,000	10,272,420,000	7,513,053,000	6,980,704,000	7,834,279,000
EBITDA	22,921,680,000	30,335,980,000	36,668,560,000	25,869,470,000	13,415,440,000	15,475,600,000
Return on Assets %	.03%	.04%	.07%	.05%	.02%	.02%
Return on Equity %	.07%	.12%	.20%	.17%	.06%	.08%
Debt to Equity	.63%	.51%	.53%	.78%	1.026	1.105

CONTACT INFORMATION:
Phone: 49 89 3822 5858   Fax: 49 89 3821 4661
Toll-Free:
Address: Petuelring 130, BMW-HAUS, Munich, BY 80788 Germany

STOCK TICKER/OTHER:
Stock Ticker: BAMXF   Exchange: PINX
Employees: 154,950   Fiscal Year Ends: 12/31
Parent Company:

SALARIES/BONUSES:
Top Exec. Salary: $ Bonus: $
Second Exec. Salary: $ Bonus: $

OTHER THOUGHTS:
Estimated Female Officers or Directors: 5
Hot Spot for Advancement for Women/Minorities: Y

Beca Group Limited

www.beca.com

NAIC Code: 541330

TYPES OF BUSINESS:
Engineering Consulting Services
Engineering Consultancy
Artificial Intelligence
Business Digital Transformation
Earthquake Engineering
Buildings and Bridges
Water and Wastewater Treatment
Environmental Advisory

BRANDS/DIVISIONS/AFFILIATES:
BEYON
CAPEXinsights
Frankly AI
Beacon

CONTACTS: Note: Officers with more than one job title may be intentionally listed here more than once.
Amelia Linzey, CEO
Craig Price, COO
Mark Fleming, CFO
Anne Henry, Chief People & Culture Officer
Stuart Tucker, CTO

GROWTH PLANS/SPECIAL FEATURES:
Beca Group Limited provides engineering consultancy services for buildings, government, industrial, power, transport and water sectors. The firm is one of the largest employee-owned consultancies in the Asia Pacific, with 24 offices worldwide while delivering projects in more than 70 countries. Beca offers a broad line of services, including advisory, artificial intelligence, analytics/insight, building tuning, decarbonization planning, electrical engineering, geographic information systems, green buildings, industrial services, intelligent transport systems, laboratory engineering, logistics and operations, operations and maintenance, surveying, valuation, water resources management, software development and engineering, structural engineering, urban design, water/wastewater treatment and much more. Markets served by Beca include airports, bioenergy, brewing, buildings, chemicals and manufacturing, consumer foods, dairy, defense and national security, education, food and beverage, government advisory, green hydrogen, healthcare, land development, leisure and hospitality, meat, minerals and metals, Pacific development, power, rail, roads, transmission and distribution, transport and infrastructure, water, wood and fiber. Beca provides digital transformation services and solutions to businesses, connecting their assets, operations, people and processes into a tailored, integrated ecosystem. Digital products and services include Industry 4.0 consultancy, which provides manufacturers with an objective review of their production facilities; CAPEXinsights, an intuitive capital project portfolio solution; Digital Twins, used with the firm's BEYON platform to assist with time asset maintenance and performance; Frankly AI, an artificial intelligence consultant; and Beacon, which assesses and manages the impact of earthquakes on buildings and structures in real time.

FINANCIAL DATA: Note: Data for latest year may not have been available at press time.

In U.S. $	2024	2023	2022	2021	2020	2019
Revenue	430,500,000	410,000,000	393,907,573	382,607,959	355,281,950	373,981,000
R&D Expense						
Operating Income						
Operating Margin %						
SGA Expense						
Net Income						
Operating Cash Flow						
Capital Expenditure						
EBITDA						
Return on Assets %						
Return on Equity %						
Debt to Equity						

CONTACT INFORMATION:
Phone: 64-9-300-9000   Fax: 64-9-300-9300
Toll-Free:
Address: 21 Pitt St., Auckland, 1010 New Zealand

STOCK TICKER/OTHER:
Stock Ticker: Private
Employees: 3,700
Parent Company:

Exchange:
Fiscal Year Ends: 03/31

SALARIES/BONUSES:
Top Exec. Salary: $ Bonus: $
Second Exec. Salary: $ Bonus: $

OTHER THOUGHTS:
Estimated Female Officers or Directors:
Hot Spot for Advancement for Women/Minorities:

Bechtel Group Inc

NAIC Code: 237000

www.bechtel.com

TYPES OF BUSINESS:

Heavy Construction
Engineering Services
Project Engineering
Digitization Solutions
Innovation and Advanced Materials
Construction and Procurement Services
Startup and Operations Services
Tunneling

BRANDS/DIVISIONS/AFFILIATES:

GROWTH PLANS/SPECIAL FEATURES:

Bechtel Group, Inc. is a world-leading engineering company, offering services and solutions that create a cleaner, greener and safer world via projects, digitization, innovation and advanced materials. Services include construction, engineering, development/investment and finance, integrated engineering/procurement/construction (EPC), master planning, modularization, procurement, startup and operations, technology licensing and consulting, tunneling and sustainability services. Bechtel's market expertise spans defense and security, environmental cleanup, energy, infrastructure, advanced materials, chemicals, water and manufacturing and related technology. In business since 1898, Bechtel has completed more than 25,000 projects in 160 countries on all seven continents.

Bechtel Group offers its employees learning and development programs.

CONTACTS: *Note: Officers with more than one job title may be intentionally listed here more than once.*

Brendan Bechtel, CEO
Craig Albert, Pres.
Keith Hennessey, CFO
Justin Zaccaria, Chief Human Resources Officer
Michael Bailey, General Counsel
Charlene Wheeless, Head-Corp. Affairs
Anette Sparks, Controller
Steve Katzman, Pres., Asia
Jose Ivo, Pres., Americas
Charlene Wheeless, Head-Sustainability Svcs.
Michael Wilkinson, Head-Risk Mgmt.
Brendan Bechtel, Chmn.
David Welch, Pres., EMEA

FINANCIAL DATA: *Note: Data for latest year may not have been available at press time.*

In U.S. $	2024	2023	2022	2021	2020	2019
Revenue	17,115,000,000	16,300,000,000	17,500,000,000	17,600,000,000	17,600,000,000	21,800,000,000
R&D Expense						
Operating Income						
Operating Margin %						
SGA Expense						
Net Income						
Operating Cash Flow						
Capital Expenditure						
EBITDA						
Return on Assets %						
Return on Equity %						
Debt to Equity						

CONTACT INFORMATION:

Phone: 571-392-6300　　Fax:
Toll-Free:
Address: 12011 Sunset Hills Rd., Reston, VA 20190-5918 United States

STOCK TICKER/OTHER:

Stock Ticker: Private　　　　Exchange:
Employees: 50,000　　　　　Fiscal Year Ends: 12/31
Parent Company:

SALARIES/BONUSES:

Top Exec. Salary: $　　　　Bonus: $
Second Exec. Salary: $　　　Bonus: $

OTHER THOUGHTS:

Estimated Female Officers or Directors: 4
Hot Spot for Advancement for Women/Minorities: Y

Beckman Coulter Inc

www.beckmancoulter.com

NAIC Code: 334510

TYPES OF BUSINESS:

Electromedical and Electrotherapeutic Apparatus Manufacturing
Chemistry Systems
Genetic Analysis/Nucleic Acid Testing
Biomedical Research Supplies
Immunoassay Systems
Cellular Systems
Discovery & Automation Systems

BRANDS/DIVISIONS/AFFILIATES:

Danaher Corporation
Access SARS-CoV-2 IgM
StoCastic LLC

CONTACTS:
Note: Officers with more than one job title may be intentionally listed here more than once.

Kevin O'Reilly, Pres.
Terry Walsh, Sr. VP-Global Oper.
Tom Coffman, CFO
Grady Davis, Sr. VP-Global Mktg.
Peggy Quirk, Sr. VP-Human Resources
Pedro Diaz, Dir.-Research
Tom Neufelder, CTO
John Blackwood, Sr. VP-Product Mgmt.
Jeff Linton, Sr. VP
Ken Hyek, Dir.-Service Oper.
Allan Harris, Sr. VP-Strategy & Bus. Dev.
Jerry Battenberg, VP-Finance
Clair O'Donovan, Sr. VP-Quality & Regulatory Affairs
Jennifer Honeycutt, Pres., Life Sciences
Richard Creager, Sr. VP
Michael K. Samoszuk, VP
Brian Burnett, Sr. VP-Global Oper.

GROWTH PLANS/SPECIAL FEATURES:

Beckman Coulter, Inc., a wholly owned subsidiary of Danaher Corporation, designs, develops, manufactures and markets clinical diagnostic products and laboratory solutions. The company's products and solutions are used in clinical settings worldwide to deliver test results. Disciplines of the firm encompass automation, blood banking, clinical chemistry, clinical centrifugation, clinical information management tools, hematology, immunoassay, microbiology, protein chemistry and urinalysis. Diagnostic solutions include sepsis diagnosis and management, early sepsis indicator, cardiovascular disease, reproductive health, anemia, drug monitoring & detection and life sciences. Beckman's Access SARS-CoV-2 Immunoglobulin M (IgM) assay is an antibody test that demonstrated 99.9% specificity against 1,400 negative samples and 98.3% sensitivity at 15-30 days post-symptom onset. Access SARS-CoV-2 IgG II received U.S. Emergency Use Authorization from the U.S. Food and Drug Administration, which measures a patient's level of antibodies in response to a previous SARS-CoV-2 infection and provides a qualitative and numerical result of antibodies in arbitrary units. Headquartered in California, the firm has additional centers in Minnesota and Florida.

Beckman offers its employees medical, dental and vision coverage; a wellness program; a 401(k) and company retirement plan; life insurance; disability income protection; credit union membership; and employee discounts.

FINANCIAL DATA:
Note: Data for latest year may not have been available at press time.

In U.S. $	2024	2023	2022	2021	2020	2019
Revenue	7,226,557,800	6,882,436,000	6,617,727,000	6,606,927,000	6,232,950,000	6,561,000,000
R&D Expense						
Operating Income						
Operating Margin %						
SGA Expense						
Net Income						
Operating Cash Flow						
Capital Expenditure						
EBITDA						
Return on Assets %						
Return on Equity %						
Debt to Equity						

CONTACT INFORMATION:

Phone: 714-993-5321   Fax: 800-232-3828
Toll-Free: 800-526-3821
Address: 250 S. Kraemer Blvd., Brea, CA 92821 United States

STOCK TICKER/OTHER:

Stock Ticker: Subsidiary
Employees: 11,000
Parent Company: Danaher Corporation

Exchange:
Fiscal Year Ends: 12/31

SALARIES/BONUSES:

Top Exec. Salary: $ Bonus: $
Second Exec. Salary: $ Bonus: $

OTHER THOUGHTS:

Estimated Female Officers or Directors: 5
Hot Spot for Advancement for Women/Minorities: Y

Becton Dickinson and Company

www.bd.com

NAIC Code: 339100

TYPES OF BUSINESS:

Medical Equipment-Injection/Infusion
Drug Delivery Systems
Infusion Therapy Products
Diabetes Care Products
Surgical Products
Microbiology Products
Diagnostic Products
Consulting Services

BRANDS/DIVISIONS/AFFILIATES:

BD Medical
BD Life Sciences
BD Interventional
V Mueller

GROWTH PLANS/SPECIAL FEATURES:

Becton, Dickinson is the world's largest manufacturer and distributor of medical surgical products, such as needles, syringes, and sharps-disposal units. The company also manufactures prefilled devices, diagnostic instruments and reagents, as well as flow cytometry and cell-imaging systems. BD Medical is nearly half of the total business, while BD Life Sciences (27% of 2024 revenue) and BD Interventional (24%) account for the remainder. International revenue accounts for 43% of the company's business.

BD offers its employees comprehensive benefits.

CONTACTS: Note: Officers with more than one job title may be intentionally listed here more than once.

Thomas Polen, CEO
Christopher DelOrefice, CFO
Pamela Spikner, Chief Accounting Officer
Antoine Ezell, Chief Marketing Officer
Michelle Quinn, Executive VP
Shana Neal, Executive VP
David Shan, Executive VP
Michael Garrison, Executive VP
Richard Byrd, Executive VP
Michael Feld, Executive VP
Pavan Kumar Mocherla, Executive VP
Roland Goette, Executive VP

FINANCIAL DATA: Note: Data for latest year may not have been available at press time.

In U.S. $	2024	2023	2022	2021	2020	2019
Revenue	20,177,999,872	19,371,999,232	18,869,999,616	19,131,000,832	16,074,000,384	17,290,000,384
R&D Expense	1,190,000,000	1,237,000,000	1,256,000,000	1,279,000,000	1,039,000,000	1,062,000,000
Operating Income	2,856,000,000	2,424,000,000	2,475,000,000	2,430,000,000	1,211,000,000	2,240,000,000
Operating Margin %	.14%	.13%	.13%	.13%	.08%	.13%
SGA Expense	4,857,000,000	4,719,000,000	4,709,000,000	4,719,000,000	4,185,000,000	4,332,000,000
Net Income	1,705,000,000	1,484,000,000	1,779,000,000	2,092,000,000	874,000,000	1,233,000,000
Operating Cash Flow	3,797,000,000	2,989,000,000	2,633,000,000	4,648,000,000	3,539,000,000	3,330,000,000
Capital Expenditure	725,000,000	874,000,000	973,000,000	1,194,000,000	769,000,000	957,000,000
EBITDA	4,819,000,000	4,402,000,000	4,410,000,000	4,391,000,000	3,057,000,000	4,068,000,000
Return on Assets %	.03%	.03%	.03%	.04%	.01%	.02%
Return on Equity %	.07%	.06%	.07%	.08%	.03%	.05%
Debt to Equity	.69%	.57%	.55%	.72%	0.725	0.858

CONTACT INFORMATION:

Phone: 201 847-6800   Fax:
Toll-Free: 800-284-6845
Address: 1 Becton Dr., Franklin Lakes, NJ 07417-1880 United States

STOCK TICKER/OTHER:

Stock Ticker: BDX   Exchange: NYS
Employees: 72,000   Fiscal Year Ends: 09/30
Parent Company:

SALARIES/BONUSES:

Top Exec. Salary: $1,354,813   Bonus: $
Second Exec. Salary: Bonus: $
$785,400

OTHER THOUGHTS:

Estimated Female Officers or Directors: 6
Hot Spot for Advancement for Women/Minorities: Y

Belden Inc

www.belden.com

NAIC Code: 334417

TYPES OF BUSINESS:

Cable & Wire Connectors Manufacturing
Electronic Products
Broadcasting Equipment
Aerospace & Automotive Electronics
Enclosures

BRANDS/DIVISIONS/AFFILIATES:

OTN Systems NV

GROWTH PLANS/SPECIAL FEATURES:

Belden Inc provides signal transmission products to distributors, end-users, installers, and original equipment manufacturers. The firm operates in two segments - Smart Infrastructure Solutions and Automation Solutions. Smart Infrastructure Solutions segment is a provider in network infrastructure and broadband solutions, as well as cabling and connectivity solutions for commercial audio/video and security applications. Automation Solutions segment provides network infrastructure and digitization solutions to enable customers to make data-based business decisions. It operates in Americas, EMEA and APAC, out of which maximum revenue from Americas.

CONTACTS: Note: Officers with more than one job title may be intentionally listed here more than once.

Ashish Chand, CEO
Jeremy Parks, CFO
David Aldrich, Chairman of the Board
Douglas Zink, Chief Accounting Officer
Brian Lieser, Executive VP, Divisional
Jay Wirts, Executive VP, Divisional
Brian Anderson, General Counsel
Leah Tate, Senior VP, Divisional

FINANCIAL DATA: Note: Data for latest year may not have been available at press time.

In U.S. $	2024	2023	2022	2021	2020	2019
Revenue	2,460,978,944	2,512,083,968	2,606,484,992	2,301,260,032	1,752,192,000	2,131,277,952
R&D Expense	112,365,000	116,427,000	104,350,000	90,227,000	73,020,000	94,360,000
Operating Income	266,460,000	305,462,000	325,443,000	272,959,000	150,114,000	207,207,000
Operating Margin %	.11%	.12%	.12%	.12%	.09%	.10%
SGA Expense	494,603,000	492,702,000	448,636,000	378,027,000	323,447,000	417,329,000
Net Income	198,433,000	242,759,000	254,663,000	63,925,000	-55,162,000	-377,015,000
Operating Cash Flow	352,076,000	319,638,000	281,296,000	272,055,000	173,364,000	276,893,000
Capital Expenditure	129,100,000	116,731,000	105,094,000	94,632,000	90,215,000	110,002,000
EBITDA	381,986,000	418,827,000	449,685,000	377,461,000	258,406,000	347,483,000
Return on Assets %	.06%	.08%	.08%	.02%	-.02%	-.11%
Return on Equity %	.16%	.21%	.24%	.07%	-.06%	-.34%
Debt to Equity	.95%	1.10%	1.07%	1.59%	2.158	1.558

CONTACT INFORMATION:

Phone: 314 854-8000   Fax: 314 854-8001
Toll-Free: 800-235-3361
Address: 1 N. Brentwood Blvd., 15/Fl, St. Louis, MO 63105 United States

STOCK TICKER/OTHER:

Stock Ticker: BDC   Exchange: NYS
Employees: 8,000   Fiscal Year Ends: 12/31
Parent Company:

SALARIES/BONUSES:

Top Exec. Salary: $937,500   Bonus: $
Second Exec. Salary: $605,034   Bonus: $

OTHER THOUGHTS:

Estimated Female Officers or Directors: 2
Hot Spot for Advancement for Women/Minorities: Y

Sales, profits and employees may be estimates. Financial information, benefits and other data can change quickly and may vary from those stated here.

Benchmark Electronics Inc

NAIC Code: 334418

www.bench.com

TYPES OF BUSINESS:

Printed Circuit Assembly (Electronic Assembly) Manufacturing
Design & Engineering
Printed Circuit Boards

BRANDS/DIVISIONS/AFFILIATES:

GROWTH PLANS/SPECIAL FEATURES:

Benchmark Electronics Inc is engaged in product designing, engineering services, technology solutions, and manufacturing services (electronic manufacturing services (EMS) and precision technology services). It serves various industries, including aerospace & defense (A&D), medical technologies, complex industrials, semiconductor capital equipment, next-generation telecommunications, and high-end computing. Its geographical segments are the Americas, Asia and Europe of which key revenue is derived from the Americas.

CONTACTS: *Note: Officers with more than one job title may be intentionally listed here more than once.*

Jeffrey Benck, CEO
Bryan Schumaker, CFO
David Scheible, Chairman of the Board
Scott Hicar, Chief Information Officer
Stephen Beaver, Chief Legal Officer
Jan Janick, Chief Technology Officer
David Valkanoff, COO
David Moezidis, Executive VP
Rhonda Turner, Other Executive Officer
David Clark, Other Executive Officer

FINANCIAL DATA: *Note: Data for latest year may not have been available at press time.*

In U.S. $	2024	2023	2022	2021	2020	2019
Revenue	2,656,104,960	2,838,976,000	2,886,330,880	2,255,319,040	2,053,131,008	2,268,094,976
R&D Expense						
Operating Income	115,747,000	118,066,000	98,636,000	62,817,000	43,754,000	49,327,000
Operating Margin %	.04%	.04%	.03%	.03%	.02%	.02%
SGA Expense	149,460,000	147,025,000	150,215,000	136,700,000	122,195,000	126,740,000
Net Income	63,327,000	64,315,000	68,229,000	35,770,000	14,055,000	23,425,000
Operating Cash Flow	189,225,000	174,294,000	-177,467,000	-2,622,000	120,438,000	93,136,000
Capital Expenditure	33,253,000	77,739,000	46,774,000	42,177,000	39,519,000	35,118,000
EBITDA	156,961,000	158,505,000	141,488,000	98,031,000	74,449,000	82,360,000
Return on Assets %	.03%	.03%	.03%	.02%	.01%	.01%
Return on Equity %	.06%	.06%	.07%	.04%	.01%	.02%
Debt to Equity	.32%	.42%	.40%	.23%	0.205	0.204

CONTACT INFORMATION:

Phone: 979 849-6550   Fax:
Toll-Free:
Address: 3000 Technology Dr., Angleton, TX 77515 United States

STOCK TICKER/OTHER:

Stock Ticker: BHE
Employees: 12,703
Parent Company:

Exchange: NYS
Fiscal Year Ends: 12/31

SALARIES/BONUSES:

Top Exec. Salary: $1,004,615   Bonus: $
Second Exec. Salary: Bonus: $
$517,377

OTHER THOUGHTS:

Estimated Female Officers or Directors: 2
Hot Spot for Advancement for Women/Minorities:

Bilfinger SE

www.bilfingerberger.com

NAIC Code: 237000

TYPES OF BUSINESS:

Heavy Construction
Industrial Services
Technology
Engineering
Digitalization
Automation
Energy Transition

GROWTH PLANS/SPECIAL FEATURES:

Bilfinger SE is an international industrial services provider. It delivers customized engineering services to customers in the chemical, pharmaceutical, energy, oil, and gas markets. Its product portfolio attempts to cover the entire value chain, from consulting and planning to installation and maintenance. Bilfinger has three operating segments: Engineering & Maintenance Europe, Engineering & Maintenance International, and Technologies. A majority of the sales are derived from Europe, with Germany being an important region for the company.

BRANDS/DIVISIONS/AFFILIATES:

Bilfinger Connected Asset Performance
PIDGraph

CONTACTS: Note: Officers with more than one job title may be intentionally listed here more than once.

Eckhard Cordes, Chairman of the Board
Stephan Bruckner, Deputy Chairman

FINANCIAL DATA: Note: Data for latest year may not have been available at press time.

In U.S. $	2024	2023	2022	2021	2020	2019
Revenue	5,717,934,063	5,091,487,243	4,894,438,144	4,242,224,822	3,928,490,283	4,911,350,997
R&D Expense						
Operating Income	264,926,200	203,291,700	146,424,500	110,896,700	-5,788,877	41,884,220
Operating Margin %	.05%	.04%	.03%	.03%	.00%	.01%
SGA Expense	357,775,300	338,025,000	349,035,200	329,966,000	351,532,400	430,760,500
Net Income	203,745,700	206,015,900	32,009,080	146,992,000	112,826,300	27,468,790
Operating Cash Flow	273,666,300	164,358,700	179,341,700	130,533,500	129,398,400	88,762,770
Capital Expenditure	71,736,660	66,515,320	58,683,320	69,580,020	41,543,700	72,190,700
EBITDA	470,147,600	356,299,600	204,767,300	280,136,200	307,037,500	183,087,400
Return on Assets %	.05%	.06%	.01%	.04%	.03%	.01%
Return on Equity %	.15%	.16%	.02%	.10%	.08%	.02%
Debt to Equity	.24%	.25%	.36%	.30%	0.431	0.473

CONTACT INFORMATION:

Phone: 49 6214590   Fax: 49 6214592366
Toll-Free:
Address: Oskar-Meixner-Street 1, Mannheim, 68163 Germany

STOCK TICKER/OTHER:

Stock Ticker: BFLBY   Exchange: PINX
Employees: 28,650   Fiscal Year Ends: 12/31
Parent Company:

SALARIES/BONUSES:

Top Exec. Salary: $ Bonus: $
Second Exec. Salary: $ Bonus: $

OTHER THOUGHTS:

Estimated Female Officers or Directors:
Hot Spot for Advancement for Women/Minorities:

Bilfinger Tebodin BV

www.tebodin.bilfinger.com

NAIC Code: 541330

TYPES OF BUSINESS:

Engineering Services
Industrial Engineering
Industrial Consultancy
Project Management
Construction Management
Engineering and Construction Technology
Digitalization Services
Energy Transition Services

BRANDS/DIVISIONS/AFFILIATES:

Bilfinger SE
Bilfinger Project Solution

CONTACTS: Note: Officers with more than one job title may be intentionally listed here more than once.

Thomas Schulz, CEO

GROWTH PLANS/SPECIAL FEATURES:

Bilfinger Tebodin BV is the global consultancy and engineering arm of industrial services provider Bilfinger SE. Bilfinger collaborates with its clients regarding project- and construction management, from start to finish. The firm delivers its services in two service lines: Engineering & Maintenance and Technologies. Product categories by the company include consultancy, design and engineering, project management, procurement, construction management, digitalization, energy transition and related solutions. Markets served by Bilfinger include chemicals and petrochemicals, energy, oil and gas, pharmaceuticals and biopharmaceuticals, nutrition and pure water. The company's network is active in 30 countries and is primarily made up of consultants and engineers specializing in technology. Bilfinger developed and offers a modular and comprehensive product, Bilfinger Project Solution, created using experiences and approaches developed throughout the firm's lifecycle. This product offers its customers advantages such as efficiency, high levels of safety, integrated processes and methods, multidisciplinary expertise and internal production.

Bilfinger Tebodin offers traineeship for senior and graduate students.

FINANCIAL DATA: Note: Data for latest year may not have been available at press time.

In U.S. $	2024	2023	2022	2021	2020	2019
Revenue	108,150,000	103,000,000	99,176,000	83,795,712	80,572,800	87,685,100
R&D Expense						
Operating Income						
Operating Margin %						
SGA Expense						
Net Income						
Operating Cash Flow						
Capital Expenditure						
EBITDA						
Return on Assets %						
Return on Equity %						
Debt to Equity						

CONTACT INFORMATION:

Phone: 31-88-996-7000   Fax:
Toll-Free:
Address: Laan van Nieuw Oost-indie 25, Den Haag, 2593 BJ Netherlands

STOCK TICKER/OTHER:

Stock Ticker: Subsidiary   Exchange:
Employees: 1,350   Fiscal Year Ends:
Parent Company: Bilfinger SE

SALARIES/BONUSES:

Top Exec. Salary: $ Bonus: $
Second Exec. Salary: $ Bonus: $

OTHER THOUGHTS:

Estimated Female Officers or Directors:
Hot Spot for Advancement for Women/Minorities:

Biogen Inc

www.biogen.com

NAIC Code: 325412

TYPES OF BUSINESS:

Drugs-Immunology, Neurology & Oncology
Autoimmune & Inflammatory Disease Treatments
Drugs-Multiple Sclerosis
Drugs-Cancer

BRANDS/DIVISIONS/AFFILIATES:

TECFIDERA
AVONEX
PLEGRIDY
SPINRAZA
FUMADERM
RITUXAN
GAZYVA
OCREVUS

GROWTH PLANS/SPECIAL FEATURES:

Biogen and Idec merged in 2003, combining forces to market Biogen's multiple sclerosis drug Avonex and Idec's cancer drug Rituxan. Today, Rituxan and next-generation antibody Gazyva (oncology) and Ocrevus (multiple sclerosis) are marketed via a collaboration with Roche. Biogen markets several multiple sclerosis drugs including Plegridy, Tysabri, Tecfidera, and Vumerity. Biogen's newer products include Spinraza (SMA, with partner Ionis), Leqembi (Alzheimers, with partner Eisai), Skyclarys (Friedreich's Ataxia, Reata), Zurzuvae (postpartum depression, Sage), and Qalsody (ALS, Ionis). Biogen has several drug candidates in phase 3 trials in neurology, immunology, and rare diseases.

Biogen offers its employees medical, dental and vision insurance; tuition reimbursement; flexible spending accounts; and an employee assistance program.

CONTACTS: Note: Officers with more than one job title may be intentionally listed here more than once.

Christopher Viehbacher, CEO
Michael Mcdonnell, CFO
Caroline Dorsa, Chairman of the Board
Robin Kramer, Chief Accounting Officer
Susan Alexander, Chief Legal Officer
Sean Godbout, Controller
Jane Grogan, Executive VP, Divisional
Rachid Izzar, Executive VP, Divisional
Nicole Murphy, Executive VP, Divisional
Adam Keeney, Executive VP, Divisional
Priya Singhal, Executive VP
Ginger Gregory, Executive VP

FINANCIAL DATA: Note: Data for latest year may not have been available at press time.

In U.S. $	2024	2023	2022	2021	2020	2019
Revenue	9,675,899,904	9,835,599,872	10,173,400,064	10,981,699,584	13,444,599,808	14,377,900,032
R&D Expense	2,041,800,000	2,462,000,000	2,231,100,000	2,501,200,000	3,990,900,000	2,280,600,000
Operating Income	2,218,900,000	1,831,100,000	2,901,900,000	2,808,000,000	4,446,300,000	7,035,700,000
Operating Margin %	.23%	.19%	.29%	.26%	.33%	.49%
SGA Expense	2,403,700,000	2,549,700,000	2,403,600,000	2,674,300,000	2,504,500,000	2,374,700,000
Net Income	1,632,200,000	1,161,100,000	3,046,900,000	1,556,100,000	4,000,600,000	5,888,500,000
Operating Cash Flow	2,875,500,000	1,547,200,000	1,384,300,000	3,639,900,000	4,229,800,000	7,078,600,000
Capital Expenditure	359,800,000	311,400,000	243,200,000	294,900,000	551,800,000	669,500,000
EBITDA	2,829,500,000	2,038,500,000	4,356,800,000	2,880,100,000	5,734,800,000	7,803,200,000
Return on Assets %	.06%	.05%	.13%	.06%	.15%	.22%
Return on Equity %	.10%	.08%	.25%	.14%	.33%	.45%
Debt to Equity	.29%	.49%	.49%	.61%	0.732	0.365

CONTACT INFORMATION:

Phone: 617-679-2000   Fax: 619 679-2617
Toll-Free:
Address: 225 Binney St., Cambridge, MA 02142 United States

STOCK TICKER/OTHER:

Stock Ticker: BIIB   Exchange: NAS
Employees: 7,570   Fiscal Year Ends: 12/31
Parent Company:

SALARIES/BONUSES:

Top Exec. Salary: $1,600,000   Bonus: $
Second Exec. Salary: Bonus: $
$992,531

OTHER THOUGHTS:

Estimated Female Officers or Directors: 4
Hot Spot for Advancement for Women/Minorities: Y

BIOS-BIOENERGYSYSTEME GmbH

www.bios-bioenergy.at

NAIC Code: 541330

TYPES OF BUSINESS:

Biomass Plant Design & Development
Biomass Fuel Energy Processing
Research and Development
Biomass Power Production
Heat, Cold and Combined Power
Computational Fluid Dynamics
Biomass Combustion, Gasification
Software and Technologies

BRANDS/DIVISIONS/AFFILIATES:

BIOBIL 2020
DATEVAL1.0

CONTACTS: *Note: Officers with more than one job title may be intentionally listed here more than once.*

Ingwald Obernberger, Managing Dir.

GROWTH PLANS/SPECIAL FEATURES:

BIOS-BIOENERGYSYSTEME GmbH is engaged in the research, development, design and optimization of processes and plants for heat, cold and power production via biomass fuels. The company specializes in computational fluid dynamics (CFD) simulation of biomass combustion, gasification and pyrolysis processes regarding new technologies as well as for the optimization and refurbishment of existing plants. BIOS operates testing and laboratory facilities for its research and development activities and works in close collaboration with national and international partners along its innovative path. BIOS partners for the planning of innovative and sustainable system solutions for heat generation, combined heat, power and cooling plants, industrial waste heat utilization, energy centers for industry and district heating networks, as well as for pellet production, biomass torrefaction and biorefinery plants based on biomass pyrolysis. Biogenic raw materials and other solid, liquid and gaseous fuels are considered. BIOS' plant monitoring services and solutions provide detailed evaluation of the performance of overall plants and of single plant components, from the start-up phase and the first year of operations through to trouble shooting. BIOS focuses on the sustainable utilization of biomass ashes and the consequent development and improvement of ash utilization processes, serving clients and customers such as municipalities and local authorities, utilities and municipal energy suppliers, heat supply companies, sawmills and wood industry, window/door/furniture industry, hotels, waste treatment/recycling/disposal companies, composting plants and other industries. BIOS' commercially available software programs and customer-specific software include: BIOBIL version 2020, offers detailed mass and energy balance calculations for combustion processes; and DATEVAL 1.0, an application for the evaluation and validation of operating data of biomass combustion and biomass combined heat and power plants. Quality management solutions and services are also provided by BIOS.

FINANCIAL DATA: *Note: Data for latest year may not have been available at press time.*

In U.S. $	2024	2023	2022	2021	2020	2019
Revenue	53,976,000	70,720,000	66,000,000	6,386,869	6,141,220	6,100,000
R&D Expense						
Operating Income						
Operating Margin %						
SGA Expense						
Net Income						
Operating Cash Flow						
Capital Expenditure						
EBITDA						
Return on Assets %						
Return on Equity %						
Debt to Equity						

CONTACT INFORMATION:

Phone: 43-316-481-300   Fax: 43-316-481-300-4
Toll-Free:
Address: Hedwig-Katschinka-Strasse 4, Graz, A-8020 Austria

STOCK TICKER/OTHER:

Stock Ticker: Private   Exchange:
Employees: 25   Fiscal Year Ends: 12/31
Parent Company:

SALARIES/BONUSES:

Top Exec. Salary: $ Bonus: $
Second Exec. Salary: $ Bonus: $

OTHER THOUGHTS:

Estimated Female Officers or Directors: 4
Hot Spot for Advancement for Women/Minorities: Y

Black & Veatch Holding Company

www.bv.com

NAIC Code: 541330

TYPES OF BUSINESS:

Heavy & Civil Engineering, Construction
Engineering and Procurement
Engineering Consulting
Construction Services
New Energy and Grid Solutions
Infrastructure and Civil Solutions
Clean Transportation
Land Services and Acquisition

BRANDS/DIVISIONS/AFFILIATES:

Diode Ventures
Black & Veatch Construction Inc
Overland Contracting Inc
Bird Electric

CONTACTS: Note: Officers with more than one job title may be intentionally listed here more than once.

Mario Azar, CEO
Jennifer Divito, Pres.-Oper.
Michael Williams, CFO
Andrea Bernica, Chief People Officer
James R. Lewis, Chief Admin. Officer
Timothy W. Triplett, General Counsel
Cindy Wallis-Lage, Pres., Water
O.H. Oskvig, CEO-Energy Business
William R. Van Dyke, Pres., Federal Svcs.
Mario Azar, Chmn.
Hoe Wai Cheong, Sr. VP-Water-Asia Pacific
John E. Murphy, Pres., Construction & Procurement

GROWTH PLANS/SPECIAL FEATURES:

Black & Veatch Holding Company (B&V) is a 100% employee-owned engineering, procurement, consulting and construction company, with global offices spanning the Americas, Europe, the Middle East, Africa and Asia Pacific. In business since 1915, B&V specializes in the following industries: commercial, connected communities, data centers, food and beverage, gas/fuels and chemicals, governments, industrial and manufacturing, management consulting, mining, power utilities, telecommunications, transportation and water. Services by the company are vast, including advisory, clean transportation, distributed energy, federal design and integrated solutions, infrastructure development, land services and acquisition, new energy, process, communications infrastructure and more. B&V holds a portfolio of four companies, including: Diode Ventures, specializing in turnkey asset development for renewable energy, data centers and specialized infrastructure; Black & Veatch Construction, Inc., which provides construction services to markets, such as power, water and communications; Overland Contracting, Inc., an industry leader in building vital infrastructure; and Bird Electric, an electrical construction service provider.

Black & Veatch offers its employees healthcare options, financial planning resources, continuing education, career development and employee ownership plans.

FINANCIAL DATA: Note: Data for latest year may not have been available at press time.

In U.S. $	2024	2023	2022	2021	2020	2019
Revenue	4,515,000,000	4,300,000,000	3,300,000,000	3,801,451,500	3,586,275,000	3,622,500,000
R&D Expense						
Operating Income						
Operating Margin %						
SGA Expense						
Net Income						
Operating Cash Flow						
Capital Expenditure						
EBITDA						
Return on Assets %						
Return on Equity %						
Debt to Equity						

CONTACT INFORMATION:

Phone: 913-458-4300   Fax: 913-458-2934
Toll-Free:
Address: 11401 Lamar Ave., Overland Park, KS 66211 United States

STOCK TICKER/OTHER:

Stock Ticker: Private   Exchange:
Employees: 12,000   Fiscal Year Ends: 12/31
Parent Company:

SALARIES/BONUSES:

Top Exec. Salary: $ Bonus: $
Second Exec. Salary: $ Bonus: $

OTHER THOUGHTS:

Estimated Female Officers or Directors: 4
Hot Spot for Advancement for Women/Minorities: Y

BMC Software Inc

NAIC Code: 511210H

www.bmc.com

TYPES OF BUSINESS:

Computer Software, Mainframe Related
Systems Management Software
eBusiness Software
Consulting & Training Services
Workload Automation
Multi-Cloud Management Solutions
Security and Compliance Solutions
Artificial Intelligence

BRANDS/DIVISIONS/AFFILIATES:

KKR & Co Inc

GROWTH PLANS/SPECIAL FEATURES:

BMC Software, Inc. is a software vendor company that provides system management, service management and automation solutions primarily for large companies. BMC's solutions are grouped into four categories: service management, automation, operations and mainframe. Service management solutions offer IT Service Management (ITSM) software and tools, which are fast, accurate and cost-effective, whether users want to operate in the cloud, a hybrid model or a data center. Automation solutions increase efficiency, productivity and reliability across applications, data and infrastructure. These solutions are spread across workload automation, data center automation and TrueSight orchestration. IT Operations Management (ITOM) solutions optimize the performance, cost and security of the apps and services delivered by users. Lastly, mainframe solutions automate and simplify mainframe management to unlock the full potential of a mainframe by leveraging DevOps, AIOps, DataOps and security. BMC Software operates as a subsidiary of KKR & Co., Inc.

CONTACTS: Note: Officers with more than one job title may be intentionally listed here more than once.

Ayman Sayed, CEO
Michelle Carbone, Sr. VP-Oper.
Marc Rothman, CFO
Martyn Etherington, CMO
Eric Olmo, Sr. VP-People & Spaces
Ram Chakravarti, CTO
Hollie Castro, Sr. VP-Admin.
Patrick K. Tagtow, General Counsel
Steve Goddard, Sr. VP-Bus. Oper.
Ken Berryman, Sr. VP-Strategy & Corp. Dev.
Ann Duhon, Mgr.-Comm.
Derrick Vializ, VP-Investor Rel.
T. Cory Bleuer, Chief Acct. Officer
Patrick K. Tagtow, Chief Compliance Officer
Paul Avenant, Sr. VP-Solutions
Bill Green, Chmn.

FINANCIAL DATA: Note: Data for latest year may not have been available at press time.

In U.S. $	2024	2023	2022	2021	2020	2019
Revenue	2,110,000,000	2,000,000,000	2,300,000,000	2,080,000,000	2,000,000,000	2,200,000,000
R&D Expense						
Operating Income						
Operating Margin %						
SGA Expense						
Net Income						
Operating Cash Flow						
Capital Expenditure						
EBITDA						
Return on Assets %						
Return on Equity %						
Debt to Equity						

CONTACT INFORMATION:

Phone: 713 918-8800   Fax: 713 918-8000
Toll-Free: 800-793-4262
Address: 2103 Citywest Blvd., Houston, TX 77042 United States

STOCK TICKER/OTHER:

Stock Ticker: Subsidiary   Exchange:
Employees: 6,000   Fiscal Year Ends: 03/31
Parent Company: KKR & Co LP

SALARIES/BONUSES:

Top Exec. Salary: $ Bonus: $
Second Exec. Salary: $ Bonus: $

OTHER THOUGHTS:

Estimated Female Officers or Directors: 2
Hot Spot for Advancement for Women/Minorities: Y

Boeing Company (The)

NAIC Code: 336411

www.boeing.com

TYPES OF BUSINESS:

Aircraft Manufacturing
Aerospace Technology & Manufacturing
Military Aircraft
Satellite Manufacturing
Communications Products & Services
Air Traffic Management Technology
Financing Services
Research & Development

BRANDS/DIVISIONS/AFFILIATES:

Boeing Capital Corporation
737
747
767
777
787

GROWTH PLANS/SPECIAL FEATURES:

Boeing is a major aerospace and defense firm. It operates in three segments: commercial airplanes; defense, space, and security; and global services. Boeing's commercial airplanes segment competes with Airbus in the production of aircraft that can carry more than 130 passengers. Boeing's defense, space, and security segment competes with defense contractors such as Lockheed Martin and Northrop Grumman to create military aircraft, satellites, and weaponry. Global services provides aftermarket support to airlines.

Boeing offers its employees health and retirement plans, tuition assistance and other programs.

CONTACTS: Note: Officers with more than one job title may be intentionally listed here more than once.

David Raymond, CEO, Divisional
Stephen Biegun, Sr. VP, Divisional
Stephanie Pope, CEO, Subsidiary
Robert Ortberg, CEO
Brian West, CFO
Steven Mollenkopf, Chairman of the Board
Michael Cleary, Chief Accounting Officer
Susan Doniz, Chief Information Officer
Brett Gerry, Chief Legal Officer
Ziad Ojakli, Executive VP, Divisional
Howard McKenzie, Executive VP, Divisional
Michael DAmbrose, Executive VP, Divisional
Brian Besanceney, Other Executive Officer
Brendan Nelson, President, Subsidiary

FINANCIAL DATA: Note: Data for latest year may not have been available at press time.

In U.S. $	2024	2023	2022	2021	2020	2019
Revenue	66,517,000,192	77,794,000,896	66,608,001,024	62,286,000,128	58,157,998,080	76,558,999,552
R&D Expense	3,812,000,000	3,377,000,000	2,852,000,000	2,249,000,000	2,476,000,000	3,219,000,000
Operating Income	-10,824,000,000	-821,000,000	-3,509,000,000	-3,357,000,000	-12,978,000,000	-2,662,000,000
Operating Margin %	-.16%	-.01%	-.05%	-.05%	-.22%	-.03%
SGA Expense	5,021,000,000	5,168,000,000	4,187,000,000	4,157,000,000	4,817,000,000	3,909,000,000
Net Income	-11,817,000,000	-2,222,000,000	-4,935,000,000	-4,202,000,000	-11,941,000,000	-636,000,000
Operating Cash Flow	-12,080,000,000	5,960,000,000	3,512,000,000	-3,416,000,000	-18,410,000,000	-2,446,000,000
Capital Expenditure	2,318,000,000	1,527,000,000	1,222,000,000	980,000,000	1,303,000,000	1,961,000,000
EBITDA	-7,649,000,000	2,315,000,000	-482,000,000	-175,000,000	-10,074,000,000	734,000,000
Return on Assets %	-.08%	-.02%	-.04%	-.03%	-.08%	-.01%
Return on Equity %						
Debt to Equity						

CONTACT INFORMATION:

Phone: 312 544-2000   Fax:
Toll-Free:
Address: 100 N. Riverside Plz., Chicago, IL 60606-1596 United States

STOCK TICKER/OTHER:

Stock Ticker: BA   Exchange: NYS
Employees: 171,000   Fiscal Year Ends: 12/31
Parent Company:

SALARIES/BONUSES:

Top Exec. Salary: $525,000   Bonus: $1,250,000
Second Exec. Salary: Bonus: $
$1,346,154

OTHER THOUGHTS:

Estimated Female Officers or Directors: 7
Hot Spot for Advancement for Women/Minorities: Y

Sales, profits and employees may be estimates. Financial information, benefits and other data can change quickly and may vary from those stated here.

Bombardier Inc

NAIC Code: 336411

TYPES OF BUSINESS:

Aircraft Manufacturing
Aircraft
Aircraft Manufacturing
Pre-Owned Aircraft
Business Jets

GROWTH PLANS/SPECIAL FEATURES:

Bombardier designs, manufactures, markets, and provides parts and maintenance for its large, long-range Global and medium-to-large Challenger aircraft families of business jets. Most of the company's revenue is generated in North America, 60% of which to customers in the US, and with operations in Europe, North America, Asia-Pacific, and other markets.

BRANDS/DIVISIONS/AFFILIATES:

Global
Challenger
Learjet
Bombarider Specialized Aircraft

CONTACTS: Note: Officers with more than one job title may be intentionally listed here more than once.

Eric Martel, CEO
Âˆve Laurier, VP, Divisional
Barton Demosky, CFO
Pierre Beaudoin, Chairman of the Board
Martin LeBlanc, Chief Compliance Officer
Paul Sislian, Executive VP, Divisional
Jean-Christophe Gallagher, Executive VP, Divisional
David Murray, Executive VP, Divisional
Eric Filion, Executive VP, Divisional
Pierre Gagnon, General Counsel
Stephen McCullough, Senior VP, Divisional
Peter Likoray, Senior VP, Divisional
Daniel Brennan, Senior VP, Divisional

FINANCIAL DATA: Note: Data for latest year may not have been available at press time.

In U.S. $	2024	2023	2022	2021	2020	2019
Revenue	8,664,999,936	8,046,000,128	6,912,999,936	6,085,000,192	6,487,000,064	7,488,000,000
R&D Expense	361,000,000	373,000,000	360,000,000	338,000,000	320,000,000	156,000,000
Operating Income	912,000,000	786,000,000	471,000,000	232,000,000	-269,000,000	290,000,000
Operating Margin %	.11%	.10%	.07%	.04%	- .04%	.04%
SGA Expense	478,000,000	447,000,000	395,000,000	355,000,000	420,000,000	557,000,000
Net Income	370,000,000	445,000,000	-148,000,000	5,041,000,000	-868,000,000	-1,797,000,000
Operating Cash Flow	405,000,000	623,000,000	1,072,000,000	-289,000,000	-2,821,000,000	-680,000,000
Capital Expenditure	173,000,000	366,000,000	355,000,000	237,000,000	364,000,000	552,000,000
EBITDA	1,167,000,000	1,295,000,000	697,000,000	678,000,000	1,182,000,000	-133,000,000
Return on Assets %	.03%	.03%	- .01%	.28%	- .04%	- .07%
Return on Equity %						
Debt to Equity						

CONTACT INFORMATION:

Phone: 514 861-9481   Fax: 514 861-2746
Toll-Free:
Address: 800 Rene-Levesque Blvd. W., Montreal, QC H3B 1Y8 Canada

STOCK TICKER/OTHER:

Stock Ticker: BBD.A   Exchange: TSE
Employees: 18,100   Fiscal Year Ends: 12/31
Parent Company:

SALARIES/BONUSES:

Top Exec. Salary: $ Bonus: $
Second Exec. Salary: $ Bonus: $

OTHER THOUGHTS:

Estimated Female Officers or Directors: 3
Hot Spot for Advancement for Women/Minorities: Y

Boston Scientific Corporation

www.bostonscientific.com

NAIC Code: 339100

TYPES OF BUSINESS:

Supplies-Surgery
Interventional Medical Products
Catheters
Guide wires
Stents
Oncology Research

BRANDS/DIVISIONS/AFFILIATES:

GROWTH PLANS/SPECIAL FEATURES:

Boston Scientific produces less invasive medical devices that are inserted into the human body through small openings or cuts. It manufactures products for use in angioplasty, blood clot filtration, kidney stone management, cardiac rhythm management, catheter-directed ultrasound imaging, upper gastrointestinal tract diagnostics, interventional oncology, neuromodulation for chronic pain, and treatment of incontinence. The firm markets its devices to healthcare professionals and institutions globally. Foreign sales account for nearly half of the firm's total sales.

The firm offers its employees comprehensive health benefits and assistance programs.

CONTACTS:
Note: Officers with more than one job title may be intentionally listed here more than once.

Michael Mahoney, CEO
Daniel Brennan, CFO
Emily Woodworth, Chief Accounting Officer
John Sorenson, Executive VP, Divisional
Wendy Carruthers, Executive VP, Divisional
Jeffrey Mirviss, Executive VP
Joseph Fitzgerald, Executive VP
Eric Thepaut, Executive VP
Arthur Butcher, Executive VP
Vance Brown, General Counsel
Jonathan Monson, Senior VP, Divisional

FINANCIAL DATA:
Note: Data for latest year may not have been available at press time.

In U.S. $	2024	2023	2022	2021	2020	2019
Revenue	16,746,999,808	14,240,000,000	12,682,000,384	11,888,000,000	9,912,999,936	10,734,999,552
R&D Expense	1,615,000,000	1,414,000,000	1,323,000,000	1,204,000,000	1,143,000,000	1,174,000,000
Operating Income	3,002,000,000	2,418,000,000	2,034,000,000	1,824,000,000	684,000,000	1,740,000,000
Operating Margin %	.18%	.17%	.16%	.15%	.07%	.16%
SGA Expense	5,984,000,000	5,190,000,000	4,520,000,000	4,359,000,000	3,787,000,000	3,941,000,000
Net Income	1,854,000,000	1,593,000,000	698,000,000	1,041,000,000	-82,000,000	4,700,000,000
Operating Cash Flow	3,435,000,000	2,503,000,000	1,526,000,000	1,870,000,000	1,508,000,000	1,836,000,000
Capital Expenditure	1,070,000,000	800,000,000	612,000,000	554,000,000	376,000,000	461,000,000
EBITDA	3,856,000,000	3,446,000,000	2,747,000,000	2,510,000,000	1,405,000,000	2,171,000,000
Return on Assets %	.05%	.05%	.02%	.03%	.00%	.18%
Return on Equity %	.09%	.09%	.04%	.06%	-.01%	.42%
Debt to Equity	.43%	.46%	.53%	.55%	0.622	0.639

CONTACT INFORMATION:

Phone: 508 683-4000   Fax: 508 647-2200
Toll-Free: 888-272-1001
Address: 300 Boston Scientific Way, Marlborough, MA 01752-1234
United States

STOCK TICKER/OTHER:

Stock Ticker: BSX
Employees: 48,000
Parent Company:

Exchange: NYS
Fiscal Year Ends: 12/31

SALARIES/BONUSES:

Top Exec. Salary: $1,400,000   Bonus: $
Second Exec. Salary: $843,146   Bonus: $

OTHER THOUGHTS:

Estimated Female Officers or Directors: 5
Hot Spot for Advancement for Women/Minorities: Y

Sales, profits and employees may be estimates. Financial information, benefits and other data can change quickly and may vary from those stated here.

Bouygues SA

NAIC Code: 237130

TYPES OF BUSINESS:

Construction & Telecommunications
Construction
Road Building
Property Development
Precasting
Cellular Phone Service
Media Operation
Research & Development

BRANDS/DIVISIONS/AFFILIATES:

Bouygues Construction
Bouygues Immobilier
Colas
Buoygues Telecom
Bbox
TF1
TMC

GROWTH PLANS/SPECIAL FEATURES:

Bouygues is a French conglomerate with a disparate range of assets: a construction business, a TV business, and a telecom business. It is one of the renowned construction companies in Europe with construction sales of around EUR 25 billion-EUR 30 billion and one of the four telecom operators in France, with both mobile and fixed operations and EUR 7.7 billion in telecom revenue in 2024. It is also the owner of TF1, one of the main media and TV companies in France.

CONTACTS: Note: Officers with more than one job title may be intentionally listed here more than once.

Martin Bouygues, Chairman of the Board

FINANCIAL DATA: Note: Data for latest year may not have been available at press time.

In U.S. $	2024	2023	2022	2021	2020	2019
Revenue	64,417,708,382	63,583,426,175	50,395,003,550	42,666,288,572	39,380,250,485	43,144,153,690
R&D Expense						
Operating Income	3,003,405,000	2,539,160,000	2,038,593,000	2,426,788,000	1,909,194,000	2,055,619,000
Operating Margin %	.05%	.04%	.04%	.06%	.05%	.05%
SGA Expense						
Net Income	1,200,908,000	1,180,477,000	1,104,427,000	1,276,958,000	790,011,300	1,343,927,000
Operating Cash Flow	6,104,426,000	6,065,834,000	3,380,250,000	4,059,024,000	3,866,062,000	3,828,604,000
Capital Expenditure	3,080,590,000	3,023,837,000	3,098,751,000	2,878,547,000	3,005,675,000	2,132,804,000
EBITDA	6,143,019,000	5,830,874,000	5,143,019,000	4,975,028,000	4,148,695,000	4,796,822,000
Return on Assets %	.02%	.02%	.02%	.03%	.02%	.03%
Return on Equity %	.08%	.08%	.08%	.10%	.07%	.12%
Debt to Equity	1.02%	1.06%	1.12%	.65%	0.665	0.547

CONTACT INFORMATION:

Phone: 33 1-44-20-10-00   Fax: 33-1-30-60-4861
Toll-Free:
Address: 32 Ave. Hoche, Paris, 75008 France

STOCK TICKER/OTHER:

Stock Ticker: BOUYY   Exchange: PINX
Employees: 83,757,123   Fiscal Year Ends: 12/31
Parent Company:

SALARIES/BONUSES:

Top Exec. Salary: $ Bonus: $
Second Exec. Salary: $ Bonus: $

OTHER THOUGHTS:

Estimated Female Officers or Directors: 5
Hot Spot for Advancement for Women/Minorities: Y

BP plc

NAIC Code: 211100

TYPES OF BUSINESS:

Oil & Gas Exploration & Production
Refining
Renewable & Alternative Energy
Fuel Stations
Convenience Stores
Retail

BRANDS/DIVISIONS/AFFILIATES:

GROWTH PLANS/SPECIAL FEATURES:

BP is an integrated oil and gas company that explores for, produces, and refines oil around the world. In 2024, it produced 1.2 million barrels of liquids and 6.9 billion cubic feet of natural gas per day. At the end of 2023, reserves stood at 6.8 billion barrels of oil equivalent, 55% of which are liquids. The company operates refineries with a capacity of 1.6 million barrels of oil per day.

CONTACTS:

Note: Officers with more than one job title may be intentionally listed here more than once.

Murray Auchincloss, CEO
Katherine Thomson, CFO
Helge Lund, Chairman of the Board
Benedict Mathews, Secretary

FINANCIAL DATA:

Note: Data for latest year may not have been available at press time.

In U.S. $	2024	2023	2022	2021	2020	2019
Revenue	189,184,999,424	210,129,993,728	241,391,992,832	157,739,008,000	105,943,998,464	159,307,005,952
R&D Expense						
Operating Income	13,615,000,000	31,049,000,000	41,447,000,000	10,672,000,000	-573,000,000	16,193,000,000
Operating Margin %	.07%	.15%	.17%	.07%	-.01%	.10%
SGA Expense	16,417,000,000	16,772,000,000	13,449,000,000	11,931,000,000	10,397,000,000	11,057,000,000
Net Income	381,000,000	15,239,000,000	-2,487,000,000	7,565,000,000	-20,305,000,000	4,026,000,000
Operating Cash Flow	27,297,000,000	32,039,000,000	40,932,000,000	23,612,000,000	12,162,000,000	25,770,000,000
Capital Expenditure	15,297,000,000	14,285,000,000	12,069,000,000	10,887,000,000	12,306,000,000	15,418,000,000
EBITDA	27,983,000,000	43,503,000,000	32,346,000,000	32,549,000,000	-7,042,000,000	29,423,000,000
Return on Assets %			-.01%	.03%	-.08%	
Return on Equity %			-.03%	.10%	-.29%	
Debt to Equity	1.09%	.81%	.74%	.83%	0.992	0.66

CONTACT INFORMATION:

Phone: 44 2074964000   Fax: 44 2074964570
Toll-Free:
Address: 1 St. James's Sq., London, SW1Y 4PD United Kingdom

STOCK TICKER/OTHER:

Stock Ticker: BP   Exchange: NYS
Employees: 87,800   Fiscal Year Ends: 12/31
Parent Company:

SALARIES/BONUSES:

Top Exec. Salary: $1,952,135   Bonus: $988,184
Second Exec. Salary: $984,145   Bonus: $498,131

OTHER THOUGHTS:

Estimated Female Officers or Directors: 3
Hot Spot for Advancement for Women/Minorities: Y

Bristol-Myers Squibb Company

www.bms.com

NAIC Code: 325412

TYPES OF BUSINESS:

Drugs-Diversified
Biopharmaceuticals
Manufacturing
Distribution
Marketing

GROWTH PLANS/SPECIAL FEATURES:

Bristol-Myers Squibb discovers, develops, and markets drugs for various therapeutic areas, such as cardiovascular, cancer, and immune disorders. A key focus for Bristol is immuno-oncology, where the firm is a leader in drug development. Bristol derives close to 70% of total sales from the US, showing a higher dependence on the US market than most of its peer group.

BMS offers its employees medical and dental insurance; pension and 401(k) plans; short- and long-term disability coverage; travel accident insurance; an employee assistance plan; and adoption assistance.

BRANDS/DIVISIONS/AFFILIATES:

MyoKardia Inc

CONTACTS: Note: Officers with more than one job title may be intentionally listed here more than once.

Christopher Boerner, CEO
David Elkins, CFO
Samit Hirawat, Chief Medical Officer
Gregory Meyers, Chief Technology Officer
Phil Holzer, Controller
Karin Shanahan, Executive VP, Divisional
Cari Gallman, Executive VP, Divisional
Robert Plenge, Executive VP
Adam Lenkowsky, Executive VP
Amanda Poole, Executive VP
Sandra Leung, General Counsel
Lynelle Hoch, President, Divisional

FINANCIAL DATA: Note: Data for latest year may not have been available at press time.

In U.S. $	2024	2023	2022	2021	2020	2019
Revenue	48,299,999,232	45,006,000,128	46,158,999,552	46,385,000,448	42,517,999,616	26,144,999,424
R&D Expense	11,159,000,000	9,299,000,000	9,509,000,000	10,195,000,000	11,143,000,000	6,148,000,000
Operating Income	5,887,000,000	8,195,000,000	9,104,000,000	8,537,000,000	2,177,000,000	5,913,000,000
Operating Margin %	.12%	.18%	.20%	.18%	.05%	.23%
SGA Expense	8,414,000,000	7,772,000,000	7,814,000,000	7,690,000,000	7,661,000,000	4,871,000,000
Net Income	-8,948,000,000	8,025,000,000	6,327,000,000	6,994,000,000	-9,015,000,000	3,439,000,000
Operating Cash Flow	15,190,000,000	13,860,000,000	13,066,000,000	16,207,000,000	14,052,000,000	8,210,000,000
Capital Expenditure	1,248,000,000	1,209,000,000	1,118,000,000	973,000,000	753,000,000	836,000,000
EBITDA	3,168,000,000	19,366,000,000	19,221,000,000	20,118,000,000	4,929,000,000	7,377,000,000
Return on Assets %	-.10%	.08%	.06%	.06%	-.07%	.04%
Return on Equity %	-.39%	.27%	.19%	.19%	-.20%	.10%
Debt to Equity	3.00%	1.30%	1.17%	1.13%	1.30	0.854

CONTACT INFORMATION:

Phone: 212 546-4000   Fax: 212 546-4020
Toll-Free:
Address: 430 E. 29th St., 14/Fl, New York, NY 10016 United States

STOCK TICKER/OTHER:

Stock Ticker: BMY   Exchange: NYS
Employees: 34,100   Fiscal Year Ends: 12/31
Parent Company:

SALARIES/BONUSES:

Top Exec. Salary: $1,536,538   Bonus: $
Second Exec. Salary: Bonus: $
$1,150,000

OTHER THOUGHTS:

Estimated Female Officers or Directors: 4
Hot Spot for Advancement for Women/Minorities: Y

Broadcom Inc

NAIC Code: 335313

www.broadcom.com

TYPES OF BUSINESS:

Electrical Switches, Sensors, MEMS, Optomechanicals
Semiconductors
Connectivity Technology
Wireless Applications
Optical Products
Mainframe Software
Enterprise Software
Security Software

BRANDS/DIVISIONS/AFFILIATES:

AppNeta Inc

GROWTH PLANS/SPECIAL FEATURES:

Broadcom is the sixth-largest semiconductor company globally and has expanded into various software businesses, with over $30 billion in annual revenue. It sells 17 core semiconductor product lines across wireless, networking, broadband, storage, and industrial markets. It is primarily a fabless designer but holds some manufacturing in-house, like for its best-of-breed FBAR filters that sell into the Apple iPhone. In software, it sells virtualization, infrastructure, and security software to large enterprises, financial institutions, and governments. Broadcom is the product of consolidation. Its businesses are an amalgamation of former companies like legacy Broadcom and Avago Technologies in chips, as well as Brocade, CA Technologies, and Symantec in software.

CONTACTS: Note: Officers with more than one job title may be intentionally listed here more than once.

Hock Tan, CEO
Kirsten Spears, CFO
Henry Samueli, Chairman of the Board
Mark Brazeal, Chief Legal Officer
Charlie Kawwas, President, Divisional

FINANCIAL DATA: Note: Data for latest year may not have been available at press time.

In U.S. $	2024	2023	2022	2021	2020	2019
Revenue	51,574,001,664	35,818,999,808	33,202,999,296	27,449,999,360	23,887,998,976	22,596,999,168
R&D Expense	9,310,000,000	5,253,000,000	4,919,000,000	4,854,000,000	4,968,000,000	4,696,000,000
Operating Income	14,996,000,000	16,451,000,000	14,282,000,000	8,667,000,000	4,212,000,000	4,180,000,000
Operating Margin %	.29%	.46%	.43%	.32%	.18%	.18%
SGA Expense	4,959,000,000	1,592,000,000	1,382,000,000	1,347,000,000	1,935,000,000	1,709,000,000
Net Income	5,895,000,000	14,082,000,000	11,495,000,000	6,736,000,000	2,960,000,000	2,724,000,000
Operating Cash Flow	19,962,000,000	18,085,000,000	16,736,000,000	13,764,000,000	12,061,000,000	9,697,000,000
Capital Expenditure	548,000,000	452,000,000	424,000,000	443,000,000	463,000,000	432,000,000
EBITDA	23,879,000,000	20,554,000,000	19,155,000,000	14,691,000,000	11,125,000,000	9,478,000,000
Return on Assets %	.05%	.19%	.15%	.08%	.04%	.05%
Return on Equity %	.13%	.60%	.47%	.26%	.11%	.10%
Debt to Equity	.98%	1.57%	1.72%	1.58%	1.685	1.203

CONTACT INFORMATION:

Phone: 408 433-8000   Fax:
Toll-Free:
Address: 1320 Ridder Park Dr., San Jose, CA 95131-2313 United States

STOCK TICKER/OTHER:

Stock Ticker: AVGO   Exchange: NAS
Employees: 37,000   Fiscal Year Ends: 10/31
Parent Company:

SALARIES/BONUSES:

Top Exec. Salary: $1,226,374   Bonus: $
Second Exec. Salary: $736,847   Bonus: $

OTHER THOUGHTS:

Estimated Female Officers or Directors: 5
Hot Spot for Advancement for Women/Minorities: Y

Burns & McDonnell Inc

www.burnsmcd.com

NAIC Code: 541330

TYPES OF BUSINESS:

Engineering Services
City Infrastructure Design and Build
Architecture Services
Buildings
Commissioning and Construction
Program and Project Management
Aviation and Environmental Solutions
Chemicals and Oil and Gas Solutions

BRANDS/DIVISIONS/AFFILIATES:

Burns & McDonnell
1898 & Co
AZCO

CONTACTS: *Note: Officers with more than one job title may be intentionally listed here more than once.*

Leslie Duke, CEO
Alissa Schuessler, CFO
Mark Taylor, Treas.
Don Greenwood, Pres., Construction
Ray Kowalik, VP
John Nobles, Pres., Process & Industrial
Leslie Duke, Chmn.

GROWTH PLANS/SPECIAL FEATURES:

Burns & McDonnell, Inc. (B&M), a 100% employee-owned company in business since 1898, specializes in the design and building of city infrastructure. The firm operates through more than 75 offices worldwide, with infrastructure services spanning architecture, aviation, buildings, chemicals, oil and gas, commissioning, construction, electric power generation, electrical transmission and distribution, environmental, federal and military, industrial, program management, sustainability, telecommunications, transportation and water. Industries served by B&M include aviation, chemicals, oil and gas, commercial, retail, institutional, environmental, government/military, municipal, manufacturing and industrial, power, telecommunications, transportation and water. B&M brands include Burns & McDonnell; 1898 & Co., a business, technology and security consultancy; and AZCO, a heavy industrial construction company.

Burns & McDonnell offers its employees comprehensive health insurance, wellness programs, an employee assistance program, an employee stock ownership program, a 401(k) program, life insurance and accident coverage, disability coverage, and more.

FINANCIAL DATA: *Note: Data for latest year may not have been available at press time.*

In U.S. $	2024	2023	2022	2021	2020	2019
Revenue	7,770,000,000	7,400,000,000	7,000,000,000	5,700,000,000	5,300,000,000	4,200,000,000
R&D Expense						
Operating Income						
Operating Margin %						
SGA Expense						
Net Income						
Operating Cash Flow						
Capital Expenditure						
EBITDA						
Return on Assets %						
Return on Equity %						
Debt to Equity						

CONTACT INFORMATION:

Phone: 816-333-9400   Fax: 816-822-3028
Toll-Free:
Address: 9400 Ward Pkwy., Kansas City, MO 64114 United States

STOCK TICKER/OTHER:

Stock Ticker: Private   Exchange:
Employees: 14,000   Fiscal Year Ends: 12/31
Parent Company:

SALARIES/BONUSES:

Top Exec. Salary: $ Bonus: $
Second Exec. Salary: $ Bonus: $

OTHER THOUGHTS:

Estimated Female Officers or Directors:
Hot Spot for Advancement for Women/Minorities:

Buro Happold Limited

www.burohappold.com

NAIC Code: 541330

TYPES OF BUSINESS:

Engineering Services
Infrastructure Engineering
Buildings and Environment Consultancy
Project Management
Cities Design
Ground and Structural Engineering
Transportation and Mobility Engineering
Technology and Digital Solutions

BRANDS/DIVISIONS/AFFILIATES:

Happold LLP

CONTACTS: Note: Officers with more than one job title may be intentionally listed here more than once.

Oliver Plunkett, CEO
Marc Barone, COO
Sam Murray, CFO
Karen O'Brien, Chief People Officer
Alain Waha, CTO
Craig Schwitter, Chmn.

GROWTH PLANS/SPECIAL FEATURES:

Buro Happold Limited provides engineering, design, planning and project management consulting services for all aspects of buildings, infrastructure and environment. The company's services are categorized into six groups, including advisory, sustainability, cities and infrastructure, engineering design, specialist consulting, and technology and digital. Through these categories, Buro offers services spanning climate change adaptation and resilience, energy and environmental consulting, ESG consulting (environmental/social/governance), building retrofit, airport consulting, bridge engineering and civil infrastructures, economics, ports/maritime, stranded assets, transport and mobility, water, waste management consulting, building services engineering, façade engineering, fire engineering, ground engineering, structural engineering, tall buildings, tensile structures, timber engineering, acoustics, asset consultancy, project and design management, environmental consultancy, health/wellbeing productivity, heritage buildings, higher education consulting, analytics, audio/visual consulting and more. Sectors served by Buro primarily include air, commercial, cultural, education, healthcare, rail, science, sport/entertainment, technology and urban development. Based in Bath, England, the firm operates through nearly 40 locations worldwide, and has 3,500+ engineers, advisors and specialist consultants across its global network. The firm is ultimately owned by Happold LLP.

FINANCIAL DATA: Note: Data for latest year may not have been available at press time.

In U.S. $	2024	2023	2022	2021	2020	2019
Revenue	386,970,150	368,543,000	264,741,309	138,569,958	121,143,007	115,418,506
R&D Expense						
Operating Income						
Operating Margin %						
SGA Expense						
Net Income		43,853,000	33,108,222	-8,394,629	-1,964,421	3,432,304
Operating Cash Flow						
Capital Expenditure						
EBITDA						
Return on Assets %						
Return on Equity %						
Debt to Equity						

CONTACT INFORMATION:

Phone: 44-1225-320-600   Fax:
Toll-Free:
Address: Camden Mill, 230 Lower Bristol Rd., Bath, BA2 3DQ United Kingdom

STOCK TICKER/OTHER:

Stock Ticker: Private   Exchange:
Employees: 2,400   Fiscal Year Ends: 04/30
Parent Company: Happold LLP

SALARIES/BONUSES:

Top Exec. Salary: $ Bonus: $
Second Exec. Salary: $ Bonus: $

OTHER THOUGHTS:

Estimated Female Officers or Directors:
Hot Spot for Advancement for Women/Minorities:

BYD Company Limited

NAIC Code: 336111

www.byd.com

TYPES OF BUSINESS:

Automobile Manufacturing
Cellular Telephone Equipment Manufacturing
Battery Manufacturing
Advanced Battery Technologies
Hybrid and Electric Cars
Contract Electronics Manufacturing

BRANDS/DIVISIONS/AFFILIATES:

SkyRail

GROWTH PLANS/SPECIAL FEATURES:

Founded in 1995, BYD is a leading Chinese manufacturer in the design, development, and production of new energy vehicles, or NEVs. In March 2022, the firm discontinued production of internal combustion engine, or ICE, vehicles. Its products primarily target the growing midpriced mass-market segment in China's passenger vehicle market. The company sold about 4.3 million passenger NEVs in 2024, accounting for 35% of the Chinese passenger NEV market. Besides automobile production, the company is also engaged in handset components and assembly services, as well as the rechargeable battery and photovoltaics business. After more than 25 years of development, the company has established over 30 industrial parks worldwide.

CONTACTS: Note: Officers with more than one job title may be intentionally listed here more than once.

Chuan-Fu Wang, Chairman of the Board
Xiang-Yang Lv, Co-Founder

FINANCIAL DATA: Note: Data for latest year may not have been available at press time.

In U.S. $	2024	2023	2022	2021	2020	2019
Revenue	107,875,453,922	83,611,941,602	58,867,059,882	30,004,357,794	21,738,508,654	17,732,348,165
R&D Expense	7,384,364,000	5,493,697,000	2,589,565,000	1,109,287,000	1,036,254,000	781,455,600
Operating Income	7,555,890,000	5,332,369,000	3,189,539,000	1,054,622,000	1,810,897,000	952,434,200
Operating Margin %	.07%	.06%	.05%	.04%	.08%	.05%
SGA Expense	1,855,914,000	2,611,087,000	1,555,099,000	604,013,200	533,868,800	432,237,500
Net Income	5,588,009,000	4,170,192,000	2,307,487,000	422,725,500	587,790,500	224,114,000
Operating Cash Flow	18,525,740,000	23,560,810,000	19,550,740,000	9,087,924,000	6,301,299,000	2,046,311,000
Capital Expenditure	13,515,240,000	16,948,720,000	13,528,720,000	5,183,948,000	1,634,451,000	2,863,412,000
EBITDA	16,221,320,000	11,435,630,000	5,925,358,000	2,846,696,000	3,122,596,000	2,181,679,000
Return on Assets %	.06%	.05%	.04%	.01%	.02%	.01%
Return on Equity %	.25%	.24%	.16%	.04%	.07%	.03%
Debt to Equity	.10%	.15%	.09%	.13%	0.43	0.396

CONTACT INFORMATION:

Phone: 86 755-89888888   Fax: 86-755-84202222
Toll-Free:
Address: BYD Rd., No. 3009, Pingshan, Shenzhen, Guangdong 518118 China

STOCK TICKER/OTHER:

Stock Ticker: BYDDF   Exchange: PINX
Employees: 703,000   Fiscal Year Ends: 12/31
Parent Company:

SALARIES/BONUSES:

Top Exec. Salary: $ Bonus: $
Second Exec. Salary: $ Bonus: $

OTHER THOUGHTS:

Estimated Female Officers or Directors:
Hot Spot for Advancement for Women/Minorities:

Cadence Design Systems Inc

www.cadence.com

NAIC Code: 511210N

TYPES OF BUSINESS:

Software-Electronic Design Automation
Training & Support Services
Design & Methodology Services

GROWTH PLANS/SPECIAL FEATURES:

Cadence Design Systems is a provider of electronic design automation software, intellectual property, and system design and analysis products. EDA software automates and aids in the chip design process, enhancing design accuracy, productivity, and complexity in a full-flow end-to-end solution. Cadence offers a portfolio of design IP, as well as system design and analysis products, which enables system-level analysis and verification solutions.

BRANDS/DIVISIONS/AFFILIATES:

CONTACTS: Note: Officers with more than one job title may be intentionally listed here more than once.

Anirudh Devgan, CEO
John Wall, CFO
Mary Krakauer, Chairman of the Board
Karna Nisewaner, General Counsel
Paul Cunningham, General Manager, Divisional
Thomas Beckley, General Manager, Divisional
Chin-Chi Teng, General Manager, Divisional

FINANCIAL DATA: Note: Data for latest year may not have been available at press time.

In U.S. $	2024	2023	2022	2021	2020	2019
Revenue	4,641,264,128	4,089,986,048	3,561,718,016	2,988,243,968	2,682,891,008	2,336,318,976
R&D Expense	1,549,093,000	1,441,796,000	1,251,544,000	1,134,277,000	1,033,732,000	935,938,000
Operating Income	1,374,528,000	1,262,238,000	1,073,741,000	778,041,000	654,767,000	500,417,000
Operating Margin %	.30%	.31%	.30%	.26%	.24%	.21%
SGA Expense	1,039,766,000	932,749,000	846,340,000	749,280,000	670,885,000	621,479,000
Net Income	1,055,484,000	1,041,144,000	848,952,000	695,955,000	590,644,000	988,979,000
Operating Cash Flow	1,260,551,000	1,349,176,000	1,241,894,000	1,100,958,000	904,922,000	729,600,000
Capital Expenditure	142,542,000	102,503,000	124,215,000	66,881,000	94,813,000	74,605,000
EBITDA	1,666,833,000	1,463,854,000	1,203,727,000	916,117,000	803,633,000	621,148,000
Return on Assets %	.14%	.19%	.18%	.17%	.16%	.34%
Return on Equity %	.26%	.34%	.31%	.27%	.26%	.58%
Debt to Equity	.55%	.12%	.29%	.17%	0.185	0.205

CONTACT INFORMATION:

Phone: 408 943-1234   Fax: 408 428-5001
Toll-Free: 800-746-6223
Address: 2655 Seely Ave., Bldg. 5, San Jose, CA 95134 United States

STOCK TICKER/OTHER:

Stock Ticker: CDNS   Exchange: NAS
Employees: 11,200   Fiscal Year Ends: 12/31
Parent Company:

SALARIES/BONUSES:

Top Exec. Salary: $750,000   Bonus: $
Second Exec. Salary: Bonus: $
$575,000

OTHER THOUGHTS:

Estimated Female Officers or Directors: 2
Hot Spot for Advancement for Women/Minorities:

CannonDesign

www.cannondesign.com

NAIC Code: 541330

TYPES OF BUSINESS:

Engineering Consulting Services
Architectural Design
Engineering
Buildings and Space Services
Immersive and Branded Experience Services
Data-Driven Facility Solutions
Sustainable Design and Engineering Services
Future Resiliency Planning

BRANDS/DIVISIONS/AFFILIATES:

SRG Partnership

GROWTH PLANS/SPECIAL FEATURES:

CannonDesign is a 100% employee-owned company that provides architectural design and engineering services to clients in the commercial, community, education, health, science and technology, sports and recreation, and wellness sectors. CannonDesign's capabilities include buildings and spaces, immersive and branded experiences, data-driven facility solutions, frameworks for fueling change, sustainable and resilient futures, and plans for growth and impact. Based in the U.S., the firm has international offices in Canada and India, with the total amount of offices summing to 18.

CannonDesign offers its employees physical, financial and well-being benefits.

CONTACTS: Note: Officers with more than one job title may be intentionally listed here more than once.

Bradley A. Lukanic, CEO
David Carlino, CFO
Charlene Miraglia, Dir.-Human Resources
Brooke Grammier, CIO

FINANCIAL DATA: Note: Data for latest year may not have been available at press time.

In U.S. $	2024	2023	2022	2021	2020	2019
Revenue	180,600,000	172,000,000	165,000,000	163,655,762	160,446,825	162,067,500
R&D Expense						
Operating Income						
Operating Margin %						
SGA Expense						
Net Income						
Operating Cash Flow						
Capital Expenditure						
EBITDA						
Return on Assets %						
Return on Equity %						
Debt to Equity						

CONTACT INFORMATION:

Phone: 212-972-9800   Fax: 212-972-9191
Toll-Free:
Address: 360 Madison Ave., Fl. 11, New York, NY 10017 United States

STOCK TICKER/OTHER:

Stock Ticker: Private   Exchange:
Employees: 1,150   Fiscal Year Ends:
Parent Company:

SALARIES/BONUSES:

Top Exec. Salary: $ Bonus: $
Second Exec. Salary: $ Bonus: $

OTHER THOUGHTS:

Estimated Female Officers or Directors:
Hot Spot for Advancement for Women/Minorities:

Canon Inc

NAIC Code: 333316

TYPES OF BUSINESS:

Photographic and Photocopying Equipment Manufacturing
Printers & Scanners
Semiconductor Lithography Equipment
Cameras, Film & Digital
Software
Analytics
Lenses

BRANDS/DIVISIONS/AFFILIATES:

Canon

GROWTH PLANS/SPECIAL FEATURES:

Canon Inc designs, manufactures and distributes an extensive range of consumer and electronic products, including copiers, cameras, lenses, and inkjet printers. The company operates four major business segments: printing, imaging, medical, industrial, and others. It generates maximum revenue from the printing segment. Printing Business Unit includes Office multifunction devices (MFDs), Document solutions, Laser multifunction printers (MFPs), Laser printers, Inkjet printers, Image scanners, Calculators, Digital continuous feed presses, Digital sheet-fed presses, and Large format printers.

Canon offers its employees medical, dental, vision and life insurance; flexible spending accounts; and employee assistance and educational assistance programs.

CONTACTS: *Note: Officers with more than one job title may be intentionally listed here more than once.*

Hiroaki Takeishi, CEO, Subsidiary
Fujio Mitarai, CEO
Toshizo Tanaka, CFO
Toshio Homma, Chief Technology Officer
Kazuto Ogawa, Director
Minoru Asada, Director

FINANCIAL DATA: *Note: Data for latest year may not have been available at press time.*

In U.S. $	2024	2023	2022	2021	2020	2019
Revenue	31,309,505,615	29,026,464,982	27,988,157,043	24,391,537,243	21,940,037,599	24,946,536,730
R&D Expense	2,342,044,000	2,304,318,000	2,129,478,000	1,994,849,000	1,890,530,000	2,072,362,000
Operating Income	3,088,406,000	2,605,985,000	2,453,478,000	1,957,220,000	767,474,400	1,210,914,000
Operating Margin %	.10%	.09%	.09%	.08%	.03%	.05%
SGA Expense	9,448,022,000	8,758,886,000	8,106,589,000	7,348,903,000	6,893,981,000	7,894,405,000
Net Income	1,110,976,000	1,836,386,000	1,693,703,000	1,490,683,000	578,436,500	867,564,600
Operating Cash Flow	4,212,934,000	3,132,394,000	1,823,126,000	3,131,269,000	2,317,447,000	2,488,621,000
Capital Expenditure	1,645,383,000	1,598,917,000	1,308,852,000	1,231,255,000	1,143,564,000	1,497,299,000
EBITDA	3,751,534,000	4,385,657,000	4,026,507,000	3,642,037,000	2,492,079,000	3,012,066,000
Return on Assets %	.03%	.05%	.05%	.05%	.02%	.03%
Return on Equity %	.05%	.08%	.08%	.08%	.03%	.05%
Debt to Equity	.09%	.03%	.03%	.09%	0.032	0.164

CONTACT INFORMATION:

Phone: 81 337582111   Fax: 81 354825135
Toll-Free:
Address: 30-2, Shimomaruko 3-chome, Ohta-ku, Tokyo, 146-8501 Japan

STOCK TICKER/OTHER:

Stock Ticker: CAJPY
Employees: 180,775
Parent Company:

Exchange: PINX
Fiscal Year Ends: 12/31

SALARIES/BONUSES:

Top Exec. Salary: $ Bonus: $
Second Exec. Salary: $ Bonus: $

OTHER THOUGHTS:

Estimated Female Officers or Directors:
Hot Spot for Advancement for Women/Minorities:

Capgemini Engineering

capgemini-engineering.com/uk/en

NAIC Code: 541512

TYPES OF BUSINESS:

Consulting-Technology & Engineering
Systems Engineering
Product Engineering
Digital and Software Solutions
Industrial Engineering Solutions
Operations Management
Product Design
Artificial Intelligence

BRANDS/DIVISIONS/AFFILIATES:

Capgemini SE

CONTACTS: *Note: Officers with more than one job title may be intentionally listed here more than once.*

William Roze, CEO
Pascal Brier, Sr. VP-Industries & Solutions Bus. Dev.
Cyril Roger, Sr, VP-Southern Europe
Michel Bailly, Exec. VP-Programs & Innovation
Michael Blickle, Sr. VP-Northern Europe

GROWTH PLANS/SPECIAL FEATURES:

Capgemini Engineering is a subsidiary and business division of Capgemini SE that offers products and systems engineering, digital and related software, industrial engineering and operations management for global innovators that engineer products and services. Capgemini Engineering's products and systems engineering solutions include mechanical and physical engineering, electrical/electronics, semiconductors, systems engineering and product design. Its digital and software solutions include software engineering, connectivity and network engineering, data science, analytics and artificial intelligence (AI). Its industrial operations include manufacturing and process engineering, industrial operations management and related product support and services. Capgemini Engineering leverages its experts, laboratories, tools and frameworks across these domains. The firm incorporates more than 55,000 engineers and scientists across the globe for its research and development services.

Capgemini offers its employees learning and development opportunities, keeping them up-to-date with the latest tools and technologies while also growing soft skills. Learning programs offered are either personalized or comprehensive.

FINANCIAL DATA: *Note: Data for latest year may not have been available at press time.*

In U.S. $	2024	2023	2022	2021	2020	2019
Revenue	7,604,748,060	7,208,292,000	6,682,799,200	6,374,959,040	5,619,303,015	3,602,590,000
R&D Expense						
Operating Income						
Operating Margin %						
SGA Expense						
Net Income						
Operating Cash Flow						
Capital Expenditure						
EBITDA						
Return on Assets %						
Return on Equity %						
Debt to Equity						

CONTACT INFORMATION:

Phone: 33 1-46-41-70-00   Fax: 33-1-46-41-70-01
Toll-Free:
Address: 96, Ave. Charles de Gaulle, Neuilly-sur-Seine, 92200 France

STOCK TICKER/OTHER:

Stock Ticker: Subsidiary   Exchange:
Employees: 55,000   Fiscal Year Ends: 12/31
Parent Company: Capgemini SE

SALARIES/BONUSES:

Top Exec. Salary: $ Bonus: $
Second Exec. Salary: $ Bonus: $

OTHER THOUGHTS:

Estimated Female Officers or Directors: 1
Hot Spot for Advancement for Women/Minorities:

Carso Infraestructura Y Construccion SAB de CV

www.ccicsa.com.mx
NAIC Code: 541330

TYPES OF BUSINESS:

Engineering Services
Large-Scale Project Design and Construction
Water Plants and Storage Dams
Community Development and Construction
Offshore Platform Engineering
Oil and Gas Wells
Energy Process Equipment Manufacturing
Telecommunication Network Construction

BRANDS/DIVISIONS/AFFILIATES:

Grupo Carso SAB de CV

CONTACTS: Note: Officers with more than one job title may be intentionally listed here more than once.

Antonio Gomez Garcia, Managing Dir.

GROWTH PLANS/SPECIAL FEATURES:

Carso Infraestructura Y Construccion SAB de CV is part of Mexican conglomerate Grupo Carso SAB de CV and is engaged in the design and execution of large-scale projects and works. The firm develops projects for strategic sectors: water, edification, hydrocarbons and energy, industry, infrastructure and telecommunications. For the water industry, Carso develops projects that integrate design, production and operation of specialized infrastructure, including lines for the transport and measurement of water, wastewater treatment plants, hydroelectric plants and water storage dams. For the edification industry, Carso offers design and flexible solutions during the various phases of its projects and primarily develops self-sustaining residential housing communities to include services such as public schools, hospitals, shopping centers, hotels, fire stations and fuel stations. For the hydrocarbons and energy industries, Carso engineers and constructs fixed offshore platforms and jack-up offshore platforms; designs, engineers and manages oil wells; drills and completes oil and geothermal wells; rents, operates and maintains drilling equipment; provides direction drilling services; cements wells and various pumping projects; offers comprehensive drilling fluid services; constructs lines for the transportation and measurement of hydrocarbons, sour gas, natural gas and oil/gas pipelines; and designs and manufactures related process equipment. For the industry sector, Carso builds metallic structures for bridges, buildings and mining companies, and also produces heat exchangers, pressure vessels, distillation towers, air coolers, surface capacitors, high-pressure feedwater heaters and large containers. For the infrastructure industry, Carso specializes in high specification highways, hydroelectric works, water storage dams, tunnels, viaducts and overpasses. Lastly, Carso serves the telecommunications industry by constructing and implementing telecommunications networks, urban fiber optic networks, laser diodes, broadband fiber optic networks, secondary copper networks, coaxial fiber networks, radio base cell sites and infrastructure for closed circuit television.

FINANCIAL DATA: Note: Data for latest year may not have been available at press time.

In U.S. $	2024	2023	2022	2021	2020	2019
Revenue						
R&D Expense						
Operating Income						
Operating Margin %						
SGA Expense						
Net Income						
Operating Cash Flow						
Capital Expenditure						
EBITDA						
Return on Assets %						
Return on Equity %						
Debt to Equity						

CONTACT INFORMATION:

Phone: 52 5553285800   Fax: 52 5552551686
Toll-Free:
Address: 245 Frisco Bldg., Mexico City, 11529 Mexico

STOCK TICKER/OTHER:

Stock Ticker: Subsidiary   Exchange:
Employees: Fiscal Year Ends: 12/31
Parent Company: Grupo Carso SAB de CV

SALARIES/BONUSES:

Top Exec. Salary: $ Bonus: $
Second Exec. Salary: $ Bonus: $

OTHER THOUGHTS:

Estimated Female Officers or Directors:
Hot Spot for Advancement for Women/Minorities:

Casio Computer Co Ltd

NAIC Code: 334111

www.casio.com

TYPES OF BUSINESS:
Computer Manufacturing
Timepieces
Calculators
Cellular Phones
Electronic Music Instruments
LCDs
Digital Cameras
Factory Automation Equipment

GROWTH PLANS/SPECIAL FEATURES:
Casio Computer is well known as a watch and calculator manufacturer. Casio, founded in 1957, has cultivated the consumer electronics market by inventing distinctive products. Milestones in its history include the Casio Mini (1972), the world's first personal electronic calculator; G-Shock (1983), a shock-resistant wristwatch; and QV-10 (1995), the world's first digital camera with an LCD display. About two thirds of its revenue and most of its profits are from the timepieces segment.

BRANDS/DIVISIONS/AFFILIATES:
Yamagata Casio Co Ltd
Casio Electronic Manufacturing Co Ltd
Casio Europe GmbH
Computer (Hong Kong) Ltd
Casio America Inc
Casio Middle East FZE
G'xEYE
G-SHOCK

CONTACTS:
Note: Officers with more than one job title may be intentionally listed here more than once.

Yuichi Masuda, CEO
Shin Takano, CFO
Kazuhiro Kashio, Chairman of the Board
Tetsuo Kashio, Director
Toshiyuki Yamagishi, Director

FINANCIAL DATA:
Note: Data for latest year may not have been available at press time.

In U.S. $	2024	2023	2022	2021	2020	2019
Revenue	1,866,342,745	1,831,650,955	1,751,749,605	1,579,005,890	1,949,111,408	2,069,987,659
R&D Expense	33,830,880	36,600,940	43,092,200	45,029,160	51,464,870	51,055,260
Operating Income	98,639,270	126,103,900	152,811,700	106,720,400	201,777,300	210,094,400
Operating Margin %	.05%	.07%	.09%	.07%	.10%	.10%
SGA Expense	213,024,200	189,780,600	182,206,300	150,069,400	189,745,900	222,403,500
Net Income	82,678,420	90,801,170	110,309,600	83,407,390	122,105,000	153,672,600
Operating Cash Flow	211,857,800	78,721,190	113,989,200	170,695,600	229,429,300	143,973,900
Capital Expenditure	68,841,990	76,687,030	76,187,180	57,803,390	68,605,940	88,399,060
EBITDA	206,720,400	194,709,800	239,676,500	202,839,500	275,590,100	273,000,600
Return on Assets %	.03%	.04%	.05%	.04%	.05%	.06%
Return on Equity %	.05%	.06%	.07%	.06%	.08%	.11%
Debt to Equity	.17%	.12%	.19%	.23%	0.187	0.279

CONTACT INFORMATION:
Phone: 81 5334-4111   Fax:
Toll-Free:
Address: 6-2, Hon-machi 1-chome, Tokyo, 151-8543 Japan

STOCK TICKER/OTHER:
Stock Ticker: CSIOY   Exchange: PINX
Employees: 13,105   Fiscal Year Ends: 03/31
Parent Company:

SALARIES/BONUSES:
Top Exec. Salary: $ Bonus: $
Second Exec. Salary: $ Bonus: $

OTHER THOUGHTS:
Estimated Female Officers or Directors:
Hot Spot for Advancement for Women/Minorities:

Caterpillar Inc

www.cat.com

NAIC Code: 333120

TYPES OF BUSINESS:

Machinery-Earth Moving & Agricultural
Diesel and Turbine Engines
Financing
Fuel Cell Manufacturing
Rail Car Maintenance
Engine & Equipment Remanufacturing
Locomotive Manufacturing and Maintenance

BRANDS/DIVISIONS/AFFILIATES:

Cat
Caterpillar Financial Services Corporation
Caterpillar Insurance Holdings Inc

GROWTH PLANS/SPECIAL FEATURES:

Caterpillar is the world's leading manufacturer of construction and mining equipment, off-highway diesel and natural gas engines, industrial gas turbines and diesel-electric locomotives. Its reporting segments are: construction industries (40% sales/47% operating profit, or OP), resource industries (20% sales/19% OP), and energy & transportation (40% sales/34% OP). Market share approaches 20% across many products. Caterpillar operates a captive finance subsidiary to facilitate sales. The firm has global reach (46% US sales/54% ex-US). Construction skews more domestic, while the other divisions are more geographically diversified. An independent network of 156 dealers operates approximately 2,800 facilities, giving Caterpillar reach into about 190 countries for sales and support services.

Caterpillar offers its employees health coverage, 401(k), an employee assistance program and flexible spending accounts.

CONTACTS:
Note: Officers with more than one job title may be intentionally listed here more than once.

D. Umpleby, CEO
Andrew Bonfield, CFO
William Schaupp, Chief Accounting Officer
Derek Owens, Chief Legal Officer
Joseph Creed, COO
Anthony Fassino, Co-President
Jason Kaiser, Co-President
Denise Johnson, Co-President
Bob De Lange, Co-President
Cheryl Johnson, Other Executive Officer

FINANCIAL DATA:
Note: Data for latest year may not have been available at press time.

In U.S. $	2024	2023	2022	2021	2020	2019
Revenue	64,809,000,960	67,059,998,720	59,427,000,320	50,971,000,832	41,748,000,768	53,800,001,536
R&D Expense	2,107,000,000	2,108,000,000	1,814,000,000	1,686,000,000	1,415,000,000	1,693,000,000
Operating Income	13,072,000,000	12,966,000,000	8,829,000,000	6,878,000,000	4,553,000,000	8,290,000,000
Operating Margin %	.20%	.19%	.15%	.13%	.11%	.15%
SGA Expense	6,667,000,000	6,371,000,000	5,651,000,000	5,365,000,000	4,642,000,000	5,162,000,000
Net Income	10,792,000,000	10,335,000,000	6,705,000,000	6,489,000,000	2,998,000,000	6,093,000,000
Operating Cash Flow	12,035,000,000	12,885,000,000	7,766,000,000	7,198,000,000	6,327,000,000	6,912,000,000
Capital Expenditure	3,215,000,000	3,092,000,000	2,599,000,000	2,472,000,000	2,115,000,000	2,669,000,000
EBITDA	16,038,000,000	15,705,000,000	11,414,000,000	11,044,000,000	6,941,000,000	10,810,000,000
Return on Assets %	.12%	.12%	.08%	.08%	.04%	.08%
Return on Equity %	.55%	.58%	.41%	.41%	.20%	.43%
Debt to Equity	1.40%	1.26%	1.62%	1.58%	1.696	1.802

CONTACT INFORMATION:

Phone: 309 675-1000   Fax: 309 675-4332
Toll-Free:
Address: 510 Lake Cook Rd., Ste. 100, Deerfield, IL 60015 United States

STOCK TICKER/OTHER:

Stock Ticker: CAT
Employees: 113,200
Parent Company:

Exchange: NYS
Fiscal Year Ends: 12/31

SALARIES/BONUSES:

Top Exec. Salary: $1,811,250   Bonus: $
Second Exec. Salary: $1,115,000   Bonus: $

OTHER THOUGHTS:

Estimated Female Officers or Directors: 11
Hot Spot for Advancement for Women/Minorities: Y

CDM Smith Inc

NAIC Code: 237000

TYPES OF BUSINESS:

Water and Sewer Line and Related Structures Construction
Water Management
Environmental Services
Design Services
Information Management & Technology
Consulting
Facilities Design
Geotechnical Services

BRANDS/DIVISIONS/AFFILIATES:

CONTACTS: *Note: Officers with more than one job title may be intentionally listed here more than once.*

Timothy Wall, CEO
Anthony Bouchard, COO
Thierry Desmaris, Exec. VP-Finance
Julia Forgas, Exec. VP-Mktg. & Communications
Carlos Echalar, Chief Human Resources Officer
Jennifer Prescott, CIO
Timothy Wall, Chmn.

GROWTH PLANS/SPECIAL FEATURES:

CDM Smith, Inc. has been in business since 1947 and is a global privately-owned engineering and construction firm. The company partners with related professionals and clients to navigate, discuss and understand challenges, and then to develop and provide solutions. CDM's solutions are divided into water, environment, transportation and energy. CDM's water solutions include planning, consulting and engineering for water and resource management. The company takes a holistic approach concerning the environment with innovative technology and broad knowledge of regulations and compliance strategies. This solutions division is committed to protecting air, water and wildlife, whether by designing remediation systems, restoring fragile ecosystems or managing greenhouse gases for cities. Transportation solutions include funding, building and/or rebuilding transportation infrastructure, for the improvement of transportation-related mobility. Energy solutions include the development and management of energy across every industry sector. CDM's energy solutions take an approach that is efficient, economical and environmentally responsible, and include solutions for urban systems, combined heat and power, minimizing energy use and utilizing renewable sources. Its design and construction teams help clients expedite project delivery, optimize water management and streamline compliance in order to drive business growth and capture market share. Based in the U.S., CDM has global offices across Canada, Europe, Asia, Africa, the Middle East and Latin America.

CDM offers its employees medical, dental, vision, disability, life and AD&D, auto and homeowners insurance; and a 401(k), profit sharing and flexible spending programs. In addition, CDM offers adoption assistance, commuter benefits and programs, such as t

FINANCIAL DATA: *Note: Data for latest year may not have been available at press time.*

In U.S. $	2024	2023	2022	2021	2020	2019
Revenue	1,664,754,000	1,585,480,000	1,524,500,000	1,510,000,000	1,495,987,500	1,459,500,000
R&D Expense						
Operating Income						
Operating Margin %						
SGA Expense						
Net Income						
Operating Cash Flow						
Capital Expenditure						
EBITDA						
Return on Assets %						
Return on Equity %						
Debt to Equity						

CONTACT INFORMATION:

Phone: 617-452-6000   Fax: 617-345-3901
Toll-Free:
Address: 75 State St., Ste. 701, Boston, MA 02109 United States

STOCK TICKER/OTHER:

Stock Ticker: Private   Exchange:
Employees: 5,000   Fiscal Year Ends: 12/31
Parent Company:

SALARIES/BONUSES:

Top Exec. Salary: $ Bonus: $
Second Exec. Salary: $ Bonus: $

OTHER THOUGHTS:

Estimated Female Officers or Directors:
Hot Spot for Advancement for Women/Minorities:

Sales, profits and employees may be estimates. Financial information, benefits and other data can change quickly and may vary from those stated here.

Celanese Corporation

www.celanese.com

NAIC Code: 325211

TYPES OF BUSINESS:
Manufacturing-Acetyl Intermediate Chemicals
Industrial Products
Technical & High-Performance Polymers
Sweeteners & Sorbates
Ethanol Production
Food Ingredients
Cellulose Derivative Fibers

BRANDS/DIVISIONS/AFFILIATES:
Celanex
Celstran
Riteflex
Thermx PCT
Sunett
Ateva
VitalDose
Elotex

CONTACTS: Note: Officers with more than one job title may be intentionally listed here more than once.
Scott Richardson, CEO
Chuck Kyrish, CFO
Edward Galante, Chairman of the Board
Aaron McGilvray, Chief Accounting Officer
Ashley Duffie, General Counsel
Mark Murray, Senior VP, Divisional
Thomas Kelly, Senior VP, Divisional

GROWTH PLANS/SPECIAL FEATURES:
Celanese is one of the world's largest producers of acetic acid and its downstream derivative chemicals, which are used in various end markets, including coatings and adhesives. The company is also one of the largest producers of specialty polymers, which are used in the automotive, electronics, medical, building, and consumer end markets. The company also makes cellulose derivatives used in cigarette filters.

FINANCIAL DATA: Note: Data for latest year may not have been available at press time.

In U.S. $	2024	2023	2022	2021	2020	2019
Revenue	10,279,999,488	10,940,000,256	9,672,999,936	8,536,999,936	5,655,000,064	6,296,999,936
R&D Expense	130,000,000	146,000,000	112,000,000	86,000,000	74,000,000	67,000,000
Operating Income	1,037,000,000	1,218,000,000	1,382,000,000	1,938,000,000	715,000,000	1,032,000,000
Operating Margin %	.10%	.11%	.14%	.23%	.13%	.16%
SGA Expense	1,030,000,000	1,075,000,000	824,000,000	633,000,000	482,000,000	483,000,000
Net Income	-1,522,000,000	1,960,000,000	1,894,000,000	1,890,000,000	1,985,000,000	852,000,000
Operating Cash Flow	966,000,000	1,899,000,000	1,819,000,000	1,757,000,000	1,343,000,000	1,454,000,000
Capital Expenditure	435,000,000	568,000,000	543,000,000	467,000,000	364,000,000	370,000,000
EBITDA	503,000,000	2,642,000,000	2,304,000,000	2,717,000,000	2,716,000,000	1,459,000,000
Return on Assets %	-.06%	.07%	.10%	.17%	.19%	.09%
Return on Equity %	-.25%	.31%	.39%	.49%	.66%	.31%
Debt to Equity	2.20%	1.78%	2.44%	.81%	0.974	1.432

CONTACT INFORMATION:
Phone: 972 443-4000   Fax: 972 332-9373
Toll-Free:
Address: 222 West Las Colinas Blvd, Ste 900N, Irving, TX 75039-5421
United States

STOCK TICKER/OTHER:
Stock Ticker: CE   Exchange: NYS
Employees: 12,410   Fiscal Year Ends: 12/31
Parent Company:

SALARIES/BONUSES:
Top Exec. Salary: $1,326,996   Bonus: $
Second Exec. Salary: Bonus: $
$800,000

OTHER THOUGHTS:
Estimated Female Officers or Directors: 1
Hot Spot for Advancement for Women/Minorities: Y

Sales, profits and employees may be estimates. Financial information, benefits and other data can change quickly and may vary from those stated here.

Celestica Inc

NAIC Code: 334418

TYPES OF BUSINESS:

Contract Electronics Manufacturing
Product Design
Engineering and Design
Distribution Services

BRANDS/DIVISIONS/AFFILIATES:

GROWTH PLANS/SPECIAL FEATURES:

Celestica Inc offers supply chain solutions. The company has two operating and reportable segments: Advanced Technology Solutions (ATS) and Connectivity & Cloud Solutions (CCS). The ATS segment consists of the ATS end market and is comprised of the Aerospace and Defense, Industrial, health tech, and Capital Equipment businesses. Its Capital Equipment business is comprised of the semiconductor, display, and robotics equipment businesses, and the CCS segment consists of Communications and Enterprise end markets, The Enterprise end market is comprised of its servers and storage businesses. The company generates a majority of its revenue from the Connectivity & Cloud Solutions segment.

CONTACTS: Note: Officers with more than one job title may be intentionally listed here more than once.

Robert Mionis, CEO
Mandeep Chawla, CFO
Michael Wilson, Chairman of the Board
Yann Etienvre, COO
Jason Phillips, President, Divisional
Todd Cooper, President, Divisional

FINANCIAL DATA: Note: Data for latest year may not have been available at press time.

In U.S. $	2024	2023	2022	2021	2020	2019
Revenue	9,646,000,128	7,960,999,936	7,249,999,872	5,634,699,776	5,748,100,096	5,888,300,032
R&D Expense	78,000,000	60,900,000	46,300,000	38,400,000	29,900,000	28,400,000
Operating Income	618,700,000	350,400,000	296,000,000	178,000,000	151,400,000	95,300,000
Operating Margin %	.06%	.04%	.04%	.03%	.03%	.02%
SGA Expense	293,500,000	303,200,000	267,300,000	245,100,000	230,700,000	231,400,000
Net Income	428,000,000	244,400,000	180,100,000	103,900,000	60,600,000	70,300,000
Operating Cash Flow	473,900,000	326,200,000	211,100,000	226,800,000	239,600,000	345,000,000
Capital Expenditure	170,900,000	125,100,000	109,000,000	52,200,000	52,800,000	80,500,000
EBITDA	736,200,000	515,700,000	406,700,000	294,000,000	252,600,000	284,700,000
Return on Assets %	.07%	.04%	.03%	.02%	.02%	.02%
Return on Equity %	.23%	.14%	.11%	.07%	.04%	.05%
Debt to Equity	.41%	.37%	.44%	.51%	0.345	0.412

CONTACT INFORMATION:

Phone: 416 448-2211   Fax: 416 448-4810
Toll-Free: 888-899-9998
Address: 844 Don Mills Rd., Toronto, ON M3C 1V7 Canada

STOCK TICKER/OTHER:

Stock Ticker: CLS   Exchange: NYS
Employees: 26,554   Fiscal Year Ends: 12/31
Parent Company:

SALARIES/BONUSES:

Top Exec. Salary: $1,112,705   Bonus: $
Second Exec. Salary: Bonus: $
$600,000

OTHER THOUGHTS:

Estimated Female Officers or Directors: 4
Hot Spot for Advancement for Women/Minorities: Y

CGI Inc

NAIC Code: 541512

TYPES OF BUSINESS:

IT Consulting
Information Technology
Business Consulting
Software
Digital Transformation
Analytics
Automation
Cloud

BRANDS/DIVISIONS/AFFILIATES:

CGI Collections360
CGI Advantage
CGI Trade360
CGI OpenGrid360
CGI All Payments

GROWTH PLANS/SPECIAL FEATURES:

CGI is a Canada-based IT-services provider with an embedded position in North America and Europe. The company generates more than CAD 14 billion in annual revenue, employs over 90,000 personnel, and operates across 400 offices in 40 countries. CGI offers a broad portfolio of services such as consulting, systems integration, application maintenance, and business process services. Its largest vertical market is government, which contributes more than a third of group revenue.

CGI provides employee wellness programs, counseling services and various savings/profit assistance programs.

CONTACTS: Note: Officers with more than one job title may be intentionally listed here more than once.

Francois Boulanger, CEO
Tara McGeehan, Pres., Geographical
Steve Perron, CFO
Serge Godin, Co-Chairman of the Board
Julie Godin, Co-Chairman of the Board
Timothy Hurlebaus, COO
Jean-Michel Baticle, Co-President
Benoit Dube, Executive VP, Divisional
Mark Boyajian, Executive VP
Torsten Strass, Executive VP
Vijay Srinivasan, President, Divisional
David Henderson, President, Divisional
Leena-Mari Lahteenmaa, President, Geographical
Dirk de Groot, President, Geographical
Caroline de Grandmaison, President, Geographical
Rakesh Aerath, President, Geographical

FINANCIAL DATA: Note: Data for latest year may not have been available at press time.

In U.S. $	2024	2023	2022	2021	2020	2019
Revenue	10,682,110,364	10,405,676,591	9,365,456,178	8,826,546,305	8,853,711,855	8,815,223,350
R&D Expense						
Operating Income	1,758,805,000	1,684,212,000	1,521,681,000	1,425,357,000	1,368,364,000	1,329,958,000
Operating Margin %	.16%	.16%	.16%	.16%	.15%	.15%
SGA Expense						
Net Income	1,232,051,000	1,187,313,000	1,067,139,000	996,485,800	813,641,400	919,431,500
Operating Cash Flow	1,604,908,000	1,537,411,000	1,357,448,000	1,540,089,000	1,410,988,000	1,189,256,000
Capital Expenditure	191,891,700	223,428,900	213,812,500	171,584,500	176,570,300	195,092,000
EBITDA	2,054,679,000	1,991,501,000	1,840,298,000	1,784,480,000	1,595,836,000	1,554,970,000
Return on Assets %	.10%	.11%	.10%	.09%	.08%	.10%
Return on Equity %	.19%	.21%	.21%	.19%	.16%	.19%
Debt to Equity	.33%	.29%	.51%	.52%	0.547	0.322

CONTACT INFORMATION:

Phone: 514 841-3200   Fax: 514 841-3299
Toll-Free:
Address: 1350 Rene-Levesque Blvd. W., 25/Fl, Montreal, QC H3G 1T4 Canada

STOCK TICKER/OTHER:

Stock Ticker: GIB   Exchange: NYS
Employees: 91,500   Fiscal Year Ends: 09/30
Parent Company:

SALARIES/BONUSES:

Top Exec. Salary: $1,921,418   Bonus: $
Second Exec. Salary: $1,301,000   Bonus: $

OTHER THOUGHTS:

Estimated Female Officers or Directors: 4
Hot Spot for Advancement for Women/Minorities: Y

Sales, profits and employees may be estimates. Financial information, benefits and other data can change quickly and may vary from those stated here.

CHA Consulting Inc   www.chacompanies.com

NAIC Code: 541330

TYPES OF BUSINESS:

Engineering Services
Engineering Design
Engineering Consulting Services
Construction Management
Infrastructure and Building Solutions
Power Sector Solutions
Sustainable and Integrated Solutions
Complex Infrastructure Solutions

BRANDS/DIVISIONS/AFFILIATES:

HIG Capital
American Fire Protection LLC
CHA Integrated Solutions
D'Huy Engineering Inc

CONTACTS: *Note: Officers with more than one job title may be intentionally listed here more than once.*

Jim Stephenson, CEO
Doug Nelson, CFO
Jennifer Chatt, Chief People Officer

GROWTH PLANS/SPECIAL FEATURES:

CHA Consulting, Inc. is a full-service engineering design, consulting and construction management firm, operating throughout the U.S., as well as in Canada and Mexico. CHA provides a wide range of planning and design services to the infrastructure, buildings and power sectors, including those engaged in aviation, transportation, water resources, building design, fire protection services, land development, project management and construction management, sports, advanced energy and manufacturing, asset management and utility infrastructure. The firm has over 1,900 employees across its 55+ office locations. CHA delivers sustainable, integrated solutions to complex infrastructure projects. Subsidiaries of CHA include American Fire, which offers comprehensive fire protection in the industrial and commercial sectors, including fire suppression, special hazards, fire alarms, inspections, testing and maintenance services; and CHA Integrated Solutions, which offers a range of geospatial and asset management technology platforms for managing, distributing and interpreting critical data that increases workflow efficiency and enhances user productivity. CHA itself is privately-owned by an equity investment firm, H.I.G. Capital.

FINANCIAL DATA: *Note: Data for latest year may not have been available at press time.*

In U.S. $	2024	2023	2022	2021	2020	2019
Revenue	336,000,000	320,000,000	319,000,000	301,514,400	279,180,000	282,000,000
R&D Expense						
Operating Income						
Operating Margin %						
SGA Expense						
Net Income						
Operating Cash Flow						
Capital Expenditure						
EBITDA						
Return on Assets %						
Return on Equity %						
Debt to Equity						

CONTACT INFORMATION:

Phone: 518-453-4500   Fax: 518-458-1735
Toll-Free:
Address: 575 Broadway, Ste. 301, Albany, NY 12207 United States

STOCK TICKER/OTHER:

Stock Ticker: Private   Exchange:
Employees: 1,500   Fiscal Year Ends:
Parent Company: H.I.G. Capital

SALARIES/BONUSES:

Top Exec. Salary: $ Bonus: $
Second Exec. Salary: $ Bonus: $

OTHER THOUGHTS:

Estimated Female Officers or Directors:
Hot Spot for Advancement for Women/Minorities:

Chevron Corporation

www.chevron.com

NAIC Code: 211100

TYPES OF BUSINESS:

Oil & Gas Exploration & Production
Power Generation
Petrochemicals
Gasoline Retailing
Coal Mining
Fuel & Oil Additives
Convenience Stores
Pipelines

BRANDS/DIVISIONS/AFFILIATES:

Texaco
Chevron
Havoline
Delo
Ursa
Taro
Caltex
Chevron Phillips Chemical Company LLC

GROWTH PLANS/SPECIAL FEATURES:

Chevron is an integrated energy company with exploration, production, and refining operations worldwide. It is the second-largest oil company in the United States with production of 3.0 million of barrels of oil equivalent a day, including 7.7 million cubic feet a day of natural gas and 1.7 million of barrels of liquids a day. Production activities take place in North America, South America, Europe, Africa, Asia, and Australia. Its refineries are in the US and Asia for total refining capacity of 1.8 million barrels of oil a day. Proven reserves at year-end 2024 stood at 9.8 billion barrels of oil equivalent, including 5.1 billion barrels of liquids and 28.4 trillion cubic feet of natural gas.

CONTACTS:
Note: Officers with more than one job title may be intentionally listed here more than once.

Eimear Bonner, CFO
Michael Wirth, Chairman of the Board
Alana Knowles, Chief Accounting Officer
Mark Nelson, Executive VP, Divisional
Andrew Hearne, Executive VP
R Pate, General Counsel
Michelle Green, Other Executive Officer
Andy Walz, President, Divisional
Jeff Gustavson, Vice President, Divisional
Balaji Krishnamurthy, Vice President

FINANCIAL DATA:
Note: Data for latest year may not have been available at press time.

In U.S. $	2024	2023	2022	2021	2020	2019
Revenue	193,414,004,736	196,913,004,544	235,717,001,216	155,606,007,808	94,470,995,968	139,864,997,888
R&D Expense						
Operating Income	18,917,000,000	26,229,000,000	39,950,000,000	16,180,000,000	-6,097,000,000	100,000,000
Operating Margin %	.10%	.13%	.17%	.10%	-.06%	.00%
SGA Expense	4,834,000,000	4,141,000,000	4,312,000,000	4,014,000,000	4,213,000,000	4,143,000,000
Net Income	17,661,000,000	21,369,000,000	35,465,000,000	15,625,000,000	-5,543,000,000	2,924,000,000
Operating Cash Flow	31,492,000,000	35,609,000,000	49,602,000,000	29,187,000,000	10,577,000,000	27,314,000,000
Capital Expenditure	16,448,000,000	15,829,000,000	11,974,000,000	8,056,000,000	8,922,000,000	14,116,000,000
EBITDA	44,725,000,000	45,042,000,000	65,485,000,000	39,364,000,000	10,436,000,000	24,299,000,000
Return on Assets %	.07%	.08%	.14%	.07%	-.02%	.01%
Return on Equity %	.11%	.13%	.24%	.12%	-.04%	.02%
Debt to Equity	.13%	.13%	.13%	.22%	0.325	0.164

CONTACT INFORMATION:

Phone: 925 842-1000   Fax:
Toll-Free:
Address: 6001 Bollinger Canyon Rd., San Ramon, CA 94583 United States

STOCK TICKER/OTHER:

Stock Ticker: CVX
Employees: 45,600
Parent Company:

Exchange: NYS
Fiscal Year Ends: 12/31

SALARIES/BONUSES:

Top Exec. Salary: $1,889,583   Bonus: $
Second Exec. Salary: $1,259,375   Bonus: $

OTHER THOUGHTS:

Estimated Female Officers or Directors: 5
Hot Spot for Advancement for Women/Minorities: Y

Sales, profits and employees may be estimates. Financial information, benefits and other data can change quickly and may vary from those stated here.

China Chengda Engineering Co Ltd

www.chengda.com

NAIC Code: 541330

TYPES OF BUSINESS:

Engineering Services
Engineering
Infrastructure Construction
Procurement
Site Management
Plant and Facility Commissioning
Startup and General Contracting Services
Integrated Digital Technology

BRANDS/DIVISIONS/AFFILIATES:

China Natl Chemical Engingeering Group Corp Ltd

CONTACTS: Note: Officers with more than one job title may be intentionally listed here more than once.

Yiheng Liu, Chmn.

GROWTH PLANS/SPECIAL FEATURES:

China Chengda Engineering Co., Ltd., a wholly owned subsidiary of China National Chemical Engineering Group Corporation Ltd., is an international engineering corporation engaged in engineering design activities. China Chengda's engineering services include front-end planning and design, feasibility studies, engineering design, procurement, site construction management, commissioning, startup and general contracting services, as well as after-project operation and maintenance. The company has made significant contributions to the capital construction of China across the chemical, energy, municipal engineering and civil construction industries, including the construction of large-scale chemical industrial bases in Dalian, Jinxi, Chuanhua and Lutianhua, and petrochemical bases in Yanshan, Qilu, Chuanwei, Shanghai and Xinjiang. China Chengda has developed several proprietary technologies, with nearly 300 authorized patents that include more than 30 invention patents, covering chlori-alkali, soda ash, natural gas chemical industry, coal chemical industry, photothermal, succinic acid, new materials, new energy and other fields. In addition, China Chengda has set up an integrated engineering design platform and a refined project management platform, enabling the firm to offer industry-leading digitalized project capabilities.

FINANCIAL DATA: Note: Data for latest year may not have been available at press time.

In U.S. $	2024	2023	2022	2021	2020	2019
Revenue						
R&D Expense						
Operating Income						
Operating Margin %						
SGA Expense						
Net Income						
Operating Cash Flow						
Capital Expenditure						
EBITDA						
Return on Assets %						
Return on Equity %						
Debt to Equity						

CONTACT INFORMATION:

Phone: 86 28 65531100   Fax: 86 28 65530000
Toll-Free:
Address: Tianfu Ave., No. 279, Middle Section, Chengdu, Sichuan 610000 China

STOCK TICKER/OTHER:

Stock Ticker: Subsidiary   Exchange:
Employees: 1,200   Fiscal Year Ends:
Parent Company: China Natl Chemical Engingeering Group Corp Ltd

SALARIES/BONUSES:

Top Exec. Salary: $ Bonus: $
Second Exec. Salary: $ Bonus: $

OTHER THOUGHTS:

Estimated Female Officers or Directors:
Hot Spot for Advancement for Women/Minorities:

China Energy Engineering Corporation Limited

www.ceecglobal.net

NAIC Code: 541330

TYPES OF BUSINESS:

Engineering Services
Energy Solutions
Project Management
Real Estate Investment
Infrastructure
Green Hydrogen
Power Planning and Consulting
Power Investment

BRANDS/DIVISIONS/AFFILIATES:

China Energy Engineering Group Co Ltd
China Energy Engineering Group Planning
China Energy Engineering Group Equipment
China Energy Engineering Group Investment

CONTACTS: Note: Officers with more than one job title may be intentionally listed here more than once.

Hailiang Song, Chmn.

GROWTH PLANS/SPECIAL FEATURES:

China Energy Engineering Corporation Limited (CEEC) provides comprehensive solutions for the power industry in China and globally. The firm offers customers one-stop integrated engineering and full lifecycle project management services. Its business activities span power planning, engineering consultation, electric power, infrastructure projects, investment, real estate and equipment manufacturing. Power planning solutions include survey, design and consulting. Engineering consultation services and solutions encompass construction and contracting, testing, evaluation and supervision. Electric power services and solutions include projects such as fossil fuel, hydro, nuclear and alternative/new energy, as well as power transmission and more. Infrastructure projects by China Energy include tunnels, railways, roads, bridges, ports and channels. The investment division invests in and operates power plants, infrastructure projects and environmental protection projects, as well as areas involving water management, cement and other building materials, and civil explosives. The real estate division engages in real estate development, as well as finance and leasing services across the group's business activities. Last, the equipment manufacturing division designs, manufactures and sells auxiliary machinery equipment for power plants, power grids, structures and more. China Energy operates through more than 10 subsidiaries, including China Energy Engineering Group Planning & Engineering Co. Ltd., China Energy Engineering Group Equipment Co. Ltd. and China Energy Engineering Group Investment Co. Ltd. China Energy Engineering Corporation Limited is itself a subsidiary of China Energy Engineering Group Co. Ltd.

FINANCIAL DATA: Note: Data for latest year may not have been available at press time.

In U.S. $	2024	2023	2022	2021	2020	2019
Revenue		57,269,980,000	54,070,626,820	50,570,815,893	41,415,500,000	34,201,755,000
R&D Expense						
Operating Income						
Operating Margin %						
SGA Expense						
Net Income		1,126,426,000	1,157,809,338	15,058,259,237	1,331,670,000	1,305,444,000
Operating Cash Flow						
Capital Expenditure						
EBITDA						
Return on Assets %						
Return on Equity %						
Debt to Equity						

CONTACT INFORMATION:

Phone: 86-10-59099999   Fax: 86-10-59098888
Toll-Free:
Address: 26 Xidawang Rd., Bldg. 1, Chaoyang Dist., Beijing, Beijing 100022 China

STOCK TICKER/OTHER:

Stock Ticker: 3996   Exchange: Hong Kong
Employees: 114,786   Fiscal Year Ends: 12/31
Parent Company: China Energy Engineering Group Co Ltd

SALARIES/BONUSES:

Top Exec. Salary: $ Bonus: $
Second Exec. Salary: $ Bonus: $

OTHER THOUGHTS:

Estimated Female Officers or Directors:
Hot Spot for Advancement for Women/Minorities:

China FAW Group Co Ltd (First Automotive Works)

www.faw.com

NAIC Code: 336111

TYPES OF BUSINESS:

Automobile Manufacturing
Parts Manufacturing
Truck Manufacturing
Passenger Vehicle Manufacturing
All-Electric Vehicles
Commercial Truck Manufacturing

BRANDS/DIVISIONS/AFFILIATES:

First Automotive Works
China FAW Group Import & Export Co Ltd
Jiefang
Hongqi
Besturne
Advanced Technical Innovation Center
New Energy Vehicle R&D Center
China FAW Group Import & Export Co Ltd

CONTACTS: *Note: Officers with more than one job title may be intentionally listed here more than once.*

Liu Yigong, Pres.
Tieqi Teng, Chief Acct.

GROWTH PLANS/SPECIAL FEATURES:

FAW Group Corporation is a state-owned Chinese vehicle manufacturer. Founded in 1953 as First Automotive Works, the firm became one of the first vehicle producers in China, starting with the 1956 rollout of Jiefang trucks and the 1958 launch of Hongqi cars. Since then, FAW grew to produce millions of vehicles annually, including light-, medium- and heavy-duty trucks; automobiles; municipal buses; luxury tourist coaches; custom bus chassis; and mini-vehicles. Current passenger vehicle models include the Hongqi, Besturne, Junpau and Senia lines; and commercial heavy duty trucks are still branded under the Jiefang name. FAW Group offers all-electric vehicles, including the Hongqi line of passenger models. Headquartered in Changchun, Jilin Province, the firm's domestic production facilities, subsidiaries and engineering development/test centers are located throughout China. FAW's Advanced Technical Innovation Center is located in Beijing, China; its New Energy Vehicle Research and Development (R&D) Center and Exterior/Interior Design Center are located in Shanghai; its forward-looking technology R&D center is located in Munich, Germany; and its artificial-intelligence (AI) R&D center is located in California, USA. Subsidiary China FAW Group Import & Export Co., Ltd. provides global marketing services and solutions for the group's passenger and commercial vehicles.

FINANCIAL DATA: *Note: Data for latest year may not have been available at press time.*

In U.S. $	2024	2023	2022	2021	2020	2019
Revenue		89,485,000,000	90,566,280,000	110,926,179,000	106,848,000,000	88,723,900,000
R&D Expense						
Operating Income						
Operating Margin %						
SGA Expense						
Net Income			7,044,044,000			2,907,032,000
Operating Cash Flow						
Capital Expenditure						
EBITDA						
Return on Assets %						
Return on Equity %						
Debt to Equity						

CONTACT INFORMATION:

Phone: 86-431-8590-0715   Fax: 86-431-8761-4780
Toll-Free:
Address: Dongfeng St., No. 3025, Changchun, Jilin 130011 China

STOCK TICKER/OTHER:

Stock Ticker: Government-Owned   Exchange:
Employees: 120,000   Fiscal Year Ends: 12/31
Parent Company:

SALARIES/BONUSES:

Top Exec. Salary: $ Bonus: $
Second Exec. Salary: $ Bonus: $

OTHER THOUGHTS:

Estimated Female Officers or Directors:
Hot Spot for Advancement for Women/Minorities:

China National Machinery Industry Corporation

www.sinomach.com.cn/en

NAIC Code: 541330

TYPES OF BUSINESS:

Engineering Services
Research and Development
Manufacturing Services
Project Contract Services
Equipment Manufacturing
Trade
Asset Management
Financial Services

BRANDS/DIVISIONS/AFFILIATES:

SINOMACH
China National Erzhong Group Company
China National Machinery & Equipment I/E Corp
China United Engineering Corporation
China National Automotive Industry International
SINOMACH Finance Co Ltd

CONTACTS: *Note: Officers with more than one job title may be intentionally listed here more than once.*
Xiaolun Zhang, Chmn.

GROWTH PLANS/SPECIAL FEATURES:

China National Machinery Industry Corporation, known as SINOMACH, is a state-owned enterprise run directly by the central government. The firm provides research and development (R&D), manufacturing and project contracting services to equipment manufacturing industries worldwide. SINOMACH undertakes projects in the fields of scientific and technological R&D, technology and equipment development, industrial planning, standards setting, consultation, engineering studies, monitoring and testing. R&D and manufacture of machinery and equipment is one of the top priority businesses for SINOMACH. It has approximately 70 state-level research institutes in all specialties and fields and holds many patents. The equipment R&D and manufacturing division offers equipment such as heavy, petrochemical, general-purpose, farming, construction, forestry, power and environmental protection as well as machine tools, electrical equipment, power plants, meters and machinery components. The company offers contractor services in relation to power engineering, automotive engineering, factory construction and transport engineering, as well as port, dock and ship engineering. In the trade and services field, SINOMACH exports mechanical and electrical products to foreign countries and introduces advanced technologies and products from outside China. Export fields include the trade of machinery, electrical products, automobiles and exhibitions. SINOMACH also provides financial and asset management services and solutions. The firm comprises over 28 wholly owned and majority-owned subsidiaries, 14 of which are publicly listed. Just a few subsidiaries include China National Erzhong Group Company, China National Machinery & Equipment I/E Corporation, China United Engineering Corporation, China National Automotive Industry International Corporation and SINOMACH Finance Co. Ltd. SINOMACH has a market presence in over 100 countries and regions worldwide.

FINANCIAL DATA: *Note: Data for latest year may not have been available at press time.*

In U.S. $	2024	2023	2022	2021	2020	2019
Revenue		51,126,400,000	41,527,855,000	32,613,327,000	31,973,850,000	42,631,800,000
R&D Expense						
Operating Income						
Operating Margin %						
SGA Expense						
Net Income						
Operating Cash Flow						
Capital Expenditure						
EBITDA						
Return on Assets %						
Return on Equity %						
Debt to Equity						

CONTACT INFORMATION:

Phone: 86-10-82688888 Fax: 86-10-82688811
Toll-Free:
Address: No.3 Danling St., Haidian Dist., Beijing, Beijing 100080 China

STOCK TICKER/OTHER:

Stock Ticker: Government-Owned Exchange:
Employees: 130,000 Fiscal Year Ends: 12/31
Parent Company:

SALARIES/BONUSES:

Top Exec. Salary: $ Bonus: $
Second Exec. Salary: $ Bonus: $

OTHER THOUGHTS:

Estimated Female Officers or Directors:
Hot Spot for Advancement for Women/Minorities:

Sales, profits and employees may be estimates. Financial information, benefits and other data can change quickly and may vary from those stated here.

China Petroleum Pipeline Engineering Co Ltd

cpp.cnpc.com.cn/gdjen/index.shtml

NAIC Code: 541330

TYPES OF BUSINESS:

Engineering Services
Pipeline Engineering
Construction

BRANDS/DIVISIONS/AFFILIATES:

China National Petroleum Corporation

CONTACTS: *Note: Officers with more than one job title may be intentionally listed here more than once.*

Dai Houliang, Chmn.-China National

GROWTH PLANS/SPECIAL FEATURES:

China Petroleum Pipeline Engineering Co., Ltd. (CPP) specializes in transportation infrastructure and constructing storage facilities, primarily for the oil and gas industry. CPP is a subsidiary of China National Petroleum Corporation. The firm has built much of the cross-country pipeline infrastructure in China and has several large-scale projects worldwide. Its business covers onshore and offshore pipelines, storage facilities, technical services for pipelines, telecommunications and electricity installation and maintenance, above-ground facilities for oilfields, liquefied natural gas (LNG) processing and receiver facilities and refinery facilities. The firm can build and manage facilities throughout the lifecycle of the products, and can also provide one-stop service, from consultation to surveying to design to procurement to startup, operation and maintenance. CPP also provides research and development services as well as machinery manufacturing for its clients. Outside of China, CPP has operations in 47 countries across Africa, the Middle East, Central and Southeast Asia, Russia, America and Oceania. The firm has worked with around 80 well-known enterprises and organizations including Fluor, Wally Parson, SinoSure and more.

FINANCIAL DATA: *Note: Data for latest year may not have been available at press time.*

In U.S. $	2024	2023	2022	2021	2020	2019
Revenue		312,000,000,000	300,000,000,000	282,555,000,000	269,100,000,000	345,000,000,000
R&D Expense						
Operating Income						
Operating Margin %						
SGA Expense						
Net Income						
Operating Cash Flow						
Capital Expenditure						
EBITDA						
Return on Assets %						
Return on Equity %						
Debt to Equity						

CONTACT INFORMATION:

Phone: 86-316-2075403   Fax: 86-316-2073756
Toll-Free:
Address: No. 22, Jinguang Rd., Langfang, 065000 China

STOCK TICKER/OTHER:

Stock Ticker: Government-Owned   Exchange:
Employees: 1,050,000   Fiscal Year Ends:
Parent Company: China National Petroleum Corporation

SALARIES/BONUSES:

Top Exec. Salary: $ Bonus: $
Second Exec. Salary: $ Bonus: $

OTHER THOUGHTS:

Estimated Female Officers or Directors:
Hot Spot for Advancement for Women/Minorities:

China Railway Construction Company Limited (CRCC)

www.crcc.cn
NAIC Code: 237990

TYPES OF BUSINESS:

Transportation Infrastructure Construction
Design and Engineering
Highway and Bridge Construction
Railway Construction
Logistics Sites
Oil Storage Capacity
Financial Services

BRANDS/DIVISIONS/AFFILIATES:

CRCC High Tech Equipment Corporation Limited

CONTACTS: Note: Officers with more than one job title may be intentionally listed here more than once.

Xu Huaxiang, Pres.
Li Chongyang, Chmn.

GROWTH PLANS/SPECIAL FEATURES:

China Railway Construction Company Limited (CRCC) is a major construction corporation under the administration of the State-owned Assets Supervision and Administration Commission of the State Council of China (SASAC). CRCC's business covers project contracting, design and survey consultation, real estate investment and development, investment services, equipment manufacturing, materials, logistics, financial services and new industries. Project contracting services include railways, highways, residential buildings, municipal works, urban rail transportation, water conservation, hydroelectricity, airports and wharfs. Design and survey consultation services span multi-industry, whole process and lifecycle integration. As for the equipment manufacturing division, CRCC operates through its subsidiary, CRCC High-Tech Equipment Corporation Limited (CRCCE), to maintain production bases in Beijing, Kunming, Changsha, Xi'an, Lanzhou, Urumqi, Changzhou, Wuxi and other core cities in China, with its primary business including large railway track maintenance machinery, track construction equipment, tunnel boring machines, special construction equipment and electrified components, among others. These products are mainly used for new and existing railway and urban rail transit projects. The materials and logistics businesses consist of regional business outlets, logistics sites and refined oil storage capacity in major cities throughout the country. Financial services cover areas such as fund settlement and deposits, integrating credit management, interbank deposits, loans and leasing services, as well as risk consulting, insurance arrangements/claims/assessments and more. Lastly, CRCC actively explores new business fields such as new rail transit, construction industrialization, new materials, new energy, water resources and water treatment, among others.

FINANCIAL DATA: Note: Data for latest year may not have been available at press time.

In U.S. $	2024	2023	2022	2021	2020	2019
Revenue		160,511,706,000	157,534,677,424	160,036,537,055	139,466,305,315	123,434,082,304
R&D Expense						
Operating Income						
Operating Margin %						
SGA Expense						
Net Income		3,680,925,000	543,900,663	4,599,467,248	3,938,697,400	3,002,033,152
Operating Cash Flow						
Capital Expenditure						
EBITDA						
Return on Assets %						
Return on Equity %						
Debt to Equity						

CONTACT INFORMATION:

Phone: 86 1052688600   Fax: 86 1052688302
Toll-Free:
Address: No. 40 Fuxing Rd. E., Beijing, Beijing 100855 China

STOCK TICKER/OTHER:

Stock Ticker: 1186   Exchange: Hong Kong
Employees: 270,000   Fiscal Year Ends: 12/31
Parent Company:

SALARIES/BONUSES:

Top Exec. Salary: $ Bonus: $
Second Exec. Salary: $ Bonus: $

OTHER THOUGHTS:

Estimated Female Officers or Directors:
Hot Spot for Advancement for Women/Minorities:

China State Construction Engineering Corp (CSCEC)

www.cscec.com.cn
NAIC Code: 531100

TYPES OF BUSINESS:

Construction & Real Estate Development
Contract Engineering
Property Development
Infrastructure Design and Construction
Real Estate Investments

BRANDS/DIVISIONS/AFFILIATES:

China State Construction International Co
China Construction Development Co Ltd
China State Decoration Group Co Ltd
China Overseas Property Holdings Limited
China Construction (South Pacific) Dev Co
China Construction America Inc

CONTACTS: *Note: Officers with more than one job title may be intentionally listed here more than once.*

Mao Zhibing, Chief Engineer
Zeng Zhaohe, General Counsel
Liu Jie, Leader-Discipline Inspection
Liu Jinzhang, VP
Kong Qingping, VP
Wang Xiangming, VP
Xuexuan Zheng, Chmn.

GROWTH PLANS/SPECIAL FEATURES:

China State Construction Engineering Corporation (CSCEC) is a Chinese state-owned enterprise that primarily engages in global investing and construction, while owning more than 100 subsidiaries and eight listed companies. The firm is a leading international contracting agent in China, and one of the largest house builders in the world. The company also conducts infrastructure and investment, real estate investment and development, investigation and design and new business. CSCEC has worked on office buildings, public facilities, airports, hotels, educational institutions, sports facilities, residential complexes, hospitals and military buildings, as well as green construction, energy conservation and other environmental segments. Its technologies are used for many applications, such as constructing high-rises, installing large industrial works, complex deep pit support and dewatering activities, concrete manufacturing, project management and general contracting of international projects. New business activities of CSCEC include energy-saving building materials, environmental protection in relation to water, ecommerce in relation to the construction industry, and financial in relation to the group's assets. Specific projects by CSCEC have included the Hada Express Way, Wuhan Railway Station, Shaanxi LanShang Expressway, the Tianjin Cihan Ferris Wheel, the Beijing Subway Line 4, Hongheyan Nuclear Station and China World Trade Center. The company has various domestic affiliated companies, such as China State Construction International Co., China Construction Development Co. Ltd., China State Decoration Group Co. Ltd. and China Overseas Property Holdings Limited. The firm also has various international affiliated companies such as China Construction (South Pacific) Development Co. Pte. Ltd. in Singapore, and China Construction America, Inc. in New Jersey, USA.

FINANCIAL DATA: *Note: Data for latest year may not have been available at press time.*

In U.S. $	2024	2023	2022	2021	2020	2019
Revenue		319,548,368,000	293,611,562,415	252,378,241,789	247,429,648,813	203,182,875,253
R&D Expense						
Operating Income						
Operating Margin %						
SGA Expense						
Net Income			7,282,749,990	7,367,673,735	10,869,952,968	9,044,859,889
Operating Cash Flow						
Capital Expenditure						
EBITDA						
Return on Assets %						
Return on Equity %						
Debt to Equity						

CONTACT INFORMATION:

Phone: 86-10-880-82888   Fax:
Toll-Free:
Address: Bldg. 3, Crtyd. 5, Anding Rd., Chaoyang Dist., Beijing, Beijing 100029 China

STOCK TICKER/OTHER:

Stock Ticker: 601668   Exchange: Shanghai
Employees: 382,492   Fiscal Year Ends: 12/31
Parent Company:

SALARIES/BONUSES:

Top Exec. Salary: $ Bonus: $
Second Exec. Salary: $ Bonus: $

OTHER THOUGHTS:

Estimated Female Officers or Directors:
Hot Spot for Advancement for Women/Minorities:

Chiyoda Corporation

www.chiyodacorp.com/en

NAIC Code: 541330

TYPES OF BUSINESS:

Engineering & Construction Services
Plant Lifecycle Engineering
Computer-Aided Engineering
Risk Management
Pollution Prevention Systems
Industrial Equipment-Online Procurement

BRANDS/DIVISIONS/AFFILIATES:

Chiyoda System Technologies Corporation
Chiyoda U-Tech Co Ltd
Chiyoda Oceania Pty Ltd
Chiyoda Almana Engineering LLC
L&T-Chiyoda Limited

GROWTH PLANS/SPECIAL FEATURES:

Chiyoda Corp offers engineering, procurement, and construction, or EPC, services to the energy and chemical industries. The Japanese firm is involved in two main areas of activity: energy and environment. Its energy segment involves constructing liquefied natural gas plants and other gas-related facilities. Chiyoda also provides EPC, operation, expansion, and improvement services to petrochemical and metal firms through this business. The environment segment includes EPC work on pharmaceutical manufacturers as well as preservation technology offerings like air pollution control and wastewater treatment. Chiyoda uses artificial intelligence technology to optimize plant operations in their digital transformation business. It earns the majority of its total revenue overseas.

CONTACTS: Note: Officers with more than one job title may be intentionally listed here more than once.

Atsushi Deguchi, CFO
Masakazu Sakakida, Chairman of the Board
Naoki Kobayashi, Director

FINANCIAL DATA: Note: Data for latest year may not have been available at press time.

In U.S. $	2024	2023	2022	2021	2020	2019
Revenue	3,512,781,355	2,986,413,602	2,159,920,853	2,189,621,119	2,679,290,485	2,374,007,326
R&D Expense						
Operating Income	-104,179,400	125,777,600	73,208,840	48,701,750	185,996,900	-1,387,087,000
Operating Margin %	-.03%	.04%	.03%	.02%	.07%	-.58%
SGA Expense						
Net Income	-109,907,000	105,436,000	-87,677,040	55,491,530	84,539,020	-1,492,280,000
Operating Cash Flow	435,622,100	306,560,700	-177,665,900	-144,446,000	-223,667,000	-263,406,000
Capital Expenditure	26,978,620	19,327,970	14,850,040	14,919,470	15,703,970	15,641,490
EBITDA	-14,100,250	173,243,600	-36,698,140	90,801,170	159,615,400	-1,326,618,000
Return on Assets %	-.04%	.04%	-.03%	.02%	.03%	-.56%
Return on Equity %	-1.17%	.80%	-.49%	.26%		-4.41%
Debt to Equity	.74%	1.06%	1.60%	1.24%	1.464	

CONTACT INFORMATION:

Phone: 81-45-225-7777   Fax:
Toll-Free:
Address: 4-6-2 Minatomirai, Nishi-ku, Yokohama, 220-8765 Japan

STOCK TICKER/OTHER:

Stock Ticker: CHYCF   Exchange: PINX
Employees: 5,943   Fiscal Year Ends: 03/31
Parent Company:

SALARIES/BONUSES:

Top Exec. Salary: $ Bonus: $
Second Exec. Salary: $ Bonus: $

OTHER THOUGHTS:

Estimated Female Officers or Directors:
Hot Spot for Advancement for Women/Minorities:

Cisco Systems Inc

NAIC Code: 334210

TYPES OF BUSINESS:

Computer Networking Equipment
Routers & Switches
Real-Time Conferencing Technology
Server Virtualization Software
Data Storage Products
Security Products
Teleconference Systems and Technology
Unified Communications Systems

BRANDS/DIVISIONS/AFFILIATES:

AppDynamics Inc
Acacia Communications Inc
Webex

GROWTH PLANS/SPECIAL FEATURES:

Cisco Systems is the largest provider of networking equipment in the world and one of the largest software companies in the world. Its largest businesses are selling networking hardware and software (where it has leading market shares) and cybersecurity software such as firewalls. It also has collaboration products, like its Webex suite, and observability tools. It primarily outsources its manufacturing to third parties and has a large sales and marketing staff, 25,000 strong across 90 countries. Overall, Cisco employs 80,000 people and sells its products globally.

CONTACTS: Note: Officers with more than one job title may be intentionally listed here more than once.

Charles Robbins, CEO
R. Herren, CFO
M. Wong, Chief Accounting Officer
Deborah Stahlkopf, Chief Legal Officer
Thimaya Subaiya, Executive VP, Divisional
Gary Steele, President, Divisional

FINANCIAL DATA: Note: Data for latest year may not have been available at press time.

In U.S. $	2024	2023	2022	2021	2020	2019
Revenue	53,802,999,808	56,997,998,592	51,556,999,168	49,818,001,408	49,301,000,192	51,904,000,000
R&D Expense	7,983,000,000	7,551,000,000	6,774,000,000	6,549,000,000	6,347,000,000	6,577,000,000
Operating Income	12,970,000,000	15,562,000,000	13,975,000,000	13,719,000,000	14,101,000,000	14,541,000,000
Operating Margin %	.24%	.27%	.27%	.28%	.29%	.28%
SGA Expense	13,177,000,000	12,358,000,000	11,186,000,000	11,411,000,000	11,094,000,000	11,398,000,000
Net Income	10,320,000,000	12,613,000,000	11,812,000,000	10,591,000,000	11,214,000,000	11,621,000,000
Operating Cash Flow	10,880,000,000	19,886,000,000	13,226,000,000	15,454,000,000	15,426,000,000	15,831,000,000
Capital Expenditure	670,000,000	849,000,000	477,000,000	692,000,000	770,000,000	909,000,000
EBITDA	15,747,000,000	17,471,000,000	16,794,000,000	15,558,000,000	16,363,000,000	17,327,000,000
Return on Assets %	.09%	.13%	.12%	.11%	.12%	.11%
Return on Equity %	.23%	.30%	.29%	.27%	.31%	.30%
Debt to Equity	.43%	.15%	.21%	.22%	0.305	0.431

CONTACT INFORMATION:

Phone: 408 526-4000   Fax: 408 526-4100
Toll-Free: 800-553-6387
Address: 170 W. Tasman Dr., San Jose, CA 95134-1706 United States

STOCK TICKER/OTHER:

Stock Ticker: CSCO   Exchange: NAS
Employees: 90,400   Fiscal Year Ends: 07/31
Parent Company:

SALARIES/BONUSES:

Top Exec. Salary: $1,390,000   Bonus: $
Second Exec. Salary: $891,238   Bonus: $

OTHER THOUGHTS:

Estimated Female Officers or Directors: 10
Hot Spot for Advancement for Women/Minorities: Y

Citrix Systems Inc

www.citrix.com

NAIC Code: 511210B

TYPES OF BUSINESS:

Computer Software: Network Management (IT), System Testing & Storage
IT Development
Cloud
Workspace Organization
Application Programming
Collaboration
Security
Delivery Management

GROWTH PLANS/SPECIAL FEATURES:

Citrix Systems, Inc. is a software company that enables users to remotely connect applications and desktops to a central server. Citrix offers digital workspaces, desktop as a service (DaaS) and virtual desktop infrastructure (VDI), secure access, Zero Trust Network Access (ZTNA) and analytics. Products include Citrix DaaS, Citrix Virtual Apps and Desktops, Citrix Analytics for Performance, Citrix Analytics for Security and Citrix Secure Private Access. Citrix has 60 offices in 40 countries. The company is owned by Cloud Software Group.

Citrix offers its employees health benefits, wellness programs, job development, a 401(k), a bonus program and flexible workstyles.

BRANDS/DIVISIONS/AFFILIATES:

Cloud Software Group
Citrix DaaS
Citrix Virtual Apps and Desktops
Citrix Analytics for Performance
Citrix Analytics for Security
Citrix Secure Private Access

CONTACTS: Note: Officers with more than one job title may be intentionally listed here more than once.

Tom Krause, CEO
Andy Nallappan, COO
Tom Berquist, CFO
Timothy Minahan, Chief Marketing Officer
Mark Schmitz, COO
Sridhar Mullapudi, Executive VP, Divisional
Hector Lima, Executive VP, Divisional
Donna Kimmel, Executive VP
Mark Ferrer, Executive VP

FINANCIAL DATA: Note: Data for latest year may not have been available at press time.

In U.S. $	2024	2023	2022	2021	2020	2019
Revenue	3,511,040,000	3,328,000,000	3,200,000,000	3,217,169,920	3,236,699,904	3,010,564,096
R&D Expense						
Operating Income						
Operating Margin %						
SGA Expense						
Net Income				307,499,008	504,446,016	681,812,992
Operating Cash Flow						
Capital Expenditure						
EBITDA						
Return on Assets %						
Return on Equity %						
Debt to Equity						

CONTACT INFORMATION:

Phone: 954 267-3000   Fax: 954 267-9319
Toll-Free: 800-424-8749
Address: 851 W. Cypress Creek Rd., Fort Lauderdale, FL 33309 United States

STOCK TICKER/OTHER:

Stock Ticker: Private   Exchange:
Employees: 9,700   Fiscal Year Ends: 12/31
Parent Company: Cloud Software Group

SALARIES/BONUSES:

Top Exec. Salary: $ Bonus: $
Second Exec. Salary: $ Bonus: $

OTHER THOUGHTS:

Estimated Female Officers or Directors: 2
Hot Spot for Advancement for Women/Minorities:

Clariant International Ltd

www.clariant.com

NAIC Code: 325510

TYPES OF BUSINESS:

Paint and Coating Manufacturing
Chemical Additives
Catalysts
Functional Materials
Textile, Leather & Paper Chemicals
Pigments

BRANDS/DIVISIONS/AFFILIATES:

GROWTH PLANS/SPECIAL FEATURES:

Clariant AG is a Switzerland-based specialty chemicals company with world-wide operations. The company reports in three business areas: care chemicals, absorbents and additives and catalysts. Care chemicals mainly targets consumer end markets such as personal care and homecare, but it also has an industrial component. Absorbents and additives encompass Clariant's coatings and adhesives, absorbents, and plastics segments. Catalysts manufacturers process catalysts, mainly for petrochemical and syngas plants.

CONTACTS: Note: Officers with more than one job title may be intentionally listed here more than once.

Gunter Au, Chairman of the Board
Ahmed Al Umar, Director

FINANCIAL DATA: Note: Data for latest year may not have been available at press time.

In U.S. $	2024	2023	2022	2021	2020	2019
Revenue	5,052,356,921	5,326,147,861	6,325,181,099	5,320,063,383	4,697,037,022	5,352,918,695
R&D Expense	153,323,000	194,695,800	194,695,800	188,611,600	209,298,000	210,514,900
Operating Income	468,486,800	292,043,700	37,722,320	485,522,800	334,633,500	160,624,100
Operating Margin %	.09%	.05%	.01%	.09%	.07%	.03%
SGA Expense	910,203,000	862,745,900	1,014,852,000	901,685,100	883,432,300	1,302,028,000
Net Income	296,911,100	163,057,800	102,215,300	418,596,000	954,009,600	12,168,490
Operating Cash Flow	508,642,900	512,293,400	610,858,200	441,716,200	449,017,300	619,376,100
Capital Expenditure	254,321,400	251,887,700	257,972,000	438,065,600	363,837,900	351,669,300
EBITDA	846,926,900	683,869,100	445,366,700	889,516,600	694,820,700	604,774,000
Return on Assets %	.04%	.02%	.01%	.05%	.11%	.00%
Return on Equity %	.11%	.06%	.04%	.15%	.33%	.00%
Debt to Equity	.67%	.45%	.45%	.51%	0.695	0.659

CONTACT INFORMATION:

Phone: 41 614695111   Fax: 41 614695901
Toll-Free:
Address: Hardstrasse 61, Pratteln, 4133 Switzerland

STOCK TICKER/OTHER:

Stock Ticker: CLZNF   Exchange: PINX
Employees: 10,481   Fiscal Year Ends: 12/31
Parent Company:

SALARIES/BONUSES:

Top Exec. Salary: $ Bonus: $
Second Exec. Salary: $ Bonus: $

OTHER THOUGHTS:

Estimated Female Officers or Directors:
Hot Spot for Advancement for Women/Minorities:

Compal Electronics Inc

NAIC Code: 334418

TYPES OF BUSINESS:

Contract Electronics Manufacturing
Personal Music Players
Monitors
Notebook Computers
LCD Televisions
Automotive Electronics
Internet of Things
Manufacturing

BRANDS/DIVISIONS/AFFILIATES:

GROWTH PLANS/SPECIAL FEATURES:

Compal Electronics Inc is a Taiwan-based original design manufacturer that produces notebook computers, monitors, and televisions for equipment manufacturers. The firm's operations are organized in two reportable segment Information technology products and strategy integrate product segment. The majority of the firm's revenue is generated from the United States, with the rest coming from China, Netherlands, United Kingdom, and Others.

Compal offers its employees company trips, an onsite fitness center, shuttle services, a pension plan and health insurance.

CONTACTS:
Note: Officers with more than one job title may be intentionally listed here more than once.

Sheng-Hsiung Hsu, Chairman of the Board
Sheng-Hua Peng, Director
Jui-Tsung Chen, Director

FINANCIAL DATA:
Note: Data for latest year may not have been available at press time.

In U.S. $	2024	2023	2022	2021	2020	2019
Revenue	30,441,209,104	31,660,583,734	35,892,111,460	41,324,395,385	35,078,899,162	32,788,520,936
R&D Expense	632,066,900	638,088,900	599,609,600			
Operating Income	496,356,000	402,906,500	308,307,000	446,411,400	384,340,300	354,035,500
Operating Margin %	.02%	.01%	.01%	.01%	.01%	.01%
SGA Expense	388,908,600	376,866,000	441,965,700			
Net Income	335,844,100	256,425,200	243,739,300	422,469,000	313,085,900	232,623,200
Operating Cash Flow	844,223,700	992,482,200	1,961,026,000	-797,083,200	476,939,400	699,654,500
Capital Expenditure	265,241,900	252,260,400	280,460,000	424,649,100	256,739,900	221,743,400
EBITDA	911,423,500	829,921,900	719,491,600	850,113,200	684,399,600	640,521,100
Return on Assets %	.02%	.02%	.01%	.03%	.02%	.02%
Return on Equity %	.08%	.07%	.06%	.12%	.09%	.07%
Debt to Equity	.13%	.20%	.18%	.10%	0.124	0.095

CONTACT INFORMATION:

Phone: 886 2-87978588   Fax: 886-2-26585001
Toll-Free:
Address: 581 Juikang Rd., Neihu, Taipei, 114 Taiwan

STOCK TICKER/OTHER:

Stock Ticker: CMPCY
Employees: 8,720
Parent Company:

Exchange: PINX
Fiscal Year Ends: 12/31

SALARIES/BONUSES:

Top Exec. Salary: $ Bonus: $
Second Exec. Salary: $ Bonus: $

OTHER THOUGHTS:

Estimated Female Officers or Directors:
Hot Spot for Advancement for Women/Minorities:

ConocoPhillips Company

www.conocophillips.com

NAIC Code: 211100

TYPES OF BUSINESS:

Oil & Gas Exploration & Production
Natural Gas Distribution
Oil Sands
Bitumen
Natural Gas Liquids
Liquefied Natural Gas

GROWTH PLANS/SPECIAL FEATURES:

ConocoPhillips is a US-based independent exploration and production firm. In 2024, it produced 2.0 million barrels per day of oil and natural gas liquids and 3.4 billion cubic feet per day of natural gas, primarily from Alaska and the Lower 48 in the United States and Norway in Europe and several countries in Asia-Pacific and the Middle East. Proven reserves at year-end 2024 were 7.8 billion barrels of oil equivalent.

BRANDS/DIVISIONS/AFFILIATES:

Concho Resources Inc

CONTACTS: *Note: Officers with more than one job title may be intentionally listed here more than once.*

Ryan Lance, CEO
William Bullock, CFO
Christopher Delk, Chief Accounting Officer
Nicholas Olds, Executive VP, Divisional
Kelly Rose, General Counsel
C. Giraud, Senior VP, Divisional
Andrew Lundquist, Senior VP, Divisional
Kirk Johnson, Senior VP, Divisional
Andrew OBrien, Senior VP, Geographical

FINANCIAL DATA: *Note: Data for latest year may not have been available at press time.*

In U.S. $	2024	2023	2022	2021	2020	2019
Revenue	54,745,001,984	56,141,000,704	78,493,999,104	45,828,001,792	18,784,000,000	32,566,999,040
R&D Expense						
Operating Income	12,783,000,000	15,026,000,000	25,462,000,000	12,071,000,000	-1,800,000,000	7,061,000,000
Operating Margin %	.23%	.27%	.32%	.26%	-.10%	.22%
SGA Expense	1,158,000,000	705,000,000	623,000,000	719,000,000	430,000,000	556,000,000
Net Income	9,245,000,000	10,957,000,000	18,680,000,000	8,079,000,000	-2,701,000,000	7,189,000,000
Operating Cash Flow	20,124,000,000	19,965,000,000	28,314,000,000	16,996,000,000	4,802,000,000	11,104,000,000
Capital Expenditure	12,118,000,000	11,248,000,000	10,159,000,000	5,324,000,000	4,715,000,000	6,636,000,000
EBITDA	24,425,000,000	25,783,000,000	37,127,000,000	21,090,000,000	3,439,000,000	16,718,000,000
Return on Assets %	.08%	.12%	.20%	.11%	-.04%	.10%
Return on Equity %	.16%	.22%	.40%	.21%	-.08%	.21%
Debt to Equity	.36%	.36%	.34%	.41%	0.494	0.423

CONTACT INFORMATION:

Phone: 281 293-1000   Fax:
Toll-Free:
Address: 925 N. Eldridge Pkwy., Houston, TX 77079 United States

STOCK TICKER/OTHER:

Stock Ticker: COP   Exchange: NYS
Employees: 9,900   Fiscal Year Ends: 12/31
Parent Company:

SALARIES/BONUSES:

Top Exec. Salary: $1,791,833   Bonus: $
Second Exec. Salary: Bonus: $
$1,084,776

OTHER THOUGHTS:

Estimated Female Officers or Directors: 1
Hot Spot for Advancement for Women/Minorities: Y

Contemporary Amperex Technology Co Limited (CATL)

www.catl.com/en

NAIC Code: 335912

TYPES OF BUSINESS:

Lithium Batteries, Primary, Manufacturing
Electric Vehicle Batteries
Energy Storage Batteries
Technology
Research and Development

BRANDS/DIVISIONS/AFFILIATES:

Contemporary Amperex Technology (USA) Inc
Contemporary Amperex Technology Canada Limited
Contemporary Amperex Technology France
Contemporary Amperex Technology GmbH
United Auto Battery Co
Guangdong Brunp Recycling Technology Limited
CATL Xiamen Institute of New Energy
EVOGO

CONTACTS:
Note: Officers with more than one job title may be intentionally listed here more than once.

Robin Zeng, CEO
Robin Zeng, Chmn.

GROWTH PLANS/SPECIAL FEATURES:

Contemporary Amperex Technology Co., Limited (CATL) is a Chinese battery products manufacturing giant engaged in related research and technology development. CATL's technologies cover the full industry chains of vehicle and energy storage batteries, including materials, batter cells, modules, battery management systems, battery recycling and reuse. The firm's business focuses on research and development (R&D), production and sales of electric vehicles and energy storage battery systems. CATL's lithium-ion battery can be applied to electric passenger vehicles, buses, trucks and diversified special vehicles. Battery and storage systems include cells, modules, electric boxes and battery cabinets, all of which provide the flow and/or storage of new energy. The company has two segments and brands: the technology brand, which is run through TECHZONE; and the service brand, run through EVOGO. The company has manufacturing facilities, branch offices and R&D centers located in China and Germany, and branch offices in China, Canada, the U.S., the U.K., Germany, Hong Kong and Japan. Subsidiaries include Contemporary Amperex Technology (USA), Inc.; Contemporary Amperex Technology Canada Limited; Contemporary Amperex Technology France; Contemporary Amperex Technology GmbH; United Auto Battery Co.; and Guangdong Brunp Recycling Technology Limited, among others. In addition, CATL Xiamen Institute of New Energy, co-established with Xiamen University, plans and organizes sci-tech industrial projects in key areas such as intelligent energy, energy storage technologies, high-power devices and next-generation power batteries.

FINANCIAL DATA:
Note: Data for latest year may not have been available at press time.

In U.S. $	2024	2023	2022	2021	2020	2019
Revenue		56,548,547,000	47,400,000,000	17,920,623,000	7,709,190,000	6,552,410,000
R&D Expense						
Operating Income						
Operating Margin %						
SGA Expense						
Net Income		6,223,214,000	4,436,738,000	2,198,318,690	7,709,190,000	717,329,000
Operating Cash Flow						
Capital Expenditure						
EBITDA						
Return on Assets %						
Return on Equity %						
Debt to Equity						

CONTACT INFORMATION:

Phone: 86-593-2583668   Fax: 86-593-2583667
Toll-Free:
Address: No. 2 Xingang Rd., Zhangman Twon, Jiaocheng Dist., Ningde, Fujian 352100 China

STOCK TICKER/OTHER:

Stock Ticker: 300750   Exchange: Shenzhen
Employees: 118,914   Fiscal Year Ends: 12/31
Parent Company:

SALARIES/BONUSES:

Top Exec. Salary: $ Bonus: $
Second Exec. Salary: $ Bonus: $

OTHER THOUGHTS:

Estimated Female Officers or Directors:
Hot Spot for Advancement for Women/Minorities:

Corning Incorporated

NAIC Code: 327212

www.corning.com

TYPES OF BUSINESS:
Glass & Optical Fiber Manufacturing
Glass Substrates for LCDs
Optical Switching Products
Photonic Modules & Components
Networking Devices
Semiconductor Materials
Laboratory Supplies
Emissions Control Products

GROWTH PLANS/SPECIAL FEATURES:
Corning is a leader in materials science, specializing in the production of glass, ceramics, and optical fiber. The firm supplies its products for a wide range of applications, from flat-panel displays in televisions to gasoline particulate filters in automobiles to optical fiber for broadband access, with a leading share in many of its end markets.

BRANDS/DIVISIONS/AFFILIATES:
Eagle XG
Iris
Vascade
LEAF
ClearCurve
InfiniCor
Gorilla

CONTACTS: Note: Officers with more than one job title may be intentionally listed here more than once.
Wendell Weeks, CEO
Avery Nelson, General Manager, Divisional
Edward Schlesinger, CFO
Stefan Becker, Chief Accounting Officer
Lewis Steverson, Chief Administrative Officer
Soumya Seetharam, Chief Information Officer
Jeffrey Evenson, Chief Strategy Officer
Jaymin Amin, Chief Technology Officer
Eric Musser, COO
Martin Curran, Executive VP
John Zhang, General Manager, Divisional
Li Fang, General Manager, Divisional
Ronald Verkleeren, General Manager, Divisional
John Bayne, General Manager, Divisional
Michael Bell, General Manager, Divisional
Jordana Kammerud, Other Executive Officer

FINANCIAL DATA: Note: Data for latest year may not have been available at press time.

In U.S. $	2024	2023	2022	2021	2020	2019
Revenue	13,118,000,128	12,588,000,256	14,188,999,680	14,081,999,872	11,303,000,064	11,502,999,552
R&D Expense	1,089,000,000	1,076,000,000	1,047,000,000	995,000,000	1,154,000,000	1,031,000,000
Operating Income	1,135,000,000	890,000,000	1,438,000,000	2,112,000,000	509,000,000	1,306,000,000
Operating Margin %	.09%	.07%	.10%	.15%	.05%	.11%
SGA Expense	1,931,000,000	1,843,000,000	1,898,000,000	1,827,000,000	1,747,000,000	1,585,000,000
Net Income	506,000,000	581,000,000	1,316,000,000	1,906,000,000	512,000,000	960,000,000
Operating Cash Flow	1,939,000,000	2,005,000,000	2,615,000,000	3,412,000,000	2,180,000,000	2,031,000,000
Capital Expenditure	965,000,000	1,390,000,000	1,604,000,000	1,637,000,000	1,377,000,000	1,978,000,000
EBITDA	2,492,000,000	2,514,000,000	3,541,000,000	4,207,000,000	2,419,000,000	2,940,000,000
Return on Assets %	.02%	.02%	.04%	.04%	.01%	.03%
Return on Equity %	.05%	.05%	.11%	.09%	.04%	.08%
Debt to Equity	.72%	.70%	.62%	.62%	0.771	0.771

CONTACT INFORMATION:
Phone: 607 974-9000   Fax: 607 974-8688
Toll-Free:
Address: 1 Riverfront Plaza, Corning, NY 14831 United States

STOCK TICKER/OTHER:
Stock Ticker: GLW   Exchange: NYS
Employees: 49,800   Fiscal Year Ends: 12/31
Parent Company:

SALARIES/BONUSES:
Top Exec. Salary: $1,623,754   Bonus: $
Second Exec. Salary: Bonus: $
$955,054

OTHER THOUGHTS:
Estimated Female Officers or Directors: 1
Hot Spot for Advancement for Women/Minorities: Y

COWI A/S

NAIC Code: 541330

www.cowi.com

TYPES OF BUSINESS:
Engineering Consulting Services
Engineering
Architecture
Consultancy
Environmental Science Services
Project Management
Sustainability and Urbanization
Digitalization and Technology

BRANDS/DIVISIONS/AFFILIATES:
Mannvit

GROWTH PLANS/SPECIAL FEATURES:
COWI A/S is a consulting group for the engineering, architecture and environmental science sectors, primarily serving in Scandinavia, the U.K., North America and India. COWI's solutions span architecture, infrastructure, buildings, environment, water, energy, industry and planning, with specialties in climate change, digitalization, technology, project complexity, sustainability and urbanization. The firm's planning and consulting services are founded on offering smarter and greener solutions.

CONTACTS: Note: Officers with more than one job title may be intentionally listed here more than once.
Jens Hojgaard Christoffersen, CEO
Natalie Shaverdian Riise-Knudsen, CFO
Jukka Pertola, Chmn.

FINANCIAL DATA: Note: Data for latest year may not have been available at press time.

In U.S. $	2024	2023	2022	2021	2020	2019
Revenue	1,221,462,900	1,163,298,000	1,051,589,000	1,061,419,390	1,061,390,000	928,010,000
R&D Expense						
Operating Income						
Operating Margin %						
SGA Expense						
Net Income		34,937,000	35,974,562	24,084,976	34,954,900	15,012,300
Operating Cash Flow						
Capital Expenditure						
EBITDA						
Return on Assets %						
Return on Equity %						
Debt to Equity						

CONTACT INFORMATION:
Phone: 45-56-40-00-00   Fax: 45-56-40-99-99
Toll-Free:
Address: Parallelvej 2, Kongens Lyngby, 2800 Denmark

STOCK TICKER/OTHER:
Stock Ticker: Private   Exchange:
Employees: 7,500   Fiscal Year Ends: 12/31
Parent Company:

SALARIES/BONUSES:
Top Exec. Salary: $ Bonus: $
Second Exec. Salary: $ Bonus: $

OTHER THOUGHTS:
Estimated Female Officers or Directors:
Hot Spot for Advancement for Women/Minorities:

CRB

NAIC Code: 541330

www.crbgroup.com

TYPES OF BUSINESS:

Engineering Consulting Services
Facility Engineering
Facility Design and Architecture
Manufacturing Facility Solutions
Virtual Design and Construction
Industry 4.0 Consulting
Multi-Modal Flexible Facilities
Technology Solutions

BRANDS/DIVISIONS/AFFILIATES:

Clark Richardson and Biskup
ONEsolution
SlateXpace

CONTACTS: *Note: Officers with more than one job title may be intentionally listed here more than once.*

Vahid Ownjazayeri, CEO
Sam Kitchell, COO
Ken Olson, CFO
Danielle David, Chief People Officer
Tracy Stanfield, VP-IT
Jeff Biskup, Chmn.

GROWTH PLANS/SPECIAL FEATURES:

CRB is a global service provider of engineers, architects, constructors and consultants that deliver solutions to life science and advanced technology clients. The firm's services include engineering, architecture, construction, consulting and the firm's very own, ONESolution, which is an integrated project delivery method. CRB launched a multi-modal manufacturing system called SlateXpace, which are highly configurable facility suites that can be produced, erected and used very swiftly for a variety of imminent business purposes. For example, SlateXpace is a quick way to deliver a need-for-space solution to the healthcare industry for purposes such as rapid equipment changeover, decontamination processes or providing therapies to patients. CRB primarily serves biotechnology, food/beverage, pharmaceuticals, science and technology industries. CRB is headquartered in Kansas City, Missouri, with offices across the U.S., as well as one office each in Puerto Rico, Germany and Switzerland. These offices have full multi-disciplinary teams to support a wide range of project types and sizes.

CRB offers its employees health, dental and vision care; life, AD&D and long-term care insurance; short- and long-term disability; a 401(k) and tax savings plans; and paid time off.

FINANCIAL DATA: *Note: Data for latest year may not have been available at press time.*

In U.S. $	2024	2023	2022	2021	2020	2019
Revenue						
R&D Expense						
Operating Income						
Operating Margin %						
SGA Expense						
Net Income						
Operating Cash Flow						
Capital Expenditure						
EBITDA						
Return on Assets %						
Return on Equity %						
Debt to Equity						

CONTACT INFORMATION:

Phone: 816-880-9800   Fax:
Toll-Free:
Address: 1251 NW Briarcliff Pkwy., Ste. 500, Kansas City, MO 64116 United States

STOCK TICKER/OTHER:

Stock Ticker: Private   Exchange:
Employees: 1,000   Fiscal Year Ends:
Parent Company:

SALARIES/BONUSES:

Top Exec. Salary: $ Bonus: $
Second Exec. Salary: $ Bonus: $

OTHER THOUGHTS:

Estimated Female Officers or Directors:
Hot Spot for Advancement for Women/Minorities:

CSL Limited

NAIC Code: 325414

www.csl.com

TYPES OF BUSINESS:

Human Blood-Plasma Collection
Plasma Products
Immunohematology Products
Vaccines
Pharmaceutical Marketing
Antivenom
Drugs-Cancer

BRANDS/DIVISIONS/AFFILIATES:

CSL Behring
CSL Plasma
Seqirus

GROWTH PLANS/SPECIAL FEATURES:

CSL is one of the largest global biotech companies and has two main segments. CSL Behring either uses plasma-derived proteins or recombinants to treat conditions including immunodeficiencies, bleeding disorders and neurological indications. Seqirus is now the world's second largest influenza vaccination business and was acquired in fiscal 2015. CSL has a strong R&D track record, and the product portfolio and pipeline include nonplasma products as the firm continues to broaden its scope. Originally formed in Australia as a government-owned entity, CSL now earns roughly half its revenue in North America and a quarter in Europe.

CSL Limited offers its employees flexible work arrangements, an employee share plan, tuition reimbursement and technology training.

CONTACTS: Note: Officers with more than one job title may be intentionally listed here more than once.

Paul McKenzie, CEO
Brian Mcnamee, Chairman of the Board

FINANCIAL DATA: Note: Data for latest year may not have been available at press time.

In U.S. $	2024	2023	2022	2021	2020	2019
Revenue	14,689,999,872	13,173,999,616	10,493,100,032	10,265,299,968	9,100,499,968	8,509,899,776
R&D Expense	1,430,000,000	1,235,000,000	1,156,200,000	1,001,400,000	921,800,000	831,800,000
Operating Income	2,764,000,000	2,102,000,000	2,316,100,000	2,590,000,000	2,246,400,000	2,099,900,000
Operating Margin %	.19%	.16%	.22%	.25%	.25%	.25%
SGA Expense	2,429,000,000	2,540,000,000	1,648,700,000	1,711,900,000	1,588,000,000	1,441,600,000
Net Income	2,642,000,000	2,194,000,000	2,254,700,000	2,375,000,000	2,102,500,000	1,918,700,000
Operating Cash Flow						
Capital Expenditure	1,258,000,000	1,692,000,000	1,247,700,000	1,667,100,000	1,367,600,000	1,284,800,000
EBITDA	4,733,000,000	3,902,000,000	3,464,900,000	3,629,200,000	3,143,300,000	2,893,200,000
Return on Assets %	.07%	.07%	.10%	.14%	.15%	.17%
Return on Equity %	.16%	.14%	.20%	.32%	.36%	.41%
Debt to Equity	1.29%	.71%	.35%	.64%	0.887	0.808

CONTACT INFORMATION:

Phone: 61-3-9389-1911   Fax: 61-3-9389-1434
Toll-Free:
Address: 45 Poplar Rd., Parkville, VIC 3052 Australia

STOCK TICKER/OTHER:

Stock Ticker: CMXHF   Exchange: PINX
Employees: 32,000   Fiscal Year Ends: 06/30
Parent Company:

SALARIES/BONUSES:

Top Exec. Salary: $ Bonus: $
Second Exec. Salary: $ Bonus: $

OTHER THOUGHTS:

Estimated Female Officers or Directors: 4
Hot Spot for Advancement for Women/Minorities: Y

Cummins Inc

NAIC Code: 336300

www.cummins.com

TYPES OF BUSINESS:

Automotive Products, Motors & Parts Manufacturing
Engines
Filtration Systems
Power Generation Systems
Alternators
Air Handling Systems
Filtration & Emissions Solutions
Fuel Systems

BRANDS/DIVISIONS/AFFILIATES:

GROWTH PLANS/SPECIAL FEATURES:

Cummins is a leading manufacturer of diesel and other engines used in heavy- and medium-duty commercial trucks, off-highway equipment, and locomotives, in addition to prime power and standby generators. The company also sells powertrain components, which include filtration products, transmissions, turbochargers, aftertreatment systems, and fuel systems. Sales are approximately 60% US and Canada and 40% rest of world. Much of Cummins' foreign sales (China, India, and so forth) are through joint ventures. The company operates 650 distributors and over 19,000 dealer locations across 190 countries. Cummins' business model is unique as it competes with many of its heavy-duty truck manufacturer customers, who also make their own engines.

Cummins offers employees life, medical and dental insurance; and various employee assistance programs.

CONTACTS: Note: Officers with more than one job title may be intentionally listed here more than once.

Jennifer Rumsey, CEO
Nathan Stoner, VP, Geographical
Mark Smith, CFO
Luther Peters, Chief Accounting Officer
Sharon Barner, Chief Administrative Officer
Nicole Lamb-Hale, Chief Legal Officer
Jonathan Wood, Chief Technology Officer
Srikanth Padmanabhan, Executive VP
Marvin Boakye, Other Executive Officer
Amy Rochelle Davis, President, Divisional
Jenny Bush, President, Divisional
Brett Merritt, President, Divisional
Bonnie Fetch, President, Divisional
Jeffrey Wiltrout, Vice President, Divisional

FINANCIAL DATA: Note: Data for latest year may not have been available at press time.

In U.S. $	2024	2023	2022	2021	2020	2019
Revenue	34,101,999,616	34,065,000,448	28,074,000,384	24,021,000,192	19,811,000,320	23,570,999,296
R&D Expense	1,463,000,000	1,500,000,000	1,278,000,000	1,090,000,000	906,000,000	1,001,000,000
Operating Income	3,382,000,000	3,323,000,000	2,580,000,000	2,200,000,000	1,847,000,000	2,489,000,000
Operating Margin %	.10%	.10%	.09%	.09%	.09%	.11%
SGA Expense	3,275,000,000	3,333,000,000	2,687,000,000	2,374,000,000	2,125,000,000	2,454,000,000
Net Income	3,946,000,000	735,000,000	2,151,000,000	2,131,000,000	1,789,000,000	2,260,000,000
Operating Cash Flow	1,487,000,000	3,966,000,000	1,962,000,000	2,256,000,000	2,722,000,000	3,181,000,000
Capital Expenditure	1,208,000,000	1,213,000,000	916,000,000	734,000,000	575,000,000	775,000,000
EBITDA	6,338,000,000	3,025,000,000	3,802,000,000	3,524,000,000	3,111,000,000	3,615,000,000
Return on Assets %	.12%	.02%	.08%	.09%	.08%	.12%
Return on Equity %	.41%	.08%	.25%	.26%	.23%	.30%
Debt to Equity	.51%	.58%	.54%	.48%	0.488	0.259

CONTACT INFORMATION:

Phone: 812 377-5000   Fax:
Toll-Free:
Address: 500 Jackson St., Columbus, IN 47202 United States

STOCK TICKER/OTHER:

Stock Ticker: CMI   Exchange: NYS
Employees: 75,500   Fiscal Year Ends: 12/31
Parent Company:

SALARIES/BONUSES:

Top Exec. Salary: $1,500,000   Bonus: $
Second Exec. Salary: $862,750   Bonus: $

OTHER THOUGHTS:

Estimated Female Officers or Directors: 2
Hot Spot for Advancement for Women/Minorities: Y

Curia Inc

NAIC Code: 541710

curiaglobal.com

TYPES OF BUSINESS:

Contract Drug Discovery & Development
Pharmaceuticals
Biotechnology
Drug Discovery
Drug Production
Chemical Process Research and Development
Active Pharmaceutical Ingredients
Product Manufacturing

BRANDS/DIVISIONS/AFFILIATES:

Carlyl Group (The)
GTCR LLC

CONTACTS: Note: Officers with more than one job title may be intentionally listed here more than once.

Philip Macnabb, CEO
Gerald Auer, CFO
Joe Sangregorio, Chief Human Resources Officer
Gregg Kuzma, CIO
Margalit Fine, Executive VP, Divisional
Lori Henderson, General Counsel
Milton Boyer, Senior VP, Divisional
Christopher Conway, Senior VP, Divisional
Steven Hagen, Senior VP

GROWTH PLANS/SPECIAL FEATURES:

Curia, Inc. is a contract research, development and manufacturing organization with more than 20 locations across the globe. The company offers products and services across the drug development spectrum to help its pharmaceutical and biotechnology partners turn ideas into products and solutions that improve patients' lives. Curia's end-to-end capabilities range from early discovery and development through manufacturing and commercialization. Solutions are customized per need and requirement and the firm continuously invests in cutting-edge technologies. Biologic capabilities include molecular biology, viral vectors, cell engineering, antibody discovery and engineering, recombinant antibody and protein production, bioanalytical assays, biological assays and functional assays, among others. R&D capabilities span chemical process R&D, clinical manufacturing, fermentation, formulation development, high potency, kilo lab and small-scale BMP API (basic metabolic panel, active pharmaceutical ingredient) manufacturing, lipid nanoparticle, method development, rare/orphan and separation science, as well as a range of discovery and consultative services. Manufacturing-wise, Curia can help streamline the path to commercialization or product at scale, and offers services including custom API manufacturing, fermentation, finished dosage form, high potency, lipid nanoparticle, rare/orphan, stability and release testing, sterile fill finish, APIs and intermediates catalog and fine chemicals catalog. Lab testing services include analytical testing, batch release and stability lot testing, method development and validation, package and device testing, pre-formulation and material science, and solid-state chemistry. Curia's integrated network of global facilities (R&D and manufacturing) enables the company to serve its partners and markets throughout the world. The firm has corporate headquarters in New York and North Carolina, and is privately owned by equity firms Carlyle Group, Inc. and GTCR LLC.

FINANCIAL DATA: Note: Data for latest year may not have been available at press time.

In U.S. $	2024	2023	2022	2021	2020	2019
Revenue	992,736,150	945,463,000	909,099,363	857,455,200	801,360,000	756,000,000
R&D Expense						
Operating Income						
Operating Margin %						
SGA Expense						
Net Income						
Operating Cash Flow						
Capital Expenditure						
EBITDA						
Return on Assets %						
Return on Equity %						
Debt to Equity						

CONTACT INFORMATION:

Phone: 518 512-2000   Fax: 518-512-2020
Toll-Free:
Address: 26 Corporate Cir., Albany, NY 12203 United States

STOCK TICKER/OTHER:

Stock Ticker: Private   Exchange:
Employees: 4,000   Fiscal Year Ends: 12/31
Parent Company: Carlyle Group Inc

SALARIES/BONUSES:

Top Exec. Salary: $ Bonus: $
Second Exec. Salary: $ Bonus: $

OTHER THOUGHTS:

Estimated Female Officers or Directors: 3
Hot Spot for Advancement for Women/Minorities: Y

Sales, profits and employees may be estimates. Financial information, benefits and other data can change quickly and may vary from those stated here.

Daelim Co Ltd

NAIC Code: 237000

www.daelim.co.kr//en/pc/index.do

TYPES OF BUSINESS:

Heavy Construction and Engineering
Petrochemicals
Construction Information Services
Information Technology Services
IT Integration
Logistics and Transportation
Infrastructure Construction

BRANDS/DIVISIONS/AFFILIATES:

DL E&C Co Ltd
DL Construction Company
DL Chemical Co Ltd
DL Motors Co Ltd
DL Energy
Daelim Education Foundation
Daelim Contemporary Art Museum

CONTACTS: *Note: Officers with more than one job title may be intentionally listed here more than once.*

Bae Weonbog, CEO

GROWTH PLANS/SPECIAL FEATURES:

Daelim Co., Ltd. is a Korea-based company that specializes in providing petrochemicals, construction information and information technology (IT) services. The firm is a petrochemical trading firm that produces and sells polyimide products, which are high-functional plastic materials and sells chemicals and polymers domestically and internationally. Daelim's logistics division offers services across its global networks, delivering freight across a range of transportation methods. Regarding construction information, Daelim provides comprehensive services, from planning to design, construction and after-sales service for houses, tunnels, roads, harbors, railways and bridges. IT services span IT integration, system integration and related IT maintenance. Daelim has 12 affiliates as well, including construction companies DL E&C Co., Ltd. and DL Construction Co.; petrochemicals companies, DL Chemical Co., Ltd., Yeochun NCC Co., Ltd. and PolyMirae Co., Ltd.; manufacturing and trading company DI Motors Co., Ltd.; education and culture companies, Daelim Education Foundation and Daelim Contemporary Art Museum; and energy company DL Energy.

FINANCIAL DATA: *Note: Data for latest year may not have been available at press time.*

In U.S. $	2024	2023	2022	2021	2020	2019
Revenue		3,873,177,000	5,447,730,176	3,435,448,932	2,306,893,669	2,661,253,625
R&D Expense						
Operating Income						
Operating Margin %						
SGA Expense						
Net Income		-103,005,000	282,714,835	746,553,106	83,269,559	123,129,799
Operating Cash Flow						
Capital Expenditure						
EBITDA						
Return on Assets %						
Return on Equity %						
Debt to Equity						

CONTACT INFORMATION:

Phone: 82 2-3708-3491   Fax: 82-2-757-7447
Toll-Free:
Address: Fl. 23, Donuimun D-Tower Bldg., 134 Tongil-ro, Seoul, 03181 South Korea

STOCK TICKER/OTHER:

Stock Ticker: 210   Exchange: Seoul
Employees: 4,200   Fiscal Year Ends: 12/31
Parent Company:

SALARIES/BONUSES:

Top Exec. Salary: $ Bonus: $
Second Exec. Salary: $ Bonus: $

OTHER THOUGHTS:

Estimated Female Officers or Directors:
Hot Spot for Advancement for Women/Minorities:

Daihatsu Motor Co Ltd

www.daihatsu.com

NAIC Code: 336111

TYPES OF BUSINESS:

Automobile Manufacturing
Industrial Engines
Compact Vehicles
Compact Commercial Vehicles
Cargo Vehicles
Vehicle Manufacture
Powertrains and Body Manufacture
Safety Vehicle Technology

BRANDS/DIVISIONS/AFFILIATES:

Toyota Motor Corporation
Daihatsu Motor Kyushu Co Ltd
Daihatsu-Chiba Co Ltd
Daihatsu Credit Co Ltd
Daihatsu Saitama Co Ltd
PT Astra Daihatsu Motor
Perodua Manufacturing Sdn Bhd
Perodua Global Manufacturing Sdn Bhd

CONTACTS: Note: Officers with more than one job title may be intentionally listed here more than once.

Masahiro Inoue, Pres.
Tatsuya Kaneko, Exec. VP
Takashi Nomoto, Sr. Managing Exec. Officer
Yasunori Nakawaki, Sr. Managing Exec. Officer
Naoto Kitagawa, Sr. Managing Exec. Officer
Sunao Matsubayashi, Chmn.

GROWTH PLANS/SPECIAL FEATURES:

Daihatsu Motor Co., Ltd, headquartered in Osaka, Japan, develops, manufactures and sells compact vehicles that offer fuel efficiency, affordability and added value. Vehicle models in Japan include the Mira e:S, Copen, Taft, Move Canbus, Hijet Cargo, Hijet Truck, Atrai, Thor, Rocky, GRANMAX, Tanto and a line of wheelchair accessible vans and smart cars. Overseas (Indonesia and Malaysia) models include AYLA, XENIA, SIGRA, TERIOS, SIRION, GRAN MAX VAN, GRAN MAX PICKUP, Rocky, MYVI, ALZA, AXIA, BEZZA, ARUZ and Ativa. Daihatsu equips vehicles with safety technology and modern body and powertrain parts. The firm has been manufacturing mini vehicles since it launched a three-wheeled car with a 500cc engine in 1931. Today, Daihatsu has manufacturing plants in Osaka, Shiga and Kyoto, and a parts center located in Hyogo. Main subsidiaries include Daihatsu Motor Kyushu Co. Ltd., which develops, designs, produces, sells and repairs automobiles, industrial vehicles and other types of vehicles and their parts; Daihatsu-Chiba Co., Ltd. and Daihatsu-Saitama Co., Ltd., which are both responsible for automobile sales; and Daihatsu Credit Co. Ltd., offering sales and lease financing. Main overseas joint ventures include PT Astra Daihatsu Motor, which is located in Indonesia; and Perodua Manufacturing Sdn Bhd and Perodua Global Manufacturing Sdn Bhd., which are both located in Malaysia. Daihatsu is a wholly owned subsidiary of Toyota Motor Corporation.

FINANCIAL DATA: Note: Data for latest year may not have been available at press time.

In U.S. $	2024	2023	2022	2021	2020	2019
Revenue	17,668,236,600	16,826,892,000	16,179,704,000	15,350,400,000	14,760,000,000	18,000,000,000
R&D Expense						
Operating Income						
Operating Margin %						
SGA Expense						
Net Income						
Operating Cash Flow						
Capital Expenditure						
EBITDA						
Return on Assets %						
Return on Equity %						
Debt to Equity						

CONTACT INFORMATION:

Phone: 81-72-751-8811   Fax:
Toll-Free:
Address: 1-1 Daihatsu-cho Ikeda-shi, Osaka, 563-0044 Japan

STOCK TICKER/OTHER:

Stock Ticker: Subsidiary   Exchange:
Employees: 12,425   Fiscal Year Ends: 03/31
Parent Company: Toyota Motor Corporation

SALARIES/BONUSES:

Top Exec. Salary: $ Bonus: $
Second Exec. Salary: $ Bonus: $

OTHER THOUGHTS:

Estimated Female Officers or Directors:
Hot Spot for Advancement for Women/Minorities:

Daimler Trucks North America LLC www.northamerica.daimlertruck.com

NAIC Code: 336120

TYPES OF BUSINESS:

Truck Manufacturing
Custom-Built Chassis
Commercial Truck Manufacturing
School Bus Manufacturing
Diesel Engines
Transmissions
Connected Vehicle Services
Used Truck Sales

BRANDS/DIVISIONS/AFFILIATES:

Daimler Truck Holding AG
Freightliner Trucks
Western Star
Thomas Built Buses
Freightliner Custom Chassis
Detroit Diesel Corporation
SelecTrucks
DTNA Parts

CONTACTS: Note: Officers with more than one job title may be intentionally listed here more than once.

John O'Leary, CEO
Jeff Allen, Sr. VP-Oper. & Specialty Vehicles
Stefan Kurschner, CFO
David Carson, Sr. VP-Sales & Mktg.
Angela Lentz, Chief People Officer
Randy DeBortoli, Sr. VP-Engineering & Technology
Friedrich Baumann, Sr. VP-Aftermarket
Albert Kirchmann, Head-Daimler Truck Asia, Finance & Control

GROWTH PLANS/SPECIAL FEATURES:

Daimler Trucks North America, LLC (DTNA), a wholly owned subsidiary of Daimler Truck Holding AG, is a leading provider of comprehensive products and technologies for the commercial transportation industry. DTNA designs, engineers, manufactures and markets medium- and heavy-duty trucks, school buses, vehicle chassis and their associated technologies and components. These trucks and products are marketed under Freightliner, Western Star, Thomas Built Buses and Freightliner Custom Chassis. Freightliner Trucks manufactures Class 5-8 models that serve a range of commercial vehicle applications. Western Star is a heavy-duty brand of DTNA, with a focus on products for small and medium fleets and owner-operators in the vocational and extreme-duty industries. Thomas Built Buses build school buses, with a focus on innovative design, reliability, safety and sustainability. Freightliner Custom Chassis manufactures premium chassis for recreational vehicle, walk-in van and delivery markets. Detroit Diesel Corporation offers a portfolio of heavy-duty and mid-range diesel engines, as well as transmissions, axles, safety systems and connected vehicle services for the on-highway and vocational commercial truck markets. Other brands within DTNA include: SelecTrucks serves as a retail distribution network for DTNA and offers late-model used trucks, primarily serving owner-operators and small fleets; and DTNA Parts, which offers more than 50 product lines that serve the commercial transportation industry with new and remanufactured parts and accessories for all makes and models to keep trucks and buses on the road.

DTNA offers its employees comprehensive health benefits, life, AD&D and short/long-term disability coverage, a 401(k) and many other plans and programs.

FINANCIAL DATA: Note: Data for latest year may not have been available at press time.

In U.S. $	2024	2023	2022	2021	2020	2019
Revenue	27,223,046,424	25,926,710,880	23,909,449,930	18,000,000,000	16,741,000,000	21,257,200,000
R&D Expense						
Operating Income						
Operating Margin %						
SGA Expense						
Net Income			258,090,573			2,758,220,000
Operating Cash Flow						
Capital Expenditure						
EBITDA						
Return on Assets %						
Return on Equity %						
Debt to Equity						

CONTACT INFORMATION:

Phone: 503-745-8000   Fax: 503-745-8921
Toll-Free:
Address: 4555 N. Channel Ave., Portland, OR 97217 United States

STOCK TICKER/OTHER:

Stock Ticker: Subsidiary   Exchange:
Employees: 28,225   Fiscal Year Ends: 12/31
Parent Company: Daimler Truck Holding AG

SALARIES/BONUSES:

Top Exec. Salary: $ Bonus: $
Second Exec. Salary: $ Bonus: $

OTHER THOUGHTS:

Estimated Female Officers or Directors:
Hot Spot for Advancement for Women/Minorities:

Dana Incorporated

www.dana.com

NAIC Code: 336300

TYPES OF BUSINESS:

Automotive Products, Motors & Parts Manufacturing
Engine Systems
Fluid Systems
Heavy Vehicle Technologies
Brake Components
Chassis & Drive Train Components
Filtration Products
Financial Services

BRANDS/DIVISIONS/AFFILIATES:

GROWTH PLANS/SPECIAL FEATURES:

Dana Inc is engaged in the designing and manufacturing of efficient propulsion and energy-management solutions that power vehicles and machines in all mobility markets across the globe. The company has four operating segments: Light Vehicles, Power Technologies, Commercial Vehicle, and Off-Highway. The Light Vehicles segment generates the majority portion of revenue by providing products to support light vehicle OEMs. Its products are designed for light trucks, SUVs, CUVs, vans, and passenger cars.

CONTACTS: Note: Officers with more than one job title may be intentionally listed here more than once.

R. McDonald, CEO
Timothy Kraus, CFO
James Kellett, Chief Accounting Officer
Douglas Liedberg, Chief Compliance Officer
Byron Foster, President, Divisional
Brian Pour, President, Divisional
Craig Price, President, Divisional
Antonio Valencia, President, Divisional

FINANCIAL DATA: Note: Data for latest year may not have been available at press time.

In U.S. $	2024	2023	2022	2021	2020	2019
Revenue	10,284,000,256	10,554,999,808	10,156,000,256	8,945,000,448	7,105,999,872	8,620,000,256
R&D Expense						
Operating Income	350,000,000	354,000,000	262,000,000	353,000,000	201,000,000	367,000,000
Operating Margin %	.03%	.03%	.03%	.04%	.03%	.04%
SGA Expense	524,000,000	549,000,000	495,000,000	470,000,000	421,000,000	767,000,000
Net Income	-57,000,000	38,000,000	-242,000,000	197,000,000	-31,000,000	226,000,000
Operating Cash Flow	450,000,000	476,000,000	649,000,000	158,000,000	386,000,000	637,000,000
Capital Expenditure	380,000,000	501,000,000	440,000,000	369,000,000	326,000,000	426,000,000
EBITDA	663,000,000	748,000,000	485,000,000	764,000,000	490,000,000	632,000,000
Return on Assets %	-.01%	.00%	-.03%	.03%	.00%	.03%
Return on Equity %	-.04%	.02%	-.14%	.11%	-.02%	.14%
Debt to Equity	1.99%	1.83%	1.69%	1.35%	1.464	1.322

CONTACT INFORMATION:

Phone: 419 887-3000   Fax: 419 535-4643
Toll-Free: 800-537-8823
Address: 3939 Technology Dr., Maumee, OH 43537 United States

STOCK TICKER/OTHER:

Stock Ticker: DAN   Exchange: NYS
Employees: 41,800   Fiscal Year Ends: 12/31
Parent Company:

SALARIES/BONUSES:

Top Exec. Salary: $1,244,930   Bonus: $
Second Exec. Salary: $277,778   Bonus: $750,000

OTHER THOUGHTS:

Estimated Female Officers or Directors:
Hot Spot for Advancement for Women/Minorities: Y

Dar Al-Handasah Consultants (Shair and Partners) www.dar.com

NAIC Code: 541330

TYPES OF BUSINESS:
Engineering Services
Building Planning
Building Project Design
Building Consultancy
Design Centers
Smart Cities
Architecture and Engineering
Project and Construction Management

BRANDS/DIVISIONS/AFFILIATES:
Dar Group
Shair and Partners

GROWTH PLANS/SPECIAL FEATURES:
Dar Al-Handasah Consultants (Dar) is a planning, design, management and consultancy for building projects, with 54 offices across the Middle East, Africa, Asia and Europe. The company's principal design centers are located in Beirut, Cairo, London, Pune and Amman. Dar works in partnership with its clients to model the project according to their specific needs, culture and environment, as well as to provide its own multidisciplinary expertise per an integrated work approach. Specialties and capabilities of Dar include digital solutions and services, smart cities, planning and strategy, architecture and design, engineering, environmental, economics and project and construction management. Markets served include civic and commercial, cities, transportation, water, power, telecommunications, oil and gas and heavy industry. Dar is a subsidiary of Dar Group, which also refers to the company as Shair and Partners.

CONTACTS: Note: Officers with more than one job title may be intentionally listed here more than once.
Talal K. Shair, CEO
Talal K. Shair, Chmn.

FINANCIAL DATA: Note: Data for latest year may not have been available at press time.

In U.S. $	2024	2023	2022	2021	2020	2019
Revenue						
R&D Expense						
Operating Income						
Operating Margin %						
SGA Expense						
Net Income						
Operating Cash Flow						
Capital Expenditure						
EBITDA						
Return on Assets %						
Return on Equity %						
Debt to Equity						

CONTACT INFORMATION:
Phone: 961-1790002   Fax: 961-1869011
Toll-Free:
Address: Verdun St., Dar Al-Handasah Bldg., Beirut, 1107 2230 Lebanon

STOCK TICKER/OTHER:
Stock Ticker: Subsidiary   Exchange:
Employees: 8,000   Fiscal Year Ends:
Parent Company: Dar Group

SALARIES/BONUSES:
Top Exec. Salary: $ Bonus: $
Second Exec. Salary: $ Bonus: $

OTHER THOUGHTS:
Estimated Female Officers or Directors:
Hot Spot for Advancement for Women/Minorities:

Dassault Aviation SA

www.dassault-aviation.com

NAIC Code: 336411

TYPES OF BUSINESS:

Aircraft Manufacturing
Business Jets
Military Aircraft
Unmanned Combat Aircraft
Aerospace Technology

GROWTH PLANS/SPECIAL FEATURES:

Dassault Aviation, a subsidiary of French multinational company Dassault Group, designs, builds, and maintains military fighter jets, and is one of the largest manufacturers of business jets. Dassault has a 26% stake in narrow-moat Thales, which contributes significantly to Dassault's net profit. In 2021, Dassault Aviation generated EUR 7.2 billion in revenue with 12,000 employees. About 70% of revenue comes from defense aircraft equipment sales and services, while Falcon business jets generate the remaining 30% of sales.

BRANDS/DIVISIONS/AFFILIATES:

Dassault Group
Dassalt Falcon Jet Corp
Dassault Procurement Services inc
Dassault Falcon Service SARL
Sogitec Industries SA
Dassault Falcon
Rafale
nEUROn Uninhabited Combat Aircraft Vehicle

CONTACTS: Note: Officers with more than one job title may be intentionally listed here more than once.

Eric Trappier, CEO
Charles Edelstenne, Director

FINANCIAL DATA: Note: Data for latest year may not have been available at press time.

In U.S. $	2024	2023	2022	2021	2020	2019
Revenue	7,082,529,134	5,453,905,949	7,888,667,613	8,224,968,508	6,233,362,313	8,366,192,754
R&D Expense						
Operating Income	613,886,500	385,074,900	679,917,100	612,134,000	327,135,100	901,365,400
Operating Margin %	.09%	.07%	.09%	.07%	.05%	.11%
SGA Expense						
Net Income	1,048,608,000	787,057,900	812,968,300	687,164,600	343,653,800	808,971,600
Operating Cash Flow	2,135,152,000	-763,456,300	5,800,194,000	1,887,431,000	-641,576,600	-75,179,340
Capital Expenditure	392,605,000	392,233,900	198,661,700	196,119,200	534,443,800	245,977,300
EBITDA	1,533,948,000	1,142,251,000	1,206,182,000	1,552,057,000	614,817,300	1,412,719,000
Return on Assets %	.04%	.03%	.04%	.04%	.02%	.04%
Return on Equity %	.15%	.12%	.13%	.12%	.07%	.16%
Debt to Equity	.03%	.04%	.03%	.03%	0.048	0.049

CONTACT INFORMATION:

Phone: 33 153769300   Fax: 33 153769320
Toll-Free:
Address: 9 Rond-Point des Champs-Elysees, Marcel Dassault, Paris, 75008 France

STOCK TICKER/OTHER:

Stock Ticker: DUAVF   Exchange: PINX
Employees: 13,533   Fiscal Year Ends: 12/31
Parent Company: Dassault Group

SALARIES/BONUSES:

Top Exec. Salary: $ Bonus: $
Second Exec. Salary: $ Bonus: $

OTHER THOUGHTS:

Estimated Female Officers or Directors:
Hot Spot for Advancement for Women/Minorities:

Sales, profits and employees may be estimates. Financial information, benefits and other data can change quickly and may vary from those stated here.

Dassault Systemes SA

NAIC Code: 511210N

www.3ds.com

TYPES OF BUSINESS:

Computer Software-Product Lifecycle Management
3D Imaging Software
Product Lifecycle Management Software
Software Development
Data Management

BRANDS/DIVISIONS/AFFILIATES:

CATIA
SOLIDWORKS
DELMIA
SIMULIA
BIOVIA
3DVIA
3DEXCITE
3DEXPERIENCE

GROWTH PLANS/SPECIAL FEATURES:

Dassault Systemes is a leading provider of computer-assisted design and product lifecycle management software, serving customers like Boeing and Volkswagen throughout the production process. The company's flagship product, Catia, primarily serves the transportation, industrial equipment, and aerospace and defense industries. In life sciences, Dassault's Medidata cloud platform optimizes clinical trial efficiency and is the leader in electronic data capture.

CONTACTS: Note: Officers with more than one job title may be intentionally listed here more than once.

Pascal Daloz, CEO
Bernard Charles, Chairman of the Board
Charles Edelstenne, Director
Herve Andorre, Director
Tanneguy de Bouaille, Director

FINANCIAL DATA: Note: Data for latest year may not have been available at press time.

In U.S. $	2024	2023	2022	2021	2020	2019
Revenue	7,052,894,736	6,755,278,028	6,430,420,129	5,516,572,192	5,053,575,415	4,560,953,540
R&D Expense	1,459,932,000	1,394,211,000	1,234,052,000	1,077,526,000	1,061,748,000	837,571,000
Operating Income	1,560,386,000	1,473,439,000	1,491,941,000	1,184,904,000	785,698,000	956,526,700
Operating Margin %	.22%	.22%	.23%	.21%	.16%	.21%
SGA Expense	2,468,558,000	2,355,392,000	2,199,546,000	1,930,420,000	1,869,467,000	1,765,948,000
Net Income	1,362,316,000	1,192,849,000	1,057,321,000	878,206,500	557,321,200	698,410,900
Operating Cash Flow	1,883,996,000	1,776,617,000	1,731,215,000	1,830,988,000	1,408,967,000	1,346,311,000
Capital Expenditure	219,523,300	164,926,200	150,170,300	117,707,200	144,154,400	111,577,800
EBITDA	2,386,039,000	2,174,801,000	2,204,767,000	1,826,447,000	1,461,975,000	1,404,200,000
Return on Assets %	.08%	.07%	.07%	.06%	.04%	.06%
Return on Equity %	.14%	.14%	.14%	.14%	.10%	.13%
Debt to Equity	.28%	.33%	.44%	.56%	0.936	1.00

CONTACT INFORMATION:

Phone: 33 161626162   Fax: 33 170734363
Toll-Free:
Address: 10 rue Marcel Dassault, CS 40501, Velizy-Villacoublay, 78140 France

STOCK TICKER/OTHER:

Stock Ticker: DASTF   Exchange: PINX
Employees: 19,789   Fiscal Year Ends: 12/31
Parent Company:

SALARIES/BONUSES:

Top Exec. Salary: $ Bonus: $
Second Exec. Salary: $ Bonus: $

OTHER THOUGHTS:

Estimated Female Officers or Directors: 2
Hot Spot for Advancement for Women/Minorities: Y

Sales, profits and employees may be estimates. Financial information, benefits and other data can change quickly and may vary from those stated here.

Deere & Company (John Deere)

www.deere.com

NAIC Code: 333111

TYPES OF BUSINESS:

Construction & Agricultural Equipment
Commercial & Consumer Equipment
Forestry Equipment
Financing

BRANDS/DIVISIONS/AFFILIATES:

John Deere

GROWTH PLANS/SPECIAL FEATURES:

Deere is the world's leading manufacturer of agricultural equipment and a major producer of construction machinery. The company is divided into four reporting segments: production & precision agriculture (PPA), small agriculture & turf (SAT), construction & forestry (CF), and financial services (FS), its captive finance subsidiary. The core PPA business is the largest contributor to sales and profits by far. Geographically, Deere sales are 60% US/Canada, 17% Europe, 14% Latin America, and 9% rest of world. Deere goes to market through a robust dealer network that includes over 2,000 dealer locations in North America with reach into over 100 countries. John Deere financial provides retail financing for machinery to its customers and wholesale financing for dealers.

CONTACTS: *Note: Officers with more than one job title may be intentionally listed here more than once.*

John May, CEO
Joshua Jepsen, CFO
Rajesh Kalathur, Chief Information Officer
Kellye Walker, Chief Legal Officer
Jahmy Hindman, Chief Technology Officer
Felecia Pryor, Other Executive Officer
Justin Rose, President, Divisional
Ryan Campbell, President, Divisional
Cory Reed, President, Divisional
Deanna Kovar, President, Divisional

FINANCIAL DATA: *Note: Data for latest year may not have been available at press time.*

In U.S. $	2024	2023	2022	2021	2020	2019
Revenue	50,517,999,616	60,247,998,464	51,282,001,920	43,033,001,984	34,722,000,896	38,378,999,808
R&D Expense	2,290,000,000	2,177,000,000	1,912,000,000	1,587,000,000	1,644,000,000	1,783,000,000
Operating Income	11,427,000,000	14,591,000,000	9,026,000,000	7,663,000,000	4,368,000,000	4,834,000,000
Operating Margin %	.23%	.24%	.18%	.18%	.13%	.13%
SGA Expense	4,507,000,000	4,309,000,000	3,645,000,000	3,200,000,000	3,446,000,000	3,484,000,000
Net Income	7,100,000,000	10,166,000,000	7,131,000,000	5,963,000,000	2,751,000,000	3,253,000,000
Operating Cash Flow	9,231,000,000	8,589,000,000	4,699,000,000	7,726,000,000	7,483,000,000	3,412,000,000
Capital Expenditure	4,802,000,000	4,468,000,000	3,788,000,000	2,580,000,000	2,656,000,000	3,449,000,000
EBITDA	14,672,000,000	17,476,000,000	12,084,000,000	10,645,000,000	7,248,000,000	7,573,000,000
Return on Assets %	.07%	.10%	.08%	.07%	.04%	.05%
Return on Equity %	.32%	.48%	.37%	.38%	.23%	.29%
Debt to Equity	1.89%	1.77%	1.66%	1.78%	2.53	2.649

CONTACT INFORMATION:

Phone: 309 765-8000   Fax: 309 765-9929
Toll-Free:
Address: 1 John Deere Pl., Moline, IL 61265 United States

STOCK TICKER/OTHER:

Stock Ticker: DE
Employees: 75,800
Parent Company:

Exchange: NYS
Fiscal Year Ends: 10/31

SALARIES/BONUSES:

Top Exec. Salary: $1,658,671   Bonus: $
Second Exec. Salary: Bonus: $
$968,764

OTHER THOUGHTS:

Estimated Female Officers or Directors: 7
Hot Spot for Advancement for Women/Minorities: Y

Dell Technologies Inc
NAIC Code: 334111

www.delltechnologies.com/en-us/index.htm

TYPES OF BUSINESS:
Computer Manufacturing
Information Technology
IT Device Development
IT Device Production
Hardware
Software
Storage Solutions
Networking Products

BRANDS/DIVISIONS/AFFILIATES:
Client Solutions Group
Infrastructure Solutions Group
Dell EMC
Virtustream

GROWTH PLANS/SPECIAL FEATURES:
Dell Technologies is a broad information technology vendor, primarily supplying hardware to enterprises. It is focused on premium and commercial personal computers and enterprise on-premises data center hardware. It holds top-three market shares in its core markets of personal computers, peripheral displays, mainstream servers, and external storage. Dell has a robust ecosystem of component and assembly partners, and also relies heavily on channel partners to fulfill its sales.

CONTACTS: Note: Officers with more than one job title may be intentionally listed here more than once.
Michael Dell, CEO
Yvonne McGill, CFO
Brunilda Rios, Chief Accounting Officer
Allison Dew, Chief Marketing Officer
Jeffrey Clarke, COO
Richard Rothberg, General Counsel
Jennifer Saavedra, Other Executive Officer
William Scannell, President, Divisional

FINANCIAL DATA: Note: Data for latest year may not have been available at press time.

In U.S. $	2024	2023	2022	2021	2020	2019
Revenue	88,424,996,864	102,300,999,680	101,196,996,608	86,670,000,128	84,815,003,648	
R&D Expense	2,801,000,000	2,779,000,000	2,577,000,000	2,455,000,000	2,454,000,000	
Operating Income	5,411,000,000	5,771,000,000	4,659,000,000	3,685,000,000	2,366,000,000	
Operating Margin %	.06%	.06%	.05%	.04%	.03%	
SGA Expense	12,857,000,000	14,136,000,000	14,655,000,000	14,000,000,000	15,819,000,000	
Net Income	3,388,000,000	2,442,000,000	5,563,000,000	3,250,000,000	4,616,000,000	
Operating Cash Flow	8,676,000,000	3,565,000,000	10,307,000,000	11,407,000,000	9,291,000,000	
Capital Expenditure	2,756,000,000	3,003,000,000	2,796,000,000	2,082,000,000	2,576,000,000	
EBITDA	8,891,000,000	7,662,000,000	12,016,000,000	9,788,000,000	8,488,000,000	
Return on Assets %	.04%	.03%	.05%	.03%	.04%	
Return on Equity %			8.79%	3.24%		
Debt to Equity				11.14%		

CONTACT INFORMATION:
Phone: 512 338-4400   Fax: 512 283-6161
Toll-Free: 800-289-3355
Address: One Dell Way, Round Rock, TX 78682 United States

STOCK TICKER/OTHER:
Stock Ticker: DELL   Exchange: NYS
Employees: 120,000   Fiscal Year Ends: 01/31
Parent Company:

SALARIES/BONUSES:
Top Exec. Salary: $1,096,974   Bonus: $
Second Exec. Salary: Bonus: $
$950,000

OTHER THOUGHTS:
Estimated Female Officers or Directors: 1
Hot Spot for Advancement for Women/Minorities: Y

Demant AS

NAIC Code: 334510

www.demant.com

TYPES OF BUSINESS:

Human Hearing Assistance Technology
Hearing Aids
Cochlear Implants
Diagnostic Instruments
Product Development
Product Manufacture
Audio Solutions

GROWTH PLANS/SPECIAL FEATURES:

Demant AS is a Denmark-based company engaged in the healthcare industry. The company develops, manufactures and sells products and equipment designed to aid the hearing and communication of individuals. The Group focuses on four business areas: Hearing Devices, including such brands as Bernafon, Oticon, Frontrow, Phonic Ear and Sonic; Hearing Implants, including Oticon Medical; Diagnostic Instruments. The Company operates through more than 90 subsidiaries and associates all around the world. More than 80% of the company's sales come from North America and Europe.

BRANDS/DIVISIONS/AFFILIATES:

William Demant Invest AS
Oticon
Bernafon
Sonic
Maico
Interacoustics
Amplivox
EPOS

CONTACTS: Note: Officers with more than one job title may be intentionally listed here more than once.

Soren Nielsen, CEO
Rene Schneider, CFO
Niels Christiansen, Chairman of the Board
Niels Jacobsen, Deputy Chairman
Charlotte Hedegaard, Director
Niels Wagner, President, Divisional

FINANCIAL DATA: Note: Data for latest year may not have been available at press time.

In U.S. $	2024	2023	2022	2021	2020	2019
Revenue	3,411,217,558	3,286,752,791	2,998,262,361	2,724,379,045	2,201,566,040	2,274,145,090
R&D Expense	212,107,500	186,545,000	199,934,900	173,307,300	191,870,500	170,416,300
Operating Income	655,037,800	675,274,800	469,405,700	539,093,800	155,961,400	309,336,100
Operating Margin %	.19%	.21%	.16%	.20%	.07%	.14%
SGA Expense	1,733,225,000	1,621,390,000	1,562,657,000	1,350,397,000	1,203,109,000	1,258,646,000
Net Income	363,199,800	273,122,600	316,791,800	382,371,600	170,568,500	222,454,200
Operating Cash Flow	620,802,400	678,317,800	398,956,800	546,701,700	398,804,600	326,986,300
Capital Expenditure	118,530,600	127,051,500	140,593,500	110,466,300	103,619,200	116,552,600
EBITDA	882,969,600	847,364,800	653,364,100	705,249,700	380,545,800	461,493,500
Return on Assets %	.08%	.06%	.08%	.11%	.05%	.07%
Return on Equity %	.25%	.20%	.25%	.31%	.14%	.20%
Debt to Equity	1.53%	1.32%	.92%	.55%	0.598	0.531

CONTACT INFORMATION:

Phone: 45 39177300   Fax: 45 39278900
Toll-Free:
Address: Kongebakken 9, Smorum, 2765 Denmark

STOCK TICKER/OTHER:

Stock Ticker: WILYY   Exchange: PINX
Employees: 21,168   Fiscal Year Ends: 12/31
Parent Company: William Demant Invest AS

SALARIES/BONUSES:

Top Exec. Salary: $ Bonus: $
Second Exec. Salary: $ Bonus: $

OTHER THOUGHTS:

Estimated Female Officers or Directors: 1
Hot Spot for Advancement for Women/Minorities:

Denso Corporation

NAIC Code: 336300

www.denso.com/global/en.html

TYPES OF BUSINESS:

Automobile Parts Manufacturer
Engine Components
Automotive Electrical Systems
Automotive Electronic Systems
Thermal Systems
Small Motors
Semiconductors
Industrial Robots

GROWTH PLANS/SPECIAL FEATURES:

Denso manufactures and sells mainly automotive components and systems. The company was founded in 1949 as a result of becoming independent from Toyota Motor, which is currently the largest shareholder. Its main businesses are powertrain control systems, thermal systems, electrification systems, mobility electronics, and sensors/semiconductor systems. The company operates globally and is headquartered in Kariya, Japan.

BRANDS/DIVISIONS/AFFILIATES:

DENSO
Electrification Innovation Center
Jeco Co Ltd

CONTACTS: *Note: Officers with more than one job title may be intentionally listed here more than once.*

Shinnosuke Hayashi, CEO
Yasushi Matsui, CFO
Koji Arima, Chairman of the Board
Yasuhiko Yamazaki, Director

FINANCIAL DATA: *Note: Data for latest year may not have been available at press time.*

In U.S. $	2024	2023	2022	2021	2020	2019
Revenue	49,602,425,567	44,441,267,937	38,291,530,380	34,273,294,419	35,778,089,113	37,231,132,022
R&D Expense						
Operating Income	2,642,315,000	2,958,199,000	2,368,641,000	1,076,833,000	424,035,000	2,195,196,000
Operating Margin %	.05%	.07%	.06%	.03%	.01%	.06%
SGA Expense	4,965,038,000	3,404,985,000	3,196,675,000	3,571,869,000	4,641,135,000	3,563,753,000
Net Income	2,171,557,000	2,184,345,000	1,832,137,000	868,196,400	472,778,400	1,767,037,000
Operating Cash Flow	6,677,493,000	4,184,393,000	2,746,716,000	3,035,511,000	4,133,019,000	3,703,742,000
Capital Expenditure	3,099,174,000	2,876,382,000	2,583,616,000	3,017,780,000	3,239,593,000	3,106,818,000
EBITDA	5,781,394,000	5,798,188,000	5,135,636,000	3,725,778,000	2,861,289,000	4,549,813,000
Return on Assets %	.04%	.04%	.04%	.02%	.01%	.04%
Return on Equity %	.06%	.07%	.06%	.03%	.02%	.07%
Debt to Equity	.09%	.13%	.17%	.19%	0.104	0.113

CONTACT INFORMATION:

Phone: 81 566255511 Fax:
Toll-Free:
Address: 1-1 Showa-cho, Kariya, 448-8661 Japan

STOCK TICKER/OTHER:

Stock Ticker: DNZOY Exchange: PINX
Employees: 206,521 Fiscal Year Ends: 03/31
Parent Company:

SALARIES/BONUSES:

Top Exec. Salary: $ Bonus: $
Second Exec. Salary: $ Bonus: $

OTHER THOUGHTS:

Estimated Female Officers or Directors:
Hot Spot for Advancement for Women/Minorities:

Desktop Metal Inc

www.desktopmetal.com

NAIC Code: 333517

TYPES OF BUSINESS:

3D Printer Equipment Manufacturing
3D Printer Software

BRANDS/DIVISIONS/AFFILIATES:

Shop System
Studio System
PureSinter Furnace

GROWTH PLANS/SPECIAL FEATURES:

Desktop Metal, Inc. is a Burlington, Massachusetts-based manufacturer of 3D metal printers. Its Desktop Metal Production System is a metal printing press for mass production, with over 400% greater productivity over the closest binder-jet alternatives and more than 100 times faster than laser powder bed fusion systems. These systems are designed to print a broad range of alloys, including reactive metals such as titanium and aluminum. This process enables the use of metal powders that are 80% lower in cost than laser powder bed fusion metals, delivering parts at 1/20th the cost. The technology is being adopted by major Fortune 500 companies. Product lines include Shop System, Studio System and PureSinter Furnace. In May 2023, Desktop Metal entered into a merger agreement with Stratasys Ltd. in a $1.8 billion transaction, which was later rejected by Stratasys shareholders.

CONTACTS: Note: Officers with more than one job title may be intentionally listed here more than once.

Ric Fulop, CEO
Jason Cole, CFO
Jonah Myerberg, Chief Technology Officer
Thomas Nogueira, COO
Meg Broderick, General Counsel

FINANCIAL DATA: Note: Data for latest year may not have been available at press time.

In U.S. $	2024	2023	2022	2021	2020	2019
Revenue	199,182,900	189,698,000	209,023,008	112,408,000		
R&D Expense						
Operating Income						
Operating Margin %						
SGA Expense						
Net Income		-323,271,008	-740,342,976	-240,334,000		
Operating Cash Flow						
Capital Expenditure						
EBITDA						
Return on Assets %						
Return on Equity %						
Debt to Equity						

CONTACT INFORMATION:

Phone: 212 503-2855   Fax:
Toll-Free:
Address: 63 3rd Ave., Burlington, MA 01803 United States

STOCK TICKER/OTHER:

Stock Ticker: Subsidiary   Exchange:
Employees: 950   Fiscal Year Ends: 12/31
Parent Company: Nano Dimension Ltd

SALARIES/BONUSES:

Top Exec. Salary: $ Bonus: $
Second Exec. Salary: $ Bonus: $

OTHER THOUGHTS:

Estimated Female Officers or Directors:
Hot Spot for Advancement for Women/Minorities:

DIC Corporation

NAIC Code: 325910

www.dic-global.com

TYPES OF BUSINESS:

Inks, Pigments & Printing Supplies
Packaging Materials
Synthetic Resins
Building Materials
Plastic Additives
Coatings & Finishes
Health Foods

BRANDS/DIVISIONS/AFFILIATES:

GROWTH PLANS/SPECIAL FEATURES:

DIC Corp manufactures and sells a variety of chemicals and chemical-based products. The company organizes itself into four segments based on product type. The printing inks segment, which generates the most revenue of any segment, sells inks used for publishing as well as inks and adhesives used for packaging. The polymers segment sells synthetic resins used in electronics and automobiles. The fine chemicals segment sells liquid crystals used for televisions and monitors as well as pigments for color filters. The application materials segment sells industrial adhesive tape as well as materials used for coating, printing, and molding.

CONTACTS: Note: Officers with more than one job title may be intentionally listed here more than once.

Takashi Ikeda, CEO
Takeshi Asai, CFO
Kaoru Ino, Chairman of the Board
Shuji Furuta, Director
Masaya Nakafuji, Director

FINANCIAL DATA: Note: Data for latest year may not have been available at press time.

In U.S. $	2024	2023	2022	2021	2020	2019
Revenue	7,436,316,564	7,211,441,720	7,318,807,655	5,938,482,682	4,868,252,104	5,335,795,789
R&D Expense	113,253,300	119,334,900	105,137,500	93,744,790	83,511,530	86,816,170
Operating Income	309,087,800	124,576,500	275,492,900	297,792,300	275,361,000	286,955,000
Operating Margin %	.04%	.02%	.04%	.05%	.06%	.05%
SGA Expense	91,127,460	98,625,380	115,947,000	110,177,700	89,655,660	90,974,740
Net Income	147,965,800	-276,707,900	122,257,700	30,304,080	91,870,320	163,149,100
Operating Cash Flow	320,792,900	618,543,400	55,088,870	311,108,000	378,103,300	351,548,200
Capital Expenditure	327,145,200	403,172,800	315,169,400	268,265,800	236,038,600	242,717,300
EBITDA	694,869,500	263,142,200	614,294,700	502,207,700	416,905,100	497,264,600
Return on Assets %	.02%	-.03%	.02%	.00%	.02%	.03%
Return on Equity %	.06%	-.11%	.05%	.01%	.04%	.08%
Debt to Equity	.97%	1.14%	.99%	.91%	0.717	0.664

CONTACT INFORMATION:

Phone: 81-3-6733-3000   Fax:
Toll-Free:
Address: 7-20, Nihonbashi 3-chome, Chuo-ku, Tokyo, 103-8233 Japan

STOCK TICKER/OTHER:

Stock Ticker: DICCF   Exchange: PINX
Employees: 20,620   Fiscal Year Ends: 12/31
Parent Company:

SALARIES/BONUSES:

Top Exec. Salary: $ Bonus: $
Second Exec. Salary: $ Bonus: $

OTHER THOUGHTS:

Estimated Female Officers or Directors:
Hot Spot for Advancement for Women/Minorities:

Sales, profits and employees may be estimates. Financial information, benefits and other data can change quickly and may vary from those stated here.

Diebold Nixdorf Incorporated

www.dieboldnixdorf.com/en-us

NAIC Code: 334118

TYPES OF BUSINESS:

Automatic Teller Machines (ATM) Manufacturing
Self-Service Terminals
Security Systems
Technical Services
Software
Electronic Voting Machines
Automated Teller Machines

BRANDS/DIVISIONS/AFFILIATES:

GROWTH PLANS/SPECIAL FEATURES:

Diebold Nixdorf Inc is engaged in providing software and hardware services for financial and retail industries. The customer segments of the company are Banking, which offers integrated solutions for financial institutions, and Retail, which offers solutions, software, and services that improve the checkout process for retailers. A majority of its revenue is generated from the Banking segment. Geographically, the company generates maximum revenue from Europe, Middle East, and Africa (EMEA), followed by the Americas and the Asia-Pacific region.

CONTACTS: Note: Officers with more than one job title may be intentionally listed here more than once.

Octavio Marquez, CEO
Thomas Timko, CFO
Patrick Byrne, Chairman of the Board
Elizabeth Radigan, Chief Legal Officer
Frank Baur, Executive VP, Divisional
James Barna, Executive VP, Divisional
Jonathan Myers, Executive VP, Divisional
Ilhami Cantadurucu, Executive VP, Divisional

FINANCIAL DATA: Note: Data for latest year may not have been available at press time.

In U.S. $	2024	2023	2022	2021	2020	2019
Revenue	3,751,099,904		3,460,699,904	3,905,200,128	3,902,299,904	4,408,699,904
R&D Expense	93,600,000		120,700,000	126,300,000	133,400,000	147,100,000
Operating Income	182,800,000		-105,000,000	141,500,000	43,000,000	11,200,000
Operating Margin %	.05%		-.03%	.04%	.01%	.00%
SGA Expense	643,600,000		741,600,000	775,600,000	858,600,000	908,800,000
Net Income	-16,500,000		-581,400,000	-78,800,000	-269,100,000	-341,300,000
Operating Cash Flow	149,200,000		-387,900,000	123,300,000	18,000,000	135,800,000
Capital Expenditure	40,400,000		53,100,000	51,300,000	44,700,000	66,000,000
EBITDA	334,900,000		-113,400,000	293,700,000	177,700,000	178,300,000
Return on Assets %	.00%		-.18%	-.02%	-.07%	-.08%
Return on Equity %	-.02%					
Debt to Equity	1.08%					

CONTACT INFORMATION:

Phone: 330 490-4000   Fax:
Toll-Free: 800-999-3600
Address: 5995 Mayfair Rd., North Canton, OH 44720 United States

STOCK TICKER/OTHER:

Stock Ticker: DBD
Employees: 21,000
Parent Company:

Exchange: NYS
Fiscal Year Ends: 12/31

SALARIES/BONUSES:

Top Exec. Salary: $850,000   Bonus: $
Second Exec. Salary: $535,832   Bonus: $247,259

OTHER THOUGHTS:

Estimated Female Officers or Directors:
Hot Spot for Advancement for Women/Minorities: Y

DLZ Corporation

dlz.com

NAIC Code: 541330

TYPES OF BUSINESS:

Engineering Services
Building and Facility Engineering
Architecture
Surveying
Consulting
Project Management

BRANDS/DIVISIONS/AFFILIATES:

DLZ Hydrokinetic Company
India Hydropower Development Company LLC

CONTACTS: *Note: Officers with more than one job title may be intentionally listed here more than once.*

Vikram Rajadhyaksha, CEO
Joseph Zwierzynski, COO
Vikram Rajadhyaksha, Chmn.

GROWTH PLANS/SPECIAL FEATURES:

DLZ Corporation provides consulting services to the engineering, architecture and surveying industries. The firm has 30 offices that partner with clients to develop the best solutions to achieve project goals. Solutions and services span compliance assistance, architecture, construction management, clean energy, environmental, geotechnical, landscape architecture and planning, materials testing and analytical services, program management, survey, transportation, water resources and water. Market sectors DLZ serves include local and state governments, federal governments, public safety, justice, design-build, education, industrial and private sector. Just a few of the company's many projects have included the I-64 Sherman-Minton Bridge over the Ohio River (rehabilitation); the Franklin County Fire Station in Kentucky; material testing for a 10th Street sinkhole in Pittsburgh, Pennsylvania; and the Hessville Youth Soccer Complex in Indiana. DLZ Hydrokinetic Company is engaged in research and development of innovative hydrokinetic technology. India Hydropower Development Company, LLC was formed in partnership with Infrastructure India Plc to develop hydropower projects in India.

DLZ offers its employees health and life insurance; healthcare and dependent care savings account; flexible work hours; short-and long-term disability; a traditional 401(k) plan or a Roth 401(k); tuition reimbursement; and an employee assistance program.

FINANCIAL DATA: *Note: Data for latest year may not have been available at press time.*

In U.S. $	2024	2023	2022	2021	2020	2019
Revenue	198,450,000	189,000,000	181,470,000	138,996,000	128,700,000	130,000,000
R&D Expense						
Operating Income						
Operating Margin %						
SGA Expense						
Net Income						
Operating Cash Flow						
Capital Expenditure						
EBITDA						
Return on Assets %						
Return on Equity %						
Debt to Equity						

CONTACT INFORMATION:

Phone: 216-771-1090   Fax: 216-771-0034
Toll-Free: 800-336-5352
Address: 6121 Huntley Rd., Columbus, OH 44113 United States

STOCK TICKER/OTHER:

Stock Ticker: Private   Exchange:
Employees: 800   Fiscal Year Ends:
Parent Company:

SALARIES/BONUSES:

Top Exec. Salary: $ Bonus: $
Second Exec. Salary: $ Bonus: $

OTHER THOUGHTS:

Estimated Female Officers or Directors:
Hot Spot for Advancement for Women/Minorities:

DNV AS

NAIC Code: 541330

www.dnv.com

TYPES OF BUSINESS:

Engineering Services
Assurance and Risk Management Services
Business-Critical Decision Solutions
Advisory Services
Certification and Classification Solutions
Digital and Software Solutions
Data and Analytics
Inspection and Testing Services

BRANDS/DIVISIONS/AFFILIATES:

Det Norske Veritas Holding AS
Veracity

CONTACTS: Note: Officers with more than one job title may be intentionally listed here more than once.

Remi Eriksen, CEO
Kjetil M. Ebbesberg, CFO
Gro Gotteberg, Chief People Officer
Adeline Yap, Sr. Comm. Officer
Tor Svensen, CEO-Maritime
Knut Orbeck-Nilssen, Pres., Maritime
Elisabeth Torstad, CEO-Oil & Gas
David Walker, CEO-Energy
Jon Fredrik Baksaas, Chmn.

GROWTH PLANS/SPECIAL FEATURES:

DNV AS provides assurance and risk management services to help businesses make critical decisions, with a focus on safeguarding life, property and the environment. Services offered by DNV include advisory, certification, classification, cyber security, data and analytics, inspection, software, testing, training and verification and assurance. Sectors served include maritime, power and renewables, oil and gas, automotive, aerospace, food and beverage, healthcare and others. As for the maritime industry, DNV has 12,000 ships and mobile offshore units in its fleet, enabling the company to have technological experience in all ship and mobile offshore unit segments. Supply chain and product assurance includes areas such as the European Union's Green Deal, supply chain governance, product assurance, digital assurance, circularity and recycling. In addition, DNV is a world-leading provider of digital solutions for managing risk and improving asset performance, and are used toward wind turbines, electric grids, pipelines, processing plants, offshore structures, ships, healthcare markets and more. Subsidiary, Veracity, offers a data-driven and platform-powered solution for trusting and scaling to industry digitalization. It enables users to take control and gain value from their data in a confident and frictionless manner. Veracity facilitates the exchange of datasets and enables the integration of application programming interfaces (APIs), applications and third-party software to onboard, expand reach and boost uptake. DNV Ventures is an arm of the firm, investing in startup companies that share DNV's purpose of safeguarding life, property and the environment. Based in Norway, DNV has offices across Europe, the Americas, Africa, the Middle East, Asia, Australia and New Zealand. The firm is wholly owned by Det Norske Veritas Holding AS.

FINANCIAL DATA: Note: Data for latest year may not have been available at press time.

In U.S. $	2024	2023	2022	2021	2020	2019
Revenue	3,257,703,750	3,102,575,000	2,340,476,096	2,435,842,040	2,440,090,000	2,447,080,000
R&D Expense						
Operating Income						
Operating Margin %						
SGA Expense						
Net Income		289,950,000	296,404,827	274,633,700	175,267,000	156,129,000
Operating Cash Flow						
Capital Expenditure						
EBITDA						
Return on Assets %						
Return on Equity %						
Debt to Equity						

CONTACT INFORMATION:

Phone: 47-6757-9900   Fax:
Toll-Free:
Address: Veritasveien 1, Hovik, 1363 Norway

STOCK TICKER/OTHER:

Stock Ticker: Private   Exchange:
Employees: 15,000   Fiscal Year Ends: 12/31
Parent Company: DNV Holding AS

SALARIES/BONUSES:

Top Exec. Salary: $ Bonus: $
Second Exec. Salary: $ Bonus: $

OTHER THOUGHTS:

Estimated Female Officers or Directors: 7
Hot Spot for Advancement for Women/Minorities: Y

Dongfeng Motor Corporation

www.dfm-global.com

NAIC Code: 336111

TYPES OF BUSINESS:

Automobile Manufacturing
Truck & Bus Manufacturing
Passenger and Commercial Vehicles
Automotive Research and Development
Cars and SUVs
Military Vehicles
Vehicle Export and Distribution

BRANDS/DIVISIONS/AFFILIATES:

GROWTH PLANS/SPECIAL FEATURES:

Dongfeng Motor Corporation (DFM) is one of China's leading automakers. Established as a state-owned company in 1969, DFM was restructured in the 1990s and has since sought out numerous joint ventures as well as integrating its development with international automotive companies. The company is engaged in research and development, automobile manufacturing and automotive services and support. DFM designs and produces passenger and commercial vehicles, including cars, mini/compact vehicles, vans, trucks, specialty trucks, new energy vehicles, buses and military vehicles. The company has overseas distributors, exclusive and non-exclusive.

CONTACTS: *Note: Officers with more than one job title may be intentionally listed here more than once.*

Jun Seki, Pres.
Cai Wei, VP
Fan Zhong, Exec. Dir.
Li Shaozhu, Exec. Dir.
Hu Xindong, Joint Sec.
Susan Lo Yee Har, Joint Sec.
Yang Qing, Chmn.

FINANCIAL DATA: *Note: Data for latest year may not have been available at press time.*

In U.S. $	2024	2023	2022	2021	2020	2019
Revenue	16,460,377,500	15,676,550,000	15,073,605,500	17,730,616,176	16,540,600,000	17,631,072,000
R&D Expense						
Operating Income						
Operating Margin %						
SGA Expense						
Net Income				1,781,879,229	1,623,970,000	1,554,378,000
Operating Cash Flow						
Capital Expenditure						
EBITDA						
Return on Assets %						
Return on Equity %						
Debt to Equity						

CONTACT INFORMATION:

Phone: 86-27-84285274   Fax:
Toll-Free:
Address: Special No. 1 Dongfeng Rd., Wuhan, Hubei 430056 China

STOCK TICKER/OTHER:

Stock Ticker: Private   Exchange:
Employees: 122,000   Fiscal Year Ends: 12/31
Parent Company:

SALARIES/BONUSES:

Top Exec. Salary: $ Bonus: $
Second Exec. Salary: $ Bonus: $

OTHER THOUGHTS:

Estimated Female Officers or Directors: 1
Hot Spot for Advancement for Women/Minorities:

Doosan Enerbility Co Ltd

www.doosanenerbility.com/en

NAIC Code: 237130

TYPES OF BUSINESS:

Power and Communication Line and Related Structures Construction
Commercial Offshore Wind Farms
New Energy Solutions
Power Plant Equipment
Plant Engineering, Procurement and Construction
Casting & Forging
3D Printing Technology
Manufacturing Facilities

BRANDS/DIVISIONS/AFFILIATES:

CONTACTS: Note: Officers with more than one job title may be intentionally listed here more than once.

Geewon Park, CEO
Yeonin Jung, COO
Sanghyun Park, CFO
Ji Taik Chung, Vice Chmn.
Geewon Park, Chmn.

GROWTH PLANS/SPECIAL FEATURES:

Doosan Enerbility Co., Ltd. established in 1962, is a heavy industrial company operating through four business units: new energy solutions, power plant equipment/services, plant engineering/procurement/construction (EPC) and material manufacturing. The new energy solutions business is engaged in commercial offshore wind farms, offering tailored solutions to customers across all stages, including site selection, wind analysis, feasibility studies, equipment procurement, EPC work and operations/maintenance services. The power plant equipment and services business designs, manufactures and supplies power plant components, including reactor and internal structures, steam generators, reactor coolant pumps, pressurizers and more. Doosan's Man-Machine Interface System (MMIS) corresponds to the neural network of connected nuclear power plants, managing the plan operation as well as the control, monitoring, instrumentation and emergency safety functions. The MMIS converges digital and human engineering technology to ensure safe operation and prevent nuclear power plant accidents. This division also specializes in combined cycle power plants, supplying related equipment such as gas turbines; and hydroelectric/pumped-storage hydro power plants, supplying the main components such as turbines, generators and instrumentation/control (I&C) systems. The EPC business engages in numerous power generation projects, from development to design and engineering, equipment supplies and construction work. Power projects span thermal power, biomass power and wind power. This division also applies seawater desalination technology to deliver solutions across all areas of the water and wastewater treatment business. Lastly, the material manufacturing business develops 3D printing technology for the 4.0 industry, providing solutions for OEM equipment as well as 3D printing fabrication and manufacturing facilities. This division also manufactures super-large castings and forgings for power plants, marine vessels, steelworks, molds and other industrial facilities.

FINANCIAL DATA: Note: Data for latest year may not have been available at press time.

In U.S. $	2024	2023	2022	2021	2020	2019
Revenue		13,577,371,000	17,155,722,096	15,014,700,000	13,902,500,000	13,523,500,000
R&D Expense						
Operating Income						
Operating Margin %						
SGA Expense						
Net Income		42,915,000	-612,771,000	416,445,000	-770,301,000	-90,130,400
Operating Cash Flow						
Capital Expenditure						
EBITDA						
Return on Assets %						
Return on Equity %						
Debt to Equity						

CONTACT INFORMATION:

Phone: 82 552786114   Fax: 82 552645551
Toll-Free:
Address: 22, Doosan Volvo-ro, Seongsan-Gu, Changwon, Gyeongnam 51711 South Korea

STOCK TICKER/OTHER:

Stock Ticker: 34020
Employees: 4,425
Parent Company: Doosan Group

Exchange: Seoul
Fiscal Year Ends: 12/31

SALARIES/BONUSES:

Top Exec. Salary: $ Bonus: $
Second Exec. Salary: $ Bonus: $

OTHER THOUGHTS:

Estimated Female Officers or Directors:
Hot Spot for Advancement for Women/Minorities:

Sales, profits and employees may be estimates. Financial information, benefits and other data can change quickly and may vary from those stated here.

Dorsch Holding GmbH

www.dorsch.de

NAIC Code: 541330

TYPES OF BUSINESS:

Engineering Consulting Services
Infrastructure Construction Consulting
Engineering
Design and Project Management
Interdisciplinary Services
Operation and Maintenance Services
Plant and Facility Lifecycle Optimization
Transport and Facility Infrastructure

BRANDS/DIVISIONS/AFFILIATES:

RAG-Stiftung
Dorsch International Consultants GmbH
Dorsch Gruppe GRE
PB Consult
BLS Energieplan GmbH
spiekermann
AHT Groupe Management & Engineering
Dorsch Gruppe DC

CONTACTS: Note: Officers with more than one job title may be intentionally listed here more than once.

Ayman Haikal, CEO
Tanja Baur, COO
Jon Grady, CFO

GROWTH PLANS/SPECIAL FEATURES:

Dorsch Holding GmbH is a consulting and engineering group that serves industrial clients, private investors and public institutions, primarily regarding infrastructure construction. It is one of Germany's largest independent planning and consulting companies, located in more than 60 countries. Dorsch's services include design and project management, construction supervision, interdisciplinary services (organizational advisory, international cooperation and feasibility study), operation and maintenance and asset management (optimizing plant/facility lifecycle). The firm specializes in transport and related infrastructure, water and environment, special engineering, industry, energy, architecture and urban development. Affiliates of the firm include Dorsch International Consultants GmbH, Dorsch Gruppe GRE (German Rail Engineering), PB Consult, BLS Energieplan GmbH, spiekermann, BPS Rail Ltd., Krebs + Kiefer, IRS Stahlwasserbau Consulting AG, Ambero Consulting GmbH, AHT Group Management & Engineering, Dorsch Gruppe DC Egypt, Dorsch Gruppe DC Abu Dhabi, Dorsch Gruppe Qatar, Dorsch Gruppe KSA, Dorsch Gruppe DC India, and Dorsch Gruppe DC Asia and more. RAG-Stiftung wholly owns Dorsch.

FINANCIAL DATA: Note: Data for latest year may not have been available at press time.

In U.S. $	2024	2023	2022	2021	2020	2019
Revenue						
R&D Expense						
Operating Income						
Operating Margin %						
SGA Expense						
Net Income						
Operating Cash Flow						
Capital Expenditure						
EBITDA						
Return on Assets %						
Return on Equity %						
Debt to Equity						

CONTACT INFORMATION:

Phone: 49-69-130257-0   Fax: 49-69-130257-32
Toll-Free:
Address: Frankfurt Airport Ctr. 1, Hugo-Eckener-Ring, Geb. 243, HBK 43, Frankfurt am Main, 60549 Germany

STOCK TICKER/OTHER:

Stock Ticker: Private
Employees: 2,500
Parent Company: RAG-Stiftung

Exchange:
Fiscal Year Ends:

SALARIES/BONUSES:

Top Exec. Salary: $ Bonus: $
Second Exec. Salary: $ Bonus: $

OTHER THOUGHTS:

Estimated Female Officers or Directors:
Hot Spot for Advancement for Women/Minorities:

Dow Inc
NAIC Code: 325199

www.dow.com/en-us.html

TYPES OF BUSINESS:
Specialty Chemicals Manufacturer
Manufacturing
Coatings & Infrastructure
Packaging Products
Industrial Intermediates
Performance Materials
Innovation

GROWTH PLANS/SPECIAL FEATURES:
Dow Chemical is a diversified global chemicals producer, formed in 2019 as a result of the DowDuPont merger and subsequent separations. The firm is a leading producer of several chemicals, including polyethylene, ethylene oxide, and silicone rubber. Its products have numerous applications in both consumer and industrial end markets.

BRANDS/DIVISIONS/AFFILIATES:

CONTACTS: *Note: Officers with more than one job title may be intentionally listed here more than once.*
James Fitterling, CEO
Jeffrey Tate, CFO
Ronald Edmonds, Chief Accounting Officer
Attiganal Sreeram, Chief Technology Officer
Andrea Dominowski, Controller
Karen Carter, COO
Amy Wilson, General Counsel
Lisa Bryant, Other Executive Officer
Mauro Gregorio, President, Divisional
Jane Palmieri, President, Divisional
John Sampson, Senior VP, Divisional

FINANCIAL DATA: *Note: Data for latest year may not have been available at press time.*

In U.S. $	2024	2023	2022	2021	2020	2019
Revenue	42,964,000,768	44,622,000,128	56,902,000,640	54,968,000,512	38,542,000,128	42,951,000,064
R&D Expense	810,000,000	829,000,000	851,000,000	857,000,000	768,000,000	765,000,000
Operating Income	1,905,000,000	2,100,000,000	5,702,000,000	7,887,000,000	2,556,000,000	3,520,000,000
Operating Margin %	.04%	.05%	.10%	.14%	.07%	.08%
SGA Expense	1,581,000,000	1,627,000,000	1,675,000,000	1,645,000,000	1,471,000,000	1,590,000,000
Net Income	1,116,000,000	589,000,000	4,582,000,000	6,311,000,000	1,225,000,000	-1,359,000,000
Operating Cash Flow	2,914,000,000	5,196,000,000	7,475,000,000	7,009,000,000	6,226,000,000	5,930,000,000
Capital Expenditure	3,065,000,000	2,477,000,000	2,058,000,000	2,324,000,000	1,387,000,000	1,970,000,000
EBITDA	5,305,000,000	4,013,000,000	9,510,000,000	11,718,000,000	5,772,000,000	2,624,000,000
Return on Assets %	.02%	.01%	.07%	.10%	.02%	-.02%
Return on Equity %	.06%	.03%	.23%	.41%	.09%	-.06%
Debt to Equity	.96%	.86%	.76%	.85%	1.448	1.308

CONTACT INFORMATION:
Phone: 989 636-1000   Fax: 989 636-3518
Toll-Free: 800-422-8193
Address: 2211 H.H. Dow Way, Midland, MI 48674 United States

STOCK TICKER/OTHER:
Stock Ticker: DOW
Employees: 35,900
Parent Company:

Exchange: NYS
Fiscal Year Ends: 12/31

SALARIES/BONUSES:
Top Exec. Salary: $1,695,200   Bonus: $
Second Exec. Salary: $953,066   Bonus: $

OTHER THOUGHTS:
Estimated Female Officers or Directors: 3
Hot Spot for Advancement for Women/Minorities: Y

Sales, profits and employees may be estimates. Financial information, benefits and other data can change quickly and may vary from those stated here.

Downer EDI Limited

NAIC Code: 541330

www.downergroup.com

TYPES OF BUSINESS:

Engineering Services
Construction Services
Railroad Infrastructure Management

BRANDS/DIVISIONS/AFFILIATES:

GROWTH PLANS/SPECIAL FEATURES:

Downer operates engineering, construction, and maintenance; transport; technology and communications; utilities; and rail units. The future of Downer is focused on urban services, and mining and high-risk construction businesses have been sold. The engineering, construction, and maintenance business had exposure to mining and energy projects through consulting services. The mining division had provided contracted mining services. The rail division services and maintains passenger rolling stock, including locomotives and wagons.

CONTACTS: Note: Officers with more than one job title may be intentionally listed here more than once.

Peter Tompkins, CEO
Mark Menhinnitt, Chairman of the Board

FINANCIAL DATA: Note: Data for latest year may not have been available at press time.

In U.S. $	2024	2023	2022	2021	2020	2019
Revenue	7,070,615,768	7,500,241,633	7,068,488,361			
R&D Expense						
Operating Income	101,717,900	104,876,400	94,562,800			
Operating Margin %	.01%	.01%	.01%			
SGA Expense	2,211,493,000	2,346,343,000	2,308,441,000			
Net Income	44,541,850	-248,622,200	97,721,340			
Operating Cash Flow						
Capital Expenditure	94,304,960	169,529,800	180,359,000			
EBITDA	330,486,300	43,574,950	416,282,600			
Return on Assets %	.01%	-.05%	.02%			
Return on Equity %	.03%	-.15%	.05%			
Debt to Equity	.81%	.87%	.63%			

CONTACT INFORMATION:

Phone: 61-2-9468-9700   Fax: 61-2-9813-8915
Toll-Free:
Address: Triniti Bus. Campus, 39 Delhi Rd., North Ryde, NSW 2113 Australia

STOCK TICKER/OTHER:

Stock Ticker: DNERF   Exchange: PINX
Employees: 30,608   Fiscal Year Ends: 06/30
Parent Company:

SALARIES/BONUSES:

Top Exec. Salary: $ Bonus: $
Second Exec. Salary: $ Bonus: $

OTHER THOUGHTS:

Estimated Female Officers or Directors: 3
Hot Spot for Advancement for Women/Minorities: Y

Dyson Singapore Pte Ltd

www.dyson.com.sg

NAIC Code: 335210

TYPES OF BUSINESS:

Vacuum Cleaner Manufacturing
Artificial Intelligence
Hair Dryers and Air Filters
Robotics
Advanced, Solid-State Battery Technologies
Research and Development
Consumer and Household Goods

BRANDS/DIVISIONS/AFFILIATES:

Dyson Airblade
Dyson Lightcycle Morph
Dyson Technology Limited

CONTACTS: Note: Officers with more than one job title may be intentionally listed here more than once.

Hanno Kirner, CEO
James Dyson, Chmn.

GROWTH PLANS/SPECIAL FEATURES:

Dyson Singapore Pte Ltd. designs and manufactures vacuum cleaners, as well as hair care, air treatment and lighting products. Owner and inventor James Dyson built an industrial cyclone tower that separated particles from the air using centrifugal force. More than 5,000 prototypes later, the Dyson bagless vacuum cleaner was invented. As of April 2025, there are Dyson machines in over 80 countries worldwide, and more than one-third of Dyson employees are engineers and scientists engaged in research, design and development. Vacuum cleaner products include uprights, cylinders, cordless, handheld and robots, along with related parts. Hair care products include dryers, straighteners, stylers and related accessories. Air treatment products include purifiers, fans, heaters, humidifiers and related filters and other accessories. Dyson's commercial hand dryers are primarily used in bathrooms and replace the need for towels after washing one's hands. Dyson Airblade hand dryers are hygienic, quiet and use 430-miles-per-hour sheets of air to scrape water from hands, drying them in just 10-12 seconds. Room fans are therefore bladeless, safe and clean; bladeless purifiers remove allergens and pollutants; bladeless heaters provide fast, even room heating; and bladeless humidifiers provide hygienic humidification with even room coverage. Lighting products include the Dyson Lightcycle Morph line of lamps, which intelligently tracks local daylight to automatically adjust lighting for visibility and reading purposes. Dyson Technology Limited is a separate company that operates Dyson's website, apps and connected products. Dyson is headquartered in Singapore, with an R&D center in the U.K.

FINANCIAL DATA: Note: Data for latest year may not have been available at press time.

In U.S. $	2024	2023	2022	2021	2020	2019
Revenue	9,490,438,650	9,038,513,000	8,090,355,000	7,624,955,520	7,331,688,000	4,671,940,000
R&D Expense						
Operating Income						
Operating Margin %						
SGA Expense						
Net Income						
Operating Cash Flow						
Capital Expenditure						
EBITDA						
Return on Assets %						
Return on Equity %						
Debt to Equity						

CONTACT INFORMATION:

Phone: 65 6643-2050   Fax: 65 6479 5531
Toll-Free: 800 397-6674
Address: 3 Sentosa Gateway, Singapore, 098544 Singapore

STOCK TICKER/OTHER:

Stock Ticker: Private   Exchange:
Employees: 1,600   Fiscal Year Ends: 12/31
Parent Company:

SALARIES/BONUSES:

Top Exec. Salary: $ Bonus: $
Second Exec. Salary: $ Bonus: $

OTHER THOUGHTS:

Estimated Female Officers or Directors:
Hot Spot for Advancement for Women/Minorities:

Eastman Chemical Company

NAIC Code: 325220

www.eastman.com

TYPES OF BUSINESS:

Chemicals, Fibers & Plastics
Coatings, Adhesives & Additives
Performance & Intermediate Chemicals
Acetate Fibers & Textiles
Gasification Services
Food Safety Diagnostics
Logistics Services
PET, Polyethylene & Polymers

BRANDS/DIVISIONS/AFFILIATES:

Estrobond
Estron
Naia
3F Feed & Food

GROWTH PLANS/SPECIAL FEATURES:

Established in 1920 to produce chemicals for Eastman Kodak, Eastman Chemical has grown into a global specialty chemical company with manufacturing sites around the world. The company generates the majority of its sales outside of the United States, with a strong presence in Asian markets. During the past several years, Eastman has sold noncore businesses, choosing to focus on higher-margin specialty product offerings.

Eastman offers its employees health, life, dependent life and disability insurance; a 401(k); and an employee stock purchase plan.

CONTACTS: Note: Officers with more than one job title may be intentionally listed here more than once.

Mark Costa, CEO
William McLain, CFO
Michelle Stewart, Chief Accounting Officer
Kellye Walker, Chief Legal Officer
Christopher Killian, Chief Technology Officer
Stephen Crawford, Executive VP, Divisional
Brad Lich, Executive VP
Adrian Holt, Other Executive Officer
Julie McAlindon, Other Executive Officer
Travis Smith, Senior VP, Divisional

FINANCIAL DATA: Note: Data for latest year may not have been available at press time.

In U.S. $	2024	2023	2022	2021	2020	2019
Revenue	9,381,999,616	9,210,000,384	10,579,999,744	10,476,000,256	8,472,999,936	9,272,999,936
R&D Expense	250,000,000	239,000,000	264,000,000	254,000,000	226,000,000	234,000,000
Operating Income	1,376,000,000	1,054,000,000	1,248,000,000	1,863,000,000	1,095,000,000	1,309,000,000
Operating Margin %	.15%	.11%	.12%	.18%	.13%	.14%
SGA Expense	664,000,000	768,000,000	625,000,000	383,000,000	654,000,000	691,000,000
Net Income	905,000,000	894,000,000	793,000,000	857,000,000	478,000,000	759,000,000
Operating Cash Flow	1,287,000,000	1,374,000,000	975,000,000	1,619,000,000	1,455,000,000	1,504,000,000
Capital Expenditure	599,000,000	828,000,000	611,000,000	578,000,000	396,000,000	431,000,000
EBITDA	1,803,000,000	1,810,000,000	1,642,000,000	1,818,000,000	1,314,000,000	1,734,000,000
Return on Assets %	.06%	.06%	.05%	.05%	.03%	.05%
Return on Equity %	.16%	.17%	.15%	.15%	.08%	.13%
Debt to Equity	.79%	.79%	.78%	.77%	0.875	0.942

CONTACT INFORMATION:

Phone: 423 229-2000   Fax: 423 229-2145
Toll-Free:
Address: 200 S. Wilcox Dr., Kingsport, TN 37662 United States

STOCK TICKER/OTHER:

Stock Ticker: EMN
Employees: 14,000
Parent Company:

Exchange: NYS
Fiscal Year Ends: 12/31

SALARIES/BONUSES:

Top Exec. Salary: $1,397,355   Bonus: $
Second Exec. Salary: Bonus: $
$852,289

OTHER THOUGHTS:

Estimated Female Officers or Directors: 2
Hot Spot for Advancement for Women/Minorities: Y

Eaton Corp plc

www.eaton.com

NAIC Code: 336300

TYPES OF BUSINESS:

Hydraulic Products
Electrical Power Distribution & Control Equipment
Truck Transmissions & Axles
Engine Components
Aerospace & Military Components

BRANDS/DIVISIONS/AFFILIATES:

HuanYu High Tech

GROWTH PLANS/SPECIAL FEATURES:

Founded in 1911 by Joseph Eaton, the eponymous company began by selling truck axles in New Jersey. Eaton has since become an industrial powerhouse largely through acquisitions in various end markets. Eaton's portfolio can broadly be divided into two parts: its electrical and industrial businesses. Its electrical portfolio (representing around 70% of company revenue) sells components within data centers, utilities, and commercial and residential buildings, while its industrial business (30% of revenue) sells components within commercial and passenger vehicles and aircraft. Eaton receives favorable tax treatment as a domiciliary of Ireland, but it generates over half of its revenue within the US.

CONTACTS: Note: Officers with more than one job title may be intentionally listed here more than once.

Craig Arnold, CEO
Olivier Leonetti, CFO
Adam Wadecki, Chief Accounting Officer
Taras Szmagala, Chief Legal Officer
Paulo Sternadt, COO, Divisional
Heath Monesmith, COO, Divisional
Earnest Marshall, Executive VP
Peter Denk, President, Divisional
Nandakumar Cheruvatath, President, Divisional
Mike Yelton, President, Geographical

FINANCIAL DATA: Note: Data for latest year may not have been available at press time.

In U.S. $	2024	2023	2022	2021	2020	2019
Revenue	24,878,000,128	23,196,000,256	20,751,998,976	19,627,999,232	17,858,000,896	21,390,000,128
R&D Expense	794,000,000	754,000,000	665,000,000	616,000,000	551,000,000	606,000,000
Operating Income	4,632,000,000	3,885,000,000	2,995,000,000	2,463,000,000	1,824,000,000	2,863,000,000
Operating Margin %	.19%	.17%	.14%	.13%	.10%	.13%
SGA Expense	4,077,000,000	3,795,000,000	3,227,000,000	3,256,000,000	3,075,000,000	3,583,000,000
Net Income	3,794,000,000	3,218,000,000	2,462,000,000	2,144,000,000	1,410,000,000	2,211,000,000
Operating Cash Flow	4,327,000,000	3,624,000,000	2,533,000,000	2,163,000,000	2,944,000,000	3,451,000,000
Capital Expenditure	808,000,000	757,000,000	598,000,000	575,000,000	389,000,000	587,000,000
EBITDA	5,617,000,000	4,904,000,000	4,009,000,000	3,962,000,000	2,706,000,000	3,674,000,000
Return on Assets %	.10%	.09%	.07%	.07%	.04%	.07%
Return on Equity %	.20%	.18%	.15%	.14%	.09%	.14%
Debt to Equity	.49%	.46%	.52%	.44%	0.491	0.507

CONTACT INFORMATION:

Phone: 353-163-72900 Fax:
Toll-Free:
Address: Eaton House, 30 Pembroke Rd., Dublin, D04 Y0C2 Ireland

STOCK TICKER/OTHER:

Stock Ticker: ETN   Exchange: NYS
Employees: 94,000   Fiscal Year Ends: 12/31
Parent Company:

SALARIES/BONUSES:

Top Exec. Salary: $1,450,000   Bonus: $
Second Exec. Salary: Bonus: $271,667
$805,076

OTHER THOUGHTS:

Estimated Female Officers or Directors: 4
Hot Spot for Advancement for Women/Minorities: Y

ECC (Environmental Chemical Corp)

NAIC Code: 541330

TYPES OF BUSINESS:

Engineering Consulting Services
Engineering
Construction
Environmental Remediation
Engineering Design

BRANDS/DIVISIONS/AFFILIATES:

CONTACTS: *Note: Officers with more than one job title may be intentionally listed here more than once.*

Manjiv S. Vohra, CEO

GROWTH PLANS/SPECIAL FEATURES:

ECC is an engineering and construction firm that delivers design-build, construction, environmental remediation, engineering and design management, energy, munitions response and international development solutions. The employee-owned firm is headquartered in the Bay Area of California, with 14 offices throughout 37 countries around the world. ECC provides cradle-to-grave environmental remediation services with a broad diversity of remedial technologies to remediate a full range of contaminants, including printed circuit boards, petroleum hydrocarbons, asbestos, metals and other inorganics and volatile/semi-volatile organic compounds as well as explosives and explosive residues. Services that the company provides are construction, environmental, contingency and disaster response, energy, munitions response, development and fuels infrastructure. Energy solutions include upgrading distribution systems; renovating facilities; installing renewable sources; and developing, constructing, owning and operating energy projects. The munitions response segment undertakes the demining operations, battlefield area clearance, range maintenance and weapons demilitarization. Markets served include defense facilities, aviation infrastructure, remote and contingency, secure and classified, cleanup and remediation, infrastructure, workforce housing and energy.

ECC offers its employees health, life and disability benefits; paid time-off and wellness benefits; educational benefits; financial benefits, such as a 401(k) plan; and many other benefits such as voluntary pet insurance.

FINANCIAL DATA: *Note: Data for latest year may not have been available at press time.*

In U.S. $	2024	2023	2022	2021	2020	2019
Revenue	13,650,000,000	13,000,000,000	11,000,000,000	11,000,000,000	8,000,000,000	
R&D Expense						
Operating Income						
Operating Margin %						
SGA Expense						
Net Income						
Operating Cash Flow						
Capital Expenditure						
EBITDA						
Return on Assets %						
Return on Equity %						
Debt to Equity						

CONTACT INFORMATION:

Phone: 650-347-1555   Fax: 650-347-8789
Toll-Free:
Address: 1240 Bayshore Hwy., Burlingame, CA 94010 United States

STOCK TICKER/OTHER:

Stock Ticker: Private   Exchange:
Employees: 350   Fiscal Year Ends:
Parent Company:

SALARIES/BONUSES:

Top Exec. Salary: $ Bonus: $
Second Exec. Salary: $ Bonus: $

OTHER THOUGHTS:

Estimated Female Officers or Directors:
Hot Spot for Advancement for Women/Minorities:

Eisai Co Ltd

NAIC Code: 325412

www.eisai.co.jp

TYPES OF BUSINESS:

Pharmaceuticals Manufacturing
Over-the-Counter Pharmaceuticals
Pharmaceutical Production Equipment
Diagnostic Products
Food Additives
Personal Health Care Products
Vitamins & Nutritional Supplements

BRANDS/DIVISIONS/AFFILIATES:

Halaven
Lenvima
Fycompa
Aricept
Pariet
Humira
Dayvigo

GROWTH PLANS/SPECIAL FEATURES:

Eisai Co Ltd is a specialty and generic drug manufacturing company. The company's business consists of a pharmaceutical business and other businesses. The pharmaceutical business is categorized by region, including Japan, Americas, China, Asia, and Europe, Middle East, and Africa. Eisai also reports a consumer healthcare business for Japan. The vast majority of the company's revenue is derived by its Japanese pharmaceutical business, followed by its Americas pharmaceuticals segment. The company utilizes licensing strategies in order to expand its research, development, manufacturing, and marketing capabilities.

CONTACTS: Note: Officers with more than one job title may be intentionally listed here more than once.

Haruo Naito, CEO
Fumihiko Ike, Chairman of the Board
Kenta Takahashi, Chief Compliance Officer

FINANCIAL DATA: Note: Data for latest year may not have been available at press time.

In U.S. $	2024	2023	2022	2021	2020	2019
Revenue	5,149,618,308	5,168,022,895	5,250,111,242	4,484,462,920	4,829,360,008	4,462,885,269
R&D Expense	1,173,431,000	1,201,048,000	1,192,294,000	1,043,592,000	972,757,600	1,005,582,000
Operating Income	370,778,900	277,978,400	373,160,300	357,622,900	871,306,600	598,125,600
Operating Margin %	.07%	.05%	.07%	.08%	.18%	.13%
SGA Expense	2,599,424,000	2,487,448,000	2,543,946,000	1,955,221,000	1,779,346,000	1,584,338,000
Net Income	294,411,300	384,837,600	332,921,400	291,183,000	845,369,400	440,058,300
Operating Cash Flow	388,732,300	-12,302,140	816,370,500	507,268,900	713,565,700	720,036,100
Capital Expenditure	172,334,100	239,926,400	280,942,800	259,358,500	348,694,800	191,766,200
EBITDA	719,307,100	605,797,000	656,401,000	620,820,700	1,133,192,000	818,196,400
Return on Assets %	.03%	.04%	.04%	.04%	.11%	.06%
Return on Equity %	.05%	.07%	.07%	.06%	.19%	.10%
Debt to Equity	.15%	.11%	.13%	.07%	0.081	0.143

CONTACT INFORMATION:

Phone: 81 338173700　　Fax:
Toll-Free:
Address: 4-6-10 Koishikawa, Tokyo, 112-8088 Japan

STOCK TICKER/OTHER:

Stock Ticker: ESAIY　　Exchange: PINX
Employees: 10,683　　Fiscal Year Ends: 03/31
Parent Company:

SALARIES/BONUSES:

Top Exec. Salary: $　　Bonus: $
Second Exec. Salary: $　　Bonus: $

OTHER THOUGHTS:

Estimated Female Officers or Directors:
Hot Spot for Advancement for Women/Minorities:

Electronic Arts Inc (EA)

NAIC Code: 511210G

TYPES OF BUSINESS:

Computer Software, Electronic Games, Apps & Entertainment
Online Interactive Games
E-Commerce Sales
Mobile Games
Apps

BRANDS/DIVISIONS/AFFILIATES:

Battlefield
Sims (The)
Apex Legends
Need for Speed
Plants vs Zombies

GROWTH PLANS/SPECIAL FEATURES:

Electronic Arts is one of the largest global developers and publishers of video games. Its most important franchises are the Madden NFL and FC soccer games, which it releases annually. In 2024, it also relaunched its American college football game. Other major franchises include Apex Legends, Battlefield, and The Sims. Typically, about three quarters of the firm's sales are from in-game spending, with the remainder coming from initial game sales.

EA offers its employees health care coverage, retirement and financial plans, and company perks.

CONTACTS: Note: Officers with more than one job title may be intentionally listed here more than once.

Andrew Wilson, CEO
Stuart Canfield, CFO
Eric Kelly, Chief Accounting Officer
Jacob Schatz, Chief Legal Officer
Vijayanthimala Singh, Executive VP
Laura Miele, President, Divisional

FINANCIAL DATA: Note: Data for latest year may not have been available at press time.

In U.S. $	2024	2023	2022	2021	2020	2019
Revenue	7,561,999,872	7,425,999,872	6,991,000,064	5,629,000,192	5,536,999,936	
R&D Expense	2,420,000,000	2,328,000,000	2,186,000,000	1,778,000,000	1,559,000,000	
Operating Income	1,580,000,000	1,443,000,000	1,129,000,000	1,046,000,000	1,450,000,000	
Operating Margin %	.21%	.19%	.16%	.19%	.26%	
SGA Expense	1,710,000,000	1,705,000,000	1,634,000,000	1,281,000,000	1,137,000,000	
Net Income	1,273,000,000	802,000,000	789,000,000	837,000,000	3,039,000,000	
Operating Cash Flow	2,315,000,000	1,550,000,000	1,899,000,000	1,934,000,000	1,797,000,000	
Capital Expenditure	199,000,000	207,000,000	188,000,000	124,000,000	140,000,000	
EBITDA	2,051,000,000	1,920,000,000	1,625,000,000	1,243,000,000	1,702,000,000	
Return on Assets %	.09%	.06%	.06%	.07%	.30%	
Return on Equity %	.17%	.11%	.10%	.11%	.48%	
Debt to Equity	.25%	.26%	.25%	.24%	0.053	

CONTACT INFORMATION:

Phone: 650 628-1500   Fax: 650 628-1414
Toll-Free:
Address: 209 Redwood Shores Pkwy., Redwood City, CA 94065 United States

STOCK TICKER/OTHER:

Stock Ticker: EA   Exchange: NAS
Employees: 13,700   Fiscal Year Ends: 03/31
Parent Company:

SALARIES/BONUSES:

Top Exec. Salary: $1,300,000   Bonus: $
Second Exec. Salary: $820,385   Bonus: $

OTHER THOUGHTS:

Estimated Female Officers or Directors: 2
Hot Spot for Advancement for Women/Minorities:

Eli Lilly and Company

www.lilly.com

NAIC Code: 325412

TYPES OF BUSINESS:
Pharmaceuticals Discovery & Development
Pharmaceuticals
Drug Development
Drug Discovery
Drug Production

GROWTH PLANS/SPECIAL FEATURES:
Eli Lilly is a drug firm with a focus on neuroscience, cardiometabolic, cancer, and immunology. Lilly's key products include Verzenio for cancer; Mounjaro, Zepbound, Jardiance, Trulicity, Humalog, and Humulin for cardiometabolic; and Taltz and Olumiant for immunology.

BRANDS/DIVISIONS/AFFILIATES:
Humalog
Trulicity
Forteo
Cymbalta
Zyprexa
Alimta
Olumiant
Promoter Technologies

CONTACTS: Note: Officers with more than one job title may be intentionally listed here more than once.
David Ricks, CEO
Jacob Van Naarden, Exec. VP
Lucas Montarce, CFO
Donald Zakrowski, Chief Accounting Officer
Alonzo Weems, Chief Compliance Officer
Diogo Rau, Chief Information Officer
Daniel Skovronsky, Chief Scientific Officer
Johna Norton, Executive VP, Divisional
Eric Dozier, Executive VP, Divisional
Patrik Jonsson, Executive VP, Divisional
Anat Hakim, Executive VP
Anne White, Executive VP
Edgardo Hernandez, Executive VP
Ilya Yuffa, Executive VP

FINANCIAL DATA: Note: Data for latest year may not have been available at press time.

In U.S. $	2024	2023	2022	2021	2020	2019
Revenue	45,042,700,288	34,124,099,584	28,541,399,040	28,318,400,512	24,539,799,552	22,319,499,264
R&D Expense	10,990,600,000	9,313,400,000	7,190,800,000	6,930,700,000	5,976,300,000	5,595,000,000
Operating Income	17,501,700,000	10,787,300,000	8,653,300,000	7,933,000,000	7,210,800,000	5,999,400,000
Operating Margin %	.39%	.32%	.30%	.28%	.29%	.27%
SGA Expense	8,132,100,000	6,941,200,000	6,067,500,000	6,141,900,000	5,869,400,000	6,003,900,000
Net Income	10,590,000,000	5,240,400,000	6,244,800,000	5,581,700,000	6,193,700,000	8,318,400,000
Operating Cash Flow	8,817,900,000	4,240,100,000	7,585,700,000	7,365,900,000	6,499,600,000	4,836,600,000
Capital Expenditure	8,403,600,000	7,392,100,000	2,985,300,000	1,978,400,000	2,029,100,000	1,353,500,000
EBITDA	15,227,600,000	8,567,800,000	8,660,500,000	8,042,900,000	8,913,400,000	6,899,100,000
Return on Assets %	.15%	.09%	.13%	.12%	.14%	.20%
Return on Equity %	.85%	.49%	.64%	.76%	1.50%	1.34%
Debt to Equity	2.01%	1.70%	1.38%	1.71%	2.94	5.301

CONTACT INFORMATION:
Phone: 317 276-2000   Fax:
Toll-Free:
Address: Lilly Corporate Center, Indianapolis, IN 46285 United States

STOCK TICKER/OTHER:
Stock Ticker: LLY   Exchange: NYS
Employees: 43,000   Fiscal Year Ends: 12/31
Parent Company:

SALARIES/BONUSES:
Top Exec. Salary: $1,690,385   Bonus: $
Second Exec. Salary: Bonus: $
$1,430,769

OTHER THOUGHTS:
Estimated Female Officers or Directors: 8
Hot Spot for Advancement for Women/Minorities: Y

Sales, profits and employees may be estimates. Financial information, benefits and other data can change quickly and may vary from those stated here.

Embraer SA

www.embraer.com

NAIC Code: 336411

TYPES OF BUSINESS:

Aircraft Manufacturing
Commuter Aircraft
Business Jets
Aircraft Maintenance
Military Aircraft
Agricultural Aircraft
Aircraft Leasing
After-Sales Service

BRANDS/DIVISIONS/AFFILIATES:

Phenom
Legacy
Praetor
Lineage
E-Jets
ERJ 145
FleetSmart
EmbraerX

GROWTH PLANS/SPECIAL FEATURES:

Embraer SA based in Sao Paulo, Brazil, manufacturer of jets. Its focus is to achieve customer satisfaction with and services addressing the commercial airline, executive jets, and defense and security markets. It has developed a customer-centric technology-driven portfolio of commercial aviation products and services that allows it to build long-term relationships with clients in the commercial aviation, executive jets, and defense and security markets. It operates through the various segments namely Commercial Aviation, Defense and Security, Executive Aviation, Service and Support, and Other Segments. The company generates maximum revenue from the Commercial Aviation segment.

CONTACTS: Note: Officers with more than one job title may be intentionally listed here more than once.

Francisco Gomes Neto, CEO
Antonio Carlos Garcia, CFO
Alexandre Silva, Chairman of the Board
Raul Calfat, Director
Luis da Silva, Executive VP, Divisional
Roberto de Deus Chaves, Executive VP, Divisional

FINANCIAL DATA: Note: Data for latest year may not have been available at press time.

In U.S. $	2024	2023	2022	2021	2020	2019
Revenue	6,394,699,776	5,268,499,968	4,540,400,128	4,197,199,872	3,771,099,904	5,462,600,192
R&D Expense	55,000,000	90,300,000	110,000,000	43,000,000	29,800,000	49,400,000
Operating Income	667,200,000	254,100,000	220,400,000	185,200,000	-147,700,000	102,100,000
Operating Margin %	.10%	.05%	.05%	.04%	-.04%	.02%
SGA Expense	508,600,000	519,600,000	459,300,000	379,600,000	337,400,000	476,700,000
Net Income	352,500,000	164,000,000	-185,400,000	-44,700,000	-731,900,000	-322,300,000
Operating Cash Flow	871,200,000	617,000,000	751,300,000	515,300,000	-1,290,200,000	893,800,000
Capital Expenditure	466,200,000	430,800,000	256,000,000	268,200,000	223,700,000	567,800,000
EBITDA	1,013,100,000	598,200,000	228,400,000	479,900,000	-123,300,000	231,800,000
Return on Assets %	.03%	.02%	-.02%	.00%	-.07%	-.03%
Return on Equity %	.12%	.06%	-.07%	-.02%	-.23%	-.09%
Debt to Equity	.80%	1.02%	1.15%	1.31%	1.476	0.035

CONTACT INFORMATION:

Phone: 55 1239271216   Fax: 55 1239226070
Toll-Free:
Address: Ave. Brigadeiro Faria Lima, 2170, Sao Paulo, SP 12227-901 Brazil

STOCK TICKER/OTHER:

Stock Ticker: ERJ   Exchange: NYS
Employees: 21,892   Fiscal Year Ends: 12/31
Parent Company:

SALARIES/BONUSES:

Top Exec. Salary: $ Bonus: $
Second Exec. Salary: $ Bonus: $

OTHER THOUGHTS:

Estimated Female Officers or Directors:
Hot Spot for Advancement for Women/Minorities:

Emerson Electric Co

www.emerson.com

NAIC Code: 334513

TYPES OF BUSINESS:
Engineering & Technology Products & Services
Industrial Automation Products
Power Products
Air Conditioning & Refrigeration Products
Appliances & Tools

BRANDS/DIVISIONS/AFFILIATES:
Mita-Teknik

GROWTH PLANS/SPECIAL FEATURES:
Founded in 1890 as the first manufacturer of electric fans in North America, Emerson Electric has become a leading industrial automation player through the acquisition of established brands. Emerson organizes its business into seven segments that sell a wide range of automation software, power tools, and automation hardware such as valves, gauges, and switches. In recent years, Emerson divested its climate technology and consumer businesses to become more of a pure-play industrial automation company. The automation of a factory is an enticing long-term proposition for manufacturers, helping reduce accident rates and raise uptime and productivity.

CONTACTS:
Note: Officers with more than one job title may be intentionally listed here more than once.

Surendralal Karsanbhai, CEO
Michael Baughman, CFO
James Turley, Chairman of the Board
Lisa Flavin, Chief Compliance Officer
Michael Tang, Chief Legal Officer
Vidya Ramnath, Chief Marketing Officer
Peter Zornio, Chief Technology Officer
Ram Krishnan, COO
Michael Train, Other Executive Officer
Nick Piazza, Other Executive Officer

FINANCIAL DATA:
Note: Data for latest year may not have been available at press time.

In U.S. $	2024	2023	2022	2021	2020	2019
Revenue	17,492,000,768	15,164,999,680	13,804,000,256	12,931,999,744	16,785,000,448	18,371,999,744
R&D Expense						
Operating Income	2,666,000,000	2,759,000,000	2,356,000,000	1,959,000,000	2,784,000,000	3,120,000,000
Operating Margin %	.15%	.18%	.17%	.15%	.17%	.17%
SGA Expense	5,142,000,000	4,186,000,000	3,614,000,000	3,494,000,000	3,986,000,000	4,457,000,000
Net Income	1,968,000,000	13,219,000,000	3,231,000,000	2,303,000,000	1,965,000,000	2,306,000,000
Operating Cash Flow	3,332,000,000	637,000,000	2,922,000,000	3,575,000,000	3,083,000,000	3,006,000,000
Capital Expenditure	419,000,000	363,000,000	299,000,000	404,000,000	538,000,000	594,000,000
EBITDA	4,032,000,000	4,215,000,000	3,502,000,000	2,689,000,000	3,364,000,000	3,882,000,000
Return on Assets %	.05%	.34%	.11%	.10%	.09%	.11%
Return on Equity %	.09%	.85%	.32%	.25%	.24%	.27%
Debt to Equity	.35%	.39%	.83%	.63%	0.797	0.519

CONTACT INFORMATION:
Phone: 314 553-2000   Fax: 314 553-3527
Toll-Free:
Address: 8000 W. Florissant Ave., (PO Box 4100), St. Louis, MO 63136
United States

STOCK TICKER/OTHER:
Stock Ticker: EMR
Employees: 73,000
Parent Company:

Exchange: NYS
Fiscal Year Ends: 09/30

SALARIES/BONUSES:
Top Exec. Salary: $1,475,000   Bonus: $
Second Exec. Salary: $900,000   Bonus: $

OTHER THOUGHTS:
Estimated Female Officers or Directors: 2
Hot Spot for Advancement for Women/Minorities: Y

Empresas ICA SAB de CV

NAIC Code: 237310

www.ica.com.mx

TYPES OF BUSINESS:

Heavy Construction
Infrastructure Engineering
Infrastructure Procurement
Infrastructure Construction
Civil and Industrial Buildings
Civil and Industrial Concessions
Airports
Landmarks

BRANDS/DIVISIONS/AFFILIATES:

GROWTH PLANS/SPECIAL FEATURES:

Empresas ICA SAB de CV is an infrastructure engineering, procurement, and construction company. Founded in 1947, the firm operates through three divisions and specialties across civil and industrial construction, concessions and airports. Empresas works in all Mexican states, as well as in other countries. The company has built many landmarks, buildings and facilities in Mexico, including the Estadio Azteca, the Basilica of Our Lady of Guadalupe, and the Infiernillo Dam (also known as Adolfo Lopez Mateos Dam). Empresas also built the Aguacapa Dam in Guatemala.

CONTACTS: *Note: Officers with more than one job title may be intentionally listed here more than once.*

Guadalupe Phillips Margain, CEO
Alonso Quintana Kawage, Pres.
Porfirio Gonzalez Alvarez, CEO-GACN
Diego Quintana Kawage, Exec. VP-Industrial Construction & Airports

FINANCIAL DATA: *Note: Data for latest year may not have been available at press time.*

In U.S. $	2024	2023	2022	2021	2020	2019
Revenue	1,207,500,000	1,150,000,000	1,075,000,000	1,051,090,425	982,327,500	992,250,000
R&D Expense						
Operating Income						
Operating Margin %						
SGA Expense						
Net Income						
Operating Cash Flow						
Capital Expenditure						
EBITDA						
Return on Assets %						
Return on Equity %						
Debt to Equity						

CONTACT INFORMATION:

Phone: 52 5552729991   Fax: 52 5252712431
Toll-Free:
Address: Av. Patriotismo 201, Torre Metropolis, Fl. 6, Mexico City, 03800 Mexico

STOCK TICKER/OTHER:

Stock Ticker: Private   Exchange:
Employees: 23,125   Fiscal Year Ends: 12/31
Parent Company:

SALARIES/BONUSES:

Top Exec. Salary: $ Bonus: $
Second Exec. Salary: $ Bonus: $

OTHER THOUGHTS:

Estimated Female Officers or Directors:
Hot Spot for Advancement for Women/Minorities: Y

Sales, profits and employees may be estimates. Financial information, benefits and other data can change quickly and may vary from those stated here.

ENERCON GmbH

www.enercon.de

NAIC Code: 333611

TYPES OF BUSINESS:

Wind Turbine Manufacturing
Wind Turbine Manufacture
Technologies
Wind Energy Conversion Solutions
Integrated Solutions
Wind Farm Data Acquisition Solutions
Wind Farm Remote Monitoring Solutions
Wind Farm Towers

BRANDS/DIVISIONS/AFFILIATES:

Aloys Wobben Stiftung
EP5
EP3
EP2

GROWTH PLANS/SPECIAL FEATURES:

ENERCON GmbH, founded in 1984, designs and manufactures wind turbines. The company's technology primarily consists of drive technology, grid technology and wind energy converter (WEC) components. Services categories include ENERCON Service, offering maintenance, repair and operational optimization through over 350 service stations around the world; SIP Service Portal, allowing customers to keep track with how their wind turbines are performing; SCADA Remote, fulfilling functions such as communication, data recording and control in the wind farm; and technical training, offered for installing, maintaining and repairing ENERCON wind turbines. Solutions include planning and implementation, energy marketing and financing, repowering and lifetime extension and reference projects. The product portfolio of wind turbines is large, with some categories including EP5, EP3 and EP2. ENERCON is owned by Aloys Wobben Stiftung.

CONTACTS:

Note: Officers with more than one job title may be intentionally listed here more than once.

Udo Bauer, CEO
Heiko Juritz, COO
Michael Jaxy, CFO
Jorg Scholle, CTO
Bernard Fink, Manager-Sales
Stefan Hartage, Head-Electrical Engineering Development

FINANCIAL DATA:

Note: Data for latest year may not have been available at press time.

In U.S. $	2024	2023	2022	2021	2020	2019
Revenue	5,540,000,000	5,300,000,000	5,150,000,000	5,038,800,000	4,845,000,000	5,100,000,000
R&D Expense						
Operating Income						
Operating Margin %						
SGA Expense						
Net Income						
Operating Cash Flow						
Capital Expenditure						
EBITDA						
Return on Assets %						
Return on Equity %						
Debt to Equity						

CONTACT INFORMATION:

Phone: 49 421 24415100   Fax: 49 421 2441539
Toll-Free:
Address: ENERCON Innovation Ctr. Borsigstr. 26, Aurich, 26607 Germany

STOCK TICKER/OTHER:

Stock Ticker: Private   Exchange:
Employees: 20,000   Fiscal Year Ends: 12/31
Parent Company: Aloys Wobben Stiftung

SALARIES/BONUSES:

Top Exec. Salary: $ Bonus: $
Second Exec. Salary: $ Bonus: $

OTHER THOUGHTS:

Estimated Female Officers or Directors:
Hot Spot for Advancement for Women/Minorities:

Eni SpA
NAIC Code: 211100

TYPES OF BUSINESS:
Oil & Gas-Exploration & Production
Hydrocarbons
Oil Refining
Biofuels
Electric Generation
Renewable Energy
Bio-Based Products
Gas Stations

BRANDS/DIVISIONS/AFFILIATES:
enjoy

GROWTH PLANS/SPECIAL FEATURES:
Eni is an integrated oil and gas company that explores for, produces, and refines oil around the world. In 2023, the company produced 0.8 million barrels of liquids and 4.6 billion cubic feet of natural gas per day. At end-2023, Eni held reserves of 6.4 billion barrels of oil equivalent, 48% of which are liquids. The Italian government owns a 30.1% stake in the company. Eni is placing its renewable and low-carbon business in a separate entity called Plentitude, which it will likely list publicly at some point.

CONTACTS: Note: Officers with more than one job title may be intentionally listed here more than once.
Claudio Descalzi, CEO
Francesco Gattei, CFO
Giuseppe Zafarana, Chairman of the Board
Giuseppe Ricci, COO, Divisional
Guido Brusco, COO, Divisional
Francesca Zarri, Other Corporate Officer
Erika Mandraffino, Other Corporate Officer
Gianfranco Cariola, Other Corporate Officer
Grazia Fimiani, Other Corporate Officer
Claudio Granata, Other Corporate Officer
Luca Franceschini, Other Corporate Officer
Lapo Pistelli, Other Corporate Officer
Stefano Speroni, Other Corporate Officer
Roberto Ulissi, Other Corporate Officer

FINANCIAL DATA: Note: Data for latest year may not have been available at press time.

In U.S. $	2024	2023	2022	2021	2020	2019
Revenue	100,791,150,819	106,375,705,104	150,410,894,545	86,918,273,110	49,928,491,931	79,320,095,468
R&D Expense						
Operating Income	7,742,339,000	10,517,590,000	22,432,460,000	12,570,940,000	305,334,800	8,972,758,000
Operating Margin %	.08%	.10%	.15%	.14%	.01%	.11%
SGA Expense	3,702,611,000	3,559,591,000	3,422,247,000	3,278,093,000	3,249,716,000	3,400,681,000
Net Income	2,978,434,000	5,415,437,000	15,762,770,000	6,607,265,000	-9,801,361,000	167,990,900
Operating Cash Flow	14,860,390,000	17,161,180,000	19,818,390,000	14,598,180,000	5,473,326,000	14,065,830,000
Capital Expenditure	9,636,776,000	10,459,700,000	9,147,559,000	5,943,246,000	5,271,282,000	9,507,378,000
EBITDA	26,185,020,000	29,307,600,000	43,799,090,000	24,930,760,000	7,132,804,000	20,353,010,000
Return on Assets %	.02%	.03%	.10%	.05%	-.07%	.00%
Return on Equity %	.05%	.09%	.28%	.14%	-.20%	.00%
Debt to Equity	.51%	.49%	.43%	.63%	0.697	0.495

CONTACT INFORMATION:
Phone: 39 252041730   Fax: 39 252041765
Toll-Free:
Address: Piazzale Enrico Mattei, 1, Rome, 00144 Italy

STOCK TICKER/OTHER:
Stock Ticker: E   Exchange: NYS
Employees: 33,142   Fiscal Year Ends: 12/31
Parent Company:

SALARIES/BONUSES:
Top Exec. Salary: $494,892   Bonus: $
Second Exec. Salary: $38,593   Bonus: $

OTHER THOUGHTS:
Estimated Female Officers or Directors: 1
Hot Spot for Advancement for Women/Minorities: Y

Enviri Corporation

www.harsco.com

NAIC Code: 541330

TYPES OF BUSINESS:

Engineering Services
Industrial Products Manufacturing
Railroad Equipment Maintenance
Rail Track Construction
Construction Equipment Rental
Water Processing
Hazardous Waste Services
Treatment Facilities

BRANDS/DIVISIONS/AFFILIATES:

GROWTH PLANS/SPECIAL FEATURES:

Enviri Corp is a market-leading, provider of environmental solutions for industrial and specialty waste streams, and equipment and technology for the rail sector. The company's current operations consist of three divisions: Harsco Environmental, Harsco Rail, and Clean Earth. The company gains its revenue from Harsco Environmental segment. Geographically company operates in USA and International Countries, with majority revenue from USA.

CONTACTS: Note: Officers with more than one job title may be intentionally listed here more than once.

F. Grasberger, CEO
Tom Vadaketh, CFO
Samuel Fenice, Chief Accounting Officer
Russell Hochman, Chief Compliance Officer
Jennifer Kozak, Other Executive Officer
Jeffrey Beswick, President, Divisional

FINANCIAL DATA: Note: Data for latest year may not have been available at press time.

In U.S. $	2024	2023	2022	2021	2020	2019
Revenue	2,342,644,992	2,366,020,096	2,133,981,056	1,848,398,976	1,534,033,024	1,204,369,024
R&D Expense	3,961,000	3,458,000	2,858,000	956,000	534,000	886,000
Operating Income	76,709,000	92,446,000	30,338,000	84,654,000	6,766,000	68,209,000
Operating Margin %	.03%	.04%	.01%	.05%	.00%	.06%
SGA Expense	359,388,000	353,985,000	304,865,000	272,233,000	284,442,000	205,177,000
Net Income	-127,973,000	-86,121,000	-180,069,000	-3,249,000	-26,341,000	503,919,000
Operating Cash Flow	78,063,000	114,448,000	150,527,000	72,197,000	53,818,000	-163,000
Capital Expenditure	137,900,000	139,528,000	137,344,000	158,684,000	120,541,000	186,284,000
EBITDA	190,347,000	225,775,000	72,759,000	267,414,000	163,678,000	203,484,000
Return on Assets %	-.05%	-.03%	-.06%	.00%	-.01%	.25%
Return on Equity %	-.27%	-.16%	-.27%	.00%	-.04%	1.00%
Debt to Equity	3.59%	2.82%	2.48%	1.92%	2.037	1.096

CONTACT INFORMATION:

Phone: 717-763-7064   Fax: 717-763-6424
Toll-Free:
Address: 350 Poplar Church Rd., Camp Hill, PA 17011 United States

STOCK TICKER/OTHER:

Stock Ticker: NVRI   Exchange: NYS
Employees: 13,000   Fiscal Year Ends: 12/31
Parent Company:

SALARIES/BONUSES:

Top Exec. Salary: $1,014,269   Bonus: $
Second Exec. Salary: Bonus: $220,000
$625,000

OTHER THOUGHTS:

Estimated Female Officers or Directors: 3
Hot Spot for Advancement for Women/Minorities: Y

Equinor ASA

NAIC Code: 211100

www.equinor.com

TYPES OF BUSINESS:

Oil & Gas Exploration & Production
Refining
Pipelines
Energy Marketing
Oil and Gas
Wind Power
Solar Power

BRANDS/DIVISIONS/AFFILIATES:

GROWTH PLANS/SPECIAL FEATURES:

Equinor is a Norway-based integrated oil and gas company. It has been publicly listed since 2001, but the government retains a 67% stake. Operating primarily on the Norwegian Continental Shelf, the firm produced 2.1 million barrels of oil equivalent per day in 2023 (53% liquids) and ended 2023 with 5.2 billion barrels of proven reserves (49% liquids). Operations also include offshore wind, solar, oil refineries and natural gas processing, marketing, and trading.

Equinox offers its employees comprehensive benefits.

CONTACTS: Note: Officers with more than one job title may be intentionally listed here more than once.

Anders Opedal, CEO
Torgrim Reitan, CFO
Jon Reinhardsen, Chairman of the Board
Hege Skryseth, Chief Technology Officer
Anne Drinkwater, Deputy Chairman
Aksel Stenerud, Executive VP, Divisional
Philippe Mathieu, Executive VP, Divisional
Jannik Lindbaek, Executive VP, Divisional
Pal Eitrheim, Executive VP, Divisional
Jannicke Nilsson, Executive VP, Divisional
Geir Tungesvik, Executive VP, Divisional
Irene Rummelhoff, Executive VP, Divisional
Siv Rygh Torstensen, Executive VP, Divisional
Kjetil Hove, Executive VP, Geographical

FINANCIAL DATA: Note: Data for latest year may not have been available at press time.

In U.S. $	2024	2023	2022	2021	2020	2019
Revenue	102,501,998,592	106,848,002,048	149,003,993,088	88,744,001,536	45,752,999,936	62,911,000,576
R&D Expense						
Operating Income	30,354,000,000	35,233,000,000	77,741,000,000	32,951,000,000	-3,888,000,000	8,679,000,000
Operating Margin %	.30%	.33%	.52%	.37%	- .08%	.14%
SGA Expense	1,255,000,000	1,218,000,000	986,000,000	780,000,000	706,000,000	809,000,000
Net Income	8,806,000,000	11,885,000,000	28,746,000,000	8,563,000,000	-5,510,000,000	1,843,000,000
Operating Cash Flow	20,110,000,000	24,701,000,000	35,136,000,000	28,816,000,000	10,386,000,000	13,749,000,000
Capital Expenditure	12,177,000,000	10,575,000,000	8,758,000,000	8,040,000,000	8,476,000,000	10,204,000,000
EBITDA	41,949,000,000	49,587,000,000	86,266,000,000	44,071,000,000	11,955,000,000	23,489,000,000
Return on Assets %	.06%	.08%	.19%	.06%	- .05%	.02%
Return on Equity %	.19%	.23%	.62%	.23%	- .15%	.04%
Debt to Equity	.51%	.51%	.49%	.77%	0.955	0.606

CONTACT INFORMATION:

Phone: 47 51990000   Fax: 47 51990050
Toll-Free:
Address: Forusbeen 50, Stavanger, 4035 Norway

STOCK TICKER/OTHER:

Stock Ticker: EQNR   Exchange: NYS
Employees: 24,564   Fiscal Year Ends: 12/31
Parent Company:

SALARIES/BONUSES:

Top Exec. Salary: $1,304,000   Bonus: $
Second Exec. Salary: Bonus: $
$1,201,000

OTHER THOUGHTS:

Estimated Female Officers or Directors: 6
Hot Spot for Advancement for Women/Minorities: Y

EssilorLuxottica SA

NAIC Code: 339100

TYPES OF BUSINESS:

Supplies-Ophthalmic Products
Corrective Lenses
Lens Treatments
Ophthalmic Instruments
Technical Consulting
Retail

BRANDS/DIVISIONS/AFFILIATES:

GROWTH PLANS/SPECIAL FEATURES:

EssilorLuxottica is a combination of the leading manufacturer of premium frames and sunglasses and the leading manufacturer of optical lenses. Both companies are significantly larger than the next biggest player in their respective fields and command over 15% of the fragmented global eyewear market. The company has a broad geographical presence, with around 37% of sales in Europe, 45% in North America, and the rest in Asia and Latin America.

CONTACTS: *Note: Officers with more than one job title may be intentionally listed here more than once.*

Francesco Milleri, CEO
Paul du Saillant, Deputy CEO

FINANCIAL DATA: *Note: Data for latest year may not have been available at press time.*

In U.S. $	2024	2023	2022	2021	2020	2019
Revenue	30,088,534,915	28,825,197,870	27,802,497,337	22,497,161,468	16,377,979,223	19,738,933,197
R&D Expense	715,096,500	673,098,800	681,044,300	657,207,700	626,560,700	622,020,400
Operating Income	3,912,599,000	3,608,400,000	3,582,293,000	2,620,885,000	519,863,800	1,876,277,000
Operating Margin %	.13%	.13%	.13%	.12%	.03%	.10%
SGA Expense	14,223,610,000	13,678,770,000	13,244,040,000	10,482,410,000	8,001,135,000	9,363,224,000
Net Income	2,677,639,000	2,598,184,000	2,442,679,000	1,643,587,000	96,481,270	1,222,474,000
Operating Cash Flow	5,532,349,000	5,517,594,000	5,429,058,000	5,158,910,000	3,351,873,000	3,744,609,000
Capital Expenditure	1,727,582,000	1,737,798,000	1,784,336,000	1,169,126,000	737,798,000	1,024,972,000
EBITDA	7,483,542,000	7,014,756,000	6,934,166,000	5,345,062,000	2,961,407,000	4,342,792,000
Return on Assets %	.04%	.04%	.04%	.03%	.00%	.02%
Return on Equity %	.06%	.06%	.06%	.04%	.00%	.03%
Debt to Equity	.28%	.27%	.30%	.33%	0.333	0.244

CONTACT INFORMATION:

Phone: 33-1-49-77-42-16   Fax: 33-1-49-77-44-20
Toll-Free:
Address: 147 rue de Paris,, Paris, 75008 France

STOCK TICKER/OTHER:

Stock Ticker: ESLOF   Exchange: PINX
Employees: 190,000   Fiscal Year Ends: 12/31
Parent Company:

SALARIES/BONUSES:

Top Exec. Salary: $ Bonus: $
Second Exec. Salary: $ Bonus: $

OTHER THOUGHTS:

Estimated Female Officers or Directors: 5
Hot Spot for Advancement for Women/Minorities: Y

Estudios Y Proyectos Tecnicos Industriales SA (Eptisa)

www.eptisa.com
NAIC Code: 541330

TYPES OF BUSINESS:

Engineering Consulting Services
Engineering
Consulting
Information Technology
Transport Infrastructure
Water Facilities
Industry and Energy
Environmental Solutions

BRANDS/DIVISIONS/AFFILIATES:

JSTI Group

CONTACTS: *Note: Officers with more than one job title may be intentionally listed here more than once.*

Mauricio Villarino, CEO
Luis Villarroya, Pres.
Chao Wong, CFO

GROWTH PLANS/SPECIAL FEATURES:

Estudios Y Proyectos Tecnicos Industriales SA (Eptisa) is a multinational engineering, consulting, information technology and institutional, economic and social development company. Eptisa is present in more than 35 countries, with services spanning transport infrastructure, water, building, industry and energy, public policy development, environmental solutions and smart tech sectors. The company offers a wide range of engineering services that cover all phases of the project lifecycle, which include transport, water treatment, building/industry and energy, environmental engineering, hydrogeology and ground engineering. Its Smart Tech sector offers auscultation, surveillance and security of infrastructures, searching technologies, Geographic Information Systems (GIS) and Smart Cities. Quality control meets the needs of customers through construction and environment care standards. The Public Policies Development division is responsible for developing cooperation and bringing together knowledge from different sectors with specific methodologies. This division covers areas such as governance, economic development and public finance management and sustainable urban development. Eptisa is an overseas company of JSTI Group, which is based in China.

FINANCIAL DATA: *Note: Data for latest year may not have been available at press time.*

In U.S. $	2024	2023	2022	2021	2020	2019
Revenue	124,950,000	119,000,000	114,126,600	118,902,000	180,180,000	182,000,000
R&D Expense						
Operating Income						
Operating Margin %						
SGA Expense						
Net Income						
Operating Cash Flow						
Capital Expenditure						
EBITDA						
Return on Assets %						
Return on Equity %						
Debt to Equity						

CONTACT INFORMATION:

Phone: 34-915-949-500   Fax: 34-914-465-546
Toll-Free:
Address: C/ Emilio Munoz 35-37, Madrid, 28037 Spain

STOCK TICKER/OTHER:

Stock Ticker: Private   Exchange:
Employees: 1,000   Fiscal Year Ends:
Parent Company: JSTI Group

SALARIES/BONUSES:

Top Exec. Salary: $ Bonus: $
Second Exec. Salary: $ Bonus: $

OTHER THOUGHTS:

Estimated Female Officers or Directors:
Hot Spot for Advancement for Women/Minorities:

Evonik Industries AG

www.evonik.com

NAIC Code: 325110

TYPES OF BUSINESS:

Petrochemicals
Industrial Engineering
Electricity Generation
Real Estate
Renewable Energy-Biomass
Paints and Coatings

BRANDS/DIVISIONS/AFFILIATES:

Evonik Nutrition & Care GmbH
Evonik Resource Efficiency GmbH
Evonik Performance Materials GmbH
Evonik Technology & Infrastructure GmbH
RAG Foundation
PeroxyChem
Porocel Group

GROWTH PLANS/SPECIAL FEATURES:

Evonik Industries AG is a German chemical company offering a mix of specialty and commodity chemical products. The company engages in the development, construction, distribution, and trade of scientific equipment, chemicals, and accessories for use in the fields of life sciences and biotechnology. The company is organized into four segments: Specialty Additives, Smart Materials, Nutrition & Care, and Technology & Infrastructure. Its geographic segments include Europe, Middle East & Africa; North America; Central & South America; and Asia-Pacific.

CONTACTS:
Note: Officers with more than one job title may be intentionally listed here more than once.

Bernd Tonjes, Chairman of the Board
Karin Erhard, Deputy Chairman
Alexander Bercht, Deputy Chairman

FINANCIAL DATA:
Note: Data for latest year may not have been available at press time.

In U.S. $	2024	2023	2022	2021	2020	2019
Revenue	17,204,313,517	17,329,171,778	20,985,244,645	16,975,028,177	13,846,765,127	14,878,546,831
R&D Expense	520,998,900	502,837,700	522,134,000	526,674,200	491,486,900	485,811,600
Operating Income	725,312,100	-112,372,300	1,426,788,000	1,396,141,000	954,597,100	1,330,306,000
Operating Margin %	.04%	-.01%	.07%	.08%	.07%	.09%
SGA Expense	3,035,187,000	2,648,127,000	2,969,353,000	2,597,049,000	2,306,470,000	2,359,818,000
Net Income	251,986,400	-527,809,300	612,939,800	846,765,100	527,809,300	2,390,465,000
Operating Cash Flow	1,944,381,000	1,809,308,000	1,872,872,000	2,060,159,000	1,960,273,000	1,499,432,000
Capital Expenditure	953,462,000	900,113,500	981,838,800	1,005,675,000	1,085,130,000	998,864,900
EBITDA	2,001,135,000	1,968,218,000	2,965,948,000	2,595,914,000	2,125,993,000	2,450,624,000
Return on Assets %	.01%	-.02%	.02%	.03%	.02%	.10%
Return on Equity %	.02%	-.05%	.05%	.09%	.05%	.25%
Debt to Equity	.33%	.37%	.37%	.37%	0.442	0.413

CONTACT INFORMATION:

Phone: 49-201-177-01   Fax: 49-201-177-3475
Toll-Free:
Address: Rellinghauser Strasse 1-11, Essen, NW 45128 Germany

STOCK TICKER/OTHER:

Stock Ticker: EVKIY   Exchange: PINX
Employees: 33,409   Fiscal Year Ends: 12/31
Parent Company:

SALARIES/BONUSES:

Top Exec. Salary: $ Bonus: $
Second Exec. Salary: $ Bonus: $

OTHER THOUGHTS:

Estimated Female Officers or Directors: 1
Hot Spot for Advancement for Women/Minorities:

Exxon Mobil Corporation (ExxonMobil)

www.exxonmobil.com

NAIC Code: 211100

TYPES OF BUSINESS:

Oil & Gas Exploration & Production
Gas Refining & Supply
Fuel Marketing
Power Generation
Chemicals
Petroleum Products
Convenience Stores

BRANDS/DIVISIONS/AFFILIATES:

ExxonMobil
Esso
Exxon
XTO
Mobil

GROWTH PLANS/SPECIAL FEATURES:

ExxonMobil is an integrated oil and gas company that explores for, produces, and refines oil worldwide. In 2023, it produced 2.4 million barrels of liquids and 7.7 billion cubic feet of natural gas per day. At the end of 2023, reserves were 16.9 billion barrels of oil equivalent, 66% of which were liquids. The company is one of the world's largest refiners, with a total global refining capacity of 4.5 million barrels of oil per day, and is one of the world's largest manufacturers of commodity and specialty chemicals.

85% of Exxon Mobil's employees are covered by its health program, its benefits vary across global offices, but build on categories such as health, finance and life.

CONTACTS:
Note: Officers with more than one job title may be intentionally listed here more than once.

Darren Woods, CEO
Kathryn Mikells, CFO
Len Fox, Chief Accounting Officer
Craig Morford, General Counsel
Jon Gibbs, President, Subsidiary
Neil Chapman, Senior VP
Jack Williams, Senior VP
James Chapman, Treasurer
Karen McKee, Vice President
Liam Mallon, Vice President
Darrin Talley, Vice President, Divisional

FINANCIAL DATA:
Note: Data for latest year may not have been available at press time.

In U.S. $	2024	2023	2022	2021	2020	2019
Revenue	339,247,005,696	334,697,005,056	398,674,984,960	276,692,008,960	178,574,000,128	255,582,994,432
R&D Expense						
Operating Income	39,652,000,000	44,461,000,000	64,028,000,000	24,019,000,000	-29,448,000,000	12,766,000,000
Operating Margin %	.12%	.13%	.16%	.09%	-.16%	.05%
SGA Expense	9,976,001,000	9,919,000,000	10,095,000,000	9,574,000,000	10,168,000,000	11,398,000,000
Net Income	33,680,000,000	36,010,000,000	55,740,000,000	23,040,000,000	-22,440,000,000	14,340,000,000
Operating Cash Flow	55,022,000,000	55,369,000,000	76,797,000,000	48,129,000,000	14,668,000,000	29,716,000,000
Capital Expenditure	24,306,000,000	21,919,000,000	18,407,000,000	12,076,000,000	17,282,000,000	24,361,000,000
EBITDA	73,311,000,000	74,273,000,000	102,591,000,000	52,788,000,000	18,284,000,000	39,884,000,000
Return on Assets %	.08%	.10%	.16%	.07%	-.06%	.04%
Return on Equity %	.14%	.18%	.31%	.14%	-.13%	.07%
Debt to Equity	.14%	.18%	.21%	.26%	0.30	0.137

CONTACT INFORMATION:

Phone: 972 444-1000   Fax: 972 444-1348
Toll-Free:
Address: 5959 Las Colinas Blvd., Irving, TX 75039 United States

STOCK TICKER/OTHER:

Stock Ticker: XOM   Exchange: NYS
Employees: 61,500   Fiscal Year Ends: 12/31
Parent Company:

SALARIES/BONUSES:

Top Exec. Salary: $1,969,000   Bonus: $4,548,000
Second Exec. Salary: Bonus: $3,118,000
$1,271,000

OTHER THOUGHTS:

Estimated Female Officers or Directors: 2
Hot Spot for Advancement for Women/Minorities: Y

ExxonMobil Product Solutions Company

www.exxonmobilchemical.com

NAIC Code: 325110

TYPES OF BUSINESS:

Plastics & Rubber Manufacturing
Petrochemicals
Polymers
Chemical Production
Oxygenated Fluids
Solvents
Plasticizers
Technologies

BRANDS/DIVISIONS/AFFILIATES:

Exxon Mobil Corporation
ExxonMobil Chemical Company

CONTACTS: *Note: Officers with more than one job title may be intentionally listed here more than once.*

Sherman J. Glass Jr., Pres., ExxonMobil Refining & Amp
Donald D. Humphreys, Sr. VP
Darren Woods, Chmn.-Corp.

GROWTH PLANS/SPECIAL FEATURES:

ExxonMobil Product Solutions Company (formerly ExxonMobil Chemical Company Inc.), a subsidiary of Exxon Mobil Corporation, is a leading chemical firm with a manufacturing capacity in every major region of the world. More than 90% of ExxonMobil Product's chemical capacity is integrated with ExxonMobil refineries or natural gas processing plants. Products by the company include higher alcohols, branched higher olefins, butyl, linear alpha olefins, neo acids, plasticizers, polymer modifiers, polyolefin plastomers and elastomers, polypropylene, solvents and fluids, synthetic base stocks, tackifiers and transformer oils. Solutions by industry span adhesives and sealants, agriculture, automotive, building and construction, compounding, consumer products, healthcare and medical, hygiene and personal care, industrial applications, energy, packaging and synthetic base stocks. ExxonMobil Product's catalysts and technology licensing services can help refineries and petrochemical manufacturers increase capacity, lower costs, improve margins, operate safe/reliable and efficient facilities.

ExxonMobil employs thousands of scientists and engineers and invests very heavily in research and development.

FINANCIAL DATA: *Note: Data for latest year may not have been available at press time.*

In U.S. $	2024	2023	2022	2021	2020	2019
Revenue	302,005,000,000	309,055,000,000	353,475,000,000	254,865,000,000	25,449,000,000	26,516,000,000
R&D Expense						
Operating Income						
Operating Margin %						
SGA Expense						
Net Income	9,662,000,000	16,493,000,000	20,924,000,000	9,902,000,000	1,963,000,000	592,000,000
Operating Cash Flow						
Capital Expenditure						
EBITDA						
Return on Assets %						
Return on Equity %						
Debt to Equity						

CONTACT INFORMATION:

Phone: 281-870-6000   Fax: 281-870-6661
Toll-Free:
Address: 22777 Springwoods Village Pkwy., Spring, TX 77389-1425 United States

STOCK TICKER/OTHER:

Stock Ticker: Subsidiary   Exchange:
Employees: 28,000   Fiscal Year Ends: 12/31
Parent Company: Exxon Mobil Corporation

SALARIES/BONUSES:

Top Exec. Salary: $ Bonus: $
Second Exec. Salary: $ Bonus: $

OTHER THOUGHTS:

Estimated Female Officers or Directors: 1
Hot Spot for Advancement for Women/Minorities: Y

Ferrari SpA

NAIC Code: 336111

www.ferrari.com

TYPES OF BUSINESS:

Automobile Manufacturing
Magazine Publication
TV Content Production
Amusement Parks
Vehicle Financing

BRANDS/DIVISIONS/AFFILIATES:

F8
Portofino
812
SF90
Roma

GROWTH PLANS/SPECIAL FEATURES:

Ferrari designs, engineers, and manufactures some of the world's most expensive luxury cars. With supply carefully controlled to be below demand and a brand steeped in decades of motor racing history, a Ferrari is viewed as a status symbol. In 2024, the company sold 13,752 vehicles at an average price over EUR 480,000 with more than 70% of its vehicles being sold to existing Ferrari clients. Eighty-six percent of revenue is generated from the sale of cars and spare parts and 10% from sponsorship, commercial, and brand activities including racing and lifestyle activities. In 2024, the Europe, Middle East, and Africa region accounted for 47% of revenue, the Americas was 33%, mainland China, Hong Kong, and Taiwan was 8%, and the rest of Asia was 12%.

CONTACTS: Note: Officers with more than one job title may be intentionally listed here more than once.

Benedetto Vigna, CEO
Marco Lovati, Other Executive Officer
Antonio Piccon, CFO
John Elkann, Chairman of the Board
Sergio Duca, Chairman of the Board
Enrico Galliera, Chief Marketing Officer
Davide Abate, Chief Technology Officer
Piero Ferrari, Director
Carlo Daneo, General Counsel
Frederic Vasseur, General Manager
Flavio Manzoni, Other Executive Officer
Michele Antoniazzi, Other Executive Officer
Francesca Montini, Other Executive Officer
Andrea Antichi, Other Executive Officer
Gianmaria Fulgenzi, Other Executive Officer
Silvia Gabrielli, Other Executive Officer
Ernesto Lasalandra, Other Executive Officer
Angelo Pesci, Other Executive Officer
Lorenzo Giorgetti, Other Executive Officer
Maria Liuni, Other Executive Officer

FINANCIAL DATA: Note: Data for latest year may not have been available at press time.

In U.S. $	2024	2023	2022	2021	2020	2019
Revenue	7,578,510,682	6,776,555,957	5,783,489,241	4,847,779,892	3,927,117,008	4,275,385,975
R&D Expense	1,014,860,000	1,000,634,000	880,331,400	871,854,700	802,934,200	793,656,100
Operating Income	2,133,378,000	1,828,867,000	1,386,160,000	1,212,931,000	828,552,800	1,043,036,000
Operating Margin %	.28%	.27%	.24%	.25%	.21%	.24%
SGA Expense	636,939,800	525,062,400	485,782,100	395,032,900	381,527,800	389,533,500
Net Income	1,727,443,000	1,421,167,000	1,058,586,000	942,981,800	689,917,200	789,804,700
Operating Cash Flow	2,186,897,000	1,948,510,000	1,592,894,000	1,455,989,000	951,431,400	1,482,512,000
Capital Expenditure	1,122,759,000	986,277,000	913,302,000	836,711,700	804,762,800	800,921,700
EBITDA	2,946,410,000	2,603,765,000	1,985,789,000	1,727,456,000	1,298,401,000	1,447,444,000
Return on Assets %	.17%	.16%	.13%	.13%	.10%	.14%
Return on Equity %	.46%	.44%	.39%	.42%	.37%	.49%
Debt to Equity	.95%	.81%	1.08%	1.19%	1.526	1.411

CONTACT INFORMATION:

Phone: 39-0-536-949-111   Fax: 39-0-536-949-714
Toll-Free:
Address: Via Abetone Inferiore n. 4, Maranello, 41053 Italy

STOCK TICKER/OTHER:

Stock Ticker: RACE   Exchange: NYS
Employees: 4,988   Fiscal Year Ends: 12/31
Parent Company: Ferrari NV

SALARIES/BONUSES:

Top Exec. Salary: $1,501,560   Bonus: $
Second Exec. Salary: Bonus: $
$513,833

OTHER THOUGHTS:

Estimated Female Officers or Directors:
Hot Spot for Advancement for Women/Minorities:

Sales, profits and employees may be estimates. Financial information, benefits and other data can change quickly and may vary from those stated here.

Ferrovial SE

www.ferrovial.com/en

NAIC Code: 488119

TYPES OF BUSINESS:

Airport Operations
Construction
Infrastructure Services
Toll Roads
Civil Engineering
Airport Development
Airport Management Solutions
Motorways

BRANDS/DIVISIONS/AFFILIATES:

Cintra
Ferrovial Construction
Webber
Budimex

GROWTH PLANS/SPECIAL FEATURES:

Ferrovial SE is a Spanish industrial company. The company organizes itself into four segments: Toll Roads, Airports, Construction, and Energy. The Toll Roads segment develops and operates toll roads globally. The Airports segment includes the Development, financing and operation of airports. The Construction segment Designs and executes all public and private works, including most notably the construction of public infrastructures. The Energy segment focuses on innovative solutions for promoting, constructing and operating energy generation and transmission infrastructures.

CONTACTS: *Note: Officers with more than one job title may be intentionally listed here more than once.*

Ignacio Fernandez, CEO
Rafael del Pino Y Calvo-Sotelo, Chairman of the Board
Oscar MartÃn, Director

FINANCIAL DATA: *Note: Data for latest year may not have been available at press time.*

In U.S. $	2024	2023	2022	2021	2020	2019
Revenue	10,382,519,657	9,664,018,026	8,570,942,193	7,843,359,972	7,414,301,647	6,871,736,816
R&D Expense						
Operating Income	1,022,702,000	670,828,600	486,946,700	384,790,000	197,502,800	-66,969,350
Operating Margin %	.10%	.07%	.06%	.05%	.03%	-.01%
SGA Expense	2,804,767,000	2,649,262,000	2,442,679,000	2,111,237,000	1,955,732,000	1,814,983,000
Net Income	3,676,504,000	387,060,200	213,393,900	1,359,818,000	-481,271,300	304,199,800
Operating Cash Flow	1,467,650,000	1,433,598,000	1,137,344,000	919,409,800	1,240,636,000	1,337,117,000
Capital Expenditure	256,526,700	97,616,340	107,832,000	140,749,200	131,668,600	229,284,900
EBITDA	5,152,100,000	1,677,639,000	1,048,808,000	1,717,367,000	131,668,600	1,157,775,000
Return on Assets %	.12%	.01%	.01%	.05%	-.02%	.01%
Return on Equity %	.66%	.09%	.05%	.33%	-.12%	.06%
Debt to Equity	1.69%	2.81%	2.65%	2.38%	2.596	1.779

CONTACT INFORMATION:

Phone: 31 20798-37-00   Fax:
Toll-Free:
Address: Kingsfordweg 151, Amsterdam, 1043 Netherlands

STOCK TICKER/OTHER:

Stock Ticker: FER   Exchange: NAS
Employees: 24,799   Fiscal Year Ends: 12/31
Parent Company:

SALARIES/BONUSES:

Top Exec. Salary: $ Bonus: $
Second Exec. Salary: $ Bonus: $

OTHER THOUGHTS:

Estimated Female Officers or Directors:
Hot Spot for Advancement for Women/Minorities:

Flex Ltd

www.flextronics.com

NAIC Code: 334418

TYPES OF BUSINESS:

Printed Circuit Assembly (Electronic Assembly) Manufacturing
Telecommunications Equipment Manufacturing
Engineering, Design & Testing Services
Logistics Services
Camera Modules
Medical Devices
LCD Displays
Original Design Manufacturing (ODM)

BRANDS/DIVISIONS/AFFILIATES:

GROWTH PLANS/SPECIAL FEATURES:

Flex Ltd is a contract manufacturing company providing comprehensive electronics design, manufacturing, and product management services to electronics and technology companies. The company's operating segments include Flex Agility Solutions (FAS) and Flex Reliability Solutions (FRS). Flex Agility Solutions segment includes markets such as Communications, Enterprise and Cloud; Lifestyle; and Consumer Devices. Flex Reliability Solutions segment includes markets such as Automotive, Health Solutions, and Industrial.

CONTACTS: Note: Officers with more than one job title may be intentionally listed here more than once.

Revathi Advaithi, CEO
Kevin Krumm, CFO
William Watkins, Chairman of the Board
Daniel Wendler, Chief Accounting Officer
D. Offer, Executive VP
Michael Hartung, Other Executive Officer
Kwang Hooi Tan, President, Divisional
Rebecca Sidelinger, President, Divisional

FINANCIAL DATA: Note: Data for latest year may not have been available at press time.

In U.S. $	2024	2023	2022	2021	2020	2019
Revenue	26,414,999,552	28,501,999,616	24,632,999,936	24,124,000,256	24,209,999,872	
R&D Expense						
Operating Income	873,000,000	1,021,000,000	890,000,000	808,000,000	441,000,000	
Operating Margin %	.03%	.04%	.04%	.03%	.02%	
SGA Expense	922,000,000	874,000,000	830,000,000	817,000,000	834,000,000	
Net Income	1,006,000,000	793,000,000	936,000,000	613,000,000	88,000,000	
Operating Cash Flow	1,326,000,000	950,000,000	1,024,000,000	144,000,000	-1,533,000,000	
Capital Expenditure	530,000,000	635,000,000	443,000,000	351,000,000	462,000,000	
EBITDA	1,410,000,000	1,538,000,000	1,614,000,000	1,444,000,000	1,067,000,000	
Return on Assets %	.05%	.04%	.05%	.04%	.01%	
Return on Equity %	.19%	.17%	.25%	.20%	.03%	
Debt to Equity	.70%	.76%	.92%	1.19%	1.137	

CONTACT INFORMATION:

Phone: 65 6890-7188   Fax: 65 6543-1888
Toll-Free:
Address: 2 Changi South Ln., Singapore, 486123 Singapore

STOCK TICKER/OTHER:

Stock Ticker: FLEX   Exchange: NAS
Employees: 148,115   Fiscal Year Ends: 03/31
Parent Company:

SALARIES/BONUSES:

Top Exec. Salary: $1,325,000   Bonus: $
Second Exec. Salary: Bonus: $
$735,000

OTHER THOUGHTS:

Estimated Female Officers or Directors: 4
Hot Spot for Advancement for Women/Minorities: Y

Fluor Corporation

www.fluor.com

NAIC Code: 237000

TYPES OF BUSINESS:

Heavy Construction and Engineering
Engineering
Procurement
Fabrication
Construction
Energy Solutions
Urban Solutions
Mission Solutions

BRANDS/DIVISIONS/AFFILIATES:

GROWTH PLANS/SPECIAL FEATURES:

Fluor is one of the largest global providers of engineering, procurement, construction, fabrication, operations, and maintenance services. The firm serves a wide range of end markets, including oil and gas, chemicals, mining, metals, and transportation. The company's business is organized into three core segments: urban solutions, mission solutions, and energy solutions. Fluor generated $16.3 billion in revenue in 2024.

Fluor offers its employees health, dental, vision, life and accident insurance; disability coverage; savings and retirement plans; a tax savings account; and educational assistance.

CONTACTS: *Note: Officers with more than one job title may be intentionally listed here more than once.*

David Constable, CEO
Joseph Brennan, CFO
John Regan, Chief Accounting Officer
Kevin Hammonds, Chief Legal Officer
James Breuer, COO
Stacy Dillow, Executive VP
John Reynolds, Executive VP
Alvin Collins, President, Divisional
Anthony Morgan, President, Divisional
Thomas DAgostino, President, Divisional
Mark Fields, President, Divisional

FINANCIAL DATA: *Note: Data for latest year may not have been available at press time.*

In U.S. $	2024	2023	2022	2021	2020	2019
Revenue	16,314,999,808	15,473,999,872	13,744,000,000	14,156,000,256	14,157,929,472	15,454,484,480
R&D Expense						
Operating Income	371,000,000	253,000,000	113,000,000	223,000,000	198,004,000	-345,871,000
Operating Margin %	.02%	.02%	.01%	.02%	.01%	-.02%
SGA Expense	203,000,000	224,000,000	242,000,000	231,000,000	201,522,000	139,819,000
Net Income	2,145,000,000	139,000,000	145,000,000	-440,000,000	-435,046,000	-1,522,164,000
Operating Cash Flow	828,000,000	212,000,000	31,000,000	25,000,000	185,884,000	219,018,000
Capital Expenditure	164,000,000	106,000,000	75,000,000	75,000,000	113,442,000	180,842,000
EBITDA	732,000,000	449,000,000	376,000,000	-182,000,000	174,438,000	-604,098,000
Return on Assets %	.27%	.01%	.02%	-.06%	-.06%	-.18%
Return on Equity %	.73%	.04%	.07%	-.38%	-.35%	-.70%
Debt to Equity	.28%	.60%	.55%	.84%	1.651	1.11

CONTACT INFORMATION:

Phone: 469 398-7000   Fax: 469 398-7255
Toll-Free:
Address: 6700 Las Colinas Blvd., Irving, TX 75039 United States

STOCK TICKER/OTHER:

Stock Ticker: FLR   Exchange: NYS
Employees: 30,187   Fiscal Year Ends: 12/31
Parent Company:

SALARIES/BONUSES:

Top Exec. Salary: $1,350,045   Bonus: $
Second Exec. Salary: Bonus: $
$685,568

OTHER THOUGHTS:

Estimated Female Officers or Directors: 3
Hot Spot for Advancement for Women/Minorities: Y

Fomento de Construcciones Y Contratas SA (FCC)   www.fcc.es

NAIC Code: 237000

TYPES OF BUSINESS:

Heavy & Civil Engineering Construction
Alternative Energy Development
Integrated Water Management
Cement Manufacturing
Logistics Services
Engineering Services
Railway Concessions

BRANDS/DIVISIONS/AFFILIATES:

Control Empresarial de Capitales SA de CV
FCC Aqualia
FCC Construction
FACC Industrial
FCC Concessiones
Cementos Portland Valderrivas

GROWTH PLANS/SPECIAL FEATURES:

Fomento de Construcciones Y Contratas SA is in the business of environmental services, end to end water management, construction and cement. The company's activities include services related to urban water treatment, waste recovery, end to end water cycle and also infrastructure construction projects, building construction, manufacturing of cement and concrete and operation of quarries and mineral deposits. The firm derives majority of its revenues from environmental services segment. It carries out international operations in European, the US and Latin American markets.

CONTACTS: Note: Officers with more than one job title may be intentionally listed here more than once.

Pablo Abril, CEO
Esther Koplowitz, Chairman of the Board
Alejandro Gonzalez, Co-Vice Chairman of the Board
Esther de Juseu, Co-Vice Chairman of the Board

FINANCIAL DATA: Note: Data for latest year may not have been available at press time.

In U.S. $	2024	2023	2022	2021	2020	2019
Revenue	10,296,726,821	9,327,232,446	8,746,523,324	7,558,777,470	6,989,810,641	7,123,985,442
R&D Expense						
Operating Income	801,923,900	812,216,800	888,337,200	765,611,800	634,606,100	648,072,600
Operating Margin %	.08%	.09%	.10%	.10%	.09%	.09%
SGA Expense						
Net Income	487,928,500	668,626,500	357,754,800	658,496,000	297,592,500	302,728,700
Operating Cash Flow	1,450,564,000	891,470,000	1,754,641,000	847,044,300	686,803,600	715,720,800
Capital Expenditure	953,440,400	916,720,800	707,053,300	439,718,500	463,034,000	372,775,300
EBITDA	1,644,855,000	1,537,488,000	1,354,258,000	1,551,923,000	1,193,806,000	1,240,431,000
Return on Assets %	.03%	.04%	.02%	.04%	.02%	.02%
Return on Equity %	.12%	.15%	.10%	.22%	.12%	.15%
Debt to Equity	1.88%	1.06%	1.23%	1.21%	1.696	2.484

CONTACT INFORMATION:

Phone: 34-934-964900   Fax: 34 913594923
Toll-Free:
Address: Federico Salmon, 13, Madrid, 28016 Spain

STOCK TICKER/OTHER:

Stock Ticker: FMOCF   Exchange: PINX
Employees: 58,640   Fiscal Year Ends: 12/31
Parent Company: Control Empresarial de Capitales SA de CV

SALARIES/BONUSES:

Top Exec. Salary: $ Bonus: $
Second Exec. Salary: $ Bonus: $

OTHER THOUGHTS:

Estimated Female Officers or Directors: 2
Hot Spot for Advancement for Women/Minorities: Y

Ford Motor Company

www.ford.com

NAIC Code: 336111

TYPES OF BUSINESS:

Automobile Manufacturing
Automobile Design
Automobile Manufacture
Automobile Distribution
Autonomous Vehicles
Automotive Parts
Automotive Financing Services
Artificial Intelligence

BRANDS/DIVISIONS/AFFILIATES:

Ford
Lincoln
Ford Credit
Argo AI
Spin
BlueOvalSK

CONTACTS: *Note: Officers with more than one job title may be intentionally listed here more than once.*

Theodore Cannis, CEO, Divisional
Marin Gjaja, Other Executive Officer
Shengpo Wu, CEO, Geographical
James Farley, CEO
John Lawler, CFO
William Ford, Chairman of the Board
Cathy OCallaghan, Chief Accounting Officer
Ashwani Kumar Galhotra, COO
Steven Croley, General Counsel
J. Field, Other Executive Officer
Jennifer Waldo, Other Executive Officer
Michael Amend, Other Executive Officer
Andrew Frick, President, Divisional
Sherry House, Vice President, Divisional

GROWTH PLANS/SPECIAL FEATURES:

Ford Motor Co. manufactures automobiles under its Ford and Lincoln brands. In March 2022, the company announced that it will run its combustion engine business, Ford Blue, and its BEV business, Ford Model e, as separate businesses but still all under Ford Motor. The company has nearly 13% market share in the United States, about 10% share in the UK, and under 2% share in China including unconsolidated affiliates. Sales in the US made up about 68% of 2024 total company revenue. Ford has about 171,000 employees, including about 56,500 UAW employees, and is based in Dearborn, Michigan.

FINANCIAL DATA: *Note: Data for latest year may not have been available at press time.*

In U.S. $	2024	2023	2022	2021	2020	2019
Revenue	184,992,006,144	176,190,996,480	158,057,005,056	136,340,996,096	127,144,001,536	155,900,002,304
R&D Expense						
Operating Income	5,219,000,000	5,458,000,000	6,276,000,000	4,523,000,000	-4,408,000,000	574,000,000
Operating Margin %	.03%	.03%	.04%	.03%	- .03%	.00%
SGA Expense	10,287,000,000	10,702,000,000	10,888,000,000	11,915,000,000	10,193,000,000	11,161,000,000
Net Income	5,879,000,000	4,347,000,000	-1,981,000,000	17,937,000,000	-1,279,000,000	47,000,000
Operating Cash Flow	15,423,000,000	14,918,000,000	6,853,000,000	15,787,000,000	24,269,000,000	17,639,000,000
Capital Expenditure	8,684,000,000	8,236,000,000	6,866,000,000	6,227,000,000	5,742,000,000	7,632,000,000
EBITDA	14,236,000,000	11,808,000,000	4,759,000,000	25,543,000,000	7,992,000,000	8,899,000,000
Return on Assets %	.02%	.02%	- .01%	.07%	.00%	.00%
Return on Equity %	.13%	.10%	- .04%	.45%	- .04%	.00%
Debt to Equity	2.35%	2.36%	2.08%	1.84%	3.628	3.086

CONTACT INFORMATION:

Phone: 313 322-3000   Fax: 313 222-4177
Toll-Free: 800-392-3673
Address: 1 American Rd., Dearborn, MI 48126 United States

STOCK TICKER/OTHER:

Stock Ticker: F   Exchange: NYS
Employees: 177,000   Fiscal Year Ends: 12/31
Parent Company:

SALARIES/BONUSES:

Top Exec. Salary: $1,700,000   Bonus: $
Second Exec. Salary: Bonus: $
$1,700,000

OTHER THOUGHTS:

Estimated Female Officers or Directors: 4
Hot Spot for Advancement for Women/Minorities: Y

Sales, profits and employees may be estimates. Financial information, benefits and other data can change quickly and may vary from those stated here.

Forvia SE

NAIC Code: 336300

TYPES OF BUSINESS:

Automobile Part Manufacturing
Vehicle Component Modules
Vehicle Seats
Vehicle Doors
Exhaust Systems
Front End Modules
Acoustic Engineering & Equipment
Vehicle Electronics

BRANDS/DIVISIONS/AFFILIATES:

Faurecia Clarion Electronics
Clarion
Parrot Automotive
Coagent Dynamics
SAS Interior Modules
Group FORVIA
Faurecia SA

GROWTH PLANS/SPECIAL FEATURES:

Forvia SE operates in automotive seating, interior systems, emission control technologies, electronics, lighting, and a segment called lifecycle solutions that does automotive-related recycling. The group's operating segments are Seating, Interiors, Clean Mobility, Electronics, Lighting, Lifecycle Solutions, and Others the majority of its revenue is generated from the seating segments.

CONTACTS: Note: Officers with more than one job title may be intentionally listed here more than once.

Patrick Koller, CEO
Michel De Rosen, Chairman of the Board

FINANCIAL DATA: Note: Data for latest year may not have been available at press time.

In U.S. $	2024	2023	2022	2021	2020	2019
Revenue	30,617,706,966	30,928,377,640	27,892,962,681	17,727,355,515	16,395,687,100	20,168,332,081
R&D Expense	1,061,067,000	1,081,725,000	1,017,026,000	375,595,900	387,854,700	476,731,000
Operating Income	1,372,872,000	1,414,188,000	988,195,300	872,985,300	370,828,600	1,392,622,000
Operating Margin %	.04%	.05%	.04%	.05%	.02%	.07%
SGA Expense	1,439,274,000	1,441,884,000	1,333,825,000	784,109,000	809,194,000	883,654,900
Net Income	-210,215,700	252,213,400	-433,371,200	-89,443,820	-429,966,000	669,353,000
Operating Cash Flow	2,986,379,000	2,967,651,000	2,797,503,000	1,580,023,000	1,254,938,000	2,023,610,000
Capital Expenditure	2,283,314,000	2,478,207,000	2,373,666,000	1,361,635,000	1,222,815,000	1,550,965,000
EBITDA	2,541,203,000	2,899,660,000	2,080,477,000	1,808,740,000	1,448,127,000	2,402,497,000
Return on Assets %	-.01%	.01%	-.01%	.00%	-.02%	.04%
Return on Equity %	-.04%	.05%	-.10%	-.02%	-.10%	.15%
Debt to Equity	2.35%	2.10%	2.22%	2.09%	1.474	0.924

CONTACT INFORMATION:

Phone: 33 172367000   Fax: 33 172367007
Toll-Free:
Address: 2 rue Hennape, Nanterre, 92000 France

STOCK TICKER/OTHER:

Stock Ticker: FURCF   Exchange: PINX
Employees: 153,000   Fiscal Year Ends: 12/31
Parent Company: Group FORVIA

SALARIES/BONUSES:

Top Exec. Salary: $ Bonus: $
Second Exec. Salary: $ Bonus: $

OTHER THOUGHTS:

Estimated Female Officers or Directors: 1
Hot Spot for Advancement for Women/Minorities:

FuelCell Energy Inc

NAIC Code: 335999A

www.fuelcellenergy.com

TYPES OF BUSINESS:

Fuel Cell Manufacturing
Fuel Cell Power Plants
Fuel Cell Technology
Thermal Energy
Power Generation Solutions

BRANDS/DIVISIONS/AFFILIATES:

GROWTH PLANS/SPECIAL FEATURES:

FuelCell Energy Inc is a fuel-cell power company. FuelCell designs manufactures, sells, installs, operates, and services fuel cell products and electrolysis platforms that decarbonize power and produce hydrogen. It serves various industries such as Industrial, Wastewater treatment, Commercial and Hospitality, Data centers and Communications, Education and Healthcare, and others. Geographically, the company operates in USA, South Korea, Europe and Canada. Majority of revenue is from USA and South Korea.

CONTACTS: *Note: Officers with more than one job title may be intentionally listed here more than once.*

Jason Few, CEO
Michael Bishop, CFO
James England, Chairman of the Board
Shankar Achanta, Chief Technology Officer
Michael Lisowski, Executive VP, Divisional
Joshua Dolger, Executive VP
Mark Feasel, Executive VP

FINANCIAL DATA: *Note: Data for latest year may not have been available at press time.*

In U.S. $	2024	2023	2022	2021	2020	2019
Revenue	112,132,000	123,394,000	130,484,000	69,585,000	70,871,000	60,752,000
R&D Expense	55,404,000	61,021,000	34,529,000	11,315,000	4,797,000	13,786,000
Operating Income	-155,926,000	-136,084,000	-143,724,000	-64,902,000	-39,166,000	-66,929,000
Operating Margin %	-1.39%	-1.10%	-1.10%	-.93%	-.55%	-1.10%
SGA Expense	64,604,000	64,528,000	79,620,000	37,948,000	26,644,000	31,874,000
Net Income	-126,009,000	-107,568,000	-142,722,000	-101,055,000	-89,107,000	-77,568,000
Operating Cash Flow	-152,906,000	-140,250,000	-112,167,000	-70,438,000	-36,781,000	-30,572,000
Capital Expenditure	59,553,000	92,362,000	46,651,000	73,230,000	31,909,000	33,826,000
EBITDA	-110,870,000	-74,853,000	-118,745,000	-73,788,000	-54,390,000	-54,483,000
Return on Assets %	-.14%	-.12%	-.16%	-.15%	-.22%	-.30%
Return on Equity %	-.19%	-.16%	-.22%	-.25%	-.68%	-1.27%
Debt to Equity	.21%	.19%	.13%	.13%	0.825	1.19

CONTACT INFORMATION:

Phone: 203 825-6000   Fax: 203 825-6100
Toll-Free:
Address: 3 Great Pasture Rd., Danbury, CT 06813 United States

STOCK TICKER/OTHER:

Stock Ticker: FCEL   Exchange: NAS
Employees: 584   Fiscal Year Ends: 10/31
Parent Company:

SALARIES/BONUSES:

Top Exec. Salary: $579,306   Bonus: $
Second Exec. Salary: Bonus: $
$441,987

OTHER THOUGHTS:

Estimated Female Officers or Directors:
Hot Spot for Advancement for Women/Minorities:

FUJIFILM Holdings Corporation

www.fujifilmholdings.com

NAIC Code: 333316

TYPES OF BUSINESS:

Copying Machines
Digital Cameras
Color Films
Flat Panel Display Materials
Office Copy Machines
Graphic Arts Equipment
Recording Media
Office Services

BRANDS/DIVISIONS/AFFILIATES:

FUJIFILM Corporation
FUJIFILM Business Innovation Corporation
FUJIFILM Business Expert Corporation
FUJIFILM Systems Corporation
FUJIFILM Intellectual Property Research Co Ltd

GROWTH PLANS/SPECIAL FEATURES:

FUJIFILM Holdings Corp offers products and services used in photo development and film and photo taking processes. The company produces color films and single use cameras, color paper and chemicals, photofinishing equipment, film and photo processing services, electronic imaging such as digital cameras, optical devices such as camera modules for mobile phones, TV camera lenses and cine lenses, x-ray imaging systems and films, inkjet printers, flat panel materials, recording storage mediums such as data cartridges and videotape products, and office products such as office printers. The document solutions segment including office printers and the information solutions segment consisting of its x-ray imaging and data storage systems form most of the group's yearly revenue stream.

CONTACTS: *Note: Officers with more than one job title may be intentionally listed here more than once.*

Teiichi Goto, CEO
Masayuki Higuchi, CFO
Kenji Sukeno, Chairman of the Board
Chisato Yoshizawa, Director

FINANCIAL DATA: *Note: Data for latest year may not have been available at press time.*

In U.S. $	2024	2023	2022	2021	2020	2019
Revenue	20,556,206,968	19,848,938,648	17,535,219,303	15,221,598,234	16,072,903,804	16,880,650,955
R&D Expense	1,090,725,000	1,070,168,000	1,045,036,000	1,056,304,000	1,096,084,000	1,083,949,000
Operating Income	1,921,168,000	1,895,855,000	1,594,710,000	1,148,799,000	1,295,265,000	1,456,727,000
Operating Margin %	.09%	.10%	.09%	.08%	.08%	.09%
SGA Expense	5,223,737,000	4,934,060,000	4,533,428,000	3,832,741,000	4,235,233,000	4,384,594,000
Net Income	1,690,565,000	1,523,341,000	1,466,121,000	1,258,019,000	867,724,300	958,803,100
Operating Cash Flow	2,832,137,000	1,461,066,000	2,248,917,000	2,921,834,000	1,774,972,000	1,731,068,000
Capital Expenditure	3,226,271,000	2,245,710,000	1,151,812,000	872,028,700	761,760,600	618,022,800
EBITDA	3,303,145,000	2,981,429,000	2,747,577,000	2,512,295,000	2,069,148,000	2,402,166,000
Return on Assets %	.05%	.05%	.06%	.05%	.04%	.04%
Return on Equity %	.08%	.08%	.09%	.09%	.06%	.07%
Debt to Equity	.08%	.12%	.12%	.22%	0.285	0.174

CONTACT INFORMATION:

Phone: 81 362711111   Fax:
Toll-Free:
Address: 7-3 Akasaka 9-chome, Minato-ku, Tokyo, 107-0052 Japan

STOCK TICKER/OTHER:

Stock Ticker: FUJIY   Exchange: PINX
Employees: 82,841   Fiscal Year Ends: 03/31
Parent Company:

SALARIES/BONUSES:

Top Exec. Salary: $ Bonus: $
Second Exec. Salary: $ Bonus: $

OTHER THOUGHTS:

Estimated Female Officers or Directors:
Hot Spot for Advancement for Women/Minorities:

Fujitsu Limited

www.fujitsu.com

NAIC Code: 334111

TYPES OF BUSINESS:

Computer Manufacturing
Information Technology
Internet of Things
Artificial Intelligence
Cyber Security
Digital Workplace
Hybrid IT
Digital Transformation

BRANDS/DIVISIONS/AFFILIATES:

GROWTH PLANS/SPECIAL FEATURES:

Fujitsu Ltd delivers total solutions in the field of information and communication technology. The company provides solutions/system integration services focused on information system consulting and construction, and infrastructure services centered on outsourcing services. Fujitsu provides services across a wide range of countries and regions, including Europe, the Americas, Asia, and Oceania. It operates in three segments namely, Technology Solutions; Ubiqitous Solutions and Device Solutions. Ubiquitous Solutions consists of PCs, mobile phones, and mobilewear. In PCs, Fujitsu's lineup includes desktop and laptop PCs known for energy efficiency, security, and other enhanced features, as well as water- and dust-resistant tablets.

CONTACTS:
Note: Officers with more than one job title may be intentionally listed here more than once.

Takahito Tokita, CEO
Takeshi Isobe, CFO
Yoshiko Kojo, Co-Chairman of the Board
Hidenori Furuta, Co-Chairman of the Board
Hiroki Hiramatsu, Director

FINANCIAL DATA:
Note: Data for latest year may not have been available at press time.

In U.S. $	2024	2023	2022	2021	2020	2019
Revenue	26,076,500,434	25,782,887,861	24,901,687,974	24,921,563,527	26,782,818,747	27,439,858,572
R&D Expense						
Operating Income	1,112,608,000	2,330,006,000	1,521,806,000	1,848,959,000	1,468,224,000	904,103,100
Operating Margin %	.04%	.09%	.06%	.07%	.05%	.03%
SGA Expense	6,280,193,000	5,921,786,000	5,920,404,000	5,793,661,000	6,003,089,000	6,479,909,000
Net Income	1,766,718,000	1,493,905,000	1,268,335,000	1,407,248,000	1,111,094,000	725,923,400
Operating Cash Flow	2,146,772,000	1,529,638,000	1,724,153,000	2,137,927,000	2,410,879,000	690,197,200
Capital Expenditure	1,359,615,000	1,167,023,000	994,522,400	893,994,800	923,146,400	837,524,300
EBITDA	2,573,778,000	3,873,688,000	2,991,565,000	3,274,632,000	3,108,130,000	2,257,130,000
Return on Assets %	.08%	.07%	.06%	.06%	.05%	.03%
Return on Equity %	.15%	.14%	.12%	.15%	.13%	.09%
Debt to Equity	.06%	.07%	.07%	.10%	0.166	0.164

CONTACT INFORMATION:

Phone: 81 362522220   Fax:
Toll-Free:
Address: Shiodome City Center, 1-5-2 Higashi-Shimbashi, Tokyo, 105-7123 Japan

STOCK TICKER/OTHER:

Stock Ticker: FJTSF   Exchange: PINX
Employees: 124,500   Fiscal Year Ends: 03/31
Parent Company:

SALARIES/BONUSES:

Top Exec. Salary: $ Bonus: $
Second Exec. Salary: $ Bonus: $

OTHER THOUGHTS:

Estimated Female Officers or Directors: 1
Hot Spot for Advancement for Women/Minorities:

Fujitsu Research and Development
www.fujitsu.com/global/about/research
NAIC Code: 541710

TYPES OF BUSINESS:
Research & Development
Technology Research and Development
Computing Technology
Network Technology
Artificial Intelligence
Data and Security Technology
Converging Technologies

BRANDS/DIVISIONS/AFFILIATES:
Fujitsu Limited
Fujitsu Consulting (Canada) Inc
Fujitsu Research of America Inc
Fujitsu R&D Center Co Ltd
Fujitsu Research of Europe Ltd
Fujitsu Research of India Private Ltd

CONTACTS: Note: Officers with more than one job title may be intentionally listed here more than once.
Indradeep Ghosh, CEO

GROWTH PLANS/SPECIAL FEATURES:
Fujitsu Research and Development is the research and development arm of Fujitsu Limited, engaged in developing new connection technologies. The division's key technologies include computing, network, artificial intelligence (AI), data and data security and converging technologies. These solutions enable business transformation and sustainable societies. Research and development activities in each technology area are complemented by advancing technology integration. Computing power is required for processing massive amounts of data, with a focus on the fields of supercomputers, high-performance computing and quantum computers. Regarding networks, Fujitsu R&D implements intelligent networks for delivering data, with a focus on the development of cloud-native, all-photonics and photonics-electronics convergence networks. The company develops AI technologies to support decision-making, such as human-sensing AI, explainable AI and more. As for data and security purposes, the firm's technologies are focused on blockchain, data trust and digital identity. Last, in the area of converging technologies, the division promotes the development of converging technologies that combine digital technologies with human knowledge and social sciences to encourage people to change behaviors and to digitize society. Fujitsu Limit subsidiaries that compose Fujitsu R&D include Fujitsu Consulting (Canada) Inc.; Fujitsu Research of America, Inc.; the Chinese Fujitsu R&D Center Co., Ltd.; Fujitsu Research of Europe Ltd.; and Fujitsu Research of India Private Ltd.

FINANCIAL DATA: Note: Data for latest year may not have been available at press time.

In U.S. $	2024	2023	2022	2021	2020	2019
Revenue						
R&D Expense						
Operating Income						
Operating Margin %						
SGA Expense						
Net Income						
Operating Cash Flow						
Capital Expenditure						
EBITDA						
Return on Assets %						
Return on Equity %						
Debt to Equity						

CONTACT INFORMATION:
Phone: 44 1235-79-7770   Fax:
Toll-Free:
Address: 3-9 Albert St., Fl. 2, Urban Bldg., Fl. 2, Slough, SL1 2BE United Kingdom

STOCK TICKER/OTHER:
Stock Ticker: Subsidiary   Exchange:
Employees: 1,200   Fiscal Year Ends: 03/31
Parent Company: Fujitsu Limited

SALARIES/BONUSES:
Top Exec. Salary: $ Bonus: $
Second Exec. Salary: $ Bonus: $

OTHER THOUGHTS:
Estimated Female Officers or Directors:
Hot Spot for Advancement for Women/Minorities:

Gannett Fleming Inc

www.gannettfleming.com

NAIC Code: 541330

TYPES OF BUSINESS:

Engineering Services
Infrastructure Engineering
Construction Management
Advanced Mobility
Technologies
Energy Solutions
Geospatial Analytics
Vertical Transportation Solutions

BRANDS/DIVISIONS/AFFILIATES:

CONTACTS: *Note: Officers with more than one job title may be intentionally listed here more than once.*

Mike Orth, CEO
Tim Rock, COO
Jim Nevada, CFO
Heather Eickhoff, Chief Human Resources Officer
Scott Nash, CIO

GROWTH PLANS/SPECIAL FEATURES:

Gannett Fleming, Inc. is an engineering infrastructure firm that provides planning, design, technology and construction management services for a diverse range of markets and disciplines. Gannett has participated in projects that span major cities, such as Toronto, New York, Houston and Los Angeles. The company offers a wide range of solutions, including advanced mobility, architecture, building systems, business and related technology, energy solutions, engineering/procurement/construction (EPC), environmental and regulatory, geospatial analytics and technology, geotechnical and geological, planning, program and construction services, rail systems, resiliency and sustainability, security and public safety, transportation, valuation and rate, and vertical transportation solutions. The firm delivers tailored solutions for complex architecture, engineering and construction industry challenges. Markets served by Gannett Fleming include civic, education, federal, industrial, life sciences, power/energy, transportation and water resources. Gannett continues to operate under its existing management team, which retains a significant ownership interest in the company.

Gannett Fleming, Inc. offers employees a comprehensive benefits program that includes medical, dental, vision and life insurance; a 401(k) plan; paid time-off; employee assistance and wellness programs; and a healthy work-life balance.

FINANCIAL DATA: *Note: Data for latest year may not have been available at press time.*

In U.S. $	2024	2023	2022	2021	2020	2019
Revenue	778,596,000	741,520,000	713,000,000	694,440,000	643,000,000	553,000,000
R&D Expense						
Operating Income						
Operating Margin %						
SGA Expense						
Net Income						
Operating Cash Flow						
Capital Expenditure						
EBITDA						
Return on Assets %						
Return on Equity %						
Debt to Equity						

CONTACT INFORMATION:

Phone: 717-763-7211   Fax:
Toll-Free: 800-233-1055
Address: 207 Senate Ave., Camp Hill, PA 17011-2316 United States

STOCK TICKER/OTHER:

Stock Ticker: Private   Exchange:
Employees: 2,800   Fiscal Year Ends:
Parent Company: OceanSound Partners

SALARIES/BONUSES:

Top Exec. Salary: $ Bonus: $
Second Exec. Salary: $ Bonus: $

OTHER THOUGHTS:

Estimated Female Officers or Directors:
Hot Spot for Advancement for Women/Minorities:

GE Aerospace
NAIC Code: 333000

www.ge.com

TYPES OF BUSINESS:
Machinery and Equipment Manufacturing
Industrial Technology
Financial Services
Power
Renewable Energy
Aviation
Healthcare

BRANDS/DIVISIONS/AFFILIATES:
General Electric Company

GROWTH PLANS/SPECIAL FEATURES:
GE Aerospace is the global leader in designing, manufacturing, and servicing large aircraft engines, along with partner Safran in their CFM joint venture. With its massive global installed base of nearly 70,000 commercial and military engines, GE Aerospace earns most of its profits on recurring service revenue of that equipment, which operates for decades. GE Aerospace is the remaining core business of the company formed in 1892 with historical ties to American inventor Thomas Edison; that company became a storied conglomerate with peak revenue of $130 billion in 2000 until GE spun off its appliance, finance, healthcare, and wind and power businesses between 2016 and 2024.

CONTACTS:
Note: Officers with more than one job title may be intentionally listed here more than once.
Scott Strazik, CEO, Subsidiary
Russell Stokes, CEO, Subsidiary
H. Culp, CEO
Rahul Ghai, CFO
Robert Giglietti, Chief Accounting Officer

FINANCIAL DATA:
Note: Data for latest year may not have been available at press time.

In U.S. $	2024	2023	2022	2021	2020	2019
Revenue	38,701,998,080	35,348,000,768	29,138,999,296	56,469,000,192	75,833,999,360	90,221,002,752
R&D Expense	1,286,000,000	1,011,000,000	808,000,000	1,682,000,000	2,565,000,000	3,118,000,000
Operating Income	6,761,000,000	4,717,000,000	3,596,000,000	1,058,000,000	409,000,000	5,151,000,000
Operating Margin %	.17%	.13%	.12%	.02%	.01%	.06%
SGA Expense	6,347,000,000	6,681,000,000	5,748,000,000	10,351,000,000	14,989,000,000	17,100,000,000
Net Income	6,556,000,000	9,482,000,000	336,000,000	-6,337,000,000	5,704,000,000	-4,979,000,000
Operating Cash Flow	4,710,000,000	5,189,000,000	5,917,000,000	3,481,000,000	3,568,000,000	8,734,000,000
Capital Expenditure	1,032,000,000	862,000,000	662,000,000	1,113,000,000	1,730,000,000	2,498,000,000
EBITDA	9,790,000,000	12,649,000,000	4,045,000,000	-1,545,000,000	12,949,000,000	6,414,000,000
Return on Assets %	.04%	.05%	.00%	-.03%	.02%	-.02%
Return on Equity %	.28%	.30%	.00%	-.17%	.16%	-.18%
Debt to Equity	.89%	.71%	.67%	.84%	2.064	2.375

CONTACT INFORMATION:
Phone: 203-373-2211   Fax:
Toll-Free:
Address: 5 Necco St., Boston, MA 02210 United States

STOCK TICKER/OTHER:
Stock Ticker: GE
Employees: 125,000
Parent Company:

Exchange: NYS
Fiscal Year Ends: 12/31

SALARIES/BONUSES:
Top Exec. Salary: $2,250,000   Bonus: $
Second Exec. Salary: $1,400,000   Bonus: $

OTHER THOUGHTS:
Estimated Female Officers or Directors: 10
Hot Spot for Advancement for Women/Minorities: Y

GE Global Research

www.ge.com/research

NAIC Code: 541710

TYPES OF BUSINESS:

Research & Development
Nuclear & Fossil Fuel Energy Technology
Wind, Solar, Hydroelectric & Biomass Technology
Fuel Cell & Energy Storage Technology
Nanotechnology
Photonics & Optoelectronics
Engine Technology
Biotechnology

BRANDS/DIVISIONS/AFFILIATES:

General Electric Company

CONTACTS: *Note: Officers with more than one job title may be intentionally listed here more than once.*

Mark M. Little, Sr. VP-Global Research
Michael Idelchik, VP-Advanced Tech. Programs
Xiangli Chen, Gen. Mgr.-GE China Tech. Center
Terry K. Lieb, Dir.-Global Tech., Chemistry & Chemical Eng.
Christine M. Furstoss, Dir.-Global Tech., Mfg. & Materials Tech.
Kenneth G. Herd, Gen. Mgr.-Brazil Tech. Center
James R. Maughan, Dir.-Global Tech. & Research, Americas
A. Nadeem Ishaque, Dir.-Global Tech., Diagnostics & Biomedical Tech.
Danielle Merfield, Dir.-Global Tech., Electrical Tech. & Systems
Michael Ming, Gen. Mgr.-Oil & Gas Tech. Center
H. Lawrence Culp, Jr, Chmn.
Gopi Katragadda, Managing Dir.-GE India Tech. Center
Carlos Hartel, Managing Dir.-GE Global Research Center-Europe

GROWTH PLANS/SPECIAL FEATURES:

GE Global Research is the research and development arm of General Electric Company. GE Global researches and develops advanced horizontal technologies across eight core areas. The aerodynamics and thermosciences division develops breakthrough aerodynamic, thermal management, and combustion technologies to grow renewable energy penetration and decarbonize industrial systems. Artificial Intelligence (AI), robotics and software researches AI and harnesses the power of industrial data to enable advanced analytics that drive asset optimization. Controls and optimization leverages controls, estimation, optimization, operations research and risk management to increase customer outcomes. The electrical and power systems division creates projects that revolutionize the operations, management and performance of electric power systems with high penetration of renewable energy through transformative analytics and modeling. Embedded systems and cybersecurity develop next generation embedded systems to enable real-time controls for industrial assets. The materials chemistry and physics teams design, make, demo and characterize material solutions for advanced applications that support the energy transition. Materials, coatings and modeling innovates world class materials solutions and coatings that enable next generation products and create market opportunities. Lastly, mechanical systems and design technology improves durability, affordability, efficiency and power density of industrial products and services. GE Global offers commercial services, digital solutions and intellectual property solutions. The firm serves GE's company-wide business divisions, related partners and government agencies.

FINANCIAL DATA: *Note: Data for latest year may not have been available at press time.*

In U.S. $	2024	2023	2022	2021	2020	2019
Revenue						
R&D Expense						
Operating Income						
Operating Margin %						
SGA Expense						
Net Income						
Operating Cash Flow						
Capital Expenditure						
EBITDA						
Return on Assets %						
Return on Equity %						
Debt to Equity						

CONTACT INFORMATION:

Phone: 518-387-5000   Fax: 518-387-6696
Toll-Free:
Address: 1 Research Cir., Niskayuna, NY 12309 United States

STOCK TICKER/OTHER:

Stock Ticker: Subsidiary   Exchange:
Employees: 1,000   Fiscal Year Ends: 12/31
Parent Company: General Electric Company (GE)

SALARIES/BONUSES:

Top Exec. Salary: $ Bonus: $
Second Exec. Salary: $ Bonus: $

OTHER THOUGHTS:

Estimated Female Officers or Directors: 2
Hot Spot for Advancement for Women/Minorities:

GE HealthCare Technologies Inc

NAIC Code: 334510

TYPES OF BUSINESS:
Imaging and Radiation Systems
MRI Equipment
CAT Scan Equipment
Pharmaceutical Imaging Agents
Radiation Therapy Equipment
Ultrasound Devices
Medical Devices and Systems
PET Scan Equipment

BRANDS/DIVISIONS/AFFILIATES:

GROWTH PLANS/SPECIAL FEATURES:
GE HealthCare Technologies is a leading medical technology firm with leading market share in imaging and ultrasound equipment. The company reports four major segments: imaging (45% of revenue), advanced visualization solutions (26%), patient care solutions (16%), and pharmaceutical diagnostics (13%). The company's sales are geographically diverse, with the United States, EMEA, China, and the rest of the world accounting for 46%, 26%, 12%, and 17% respectively. We estimate approximately half of its revenue is recurring, which consists of servicing (about one third of revenue), pharmaceutical diagnostics (about 10%-15%), and digital solutions (just over 5%).

CONTACTS:
Note: Officers with more than one job title may be intentionally listed here more than once.
Kevin O'Neill, CEO, Divisional
Thomas Westrick, CEO, Divisional
Roland Rott, CEO, Divisional
Peter Arduini, CEO
James Saccaro, CFO
H. Culp, Chairman of the Board
George Newcomb, Chief Accounting Officer
Taha Kass-Hout, Chief Scientific Officer
Frank Jimenez, General Counsel
Kenneth Stacherski, Other Executive Officer

FINANCIAL DATA:
Note: Data for latest year may not have been available at press time.

In U.S. $	2024	2023	2022	2021	2020	2019
Revenue	19,672,000,512	19,552,000,000	18,340,999,168	17,585,000,448	17,164,000,256	16,632,999,936
R&D Expense	1,311,000,000	1,205,000,000	1,026,000,000	816,000,000	810,000,000	833,000,000
Operating Income	2,625,000,000	2,435,000,000	2,522,000,000	2,795,000,000	2,720,000,000	2,124,000,000
Operating Margin %	.13%	.12%	.14%	.16%	.16%	.13%
SGA Expense	4,269,000,000	4,282,000,000	3,631,000,000	3,563,000,000	3,237,000,000	3,591,000,000
Net Income	1,993,000,000	1,568,000,000	1,916,000,000	2,247,000,000	13,846,000,000	1,524,000,000
Operating Cash Flow	1,951,000,000	2,101,000,000	2,113,000,000	1,607,000,000	1,687,000,000	1,989,000,000
Capital Expenditure	401,000,000	387,000,000	310,000,000	248,000,000	259,000,000	331,000,000
EBITDA	3,666,000,000	3,513,000,000	3,231,000,000	3,540,000,000	3,406,000,000	2,838,000,000
Return on Assets %	.06%	.05%	.07%	.09%	.57%	
Return on Equity %	.26%	.17%	.15%	.14%	.94%	
Debt to Equity	.92%	1.23%	.91%	.02%	0.023	

CONTACT INFORMATION:
Phone: 617-443-3400 Fax:
Toll-Free:
Address: 500 W. Monroe St., Chicago, IL 60661 United States

STOCK TICKER/OTHER:
Stock Ticker: GEHC
Employees: 51,000
Parent Company:
Exchange: NAS
Fiscal Year Ends: 12/31

SALARIES/BONUSES:
Top Exec. Salary: $1,282,427 Bonus: $
Second Exec. Salary: $897,124 Bonus: $

OTHER THOUGHTS:
Estimated Female Officers or Directors: 4
Hot Spot for Advancement for Women/Minorities: Y

GE Vernova Inc

www.gevernova.com

NAIC Code: 333611

TYPES OF BUSINESS:

Generation Equipment-Turbines & Generators
Digital Energy Software
Energy Consulting Services
Energy Financial Services
Renewable Power Equipment
Grid Solutions
Nuclear Reactors
Power Conversion Solutions

BRANDS/DIVISIONS/AFFILIATES:

General Electric Company (GE)
GE Digital
GE Energy Consulting
GE Energy Financial Services
GE Gas Power
GE Grid Solutions
GE Hitachi Nuclear Energy
GE Power Conversion

GROWTH PLANS/SPECIAL FEATURES:

GE Vernova is a global leader in the electric power industry, with products and services that generate, transfer, convert, and store electricity. The company has three business segments: power, wind, and electrification. Power includes gas, nuclear, hydroelectric, and steam technologies, providing dispatchable power. The wind segment includes wind generation technologies, inclusive of onshore and offshore wind turbines and blades. Electrification includes grid solutions, power conversion, electrification software, and solar and storage solutions technologies required for the transmission, distribution, conversion, and storage of electricity from the point of generation to point of consumption.

CONTACTS: Note: Officers with more than one job title may be intentionally listed here more than once.

Mavi Zingoni, CEO, Divisional
Victor Abate, CEO, Divisional
Scott Strazik, CEO
Kenneth Parks, CFO
Stephen Angel, Chairman of the Board
Rachel Gonzalez, General Counsel
Steven Baert, Other Executive Officer
Jessica Uhl, President

FINANCIAL DATA: Note: Data for latest year may not have been available at press time.

In U.S. $	2024	2023	2022	2021	2020	2019
Revenue	34,935,001,088	33,238,999,040	29,653,999,616	33,006,000,128		
R&D Expense	982,000,000	896,000,000	979,000,000	1,008,000,000		
Operating Income	471,000,000	-923,000,000	-2,881,000,000	-884,000,000		
Operating Margin %	.01%	- .03%	- .10%	- .03%		
SGA Expense	4,632,000,000	4,845,000,000	5,360,000,000	4,821,000,000		
Net Income	1,552,000,000	-438,000,000	-2,736,000,000	-633,000,000		
Operating Cash Flow	2,583,000,000	1,186,000,000	-114,000,000	-1,660,000,000		
Capital Expenditure	883,000,000	744,000,000	513,000,000	577,000,000		
EBITDA	1,643,000,000	932,000,000	-526,000,000	484,000,000		
Return on Assets %	.03%	- .01%	- .06%			
Return on Equity %	.18%	- .05%	- .26%			
Debt to Equity	.09%	.11%	.08%			

CONTACT INFORMATION:

Phone: 617 674-7555   Fax:
Toll-Free:
Address: 58 Charles St., Cambridge, MA 02141 United States

STOCK TICKER/OTHER:

Stock Ticker: GEV   Exchange: NYS
Employees: 32,000   Fiscal Year Ends: 12/31
Parent Company:

SALARIES/BONUSES:

Top Exec. Salary: $1,114,460   Bonus: $506,376
Second Exec. Salary: $1,390,159   Bonus: $

OTHER THOUGHTS:

Estimated Female Officers or Directors:
Hot Spot for Advancement for Women/Minorities:

Gen Digital Inc

www.gendigital.com

NAIC Code: 511210E

TYPES OF BUSINESS:

Computer Software: Network Security, Managed Access, Digital ID,
Cybersecurity & Anti-Virus
Cybersecurity
Identity Security

GROWTH PLANS/SPECIAL FEATURES:

Gen is a cybersecurity pure-play that offers security, identity
protection, and privacy solutions to individual consumers. The
firm's cyber safety offerings, via brands such as Norton, Avast,
and LifeLock, have long maintained their positions as some of
the most recognizable consumer-focused security and identity-
protection products.

BRANDS/DIVISIONS/AFFILIATES:

NortonLifeLock
Norton 360
Avast

CONTACTS: Note: Officers with more than one job title may be intentionally listed here more than once.

Vincent Pilette, CEO
Natalie Derse, CFO
Frank Dangeard, Chairman of the Board
Bryan Ko, Chief Legal Officer

FINANCIAL DATA: Note: Data for latest year may not have been available at press time.

In U.S. $	2024	2023	2022	2021	2020	2019
Revenue	3,800,000,000	3,316,999,936	2,796,000,000	2,551,000,064	2,489,999,872	
R&D Expense	332,000,000	313,000,000	253,000,000	267,000,000	328,000,000	
Operating Income	1,167,000,000	1,275,000,000	1,036,000,000	1,057,000,000	621,000,000	
Operating Margin %	.31%	.38%	.37%	.41%	.25%	
SGA Expense	1,337,000,000	968,000,000	1,014,000,000	791,000,000	1,069,000,000	
Net Income	607,000,000	1,334,000,000	836,000,000	554,000,000	3,887,000,000	
Operating Cash Flow	2,064,000,000	757,000,000	974,000,000	706,000,000	-861,000,000	
Capital Expenditure	20,000,000	6,000,000	6,000,000	6,000,000	89,000,000	
EBITDA	1,601,000,000	1,513,000,000	1,308,000,000	1,166,000,000	1,376,000,000	
Return on Assets %	.04%	.12%	.13%	.08%	.33%	
Return on Equity %	.28%	1.27%			1.35%	
Debt to Equity	3.96%	4.35%			353.80	

CONTACT INFORMATION:

Phone: 650 527-2900   Fax:
Toll-Free:
Address: 60 E. Rio Salado Pkwy, Ste. 1000, Tempe, AZ 85281 United
States

STOCK TICKER/OTHER:

Stock Ticker: GEN   Exchange: NAS
Employees: 3,400   Fiscal Year Ends: 03/31
Parent Company:

SALARIES/BONUSES:

Top Exec. Salary: $950,000   Bonus: $
Second Exec. Salary: Bonus: $
$759,121

OTHER THOUGHTS:

Estimated Female Officers or Directors: 3
Hot Spot for Advancement for Women/Minorities: Y

Genentech Inc

www.gene.com

NAIC Code: 325412

TYPES OF BUSINESS:

Drug Development & Manufacturing
Genetically Engineered Drugs
Biotechnology

BRANDS/DIVISIONS/AFFILIATES:

Roche Holding AG
www.gene.com

CONTACTS: Note: Officers with more than one job title may be intentionally listed here more than once.

Ashley Magargee, CEO
Matteo Pietra, CFO
Cori Davis, Chief People Officer
Richard H. Scheller, Exec. VP-Research
Frederick C. Kentz, Sec.
Timothy Moore, Head-Pharmaceutical Technical Operation Biologics
Thomas Schinecker, Chmn.

GROWTH PLANS/SPECIAL FEATURES:

Genentech, Inc., a wholly-owned subsidiary of Roche Holding AG, is a biotechnology company that discovers, develops, manufactures and commercializes medicines to treat patients with serious/life-threatening medical conditions. The firm makes medicines by splicing genes into fast-growing bacteria that then produce therapeutic proteins and combat diseases on a molecular level. Genentech uses cutting-edge technologies such as computer visualization of molecules, micro arrays and sensitive assaying techniques to develop, manufacture and market pharmaceuticals for unmet medical needs. For patients, the company's website (www.gene.com) provides access to viewing medicine information, investigational medicines, finding open clinical trials and information on diseases in general. Genentech's range of programs and services help make sure that price is not a barrier for patients. For medical professionals, the website offers information on the medicines that are on the market by Genentech, as well as what is on the current pipeline, compliance, product security and various types of medical resources. As of May 2025, there were more than 45 medicines on the market by the company, and 39 Food and Drug Administration (FDA) breakthrough therapy designations. These medicines and molecules are in various phases in relation to oncology, metabolism, immunology, infectious disease, neuroscience, ophthalmology or other conditions. Approximately half of Genentech's marketed and pipeline products are derived from collaborations with companies and institutions worldwide; therefore, the firm is open to having partners.

Genentech provides employees benefits including a 401(k); disability, life, AD&D, medical, dental and vision coverage; flexible spending accounts; and paid vacations.

FINANCIAL DATA: Note: Data for latest year may not have been available at press time.

In U.S. $	2024	2023	2022	2021	2020	2019
Revenue	26,550,888,000	25,286,560,000	24,314,000,000	23,587,200,000	21,840,000,000	21,000,000,000
R&D Expense						
Operating Income						
Operating Margin %						
SGA Expense						
Net Income						
Operating Cash Flow						
Capital Expenditure						
EBITDA						
Return on Assets %						
Return on Equity %						
Debt to Equity						

CONTACT INFORMATION:

Phone: 650-225-1000   Fax: 650-225-6000
Toll-Free: 800-626-3553
Address: 1 DNA Way, San Francisco, CA 94080-4990 United States

STOCK TICKER/OTHER:

Stock Ticker: Subsidiary   Exchange:
Employees: 13,500   Fiscal Year Ends: 12/31
Parent Company: Roche Holding AG

SALARIES/BONUSES:

Top Exec. Salary: $ Bonus: $
Second Exec. Salary: $ Bonus: $

OTHER THOUGHTS:

Estimated Female Officers or Directors: 1
Hot Spot for Advancement for Women/Minorities: Y

General Dynamics Corporation

www.generaldynamics.com

NAIC Code: 336411

TYPES OF BUSINESS:

Aircraft Manufacturing
Combat Vehicles & Systems
Telecommunications Systems
Naval Vessels & Submarines
Ship Management Services
Information Systems & Technology
Defense Systems & Services
Business Jets

BRANDS/DIVISIONS/AFFILIATES:

Bath Iron Works
Electric Boat Corporation
General Dynamics NASSCO
Jet Aviation
Gulfstream Aerospace Corporation

GROWTH PLANS/SPECIAL FEATURES:

General Dynamics is a defense contractor and business jet manufacturer. The firm's segments are aerospace, marine, combat systems, and technologies. General Dynamics' aerospace segment manufactures Gulfstream business jets and operates a global aircraft servicing operation. Combat systems produces land-based combat vehicles such as the M1 Abrams tank and Stryker armored personnel carrier, as well as munitions. The marine segment builds and services nuclear-powered submarines, destroyers, and other ships. The technologies segment contains two main units: an IT business that primarily serves the government market and a mission systems business that focuses on products that provide command, control, computing, intelligence, surveillance, and reconnaissance capabilities to the military.

CONTACTS: Note: Officers with more than one job title may be intentionally listed here more than once.

Phebe Novakovic, CEO
Christopher Brady, Pres., Subsidiary
Kimberly Kuryea, CFO
William Moss, Chief Accounting Officer
Robert Smith, Executive VP, Divisional
Danny Deep, Executive VP, Divisional
Jason Aiken, Executive VP, Divisional
Gregory Gallopoulos, General Counsel
Jeremie Caillet, President, Divisional
David Paddock, President, Subsidiary
Marguerite Gilliland, President, Subsidiary
Mark Burns, President, Subsidiary
Kevin Graney, President, Subsidiary

FINANCIAL DATA: Note: Data for latest year may not have been available at press time.

In U.S. $	2024	2023	2022	2021	2020	2019
Revenue	47,715,999,744	42,271,997,952	39,407,001,600	38,469,001,216	37,924,999,168	39,350,001,664
R&D Expense						
Operating Income	4,796,000,000	4,245,000,000	4,211,000,000	4,163,000,000	4,133,000,000	4,570,000,000
Operating Margin %	.10%	.10%	.11%	.11%	.11%	.12%
SGA Expense	2,568,000,000	2,427,000,000	2,411,000,000	2,245,000,000	2,192,000,000	2,417,000,000
Net Income	3,782,000,000	3,315,000,000	3,390,000,000	3,257,000,000	3,167,000,000	3,484,000,000
Operating Cash Flow	4,112,000,000	4,710,000,000	4,579,000,000	4,271,000,000	3,858,000,000	2,981,000,000
Capital Expenditure	916,000,000	904,000,000	1,114,000,000	887,000,000	967,000,000	987,000,000
EBITDA	5,819,000,000	5,246,000,000	5,311,000,000	5,194,000,000	5,105,000,000	5,503,000,000
Return on Assets %	.07%	.06%	.07%	.06%	.06%	.07%
Return on Equity %	.17%	.17%	.19%	.20%	.21%	.27%
Debt to Equity	.40%	.48%	.57%	.67%	0.728	0.734

CONTACT INFORMATION:

Phone: 703 876-3000   Fax: 703 876-3125
Toll-Free:
Address: 11011 Sunset Hills Rd., Renton, VA 20190 United States

STOCK TICKER/OTHER:

Stock Ticker: GD   Exchange: NYS
Employees: 111,600   Fiscal Year Ends: 12/31
Parent Company:

SALARIES/BONUSES:

Top Exec. Salary: $1,700,000   Bonus: $
Second Exec. Salary: Bonus: $
$1,100,000

OTHER THOUGHTS:

Estimated Female Officers or Directors: 3
Hot Spot for Advancement for Women/Minorities: Y

General Motors Company (GM)

www.gm.com

NAIC Code: 336111

TYPES OF BUSINESS:

Automobile Manufacturing
Security & Information Services
Automotive Electronics
Financing & Insurance
Parts & Service
Transmissions
Engines
Locomotives

BRANDS/DIVISIONS/AFFILIATES:

Cruise
Buick
Cadillac
Chevrolet
GMC
Baojun
Wuling
Ultium Cells LLC

GROWTH PLANS/SPECIAL FEATURES:

General Motors Co. emerged from the bankruptcy of General Motors Corp. (old GM) in July 2009. GM has eight brands and operates under three segments: GM North America, GM International, and GM Financial. The United States now has four brands instead of eight under old GM. The company regained its US market share leadership in 2022, after losing it to Toyota due to the chip shortage in 2021. 2024's share was 17.0%. The Cruise autonomous vehicle arm, which GM now owns outright, previously operated driverless geofenced AV robotaxi services in San Francisco and other cities, but after a 2023 accident, GM decided that it will focus on personal AVs. GM Financial became the company's captive finance arm in 2010 via the purchase of AmeriCredit.

CONTACTS:
Note: Officers with more than one job title may be intentionally listed here more than once.

Mary Barra, CEO
Paul Jacobson, CFO
Christopher Hatto, Chief Accounting Officer
Grant Dixton, Chief Legal Officer
Michael Abbott, Executive VP, Divisional
Gerald Johnson, Executive VP, Divisional
Rory Harvey, Executive VP
Julian Blissett, Executive VP
Mark Reuss, President

FINANCIAL DATA:
Note: Data for latest year may not have been available at press time.

In U.S. $	2024	2023	2022	2021	2020	2019
Revenue	187,442,003,968	171,841,994,752	156,734,996,480	127,004,000,256	122,484,998,144	137,236,996,096
R&D Expense						
Operating Income	12,784,000,000	9,298,000,000	10,314,000,000	9,324,000,000	6,634,000,000	5,481,000,000
Operating Margin %	.07%	.05%	.07%	.07%	.05%	.04%
SGA Expense	10,621,000,000	9,840,000,000	10,667,000,000	8,554,000,000	7,038,000,000	8,491,000,000
Net Income	6,008,000,000	10,127,000,000	9,934,000,000	10,019,000,000	6,427,000,000	6,732,000,000
Operating Cash Flow	20,129,000,000	20,930,000,000	16,043,000,000	15,188,000,000	16,670,000,000	15,021,000,000
Capital Expenditure	26,109,000,000	24,610,000,000	21,187,000,000	22,111,000,000	20,533,000,000	23,996,000,000
EBITDA	21,754,000,000	23,202,000,000	23,874,000,000	25,717,000,000	22,008,000,000	22,336,000,000
Return on Assets %	.03%	.04%	.04%	.04%	.03%	.03%
Return on Equity %	.11%	.15%	.14%	.19%	.14%	.16%
Debt to Equity	1.45%	1.30%	1.13%	1.28%	1.642	1.602

CONTACT INFORMATION:

Phone: 313 556-5000   Fax:
Toll-Free:
Address: 300 Renaissance Ctr., Detroit, MI 48265-3000 United States

STOCK TICKER/OTHER:

Stock Ticker: GM
Employees: 87,000
Parent Company:

Exchange: NYS
Fiscal Year Ends: 12/31

SALARIES/BONUSES:

Top Exec. Salary: $2,100,000   Bonus: $
Second Exec. Salary: Bonus: $
$1,350,000

OTHER THOUGHTS:

Estimated Female Officers or Directors: 8
Hot Spot for Advancement for Women/Minorities: Y

Georg Fischer AG

www.georgfischer.com

NAIC Code: 336300

TYPES OF BUSINESS:

Automotive Components
Iron Casting
Manufacturing Technology
Machine Tools
Metal and Plastic Piping Systems
Product Design
Control systems
Production Facilities

BRANDS/DIVISIONS/AFFILIATES:

GROWTH PLANS/SPECIAL FEATURES:

Georg Fischer AG provides transportation of liquids and gases, lightweight casting components in vehicles, and high-precision manufacturing technologies. It supplies plastic and metal piping systems, valves and fittings, electrical discharge machines, and other additive manufacturing solutions. The company is one of the world's providers for the tool and mold-making industry and services customers in utilities, automotive, aerospace, water and gas, and other industrial Applications. The Group comprises four divisions, GF Piping Systems, GF Uponor, GF Casting Solutions and GF Machining Solutions, which operate across three main geographical regions-Europe, North/South America and Asia.

CONTACTS: Note: Officers with more than one job title may be intentionally listed here more than once.

Andreas Muller, CEO
Mads Joergensen, CFO
Beat Romer, Head-Corp. Comm.
Daniel Bosiger, Head-Investor Rel.
Josef Edbauer, Head-Automotive
Pietro Lori, Head-Piping Systems
Pascal Boillat, Head-GF AgieCharmilles
Yves Serra, Chmn.

FINANCIAL DATA: Note: Data for latest year may not have been available at press time.

In U.S. $	2024	2023	2022	2021	2020	2019
Revenue	4,735,976,189	3,819,688,993	4,864,962,336	4,529,111,709	3,874,447,119	4,526,678,166
R&D Expense						
Operating Income	405,210,700	372,355,800	484,305,900	344,368,300	187,394,700	288,393,200
Operating Margin %	.09%	.10%	.10%	.08%	.05%	.06%
SGA Expense	414,945,500	299,344,800	278,658,400	250,670,900	214,165,400	282,309,000
Net Income	260,405,700	285,959,500	335,850,300	260,405,700	141,154,500	210,514,900
Operating Cash Flow	478,221,600	411,294,900	396,692,800	350,452,500	416,162,300	386,958,000
Capital Expenditure	285,959,500	251,887,700	200,780,100	176,443,100	176,443,100	226,333,900
EBITDA	629,110,900	498,908,100	605,990,800	497,691,200	365,054,700	447,800,400
Return on Assets %	.05%	.06%	.07%	.06%	.03%	.05%
Return on Equity %	6.58%	.30%	.18%	.15%	.08%	.12%
Debt to Equity	21.31%		.39%	.42%	0.573	0.411

CONTACT INFORMATION:

Phone: 41 526311111   Fax: 41 526312847
Toll-Free:
Address: Amsler-Laffon-Strasse 9, Schaffhausen, 8201 Switzerland

STOCK TICKER/OTHER:

Stock Ticker: FCHRF   Exchange: PINX
Employees: 15,464   Fiscal Year Ends: 12/31
Parent Company:

SALARIES/BONUSES:

Top Exec. Salary: $ Bonus: $
Second Exec. Salary: $ Bonus: $

OTHER THOUGHTS:

Estimated Female Officers or Directors: 2
Hot Spot for Advancement for Women/Minorities: Y

Geosyntec Consultants Inc

www.geosyntec.com

NAIC Code: 541330

TYPES OF BUSINESS:

Engineering Consulting Services
Consulting
Engineering
Environment
Natural Resources
Civil Infrastructure

BRANDS/DIVISIONS/AFFILIATES:

SiREM
Savron
Geosyntec Europe
Blackstone Energy Partners II Q LP

CONTACTS: Note: Officers with more than one job title may be intentionally listed here more than once.

Majdi Othman, CEO
Rudy Bonaparte, Chmn.

GROWTH PLANS/SPECIAL FEATURES:

Geosyntec Consultants, Inc. is a specialized consulting and engineering firm primarily for private and public sector clients. The company offers expertise in environment, natural resources and civil infrastructure. Geosyntec's companies deliver seamless solutions from more than 130 offices in the U.S., Canada, the U.K., Ireland, Sweden, Spain, the United Arab Emirates and Australia. These integrated divisions include SiREM, Savron and Geosyntec Europe. SiREM offers leading-edge remediation technology development and testing services and solutions. Savron is the exclusive vendor of STAR and STARx technology for the safe and effective treatment of contaminated soil and liquid organic waste. Geosyntec Europe offers specialized consulting and engineering services in the U.K. and Europe. Geosyntec Consultations also provides COVID-19 services, and transactional due diligence and consultation, among other services and solutions. Market sectors served by the group include aerospace, agribusiness, biotechnology, chemicals, coastal, dams, electric power utilities, electronics, energy transition, finance, food and beverage, industrial water, insurance, government agencies, federal departments, state departments and agencies, municipalities, counties and local government bodies, legal counsel, manufacturing, mining, oil and gas, petrochemicals, pharmaceuticals, real estate, resilience/adaptation and solid and hazardous waste management. Geosyntec is owned by Blackstone Energy Partners II Q L.P.

FINANCIAL DATA: Note: Data for latest year may not have been available at press time.

In U.S. $	2024	2023	2022	2021	2020	2019
Revenue						
R&D Expense						
Operating Income						
Operating Margin %						
SGA Expense						
Net Income						
Operating Cash Flow						
Capital Expenditure						
EBITDA						
Return on Assets %						
Return on Equity %						
Debt to Equity						

CONTACT INFORMATION:

Phone: 561-995-0900   Fax:
Toll-Free: 866-676-1101
Address: 900 Broken Sound Pkwy. NW, Ste. 200, Boca Raton, FL 33487 United States

STOCK TICKER/OTHER:

Stock Ticker: Private   Exchange:
Employees: 1,700   Fiscal Year Ends:
Parent Company: Blackstone Energy Partners II Q LP

SALARIES/BONUSES:

Top Exec. Salary: $ Bonus: $
Second Exec. Salary: $ Bonus: $

OTHER THOUGHTS:

Estimated Female Officers or Directors:
Hot Spot for Advancement for Women/Minorities:

Ghafari Associates LLC

www.ghafari.com

NAIC Code: 541330

TYPES OF BUSINESS:

Engineering Consulting Services
Architecture
Engineering
Consulting
Business Spaces
Civil and Structural Engineering
MEP Engineering
Laser Scanning and Virtual Planning

BRANDS/DIVISIONS/AFFILIATES:

vPlanner

CONTACTS: *Note: Officers with more than one job title may be intentionally listed here more than once.*

Kouhaila Hammer, CEO
Keith Sherman, CFO
Christine McDermott, Chief Human Resources Officer
Bob Bell, CIO
Yousif B. Ghafari, Chmn.

GROWTH PLANS/SPECIAL FEATURES:

Ghafari Associates, LLC is an architecture, engineering and consulting firm that designs business spaces. With offices in the U.S., the Middle East and India, and a portfolio spanning more than 40 countries, Ghafari serves a diverse range of clients within markets such as automotive, aviation, commercial, education, government/institutional, health/wellness, industrial/manufacturing and workplace. The company offers in-house services from planning to start-up and commissioning, regardless of size or scope of complexity. Ghafari's capabilities include architecture and design, interior design, civil and structural engineering, mechanical/electrical/plumbing (MEP) engineering, information/communications/technology (ICT) and security engineering, operations and systems engineering, laser scanning and virtual planning and production management software (vPlanner).

Ghafari offers its employees comprehensive health coverage, flexible spending accounts, an employee assistance program, 401(k) planning, life and AD&D insurance, short-term disability, educational reimbursement and many other benefits and perks.

FINANCIAL DATA: *Note: Data for latest year may not have been available at press time.*

In U.S. $	2024	2023	2022	2021	2020	2019
Revenue						
R&D Expense						
Operating Income						
Operating Margin %						
SGA Expense						
Net Income						
Operating Cash Flow						
Capital Expenditure						
EBITDA						
Return on Assets %						
Return on Equity %						
Debt to Equity						

CONTACT INFORMATION:

Phone: 313-441-3000   Fax: 313-441-1545
Toll-Free:
Address: 17101 Michigan Ave., Dearborn, MI 48126 United States

STOCK TICKER/OTHER:

Stock Ticker: Private   Exchange:
Employees: 600   Fiscal Year Ends:
Parent Company:

SALARIES/BONUSES:

Top Exec. Salary: $ Bonus: $
Second Exec. Salary: $ Bonus: $

OTHER THOUGHTS:

Estimated Female Officers or Directors:
Hot Spot for Advancement for Women/Minorities:

Sales, profits and employees may be estimates. Financial information, benefits and other data can change quickly and may vary from those stated here.

GHD Group Pty Ltd

www.ghd.com

NAIC Code: 541330

TYPES OF BUSINESS:

Engineering Services
Engineering
Architecture and Design
Buildings
Project Management
Future Communities
Energy and Water Resource Solutions
Urbanization

BRANDS/DIVISIONS/AFFILIATES:

GROWTH PLANS/SPECIAL FEATURES:

GHD Group Pty. Ltd. (Gutteridge, Haskins and Davey or GHD) is an employee-owned global professional services company that specializes in engineering and architecture. The firm specializes in a wide range of capabilities, including advisory, architecture and design, buildings, digital, energy/resources, environmental, sustainability and resilience, transportation and water. GHD is committed to solving global challenges in the areas of water, energy and urbanization, and operates from 160 offices across five continents, including Asia, Australia, Europe, North and South America and the Pacific region. The firm has been in business since 1928.

CONTACTS: *Note: Officers with more than one job title may be intentionally listed here more than once.*

Jim Giannopoulos, CEO
Marc Armstrong, CFO
Jan Sipsma, Chief People Officer
Paul Murphy, CIO
Robert Knott, Chmn.

FINANCIAL DATA: *Note: Data for latest year may not have been available at press time.*

In U.S. $	2024	2023	2022	2021	2020	2019
Revenue	1,860,701,850	1,772,097,000	1,552,040,000	1,656,716,600	1,499,790,600	1,514,940,000
R&D Expense						
Operating Income						
Operating Margin %						
SGA Expense						
Net Income						
Operating Cash Flow						
Capital Expenditure						
EBITDA						
Return on Assets %						
Return on Equity %						
Debt to Equity						

CONTACT INFORMATION:

Phone: 61 2-9239-7100   Fax: 61-2-9239-7199
Toll-Free:
Address: 133 Castlereagh St., Level 15, Sydney, NSW 2000 Australia

STOCK TICKER/OTHER:

Stock Ticker: Private   Exchange:
Employees: 11,000   Fiscal Year Ends: 06/30
Parent Company:

SALARIES/BONUSES:

Top Exec. Salary: $ Bonus: $
Second Exec. Salary: $ Bonus: $

OTHER THOUGHTS:

Estimated Female Officers or Directors:
Hot Spot for Advancement for Women/Minorities:

Gilead Sciences Inc

NAIC Code: 325412

www.gilead.com

TYPES OF BUSINESS:

Viral & Bacterial Infections Drugs
Biopharmaceuticals
Drug Development
Drug Commercialization

BRANDS/DIVISIONS/AFFILIATES:

MYR GmbH
Hepcludex

GROWTH PLANS/SPECIAL FEATURES:

Gilead Sciences develops and markets therapies to treat life-threatening infectious diseases, with the core of its portfolio focused on HIV and hepatitis B and C. Gilead's acquisition of Pharmasset brought rights to hepatitis C drug Sovaldi, which is also part of newer combination regimens that remain standards of care. Gilead is also growing its presence in the oncology market via acquisitions, led by CAR-T cell therapy Yescarta/Tecartus (from Kite) and breast and bladder cancer therapy Trodelvy (from Immunomedics).

Gilead offers its employees comprehensive benefits.

CONTACTS: Note: Officers with more than one job title may be intentionally listed here more than once.

Sandra Patterson, Assistant Controller
Daniel ODay, CEO
Andrew Dickinson, CFO
Merdad Parsey, Chief Medical Officer
Deborah Telman, Executive VP, Divisional
Johanna Mercier, Other Executive Officer

FINANCIAL DATA: Note: Data for latest year may not have been available at press time.

In U.S. $	2024	2023	2022	2021	2020	2019
Revenue	28,753,999,872	27,115,999,232	27,281,000,448	27,305,000,960	24,689,000,448	22,449,000,448
R&D Expense	5,907,000,000	5,718,000,000	4,977,000,000	4,601,000,000	5,039,000,000	4,055,000,000
Operating Income	10,505,000,000	8,810,000,000	10,974,000,000	10,857,000,000	9,927,000,000	9,338,000,000
Operating Margin %	.37%	.32%	.40%	.40%	.40%	.42%
SGA Expense	6,091,000,000	6,090,000,000	5,673,000,000	5,246,000,000	5,151,000,000	4,381,000,000
Net Income	480,000,000	5,665,000,000	4,592,000,000	6,225,000,000	123,000,000	5,386,000,000
Operating Cash Flow	10,828,000,000	8,006,000,000	9,072,000,000	11,384,000,000	8,168,000,000	9,144,001,000
Capital Expenditure	523,000,000	585,000,000	728,000,000	579,000,000	650,000,000	825,000,000
EBITDA	4,434,000,000	10,496,000,000	8,852,000,000	11,329,000,000	4,133,000,000	7,559,000,000
Return on Assets %	.01%	.09%	.07%	.09%	.00%	.09%
Return on Equity %	.02%	.26%	.22%	.32%	.01%	.25%
Debt to Equity	1.29%	1.02%	1.08%	1.20%	1.574	0.981

CONTACT INFORMATION:

Phone: 650 574-3000   Fax: 650 578-9264
Toll-Free: 800-445-3235
Address: 333 Lakeside Dr., Foster City, CA 94404 United States

STOCK TICKER/OTHER:

Stock Ticker: GILD
Employees: 18,000
Parent Company:

Exchange: NAS
Fiscal Year Ends: 12/31

SALARIES/BONUSES:

Top Exec. Salary: $1,771,201   Bonus: $
Second Exec. Salary: Bonus: $
$1,148,038

OTHER THOUGHTS:

Estimated Female Officers or Directors: 4
Hot Spot for Advancement for Women/Minorities: Y

GKN Aerospace

NAIC Code: 336300

www.gknaerospace.com

TYPES OF BUSINESS:

Aerospace Engineering

BRANDS/DIVISIONS/AFFILIATES:

Melrose Industries plc

GROWTH PLANS/SPECIAL FEATURES:

GKN Aerospace is a global aerospace engineering company. The firm is a leading global tier one supplier of airframe and engine structures, landing gear, electrical interconnection systems, transparencies and aftermarket services. It supplies products and services to a wide range of commercial and military aircraft, as well as engine prime contractors and other tier one suppliers. With 32 manufacturing locations in 12 countries, GKN Aerospace serves more than 90% of the world's aircraft and engine manufacturers. GKN Aerospace operates as a subsidiary of Melrose Industries PLC.

CONTACTS: Note: Officers with more than one job title may be intentionally listed here more than once.

Peter Dilnot, CEO
Matthew Gregory, CFO
Zareena Brown, Chief Human Resources Officer
Russ Dunn, CTO
Judith Felton, Corp. Sec.
William Seeger, Jr., Dir.-Finance
Andrew Reynolds Smith, CEO-Automotive & Power Metallurgy
Marcus Bryson, CEO-Aerospace & Land Systems

FINANCIAL DATA: Note: Data for latest year may not have been available at press time.

In U.S. $	2024	2023	2022	2021	2020	2019
Revenue	4,477,883,025	4,264,650,500	10,356,104,500	9,678,644,500	10,189,688,600	10,492,800,000
R&D Expense						
Operating Income						
Operating Margin %						
SGA Expense						
Net Income						
Operating Cash Flow						
Capital Expenditure						
EBITDA						
Return on Assets %						
Return on Equity %						
Debt to Equity						

CONTACT INFORMATION:

Phone: 44 1527517715   Fax: 44 1527517700
Toll-Free:
Address: Ipsley House, Ipsley Church Ln., P.O. Box 55, Worcestershire, B98 0TL United Kingdom

STOCK TICKER/OTHER:

Stock Ticker: Subsidiary   Exchange:
Employees: 16,000   Fiscal Year Ends: 12/31
Parent Company: Melrose Industries PLC

SALARIES/BONUSES:

Top Exec. Salary: $ Bonus: $
Second Exec. Salary: $ Bonus: $

OTHER THOUGHTS:

Estimated Female Officers or Directors:
Hot Spot for Advancement for Women/Minorities:

Globalvia Inversiones SAU

www.globalvia.com

NAIC Code: 488490

TYPES OF BUSINESS:
Bridge, Tunnel and Highway Operations
Transport Infrastructure Concessions Management
Highway, Bus and Railway Transport Management
Mobility Innovation and Technology

BRANDS/DIVISIONS/AFFILIATES:
Openvia

GROWTH PLANS/SPECIAL FEATURES:
Globalvia Inversiones S.A.U. manages transport infrastructure concessions and mobility services. Through its products and services, the company connects people with highways, buses and railways. Globalvia manages highways in 11 countries. Openvia is Globalvia's technology and innovation arm and engaged in continuously developing mobility solutions for mobility transformation purposes. Globalvia has international offices in Spain, the U.S., Ireland, Portugal, Costa Rica and Chile. The firm was established in 2007 and is led by three international pension funds.

CONTACTS: *Note: Officers with more than one job title may be intentionally listed here more than once.*
Javier Perez Fortea, CEO
Javier Perez Fortea, Dir.-Dev., Construction & Oper.
Jose Felipe Gomez de Barreda, General Counsel
Rafael Nevada, Dir.-Bus. Dev. & Contract Bids
Patricia Coba, Chief Comm. Officer
Carmen Rubio, Dir.-Audit & Risk Control
Luis Sanchez Salmeron, Dir.-Bus. Managing
Maria Luisa Castro, Dir.-Spanish Highways
Javier Galera, Dir.-European Highways
Juan Bejar Ochoa, Chmn.
Pablo Pajares, Construction Department

FINANCIAL DATA: *Note: Data for latest year may not have been available at press time.*

In U.S. $	2024	2023	2022	2021	2020	2019
Revenue		490,366,000	471,506,000	484,380,000	465,750,000	507,521,000
R&D Expense						
Operating Income						
Operating Margin %						
SGA Expense						
Net Income						
Operating Cash Flow						
Capital Expenditure						
EBITDA						
Return on Assets %						
Return on Equity %						
Debt to Equity						

CONTACT INFORMATION:
Phone: 34-914-565-850   Fax: 34-915-720-068
Toll-Free:
Address: Pasea de la Castellana, 259 C, Plants 21-22, Madrid, 28046 Spain

STOCK TICKER/OTHER:
Stock Ticker: Joint Venture   Exchange:
Employees: 28,000   Fiscal Year Ends:
Parent Company:

SALARIES/BONUSES:
Top Exec. Salary: $ Bonus: $
Second Exec. Salary: $ Bonus: $

OTHER THOUGHTS:
Estimated Female Officers or Directors: 3
Hot Spot for Advancement for Women/Minorities: Y

GM Korea

NAIC Code: 336111

TYPES OF BUSINESS:

Automobile Manufacturing
Auto Manufacture
Vehicle Kits
Manufacturing Facilities
Vehicle Painting Facility

BRANDS/DIVISIONS/AFFILIATES:

General Motors Company (GM)
Chevrolet
GMC
Cadillac

GROWTH PLANS/SPECIAL FEATURES:

GM Korea designs, develops, produces and sells vehicles in South Korea. General Motors Company holds a leading equity stake in the firm. GM Korea manufactures passenger vehicles, sport utility and crossover vehicles (SUV/CUV), trucks and electric vehicles under the Chevrolet and GMC brands. The firm's luxury division also offers Cadillac vehicles. GM Korea offers vehicle kits for assembly at GM facilities throughout the world. The firm exports to automakers internationally. It has three manufacturing facilities in South Korea and has a global state-of-the-art painting factory to produce next-generation global new cars. The painting factory is located within GM Korea's Changwon factory, taking up three floors with an area of 80,000 square meters (861,113 square feet). GM Korea partners with SupplyPower, which is the portal for suppliers with an active relationship with GM.

CONTACTS: Note: Officers with more than one job title may be intentionally listed here more than once.

Hector Villareal, CEO

FINANCIAL DATA: Note: Data for latest year may not have been available at press time.

In U.S. $	2024	2023	2022	2021	2020	2019
Revenue	10,255,714,350	9,767,347,000	9,443,381,000	8,469,400,000	9,964,000,000	9,400,000,000
R&D Expense						
Operating Income						
Operating Margin %						
SGA Expense						
Net Income						
Operating Cash Flow						
Capital Expenditure						
EBITDA						
Return on Assets %						
Return on Equity %						
Debt to Equity						

CONTACT INFORMATION:

Phone: 8280-3000-5000   Fax: 833-2520-4613
Toll-Free:
Address: 233 Chongcheon-dong, Bupyeong-gu, Incheon, 403-714 South Korea

STOCK TICKER/OTHER:

Stock Ticker: Subsidiary   Exchange:
Employees: 10,000   Fiscal Year Ends: 12/31
Parent Company: General Motors Company (GM)

SALARIES/BONUSES:

Top Exec. Salary: $ Bonus: $
Second Exec. Salary: $ Bonus: $

OTHER THOUGHTS:

Estimated Female Officers or Directors:
Hot Spot for Advancement for Women/Minorities:

Golder Associates Corporation

www.golder.com

NAIC Code: 541330

TYPES OF BUSINESS:

Engineering & Environmental Services
Engineering
Environmental Solutions
Tunneling
Remediation
Regulatory Compliance
Construction Support
Waste Solutions

BRANDS/DIVISIONS/AFFILIATES:

WSP Global Inc
Communica Public Affairs Inc
Proxion Plan Oy
Proxion Pro Oy
1A Ingenieros SL
AKF LLC

CONTACTS: Note: Officers with more than one job title may be intentionally listed here more than once.

Alexandre L'Heureux, CEO
Christopher Cole, Chmn.

GROWTH PLANS/SPECIAL FEATURES:

Golder Associates Corporation develops comprehensive and sustainable engineering solutions, primarily serving mining, oil and gas, manufacturing, transportation, government and power sectors. The firm operates within markets of property and buildings, transport and infrastructure, Earth and environment, energy and resources, industry, water and services. Services offered by Golder span advisory, design, digital solutions, planning services, project delivery and safety and security. Those acquisitions, in order of when they were acquired, were: Communica Public Affairs, Inc., a stakeholder engagement and information management consulting firm; Proxion Plan Oy and Proxion Pro Oy, which combine to form one of Finland's largest rail consultancies; 1A Ingenieros, S.L., which will enhance the firm's capabilities in Spain's Power & Energy sector; and AKF LLC, a specialized mechanical, electrical and plumbing firm that designs complex healthcare, science, technology and mission-critical facilities. Golder has locations throughout North America, Latin America, Africa, Europe and Asia Pacific. Golder is a subsidiary of WSP Global, Inc.

Golder offers a variety of internships and full-time opportunities.

FINANCIAL DATA: Note: Data for latest year may not have been available at press time.

In U.S. $	2024	2023	2022	2021	2020	2019
Revenue	1,155,000,000	1,100,000,000	1,086,618,010	930,323,639	869,461,345	878,243,783
R&D Expense						
Operating Income						
Operating Margin %						
SGA Expense						
Net Income						
Operating Cash Flow						
Capital Expenditure						
EBITDA						
Return on Assets %						
Return on Equity %						
Debt to Equity						

CONTACT INFORMATION:

Phone: 905-567-4444   Fax: 905-567-6561
Toll-Free:
Address: 2390 Argentia Rd., Mississauga, ON L5N 5Z7 Canada

STOCK TICKER/OTHER:

Stock Ticker: Subsidiary   Exchange:
Employees: 7,500   Fiscal Year Ends:
Parent Company: WSP Global Inc

SALARIES/BONUSES:

Top Exec. Salary: $ Bonus: $
Second Exec. Salary: $ Bonus: $

OTHER THOUGHTS:

Estimated Female Officers or Directors:
Hot Spot for Advancement for Women/Minorities:

Granite Construction Incorporated

www.graniteconstruction.com

NAIC Code: 237310

TYPES OF BUSINESS:

Construction, Heavy & Civil Engineering
Infrastructure Projects
Site Preparation Services
Construction Materials Processing
Heavy Construction Equipment
Civil Contractor

BRANDS/DIVISIONS/AFFILIATES:

GROWTH PLANS/SPECIAL FEATURES:

Granite Construction Inc engages in the construction and development of various infrastructure projects on behalf of public and private clients in the United States. It focuses on heavy civil infrastructure projects, including roads, highways, transit facilities, airports, bridges, and other infrastructure projects. In addition, the company performs site preparation and infrastructure services for residential development, energy development, and other facilities. The majority of revenue is derived from the company's Construction operating segment, with the remainder derived from its Materials segment.

Granite Construction offers employees comprehensive benefits, retirement plans and employee assistance programs.

CONTACTS: Note: Officers with more than one job title may be intentionally listed here more than once.

Kyle Larkin, CEO
Staci Woolsey, CFO
Michael McNally, Chairman of the Board
James Radich, COO
Bradley Williams, Senior VP, Divisional
Bradly Estes, Senior VP, Divisional
Michael Tatusko, Senior VP, Divisional
Brian Dowd, Senior VP, Divisional

FINANCIAL DATA: Note: Data for latest year may not have been available at press time.

In U.S. $	2024	2023	2022	2021	2020	2019
Revenue	4,007,574,016	3,509,137,920	3,301,255,936	3,501,864,960	3,562,458,880	2,914,876,928
R&D Expense						
Operating Income	198,599,000	51,716,000	72,764,000	-41,721,000	-8,585,000	-55,097,000
Operating Margin %	.05%	.01%	.02%	-.01%	.00%	-.02%
SGA Expense	334,162,000	294,466,000	272,610,000	303,015,000	316,284,000	238,147,000
Net Income	126,346,000	43,599,000	83,302,000	10,096,000	-145,117,000	-60,191,000
Operating Cash Flow	456,343,000	183,707,000	55,647,000	21,931,000	268,460,000	111,438,000
Capital Expenditure	136,405,000	140,384,000	121,612,000	94,810,000	93,253,000	106,828,000
EBITDA	351,711,000	170,586,000	187,010,000	151,916,000	-29,305,000	99,821,000
Return on Assets %	.04%	.02%	.04%	.00%	-.06%	-.02%
Return on Equity %	.13%	.05%	.09%	.01%	-.14%	-.05%
Debt to Equity	.80%	.69%	.33%	.38%	0.38	0.363

CONTACT INFORMATION:

Phone: 831 724-1011   Fax: 831 7617871
Toll-Free:
Address: 585 W. Beach St., Watsonville, CA 95076 United States

STOCK TICKER/OTHER:

Stock Ticker: GVA   Exchange: NYS
Employees: 4,100   Fiscal Year Ends: 12/31
Parent Company:

SALARIES/BONUSES:

Top Exec. Salary: $975,000   Bonus: $
Second Exec. Salary: Bonus: $
$546,000

OTHER THOUGHTS:

Estimated Female Officers or Directors: 2
Hot Spot for Advancement for Women/Minorities:

Group Lotus plc
NAIC Code: 336111

www.lotuscars.com

TYPES OF BUSINESS:
Automobile Manufacturing
Sports Car Design & Manufacturing
Design & Engineering Services
Consulting Services
All-Electric Vehicles
Hypercars
Sports Utility Vehicles
Technology Innovation

BRANDS/DIVISIONS/AFFILIATES:
Zhejiang Geely Holding Group
Etika Automotive Sdn Bhd
Lotus Cars
Lotus Engineering
Lotus Technology
Emira
Evija
Eletre

CONTACTS: *Note: Officers with more than one job title may be intentionally listed here more than once.*
Feng Qingfeng, CEO
Alexious Kuen Long Lee, CFO
Caudio Berro, Dir.-Motorsport
Donato Coco, Dir.-Design
Russell Carr, Head-Lotus Design
Li Daniel, Chmn.

GROWTH PLANS/SPECIAL FEATURES:
Group Lotus plc is the parent company or is affiliated with Lotus companies, which specializes in the design and production of luxury sports cars. Operating in three segments, Group Lotus comprises: Lotus Cars, Lotus Engineering and Lotus Technology. Lotus Cars is based in the U.K. and is the global headquarters for the group's sports car and hypercar manufacturing operations. Lotus Cars builds high-performance cars, including Formula 1 race cars. Models include the Lotus Emira, the firm's last petroleum-powered sports car; the Evija all-electric British sportscar; the Eletre all-electric hyper-SUV; the Emeya high performance electric sedan; and the Evija, which is all-electric and delivers enhanced driving dynamics and road handling. Lotus Engineering provides consultancy services to global original equipment manufacturers (OEMs) and Tire 1 suppliers, specializing in innovative engineering and vehicle development. Lotus Engineering has offices worldwide, and is headquartered at the Lotus Advanced Technology Centre on the University of Warwick's Wellesbourne campus in the U.K. Lotus Technology is an affiliate company of Group Lotus, with operational assets across China, the U.K. and Europe. Lotus Technology delivers smart lifestyle battery electric vehicles such as the Eletre. The unit focuses on research and development in next generation automobility technologies such as electrification and digitalization. Group Lotus is 51%-owned by Zhejiang Geely Holding Group and 49%-owned by Etika Automotive Sdn Bhd.

FINANCIAL DATA: *Note: Data for latest year may not have been available at press time.*

In U.S. $	2024	2023	2022	2021	2020	2019
Revenue	127,050,000	121,000,000	116,421,000	113,694,172	108,280,164	124,174,500
R&D Expense						
Operating Income						
Operating Margin %						
SGA Expense						
Net Income						
Operating Cash Flow						
Capital Expenditure						
EBITDA						
Return on Assets %						
Return on Equity %						
Debt to Equity						

CONTACT INFORMATION:
Phone: 44-1953-608-000   Fax: 44-1953-608-300
Toll-Free:
Address: Potash Ln., Norwich, Norfolk NR14 8EZ United Kingdom

STOCK TICKER/OTHER:
Stock Ticker: Subsidiary   Exchange:
Employees: 1,100   Fiscal Year Ends: 03/31
Parent Company: Zhejiang Geely Holding Group

SALARIES/BONUSES:
Top Exec. Salary: $ Bonus: $
Second Exec. Salary: $ Bonus: $

OTHER THOUGHTS:
Estimated Female Officers or Directors:
Hot Spot for Advancement for Women/Minorities:

GS Engineering & Construction Corporation

www.gsenc.com

NAIC Code: 237000

TYPES OF BUSINESS:

Heavy Construction and Civil Engineering
Plant and Facility Construction
Architecture
Infrastructure
Engineering
Artificial Intelligence
Robotics

BRANDS/DIVISIONS/AFFILIATES:

Kangchon Resort
Jeju Elysian Resort
Konjiam Resort

CONTACTS:
Note: Officers with more than one job title may be intentionally listed here more than once.

Chang-Soo Huh, Chmn.

GROWTH PLANS/SPECIAL FEATURES:

GS Engineering & Construction Corporation (GS E&C) operates through five main construction divisions: plant, power, architecture, infrastructure and leisure. The plant business constructs refinery, gas, petrochemical, waste and water treatment plants. This division seeks to enter the liquid natural gas (LNG) and unconventional oil and gas business. The power business engages in developing a country's power, communication and railway infrastructure. This division has completed projects for high-voltage substations in South Korea, Asia, Saudi Arabia, Ghana and Tanzania. The architecture business markets and builds various types of buildings for residencies, offices and factories, including public and private sectors. This division also specializes in environmentally friendly and energy-saving buildings. The infrastructure business constructs roads, railways, water reservoirs, ports, industrial parks and underground structures. This division has also been working on new construction methods for projects such as marine suspension bridges and deep underground tunnels. Lastly, the leisure business provides cultural space, services and facilities, including recreational facilities, stadiums, arenas, high-class hotels, sports facilities and arts centers. For this division, the firm is operating Kangchon and Jeju Elysian resorts, whilst constructing Konjiam Resort. GS E&C also has a technology division for research and development purposes, including developments in artificial intelligence, robotics and more; a finance division; a procurement and sub-contract management division; and various company and administrative departments.

FINANCIAL DATA:
Note: Data for latest year may not have been available at press time.

In U.S. $	2024	2023	2022	2021	2020	2019
Revenue		10,371,576,000	9,191,891,331	2,907,637,049	2,134,872,519	2,855,458,608
R&D Expense						
Operating Income						
Operating Margin %						
SGA Expense						
Net Income		-372,006,000	961,863,903	-3,689,593	-59,467,232	-22,786,686
Operating Cash Flow						
Capital Expenditure						
EBITDA						
Return on Assets %						
Return on Equity %						
Debt to Equity						

CONTACT INFORMATION:
Phone: 82 2-2154 1112 Fax:
Toll-Free:
Address: Gran Seoul, 33 Jong-ro, Jongno-gu, Seoul, 110-130 South Korea

STOCK TICKER/OTHER:
Stock Ticker: 6360
Employees: 3,842
Parent Company:

Exchange: Seoul
Fiscal Year Ends: 12/31

SALARIES/BONUSES:
Top Exec. Salary: $ Bonus: $
Second Exec. Salary: $ Bonus: $

OTHER THOUGHTS:
Estimated Female Officers or Directors:
Hot Spot for Advancement for Women/Minorities:

GSK PLC

NAIC Code: 325412

www.gsk.com

TYPES OF BUSINESS:

Prescription Medications
Pharmaceuticals
Vaccines
Consumer Healthcare
Drug Development
Commercialization

GROWTH PLANS/SPECIAL FEATURES:

In the pharmaceutical industry, GSK ranks as one of the largest firms by total sales. The company wields its might across several therapeutic classes, including respiratory, antiviral, and vaccines, and has been growing its presence in oncology and immunology, as well. GSK uses joint ventures to gain additional scale in certain markets like HIV.

BRANDS/DIVISIONS/AFFILIATES:

GlaxoSmithKline

CONTACTS:
Note: Officers with more than one job title may be intentionally listed here more than once.

Emma Walmsley, CEO
Julie Brown, CFO
Jonathan Symonds, Chairman of the Board
Hal Barron, Chief Scientific Officer
Victoria Whyte, Secretary

FINANCIAL DATA:
Note: Data for latest year may not have been available at press time.

In U.S. $	2024	2023	2022	2021	2020	2019
Revenue	42,241,507,607	40,830,587,269	39,478,900,339	33,248,225,635	32,787,791,550	45,443,009,538
R&D Expense	8,617,667,000	8,378,025,000	7,388,494,000	6,757,080,000	6,452,816,000	6,149,898,000
Operating Income	7,461,195,000	9,888,573,000	9,059,252,000	6,567,251,000	6,163,361,000	8,470,919,000
Operating Margin %	.18%	.24%	.23%	.20%	.19%	.19%
SGA Expense	14,829,490,000	12,635,030,000	11,271,220,000	9,518,341,000	10,012,430,000	15,350,510,000
Net Income	3,466,723,000	6,634,567,000	20,135,260,000	5,903,525,000	7,739,879,000	6,253,564,000
Operating Cash Flow	8,823,650,000	9,111,759,000	9,966,659,000	10,705,780,000	11,364,120,000	10,797,330,000
Capital Expenditure	4,014,667,000	3,155,727,000	3,039,945,000	3,573,080,000	2,618,553,000	2,912,047,000
EBITDA	8,977,128,000	12,228,440,000	11,579,530,000	8,730,756,000	10,860,600,000	12,700,990,000
Return on Assets %	.04%	.08%	.21%	.05%	.07%	.07%
Return on Equity %	.19%	.41%	1.17%	.30%	.44%	.61%
Debt to Equity	1.07%	1.14%	1.61%	1.37%	1.606	2.068

CONTACT INFORMATION:

Phone: 44 20-8047-5000   Fax: 44 20-8047-7807
Toll-Free: 888-825-5249
Address: 980 Great W. Rd., Brentford, Middlesex, TW8 9GS United Kingdom

STOCK TICKER/OTHER:

Stock Ticker: GSK
Employees: 70,212
Parent Company:

Exchange: NYS
Fiscal Year Ends: 12/31

SALARIES/BONUSES:

Top Exec. Salary: $1,835,007   Bonus: $3,843,687
Second Exec. Salary: $1,332,837   Bonus: $2,632,017

OTHER THOUGHTS:

Estimated Female Officers or Directors: 8
Hot Spot for Advancement for Women/Minorities: Y

Gulf Interstate Engineering Company
gulfcompanies.com

NAIC Code: 541330

TYPES OF BUSINESS:
Engineering Consulting Services
Engineering
Field Services
Project Management
Geospatial
Survey
Construction Services
Materials Management

BRANDS/DIVISIONS/AFFILIATES:

GROWTH PLANS/SPECIAL FEATURES:
Gulf Interstate Engineering Company (GIE) has served the global energy industry since 1953, supporting the complete lifecycle of projects. The firm provides field services, engineering, project management, geospatial services, survey, integrity services, construction services, materials management, carbon management, renewable services and underground storage. GIE's worldwide experience and multi-disciplined capabilities encompass all aspects of the engineering, procurement, geographic information system (GIS) integrity, construction management, field inspection, staffing services, and more. The company has completed over 2,500 projects in 36 countries (as of May 2025).

CONTACTS:
Note: Officers with more than one job title may be intentionally listed here more than once.
Kent Wilfur, CEO
Bill Olson, Sr. VP-Oper.
Karey Cox, CFO

FINANCIAL DATA:
Note: Data for latest year may not have been available at press time.

In U.S. $	2024	2023	2022	2021	2020	2019
Revenue						
R&D Expense						
Operating Income						
Operating Margin %						
SGA Expense						
Net Income						
Operating Cash Flow						
Capital Expenditure						
EBITDA						
Return on Assets %						
Return on Equity %						
Debt to Equity						

CONTACT INFORMATION:
Phone: 713-850-3400 Fax: 713-850-3579
Toll-Free:
Address: 1080 Eldridge Pkwy., Houston, TX 77077 United States

STOCK TICKER/OTHER:
Stock Ticker: Private Exchange:
Employees: 1,200 Fiscal Year Ends:
Parent Company:

SALARIES/BONUSES:
Top Exec. Salary: $ Bonus: $
Second Exec. Salary: $ Bonus: $

OTHER THOUGHTS:
Estimated Female Officers or Directors:
Hot Spot for Advancement for Women/Minorities:

Gulfstream Aerospace Corporation
www.gulfstream.com

NAIC Code: 336411

TYPES OF BUSINESS:
Aircraft Manufacturing
Business Jets
Support Services
Leasing & Financing
Aircraft Manufacture
Aircraft Maintenance
Technology-Advanced Jets
Sustainable Aviation Fuel Capabilities

BRANDS/DIVISIONS/AFFILIATES:
General Dynamics Corporation
G280
G400
G500
G600
G650
G700
G800

CONTACTS: *Note: Officers with more than one job title may be intentionally listed here more than once.*
Mark Burns, Pres.
Amy Ariano, Chief People Officer
Dan Nale, Sr. VP-Programs, Eng. & Test
Ira Berman, Sr. VP-Admin.
Ira Berman, General Counsel
Dennis Stuligross, Sr. VP-Oper.
Joe Lombardo, Exec. VP-Aerospace Group, General Dynamics
Mark Burns, Pres., Product Support
Scott Neal, Sr. VP-Worldwide Sales & Mktg.
Buddy Sams, Sr. VP-Gov't Programs & Sales

GROWTH PLANS/SPECIAL FEATURES:
Gulfstream Aerospace Corporation, a subsidiary of General Dynamics Corporation, designs, develops, manufactures, markets and provides maintenance and support services for technologically advanced business jet aircraft. Established in 1958, Gulfstream operates facilities on four continents. The company is also a leading provider of land and expeditionary combat systems, armaments and munitions; shipbuilding and marine systems; and information systems and technologies. Gulfstream's current aircraft includes: the mid-size G280 with a maximum operating speed of Mach 0.84; the G400 4,200-nautical-mile (nm) range; the G500 and G600, offering an nm ranging from 5,300 to 6,600; the G650 and extended reach G650ER, offering a maximum range of 7,500 nm at Mach 0.85; the spacious G700, offering five living areas and a nonstop reach to 7,750 nm at Mach 0.9; and the G800, offering 8,000 nm and four living areas. Gulfstream also routinely accepts aircraft trade-ins for the sale of new Gulfstream models and resells the used planes on the pre-owned market. The group offers several product enhancements for its planes, including the ultra-high-speed broadband multi-link (BBML) system, which allows customers to access the internet; and the enhanced vision system (EVS), a forward-looking infrared (FLIR) camera that projects an infrared real-world image on the pilot's heads-up display, which allows the flight crew to see in conditions of low light and reduced visibility.

FINANCIAL DATA: *Note: Data for latest year may not have been available at press time.*

In U.S. $	2024	2023	2022	2021	2020	2019
Revenue	9,450,000,000	9,000,000,000	8,567,000,000	9,600,000,000	9,313,258,500	9,313,258,500
R&D Expense						
Operating Income						
Operating Margin %						
SGA Expense						
Net Income						
Operating Cash Flow						
Capital Expenditure						
EBITDA						
Return on Assets %						
Return on Equity %						
Debt to Equity						

CONTACT INFORMATION:
Phone: 912-965-3000   Fax: 912-965-3084
Toll-Free:
Address: 500 Gulfstream Rd., Savannah, GA 31408 United States

STOCK TICKER/OTHER:
Stock Ticker: Subsidiary   Exchange:
Employees: 16,000   Fiscal Year Ends: 12/31
Parent Company: General Dynamics Corporation

SALARIES/BONUSES:
Top Exec. Salary: $ Bonus: $
Second Exec. Salary: $ Bonus: $

OTHER THOUGHTS:
Estimated Female Officers or Directors:
Hot Spot for Advancement for Women/Minorities:

Sales, profits and employees may be estimates. Financial information, benefits and other data can change quickly and may vary from those stated here.

Halliburton Company

www.halliburton.com

NAIC Code: 213112

TYPES OF BUSINESS:

Oil Field Services
Software Information Systems
Project Management Consulting
Well Drilling Services
Oil and Natural Gas Services
Well Completion Services
Well Production Services
Advanced Technology

BRANDS/DIVISIONS/AFFILIATES:

Baroid
Landmark
Sperry
Halliburton Labs

GROWTH PLANS/SPECIAL FEATURES:

Halliburton is North America's largest oilfield service company as measured by market share. Despite industry fragmentation, it holds a leading position in the hydraulic fracturing and completions market, which makes up nearly half of its revenue. It also holds strong positions in other service offerings like drilling and completions fluids, which leverages its expertise in material science, as well as the directional drilling market. While we consider SLB the global leader in reservoir evaluation, we think Halliburton leads in any activity from the reservoir to the wellbore. The firm's innovations have helped multiple producers lower their development costs per barrel of oil equivalent, with techniques that have been homed in over a century of operations.

Employee benefits include retirement and savings plans; an employee stock purchase program; life, disability and AD&D insurance; comprehensive health benefits; and a wellness program.

CONTACTS: *Note: Officers with more than one job title may be intentionally listed here more than once.*

Jefferey Miller, CEO
Eric Carre, CFO
Charles Geer, Chief Accounting Officer
Van Beckwith, Chief Legal Officer
Lawrence Pope, Executive VP, Divisional
Mark Richard, President, Geographical
Shannon Slocum, President, Geographical
Jill Sharp, Senior VP, Divisional
Myrtle Jones, Senior VP, Divisional
Lance Loeffler, Senior VP, Geographical
Timothy McKeon, Senior VP

FINANCIAL DATA: *Note: Data for latest year may not have been available at press time.*

In U.S. $	2024	2023	2022	2021	2020	2019
Revenue	22,944,000,000	23,018,000,384	20,297,000,960	15,294,999,552	14,444,999,680	22,407,999,488
R&D Expense						
Operating Income	3,938,000,000	4,185,000,000	3,073,000,000	1,776,000,000	1,363,000,000	2,058,000,000
Operating Margin %	.17%	.18%	.15%	.12%	.09%	.09%
SGA Expense	239,000,000	226,000,000	240,000,000	204,000,000	182,000,000	227,000,000
Net Income	2,501,000,000	2,638,000,000	1,572,000,000	1,457,000,000	-2,945,000,000	-1,131,000,000
Operating Cash Flow	3,865,000,000	3,458,000,000	2,242,000,000	1,911,000,000	1,881,000,000	2,445,000,000
Capital Expenditure	1,442,000,000	1,379,000,000	1,011,000,000	799,000,000	728,000,000	1,530,000,000
EBITDA	4,763,000,000	4,939,000,000	3,542,000,000	2,685,000,000	-1,619,000,000	1,095,000,000
Return on Assets %	.10%	.11%	.07%	.07%	-.13%	-.04%
Return on Equity %	.25%	.30%	.21%	.25%	-.45%	-.13%
Debt to Equity	.76%	.91%	1.10%	1.49%	1.988	1.391

CONTACT INFORMATION:

Phone: 281 871-2699   Fax: 713 759-2635
Toll-Free: 888-669-3920
Address: 3000 N. Sam Houston Pkwy. E., Houston, TX 77032 United States

STOCK TICKER/OTHER:

Stock Ticker: HAL
Employees: 48,000
Parent Company:

Exchange: NYS
Fiscal Year Ends: 12/31

SALARIES/BONUSES:

Top Exec. Salary: $1,650,000   Bonus: $
Second Exec. Salary: $950,000   Bonus: $

OTHER THOUGHTS:

Estimated Female Officers or Directors:
Hot Spot for Advancement for Women/Minorities: Y

Hanwha Ocean Co Ltd

www.hanwhaocean.com/epub/main/index.do

NAIC Code: 336611

TYPES OF BUSINESS:

Ship Building
Ship Building
Floating Units
Offshore Platforms
Submarine Building
Carriers and Tankers
Warships
Research and Development

BRANDS/DIVISIONS/AFFILIATES:

Hanwha Group
Daewoo Shipbuilding & Marine Engineering Co Ltd

CONTACTS: Note: Officers with more than one job title may be intentionally listed here more than once.

Hyek Woong Kwon, CEO
Kim Gap-Jung, VP
Mun Gyu-Sang, VP
Ryu Wan-Soo, VP
Jung Bang-Eon, VP

GROWTH PLANS/SPECIAL FEATURES:

Hanwha Ocean Co. Ltd., formerly Daewoo Shipbuilding & Marine Engineering Co., Ltd., is a leading shipbuilder based in South Korea. Through its domestic and international subsidiaries, Hanwha Ocean operates through two primary business areas: commercial and specialty ship, and offshore operations and floating power plants. The commercial and specialty ship business builds gas carriers, tankers, containerships, roll-on/roll-off ships, bulk carriers, submarines, warships, cruise ships, ferries and multi-functional support and salvage vessels. The offshore and floating power plants business utilizes innovative technology hardware and software regarding the vessels and plants it builds, which include floating LNG vessels which produce and process LNG, floating production storage and offloading (FPSO) vessels, floating production units (FPU) for supporting offshore deepwater projects, fixed platforms, onshore modules, drilling rigs, drill ships, floating power plants and offshore support vessels (OSVs). The company's state-of-the-art research and development facilities are located in Siheung and Okpo, with a current focus on ship and ocean R&D, naval and energy system R&D and industrial application R&D. Hanwha Ocean is part of the Hanwha Group.

FINANCIAL DATA: Note: Data for latest year may not have been available at press time.

In U.S. $	2024	2023	2022	2021	2020	2019
Revenue		5,718,365,000	3,617,361,044	7,104,680,000	6,458,797,527	8,343,657,000
R&D Expense						
Operating Income						
Operating Margin %						
SGA Expense						
Net Income		123,414,000	-1,298,620,818		79,536,800	-40,143,981
Operating Cash Flow						
Capital Expenditure						
EBITDA						
Return on Assets %						
Return on Equity %						
Debt to Equity						

CONTACT INFORMATION:

Phone: 82 55-735-2114   Fax:
Toll-Free:
Address: 3370, Geoje-daero, Geoje-si, Gyeongsangnam-do, 53302
South Korea

STOCK TICKER/OTHER:

Stock Ticker: 42660   Exchange: Seoul
Employees: 35,000   Fiscal Year Ends: 12/31
Parent Company: Hanwha Group

SALARIES/BONUSES:

Top Exec. Salary: $ Bonus: $
Second Exec. Salary: $ Bonus: $

OTHER THOUGHTS:

Estimated Female Officers or Directors:
Hot Spot for Advancement for Women/Minorities:

Hatch Ltd
www.hatch.ca

NAIC Code: 541330

TYPES OF BUSINESS:

Engineering Services
Mining and Metal Engineering
Construction Management
Project Management
Consulting
Energy Engineering
Infrastructure Engineering
Sustainable Urban Development

BRANDS/DIVISIONS/AFFILIATES:

CONTACTS: Note: Officers with more than one job title may be intentionally listed here more than once.

John Bianchini, CEO

GROWTH PLANS/SPECIAL FEATURES:

Hatch Ltd. is an employee-owned company that supplies engineering, project and construction management services, process and business consulting and operational services to mining, metallurgical, energy and infrastructure sectors globally. It has project experience in more than 150 countries, specializing in sustainable business, sustainable urban development, energy transformation, battery market solutions, mining innovation, water development, analytics and optimization and more. The metals and minerals industry spans alumina/bauxite, aluminum, coal, copper, diamonds, gold, iron ore, iron and steel, lead/zinc/tin, lithium, magnesium, nickel, phosphates, potash, rare earths and related elements, silver, titanium dioxide, titanium and uranium. The energy industry consists of upstream/midstream/downstream oil and gas, smart grid and grid modernization, nuclear, renewable power, thermal power, transmission, distribution and hydropower. The infrastructure industry includes aviation, highways, bridges, ports, terminals, rail and transit, transportation, logistics, tunnels, urban solutions and water. Hatch's services across these industry sectors are vast, with some including advisory, asset and maintenance management, commissioning, corrosion control, digital mining, digital underground operations management, electrometallurgy, engineering, mine-to-process integration and optimization, non-destructive testing, pipelines, remote services, site deployment, strategy and technology, tailings and mine waste management, and unmanned aircraft systems (UAS) solutions. Headquartered in Canada, Hatch has offices located throughout North and South America, Europe, the Middle East, Africa and Asia Pacific.

Hatch offers its employees comprehensive health benefits, career development opportunities and many other programs, plans and company perks.

FINANCIAL DATA: Note: Data for latest year may not have been available at press time.

In U.S. $	2024	2023	2022	2021	2020	2019
Revenue						
R&D Expense						
Operating Income						
Operating Margin %						
SGA Expense						
Net Income						
Operating Cash Flow						
Capital Expenditure						
EBITDA						
Return on Assets %						
Return on Equity %						
Debt to Equity						

CONTACT INFORMATION:

Phone: 905-855-7600   Fax: 905-855-8270
Toll-Free:
Address: 2800 Speakman Dr., Sheridan Science & Technology Park, Mississauga, ON L5K 2R7 Canada

STOCK TICKER/OTHER:

Stock Ticker: Private   Exchange:
Employees: 9,000   Fiscal Year Ends:
Parent Company:

SALARIES/BONUSES:

Top Exec. Salary: $ Bonus: $
Second Exec. Salary: $ Bonus: $

OTHER THOUGHTS:

Estimated Female Officers or Directors:
Hot Spot for Advancement for Women/Minorities:

HDR Inc

NAIC Code: 541330

TYPES OF BUSINESS:

Engineering Services
Engineering
Architecture
Environmental
Construction
Asset Management
Finance
Consulting

BRANDS/DIVISIONS/AFFILIATES:

GROWTH PLANS/SPECIAL FEATURES:

HDR, Inc., a 100% employee-owned company, specializes in engineering, architecture, environmental and construction services, with more than 200 offices in 15 countries across the globe. HDR also offers asset management, commissioning, operations, economic and finance, planning and consulting, project delivery, research and sustainability/resiliency services. The company serves a wide range of markets, which are grouped into categories such as civic, culture, commercial and real estate, defense and intelligence, education, finance, health, hospitality, industrial, power, science, technology/media/telecommunications/data, transportation, urban and community, waste and water.

HDR offers its employees comprehensive health benefits, life and disability insurance, 401(k), employee stock ownership plans and retiree insurance.

CONTACTS: Note: Officers with more than one job title may be intentionally listed here more than once.

John W. Henderson, CEO
Neil Graff, COO
Eric L. Keen, Vice Chmn.
Doug S. Wignall, Pres., HDR Architecture
Eric L. Keen, Chmn.

FINANCIAL DATA: Note: Data for latest year may not have been available at press time.

In U.S. $	2024	2023	2022	2021	2020	2019
Revenue	3,255,000,000	3,100,000,000	2,800,000,000	2,675,000,000	2,500,000,000	2,200,000,000
R&D Expense						
Operating Income						
Operating Margin %						
SGA Expense						
Net Income						
Operating Cash Flow						
Capital Expenditure						
EBITDA						
Return on Assets %						
Return on Equity %						
Debt to Equity						

CONTACT INFORMATION:

Phone: 402-399-1000   Fax: 402-970-9074
Toll-Free: 800-366-4411
Address: 1917 S. 67th St., Omaha, NE 68106-2973 United States

STOCK TICKER/OTHER:

Stock Ticker: Private   Exchange:
Employees: 12,000   Fiscal Year Ends: 12/31
Parent Company:

SALARIES/BONUSES:

Top Exec. Salary: $ Bonus: $
Second Exec. Salary: $ Bonus: $

OTHER THOUGHTS:

Estimated Female Officers or Directors: 1
Hot Spot for Advancement for Women/Minorities:

Hewlett Packard Enterprise Company

www.hpe.com

NAIC Code: 334111

TYPES OF BUSINESS:

Computer Manufacturing
Hybrid IT
Intelligent Edge
Financial Services
Computer Servers
Artificial Intelligence
Hardware and Software
Storage

GROWTH PLANS/SPECIAL FEATURES:

Hewlett Packard Enterprise is an information technology vendor that provides hardware and software to enterprises. Its primary product lines are compute servers, storage arrays, and networking equipment; it also has a high-performance computing business. HPE's stated goal is to be a complete edge-to-cloud company. Its portfolio enables hybrid clouds and hyperconverged infrastructure. It uses a primarily outsourced manufacturing model and employs 60,000 people worldwide.

BRANDS/DIVISIONS/AFFILIATES:

HPE Apollo
HPE Cray
HPE Superdome
HPE Nonstop
HPE Integrity
HPE Edgeline
Aruba
Hewlett Packard Labs

CONTACTS: *Note: Officers with more than one job title may be intentionally listed here more than once.*

Gerri Gold, CEO, Divisional
Antonio Neri, CEO
Marie Myers, CFO
Patricia Russo, Chairman of the Board
Jeremy Cox, Chief Accounting Officer
John Schultz, Chief Legal Officer
Fidelma Russo, Chief Technology Officer
Philip Mottram, Executive VP
Neil MacDonald, Executive VP
Kristin Major, Executive VP
Kirt Karros, Senior VP, Divisional

FINANCIAL DATA: *Note: Data for latest year may not have been available at press time.*

In U.S. $	2024	2023	2022	2021	2020	2019
Revenue	30,126,999,552	29,134,999,552	28,495,998,976	27,783,999,488	26,982,000,640	29,134,999,552
R&D Expense	2,246,000,000	2,349,000,000	2,045,000,000	1,979,000,000	1,874,000,000	1,842,000,000
Operating Income	2,494,000,000	2,442,000,000	2,227,000,000	2,114,000,000	1,592,000,000	2,477,000,000
Operating Margin %	.08%	.08%	.08%	.08%	.06%	.09%
SGA Expense	4,871,000,000	5,160,000,000	4,941,000,000	4,929,000,000	4,624,000,000	4,907,000,000
Net Income	2,579,000,000	2,025,000,000	868,000,000	3,427,000,000	-322,000,000	1,049,000,000
Operating Cash Flow	4,341,000,000	4,428,000,000	4,593,000,000	5,871,000,000	2,240,000,000	3,997,000,000
Capital Expenditure	2,367,000,000	2,828,000,000	3,122,000,000	2,502,000,000	2,383,000,000	2,856,000,000
EBITDA	5,058,000,000	5,058,000,000	4,707,000,000	4,711,000,000	4,217,000,000	5,012,000,000
Return on Assets %	.04%	.04%	.02%	.06%	-.01%	.02%
Return on Equity %	.11%	.10%	.04%	.19%	-.02%	.05%
Debt to Equity	.60%	.40%	.44%	.54%	0.815	0.549

CONTACT INFORMATION:

Phone: 650-687-5817   Fax:
Toll-Free:
Address: 11445 Compaq Center West Dr., Houston, TX 77070 United States

STOCK TICKER/OTHER:

Stock Ticker: HPE
Employees: 61,000
Parent Company:

Exchange: NYS
Fiscal Year Ends: 10/31

SALARIES/BONUSES:

Top Exec. Salary: $1,300,000   Bonus: $
Second Exec. Salary: $676,136   Bonus: $500,000

OTHER THOUGHTS:

Estimated Female Officers or Directors:
Hot Spot for Advancement for Women/Minorities:

Hewlett Packard Laboratories (HP Labs)

www.hpe.com/us/en/hewlett-packard-labs.html

NAIC Code: 541710

TYPES OF BUSINESS:

Electronics Research
Innovation
Research and Development
Advanced Technologies
Next-Generation Products and Solutions
Artificial Intelligence Development
Edge and Cloud Solutions
Innovation Podcasts and Publications

BRANDS/DIVISIONS/AFFILIATES:

Hewlett Packard Enterprise Company
From Research to Reality
Labs Publications

CONTACTS: *Note: Officers with more than one job title may be intentionally listed here more than once.*

Antonio Neri, CEO
John Sontag, Dir.-Systems Research
Martin Sadler, Dir.-Security & Cloud Lab
Chandrakant D. Patel, Chief Engineer
Jaap Suermondt, Dir.-Analytics Lab
Laurel Krieger, VP-Strategy & Oper.
Ruth Bergman, Head-HP Labs Israel
David Lee, Dir.-Networking & Mobility
David Lee, Head-HP Labs China
Eric Hanson, Dir.-Printing & Content Lab

GROWTH PLANS/SPECIAL FEATURES:

Hewlett-Packard Laboratories (HP Labs) is the innovation and research arm of Hewlett Packard Enterprise Company. HP Labs is focused on the transfer of advanced technologies into next-generation products and solutions. The company is responsible for solving complex challenges for Hewlett Packard Enterprise businesses, working alongside them to integrate key technologies into their products and accelerate technology from research and development through to commercialization. HP Labs develops artificial intelligence (AI) where accuracy, equity, sustainability, privacy and compliance are engineered from edge to cloud. HP Labs' podcast, From Research to Reality, covers the many phases of technology innovation, such as ideas, research, development, management and marketing. The podcast engages in conversations across diverse backgrounds, including engineers, scientists, mathematicians, business leaders and technologists. Labs Publications offers recent papers, technical essays and studies authored by HP Labs researchers, which can be explored on the firm's website.

FINANCIAL DATA: *Note: Data for latest year may not have been available at press time.*

In U.S. $	2024	2023	2022	2021	2020	2019
Revenue						
R&D Expense						
Operating Income						
Operating Margin %						
SGA Expense						
Net Income						
Operating Cash Flow						
Capital Expenditure						
EBITDA						
Return on Assets %						
Return on Equity %						
Debt to Equity						

CONTACT INFORMATION:

Phone: 650-857-1501   Fax: 650-857-5518
Toll-Free: 800-752-0900
Address: 1501 Page Mill Rd., Palo Alto, CA 94304 United States

STOCK TICKER/OTHER:

Stock Ticker: Subsidiary   Exchange:
Employees: 155   Fiscal Year Ends: 10/31
Parent Company: Hewlett Packard Enterprise Company

SALARIES/BONUSES:

Top Exec. Salary: $ Bonus: $
Second Exec. Salary: $ Bonus: $

OTHER THOUGHTS:

Estimated Female Officers or Directors: 2
Hot Spot for Advancement for Women/Minorities: Y

Hill-Rom Holdings Inc

www.hillrom.com

NAIC Code: 339100

TYPES OF BUSINESS:

Equipment-Hospital Beds & Related Products
Hospital Equipment
Medical Supplies
Smart Beds
Patient Monitoring Devices
Care Communication Strategies
Patient Handling and Mobility Services
Diagnostic Systems and Devices

BRANDS/DIVISIONS/AFFILIATES:

Baxter International Inc
Baxter Hillrom/Welch Allyn
SmartCare

CONTACTS: Note: Officers with more than one job title may be intentionally listed here more than once.

Barbara Bodem, CFO
Paul Johnson, President, Divisional
Amy Dodrill, President, Divisional
Andreas Frank, President, Divisional
Mary Ladone, Senior VP, Divisional
Robert L. Parkinson, Jr., Chmn.-Baxter

GROWTH PLANS/SPECIAL FEATURES:

Hill-Rom Holdings, Inc. is a subsidiary of Baxter International, Inc. and therefore does business as Baxter Hillrom/Welch Allyn and is a global provider of hospital equipment and medical supplies. Baxter Hillrom/Welch Allyn products span areas such as smart beds and surfaces, patient monitoring, care communications, safe patient handling and mobility, healthcare furniture, non-invasive respiratory therapy, surgical workflow and precision positioning, procedural connectivity, diagnostic cardiology, physical exam and diagnostics, vision screening and diagnostics, veterinary and animal health, as well as related interactive economic and clinical impact tools, construction solutions, rental therapy solutions and new/refurbished parts. The company's products and services provide solutions across hospital care, surgical care, primary care and home healthcare. Services offered include care communications, financial services, customer experience centers, smart care, equipment maintenance/repair and more. SmartCare is the firm's on-call, ready-to-go repair service for technical or functional impairments in equipment. Hill-Rom has offices in more than 100 countries across North and Latin America, Europe, the Middle East, Africa and Asia Pacific.

Parent Baxter offers Hill-Rom employees healthcare and retirement benefits, insurance coverage and more.

FINANCIAL DATA: Note: Data for latest year may not have been available at press time.

In U.S. $	2024	2023	2022	2021	2020	2019
Revenue	3,209,388,000	3,056,560,000	2,939,000,000	3,018,700,032	2,880,999,936	2,907,300,096
R&D Expense						
Operating Income						
Operating Margin %						
SGA Expense						
Net Income				248,500,000	223,000,000	152,200,000
Operating Cash Flow						
Capital Expenditure						
EBITDA						
Return on Assets %						
Return on Equity %						
Debt to Equity						

CONTACT INFORMATION:

Phone: 3120819-7200   Fax:
Toll-Free:
Address: 130 E. Randolph St., Ste. 1000, Chicago, IL 60601 United States

STOCK TICKER/OTHER:

Stock Ticker: Subsidiary   Exchange:
Employees: 10,000   Fiscal Year Ends: 09/30
Parent Company: Baxter International Inc

SALARIES/BONUSES:

Top Exec. Salary: $ Bonus: $
Second Exec. Salary: $ Bonus: $

OTHER THOUGHTS:

Estimated Female Officers or Directors: 1
Hot Spot for Advancement for Women/Minorities: Y

Hitachi High Technologies America Inc www.hitachi-hightech.com/us

NAIC Code: 541710

TYPES OF BUSINESS:

Research & Development
Semiconductor Manufacturing Equipment
Analytical Instrumentation Products
Scientific Instrument Products
Bio-Based Products
Technology Solutions
Product Innovation
Molecular Research and Diagnostic Solutions

BRANDS/DIVISIONS/AFFILIATES:

Hitachi Limited

CONTACTS: Note: Officers with more than one job title may be intentionally listed here more than once.

Craig Kerkove, CEO
Masahiro Miyazaki, Pres.
Greg Rigby, VP
Tom Grossi, Asst. Dir.-Corp. Business. Dev.
Steve Keough, Head-Media, Central & Eastern U.S.
Monica Degnan, Head-Media, Western U.S.
Phil Bryson, Gen. Mgr.-Nanotechnology Systems Division

GROWTH PLANS/SPECIAL FEATURES:

Hitachi High Technologies America, Inc. (Hitachi Hi-Tech), a subsidiary of Hitachi Limited of Japan, sells and services semiconductor manufacturing equipment, analytical instrumentation, scientific instruments and bio-related products. Hitachi Hi-Tech also sells and services industrial equipment, electronic devices, and electronic and industrial materials. The firm operates through seven divisions. The analytical systems division assists researchers in finding solutions to scientific instrument requirements through its wide range of analytical instrumentation, products, services and solutions. The industrial solutions division offers essential technologies and services to leading manufacturers of automotive, communications and electronics for the observation, measurement and analysis field. The innovative production business division services automated production line equipment, provides thin-film R&D solutions and supports industries with a range of products, services and solutions for their current and long-term needs. The molecular research and diagnostic division develops solutions in the areas of molecular life sciences and clinical diagnostics, primarily focusing on identifying and enabling new technologies that advance the understanding and treatment of constitutional disorders and cancer via R&D, collaboration and partnership. The systems products division designs and builds in-flight entertainment tablets for the aerospace industry. The metrology and analysis systems division provides equipment, technologies and services to semiconductor and equipment manufacturers, as well as to the fields of materials science, biological research and industrial manufacturing. Lastly, the semiconductor equipment division supplies state-of-the-art dry-plasma etch systems to global semiconductor manufacturers. Based in Illinois, Hitachi Hi-Tech has offices and innovation labs throughout the U.S., as well as in Mexico City, Mexico.

Hitachi Hi-Tech offers its employees comprehensive health coverage, and retirement and savings protection plans.

FINANCIAL DATA: Note: Data for latest year may not have been available at press time.

In U.S. $	2024	2023	2022	2021	2020	2019
Revenue						
R&D Expense						
Operating Income						
Operating Margin %						
SGA Expense						
Net Income						
Operating Cash Flow						
Capital Expenditure						
EBITDA						
Return on Assets %						
Return on Equity %						
Debt to Equity						

CONTACT INFORMATION:

Phone: 847-273-4141   Fax: 847-273-4407
Toll-Free:
Address: 10 N. Martingale Rd., Ste. 500, Schaumburg, IL 60173-2295
United States

STOCK TICKER/OTHER:

Stock Ticker: Subsidiary   Exchange:
Employees: 800   Fiscal Year Ends: 03/31
Parent Company: Hitachi Limited

SALARIES/BONUSES:

Top Exec. Salary: $ Bonus: $
Second Exec. Salary: $ Bonus: $

OTHER THOUGHTS:

Estimated Female Officers or Directors:
Hot Spot for Advancement for Women/Minorities:

Hitachi Limited

NAIC Code: 334111

www.hitachi.com

TYPES OF BUSINESS:
Computer & Electronics Manufacturing
Information Technology
Nuclear Energy
Industrial Manufacturing
Transportation Mobility
Smart Life Products and Solutions
Automotive Systems
Automotive Components

BRANDS/DIVISIONS/AFFILIATES:
Hitachi Astemo Ltd
Hitachi Solutions Technology Ltd
Hitachi GE Nuclear Ltd
Hitachi Industry & Control Solutions Ltd
Hitachi Rail STS Mobilinx Hurontario GP Inc
Hitachi High-tech Amata Smart Services Co Ltd

GROWTH PLANS/SPECIAL FEATURES:
Hitachi Ltd provides IT services and has an expertise in the range of business fields, including financial services. The company's main products and services include system integration, consulting, cloud services, servers, storage, software, telecommunications and networks, and ATMs. Hitachi operates in various segments namely, Information and Telecommunication Systems; Social Infrastructure and Industrial Systems; Electronic Systems and Equipment; Construction Machinery; High Functional Materials and Components; Automotive Systems; Smart Life and Ecofriendly Systems; Financial Services; and Others.

CONTACTS:
Note: Officers with more than one job title may be intentionally listed here more than once.
Keiji Kojima, CEO
Katsumi Ihara, Chairman of the Board
Toshiaki Higashihara, Director

FINANCIAL DATA:
Note: Data for latest year may not have been available at press time.

In U.S. $	2024	2023	2022	2021	2020	2019
Revenue	67,541,771,417	75,542,557,975	71,262,163,446	60,602,584,376	60,866,864,993	65,819,352,061
R&D Expense						
Operating Income	5,247,265,000	5,194,001,000	5,125,215,000	3,437,795,000	4,595,133,000	5,241,433,000
Operating Margin %	.08%	.07%	.07%	.06%	.08%	.08%
SGA Expense	12,678,920,000	13,475,030,000	12,638,050,000	11,803,150,000	11,861,180,000	12,225,830,000
Net Income	4,095,363,000	4,506,554,000	4,050,750,000	3,482,456,000	608,136,600	1,545,029,000
Operating Cash Flow	6,641,294,000	5,741,773,000	5,067,641,000	5,506,304,000	3,894,196,000	4,235,109,000
Capital Expenditure	2,673,875,000	2,850,493,000	3,053,742,000	2,589,177,000	2,924,716,000	3,278,596,000
EBITDA	9,360,233,000	9,702,819,000	9,766,003,000	9,434,074,000	4,425,229,000	6,283,477,000
Return on Assets %	.05%	.05%	.05%	.05%	.01%	.02%
Return on Equity %	.11%	.14%	.15%	.15%	.03%	.07%
Debt to Equity	.17%	.26%	.36%	.48%	0.339	0.217

CONTACT INFORMATION:
Phone: 81 332581111   Fax: 81 332582375
Toll-Free:
Address: 6-6, Marunouchi 1-chome, Chiyoda-ku, Tokyo, 100-8280 Japan

STOCK TICKER/OTHER:
Stock Ticker: HTHIF   Exchange: PINX
Employees: 268,600   Fiscal Year Ends: 03/31
Parent Company:

SALARIES/BONUSES:
Top Exec. Salary: $ Bonus: $
Second Exec. Salary: $ Bonus: $

OTHER THOUGHTS:
Estimated Female Officers or Directors: 1
Hot Spot for Advancement for Women/Minorities:

HKS Inc

www.hksinc.com

NAIC Code: 541330

TYPES OF BUSINESS:

Engineering Consulting Services
Architecture
Consulting
Experiential Branding
Interior Design
Structural Engineering
Planning and Urban Design
Sustainable Design

BRANDS/DIVISIONS/AFFILIATES:

Citizen HKS
LINE

GROWTH PLANS/SPECIAL FEATURES:

HKS, Inc. is an architectural consulting firm that has worked on projects in more than 200 worldwide locations since its 1939 inception. Headquartered in Dallas, Texas, HKS has additional offices across the Americas, Europe, Middle East and Asia Pacific. The company's services include advisory, alternative project delivery, architecture, diversity and inclusion, experiential branding, interior design, mixed-use, planning and urban design, research, structural engineering and sustainable design. HKS has two of its own service teams: Citizen HKS, its public-interest design initiative; and LINE (Laboratory for Intensive Exploration), its design research team. Types of practices HKS engages in span aviation, cities and communities, cultural, commercial, education, government, health, hospitality, life science, mission critical, residential mixed-use, senior living and sports and entertainment.

CONTACTS: *Note: Officers with more than one job title may be intentionally listed here more than once.*

Dan Noble, CEO
Sam Mudro, CFO
Ann Kifer, CMO

FINANCIAL DATA: *Note: Data for latest year may not have been available at press time.*

In U.S. $	2024	2023	2022	2021	2020	2019
Revenue	423,150,000	403,000,000	387,000,000	463,320,000	445,500,000	450,000,000
R&D Expense						
Operating Income						
Operating Margin %						
SGA Expense						
Net Income						
Operating Cash Flow						
Capital Expenditure						
EBITDA						
Return on Assets %						
Return on Equity %						
Debt to Equity						

CONTACT INFORMATION:

Phone: 214-969-5599   Fax: 214-969-3367
Toll-Free:
Address: 350 N. Saint Paul St., Ste. 100, Dallas, TX 75201 United States

STOCK TICKER/OTHER:

Stock Ticker: Private   Exchange:
Employees: 1,500   Fiscal Year Ends:
Parent Company:

SALARIES/BONUSES:

Top Exec. Salary: $ Bonus: $
Second Exec. Salary: $ Bonus: $

OTHER THOUGHTS:

Estimated Female Officers or Directors:
Hot Spot for Advancement for Women/Minorities:

HNTB Corporation

www.hntb.com

NAIC Code: 541330

TYPES OF BUSINESS:

Engineering Design Services
Infrastructure Services
Architecture Services
Planning and Design
Program and Construction Management
Design-Build
Environmental Planning
Mobility Solutions

BRANDS/DIVISIONS/AFFILIATES:

GROWTH PLANS/SPECIAL FEATURES:

HNTB Corporation was founded in 1914 and is an employee-owned provider of infrastructure and architecture services to public and private property owners, as well as to contractors. The firm addresses the full lifecycle of infrastructure, delivering a range of related services such as planning, design, program and construction management. HNTB's expertise includes the following industries and applications: architecture, aviation, bridges, construction management, design-build, digital infrastructure solutions, environmental planning, highways, infrastructure and mobility equity, program management, tolls, transit and rail, tunnels and water. Based in Missouri, the firm has offices throughout the U.S.

HNTB offers its employees a 401(k), life and disability insurance, flexible spending accounts, adoption assistance and paid time off.

CONTACTS: Note: Officers with more than one job title may be intentionally listed here more than once.

Rob Slimp, CEO
Craig Denson, CFO
Lindsay Jordan, Chief People Officer
Marty Williams, CIO
Paul Yarossi, Exec. VP
Rob Slimp, CEO-HNTB Infrastructure
Rob Slimp, Chmn.

FINANCIAL DATA: Note: Data for latest year may not have been available at press time.

In U.S. $	2024	2023	2022	2021	2020	2019
Revenue	756,756,000	720,720,000	693,000,000	648,648,000	623,700,000	630,000,000
R&D Expense						
Operating Income						
Operating Margin %						
SGA Expense						
Net Income						
Operating Cash Flow						
Capital Expenditure						
EBITDA						
Return on Assets %						
Return on Equity %						
Debt to Equity						

CONTACT INFORMATION:

Phone: 816-472-1201   Fax: 816-472-4060
Toll-Free:
Address: 715 Kirk Dr., Kansas City, MO 64105 United States

STOCK TICKER/OTHER:

Stock Ticker: Private   Exchange:
Employees: 5,500   Fiscal Year Ends: 12/31
Parent Company:

SALARIES/BONUSES:

Top Exec. Salary: $ Bonus: $
Second Exec. Salary: $ Bonus: $

OTHER THOUGHTS:

Estimated Female Officers or Directors:
Hot Spot for Advancement for Women/Minorities:

HOCHTIEF AG

NAIC Code: 237000

www.hochtief.de

TYPES OF BUSINESS:

Heavy Construction
Airport Management & Consulting Services
Infrastructure Development
Geothermal Plant Construction
Green Building Engineering Services

BRANDS/DIVISIONS/AFFILIATES:

Turner
Flatiron
HOCHTIEF PPP
HOCHTIEF Infrastructure
CIMIC Group
CPB Contractors
Leighton Asia
Abertis

GROWTH PLANS/SPECIAL FEATURES:

Hochtief AG develops and constructs building and infrastructure projects. It works on complex projects in transportation, energy, urban infrastructure, and mining markets. It expands transportation networks with roads, bridges, and tunnels, or designs and constructs office buildings, hospitals, and power plants. The company leans on expertise and technical know-how in developing, financing, building, and operating in designated business areas. Also, it will partner with external groups to work on specific components of a project. Hochtief reports operating segments by regional divisions: Americas, Asia Pacific, and Europe. The Americas and the Asia Pacific account for the majority of sales and are where the company's assets are located.

CONTACTS: Note: Officers with more than one job title may be intentionally listed here more than once.

Pedro Jimenez, Chairman of the Board

FINANCIAL DATA: Note: Data for latest year may not have been available at press time.

In U.S. $	2024	2023	2022	2021	2020	2019
Revenue	37,799,399,051	31,505,160,461	29,760,875,837	24,265,464,180	26,054,202,725	29,343,762,629
R&D Expense			13,256,530	25,163,450	28,438,140	
Operating Income	646,846,800	625,702,700	228,625,400	427,617,500	-712,155,500	1,013,986,000
Operating Margin %	.02%	.02%	.01%	.02%	-.03%	.03%
SGA Expense	790,816,100	626,463,100	603,038,600	451,970,500	619,438,100	565,393,900
Net Income	880,391,600	593,358,700	546,849,000	236,005,700	484,950,000	-234,105,600
Operating Cash Flow	2,416,994,000	1,515,623,000	1,192,754,000	439,496,000	802,869,400	1,267,891,000
Capital Expenditure	537,689,000	239,261,100	212,870,600	89,939,840	450,914,900	668,548,200
EBITDA	2,305,432,000	1,477,952,000	1,375,887,000	1,019,153,000	2,021,973,000	3,086,254,000
Return on Assets %	.04%	.03%	.03%	.01%	.02%	-.01%
Return on Equity %	.67%	.44%	.50%	.28%	.44%	-.13%
Debt to Equity	6.65%	3.93%	4.46%	5.22%	6.25	2.827

CONTACT INFORMATION:

Phone: 49 2018240   Fax: 49 2018242777
Toll-Free:
Address: Alfredstrasse 236, Essen, NW 45133 Germany

STOCK TICKER/OTHER:

Stock Ticker: HOCFF   Exchange: PINX
Employees: 41,575   Fiscal Year Ends: 12/31
Parent Company: ACS Group

SALARIES/BONUSES:

Top Exec. Salary: $ Bonus: $
Second Exec. Salary: $ Bonus: $

OTHER THOUGHTS:

Estimated Female Officers or Directors: 1
Hot Spot for Advancement for Women/Minorities:

HOK Group Inc

www.hok.com

NAIC Code: 541330

TYPES OF BUSINESS:
Engineering Services
Engineering
Architecture
Consultancy
Interior Design
Planning and Urban Design
Renovation and Restoration
Tall Buildings and Facilities

BRANDS/DIVISIONS/AFFILIATES:

CONTACTS: Note: Officers with more than one job title may be intentionally listed here more than once.
Tom Robson, COO
John Bartolomi, CIO

GROWTH PLANS/SPECIAL FEATURES:
HOK Group, Inc. is a global design, architecture, engineering and planning firm. Founded in St. Louis in 1955, the company now has a network of 27 offices on the continents of North America, Europe and Asia. HOK offers a multitude of services across various strategic practice areas, including architecture, consulting, engineering, interior design, landscape architecture, lighting design, onsite space management, planning and urban design and sustainable design. The strategic practice areas of the firm are aviation and transportation, civic and cultural, corporate, government, healthcare, higher education, justice, lifestyle, mixed-use, renovation, refurbishment, science and technology, sports and recreation, entertainment and more. HOK projects include the LG North American Headquarters in New Jersey, the New York-Presbyterian David H. Koch Center, the Central + Wolfe Campus in California, the LG Science Park in South Korea, the Francis Crick Institute in the U.K., the King Abdullah University of Science and Technology in Saudi Arabia, among others.

HOK offers its employees health and retirement plans, and professional development opportunities.

FINANCIAL DATA: Note: Data for latest year may not have been available at press time.

In U.S. $	2024	2023	2022	2021	2020	2019
Revenue	521,976,000	497,120,000	478,000,000	477,454,040	459,090,423	463,727,700
R&D Expense						
Operating Income						
Operating Margin %						
SGA Expense						
Net Income						
Operating Cash Flow						
Capital Expenditure						
EBITDA						
Return on Assets %						
Return on Equity %						
Debt to Equity						

CONTACT INFORMATION:
Phone: 314-421-2000   Fax:
Toll-Free:
Address: 10 S. Broadway, Ste. 200, St. Louis, MO 63102 United States

STOCK TICKER/OTHER:
Stock Ticker: Private   Exchange:
Employees: 1,600   Fiscal Year Ends:
Parent Company:

SALARIES/BONUSES:
Top Exec. Salary: $ Bonus: $
Second Exec. Salary: $ Bonus: $

OTHER THOUGHTS:
Estimated Female Officers or Directors:
Hot Spot for Advancement for Women/Minorities:

Hon Hai Precision Industry Company Ltd

www.foxconn.com

NAIC Code: 334418

TYPES OF BUSINESS:

Contract Manufacturing of Electronics
Technology Solutions
Cloud Computing
Mobile Devices
Internet of Things
Artificial Intelligence
Smart Networks
Robotics

BRANDS/DIVISIONS/AFFILIATES:

Foxconn Technology Group
Foxconn Industrial Internet
Foxconn Interconnect Technology Limited
FIH Mobile Limited

GROWTH PLANS/SPECIAL FEATURES:

Hon Hai Precision is the world's largest contract manufacturer of consumer electronics, communications, and computer products. It is the biggest supplier to Apple, whose business accounted for around 54% of overall revenue in 2023. Hon Hai is also involved in the production of upstream components such as electronic connectors, semiconductor packaging, and metal casings for smartphones, as well as producing servers. These upstream activities are mainly conducted through its listed majority-owned subsidiaries Foxconn Industrial Internet and FIH Mobile. In response to its traditional end markets of computers, smartphones, and telecom equipment maturing in 2019 it started on a strategy to develop expertise in three new growth areas, electric vehicles, digital health, and robotics.

CONTACTS:
Note: Officers with more than one job title may be intentionally listed here more than once.

Young-Way Liu, CEO

FINANCIAL DATA:
Note: Data for latest year may not have been available at press time.

In U.S. $	2024	2023	2022	2021	2020	2019
Revenue	229,403,230,402	206,080,567,417	221,623,860,390	200,460,628,557	179,186,111,327	178,677,375,578
R&D Expense	3,871,705,000	3,679,345,000	3,821,085,000	3,513,770,000	3,147,298,000	3,061,606,000
Operating Income	6,708,823,000	5,569,143,000	5,811,914,000	4,981,590,000	3,706,356,000	3,842,448,000
Operating Margin %	.03%	.03%	.03%	.02%	.02%	.02%
SGA Expense	3,764,530,000	3,725,477,000	3,746,882,000	3,615,102,000	3,276,729,000	3,659,400,000
Net Income	5,106,851,000	4,752,131,000	4,731,547,000	4,659,231,000	3,404,281,000	3,856,221,000
Operating Cash Flow	5,552,433,000	14,900,430,000	3,668,931,000	-3,284,475,000	12,628,720,000	8,294,352,000
Capital Expenditure	4,817,116,000	3,978,014,000	3,399,764,000	3,160,289,000	2,258,590,000	2,608,929,000
EBITDA	11,255,170,000	11,443,150,000	9,989,565,000	9,732,172,000	8,390,843,000	9,948,749,000
Return on Assets %	.04%	.04%	.04%	.04%	.03%	.03%
Return on Equity %	.10%	.10%	.10%	.10%	.08%	.09%
Debt to Equity	.19%	.19%	.22%	.21%	0.196	0.192

CONTACT INFORMATION:

Phone: 886 222683466   Fax: 886 222686204
Toll-Free:
Address: 66 Zhonngshan Rd., Tu-Chen Industrial Zone, Tu-Chen City, Taipei, 236 Taiwan

STOCK TICKER/OTHER:

Stock Ticker: HNHAF
Employees: 1,200,000
Parent Company:

Exchange: PINX
Fiscal Year Ends: 12/31

SALARIES/BONUSES:

Top Exec. Salary: $173,901   Bonus: $5,020,066
Second Exec. Salary: $173,901   Bonus: $5,020,066

OTHER THOUGHTS:

Estimated Female Officers or Directors:
Hot Spot for Advancement for Women/Minorities:

Honda Motor Co Ltd

NAIC Code: 336111

global.honda

TYPES OF BUSINESS:

Automobile Manufacturing
Motorcycles
ATVs & Personal Watercraft
Generators
Marine Engines
Lawn & Garden Equipment
Fuel Cell & Hybrid Vehicles
Airplanes

BRANDS/DIVISIONS/AFFILIATES:

Fit/Jazz
Civic
Accord
CR-V
HR-V
NSX
Clarity Fuel Cell
HondaJet

CONTACTS: *Note: Officers with more than one job title may be intentionally listed here more than once.*

Toshihiro Mibe, CEO
Keiji Ohtsu, Other Corporate Officer
Kazuhiro Takizawa, CEO
Eiji Fujimura, CFO
Noriya Kaihara, Chief Compliance Officer
Shinji Aoyama, COO
Ayumu Matsuo, Other Corporate Officer
Minoru Kato, Other Corporate Officer
Yutaka Tamagawa, Other Corporate Officer
Katsuto Hayashi, Other Corporate Officer
Takashi Onuma, Other Corporate Officer
Hironao Ito, Other Corporate Officer
Katsushi Inoue, Other Corporate Officer
Manabu Ozawa, Other Corporate Officer
Masayuki Igarashi, Other Corporate Officer
Kensuke Oe, Other Corporate Officer

GROWTH PLANS/SPECIAL FEATURES:

Incorporated in 1948, Honda Motor was originally a motorcycle manufacturer. Today, the firm makes automobiles, motorcycles, and power products such as boat engines, generators, and lawnmowers. Including joint ventures, Honda sold 3.7 million light vehicles and 20.6 million motorcycles in fiscal 2025, and consolidated sales were JPY 21.7 trillion. Automobiles constitute 65% of revenue and motorcycles 17%, with the rest split between power products and financial services. Honda also makes robots and private jets.

Employee benefits vary by location.

FINANCIAL DATA: *Note: Data for latest year may not have been available at press time.*

In U.S. $	2024	2023	2022	2021	2020	2019
Revenue	141,827,290,269	117,382,154,004	101,032,324,647	91,436,543,580	103,658,773,204	110,306,981,123
R&D Expense	6,412,296,000	6,115,767,000	5,464,149,000	5,129,784,000	5,582,637,000	5,601,951,000
Operating Income	9,594,398,000	5,420,501,000	6,048,542,000	4,583,505,000	4,399,035,000	5,042,835,000
Operating Margin %	.07%	.05%	.06%	.05%	.04%	.05%
SGA Expense	14,624,680,000	11,593,360,000	9,209,143,000	9,245,543,000	11,396,770,000	12,318,750,000
Net Income	7,686,573,000	4,522,466,000	4,908,824,000	4,564,184,000	3,164,024,000	4,237,129,000
Operating Cash Flow	5,187,990,000	14,780,770,000	11,660,800,000	7,445,008,000	6,799,605,000	5,387,309,000
Capital Expenditure	4,225,667,000	4,391,058,000	3,118,759,000	3,826,277,000	4,174,243,000	4,219,710,000
EBITDA	17,331,170,000	11,367,030,000	11,789,220,000	10,775,960,000	10,514,330,000	11,901,470,000
Return on Assets %	.04%	.03%	.03%	.03%	.02%	.03%
Return on Equity %	.09%	.06%	.07%	.08%	.06%	.08%
Debt to Equity						

CONTACT INFORMATION:

Phone: 81 3 3423 1111   Fax:
Toll-Free:
Address: 2-1-1, Minami-Aoyama, Minato-ku, Tokyo, 107-8556 Japan

STOCK TICKER/OTHER:

Stock Ticker: HMC
Employees: 194,993
Parent Company:

Exchange: NYS
Fiscal Year Ends: 03/31

SALARIES/BONUSES:

Top Exec. Salary: $708,137   Bonus: $367,953
Second Exec. Salary: $ Bonus: $

OTHER THOUGHTS:

Estimated Female Officers or Directors:
Hot Spot for Advancement for Women/Minorities:

Honeywell International Inc

www.honeywell.com

NAIC Code: 336412

TYPES OF BUSINESS:

Aircraft Engine and Engine Parts Manufacturing
Automation & Control Systems
Turboprop Engines
Performance Polymers
Specialty Chemicals
Nuclear Services
Warehouse Automation
Quantum Computing

BRANDS/DIVISIONS/AFFILIATES:

Sparta Systems

GROWTH PLANS/SPECIAL FEATURES:

Honeywell traces its roots to 1885 with Albert Butz's firm, Butz Thermo-Electric Regulator, which produced a predecessor to the modern thermostat. Other inventions by Honeywell include biodegradable detergent and autopilot. Today, Honeywell is a global multi-industry behemoth with one of the largest installed bases of equipment. It operates through four business segments: aerospace technologies (37% of 2023 company revenue), industrial automation (29%), energy and sustainability solutions (17%), and building automation (17%). Recently, Honeywell has made several portfolio changes to focus on fewer end markets and align with a set of secular growth trends. The firm is working diligently to expand its installed base, deriving around 30% of its revenue from recurring aftermarket services.

CONTACTS: Note: Officers with more than one job title may be intentionally listed here more than once.

Kenneth West, CEO, Divisional
Lucian Boldea, CEO, Divisional
Kevin Dehoff, CEO, Divisional
Billal Hammoud, CEO, Divisional
James Currier, CEO, Divisional
Vimal Kapur, CEO
Gregory Lewis, CFO
Robert Mailloux, Chief Accounting Officer
Anne Madden, General Counsel
Karen Mattimore, Other Executive Officer
Michael Stepniak, Vice President, Divisional

FINANCIAL DATA: Note: Data for latest year may not have been available at press time.

In U.S. $	2024	2023	2022	2021	2020	2019
Revenue	38,498,000,896	36,662,001,664	35,465,998,336	34,391,998,464	32,636,999,680	36,708,999,168
R&D Expense	1,536,000,000	1,456,000,000	1,478,000,000	1,333,000,000		
Operating Income	7,660,000,000	7,084,000,000	6,427,000,000	6,200,000,000	5,696,000,000	6,851,000,000
Operating Margin %	.20%	.19%	.18%	.18%	.17%	.19%
SGA Expense	5,466,000,000	5,127,000,000	5,214,000,000	4,798,000,000	4,772,000,000	5,519,000,000
Net Income	5,705,000,000	5,658,000,000	4,966,000,000	5,542,000,000	4,779,000,000	6,143,000,000
Operating Cash Flow	6,097,000,000	5,340,000,000	5,274,000,000	6,038,000,000	6,208,000,000	6,897,000,000
Capital Expenditure	1,164,000,000	1,039,000,000	766,000,000	895,000,000	906,000,000	839,000,000
EBITDA	9,605,000,000	9,100,000,000	7,997,000,000	8,801,000,000	7,373,000,000	9,004,000,000
Return on Assets %	.08%	.09%	.08%	.09%	.08%	.11%
Return on Equity %	.33%	.35%	.28%	.31%	.27%	.34%
Debt to Equity	1.42%	1.10%	.95%	.81%	0.968	0.63

CONTACT INFORMATION:

Phone: 704-627-6200   Fax:
Toll-Free:
Address: 300 S. Tryon St., Charlotte, NC 28202 United States

STOCK TICKER/OTHER:

Stock Ticker: HON
Employees: 95,000
Parent Company:

Exchange: NAS
Fiscal Year Ends: 12/31

SALARIES/BONUSES:

Top Exec. Salary: $1,555,769   Bonus: $
Second Exec. Salary: $1,000,961   Bonus: $

OTHER THOUGHTS:

Estimated Female Officers or Directors: 2
Hot Spot for Advancement for Women/Minorities: Y

Hoya Corp

NAIC Code: 339115

www.hoya.co.jp

TYPES OF BUSINESS:

Ophthalmic Goods Manufacturing
Glass Semiconductor Components
Medical Equipment
Eyeglass Lenses
Optical Glass
Bio-Compatible Bone Replacement
Laser & UV Light Sources
Nanoimprint Technology

GROWTH PLANS/SPECIAL FEATURES:

Founded in 1941 in Tokyo as an optical glass production plant, Hoya is one of the largest eyeglass lens manufacturers in the world. Leveraging its technology know-how in glass manufacturing, Hoya entered the mask blanks business in 1974. Now although its life care business accounts for 67% of its total revenue, almost half of its profit before tax comes from its higher-margin IT business.

BRANDS/DIVISIONS/AFFILIATES:

ViXion Inc

CONTACTS: *Note: Officers with more than one job title may be intentionally listed here more than once.*

Eiichiro Ikeda, CEO
Ryo Hirooka, CFO

FINANCIAL DATA: *Note: Data for latest year may not have been available at press time.*

In U.S. $	2024	2023	2022	2021	2020	2019
Revenue	5,502,832,517	5,096,466,535	4,653,742,268	3,875,757,034	4,043,807,468	3,973,604,688
R&D Expense						
Operating Income	3,009,254,000	2,783,005,000	2,523,410,000	2,114,378,000	2,104,325,000	2,163,475,000
Operating Margin %	.55%	.55%	.54%	.55%	.52%	.54%
SGA Expense	126,749,500	111,108,000	91,544,020	69,418,220	84,795,890	88,301,860
Net Income	1,259,206,000	1,170,772,000	1,142,092,000	870,910,800	794,265,500	847,702,000
Operating Cash Flow	1,546,807,000	1,401,201,000	1,319,460,000	1,053,957,000	1,134,171,000	1,017,690,000
Capital Expenditure	285,156,900	232,386,800	200,444,300	216,925,900	313,642,000	185,170,800
EBITDA	1,983,505,000	1,855,478,000	1,773,042,000	1,371,591,000	1,266,544,000	1,190,392,000
Return on Assets %	.16%	.17%	.18%	.15%	.15%	.17%
Return on Equity %	.20%	.21%	.22%	.19%	.18%	.21%
Debt to Equity	.02%	.02%	.02%	.02%	0.022	0.001

CONTACT INFORMATION:

Phone: 81 3-39521151   Fax: 81339520726
Toll-Free:
Address: Fl. 20, Nittochi Nishishinjuku Bldg, 6-10-1 Nishi-S, Tokyo, 160-8347 Japan

STOCK TICKER/OTHER:

Stock Ticker: HOCPF
Employees: 37,412
Parent Company:

Exchange: PINX
Fiscal Year Ends: 03/31

SALARIES/BONUSES:

Top Exec. Salary: $ Bonus: $
Second Exec. Salary: $ Bonus: $

OTHER THOUGHTS:

Estimated Female Officers or Directors:
Hot Spot for Advancement for Women/Minorities:

Sales, profits and employees may be estimates. Financial information, benefits and other data can change quickly and may vary from those stated here.

HP Inc

NAIC Code: 334111

www.hp.com

TYPES OF BUSINESS:

Computer Manufacturing
Computer Software
Printers & Supplies
Scanners
Computing Devices

BRANDS/DIVISIONS/AFFILIATES:

HP Labs

GROWTH PLANS/SPECIAL FEATURES:

HP (formerly Hewlett-Packard) is a behemoth in the PC and printing markets. It has focused on these markets since it exited IT infrastructure in 2015 with the split from Hewlett Packard Enterprise. HP focuses on the commercial market, but maintains sales of consumer devices and printers. The firm has a broad and global customer base, with only one third of sales coming from the US. HP completely outsources manufacturing and relies heavily on channel partners for its sales and marketing.

CONTACTS: *Note: Officers with more than one job title may be intentionally listed here more than once.*

Enrique Lores, CEO
Karen Parkhill, CFO
Charles Bergh, Chairman of the Board
Stephanie Liebman, Chief Accounting Officer
Julie Jacobs, Chief Legal Officer
David McQuarrie, Other Executive Officer
Kristen Ludgate, Other Executive Officer
Alexander Cho, President, Divisional
Anneliese Olson, President, Divisional

FINANCIAL DATA: *Note: Data for latest year may not have been available at press time.*

In U.S. $	2024	2023	2022	2021	2020	2019
Revenue	53,559,001,088	53,717,999,616	62,910,001,152	63,459,999,744	56,638,001,152	58,756,001,792
R&D Expense	1,640,000,000	1,578,000,000	1,653,000,000	1,848,000,000	1,477,000,000	1,499,000,000
Operating Income	4,202,000,000	4,223,000,000	5,117,000,000	5,678,000,000	3,931,000,000	3,001,000,000
Operating Margin %	.08%	.08%	.08%	.09%	.07%	.05%
SGA Expense	5,658,000,000	5,357,000,000	5,264,000,000	5,727,000,000	4,901,000,000	5,368,000,000
Net Income	2,775,000,000	3,263,000,000	3,132,000,000	6,541,000,000	2,815,000,000	3,152,000,000
Operating Cash Flow	3,749,000,000	3,571,000,000	4,463,000,000	6,409,000,000	4,316,000,000	4,654,000,000
Capital Expenditure	592,000,000	593,000,000	765,000,000	582,000,000	580,000,000	671,000,000
EBITDA	4,716,000,000	4,471,000,000	5,463,000,000	8,607,000,000	4,239,000,000	3,509,000,000
Return on Assets %	.07%	.09%	.08%	.18%	.08%	.09%
Return on Equity %						
Debt to Equity						

CONTACT INFORMATION:

Phone: 650 857-1501   Fax:
Toll-Free:
Address: 1501 Page Mill Rd., Palo Alto, CA 94304 United States

STOCK TICKER/OTHER:

Stock Ticker: HPQ   Exchange: NYS
Employees: 58,000   Fiscal Year Ends: 10/31
Parent Company:

SALARIES/BONUSES:

Top Exec. Salary: $1,400,000   Bonus: $
Second Exec. Salary: Bonus: $
$861,000

OTHER THOUGHTS:

Estimated Female Officers or Directors: 6
Hot Spot for Advancement for Women/Minorities: Y

HTC Corporation

NAIC Code: 334418

TYPES OF BUSINESS:

Contract Electronics Manufacturing
Innovative Technology
Virtual Reality Products
Augmented Reality Products
5G Connectivity
Artificial Intelligence
Blockchain Solutions
Virtual and Metaverse Creation

BRANDS/DIVISIONS/AFFILIATES:

VIVE
VIVE Flow
VIVERSE
VIVE Avatar
VIVERSE Market

GROWTH PLANS/SPECIAL FEATURES:

HTC Corporation is an innovation company that creates products, solutions and platforms in mobile and immersive technologies. HTC's technologies include virtual reality (VR), augmented reality (AR), 5G, artificial intelligence (AI) and blockchain, which are marketed under the VIVE and other brand names and can be embedded to support, develop and deploy products and solutions for customers across a range of industries. VIVE VR/AR and XR are the firm's virtual reality headsets, VIVE Flow virtual reality glasses, VIVERSE offers AI collaboration and exhibitions with partners, VIVE Avatar is an open-platform Avatar creator built for the VIVERSE, and VIVERSE connects individuals and communities in the metaverse, enabling the creation and exploration of virtual worlds from any device. VIVERSE Market is a digital platform for buying, selling and/or trading digital artifacts. VIVE accessories span trackers, wireless adapters and a base station.

CONTACTS: Note: Officers with more than one job title may be intentionally listed here more than once.

Cher Wang, CEP
Fred Liu, Pres., Eng.
Fred Liu, Pres., Oper.
Cher Wang, Chmn.

FINANCIAL DATA: Note: Data for latest year may not have been available at press time.

In U.S. $	2024	2023	2022	2021	2020	2019
Revenue		143,423,000	130,386,501	189,564,047	206,480,000	350,381,888
R&D Expense						
Operating Income						
Operating Margin %						
SGA Expense						
Net Income		-110,239,000	-130,090,840	-111,928,756	-214,194,000	-327,400,128
Operating Cash Flow						
Capital Expenditure						
EBITDA						
Return on Assets %						
Return on Equity %						
Debt to Equity						

CONTACT INFORMATION:

Phone: 886 33753252 Fax: 886 33753251
Toll-Free:
Address: NO. 23, Xinghua Rd., Taoyuan, 330 Taiwan

STOCK TICKER/OTHER:

Stock Ticker: 2498 Exchange: TWSE
Employees: 3,905 Fiscal Year Ends: 12/31
Parent Company:

SALARIES/BONUSES:

Top Exec. Salary: $ Bonus: $
Second Exec. Salary: $ Bonus: $

OTHER THOUGHTS:

Estimated Female Officers or Directors:
Hot Spot for Advancement for Women/Minorities:

Huawei Technologies Co Ltd

NAIC Code: 334210

www.huawei.com

TYPES OF BUSINESS:

Telecommunications Equipment Manufacturing
Network Equipment
Software
Wireless Technology
Smartphones
5G Wireless Technology
Watches

BRANDS/DIVISIONS/AFFILIATES:

Union of Huawei Investment & Holding Co
Huaewi

CONTACTS: Note: Officers with more than one job title may be intentionally listed here more than once.

Ren Zhengfei, CEO
Ren Zhengfei, Pres.
Meng Wanzhou, CFO
Ding Yun (Ryan Ding), Chief Prod. & Solutions Officer
Yu Chengdong (Richard Yu), Chief Strategy Officer
Chen Lifang, Corp. Sr. VP-Public Affairs & Comm. Dept.
Guo Ping, Chmn.-Finance Committee
Zhang Ping'an (Alex Zhang), CEO-Huawei Symantec
Hu Houkun (Ken Hu), Chmn.-Huawei USA
Liang Hua, Chmn.
Wan Biao, Pres., Russia

GROWTH PLANS/SPECIAL FEATURES:

Huawei Technologies Co., Ltd., founded in 1987, is a leading global information and communications technology (ICT) solutions provider. Huawei is one of the world's leading manufacturers of smartphones. The company's ICT portfolio of end-to-end solutions in telecom, enterprise networks, and consumers are used in more than 170 countries and regions, serving more than one-third of the world's population. Huawei's consumer products include the Huawei brand of mobile smart phones, laptops, tablets, watches, ear buds, speakers, Wi-Fi connection devices and more. The company's business products include switches, routers, WLAN (wireless local area network), servers, storage, cloud computing, network energy services and more. Huawei's smart city solutions sense, process and deliver informed decisions for improving the environment for citizens, with recent information and communications technology (ICT) offering real-time situation reporting and analysis, empowered by a combination of cloud computing, IoT technologies, big data analytics and artificial intelligence (AI). The company has global joint innovation centers and research and development centers. Huawei Technologies operates as a subsidiary of the Union of Huawei Investment & Holding Co., Ltd.

FINANCIAL DATA: Note: Data for latest year may not have been available at press time.

In U.S. $	2024	2023	2022	2021	2020	2019
Revenue						
R&D Expense						
Operating Income						
Operating Margin %						
SGA Expense						
Net Income						
Operating Cash Flow						
Capital Expenditure						
EBITDA						
Return on Assets %						
Return on Equity %						
Debt to Equity						

CONTACT INFORMATION:

Phone: 86 755-28780808   Fax: 86-755-28789251
Toll-Free:
Address: Section H, Bantian, Longgang Distr., Shenzhen, Guangdong 518129 China

STOCK TICKER/OTHER:

Stock Ticker: Subsidiary   Exchange:
Employees: 208,000   Fiscal Year Ends: 12/31
Parent Company: Union of Huawei Investment & Holding Co Ltd

SALARIES/BONUSES:

Top Exec. Salary: $ Bonus: $
Second Exec. Salary: $ Bonus: $

OTHER THOUGHTS:

Estimated Female Officers or Directors: 3
Hot Spot for Advancement for Women/Minorities: Y

Huntsman Corporation

www.huntsman.com

NAIC Code: 325211

TYPES OF BUSINESS:

Chemicals Manufacturing
Polyurethane Manufacturing
Advanced Materials & Surface Technologies
Performance Chemicals
Textile
Specialty Additives

BRANDS/DIVISIONS/AFFILIATES:

Huntsman International LLC
Gabriel Performance Products

GROWTH PLANS/SPECIAL FEATURES:

Huntsman Corp is a USA-based manufacturer of differentiated organic chemical products. Its product portfolio comprises Methyl diphenyl diisocyanate (MDI), Amines, Maleic anhydride, and Epoxy-based polymer formulations. The company's products are used in adhesives, aerospace, automotive, and construction products, among others. Its operating segments are Polyurethanes, Performance Products, and Advanced Materials. It derives the majority of its revenue from the Polyurethanes segment which includes MDI, polyols, TPU (thermoplastic polyurethane), and other polyurethane-related products. Its geographical segments are the United States & Canada, Europe, Asia-Pacific, and the Rest of the world.

CONTACTS: Note: Officers with more than one job title may be intentionally listed here more than once.

Rachel Muir, Assistant Secretary
Pierre Poukens, VP, Divisional
Anthony Hankins, CEO, Geographical
Peter Huntsman, CEO
Philip Lister, CFO
Steven Jorgensen, Chief Accounting Officer
R. Rogers, Chief Compliance Officer
Twila Day, Chief Information Officer
David Stryker, Executive VP
Brittany Benko, Other Corporate Officer
Chuck Hirsch, President, Divisional
Scott Wright, President, Divisional
Claire Mei, Treasurer
Nooshin Vaughn, Vice President, Divisional
Ivan Marcuse, Vice President, Divisional
Kevin Hardman, Vice President, Divisional

FINANCIAL DATA: Note: Data for latest year may not have been available at press time.

In U.S. $	2024	2023	2022	2021	2020	2019
Revenue	6,035,999,744	6,111,000,064	8,023,000,064	7,670,000,128	6,017,999,872	6,797,000,192
R&D Expense	121,000,000	115,000,000	125,000,000	135,000,000	135,000,000	137,000,000
Operating Income	73,000,000	102,000,000	758,000,000	743,000,000	235,000,000	428,000,000
Operating Margin %	.01%	.02%	.09%	.10%	.04%	.06%
SGA Expense	671,000,000	689,000,000	711,000,000	739,000,000	775,000,000	786,000,000
Net Income	-189,000,000	101,000,000	460,000,000	1,045,000,000	1,034,000,000	562,000,000
Operating Cash Flow	263,000,000	209,000,000	914,000,000	952,000,000	253,000,000	897,000,000
Capital Expenditure	184,000,000	230,000,000	272,000,000	326,000,000	249,000,000	274,000,000
EBITDA	329,000,000	442,000,000	1,040,000,000	1,591,000,000	706,000,000	772,000,000
Return on Assets %	-.03%	.01%	.05%	.12%	.12%	.07%
Return on Equity %	-.06%	.03%	.11%	.26%	.33%	.22%
Debt to Equity	.63%	.62%	.55%	.43%	0.551	0.953

CONTACT INFORMATION:

Phone: 281-719-6000   Fax:
Toll-Free:
Address: 10003 Woodloch Forest Dr., The Woodlands, TX 77380 United States

STOCK TICKER/OTHER:

Stock Ticker: HUN   Exchange: NYS
Employees: 6,000   Fiscal Year Ends: 12/31
Parent Company:

SALARIES/BONUSES:

Top Exec. Salary: $1,300,000   Bonus: $
Second Exec. Salary: Bonus: $
$1,097,040

OTHER THOUGHTS:

Estimated Female Officers or Directors: 2
Hot Spot for Advancement for Women/Minorities:

Hyundai Engineering & Construction Company Ltd www.hdec.kr
NAIC Code: 237000

TYPES OF BUSINESS:
Construction, Heavy & Civil Engineering
Construction
Infrastructure and Buildings
Housing
Plant and Facility
Energy Facilities and Plants
Substations
Highways, Railways and Bridges

BRANDS/DIVISIONS/AFFILIATES:

CONTACTS: *Note: Officers with more than one job title may be intentionally listed here more than once.*
Young-Joon Yoon, CEO

GROWTH PLANS/SPECIAL FEATURES:

Hyundai Engineering & Construction Company Ltd. (Hyundai E&C) is an international construction company based in South Korea and in business since 1947, operating in more than 60 countries. Hyundai E&C is organized into five divisions, civil engineering, construction, housing, plant and new energy. The civil engineering division applies technology to marine, port, dredging and reclamation; road and railways; bridges; environment and water treatment; and underground space. The construction division provides future-oriented architectural spaces, such as hospital/medical facilities, production and logistics facilities, hotels, public and commercial office buildings, transportation facilities, culture and sport facilities, data centers, education facilities, research facilities, complex developments and special projects. The housing division primarily engages in building apartments and residential developments in Korea and utilizes advanced technologies in its construction processes. The plant division designs and builds facilities and factories where oil and gas processing/refining happens, as well as other processes, such as petrochemicals and fertilizers, LNG-GTL and thermal power generation/ generation desalination. Last, the firm's energy division engages in a variety of related projects, such as nuclear power generation, renewable energy and transmission lines and substation projects.

Hyundai E&C offers its employees welfare benefits (medical, insurance, life event support), and a variety of training opportunities, including internal job training, overseas placement training, external training.

FINANCIAL DATA: *Note: Data for latest year may not have been available at press time.*

In U.S. $	2024	2023	2022	2021	2020	2019
Revenue		22,887,438,000	15,873,431,475	16,839,036,000	15,591,700,000	14,922,000,000
R&D Expense						
Operating Income						
Operating Margin %						
SGA Expense						
Net Income		413,656,000	305,588,721	304,558,846	504,380,000	494,837,000
Operating Cash Flow						
Capital Expenditure						
EBITDA						
Return on Assets %						
Return on Equity %						
Debt to Equity						

CONTACT INFORMATION:
Phone: 82-2-746-1114   Fax: 82-2-743-8963
Toll-Free:
Address: 75 Yulgok-ro, Jongno-gu, Seoul, 03058 South Korea

STOCK TICKER/OTHER:
Stock Ticker: 720   Exchange: Seoul
Employees: 4,552   Fiscal Year Ends: 12/31
Parent Company: Hyundai Motor Group

SALARIES/BONUSES:
Top Exec. Salary: $ Bonus: $
Second Exec. Salary: $ Bonus: $

OTHER THOUGHTS:
Estimated Female Officers or Directors:
Hot Spot for Advancement for Women/Minorities:

Hyundai Motor Company

worldwide.hyundai.com

NAIC Code: 336111

TYPES OF BUSINESS:

Automobile Manufacturing
Trucks
Buses
Light Commercial Vehicles
Machine Tools
Factory Automation Equipment
Material Handling Equipment
Specialty Vehicle Manufacturing

BRANDS/DIVISIONS/AFFILIATES:

Accent
Sonata
Elantra
Xcient
Kia Motors Corporation
Hyundai Capital
Hyundai Mobis
Boston Dynamics

GROWTH PLANS/SPECIAL FEATURES:

Hyundai Motor Co is engaged in the manufacturing and distribution of motor vehicles and parts. The business of the group is operated through a vehicle, finance, and other segments. Its vehicle segment is engaged in the manufacturing and sale of motor vehicles. The finance segment operates vehicle financing, credit card processing, and other financing activities. Others segment includes the research and development, train manufacturing and other activities. The company derives majority of the revenue from vehicle segment.

CONTACTS: *Note: Officers with more than one job title may be intentionally listed here more than once.*

Jae Hoon Chang, CEO
Eui-Seon Jeong, Chairman of the Board
Dong Seock Lee, Co-CEO
Jose Munoz, COO
Gang Hyun Seo, Director
Seung Jo Lee, Director

FINANCIAL DATA: *Note: Data for latest year may not have been available at press time.*

In U.S. $	2024	2023	2022	2021	2020	2019
Revenue	126,797,171,543	117,703,279,208	102,860,727,931	85,102,983,997	75,252,606,745	76,518,054,436
R&D Expense	1,717,449,000	1,565,468,000	1,273,323,000	1,110,720,000	968,083,400	933,237,100
Operating Income	10,303,760,000	10,945,820,000	7,109,312,000	4,832,884,000	1,732,783,000	2,608,942,000
Operating Margin %	.08%	.09%	.07%	.06%	.02%	.03%
SGA Expense	10,088,470,000	8,434,812,000	9,196,644,000	7,351,831,000	8,258,174,000	6,826,875,000
Net Income	9,064,307,000	8,655,492,000	5,328,850,000	3,576,286,000	1,030,721,000	2,156,362,000
Operating Cash Flow	-4,096,760,000	-1,822,573,000	7,689,917,000	-851,254,000	-296,536,100	303,755,500
Capital Expenditure	7,501,885,000	6,404,710,000	4,148,904,000	4,241,253,000	4,623,402,000	3,837,534,000
EBITDA	16,295,420,000	16,731,570,000	12,122,100,000	9,276,430,000	4,805,428,000	6,015,005,000
Return on Assets %	.04%	.04%	.03%	.02%	.01%	.02%
Return on Equity %	.12%	.14%	.09%	.07%	.02%	.04%
Debt to Equity	1.12%	.99%	.93%	1.00%	0.899	0.769

CONTACT INFORMATION:

Phone: 82 234641114   Fax: 82 234643477
Toll-Free:
Address: 12 Heolleung-ro Seocho-gu, Seoul, 06797 South Korea

STOCK TICKER/OTHER:

Stock Ticker: HYMLF   Exchange: PINX
Employees: 62,000   Fiscal Year Ends: 12/31
Parent Company: Hyundai Motor Group

SALARIES/BONUSES:

Top Exec. Salary: $ Bonus: $
Second Exec. Salary: $ Bonus: $

OTHER THOUGHTS:

Estimated Female Officers or Directors:
Hot Spot for Advancement for Women/Minorities:

IBM Research

NAIC Code: 541710

www.research.ibm.com

TYPES OF BUSINESS:

Research & Development
Hybrid Cloud
Artificial Intelligence
Quantum Computing
Science Innovation
Research and Development
Semiconductor Research
Chiplets

BRANDS/DIVISIONS/AFFILIATES:

International Business Machines Corporation (IBM)

CONTACTS:
Note: Officers with more than one job title may be intentionally listed here more than once.

Arvind Krishna, CEO
T.C. Chen, VP-Science

GROWTH PLANS/SPECIAL FEATURES:

IBM Research is the research and development arm of International Business Machines Corporation (IBM). The company often works with private customers and academic and government research centers. Featured research areas include hybrid cloud, artificial intelligence (AI), quantum computing and semiconductors. Hybrid cloud focuses on open standards and opensource code to build a seamless hybrid cloud platform, encompassing security, compliance and reliability for the enterprise. AI focuses on providing enterprises with AI that is adaptable to new challenges and domains and therefore engages in algorithm development and improving AI engineering tools and hardware. Quantum computing is engaged in innovating across the entire stack to make quantum frictionless and is therefore building libraries of circuits to empower researchers, developers and businesses to tap into quantum-as-a-service through the cloud via easy-to-use coding language. Last, the semiconductor research area develops new designs and methods to make semiconductors of the future smaller, faster, more energy efficient and reliable. This division is engaged in logic scaling, AI hardware and chiplet technology. IBM Research has lab locations worldwide, including Africa, Brazil, the U.S., the U.K., India, Canada, Ireland, Israel, Japan and Switzerland.

FINANCIAL DATA:
Note: Data for latest year may not have been available at press time.

In U.S. $	2024	2023	2022	2021	2020	2019
Revenue						
R&D Expense						
Operating Income						
Operating Margin %						
SGA Expense						
Net Income						
Operating Cash Flow						
Capital Expenditure						
EBITDA						
Return on Assets %						
Return on Equity %						
Debt to Equity						

CONTACT INFORMATION:

Phone: 914-945-3000   Fax: 914-945-2141
Toll-Free:
Address: 1101 Kitchawan Rd., Rte. 134, Yorktown Heights, NY 10598 United States

STOCK TICKER/OTHER:

Stock Ticker: Subsidiary   Exchange:
Employees: 3,000   Fiscal Year Ends: 12/31
Parent Company: International Business Machines Corporation (IBM)

SALARIES/BONUSES:

Top Exec. Salary: $ Bonus: $
Second Exec. Salary: $ Bonus: $

OTHER THOUGHTS:

Estimated Female Officers or Directors:
Hot Spot for Advancement for Women/Minorities: Y

IDOM

NAIC Code: 541330

www.idom.com

TYPES OF BUSINESS:

Engineering Consulting Services
Engineering Services
Architecture Services
Consulting Services
Renewable Energy Plants
Smart Cities and Urbanization
Nuclear Power Facilities
Telecommunication Networks

BRANDS/DIVISIONS/AFFILIATES:

CONTACTS: *Note: Officers with more than one job title may be intentionally listed here more than once.*

Ignacio Rey Gomez, CEO
Luis Rodriguez Llopis, Pres.

GROWTH PLANS/SPECIAL FEATURES:

IDOM is a consulting, engineering and architecture professional services firm in business since 1957, with operations in 125 countries. Through these core services, the company's capabilities are vast, and include architecture, city and territory, competitiveness and innovation, digital transformation, energy, environment, health, infrastructures, metals and minerals, manufacturing, oil and gas, rail and transit, science and technology, strategy and operations, supply chain, telecommunications and security and water cycle. IDOM's expertise spans areas such as airport infrastructure, leisure and culture architecture, urban renewal and smart growth, business industry entrepreneurship, Industry 4.0, hydroelectric power plants, offshore marine facilities, environmental consulting, waste and circular economy, healthcare facilities, medical equipment and technology, agro-industry, pharmaceutical facilities, bridge/tunnel/road infrastructure, mobility, mining, biofuels, metro systems and urban light rail systems, precision instruments, nuclear technology, financial advisory, ports and waterborne transport, communication networks and operators, water and wastewater treatment and desalination.

FINANCIAL DATA: *Note: Data for latest year may not have been available at press time.*

In U.S. $	2024	2023	2022	2021	2020	2019
Revenue	336,000,000	320,000,000	306,113,215	383,211,920	368,473,000	335,958,000
R&D Expense						
Operating Income						
Operating Margin %						
SGA Expense						
Net Income						
Operating Cash Flow						
Capital Expenditure						
EBITDA						
Return on Assets %						
Return on Equity %						
Debt to Equity						

CONTACT INFORMATION:

Phone: 34-94-479-7600   Fax: 34-94-476-1804
Toll-Free:
Address: Avda, Zarandoa 23, Bilbao, 48015 Spain

STOCK TICKER/OTHER:

Stock Ticker: Private   Exchange:
Employees: 4,300   Fiscal Year Ends:
Parent Company:

SALARIES/BONUSES:

Top Exec. Salary: $ Bonus: $
Second Exec. Salary: $ Bonus: $

OTHER THOUGHTS:

Estimated Female Officers or Directors:
Hot Spot for Advancement for Women/Minorities:

ILF Consulting Engineers Austria GmbH   www.ilf.com

NAIC Code: 541330

TYPES OF BUSINESS:

Engineering Consulting Services
Engineering
Consulting
Industrial and Infrastructure Projects
Oil and Gas Pipelines and Storage
Water and Environment Systems
Bioenergy and Hybrid Power
Transportation and Urban Spaces

BRANDS/DIVISIONS/AFFILIATES:

CONTACTS: Note: Officers with more than one job title may be intentionally listed here more than once.

Klaus Lasser, CEO
Markus Steiner, CFO
Hans Georg Wechsler, Chmn.

GROWTH PLANS/SPECIAL FEATURES:

ILF Consulting Engineers Austria GmbH is an international engineering and consulting firm that helps clients execute technically demanding industrial and infrastructure projects. ILF's main offices are in Austria and Germany, with more than 45 subsidiary offices strategically located worldwide. Business areas of focus include resources and sustainable energy; water and environment; energy and climate protection; and transportation and urban spaces. The resources and sustainable energy business division provides services regarding carbon management, fuels and chemicals, industrial, LNG (liquefied natural gas), mining, pipelines, refining, tank farms and terminals, underground storage and upstream. The water and environment business division engages in desalination, industrial water, urban water systems, wastewater treatment, water transmission and water treatment. The energy and climate protection business division specializes in bioenergy, energy storage, heating and cooling, hybrid power, hydrogen, hydropower, power transmission and distribution, solar power, thermal power, waste-to-energy and wind power. Last, the transportation and urban spaces business division is engaged in airports, buildings, railways, roads, ski resorts, structures, tunnels and caverns, urban development and urban transportation. ILF has successfully executed over 11,000 projects in more than 150 countries.

ILF offers its employees health benefits, and professional and personal development opportunities.

FINANCIAL DATA: Note: Data for latest year may not have been available at press time.

In U.S. $	2024	2023	2022	2021	2020	2019
Revenue						
R&D Expense						
Operating Income						
Operating Margin %						
SGA Expense						
Net Income						
Operating Cash Flow						
Capital Expenditure						
EBITDA						
Return on Assets %						
Return on Equity %						
Debt to Equity						

CONTACT INFORMATION:

Phone: 43-512-24120   Fax: 43-512-24125900
Toll-Free:
Address: Feldkreuzstrasse 3, Rum/Innsbruck, 6063 Austria

STOCK TICKER/OTHER:

Stock Ticker: Private   Exchange:
Employees: 2,500   Fiscal Year Ends:
Parent Company:

SALARIES/BONUSES:

Top Exec. Salary: $ Bonus: $
Second Exec. Salary: $ Bonus: $

OTHER THOUGHTS:

Estimated Female Officers or Directors:
Hot Spot for Advancement for Women/Minorities:

Illinois Tool Works Inc

www.itw.com

NAIC Code: 333249

TYPES OF BUSINESS:

Industrial Products & Equipment
Steel, Plastic & Paper Products
Power Systems & Electronics
Transportation-Related Components, Fasteners, Fluids & Polymers
Construction-Related Fasteners & Tools
Food Equipment & Adhesives
Decorative Surfacing Materials
Adhesives, Sealants & Lubrication

BRANDS/DIVISIONS/AFFILIATES:

GROWTH PLANS/SPECIAL FEATURES:

Founded in 1912, Illinois Tool Works has become a diversified industrial manufacturer through acquisitions and innovations that follow customer needs. ITW operates through seven business segments, with no segment representing more than one fifth of revenue. ITW's automotive OEM segment sells vehicle components; its food equipment segment sells commercial kitchen appliances; its test & measurement and electronics segment sells inspection and analysis equipment; its welding segment sells welding equipment and consumables; its polymers & fluids segment sells industrial and consumer adhesives, solvents, and coatings; its construction products segment sells building fasteners and tools; and its specialty products segment sells medical, packaging, HVAC, and airport ground equipment.

CONTACTS: Note: Officers with more than one job title may be intentionally listed here more than once.

Christopher OHerlihy, CEO
Michael Larsen, CFO
E. Santi, Chairman of the Board
Randall Scheuneman, Chief Accounting Officer
Guilherme de Figueiredo Silva, Executive VP
Kenneth Escoe, Executive VP
Axel Beck, Executive VP
Sharon Szafranski, Executive VP
Javier Carbonell, Executive VP
Patricia Hartzell, Executive VP
Michael Zimmerman, Executive VP
Jennifer Schott, General Counsel
Mary Lawler, Other Executive Officer

FINANCIAL DATA: Note: Data for latest year may not have been available at press time.

In U.S. $	2024	2023	2022	2021	2020	2019
Revenue	15,898,000,384	16,106,999,808	15,932,000,256	14,455,000,064	12,574,000,128	14,108,999,680
R&D Expense						
Operating Income	4,264,000,000	4,040,000,000	3,790,000,000	3,477,000,000	2,882,000,000	3,402,000,000
Operating Margin %	.27%	.25%	.24%	.24%	.23%	.24%
SGA Expense	2,675,000,000	2,638,000,000	2,579,000,000	2,356,000,000	2,163,000,000	2,361,000,000
Net Income	3,488,000,000	2,957,000,000	3,034,000,000	2,694,000,000	2,109,000,000	2,521,000,000
Operating Cash Flow	3,281,000,000	3,539,000,000	2,348,000,000	2,557,000,000	2,807,000,000	2,995,000,000
Capital Expenditure	437,000,000	455,000,000	412,000,000	296,000,000	236,000,000	326,000,000
EBITDA	5,107,000,000	4,484,000,000	4,455,000,000	3,938,000,000	3,337,000,000	3,935,000,000
Return on Assets %	.23%	.19%	.19%	.17%	.14%	.17%
Return on Equity %	1.10%	.97%	.90%	.79%	.68%	.80%
Debt to Equity	1.95%	2.15%	2.04%	1.94%	2.485	2.605

CONTACT INFORMATION:

Phone: 847 724-7500   Fax: 847 657-4261
Toll-Free:
Address: 155 Harlem Ave., Glenview, IL 60025 United States

STOCK TICKER/OTHER:

Stock Ticker: ITW   Exchange: NYS
Employees: 45,000   Fiscal Year Ends: 12/31
Parent Company:

SALARIES/BONUSES:

Top Exec. Salary: $1,300,000   Bonus: $
Second Exec. Salary: $942,227   Bonus: $

OTHER THOUGHTS:

Estimated Female Officers or Directors: 4
Hot Spot for Advancement for Women/Minorities: Y

Sales, profits and employees may be estimates. Financial information, benefits and other data can change quickly and may vary from those stated here.

IMI plc

NAIC Code: 333996

www.imiplc.com

TYPES OF BUSINESS:

Fluid Power Pump and Motor Manufacturing
Fluid Controls
HVAC Components
Engineering

BRANDS/DIVISIONS/AFFILIATES:

IMI CCI
IMI Bopp & Reuther
IMI Fluid Kinetics
Norgren
Bimba
IMI TA
IMI Flow Design
IMI Heimeier

GROWTH PLANS/SPECIAL FEATURES:

IMI PLC is engaged in designing, building, and servicing engineered products in fluid and motion control applications It develops technologies centered around valves and actuators to improve processes. It focuses on five market sectors: Process Automation, Industrial Automation, Life Science and Fluid Control, Climate Control, and Transport. Solutions can help with power generation in nuclear power plants, fuel delivery, or provide heating and cooling systems to various buildings. Customers work in energy, transportation, infrastructure, and other industrial sectors. It operates a service network to provide maintenance and repairs. Geographic Revenue based on Europe, the Americas, Asia Pacific, and the Middle East and Africa.

CONTACTS: Note: Officers with more than one job title may be intentionally listed here more than once.

Roy Twite, CEO
Daniel Shook, CFO
James Pike, Chairman of the Board
Louise Waldek, Secretary

FINANCIAL DATA: Note: Data for latest year may not have been available at press time.

In U.S. $	2024	2023	2022	2021	2020	2019
Revenue	2,975,322,841	2,956,474,813	2,758,568,626	2,512,195,811	2,456,997,425	2,521,619,825
R&D Expense						
Operating Income	479,552,100	428,931,200	401,466,700	337,248,200	305,340,800	356,769,500
Operating Margin %	.16%	.15%	.15%	.13%	.12%	.14%
SGA Expense						738,176,300
Net Income	334,555,600	319,477,000	304,667,700	264,278,700	229,140,300	210,157,400
Operating Cash Flow	500,285,100	488,976,200	381,945,300	362,424,000	443,202,000	423,815,200
Capital Expenditure	123,186,400	107,569,400	95,991,190	77,412,250	68,257,410	88,586,540
EBITDA	638,011,600	616,066,900	580,793,800	482,783,200	458,011,300	430,681,400
Return on Assets %	.10%	.09%	.10%	.10%	.09%	.09%
Return on Equity %	.23%	.25%	.27%	.25%	.23%	.23%
Debt to Equity	.42%	.59%	.75%	.64%	0.531	0.595

CONTACT INFORMATION:

Phone: 44 1217173700   Fax: 44 1217173701
Toll-Free:
Address: Lakeside, Solihull Parkway, Birmingham, B37 7XZ United Kingdom

STOCK TICKER/OTHER:

Stock Ticker: IMIUY
Employees: 10,772
Parent Company:

Exchange: PINX
Fiscal Year Ends: 12/31

SALARIES/BONUSES:

Top Exec. Salary: $1,117,429   Bonus: $2,181,006
Second Exec. Salary: $776,815   Bonus: $1,145,701

OTHER THOUGHTS:

Estimated Female Officers or Directors: 3
Hot Spot for Advancement for Women/Minorities: Y

Infineon Technologies AG

NAIC Code: 334413

www.infineon.com

TYPES OF BUSINESS:

Semiconductor Manufacturing
Semiconductor Production
Automotive
Power Systems
Sensors
Security Systems
Mobility
Internet of Things

BRANDS/DIVISIONS/AFFILIATES:

GROWTH PLANS/SPECIAL FEATURES:

Infineon Technologies headquartered in Munich, was spun off from German industrial conglomerate Siemens in 2000 and today is one of Europe's largest chipmakers. The company is a leader in the automotive semiconductor market with prominent products used in active safety and powertrain content within vehicles. Infineon is also the market leader in power semiconductors used to deliver voltage within a wide variety of electrical systems. The company operates in four segments: automotive, or ATV, green industrial power, or GIP, power and sensor systems, or PSS, and connected secure systems, or CSS.

CONTACTS: *Note: Officers with more than one job title may be intentionally listed here more than once.*

Peter Gruber, CFO, Divisional
Herbert Diess, Chairman of the Board
Johann Dechant, Director

FINANCIAL DATA: *Note: Data for latest year may not have been available at press time.*

In U.S. $	2024	2023	2022	2021	2020	2019
Revenue	16,975,028,177	18,511,918,512	16,138,479,454	12,553,915,727	9,724,177,155	9,113,507,606
R&D Expense	2,253,121,000	2,253,121,000	2,040,863,000	1,643,587,000	1,263,337,000	1,072,645,000
Operating Income	2,485,812,000	4,481,271,000	3,229,285,000	1,668,558,000	659,477,900	1,317,821,000
Operating Margin %	.15%	.24%	.20%	.13%	.07%	.14%
SGA Expense	1,763,905,000	1,814,983,000	1,776,390,000	1,536,890,000	1,182,747,000	981,838,800
Net Income	1,476,731,000	3,560,726,000	2,473,326,000	1,326,901,000	417,707,100	987,514,200
Operating Cash Flow	3,155,505,000	4,494,892,000	4,517,594,000	3,479,001,000	2,055,619,000	1,817,253,000
Capital Expenditure	3,086,266,000	3,398,411,000	2,622,021,000	1,699,205,000	1,247,446,000	1,646,992,000
EBITDA	4,744,608,000	6,620,886,000	5,140,749,000	3,390,466,000	2,059,024,000	2,372,304,000
Return on Assets %	.04%	.11%	.09%	.05%	.02%	.07%
Return on Equity %	.07%	.19%	.16%	.11%	.04%	.12%
Debt to Equity	.27%	.28%	.35%	.53%	0.662	0.178

CONTACT INFORMATION:

Phone: 49 89-234-0   Fax: 49-89-2349553431
Toll-Free: 49-800-951-951-951
Address: Biberger Strasse 93, Neubiberg, 82008 Germany

STOCK TICKER/OTHER:

Stock Ticker: IFNNY   Exchange: PINX
Employees: 58,065   Fiscal Year Ends: 09/30
Parent Company:

SALARIES/BONUSES:

Top Exec. Salary: $ Bonus: $
Second Exec. Salary: $ Bonus: $

OTHER THOUGHTS:

Estimated Female Officers or Directors:
Hot Spot for Advancement for Women/Minorities:

Innolux Corporation

NAIC Code: 334419

www.innolux.com

TYPES OF BUSINESS:

LCD (Liquid Crystal Display) Unit Screens Manufacturing
Liquid Crystal Displays
Touch Panels and Sensors
Computer Monitor and Laptop Panels
Medical and Automotive Panels
Tablet and Smartphone Display Applications
Consumer Electronic Applications
Fabrication and Manufacturing Facilities

BRANDS/DIVISIONS/AFFILIATES:

InnoCare Optoelectronics Corporation

CONTACTS: *Note: Officers with more than one job title may be intentionally listed here more than once.*

Hung Jinyang, CEO
Hung-Wen Yang, Pres.
Wen-Jyh Sah, VP
Ching-Lung Ting, VP
Chih-Hung Shiao, VP
Hung-Wen Yang, Associate VP
Hung Jinyang, Chmn.

GROWTH PLANS/SPECIAL FEATURES:

Innolux Corporation manufactures thin-film transistor liquid-crystal displays (TFT-LCD) and touch panels used to enhance resolution, color and brightness in a variety of LCD display products. The company's LCD TV panels are produced with light-emitting diode (LED) technology and range from 18.5 to 100 inches in size. They feature environmentally friendly components for low-energy consumption, low weight, reduced materials use, mercury-free lighting and low electromagnetic radiation. Other product lines by Innolux include desktop and laptop applications, commercial/automotive and industrial display applications, smartphone and mobile phone panel applications, smart retail solutions and many more. The firm owns several TFT-LCD and touch sensor fabrication facilities in Jhunan and Tainan, Taiwan, with production lines spanning all generations from G3.5, G4, G5, G6, G7.5 to G8.6. Innolux integrates the product manufacturing supply chain process and provides customers with solutions through its innovative operation approach of panel-centric and vertical integration. The company also focuses on process technology and components. Affiliate, InnoCare Optoelectronics Corporation, provides X-ray tablet detector solutions, with a focus on the manufacture of X-ray FPD key parts, substrates and assembly. InnoCare integrates with Innolux TFT manufacturing and the X-ray supply chain in Taiwan.

Innolux offers its employees labor and health insurance, an employee stock ownership program, various insurance options, a retirement plan, all of which may vary depending on location.

FINANCIAL DATA: *Note: Data for latest year may not have been available at press time.*

In U.S. $	2024	2023	2022	2021	2020	2019
Revenue		6,873,903,000	6,614,409,628	12,632,529,622	9,599,380,000	8,379,760,000
R&D Expense						
Operating Income						
Operating Margin %						
SGA Expense						
Net Income		-605,208,000	-827,555,139	1,701,055,997	58,320,300	578,602,000
Operating Cash Flow						
Capital Expenditure						
EBITDA						
Return on Assets %						
Return on Equity %						
Debt to Equity						

CONTACT INFORMATION:

Phone: 886 37586000   Fax:
Toll-Free:
Address: No. 160, Kesyue Rd., Chu-Nan Site Hsinchu, Taipei City, 35053 Taiwan

STOCK TICKER/OTHER:

Stock Ticker: 3481
Employees: 29,785
Parent Company:

Exchange: TWSE
Fiscal Year Ends: 12/31

SALARIES/BONUSES:

Top Exec. Salary: $ Bonus: $
Second Exec. Salary: $ Bonus: $

OTHER THOUGHTS:

Estimated Female Officers or Directors:
Hot Spot for Advancement for Women/Minorities: Y

Integrated Design & Engineering Holdings Co Ltd www.id-and-e-hd.co.jp/english

NAIC Code: 541330

TYPES OF BUSINESS:

Engineering Consulting Services
Consultancy
Technical Assistance
Water Resources
Land Development
Disaster Prevention
Power Generation
Engineering

BRANDS/DIVISIONS/AFFILIATES:

Nippon Koei Urban Space Co Ltd
Nippon Koei Co Ltd
Nippon Koei Energy Solutions Co Ltd

CONTACTS: Note: Officers with more than one job title may be intentionally listed here more than once.

Hiroaki Shinya, Pres.

GROWTH PLANS/SPECIAL FEATURES:

Integrated Design & Engineering Holdings Co, Ltd. (IDE), formerly Nippon Koei Group, is a Japanese consulting firm that provides technical assistance and other services to developing countries. IDE's global network spans more than 160 countries and regions, with more than 80 subsidiaries, as well. The company's services address fields such as water, energy, transportation, disaster prevention and environmental management. IDE's business is divided into three businesses: consulting, which is operated by Nippon Koei Co., Ltd; energy, operated by Nippon Koei Energy Solutions Co., Ltd; and urban and spatial development, operated by Nippon Koei Urban Space Co., Ltd. The domestic and international consulting business segments offer consultancy services regarding river and water resources, water environment, rural/urban/regional development, transportation, disaster prevention, environmental geohazard management, railway, sustainable regional development and more. The energy segment is engaged in the generation of power, energy management and energy storage and solutions. The urban and spatial development segment is engaged in architecture, landscape and urban design, the revitalization of historic buildings and much more.

FINANCIAL DATA: Note: Data for latest year may not have been available at press time.

In U.S. $	2024	2023	2022	2021	2020	2019
Revenue		978,877,000	956,656,000	1,066,459,000	1,039,540,000	1,005,960,000
R&D Expense						
Operating Income						
Operating Margin %						
SGA Expense						
Net Income		21,393,000	38,337,000	40,887,000	25,253,400	30,737,600
Operating Cash Flow						
Capital Expenditure						
EBITDA						
Return on Assets %						
Return on Equity %						
Debt to Equity						

CONTACT INFORMATION:

Phone: 81 3-3238-8030   Fax: 81 3-3238-8326
Toll-Free:
Address: 5-4 Kojimachi, Chiyoda-ku, Tokyo, 102-8539 Japan

STOCK TICKER/OTHER:

Stock Ticker: 9161   Exchange: Tokyo
Employees: 6,335   Fiscal Year Ends: 06/30
Parent Company:

SALARIES/BONUSES:

Top Exec. Salary: $ Bonus: $
Second Exec. Salary: $ Bonus: $

OTHER THOUGHTS:

Estimated Female Officers or Directors:
Hot Spot for Advancement for Women/Minorities:

Intel Corporation

NAIC Code: 334413

TYPES OF BUSINESS:

Microprocessors
Processors
Chipsets
Technologies
Graphics Processing Units
Memory and Storage Products
Programmable Devices
Internet of Things

BRANDS/DIVISIONS/AFFILIATES:

Mobileye

GROWTH PLANS/SPECIAL FEATURES:

Intel is a leading digital chipmaker, focused on the design and manufacturing of microprocessors for the global personal computer and data center markets. Intel pioneered the x86 architecture for microprocessors and was the prime proponent of Moore's law for advances in semiconductor manufacturing. Intel remains the market share leader in central processing units in both the PC and server end markets. Intel has also been expanding into new adjacencies, such as communications infrastructure, automotive, and the Internet of Things. Further, Intel expects to leverage its chip manufacturing capabilities into an outsourced foundry model where it constructs chips for others.

CONTACTS: Note: Officers with more than one job title may be intentionally listed here more than once.

Michelle Holthaus, CEO, Divisional
David Zinsner, CFO
Frank Yeary, Chairman of the Board
Scott Gawel, Chief Accounting Officer
April Boise, Chief Legal Officer
Ann Kelleher, Executive VP, Divisional
Christoph Schell, Executive VP

FINANCIAL DATA: Note: Data for latest year may not have been available at press time.

In U.S. $	2024	2023	2022	2021	2020	2019
Revenue	53,100,998,656	54,228,000,768	63,054,000,128	79,023,996,928	77,866,999,808	71,964,999,680
R&D Expense	16,546,000,000	16,046,000,000	17,528,000,000	15,190,000,000	13,556,000,000	13,362,000,000
Operating Income	-4,708,000,000	31,000,000	2,336,000,000	22,082,000,000	23,876,000,000	22,428,000,000
Operating Margin %	-.09%	.00%	.04%	.28%	.31%	.31%
SGA Expense	5,507,000,000	5,634,000,000	7,002,000,000	6,543,000,000	6,180,000,000	6,350,000,000
Net Income	-18,756,000,000	1,689,000,000	8,014,000,000	19,868,000,000	20,899,000,000	21,048,000,000
Operating Cash Flow	8,288,000,000	11,471,000,000	15,433,000,000	29,456,000,000	35,864,000,000	33,145,000,000
Capital Expenditure	23,944,000,000	25,750,000,000	24,844,000,000	20,329,000,000	14,453,000,000	16,213,000,000
EBITDA	1,203,000,000	11,242,000,000	21,299,000,000	34,092,000,000	37,946,000,000	35,373,000,000
Return on Assets %	-.10%	.01%	.05%	.12%	.14%	.16%
Return on Equity %	-.18%	.02%	.08%	.23%	.26%	.28%
Debt to Equity	.47%	.44%	.37%	.35%	0.418	0.327

CONTACT INFORMATION:

Phone: 408 765-8080   Fax: 408 765-2633
Toll-Free: 800-628-8686
Address: 2200 Mission College Blvd., Santa Clara, CA 95054-1549 United States

STOCK TICKER/OTHER:

Stock Ticker: INTC   Exchange: NAS
Employees: 124,800   Fiscal Year Ends: 12/31
Parent Company:

SALARIES/BONUSES:

Top Exec. Salary: $721,900   Bonus: $1,500,000
Second Exec. Salary: $1,145,800   Bonus: $

OTHER THOUGHTS:

Estimated Female Officers or Directors: 10
Hot Spot for Advancement for Women/Minorities: Y

Intellectual Ventures Management LLC www.intellectualventures.com

NAIC Code: 541710

TYPES OF BUSINESS:

Research & Engineering
Invention Creation and Incubation
Invention Commercialization
Patent Licensing
Technologies
Advanced Chemistry and Physical Sciences
Metamaterials
Cold-Chain Technologies

BRANDS/DIVISIONS/AFFILIATES:

Invention Investment Fund
Enterprise Science Fund
Intellectual Ventures Lab (IV Lab)
Deep Science Fund

CONTACTS: Note: Officers with more than one job title may be intentionally listed here more than once.

Nathan Myhrvold, CEO
Larry Froeber, CFO
Nicole Grogan, Chief People Officer
David Kris, General Counsel
Shelby Barnes, Sr. VP-Corp. Comm.
Andy Elder, Exec. VP-Global Licensing
Jim Wallace, Sr. VP-Systems & Tech. Group
Loria Yeadon, Exec. VP-Invention Investment Fund
Casey Tegreene, Exec. VP-Invention Science Fund
Maurizio Vecchione, VP-Global Good

GROWTH PLANS/SPECIAL FEATURES:

Intellectual Ventures Management, LLC (IVM) is a global business that creates, incubates and commercializes inventions. The Invention Investment Fund (IIF) is a pioneer in patent licensing, having invested over $3 billion in patents acquired across more than 1,000 distinct transactions. The fund's patents have generated billions of dollars in licensing revenue. It offers licenses which grant companies rights to patents in divers technical categories acquired from a variety of sources, from independent inventors, universities, startups and small/medium-sized businesses to Fortune 500 firms, all while generating a return for IVM's investors. IIF has 16 technology areas in which some include fields such as wireless communication, hybrid cloud infrastructure, memory, storage, networking, security, data acquisition, autonomous vehicle engineering, digital payments and many others. The Enterprise Science Fund investigates applications for the company's inventions and ideas in areas such as advanced chemistry, physical sciences and biomedical devices; meanwhile, the Deep Science Fund is responsible for leveraging a multidisciplinary approach to identify, develop and commercialize impactful technologies. Intellectual Ventures Laboratory (IV Lab), an 87,000+ sq. ft. facility and team, engages in research and development to provide advanced solutions to very complex problems that affect the world. IV Lab comprises scientists, engineers and inventors that translate scientific research into technological solutions by developing early-stage ideas into proofs-of-concept and prototypes, and then works with partners to introduce them to the world. Areas of invention by IV Lab include metamaterials as disruptive technology in satellite communications, cold-chain technologies for creating a super-insulated container for safely storing vaccines between 0- to-10 degrees Celsius for 35 days or more, sodium-cooled traveling wave reactor (TWR) energy for leading to key advancements in fuel/materials/engineering, among others. Based in Washington state, USA, the firm has an international office in Dublin, Ireland.

FINANCIAL DATA: Note: Data for latest year may not have been available at press time.

In U.S. $	2024	2023	2022	2021	2020	2019
Revenue						
R&D Expense						
Operating Income						
Operating Margin %						
SGA Expense						
Net Income						
Operating Cash Flow						
Capital Expenditure						
EBITDA						
Return on Assets %						
Return on Equity %						
Debt to Equity						

CONTACT INFORMATION:

Phone: 425-467-2300   Fax:
Toll-Free:
Address: 3150 139th Ave. SE, Bldg. 4, Bellevue, WA 98005 United States

STOCK TICKER/OTHER:

Stock Ticker: Private   Exchange:
Employees: 650   Fiscal Year Ends:
Parent Company:

SALARIES/BONUSES:

Top Exec. Salary: $ Bonus: $
Second Exec. Salary: $ Bonus: $

OTHER THOUGHTS:

Estimated Female Officers or Directors: 4
Hot Spot for Advancement for Women/Minorities: Y

Sales, profits and employees may be estimates. Financial information, benefits and other data can change quickly and may vary from those stated here.

International Business Machines Corporation (IBM)

www.ibm.com
NAIC Code: 541513

TYPES OF BUSINESS:

Computer Facilities and Business Process Outsourcing
Computer Facilities Management
Business Process Outsourcing
Software & Hardware
Cloud-Based Computer Services
IT Consulting & Outsourcing
Financial Services
Data Analytics and Health Care Analytics

BRANDS/DIVISIONS/AFFILIATES:

Aspera
Cognos
IBM
Red Hat OpenShift
Watson
Kyndryl Holdings Inc

GROWTH PLANS/SPECIAL FEATURES:

IBM looks to be a part of every aspect of an enterprise's IT needs. The company primarily sells software, IT services, consulting, and hardware. IBM operates in 175 countries and employs approximately 300,000 people. The company has a robust roster of business partners to service its clients, which include 95% of all Fortune 500 companies. Primary products include its mainframes, Red Hat software, transaction processing software, and IT consulting.

IBM offers employees medical, vision, dental and disability insurance; a flexible spending account; and 401(k) and stock purchase options.

CONTACTS: Note: Officers with more than one job title may be intentionally listed here more than once.

Arvind Krishna, CEO
James Kavanaugh, CFO, Divisional
Nicolas Fehring, Chief Accounting Officer
Nickle Lamoreaux, Other Executive Officer
Robert Thomas, Other Executive Officer
Michelle Browdy, Senior VP, Divisional
Gary Cohn, Vice Chairman

FINANCIAL DATA: Note: Data for latest year may not have been available at press time.

In U.S. $	2024	2023	2022	2021	2020	2019
Revenue	62,753,001,472	61,859,999,744	60,529,999,872	57,351,000,064	55,179,001,856	57,713,999,872
R&D Expense	7,479,000,000	6,775,000,000	6,567,000,000	6,488,000,000	6,262,000,000	5,910,000,000
Operating Income	10,074,000,000	9,821,000,000	8,174,000,000	6,865,000,000	4,662,000,000	7,538,000,000
Operating Margin %	.16%	.16%	.14%	.12%	.08%	.13%
SGA Expense	17,910,000,000	17,559,000,000	18,609,000,000	18,745,000,000	20,561,000,000	18,724,000,000
Net Income	6,023,000,000	7,502,000,000	1,640,000,000	5,742,000,000	5,590,000,000	9,431,000,000
Operating Cash Flow	13,445,000,000	13,931,000,000	10,435,000,000	12,796,000,000	18,197,000,000	14,770,000,000
Capital Expenditure	1,685,000,000	1,810,000,000	1,972,000,000	2,768,000,000	3,230,000,000	2,907,000,000
EBITDA	12,176,000,000	14,693,000,000	7,174,000,000	12,409,000,000	10,555,000,000	14,609,000,000
Return on Assets %	.04%	.06%	.01%	.04%	.04%	.07%
Return on Equity %	.24%	.34%	.08%	.29%	.27%	.50%
Debt to Equity	1.92%	2.34%	2.20%	2.51%	2.764	2.782

CONTACT INFORMATION:

Phone: 914 499-1900   Fax: 800-314-1092
Toll-Free: 800-426-4968
Address: 1 New Orchard Rd., Armonk, NY 10504 United States

STOCK TICKER/OTHER:

Stock Ticker: IBM   Exchange: NYS
Employees: 282,200   Fiscal Year Ends: 12/31
Parent Company:

SALARIES/BONUSES:

Top Exec. Salary: $1,500,000   Bonus: $
Second Exec. Salary: $467,500   Bonus: $750,000

OTHER THOUGHTS:

Estimated Female Officers or Directors: 6
Hot Spot for Advancement for Women/Minorities: Y

Intertek Group plc

www.intertek.com

NAIC Code: 541380

TYPES OF BUSINESS:
Testing Laboratories, Safety and Compliance Services
Quality Assurance
Operations Testing
Operations Inspection
Operations Certification

BRANDS/DIVISIONS/AFFILIATES:

GROWTH PLANS/SPECIAL FEATURES:
Intertek is one of the largest and oldest companies in the testing, inspection, and certification industry. Its primary activities involve testing products and materials, inspecting sites/industrial equipment, and certifying products and systems to ensure global/company standards. Intertek is one of only three TIC companies that operate globally across numerous industries. The firm was listed in 2002 following a divestment by Charterhouse. It employs over 40,000 people worldwide.

CONTACTS:
Note: Officers with more than one job title may be intentionally listed here more than once.
Andre Lacroix, CEO
Colm Deasy, CFO
Andrew Martin, Chairman of the Board
Fiona Evans, Secretary

FINANCIAL DATA:
Note: Data for latest year may not have been available at press time.

In U.S. $	2024	2023	2022	2021	2020	2019
Revenue	4,568,265,352	4,481,428,700	4,298,601,418	3,751,195,577	3,691,150,855	4,021,398,204
R&D Expense						
Operating Income	721,212,900	654,571,100	609,066,100	598,565,000	537,981,500	666,553,200
Operating Margin %	.16%	.15%	.14%	.16%	.15%	.17%
SGA Expense						
Net Income	465,012,000	400,389,600	388,811,500	387,869,000	332,940,000	421,526,500
Operating Cash Flow	803,875,800	720,270,500	753,793,400	740,734,300	752,312,400	757,697,700
Capital Expenditure	181,750,500	157,382,500	156,844,000	130,725,700	107,434,700	157,247,800
EBITDA	976,471,400	910,368,100	908,617,900	860,016,400	774,257,200	917,368,800
Return on Assets %	.10%	.08%	.08%	.10%	.09%	.11%
Return on Equity %	.25%	.23%	.24%	.28%	.26%	.34%
Debt to Equity	.69%	.79%	.82%	.71%	0.775	0.839

CONTACT INFORMATION:
Phone: 44 2073963400   Fax: 44 2073963480
Toll-Free:
Address: 33 Cavendish Square, London, W1G 0PS United Kingdom

STOCK TICKER/OTHER:
Stock Ticker: IKTSF   Exchange: PINX
Employees: 43,908   Fiscal Year Ends: 12/31
Parent Company:

SALARIES/BONUSES:
Top Exec. Salary: $1,414,961   Bonus: $2,726,258
Second Exec. Salary: $647,570   Bonus: $1,287,063

OTHER THOUGHTS:
Estimated Female Officers or Directors: 4
Hot Spot for Advancement for Women/Minorities: Y

Introba Inc

NAIC Code: 541330

TYPES OF BUSINESS:

Engineering Consulting Services
Building Engineering
Consultancy
Digital Solutions and Technologies
Baggage Handling Systems
Design Analytics
Medical Equipment Planning
Sustainable Strategies

BRANDS/DIVISIONS/AFFILIATES:

Ross & Baruzzini
Introba

GROWTH PLANS/SPECIAL FEATURES:

Introba Inc., product of the merger of Integral Group, Inc. and Ross & Baruzzini, is a building engineering and consulting firm with offices across the U.S., Canada, the U.K., Singapore, Serbia and Australia. Introba combines digital solutions with emerging technologies and sustainable strategies to transform the built environment. The company collaborates with clients to create smart, safe, resilient and connected living systems and spaces for the benefit of communities, the planet and the future. As a result, Introba's solutions include baggage handling systems, climate and sustainability, design analytics, digital advisory, engineering, medical equipment planning, security and resilience, technology and wireless systems. Sectors served span aviation, commercial, culture, entertainment, education, government, healthcare, industrial, utilities, mobility, science and technology.

CONTACTS: Note: Officers with more than one job title may be intentionally listed here more than once.

Matthew Cummings, CEO
William Harnagel, CFO
Preethi Santhanam, Chief People Officer
Stephen Cayea, CIO

FINANCIAL DATA: Note: Data for latest year may not have been available at press time.

In U.S. $	2024	2023	2022	2021	2020	2019
Revenue						
R&D Expense						
Operating Income						
Operating Margin %						
SGA Expense						
Net Income						
Operating Cash Flow						
Capital Expenditure						
EBITDA						
Return on Assets %						
Return on Equity %						
Debt to Equity						

CONTACT INFORMATION:

Phone: Fax:
Toll-Free: 800 404-7677
Address: 600 Riveredge Pkwy. NW, Ste. 900, Atlanta, GA 30328 United States

STOCK TICKER/OTHER:

Stock Ticker: Private   Exchange:
Employees: 500   Fiscal Year Ends:
Parent Company:

SALARIES/BONUSES:

Top Exec. Salary: $ Bonus: $
Second Exec. Salary: $ Bonus: $

OTHER THOUGHTS:

Estimated Female Officers or Directors:
Hot Spot for Advancement for Women/Minorities:

Intuit Inc

NAIC Code: 511210Q

www.intuit.com

TYPES OF BUSINESS:

Computer Software-Financial Management
Business Accounting Software
Consumer Finance Software
Tax Preparation Software
Online Financial Services

GROWTH PLANS/SPECIAL FEATURES:

Intuit serves small and midsize businesses with accounting software QuickBooks and online marketing platform Mailchimp. The company also operates retail tax filing tool TurboTax, personal finance platform Credit Karma, and a suite of professional tax offerings for accountants. Founded in the mid-1980s, Intuit enjoys a dominant market share for small business accounting and do-it-yourself tax filing in the US.

BRANDS/DIVISIONS/AFFILIATES:

Credit Karma
ProConnect
QuickBooks
TurboTax
Mint
Lacerte
ProFile
Rocket Science Group LLC (The)

CONTACTS:
Note: Officers with more than one job title may be intentionally listed here more than once.

Sasan Goodarzi, CEO
Sandeep Aujla, CFO
Suzanne Johnson, Chairman of the Board
Lauren Hotz, Chief Accounting Officer
Alex Balazs, Chief Technology Officer
Kerry McLean, Executive VP
Marianna Tessel, Executive VP
Mark Notarainni, Executive VP
Laura Fennell, Executive VP
Scott Cook, Founder

FINANCIAL DATA:
Note: Data for latest year may not have been available at press time.

In U.S. $	2024	2023	2022	2021	2020	2019
Revenue	16,284,999,680	14,368,000,000	12,725,999,616	9,633,000,448	7,679,000,064	6,784,000,000
R&D Expense	2,754,000,000	2,539,000,000	2,347,000,000	1,678,000,000	1,392,000,000	1,233,000,000
Operating Income	3,877,000,000	3,153,000,000	2,559,000,000	2,528,000,000	2,181,000,000	1,857,000,000
Operating Margin %	.24%	.22%	.20%	.26%	.28%	.27%
SGA Expense	5,706,000,000	5,050,000,000	4,998,000,000	3,598,000,000	2,722,000,000	2,521,000,000
Net Income	2,963,000,000	2,384,000,000	2,066,000,000	2,062,000,000	1,826,000,000	1,557,000,000
Operating Cash Flow	4,884,000,000	5,046,000,000	3,889,000,000	3,250,000,000	2,414,000,000	2,324,000,000
Capital Expenditure	250,000,000	260,000,000	229,000,000	125,000,000	137,000,000	155,000,000
EBITDA	4,581,000,000	4,043,000,000	3,369,000,000	2,948,000,000	2,430,000,000	2,121,000,000
Return on Assets %	.10%	.09%	.10%	.16%	.21%	.27%
Return on Equity %	.17%	.14%	.16%	.28%	.41%	.47%
Debt to Equity	.33%	.38%	.42%	.24%	0.441	0.103

CONTACT INFORMATION:

Phone: 650 944-6000   Fax: 650 944-3060
Toll-Free: 800-446-8848
Address: 2700 Coast Ave., Mountain View, CA 94043 United States

STOCK TICKER/OTHER:

Stock Ticker: INTU   Exchange: NAS
Employees: 18,800   Fiscal Year Ends: 07/31
Parent Company:

SALARIES/BONUSES:

Top Exec. Salary: $1,200,000   Bonus: $
Second Exec. Salary: $770,000   Bonus: $

OTHER THOUGHTS:

Estimated Female Officers or Directors: 5
Hot Spot for Advancement for Women/Minorities: Y

IPS - Integrated Project Services LLC

www.ipsdb.com

NAIC Code: 541330

TYPES OF BUSINESS:

Engineering Consulting Services
Architectural Services
Engineering Services
Consultancy
Development and Manufacturing Facilities
Project Management
Technology Solutions
Commissioning, Qualification and Validation

BRANDS/DIVISIONS/AFFILIATES:

Berkshire Hathaway Inc
Springfield

CONTACTS: *Note: Officers with more than one job title may be intentionally listed here more than once.*

Dave Goswami, CEO
John Williamson, CFO
Rebecca J. Savikas, Chief People Officer
Dave Goswami, Chmn.

GROWTH PLANS/SPECIAL FEATURES:

IPS-Integrated Project Services, LLC, owned by Berkshire Hathway, Inc., is an architectural, engineering and consulting (AEC) firm with offices spanning 17 countries on five continents. IPS provides technical and business consulting solutions; designs innovative, compliant, safe, efficient and sustainable solutions for technically-complex development and manufacturing facilities; creates high-performance systems and facilities through its engineering capabilities; evaluates the global supply chain, the local labor market and schedules to implement a procurement strategy for each client project; develops and executes project plans that maximize value and meet/exceed expectations; provides management teams to administer construction development and facility manufacturing for clients; to provide commissioning, qualification and validation services for client projects; and applies a lean integrated project delivery model that addresses the entire project lifecycle. Industries served by IPS include cell and gene therapy, pharmaceutical, biotechnology, biomanufacturing, animal health, medical device and diagnostics, consumer goods and science and technology. Springtide is a division of IPS that provides engineering, procurement and construction management (EPCM) services.

IPS offers its employees health and insurance coverage, disability benefits, retirement and savings plans, and a variety of employee assistance programs, plans and perks.

FINANCIAL DATA: *Note: Data for latest year may not have been available at press time.*

In U.S. $	2024	2023	2022	2021	2020	2019
Revenue						
R&D Expense						
Operating Income						
Operating Margin %						
SGA Expense						
Net Income						
Operating Cash Flow						
Capital Expenditure						
EBITDA						
Return on Assets %						
Return on Equity %						
Debt to Equity						

CONTACT INFORMATION:

Phone: 610-828-4090   Fax: 610-828-3656
Toll-Free:
Address: 721 Arbor Way, Ste. 100, Blue Bell, PA 19422 United States

STOCK TICKER/OTHER:

Stock Ticker: Subsidiary   Exchange:
Employees: 2,500   Fiscal Year Ends:
Parent Company: Berkshire Hathaway Inc

SALARIES/BONUSES:

Top Exec. Salary: $ Bonus: $
Second Exec. Salary: $ Bonus: $

OTHER THOUGHTS:

Estimated Female Officers or Directors:
Hot Spot for Advancement for Women/Minorities:

IQVIA Holdings Inc

NAIC Code: 541710

www.iqvia.com

TYPES OF BUSINESS:

Contract Research
Pharmaceutical, Biotech & Medical Device Research
Consulting & Training Services
Sales & Marketing Services

BRANDS/DIVISIONS/AFFILIATES:

IQVIA CORE
Q2 Solutions

GROWTH PLANS/SPECIAL FEATURES:

Iqvia is the result of the 2016 merger of Quintiles, a leading global contract research organization, and IMS Health, a leading healthcare data and analytics provider. The research and development segment focuses primarily on providing outsourced late-stage clinical trials for pharmaceutical, device, and diagnostic firms. The technology and analytics segment provides aggregated information and technology services to clients in the healthcare industry, including pharmaceutical companies, providers, payers, and policymakers, as well as data and analytics capabilities for clinical trials, including virtual trials. The company also has a small contract sales business.

CONTACTS: Note: Officers with more than one job title may be intentionally listed here more than once.

Ari Bousbib, CEO
Ronald Bruehlman, CFO
Keriann Cherofsky, Chief Accounting Officer
Eric Sherbet, Executive VP
W. Staub, President, Divisional

FINANCIAL DATA: Note: Data for latest year may not have been available at press time.

In U.S. $	2024	2023	2022	2021	2020	2019
Revenue	15,404,999,680	14,983,999,488	14,410,000,384	13,873,999,872	11,358,999,552	11,088,000,000
R&D Expense						
Operating Income	2,269,000,000	2,061,000,000	1,827,000,000	1,413,000,000	783,000,000	852,000,000
Operating Margin %	.15%	.14%	.13%	.10%	.07%	.08%
SGA Expense	1,992,000,000	2,053,000,000	2,071,000,000	1,964,000,000	1,789,000,000	1,734,000,000
Net Income	1,373,000,000	1,358,000,000	1,091,000,000	966,000,000	279,000,000	191,000,000
Operating Cash Flow	2,716,000,000	2,149,000,000	2,260,000,000	2,942,000,000	1,959,000,000	1,417,000,000
Capital Expenditure	602,000,000	649,000,000	674,000,000	640,000,000	616,000,000	582,000,000
EBITDA	3,453,000,000	3,256,000,000	2,909,000,000	2,767,000,000	2,076,000,000	2,001,000,000
Return on Assets %	.05%	.05%	.04%	.04%	.01%	.01%
Return on Equity %	.23%	.23%	.18%	.16%	.05%	.03%
Debt to Equity	2.14%	2.16%	2.23%	2.04%	2.125	1.989

CONTACT INFORMATION:

Phone: 919-998-2000   Fax:
Toll-Free: 866-267-4479
Address: 4820 Emperor Blvd., Durham, NC 27703 United States

STOCK TICKER/OTHER:

Stock Ticker: IQV
Employees: 87,000
Parent Company:

Exchange: NYS
Fiscal Year Ends: 12/31

SALARIES/BONUSES:

Top Exec. Salary: $1,800,000   Bonus: $
Second Exec. Salary: $905,000   Bonus: $

OTHER THOUGHTS:

Estimated Female Officers or Directors: 3
Hot Spot for Advancement for Women/Minorities: Y

Sales, profits and employees may be estimates. Financial information, benefits and other data can change quickly and may vary from those stated here.

Isuzu Motors Limited

www.isuzu.co.jp

NAIC Code: 336111

TYPES OF BUSINESS:

Automobile Manufacturing
Trucks & Buses
Diesel Engines
Logistics Services
Sport Utility Vehicles
Passenger Pickup Trucks
Commercial Trucks

BRANDS/DIVISIONS/AFFILIATES:

D-MAX
TRAGA
Erga
GALA
UD Trucks Corporation

GROWTH PLANS/SPECIAL FEATURES:

Isuzu Motors is a Japanese automobile manufacturing company focused on the production of commercial vehicles, passenger vehicles, and diesel engines. The company primarily manufactures light- to heavy-duty trucks, buses, pickup trucks, and industrial diesel engines. Isuzu derives the vast majority of revenue from vehicle sales. While Isuzu conducts sales across the globe, by individual country, Japan contributes the largest portion of consolidated revenue, followed by Thailand. The company mainly conducts manufacturing operations domestically.

CONTACTS: Note: Officers with more than one job title may be intentionally listed here more than once.

Masanori Katayama, CEO
Naohiro Yamaguchi, CFO
Shinsuke Minami, COO
Shinichi Takahashi, Director
Tetsuya Ikemoto, Director
Shun Fujimori, Director

FINANCIAL DATA: Note: Data for latest year may not have been available at press time.

In U.S. $	2024	2023	2022	2021	2020	2019
Revenue	23,512,053,558	22,185,066,901	17,455,505,976	13,247,362,114	14,439,989,047	14,920,634,018
R&D Expense						
Operating Income	2,034,796,000	1,760,282,000	1,299,660,000	664,655,700	976,027,600	1,227,361,000
Operating Margin %	.09%	.08%	.07%	.05%	.07%	.08%
SGA Expense	590,072,200	626,062,300	446,369,100	314,253,000	383,719,800	398,882,300
Net Income	1,224,951,000	1,053,478,000	876,097,000	296,501,000	563,954,500	787,586,800
Operating Cash Flow	2,072,813,000	1,576,541,000	1,194,502,000	1,547,612,000	858,796,200	1,086,823,000
Capital Expenditure						
EBITDA	2,981,686,000	2,662,747,000	2,145,793,000	1,209,726,000	1,562,212,000	1,811,275,000
Return on Assets %	.06%	.05%	.05%	.02%	.04%	.05%
Return on Equity %	.13%	.12%	.11%	.04%	.09%	.12%
Debt to Equity	.23%	.30%	.32%	.25%	0.263	0.239

CONTACT INFORMATION:

Phone: 81 354711141   Fax: 81 354711043
Toll-Free:
Address: 6-26-1 Minami-Oi, Shinagawa-Ku, Tokyo, 140-8722 Japan

STOCK TICKER/OTHER:

Stock Ticker: ISUZF   Exchange: PINX
Employees: 47,255   Fiscal Year Ends: 03/31
Parent Company:

SALARIES/BONUSES:

Top Exec. Salary: $ Bonus: $
Second Exec. Salary: $ Bonus: $

OTHER THOUGHTS:

Estimated Female Officers or Directors:
Hot Spot for Advancement for Women/Minorities:

ITT Inc

NAIC Code: 336000

TYPES OF BUSINESS:

Industrial and Transportation Equipment Manufacturing
Shock Absorbers
Industrial Pumps
Connectors
Controls
Motion Technologies
Fluid Handling Equipment
Industrial Process Equipment

BRANDS/DIVISIONS/AFFILIATES:

Axtone
biw
Compact Automation Products
Enidine
Goulds Pumps
Rheinhutte Pumpen
Veam
Wolverine Advanced Materials

CONTACTS: *Note: Officers with more than one job title may be intentionally listed here more than once.*

Luca Savi, CEO
Emmanuel Caprais, CFO
Timothy Powers, Chairman of the Board
Cheryl de Mesa Graziano, Chief Accounting Officer
Lori Marino, Chief Compliance Officer
Bartek Makowiecki, Chief Strategy Officer
Maurine Lembesis, Other Executive Officer
Fernando Roland, President, Divisional
Davide Barbon, President, Geographical

GROWTH PLANS/SPECIAL FEATURES:

ITT began its journey as International Telephone & Telegraph in 1920. Through decades of acquisitions in the mid-1900s, ITT went from manufacturing telephone switching equipment to operating hotels, car rentals, insurance agencies, and bread bakeries. In 1995, the firm split into three separate entities, one of which is the ITT in current operation. After a few more spinoffs in 2011, today ITT Inc. sells automotive, industrial, and aerospace products such as brake pads, seals, pumps, valves, connectors, and regulators. It has operations around the globe with notable exposures to North America, Europe, and Asia.

ITT offers its employees health and retirement benefits, as well as a range of employee assistance plans and programs.

FINANCIAL DATA: *Note: Data for latest year may not have been available at press time.*

In U.S. $	2024	2023	2022	2021	2020	2019
Revenue	3,630,700,032	3,283,000,064	2,987,699,968	2,764,999,936	2,477,799,936	2,846,400,000
R&D Expense	116,300,000	102,600,000	96,500,000	94,900,000	84,900,000	97,900,000
Operating Income	628,700,000	536,200,000	451,700,000	408,500,000	321,300,000	357,100,000
Operating Margin %	.17%	.16%	.15%	.15%	.13%	.13%
SGA Expense	502,300,000	468,500,000	374,100,000	381,700,000	345,200,000	407,200,000
Net Income	518,300,000	410,500,000	367,000,000	316,300,000	72,500,000	325,100,000
Operating Cash Flow	562,100,000	537,700,000	277,800,000	-7,600,000	436,900,000	358,600,000
Capital Expenditure	123,900,000	107,600,000	103,900,000	88,400,000	63,700,000	91,400,000
EBITDA	821,500,000	647,900,000	580,100,000	521,600,000	433,500,000	470,500,000
Return on Assets %	.12%	.11%	.10%	.08%	.02%	.08%
Return on Equity %	.20%	.17%	.16%	.15%	.03%	.17%
Debt to Equity	.11%	.03%	.03%	.03%	0.04	0.043

CONTACT INFORMATION:

Phone: 914 641-2000   Fax: 914 696-2950
Toll-Free:
Address: 1133 Westchester Ave., White Plains, NY 10604 United States

STOCK TICKER/OTHER:

Stock Ticker: ITT   Exchange: NYS
Employees: 10,600   Fiscal Year Ends: 12/31
Parent Company:

SALARIES/BONUSES:

Top Exec. Salary: $1,140,393   Bonus: $
Second Exec. Salary: $616,157   Bonus: $

OTHER THOUGHTS:

Estimated Female Officers or Directors: 5
Hot Spot for Advancement for Women/Minorities: Y

Jabil Inc

NAIC Code: 334418

www.jabil.com

TYPES OF BUSINESS:

Contract Electronics Manufacturing
Electronic Manufacturing Services
Engineering Solutions

BRANDS/DIVISIONS/AFFILIATES:

GROWTH PLANS/SPECIAL FEATURES:

Jabil Inc is a United States-based company engaged in providing manufacturing services and solutions. It provides comprehensive electronics design, production and product management services to companies in various industries and end markets. The Company derives its revenue from providing comprehensive electronics design, production and product management services. It operates in two segments. The Electronics Manufacturing Services (EMS) segment, which is the key revenue driver, is focused on leveraging IT, supply chain design and engineering, technologies largely centered on core electronics. The Diversified Manufacturing Services (DMS) segment is focused on providing engineering solutions, with an emphasis on material sciences, technologies, and healthcare.

CONTACTS:
Note: Officers with more than one job title may be intentionally listed here more than once.

Meheryar Dastoor, CEO
Gregory Hebard, CFO
Mark Mondello, Chairman of the Board
May Yee Yap, Chief Information Officer
Matthew Crowley, Executive VP, Divisional
Andrew Priestley, Executive VP, Divisional
Steven Borges, Executive VP, Divisional
Frederic McCoy, Executive VP, Divisional
Kristine Melachrino, General Counsel
Gary Schick, Other Executive Officer
Francis McKay, Other Executive Officer
Adam Berry, Senior VP, Divisional

FINANCIAL DATA:
Note: Data for latest year may not have been available at press time.

In U.S. $	2024	2023	2022	2021	2020	2019
Revenue	28,882,999,296	34,702,000,128	33,478,000,640	29,284,999,168	27,266,000,896	25,282,000,896
R&D Expense	39,000,000	34,000,000	33,000,000	34,000,000	43,000,000	43,000,000
Operating Income	1,437,000,000	1,594,000,000	1,411,000,000	1,065,000,000	657,000,000	727,000,000
Operating Margin %	.05%	.05%	.04%	.04%	.02%	.03%
SGA Expense	1,160,000,000	1,206,000,000	1,154,000,000	1,213,000,000	1,175,000,000	1,111,000,000
Net Income	1,388,000,000	818,000,000	996,000,000	696,000,000	54,000,000	287,000,000
Operating Cash Flow	1,716,000,000	1,734,000,000	1,651,000,000	1,433,000,000	1,257,000,000	1,193,000,000
Capital Expenditure	784,000,000	1,030,000,000	1,385,000,000	1,159,000,000	983,000,000	1,005,000,000
EBITDA	2,620,000,000	2,392,000,000	2,302,000,000	1,944,000,000	1,230,000,000	1,411,000,000
Return on Assets %	.08%	.04%	.05%	.04%	.00%	.02%
Return on Equity %	.60%	.31%	.43%	.35%	.03%	.15%
Debt to Equity	1.82%	1.10%	1.22%	1.50%	1.646	1.124

CONTACT INFORMATION:

Phone: 727 577-9749   Fax: 727 579-8529
Toll-Free:
Address: 10560 Dr. Martin Luther King Jr. St. N., St. Petersburg, FL 33716 United States

STOCK TICKER/OTHER:

Stock Ticker: JBL   Exchange: NYS
Employees: 138,000   Fiscal Year Ends: 08/31
Parent Company:

SALARIES/BONUSES:

Top Exec. Salary: $1,049,039   Bonus: $
Second Exec. Salary: Bonus: $
$877,692

OTHER THOUGHTS:

Estimated Female Officers or Directors:
Hot Spot for Advancement for Women/Minorities: Y

Jacobs Solutions Inc

www.jacobs.com

NAIC Code: 237000

TYPES OF BUSINESS:

Engineering & Design Services
Facility Management
Construction & Field Services
Technical Consulting Services
Environmental Services

GROWTH PLANS/SPECIAL FEATURES:

Jacobs Solutions is a global provider of engineering, design, procurement, construction, and maintenance services as well as cyber engineering and security solutions. The firm serves industrial, commercial, and government clients in a wide variety of sectors, including water, transportation, healthcare, technology, and chemicals. Jacobs Solutions employs approximately 60,000 workers. The company generated $11.5 billion in revenue in fiscal 2024.

Jacobs offers its employees medical, disability, life and AD&D insurance; an employee stock purchase plan; and tuition reimbursement.

BRANDS/DIVISIONS/AFFILIATES:

PA Consulting

CONTACTS: Note: Officers with more than one job title may be intentionally listed here more than once.

Robert Pragada, CEO
Venkatesh Nathamuni, CFO
William Allen, Chief Accounting Officer
Joanne Caruso, Chief Administrative Officer
Shannon Miller, Executive VP
Patrick Hill, Executive VP

FINANCIAL DATA: Note: Data for latest year may not have been available at press time.

In U.S. $	2024	2023	2022	2021	2020	2019
Revenue	11,500,941,312	10,851,420,160	9,783,073,792	14,092,632,064	13,566,974,976	12,737,867,776
R&D Expense						
Operating Income	692,436,000	676,484,000	539,884,000	688,089,000	535,973,000	404,851,000
Operating Margin %	.06%	.06%	.06%	.05%	.04%	.03%
SGA Expense	2,140,320,000	2,034,376,000	2,040,075,000	2,355,683,000	2,050,695,000	2,072,177,000
Net Income	806,093,000	665,777,000	644,039,000	477,030,000	491,845,000	847,979,000
Operating Cash Flow	1,054,673,000	974,763,000	474,709,000	726,276,000	806,849,000	-366,436,000
Capital Expenditure	121,114,000	137,486,000	127,615,000	92,814,000	118,269,000	135,977,000
EBITDA	1,255,083,000	996,312,000	878,740,000	1,019,116,000	685,042,000	604,095,000
Return on Assets %	.06%	.05%	.04%	.04%	.04%	.07%
Return on Equity %	.15%	.11%	.11%	.08%	.09%	.15%
Debt to Equity	.39%	.50%	.65%	.61%	0.415	0.21

CONTACT INFORMATION:

Phone: 214-583-8500   Fax:
Toll-Free:
Address: 1999 Bryan St., Ste. 1200, Dallas, TX 75201 United States

STOCK TICKER/OTHER:

Stock Ticker: J   Exchange: NYS
Employees: 45,000   Fiscal Year Ends: 09/30
Parent Company:

SALARIES/BONUSES:

Top Exec. Salary: $1,338,462   Bonus: $
Second Exec. Salary: Bonus: $
$1,250,000

OTHER THOUGHTS:

Estimated Female Officers or Directors: 1
Hot Spot for Advancement for Women/Minorities: Y

Jaguar Land Rover Limited

www.jaguarlandrover.com

NAIC Code: 336111

TYPES OF BUSINESS:

Automobile Manufacturing
Vehicle Design and Manufacture
Vehicle Distribution
Sedans
Sports Cars
Electric and Hybrid Vehicles
Sport Utility Vehicles

BRANDS/DIVISIONS/AFFILIATES:

Tata Group
Tata Motors Limited
XE
XF
F-Type
Range Rover
Defender
Discovery

CONTACTS: Note: Officers with more than one job title may be intentionally listed here more than once.

Adrian Merdell Thierry Bollore, CEO
Richard Molyneux, CFO
Dave Williams, Chief People Officer
Ian Callum, Dir.-Jaguar Design

GROWTH PLANS/SPECIAL FEATURES:

Jaguar Land Rover Limited, founded in 1922 and based in the U.K., manufactures a distinctive line of luxury sedans, sports cars, electric/hybrid vehicles and sports utility vehicles (SUV). The company is part of India-based Tata Motors Limited, itself part of the Tata Group. Jaguar's current line includes six models: the XE, XF, F-Type, I-Pace, E-Pace and F-Pace. The XE, XF and F-Type are all luxury sports cars with various differing characteristics such as a lightweight aluminum intensive architecture, a supercharged engine, a monocoque alloy body shell or a convertible. The I-Pace is an all-electric performance sport utility vehicle (SUV). The E-Pace is a compact SUV. The F-Pace is a sports car based on the C-X17 crossover concept vehicle and includes lightweight aluminum intensive architecture. Land Rovers' current line includes the Range Rover, Range Rover Sport, Range Rover Velar, Range Rover Evoque, Land Rover Defender, Land Rover Discovery and Land Rover Discovery Sport. All of Land Rovers' models are SUVs of varying sizes and interior packages, and available as plug-in hybrids. The firm operates research, engineering and/or production facilities in the U.S., Brazil, The U.K., Austria, Hungary, Slovakia, India and China.

FINANCIAL DATA: Note: Data for latest year may not have been available at press time.

In U.S. $	2024	2023	2022	2021	2020	2019
Revenue	29,579,726,400	28,171,168,000	22,869,327,000	23,110,900,000	22,170,100,000	31,759,200,000
R&D Expense						
Operating Income						
Operating Margin %						
SGA Expense						
Net Income		-74,105,000	-499,876,000	-2,317,910,000	-6,176,680,000	-4,355,840,000
Operating Cash Flow						
Capital Expenditure						
EBITDA						
Return on Assets %						
Return on Equity %						
Debt to Equity						

CONTACT INFORMATION:

Phone: 44-24-7640-2121   Fax:
Toll-Free:
Address: Abbey Rd., Whitley, Coventry, CV3 4LF United Kingdom

STOCK TICKER/OTHER:

Stock Ticker: Subsidiary   Exchange:
Employees: 33,000   Fiscal Year Ends: 03/31
Parent Company: Tata Group

SALARIES/BONUSES:

Top Exec. Salary: $ Bonus: $
Second Exec. Salary: $ Bonus: $

OTHER THOUGHTS:

Estimated Female Officers or Directors: 4
Hot Spot for Advancement for Women/Minorities: Y

JGC Holdings Corp

NAIC Code: 541330

TYPES OF BUSINESS:
Engineering Services
Engineering
Procurement
Construction
Functional Materials
Manufacturing

BRANDS/DIVISIONS/AFFILIATES:
JGC Corporation
JGC Japan Corporation
JGC Catalysts and Chemicals Ltd
Japan Fine Ceramics Co Ltd
Japan Nus Co Ltd
Nikki-Universal Co Ltd
PT JGC Indonesia
JGC America Inc

GROWTH PLANS/SPECIAL FEATURES:
JGC Holdings Corp offers planning, consulting, materials procurement, construction, operation, and maintenance for various plants and facilities. In addition, it invests in oil and gas field development projects and utility businesses. The company has two operating segments: total engineering the (majority of total revenue); and catalysts and fine products. It constructs and performs tests on machinery and plants for multiple energy and industrial markets. The company utilizes engineering technology and project management capabilities. Additional sales are generated from providing operational support after completion of projects. Asia is an important region for the company, but the company also sells to Australia, the Middle East, and North America.

CONTACTS:
Note: Officers with more than one job title may be intentionally listed here more than once.
Masayuki Sato, CEO
Kiyotaka Terajima, CFO
Tadashi Ishizuka, COO
Masaki Ishikawa, Director

FINANCIAL DATA:
Note: Data for latest year may not have been available at press time.

In U.S. $	2024	2023	2022	2021	2020	2019
Revenue	5,780,304,051	4,213,343,427	2,974,180,883	3,012,843,666	3,338,024,218	4,299,090,762
R&D Expense						
Operating Income	-131,880,000	254,783,400	143,633,700	158,851,700	140,481,800	161,413,500
Operating Margin %	-.02%	.06%	.05%	.05%	.04%	.04%
SGA Expense						
Net Income	-54,359,900	212,892,300	-246,813,400	35,691,480	28,582,340	166,655,100
Operating Cash Flow	76,992,500	769,015,600	134,066,900	86,552,350	641,780,100	-383,636,500
Capital Expenditure	131,817,600	84,268,260	68,078,310	70,855,320	46,292,700	67,092,480
EBITDA	96,327,420	401,360,700	-136,344,100	201,721,700	230,102,800	279,082,200
Return on Assets %	-.01%	.04%	-.05%	.01%	.01%	.03%
Return on Equity %	-.02%	.08%	-.09%	.01%	.01%	.06%
Debt to Equity	.09%	.06%	.08%	.16%	0.078	0.132

CONTACT INFORMATION:
Phone: 81 456821111 Fax: 81 456821112
Toll-Free:
Address: 2-3-1, Minato Mirai, Nishi-ku, Yokohama-shi, Kanagawa, 220-6001 Japan

STOCK TICKER/OTHER:
Stock Ticker: JGCCY Exchange: PINX
Employees: 10,403 Fiscal Year Ends: 03/31
Parent Company:

SALARIES/BONUSES:
Top Exec. Salary: $ Bonus: $
Second Exec. Salary: $ Bonus: $

OTHER THOUGHTS:
Estimated Female Officers or Directors:
Hot Spot for Advancement for Women/Minorities:

Johnson & Johnson

www.jnj.com

NAIC Code: 325412

TYPES OF BUSINESS:

Personal Health Care & Hygiene Products
Sterilization Products
Surgical Products
Pharmaceuticals
Contact Lenses
Medical Equipment

BRANDS/DIVISIONS/AFFILIATES:

Johnson & Johnson Innovative Medicine
Johnson & Johnson MedTech

GROWTH PLANS/SPECIAL FEATURES:

Johnson & Johnson is the world's largest and most diverse healthcare firm. It has two divisions: pharmaceutical and medical devices. These now represent all of the company's sales following the divestment of the consumer business, Kenvue, in 2023. The drug division focuses on the following therapeutic areas: immunology, oncology, neurology, pulmonary, cardiology, and metabolic diseases. Geographically, just over half of total revenue is generated in the United States.

CONTACTS: Note: Officers with more than one job title may be intentionally listed here more than once.

Joaquin Duato, CEO
Joseph Wolk, CFO
Timothy Schmid, Chairman, Divisional
Jennifer Taubert, Chairman, Divisional
Robert Decker, Chief Accounting Officer
James Swanson, Chief Information Officer
William Hait, Chief Medical Officer
Kathryn Wengel, Chief Risk Officer
John Reed, Executive VP, Divisional
Vanessa Broadhurst, Executive VP, Divisional
Elizabeth Forminard, Executive VP
Kristen Mulholland, Other Executive Officer

FINANCIAL DATA: Note: Data for latest year may not have been available at press time.

In U.S. $	2024	2023	2022	2021	2020	2019
Revenue	88,820,998,144	85,159,002,112	79,989,997,568	78,739,996,672	82,584,002,560	82,059,001,856
R&D Expense	17,232,000,000	15,085,000,000	14,135,000,000	14,277,000,000	12,340,000,000	11,355,000,000
Operating Income	22,149,000,000	23,409,000,000	21,013,000,000	20,943,000,000	19,733,000,000	20,970,000,000
Operating Margin %	.25%	.27%	.26%	.27%	.24%	.26%
SGA Expense	21,969,000,000	20,112,000,000	20,246,000,000	20,118,000,000	22,084,000,000	22,178,000,000
Net Income	14,066,000,000	35,153,000,000	17,941,000,000	20,878,000,000	14,714,000,000	15,119,000,000
Operating Cash Flow	24,266,000,000	22,791,000,000	21,194,000,000	23,410,000,000	23,536,000,000	23,416,000,000
Capital Expenditure	6,207,000,000	5,013,000,000	4,009,000,000	3,652,000,000	3,347,000,000	3,498,000,000
EBITDA	24,781,000,000	23,320,000,000	26,605,000,000	26,751,000,000	23,929,000,000	24,655,000,000
Return on Assets %	.08%	.20%	.10%	.12%	.09%	.10%
Return on Equity %	.20%	.48%	.24%	.30%	.24%	.25%
Debt to Equity	.43%	.38%	.35%	.41%	0.516	0.445

CONTACT INFORMATION:

Phone: 732 524-0400   Fax: 732 214-0332
Toll-Free:
Address: 1 Johnson & Johnson Plaza, New Brunswick, NJ 08933 United States

STOCK TICKER/OTHER:

Stock Ticker: JNJ
Employees: 131,900
Parent Company:

Exchange: NYS
Fiscal Year Ends: 12/31

SALARIES/BONUSES:

Top Exec. Salary: $1,600,000   Bonus: $
Second Exec. Salary: $1,212,308   Bonus: $

OTHER THOUGHTS:

Estimated Female Officers or Directors: 4
Hot Spot for Advancement for Women/Minorities: Y

Johnson Controls International plc

www.johnsoncontrols.com

NAIC Code: 561600

TYPES OF BUSINESS:
Fire & Security Systems & Services
Security Monitoring Services
Fire Detection Systems
Raw Materials
Intelligent Buildings

BRANDS/DIVISIONS/AFFILIATES:

GROWTH PLANS/SPECIAL FEATURES:

Johnson Controls manufactures, installs, and services commercial HVAC systems, building management platforms and controls, fire and security solutions, and industrial refrigeration units. Commercial HVAC and fire and security each account for approximately 45% of sales, while industrial refrigeration and other solutions account for the remaining 10% of revenue. In fiscal 2024, Johnson Controls generated nearly $23 billion in pro forma revenue.

CONTACTS: Note: Officers with more than one job title may be intentionally listed here more than once.
George Oliver, CEO
Marc Vandiepenbeeck, CFO
Daniel Mcconeghy, Chief Accounting Officer
John Donofrio, Executive VP
Marlon Sullivan, Executive VP
Nathan Manning, President, Divisional
Julie M Brandt, President, Divisional
Lei Schlitz, President, Divisional
Anuruddha Rathninde, President, Geographical
Richard Lek, President

FINANCIAL DATA: Note: Data for latest year may not have been available at press time.

In U.S. $	2024	2023	2022	2021	2020	2019
Revenue	22,951,999,488	22,331,000,832	20,636,999,680	23,668,000,768	22,317,000,704	23,968,000,000
R&D Expense						
Operating Income	2,416,000,000	2,417,000,000	2,012,000,000	2,801,000,000	1,746,000,000	1,449,000,000
Operating Margin %	.11%	.11%	.10%	.12%	.08%	.06%
SGA Expense	5,661,000,000	5,387,000,000	5,078,000,000	5,258,000,000	5,665,000,000	6,244,000,000
Net Income	1,705,000,000	1,849,000,000	1,532,000,000	1,637,000,000	631,000,000	5,674,000,000
Operating Cash Flow	2,098,000,000	2,221,000,000	1,990,000,000	2,487,000,000	2,219,000,000	1,202,000,000
Capital Expenditure	494,000,000	446,000,000	487,000,000	552,000,000	443,000,000	586,000,000
EBITDA	2,719,000,000	2,155,000,000	2,050,000,000	3,665,000,000	1,965,000,000	2,216,000,000
Return on Assets %	.04%	.04%	.04%	.04%	.02%	.12%
Return on Equity %	.10%	.11%	.09%	.09%	.03%	.28%
Debt to Equity	.50%	.47%	.46%	.43%	0.431	0.339

CONTACT INFORMATION:
Phone: 353-21735-5800 Fax:
Toll-Free:
Address: One Albert Quay, Cork, T12 X8N6 Ireland

STOCK TICKER/OTHER:
Stock Ticker: JCI
Employees: 94,000
Parent Company:

Exchange: NYS
Fiscal Year Ends: 09/30

SALARIES/BONUSES:
Top Exec. Salary: $1,500,000 Bonus: $
Second Exec. Salary: Bonus: $
$775,000

OTHER THOUGHTS:
Estimated Female Officers or Directors: 2
Hot Spot for Advancement for Women/Minorities: Y

Juniper Networks Inc

NAIC Code: 334210

www.juniper.net

TYPES OF BUSINESS:

Networking Equipment
Network Product Development
Network Security Solutions
Artificial Intelligence
Machine Learning
Automated WAN Solutions
Cloud-Based Data Center Solutions

BRANDS/DIVISIONS/AFFILIATES:

Mist
EX
128 Technology
SRX
MX
PTX
ACX
Apstra

GROWTH PLANS/SPECIAL FEATURES:

Juniper Networks Inc is engaged in designing, developing, and selling products and services for high-performance networks to enable customers to build scalable, reliable, secure, and cost-effective networks for their businesses while achieving agility and improved operating efficiency through automation. The company's high-performance network and service offerings include routing, switching, Wi-Fi, network security, artificial intelligence (AI) or AI-enabled enterprise networking operations (AIOps), and software-defined networking (SDN) technologies. In addition to the company's products, the company offers its customers a variety of services, including maintenance and support, professional services, Software-as-a-Service (SaaS), and education and training programs.

Juniper Networks offers medical, dental, prescription and vision insurance; paid time off; and stock/savings plans.

CONTACTS: Note: Officers with more than one job title may be intentionally listed here more than once.

Rami Rahim, CEO
Kenneth Miller, CFO
Scott Kriens, Chairman of the Board
Thomas Austin, Chief Accounting Officer
Manoj Leelanivas, COO
Christopher Kaddaras, Executive VP
Robert Mobassaly, General Counsel

FINANCIAL DATA: Note: Data for latest year may not have been available at press time.

In U.S. $	2024	2023	2022	2021	2020	2019
Revenue	5,073,600,000	5,564,499,968	5,301,199,872	4,735,399,936	4,445,100,032	4,445,400,064
R&D Expense	1,150,500,000	1,144,400,000	1,036,100,000	1,007,200,000	958,400,000	955,700,000
Operating Income	363,800,000	569,700,000	539,300,000	430,400,000	421,100,000	477,500,000
Operating Margin %	.07%	.10%	.10%	.09%	.09%	.11%
SGA Expense	1,467,200,000	1,487,800,000	1,382,900,000	1,302,500,000	1,194,200,000	1,183,600,000
Net Income	287,900,000	310,200,000	471,000,000	252,700,000	257,800,000	345,000,000
Operating Cash Flow	788,100,000	872,800,000	97,600,000	689,700,000	612,000,000	528,900,000
Capital Expenditure	115,500,000	159,400,000	105,100,000	100,000,000	100,400,000	109,600,000
EBITDA	536,200,000	623,700,000	812,600,000	598,300,000	554,600,000	713,400,000
Return on Assets %	.03%	.03%	.05%	.03%	.03%	.04%
Return on Equity %	.06%	.07%	.11%	.06%	.06%	.07%
Debt to Equity	.28%	.38%	.38%	.42%	0.411	0.40

CONTACT INFORMATION:

Phone: 408 745-2000 Fax: 408 745-2100
Toll-Free: 888-586-4737
Address: 1133 Innovation Way, Sunnyvale, CA 94089 United States

STOCK TICKER/OTHER:

Stock Ticker: JNPR Exchange: NYS
Employees: 11,144 Fiscal Year Ends: 12/31
Parent Company:

SALARIES/BONUSES:

Top Exec. Salary: $1,000,000 Bonus: $
Second Exec. Salary: $665,000 Bonus: $

OTHER THOUGHTS:

Estimated Female Officers or Directors: 3
Hot Spot for Advancement for Women/Minorities: Y

Jutal Offshore Oil Services Ltd

www.jutal.com

NAIC Code: 541330

TYPES OF BUSINESS:

Engineering Services

BRANDS/DIVISIONS/AFFILIATES:

GROWTH PLANS/SPECIAL FEATURES:

Jutal Offshore Oil Services Ltd is an investment holding company. The company's operating segments include Fabrication of facilities and provision of integrated services for oil and gas industries, Fabrication of facilities and provision of integrated services for new energy and refining and chemical industries, and Others. It generates maximum revenue from the Fabrication of facilities and provision of integrated services for oil and gas industries segment. Geographically, it derives a majority of revenue from the United States and also has an international presence.

CONTACTS: Note: Officers with more than one job title may be intentionally listed here more than once.

Cao Yunsheng, CEO
Wang Lishan, Chmn.

FINANCIAL DATA: Note: Data for latest year may not have been available at press time.

In U.S. $	2024	2023	2022	2021	2020	2019
Revenue	288,604,731	359,783,565	243,059,391	552,717,622	506,293,018	244,405,508
R&D Expense						
Operating Income	35,532,850	61,129,000	-18,301,840	-979,358	29,776,360	16,351,600
Operating Margin %	.12%	.17%	-.08%	.00%	.06%	.07%
SGA Expense	43,482,100	27,476,440	23,325,100	41,873,200	35,601,840	30,634,810
Net Income	25,690,410	35,396,950	-28,906,530	1,530,325	20,366,200	614,129
Operating Cash Flow	66,266,780	39,859,930	-17,402,450	10,903,560	110,822,500	20,649,670
Capital Expenditure	19,319,100	3,549,704	6,462,096	11,535,740	21,384,980	20,131,740
EBITDA	47,835,280	75,353,500	-2,002,582	29,705,710	50,294,020	23,782,500
Return on Assets %	.05%	.07%	-.06%	.00%	.03%	.00%
Return on Equity %	.09%	.14%	-.12%	.01%	.07%	.00%
Debt to Equity	.02%	.12%	.16%	.12%	0.235	0.20

CONTACT INFORMATION:

Phone: 86 75526694111   Fax:
Toll-Free:
Address: 10th Floor, Chiwan Petroleum Building, Shenzhen, Guangdong 518068 China

STOCK TICKER/OTHER:

Stock Ticker: JUTOF
Employees: 2,739
Parent Company:

Exchange: PINX
Fiscal Year Ends: 12/31

SALARIES/BONUSES:

Top Exec. Salary: $ Bonus: $
Second Exec. Salary: $ Bonus: $

OTHER THOUGHTS:

Estimated Female Officers or Directors:
Hot Spot for Advancement for Women/Minorities:

Kaneka Corp
NAIC Code: 325211

www.kaneka.co.jp

TYPES OF BUSINESS:
Plastics Material and Resin Manufacturing
Functional & Expandable Plastics
PVC
Food Products
Specialty Fibers
Medical devices
Biopharmaceuticals

BRANDS/DIVISIONS/AFFILIATES:

GROWTH PLANS/SPECIAL FEATURES:
Kaneka Corp manufactures and sells a variety of chemicals, plastics, and chemical-based products. The company organizes itself into seven segments based on product type. The foodstuffs segment, which generates more revenue than any other segment, sells margarine, shortening, bakery yeast and spices. The chemicals segment sells polyvinyl chloride used in pipes and flooring. The functional and expandable products segments sell polystyrene- and silicone-based products. The life science products segment sells medical devices, which include balloon catheters for vessel stenosis, and pharmaceutical ingredients. The electronic products segment sells heat resistant films and optical materials. The synthetic fibers segment sells fibers used to make apparel. The majority of revenue comes from Japan.

CONTACTS:
Note: Officers with more than one job title may be intentionally listed here more than once.
Kimikazu Sugawara, Chairman of the Board
Shinichiro Kametaka, Director
Mamoru Kadokura, Director
Jun Enoki, Director
Masaaki Kimura, Director
Toshio Komori, Director
Kazuhiko Fujii, Director
Katsunobu Doro, Director

FINANCIAL DATA:
Note: Data for latest year may not have been available at press time.

In U.S. $	2024	2023	2022	2021	2020	2019
Revenue	5,292,293,788	5,247,299,437	4,800,958,041	4,008,789,568	4,176,020,574	4,311,601,022
R&D Expense						
Operating Income	226,180,200	243,599,000	302,436,800	191,231,600	180,609,600	250,222,200
Operating Margin %	.04%	.05%	.06%	.05%	.04%	.06%
SGA Expense						
Net Income	161,205,200	159,733,400	183,886,400	109,907,000	97,216,060	154,387,700
Operating Cash Flow	429,818,100	199,319,600	236,781,500	514,023,900	277,582,600	285,427,700
Capital Expenditure	453,110,300	291,523,200	277,214,700	294,334,900	321,258,000	317,939,500
EBITDA	561,982,800	512,316,100	523,618,500	414,620,900	387,746,500	458,712,900
Return on Assets %	.03%	.03%	.04%	.02%	.02%	.03%
Return on Equity %	.05%	.06%	.07%	.05%	.04%	.07%
Debt to Equity	.16%	.14%	.11%	.10%	0.13	0.134

CONTACT INFORMATION:
Phone: 81 662265050   Fax: 81 662265037
Toll-Free:
Address: 2-3-18, Nakanoshima, Kita-ku, Osaka, 530-8288 Japan

STOCK TICKER/OTHER:
Stock Ticker: KANKF   Exchange: PINX
Employees: 12,287   Fiscal Year Ends: 03/31
Parent Company:

SALARIES/BONUSES:
Top Exec. Salary: $ Bonus: $
Second Exec. Salary: $ Bonus: $

OTHER THOUGHTS:
Estimated Female Officers or Directors:
Hot Spot for Advancement for Women/Minorities:

Kawasaki Heavy Industries Ltd

www.khi.co.jp

NAIC Code: 336999

TYPES OF BUSINESS:

Recreational Vehicle & Machinery Manufacturing
Manufacturing
Rail Cars
Ships
Motorcycles
Engines
Gas Turbines
Boilers

BRANDS/DIVISIONS/AFFILIATES:

Kawasaki
Kawasaki Motors Ltd

GROWTH PLANS/SPECIAL FEATURES:

Kawasaki Heavy Industries Ltd is a diversified industrial company serving land, sea, and air markets. It produces heavy machinery, including multiple land vehicles, large tankers, submarines, energy systems, and aerospace equipment. In addition, the company works to produce environmental plants, industrial plants, precision machinery, robots, and infrastructure equipment. One aspect of the company focuses on manufacturing motorcycles under its well-known Kawasaki brand. Another focus and revenue generator is the division geared towards manufacturing commercial aircraft and jet engines. Sales generated in Asia account for the majority of total revenue, but the company does have a presence in the Americas and Europe.

CONTACTS: *Note: Officers with more than one job title may be intentionally listed here more than once.*

Yasuhiko Hashimoto, CEO
Katsuya Yamamoto, CFO
Yoshinori Kanehana, Chairman of the Board
Hiroshi Nakatani, Director
Atsuko Kakihara, Director

FINANCIAL DATA: *Note: Data for latest year may not have been available at press time.*

In U.S. $	2024	2023	2022	2021	2020	2019
Revenue	12,838,704,829	11,980,068,545	10,419,876,729	10,333,838,205	11,394,994,567	11,071,529,535
R&D Expense				312,059,200	365,231,900	338,336,600
Operating Income	241,905,000	548,743,400	310,865,100	-36,830,050	430,880,300	444,494,600
Operating Margin %	.02%	.05%	.03%	.00%	.04%	.04%
SGA Expense	1,916,440,000	1,751,673,000	1,465,801,000			
Net Income	176,180,200	368,154,700	87,739,520	-134,212,700	129,561,200	190,592,900
Operating Cash Flow	219,814,000	163,961,400	1,089,211,000	240,218,000	-107,338,200	762,024,500
Capital Expenditure	670,251,300	485,587,400	469,612,600	358,872,500	499,493,200	575,090,200
EBITDA	904,075,300	1,124,826,000	763,114,400	349,625,100	723,556,000	696,403,800
Return on Assets %	.01%	.02%	.01%	-.01%	.01%	.02%
Return on Equity %	.04%	.10%	.03%	-.04%	.04%	.06%
Debt to Equity				.86%	0.768	0.691

CONTACT INFORMATION:

Phone: 81 783719530   Fax: 81 783719568
Toll-Free:
Address: Kobe Crystal Tower, 1-3, Kobe, 650-8680 Japan

STOCK TICKER/OTHER:

Stock Ticker: KWHIY   Exchange: PINX
Employees: 35,691   Fiscal Year Ends: 03/31
Parent Company:

SALARIES/BONUSES:

Top Exec. Salary: $ Bonus: $
Second Exec. Salary: $ Bonus: $

OTHER THOUGHTS:

Estimated Female Officers or Directors: 1
Hot Spot for Advancement for Women/Minorities:

KBR Inc

NAIC Code: 237000

www.kbr.com

TYPES OF BUSINESS:

Heavy Construction and Engineering
Engineering
Technology
Test and Evaluation
Software
Petrochemicals
Licensing
Energy

BRANDS/DIVISIONS/AFFILIATES:

GROWTH PLANS/SPECIAL FEATURES:

KBR, formerly Kellogg Brown & Root, is a global provider of technology, integrated engineering, procurement, and construction delivery, and operations and maintenance services. The company's business is organized into two segments: mission technology solutions and sustainable technology solutions. KBR has operations in over 30 countries and employs approximately 34,000 people. The firm generated $7.7 billion in revenue in 2024.

CONTACTS: Note: Officers with more than one job title may be intentionally listed here more than once.

Stuart Bradie, CEO
Shad Evans, CFO, Divisional
Mark Sopp, CFO
Lester Lyles, Chairman of the Board
Alison Vasquez, Chief Accounting Officer
Sonia Galindo, Executive VP
Jenni Myles, Executive VP
Gregory Conlon, Other Executive Officer
Paul Kahn, President, Divisional
J. Ibrahim, President, Divisional
William Bright, President, Geographical

FINANCIAL DATA: Note: Data for latest year may not have been available at press time.

In U.S. $	2024	2023	2022	2021	2020	2019
Revenue	7,742,000,128	6,956,000,256	6,563,999,744	7,338,999,808	5,767,000,064	5,639,000,064
R&D Expense						
Operating Income	548,000,000	485,000,000	404,000,000	399,000,000	331,000,000	312,000,000
Operating Margin %	.07%	.07%	.06%	.05%	.06%	.06%
SGA Expense	544,000,000	488,000,000	420,000,000	393,000,000	335,000,000	341,000,000
Net Income	375,000,000	-265,000,000	190,000,000	27,000,000	-72,000,000	202,000,000
Operating Cash Flow	462,000,000	331,000,000	396,000,000	278,000,000	367,000,000	256,000,000
Capital Expenditure	77,000,000	80,000,000	71,000,000	30,000,000	20,000,000	20,000,000
EBITDA	811,000,000	90,000,000	508,000,000	372,000,000	173,000,000	471,000,000
Return on Assets %	.06%	-.05%	.03%	.00%	-.01%	.04%
Return on Equity %	.26%	-.18%	.12%	.02%	-.04%	.11%
Debt to Equity	1.90%	1.43%	.97%	1.24%	1.122	0.751

CONTACT INFORMATION:

Phone: 713 753-2000   Fax: 713 753-5353
Toll-Free:
Address: 601 Jefferson St., Ste. 3400, Houston, TX 77002 United States

STOCK TICKER/OTHER:

Stock Ticker: KBR   Exchange: NYS
Employees: 34,000   Fiscal Year Ends: 12/31
Parent Company:

SALARIES/BONUSES:

Top Exec. Salary: $1,284,698   Bonus: $
Second Exec. Salary: Bonus: $
$768,458

OTHER THOUGHTS:

Estimated Female Officers or Directors: 2
Hot Spot for Advancement for Women/Minorities: Y

Sales, profits and employees may be estimates. Financial information, benefits and other data can change quickly and may vary from those stated here.

Keller Group PLC

NAIC Code: 541330

www.keller.co.uk

TYPES OF BUSINESS:
Engineering Services, Incl Civil, Mechanical, Electronic, Computer & Environmental

BRANDS/DIVISIONS/AFFILIATES:

GROWTH PLANS/SPECIAL FEATURES:
Keller Group PLC is a UK-based company that provides specialist ground engineering services. Its Techniques Ground improvement, Grouting, Deep foundations, Earth retention, Marine, and instrumentation and monitoring. Its solutions are to Improve bearing capacity Low-impact, low-carbon construction, Containment, Excavation support, Stabilisation, Marine structures, Seepage control, Slope stabilization, and Monitoring. Its markets are Commercial, Industrial, Infrastructure, Power, Institutional, public, and Residential. It offers marketed under brands including Franki, Resource Piling, and Keller Foundations. Its geographical segments are North America, Europe, Asia-Pacific, and Middle East. it generates revenue from North America.

CONTACTS: *Note: Officers with more than one job title may be intentionally listed here more than once.*
Michael Speakman, CEO
David Burke, CFO
Peter Hill, Chairman of the Board
Kerry Porritt, Secretary

FINANCIAL DATA: *Note: Data for latest year may not have been available at press time.*

In U.S. $	2024	2023	2022	2021	2020	2019
Revenue	4,020,994,271	3,993,125,990	3,964,315,084	2,992,151,892	2,776,743,719	3,097,163,121
R&D Expense						
Operating Income	280,030,400	258,355,000	134,226,100	115,108,600	145,669,700	135,572,400
Operating Margin %	.07%	.06%	.03%	.04%	.05%	.04%
SGA Expense					3,635,010	2,827,230
Net Income	191,578,500	120,359,200	61,929,800	76,065,950	57,217,750	28,810,820
Operating Cash Flow	357,981,200	265,221,100	73,777,240	206,387,800	283,396,200	220,658,600
Capital Expenditure	119,820,700	127,225,400	109,992,700	113,627,700	98,279,900	84,682,270
EBITDA	435,931,900	366,462,800	248,527,000	229,678,800	238,564,400	233,986,900
Return on Assets %	.08%	.05%	.03%	.04%	.03%	.01%
Return on Equity %	.26%	.18%	.10%	.14%	.11%	.05%
Debt to Equity	.52%	.59%	.74%	.58%	0.482	0.887

CONTACT INFORMATION:
Phone: 44 20 7616 7575   Fax:
Toll-Free:
Address: 2 Kingdom St., London, W2 6BD United Kingdom

STOCK TICKER/OTHER:
Stock Ticker: KLRGF
Employees: 9,489
Parent Company:

Exchange: PINX
Fiscal Year Ends: 12/31

SALARIES/BONUSES:
Top Exec. Salary: $869,710   Bonus: $1,029,920
Second Exec. Salary: $570,831   Bonus: $675,843

OTHER THOUGHTS:
Estimated Female Officers or Directors:
Hot Spot for Advancement for Women/Minorities:

KEO International Consultants WLL
www.keoic.com

NAIC Code: 541330

TYPES OF BUSINESS:
Engineering Consulting Services
Consulting
Engineering
Architecture
Project Management
Construction Management
Real Estate Investment Consulting

BRANDS/DIVISIONS/AFFILIATES:
InSite
C-Quest
iCRBN

CONTACTS: Note: Officers with more than one job title may be intentionally listed here more than once.
Donna Sultan, CEO
Ayub Ibrahim, CFO
Ann de Villiers, VP-Human Resources
Abdul Aziz Sultan, Chmn.

GROWTH PLANS/SPECIAL FEATURES:
KEO International Consultants WLL provides architectural design, infrastructure engineering and project and construction management services. KEO is well positioned with 11 offices in two continents. The firm offers end-to-end planning and development solutions through two firms: InSite, for inspired planning, urban design and landscape architecture; and C-Quest, for surveying purposes. In addition, KEO sponsors Black Mule Investment & Advisory, a professional services practice in the United Arab Emirates focused on real estate investment services for the Gulf Cooperation Council and the management consulting sector. Sectors include commercial, retail, education, government, civic, healthcare, industrial, leisure/hospitality, residential, sports, tall buildings, transportation and water. Services offered by KEO cover areas such as architecture, digital advisory services, engineering, infrastructure, investment and advisory, landscape architecture, project and construction management, quantity surveying, specialist services, sustainability, environment and iCRBN. iCRBN is a scenario analysis tool developed by KEO that allows clients to examine the most efficient ways to reduce carbon emissions through design. Based in Kuwait, the firm has offices in Bahrain, Oman, Qatar, Saudi Arabia, Dubai, Abu Dhabi and Portugal.

FINANCIAL DATA: Note: Data for latest year may not have been available at press time.

In U.S. $	2024	2023	2022	2021	2020	2019
Revenue						
R&D Expense						
Operating Income						
Operating Margin %						
SGA Expense						
Net Income						
Operating Cash Flow						
Capital Expenditure						
EBITDA						
Return on Assets %						
Return on Equity %						
Debt to Equity						

CONTACT INFORMATION:
Phone: 965-24651-6000   Fax: 965-2461-6001
Toll-Free:
Address: Free Trade Zone, Future Zone, Flamingo Complex, Bldg. 6, Safat, 13037 Kuwait

STOCK TICKER/OTHER:
Stock Ticker: Private   Exchange:
Employees: 2,500   Fiscal Year Ends:
Parent Company:

SALARIES/BONUSES:
Top Exec. Salary: $ Bonus: $
Second Exec. Salary: $ Bonus: $

OTHER THOUGHTS:
Estimated Female Officers or Directors:
Hot Spot for Advancement for Women/Minorities:

KEPCO Engineering & Construction Company Inc   www.kepco-enc.com

NAIC Code: 541330

TYPES OF BUSINESS:

Engineering Services
Power Plant
Power Plant Development
Engineering
Technology
Power Plant Pipe Maintenance
Procurement
Construction

BRANDS/DIVISIONS/AFFILIATES:

Korea Electric Power Corporation (KEPCO)
ToSPACE

GROWTH PLANS/SPECIAL FEATURES:

KEPCO Engineering & Construction Company, Inc. (KEPCO E&C) designs and develops power plant engineering technology. KEPCO stands for Korea Electric Power Corporation, of which KEPCO E&C is a wholly-owned subsidiary. In business since 1975, the firm developed the Korean-model nuclear reactor, as well as various unique technologies in both thermal and nuclear power, and in architectural design. KEPCO E&C specializes and performs R&D in nuclear power, thermal power, new energy, future technology development and overseas projects. Core engineering services consist of the engineering, procurement and construction of power plants. In addition, KEPCO E&C offers ToSPACE (Total Solution for Piping and Component Engineering), a program to manage pipe thickness at power plants because the pipes become thinner over time. The ToSPACE solution reduces human damage and economic losses caused by pipe rupture.

CONTACTS: Note: Officers with more than one job title may be intentionally listed here more than once.

Kim Tae-kyun, CEO

FINANCIAL DATA: Note: Data for latest year may not have been available at press time.

In U.S. $	2024	2023	2022	2021	2020	2019
Revenue		420,748,000	377,638,829	364,189,207	396,634,713	387,436,000
R&D Expense						
Operating Income						
Operating Margin %						
SGA Expense						
Net Income		25,206,000	13,418,263	13,833,450	18,521,496	22,796,900
Operating Cash Flow						
Capital Expenditure						
EBITDA						
Return on Assets %						
Return on Equity %						
Debt to Equity						

CONTACT INFORMATION:

Phone: 82-544213114   Fax: 82-544216114
Toll-Free:
Address: 269, Hyeoksin-ro, Gimcheon-si, Gyeongshangbuk-do, 39660 South Korea

STOCK TICKER/OTHER:

Stock Ticker: 52690   Exchange: Seoul
Employees: 2,080   Fiscal Year Ends: 12/31
Parent Company: Korea Electric Power Corporation (KEPCO)

SALARIES/BONUSES:

Top Exec. Salary: $ Bonus: $
Second Exec. Salary: $ Bonus: $

OTHER THOUGHTS:

Estimated Female Officers or Directors:
Hot Spot for Advancement for Women/Minorities:

Khatib & Alami

www.khatibalami.com

NAIC Code: 541330

TYPES OF BUSINESS:

Engineering Consulting Services
Engineering
Design-Build
Project Management
Geographic Information System (GIS)
Architecture and Planning
Buildings and Cities
Transportation and Water Infrastructure

BRANDS/DIVISIONS/AFFILIATES:

GROWTH PLANS/SPECIAL FEATURES:

Khatib & Alami (K&A) is a technology-enabled consulting company, with more than 30 offices worldwide. The firm's services include engineering, design, tendering, supervision, project management, design/build projects, geographic information systems (GIS) and client engineer representation/integrates with the client organization. K&A business divisions include architecture and planning regarding buildings, interior design and city/regional planning; infrastructure in the areas of transportation, water, environment, geotechnical and heavy civil; energy, including oil and gas, power and renewables; digital services, including geospatial systems integration, energy and utilities; and project management services, including project management consultancy, other areas of consulting and sustainability.

CONTACTS: *Note: Officers with more than one job title may be intentionally listed here more than once.*

Najib Khatib, CEO

FINANCIAL DATA: *Note: Data for latest year may not have been available at press time.*

In U.S. $	2024	2023	2022	2021	2020	2019
Revenue						
R&D Expense						
Operating Income						
Operating Margin %						
SGA Expense						
Net Income						
Operating Cash Flow						
Capital Expenditure						
EBITDA						
Return on Assets %						
Return on Equity %						
Debt to Equity						

CONTACT INFORMATION:

Phone: 961-1-843-843   Fax: 961-1-844-400
Toll-Free:
Address: Al Akhtal Assaghir St., Jnah, K&A Bldg., Beirut, 1105 2100
Lebanon

STOCK TICKER/OTHER:

Stock Ticker: Private   Exchange:
Employees: 6,000   Fiscal Year Ends:
Parent Company:

SALARIES/BONUSES:

Top Exec. Salary: $ Bonus: $
Second Exec. Salary: $ Bonus: $

OTHER THOUGHTS:

Estimated Female Officers or Directors:
Hot Spot for Advancement for Women/Minorities:

Kia Corporation

www.kia.com

NAIC Code: 336111

TYPES OF BUSINESS:

Automobile Manufacturing
Automobile Manufacture
Mobility Solutions
Electric Vehicles
Augmented Reality Technology
Driver Assistance Systems

BRANDS/DIVISIONS/AFFILIATES:

Hyundai Motor Group
Hyundai Motor Company
Kia EV6
Kia Sportage
Kia Niro
LX
GT
Kia Motor Corporation

CONTACTS: Note: Officers with more than one job title may be intentionally listed here more than once.

Jun-Young Choi, Co-CEO
Ho-Seong Song, Co-CEO
Eui-Seon Jeong, Director
Woo-Jeong Joo, Director

GROWTH PLANS/SPECIAL FEATURES:

Kia Corp is a Korean motor-vehicle manufacturer. While the company has factories in several countries, the majority of vehicles are manufactured domestically. The company's consolidated revenue is principally derived from the manufacture of passenger vehicles, with another third from recreational vehicles, and a small footprint in commercial vehicles. The three largest individual countries together constitute more than half of total retail sales, with the United States contributing the largest portion, followed closely by China and then Korea.

FINANCIAL DATA: Note: Data for latest year may not have been available at press time.

In U.S. $	2024	2023	2022	2021	2020	2019
Revenue	77,749,856,161	72,221,319,416	62,634,064,186	50,552,369,946	42,814,000,950	42,074,384,542
R&D Expense	1,243,349,000	1,088,177,000	909,724,400	757,471,200	648,757,600	661,377,900
Operating Income	9,166,028,000	8,401,423,000	5,234,166,000	3,666,366,000	1,496,074,000	1,454,279,000
Operating Margin %	.12%	.12%	.08%	.07%	.03%	.03%
SGA Expense	5,793,478,000	5,330,998,000	5,513,770,000	3,711,001,000	3,899,041,000	3,460,988,000
Net Income	7,071,706,000	6,351,011,000	3,914,260,000	3,444,659,000	1,076,416,000	1,321,769,000
Operating Cash Flow	9,091,570,000	8,174,160,000	6,753,488,000	5,325,453,000	3,924,728,000	2,612,670,000
Capital Expenditure	3,388,327,000	2,264,979,000	1,516,922,000	1,376,748,000	1,678,621,000	1,743,772,000
EBITDA	11,686,820,000	11,007,920,000	7,350,015,000	6,355,618,000	3,108,152,000	3,508,915,000
Return on Assets %	.11%	.11%	.08%	.07%	.03%	.03%
Return on Equity %	.19%	.20%	.15%	.15%	.05%	.06%
Debt to Equity	.04%	.06%	.11%	.15%	0.171	0.144

CONTACT INFORMATION:

Phone: 82 234641114   Fax: 82 234646816
Toll-Free:
Address: 12 Heolleung-ro Seocho-gu, Seoul, 06797 South Korea

STOCK TICKER/OTHER:

Stock Ticker: KIMTF   Exchange: PINX
Employees: 51,899   Fiscal Year Ends: 12/31
Parent Company: Hyundai Motor Group

SALARIES/BONUSES:

Top Exec. Salary: $ Bonus: $
Second Exec. Salary: $ Bonus: $

OTHER THOUGHTS:

Estimated Female Officers or Directors:
Hot Spot for Advancement for Women/Minorities:

Kiewit Corporation

NAIC Code: 237310

www.kiewit.com

TYPES OF BUSINESS:

Construction & Engineering Services
Building Engineering
Construction Engineering
Industrial Engineering
Mining Engineering
Oil and Gas Engineering
Transportation Engineering
Water Engineering

BRANDS/DIVISIONS/AFFILIATES:

CONTACTS: *Note: Officers with more than one job title may be intentionally listed here more than once.*

Rick Lanoha, CEO

GROWTH PLANS/SPECIAL FEATURES:

Kiewit Corporation, based in Omaha, Nebraska and employee-owned, is one of the largest general contractors in the world. The firm is organized into seven business divisions: building, industrial, mining, oil/gas/chemical, power, transportation and water/wastewater. The building division focuses on office buildings, industrial complexes, education and sports facilities, hotels, hospitals, transportation terminals, science and technology facilities and manufacturing plants, as well as retail and special-use facilities. The segment is Leadership in Energy and Environmental Design (LEED) certified. The industrial division has extensive experience in industrial engineering and construction with work including mineral processing; cement; bulk manufacturing; industrial water; metals; pulp and paper; specialty chemicals; food and beverage; pharmaceuticals and advanced manufacturing. The mining division specializes in mine management, production, maintenance, contract mining, ore processing and mine infrastructure. The oil, gas and chemical division partners with domestic and international oil and gas firms to develop energy sources. It offers clients a fully integrated delivery model for engineer-procure-construct (EPC) and startup services for their energy needs. This division focuses on the market sectors of offshore, oil sands, midstream and downstream. The power division helps clients meet the challenge of changing power consumption trends by building run-of-the-river hydroelectric, nuclear and geothermal power plants, as well as cogeneration, combined-cycle and waste-to-energy generation and resource facilities. The transportation division builds highways, bridges, rails and runways in order to connect the world. Its transportation projects deliver engineering solutions and construction services for air, bridge, marine/port, rail, roads and tunnels sectors, among others. Lastly, water/wastewater performs water supply projects such as roller-compacted concrete, earth-fill and rock-fill dams, reservoirs, water tunnels and canals across North America. Kiewet has hundreds of subsidiaries and offices located in the U.S., Canada and Mexico.

FINANCIAL DATA: *Note: Data for latest year may not have been available at press time.*

In U.S. $	2024	2023	2022	2021	2020	2019
Revenue	17,955,000,000	17,100,000,000	13,700,000,000	12,100,000,000	12,500,000,000	10,300,000,000
R&D Expense						
Operating Income						
Operating Margin %						
SGA Expense						
Net Income						
Operating Cash Flow						
Capital Expenditure						
EBITDA						
Return on Assets %						
Return on Equity %						
Debt to Equity						

CONTACT INFORMATION:

Phone: 402-342-2052   Fax: 402-271-2829
Toll-Free:
Address: 1550 Mike Fahey St., Omaha, NE 68102 United States

STOCK TICKER/OTHER:

Stock Ticker: Private   Exchange:
Employees: 31,100   Fiscal Year Ends:
Parent Company:

SALARIES/BONUSES:

Top Exec. Salary: $ Bonus: $
Second Exec. Salary: $ Bonus: $

OTHER THOUGHTS:

Estimated Female Officers or Directors:
Hot Spot for Advancement for Women/Minorities:

Kimley-Horn and Associates Inc

www.kimley-horn.com

NAIC Code: 541330

TYPES OF BUSINESS:

Engineering
Project Consulting
Planning and Design
Community Development
Mixed-Use Development
Energy and Environmental Services
Landscape Architecture
Project Management

BRANDS/DIVISIONS/AFFILIATES:

CONTACTS: Note: Officers with more than one job title may be intentionally listed here more than once.

Steve Lefton, CEO
John Atz, Pres.
Julie Beauvais, Dir.-Corp. Comm.
Varner Olmsted, Controller
Richard Adams, VP
Kurt Cooper, Sr. VP

GROWTH PLANS/SPECIAL FEATURES:

Kimley-Horn and Associates, Inc. is a planning and design consultancy with more than 120 offices across the U.S. The company taps into a variety of markets for clients in both private and public sectors across industries including education, institutions, energy, healthcare, hospitality/resorts, industrial, mixed-use development, office/corporate, residential, retail, sports and entertainment, telecommunications, water, aerospace, government, parks and recreation, transit and more. Services by Kimley-Horn include aviation, community planning, development management, development services, energy, environmental, forensics, grants/funding, landscape architecture, mechanical/electrical/plumbing, parking, pavement and asset management, resilience, roadway and bridge, Safety Act designated TMCS, streetscape/landscape/irrigation, structural, surface water, sustainable and green design, technology and software, transit and rail, transportation planning, transportation systems management/operations, urban design and water/wastewater.

Kimley-Horn offers its employees comprehensive health coverage, a health savings account, life and short-/long-term disability insurance coverage, an employee assistance program, a 401(k), internal trainings, tuition reimbursement and more.

FINANCIAL DATA: Note: Data for latest year may not have been available at press time.

In U.S. $	2024	2023	2022	2021	2020	2019
Revenue	1,638,000,000	1,560,000,000	1,500,000,000	944,143,200	907,830,000	917,000,000
R&D Expense						
Operating Income						
Operating Margin %						
SGA Expense						
Net Income						
Operating Cash Flow						
Capital Expenditure						
EBITDA						
Return on Assets %						
Return on Equity %						
Debt to Equity						

CONTACT INFORMATION:

Phone: 919-677-2000   Fax: 919-677-2050
Toll-Free: 888-524-4636
Address: 421 Fayetteville St., Ste. 600, Raleigh, NC 27601 United States

STOCK TICKER/OTHER:

Stock Ticker: Private   Exchange:
Employees: 7,000   Fiscal Year Ends: 12/31
Parent Company:

SALARIES/BONUSES:

Top Exec. Salary: $ Bonus: $
Second Exec. Salary: $ Bonus: $

OTHER THOUGHTS:

Estimated Female Officers or Directors: 1
Hot Spot for Advancement for Women/Minorities:

Kleinfelder Group Inc (The)

NAIC Code: 541330

TYPES OF BUSINESS:

Engineering Consulting Services
Engineering
Construction Management
Construction Materials Inspection and Testing
Environmental Professional Services
Natural Resources
Remediation
Electrical and Mechanical Engineering

BRANDS/DIVISIONS/AFFILIATES:

Lindsay Goldberg

CONTACTS: Note: Officers with more than one job title may be intentionally listed here more than once.

Louis Armstrong, CEO
John A. Murphy, COO
Erik Soderquist, CFO
Patrick Schaffner, Sr. VP-Human Resources
George J. Pierson, Chmn.

GROWTH PLANS/SPECIAL FEATURES:

The Kleinfelder Group, Inc. (Kleinfelder) was founded in 1961 and is a leading engineering, design, construction management, construction materials inspection and testing, and environmental professional services firm. Markets Kleinfelder serves are grouped into five categories, including energy, facilities, government, transportation and water; and its services are grouped into environmental, geotechnical, design, construction materials engineering and testing and construction management. Services by the firm are very vast, and include, but are not limited to, air quality, data management and analysis, environmental remediation, graphic design and visualization, hydrogeology, natural resources, earthquake and seismic design, foundation design, rock engineering, tunnel engineering, architecture, urban planning and landscape design, bridge engineering, electrical engineering, mechanical engineering, water and wastewater services, construction observation and inspection, laboratory testing, construction management, design-build and project controls. Kleinfelder is headquartered in San Diego, California, with more than 100 office locations in the U.S., Canada and Australia. The firm is owned by Lindsay Goldberg, a private investment company.

Kleinfelder Group offers its U.S. and Canadian employees health, financial and other types of benefits.

FINANCIAL DATA: Note: Data for latest year may not have been available at press time.

In U.S. $	2024	2023	2022	2021	2020	2019
Revenue						
R&D Expense						
Operating Income						
Operating Margin %						
SGA Expense						
Net Income						
Operating Cash Flow						
Capital Expenditure						
EBITDA						
Return on Assets %						
Return on Equity %						
Debt to Equity						

CONTACT INFORMATION:

Phone: 619-831-4600   Fax: 619-232-1039
Toll-Free:
Address: 770 First Ave., Ste. 400, San Diego, CA 92101 United States

STOCK TICKER/OTHER:

Stock Ticker: Private   Exchange:
Employees: 1,900   Fiscal Year Ends:
Parent Company: Lindsay Goldberg

SALARIES/BONUSES:

Top Exec. Salary: $ Bonus: $
Second Exec. Salary: $ Bonus: $

OTHER THOUGHTS:

Estimated Female Officers or Directors:
Hot Spot for Advancement for Women/Minorities:

Konami Group Corp

NAIC Code: 511210G

www.konami.com/en

TYPES OF BUSINESS:
Computer Software, Electronic Games, Apps & Entertainment
Toys
Arcade Games
Mobile Phone Media Content
Sports Clubs
Health & Fitness Products
Casino Games
Casino Management Systems

BRANDS/DIVISIONS/AFFILIATES:
Konami Digital Entertainment Co Ltd
Konami Gaming inc
Konami Australia Pty Ltd
Konami Amusement Co Ltd
Internet Revolution Inc
Konami Real Estate Inc
Konami Corporation of America
Konami Digital Entertainment BV

GROWTH PLANS/SPECIAL FEATURES:
Konami Group Corp is a Japan-based company that develops, publishes, markets, and distributes video game software products for stationary consoles and for portable consoles. It also produces gaming machines for casinos and operates Health & Fitness clubs. The company operates through four business operations namely Digital Entertainment, Amusement, Gaming & Systems, and Sports. The company generates the majority of its revenue from the Digital Entertainment segment which is involved in the production, manufacture, and sale of digital content and related products including mobile games, card games, and computer and video games. Geographically, the company derives a majority of its revenue from Japan and the rest from the United States, Europe, Asia, and Oceania regions.

CONTACTS:
Note: Officers with more than one job title may be intentionally listed here more than once.
Kagemasa Kozuki, Chairman of the Board
Kimihiko Higashio, Director

FINANCIAL DATA:
Note: Data for latest year may not have been available at press time.

In U.S. $	2024	2023	2022	2021	2020	2019
Revenue	2,501,485,860	2,182,178,706	2,079,436,327	1,892,918,745	1,824,562,634	1,822,750,657
R&D Expense						
Operating Income	557,220,200	320,640,100	516,766,200	253,749,000	215,023,600	350,749,800
Operating Margin %	.22%	.15%	.25%	.13%	.12%	.19%
SGA Expense	498,646,200	456,678,700	378,533,700	342,106,400	385,101,300	365,391,600
Net Income	410,795,600	242,259,100	380,491,600	223,972,500	138,100,500	237,406,300
Operating Cash Flow	715,502,700	250,610,900	670,244,400	484,379,400	355,220,800	341,092,800
Capital Expenditure	203,526,800	303,936,400	160,566,500	163,572,600	434,358,500	165,294,400
EBITDA	740,190,300	497,896,400	652,089,700	387,788,100	401,853,700	452,790,900
Return on Assets %	.10%	.06%	.11%	.07%	.05%	.09%
Return on Equity %	.15%	.10%	.17%	.11%	.07%	.13%
Debt to Equity	.14%	.16%	.17%	.23%	0.037	0.036

CONTACT INFORMATION:
Phone: 81 36636-0573   Fax: 81 36893-1573
Toll-Free:
Address: 1-11-1, Ginza, Chuo-ku, Tokyo, 104-0061 Japan

STOCK TICKER/OTHER:
Stock Ticker: KONMY   Exchange: PINX
Employees: 9,045   Fiscal Year Ends: 03/31
Parent Company:

SALARIES/BONUSES:
Top Exec. Salary: $ Bonus: $
Second Exec. Salary: $ Bonus: $

OTHER THOUGHTS:
Estimated Female Officers or Directors:
Hot Spot for Advancement for Women/Minorities:

Koninklijke Philips NV (Royal Philips)

www.philips.com

NAIC Code: 334310

TYPES OF BUSINESS:

Manufacturing-Electrical & Electronic Equipment
Consumer Electronics & Appliances
Lighting Systems
Medical Imaging Equipment
Semiconductors
Consulting Services
Nanotech Research
MEMS

BRANDS/DIVISIONS/AFFILIATES:

BioTelemetry Inc

GROWTH PLANS/SPECIAL FEATURES:

Koninklijke Philips is a diversified global healthcare company operating in three segments: diagnosis and treatment, connected care, and personal health. Nearly 50% of the company's revenue comes from the diagnosis and treatment segment, which features imaging systems, ultrasound equipment, and image-guided therapy solutions. The connected care segment (around 30% of revenue) encompasses monitoring and analytics systems for hospitals, informatics business, and also houses the sleep and respiratory care segment. Personal health business (remainder of revenue) is mainly oral health and personal care product lines, which include electric toothbrushes and men's grooming and personal care products.

CONTACTS:
Note: Officers with more than one job title may be intentionally listed here more than once.

Roy Jakobs, CEO
Abhijit Bhattacharya, CFO
Feike Sijbesma, Chairman of the Board
Marnix Van Ginneken, Chief Legal Officer
Shez Partovi, Chief Strategy Officer
Willem Appelo, COO
Paulus Stoffels, Director
Andy Ho, Executive VP
Bert van Meurs, Executive VP
Edwin Paalvast, Executive VP
Deeptha Khanna, Executive VP
Jeff DiLullo, Executive VP
Heidi Sichien, Executive VP
Steve de Baca, Executive VP
Julia Strandberg, Executive VP

FINANCIAL DATA:
Note: Data for latest year may not have been available at press time.

In U.S. $	2024	2023	2022	2021	2020	2019
Revenue	20,455,163,663	20,623,155,455	20,234,960,657	19,473,325,496	19,650,397,297	19,463,109,905
R&D Expense	1,982,974,000	2,145,289,000	2,373,439,000	2,049,943,000	2,068,104,000	2,031,782,000
Operating Income	582,292,900	-190,692,400	-200,908,100	707,151,000	1,593,644,000	1,578,888,000
Operating Margin %	.03%	-.01%	-.01%	.04%	.08%	.08%
SGA Expense	5,752,554,000	5,825,199,000	6,006,811,000	5,513,053,000	5,316,686,000	5,347,333,000
Net Income	-796,821,800	-528,944,400	-1,825,199,000	3,767,310,000	1,347,333,000	1,324,631,000
Operating Cash Flow	1,780,931,000	2,424,518,000	-196,367,800	1,849,035,000	2,850,170,000	2,057,889,000
Capital Expenditure	767,309,900	730,987,500	914,869,400	866,061,300	1,015,891,000	1,079,455,000
EBITDA	2,098,751,000	1,181,612,000	130,533,500	2,265,607,000	3,240,636,000	3,188,422,000
Return on Assets %	-.02%	-.02%	-.05%	.11%	.04%	.04%
Return on Equity %	-.06%	-.04%	-.12%	.25%	.10%	.09%
Debt to Equity	.59%	.58%	.53%	.40%	0.471	0.387

CONTACT INFORMATION:

Phone: 31 402791111   Fax:
Toll-Free: 877-248-4237
Address: Breitner Ctr., Amstelplein 2, Amsterdam, 1096 BC Netherlands

STOCK TICKER/OTHER:

Stock Ticker: PHG
Employees: 69,656
Parent Company:

Exchange: NYS
Fiscal Year Ends: 12/31

SALARIES/BONUSES:

Top Exec. Salary: $1,182,576   Bonus: $236,515
Second Exec. Salary: $915,153   Bonus: $

OTHER THOUGHTS:

Estimated Female Officers or Directors: 3
Hot Spot for Advancement for Women/Minorities: Y

Kumho Engineering & Construction Co Ltd   www.kumhoenc.com

NAIC Code: 236220

TYPES OF BUSINESS:

Commercial and Institutional Building Construction
Architecture
Building Construction
Civil Engineering
Technology
Housing Developments
Plant Engineering
Environmental Engineering

BRANDS/DIVISIONS/AFFILIATES:

GROWTH PLANS/SPECIAL FEATURES:

Kumho Industrial Co., Ltd. provides engineering and construction services in South Korea and internationally. The firm's business activities are divided into four divisions: buildings, civil works, housing and environment/plant. The buildings division is focused on architecture, designing, developing and constructing buildings in relation to city/urban development, including public, business, education, research, correction, military, airport, sales, culture, medical and various types of overseas buildings and facilities. The civil works division designs, develops and constructs buildings in relation to cities and its respective country, including airports, railways, roads, housing, harbors and various related overseas construction. The housing division designs, develops and constructs residential complexes such as apartments and various types of residential living spaces. Last, the environment/plant division is engaged in industrial development, including energy storage, petrochemicals, industrial facilities and solutions, as well as environmental facilities and solutions.

CONTACTS: Note: Officers with more than one job title may be intentionally listed here more than once.

Jae-Hwan Seo, CEO
Bak Sam Koo, CEO-Kumho Asiana Group

FINANCIAL DATA: Note: Data for latest year may not have been available at press time.

In U.S. $	2024	2023	2022	2021	2020	2019
Revenue		1,711,752,000	1,530,990,628	1,736,392,309	1,680,880,000	1,379,790,000
R&D Expense						
Operating Income						
Operating Margin %						
SGA Expense						
Net Income			15,838,991	124,548,981	24,276,400	47,909,400
Operating Cash Flow						
Capital Expenditure						
EBITDA						
Return on Assets %						
Return on Equity %						
Debt to Equity						

CONTACT INFORMATION:

Phone: 82 2-6303-0102   Fax: 82-2-6303-0734
Toll-Free:
Address: 26 Centropolis A, Ujeongguk-ro, Jongno-gu, Seoul, 03161 South Korea

STOCK TICKER/OTHER:

Stock Ticker: 2990   Exchange: Seoul
Employees: 868   Fiscal Year Ends: 12/31
Parent Company:

SALARIES/BONUSES:

Top Exec. Salary: $ Bonus: $
Second Exec. Salary: $ Bonus: $

OTHER THOUGHTS:

Estimated Female Officers or Directors:
Hot Spot for Advancement for Women/Minorities:

L3Harris Technologies Inc

www.l3harris.com

NAIC Code: 334220

TYPES OF BUSINESS:

Communications Equipment Manufacturing
Aerospace and Defense Technology
Communication Systems
Electronic Systems
Space Systems
Intelligence Systems
Command and Control Systems
Signals Intelligence Systems

BRANDS/DIVISIONS/AFFILIATES:

GROWTH PLANS/SPECIAL FEATURES:

L3Harris Technologies provides products primarily for the command, control, communications, computers, intelligence, surveillance, and reconnaissance, or C4ISR, market. The firm produces uncrewed aerial vehicles, sensors, and avionics, provides military and commercial training services, and maintains the US Federal Aviation Administration's communications infrastructure. In July 2023, the company acquired Aerojet Rocketdyne, a key supplier of rocket motors used in the space industry and to propel munitions.

CONTACTS: Note: Officers with more than one job title may be intentionally listed here more than once.

Christopher Kubasik, CEO
Kenneth Bedingfield, CFO
John Cantillon, Chief Accounting Officer
Scott Mikuen, General Counsel
Melanie Rakita, Other Executive Officer
Ross Niebergall, President, Divisional
Jonathan Rambeau, President, Divisional
Samir Mehta, President, Divisional
Edward Zoiss, President, Divisional

FINANCIAL DATA: Note: Data for latest year may not have been available at press time.

In U.S. $	2024	2023	2022	2021	2020	2019
Revenue	21,325,000,704	19,419,000,832	17,061,999,616	17,813,999,616	18,193,999,872	6,800,999,936
R&D Expense	515,000,000	480,000,000				
Operating Income	2,077,000,000	2,025,000,000	1,929,000,000	2,096,000,000	1,993,000,000	1,092,000,000
Operating Margin %	.10%	.10%	.11%	.12%	.11%	.16%
SGA Expense	2,153,000,000	1,921,000,000	2,998,000,000	3,280,000,000	3,315,000,000	1,242,000,000
Net Income	1,502,000,000	1,227,000,000	1,062,000,000	1,846,000,000	1,119,000,000	949,000,000
Operating Cash Flow	2,559,000,000	2,096,000,000	2,158,000,000	2,687,000,000	2,790,000,000	1,185,000,000
Capital Expenditure	408,000,000	449,000,000	252,000,000	342,000,000	368,000,000	161,000,000
EBITDA	3,561,000,000	2,930,000,000	2,490,000,000	3,515,000,000	2,608,000,000	1,538,000,000
Return on Assets %	.04%	.03%	.03%	.05%	.03%	.10%
Return on Equity %	.08%	.07%	.06%	.09%	.05%	.29%
Debt to Equity	.57%	.59%	.34%	.41%	0.37	0.822

CONTACT INFORMATION:

Phone: 321 727-9100   Fax: 321 724-3973
Toll-Free: 800-442-7747
Address: 1025 West NASA Blvd., Melbourne, FL 32919 United States

STOCK TICKER/OTHER:

Stock Ticker: LHX   Exchange: NYS
Employees: 50,000   Fiscal Year Ends: 06/30
Parent Company:

SALARIES/BONUSES:

Top Exec. Salary: $1,582,788   Bonus: $
Second Exec. Salary: Bonus: $
$889,664

OTHER THOUGHTS:

Estimated Female Officers or Directors: 2
Hot Spot for Advancement for Women/Minorities: Y

Langan Engineering and Environmental Services Inc

www.langan.com

NAIC Code: 541330

TYPES OF BUSINESS:

Engineering Consulting Services
Engineering
Consulting
Environmental Services
Infrastructure Engineering
Buildings
Resorts and Casinos
Residential Properties

BRANDS/DIVISIONS/AFFILIATES:

CONTACTS: Note: Officers with more than one job title may be intentionally listed here more than once.

David T. Gockel, CEO
Eric Vervoordt, COO
Shekhar Yadavalli, CFO
Sam Ishak, CIO

GROWTH PLANS/SPECIAL FEATURES:

Langan Engineering and Environmental Services, Inc. provides integrated site engineering and environmental consulting services regarding land development projects, corporate real estate portfolios and the energy industry. Clients of Langan include developers, property owners, public agencies, corporations, institutions and energy companies worldwide. The company's services include site/civil, geotechnical, environmental, energy, earthquake/seismic, traffic and transportation, surveying, geospatial, environmental compliance, EHS management and compliance, landscape architecture, land use planning, natural resources and permitting, sustainable design, waterfront and marine, geologic hazards, PFAS, demolition, ESG (environmental, social and governance) consulting and digital solutions. Langan's portfolio spans tall buildings, land recycling, colleges/universities, environmental remediation, warehouse and distribution centers, residential, hospitals and healthcare, government (federal, state and local), retail, stadium and arena, infrastructure, mixed-use, resorts and casinos, data centers, office buildings, renewable energy, waterfront and marine, airports, entertainment and cultural/parks. Langan is headquartered in New Jersey, with offices throughout the U.S., as well as in Athens, Greece; Alberta and British Columbia, Canada; Dubai, UAE; London, U.K.; and Panama City, Panama.

LEES offers its employees health and financial benefits, and company training and development programs.

FINANCIAL DATA: Note: Data for latest year may not have been available at press time.

In U.S. $	2024	2023	2022	2021	2020	2019
Revenue						
R&D Expense						
Operating Income						
Operating Margin %						
SGA Expense						
Net Income						
Operating Cash Flow						
Capital Expenditure						
EBITDA						
Return on Assets %						
Return on Equity %						
Debt to Equity						

CONTACT INFORMATION:

Phone: 973-560-4900   Fax: 973-560-4901
Toll-Free:
Address: 300 Kimball Dr., Fl. 4, Parsippany, NJ 07054 United States

STOCK TICKER/OTHER:

Stock Ticker: Private   Exchange:
Employees: 1,300   Fiscal Year Ends:
Parent Company:

SALARIES/BONUSES:

Top Exec. Salary: $ Bonus: $
Second Exec. Salary: $ Bonus: $

OTHER THOUGHTS:

Estimated Female Officers or Directors:
Hot Spot for Advancement for Women/Minorities:

Lanxess AG

www.lanxess.com

NAIC Code: 325211

TYPES OF BUSINESS:

Plastics Material and Resin Manufacturing
Performance Chemicals
Chemical Intermediates
Engineering Plastics
Performance Rubber

GROWTH PLANS/SPECIAL FEATURES:

Lanxess AG is a German chemical company that was originally spun out of Bayer. Lanxess has visibly decommoditised its portfolio by divesting its synthetic rubber business. It has business segments namely: specialty chemicals company in the fields of consumer protection chemicals, specialty additives, intermediates, and others. Geographically, it operates in EMEA (excluding Germany), Germany, Americas, and Asia-Pacific.

BRANDS/DIVISIONS/AFFILIATES:

CONTACTS: Note: Officers with more than one job title may be intentionally listed here more than once.

Matthias Wolfgruber, Chairman of the Board
Ralf Sikorski, Director

FINANCIAL DATA: Note: Data for latest year may not have been available at press time.

In U.S. $	2024	2023	2022	2021	2020	2019
Revenue	7,225,879,835	7,620,885,220	9,180,476,741	6,925,085,356	6,928,490,359	7,720,771,713
R&D Expense	118,047,700	112,372,300	115,777,500	107,832,000	122,588,000	129,398,400
Operating Income	56,753,690	-56,753,690	483,541,400	412,031,800	468,785,500	661,748,000
Operating Margin %	.01%	-.01%	.05%	.06%	.07%	.09%
SGA Expense	1,303,065,000	1,375,709,000	1,569,807,000	1,239,501,000	1,180,477,000	1,232,690,000
Net Income	-200,908,100	502,837,700	283,768,400	303,064,700	1,004,540,000	232,690,100
Operating Cash Flow	576,617,500	951,191,800	180,476,700	461,975,000	664,018,200	729,852,400
Capital Expenditure	363,223,600	370,034,000	461,975,000	481,271,300	517,593,600	576,617,500
EBITDA	505,107,800	164,585,700	1,013,621,000	793,416,600	1,889,898,000	1,082,860,000
Return on Assets %	-.02%	.04%	.02%	.03%	.10%	.02%
Return on Equity %	-.04%	.10%	.06%	.08%	.31%	.08%
Debt to Equity	.53%	.65%	.77%	.75%	0.754	1.039

CONTACT INFORMATION:

Phone: 49 221 8885-0   Fax:
Toll-Free:
Address: Kennedyplatz 1, Cologne, 50569 Germany

STOCK TICKER/OTHER:

Stock Ticker: LNXSY   Exchange: PINX
Employees: 12,787   Fiscal Year Ends: 12/31
Parent Company:

SALARIES/BONUSES:

Top Exec. Salary: $ Bonus: $
Second Exec. Salary: $ Bonus: $

OTHER THOUGHTS:

Estimated Female Officers or Directors: 3
Hot Spot for Advancement for Women/Minorities: Y

Larsen & Toubro Limited (L&T)

www.larsentoubro.com

NAIC Code: 237000

TYPES OF BUSINESS:

Heavy Construction and Engineering
Engineering
Construction
Manufacturing
Hydrocarbon
Shipbuilding
Infrastructure
Artificial Intelligence

BRANDS/DIVISIONS/AFFILIATES:

L&T Hydrocarbon Engineering
L&T Heavy Engineering
L&T Valves
L&T Infotech
L&T Technology Services
L&T Infrastructure Development Projects Ltd
L&T Metro Rail
L&T NxT

GROWTH PLANS/SPECIAL FEATURES:

Larsen & Toubro Ltd is a technology, engineering, manufacturing, and financial services conglomerate operating globally. It enters into contracts to construct various facilities, develop solutions for offshore and onshore hydrocarbon projects, serve power plants, build ships, and perform other engineering projects. Its integrated capabilities help customers throughout the entire value chain, from design to delivering a project. The company's operating segments are: Infrastructure projects, Energy projects, Hi-Tech Manufacturing, IT & Technology services, Financial services, Development projects, and other segments. A majority of its revenue is generated from the Infrastructure projects segment. Geographically, the group generates maximum revenue from its operations in India.

CONTACTS: Note: Officers with more than one job title may be intentionally listed here more than once.

Ramamurthi Raman, CFO
Sekharipuram Subrahmanyan, Chairman of the Board
Anil Parab, Director
Subramanian Sarma, Director
Maddur Satish, Director
Tharayil Madhava Das, Director
Sudhindra Desai, Director
A Sivaram Nair, Other Corporate Officer

FINANCIAL DATA: Note: Data for latest year may not have been available at press time.

In U.S. $	2024	2023	2022	2021	2020	2019
Revenue	25,622,890,369	21,243,073,150	18,203,983,648	15,725,405,985	16,875,054,858	
R&D Expense						
Operating Income	2,541,183,000	2,280,459,000	2,261,699,000	1,826,799,000	1,821,631,000	
Operating Margin %	.10%	.11%	.12%	.12%	.11%	
SGA Expense	614,921,700	542,358,400	455,059,600	367,616,000	501,550,600	
Net Income	1,527,103,000	1,224,422,000	1,013,772,000	1,354,482,000	1,116,642,000	
Operating Cash Flow	2,136,017,000	2,663,486,000	2,240,945,000	2,698,200,000	782,767,100	
Capital Expenditure	528,152,800	484,565,400	363,750,000	211,388,300	401,893,900	
EBITDA	3,242,487,000	2,768,023,000	2,395,869,000	2,216,417,000	2,176,969,000	
Return on Assets %	.04%	.03%	.03%	.04%	.03%	
Return on Equity %	.15%	.12%	.11%	.16%	.15%	
Debt to Equity	.67%	.70%	.76%	1.09%	1.239	

CONTACT INFORMATION:

Phone: 91-22-67525656   Fax: 91-22-67525893
Toll-Free:
Address: L&T House, N.M. Marg, Ballard Estate, PO Box 278, Mumbai, Maharashtra 400 001 India

STOCK TICKER/OTHER:

Stock Ticker: LTOUF   Exchange: PINX
Employees: 59,018   Fiscal Year Ends: 03/31
Parent Company:

SALARIES/BONUSES:

Top Exec. Salary: $4,630,734   Bonus: $
Second Exec. Salary: Bonus: $
$2,806,506

OTHER THOUGHTS:

Estimated Female Officers or Directors:
Hot Spot for Advancement for Women/Minorities:

Layne-A Granite Company   www.graniteconstruction.com/company/our-brands/layne

NAIC Code: 237110

TYPES OF BUSINESS:

Construction & Civil Engineering Services
Water Well Drilling
Water Well Management
Rehabilitation Services
Maintenance
Repair
Mineral Underground Development
Mineral Drilling Services

BRANDS/DIVISIONS/AFFILIATES:

Granite Construction Inc

GROWTH PLANS/SPECIAL FEATURES:

Layne, a Granite Company, provides sustainable solutions for water resources and mineral exploration. The company delivers water and mineral solutions throughout North and South America. Its water resources division offers services that range from water well drilling and management to infrastructure, with specialties including water well rehabilitation and maintenance, and the repair of wells and pumps. The mineral services division identifies and develops underground bases and mineral deposits. It is one of the largest providers of drilling services for the global mineral services industry. Layne operates as a subsidiary of Granite Construction, Inc.

CONTACTS: Note: Officers with more than one job title may be intentionally listed here more than once.

Kyle Larkin, Pres.
Lisa Curtis, Chief Accounting Officer
Michael Caliel, Director
Steven Crooke, General Counsel
Larry Purlee, President, Subsidiary
Kevin Maher, Senior VP, Divisional
J. Anderson, Senior VP

FINANCIAL DATA: Note: Data for latest year may not have been available at press time.

In U.S. $	2024	2023	2022	2021	2020	2019
Revenue	543,074,700	517,214,000	497,321,000	533,843,916	494,299,922	499,292,850
R&D Expense						
Operating Income						
Operating Margin %						
SGA Expense						
Net Income						
Operating Cash Flow						
Capital Expenditure						
EBITDA						
Return on Assets %						
Return on Equity %						
Debt to Equity						

CONTACT INFORMATION:

Phone: 913-321-5000   Fax:
Toll-Free:
Address: 620 S. 38th St., Kansas City, KS 66106 United States

STOCK TICKER/OTHER:

Stock Ticker: Subsidiary   Exchange:
Employees: 2,300   Fiscal Year Ends: 12/31
Parent Company: Granite Construction Inc

SALARIES/BONUSES:

Top Exec. Salary: $ Bonus: $
Second Exec. Salary: $ Bonus: $

OTHER THOUGHTS:

Estimated Female Officers or Directors: 2
Hot Spot for Advancement for Women/Minorities: Y

Lear Corporation

www.lear.com

NAIC Code: 336300

TYPES OF BUSINESS:
Automobile Components
Automotive Interiors
Electrical Systems
Instrument Panels
Seat Systems
Flooring Systems
Entertainment & Wireless Systems
Keyless Entry Systems

BRANDS/DIVISIONS/AFFILIATES:

GROWTH PLANS/SPECIAL FEATURES:
Lear Corp designs, develops, and manufactures automotive seating and electrical systems and components. The company has two reporting segments Seating and E-Systems. Seating components include frames and mechanisms, covers (leather and woven fabric), seat heating and cooling, foam, and headrests. Automotive electrical distribution and connection systems and electronic systems include wiring harnesses, terminals and connectors, on-board battery chargers, high-voltage battery management systems. The company earns most of its revenue from the seating segment.

CONTACTS: *Note: Officers with more than one job title may be intentionally listed here more than once.*
Raymond Scott, CEO
Jason Cardew, CFO
Gregory Smith, Chairman of the Board
Amy Doyle, Chief Accounting Officer
Harry Kemp, Chief Administrative Officer
Alicia Davis, Chief Strategy Officer
Frank Orsini, President, Divisional
Nicholas Roelli, President, Divisional
Carl Esposito, Senior VP, Divisional
Marianne Vldershain, Treasurer

FINANCIAL DATA: *Note: Data for latest year may not have been available at press time.*

In U.S. $	2024	2023	2022	2021	2020	2019
Revenue	23,306,000,384	23,466,899,456	20,891,500,544	19,263,100,928	17,045,499,904	19,810,299,904
R&D Expense						
Operating Income	887,700,000	933,200,000	654,300,000	675,400,000	454,100,000	1,070,200,000
Operating Margin %	.04%	.04%	.03%	.04%	.03%	.05%
SGA Expense	702,500,000	714,700,000	684,800,000	643,200,000	588,900,000	605,000,000
Net Income	506,600,000	572,500,000	327,700,000	373,900,000	158,500,000	753,600,000
Operating Cash Flow	1,120,100,000	1,249,300,000	1,021,400,000	670,100,000	663,100,000	1,284,300,000
Capital Expenditure	558,700,000	626,500,000	638,200,000	585,100,000	452,300,000	603,900,000
EBITDA	1,459,800,000	1,482,700,000	1,184,400,000	1,249,200,000	938,800,000	1,555,500,000
Return on Assets %	.04%	.04%	.02%	.03%	.01%	.07%
Return on Equity %	.11%	.12%	.07%	.08%	.04%	.18%
Debt to Equity	.61%	.56%	.55%	.56%	0.515	0.527

CONTACT INFORMATION:
Phone: 248 447-1500 Fax:
Toll-Free: 800-413-5327
Address: 21557 Telegraph Rd., Southfield, MI 48033 United States

STOCK TICKER/OTHER:
Stock Ticker: LEA Exchange: NYS
Employees: 186,600 Fiscal Year Ends: 12/31
Parent Company:

SALARIES/BONUSES:
Top Exec. Salary: $1,323,333 Bonus: $
Second Exec. Salary: Bonus: $
$866,667

OTHER THOUGHTS:
Estimated Female Officers or Directors: 1
Hot Spot for Advancement for Women/Minorities:

Leidos Holdings Inc

NAIC Code: 541512

www.leidos.com

TYPES OF BUSINESS:

Computer Systems Design and Related Services
Consultancy
Defense Solutions
Civil Protection
Digital Protection
Health Solutions

BRANDS/DIVISIONS/AFFILIATES:

Leidos Inc

GROWTH PLANS/SPECIAL FEATURES:

Leidos Holdings Inc is a technology, engineering, and science company that provides services and solutions in the defense, intelligence, civil, and health markets, both domestically and internationally. Company customer includes the U.S. Department of Defense ("DoD"), the U.S. Intelligence Community, the U.S. Department of Homeland Security ("DHS"), the Federal Aviation Administration ("FAA"), the Department of Veterans Affairs ("VA"), and many other U.S. civilian, state and local government agencies, etc. The company is engaged in four reportable segments; National Security & Digital, Health & Civil, Commercial & International and Defense Systems. It provides a wide array of scientific, engineering and technical services and solutions across these reportable segments.

CONTACTS: Note: Officers with more than one job title may be intentionally listed here more than once.

Thomas Bell, CEO
Cindy Gruensfelder, Pres., Divisional
Christopher Cage, CFO
Robert Shapard, Chairman of the Board
Carly Kimball, Chief Accounting Officer
James Carlini, Chief Technology Officer
Mary Schmanske, Executive VP, Divisional
Gerard Fasano, Executive VP
Jerald Howe,, General Counsel
Thomas Sanglier, Other Corporate Officer
Maureen Waterston, Other Executive Officer
Elizabeth Porter, President, Divisional
Roy Stevens, President, Divisional
Steve Hull, President, Divisional
Steve Cook, President, Subsidiary

FINANCIAL DATA: Note: Data for latest year may not have been available at press time.

In U.S. $	2024	2023	2022	2021	2020	2019
Revenue	16,661,999,616	15,438,000,128	14,396,000,256	13,736,999,936	12,296,999,936	11,093,999,616
R&D Expense						
Operating Income	1,815,000,000	1,302,000,000	1,133,000,000	1,163,000,000	967,000,000	859,000,000
Operating Margin %	.11%	.08%	.08%	.08%	.08%	.08%
SGA Expense	983,000,000	942,000,000	951,000,000	851,000,000	770,000,000	689,000,000
Net Income	1,254,000,000	199,000,000	685,000,000	753,000,000	628,000,000	667,000,000
Operating Cash Flow	1,392,000,000	1,165,000,000	992,000,000	1,033,000,000	1,334,000,000	992,000,000
Capital Expenditure	149,000,000	207,000,000	129,000,000	104,000,000	183,000,000	121,000,000
EBITDA	2,122,000,000	946,000,000	1,418,000,000	1,476,000,000	1,245,000,000	1,247,000,000
Return on Assets %	.10%	.02%	.05%	.06%	.06%	.07%
Return on Equity %	.29%	.05%	.16%	.18%	.17%	.20%
Debt to Equity	1.06%	1.23%	1.05%	1.21%	1.349	0.953

CONTACT INFORMATION:

Phone: 571 526-6000   Fax:
Toll-Free:
Address: 1750 Presidents St., Reston, VA 20190 United States

STOCK TICKER/OTHER:

Stock Ticker: LDOS   Exchange: NYS
Employees: 47,000   Fiscal Year Ends: 01/31
Parent Company:

SALARIES/BONUSES:

Top Exec. Salary: $1,306,539   Bonus: $
Second Exec. Salary: Bonus: $5,000
$807,003

OTHER THOUGHTS:

Estimated Female Officers or Directors:
Hot Spot for Advancement for Women/Minorities:

Lenovo Group Limited

www.lenovo.com

NAIC Code: 334111

TYPES OF BUSINESS:
Computer Manufacturing
Servers
Notebook Computers
Handheld Computers
Peripherals
Cellular Phones
Artificial Intelligence

BRANDS/DIVISIONS/AFFILIATES:
ThinkPad
ThinkBook
IdeaPad
Legion
Lenovo
ThinkCentre
IdeaCentre

GROWTH PLANS/SPECIAL FEATURES:
Lenovo is a global technology hardware company with a leading market share in personal computers. The firm has been actively growing its data center business, which primarily sells network servers to enterprise and hyperscale customers, as well as storage equipment through its mainland China joint venture with NetApp. Server-related revenue contribution has jumped to 13% of overall sales in fiscal 2024, from 6% in 2015.

Lenovo Group offers its employees comprehensive health and retirement benefits and employee assistance plans and programs.

CONTACTS:
Note: Officers with more than one job title may be intentionally listed here more than once.
Yuanqing Yang, CEO
Chuanzhi Liu, Other Corporate Officer

FINANCIAL DATA:
Note: Data for latest year may not have been available at press time.

In U.S. $	2024	2023	2022	2021	2020	2019
Revenue	56,863,784,960	61,946,855,424	71,618,215,936	60,742,311,936	50,716,348,416	51,037,941,760
R&D Expense	2,027,532,000	2,195,329,000	2,073,461,000	1,453,912,000	1,335,744,000	1,266,341,000
Operating Income	2,005,784,000	2,668,823,000	3,080,569,000	2,180,407,000	1,438,596,000	1,177,817,000
Operating Margin %	.04%	.04%	.04%	.04%	.03%	.02%
SGA Expense	5,800,728,000	5,596,897,000	6,690,524,000	6,029,323,000	5,497,078,000	4,867,305,000
Net Income	1,010,506,000	1,607,722,000	2,029,818,000	1,210,839,000	718,851,000	650,103,000
Operating Cash Flow	2,010,991,000	2,801,402,000	4,076,979,000	3,652,773,000	2,209,923,000	1,472,573,000
Capital Expenditure	1,285,897,000	1,578,146,000	1,284,081,000	843,750,000	953,080,000	700,821,000
EBITDA	3,538,612,000	4,142,962,000	4,390,301,000	3,238,051,000	2,438,559,000	1,989,412,000
Return on Assets %	.03%	.04%	.05%	.03%	.02%	.02%
Return on Equity %	.18%	.30%	.47%	.29%	.16%	.13%
Debt to Equity	.68%	.71%	.58%	1.02%	0.456	0.553

CONTACT INFORMATION:
Phone: 852 3422-3302   Fax:
Toll-Free:
Address: New Town Plaza Phase 1, Hong Kong, 999077 Hong Kong

STOCK TICKER/OTHER:
Stock Ticker: LNVGF   Exchange: PINX
Employees: 69,500   Fiscal Year Ends: 03/31
Parent Company:

SALARIES/BONUSES:
Top Exec. Salary: $ Bonus: $
Second Exec. Salary: $ Bonus: $

OTHER THOUGHTS:
Estimated Female Officers or Directors: 2
Hot Spot for Advancement for Women/Minorities:

Leo A Daly Company

www.leoadaly.com

NAIC Code: 541330

TYPES OF BUSINESS:

Engineering Services
Engineering
Design
Architecture
Management

BRANDS/DIVISIONS/AFFILIATES:

Lockwood Andrews & Newman Inc

GROWTH PLANS/SPECIAL FEATURES:

Leo A Daly Company is an architecture, engineering, planning, interior design and program management firm, with a project portfolio spanning more than 90 countries, all 50 U.S. states and Washington DC. Leo A Daly's services include engineering, small business program, preservation and sustainability. Markets served by the company include aviation, civic, commercial, education, federal, healthcare, hospitality, industrial, residential, science, senior living, technology, venues and workplace. Subsidiary Lockwood, Andrews & Newnam, Inc. is a national, full-service civil engineering firm that offers planning, engineering and program management services. Based in Nebraska, Leo A Daly has office locations across the U.S. as well as in Abu Dhabi.

CONTACTS: Note: Officers with more than one job title may be intentionally listed here more than once.

Edward Benes, CEO
Steven A. Lichtenberger, Pres.
James B. Brader, CFO
Samantha G. Holy, Chief Human Resources Officer
Stephen W. Held, CIO
Leo A. Daly III, Chmn.

FINANCIAL DATA: Note: Data for latest year may not have been available at press time.

In U.S. $	2024	2023	2022	2021	2020	2019
Revenue	218,400,000	208,000,000	200,000,000	178,161,984	171,309,600	173,040,000
R&D Expense						
Operating Income						
Operating Margin %						
SGA Expense						
Net Income						
Operating Cash Flow						
Capital Expenditure						
EBITDA						
Return on Assets %						
Return on Equity %						
Debt to Equity						

CONTACT INFORMATION:

Phone: 402-391-8111   Fax: 402-391-8564
Toll-Free:
Address: 8600 Indian Hills Dr., Omaha, NE 68114-4039 United States

STOCK TICKER/OTHER:

Stock Ticker: Private   Exchange:
Employees: 1,200   Fiscal Year Ends:
Parent Company:

SALARIES/BONUSES:

Top Exec. Salary: $ Bonus: $
Second Exec. Salary: $ Bonus: $

OTHER THOUGHTS:

Estimated Female Officers or Directors:
Hot Spot for Advancement for Women/Minorities:

LG Display Co Ltd

www.lgdisplay.com

NAIC Code: 334419

TYPES OF BUSINESS:

LCD (Liquid Crystal Display) Unit Screens Manufacturing
Digital Displays
Manufacturing
Technology
Innovation
Liquid Crystal Display
Organic Light Emitting Diode
Panels

BRANDS/DIVISIONS/AFFILIATES:

GROWTH PLANS/SPECIAL FEATURES:

LG Display Co Ltd is a South Korea-based company that is principally engaged in developing, manufacturing, and selling TFT-LCD and OLED display panels. The company's products consist of panels for notebook computers, monitors, televisions, smartphones, tablets, and others. The company conducts direct sales through overseas subsidiaries in several countries, including the United States, Germany, Japan, Taiwan, China, and Singapore. These subsidiaries conduct sales activities and offer technical support to clients. The company generates the majority of its revenue from overseas markets, with the rest from South Korea.

CONTACTS: Note: Officers with more than one job title may be intentionally listed here more than once.

Cheoldong Jeong, CEO
Sunghyun Kim, CFO
Myoung Kyu Kim, Other Executive Officer

FINANCIAL DATA: Note: Data for latest year may not have been available at press time.

In U.S. $	2024	2023	2022	2021	2020	2019
Revenue	19,258,849,968	15,434,968,857	18,923,414,612	21,619,735,491	17,555,652,650	16,986,908,039
R&D Expense	1,047,559,000	998,316,200	1,000,308,000	884,270,400	795,044,800	884,222,600
Operating Income	-405,646,900	-1,816,353,000	-1,508,739,000	1,614,067,000	-26,386,050	-983,648,100
Operating Margin %	-.02%	-.12%	-.08%	.07%	.00%	-.06%
SGA Expense	983,203,800	828,649,500	1,080,427,000	1,093,263,000	922,418,500	1,451,346,000
Net Income	-1,854,300,000	-1,978,134,000	-2,222,583,000	858,320,600	-68,635,580	-2,047,573,000
Operating Cash Flow	1,745,149,000	1,217,635,000	2,178,772,000	4,163,190,000	1,648,927,000	1,958,455,000
Capital Expenditure	2,110,417,000	3,006,433,000	4,276,373,000	2,733,205,000	2,133,673,000	5,403,827,000
EBITDA	2,781,326,000	1,156,117,000	1,113,336,000	4,814,596,000	2,823,528,000	378,847,000
Return on Assets %	-.07%	-.08%	-.08%	.03%	.00%	-.08%
Return on Equity %	-.37%	-.32%	-.27%	.10%	-.01%	-.22%
Debt to Equity	1.24%	1.57%	.97%	.66%	0.967	1.022

CONTACT INFORMATION:

Phone: 82 2-3777-1010   Fax: 82-2-3777-0785
Toll-Free:
Address: LG Twin Towers, 128, Yeoui-daero, Yeongdeungpo-gu, Seoul, 07336 South Korea

STOCK TICKER/OTHER:

Stock Ticker: LPL
Employees: 66,418
Parent Company: LG Corporation

Exchange: NYS
Fiscal Year Ends: 12/31

SALARIES/BONUSES:

Top Exec. Salary: $1,030,406   Bonus: $
Second Exec. Salary: $253,983   Bonus: $

OTHER THOUGHTS:

Estimated Female Officers or Directors:
Hot Spot for Advancement for Women/Minorities:

LG Electronics Inc

www.lg.com

NAIC Code: 334220

TYPES OF BUSINESS:

Manufacturing-Electronics
Technology
Home Appliances
Home Entertainment
Mobile Communications
Vehicle Component Solutions
Commercial Displays
Energy Management

BRANDS/DIVISIONS/AFFILIATES:

LG Corporation
LG Signature
LG ThinQ

GROWTH PLANS/SPECIAL FEATURES:

LG Electronics Inc is a South Korea-based company that produces a broad range of electronic products. Its businesses are the home entertainment segment, which produces and sells TVs and digital media products; the mobile communications segment, which produces and sells mobile communications equipment; the home appliance and air solutions segment, which produces and sells washing machines, refrigerators, and other products; the vehicle components segment, which designs and produces vehicle parts; the business solutions segment, which manufactures and sells PCs, solar panels, and other products; and Innotek, which sells substrates, sensors, and other items. The company generates the majority of total revenue from the home entertainment and home appliance and air solutions segments.

CONTACTS: Note: Officers with more than one job title may be intentionally listed here more than once.

Doo-Yong Bae, CFO
Young Kwon, Chairman of the Board

FINANCIAL DATA: Note: Data for latest year may not have been available at press time.

In U.S. $	2024	2023	2022	2021	2020	2019
Revenue	63,480,063,277	59,525,220,567	60,396,907,865	53,479,775,428	42,010,670,869	45,084,715,223
R&D Expense	1,944,525,000	1,842,912,000	1,734,709,000	1,514,458,000	1,320,120,000	1,796,991,000
Operating Income	2,474,475,000	2,643,522,000	2,569,481,000	2,936,364,000	2,825,734,000	1,762,789,000
Operating Margin %	.04%	.04%	.04%	.05%	.07%	.04%
SGA Expense	11,051,000,000	9,841,747,000	10,338,740,000	9,223,197,000	7,076,248,000	7,537,030,000
Net Income	265,933,700	515,855,500	865,744,800	746,544,800	1,424,284,000	22,637,810
Operating Cash Flow	2,780,547,000	4,279,075,000	2,248,831,000	1,937,352,000	3,349,235,000	2,669,477,000
Capital Expenditure	2,654,181,000	2,993,971,000	2,715,515,000	2,358,277,000	2,230,887,000	1,841,271,000
EBITDA	3,937,104,000	4,173,107,000	4,260,929,000	4,925,793,000	4,406,807,000	2,490,778,000
Return on Assets %	.01%	.01%	.02%	.02%	.04%	.00%
Return on Equity %	.02%	.04%	.07%	.06%	.13%	.00%
Debt to Equity	.57%	.59%	.51%	.51%	0.59	0.656

CONTACT INFORMATION:

Phone: 82 237771114   Fax:
Toll-Free: 800-243-0000
Address: LG Twin Towers, 20 Yoido Dong, Seoul, 150-721 South Korea

STOCK TICKER/OTHER:

Stock Ticker: LGEJY
Employees: 100,000
Parent Company: LG Corporation

Exchange: PINX
Fiscal Year Ends: 12/31

SALARIES/BONUSES:

Top Exec. Salary: $ Bonus: $
Second Exec. Salary: $ Bonus: $

OTHER THOUGHTS:

Estimated Female Officers or Directors:
Hot Spot for Advancement for Women/Minorities:

LITE-ON Technology Corporation

www.liteon.com

NAIC Code: 335313

TYPES OF BUSINESS:

Switchgear and Switchboard Apparatus Manufacturing
Optoelectronic Components
Electronic Modules
Cloud Computing
Internet of Things
Smart Industries
Integrated Circuit Chips
Automotive Electronics

BRANDS/DIVISIONS/AFFILIATES:

CONTACTS: Note: Officers with more than one job title may be intentionally listed here more than once.

Anson Chiu, Pres.
Warren Chen, CEO-Lite-On Group
Tom Soong, Chmn.
Danny Liao, Sr. VP-Procurement

GROWTH PLANS/SPECIAL FEATURES:

LITE-ON Technology Corporation was founded in 1975 and manufactures and markets optoelectronic components and key electronic modules. The firm is also engaged in the fields of cloud computing, automotive electronics, 5G, Internet of Things (IoT), smart industries, smart life and smart cities. LITE-ON groups its products and services into four categories: optoelectronics, information and communication technologies (ICT), IoT and smart life applications and automotive electronics. The optoelectronics category offers image and video solutions, light-emitting diode (LED) components, surface-mounted color chips, plastic leaded chip carriers (PLCCs), photocouplers, infrared emitters and detectors and automotive LED products. The ICT category offers cloud infrastructure power solutions, power module solutions, human input solutions, magnetic components, enclosures, image technical solutions, system solutions and optical disc storage. The IoT and smart life applications category offers products, services and solutions regarding wired access network, wireless access network, radio access network, connected video intelligence, intelligent communication, outdoor lighting, 5G total solution and smart connection. Lastly, the automotive electronics category offers automotive vision solutions, vehicle lighting solutions, vehicle control and related applications and electric vehicle charging solutions. LITE-ON has offices, factories and operation centers throughout Taiwan, and international offices in Japan and Singapore.

FINANCIAL DATA: Note: Data for latest year may not have been available at press time.

In U.S. $	2024	2023	2022	2021	2020	2019
Revenue		4,815,468,000	5,645,601,000	5,947,874,067	5,588,457,302	6,225,873,920
R&D Expense						
Operating Income						
Operating Margin %						
SGA Expense						
Net Income		473,018,000	460,583,000	501,095,000	349,575,640	327,988,608
Operating Cash Flow						
Capital Expenditure						
EBITDA						
Return on Assets %						
Return on Equity %						
Debt to Equity						

CONTACT INFORMATION:

Phone: 886 287982888   Fax: 886 287982866
Toll-Free:
Address: No. 392, Ruiguang Rd., Fl. 22, Neihu Dist., Taipei, 114 Taiwan

STOCK TICKER/OTHER:

Stock Ticker: 2301   Exchange: TWSE
Employees: 38,676   Fiscal Year Ends: 12/31
Parent Company:

SALARIES/BONUSES:

Top Exec. Salary: $ Bonus: $
Second Exec. Salary: $ Bonus: $

OTHER THOUGHTS:

Estimated Female Officers or Directors:
Hot Spot for Advancement for Women/Minorities:

LM Ericsson Telephone Company (Ericsson)   www.ericsson.com

NAIC Code: 334220

TYPES OF BUSINESS:

Wireless Telecommunications Equipment
Information Technology
Communications
Networks
Digital
Internet of Things
Telecommunications
Artificial Intelligence

BRANDS/DIVISIONS/AFFILIATES:

GROWTH PLANS/SPECIAL FEATURES:

Ericsson provides telecom equipment and services that are primarily used to build and operate mobile networks. The firm divides its business into three segments: networks, cloud and software services, and enterprise. Wireless carriers have traditionally been the firm's primary customers, but it is pushing to cater more to enterprises as well, as both try to take advantage of 5G capabilities and utilize as-a-service communications platforms. The company also licenses its patents to handset manufacturers.

CONTACTS: Note: Officers with more than one job title may be intentionally listed here more than once.

Niklas Heuveldop, CEO, Subsidiary
Fredrik Jejdling, Executive VP, Divisional
Ã...sa Tamsons, CEO, Subsidiary
E. Ekholm, CEO
Carl Mellander, CFO
Jan Carlson, Chairman of the Board
Scott Dresser, Chief Legal Officer
Stella Medlicott, Chief Marketing Officer
Erik Ekudden, Chief Technology Officer
Chris Houghton, COO, Divisional
Helena Stjernholm, Deputy Chairman
Jacob Wallenberg, Deputy Chairman
MajBritt Arfert, Other Executive Officer
Moti Gyamlani, Senior VP, Divisional
Per Narvinger, Senior VP, Divisional

FINANCIAL DATA: Note: Data for latest year may not have been available at press time.

In U.S. $	2024	2023	2022	2021	2020	2019
Revenue	25,856,117,587	27,469,880,700	28,324,694,545	24,232,442,280	24,240,370,326	23,700,675,347
R&D Expense	5,581,992,000	5,284,712,000	4,933,607,000	4,388,697,000	4,142,528,000	4,048,754,000
Operating Income	650,575,300	1,249,935,000	2,790,892,000	3,256,632,000	2,927,432,000	975,289,200
Operating Margin %	.03%	.05%	.10%	.13%	.12%	.04%
SGA Expense	5,388,290,000	4,094,650,000	3,722,997,000	2,811,858,000	2,783,382,000	2,726,324,000
Net Income	2,086,180	-2,758,556,000	1,953,082,000	2,367,189,000	1,823,634,000	231,878,900
Operating Cash Flow	4,825,439,000	748,625,700	3,219,289,000	4,074,832,000	3,017,972,000	1,760,006,000
Capital Expenditure	379,684,800	570,570,300	646,402,900	482,429,200	553,880,800	695,010,900
EBITDA	1,685,946,000	-928,245,900	3,812,286,000	4,059,811,000	3,840,136,000	1,995,848,000
Return on Assets %	.00%	-.08%	.06%	.08%	.06%	.01%
Return on Equity %	.00%	-.23%	.15%	.23%	.21%	.03%
Debt to Equity	.40%	.35%	.25%	.27%	0.338	0.434

CONTACT INFORMATION:

Phone: 46 87190000   Fax: 46 87191976
Toll-Free:
Address: Torshamnsgatan 21, Kista, Stockholm, 164 83 Sweden

STOCK TICKER/OTHER:

Stock Ticker: ERIC   Exchange: NAS
Employees: 99,952   Fiscal Year Ends: 12/31
Parent Company:

SALARIES/BONUSES:

Top Exec. Salary: $1,602,457   Bonus: $1,914,202
Second Exec. Salary: $ Bonus: $

OTHER THOUGHTS:

Estimated Female Officers or Directors: 10
Hot Spot for Advancement for Women/Minorities: Y

Sales, profits and employees may be estimates. Financial information, benefits and other data can change quickly and may vary from those stated here.

Lockheed Martin Corporation

www.lockheedmartin.com

NAIC Code: 336411

TYPES OF BUSINESS:

Aircraft Manufacturing
Military Aircraft
Defense Electronics
Systems Integration & Technology Services
Communications Satellites & Launch Services
Undersea, Shipboard, Land & Airborne Systems & Subsystems
Cyber Resilient Systems

BRANDS/DIVISIONS/AFFILIATES:

F-35 Lightning
F-22
F-16
C-130

GROWTH PLANS/SPECIAL FEATURES:

Lockheed Martin is the world's largest defense contractor and has dominated the Western market for high-end fighter aircraft since it won the F-35 Joint Strike Fighter program in 2001. Aeronautics is Lockheed's largest segment, which derives upward of two-thirds of its revenue from the F-35. Lockheed's remaining segments are rotary and mission systems, mainly encompassing the Sikorsky helicopter business; missiles and fire control, which creates missiles and missile defense systems; and space systems, which produces satellites and receives equity income from the United Launch Alliance joint venture.

CONTACTS: Note: Officers with more than one job title may be intentionally listed here more than once.

James Taiclet, CEO
Jesus Malave, CFO
H. Paul, Chief Accounting Officer
Frank St John, COO
Stephanie Hill, Executive VP, Divisional
Gregory Ulmer, Executive VP, Divisional
Robert Lightfoot, Executive VP, Divisional
Timothy Cahill, Executive VP, Divisional
Maryanne Lavan, General Counsel
Maria Lee, Treasurer

FINANCIAL DATA: Note: Data for latest year may not have been available at press time.

In U.S. $	2024	2023	2022	2021	2020	2019
Revenue	71,042,998,272	67,570,999,296	65,984,000,000	67,043,999,744	65,398,001,664	59,811,999,744
R&D Expense						
Operating Income	7,013,000,000	8,507,000,000	8,348,000,000	9,123,000,000	8,644,000,000	8,545,000,000
Operating Margin %	.10%	.13%	.13%	.14%	.13%	.14%
SGA Expense						
Net Income	5,336,000,000	6,920,000,000	5,732,000,000	6,315,000,000	6,833,000,000	6,230,000,000
Operating Cash Flow	6,972,000,000	7,920,000,000	7,802,000,000	9,221,000,000	8,183,000,000	7,311,000,000
Capital Expenditure	1,685,000,000	1,691,000,000	1,670,000,000	1,522,000,000	1,766,000,000	1,484,000,000
EBITDA	8,815,000,000	10,444,000,000	8,707,000,000	9,483,000,000	10,116,000,000	9,083,000,000
Return on Assets %	.10%	.13%	.11%	.12%	.14%	.13%
Return on Equity %	.81%	.86%	.57%	.74%	1.49%	2.76%
Debt to Equity	3.10%	2.53%	1.67%	1.06%	1.94	3.647

CONTACT INFORMATION:

Phone: 301 897-6000   Fax: 301 897-6083
Toll-Free:
Address: 6801 Rockledge Dr., Bethesda, MD 20817 United States

STOCK TICKER/OTHER:

Stock Ticker: LMT   Exchange: NYS
Employees: 122,000   Fiscal Year Ends: 12/31
Parent Company:

SALARIES/BONUSES:

Top Exec. Salary: $1,751,000   Bonus: $
Second Exec. Salary: Bonus: $
$1,069,615

OTHER THOUGHTS:

Estimated Female Officers or Directors: 5
Hot Spot for Advancement for Women/Minorities: Y

Luxshare Precision Industry Co Ltd   www.luxshare-ict.com

NAIC Code: 334417

TYPES OF BUSINESS:

Connectors for Electronics Manufacturing
Electronics Components Manufacturing
Automotive Parts
Electronics Components Solutions
Medical Devices
Custom Electronics Parts
Interconnect Cables

BRANDS/DIVISIONS/AFFILIATES:

GROWTH PLANS/SPECIAL FEATURES:

Established in 2004, Luxshare ICT is a prominent Chinese multinational enterprise specializing in the research, development, design, and manufacturing of a diverse array of solutions. Luxshare's solutions covers areas such as communications and data centers, automotive industry and consumer electronics. With its strong focus on meeting consumer demands, Luxshare invests significantly in research and development, enabling consumers to design prototypes and request effective custom-made parts. The company maintains a global presence, with manufacturing facilities and offices strategically located in the United States, Vietnam, Europe, and Mexico.

CONTACTS: Note: Officers with more than one job title may be intentionally listed here more than once.

Wu Tiansong, CFO

FINANCIAL DATA: Note: Data for latest year may not have been available at press time.

In U.S. $	2024	2023	2022	2021	2020	2019
Revenue		32,709,801,000	30,901,847,000	24,153,681,000	14,171,656,000	
R&D Expense						
Operating Income						
Operating Margin %						
SGA Expense						
Net Income			1,322,987,000	1,109,343,000	1,106,977,000	
Operating Cash Flow						
Capital Expenditure						
EBITDA						
Return on Assets %						
Return on Equity %						
Debt to Equity						

CONTACT INFORMATION:

Phone: 86 769-3880-0888   Fax:
Toll-Free:
Address: 313 Beihuan Rd., Qingxi Town, Dongguan, Guangdong 523642 China

STOCK TICKER/OTHER:

Stock Ticker: 2475   Exchange: Shenzhen
Employees: 236,932   Fiscal Year Ends: 12/31
Parent Company:

SALARIES/BONUSES:

Top Exec. Salary: $ Bonus: $
Second Exec. Salary: $ Bonus: $

OTHER THOUGHTS:

Estimated Female Officers or Directors:
Hot Spot for Advancement for Women/Minorities:

LyondellBasell Industries NV

www.lyondellbasell.com

NAIC Code: 325110

TYPES OF BUSINESS:

Polymers & Petrochemicals
Intermediate & Performance Chemicals
Petroleum Products
Refining
Biofuels
Automotive Parts
Medical Applications
Durable Textiles

BRANDS/DIVISIONS/AFFILIATES:

Lyondell Chemical Co
Basell AF SCA
Bora Lyondell Basell Petrochemical Co Ltd
PolyPacific Polymers Sdn Bhd

GROWTH PLANS/SPECIAL FEATURES:

LyondellBasell is a petrochemical producer with operations in the United States, Europe, and Asia. The company is the world's largest producer of polypropylene and also a major producer of polyethylene and propylene oxide. Its chemicals are used in various consumer and industrial end products. Well over half of LyondellBasell's production comes from its North American operations.

CONTACTS: Note: Officers with more than one job title may be intentionally listed here more than once.

Peter Vanacker, CEO
Agustin Izquierdo, Sr. VP, Divisional
Michael McMurray, CFO
Jacques Aigrain, Chairman of the Board
Chukwuemeka Oyolu, Chief Accounting Officer
James Seward, Chief Information Officer
Aaron Ledet, Executive VP, Divisional
Kimberly Foley, Executive VP, Divisional
Dale Friedrichs, Executive VP, Divisional
Torkel Rhenman, Executive VP, Divisional
Tracey Campbell, Executive VP, Divisional
Yvonne van der Laan, Executive VP, Divisional
Trisha Conley, Executive VP, Divisional
Jeffrey Kaplan, Executive VP

FINANCIAL DATA: Note: Data for latest year may not have been available at press time.

In U.S. $	2024	2023	2022	2021	2020	2019
Revenue	40,301,998,080	41,107,001,344	50,451,001,344	46,172,999,680	27,753,000,960	34,726,998,016
R&D Expense	135,000,000	130,000,000	124,000,000	124,000,000	113,000,000	111,000,000
Operating Income	2,766,000,000	3,571,000,000	5,170,000,000	7,397,000,000	2,141,000,000	4,116,000,000
Operating Margin %	.07%	.09%	.10%	.16%	.08%	.12%
SGA Expense	1,663,000,000	1,557,000,000	1,310,000,000	1,255,000,000	1,140,000,000	1,199,000,000
Net Income	1,360,000,000	2,114,000,000	3,882,000,000	5,610,000,000	1,420,000,000	3,390,000,000
Operating Cash Flow	3,819,000,000	4,942,000,000	6,119,000,000	7,695,000,000	3,404,000,000	4,961,000,000
Capital Expenditure	1,839,000,000	1,531,000,000	1,890,000,000	1,959,000,000	1,947,000,000	2,694,000,000
EBITDA	3,606,000,000	4,638,000,000	6,330,000,000	8,698,000,000	3,297,000,000	5,711,000,000
Return on Assets %	.04%	.06%	.11%	.16%	.04%	.12%
Return on Equity %	.11%	.16%	.32%	.56%	.18%	.37%
Debt to Equity	.96%	.91%	.96%	1.09%	2.071	1.595

CONTACT INFORMATION:

Phone: 31-10-275-5500   Fax: 31-10-275-5589
Toll-Free:
Address: Delftseplein 27E, Rotterdam, 3013 AK Netherlands

STOCK TICKER/OTHER:

Stock Ticker: LYB   Exchange: NYS
Employees: 20,000   Fiscal Year Ends: 12/31
Parent Company:

SALARIES/BONUSES:

Top Exec. Salary: $1,450,000   Bonus: $
Second Exec. Salary: $872,313   Bonus: $

OTHER THOUGHTS:

Estimated Female Officers or Directors: 3
Hot Spot for Advancement for Women/Minorities: Y

Magna International Inc

NAIC Code: 336300

TYPES OF BUSINESS:

Automobile Parts Manufacturer
Vehicle Manufacturing
Vehicle Engineering
Body Structures
Seating
Lighting
Transmissions
Automated Driving Technologies

BRANDS/DIVISIONS/AFFILIATES:

GROWTH PLANS/SPECIAL FEATURES:

Magna International prides itself on an entrepreneurial culture and a corporate constitution that outlines the distribution of profits to various stakeholders. This automotive supplier's product groups include exteriors, interiors, seating, roof systems, body and chassis, powertrain, vision and electronic systems, closure systems, electric vehicle systems, tooling and engineering, and contract vehicle assembly. In 2024, 48% of Magna's USD 42.8 billion of revenue came from North America, while Europe accounted for approximately 37% and Asia the remainder. The firm's top six customers constituted 72.9% of revenue, with the top three being GM, Mercedes, and Ford. GM was the largest contributor at 15.4%. Magna was founded in 1957, has over 170,000 employees, and is based in Aurora, Ontario.

CONTACTS: Note: Officers with more than one job title may be intentionally listed here more than once.

Seetarama Kotagiri, CEO
Patrick McCann, CFO
Robert Maclellan, Chairman of the Board
Bruce Cluney, Chief Legal Officer
Eric Wilds, Chief Marketing Officer
Matteo Del Sorbo, Executive VP, Divisional
Boris Shulkin, Executive VP
Aaron McCarthy, Executive VP
Uwe Geissinger, Executive VP
Indira Samarasekera, Independent Director
Tom Rucker, President, Divisional
John Farrell, President, Divisional

FINANCIAL DATA: Note: Data for latest year may not have been available at press time.

In U.S. $	2024	2023	2022	2021	2020	2019
Revenue	42,836,000,768	42,796,998,656	37,839,998,976	36,242,001,920	32,647,000,064	39,431,000,064
R&D Expense						
Operating Income	2,116,000,000	2,038,000,000	1,573,000,000	1,916,000,000	1,487,000,000	2,367,000,000
Operating Margin %	.05%	.05%	.04%	.05%	.05%	.06%
SGA Expense	2,061,000,000	2,050,000,000	1,660,000,000	1,717,000,000	1,587,000,000	1,697,000,000
Net Income	1,009,000,000	1,213,000,000	592,000,000	1,514,000,000	757,000,000	1,765,000,000
Operating Cash Flow	3,634,000,000	3,149,000,000	2,095,000,000	2,940,000,000	3,278,000,000	3,960,000,000
Capital Expenditure	2,178,000,000	2,548,000,000	1,681,000,000	1,413,000,000	1,145,000,000	1,441,000,000
EBITDA	3,779,000,000	3,596,000,000	2,423,000,000	3,582,000,000	2,477,000,000	3,672,000,000
Return on Assets %	.03%	.04%	.02%	.05%	.03%	.07%
Return on Equity %	.09%	.11%	.05%	.13%	.07%	.16%
Debt to Equity	.50%	.46%	.38%	.42%	0.495	0.431

CONTACT INFORMATION:

Phone: 905 726-2462   Fax:
Toll-Free:
Address: 337 Magna Dr., Aurora, ON L4G 7K1 Canada

STOCK TICKER/OTHER:

Stock Ticker: MG   Exchange: TSE
Employees: 179,000   Fiscal Year Ends: 12/31
Parent Company:

SALARIES/BONUSES:

Top Exec. Salary: $325,000   Bonus: $
Second Exec. Salary: Bonus: $
$325,000

OTHER THOUGHTS:

Estimated Female Officers or Directors: 2
Hot Spot for Advancement for Women/Minorities:

Marelli Corporation

www.marelli.com

NAIC Code: 336300

TYPES OF BUSINESS:

Automobile Parts Manufacturing
Electrification and Green Technology
Powertrain
Thermal Solutions
Cockpit Modules
Exhaust Systems
Climate Control Systems
Compressors

BRANDS/DIVISIONS/AFFILIATES:

Marelli Holdings Co Ltd

GROWTH PLANS/SPECIAL FEATURES:

Marelli Corporation innovates and manufactures automobile parts and related accessories. The company develops and innovates a broad range of products across technological domains, including lighting, interiors, electronics, propulsion, exhaust, chassis and thermal. Just a few of the firm's many products include cockpit modules, interior solutions, exhaust systems, climate control systems, heat exchanges and compressors. Marelli Corporation operates as a subsidiary of Marelli Holdings Co., Ltd., which has a global footprint including 170 facilities and research and development centers across Asia, the Americas, Europe and Africa.

CONTACTS: Note: Officers with more than one job title may be intentionally listed here more than once.

David Slump, CEO
Alanna Abrahamson, CFO
Juan Molla, CMO
Sherry Vasa, Chief Human Resources Officer
Joachim Fetzer, CTO
Shigeo Shingyoji, Exec. VP
Kosaku Hosokawa, Exec. VP
Koji Furukawa, Sr. VP
Akira Fujisaki, Exec. VP
Dinesh Paliwal, Chmn.

FINANCIAL DATA: Note: Data for latest year may not have been available at press time.

In U.S. $	2024	2023	2022	2021	2020	2019
Revenue	14,242,999,680	13,564,761,600	13,043,040,000	12,521,692,200	11,740,300,000	13,896,900,000
R&D Expense						
Operating Income						
Operating Margin %						
SGA Expense						
Net Income			823,885,360			
Operating Cash Flow						
Capital Expenditure						
EBITDA						
Return on Assets %						
Return on Equity %						
Debt to Equity						

CONTACT INFORMATION:

Phone: 81 486602111   Fax:
Toll-Free:
Address: 2-1917 Nisshin, Kita-ku, Saitama, 331-8501 Japan

STOCK TICKER/OTHER:

Stock Ticker: Subsidiary   Exchange:
Employees: 50,000   Fiscal Year Ends: 03/31
Parent Company: Marelli Holdings Co Ltd

SALARIES/BONUSES:

Top Exec. Salary: $ Bonus: $
Second Exec. Salary: $ Bonus: $

OTHER THOUGHTS:

Estimated Female Officers or Directors:
Hot Spot for Advancement for Women/Minorities:

Mason & Hanger

NAIC Code: 541330

TYPES OF BUSINESS:

Engineering Consulting Services
Architecture and Engineering Services
Government Facilities
Munitions Modernization
Office Buildings and Data Centers
Command and Control Centers
Construction Contract Administration
Energy and Sustainability Services

BRANDS/DIVISIONS/AFFILIATES:

Day & Zimmermann Company

GROWTH PLANS/SPECIAL FEATURES:

Mason & Hanger, a Day & Zimmermann Company, provides architectural and engineering services for U.S. federal projects and government agencies. The firm has served in the U.S. for nearly two centuries, being founded in 1827 as a railroad-engineering and construction company. Today, Mason & Hanger has served the federal government on thousands of projects in more than 175 countries. The company specializes in the design of secure, mission-driven facilities, including office buildings, data centers, command and control centers, communications facilities, headquarters facilities, embassies, SCIF spaces, training facilities and more. Mason & Hanger's services include architecture and planning, engineering, commissioning, construction contract administration, energy and sustainability services, munitions modernization and security design services.

CONTACTS:
Note: Officers with more than one job title may be intentionally listed here more than once.

Benjamin A. Lilly, Pres.
Jon Miller, VP-Operations

FINANCIAL DATA:
Note: Data for latest year may not have been available at press time.

In U.S. $	2024	2023	2022	2021	2020	2019
Revenue						
R&D Expense						
Operating Income						
Operating Margin %						
SGA Expense						
Net Income						
Operating Cash Flow						
Capital Expenditure						
EBITDA						
Return on Assets %						
Return on Equity %						
Debt to Equity						

CONTACT INFORMATION:

Phone: 859-252-9980   Fax: 859-259-2712
Toll-Free:
Address: 300 W. Vine St., Ste. 1300, Lexington, KY 40507 United States

STOCK TICKER/OTHER:

Stock Ticker: Private   Exchange:
Employees: 250   Fiscal Year Ends:
Parent Company: Day & Zimmermann Company

SALARIES/BONUSES:

Top Exec. Salary: $ Bonus: $
Second Exec. Salary: $ Bonus: $

OTHER THOUGHTS:

Estimated Female Officers or Directors:
Hot Spot for Advancement for Women/Minorities:

Matrix Service Company

www.matrixservice.com

NAIC Code: 237100

TYPES OF BUSINESS:

Heavy Construction for Utilities and Energy
Plant Maintenance Services
Storage Tank Services
Petrochemical Industry Services

BRANDS/DIVISIONS/AFFILIATES:

Matrix PDM Engineering Inc
Matrix Service Inc
Matrix Applied Technologies Inc

GROWTH PLANS/SPECIAL FEATURES:

Matrix Service Co is an engineering and construction provider for large industrial projects, primarily in the oil and gas, power, petrochemical, industrial, mining, and minerals markets. It offers engineering, fabrication, construction, and maintenance services, operating across three segments namely Utility and Power Infrastructure; Process and Industrial Facilities; and Storage and Terminal Solutions.

Matrix offers its employees comprehensive health benefits, retirement options and a variety of employee assistance plans and programs.

CONTACTS: *Note: Officers with more than one job title may be intentionally listed here more than once.*

John Hewitt, CEO
Kevin Cavanah, CFO
John Chandler, Chairman of the Board
Nancy Austin, Chief Administrative Officer
Kevin Durkin, Chief Strategy Officer
Alan Updyke, COO
Justin Sheets, General Counsel
Glyn Rodgers, President, Subsidiary
Shawn Payne, President, Subsidiary
Douglas Montalbano, President, Subsidiary

FINANCIAL DATA: *Note: Data for latest year may not have been available at press time.*

In U.S. $	2024	2023	2022	2021	2020	2019
Revenue	728,212,992	795,020,032	707,779,968	673,398,016	1,100,937,984	1,416,679,936
R&D Expense						
Operating Income	-29,612,000	-37,429,000	-68,896,000	-36,991,000	15,900,000	37,930,000
Operating Margin %	-.04%	-.05%	-.10%	-.05%	.01%	.03%
SGA Expense	70,085,000	68,249,000	67,690,000	69,756,000	86,276,000	94,021,000
Net Income	-24,976,000	-52,361,000	-63,900,000	-31,224,000	-33,074,000	27,982,000
Operating Cash Flow	72,571,000	10,247,000	-54,196,000	-2,971,000	44,085,000	41,394,000
Capital Expenditure	6,994,000	9,009,000	3,345,000	4,354,000	18,539,000	19,558,000
EBITDA	-12,859,000	-37,043,000	-40,078,000	-23,846,000	-15,923,000	57,932,000
Return on Assets %	-.06%	-.12%	-.14%	-.06%	-.06%	.05%
Return on Equity %	-.14%	-.26%	-.25%	-.11%	-.10%	.08%
Debt to Equity	.12%	.17%	.15%	.07%	0.095	0.015

CONTACT INFORMATION:

Phone: 866-367-5879   Fax: 918-838-8810
Toll-Free:
Address: 5100 E. Skelly Dr., Ste. 500, Tulsa, OK 74135 United States

STOCK TICKER/OTHER:

Stock Ticker: MTRX   Exchange: NAS
Employees: 2,064   Fiscal Year Ends: 06/30
Parent Company:

SALARIES/BONUSES:

Top Exec. Salary: $800,000   Bonus: $
Second Exec. Salary: Bonus: $
$505,000

OTHER THOUGHTS:

Estimated Female Officers or Directors: 1
Hot Spot for Advancement for Women/Minorities:

Mayville Engineering Company Inc

NAIC Code: 332700

TYPES OF BUSINESS:

Rapid Prototyping
Process Engineering
Manufacturing
Fabrication
Assembly
Aftermarket

BRANDS/DIVISIONS/AFFILIATES:

GROWTH PLANS/SPECIAL FEATURES:

Mayville Engineering Co Inc is involved in a manufacturing partner providing a full suite of manufacturing solutions from concept to production, including design, prototyping and tooling, fabrication, aluminum extrusion, coating, assembly and aftermarket components. Its customers operate in diverse end markets, including heavy- and medium-duty commercial vehicles, construction, power sports, agriculture, military, and other end markets. Its services comprise stamping, shearing, fiber laser cutting, forming, drilling, tapping, grinding, tube bending, machining, welding, assembly and logistic services.

CONTACTS: Note: Officers with more than one job title may be intentionally listed here more than once.

Jagadeesh Reddy, CEO
Todd Butz, CFO
Timothy Christen, Chairman of the Board
Ryan Raber, Executive VP, Divisional
Sean Leuba, General Counsel
Rachele Lehr, Other Executive Officer

FINANCIAL DATA: Note: Data for latest year may not have been available at press time.

In U.S. $	2024	2023	2022	2021	2020	2019
Revenue	581,603,968	588,425,024	539,392,000	454,825,984	357,606,016	519,704,000
R&D Expense						
Operating Income	19,053,000	20,191,000	21,428,000	8,760,000	-6,498,000	-8,012,000
Operating Margin %	.03%	.03%	.04%	.02%	- .02%	- .02%
SGA Expense	45,111,000	41,770,000	32,689,000	31,909,000	27,293,000	56,024,000
Net Income	25,968,000	7,844,000	18,727,000	-7,451,000	-7,092,000	-4,753,000
Operating Cash Flow	89,807,000	40,363,000	52,426,000	14,457,000	36,523,000	33,402,000
Capital Expenditure	12,098,000	16,598,000	58,610,000	39,309,000	7,794,000	25,797,000
EBITDA	82,141,000	55,055,000	55,085,000	24,392,000	25,591,000	30,890,000
Return on Assets %	.06%	.02%	.05%	- .02%	- .02%	- .01%
Return on Equity %	.11%	.04%	.09%	- .04%	- .04%	- .03%
Debt to Equity	.42%	.77%	.48%	.34%	0.236	0.375

CONTACT INFORMATION:

Phone: 920-387-4500   Fax:
Toll-Free:
Address: 715 South St, Mayville, WI 53050 United States

STOCK TICKER/OTHER:

Stock Ticker: MEC   Exchange: NYS
Employees: 2,500   Fiscal Year Ends:
Parent Company:

SALARIES/BONUSES:

Top Exec. Salary: $715,000   Bonus: $
Second Exec. Salary: Bonus: $
$473,800

OTHER THOUGHTS:

Estimated Female Officers or Directors:
Hot Spot for Advancement for Women/Minorities:

Mazda Motor Corporation

NAIC Code: 336111

www.mazda.com

TYPES OF BUSINESS:

Automobile Manufacturing
Commercial Vans & Trucks
Hydrogen Engine Technology

BRANDS/DIVISIONS/AFFILIATES:

Mazda
CX
Flair
Scrum
Carol
Bongo
Titan
Mazda BT-50

GROWTH PLANS/SPECIAL FEATURES:

Mazda Motor Corp is a Japanese automobile manufacturer. The company primarily manufactures passenger cars and commercial vehicles. Also, Mazda manufactures diesel and petroleum gasoline engines, along with manual and automatic transmissions for vehicles. The vast majority of Mazda's production is manufactured locally. The company segments itself across four geographic areas: Japan, North America, Europe, and other markets. The company derives more than half its consolidated revenue from operations in Japan, followed by North America, and then Europe.

CONTACTS: Note: Officers with more than one job title may be intentionally listed here more than once.

Masahiro Moro, CEO
Jeffrey Guyton, CFO
Kiyotaka Shobuda, Chairman of the Board
Ichiro Hirose, Chief Technology Officer
Takeshi Mukai, Director
Yasuhiro Aoyama, Director
Takeji Kojima, Director

FINANCIAL DATA: Note: Data for latest year may not have been available at press time.

In U.S. $	2024	2023	2022	2021	2020	2019
Revenue	33,516,123,372	26,567,287,015	21,663,073,827	20,008,789,347	23,814,809,505	24,744,321,492
R&D Expense						
Operating Income	1,739,121,000	985,622,100	723,597,600	61,232,990	302,714,500	571,417,700
Operating Margin %	.05%	.04%	.03%	.00%	.01%	.02%
SGA Expense						
Net Income	1,441,933,000	991,488,500	566,210,800	-219,737,600	84,219,660	438,454,600
Operating Cash Flow	2,908,185,000	954,068,400	1,313,212,000	833,504,600	241,835,600	1,018,398,000
Capital Expenditure	800,076,400	688,197,800	967,446,600	597,327,200	849,472,400	837,635,400
EBITDA	2,912,448,000	1,974,486,000	1,454,193,000	694,258,600	1,025,292,000	1,402,076,000
Return on Assets %	.06%	.05%	.03%	-.01%	.00%	.02%
Return on Equity %	.13%	.10%	.07%	-.03%	.01%	.05%
Debt to Equity	.24%	.29%	.47%	.62%	0.389	0.359

CONTACT INFORMATION:

Phone: 81 822821111   Fax:
Toll-Free:
Address: 3-1 Shinchi, Fuchu-cho, Aki-gun, Hiroshima, 100-0011 Japan

STOCK TICKER/OTHER:

Stock Ticker: MZDAF   Exchange: PINX
Employees: 49,998   Fiscal Year Ends: 03/31
Parent Company:

SALARIES/BONUSES:

Top Exec. Salary: $ Bonus: $
Second Exec. Salary: $ Bonus: $

OTHER THOUGHTS:

Estimated Female Officers or Directors:
Hot Spot for Advancement for Women/Minorities:

McAfee Corp

www.mcafee.com

NAIC Code: 511210E

TYPES OF BUSINESS:

Computer Software: Network Security, Managed Access, Digital ID,
Cybersecurity & Anti-Virus
Virus Protection Software
Identity Protection Software
Cybersecurity
Malware Protection
Software Design and Development
Software Technology
Virtual Private Network Solution

BRANDS/DIVISIONS/AFFILIATES:

Advent International Corporation
McAfee+
McAfee+ Antivirus
Total Protection
McAfee Assist

CONTACTS: *Note: Officers with more than one job title may be intentionally listed here more than once.*

Craig Boundy, CEO
Jennifer Biry, CFO
Justin Hastings, Chief People Officer
Steve Grobman, CTO
Lynne Doherty McDonald, Executive VP, Divisional
Gagan Singh, Executive VP
Ashish Agarwal, Senior VP, Divisional

GROWTH PLANS/SPECIAL FEATURES:

McAfee Corp. is an online protection company offering products and solutions that protect user privacy and identity across devices and locations. All-in-one protection products include McAfee+, offering privacy, identity and device protection for individuals and families; McAfee+ Antivirus, offering privacy, identity and device protection as well as $2 million in ID theft coverage; and Total Protection, which protects devices with identity monitoring and virtual private network (VPN), enabling users to securely send/receive data across shared or public networks. Protection products for devices are available for antivirus, text scam detection, VPN, mobile security, PC optimization, TechMaster concierge and McAfee Assist. Security features span personal data cleanup, identity monitoring, credit monitoring, security freeze, identity theft coverage and restoration, password manager, antivirus, web protection, parental controls and more. McAfee offers free tools and downloads on its website, as well as services regarding PC optimizing, technical and virus removal. McAfee serves more than 100 million customers in over 180 countries. The firm is privately-owned by Advent International Corporation.

McAfee offers its employees health and retirement plans, as well as skill and learning development opportunities.

FINANCIAL DATA: *Note: Data for latest year may not have been available at press time.*

In U.S. $	2024	2023	2022	2021	2020	2019
Revenue	2,194,400,000	2,080,000,000	2,000,000,000	1,920,000,000	1,558,000,000	1,303,000,000
R&D Expense						
Operating Income						
Operating Margin %						
SGA Expense						
Net Income				2,688,000,000	-289,000,000	-236,000,000
Operating Cash Flow						
Capital Expenditure						
EBITDA						
Return on Assets %						
Return on Equity %						
Debt to Equity						

CONTACT INFORMATION:

Phone: 866 622-3911   Fax:
Toll-Free:
Address: 6220 America Center Dr., San Jose, CA 95002 United States

STOCK TICKER/OTHER:

Stock Ticker: Private   Exchange:
Employees: 6,900   Fiscal Year Ends: 12/31
Parent Company: Advent International Corporation

SALARIES/BONUSES:

Top Exec. Salary: $ Bonus: $
Second Exec. Salary: $ Bonus: $

OTHER THOUGHTS:

Estimated Female Officers or Directors:
Hot Spot for Advancement for Women/Minorities:

McDermott International Ltd

www.mcdermott.com

NAIC Code: 541330

TYPES OF BUSINESS:
Engineering Services
Energy Engineering Services
Energy Construction Services
Energy Transformation Services
Consulting Services
Procurement and Supply Chain Management
Commissioning Services
Storage Tanks and Terminals

BRANDS/DIVISIONS/AFFILIATES:

GROWTH PLANS/SPECIAL FEATURES:

McDermott International Ltd. is a fully integrated provider of engineering and construction solutions to the energy industry. The firm designs and builds infrastructure solutions so that customers can transport and transform global energy resources into products. McDermott offers technology, engineering and fabrication services, storage facilities/tanks/terminals, onshore construction, marine construction vessels, procurement, supply chain management, startup/commissioning and related operations, and consulting services. Markets served by McDermott are categorized into energy transition, upstream, refining, chemicals, petrochemicals, liquefied natural gas (LNG), industrial storage, water and wastewater. McDermott operates in over 54 countries, and its globally integrated resources include a diversified fleet of specialty marine construction vessels and fabrication facilities.

CONTACTS: Note: Officers with more than one job title may be intentionally listed here more than once.
Michael McKelvy, CEO
Maurizio Boratella, COO
Gary Luquette, Chairman of the Board
Travis Brantley, CFO
Linda Borne, Chief Human Resources Officer
David Dickson, Director
Daniel McCarthy, Executive VP, Divisional
Samik Mukherjee, Executive VP
John Freeman, Executive VP
Brian McLaughlin, Other Executive Officer
Stephen Allen, Other Executive Officer
Scott Munro, Other Executive Officer
Neil Gunnion, Senior VP, Divisional
Mark Coscio, Senior VP, Geographical
Linh Austin, Senior VP, Geographical
Ian Prescott, Senior VP, Geographical

FINANCIAL DATA: Note: Data for latest year may not have been available at press time.

In U.S. $	2024	2023	2022	2021	2020	2019
Revenue	8,873,592,000	8,451,040,000	8,126,000,000	6,507,280,000	6,257,000,000	7,847,000,000
R&D Expense						
Operating Income						
Operating Margin %						
SGA Expense						
Net Income						
Operating Cash Flow						
Capital Expenditure						
EBITDA						
Return on Assets %						
Return on Equity %						
Debt to Equity						

CONTACT INFORMATION:
Phone: 281 58806600   Fax:
Toll-Free:
Address: 915 N. Eldridge Pkwy., Houston, TX 77079 United States

STOCK TICKER/OTHER:
Stock Ticker: Private   Exchange:
Employees: 32,000   Fiscal Year Ends: 12/31
Parent Company:

SALARIES/BONUSES:
Top Exec. Salary: $ Bonus: $
Second Exec. Salary: $ Bonus: $

OTHER THOUGHTS:
Estimated Female Officers or Directors: 4
Hot Spot for Advancement for Women/Minorities: Y

Medtronic plc

NAIC Code: 334510

www.medtronic.com

TYPES OF BUSINESS:

Equipment-Defibrillators & Pacing Products
Neurological Devices
Diabetes Management Devices
Ear, Nose & Throat Surgical Equipment
Pain Management Devices
Cardiac Surgery Equipment

BRANDS/DIVISIONS/AFFILIATES:

GROWTH PLANS/SPECIAL FEATURES:

One of the largest medical-device companies, Medtronic develops and manufactures therapeutic medical devices for chronic diseases. Its portfolio includes pacemakers, defibrillators, transcatheter heart valves, stents, insulin pumps, spinal fixation devices, neurovascular products, advanced energy, and surgical tools. The company primarily markets its products to healthcare institutions and physicians in the United States, Western Europe, and Japan. Foreign sales account for roughly 50% of the company's total sales.

Medtronic offers its employees healthcare and disability, adoption and elder care assistance, retirement plans and stock options.

CONTACTS: Note: Officers with more than one job title may be intentionally listed here more than once.

Geoffrey Martha, CEO
Gary Corona, CFO
Jennifer Kirk, Chief Accounting Officer
Gregory Smith, Executive VP, Divisional
Ivan Fong, Executive VP
Brett Wall, Executive VP
Sean Salmon, Executive VP
Michael Marinaro, Executive VP

FINANCIAL DATA: Note: Data for latest year may not have been available at press time.

In U.S. $	2024	2023	2022	2021	2020	2019
Revenue	32,363,999,232	31,227,000,832	31,686,000,640	30,116,999,168	28,913,000,448	30,556,999,680
R&D Expense	2,735,000,000	2,696,000,000	2,746,000,000	2,493,000,000	2,331,000,000	2,330,000,000
Operating Income	5,520,000,000	5,830,000,000	5,908,000,000	4,895,000,000	5,222,000,000	6,632,000,000
Operating Margin %	.17%	.19%	.19%	.16%	.18%	.22%
SGA Expense	10,736,000,000	10,415,000,000	10,292,000,000	10,148,000,000	10,109,000,000	10,418,000,000
Net Income	3,676,000,000	3,758,000,000	5,039,000,000	3,606,000,000	4,789,000,000	4,631,000,000
Operating Cash Flow	6,787,000,000	6,039,000,000	7,346,000,000	6,240,000,000	7,234,000,000	7,007,000,000
Capital Expenditure	1,587,000,000	1,459,000,000	1,368,000,000	1,355,000,000	1,213,000,000	1,134,000,000
EBITDA	8,203,000,000	8,697,000,000	8,777,000,000	7,522,000,000	7,810,000,000	9,300,000,000
Return on Assets %	.04%	.04%	.05%	.04%	.05%	.05%
Return on Equity %	.07%	.07%	.10%	.07%	.09%	.09%
Debt to Equity	.48%	.47%	.39%	.51%	0.434	0.489

CONTACT INFORMATION:

Phone: 3531-438-1700   Fax:
Toll-Free:
Address: 20 On Hatch, Lower Hatch St., Dublin, 2 Ireland

STOCK TICKER/OTHER:

Stock Ticker: MDT   Exchange: NYS
Employees: 95,000   Fiscal Year Ends: 04/30
Parent Company:

SALARIES/BONUSES:

Top Exec. Salary: $1,350,000   Bonus: $
Second Exec. Salary: Bonus: $
$911,233

OTHER THOUGHTS:

Estimated Female Officers or Directors: 5
Hot Spot for Advancement for Women/Minorities: Y

Mercedes-Benz Group AG

group.mercedes-benz.com/en

NAIC Code: 336111

TYPES OF BUSINESS:

Automobile Manufacturing
Financial Services & Insurance
Commercial Vehicles, Trucks & Buses
Aerospace & Defense Technology
Automotive Manufacture
Vehicle Distribution
Vehicle Development

BRANDS/DIVISIONS/AFFILIATES:

Mercedes-Benz
Daimler
Maybach
Freightliner
BharatBenz
car2go
Citan
eActros

GROWTH PLANS/SPECIAL FEATURES:

Mercedes-Benz Group is a premium automotive original equipment manufacturer, selling around 2 million passenger cars, including its Chinese joint venture, and just under 400,000 vans per year. The company's financial profile improved significantly following the spinoff of Daimler Truck in 2021. Unlike most automotive OEMs, Mercedes operates under its own brand alone. In 2024, 14% of its passenger cars sold were top end (G Class, Maybach, AMG, S Class), 59% were core (C and E Class), and 27% entry (A and B Class). In volume terms, Asia and Europe are Mercedes' largest markets, each at just under 40% of 2024 vehicle sales followed by North America at 16%.

CONTACTS: *Note: Officers with more than one job title may be intentionally listed here more than once.*

Bernd Pischetsrieder, Chairman of the Board
Ergun Lumali, Deputy Chairman

FINANCIAL DATA: *Note: Data for latest year may not have been available at press time.*

In U.S. $	2024	2023	2022	2021	2020	2019
Revenue	165,259,940,645	172,973,884,917	170,280,362,752	151,978,430,492	138,227,019,408	196,078,319,066
R&D Expense	6,333,712,000	7,071,510,000	6,358,683,000	6,205,448,000	5,492,622,000	7,475,596,000
Operating Income	13,962,540,000	19,888,760,000	20,299,660,000	16,998,860,000	6,459,705,000	4,572,077,000
Operating Margin %	.08%	.11%	.12%	.11%	.05%	.02%
SGA Expense	14,213,390,000	14,802,500,000	13,695,800,000	13,623,160,000	13,022,700,000	19,127,130,000
Net Income	11,585,700,000	16,187,290,000	16,459,710,000	26,113,510,000	4,116,913,000	2,698,070,000
Operating Cash Flow	20,130,530,000	16,424,520,000	19,175,940,000	27,864,930,000	25,348,470,000	8,953,462,000
Capital Expenditure	9,835,415,000	9,322,361,000	7,830,874,000	8,308,740,000	9,716,231,000	12,298,520,000
EBITDA	24,409,760,000	31,144,160,000	30,933,030,000	26,356,410,000	17,471,060,000	14,414,300,000
Return on Assets %	.04%	.05%	.06%	.08%	.01%	.01%
Return on Equity %	.11%	.16%	.18%	.35%	.06%	.04%
Debt to Equity	.68%	.60%	.60%	.87%	1.238	1.447

CONTACT INFORMATION:

Phone: 49 7111792543   Fax: 49 7111794116
Toll-Free:
Address: Mercedesstrasse 137, Stuttgart, BW 70372 Germany

SALARIES/BONUSES:

Top Exec. Salary: $ Bonus: $
Second Exec. Salary: $ Bonus: $

STOCK TICKER/OTHER:

Stock Ticker: MBGYY   Exchange: PINX
Employees: 166,056   Fiscal Year Ends: 12/31
Parent Company:

OTHER THOUGHTS:

Estimated Female Officers or Directors: 6
Hot Spot for Advancement for Women/Minorities: Y

Merck & Co Inc

NAIC Code: 325412

www.merck.com

TYPES OF BUSINESS:

Drugs-Diversified
Prescription Medicines
Vaccines
Biologic Therapies
Animal Health Products

GROWTH PLANS/SPECIAL FEATURES:

Merck makes pharmaceutical products to treat several conditions in a number of therapeutic areas, including cardiometabolic disease, cancer, and infections. Within cancer, the firm's immuno-oncology platform is growing as a major contributor to overall sales. The company also has a substantial vaccine business, with treatments to prevent pediatric diseases as well as human papillomavirus, or HPV. Additionally, Merck sells animal health-related drugs. From a geographical perspective, just under half of the company's sales are generated in the United States.

BRANDS/DIVISIONS/AFFILIATES:

CONTACTS: Note: Officers with more than one job title may be intentionally listed here more than once.

Robert Davis, CEO
Chirfi Guindo, Other Executive Officer
Caroline Litchfield, CFO
Dalton Smart, Chief Accounting Officer
David Williams, Chief Information Officer
Michael Klobuchar, Chief Strategy Officer
Jennifer Zachary, Executive VP
Cristal Downing, Executive VP
Sanat Chattopadhyay, Executive VP
Dean Li, Executive VP
Richard DeLuca, Executive VP
Betty Larson, Other Executive Officer
Dean Li, President, Divisional
Jannie Oosthuizen, President, Geographical
Joseph Romanelli, President, Subsidiary

FINANCIAL DATA: Note: Data for latest year may not have been available at press time.

In U.S. $	2024	2023	2022	2021	2020	2019
Revenue	64,168,001,536	60,115,001,344	59,283,001,344	48,704,000,000	41,517,998,080	39,120,998,400
R&D Expense	17,938,000,000	30,531,000,000	13,548,000,000	12,245,000,000	13,397,000,000	9,724,000,000
Operating Income	20,221,000,000	2,954,000,000	18,282,000,000	13,199,000,000	5,548,000,000	7,926,000,000
Operating Margin %	.32%	.05%	.31%	.27%	.13%	.20%
SGA Expense	10,816,000,000	10,504,000,000	10,042,000,000	9,634,000,000	8,955,000,000	9,455,000,000
Net Income	17,117,000,000	365,000,000	14,519,000,000	13,049,000,000	7,067,000,000	9,843,000,000
Operating Cash Flow	21,468,000,000	13,006,000,000	19,095,000,000	14,109,000,000	10,253,000,000	13,440,000,000
Capital Expenditure	3,372,000,000	3,863,000,000	4,388,000,000	4,448,000,000	4,429,000,000	3,369,000,000
EBITDA	25,706,000,000	6,907,000,000	21,315,000,000	17,899,000,000	10,180,000,000	11,374,000,000
Return on Assets %	.15%	.00%	.14%	.13%	.08%	.12%
Return on Equity %	.41%	.01%	.34%	.41%	.28%	.37%
Debt to Equity	.74%	.90%	.63%	.80%	1.002	0.878

CONTACT INFORMATION:

Phone: 908 423-1000   Fax: 908 735-1253
Toll-Free:
Address: 2000 Galloping Hill Rd., Kenilworth, NJ 07033 United States

STOCK TICKER/OTHER:

Stock Ticker: MRK   Exchange: NYS
Employees: 72,000   Fiscal Year Ends: 12/31
Parent Company:

SALARIES/BONUSES:

Top Exec. Salary: $1,623,874   Bonus: $
Second Exec. Salary: Bonus: $
$1,451,077

OTHER THOUGHTS:

Estimated Female Officers or Directors: 4
Hot Spot for Advancement for Women/Minorities: Y

Merck KGaA

NAIC Code: 325412

www.emdgroup.com/en

TYPES OF BUSINESS:

Pharmaceuticals
Drug Development
Therapeutics
Laboratory Materials
Manufacturing
Gene Editing Tools
Semiconductor Solutions
Performance Materials

BRANDS/DIVISIONS/AFFILIATES:

GROWTH PLANS/SPECIAL FEATURES:

Merck KGaA operates in three main segments: Life Science, Electronics, and Healthcare. The Life Science segment provides laboratory consumables and instruments to researchers in academia and applied fields, including the biopharmaceutical industry. The Electronics segment offers specialty materials to manufacture a variety of products, such as semiconductors and flat-screen televisions. In the healthcare segment, Merck develops, manufactures, and sells branded pharmaceuticals with significant therapeutic concentrations in oncology, multiple sclerosis, and fertility. In 1995, the E. Merck KG family publicly sold part of the company, resulting in the current 30% public ownership of the firm.

Merck offers its employees health benefits and retirement plans.

CONTACTS: *Note: Officers with more than one job title may be intentionally listed here more than once.*

Sascha Held, Director

FINANCIAL DATA: *Note: Data for latest year may not have been available at press time.*

In U.S. $	2024	2023	2022	2021	2020	2019
Revenue	24,013,620,621	23,828,603,231	25,234,960,881	22,346,197,599	19,902,382,659	18,333,712,292
R&D Expense	2,586,833,000	2,775,255,000	2,861,521,000	2,753,689,000	2,597,049,000	2,574,347,000
Operating Income	4,560,727,000	4,055,619,000	5,393,871,000	4,777,525,000	3,189,557,000	2,615,210,000
Operating Margin %	.19%	.17%	.21%	.21%	.16%	.14%
SGA Expense	6,083,996,000	6,048,808,000	6,143,019,000	5,608,400,000	5,402,951,000	5,456,300,000
Net Income	3,152,100,000	3,205,448,000	3,775,256,000	3,467,651,000	2,255,392,000	1,498,297,000
Operating Cash Flow	5,205,448,000	4,295,119,000	4,834,279,000	5,239,501,000	3,946,651,000	3,241,771,000
Capital Expenditure	2,479,001,000	2,296,254,000	2,049,943,000	1,612,940,000	1,774,120,000	1,158,910,000
EBITDA	6,767,310,000	6,452,895,000	7,437,003,000	6,768,445,000	5,624,290,000	4,716,232,000
Return on Assets %	.06%	.06%	.07%	.07%	.05%	.03%
Return on Equity %	.10%	.11%	.14%	.16%	.11%	.08%
Debt to Equity	.23%	.35%	.35%	.39%	0.575	0.481

CONTACT INFORMATION:

Phone: 49 6151720   Fax: 49 6151722000
Toll-Free:
Address: Frankfurter Strasse 250, Darmstadt, HE 64293 Germany

STOCK TICKER/OTHER:

Stock Ticker: MKKGY   Exchange: PINX
Employees: 62,908   Fiscal Year Ends: 12/31
Parent Company:

SALARIES/BONUSES:

Top Exec. Salary: $ Bonus: $
Second Exec. Salary: $ Bonus: $

OTHER THOUGHTS:

Estimated Female Officers or Directors:
Hot Spot for Advancement for Women/Minorities:

Merck Serono SA

NAIC Code: 325412

TYPES OF BUSINESS:

Biopharmaceuticals Development
Therapy Development
Drug Development Pipeline
Healthcare Science and Technology
Research and Development
Oncology
Immunology
Fertility and Endocrinology

BRANDS/DIVISIONS/AFFILIATES:

Merck KGaA
EMD Serono

CONTACTS: *Note: Officers with more than one job title may be intentionally listed here more than once.*

Helene von Roeder, CFO
Khadija Ben Hammada, Chief People Officer
Thierry Hulot, Head-Global Mfg. & Supply
Thomas Gunning, Head-Legal
Meeta Gulyani, Head-Strategy & Global Franchises
Patrice Grand, Head-Communications
Susan Herbert, Head-Global Bus. Dev. & Strategy
Sascha Becker, Sr. VP
Elchin Ergun, Head-Global Commercial
Belen Garijo, Chmn.
Annalisa Jenkins, Head-Global Dev. & Medical

GROWTH PLANS/SPECIAL FEATURES:

Merck Serono SA is the healthcare business and subsidiary of Merck KGaA and branded as EMD Serono in the U.S. EMD Serono develops and delivers therapies to support the needs of individual patients, specializing in neurology, immunology, fertility, endocrinology and oncology. The company is known for integrating cutting-edge science and innovative technology to develop products and devices for people living with difficult-to-treat diseases. More than 20% of global revenues goes toward continued research and development investments in oncology, immune-oncology and immunology. EMD Serono's R&D operating model strives to advance its development and regulatory capabilities, as well as to continue its focus on high-priority programs. As of May 2025, the firm's healthcare development pipeline had three drugs in Phase 3 trials, xevinapant for the treatment of squamous cell carcinoma of the head and neck; xevinapant, also for the treatment of squamous cell carcinoma of the head and neck; and pimicotinib for the treatment of tenosynovial giant cell tumor. Drugs in Phase 2 trials included avelumab for the treatment of metastatic urothelial carcinoma and ompenaclid for the treatment of mutated advanced or metastatic colorectal cancer. Drugs in Phase 1 trials included tuvusertib, lartesertib and M9140 for the treatment of solid tumors. The company has 24 connected R&D hubs on three continents to drive its innovation and deliver a potentially transformative pipeline, they are located in Asia, Europe and North America.

FINANCIAL DATA: *Note: Data for latest year may not have been available at press time.*

In U.S. $	2024	2023	2022	2021	2020	2019
Revenue	9,235,636,200	8,795,844,000	8,457,541,904	8,507,772,000	8,180,550,000	7,717,500,000
R&D Expense						
Operating Income						
Operating Margin %						
SGA Expense						
Net Income						
Operating Cash Flow						
Capital Expenditure						
EBITDA						
Return on Assets %						
Return on Equity %						
Debt to Equity						

CONTACT INFORMATION:

Phone: 49-6151-72-0   Fax: 49-6151-72-2000
Toll-Free:
Address: Frankfurter St. 250, Darmstadt, 64293 Germany

STOCK TICKER/OTHER:

Stock Ticker: Subsidiary   Exchange:
Employees: 4,775   Fiscal Year Ends: 12/31
Parent Company: Merck KGaA

SALARIES/BONUSES:

Top Exec. Salary: $ Bonus: $
Second Exec. Salary: $ Bonus: $

OTHER THOUGHTS:

Estimated Female Officers or Directors: 5
Hot Spot for Advancement for Women/Minorities: Y

Meta Platforms Inc (Facebook)

NAIC Code: 519130

investor.fb.com

TYPES OF BUSINESS:

Social Networking
Advertising Services
Metaverse Technologies and Platforms
Online Video
3-D Headset Manufacturing
In-App Merchandising and Ecommerce
Virtual Reality (VR) and Augmented Reality (AR)
Instant Messaging

BRANDS/DIVISIONS/AFFILIATES:

Facebook
Instagram
Meta Quest
WhatsApp Messenger
Oculus
Llama
Meta Spark
Meta Horizon

GROWTH PLANS/SPECIAL FEATURES:

Meta is the largest social media company in the world, boasting close to 4 billion monthly active users worldwide. The firm's "Family of Apps," its core business, consists of Facebook, Instagram, Messenger, and WhatsApp. End users can leverage these applications for a variety of different purposes, from keeping in touch with friends to following celebrities and running digital businesses for free. Meta packages customer data, gleaned from its application ecosystem and sells ads to digital advertisers. While the firm has been investing heavily in its Reality Labs business, it remains a very small part of Meta's overall sales.

CONTACTS: Note: Officers with more than one job title may be intentionally listed here more than once.

Mark Zuckerberg, CEO
Susan Li, CFO
Aaron Anderson, Chief Accounting Officer
Jennifer Newstead, Chief Legal Officer
Andrew Bosworth, Chief Technology Officer
Javier Olivan, COO
Christopher Cox, Other Executive Officer
Nick Clegg, President, Divisional

FINANCIAL DATA: Note: Data for latest year may not have been available at press time.

In U.S. $	2024	2023	2022	2021	2020	2019
Revenue	164,500,996,096	134,901,997,568	116,608,999,424	117,929,000,960	85,964,996,608	70,697,000,960
R&D Expense	43,873,000,000	38,483,000,000	35,338,000,000	24,655,000,000	18,447,000,000	13,600,000,000
Operating Income	69,380,000,000	46,751,000,000	28,944,000,000	46,753,000,000	32,671,000,000	28,986,000,000
Operating Margin %	.42%	.35%	.25%	.40%	.38%	.41%
SGA Expense	21,087,000,000	23,709,000,000	27,078,000,000	23,872,000,000	18,155,000,000	15,341,000,000
Net Income	62,360,000,000	39,098,000,000	23,200,000,000	39,370,000,000	29,146,000,000	18,485,000,000
Operating Cash Flow	91,328,000,000	71,113,000,000	50,475,000,000	57,683,000,000	38,747,000,000	36,314,000,000
Capital Expenditure	37,256,000,000	27,045,000,000	31,186,000,000	18,690,000,000	15,163,000,000	15,102,000,000
EBITDA	86,876,000,000	59,052,000,000	37,690,000,000	55,274,000,000	39,533,000,000	34,727,000,000
Return on Assets %	.25%	.19%	.13%	.24%	.20%	.16%
Return on Equity %	.37%	.28%	.19%	.31%	.25%	.20%
Debt to Equity	.26%	.23%	.20%	.10%	0.075	0.094

CONTACT INFORMATION:

Phone: 650 543-4800   Fax:
Toll-Free:
Address: 1601 Willow Rd., Menlo Park, CA 94025 United States

STOCK TICKER/OTHER:

Stock Ticker: META   Exchange: NAS
Employees: 67,317   Fiscal Year Ends: 12/31
Parent Company:

SALARIES/BONUSES:

Top Exec. Salary: $1,082,979   Bonus: $1,015,293
Second Exec. Salary: Bonus: $923,799
$996,289

OTHER THOUGHTS:

Estimated Female Officers or Directors: 2
Hot Spot for Advancement for Women/Minorities: Y

Sales, profits and employees may be estimates. Financial information, benefits and other data can change quickly and may vary from those stated here.

Michael Baker International LLC   www.mbakerintl.com

NAIC Code: 541330

TYPES OF BUSINESS:

Engineering Services
Infrastructure Projects
Facilities Management
Consulting Services
Regulatory Compliance Services
Engineering Services
Architecture and Planning
Technology Development

BRANDS/DIVISIONS/AFFILIATES:

DC Capital Partners LLC
OMTR
OTMRdata

CONTACTS: Note: Officers with more than one job title may be intentionally listed here more than once.

Brian A. Lutes, CEO
James E. Koch, COO
Stephanie Long, CFO
Devendra Kumar, CIO
James McKnight, Chief Legal Officer
Nicholas Gross, COO-Intl

GROWTH PLANS/SPECIAL FEATURES:

Michael Baker International, LLC is a provider of engineering and consulting services, operating through more than 90 offices in the U.S. The firm's services include design, planning, architectural, environmental, construction and program management. Michael Baker's practices, services and solutions span all key areas of infrastructure, including bridge, highway, intelligent transportation, federal, design-build, construction services, planning, water, environmental, architecture, aviation, land development, railroad and transit, cold regions engineering, energy and cost management. The company partners with its clients on projects ranging from tunnels, mass transit and airports, to water treatment plants, arctic oil pipelines, environmental restoration and specialized overseas construction. Signature projects by Michael Baker include Route 52 Causeway in New Jersey, Padre Dam Municipal Water District-Eastern Service Area Secondary Connection in California, Jacksonville Regional Transportation Center at La Villa in Florida, Fort Lee Lodge in Virginia and Trans-Alaska Pipeline in Alaska. Michael Baker develops and utilizes updated technology for its projects, including the DATAMARK public safety geographic information system (GIS), OTMR data technology for electric utilities and communications providers in relation to LiDAR and GIS, aerial technologies, geospatial solutions, indoor spatial data (2D and 3D), mobility technology solutions, virtual design and construction, and more. Michael Baker is privately-owned by DC Capital Partners, LLC.

Michael Baker International offers its employees medical benefits, life and accident insurance, a 401(k), spending accounts, tuition reimbursement and wellness programs.

FINANCIAL DATA: Note: Data for latest year may not have been available at press time.

In U.S. $	2024	2023	2022	2021	2020	2019
Revenue	1,791,972,000	1,706,640,000	1,641,000,000	1,597,776,887	1,493,249,427	1,659,166,031
R&D Expense						
Operating Income						
Operating Margin %						
SGA Expense						
Net Income						
Operating Cash Flow						
Capital Expenditure						
EBITDA						
Return on Assets %						
Return on Equity %						
Debt to Equity						

CONTACT INFORMATION:

Phone: 412 918-4000   Fax: 412 375-3909
Toll-Free: 800-553-1153
Address: 500 Grant St., Ste. 5400, Pittsburgh, PA 15219 United States

STOCK TICKER/OTHER:

Stock Ticker: Private   Exchange:
Employees: 3,000   Fiscal Year Ends: 12/31
Parent Company: DC Capital Partners LLC

SALARIES/BONUSES:

Top Exec. Salary: $ Bonus: $
Second Exec. Salary: $ Bonus: $

OTHER THOUGHTS:

Estimated Female Officers or Directors: 1
Hot Spot for Advancement for Women/Minorities:

Micron Technology Inc

NAIC Code: 334413

www.micron.com

TYPES OF BUSINESS:

Components-Semiconductor Memory
Storage
Memory
Artificial Intelligence
5G
Machine Learning
Autonomous
Security

BRANDS/DIVISIONS/AFFILIATES:

3D Xpoint
Authenta

GROWTH PLANS/SPECIAL FEATURES:

Micron is one of the largest semiconductor companies in the world, specializing in memory and storage chips. Its primary revenue stream comes from dynamic random access memory, or DRAM, and it also has minority exposure to not-and or NAND, flash chips. Micron serves a global customer base, selling chips into data centers, mobile phones, consumer electronics, and industrial and automotive applications. The firm is vertically integrated.

Micron offers its employees health insurance, a retirement plan, a stock purchase program, tuition support, training and more.

CONTACTS: Note: Officers with more than one job title may be intentionally listed here more than once.

Sanjay Mehrotra, CEO
Mark Murphy, CFO
Scott Allen, Chief Accounting Officer
Michael Ray, Chief Legal Officer
Scott Deboer, Executive VP, Divisional
Manish Bhatia, Executive VP, Divisional
April Arnzen, Executive VP
Sumit Sadana, Executive VP
Michael Bokan, Senior VP, Divisional

FINANCIAL DATA: Note: Data for latest year may not have been available at press time.

In U.S. $	2024	2023	2022	2021	2020	2019
Revenue	25,110,999,040	15,539,999,744	30,758,000,640	27,704,999,936	21,435,000,832	23,406,000,128
R&D Expense	3,430,000,000	3,114,000,000	3,116,000,000	2,663,000,000	2,600,000,000	2,441,000,000
Operating Income	1,246,000,000	-5,459,000,000	9,709,000,000	6,747,000,000	3,060,000,000	7,390,000,000
Operating Margin %	.05%	-.35%	.32%	.24%	.14%	.32%
SGA Expense	1,129,000,000	920,000,000	1,066,000,000	894,000,000	881,000,000	836,000,000
Net Income	778,000,000	-5,833,000,000	8,687,000,000	5,861,000,000	2,687,000,000	6,313,000,000
Operating Cash Flow	8,507,000,000	1,559,000,000	15,181,000,000	12,468,000,000	8,306,000,000	13,189,000,000
Capital Expenditure	8,386,000,000	7,676,000,000	12,067,000,000	10,030,000,000	8,223,000,000	9,780,000,000
EBITDA	9,582,000,000	2,486,000,000	16,876,000,000	12,615,000,000	8,827,000,000	12,600,000,000
Return on Assets %	.01%	-.09%	.14%	.10%	.05%	.14%
Return on Equity %	.02%	-.12%	.19%	.14%	.07%	.19%
Debt to Equity	.30%	.31%	.15%	.16%	0.177	0.127

CONTACT INFORMATION:

Phone: 208 368-4000   Fax: 208 368-4435
Toll-Free:
Address: 8000 S. Federal Way, Boise, ID 83716-9632 United States

STOCK TICKER/OTHER:

Stock Ticker: MU
Employees: 48,000
Parent Company:

Exchange: NAS
Fiscal Year Ends: 08/31

SALARIES/BONUSES:

Top Exec. Salary: $1,416,909   Bonus: $
Second Exec. Salary: $819,452   Bonus: $

OTHER THOUGHTS:

Estimated Female Officers or Directors: 2
Hot Spot for Advancement for Women/Minorities:

Microsoft Corporation

www.microsoft.com

NAIC Code: 511210H

TYPES OF BUSINESS:

Computer Software, Operating Systems, Languages & Development Tools
Enterprise Software
Game Consoles
Operating Systems
Software as a Service (SAAS)
Search Engine and Advertising
E-Mail Services
Instant Messaging

BRANDS/DIVISIONS/AFFILIATES:

Office 365
Exchange
SharePoint
Microsoft Teams
Skype for Business
Outlook.com
OneDrive
LinkedIn

GROWTH PLANS/SPECIAL FEATURES:

Microsoft develops and licenses consumer and enterprise software. It is known for its Windows operating systems and Office productivity suite. The company is organized into three equally sized broad segments: productivity and business processes (legacy Microsoft Office, cloud-based Office 365, Exchange, SharePoint, Skype, LinkedIn, Dynamics), intelligence cloud (infrastructure- and platform-as-a-service offerings Azure, Windows Server OS, SQL Server), and more personal computing (Windows Client, Xbox, Bing search, display advertising, and Surface laptops, tablets, and desktops).

Microsoft offers its employees comprehensive benefits, a 401(k) and employee stock purchase plans; and employee assistance programs.

CONTACTS: Note: Officers with more than one job title may be intentionally listed here more than once.

Satya Nadella, CEO
Amy Hood, CFO
Alice Jolla, Chief Accounting Officer
Takeshi Numoto, Chief Marketing Officer
Kathleen Hogan, Executive VP
Judson Althoff, Executive VP
Bradford Smith, President

FINANCIAL DATA: Note: Data for latest year may not have been available at press time.

In U.S. $	2024	2023	2022	2021	2020	2019
Revenue	245,122,007,040	211,914,997,760	198,269,992,960	168,087,994,368	143,015,002,112	125,842,997,248
R&D Expense	29,510,000,000	27,195,000,000	24,512,000,000	20,716,000,000	19,269,000,000	16,876,000,000
Operating Income	109,433,000,000	88,523,000,000	83,383,000,000	69,916,000,000	52,959,000,000	42,959,000,000
Operating Margin %	.45%	.42%	.42%	.42%	.37%	.34%
SGA Expense	32,065,000,000	30,334,000,000	27,725,000,000	25,224,000,000	24,709,000,000	23,098,000,000
Net Income	88,136,000,000	72,361,000,000	72,738,000,000	61,271,000,000	44,281,000,000	39,240,000,000
Operating Cash Flow	118,548,000,000	87,582,000,000	89,035,000,000	76,740,000,000	60,675,000,000	52,185,000,000
Capital Expenditure	44,477,000,000	28,107,000,000	23,886,000,000	20,622,000,000	15,441,000,000	13,925,000,000
EBITDA	133,009,000,000	105,140,000,000	100,239,000,000	85,134,000,000	68,423,000,000	58,056,000,000
Return on Assets %	.19%	.19%	.21%	.19%	.15%	.14%
Return on Equity %	.37%	.39%	.47%	.47%	.40%	.42%
Debt to Equity	.22%	.27%	.35%	.42%	0.568	0.712

CONTACT INFORMATION:

Phone: 425 882-8080   Fax: 425 936-7329
Toll-Free: 800-642-7676
Address: One Microsoft Way, Redmond, WA 98052 United States

STOCK TICKER/OTHER:

Stock Ticker: MSFT   Exchange: NAS
Employees: 221,400   Fiscal Year Ends: 06/30
Parent Company:

SALARIES/BONUSES:

Top Exec. Salary: $2,500,000   Bonus: $
Second Exec. Salary: $1,000,000   Bonus: $

OTHER THOUGHTS:

Estimated Female Officers or Directors: 4
Hot Spot for Advancement for Women/Minorities: Y

Middough Inc

www.middough.com

NAIC Code: 541330

TYPES OF BUSINESS:

Engineering Services
Engineering
Construction Management
Consulting and Planning
Architecture and Design
Commissioning and Startup Services
Project Estimating and Scheduling
Procurement

BRANDS/DIVISIONS/AFFILIATES:

GROWTH PLANS/SPECIAL FEATURES:

Middough, Inc., founded in 1950 by Willian Vance Middough, is a private engineering, procurement and construction management (EPCM) company that provides related solutions and consulting services for major projects. As a full-service project solutions firm, Middough serves multiple core industries, including agribusiness, chemicals, food and consumer products, manufacturing, metals, oil and gas, pharmaceuticals, biopharmaceuticals, power and refining. In addition to what is mentioned above, the company specializes in consulting and planning, design, architecture, estimating and scheduling, project delivery, commissioning and startup and asset integrity. Based in Cleveland, Ohio, the firm has additional offices in Illinois, Indiana, Kentucky, New York, Ohio, Pennsylvania and Wisconsin.

Middough offers its employees comprehensive health coverage, health savings account options, life and short-/long-term disability insurance, AD&D and travel accident insurance, flexible spending accounts, a 401(k), tuition assistance and other benefits, p

CONTACTS: *Note: Officers with more than one job title may be intentionally listed here more than once.*

Samuel R. Barnes, CEO
Ronald R. Ledin, Chmn.

FINANCIAL DATA: *Note: Data for latest year may not have been available at press time.*

In U.S. $	2024	2023	2022	2021	2020	2019
Revenue						
R&D Expense						
Operating Income						
Operating Margin %						
SGA Expense						
Net Income						
Operating Cash Flow						
Capital Expenditure						
EBITDA						
Return on Assets %						
Return on Equity %						
Debt to Equity						

CONTACT INFORMATION:

Phone: 216-367-6000   Fax: 216-367-6020
Toll-Free:
Address: 1901 E. 13th St., Ste. 400, Cleveland, OH 44114 United States

STOCK TICKER/OTHER:

Stock Ticker: Private   Exchange:
Employees: 600   Fiscal Year Ends:
Parent Company:

SALARIES/BONUSES:

Top Exec. Salary: $ Bonus: $
Second Exec. Salary: $ Bonus: $

OTHER THOUGHTS:

Estimated Female Officers or Directors:
Hot Spot for Advancement for Women/Minorities:

Mitsubishi Corporation

www.mitsubishicorp.com

NAIC Code: 336000

TYPES OF BUSINESS:

Transportation Equipment Manufacturing, Automobiles (Cars),
Components, Trucks, Aircraft
Automobile Manufacturing
Metals Mining & Production
Chemicals
Food Products & Commodities
Petroleum Exploration & Production
IT Services & Equipment
Machinery Manufacturing

BRANDS/DIVISIONS/AFFILIATES:

GROWTH PLANS/SPECIAL FEATURES:

Mitsubishi Corp is a conglomerate that operates businesses in
various industries. Its operating segments include Natural Gas,
Industrial materials, Petroleum & chemicals, Mineral resource,
Industrial Infrastructure, Automotive, Food & Consumer
Industry, Power Solution, and Urban Development.

CONTACTS: Note: Officers with more than one job title may be intentionally listed here more than once.

Katsuya Nakanishi, CEO
Yuzo Nouchi, CFO
Takehiko Kakiuchi, Chairman of the Board
Kotaro Tsukamoto, Chief Compliance Officer
Yoshiyuki Nojima, Director
Yutaka Kashiwagi, Director

FINANCIAL DATA: Note: Data for latest year may not have been available at press time.

In U.S. $	2024	2023	2022	2021	2020	2019
Revenue	135,848,383,103	149,763,767,464	119,861,347,659	89,450,997,449	102,608,544,665	111,800,634,151
R&D Expense						
Operating Income	4,633,623,000	6,612,358,000	4,989,760,000	1,439,871,000	2,484,720,000	4,057,824,000
Operating Margin %	.03%	.04%	.04%	.02%	.02%	.04%
SGA Expense	11,748,700,000	11,160,220,000	9,941,955,000	9,703,603,000	9,936,351,000	9,742,586,000
Net Income	6,692,822,000	8,196,987,000	6,508,810,000	1,197,931,000	3,716,697,000	4,101,201,000
Operating Cash Flow	9,354,208,000	13,400,010,000	7,330,214,000	7,064,357,000	5,899,250,000	4,531,249,000
Capital Expenditure	3,613,871,000	3,158,525,000	2,734,192,000	2,700,507,000	2,263,357,000	2,190,461,000
EBITDA	14,947,690,000	16,518,340,000	13,085,540,000	5,718,252,000	8,104,103,000	8,132,950,000
Return on Assets %	.04%	.05%	.05%	.01%	.03%	.04%
Return on Equity %	.11%	.16%	.15%	.03%	.10%	.11%
Debt to Equity	.42%	.61%	.78%	1.01%	1.068	0.667

CONTACT INFORMATION:

Phone: 81 332102121   Fax:
Toll-Free:
Address: 3-1 Marunouchi 2-chome, Chiyoda-ku, Tokyo, 100-8086
Japan

STOCK TICKER/OTHER:

Stock Ticker: MTSUY   Exchange: PINX
Employees: 104,168   Fiscal Year Ends: 03/31
Parent Company:

SALARIES/BONUSES:

Top Exec. Salary: $ Bonus: $
Second Exec. Salary: $ Bonus: $

OTHER THOUGHTS:

Estimated Female Officers or Directors: 1
Hot Spot for Advancement for Women/Minorities:

Mitsubishi Electric Corporation

www.mitsubishielectric.com/en/index.html

NAIC Code: 335311

TYPES OF BUSINESS:

Electrical and Electronic Equipment Manufacturer
Power Plant Manufacturing, Nuclear & Fossil
Wind & Solar Generation Systems
Consumer Electronics
Telecommunications & Computer Equipment
Industrial Automation Systems
Chips & Memory Devices
Semiconductors

BRANDS/DIVISIONS/AFFILIATES:

Mitsubishi Corporation

GROWTH PLANS/SPECIAL FEATURES:

Mitsubishi Electric is a diversified industrials company that develops, manufactures and sells electrical equipment worldwide. The company's core segments include: industrial automation systems, energy and electric systems, electric devices, information and communication systems, and home appliances (which includes commercial air conditioning). Mitsubishi Electric was founded in 1921 and is headquartered in Tokyo.

CONTACTS: Note: Officers with more than one job title may be intentionally listed here more than once.

Kei Uruma, CEO
Kuniaki Masuda, CFO
Hiroyuki Yanagi, Chairman of the Board
Satoshi Takeda, Chief Strategy Officer

FINANCIAL DATA: Note: Data for latest year may not have been available at press time.

In U.S. $	2024	2023	2022	2021	2020	2019
Revenue	36,503,152,797	34,738,226,947	31,079,963,994	29,099,091,466	30,981,039,391	31,379,624,224
R&D Expense						
Operating Income	2,280,790,000	1,821,383,000	1,749,868,000	1,598,132,000	1,802,701,000	2,016,641,000
Operating Margin %	.06%	.05%	.06%	.05%	.06%	.06%
SGA Expense	8,589,288,000	7,969,876,000	7,037,448,000	6,620,398,000	7,061,060,000	7,243,085,000
Net Income	1,978,263,000	1,485,060,000	1,412,677,000	1,340,822,000	1,540,086,000	1,573,507,000
Operating Cash Flow	2,884,470,000	1,157,394,000	1,960,365,000	3,763,670,000	2,748,084,000	1,664,933,000
Capital Expenditure	1,451,014,000	1,218,800,000	1,083,463,000	1,307,685,000	1,507,894,000	1,513,656,000
EBITDA	4,015,336,000	3,542,891,000	3,396,334,000	3,297,015,000	3,469,036,000	3,447,563,000
Return on Assets %	.05%	.04%	.04%	.04%	.05%	.05%
Return on Equity %	.08%	.07%	.07%	.07%	.09%	.10%
Debt to Equity	.06%	.07%	.05%	.08%	0.10	0.081

CONTACT INFORMATION:

Phone: 81 332182111   Fax: 81 332182431
Toll-Free:
Address: Tokyo Bldg. 2-7-3 Marunouchi, Chiyoda-ku, Tokyo, 100-8310 Japan

STOCK TICKER/OTHER:

Stock Ticker: MIELY   Exchange: PINX
Employees: 149,314   Fiscal Year Ends: 03/31
Parent Company: Mitsubishi Corporation

SALARIES/BONUSES:

Top Exec. Salary: $ Bonus: $
Second Exec. Salary: $ Bonus: $

OTHER THOUGHTS:

Estimated Female Officers or Directors:
Hot Spot for Advancement for Women/Minorities:

Mitsubishi Motors Corp

NAIC Code: 336111

www.mitsubishi-motors.co.jp

TYPES OF BUSINESS:

Automobile Manufacturing
Automobile Parts
Agricultural Machinery & Industrial Engines
Automotive Sales
Financial Services
Plug-In Hybrid Electric Vehicles
Electric Vehicles

BRANDS/DIVISIONS/AFFILIATES:

Nissan Motor Co Ltd
Mitsubishi Corporation
Renault-Nissan
Eclipse Cross
Xpander
Outlander
i-MiEV
eK

GROWTH PLANS/SPECIAL FEATURES:

Mitsubishi Motors is a Japanese automobile manufacturer. The company principally produces small passenger vehicles, electric and hybrid vehicles, and sport utility vehicles, or SUVs. Mitsubishi Motors is organized into two business segments: automobile business and automobile financing business. The company derives the vast majority of company revenue from the automotive business. Geographically, the company is separated into five regions: Japan, North America, Europe, Asia (excluding Japan), and other. With more than half of its products manufactures in Japan where it also generates the majority of its consolidated revenue, followed by Asia, and North America.

CONTACTS: Note: Officers with more than one job title may be intentionally listed here more than once.

Takao Kato, CEO
Tomofumi Hiraku, Chairman of the Board

FINANCIAL DATA: Note: Data for latest year may not have been available at press time.

In U.S. $	2024	2023	2022	2021	2020	2019
Revenue	19,366,767,658	17,065,684,149	14,155,158,590	10,104,666,031	15,761,428,530	17,457,609,825
R&D Expense	400,180,500	423,667,100	399,243,300	388,711,500	512,538,200	457,650,700
Operating Income	1,325,840,000	1,322,535,000	606,338,600	-661,753,700	88,801,730	776,305,200
Operating Margin %	.07%	.08%	.04%	-.07%	.01%	.04%
SGA Expense	1,087,212,000	862,829,800	617,856,200	444,341,900	690,537,400	880,804,000
Net Income	1,074,070,000	1,171,411,000	514,003,100	-2,168,266,000	-178,971,100	922,459,100
Operating Cash Flow	977,547,900	1,205,054,000	820,008,400	-288,371,300	130,422,100	1,013,975,000
Capital Expenditure	880,623,500	552,915,900	605,324,900	637,739,500	898,215,800	961,975,800
EBITDA	1,767,724,000	1,609,414,000	1,065,010,000	-1,575,930,000	572,611,800	1,279,089,000
Return on Assets %	.07%	.08%	.04%	-.16%	-.01%	.07%
Return on Equity %	.17%	.24%	.13%	-.49%	-.03%	.16%
Debt to Equity	.15%	.34%	.20%	.73%	0.155	0.097

CONTACT INFORMATION:

Phone: 81 334561111   Fax:
Toll-Free:
Address: 1-21, Shibaura 3 chome, Minato-ku, Tokyo, 108-8410 Japan

STOCK TICKER/OTHER:

Stock Ticker: MMTOY
Employees: 39,996
Parent Company: Nissan Motor Co Ltd

Exchange: PINX
Fiscal Year Ends: 03/31

SALARIES/BONUSES:

Top Exec. Salary: $ Bonus: $
Second Exec. Salary: $ Bonus: $

OTHER THOUGHTS:

Estimated Female Officers or Directors:
Hot Spot for Advancement for Women/Minorities:

Mitsui Chemicals Inc

jp.mitsuichemicals.com/en

NAIC Code: 325110

TYPES OF BUSINESS:

Petrochemical Producer
Agrochemicals
Industrial Products
Pharmaceuticals & Medical
Packaging
Dyes & Pigments
Phenols

GROWTH PLANS/SPECIAL FEATURES:

Mitsui Chemicals Inc manufactures and sells a variety of chemicals, plastics, and chemical-based products. The firm organizes itself into five segments based on the product type. The basic materials segment, which generates more revenue than any other segment, sells petrochemicals, industrial chemicals, phenols, and polyesters. The mobility segment sells elastomers, performance compounds, and performance polymers to the automotive industry. The other three segments are healthcare, food and packaging, and others. The majority of revenue comes from Asia.

BRANDS/DIVISIONS/AFFILIATES:

Chiba Chemicals Manufacturing LLP
Chiba Phenol Co Ltd
DM NovaFoam Ltd
Mitsui Chemicals Europe GmbH
Mitsui Chemicals Asia Pacific Ltd
Mitsui Chemicals America Inc
COTEC GmbH

CONTACTS: Note: Officers with more than one job title may be intentionally listed here more than once.

Osamu Hashimoto, CEO
Hajime Nakajima, CFO
Tsutomu Tannowa, Chairman of the Board
Tadashi Yoshino, Chief Technology Officer
Yoshinori Andou, Director

FINANCIAL DATA: Note: Data for latest year may not have been available at press time.

In U.S. $	2024	2023	2022	2021	2020	2019
Revenue	12,147,619,406	13,048,785,844	11,196,112,547	8,412,420,353	9,369,078,550	10,295,119,913
R&D Expense						
Operating Income	429,200,300	744,966,700	843,453,200	500,451,300	416,946,700	648,618,400
Operating Margin %	.04%	.06%	.08%	.06%	.04%	.06%
SGA Expense	1,962,351,000	1,975,764,000	1,661,733,000	1,471,674,000	1,573,119,000	
Net Income	347,118,900	575,784,500	763,607,400	401,784,200	235,837,300	528,429,600
Operating Cash Flow	1,120,099,000	702,867,300	642,766,000	1,210,240,000	987,447,900	760,150,000
Capital Expenditure	1,069,085,000	957,102,300	806,831,400	531,664,900	692,661,800	387,080,000
EBITDA	1,272,167,000	1,574,257,000	1,650,285,000	1,103,805,000	1,013,496,000	1,113,128,000
Return on Assets %	.02%	.04%	.06%	.04%	.02%	.05%
Return on Equity %	.06%	.11%	.17%	.10%	.06%	.14%
Debt to Equity	.50%	.47%	.45%	.48%	0.592	0.585

CONTACT INFORMATION:

Phone: 81-3-6253-2100   Fax: 81-3-6253-4245
Toll-Free:
Address: 1-5-2, Higashi-Shimbashi, Tokyo, 105-7122 Japan

STOCK TICKER/OTHER:

Stock Ticker: MITUY   Exchange: PINX
Employees: 17,979   Fiscal Year Ends: 03/31
Parent Company:

SALARIES/BONUSES:

Top Exec. Salary: $ Bonus: $
Second Exec. Salary: $ Bonus: $

OTHER THOUGHTS:

Estimated Female Officers or Directors:
Hot Spot for Advancement for Women/Minorities:

Molex LLC

NAIC Code: 334417

TYPES OF BUSINESS:

Electronic Connector Manufacturing
Transportation Products
Commercial Products
Micro Products
Automation & Electrical Products
Integrated Products
Global Sales & Marketing Organization
Product Manufacturing

BRANDS/DIVISIONS/AFFILIATES:

Koch Industries Inc

GROWTH PLANS/SPECIAL FEATURES:

Molex, LLC, a subsidiary of Koch Industries, Inc., manufactures and supplies electronic components. The firm designs, manufactures and sells thousands of products, with some categories including advanced packaging, antennas, automotive connectivity, building infrastructure, connectors, electrical products, industrial solutions, printed electronics, optical solutions, sensors and more. Molex also provides manufacturing services to integrate specific components into a customer's product. The company's products are utilized across a wide range of industries, including aerospace, automotive, charging infrastructure, defense, diagnostics, drug delivery solutions, home energy storage, industrial automation, MedTech, mobile devices, networking, server and storage, telecommunications, wireless infrastructure and more. Molex has over 100,000 products in its portfolio and has a presence in 38 countries.

CONTACTS: *Note: Officers with more than one job title may be intentionally listed here more than once.*

Joseph Nelligan, CEO
Travis George, CFO
Murat Dogansoysal, Sr. VP-Mktg. & Sales
Bryn Wiley, Sr. VP-Human Resources
Robert J. Zeitler, General Counsel
Tim Ruff, Sr. VP-Bus. Dev. & Corp. Strategy
David D. Johnson, Treas.
John H. Krehbiel, Jr., Co-Chmn.
Junichi Kaji, Pres., Global Micro Prod. Div.
J. Michael Nauman, Pres., Global Integrated Prod. Div.
Joseph Nelligan, Pres., Commercial Prod. Division

FINANCIAL DATA: *Note: Data for latest year may not have been available at press time.*

In U.S. $	2024	2023	2022	2021	2020	2019
Revenue	5,156,840,000	4,888,000,000	4,700,000,000	4,674,600,000	4,452,000,000	4,200,000,000
R&D Expense						
Operating Income						
Operating Margin %						
SGA Expense						
Net Income						
Operating Cash Flow						
Capital Expenditure						
EBITDA						
Return on Assets %						
Return on Equity %						
Debt to Equity						

CONTACT INFORMATION:

Phone: 630 969-4550   Fax: 630 969-1352
Toll-Free: 800-786-6539
Address: 2222 Wellington Ct., Lisle, IL 60532 United States

STOCK TICKER/OTHER:

Stock Ticker: Subsidiary   Exchange:
Employees: 45,000   Fiscal Year Ends: 06/30
Parent Company: Koch Industries Inc

SALARIES/BONUSES:

Top Exec. Salary: $ Bonus: $
Second Exec. Salary: $ Bonus: $

OTHER THOUGHTS:

Estimated Female Officers or Directors: 1
Hot Spot for Advancement for Women/Minorities:

Mott MacDonald Limited

www.mottmac.com

NAIC Code: 541330

TYPES OF BUSINESS:

Engineering & Development Consultancy
Civil Engineering
Global Development
Consultancy Services
Environmental Solutions
Highway and Transportation Engineering
Planning and Development
Water/Wastewater Solutions

BRANDS/DIVISIONS/AFFILIATES:

CONTACTS: *Note: Officers with more than one job title may be intentionally listed here more than once.*

James Harris, Chmn.

GROWTH PLANS/SPECIAL FEATURES:

Mott MacDonald Limited is an employee-owned global development, engineering and management consultancy for public and private clients worldwide. Through its civil engineering services, the firm strives to save customers money and time, reduce risks, increase efficiency, maximize sustainable outcomes and advance best practice through innovative thinking and cross-sector mobilization strategies. Mott MacDonald consists of designers, engineers, project and program managers, consultants, environmentalists, planners, economists, infrastructure finance advisors, public/private partnership experts, technology experts, safety advisors and health and education specialists. The company has offices in 50 countries. Its wide range of business sectors include advisory, aviation, buildings, bridges, cities, coastal, digital delivery, education, energy, environment, health, highways, industry, international development, ports, rail/metros, transportation planning, tunnels, wastewater and water. Projects of Mott MacDonald include, but not limited to, London's Elizabeth Line underground network extension, the New Hospital Programme which is a pipeline of 40 hospital construction projects throughout England, the Bangladesh Delta Plan 2100 to attract private capital investment into climate resilient projects and the White Pine Energy Pumped Storage Project, a 1-gigawatt pumped-hydro storage project in Nevada in the U.S.

Mott MacDonald offers its employees professional training and development opportunities.

FINANCIAL DATA: *Note: Data for latest year may not have been available at press time.*

In U.S. $	2024	2023	2022	2021	2020	2019
Revenue	3,167,935,050	3,017,081,000	2,470,725,000	2,403,811,000	2,452,042,000	2,339,894,000
R&D Expense						
Operating Income						
Operating Margin %						
SGA Expense						
Net Income		483,751,000			61,590,252	28,806,671
Operating Cash Flow						
Capital Expenditure						
EBITDA						
Return on Assets %						
Return on Equity %						
Debt to Equity						

CONTACT INFORMATION:

Phone: 4420-8774-2000   Fax: 4420-8681-5706
Toll-Free:
Address: Mott MacDonald House, 8-10 Sydenham Rd., Croydon, CR0 2EE United Kingdom

STOCK TICKER/OTHER:

Stock Ticker: Private   Exchange:
Employees: 16,000   Fiscal Year Ends: 12/31
Parent Company:

SALARIES/BONUSES:

Top Exec. Salary: $ Bonus: $
Second Exec. Salary: $ Bonus: $

OTHER THOUGHTS:

Estimated Female Officers or Directors:
Hot Spot for Advancement for Women/Minorities:

NCR Voyix Corp

www.ncrvoyix.com

NAIC Code: 334118

TYPES OF BUSINESS:

Computer Manufacturing
Barcode Scanning Equipment
Automatic Teller Machines (ATMs)
Transaction Processing Equipment
Point-of-Sale & Store Automation
Data Warehousing
Printer Consumables

BRANDS/DIVISIONS/AFFILIATES:

GROWTH PLANS/SPECIAL FEATURES:

NCR Voyix Corp is a company providing services of digital commerce solutions for retail, restaurant, and digital banking. The company operates in three reportable segments: Retail, Restaurants, and Digital Banking. The Retail segment provides software solutions for retailers of all sizes, enhancing operational efficiency and customer experience. The Restaurants segment offers end-to-end technology solutions for food service establishments, improving operational efficiency, and customer satisfaction, and reducing costs. The Digital Banking segment serves financial institutions with cloud-based software solutions for a fully integrated digital banking experience across channels. Revenue sources include software sales and service support within each segment.

CONTACTS: Note: Officers with more than one job title may be intentionally listed here more than once.

David Wilkinson, CEO
Brian Webb-Walsh, CFO
James Kelly, Chairman of the Board
Anthony Radesca, Chief Accounting Officer
Kelli Sterrett, Executive VP
Eric Schoch, Executive VP
Beimnet Tadele, Executive VP
Brendan Tansill, Executive VP

FINANCIAL DATA: Note: Data for latest year may not have been available at press time.

In U.S. $	2024	2023	2022	2021	2020	2019
Revenue	2,825,999,872	3,177,999,872	3,174,000,128	3,692,000,000	6,207,000,064	6,914,999,808
R&D Expense	157,000,000	139,000,000	116,000,000	195,000,000	234,000,000	259,000,000
Operating Income	-37,000,000	-129,000,000	-50,000,000	26,000,000	221,000,000	611,000,000
Operating Margin %	- .01%	- .04%	- .02%	.01%	.04%	.09%
SGA Expense	459,000,000	659,000,000	618,000,000	704,000,000	1,069,000,000	1,051,000,000
Net Income	958,000,000	-423,000,000	60,000,000	97,000,000	-79,000,000	564,000,000
Operating Cash Flow	-132,000,000	694,000,000	427,000,000	1,009,000,000	641,000,000	634,000,000
Capital Expenditure	217,000,000	377,000,000	377,000,000	348,000,000	263,000,000	329,000,000
EBITDA	232,000,000	308,000,000	578,000,000	488,000,000	523,000,000	871,000,000
Return on Assets %	.20%	- .05%	.00%	.01%	- .01%	.05%
Return on Equity %	1.97%	- .58%	.03%	.07%	- .10%	.61%
Debt to Equity	1.44%	112.56%	3.94%	4.69%	3.43	3.303

CONTACT INFORMATION:

Phone: 937 821-9817   Fax:
Toll-Free: 800-225-5627
Address: 864 Spring St. NW, Atlanta, GA 30308 United States

STOCK TICKER/OTHER:

Stock Ticker: VYX   Exchange: NYS
Employees: 15,500   Fiscal Year Ends: 12/31
Parent Company:

SALARIES/BONUSES:

Top Exec. Salary: $316,058   Bonus: $4,000,000
Second Exec. Salary: Bonus: $131,760
$800,000

OTHER THOUGHTS:

Estimated Female Officers or Directors: 3
Hot Spot for Advancement for Women/Minorities: Y

NEC Corp

NAIC Code: 334111

www.nec.com

TYPES OF BUSINESS:

Computer Manufacturing
Computer Integration Products
Network Technology
Security Solutions
5G Solutions
Artificial Intelligence Solutions
Biometric Authentication Solutions
Smart City

BRANDS/DIVISIONS/AFFILIATES:

GROWTH PLANS/SPECIAL FEATURES:

NEC Corp is a leading Japanese technology firm. It manufactures PCs, computer platforms, semiconductors, and display panels; builds broadband and mobile communication networks; and provides systems-integration services. The firm's research and development has funded accomplishments such as breakthroughs in quantum computing and PDA speech-translation software.

CONTACTS: *Note: Officers with more than one job title may be intentionally listed here more than once.*

Takayuki Morita, CEO
Osamu Fujikawa, CFO
Daisuke Horikawa, Chief Human Resources Officer
Hiroshi Kodama, CIO
Takashi Niino, Chief Strategy Officer
Toshiyuki Mineno, Exec. VP
Kuniaki Okada, Exec. VP
Manabu Kinoshita, Exec. VP
Tomonori Nishimura, Exec. VP
Takashi Niino, Chmn.
Junji Yasui, Chief Supply Chain Officer

FINANCIAL DATA: *Note: Data for latest year may not have been available at press time.*

In U.S. $	2024	2023	2022	2021	2020	2019
Revenue	24,140,948,027	23,000,681,648	20,925,403,426	20,786,052,520	21,488,712,755	20,226,645,141
R&D Expense						
Operating Income	1,305,276,000	1,183,331,000	920,057,000	1,067,474,000	885,927,600	401,138,600
Operating Margin %	.05%	.05%	.04%	.05%	.04%	.02%
SGA Expense	5,651,299,000	5,510,275,000	5,296,931,000	5,088,788,000	5,225,563,000	5,158,435,000
Net Income	1,038,052,000	794,918,100	980,817,900	1,038,642,000	694,022,500	275,444,300
Operating Cash Flow	1,883,005,000	1,056,144,000	1,024,139,000	1,908,546,000	1,817,988,000	445,952,500
Capital Expenditure	692,634,000	539,530,700	493,654,600	492,474,300	619,251,600	421,362,100
EBITDA	2,713,017,000	2,558,963,000	2,335,060,000	2,333,081,000	2,122,973,000	1,282,748,000
Return on Assets %	.04%	.03%	.04%	.04%	.03%	.01%
Return on Equity %	.08%	.07%	.10%	.13%	.11%	.05%
Debt to Equity	.21%	.27%	.24%	.46%	0.52	0.452

CONTACT INFORMATION:

Phone: 81 334541111 Fax:
Toll-Free: 800-268-3997
Address: 7-1, Shiba 5-Chome, Minato-ku, Tokyo, 108-8001 Japan

STOCK TICKER/OTHER:

Stock Ticker: NECPY Exchange: PINX
Employees: 118,527 Fiscal Year Ends: 03/31
Parent Company:

SALARIES/BONUSES:

Top Exec. Salary: $ Bonus: $
Second Exec. Salary: $ Bonus: $

OTHER THOUGHTS:

Estimated Female Officers or Directors:
Hot Spot for Advancement for Women/Minorities:

NEC Laboratories America Inc

www.nec-labs.com

NAIC Code: 541710

TYPES OF BUSINESS:

Communications Technology
Electronics
Broadband & Mobile Networking
Internet of Things
Software
Storage Technologies
Security Systems
Quantum Computing

BRANDS/DIVISIONS/AFFILIATES:

NEC Corporation

CONTACTS: Note: Officers with more than one job title may be intentionally listed here more than once.

Christopher White, Pres.
Kaoru Yano, Chmn.-NEC Corp.

GROWTH PLANS/SPECIAL FEATURES:

NEC Laboratories America, Inc. is the U.S.-based facility in NEC Corporation's global network of research laboratories. NEC Laboratories is engaged in five areas of research. The data science and system security department focuses on building novel big data solutions and service platforms to support complex computer systems management, and to develop new information technology that supports innovative applications, from big data analytics to the Internet of Things (IoT). The integrated systems department focuses on accelerating enterprise workloads on computing clusters that include various types of heterogeneity in computing, interconnect, networking and storage units. The machine learning department develops solutions such as deep learning, support vector machines and semantic analysis in order to interpret multi-modal data and complex situations. The media analytics department aims to solve challenges in computer vision, including image-based recognition, object detection, tracking, segmentation and 3D reconstruction. Last, the optical networking and sensing department conducts research into the next-generation of optical networks and sensing systems that will power ICT-based (information and communication technologies) social solutions for the future. These solutions include optics, photonics, multi-dimensional optical processing, optical transmission systems and software. Other current areas of research include big data analytics, deep learning and agile digital signal processing (DSP)-based optical transmission systems.

NEC Labs offers employees medical, dental, vision, life, AD&D and disability insurance; a 401(k); and various employee-assistance programs.

FINANCIAL DATA: Note: Data for latest year may not have been available at press time.

In U.S. $	2024	2023	2022	2021	2020	2019
Revenue						
R&D Expense						
Operating Income						
Operating Margin %						
SGA Expense						
Net Income						
Operating Cash Flow						
Capital Expenditure						
EBITDA						
Return on Assets %						
Return on Equity %						
Debt to Equity						

CONTACT INFORMATION:

Phone: 609-520-1555   Fax: 609-951-2481
Toll-Free:
Address: 4 Independence Way, Ste. 200, Princeton, NJ 08540 United States

STOCK TICKER/OTHER:

Stock Ticker: Subsidiary   Exchange:
Employees: 2,800   Fiscal Year Ends: 03/31
Parent Company: NEC Corporation

SALARIES/BONUSES:

Top Exec. Salary: $ Bonus: $
Second Exec. Salary: $ Bonus: $

OTHER THOUGHTS:

Estimated Female Officers or Directors:
Hot Spot for Advancement for Women/Minorities:

NetApp Inc

www.netapp.com

NAIC Code: 334112

TYPES OF BUSINESS:

Data Management Solutions
Storage Solutions
Data Protection Software Products
Data Protection Platform Products
Storage Security Products
Data Retention & Archive Software Products
Storage Management & Application Software
Management Tools

BRANDS/DIVISIONS/AFFILIATES:

NetApp Keystone

GROWTH PLANS/SPECIAL FEATURES:

NetApp Inc is a provider of enterprise data management and storage solutions. The company's segments include Hybrid Cloud and Public Cloud. It generates maximum revenue from the Hybrid Cloud segment. The Hybrid Cloud segment offers a portfolio of storage management and infrastructure solutions that help customers recast their traditional data centers with the power of cloud. This portfolio is designed to operate with public clouds to unlock the potential of hybrid, multi-cloud operations. Hybrid Cloud is composed of software, hardware, and related support, as well as professional and other services.

NetApp offers employees healthcare, insurance, financial, saving and income protection programs.

CONTACTS: *Note: Officers with more than one job title may be intentionally listed here more than once.*

George Kurian, CEO
Michael Berry, CFO
T. Nevens, Chairman of the Board
Daniel De Lorenzo, Chief Accounting Officer
Elizabeth OCallahan, Chief Legal Officer
Harvinder Bhela, Executive VP
Cesar Cernuda, President

FINANCIAL DATA: *Note: Data for latest year may not have been available at press time.*

In U.S. $	2024	2023	2022	2021	2020	2019
Revenue	6,268,000,256	6,361,999,872	6,318,000,128	5,744,000,000	5,411,999,744	6,145,999,872
R&D Expense	1,029,000,000	956,000,000	881,000,000	881,000,000	847,000,000	827,000,000
Operating Income	1,268,000,000	1,159,000,000	1,203,000,000	933,000,000	928,000,000	1,183,000,000
Operating Margin %	.20%	.18%	.19%	.16%	.17%	.19%
SGA Expense	2,136,000,000	2,094,000,000	2,136,000,000	2,001,000,000	1,848,000,000	1,935,000,000
Net Income	986,000,000	1,274,000,000	937,000,000	730,000,000	819,000,000	1,169,000,000
Operating Cash Flow	1,685,000,000	1,107,000,000	1,211,000,000	1,333,000,000	1,060,000,000	1,341,000,000
Capital Expenditure	155,000,000	239,000,000	226,000,000	162,000,000	124,000,000	173,000,000
EBITDA	1,582,000,000	1,381,000,000	1,362,000,000	1,243,000,000	1,192,000,000	1,523,000,000
Return on Assets %	.10%	.13%	.10%	.09%	.10%	.12%
Return on Equity %	.86%	1.28%	1.23%	1.57%	1.23%	.69%
Debt to Equity	1.93%	2.28%	3.15%	3.95%	5.12	1.05

CONTACT INFORMATION:

Phone: 408 822-6000   Fax: 408 822-4501
Toll-Free: 877-263-8277
Address: 1395 Crossman Ave., Sunnyvale, CA 94089 United States

STOCK TICKER/OTHER:

Stock Ticker: NTAP   Exchange: NAS
Employees: 11,800   Fiscal Year Ends: 04/30
Parent Company:

SALARIES/BONUSES:

Top Exec. Salary: $1,000,000   Bonus: $
Second Exec. Salary: Bonus: $
$717,938

OTHER THOUGHTS:

Estimated Female Officers or Directors: 4
Hot Spot for Advancement for Women/Minorities: Y

Nidec Corp

NAIC Code: 334112

TYPES OF BUSINESS:

Motor Manufacturing
Brushless DC Motors
Brushless DC Fans
Camera Shutters
Hard Drive Pivot Assemblies
Card Readers

BRANDS/DIVISIONS/AFFILIATES:

GROWTH PLANS/SPECIAL FEATURES:

Nidec is a global leader of brushless DC motors, which have advantages in power efficiency, silence, and durability. Nidec possesses the number-one market share in a wide variety of products, such as hard disk drive motors, optical disk drive motors, vibration motors on handsets, brushless motors for inverter air conditioners, and brushless motors for electric power steering on automobiles. It continues to benefit from the growing demand for power-efficient motors, driven by strengthening environmental regulations.

CONTACTS: Note: Officers with more than one job title may be intentionally listed here more than once.

Mitsuya Kishida, CEO
Shigenobu Nagamori, Chairman of the Board
Hiroshi Kobe, Director

FINANCIAL DATA: Note: Data for latest year may not have been available at press time.

In U.S. $	2024	2023	2022	2021	2020	2019
Revenue	16,302,430,867	15,570,842,702	13,316,953,850	11,233,435,855	10,655,374,102	10,243,238,003
R&D Expense	562,725,600	564,683,500	541,620,400	467,092,500	545,890,000	436,149,700
Operating Income	1,132,366,000	694,446,000	1,182,824,000	1,110,594,000	753,665,700	897,125,800
Operating Margin %	.07%	.04%	.09%	.10%	.07%	.09%
SGA Expense	1,759,588,000	1,609,213,000	1,075,673,000	966,863,400	1,009,157,000	997,618,800
Net Income	870,501,200	312,163,300	942,509,100	846,605,100	405,852,500	763,399,100
Operating Cash Flow	2,231,929,000	996,146,900	659,497,300	1,521,494,000	1,166,683,000	1,181,845,000
Capital Expenditure	891,696,800	1,067,329,000	799,923,600	693,737,900	996,514,900	912,586,800
EBITDA	2,474,146,000	1,757,901,000	1,948,188,000	1,213,087,000	886,163,600	1,044,508,000
Return on Assets %	.04%	.02%	.06%	.06%	.03%	.06%
Return on Equity %	.08%	.03%	.11%	.12%	.06%	.11%
Debt to Equity	.25%	.36%	.25%	.39%	0.392	0.261

CONTACT INFORMATION:

Phone: 81 759221111   Fax: 81 759356101
Toll-Free:
Address: 338 Kuzetonoshiro-cho, Minami-ku, Kyoto, 601-8205 Japan

STOCK TICKER/OTHER:

Stock Ticker: NJDCY   Exchange: PINX
Employees: 101,100   Fiscal Year Ends: 03/31
Parent Company:

SALARIES/BONUSES:

Top Exec. Salary: $ Bonus: $
Second Exec. Salary: $ Bonus: $

OTHER THOUGHTS:

Estimated Female Officers or Directors:
Hot Spot for Advancement for Women/Minorities:

Sales, profits and employees may be estimates. Financial information, benefits and other data can change quickly and may vary from those stated here.

Nikon Corp
NAIC Code: 333316

TYPES OF BUSINESS:
Digital Cameras and Equipment
Lenses
Semiconductor Testing Equipment
Image Processing Software
Microscopes and Binoculars
Measurement Systems
Surveying Instruments

BRANDS/DIVISIONS/AFFILIATES:

GROWTH PLANS/SPECIAL FEATURES:
Nikon manufactures photography and videography equipment. The company organizes itself into various segments based on product type: imaging products, precision equipment, instruments, medical, and other business. The imaging products and precision equipment businesses collectively constitute the vast majority of company revenue. The imaging products business, which contributes more than half of consolidated revenue, principally produces digital cameras and interchangeable lenses. The precision equipment business produces semiconductor lithography systems for the production of semiconductors, and FPD lithography systems for the production of LCD and OLED panels.

Nikon offers its U.S. employees benefits including health coverage, life and disability insurance and an employee assistance program.

CONTACTS: Note: Officers with more than one job title may be intentionally listed here more than once.
Toshikazu Umatate, Chairman of the Board
Yasuhiro Ohmura, Director
Muneaki Tokunari, Director

FINANCIAL DATA: Note: Data for latest year may not have been available at press time.

In U.S. $	2024	2023	2022	2021	2020	2019
Revenue	4,979,484,953	4,360,629,268	3,746,264,964	3,132,622,949	4,103,110,179	4,919,883,317
R&D Expense						
Operating Income	276,138,600	381,199,700	346,660,700	-390,447,100	46,868,930	573,826,800
Operating Margin %	.06%	.09%	.09%	-.12%	.01%	.12%
SGA Expense	1,860,983,000	1,605,304,000	1,315,364,000	1,258,949,000	1,428,062,000	1,656,214,000
Net Income	226,117,700	312,024,400	296,299,600	-239,496,000	53,408,780	461,767,600
Operating Cash Flow	213,600,400	104,138	217,654,800	34,476,540	113,989,200	478,346,300
Capital Expenditure	383,331,000	229,262,700	165,405,500	160,365,200	176,555,100	197,118,900
EBITDA	598,229,700	638,954,500	594,251,600	-104,672,300	332,386,800	829,998,700
Return on Assets %	.03%	.04%	.04%	-.03%	.01%	.06%
Return on Equity %	.05%	.07%	.08%	-.06%	.01%	.11%
Debt to Equity	.11%	.18%	.16%	.19%	0.19	0.182

CONTACT INFORMATION:
Phone: 81-3-6433-3600 Fax:
Toll-Free:
Address: Shinagawa Intercity Tower C, 2-15-3, Konan, Minato, Tokyo, 108-6290 Japan

STOCK TICKER/OTHER:
Stock Ticker: NINOY
Employees: 20,917
Parent Company:

Exchange: PINX
Fiscal Year Ends: 03/31

SALARIES/BONUSES:
Top Exec. Salary: $ Bonus: $
Second Exec. Salary: $ Bonus: $

OTHER THOUGHTS:
Estimated Female Officers or Directors:
Hot Spot for Advancement for Women/Minorities:

Nintendo Co Ltd

NAIC Code: 334111

TYPES OF BUSINESS:

Video Game Hardware & Software
Electronic Games
Online Games

BRANDS/DIVISIONS/AFFILIATES:

Nintendo DS
Nintendo Switch
Animal Crossing
Mario Brothers
Donkey Kong
Pokemon
Legend of Zelda (The)
Super Nintendo World

GROWTH PLANS/SPECIAL FEATURES:

Nintendo started its video game console business in 1983 by launching the NES, and started its portable console business in 1989 by launching the Game Boy. Since then, the firm has focused on expanding the gaming population by delivering unique entertainment experiences on its original console systems; the Wii and Nintendo DS are its most popular hardware. However, Nintendo not only makes game consoles, but also owns world-renowned IPs such as Super Mario, Pokemon, and Zelda, which have been a source of cash flow for 40 years.

CONTACTS: Note: Officers with more than one job title may be intentionally listed here more than once.

Shinya Takahashi, Director
Satoru Shibata, Director
Ko Shiota, Director
Yusuke Beppu, Director
Shuntaro Furukawa, Director

FINANCIAL DATA: Note: Data for latest year may not have been available at press time.

In U.S. $	2024	2023	2022	2021	2020	2019
Revenue	11,606,950,119	11,119,668,741	11,769,952,952	12,211,260,852	9,084,414,617	8,334,907,333
R&D Expense						
Operating Income	3,672,188,000	3,501,631,000	4,115,253,000	4,447,612,000	2,446,334,000	1,733,553,000
Operating Margin %	.32%	.31%	.35%	.36%	.27%	.21%
SGA Expense						
Net Income	3,406,012,000	3,004,499,000	3,316,377,000	3,335,018,000	1,795,619,000	1,346,911,000
Operating Cash Flow	3,208,116,000	2,241,343,000	2,010,976,000	4,249,556,000	2,414,281,000	1,183,900,000
Capital Expenditure	111,934,200	154,054,400	52,672,870	48,673,980	68,335,190	74,541,800
EBITDA	4,851,041,000	4,248,258,000	4,756,991,000	4,806,165,000	2,575,333,000	1,799,951,000
Return on Assets %	.16%	.16%	.19%	.22%	.14%	.12%
Return on Equity %	.20%	.20%	.24%	.28%	.18%	.14%
Debt to Equity						

CONTACT INFORMATION:

Phone: 81 756629614   Fax: 81 756629540
Toll-Free: 1-800-255-3700
Address: 11-1 Hokotate-cho, Kyoto, 601-8501 Japan

STOCK TICKER/OTHER:

Stock Ticker: NTDOF   Exchange: PINX
Employees: 5,944   Fiscal Year Ends: 03/31
Parent Company:

SALARIES/BONUSES:

Top Exec. Salary: $ Bonus: $
Second Exec. Salary: $ Bonus: $

OTHER THOUGHTS:

Estimated Female Officers or Directors:
Hot Spot for Advancement for Women/Minorities:

Nissan Motor Co Ltd

NAIC Code: 336111

www.nissan-global.com

TYPES OF BUSINESS:

Automobile Manufacturing
Research & Development
Industrial Machinery
Marine Equipment
Logistics Services
Alternative Fuels Research
Financial Services

BRANDS/DIVISIONS/AFFILIATES:

Nissan
Infiniti
Datsun
Nissan Motorsport International Limited
Renault SA
Versa
Q50
QX55

GROWTH PLANS/SPECIAL FEATURES:

While Nissan sold 3.3 million vehicles last fiscal year, total calendar 2024 Renault-Nissan-Mitsubishi alliance sales volume of 6.5 million vehicles makes the group the fourth-largest vehicle seller in the world, behind Toyota at 10.8 million, Volkswagen at 9.0 million, and Hyundai/Kia with 7.2 million vehicles sold. Nissan's financial services subsidiary provides consumers with auto loans and leases but also finances Nissan's sales to its dealerships (known as floor-plan financing). Under a new alliance agreement, Nissan and Renault will have cross-shareholding capped at 15% voting rights for each company. Renault holds the remaining stake in Nissan through a French trust where the voting rights of such shares are neutralized for most decisions but retain the economic benefit.

CONTACTS: *Note: Officers with more than one job title may be intentionally listed here more than once.*

Makoto Uchida, CEO
Yasushi Kimura, Chairman of the Board
Hideyuki Sakamoto, Director
Jean-Dominique Senard, Director

FINANCIAL DATA: *Note: Data for latest year may not have been available at press time.*

In U.S. $	2024	2023	2022	2021	2020	2019
Revenue	88,070,792,136	73,567,727,645	58,487,818,938	54,586,033,592	68,584,188,777	80,354,396,521
R&D Expense						
Operating Income	3,948,334,000	2,618,085,000	1,716,933,000	-1,045,897,000	-280,956,700	2,209,275,000
Operating Margin %	.04%	.04%	.03%	-.02%	.00%	.03%
SGA Expense	3,812,233,000	3,279,825,000	2,707,415,000	3,122,112,000	3,961,670,000	4,676,749,000
Net Income	2,962,018,000	1,540,544,000	1,496,341,000	-3,115,086,000	-4,659,928,000	2,215,621,000
Operating Cash Flow	6,671,057,000	8,477,167,000	5,881,610,000	9,183,484,000	8,232,810,000	10,072,810,000
Capital Expenditure	8,744,135,000	5,628,832,000	5,614,302,000	5,692,363,000	7,739,864,000	9,016,260,000
EBITDA	9,138,107,000	7,761,921,000	7,533,629,000	2,448,799,000	1,808,220,000	9,419,419,000
Return on Assets %	.02%	.01%	.01%	-.03%	-.04%	.02%
Return on Equity %	.08%	.05%	.05%	-.11%	-.14%	.06%
Debt to Equity	.90%	.81%	.90%	1.09%	0.791	0.801

CONTACT INFORMATION:

Phone: 81 455235523   Fax:
Toll-Free:
Address: 1-1, Takashima 1-chome, Nishi-ku, Yokohama-shi, Kanagawa, 220-8686 Japan

STOCK TICKER/OTHER:

Stock Ticker: NSANF
Employees: 158,133
Parent Company:

Exchange: PINX
Fiscal Year Ends: 03/31

SALARIES/BONUSES:

Top Exec. Salary: $ Bonus: $
Second Exec. Salary: $ Bonus: $

OTHER THOUGHTS:

Estimated Female Officers or Directors:
Hot Spot for Advancement for Women/Minorities:

Nitto Denko Corp

www.nitto.com

NAIC Code: 322220

TYPES OF BUSINESS:

Industrial Adhesive Tapes
Semiconductor Materials
Drug Delivery Systems
Water Treatment Membranes
Semiconductor Machinery

BRANDS/DIVISIONS/AFFILIATES:

GROWTH PLANS/SPECIAL FEATURES:

Nitto Denko Corp manufactures and sells a variety of industrial and electronics products. The company sells tape products, which include masking tape for painting and printed-circuit boards, double sided tapes, electrical tape, and sealant materials used in the construction industry. Nitto Denko also sells film products, which include surface protective film, fluoroplastic films used to seal pipes and air filters, and porous film that allows air to pass through but seals water and other liquids. The firm also produces electronics, which include flexible printed circuit boards for smartphones and tablets, and medical products such as drug delivery patches and adhesive sheets.

CONTACTS: Note: Officers with more than one job title may be intentionally listed here more than once.

Hideo Takasaki, CEO
Yasuhiro Iseyama, CFO
Yosuke Miki, Chief Technology Officer
Yasuhito Ohwaki, Director
Tatsuya Akagi, Director

FINANCIAL DATA: Note: Data for latest year may not have been available at press time.

In U.S. $	2024	2023	2022	2021	2020	2019
Revenue	6,353,367,343	6,449,847,312	5,925,076,556	5,285,483,576	5,144,529,303	5,599,104,558
R&D Expense	301,895,300	278,915,600	258,754,500	244,800,100	234,414,000	222,091,100
Operating Income	965,926,100	1,021,758,000	918,224,100	651,277,400	484,129,400	644,105,800
Operating Margin %	.15%	.16%	.15%	.12%	.09%	.12%
SGA Expense	1,014,600,000	1,009,692,000	899,923,600	747,861,700	773,174,100	837,100,900
Net Income	712,850,600	757,935,300	674,340,500	487,607,600	327,381,300	462,093,900
Operating Cash Flow	1,079,707,000	1,261,469,000	1,003,117,000	807,477,100	858,379,600	684,316,900
Capital Expenditure	470,522,100	457,657,600	409,316,900	400,749,800	415,141,600	413,968,400
EBITDA	1,403,582,000	1,431,116,000	1,277,236,000	988,218,600	833,261,600	970,084,700
Return on Assets %	.09%	.10%	.09%	.07%	.05%	.07%
Return on Equity %	.11%	.13%	.13%	.10%	.07%	.10%
Debt to Equity						

CONTACT INFORMATION:

Phone: 816 76322101   Fax:
Toll-Free: 800-356-4880
Address: 33/Fl, Grand Front Osaka, 4-20, Ofuka-cho, Kita-ku, Osaka, 530-0001 Japan

STOCK TICKER/OTHER:

Stock Ticker: NDEKY   Exchange: PINX
Employees: 29,046   Fiscal Year Ends: 03/31
Parent Company:

SALARIES/BONUSES:

Top Exec. Salary: $ Bonus: $
Second Exec. Salary: $ Bonus: $

OTHER THOUGHTS:

Estimated Female Officers or Directors:
Hot Spot for Advancement for Women/Minorities:

Sales, profits and employees may be estimates. Financial information, benefits and other data can change quickly and may vary from those stated here.

Nokia Bell Labs

www.bell-labs.com

NAIC Code: 541710

TYPES OF BUSINESS:

Research & Development-Communications
Research and Science Development
Computer Science & Software
Consulting Services
Next-Generation Innovation
Lunar Network Research
Artificial Intelligence Research
Next-Generation Technology Research

BRANDS/DIVISIONS/AFFILIATES:

Nokia Corporation

GROWTH PLANS/SPECIAL FEATURES:

Nokia Bell Labs is a research and scientific development company headquartered in the U.S., with global locations throughout Europe as well as in China. Winner of Nobel prizes, U.S. Medals of Science and U.S. Medals of Technology & Innovation, the firm designs products and services at the forefront of communications technology and conducts fundamental research in fields such as physical technologies, computer science and software, mathematical/algorithmic sciences, optical and wireless networking, security solutions and government research. Nokia Bell Labs offers consulting services in relation to communications service providers, enterprises, industry entities and webscalers. Bell Labs Institute offers blogs, white papers, media, publications, podcasts and more, which can be obtained from the firm's website. ASTaR is the company's first end-to-end 5G testing lab in the U.S. and focuses solely on cybersecurity. Nokia Bell Labs operates as a subsidiary of Nokia Corporation.

CONTACTS: Note: Officers with more than one job title may be intentionally listed here more than once.

Peter Vetter, Pres.

FINANCIAL DATA: Note: Data for latest year may not have been available at press time.

In U.S. $	2024	2023	2022	2021	2020	2019
Revenue						
R&D Expense						
Operating Income						
Operating Margin %						
SGA Expense						
Net Income						
Operating Cash Flow						
Capital Expenditure						
EBITDA						
Return on Assets %						
Return on Equity %						
Debt to Equity						

CONTACT INFORMATION:

Phone: 908-582-3000   Fax: 908-508-2576
Toll-Free:
Address: 600 Mountain Ave., Murray Hill, NJ 07974-0636 United States

STOCK TICKER/OTHER:

Stock Ticker: Subsidiary   Exchange:
Employees: 750   Fiscal Year Ends: 12/31
Parent Company: Nokia Corporation

SALARIES/BONUSES:

Top Exec. Salary: $ Bonus: $
Second Exec. Salary: $ Bonus: $

OTHER THOUGHTS:

Estimated Female Officers or Directors:
Hot Spot for Advancement for Women/Minorities:

Nokia Corporation

www.nokia.com

NAIC Code: 334220

TYPES OF BUSINESS:

Smartphones and Cellphones
Network Systems & Services
Internet Software & Services
Multimedia Equipment
Brand Licensing
Collaboration Devices
5G
Innovation

BRANDS/DIVISIONS/AFFILIATES:

Nokia Bell Labs

GROWTH PLANS/SPECIAL FEATURES:

Nokia provides telecom equipment and services that are used to build wireless and fixed-line networks. It operates in four segments. The mobile networks segment, which sells equipment and services to telecom carriers to power public wireless networks, is the largest. Network infrastructure focuses on fixed networks, including infrastructure, solutions, and components for IP networks, optical networks, and submarine networks. Cloud and network services is a nascent segment catering to enterprises, offering as-a-service platforms. Nokia also has a sizable research division and patent business, where it licenses technology used by handset providers, consumer electronics firms, and other firms making electronic and Internet of Things products.

CONTACTS: Note: Officers with more than one job title may be intentionally listed here more than once.

Pekka Lundmark, CEO
Marco Wiren, CFO
Sari Baldauf, Chairman of the Board
Esa Niinimaki, Chief Legal Officer
Nishant Batra, Chief Strategy Officer
Soren Skou, Director
Melissa Schoeb, Other Executive Officer
Amy Hanlon-Rodemich, Other Executive Officer
Ricky Corker, Other Executive Officer
Tommi Uitto, President, Divisional
Jenni Lukander, President, Divisional
Federico Guillen, President, Divisional
Raghav Sahgal, President, Divisional

FINANCIAL DATA: Note: Data for latest year may not have been available at press time.

In U.S. $	2024	2023	2022	2021	2020	2019
Revenue	21,816,118,943	23,993,189,438	26,970,488,619	25,200,907,360	24,803,632,553	26,464,244,405
R&D Expense	5,121,453,000	4,854,710,000	5,111,237,000	4,783,201,000	4,639,047,000	5,144,154,000
Operating Income	1,784,336,000	1,651,532,000	2,774,120,000	2,007,945,000	1,153,235,000	573,212,300
Operating Margin %	.08%	.07%	.10%	.08%	.05%	.02%
SGA Expense	3,280,363,000	3,266,743,000	3,355,278,000	3,169,126,000	3,289,444,000	3,653,802,000
Net Income	1,449,489,000	754,824,100	4,824,063,000	1,842,225,000	-2,863,791,000	7,945,517
Operating Cash Flow	2,829,739,000	1,494,892,000	1,673,099,000	2,979,569,000	1,996,595,000	442,678,800
Capital Expenditure	535,754,800	740,068,100	682,179,300	635,641,300	543,700,400	783,200,900
EBITDA	3,895,573,000	3,306,470,000	4,005,675,000	3,662,883,000	2,405,221,000	2,415,437,000
Return on Assets %	.03%	.02%	.10%	.04%	-.07%	.00%
Return on Equity %	.06%	.03%	.22%	.11%	-.18%	.00%
Debt to Equity	.17%	.22%	.24%	.31%	0.46	0.31

CONTACT INFORMATION:

Phone: 358 10-44-88-000   Fax: 358-10-44-81-002
Toll-Free:
Address: Karakaari 7A, Espoo, FI-02610 Finland

STOCK TICKER/OTHER:

Stock Ticker: NOK
Employees: 91,000
Parent Company:

Exchange: NYS
Fiscal Year Ends: 12/31

SALARIES/BONUSES:

Top Exec. Salary: $1,601,022   Bonus: $
Second Exec. Salary: $ Bonus: $

OTHER THOUGHTS:

Estimated Female Officers or Directors: 4
Hot Spot for Advancement for Women/Minorities: Y

Sales, profits and employees may be estimates. Financial information, benefits and other data can change quickly and may vary from those stated here.

NORR Group Inc

norr.com

NAIC Code: 541330

TYPES OF BUSINESS:

Engineering Consulting Services
Urban Design
Architecture
Project Planning
Interior Design
Structural Engineering
Mechanical Engineering
Electrical Engineering

BRANDS/DIVISIONS/AFFILIATES:

GROWTH PLANS/SPECIAL FEATURES:

NORR is an employee-owned global design firm specializing in architecture, engineering, planning and interior design. The company's team of 750 professionals work collaboratively across 12 market sectors from offices in Canada, the U.S., the U.K. and the United Arab Emirates. Markets include commercial, education, health sciences, hospitality, industrial, justice, public buildings, residential, restaurants, retail, science and research, and transportation. NORR's engineering services include structural, mechanical and electrical engineering, and other services such as master planning and urban design.

CONTACTS: Note: Officers with more than one job title may be intentionally listed here more than once.

Brian Gerstmar, CEO
Jonathan Hughes, COO
Daniela Ciolac, VP-Finance
Melanie Kurzuk, VP-Global Mktg.
Jacqui Souter, VP-Human Resources
Ashroff Khan, VP-IT
Silvio Baldassarra, Chmn.

FINANCIAL DATA: Note: Data for latest year may not have been available at press time.

In U.S. $	2024	2023	2022	2021	2020	2019
Revenue						
R&D Expense						
Operating Income						
Operating Margin %						
SGA Expense						
Net Income						
Operating Cash Flow						
Capital Expenditure						
EBITDA						
Return on Assets %						
Return on Equity %						
Debt to Equity						

CONTACT INFORMATION:

Phone: 416-929-0200   Fax:
Toll-Free:
Address: 175 Bloor St. E., N. Tower, Fl. 15, Toronto, ON M4W 3R8 Canada

STOCK TICKER/OTHER:

Stock Ticker: Private   Exchange:
Employees: Fiscal Year Ends:
Parent Company:

SALARIES/BONUSES:

Top Exec. Salary: $ Bonus: $
Second Exec. Salary: $ Bonus: $

OTHER THOUGHTS:

Estimated Female Officers or Directors:
Hot Spot for Advancement for Women/Minorities:

Sales, profits and employees may be estimates. Financial information, benefits and other data can change quickly and may vary from those stated here.

Northrop Grumman Corporation

www.northropgrumman.com

NAIC Code: 336411

TYPES OF BUSINESS:

Aircraft Manufacturing
Aeronautics Systems
Defense Systems
Mission Systems
Space Systems
Product Design and Engineering
System Production
System Integration Services

BRANDS/DIVISIONS/AFFILIATES:

GROWTH PLANS/SPECIAL FEATURES:

Northrop Grumman is a diversified defense contractor providing aeronautics, defense, and space systems. The company's aerospace segment creates the fuselage for the massive F-35 program, produces autonomous and piloted aircraft such as Global Hawk drones and the new B-21 bomber, and maintains and upgrades numerous military aircraft. Defense systems makes artillery and missile ammunition and guidance systems, long-range missiles, and missile defense systems. Mission systems creates and integrates a variety of radar, navigation, and communication systems for avionics, weapons control, and countermeasures on a range of platforms from helicopters to destroyers. Space systems produces satellites, sensors, space structures, and rocket motors.

CONTACTS:
Note: Officers with more than one job title may be intentionally listed here more than once.

Kathy Warden, CEO
Kenneth Crews, CFO
Michael Hardesty, Chief Accounting Officer
Kathryn Simpson, General Counsel
Roshan Roeder, President, Divisional
Benjamin Davies, President, Divisional
Thomas Jones, President, Divisional
Robert Fleming, President, Divisional
Jennifer McGarey, Secretary

FINANCIAL DATA:
Note: Data for latest year may not have been available at press time.

In U.S. $	2024	2023	2022	2021	2020	2019
Revenue	41,032,998,912	39,289,999,360	36,601,999,360	35,667,001,344	36,799,000,576	33,841,000,448
R&D Expense						
Operating Income	4,370,000,000	2,537,000,000	3,601,000,000	3,671,000,000	4,065,000,000	3,969,000,000
Operating Margin %	.11%	.06%	.10%	.10%	.11%	.12%
SGA Expense	3,992,000,000	4,014,000,000	3,873,000,000	3,597,000,000	3,413,000,000	3,290,000,000
Net Income	4,174,000,000	2,056,000,000	4,896,000,000	7,005,000,000	3,189,000,000	2,248,000,000
Operating Cash Flow	4,388,000,000	3,875,000,000	2,901,000,000	3,567,000,000	4,305,000,000	4,297,000,000
Capital Expenditure	1,767,000,000	1,775,000,000	1,435,000,000	1,415,000,000	1,420,000,000	1,264,000,000
EBITDA	7,007,000,000	4,229,000,000	7,684,000,000	10,733,000,000	5,588,000,000	4,341,000,000
Return on Assets %	.09%	.05%	.11%	.16%	.07%	.06%
Return on Equity %	.28%	.14%	.35%	.60%	.33%	.26%
Debt to Equity	1.08%	1.06%	.89%	1.11%	1.475	1.596

CONTACT INFORMATION:

Phone: 703 280-2900   Fax: 310 201-3023
Toll-Free:
Address: 2980 Fairview Park Dr., Falls Church, VA 22042 United States

STOCK TICKER/OTHER:

Stock Ticker: NOC   Exchange: NYS
Employees: 101,000   Fiscal Year Ends: 12/31
Parent Company:

SALARIES/BONUSES:

Top Exec. Salary: $1,790,385   Bonus: $
Second Exec. Salary: Bonus: $
$875,192

OTHER THOUGHTS:

Estimated Female Officers or Directors: 9
Hot Spot for Advancement for Women/Minorities: Y

Novartis AG

NAIC Code: 325412

www.novartis.com

TYPES OF BUSINESS:

Pharmaceuticals, Biopharmaceuticals, Generics and Drug Manufacturing
Therapeutic Drug Discovery
Therapeutic Drug Manufacturing
Generic Drugs
Over-the-Counter Drugs
Ophthalmic Products
Nutritional Products
Veterinary Products

BRANDS/DIVISIONS/AFFILIATES:

Sandoz
Novartis Institute for BioMedical Research
Global Drug Development
Novartis Technical Operations
Novartis Business Services
Tasigna
Cosentyx
Gilenya

CONTACTS: *Note: Officers with more than one job title may be intentionally listed here more than once.*

Vasant Narasimhan, CEO
Victor Bulto, Pres., Geographical
Harry Kirsch, CFO
Joerg Reinhardt, Chairman of the Board
Klaus Moosmayer, Chief Compliance Officer
Karen Hale, Chief Legal Officer
Shreeram Aradhye, Chief Medical Officer
Aharon Gal, Chief Strategy Officer
Simon Moroney, Director
Robert Kowalski, Other Executive Officer
Steffen Lang, President, Divisional
Fiona Marshall, President, Divisional
Patrick Horber, President, Divisional

GROWTH PLANS/SPECIAL FEATURES:

Novartis develops and manufactures innovative drugs. Key areas of drug development include oncology, rare diseases, neuroscience, immunology, respiratory, cardio-metabolic, and established medicines. The company sells its products globally, with the United States comprising close to one third of total revenue.

FINANCIAL DATA: *Note: Data for latest year may not have been available at press time.*

In U.S. $	2024	2023	2022	2021	2020	2019
Revenue	51,721,998,336	46,660,001,792	43,461,001,216	43,974,000,640	49,898,000,384	48,676,999,168
R&D Expense	10,022,000,000	11,371,000,000	9,172,000,000	8,641,000,000	8,980,000,000	9,402,000,000
Operating Income	14,544,000,000	9,769,000,000	7,946,000,000	10,056,000,000	10,152,000,000	9,086,000,000
Operating Margin %	.28%	.21%	.18%	.23%	.20%	.19%
SGA Expense	12,566,000,000	12,517,000,000	12,193,000,000	12,827,000,000	14,197,000,000	14,369,000,000
Net Income	11,941,000,000	14,850,000,000	6,955,000,000	24,021,000,000	8,072,000,000	11,732,000,000
Operating Cash Flow	17,619,000,000	14,458,000,000	14,236,000,000	15,071,000,000	13,650,000,000	13,625,000,000
Capital Expenditure	3,814,000,000	2,753,000,000	2,239,000,000	2,556,000,000	2,585,000,000	2,257,000,000
EBITDA	20,715,000,000	18,255,000,000	14,682,000,000	30,914,000,000	17,211,000,000	15,616,000,000
Return on Assets %	.12%	.14%	.06%	.19%	.07%	.09%
Return on Equity %	.26%	.28%	.11%	.39%	.14%	.17%
Debt to Equity	.52%	.43%	.37%	.36%	0.494	0.398

CONTACT INFORMATION:

Phone: 41 613241111   Fax: 41 613248001
Toll-Free:
Address: Lichtstrasse 35, Basel, 4056 Switzerland

STOCK TICKER/OTHER:

Stock Ticker: NVS   Exchange: NYS
Employees: 76,057   Fiscal Year Ends: 12/31
Parent Company:

SALARIES/BONUSES:

Top Exec. Salary: $2,270,011   Bonus: $
Second Exec. Salary: Bonus: $
$1,375,121

OTHER THOUGHTS:

Estimated Female Officers or Directors: 4
Hot Spot for Advancement for Women/Minorities: Y

Novo Nordisk AS

www.novonordisk.com

NAIC Code: 325412

TYPES OF BUSINESS:

Drugs-Diabetes and Obesity
Pharmaceuticals
Drug Research and Development
Insulin
Diabetes
Obesity
Fertility
Hemophilia

BRANDS/DIVISIONS/AFFILIATES:

Ozempic
Wegovy
NovoFine
Tresiba
Saxenda
NovoSeven
Norditropin
Emisphere Technologies Inc

CONTACTS: *Note: Officers with more than one job title may be intentionally listed here more than once.*

Lars Jorgensen, CEO
Karsten Knudsen, CFO
Helge Lund, Chairman of the Board
Marcus Schindler, Chief Scientific Officer
Henrik Poulsen, Director
Tania Sabroe, Executive VP, Divisional
Martin Lange, Executive VP, Divisional
Maziar Doustdar, Executive VP, Divisional
Henrik Wulff, Executive VP, Divisional
David Moore, Executive VP, Divisional
Camilla Sylvest, Executive VP, Divisional
Ludovic Helfgott, Executive VP, Divisional
Doug Langa, Executive VP, Geographical

GROWTH PLANS/SPECIAL FEATURES:

With roughly one third of the global branded diabetes treatment market, Novo Nordisk is the leading provider of diabetes-care products in the world. Based in Denmark, the company manufactures and markets a variety of human and modern insulins, injectable diabetes treatments such as GLP-1 therapy, oral antidiabetic agents, and obesity treatments. Novo also has a biopharmaceutical segment (constituting less than 10% of revenue) that specializes in protein therapies for hemophilia and other disorders.

About 28% of the firm's outstanding stock (and 75% of the vote) are held by the Novo Nordisk Foundation, one of the world's largest charitable foundations.

FINANCIAL DATA: *Note: Data for latest year may not have been available at press time.*

In U.S. $	2024	2023	2022	2021	2020	2019
Revenue	44,186,976,078	35,340,238,292	26,924,867,679	21,423,767,662	19,315,778,614	18,566,403,578
R&D Expense	7,312,991,000	4,936,444,000	3,658,930,000	2,704,142,000	2,352,658,000	2,163,679,000
Operating Income	19,527,730,000	15,607,400,000	11,382,750,000	8,923,121,000	8,235,674,000	7,985,679,000
Operating Margin %	.44%	.44%	.42%	.42%	.43%	.43%
SGA Expense	10,251,910,000	9,372,594,000	7,711,947,000	6,247,280,000	5,612,479,000	5,451,802,000
Net Income	15,366,080,000	12,732,990,000	8,448,542,000	7,266,583,000	6,411,611,000	5,926,684,000
Operating Cash Flow	18,406,180,000	16,571,160,000	12,003,240,000	8,368,659,000	7,904,732,000	7,118,230,000
Capital Expenditure	7,807,046,000	5,918,316,000	2,244,779,000	1,123,683,000	3,359,788,000	1,708,880,000
EBITDA	20,902,780,000	17,441,650,000	11,686,000,000	9,950,183,000	9,018,828,000	8,282,538,000
Return on Assets %	.26%	.30%	.25%	.28%	.31%	.33%
Return on Equity %	.81%	.88%	.72%	.71%	.70%	.71%
Debt to Equity	.62%	.19%	.29%	.18%	0.046	0.052

CONTACT INFORMATION:

Phone: 45 44448888   Fax: 45 44490555
Toll-Free:
Address: Novo Alle 1, Bagsvaerd, 2880 Denmark

STOCK TICKER/OTHER:

Stock Ticker: NVO   Exchange: NYS
Employees: 64,319   Fiscal Year Ends: 12/31
Parent Company:

SALARIES/BONUSES:

Top Exec. Salary: $2,799,697   Bonus: $45,647
Second Exec. Salary: Bonus: $60,863
$1,384,633

OTHER THOUGHTS:

Estimated Female Officers or Directors: 3
Hot Spot for Advancement for Women/Minorities: Y

Novonesis AS

www.novozymes.com

NAIC Code: 325414

TYPES OF BUSINESS:

Industrial Enzyme & Microorganism Production
Biopharmaceuticals
Enzymes
Microbiology

BRANDS/DIVISIONS/AFFILIATES:

PrecisionBiotics Group Limited
Microbiome Labs
Novozymes A/S
Chr Hansen

GROWTH PLANS/SPECIAL FEATURES:

Novonesis was formed in 2024 through the merger of Novozymes and Chr. Hansen. Following the merger, the company became the world leader in industrial enzymes and microbial solutions, with a nearly 50% market share in both. The firm supplies a wide range of industry groups: household care, food and beverages, bioenergy, agriculture and feed, technical and pharmaceuticals. Its biological solutions create value for its customers by improving yield efficiency and performance, while saving energy and generating less waste. The company is headquartered in Denmark, employs around 10,000 people, and works across more than 30 research and development and application centers and 23 manufacturing sites.

CONTACTS: Note: Officers with more than one job title may be intentionally listed here more than once.

Ester Baiget, CEO
Rainer Lehmann, CFO
Cees Jong, Chairman of the Board
Kim Stratton, Director

FINANCIAL DATA: Note: Data for latest year may not have been available at press time.

In U.S. $	2024	2023	2022	2021	2020	2019
Revenue	4,351,305,231	2,726,674,309	2,674,028,679	2,281,815,321	2,137,318,577	2,183,645,133
R&D Expense	469,012,500	307,264,500	304,832,900	306,612,700	295,460,100	298,667,500
Operating Income	748,013,600	693,416,500	674,562,700	592,927,000	550,650,900	538,543,400
Operating Margin %	.17%	.25%	.25%	.26%	.26%	.25%
SGA Expense	868,899,000	506,356,400	490,992,700	426,571,700	353,880,900	375,081,400
Net Income	347,105,600	460,726,400	560,002,800	480,141,200	430,911,000	479,144,100
Operating Cash Flow	1,157,662,000	632,349,600	610,275,100	619,940,700	664,289,300	485,524,500
Capital Expenditure	408,399,600	313,053,300	440,263,400	189,248,300	143,382,800	151,460,600
EBITDA	1,177,753,000	833,371,200	931,560,800	824,145,700	739,794,200	769,759,900
Return on Assets %	.03%	.11%	.14%	.14%	.14%	.16%
Return on Equity %	.05%	.22%	.29%	.27%	.25%	.28%
Debt to Equity			.28%	.03%	0.034	0.281

CONTACT INFORMATION:

Phone: 45 44460000   Fax: 45 44469999
Toll-Free:
Address: Krogshoejvej 36, Bagsvaerd, 2880 Denmark

STOCK TICKER/OTHER:

Stock Ticker: NVZMY   Exchange: PINX
Employees: 6,756   Fiscal Year Ends: 12/31
Parent Company:

SALARIES/BONUSES:

Top Exec. Salary: $ Bonus: $
Second Exec. Salary: $ Bonus: $

OTHER THOUGHTS:

Estimated Female Officers or Directors: 3
Hot Spot for Advancement for Women/Minorities: Y

NTT Data Corp
NAIC Code: 541512

www.nttdata.com/global/en/about-us

TYPES OF BUSINESS:
IT Services
Information Technology Solutions
IT Services
Business Services
Consulting Services
Business Process Services
IT Modernization
System and Software Development

BRANDS/DIVISIONS/AFFILIATES:
Nippon Telegraph and Telephone Corporation (NTT)

GROWTH PLANS/SPECIAL FEATURES:
NTT Data Group Corp Formerly NTT Data Corp provides IT services to a wide range of business fields. The company's operations are divided into three segments: global, public and social infrastructure; enterprise and solutions; and financial. Each segment contributes approximately an even proportion of the company's revenue. The services the company provides include system integration by constructing systems tailored to individual customer needs, multiple Internet and computer network-based information and processing services, consulting that evaluates customers' management issues, system support for large-scale systems, and new IT-based business models. The company is based in Japan but has a global presence.

CONTACTS: Note: Officers with more than one job title may be intentionally listed here more than once.
Tadaoki Nishimura, Director
Kazuhiko Nakayama, Director
Yutaka Sasaki, Director

FINANCIAL DATA: Note: Data for latest year may not have been available at press time.

In U.S. $	2024	2023	2022	2021	2020	2019
Revenue	30,320,654,518	24,230,645,539	17,716,649,018	16,097,320,105	15,737,350,738	15,021,001,832
R&D Expense						
Operating Income	2,149,056,000	1,798,875,000	1,475,916,000	966,210,800	909,032,300	1,025,521,000
Operating Margin %	.07%	.07%	.08%	.06%	.06%	.07%
SGA Expense	6,147,015,000	4,603,749,000	3,217,238,000	3,092,210,000	3,063,691,000	2,758,067,000
Net Income	929,387,700	1,041,114,000	992,634,000	533,483,800	521,716,200	649,930,600
Operating Cash Flow	3,462,851,000	2,433,824,000	2,154,985,000	2,447,181,000	1,944,106,000	1,680,151,000
Capital Expenditure	4,543,689,000	2,546,244,000	1,214,899,000	1,132,422,000	1,328,062,000	1,249,556,000
EBITDA	4,708,713,000	3,811,122,000	3,068,516,000	2,456,672,000	2,335,837,000	2,171,460,000
Return on Assets %	.02%	.03%	.05%	.03%	.03%	.04%
Return on Equity %	.08%	.11%	.12%	.08%	.08%	.11%
Debt to Equity	.95%	1.14%	.41%	.55%	0.599	0.482

CONTACT INFORMATION:
Phone: 81 355468202   Fax: 81 355462405
Toll-Free:
Address: Toyosu Ctr. Bldg., 3-3 Toyosu 3-chome, Koto-ku, Tokyo, 135-6033 Japan

STOCK TICKER/OTHER:
Stock Ticker: NTDTY   Exchange: PINX
Employees: 126,953   Fiscal Year Ends: 03/31
Parent Company: Nippon Telegraph and Telephone Corporation (NTT)

SALARIES/BONUSES:
Top Exec. Salary: $ Bonus: $
Second Exec. Salary: $ Bonus: $

OTHER THOUGHTS:
Estimated Female Officers or Directors:
Hot Spot for Advancement for Women/Minorities:

NV5 Global Inc

NAIC Code: 541330

www.nv5.com

TYPES OF BUSINESS:

Construction Engineering Services
Technical Engineering
Geospatial
Consulting

BRANDS/DIVISIONS/AFFILIATES:

Geodynamics LLC

GROWTH PLANS/SPECIAL FEATURES:

NV5 Global Inc is a provider of technology, conformity assessment, and consulting solutions to public and private sector clients in the infrastructure, utility services, construction, real estate, environmental, and geospatial markets, operating nationwide and abroad. The Company's clients include the U.S. Federal, state and local governments, and the private sector. It also serve quasi-public and private sector clients from the education, healthcare, utility services, and public utilities, including schools, universities, hospitals, health care providers, and insurance providers. The operating business segments are Infrastructure, Building, Technology & Sciences, and Geospatial Solutions. The maximum revenue derives from the infrastructure segment.

NV5 offers its employees medical, dental, vision, life and disability insurance plans; 401(k) and financial consulting; paid time off; and an employee assistance program.

CONTACTS:

Note: Officers with more than one job title may be intentionally listed here more than once.

Benjamin Heraud, CEO
Alexander Hockman, CEO, Divisional
Edward Codispoti, CFO
Dickerson Wright, Chairman of the Board
MaryJo OBrien, Chief Administrative Officer
Richard Tong, Director
Donald Alford, Executive VP

FINANCIAL DATA:

Note: Data for latest year may not have been available at press time.

In U.S. $	2024	2023	2022	2021	2020	2019
Revenue	941,265,024	857,155,008	786,777,984	706,705,984	659,296,000	508,937,984
R&D Expense						
Operating Income	43,434,000	59,973,000	66,182,000	68,344,000	44,149,000	31,207,000
Operating Margin %	.05%	.07%	.08%	.10%	.07%	.06%
SGA Expense	355,342,000	293,805,000	259,602,000	230,824,000	227,030,000	188,359,000
Net Income	27,979,000	43,724,000	49,973,000	47,147,000	21,018,000	23,756,000
Operating Cash Flow	57,320,000	62,207,000	93,980,000	101,442,000	96,009,000	39,900,000
Capital Expenditure	16,921,000	17,166,000	15,689,000	13,903,000	9,855,000	2,625,000
EBITDA	110,045,000	115,084,000	110,245,000	113,315,000	89,637,000	57,023,000
Return on Assets %	.02%	.04%	.05%	.05%	.02%	.04%
Return on Equity %	.03%	.06%	.08%	.09%	.06%	.07%
Debt to Equity	.29%	.27%	.06%	.18%	0.719	1.032

CONTACT INFORMATION:

Phone: 954 495-2112   Fax: 954 495-2101
Toll-Free:
Address: 200 South Park Rd., Ste. 350, Hollywood, FL 33021 United States

STOCK TICKER/OTHER:

Stock Ticker: NVEE   Exchange: NAS
Employees: 4,106   Fiscal Year Ends: 12/31
Parent Company:

SALARIES/BONUSES:

Top Exec. Salary: $749,014   Bonus: $
Second Exec. Salary: $475,010   Bonus: $

OTHER THOUGHTS:

Estimated Female Officers or Directors:
Hot Spot for Advancement for Women/Minorities:

NVIDIA Corporation

www.nvidia.com

NAIC Code: 334413

TYPES OF BUSINESS:

Printed Circuit & Chips Manufacturing
Graphics Processors
Graphics Software
Artificial Intelligence (AI) Server Chips
Processing Software

BRANDS/DIVISIONS/AFFILIATES:

GeForce
Quadro
NVIDIA RTX
AI Cockpit
Jetson
Cuda

GROWTH PLANS/SPECIAL FEATURES:

Nvidia is a leading developer of graphics processing units. Traditionally, GPUs were used to enhance the experience on computing platforms, most notably in gaming applications on PCs. GPU use cases have since emerged as important semiconductors used in artificial intelligence. Nvidia not only offers AI GPUs, but also a software platform, Cuda, used for AI model development and training. Nvidia is also expanding its data center networking solutions, helping to tie GPUs together to handle complex workloads.

NVIDIA offers its employees medical benefits, an employee stock purchase plan and flexible paid leave of absence. Time off includes two free days per quarter and a vacation policy that operates on somewhat of a take-what-you-want basis.

CONTACTS:
Note: Officers with more than one job title may be intentionally listed here more than once.

Jen-Hsun Huang, CEO
Colette Kress, CFO
Donald Robertson, Chief Accounting Officer
Ajay Puri, Executive VP, Divisional
Debora Shoquist, Executive VP, Divisional
Timothy Teter, Executive VP

FINANCIAL DATA:
Note: Data for latest year may not have been available at press time.

In U.S. $	2024	2023	2022	2021	2020	2019
Revenue	60,921,999,360	26,973,999,104	26,914,000,896	16,675,000,320	10,917,999,616	
R&D Expense	8,675,000,000	7,339,000,000	5,268,000,000	3,924,000,000	2,829,000,000	
Operating Income	32,972,000,000	5,577,000,000	10,041,000,000	4,532,000,000	2,846,000,000	
Operating Margin %	.54%	.21%	.37%	.27%	.26%	
SGA Expense	2,654,000,000	2,440,000,000	2,166,000,000	1,940,000,000	1,093,000,000	
Net Income	29,760,000,000	4,368,000,000	9,752,001,000	4,332,000,000	2,796,000,000	
Operating Cash Flow	28,090,000,000	5,641,000,000	9,108,000,000	5,822,000,000	4,761,000,000	
Capital Expenditure	1,069,000,000	1,833,000,000	976,000,000	1,128,000,000	489,000,000	
EBITDA	35,583,000,000	5,986,000,000	11,351,000,000	5,691,000,000	3,402,000,000	
Return on Assets %	.56%	.10%	.27%	.19%	.18%	
Return on Equity %	.91%	.18%	.45%	.30%	.26%	
Debt to Equity	.22%	.48%	.44%	.39%	0.209	

CONTACT INFORMATION:

Phone: 408 486-2000   Fax: 408 486-2200
Toll-Free:
Address: 2788 San Tomas Expressway, Santa Clara, CA 95051 United States

STOCK TICKER/OTHER:

Stock Ticker: NVDA   Exchange: NAS
Employees: 29,600   Fiscal Year Ends: 01/31
Parent Company:

SALARIES/BONUSES:

Top Exec. Salary: $1,486,199   Bonus: $
Second Exec. Salary: $943,391   Bonus: $

OTHER THOUGHTS:

Estimated Female Officers or Directors: 3
Hot Spot for Advancement for Women/Minorities: Y

Opel Automobile GmbH

www.opel.com

NAIC Code: 336111

TYPES OF BUSINESS:

Automobile Manufacturing
Automobile Manufacture
Passenger Vehicles
Light Commercial Vehicles
Electric Vehicles
Hybrid Vehicles

BRANDS/DIVISIONS/AFFILIATES:

Stellantis NV
Opel Group GmbH
Astra
Grandland
Mokka
Combo
Insignia
Mocha-e

CONTACTS: *Note: Officers with more than one job title may be intentionally listed here more than once.*

Florian Heuttl, CEO
Stephen J. Girsky, Pres., GM Europe
Ralph Wangemann, Dir.-Human Resources
Michael F. Ableson, VP-Eng.
Peter Thom, VP-Mfg.
Johan Willems, Communications
Susanna Webber, VP-Supply Chain & Purchasing

GROWTH PLANS/SPECIAL FEATURES:

Opel Automobile GmbH, along with its Vauxhall sister brand in the U.K., is a European manufacturer of passenger cars, trucks, commercial vehicles, automobile parts and accessories. Beginning with the manufacturing of sewing machines and bikes, the firm's founder, Adam Opel, began making automobiles in 1899. Opel operates plants, development and test centers throughout Europe, while its cars are sold in more than 60 countries, including locations in the Middle East, Asia Pacific and South America. Intending to cut carbon dioxide emissions, the company offers compressed natural gas (CNG) and liquefied petroleum gas (LPG) powered models for several of its vehicles. Subsidiary Opel Group GmbH is responsible for Opel/Vauxhall. Opel has a broad range of vehicle models, including the Astra hatchback, Combo Life van, Corsa hatchback, Crossland sport utility vehicle (SUV), Grandland SUV, Insignia family car, Mokka subcompact crossover SUV, and the Zafira Life minibus. Light commercial vehicle models include the Combo panel van, the Vivaro van and the Movano van. Box vans include the Combo Cargo, the Movano Cargo and the Vivaro Double Cab models. Sports tourers include the Astra and the Insignia lines. Some of these models come as electric or hybrid. Services and accessories include, but are not limited to, wheels, tires, equipment, original parts, replacement parts, warranties, inspections, accident and glass service, services for company/commercial customers, as well as vehicle and lease financing. The firm is a subsidiary of Stellantis NV.

FINANCIAL DATA: *Note: Data for latest year may not have been available at press time.*

In U.S. $	2024	2023	2022	2021	2020	2019
Revenue	9,828,000,000	9,360,000,000	9,000,000,000	8,832,358,319	8,411,769,828	9,558,829,350
R&D Expense						
Operating Income						
Operating Margin %						
SGA Expense						
Net Income						
Operating Cash Flow						
Capital Expenditure						
EBITDA						
Return on Assets %						
Return on Equity %						
Debt to Equity						

CONTACT INFORMATION:

Phone: 49 061-42-7-70   Fax: 49-061-42-7-88-00
Toll-Free:
Address: Bahnhofsplatz 1, Russelsheim, D-65423 Germany

STOCK TICKER/OTHER:

Stock Ticker: Subsidiary   Exchange:
Employees: 37,000   Fiscal Year Ends: 12/31
Parent Company: Stellantis NV

SALARIES/BONUSES:

Top Exec. Salary: $ Bonus: $
Second Exec. Salary: $ Bonus: $

OTHER THOUGHTS:

Estimated Female Officers or Directors: 1
Hot Spot for Advancement for Women/Minorities: Y

Oracle Corporation

NAIC Code: 511210H

TYPES OF BUSINESS:

Computer Software, Data Base & File Management
Enterprise Software
Servers
Operating Systems
Infrastructure Technologies
Software
Cloud Deployment

BRANDS/DIVISIONS/AFFILIATES:

GROWTH PLANS/SPECIAL FEATURES:

Oracle provides enterprise applications and infrastructure offerings around the world through a variety of flexible IT deployment models, including on-premises, cloud-based, and hybrid. Founded in 1977, Oracle pioneered the first commercial SQL-based relational database management system, which is commonly used for running online transaction processing and data warehousing workloads. Besides database systems, Oracle also sells enterprise resource planning, or ERP, customer relationship management, or CRM, and human capital management, or HCM, applications. Today, Oracle has more than 159,000 full-time employees in over 170 countries.

Oracle offers employees health, life and disability benefits, a 401(k) plan and an employee stock purchase plan.

CONTACTS: *Note: Officers with more than one job title may be intentionally listed here more than once.*

Safra Catz, CEO
Lawrence Ellison, Chairman of the Board
Maria Smith, Chief Accounting Officer
Stuart Levey, Chief Legal Officer
Jeffrey Henley, Director
Edward Screven, Executive VP

FINANCIAL DATA: *Note: Data for latest year may not have been available at press time.*

In U.S. $	2024	2023	2022	2021	2020	2019
Revenue	52,961,001,472	49,954,000,896	42,439,999,488	40,478,998,528	39,068,000,256	39,506,001,920
R&D Expense	8,915,000,000	8,623,000,000	7,219,000,000	6,527,000,000	6,067,000,000	6,026,000,000
Operating Income	16,071,000,000	13,773,000,000	15,830,000,000	15,782,000,000	14,202,000,000	14,022,000,000
Operating Margin %	.30%	.28%	.37%	.39%	.36%	.35%
SGA Expense	9,822,000,000	10,412,000,000	9,364,000,000	8,935,999,000	9,275,000,000	9,774,000,000
Net Income	10,467,000,000	8,503,000,000	6,717,000,000	13,746,000,000	10,135,000,000	11,083,000,000
Operating Cash Flow	18,673,000,000	17,165,000,000	9,539,000,000	15,887,000,000	13,139,000,000	14,551,000,000
Capital Expenditure	6,866,000,000	8,695,000,000	4,511,000,000	2,135,000,000	1,564,000,000	1,660,000,000
EBITDA	21,394,000,000	18,739,000,000	13,526,000,000	18,411,000,000	17,026,000,000	17,269,000,000
Return on Assets %	.08%	.07%	.06%	.11%	.09%	.09%
Return on Equity %	2.14%			1.59%	.60%	.33%
Debt to Equity	8.76%	80.54%		14.51%	5.733	2.372

CONTACT INFORMATION:

Phone: 737-867-1000   Fax:
Toll-Free:
Address: 2300 Oracle Way, Austin, TX 78741 United States

STOCK TICKER/OTHER:

Stock Ticker: ORCL   Exchange: NYS
Employees: 159,500   Fiscal Year Ends: 05/31
Parent Company:

SALARIES/BONUSES:

Top Exec. Salary: $950,000   Bonus: $1,000,000
Second Exec. Salary: Bonus: $
$950,000

OTHER THOUGHTS:

Estimated Female Officers or Directors: 6
Hot Spot for Advancement for Women/Minorities: Y

Orano SA

NAIC Code: 332410

TYPES OF BUSINESS:

Nuclear Power Generation Equipment
Nuclear Power Plant Design, Construction & Maintenance
Electrical Transmission & Distribution Products
Electrical & Electronic Interconnect Systems
Uranium Mining & Processing
Forged Steel Equipment
Solar Thermal Technology (CSP)

BRANDS/DIVISIONS/AFFILIATES:

Orano Med
Societe de Transports Speciaux Industriels
Orano Projects
INEVO

CONTACTS: Note: Officers with more than one job title may be intentionally listed here more than once.

Luc Oursel, Pres.
Olivier Wantz, Sr. VP-Mining
Claude Imauven, Chmn.

GROWTH PLANS/SPECIAL FEATURES:

Orano SA processes nuclear materials, allowing them to contribute to the fields of energy, medical radiological research and more. The firm offers high value-added products and services for the entire nuclear fuel cycle, from raw materials to waste processing. Its activities range from mining to dismantling, conversion, enrichment, recycling, logistics and engineering. Orano also provides nuclear facility supervision and management, whether during the operational stage, for maintenance or at the end-of-life cycle. It offers operational assistance services and implements site assistance, specialized maintenance and handling operations on all equipment. Orano draws ore where the uranium content is high, including mines in Canada, Kazakhstan and Niger. The company's uranium conversion and enrichment facilities include the Tricastin and Malvesi plants and the Comurhex II and Georges Besse II plants. Malvesi is responsible for the first phase of conversion, purifying the natural uranium ore from the mines into uranium tetrafluoride (UF4). The group also has facilities that are global benchmarks, such as the used-fuel recycling sites of La Hague and Melox. Subsidiary Orano Med specializes in nuclear medicine, with laboratories located in France and the U.S. Orano Med develops new therapies based on the use of radioactive elements to destroy cancer cells.

FINANCIAL DATA: Note: Data for latest year may not have been available at press time.

In U.S. $	2024	2023	2022	2021	2020	2019
Revenue		5,269,881,000	4,522,955,130	4,819,400,192	3,756,806,912	3,861,842,432
R&D Expense						
Operating Income						
Operating Margin %						
SGA Expense						
Net Income		239,490,000	-285,019,830	691,399,296	-72,403,176	416,063,296
Operating Cash Flow						
Capital Expenditure						
EBITDA						
Return on Assets %						
Return on Equity %						
Debt to Equity						

CONTACT INFORMATION:

Phone: 33-1-34-96-00-00   Fax: 33-1-34-96-00-01
Toll-Free:
Address: 111 quai du President Roosevelt, Issy-les-Moulineaux, 92130 France

STOCK TICKER/OTHER:

Stock Ticker: Government-Owned   Exchange:
Employees: 19,102   Fiscal Year Ends: 12/31
Parent Company:

SALARIES/BONUSES:

Top Exec. Salary: $ Bonus: $
Second Exec. Salary: $ Bonus: $

OTHER THOUGHTS:

Estimated Female Officers or Directors: 3
Hot Spot for Advancement for Women/Minorities: Y

Oriental Consultants Global Co Ltd

www.ocglobal.jp

NAIC Code: 541330

TYPES OF BUSINESS:

Engineering Consulting Services
Civil Engineering
Planning and Feasibility
Construction Supervision
Operation and Maintenance
Project Management
Project Formulation
Project Financing

BRANDS/DIVISIONS/AFFILIATES:

OC Latin America SA
Oriental Consultants Philippines Inc
OCG East Africa Limited
Taiseikiso Engineering Co Ltd
Chuou Sekkei Engineering Co Ltd
A-TEC Co Ltd
Research and Solutions Co Ltd

CONTACTS: Note: Officers with more than one job title may be intentionally listed here more than once.

Eiji Yonezawa, CEO

GROWTH PLANS/SPECIAL FEATURES:

Oriental Consultants Global Co., Ltd. (OC Global) provides engineering services, having worked on more than 3,000 civil projects in over 150 countries worldwide. OC Global's wide range of services include capacity building and training, studies and investigations, planning, feasibility studies, design, design review, tender assistance, construction supervision, environmental and social safeguards, operation and maintenance, asset management, project management, project formulation and project financing. The company serves many industries, including agriculture and forestry, airports and aviation, architecture, disaster recovery and resilience, energy and power, environmental management, ports and marine, post-conflict reconstruction, railways and mass transit, roads/bridges/tunnels, smart cities, tourism, transportation and logistics, urban and regional development, water and sanitation, and water resource management. Just a few of OC Global's many subsidiaries include OC Latin America SA, Oriental Consultants Philippines Inc., and OCG East Africa Limited, and other group companies include Asano Taiseikiso Engineering Co. Ltd., Chuou Sekkei Engineering Co. Ltd., A-TEC Co. Ltd. and Research and Solutions Co. Ltd.

FINANCIAL DATA: Note: Data for latest year may not have been available at press time.

In U.S. $	2024	2023	2022	2021	2020	2019
Revenue	241,500,000	230,000,000	220,000,000	202,800,000	195,000,000	206,515,000
R&D Expense						
Operating Income						
Operating Margin %						
SGA Expense						
Net Income						
Operating Cash Flow						
Capital Expenditure						
EBITDA						
Return on Assets %						
Return on Equity %						
Debt to Equity						

CONTACT INFORMATION:

Phone: 81-3-6311-7551   Fax: 81-3-6311-8011
Toll-Free:
Address: Tokyo Opera City Tower, Fl. 9, 20-2, Nishishinjuku 3-chome, Shinjuku-ku, Tokyo, 151-0071 Japan

STOCK TICKER/OTHER:

Stock Ticker: Private   Exchange:
Employees: 1,449   Fiscal Year Ends: 03/31
Parent Company:

SALARIES/BONUSES:

Top Exec. Salary: $ Bonus: $
Second Exec. Salary: $ Bonus: $

OTHER THOUGHTS:

Estimated Female Officers or Directors:
Hot Spot for Advancement for Women/Minorities:

OYO Corporation

NAIC Code: 541620

TYPES OF BUSINESS:
Geological Research
Environmental Services
Disaster Prevention
Engineering Consultation
Equipment Manufacturing
Surveying

BRANDS/DIVISIONS/AFFILIATES:
McSEIS-3
SonicViewer-SX
Geometrics Inc
McSEIS-SX48
Optical Borehole Camera
Acoustic Borehole Televiewer
OYO Corporation USA

GROWTH PLANS/SPECIAL FEATURES:
OYO Corp is a Japanese based company, engages in the geological, geophysical, and geotechnical research and consulting business. The company offers survey and analysis services primarily for ground and groundwater, and ocean water, as well as advisory and consulting services in the areas of disaster management, construction, and environmental investigation. It's products which include Remote Monitoring for underground deformation, Sensor for Deformation Measurement and Standalone with data logger for automatic monitoring of water level with multi-parameters.

CONTACTS: Note: Officers with more than one job title may be intentionally listed here more than once.
Masaru Narita, Chairman of the Board
Munehiro Igarashi, Director
Yuichi Hirashima, Director
Wataru Nakagawa, Director
Hirofumi Amano, Director

FINANCIAL DATA: Note: Data for latest year may not have been available at press time.

In U.S. $	2024	2023	2022	2021	2020	2019
Revenue	514,336,306	455,442,939	409,684,811	358,754,530	344,404,340	374,083,592
R&D Expense	17,543,740	15,627,600	14,822,270	10,094,420	9,906,971	11,191,340
Operating Income	30,442,930	19,772,290	17,071,650	25,492,920	17,550,680	17,967,230
Operating Margin %	.06%	.04%	.04%	.07%	.05%	.05%
SGA Expense	4,005,832	3,499,028	2,804,777	2,006,387	2,013,330	3,596,224
Net Income	27,839,490	27,811,720	12,552,070	19,897,250	12,364,620	15,106,920
Operating Cash Flow	9,059,983	6,039,989	-28,714,250	16,016,390	34,191,890	17,460,430
Capital Expenditure	10,816,440	11,732,850	11,323,240	7,643,710	6,199,667	7,990,837
EBITDA	53,096,360	40,717,860	31,519,030	36,823,100	28,853,100	30,283,250
Return on Assets %	.04%	.04%	.02%	.03%	.02%	.03%
Return on Equity %	.05%	.06%	.03%	.04%	.03%	.03%
Debt to Equity	.08%	.08%	.04%	.04%	0.039	0.029

CONTACT INFORMATION:
Phone: 81-3-5577-4936 Fax: 81-3-5577-4937
Toll-Free:
Address: 7 Kanda-Mltoshiro-cho, Chiyoda-ku, Tokyo, 102-0073 Japan

STOCK TICKER/OTHER:
Stock Ticker: OYOCF
Employees: 2,372
Parent Company:

Exchange: PINX
Fiscal Year Ends: 12/31

SALARIES/BONUSES:
Top Exec. Salary: $ Bonus: $
Second Exec. Salary: $ Bonus: $

OTHER THOUGHTS:
Estimated Female Officers or Directors:
Hot Spot for Advancement for Women/Minorities:

PACCAR Inc

NAIC Code: 336120

www.paccar.com

TYPES OF BUSINESS:

Truck Manufacturing
Premium Truck Manufacturer
Parts Distribution
Finance, Lease and Insurance Services

BRANDS/DIVISIONS/AFFILIATES:

Kenworth Truck Company
Peterbilt Motors
DAF Trucks
PACCAR Financial Services
Braden
Carco
Gearmatic

GROWTH PLANS/SPECIAL FEATURES:

Paccar is a leading manufacturer of medium- and heavy-duty trucks under the premium nameplates Kenworth and Peterbilt, which are primarily sold in the Americas and Australia, and DAF, which primarily services Europe and South America. The trucks segment (74% sales) goes to market through a network of 2,200 independent dealers. Paccar maintains an internal finance subsidiary that provides retail and wholesale financing for customers and dealers (6% sales). In recent years, Paccar has aggressively grown its parts business (20% sales), which include engines, axles, and transmissions for its own truck brands as well as independent producers. The company commands approximately 30% of the Class 8 market share in North America and 15% of the heavy-duty market share in Europe.

CONTACTS: Note: Officers with more than one job title may be intentionally listed here more than once.

R. Feight, CEO
James Walenczak, General Manager, Subsidiary
Harrie Schippers, CFO
Mark Pigott, Chairman of the Board
A Ley, Chief Information Officer
John Rich, Chief Technology Officer
Brice Poplawski, Controller
Darrin Siver, Executive VP
Michael Dozier, Executive VP
Michael Walton, General Counsel
Harry Wolters, General Manager, Divisional
Jason Skoog, General Manager, Subsidiary
Laura Bloch, General Manager
Paulo Bolgar, Other Executive Officer
Harald Seidel, President, Subsidiary

FINANCIAL DATA: Note: Data for latest year may not have been available at press time.

In U.S. $	2024	2023	2022	2021	2020	2019
Revenue	33,663,799,296	35,127,398,400	28,819,699,712	23,522,299,904	18,728,499,200	25,599,700,992
R&D Expense	452,900,000	410,900,000	341,200,000	324,100,000	273,900,000	326,600,000
Operating Income	4,892,400,000	5,946,400,000	3,678,600,000	2,308,200,000	1,571,600,000	2,974,900,000
Operating Margin %	.15%	.17%	.13%	.10%	.08%	.12%
SGA Expense	744,000,000	753,300,000	726,300,000	676,800,000	581,400,000	698,500,000
Net Income	4,162,000,000	4,600,800,000	3,011,600,000	1,865,500,000	1,301,200,000	2,387,900,000
Operating Cash Flow	4,640,900,000	4,190,000,000	3,027,000,000	2,186,700,000	2,987,200,000	2,860,300,000
Capital Expenditure	1,745,600,000	1,262,500,000	1,390,500,000	1,632,800,000	1,638,400,000	1,970,800,000
EBITDA	5,809,300,000	6,870,300,000	4,468,800,000	3,277,600,000	2,620,600,000	4,052,200,000
Return on Assets %	.10%	.12%	.10%	.06%	.05%	.09%
Return on Equity %	.25%	.32%	.24%	.17%	.13%	.26%
Debt to Equity	.59%	.58%	.62%	.64%	0.745	0.765

CONTACT INFORMATION:

Phone: 425 468-7400   Fax: 425 468-8216
Toll-Free:
Address: 777 106th Ave. NE, Bellevue, WA 98004 United States

STOCK TICKER/OTHER:

Stock Ticker: PCAR   Exchange: NAS
Employees: 32,400   Fiscal Year Ends: 12/31
Parent Company:

SALARIES/BONUSES:

Top Exec. Salary: $1,646,154   Bonus: $
Second Exec. Salary: Bonus: $
$1,103,365

OTHER THOUGHTS:

Estimated Female Officers or Directors:
Hot Spot for Advancement for Women/Minorities:

Sales, profits and employees may be estimates. Financial information, benefits and other data can change quickly and may vary from those stated here.

Page Southerland Page Inc

NAIC Code: 541330

pagethink.com

TYPES OF BUSINESS:

Engineering Consulting Services
Architecture and Design
Engineering
Complex Building Projects
Urban Planning and Design
Interiors
Advanced Manufacturing Facilities
Aviation Branding and Graphics

BRANDS/DIVISIONS/AFFILIATES:

Stantec

GROWTH PLANS/SPECIAL FEATURES:

Page Southerland Page, Inc. is a full-service design, architecture and engineering firm with offices in the U.S., Mexico City and Dubai. The company's work primarily consists of complex projects, with services addressing a wide range of sectors including academic, advanced manufacturing, architecture, aviation, branding and graphics, building sciences, civic/community/culture, commissioning, corporate/commercial, engineering, government, healthcare, housing, hospitality, interiors, lab design and planning, mission-critical, urban planning and design, science, technology, and strategies and analytics. As of April 2025, Page is a subsidiary of Stantec.

CONTACTS: *Note: Officers with more than one job title may be intentionally listed here more than once.*

Thomas McCarthy, CEO
Mattia J. Flabiano III, Pres.
Catherine J. Britt, CFO
John F. Gloetzner, CMO
Lisa Rosenfeld, Chief Human Resources Officer
Zoltan Karl, CIO

FINANCIAL DATA: *Note: Data for latest year may not have been available at press time.*

In U.S. $	2024	2023	2022	2021	2020	2019
Revenue	178,500,000	170,000,000	163,000,000	154,720,800	148,770,000	165,300,000
R&D Expense						
Operating Income						
Operating Margin %						
SGA Expense						
Net Income						
Operating Cash Flow						
Capital Expenditure						
EBITDA						
Return on Assets %						
Return on Equity %						
Debt to Equity						

CONTACT INFORMATION:

Phone: 713-871-8484   Fax:
Toll-Free:
Address: 1100 Louisiana, Ste. One, Houston, TX 77002 United States

STOCK TICKER/OTHER:

Stock Ticker: Private   Exchange:
Employees: 1,300   Fiscal Year Ends:
Parent Company:

SALARIES/BONUSES:

Top Exec. Salary: $ Bonus: $
Second Exec. Salary: $ Bonus: $

OTHER THOUGHTS:

Estimated Female Officers or Directors:
Hot Spot for Advancement for Women/Minorities: Y

Palo Alto Research Center Inc (PARC)

www.parc.com

NAIC Code: 541710

TYPES OF BUSINESS:

Research & Development-Office Technology
Research and Development Services
Technology and Software Solutions
New Business Creation
Technology Development
Artificial Intelligence Solutions
Digital Workplace Solutions
Internet of Things and Machine Intelligence

BRANDS/DIVISIONS/AFFILIATES:

SRI International
Xerox Corporation

GROWTH PLANS/SPECIAL FEATURES:

Palo Alto Research Center Incorporated (PARC) is a research and development (R&D) firm owned and operated by Xerox Corporation. The company practices open innovation, and provides custom R&D services, technology, expertise and best practice to Fortune 500 and Global 1000 companies, startups and government agencies and partners worldwide. PARC's current (March 2025) focus areas are led by experts with a diverse range of capabilities and experiences, all of which are linked to its competencies, including: advanced technology and systems, biosciences, education, information and computing sciences and integrated systems and solutions. Services include licensing, commercialization and cleanroom. The firm is owned by nonprofit SRI International.

CONTACTS: Note: Officers with more than one job title may be intentionally listed here more than once.

Stephen Hoover, CEO
Walt Johnson, VP-Intelligent Systems Laboratory
Mike Steep, Sr. VP-Global Bus. Oper.
John Pauksta, VP-Finance
Rob McHenry, VP-Public Sector Oper.
Scott Elrod, VP-Hardware Systems Laboratory
Teresa Lunt, VP

FINANCIAL DATA: Note: Data for latest year may not have been available at press time.

In U.S. $	2024	2023	2022	2021	2020	2019
Revenue						
R&D Expense						
Operating Income						
Operating Margin %						
SGA Expense						
Net Income						
Operating Cash Flow						
Capital Expenditure						
EBITDA						
Return on Assets %						
Return on Equity %						
Debt to Equity						

CONTACT INFORMATION:

Phone: 650-812-4000   Fax: 650-812-4028
Toll-Free:
Address: 3333 Coyote Hill Rd., Palo Alto, CA 94304 United States

STOCK TICKER/OTHER:

Stock Ticker: Subsidiary   Exchange:
Employees: 142   Fiscal Year Ends: 12/31
Parent Company: SRI International

SALARIES/BONUSES:

Top Exec. Salary: $ Bonus: $
Second Exec. Salary: $ Bonus: $

OTHER THOUGHTS:

Estimated Female Officers or Directors:
Hot Spot for Advancement for Women/Minorities: Y

Panasonic Corporation

www.panasonic.com/global/home.html

NAIC Code: 334310

TYPES OF BUSINESS:

Audio & Video Equipment, Manufacturing
Appliances
Automotive Systems
Digital Cameras
Housing Construction Systems
Industrial Connected Systems
Batteries
Business-to-Business Solutions

BRANDS/DIVISIONS/AFFILIATES:

Blue Yonder

GROWTH PLANS/SPECIAL FEATURES:

Panasonic Holdings is a conglomerate that has diversified from its consumer electronics roots. It has five main business units: lifestyle (white appliances and housing products); automotive (cockpit systems); connect (BtoB businesses); industry (FA products, electronic materials, and devices); and energy (rechargeable batteries). After the crisis in 2012, former president Kazuhiro Tsuga has focused on shifting the business portfolio to increase the proportion of B2B businesses to mitigate the tough competition in consumer electronics products.

CONTACTS: Note: Officers with more than one job title may be intentionally listed here more than once.

Yuki Kusumi, CEO
Hirokazu Umeda, CFO
Kazuhiro Tsuga, Chairman of the Board
Mototsugu Sato, Chief Risk Officer
Yoshiyuki Miyabe, Director
Tetsuro Homma, Director
Ayako Shotoku, Director

FINANCIAL DATA: Note: Data for latest year may not have been available at press time.

In U.S. $	2024	2023	2022	2021	2020	2019
Revenue	58,986,533,173	58,170,942,085	51,296,799,663	46,506,487,355	52,003,620,278	55,559,103,999
R&D Expense						
Operating Income	2,476,166,000	1,993,460,000	2,569,863,000	1,939,413,000	2,002,590,000	2,781,484,000
Operating Margin %	.04%	.03%	.05%	.04%	.04%	.05%
SGA Expense	14,609,530,000	13,519,650,000	11,972,450,000	11,578,010,000	12,943,500,000	13,464,780,000
Net Income	3,082,436,000	1,843,252,000	1,772,660,000	1,146,050,000	1,566,974,000	1,972,709,000
Operating Cash Flow	6,018,454,000	3,615,260,000	1,753,888,000	3,499,292,000	2,987,385,000	1,414,031,000
Capital Expenditure	4,493,190,000	2,567,940,000	2,067,315,000	2,057,949,000	2,397,168,000	2,769,113,000
EBITDA	5,900,569,000	4,997,438,000	4,990,295,000	4,144,807,000	4,846,473,000	5,089,850,000
Return on Assets %	.05%	.03%	.03%	.03%	.04%	.05%
Return on Equity %	.11%	.08%	.09%	.07%	.12%	.16%
Debt to Equity	.29%	.34%	.44%	.42%	0.579	0.318

CONTACT INFORMATION:

Phone: 81 669081121   Fax:
Toll-Free:
Address: 1006 Oaza Kadoma, Kadoma City, Osaka, 571-8501 Japan

STOCK TICKER/OTHER:

Stock Ticker: PCRFF   Exchange: PINX
Employees: 219,000   Fiscal Year Ends: 03/31
Parent Company:

SALARIES/BONUSES:

Top Exec. Salary: $ Bonus: $
Second Exec. Salary: $ Bonus: $

OTHER THOUGHTS:

Estimated Female Officers or Directors:
Hot Spot for Advancement for Women/Minorities:

Parsons Corporation

www.parsons.com

NAIC Code: 541330

TYPES OF BUSINESS:

Civil Engineering
Construction Management
Facility Operations and Maintenance
Environmental Services
Analytical, Technical and Training Services
Transportation Infrastructure Project Design and Construction

BRANDS/DIVISIONS/AFFILIATES:

Braxton Science and Technology Group LLC

GROWTH PLANS/SPECIAL FEATURES:

Parsons Corp is a provider of technology-driven solutions in the defense, intelligence, and critical infrastructure markets. The business activities of the group are carried out through Federal Solutions and Critical Infrastructure segments. The Federal Solutions segment is a high-end service and technology provider to the U.S. government, delivering timely, cost-effective solutions for mission-critical projects, whereas the Critical Infrastructure segment provides integrated design and engineering services for complex physical and digital infrastructure around the globe.

Parsons offers its employees medical and life insurance, tuition reimbursement, an ESOP for eligible employees, a 401(k) and membership to a Federal Credit Union.

CONTACTS: Note: Officers with more than one job title may be intentionally listed here more than once.

Carey Smith, CEO
Matthew Ofilos, CFO
Michael Kolloway, Chief Legal Officer
Susan Balaguer, Other Executive Officer

FINANCIAL DATA: Note: Data for latest year may not have been available at press time.

In U.S. $	2024	2023	2022	2021	2020	2019
Revenue	6,750,576,128	5,442,748,928	4,195,271,936	3,660,771,072	3,918,946,048	3,954,811,904
R&D Expense						
Operating Income	451,427,000	336,109,000	169,319,000	95,584,000	147,756,000	50,342,000
Operating Margin %	.07%	.06%	.04%	.03%	.04%	.01%
SGA Expense	954,995,000	869,905,000	777,403,000	757,237,000	729,103,000	781,408,000
Net Income	235,053,000	161,149,000	96,664,000	64,072,000	98,541,000	120,534,000
Operating Cash Flow	523,606,000	407,699,000	237,526,000	205,574,000	289,161,000	220,240,000
Capital Expenditure	49,213,000	40,396,000	30,593,000	21,105,000	34,036,000	67,597,000
EBITDA	518,484,000	415,523,000	309,908,000	274,494,000	310,349,000	216,671,000
Return on Assets %	.05%	.04%	.02%	.02%	.03%	.04%
Return on Equity %	.10%	.07%	.05%	.03%	.06%	.09%
Debt to Equity	.37%	.38%	.42%	.39%	0.399	0.279

CONTACT INFORMATION:

Phone: 703-988-8500 Fax:
Toll-Free:
Address: 5875 Trinity Pkwy. #300, Centreville, VA 20120 United States

STOCK TICKER/OTHER:

Stock Ticker: PSN   Exchange: NYS
Employees: 18,500   Fiscal Year Ends: 12/31
Parent Company:

SALARIES/BONUSES:

Top Exec. Salary: $1,028,846   Bonus: $
Second Exec. Salary: Bonus: $
$576,044

OTHER THOUGHTS:

Estimated Female Officers or Directors:
Hot Spot for Advancement for Women/Minorities:

PCL Construction Group Inc

www.pcl.com

NAIC Code: 237000

TYPES OF BUSINESS:

Heavy Construction
Construction
Buildings
Civil Infrastructure
Industrial Facilities

BRANDS/DIVISIONS/AFFILIATES:

CONTACTS: Note: Officers with more than one job title may be intentionally listed here more than once.

Chris Gower, CEO
Gordon Stephenson, CFO
Steve Richards, General Counsel
Lee Clayton, VP-Global Strategic Initiatives
Gordon Stephenson, VP-Corp. Finance
Luis Ventoza, COO-Civil Infrastructure
Ian Johnson, COO-Heavy Industrial
Rob Hoimberg, COO-Buildings
Dave Filipchuk, Chmn.

GROWTH PLANS/SPECIAL FEATURES:

PCL Construction Group, Inc. (PCL) is an employee-owned group of construction companies founded in 1906, with more than 32 offices across Canada, the U.S., the Caribbean and Australia. The firm focuses on three main areas of construction: buildings, civil and industrial. Services relating to buildings include constructability and budget control, smart construction, pre-fabrication and modular construction, sustainable construction services, construction services, emergency response, self-perform capabilities, delivery methods, preconstruction services and special projects. PCL expertise ranges from public-private partnerships (P3s) and engineering/procurement/construction (EPC) to pre-construction. Civil services include construction services, pre-fabrication and modular construction, sustainable construction services, delivery methods, self-perform capabilities, emergency response and special projects. Industrial services include industrial construction services, industrial construction engineering, industrial modular construction, industrial fabrication (U.S. and Canada), industrial site execution, people/teams/craft labor solutions, industrial maintenance and turnaround, and industrial special projects. PCL serves many sectors, such as agribusiness, food and beverage, buildings, cultural and civic, entertainment, hospitality, gaming, multi-family residential, sports facilities, aviation and transportation, commercial and retail, data centers, mission critical, government, public, manufacturing, parking structures, building revitalization, convention centers, education, healthcare, mass timber and renewable energy.

FINANCIAL DATA: Note: Data for latest year may not have been available at press time.

In U.S. $	2024	2023	2022	2021	2020	2019
Revenue	8,736,000,000	8,320,000,000	8,000,000,000	10,122,735,000	9,460,500,000	8,925,000,000
R&D Expense						
Operating Income						
Operating Margin %						
SGA Expense						
Net Income						
Operating Cash Flow						
Capital Expenditure						
EBITDA						
Return on Assets %						
Return on Equity %						
Debt to Equity						

CONTACT INFORMATION:

Phone: 780-733-5000   Fax: 780-733-5075
Toll-Free:
Address: 9915 56th Ave. NW, Edmonton, AB T6E 5L7 Canada

STOCK TICKER/OTHER:

Stock Ticker: Private   Exchange:
Employees: 9,800   Fiscal Year Ends:
Parent Company:

SALARIES/BONUSES:

Top Exec. Salary: $ Bonus: $
Second Exec. Salary: $ Bonus: $

OTHER THOUGHTS:

Estimated Female Officers or Directors:
Hot Spot for Advancement for Women/Minorities:

Sales, profits and employees may be estimates. Financial information, benefits and other data can change quickly and may vary from those stated here.

Petrobras (Petroleo Brasileiro SA)

www.petrobras.com.br

NAIC Code: 211100

TYPES OF BUSINESS:

Oil & Gas Exploration & Production
Oil Refineries
Service Stations
Transportation & Pipelines
Energy Trading

BRANDS/DIVISIONS/AFFILIATES:

Petrobras
Petrobras Distribuidora SA

GROWTH PLANS/SPECIAL FEATURES:

Petrobras is a Brazil-based integrated energy company controlled by the Brazilian government. The company focuses on exploration and production of oil and gas in Brazilian offshore fields. Production in 2024 was 2.7 million barrels of oil equivalent a day (80% oil production), and reserves stood at 10.9 billion boe (85% oil). At end-2023, Petrobras operated 10 refineries in Brazil with capacity of 1.8 million barrels a day and distributes refined products and natural gas throughout Brazil.

CONTACTS: Note: Officers with more than one job title may be intentionally listed here more than once.

Jean Prates, CEO
Sergio Leite, CFO
Pietro Mendes, Chairman of the Board
Mario Spinelli, Chief Compliance Officer
Carlos Travassos, Chief Technology Officer
Clarice Coppetti, Other Executive Officer
Claudio Schlosser, Other Executive Officer
Joelson Mendes, Other Executive Officer
Mauricio Tolmasquim, Other Executive Officer
William da Silva, Other Executive Officer

FINANCIAL DATA: Note: Data for latest year may not have been available at press time.

In U.S. $	2024	2023	2022	2021	2020	2019
Revenue	91,416,002,560	102,409,003,008	124,473,999,360	83,966,001,152	53,682,999,296	76,588,998,656
R&D Expense	789,000,000	726,000,000	792,000,000	563,000,000	355,000,000	576,000,000
Operating Income	25,691,000,000	39,473,000,000	53,265,000,000	31,001,000,000	20,133,000,000	20,918,000,000
Operating Margin %	.28%	.39%	.43%	.37%	.38%	.27%
SGA Expense	9,033,000,000	8,061,000,000	7,004,000,000	6,782,000,000	4,516,000,000	7,258,000,000
Net Income	7,528,000,000	24,884,000,000	36,623,000,000	19,875,000,000	1,141,000,000	10,151,000,000
Operating Cash Flow	37,984,000,000	43,212,000,000	49,717,000,000	37,791,000,000	28,890,000,000	25,600,000,000
Capital Expenditure	14,644,000,000	12,114,000,000	9,581,000,000	6,325,000,000	5,874,000,000	23,897,000,000
EBITDA	27,462,000,000	52,292,000,000	69,933,000,000	44,897,000,000	16,990,000,000	33,523,000,000
Return on Assets %	.04%	.12%	.20%	.11%	.01%	.04%
Return on Equity %	.11%	.34%	.53%	.31%	.02%	.14%
Debt to Equity	.83%	.65%	.64%	.72%	1.106	1.049

CONTACT INFORMATION:

Phone: 55 2132244477   Fax: 55 2 132246055
Toll-Free:
Address: 65 Ave. Republica do Chile, Rio de Janeiro, RJ 20031-912 Brazil

STOCK TICKER/OTHER:

Stock Ticker: PBR
Employees: 40,213
Parent Company:

Exchange: NYS
Fiscal Year Ends: 12/31

SALARIES/BONUSES:

Top Exec. Salary: $ Bonus: $
Second Exec. Salary: $ Bonus: $

OTHER THOUGHTS:

Estimated Female Officers or Directors: 1
Hot Spot for Advancement for Women/Minorities:

PetroChina Company Limited
www.petrochina.com.cn

NAIC Code: 211100

TYPES OF BUSINESS:
Oil & Gas Exploration & Production
Chemicals, Lubricants & Petroleum Products
Oil Refining, Transportation & Marketing
Gas Stations

BRANDS/DIVISIONS/AFFILIATES:
China National Petroleum Corporation (CNPC)

GROWTH PLANS/SPECIAL FEATURES:
PetroChina, the national champion that inherited the majority of Chinese onshore oil and gas assets, has developed into an international supermajor. In 2024, it produced more than 1.7 billion barrels of oil equivalent of oil and gas, and processed 1.4 billion barrels of crude oil. It also has more than 22,000 service stations. The fluctuations in the prices of crude oil, refined products, chemical products, and natural gas have a significant impact on PetroChina's revenue. State-owned China National Petroleum Corp is PetroChina's controlling shareholder with a stake of more than 82%.

CONTACTS:
Note: Officers with more than one job title may be intentionally listed here more than once.

Houliang Dai, Chairman of the Board
Yongzhang Huang, Director
Daowei Zhang, Director
Lixin Ren, Director
Qijun Hou, Director

FINANCIAL DATA:
Note: Data for latest year may not have been available at press time.

In U.S. $	2024	2023	2022	2021	2020	2019
Revenue	407,843,317,528	418,231,187,671	449,653,204,823	362,917,520,428	268,450,376,797	349,377,386,683
R&D Expense	3,194,747,000	3,049,405,000	2,778,572,000	2,322,279,000	2,185,821,000	2,174,716,000
Operating Income	36,875,210,000	40,054,970,000	43,546,650,000	26,473,480,000	8,284,631,000	20,439,220,000
Operating Margin %	.09%	.10%	.10%	.07%	.03%	.06%
SGA Expense	5,906,826,000	4,582,923,000	4,409,540,000	4,756,028,000	5,147,910,000	5,553,812,000
Net Income	22,859,920,000	22,407,100,000	20,647,440,000	12,793,560,000	2,637,811,000	6,340,769,000
Operating Cash Flow	56,433,770,000	63,418,380,000	54,661,910,000	47,401,890,000	44,223,800,000	49,920,180,000
Capital Expenditure	42,013,270,000	39,217,070,000	33,837,050,000	36,864,800,000	35,638,210,000	45,360,300,000
EBITDA	68,272,830,000	67,269,320,000	62,048,250,000	52,646,280,000	38,535,060,000	47,577,770,000
Return on Assets %	.06%	.06%	.06%	.04%	.01%	.02%
Return on Equity %	.11%	.11%	.11%	.07%	.02%	.04%
Debt to Equity	.14%	.18%	.25%	.32%	0.308	0.37

CONTACT INFORMATION:
Phone: 86 1059986223   Fax: 86 1062099557
Toll-Free:
Address: 9 Dongzhimen N. St., Dongcheng Dist., Beijing, Beijing 100007 China

STOCK TICKER/OTHER:
Stock Ticker: PCCYF   Exchange: PINX
Employees: 375,803   Fiscal Year Ends: 12/31
Parent Company: China National Petroleum Corporation (CNPC)

SALARIES/BONUSES:
Top Exec. Salary: $793,000   Bonus: $
Second Exec. Salary: $646,000   Bonus: $

OTHER THOUGHTS:
Estimated Female Officers or Directors:
Hot Spot for Advancement for Women/Minorities:

Sales, profits and employees may be estimates. Financial information, benefits and other data can change quickly and may vary from those stated here.

Petroleos Mexicanos (Pemex)

www.pemex.com

NAIC Code: 211100

TYPES OF BUSINESS:

Oil & Gas Exploration & Production
Oil & Gas Transportation & Storage
Gas Stations
Refining
Petrochemicals
Pipeline Construction

BRANDS/DIVISIONS/AFFILIATES:

Pemex Transformacion Industrial
Pemex Logistica
Pemex Exploracion Y Produccion
PMI
Petroleos Mexicanos

GROWTH PLANS/SPECIAL FEATURES:

Petroleos Mexicanos (Pemex) is Mexico's national petroleum company and an essential source of revenue for the country's government. Pemex, under Mexican Law, has the exclusive right to explore, exploit, refine/produce, transport and sell crude oil and other petroleum derivatives in Mexico. Pemex stores, markets, transports and distributes its petroleum products, and also offers Pemex gas station franchise opportunities. The company's services include pipeline carriage for natural gas and liquefied petroleum gas, logistics and fuel commercialization, shipping terminals for the delivery of petrochemical products, petrochemical distribution and technical assistance for polyethylene. Pemex also builds energy pipelines. Subsidiaries include Pemex Transformacion Industrial, Pemex Logistica, Pemex Exploracion Y Produccion, PMI and Petroleos Mexicanos.

CONTACTS:
Note: Officers with more than one job title may be intentionally listed here more than once.

Octavio Romero Oropeza, CEO
Victor Diaz Solis, Dir.-Admin.
Marco Sanchez, General Counsel
Elena del Carmen Tanus Meouchi, Dir.-Finance
Tame Miguel Dominguez, CEO-Pemex Refining
Gustavo Hernandez Garcia, CEO-Pemex Exploration & Prod.
Alejandro Martinez Sibaja, CEO-Pemex Gas & Basic Petrochemicals
Manuel Sanchez Guzman, CEO-Pemex Petrochemicals
Jose Manuel Carrera Panizzo, CEO-Pemex Int'l
Francisco Arturo Heriquez Autrey, Dir.-Procurement & Supply

FINANCIAL DATA:
Note: Data for latest year may not have been available at press time.

In U.S. $	2024	2023	2022	2021	2020	2019
Revenue		101,243,289,000	135,781,280,000	52,586,286,500	47,805,715,000	74,398,000,000
R&D Expense						
Operating Income						
Operating Margin %						
SGA Expense						
Net Income			125,000,000		-25,518,054,000	-18,462,000,000
Operating Cash Flow						
Capital Expenditure						
EBITDA						
Return on Assets %						
Return on Equity %						
Debt to Equity						

CONTACT INFORMATION:

Phone: 52-55-1944--2500   Fax: 52-55-1944-8768
Toll-Free:
Address: Avenida Marina Nacional 329, Mexico City, 11311 Mexico

STOCK TICKER/OTHER:

Stock Ticker: Government-Owned   Exchange:
Employees: 123,800   Fiscal Year Ends: 12/31
Parent Company:

SALARIES/BONUSES:

Top Exec. Salary: $ Bonus: $
Second Exec. Salary: $ Bonus: $

OTHER THOUGHTS:

Estimated Female Officers or Directors:
Hot Spot for Advancement for Women/Minorities:

Pfizer Inc

NAIC Code: 325412

TYPES OF BUSINESS:

Pharmaceuticals
Biopharmaceutical
Therapeutics
Drug Development

BRANDS/DIVISIONS/AFFILIATES:

Seagen Inc

GROWTH PLANS/SPECIAL FEATURES:

Pfizer is one of the world's largest pharmaceutical firms, with annual sales close to $50 billion (excluding covid-19-related product sales). While it historically sold many types of healthcare products and chemicals, now prescription drugs and vaccines account for the majority of sales. Top sellers include pneumococcal vaccine Prevnar 13, cancer drug Ibrance, and cardiovascular treatment Eliquis. Pfizer sells these products globally, with international sales representing close to 50% of total sales. Within international sales, emerging markets are a major contributor.

CONTACTS: Note: Officers with more than one job title may be intentionally listed here more than once.

Albert Bourla, CEO
Michael McDermott, Exec. VP
David Denton, CFO
Jennifer Damico, Chief Accounting Officer
Rady Johnson, Chief Compliance Officer
G. Dolsten, Chief Scientific Officer
Lidia Fonseca, Chief Technology Officer
Douglas Lankler, Executive VP
Sally Susman, Executive VP
Payal Sahni, Executive VP
Aamir Malik, Executive VP
Chris Boshoff, Executive VP
Alexandre de Germay, Executive VP
Margaret Madden, Other Corporate Officer

FINANCIAL DATA: Note: Data for latest year may not have been available at press time.

In U.S. $	2024	2023	2022	2021	2020	2019
Revenue	63,627,001,856	59,553,001,472	101,175,001,088	81,288,003,584	41,650,999,296	40,904,998,912
R&D Expense	10,822,000,000	10,679,000,000	11,428,000,000	10,360,000,000	9,393,000,000	8,385,000,000
Operating Income	14,938,000,000	4,416,000,000	38,117,000,000	23,704,000,000	8,829,000,000	7,311,000,000
Operating Margin %	.23%	.07%	.38%	.29%	.21%	.18%
SGA Expense	14,730,000,000	14,771,000,000	13,677,000,000	12,703,000,000	11,597,000,000	12,726,000,000
Net Income	8,031,000,000	2,119,000,000	31,372,000,000	21,979,000,000	9,159,000,000	16,026,000,000
Operating Cash Flow	12,744,000,000	8,700,000,000	29,267,000,000	32,580,000,000	14,403,000,000	12,588,000,000
Capital Expenditure	2,909,000,000	3,907,000,000	3,236,000,000	2,711,000,000	2,226,000,000	2,046,000,000
EBITDA	18,127,000,000	9,557,000,000	41,031,000,000	30,793,000,000	13,262,000,000	18,649,000,000
Return on Assets %	.04%	.01%	.17%	.13%	.06%	.10%
Return on Equity %	.09%	.02%	.36%	.31%	.14%	.25%
Debt to Equity	.64%	.68%	.33%	.45%	0.562	0.549

CONTACT INFORMATION:

Phone: 212 733-2323   Fax: 212 573-7851
Toll-Free:
Address: 235 E. 42nd St., New York, NY 10017 United States

STOCK TICKER/OTHER:

Stock Ticker: PFE   Exchange: NYS
Employees: 88,000   Fiscal Year Ends: 12/31
Parent Company:

SALARIES/BONUSES:

Top Exec. Salary: $1,800,000   Bonus: $
Second Exec. Salary: Bonus: $
$1,654,300

OTHER THOUGHTS:

Estimated Female Officers or Directors: 7
Hot Spot for Advancement for Women/Minorities: Y

Pininfarina SpA

NAIC Code: 541330

www.pininfarina.it

TYPES OF BUSINESS:

Automotive Design & Engineering Services
Automotive Design
Manufacturing Design
Product Development Services
Engineering Services
Manufacturing Services
Prototype Testing
Aerodynamics Testing and Validation

BRANDS/DIVISIONS/AFFILIATES:

Mahindra Group
Pininfarina Deutschland GmbH
Pininfarina Shanghai Co Ltd
Pininfarina of America Corp
Pininfarina Wind Tunnel
Signature SRL (Pininfarina Segno)
GOODMIND SRL

CONTACTS: *Note: Officers with more than one job title may be intentionally listed here more than once.*

Silvio Pietro Angori, CEO
Marco Busi, Sr. VP-Oper.
Roberta Miniotti, Sr. VP-Finance
Roberto Mattio, Sr. VP-Human Resources & Organization
Andrea Maria Benedetto, VP-Prod. Dev.
Gabriella Isoardi, Dir.-Legal
Silvio Pietro Angori, Interim Dir.-Comm. & Image
Gianfranco Albertini, Gen. Mgr.-Investor Rel.
Fabio Filippini, Dir.-Design
Lucia Morselli, Chmn.

GROWTH PLANS/SPECIAL FEATURES:

Pininfarina SpA specializes in providing automotive and general manufacturers with services through all stages of product development, from planning, designing and development to engineering, manufacturing and end-product consultation. Wholly owned subsidiaries engaged in these business activities include Pininfarina Deutschland GmbH, Pininfarina Shanghai Co. Ltd., and Pininfarina of America Corp. From ideation to execution, Pininfarina offers a range of competencies and capabilities, including product design, product branding and low-/mid-/high-fidelity model prototyping. Pininfarina's Wind Tunnel is active in the aerodynamic and aeroacoustics field, primarily on full-scale passenger cars, supporting the realization of aerodynamic vehicles sculpted by the wind. The Wind Tunnel is a strategic tool for automotive original equipment manufacturers (OEMs) to achieve high-level standards in vehicle performance, energy consumptions and overall comfort via aerodynamic and aeroacoustics testing and validation. Pininfarina designs across other industries including nautical, architecture, consumer electronics, furniture, home appliances, industrial and vending machines, lifestyle products and transportation. Additional subsidiaries include Signature SRL (also referred to as Pininfarina Segno) creates writing instruments such as pens and related accessories; and minority owned GOODMIND SRL, is an advertising agency offering brand strategy and communication services and solutions. Moreover, Pininfarina, Bosch and Benteler have a strategic collaboration to provide car manufacturers with new modular electric vehicle platforms. These entities combine their vehicle integration expertise in order to offer a complete package for a modular, scalable and tailor-made eMobility plan. The Mahindra Group owns a majority stake in Pininfarina SpA (76.06%). Headquartered in Torino, Italy, the firm has global offices in Germany, China and the U.S.

FINANCIAL DATA: *Note: Data for latest year may not have been available at press time.*

In U.S. $	2024	2023	2022	2021	2020	2019
Revenue		99,787,000	79,127,776	75,031,692	82,287,615	101,235,000
R&D Expense						
Operating Income						
Operating Margin %						
SGA Expense						
Net Income		-1,756,000	-347,814	445,637	-30,015,347	-25,868,800
Operating Cash Flow						
Capital Expenditure						
EBITDA						
Return on Assets %						
Return on Equity %						
Debt to Equity						

CONTACT INFORMATION:

Phone: 39-011-9438111   Fax:
Toll-Free:
Address: Via Nazionale, 30, Cambiano, TO 10020 Italy

STOCK TICKER/OTHER:

Stock Ticker: PINF   Exchange: Milan
Employees: 467   Fiscal Year Ends: 12/31
Parent Company: Mahindra Group

SALARIES/BONUSES:

Top Exec. Salary: $ Bonus: $
Second Exec. Salary: $ Bonus: $

OTHER THOUGHTS:

Estimated Female Officers or Directors: 2
Hot Spot for Advancement for Women/Minorities: Y

Pioneer Corporation

NAIC Code: 334310

global.pioneer/en

TYPES OF BUSINESS:

Consumer Electronics
Audio/Video Equipment
CD/DVD Players
Automotive Electronics
Artificial Intelligent Vehicle Assistant
Personalized Driver Safety Device
Navigation Systems
Digital Accounting and Audio Solutions

BRANDS/DIVISIONS/AFFILIATES:

Pioneer Green Mobility Program

CONTACTS: Note: Officers with more than one job title may be intentionally listed here more than once.

Shiro Yahara, CEO
Masanori Koshoubu, Gen. Mgr.-R&D
Hideki Okayasu, Sr. Mgr. Dir.-Gen. Admin. Div.
Masanori Koshoubu, Mgr. Dir.-Legal & Intellectual Property Div.
Mikio Ono, Gen. Mgr.-Corp. Planning Div.
Hideki Okayasu, Sr. Mgr. Dir.-Corp. Comm.
Hideki Okayasu, Sr. Mgr. Dir.-Finance & Acct. Div.
Satoshi Matsumoto, Mgr. Dir.-Quality Assurance Div.
Mikio Ono, Gen. Mgr.-Home Audiovisual Bus.
Sanjay Dhawan, Chmn.
Tatsuo Takeuchi, Gen. Mgr.-Intl Bus. Div.

GROWTH PLANS/SPECIAL FEATURES:

Pioneer Corporation, headquartered in Japan, is a leading manufacturer of consumer electronics, primarily serving the automotive industry across six business segments. The firm operates through subsidiaries and affiliates worldwide, with products and services grouped into five business categories. The sound business develops in-car sound solutions that meet the transformative needs of the mobility industry. This division's technology expertise in speaker and enclosure design, as well as digital acoustic correction, have allowed it to develop and provide gaming speakers, PC speaker units and commercial and professional sound solutions. The original equipment (OE) solutions business supplies navigation systems, audio/video systems and speakers to leading automakers worldwide; and uses its proprietary technologies to develop and offer software applications and solutions to be incorporated into next-generation vehicles. The consumer business produces a broad range of in-car products such as navigation systems, audio/video systems, speakers and dash cams, as well as on-board/in-car Wi-Fi routers for internet connectivity. The mobility services business division provides solutions and services that help achieve a safer and more secure mobility society. This division's Pioneer Green Mobility Program is an initiative to assist drivers, businesses and municipalities in achieving carbon neutrality in the mobility environment. Last, the optical storage business offers Blu-ray and DVD drives for PCs, with high-precision reading and writing capabilities, including those capable of reading Ultra HD Blu-ray discs.

FINANCIAL DATA: Note: Data for latest year may not have been available at press time.

In U.S. $	2024	2023	2022	2021	2020	2019
Revenue	2,106,359,840	2,025,346,000	1,983,605,759	2,547,892,152	3,193,021,383	3,433,356,326
R&D Expense						
Operating Income						
Operating Margin %						
SGA Expense						
Net Income						
Operating Cash Flow						
Capital Expenditure						
EBITDA						
Return on Assets %						
Return on Equity %						
Debt to Equity						

CONTACT INFORMATION:

Phone: 81 3-6634-8777   Fax:
Toll-Free:
Address: 28-8, Honkomagome 2-chome, Bunkyo-ku, Tokyo, 113-0021 Japan

STOCK TICKER/OTHER:

Stock Ticker: Private
Employees: 8,368
Parent Company:

Exchange:
Fiscal Year Ends: 03/31

SALARIES/BONUSES:

Top Exec. Salary: $ Bonus: $
Second Exec. Salary: $ Bonus: $

OTHER THOUGHTS:

Estimated Female Officers or Directors:
Hot Spot for Advancement for Women/Minorities:

PJSC Lukoil Oil Company

www.lukoil.com

NAIC Code: 211100

TYPES OF BUSINESS:

Oil & Gas Exploration & Production
Petroleum Refining
Pipeline Operations
Gas Stations
Ocean Terminals & Oil Tankers
Natural Gas & Petrochemical Processing Plants
Solar Power
Hydroelectricity

BRANDS/DIVISIONS/AFFILIATES:

GROWTH PLANS/SPECIAL FEATURES:

PJSC Lukoil Oil Company (Lukoil) directs the financial decisions and operations of the main group's subsidiaries. Altogether, Lukoil is an integrated oil company that has exposure to the entire range of activities in the oil and gas cycle from exploration to sales of refined products. Exploration and production activities are conducted with assets located in Russia, Iraq and Uzbekistan, on offshore and onshore fields. Lukoil brings an array of petroleum products to the market through its refinery unit, including gasoline, medium distillates, dark petroleum products, lubricants, and other related products. Russia constitutes a significant portion of the group's distribution network; however, its products penetrate several different markets in Europe and the Americas.

CONTACTS: Note: Officers with more than one job title may be intentionally listed here more than once.

Vadim Vorobyev, Pres.
Ivan Maslyaev, General Counsel
Lyubov Khoba, Chief Acct.
Sergei Kukura, First VP-Finance & Economics
Gennady Fedotov, VP-Economics & Planning
Sergei Malyukov, VP-Internal Control & Audit
Ravil Maganov, First Exec. VP-OAO LUKOIL Exploration & Production
Valery Subbotin, VP-Supplies & Sales

FINANCIAL DATA: Note: Data for latest year may not have been available at press time.

In U.S. $	2024	2023	2022	2021	2020	2019
Revenue		88,828,710,000	125,135,500,000	153,129,779,200	84,008,747,008	119,914,012,672
R&D Expense						
Operating Income						
Operating Margin %						
SGA Expense						
Net Income		12,936,860,000	10,309,210,000	12,844,673,024	245,391,328	10,352,165,888
Operating Cash Flow						
Capital Expenditure						
EBITDA						
Return on Assets %						
Return on Equity %						
Debt to Equity						

CONTACT INFORMATION:

Phone: 7 4956274444   Fax: 7 4956257016
Toll-Free:
Address: 11 Sretensky Blvd., Moscow, 101000 Russia

SALARIES/BONUSES:

Top Exec. Salary: $ Bonus: $
Second Exec. Salary: $ Bonus: $

STOCK TICKER/OTHER:

Stock Ticker: LKOH   Exchange: Moscow
Employees: 102,424   Fiscal Year Ends: 12/31
Parent Company:

OTHER THOUGHTS:

Estimated Female Officers or Directors: 1
Hot Spot for Advancement for Women/Minorities:

Plexus Corp

NAIC Code: 334418

www.plexus.com

TYPES OF BUSINESS:

Telephone Apparatus Manufacturing
Hardware & Software Design
Printed Circuit Board Design
Prototyping Services
Material Procurement & Management
Logistics Services

BRANDS/DIVISIONS/AFFILIATES:

GROWTH PLANS/SPECIAL FEATURES:

Plexus Corp is a U.S based Electronic Manufacturing Services company that provides a range of services, from conceptualization and design to fulfilling orders and providing sustaining solutions, such as replenishment and refurbishment. The company's segments comprise AMER, APAC, and EMEA.

Plexus offers employees medical, dental and vision coverage; flexible spending accounts; tuition reimbursement; employee assistance programs; a 401(k); and performance-based salary increases.

CONTACTS: *Note: Officers with more than one job title may be intentionally listed here more than once.*

Todd Kelsey, CEO
Patrick Jermain, CFO
Dean Foate, Chairman of the Board
Angelo Ninivaggi, Chief Administrative Officer
Oliver Mihm, COO
Victor Tan, President, Geographical
Frank Zycinski, President, Geographical
Michael Running, President, Geographical

FINANCIAL DATA: *Note: Data for latest year may not have been available at press time.*

In U.S. $	2024	2023	2022	2021	2020	2019
Revenue	3,960,826,880	4,210,305,024	3,811,367,936	3,368,865,024	3,390,394,112	3,164,433,920
R&D Expense						
Operating Income	187,989,000	218,914,000	180,206,000	179,535,000	159,375,000	143,733,000
Operating Margin %	.05%	.05%	.05%	.05%	.05%	.05%
SGA Expense	190,541,000	175,640,000	167,023,000	143,761,000	153,331,000	148,105,000
Net Income	111,815,000	139,094,000	138,243,000	138,912,000	117,479,000	108,616,000
Operating Cash Flow	436,502,000	165,822,000	-26,240,000	142,577,000	210,368,000	115,300,000
Capital Expenditure	95,182,000	104,049,000	101,612,000	57,099,000	50,088,000	90,600,000
EBITDA	236,255,000	262,313,000	236,850,000	235,678,000	208,249,000	191,014,000
Return on Assets %	.03%	.04%	.05%	.06%	.05%	.06%
Return on Equity %	.09%	.12%	.13%	.14%	.13%	.12%
Debt to Equity	.09%	.19%	.20%	.22%	0.23	0.216

CONTACT INFORMATION:

Phone: 920 722-3451   Fax: 920 751-5395
Toll-Free: 888 208-9005
Address: One Plexus Way, P.O. Box 156, Neenah, WI 54956 United States

STOCK TICKER/OTHER:

Stock Ticker: PLXS
Employees: 25,000
Parent Company:

Exchange: NAS
Fiscal Year Ends: 10/31

SALARIES/BONUSES:

Top Exec. Salary: $1,049,231   Bonus: $
Second Exec. Salary: $635,053   Bonus: $

OTHER THOUGHTS:

Estimated Female Officers or Directors: 2
Hot Spot for Advancement for Women/Minorities:

PM Group

NAIC Code: 541330

TYPES OF BUSINESS:

Engineering Consulting Services
High-Tech Facilities
Construction Management
Facility Design
Facility Commissioning Management
Project Management
Location Selection
Procurement Services

BRANDS/DIVISIONS/AFFILIATES:

CONTACTS: Note: Officers with more than one job title may be intentionally listed here more than once.

Anthony O'Rourke, CEO
Rosita Fennell, CFO
Brendan Jennings, Chmn.

GROWTH PLANS/SPECIAL FEATURES:

PM Group is an employee-owned company that manages the design, construction and commissioning of high-tech facilities for a range of customers. The firm has been in operation since 1973 and has network offices in Europe, Asia and the U.S. PM Group collaborates with many of the world's leading private companies and major public-sector organizations, which are engaged in pharmaceuticals, medical technologies, food/beverage, consumer health, advanced manufacturing, data centers, mission-critical facilities, energy and buildings and infrastructure. Services by PM Group are offered across the complete lifecycle, and include project management, location selection, strategic project planning, architecture, master planning, engineering consulting and design, procurement, construction services, commissioning, qualification, verification, sustainability, environment, health and safety, managed services and outsourced technical services. PM Group's innovations help to improve client performance, flexibility and competitiveness. The firm focuses on service innovations and eventual client assets, with solutions including virtual reality, 4D, building information modeling (BIM), energy efficiency and food safety.

FINANCIAL DATA: Note: Data for latest year may not have been available at press time.

In U.S. $	2024	2023	2022	2021	2020	2019
Revenue	563,784,900	536,938,000	516,287,000	508,393,100	488,839,520	311,992,996
R&D Expense						
Operating Income						
Operating Margin %						
SGA Expense						
Net Income						
Operating Cash Flow						
Capital Expenditure						
EBITDA						
Return on Assets %						
Return on Equity %						
Debt to Equity						

CONTACT INFORMATION:

Phone: 353-1-404-0700   Fax: 353-1-459-9785
Toll-Free:
Address: Killakee House, Belgard Square, Tallaght, Dublin, D24 XFW2 Ireland

STOCK TICKER/OTHER:

Stock Ticker: Private   Exchange:
Employees: 3,500   Fiscal Year Ends: 12/31
Parent Company:

SALARIES/BONUSES:

Top Exec. Salary: $ Bonus: $
Second Exec. Salary: $ Bonus: $

OTHER THOUGHTS:

Estimated Female Officers or Directors:
Hot Spot for Advancement for Women/Minorities:

Porsche Automobil Holding SE

www.porsche-se.com

NAIC Code: 336111

TYPES OF BUSINESS:

Automobile Manufacturing
Sports Cars
Apparel & Accessories

BRANDS/DIVISIONS/AFFILIATES:

Volkswagen Group
Audi
SEAT
SKODA
Bentley
Bugatti
Lamborghini
Porsche

GROWTH PLANS/SPECIAL FEATURES:

Porsche Automobil Holding SE is an automotive holdings company. The company's core investment is a controlling stake in Volkswagen AG. Through this stake, Porsche SE has an interest in passenger and luxury car manufacturers which include Volkswagen, Audi, SEAT, SKODA, Bentley, Bugatti, Lamborghini, and Porsche; motorcycles under the Ducati brand name; and commercial vehicles under Volkswagen Commercial Vehicles, Scania, and MAN. In addition to the automobile manufacturers, this core investment provides Porsche Automobil exposure to the Volkswagen Financial Services financing business. Porsche SE also has a minority stake in technology company INRIX, a company that provides connected-car services and real-time traffic information.

CONTACTS:
Note: Officers with more than one job title may be intentionally listed here more than once.

Frank-Steffen Walliser, CEO
Karsten Hoeldtke, Head-Investor Rel.

FINANCIAL DATA:
Note: Data for latest year may not have been available at press time.

In U.S. $	2024	2023	2022	2021	2020	2019
Revenue	-22,544,835,003	6,157,775,189	6,174,801,369	5,256,526,753	2,998,864,784	5,132,803,492
R&D Expense						
Operating Income	-22,578,890,000	6,118,048,000	6,127,129,000	5,208,854,000	2,952,327,000	4,986,379,000
Operating Margin %		.99%	.99%	.99%	.98%	.97%
SGA Expense	9,080,590	11,350,740	17,026,110	26,106,700	23,836,550	47,673,100
Net Income	-22,720,770,000	5,759,364,000	6,233,825,000	5,182,747,000	2,977,299,000	5,002,270,000
Operating Cash Flow	1,624,291,000	2,125,993,000	897,843,400	832,009,100	877,412,000	819,523,300
Capital Expenditure						6,810,443
EBITDA	-22,461,980,000	6,178,206,000	6,138,479,000	5,209,989,000	3,017,026,000	5,010,216,000
Return on Assets %	-.19%	.04%	.05%	.12%	.07%	.13%
Return on Equity %	-.22%	.05%	.06%	.12%	.07%	.13%
Debt to Equity	.21%	.12%	.06%		0.001	0.001

CONTACT INFORMATION:

Phone: 49-711-911-0   Fax: 49-711-911-25777
Toll-Free:
Address: Porscheplatz 1, Stuttgart, BW 70435 Germany

STOCK TICKER/OTHER:

Stock Ticker: POAHY   Exchange: PINX
Employees: 42   Fiscal Year Ends: 07/31
Parent Company:

SALARIES/BONUSES:

Top Exec. Salary: $ Bonus: $
Second Exec. Salary: $ Bonus: $

OTHER THOUGHTS:

Estimated Female Officers or Directors:
Hot Spot for Advancement for Women/Minorities:

Power Construction Corporation of China Ltd (PowerChina)

ec.powerchina.cn/indexEn.html
NAIC Code: 541330

TYPES OF BUSINESS:

Engineering Consulting Services
Hydropower Engineering
Thermal Power
New Energy
Infrastructure Construction
Planning and Design
Consulting Services
Equipment Manufacturing

BRANDS/DIVISIONS/AFFILIATES:

GROWTH PLANS/SPECIAL FEATURES:

Power Construction Corporation of China (PowerChina) provides a range of services in the fields of hydropower, thermal power, new energy and infrastructure. The state-owned company's services include planning, investigation, design, consultancy, construction, mechanical/electrical installation and equipment manufacturing. PowerChina provides global engineering, procurement and construction (EPC) services, particularly in relation to the development of hydropower, water works, thermal power, new energy and transmission and distribution projects. The firm possesses state-of-the-art technology in dam engineering and construction and specializes in the installation of turbine-generator units, foundation design, construction of extra-large underground caverns, engineering/treatment of high earth/rock slopes, dredging and hydraulic fill works, construction of airport runways, design and construction of thermal and hydropower plants, design and installation of power grids, and much more. PowerChina is also engaged in real estate and investment.

CONTACTS:
Note: Officers with more than one job title may be intentionally listed here more than once.

Yanzhang Ding, Chmn.

FINANCIAL DATA:
Note: Data for latest year may not have been available at press time.

In U.S. $	2024	2023	2022	2021	2020	2019
Revenue		85,828,224,000	82,013,948,048	64,660,575,000	61,581,500,000	61,224,000,000
R&D Expense						
Operating Income						
Operating Margin %						
SGA Expense						
Net Income		1,831,986,000	1,643,849,860	1,418,009,184	527,707,000	808,300,000
Operating Cash Flow						
Capital Expenditure						
EBITDA						
Return on Assets %						
Return on Equity %						
Debt to Equity						

CONTACT INFORMATION:

Phone: 8610-58368779   Fax: 8610-68599504
Toll-Free:
Address: No.22, Chegongzhuang West Rd., Haidian Dist., Beijing, Beijing 100048 China

STOCK TICKER/OTHER:

Stock Ticker: 601669   Exchange: Shanghai
Employees: 164,165   Fiscal Year Ends: 12/31
Parent Company:

SALARIES/BONUSES:

Top Exec. Salary: $ Bonus: $
Second Exec. Salary: $ Bonus: $

OTHER THOUGHTS:

Estimated Female Officers or Directors:
Hot Spot for Advancement for Women/Minorities:

Sales, profits and employees may be estimates. Financial information, benefits and other data can change quickly and may vary from those stated here.

POWER Engineers Incorporated

www.powereng.com

NAIC Code: 541330

TYPES OF BUSINESS:

Engineering Consulting Services
Engineering Consulting
Power Delivery
Air Quality and Environmental Consulting
Water/Wastewater
Buildings
Infrastructure
Power Plant Engineering

BRANDS/DIVISIONS/AFFILIATES:

WSP Global Inc

CONTACTS: *Note: Officers with more than one job title may be intentionally listed here more than once.*

Jim Haynes, CEO

GROWTH PLANS/SPECIAL FEATURES:

POWER Engineers Incorporated (POWER) has been in business since 1976 and is an employee-owned engineering and environmental consulting firm. POWER's services include advanced distribution management systems, environmental/air quality, water/wastewater, architecture, buildings, infrastructure, asset management solutions, construction support, distributed energy resources, environmental/health/safety (EHS) compliance, corrective action, electrical studies, environmental planning and permitting, geospatial, international development, mission-critical infrastructure, owner's engineering, power plant engineering, process/packaging/controls engineering, program and project services, protection and control, routing and siting, testing and commissioning, transmission and distribution engineering, and visualization services. Industries served by the company include power delivery, power generation, renewables and storage, food and beverage, government, oil/gas/petrochemical, campus energy and agribusiness. POWER is headquartered in Idaho, with locations throughout the U.S., as well as in Canada. The firm is owned by WSP Global, Inc.

POWER offers its employees comprehensive health benefits, a wellness program, a 401(k), life and disability insurance, training and education opportunities and other company programs and perks.

FINANCIAL DATA: *Note: Data for latest year may not have been available at press time.*

In U.S. $	2024	2023	2022	2021	2020	2019
Revenue						
R&D Expense						
Operating Income						
Operating Margin %						
SGA Expense						
Net Income						
Operating Cash Flow						
Capital Expenditure						
EBITDA						
Return on Assets %						
Return on Equity %						
Debt to Equity						

CONTACT INFORMATION:

Phone: 208-788-3456   Fax: 208-788-2082
Toll-Free:
Address: 3940 Glenbrook Dr., P.O. Box 1066, Hailey, ID 83333 United States

STOCK TICKER/OTHER:

Stock Ticker: Private   Exchange:
Employees: 3,800   Fiscal Year Ends:
Parent Company: WSP Global Inc

SALARIES/BONUSES:

Top Exec. Salary: $ Bonus: $
Second Exec. Salary: $ Bonus: $

OTHER THOUGHTS:

Estimated Female Officers or Directors:
Hot Spot for Advancement for Women/Minorities:

PPD Inc

NAIC Code: 541710

www.ppd.com

TYPES OF BUSINESS:

Contract Research
Clinical Development
Clinical Trials
Laboratory Services
Outsourced Trial Services
Bio-analytics
Clinical Software and Data Integration
Pharmaceutical Development

BRANDS/DIVISIONS/AFFILIATES:

Thermo Fisher Scientific Inc
Preclarus

CONTACTS: Note: Officers with more than one job title may be intentionally listed here more than once.

David Johnston, Pres.
David Simmons, CEO
William Sharbaugh, COO
Christopher Fikry, Executive VP, Divisional
David Johnston, Executive VP, Divisional
Julia James, Executive VP
Ronald Garrow, Executive VP
Anshul Thakral, Executive VP

GROWTH PLANS/SPECIAL FEATURES:

PPD, Inc. is a global contract research organization that provides clinical trial and laboratory services to pharmaceutical, device, and diagnostic firms. PPD's clinical development division offers outsourced trial services, spanning early- and late-stage trials, as well as peri- and post-approval trials. The laboratory division offers advanced testing services, including bioanalytical, biomarkers, central lab, good manufacturing practice (GMP) and vaccine sciences. This division's Preclarus solutions enable PPD to integrate laboratory and clinical data in real-time, delivering clean data quickly. Together its laboratory services and data integration capabilities accelerate pharmaceutical development for small molecules, biologics, vaccines and cell and gene therapies. Therapeutic areas by PPD include biosimilar development, cardiovascular, cell and gene therapy, critical care, dermatology, gastroenterology, immunology, rheumatology, infectious diseases, metabolic, endocrine, nephrology, renal diseases, neuroscience research, oncology, hematology, ophthalmology, pediatrics, rare diseases, respiratory, urology, vaccine development and women's health. PPD operates as a subsidiary of Thermo Fisher Scientific, Inc.

FINANCIAL DATA: Note: Data for latest year may not have been available at press time.

In U.S. $	2024	2023	2022	2021	2020	2019
Revenue	5,395,790,400	5,138,848,000	4,941,200,000	4,868,733,009	4,681,474,048	4,031,016,960
R&D Expense						
Operating Income						
Operating Margin %						
SGA Expense						
Net Income						
Operating Cash Flow						
Capital Expenditure						
EBITDA						
Return on Assets %						
Return on Equity %						
Debt to Equity						

CONTACT INFORMATION:

Phone: 910-251-0081   Fax: 910-762-5820
Toll-Free:
Address: 929 N. Front St., Wilmington, NC 28401-3331 United States

STOCK TICKER/OTHER:

Stock Ticker: Subsidiary   Exchange:
Employees: 25,000   Fiscal Year Ends: 12/31
Parent Company: Thermo Fisher Scientific Inc

SALARIES/BONUSES:

Top Exec. Salary: $ Bonus: $
Second Exec. Salary: $ Bonus: $

OTHER THOUGHTS:

Estimated Female Officers or Directors: 2
Hot Spot for Advancement for Women/Minorities:

Primoris Services Corp

www.primoriscorp.com

NAIC Code: 541330

TYPES OF BUSINESS:

Industrial Engineering Services
Infrastructure Construction Services

BRANDS/DIVISIONS/AFFILIATES:

ARB Inc
James Construction Group LLC

GROWTH PLANS/SPECIAL FEATURES:

Primoris Services Corp is a provider of infrastructure services operating mainly in the United States and Canada. It provides a wide range of construction services, maintenance, replacement, fabrication and engineering services to a diversified base of customers. The reportable segments are the Utilities segment and the Energy segment. The Utilities segment operates in a range of services, including the installation and maintenance of new and existing natural gas and electric utility distribution and transmission systems, and communication systems. The Energy segment operates in a range of services that include engineering, procurement, and construction, retrofits, highway and bridge construction, demolition, site work, outages, pipeline construction and maintenance, and others.

CONTACTS: Note: Officers with more than one job title may be intentionally listed here more than once.

Thomas McCormick, CEO
Kenneth Dodgen, CFO
David King, Chairman of the Board
Travis Stricker, Chief Accounting Officer
John Perisich, Chief Administrative Officer
Jeremy Kinch, Other Executive Officer
Heath Moncrief, President, Divisional

FINANCIAL DATA: Note: Data for latest year may not have been available at press time.

In U.S. $	2024	2023	2022	2021	2020	2019
Revenue	6,366,837,760	5,715,309,056	4,420,598,784	3,497,632,000	3,491,496,960	3,106,329,088
R&D Expense						
Operating Income	319,894,000	258,758,000	175,308,000	186,550,000	167,379,000	141,797,000
Operating Margin %	.05%	.05%	.04%	.05%	.05%	.05%
SGA Expense	383,351,000	328,733,000	281,577,000	230,110,000	202,835,000	189,129,000
Net Income	180,888,000	126,145,000	133,021,000	115,739,000	104,983,000	82,327,000
Operating Cash Flow	508,313,000	198,552,000	83,346,000	79,747,000	313,001,000	118,946,000
Capital Expenditure	126,555,000	103,005,000	94,690,000	133,842,000	64,357,000	94,494,000
EBITDA	415,754,000	362,881,000	297,655,000	275,914,000	248,059,000	222,451,000
Return on Assets %	.05%	.03%	.04%	.05%	.06%	.05%
Return on Equity %	.14%	.11%	.13%	.14%	.16%	.13%
Debt to Equity	.70%	.93%	1.08%	.70%	0.569	0.743

CONTACT INFORMATION:

Phone: 214 740-5600   Fax:
Toll-Free:
Address: 2300 N. Field St., Ste. 1900, Dallas, TX 75201 United States

STOCK TICKER/OTHER:

Stock Ticker: PRIM   Exchange: NYS
Employees: 14,058   Fiscal Year Ends: 12/31
Parent Company:

SALARIES/BONUSES:

Top Exec. Salary: $929,769   Bonus: $
Second Exec. Salary: $575,673   Bonus: $

OTHER THOUGHTS:

Estimated Female Officers or Directors:
Hot Spot for Advancement for Women/Minorities:

PTC Inc

NAIC Code: 511210N

www.ptc.com

TYPES OF BUSINESS:

Computer Software-Engineering & Manufacturing
Engineering Consulting Services
Enterprise Publishing Software
Product Data Management

GROWTH PLANS/SPECIAL FEATURES:

PTC offers high-end computer-assisted design (Creo) and product lifecycle management (Windchill) software as well as Internet of Things and AR industrial solutions. Founded in 1985, PTC has 28,000 customers, with revenue stemming mostly from North America and Europe.

PTC offers its employees health and wealth benefits programs.

BRANDS/DIVISIONS/AFFILIATES:

Creo
Windchill
Onshape
ThingWorx
Vuforia
Arena Solutions

CONTACTS: Note: Officers with more than one job title may be intentionally listed here more than once.

Neil Barua, CEO
Kristian Talvitie, CFO
Janice Chaffin, Chairman of the Board
Alice Christenson, Chief Accounting Officer
Catherine Kniker, Chief Marketing Officer
Aaron Von Staats, Executive VP
Robert Dahdah, Executive VP

FINANCIAL DATA: Note: Data for latest year may not have been available at press time.

In U.S. $	2024	2023	2022	2021	2020	2019
Revenue	2,298,471,936	2,097,053,056	1,933,346,944	1,807,159,040	1,458,414,976	1,255,630,976
R&D Expense	433,047,000	394,370,000	338,822,000	299,917,000	256,575,000	246,888,000
Operating Income	587,260,000	458,014,000	483,596,000	382,959,000	243,579,000	114,156,000
Operating Margin %	.26%	.22%	.25%	.21%	.17%	.09%
SGA Expense	791,331,000	763,641,000	689,979,000	723,785,000	595,277,000	545,368,000
Net Income	376,333,000	245,540,000	313,081,000	476,923,000	130,695,000	-27,460,000
Operating Cash Flow	749,984,000	610,861,000	435,326,000	368,809,000	233,808,000	285,145,000
Capital Expenditure	18,368,000	24,614,000	25,947,000	25,263,000	31,246,000	64,411,000
EBITDA	730,022,000	599,145,000	573,406,000	564,767,000	330,638,000	141,171,000
Return on Assets %	.06%	.04%	.07%	.12%	.04%	- .01%
Return on Equity %	.13%	.10%	.14%	.27%	.10%	- .03%
Debt to Equity	.43%	.69%	.66%	.79%	0.824	0.557

CONTACT INFORMATION:

Phone: 781 370-5000   Fax: 781 370-6000
Toll-Free: 877-275-4782
Address: 121 Seaport Blvd., Boston, MA 02210 United States

STOCK TICKER/OTHER:

Stock Ticker: PTC   Exchange: NAS
Employees: 7,501   Fiscal Year Ends: 09/30
Parent Company:

SALARIES/BONUSES:

Top Exec. Salary: $800,000   Bonus: $
Second Exec. Salary: $575,000   Bonus: $

OTHER THOUGHTS:

Estimated Female Officers or Directors: 1
Hot Spot for Advancement for Women/Minorities:

Qualcomm Incorporated

NAIC Code: 334413

www.qualcomm.com

TYPES OF BUSINESS:

Telecommunications Equipment
Digital Wireless Communications Products
Integrated Circuits
Mobile Communications Systems
Wireless Software & Services
E-Mail Software
Code Division Multiple Access

BRANDS/DIVISIONS/AFFILIATES:

GROWTH PLANS/SPECIAL FEATURES:

Qualcomm develops and licenses wireless technology and designs chips for smartphones. The company's key patents revolve around CDMA and OFDMA technologies, which are standards in wireless communications that are the backbone of all 3G, 4G, and 5G networks. Qualcomm's IP is licensed by virtually all wireless device makers. The firm is also the world's largest wireless chip vendor, supplying nearly every premier handset maker with leading-edge processors. Qualcomm also sells RF-front end modules into smartphones, as well as chips into automotive and Internet of Things markets.

U.S. employees of the company receive medical, dental and vision insurance; dependent/health care reimbursement accounts; tuition reimbursement; a 401(k); and an employee stock purchase plan.

CONTACTS: Note: Officers with more than one job title may be intentionally listed here more than once.

Cristiano Amon, CEO
Akash Palkhiwala, CFO
Mark McLaughlin, Chairman of the Board
Neil Martin, Chief Accounting Officer
Baaziz Achour, Chief Technology Officer
Ann Chaplin, General Counsel
James Thompson, Other Executive Officer
Heather Ace, Other Executive Officer
Alexander Rogers, President, Divisional

FINANCIAL DATA: Note: Data for latest year may not have been available at press time.

In U.S. $	2024	2023	2022	2021	2020	2019
Revenue	38,961,999,872	35,819,999,232	44,200,001,536	33,565,999,104	23,530,999,808	24,273,000,448
R&D Expense	8,893,000,000	8,818,000,000	8,194,000,000	7,176,000,000	5,975,000,000	5,398,000,000
Operating Income	10,071,000,000	7,788,000,000	15,860,000,000	9,789,000,000	6,255,000,000	7,667,000,000
Operating Margin %	.26%	.22%	.36%	.29%	.27%	.32%
SGA Expense	2,759,000,000	2,483,000,000	2,570,000,000	2,339,000,000	2,074,000,000	2,195,000,000
Net Income	10,142,000,000	7,232,000,000	12,936,000,000	9,043,000,000	5,198,000,000	4,386,000,000
Operating Cash Flow	12,202,000,000	11,299,000,000	9,095,999,000	10,536,000,000	5,814,000,000	7,286,000,000
Capital Expenditure	1,041,000,000	1,450,000,000	2,262,000,000	1,888,000,000	1,407,000,000	887,000,000
EBITDA	12,739,000,000	9,946,000,000	17,250,000,000	12,415,000,000	7,714,000,000	9,509,000,000
Return on Assets %	.19%	.14%	.29%	.24%	.15%	.13%
Return on Equity %	.42%	.37%	.93%	1.13%	.95%	1.53%
Debt to Equity	.51%	.67%	.75%	1.38%	2.506	2.737

CONTACT INFORMATION:

Phone: 858 587-1121   Fax: 858 658-2100
Toll-Free:
Address: 5775 Morehouse Dr., San Diego, CA 92121-1714 United States

STOCK TICKER/OTHER:

Stock Ticker: QCOM   Exchange: NAS
Employees: 49,000   Fiscal Year Ends: 09/30
Parent Company:

SALARIES/BONUSES:

Top Exec. Salary: $1,350,000   Bonus: $
Second Exec. Salary: $900,058   Bonus: $

OTHER THOUGHTS:

Estimated Female Officers or Directors: 2
Hot Spot for Advancement for Women/Minorities: Y

QuTech
NAIC Code: 334111

qutech.nl

TYPES OF BUSINESS:
Electronic Computer Manufacturing
Quantum Technology
Quantum Engineering
Qubit Research and Development
Quantum Computing
Quantum Internet
Quantum Hardware and Software
Quantum Stack Development

BRANDS/DIVISIONS/AFFILIATES:
Delft Univeristy of Technology
Netherlands Organization for Applied Scientific
Qubit Research
QuTech Academy
Quantum for Business

CONTACTS: Note: Officers with more than one job title may be intentionally listed here more than once.
Charlotte van Hees, Dir.-Ops.
Kees Eijkel, Dir.-Bus. Dev.

GROWTH PLANS/SPECIAL FEATURES:
QuTech, which stands for quantum technology, is engaged in the researching and engineering of quantum computing and quantum internet technologies. Quantum technology is an energy technology based on the fields of physics and engineering, and transitions some of the properties of quantum mechanics into practical computing/internet applications. Founded in 2015 by Delft University of Technology and the Netherlands Organization for Applied Scientific Research (TNO), the center has transformed from a being university-based research division to a quantum science technology engineering entity. Currently, QuTech operates through three divisions: Qubit Research, quantum internet and quantum computing. Qubit Research works to develop novel qubits that are protected from noise by design so that QuTech can eventually build a scalable quantum computer. Qubit Research has four research labs: Andersen Lab, engaged in protected superconducting qubits; Goswami Lab, engaged in topological qubits in two dimensional structures; Kouwenhoven Lab, engaged in superconductor-semiconductor hybrid devices; and Wimmer Group, engaged in quantum device theory. The quantum internet division aims to develop technologies that will enable quantum communication between any two places on earth, with some applications having been identified. This division's goals are to develop a full control stack and novel applications for a quantum internet. The quantum computing division aims to develop different layers of hardware and software to create a quantum computing stack. The basis of the stack (the quantum chip) contains the qubits; therefore, this division investigates various types of approaches for the stack, such as electronic spins in quantum dots and superconducting quantum circuits and develops the system architecture that connects and translates quantum algorithms to the low-level pulses that operate on the qubits of quantum processors. QuTech Academy offers bachelor's and master's degrees, as well as scholarships. Quantum for Business is a collaboration platform for inspiration, education and community building.

FINANCIAL DATA: Note: Data for latest year may not have been available at press time.

In U.S. $	2024	2023	2022	2021	2020	2019
Revenue						
R&D Expense						
Operating Income						
Operating Margin %						
SGA Expense						
Net Income						
Operating Cash Flow						
Capital Expenditure						
EBITDA						
Return on Assets %						
Return on Equity %						
Debt to Equity						

CONTACT INFORMATION:
Phone: 31 15-27-86-133   Fax:
Toll-Free:
Address: Lorentzweg 1, Bldg. 22, Delft, 2628 CJ Netherlands

STOCK TICKER/OTHER:
Stock Ticker: Private   Exchange:
Employees: 306   Fiscal Year Ends:
Parent Company:

SALARIES/BONUSES:
Top Exec. Salary: $ Bonus: $
Second Exec. Salary: $ Bonus: $

OTHER THOUGHTS:
Estimated Female Officers or Directors:
Hot Spot for Advancement for Women/Minorities:

Ramboll Group A/S

www.ramboll.com

NAIC Code: 541330

TYPES OF BUSINESS:

Engineering Consulting Services
Engineering
Consulting
Buildings
Transportation Structures
Water/Wastewater
Power Generation and Transmission
Architecture and Landscape

BRANDS/DIVISIONS/AFFILIATES:

Ramboll Foundation
Opseyes
SafetyWize
HABAlert
BloomOptix
EHS Compass
Galago

CONTACTS: Note: Officers with more than one job title may be intentionally listed here more than once.

Jens-Peter Saul, CEO
Eva Kienle, CFO
Lone Tvis, Chief People Officer
Claus Hemmingsen, Chmn.

GROWTH PLANS/SPECIAL FEATURES:

Ramboll Group A/S (Ramboll) was founded in 1945 and is a global engineering, architecture and consultancy that operates across 35 countries. The firm offers its services in the sectors of energy, water, resources and waste, transport, real estate, industrial, government and public, finance and investment, technology and healthcare facilities. Services offered by Ramboll include engineering and design, architecture and landscape, environmental and nature-based services, management consulting, ESG and sustainability advisory, planning and project management, health, safety and risk, society and social value, operations and asset management. Ramboll is privately-owned by Ramboll Foundation. Products that the firm holds are Opseyes, a wastewater testing agent; Galago, geospatial intelligence for sustainable land management and biodiversity restoration; EHS Compass, helping customers navigate environment, health and safety related issues within their organization; SafetyWize, which provides users with safer road environments by showing dangerous locations in real time based on real-world data and expert knowledge; and BloomOptix, which enables intelligent and timely algal bloom decision-making while utilizing its newest innovation, the HABAlert system.

FINANCIAL DATA: Note: Data for latest year may not have been available at press time.

In U.S. $	2024	2023	2022	2021	2020	2019
Revenue	2,644,789,350	2,518,847,000	2,335,088,000	2,164,145,396	2,247,180,000	2,127,010,000
R&D Expense						
Operating Income						
Operating Margin %						
SGA Expense						
Net Income		57,814,000	55,957,000	48,179,470	21,343,900	25,769,100
Operating Cash Flow						
Capital Expenditure						
EBITDA						
Return on Assets %						
Return on Equity %						
Debt to Equity						

CONTACT INFORMATION:

Phone: 45-5161-1000   Fax: 45-5161-1001
Toll-Free:
Address: Hannemanns Alle 53, Copenhagen, DK-2300 Denmark

STOCK TICKER/OTHER:

Stock Ticker: Private   Exchange:
Employees: 18,300   Fiscal Year Ends: 12/31
Parent Company: Ramboll Foundation

SALARIES/BONUSES:

Top Exec. Salary: $ Bonus: $
Second Exec. Salary: $ Bonus: $

OTHER THOUGHTS:

Estimated Female Officers or Directors:
Hot Spot for Advancement for Women/Minorities:

Reality Labs

NAIC Code: 511210G

TYPES OF BUSINESS:

Computer Software, Electronic Games, Apps & Entertainment
Virtual Reality Technology
Augmented Reality Technology
Software Development
Hardware Development
VR/AR Products
Artificial Intelligence
Machine Learning

BRANDS/DIVISIONS/AFFILIATES:

Meta Platforms Inc
Oculus
Spark AR

CONTACTS: Note: Officers with more than one job title may be intentionally listed here more than once.

Mark Zuckerberg, CEO
Javier Olivan, COO
Susan Li, CFO
Chris Cox, Chief Product Officer
Lori Goler, Head of People
Andrew Bosworth, CTO
Mark Zuckerberg, Chmn.

GROWTH PLANS/SPECIAL FEATURES:

Reality Labs is the virtual reality/augmented reality (VR/AR) division of Meta Platforms, Inc. It builds VR/AR software and hardware that enables people to feel connected to/with almost anything, anywhere at any time. Reality Labs' primary technologies include Oculus, a VR headset that allows users to connect with friends and other users, no matter the location of other users; and Spark AR, the firm's AR creation platform that makes it both easy and scalable to help create big ideas. The business comprises a team of scientists and engineers which create solutions via computer science and related fields such as artificial intelligence, machine learning, neural control interface, life-like haptic interaction, audio enhancement and full-body tracking. These technologies, along with software and hardware products expand the possibilities of human connection and collaboration. Oculus and Spark AR can teleport users into a room with another real person or into virtual experiences, all of which is referred to as the Metaverse.

FINANCIAL DATA: Note: Data for latest year may not have been available at press time.

In U.S. $	2024	2023	2022	2021	2020	2019
Revenue						
R&D Expense						
Operating Income						
Operating Margin %						
SGA Expense						
Net Income						
Operating Cash Flow						
Capital Expenditure						
EBITDA						
Return on Assets %						
Return on Equity %						
Debt to Equity						

CONTACT INFORMATION:

Phone: 949-274-9947   Fax:
Toll-Free:
Address: 1601 Willow Rd., Menlo Park, CA 94025 United States

STOCK TICKER/OTHER:

Stock Ticker: Subsidiary   Exchange:
Employees: Fiscal Year Ends:
Parent Company: Meta Platforms Inc

SALARIES/BONUSES:

Top Exec. Salary: $ Bonus: $
Second Exec. Salary: $ Bonus: $

OTHER THOUGHTS:

Estimated Female Officers or Directors:
Hot Spot for Advancement for Women/Minorities:

Regulus Group LLC

www.regulus-group.com

NAIC Code: 541330

TYPES OF BUSINESS:

Engineering Services
Air Traffic Systems Engineering
Air Traffic Program Management
Aviation Test Tools and Data Analytics
Air Safety Strategy Development
National Airspace System Solutions
Planning, Development and Deployment
Aviation Radar and Networking Solutions

BRANDS/DIVISIONS/AFFILIATES:

CONTACTS: *Note: Officers with more than one job title may be intentionally listed here more than once.*

Karl Roulston, Managing Dir.

GROWTH PLANS/SPECIAL FEATURES:

Regulus Group, LLC is a provider of systems engineering, program management and air traffic support for multiple Federal Aviation Administration (FAA) and Department of Defense (DOD) programs. The firm's integrated service offerings enable collaboration across critical disciplines. Regulus' systems engineering division solves complex problems and programs in the aviation industry, with expertise in specialized areas such as radar, networking, automation, safety and human factors. This division develops test tools, data analysis capabilities, modeling and simulation tools; works with U.S. and international standards bodies to maintain existing standards documents and develop requirements for advanced surveillance applications; and develops, coordinates, assesses and implements project-specific safety strategies and products. The program management division offers data-driven, informed decision-making solutions and baseline management for customers faced with time-sensitive, critical decisions on a daily basis. This division develops an understanding of the strategic and technological aspects of the current situation and develops processes, dashboards, analysis and data deliverables to provide a comprehensive grasp across the entire political, technical and financial spectrum. Last, the air traffic support division consists of air traffic controllers (ATC) with diverse experience in all domains and levels of ATC functionality, which provide expertise during the planning, development and deployment of national airspace system (NAS) enhancements. This division's focus is air traffic operations and utilizes an integrated approach that blends communication with knowledge of air traffic systems and operations. Based in Virginia, Regulus has additional strategic locations: Washington DC, located next to FAA headquarters; New Jersey, located near the FAA Technical Center; and Oklahoma, located near the Mike Monroney Aeronautical Center.

FINANCIAL DATA: *Note: Data for latest year may not have been available at press time.*

In U.S. $	2024	2023	2022	2021	2020	2019
Revenue						
R&D Expense						
Operating Income						
Operating Margin %						
SGA Expense						
Net Income						
Operating Cash Flow						
Capital Expenditure						
EBITDA						
Return on Assets %						
Return on Equity %						
Debt to Equity						

CONTACT INFORMATION:

Phone: 540-459-2142   Fax:
Toll-Free:
Address: 102 N. Main St., Woodstock, VA 22664 United States

STOCK TICKER/OTHER:

Stock Ticker: Private   Exchange:
Employees: Fiscal Year Ends:
Parent Company:

SALARIES/BONUSES:

Top Exec. Salary: $ Bonus: $
Second Exec. Salary: $ Bonus: $

OTHER THOUGHTS:

Estimated Female Officers or Directors:
Hot Spot for Advancement for Women/Minorities:

Renault SA

NAIC Code: 336111

TYPES OF BUSINESS:

Automobile Manufacturing
Automobile
Manufacture
Electric Vehicles
Mobility
Sport Cars

BRANDS/DIVISIONS/AFFILIATES:

Renault
Dacia
LADA
Alpine
Mobilize
Twingo
Sandero
Mobilize EZ-1

GROWTH PLANS/SPECIAL FEATURES:

Renault manufactures and sells around 2.3 million vehicles per year. On a global scale, it is relatively small, with just over 2% market share. With around 80% of its revenue sourced from only three brands, Renault, Dacia, and Alpine, in Europe, the company is the third-largest player, with Renault being the third-largest single brand in Europe. Its alliance with Nissan allows it to leverage the scale of 6 million vehicles by sharing platform infrastructure, capacity, and R&D.

CONTACTS: Note: Officers with more than one job title may be intentionally listed here more than once.

Luca de Meo, CEO
Jean-Dominique Senard, Chairman of the Board

FINANCIAL DATA: Note: Data for latest year may not have been available at press time.

In U.S. $	2024	2023	2022	2021	2020	2019
Revenue	63,827,470,597	59,450,622,611	52,585,698,708	47,286,037,263	49,346,199,735	63,038,593,085
R&D Expense	2,581,158,000	2,433,598,000	2,412,032,000	2,625,426,000	2,916,004,000	3,017,026,000
Operating Income	4,624,290,000	4,468,785,000	2,994,325,000	1,116,913,000	-624,290,600	2,934,166,000
Operating Margin %	.07%	.08%	.06%	.02%	-.01%	.05%
SGA Expense	5,896,708,000	5,335,982,000	5,132,804,000	5,077,185,000	5,658,343,000	6,301,929,000
Net Income	853,575,500	2,494,892,000	-401,816,100	1,007,946,000	-9,089,671,000	-160,045,400
Operating Cash Flow	8,128,263,000	5,064,699,000	4,101,021,000	2,734,393,000	6,530,079,000	6,355,278,000
Capital Expenditure	3,362,088,000	3,477,866,000	3,046,538,000	2,796,822,000	4,549,375,000	5,812,713,000
EBITDA	5,788,877,000	7,257,661,000	6,844,495,000	6,045,403,000	-2,843,360,000	6,465,380,000
Return on Assets %	.01%	.02%	.00%	.01%	-.07%	.00%
Return on Equity %	.03%	.07%	-.01%	.03%	-.27%	.00%
Debt to Equity	.22%	.28%	.36%	.47%	0.521	0.241

CONTACT INFORMATION:

Phone: 33 176840404   Fax:
Toll-Free:
Address: 13-15, quai Le Gallo, Billancourt, 92100 France

STOCK TICKER/OTHER:

Stock Ticker: RNSDF   Exchange: PINX
Employees: 183,002   Fiscal Year Ends: 12/31
Parent Company:

SALARIES/BONUSES:

Top Exec. Salary: $ Bonus: $
Second Exec. Salary: $ Bonus: $

OTHER THOUGHTS:

Estimated Female Officers or Directors: 7
Hot Spot for Advancement for Women/Minorities: Y

Resonac Holdings Corp

NAIC Code: 325110

TYPES OF BUSINESS:

Petrochemical Manufacturing
Aluminum
Electronic Components
Basic & Specialty Chemicals
Ceramic Materials
Carbon Nanofiber
Graphite

BRANDS/DIVISIONS/AFFILIATES:

Showa Denko Gas Products Co Ltd
Union Showa KK
Showa Denko Kenzai KK
Showa Denko Packaging Co Ltd
Showa Denko Aluminum Trading KK
Showa Denko Photonics Co Ltd

GROWTH PLANS/SPECIAL FEATURES:

Resonac Holdings Corp manufactures and sells chemicals, aluminum, and electronics. The firm organizes itself into four segments, which are the Semiconductor and Electronic materials segment, the Mobility segment, the Chemicals segment, and the Innovations Enabling segment. Geographically the company derives sales from Japan, China, Asia excluding Japan and China, and the rest of the world. The majority of sales are derived from Japan.

CONTACTS: Note: Officers with more than one job title may be intentionally listed here more than once.

Hidehito Takahashi, CEO
Hideki Somemiya, CFO
Kohei Morikawa, Chairman of the Board
Tomomitsu Maoka, Chief Strategy Officer
Nori Imai, Director

FINANCIAL DATA: Note: Data for latest year may not have been available at press time.

In U.S. $	2024	2023	2022	2021	2020	2019
Revenue	9,660,372,521	8,993,301,192	9,668,293,805	9,855,839,425	6,759,928,058	6,293,071,400
R&D Expense						
Operating Income	618,133,800	-65,308,250	428,540,700	605,373,500	-135,025,000	838,642,100
Operating Margin %	.06%	-.01%	.04%	.06%	-.02%	.13%
SGA Expense	1,686,587,000	1,711,164,000				
Net Income	510,295,700	-45,161,070	225,090,300	-83,962,790	-529,741,800	507,414,600
Operating Cash Flow	1,136,164,000	824,180,800	689,919,500	800,354,100	758,719,800	545,362,400
Capital Expenditure	613,107,500	593,994,800	609,948,600	470,293,000	447,792,300	282,616,000
EBITDA	1,378,888,000	674,375,200	1,218,384,000	1,030,117,000	115,877,500	957,650,600
Return on Assets %	.03%	.00%	.02%	-.01%	-.05%	.07%
Return on Equity %	.12%	-.01%	.06%	-.03%	-.17%	.15%
Debt to Equity	1.33%	1.61%	1.77%	1.33%	2.233	0.428

CONTACT INFORMATION:

Phone: 81-3-5470-3235   Fax: 81-3-3431-6215
Toll-Free:
Address: 13-9, Shiba Daimon 1-Chome, Tokyo, 105-8518 Japan

STOCK TICKER/OTHER:

Stock Ticker: SHWDY   Exchange: PINX
Employees: 25,803   Fiscal Year Ends: 12/31
Parent Company:

SALARIES/BONUSES:

Top Exec. Salary: $ Bonus: $
Second Exec. Salary: $ Bonus: $

OTHER THOUGHTS:

Estimated Female Officers or Directors:
Hot Spot for Advancement for Women/Minorities:

Sales, profits and employees may be estimates. Financial information, benefits and other data can change quickly and may vary from those stated here.

Rheinmetall AG

NAIC Code: 336300

TYPES OF BUSINESS:

Automotive Components Manufacturing
Military Vehicles
Weapons & Ammunition
Defense Electronics
Air Defense Systems
Command & Control Systems
Reconnaissance Systems
Training & Simulator Operations

BRANDS/DIVISIONS/AFFILIATES:

Rheinmetall Defence AG
Rheinmetall Automotive AG

GROWTH PLANS/SPECIAL FEATURES:

Rheinmetall is an international group active in various markets with leading technological products and services. The sales focus is on the security technology and mobility segments. Since February 2021, the group structure has been made up of five divisions, vehicle systems, weapons and ammunition, electronic solutions, sensors and actuators, and materials and trade. The vehicle systems, weapons and ammunition, and electronic solutions divisions are among the defense and security industry's leading suppliers of innovative products to German and international defense forces. The sensors and actuators and materials and trade divisions' core area of expertise is the reduction of emissions, pollutants, and fuel consumption.

CONTACTS: Note: Officers with more than one job title may be intentionally listed here more than once.

Ulrich Grillo, Chairman of the Board
Daniel Hay, Deputy Chairman

FINANCIAL DATA: Note: Data for latest year may not have been available at press time.

In U.S. $	2024	2023	2022	2021	2020	2019
Revenue	11,068,104,511	8,145,289,453	7,275,822,791	6,422,247,308	6,135,074,004	7,099,886,573
R&D Expense						
Operating Income	1,597,049,000	969,353,000	855,845,600	696,935,300	494,892,200	547,105,500
Operating Margin %	.14%	.12%	.12%	.11%	.08%	.08%
SGA Expense	362,088,500	299,659,500	265,607,300	179,341,700	171,396,100	202,043,100
Net Income	813,847,900	607,264,400	538,025,000	330,306,500	-30,646,990	380,249,700
Operating Cash Flow	1,952,327,000	843,359,800	197,502,800	783,200,900	514,188,400	683,314,400
Capital Expenditure	830,874,000	451,759,400	396,140,700	307,605,000	269,012,500	326,901,200
EBITDA	2,005,675,000	1,400,681,000	1,135,074,000	984,109,000	805,902,400	911,464,300
Return on Assets %	.06%	.05%	.06%	.04%	.00%	.05%
Return on Equity %	.19%	.17%	.18%	.14%	-.01%	.16%
Debt to Equity	.46%	.45%	.18%	.29%	0.462	0.414

CONTACT INFORMATION:

Phone: 49-211-473-01   Fax: 49-21-473-4727
Toll-Free:
Address: Rheinmetall Platz 1, Dusseldorf, 40476 Germany

STOCK TICKER/OTHER:

Stock Ticker: RNMBY   Exchange: PINX
Employees: 24,753   Fiscal Year Ends: 12/31
Parent Company:

SALARIES/BONUSES:

Top Exec. Salary: $ Bonus: $
Second Exec. Salary: $ Bonus: $

OTHER THOUGHTS:

Estimated Female Officers or Directors:
Hot Spot for Advancement for Women/Minorities:

Ricardo plc

NAIC Code: 541330

www.ricardo.com

TYPES OF BUSINESS:

Engineering Services, Incl Civil, Mechanical, Electronic, Computer &
Environmental
Consulting and Technical Services
Software

GROWTH PLANS/SPECIAL FEATURES:

Ricardo PLC is a provider of business solutions in the United
Kingdom. The company's operating segments include Energy
& Environment, Rail, Automotive and Industrial, Defense, and
Performance Products. Its Automotive and Industrial segment
generates majority of the revenue for the company. The
company operates in the UK, Mainland Europe, North America,
China, Australia, the Rest of Asia, and the Rest of the World.

BRANDS/DIVISIONS/AFFILIATES:

Ricardo Certification

CONTACTS: Note: Officers with more than one job title may be intentionally listed here more than once.

Peter Gilchrist,
Graham Ritchie, CEO
Judith Cottrell, CFO
Mark Clare, Chairman of the Board
Harpreet Sagoo, General Counsel

FINANCIAL DATA: Note: Data for latest year may not have been available at press time.

In U.S. $	2024	2023	2022	2021	2020	2019
Revenue	639,088,613	599,372,763	511,863,262	462,723,312	473,897,602	517,517,722
R&D Expense						
Operating Income	46,043,460	42,004,560	33,253,610	20,733,020	18,848,200	47,928,280
Operating Margin %	.07%	.07%	.06%	.04%	.04%	.09%
SGA Expense	130,321,800	123,455,700	122,244,000	126,282,900	129,783,300	129,648,700
Net Income	942,410	-7,000,760	11,578,180	2,288,710	-8,750,950	26,656,740
Operating Cash Flow	34,869,170	13,328,370	58,698,680	34,869,170	31,907,310	33,926,760
Capital Expenditure	15,213,190	14,270,780	18,982,830	18,040,420	42,004,560	22,483,210
EBITDA	44,697,160	49,139,950	56,409,930	43,081,600	39,985,110	60,448,870
Return on Assets %	.00%	-.01%	.02%	.00%	-.02%	.06%
Return on Equity %	.00%	-.03%	.05%	.01%	-.04%	.12%
Debt to Equity	.73%	.67%	.47%	.52%	1.021	0.465

CONTACT INFORMATION:

Phone: 44 1273455611   Fax: 44 1273464124
Toll-Free:
Address: Shoreham Technical Ctr., Shoreham-by-Sea, West Sussex,
BN43 5FG United Kingdom

STOCK TICKER/OTHER:

Stock Ticker: RCDOF   Exchange: PINX
Employees: 2,933   Fiscal Year Ends: 06/30
Parent Company:

SALARIES/BONUSES:

Top Exec. Salary: $661,033   Bonus: $484,668
Second Exec. Salary: Bonus: $298,879
$498,131

OTHER THOUGHTS:

Estimated Female Officers or Directors:
Hot Spot for Advancement for Women/Minorities:

Ricoh Company Ltd

www.ricoh.com

NAIC Code: 333316

TYPES OF BUSINESS:

Photographic and Photocopying Equipment Manufacturing
Network Systems
Printers, Copiers & Fax Machines
PCs & Servers
Accessories
Digital Cameras
Electronic Devices
Managed Print Services

BRANDS/DIVISIONS/AFFILIATES:

GROWTH PLANS/SPECIAL FEATURES:

Ricoh Co Ltd provides products, services, and solutions in offices and other environments. The company's Imaging and Solutions segment is engaged in office imaging, production printing, and network system solutions. Industrial Products segment manufactures and sales of thermal media, optical equipment, semiconductors, electronic component and the Inkjet head. Its Other segment is engaged in manufacturing and sales of digital cameras, financing business and logistics services provided by the company's subsidiaries. The company's revenue is majorly derived from Japan.

CONTACTS: Note: Officers with more than one job title may be intentionally listed here more than once.

Yoshinori Yamashita, CEO
Mutsuko Hatano, Chairman of the Board
Seiji Sakata, Chief Technology Officer
Akira Oyama, Director

FINANCIAL DATA: Note: Data for latest year may not have been available at press time.

In U.S. $	2024	2023	2022	2021	2020	2019
Revenue	16,307,879,764	14,816,579,008	12,209,018,687	11,677,791,243	13,944,598,931	13,976,868,269
R&D Expense						
Operating Income	434,893,100	547,139,700	280,186,000	-289,100,300	548,826,700	606,914,800
Operating Margin %	.03%	.04%	.02%	-.02%	.04%	.04%
SGA Expense	5,344,418,000	4,777,534,000	4,167,377,000	4,302,555,000	4,571,196,000	4,879,978,000
Net Income	306,692,600	377,443,800	210,851,200	-227,228,500	274,548,700	343,835,100
Operating Cash Flow	872,098,000	463,121,400	572,493,800	881,435,700	810,198,600	568,918,400
Capital Expenditure	613,753,200	559,670,900	493,210,200	464,690,400	789,947,300	708,490,700
EBITDA	1,292,183,000	1,297,424,000	962,697,900	466,585,700	1,422,508,000	1,292,815,000
Return on Assets %	.02%	.03%	.02%	-.01%	.01%	.02%
Return on Equity %	.04%	.06%	.03%	-.04%	.04%	.05%
Debt to Equity	.24%	.26%	.18%	.20%	0.181	0.715

CONTACT INFORMATION:

Phone: 81 3-3777-8111   Fax:
Toll-Free:
Address: 3-6, Nakamagome 1-chome, Ohta-ku, Tokyo, 143-8555 Japan

STOCK TICKER/OTHER:

Stock Ticker: RICOY   Exchange: PINX
Employees: 92,663   Fiscal Year Ends: 03/31
Parent Company:

SALARIES/BONUSES:

Top Exec. Salary: $ Bonus: $
Second Exec. Salary: $ Bonus: $

OTHER THOUGHTS:

Estimated Female Officers or Directors:
Hot Spot for Advancement for Women/Minorities:

Sales, profits and employees may be estimates. Financial information, benefits and other data can change quickly and may vary from those stated here.

RIZZO International Inc

www.rizzointl.com

NAIC Code: 541330

TYPES OF BUSINESS:

Engineering Consulting Services
Engineering Consultancy
Earth Sciences Consultancy
Design
Analysis
Testing
Quality Assurance

BRANDS/DIVISIONS/AFFILIATES:

GROWTH PLANS/SPECIAL FEATURES:

RIZZO International, Inc. was founded in 1984 and provides economical and technical solutions regarding complex engineering and engineering-related issues. As a consultancy, RIZZO has expertise in special civil, geotechnical and structural analysis and design, as well as modeling techniques and strategies. Services by RIZZO include dams and water resources engineering, geotechnical engineering, nuclear engineering, structural and seismic engineering, seismic hazard analysis, hydrologic and hydraulic engineering, geologic and hydrogeologic investigation, testing and inspection and construction support services. Clients of the firm include FirstEnergy, Orange & Rockland, Nuscale, ConsolEnergy, Entergy Nuclear, Duke Energy, Eskom, Curtiss-Wright and many others. Headquartered in Pennsylvania, RIZZO has office locations in Colorado, Florida, South Carolina, New Mexico and New York, as well as collaborative relationships with firms worldwide.

CONTACTS: Note: Officers with more than one job title may be intentionally listed here more than once.

Rachelle Rizzo, CEO
Michael Edwards, COO
John Paul Giunta, Sr. VP-Finance
Paul Rizzo, CTO

FINANCIAL DATA: Note: Data for latest year may not have been available at press time.

In U.S. $	2024	2023	2022	2021	2020	2019
Revenue						
R&D Expense						
Operating Income						
Operating Margin %						
SGA Expense						
Net Income						
Operating Cash Flow						
Capital Expenditure						
EBITDA						
Return on Assets %						
Return on Equity %						
Debt to Equity						

CONTACT INFORMATION:

Phone: 412-856-9700   Fax: 412-856-9749
Toll-Free:
Address: 500 Penn Center Blvd., Ste. 100, Pittsburgh, PA 15235 United States

STOCK TICKER/OTHER:

Stock Ticker: Private   Exchange:
Employees: Fiscal Year Ends:
Parent Company:

SALARIES/BONUSES:

Top Exec. Salary: $ Bonus: $
Second Exec. Salary: $ Bonus: $

OTHER THOUGHTS:

Estimated Female Officers or Directors:
Hot Spot for Advancement for Women/Minorities:

Robert Bosch GmbH

www.bosch.com

NAIC Code: 336300

TYPES OF BUSINESS:

Automobile Components Manufacturing
Technology Solutions and Services
Mobility Hardware and Software
Automotive Solutions
Smart Home Products Solutions
Technology Business Process Outsourcing
Factory Automation Solutions
Power Tools

BRANDS/DIVISIONS/AFFILIATES:

Robert Bosch Stiftung GmbH

CONTACTS: *Note: Officers with more than one job title may be intentionally listed here more than once.*

Volkmar Denner, Dir.-Research
Volkmar Denner, Dir.-Prod. Planning
Volkmar Denner, Dir.-Eng.
Stefan Asenkerschbaumer, Dir.-Bus. Admin.
Christoph Kubel, Dir.-Legal Svcs., Taxes & Internal Auditing
Stefan Asenkerschbaumer, Dir.-Corp. Planning
Volkmar Denner, Dir.-Corp. Comm.
Stefan Asenkerschbaumer, Dir.-Finance & Controlling
Wolf-Henning Scheider, Dir.-Coordination Automotive Tech.
Uwe Raschke, Dir.-Consumer Goods & User Experience
Werner Struth, Dir.-North & South America
Stefan Hartung, Chmn.
Peter Tyroller, Dir.-Asia Pacific
Stefan Asenkerschbaumer, Dir.-Purchasing & Logistics

GROWTH PLANS/SPECIAL FEATURES:

Robert Bosch GmbH, majority-owned by Robert Bosch Stiftung GmbH, is a global supplier of technology and services, with products and services grouped into four categories: mobility, at home, industry and trades, and market-specific solutions. The mobility division develops vehicle technology hardware and software, with solutions spanning areas such as mobility, mobility aftermarket, car service, motorsport and eBike systems. These solutions are designed for passenger vehicles, commercial vehicles, two-wheelers, off-highway applications and ship and rail transport. The at home division develops technology for home and garden purposes, including home appliances, power tools, garden tools, measuring tools, cleaning tools, heating/cooling systems and smart home products and systems. The industry and trades division offers innovative products and services such as business process outsourcing solutions for complex, technology-driven services; drive and control technology solutions for mobile applications, factory automation and process plan engineering; energy and building solutions for connecting, integrating and securing from a single source; and thermal plants and system solutions for energy management via heat and steam systems, as well as air conditioning appliances and waste heat recovery systems. Other industry/trades solutions include power tools for professionals, safety/security solutions, industrial software solutions and production equipment and automation. Lastly, the market-specific division offers a range of products and solutions that cover hydrogen technology, smart buildings, product authentication and carbon neutrality. Bosch has approximately 468 subsidiaries and regional companies in 60 countries worldwide, including engineering locations.

FINANCIAL DATA: *Note: Data for latest year may not have been available at press time.*

In U.S. $	2024	2023	2022	2021	2020	2019
Revenue	103,725,726,000	99,253,000,000	95,866,344,000	85,056,714,000	87,812,100,000	84,327,290,000
R&D Expense						
Operating Income						
Operating Margin %						
SGA Expense						
Net Income		5,008,918,300	4,130,296,000	3,650,000,000	2,158,862,000	2,235,170,000
Operating Cash Flow						
Capital Expenditure						
EBITDA						
Return on Assets %						
Return on Equity %						
Debt to Equity						

CONTACT INFORMATION:

Phone: 49-711-400-40990   Fax: 49-711-400-40999
Toll-Free:
Address: Robert-Bosch-Platz   1,   Gerlingen-Schillerhohe,   70839
Germany

STOCK TICKER/OTHER:

Stock Ticker: Private   Exchange:
Employees: 427,600   Fiscal Year Ends: 12/31
Parent Company: Robert Bosch Stiftung GmbH

SALARIES/BONUSES:

Top Exec. Salary: $ Bonus: $
Second Exec. Salary: $ Bonus: $

OTHER THOUGHTS:

Estimated Female Officers or Directors: 3
Hot Spot for Advancement for Women/Minorities: Y

Roche Holding AG

www.roche.com

NAIC Code: 325412

TYPES OF BUSINESS:

Pharmaceuticals Manufacturing
Antibiotics
Diagnostics
Cancer Drugs
Virology Products
HIV/AIDS Treatments
Transplant Drugs

BRANDS/DIVISIONS/AFFILIATES:

F Hoffmann-La Roche Ltd
Genentech Inc
Chugai Pharmaceutical Co Ltd
GenMark Diagnositcs Inc

GROWTH PLANS/SPECIAL FEATURES:

Roche is a Swiss biopharmaceutical and diagnostic company. The firm's bestselling pharmaceutical products include a variety of oncology therapies from acquired partner Genentech, and its diagnostics group was bolstered by the acquisition of Ventana in 2008. Oncology products account for 50% of pharmaceutical sales, and centralized and point-of-care diagnostics for more than half of diagnostic-related sales.

CONTACTS: *Note: Officers with more than one job title may be intentionally listed here more than once.*

Severin Schwan, Chairman of the Board
Andre Hoffmann, Director

FINANCIAL DATA: *Note: Data for latest year may not have been available at press time.*

In U.S. $	2024	2023	2022	2021	2020	2019
Revenue	75,925,289,970	73,547,570,977	80,085,697,609	76,419,330,184	70,970,284,081	74,794,840,470
R&D Expense	18,622,660,000	17,279,260,000	18,526,530,000	18,008,150,000	15,829,990,000	15,544,030,000
Operating Income	16,326,460,000	18,733,390,000	21,265,650,000	22,091,890,000	22,564,030,000	21,353,270,000
Operating Margin %	.22%	.25%	.27%	.29%	.32%	.29%
SGA Expense	18,126,180,000	18,107,930,000	17,280,470,000	16,122,030,000	15,349,330,000	18,347,650,000
Net Income	10,071,860,000	13,991,330,000	15,114,480,000	16,950,710,000	17,394,860,000	16,423,810,000
Operating Cash Flow	24,451,360,000	19,585,180,000	21,663,560,000	25,524,630,000	22,592,020,000	27,239,160,000
Capital Expenditure	6,095,196,000	5,657,131,000	5,539,097,000	5,535,446,000	8,140,720,000	5,957,692,000
EBITDA	20,222,810,000	22,560,380,000	25,384,690,000	27,087,060,000	28,080,010,000	26,401,970,000
Return on Assets %	.09%	.13%	.14%	.16%	.17%	.17%
Return on Equity %	.27%	.40%	.47%	.46%	.41%	.45%
Debt to Equity	1.01%	.89%	.80%	.70%	0.305	0.414

CONTACT INFORMATION:

Phone: 41-61-688-1111   Fax: 41-61-691-9391
Toll-Free:
Address: F. Hoffmann-La Roche Ltd, Basel, CH-4070 Switzerland

STOCK TICKER/OTHER:

Stock Ticker: RHHBF   Exchange: PINX
Employees: 103,605   Fiscal Year Ends: 12/31
Parent Company:

SALARIES/BONUSES:

Top Exec. Salary: $ Bonus: $
Second Exec. Salary: $ Bonus: $

OTHER THOUGHTS:

Estimated Female Officers or Directors: 4
Hot Spot for Advancement for Women/Minorities: Y

Rockwell Automation Inc

www.rockwellautomation.com

NAIC Code: 334513

TYPES OF BUSINESS:

Architecture & Software Products
Industrial Automation
Digital Transformation
Intelligent Devices
Software
Control Systems
Security Infrastructure
Digital Oilfield Automation Solutions

BRANDS/DIVISIONS/AFFILIATES:

Sensia
Allen-Bradley
PlantPAx
ControlLogix
PowerFlex
Rockwell Software
FactoryTalk
Fiix Inc

GROWTH PLANS/SPECIAL FEATURES:

With roots tracing back to the early 1900s, Rockwell Automation is the successor to Rockwell International, which spun off its avionics segment in 2001. It is a pure-play industrial automation company that operates through three segments. Its largest segment by revenue, intelligent devices, sells factory floor-level devices such as motors, drives, sensors, relays, and actuators. Its software and control segment sells visualization, simulation, and human-machine interface software and control products such as programmable controllers, computers, and operator terminals. Its smallest segment, lifecycle services, offers digital consulting, engineered-to-order services, and other outsourced services such as remote monitoring, cybersecurity, and asset and plant maintenance and optimization.

CONTACTS:

Note: Officers with more than one job title may be intentionally listed here more than once.

Blake Moret, CEO
Isaac Woods, Treasurer
Christian Rothe, CFO
Terry Riesterer, Chief Accounting Officer
Christopher Nardecchia, Chief Information Officer
Rebecca House, Chief Legal Officer
Cyril Perducat, Chief Technology Officer
John Miller, Other Corporate Officer
Scott Genereux, Other Executive Officer
Robert Buttermore, Other Executive Officer
Matthew Fordenwalt, Senior VP, Divisional
Matheus De A G Viera Bulho, Senior VP, Divisional
Veena Lakkundi, Senior VP, Divisional
Tessa Myers, Senior VP, Divisional

FINANCIAL DATA:

Note: Data for latest year may not have been available at press time.

In U.S. $	2024	2023	2022	2021	2020	2019
Revenue	8,264,200,192	9,057,999,872	7,760,399,872	6,997,400,064	6,329,800,192	6,694,799,872
R&D Expense						
Operating Income	1,190,800,000	1,693,300,000	1,335,300,000	1,217,700,000	1,115,400,000	1,361,600,000
Operating Margin %	.14%	.19%	.17%	.17%	.18%	.20%
SGA Expense	2,002,600,000	2,023,700,000	1,766,700,000	1,680,000,000	1,479,800,000	1,538,500,000
Net Income	952,500,000	1,387,400,000	932,200,000	1,344,300,000	1,023,400,000	695,800,000
Operating Cash Flow	863,800,000	1,374,600,000	823,100,000	1,261,000,000	1,120,500,000	1,182,000,000
Capital Expenditure	224,700,000	160,500,000	141,100,000	120,300,000	113,900,000	132,800,000
EBITDA	1,571,100,000	1,994,200,000	1,435,700,000	1,810,600,000	1,412,300,000	1,151,400,000
Return on Assets %	.08%	.13%	.09%	.15%	.15%	.11%
Return on Equity %	.27%	.44%	.36%	.79%	1.43%	.69%
Debt to Equity	.83%	.88%	1.15%	1.58%	2.189	4.84

CONTACT INFORMATION:

Phone: 414 382-2000   Fax: 414 382-8520
Toll-Free:
Address: 1201 S. Second St., Milwaukee, WI 53204 United States

STOCK TICKER/OTHER:

Stock Ticker: ROK   Exchange: NYS
Employees: 27,000   Fiscal Year Ends: 09/30
Parent Company:

SALARIES/BONUSES:

Top Exec. Salary: $1,210,456   Bonus: $
Second Exec. Salary: Bonus: $
$899,177

OTHER THOUGHTS:

Estimated Female Officers or Directors: 1
Hot Spot for Advancement for Women/Minorities:

Rohm Co Ltd
NAIC Code: 334418

www.rohm.com/company

TYPES OF BUSINESS:
Electronic Components Manufacturing
Integrated Circuits
Discrete Semiconductor Devices
Passive Components
Resistors & Capacitors
Display Devices
LED Displays
Foundry Services

BRANDS/DIVISIONS/AFFILIATES:

GROWTH PLANS/SPECIAL FEATURES:

Rohm Co Ltd is a Japan-based company that manufactures and distributes electronic components for use in automotive, transportation, medical, healthcare, audiovisual, telecommunications, digital power, computer and peripherals, and home appliance end markets. Its product portfolio includes integrated circuits in memory, amplifiers, switches, data converters, and microcontrollers; discrete semiconductors, such as transistors and diodes; power devices; passive devices, such as resistors and capacitors; and optoelectronic devices.

CONTACTS: Note: Officers with more than one job title may be intentionally listed here more than once.
Isao Matsumoto, CEO
Tetsuo Aoki, Director
Koji Yamamoto, Director
Tetsuo Tateishi, Director
Kazuhide Ino, Director
Katsumi Azuma, Director

FINANCIAL DATA: Note: Data for latest year may not have been available at press time.

In U.S. $	2024	2023	2022	2021	2020	2019
Revenue	3,247,570,294	3,525,979,097	3,138,878,079	2,498,528,232	2,519,334,912	2,769,987,598
R&D Expense						
Operating Income	300,798,400	640,912,300	496,244,100	267,210,500	204,734,800	388,156,100
Operating Margin %	.09%	.18%	.16%	.11%	.08%	.14%
SGA Expense						
Net Income	374,652,900	558,004,700	463,947,600	256,887,000	177,950,600	315,474,900
Operating Cash Flow	575,243,000	684,726,500	639,968,100	319,182,200	549,361,300	458,136,600
Capital Expenditure	1,154,353,000	699,590,400	462,225,800	224,777,800	290,752,600	376,791,200
EBITDA	1,001,028,000	1,150,930,000	874,757,000	560,774,800	572,431,200	738,260,200
Return on Assets %	.04%	.07%	.07%	.04%	.03%	.05%
Return on Equity %	.06%	.09%	.08%	.05%	.03%	.06%
Debt to Equity		.04%	.05%	.05%	0.057	

CONTACT INFORMATION:
Phone: 81 753112121   Fax: 81 753150172
Toll-Free:
Address: 21, Saiin Mizosaki-cho, Kyoto, 615-8585 Japan

STOCK TICKER/OTHER:
Stock Ticker: ROHCF
Employees: 22,899
Parent Company:

Exchange: PINX
Fiscal Year Ends: 03/31

SALARIES/BONUSES:
Top Exec. Salary: $ Bonus: $
Second Exec. Salary: $ Bonus: $

OTHER THOUGHTS:
Estimated Female Officers or Directors:
Hot Spot for Advancement for Women/Minorities:

Rolls-Royce Holdings plc

www.rolls-royce.com

NAIC Code: 336412

TYPES OF BUSINESS:

Aircraft Engine and Engine Parts Manufacturing
Engines
Power Systems
Nuclear
Artificial Intelligence Technology
Machine Learning

BRANDS/DIVISIONS/AFFILIATES:

GROWTH PLANS/SPECIAL FEATURES:

Rolls-Royce operates three core business segments: civil aerospace, power systems, and defense. The civil aerospace segment builds engines powering wide-body aircraft, regional and business jets, and offers aftermarket services. Twenty years ago, the firm pioneered full-service flight hour contracts with the TotalCare package. Power systems provides power solutions to multiple end markets (defense, agriculture, marine, and power generation) while the defense business provides military, ground vehicle and naval propulsion solutions.

CONTACTS: Note: Officers with more than one job title may be intentionally listed here more than once.

Tufan Erginbilgic, CEO
Helen McCabe, CFO
Anita Frew, Chairman of the Board
Pamela Coles, Other Executive Officer

FINANCIAL DATA: Note: Data for latest year may not have been available at press time.

In U.S. $	2024	2023	2022	2021	2020	2019
Revenue	25,457,186,381	22,195,101,380	18,201,976,080	15,102,793,294	15,470,333,799	22,331,077,940
R&D Expense	273,298,900	994,915,700	1,199,553,000	1,047,421,000	1,620,945,000	1,036,651,000
Operating Income	3,680,784,000	2,384,297,000	1,062,231,000	630,068,400	-2,910,701,000	-1,287,063,000
Operating Margin %	.14%	.11%	.06%	.04%	- .19%	- .06%
SGA Expense	1,728,649,000	1,494,393,000	1,449,965,000	1,198,207,000	1,037,997,000	1,518,626,000
Net Income	3,394,022,000	3,247,276,000	-1,708,455,000	161,556,000	-4,267,771,000	-1,770,385,000
Operating Cash Flow	5,091,707,000	3,345,555,000	2,051,761,000	-348,691,700	-4,051,017,000	3,092,451,000
Capital Expenditure	1,192,822,000	959,911,900	802,394,800	752,581,700	1,278,985,000	1,867,318,000
EBITDA	4,689,163,000	5,040,547,000	-278,684,100	1,309,950,000	-223,485,800	815,857,800
Return on Assets %	.08%	.08%	- .04%	.00%	- .10%	- .04%
Return on Equity %						
Debt to Equity						

CONTACT INFORMATION:

Phone: 44 2072229020   Fax: 44 2072279170
Toll-Free:
Address: 90 York Way, London, N1C 4 United Kingdom

STOCK TICKER/OTHER:

Stock Ticker: RYCEF
Employees: 41,400
Parent Company:

Exchange: PINX
Fiscal Year Ends: 12/31

SALARIES/BONUSES:

Top Exec. Salary: $1,529,397   Bonus: $3,441,143
Second Exec. Salary: $928,947   Bonus: $1,996,563

OTHER THOUGHTS:

Estimated Female Officers or Directors: 4
Hot Spot for Advancement for Women/Minorities: Y

Royal HaskoningDHV

www.royalhaskoningdhv.com

NAIC Code: 541330

TYPES OF BUSINESS:

Engineering Consulting Services
Engineering
Consultancy
Environmental Sustainability
Buildings
Infrastructure
Maritime
Urban Development

BRANDS/DIVISIONS/AFFILIATES:

NACO
Aurea
Twinn

CONTACTS: Note: Officers with more than one job title may be intentionally listed here more than once.

Marije Hulshof, CEO
Jasper de Wit, CFO
Erik Oostwegel, Chief Commercial Officer
Daan Sperling, Chmn.

GROWTH PLANS/SPECIAL FEATURES:

Royal HaskoningDHV (RHDHV) is an independent consultancy, specializing in engineering since 1881. Present in 25 different countries around the world, the company offers related digital technologies and software solutions as well as a range of engineering services across aviation, which is run by the RHDHV's airport consultancy and engineering firm, NACO; buildings; data centers; energy, which guides clients towards low-carbon and sustainable sources of energy; industry; infrastructure, which offers smart planning, novel technologies and stakeholder management; maritime, offering consulting and master planning, as well as other services and support end-to-end; urban development, which provides master planning to avoid future industrial, transport and water challenges in the urban setting; and water, accompanied by the firm's Aurea anti-micro-pollutant for wastewater treatment plants, drinking water production sites and industrial wastewater treatment plants. Services for all markets include environmental and social sustainability, health and safety, architecture, legal consulting, permits and licenses, project management, and strategy and management consultancy. Twinn is RHDHV's provider of digital solutions for decision intelligence that helps connect and understand the dynamics across customer's organizations. Headquartered in the Netherlands, RHDHV has offices throughout the world, including Europe, Africa, Asia, Australia, the Middle East and the Americas.

FINANCIAL DATA: Note: Data for latest year may not have been available at press time.

In U.S. $	2024	2023	2022	2021	2020	2019
Revenue	853,242,955	812,612,339	759,917,048	706,277,880	729,454,000	713,575,000
R&D Expense						
Operating Income						
Operating Margin %						
SGA Expense						
Net Income		27,358,132	14,898,202	17,212,480	15,967,200	10,302,700
Operating Cash Flow						
Capital Expenditure						
EBITDA						
Return on Assets %						
Return on Equity %						
Debt to Equity						

CONTACT INFORMATION:

Phone: 31-88-348-20-00   Fax: 31-88-348-28-01
Toll-Free:
Address: Laan 1914 no 35, Amersfoort, 3818 EX Netherlands

STOCK TICKER/OTHER:

Stock Ticker: Private   Exchange:
Employees: 6,000   Fiscal Year Ends: 12/31
Parent Company:

SALARIES/BONUSES:

Top Exec. Salary: $ Bonus: $
Second Exec. Salary: $ Bonus: $

OTHER THOUGHTS:

Estimated Female Officers or Directors:
Hot Spot for Advancement for Women/Minorities:

RTX Corp (Raytheon Technologies)

NAIC Code: 336412

www.rtx.com

TYPES OF BUSINESS:

Aircraft Engine and Engine Parts Manufacturing
Advanced Aerospace Products
Defense Products
Aftermarket Aircraft Solutions
Avionic Systems
Aircraft Engines
Sensors
Communication Systems

BRANDS/DIVISIONS/AFFILIATES:

Collins Aerospace Systems
Pratt & Whitney
Raytheon Intelligence & Space
Raytheon Missiles & Defense

GROWTH PLANS/SPECIAL FEATURES:

RTX is an aerospace and defense manufacturer formed from the merger of United Technologies and Raytheon, with roughly equal exposure as a supplier to commercial aerospace and to the defense market across three segments: Collins Aerospace, a diversified aerospace supplier; Pratt & Whitney, a commercial and military aircraft engine manufacturer; and Raytheon, a defense prime contractor providing a mix of missiles, missile defense systems, sensors, hardware, and communications technology to the military.

CONTACTS:
Note: Officers with more than one job title may be intentionally listed here more than once.

Christopher Calio, CEO
Kevin DaSilva, Treas.
Neil Mitchill, CFO
Gregory Hayes, Chairman of the Board
Amy Johnson, Chief Accounting Officer
Ramsaran Maharajh, Executive VP
Dantaya Williams, Executive VP
Heather Robertson, President, Divisional
Nathan Boelkins, President, Divisional
Phil Jasper, President, Divisional
Troy Brunk, President, Subsidiary
Stephen Timm, President, Subsidiary
Shane Eddy, President, Subsidiary
Philip Jasper, President, Subsidiary

FINANCIAL DATA:
Note: Data for latest year may not have been available at press time.

In U.S. $	2024	2023	2022	2021	2020	2019
Revenue	80,738,000,896	68,920,000,512	67,073,998,848	64,388,001,792	56,587,001,856	45,348,999,168
R&D Expense	2,934,000,000	2,805,000,000	2,711,000,000	2,732,000,000	2,582,000,000	2,452,000,000
Operating Income	6,538,000,000	3,561,000,000	5,504,000,000	5,136,000,000	1,294,000,000	4,914,000,000
Operating Margin %	.08%	.05%	.08%	.08%	.02%	.11%
SGA Expense	5,806,000,000	5,809,000,000	5,573,000,000	5,046,000,000	5,540,000,000	3,711,000,000
Net Income	4,774,000,000	3,195,000,000	5,197,000,000	3,864,000,000	-3,519,000,000	5,537,000,000
Operating Cash Flow	7,159,000,000	7,883,000,000	7,168,000,000	7,071,000,000	3,606,000,000	8,883,000,000
Capital Expenditure	3,236,000,000	3,166,000,000	2,775,000,000	2,442,000,000	1,967,000,000	2,219,000,000
EBITDA	12,528,000,000	9,700,000,000	11,525,000,000	10,996,000,000	3,211,000,000	8,571,000,000
Return on Assets %	.03%	.02%	.03%	.02%	-.02%	.04%
Return on Equity %	.08%	.05%	.07%	.05%	-.06%	.14%
Debt to Equity	.67%	.73%	.44%	.45%	0.451	0.929

CONTACT INFORMATION:

Phone: 781-522-3000　Fax:
Toll-Free:
Address: 870 Winter St., Waltham, MA 02451 United States

STOCK TICKER/OTHER:

Stock Ticker: RTX
Employees: 185,000
Parent Company:

Exchange: NYS
Fiscal Year Ends: 12/31

SALARIES/BONUSES:

Top Exec. Salary: $1,182,500　Bonus: $2,760,000
Second Exec. Salary: $1,200,000　Bonus: $2,320,000

OTHER THOUGHTS:

Estimated Female Officers or Directors: 2
Hot Spot for Advancement for Women/Minorities: Y

Sales, profits and employees may be estimates. Financial information, benefits and other data can change quickly and may vary from those stated here.

Saab AB

NAIC Code: 336411

TYPES OF BUSINESS:

Aircraft Manufacturing
Aeronautics
Advanced Weapon Systems
Command and Control Systems
Sensors
Underwater Systems
Security
Defense

BRANDS/DIVISIONS/AFFILIATES:

GROWTH PLANS/SPECIAL FEATURES:

Saab supplies products and services for military, defense, and civil security. The company operates in four segments: aeronautics, dynamics, surveillance, and Kockums. Aeronautics involves the manufacturing and support of defense and commercial aerial systems. Dynamics produces combat weapons and defense training and management systems. Surveillance supplies security services, and creates traffic management technology and aviation parts. Kockums offers solutions for naval missions. Over three fourths of Saab's sales are from the defense sector. The company sells to multiple geographic regions, but over half of its sales come from Europe.

CONTACTS: Note: Officers with more than one job title may be intentionally listed here more than once.

Micael Johansson, CEO
Anna Wijkander, CFO
Marcus Wallenberg, Chairman of the Board
Bert Nordberg, Deputy Chairman

FINANCIAL DATA: Note: Data for latest year may not have been available at press time.

In U.S. $	2024	2023	2022	2021	2020	2019
Revenue	6,649,803,545	5,383,283,776	4,381,604,130	4,084,114,867	3,695,772,239	3,695,981,164
R&D Expense	293,004,000	220,822,200	189,529,500	173,048,700	138,835,300	118,599,300
Operating Income	583,921,900	471,476,700	342,133,500	307,294,300	72,181,830	299,575,500
Operating Margin %	.09%	.09%	.08%	.08%	.02%	.08%
SGA Expense	575,264,100	492,129,900	404,301,700	385,943,300	390,950,200	427,354,000
Net Income	435,072,900	352,668,700	228,958,300	200,899,200	111,923,600	206,844,800
Operating Cash Flow	702,208,300	674,044,800	485,454,100	595,917,400	604,992,300	124,545,000
Capital Expenditure	504,751,300	369,045,200	240,953,800	262,858,700	301,557,300	292,169,500
EBITDA	885,896,400	751,963,600	547,935,200	501,413,400	303,956,400	444,773,600
Return on Assets %	.05%	.04%	.03%	.03%	.02%	.03%
Return on Equity %	.12%	.11%	.08%	.09%	.05%	.10%
Debt to Equity	.27%	.28%	.30%	.34%	0.344	0.421

CONTACT INFORMATION:

Phone: 46 84630000   Fax: 46 84630152
Toll-Free:
Address: Olof Palmes gata 17, 5tr, Stockholm, SE-111 22 Sweden

STOCK TICKER/OTHER:

Stock Ticker: SAABY   Exchange: PINX
Employees: 21,600   Fiscal Year Ends: 12/31
Parent Company:

SALARIES/BONUSES:

Top Exec. Salary: $ Bonus: $
Second Exec. Salary: $ Bonus: $

OTHER THOUGHTS:

Estimated Female Officers or Directors: 7
Hot Spot for Advancement for Women/Minorities: Y

Safran SA

NAIC Code: 336412

TYPES OF BUSINESS:

Aircraft Engine and Engine Parts Manufacturing
Aircraft Equipment
Defense Security Equipment
Defense Electronics
Aerospace Propulsion

BRANDS/DIVISIONS/AFFILIATES:

Ariane 5
ArianeGroup
Ariane 6
OXIS Energy

GROWTH PLANS/SPECIAL FEATURES:

Safran is a key player in the global commercial and military aerospace propulsion and equipment sectors. The group has three reportable segments: aerospace propulsion (commercial and military aircraft engines and spare parts); aircraft equipment, defense, and aerosystems (diversified business supplying components ranging from landing gear to avionics); and aircraft interiors (seats, cabins, and in-flight entertainment systems). Safran is a partner to the CFM joint venture with GE Aviation, which produces narrow-body engines.

CONTACTS: *Note: Officers with more than one job title may be intentionally listed here more than once.*

Olivier Andries, CEO
Ross McInnes, Chairman of the Board

FINANCIAL DATA: *Note: Data for latest year may not have been available at press time.*

In U.S. $	2024	2023	2022	2021	2020	2019
Revenue	31,459,704,624	26,845,630,358	22,160,045,790	17,177,071,165	18,877,412,125	28,488,082,192
R&D Expense						
Operating Income	4,528,945,000	3,602,724,000	3,081,725,000	1,339,387,000	1,712,826,000	4,056,754,000
Operating Margin %	.14%	.13%	.14%	.08%	.09%	.14%
SGA Expense						
Net Income	-757,094,200	3,909,194,000	-2,791,146,000	48,808,170	399,546,000	2,777,526,000
Operating Cash Flow	5,372,304,000	4,846,765,000	4,023,836,000	2,765,040,000	2,118,048,000	3,569,807,000
Capital Expenditure	1,752,554,000	1,503,973,000	997,729,900	858,115,800	900,113,500	1,318,956,000
EBITDA	767,309,900	7,255,392,000	-1,594,779,000	2,297,389,000	2,553,916,000	5,897,844,000
Return on Assets %	- .01%	.07%	- .06%	.00%	.01%	.06%
Return on Equity %	- .06%	.31%	- .21%	.00%	.03%	.20%
Debt to Equity	.40%	.43%	.55%	.42%	0.364	0.303

CONTACT INFORMATION:

Phone: 33 140608080   Fax: 33 40608102
Toll-Free:
Address: 2, boulevard du General-Martial-Valin, Paris, 75015 France

STOCK TICKER/OTHER:

Stock Ticker: SAFRY   Exchange: PINX
Employees: 76,765   Fiscal Year Ends: 12/31
Parent Company:

SALARIES/BONUSES:

Top Exec. Salary: $ Bonus: $
Second Exec. Salary: $ Bonus: $

OTHER THOUGHTS:

Estimated Female Officers or Directors: 5
Hot Spot for Advancement for Women/Minorities: Y

SAIC Motor Corporation Limited

www.saicmotor.com

NAIC Code: 336111

TYPES OF BUSINESS:

Automobile Manufacturing
Automotive Manufacturing
Passenger Cars and Trucks
Commercial Trucks and Buses
Automotive Parts
Mobility Technology
Auto Finance and Insurance
Overseas Automobile Sales and Trade

BRANDS/DIVISIONS/AFFILIATES:

MG Motor India Private Limited
SAIC USA Inc
SAIC Europe GmbH
SAIC Motor CP Co Ltd
SAIC Hong Kong Co Ltd
MG Motor UK Ltd
SASAC

CONTACTS: Note: Officers with more than one job title may be intentionally listed here more than once.

Jia Jianxu, Pres.
Wei Yong, CFO
Wang Jianzhang, Sec.
Chen Demei, VP
Chen Zhixin, Exec. VP
Xiao Guopu, Exec. VP
Yu Jianwei, VP-Nanjing Automotive Group
Zhu Genlin, VP
Wang Xiaoqiu, Chmn.

GROWTH PLANS/SPECIAL FEATURES:

SAIC Motor Corporation Limited is a state-owned entity and one of China's largest automotive companies. The group operates manufacturing facilities, mainly near Shanghai, which produce passenger cars, trucks, buses and automotive parts. SAIC also has operations in India, Germany, Thailand, Hong Kong, the U.K. and the U.S. The company's business covers complete vehicles, components, mobility services, finance, international operations and innovative technology. SAIC has 15 domestic-based complete vehicle manufacturing bases, along with corresponding parts and logistics bases, as well as four more overseas vehicle manufacturing bases. The firm's products reach over 100 countries around the world. Subsidiaries include MG Motor India Private Limited, General Motors India Private Limited, SAIC USA, Inc., SAIC Europe GmbH, SAIC Motor CP Co. Ltd., SAIC Hong Kong Co. Ltd., and MG Motor UK Ltd. SAIC is part of the State Assets Supervision Administration Commission (SASAC).

FINANCIAL DATA: Note: Data for latest year may not have been available at press time.

In U.S. $	2024	2023	2022	2021	2020	2019
Revenue		105,039,169,000	106,753,264,440	115,971,960,000	113,698,000,000	188,775,450,000
R&D Expense						
Operating Income						
Operating Margin %						
SGA Expense						
Net Income		1,989,648,000		3,849,170,000	4,471,750,000	4,972,243,000
Operating Cash Flow						
Capital Expenditure						
EBITDA						
Return on Assets %						
Return on Equity %						
Debt to Equity						

CONTACT INFORMATION:

Phone: 86-21-2201-1888   Fax: 86-21-2201-1777
Toll-Free:
Address: 489 Weihai Rd., Shanghai, Shanghai 200041 China

STOCK TICKER/OTHER:

Stock Ticker: 600104
Employees: 205,000
Parent Company: SASAC

Exchange: Shanghai
Fiscal Year Ends: 12/31

SALARIES/BONUSES:

Top Exec. Salary: $ Bonus: $
Second Exec. Salary: $ Bonus: $

OTHER THOUGHTS:

Estimated Female Officers or Directors: 1
Hot Spot for Advancement for Women/Minorities:

SAIC-GM-Wuling Automobile Company

www.sgmw.com.cn

NAIC Code: 336111

TYPES OF BUSINESS:

Automobile Manufacturing
Gasoline Engine Manufacturing
Electric Vehicle Manufacturing
Vehicle Manufacture
Technology
Small Vehicles

BRANDS/DIVISIONS/AFFILIATES:

Shanghai Automotive Industry Corporation
General Motors China
Liuzhou Wuling Motors Co Ltd
Hongguang Mini EV
Nano EV

GROWTH PLANS/SPECIAL FEATURES:

SAIC-GM-Wuling Automobile Company (SGMW) is a Chinese automaker. SGMW is a three-way joint venture between Shanghai Automobile Industry Corporation (SAIC), General Motors China and Liuzhou Wuling Motors Co., Ltd. The firm manufactures the Hongguang Mini electric vehicle (EV), which is very popular in China. The smaller Nano EV model (42 centimeters/16 ½ inches shorter) is a neighborhood electric vehicle (NEV) launched by SGMW in 2022. The company plans to enhance its core technologies across batteries, motors and electric control systems, and is planning a battery production facility for battery systems and cells. In addition to its electric vehicles, the firm also manufactures various SUVs, MPV, pickups and vans. SGMW has six manufacturing facilities, four in China and one each in India and Indonesia.

CONTACTS: Note: Officers with more than one job title may be intentionally listed here more than once.

Shen Yang, Pres.
Ray Bierzynski, Exec. VP
Matthew Tsien, Exec. VP

FINANCIAL DATA: Note: Data for latest year may not have been available at press time.

In U.S. $	2024	2023	2022	2021	2020	2019
Revenue		10,720,954,000	11,714,870,000	12,385,893,000	11,172,748,000	12,267,726,000
R&D Expense						
Operating Income						
Operating Margin %						
SGA Expense						
Net Income		119,707,000	210,857,374	178,115,000	21,807,000	243,068,000
Operating Cash Flow						
Capital Expenditure						
EBITDA						
Return on Assets %						
Return on Equity %						
Debt to Equity						

CONTACT INFORMATION:

Phone: 86-772-2650-226   Fax: 86-772-2650-222
Toll-Free:
Address: Hexi Rd., No. 18, Liuzhou, Guangxi 545007 China

STOCK TICKER/OTHER:

Stock Ticker: Joint Venture   Exchange:
Employees: 20,000   Fiscal Year Ends: 12/31
Parent Company: SAIC Motor Corporation Limited

SALARIES/BONUSES:

Top Exec. Salary: $ Bonus: $
Second Exec. Salary: $ Bonus: $

OTHER THOUGHTS:

Estimated Female Officers or Directors:
Hot Spot for Advancement for Women/Minorities:

Samsung Electronics Co Ltd

www.samsung.com

NAIC Code: 334310

TYPES OF BUSINESS:

Consumer Electronics
Semiconductors and Memory Products
Smartphones
Computers & Accessories
Digital Cameras
Fuel-Cell Technology
LCD Displays
Solar Energy Panels

BRANDS/DIVISIONS/AFFILIATES:

Samsung Group

GROWTH PLANS/SPECIAL FEATURES:

Samsung Electronics is a diversified electronics conglomerate that manufactures and sells a wide range of products, including smartphones, semiconductor chips, printers, home appliances, medical equipment, and telecom network equipment. More than half of its profit is generated from semiconductor business, and a further 20-25% is generated from its mobile handset business, although these percentages vary with the fortunes of each of these businesses. It is the largest smartphone and television manufacturer in the world, which helps provide a base demand for its component businesses, such as memory chips and displays, and is also the largest manufacturer of these globally.

CONTACTS:
Note: Officers with more than one job title may be intentionally listed here more than once.

Jong-Hee Han, CEO, Divisional
Han-Jo Kim, Chairman of the Board
Tae-Moon Roh, Director
Hark-Kyu Park, Director
Jung-Bae Lee, Director

FINANCIAL DATA:
Note: Data for latest year may not have been available at press time.

In U.S. $	2024	2023	2022	2021	2020	2019
Revenue	217,710,030,352	187,365,580,968	218,694,437,405	202,321,883,898	171,353,402,896	166,717,956,242
R&D Expense	25,324,640,000	20,506,610,000	18,031,520,000	16,209,880,000	15,276,260,000	14,404,870,000
Operating Income	23,680,490,000	4,751,860,000	31,387,300,000	37,362,230,000	26,045,150,000	20,093,280,000
Operating Margin %	.11%	.03%	.14%	.18%	.15%	.12%
SGA Expense	25,382,590,000	23,645,900,000	24,284,690,000	21,366,460,000	18,874,940,000	19,553,230,000
Net Income	24,328,400,000	10,472,950,000	39,602,610,000	28,396,790,000	18,879,320,000	15,561,050,000
Operating Cash Flow	52,810,180,000	31,937,820,000	44,994,390,000	47,110,270,000	47,241,650,000	32,839,050,000
Capital Expenditure	38,887,420,000	43,802,490,000	38,442,480,000	36,056,250,000	29,140,660,000	20,707,730,000
EBITDA	58,658,210,000	36,616,360,000	62,454,700,000	63,698,990,000	48,672,010,000	43,934,200,000
Return on Assets %	.07%	.03%	.13%	.10%	.07%	.06%
Return on Equity %	.09%	.04%	.17%	.14%	.10%	.09%
Debt to Equity	.01%	.01%	.01%	.01%	0.011	0.012

CONTACT INFORMATION:

Phone: 82 31-200-1114   Fax: 82-31-200-7538
Toll-Free:
Address: 129, Samsung-ro, Suwon-si, 443-742 South Korea

STOCK TICKER/OTHER:

Stock Ticker: SSNHZ   Exchange: PINX
Employees: 117,904   Fiscal Year Ends: 12/31
Parent Company: Samsung Group

SALARIES/BONUSES:

Top Exec. Salary: $ Bonus: $
Second Exec. Salary: $ Bonus: $

OTHER THOUGHTS:

Estimated Female Officers or Directors:
Hot Spot for Advancement for Women/Minorities:

Sanmina Corporation

www.sanmina.com

NAIC Code: 334418

TYPES OF BUSINESS:

Printed Circuit Assembly (Electronic Assembly) Manufacturing
Assembly & Testing
Logistics Services
Support Services
Product Design & Engineering
Repair & Maintenance Services
Printed Circuit Boards

BRANDS/DIVISIONS/AFFILIATES:

GROWTH PLANS/SPECIAL FEATURES:

Sanmina Corp is a provider of integrated manufacturing solutions, components, and after-market services to original equipment manufacturers in the communications networks, storage, industrial, defense and aerospace end markets. The operations are managed as two businesses: Integrated Manufacturing Solutions, which consists of printed circuit board assembly and represents a majority of the firm's revenue; and Components, Products, and Services, which includes interconnect systems and mechanical systems. The firm generates revenue primarily in the United States, China, and Mexico, but has a presence around the world.

CONTACTS: Note: Officers with more than one job title may be intentionally listed here more than once.

Jure Sola, CEO
Jonathan Faust, CFO
Vishnu Venkatesh, Chief Accounting Officer
Alan Reid, Executive VP, Divisional
Charles Mason, Executive VP, Divisional

FINANCIAL DATA: Note: Data for latest year may not have been available at press time.

In U.S. $	2024	2023	2022	2021	2020	2019
Revenue	7,568,328,192	8,935,048,192	7,919,622,144	6,738,356,224	6,950,208,000	8,233,859,072
R&D Expense	28,514,000	26,427,000	21,343,000	20,911,000	22,564,000	27,552,000
Operating Income	345,721,000	461,712,000	356,294,000	270,993,000	253,669,000	304,354,000
Operating Margin %	.05%	.05%	.04%	.04%	.04%	.04%
SGA Expense	266,194,000	255,072,000	244,569,000	234,537,000	240,931,000	260,032,000
Net Income	222,536,000	309,970,000	240,384,000	249,546,000	133,169,000	141,515,000
Operating Cash Flow	340,216,000	235,168,000	330,854,000	338,342,000	300,555,000	382,965,000
Capital Expenditure	111,227,000	191,367,000	138,639,000	73,296,000	65,982,000	134,674,000
EBITDA	469,136,000	567,334,000	433,576,000	410,848,000	335,336,000	393,331,000
Return on Assets %	.05%	.06%	.05%	.06%	.03%	.04%
Return on Equity %	.10%	.16%	.13%	.14%	.08%	.09%
Debt to Equity	.14%	.14%	.18%	.17%	0.202	0.211

CONTACT INFORMATION:

Phone: 408 964-3500   Fax: 408-964-3636
Toll-Free:
Address: 2700 N. First St., San Jose, CA 95134 United States

STOCK TICKER/OTHER:

Stock Ticker: SANM   Exchange: NAS
Employees: 37,000   Fiscal Year Ends: 09/30
Parent Company:

SALARIES/BONUSES:

Top Exec. Salary: $1,230,769   Bonus: $
Second Exec. Salary: Bonus: $
$487,500

OTHER THOUGHTS:

Estimated Female Officers or Directors:
Hot Spot for Advancement for Women/Minorities:

Sanofi SA

NAIC Code: 325412

en.sanofi.com

TYPES OF BUSINESS:

Pharmaceuticals Development & Manufacturing
Pharmaceuticals
Research
Development
Vaccines
Diabetes
Cardiovascular
Specialty Care

BRANDS/DIVISIONS/AFFILIATES:

GROWTH PLANS/SPECIAL FEATURES:

Sanofi develops and markets drugs with a concentration in vaccines, immunology, oncology, cardiovascular disease, diabetes, and over-the-counter treatments. However, the company's decision in late 2019 to pull back from the cardio-metabolic area will likely reduce the firm's footprint in this large therapeutic area. The company offers a diverse array of drugs with its highest revenue generator, Dupixent, representing about 30% of total sales, but profits are shared with Regeneron. Just over 40% of total revenue comes from the United States and 25% from Europe. Emerging markets represent the majority of the remainder of revenue.

CONTACTS: *Note: Officers with more than one job title may be intentionally listed here more than once.*

Paul Hudson, CEO
Roy Papatheodorou, Exec. VP
Jean-Baptiste De Chatillon, CFO
Frederic Oudea, Chairman of the Board
Olivier Charmeil, Executive VP, Divisional
Julie Van Ongevalle, Executive VP, Divisional
Thomas Triomphe, Executive VP, Divisional
Brendan OCallaghan, Executive VP, Divisional
Madeleine Roach, Executive VP, Divisional
Brian Foard, Executive VP, Divisional
Houman Ashrafian, Executive VP
Emmanuel Frenehard, Executive VP
Natalie Bickford, Executive VP

FINANCIAL DATA: *Note: Data for latest year may not have been available at press time.*

In U.S. $	2024	2023	2022	2021	2020	2019
Revenue	50,267,878,774	47,239,502,798	46,039,728,140	44,466,515,444	42,416,572,050	42,713,962,107
R&D Expense	8,392,735,000	7,385,925,000	7,379,115,000	6,460,840,000	6,276,958,000	6,833,144,000
Operating Income	10,740,070,000	10,414,300,000	12,401,820,000	10,382,520,000	8,955,732,000	8,147,559,000
Operating Margin %	.21%	.22%	.27%	.23%	.21%	.19%
SGA Expense	10,423,380,000	10,139,610,000	9,919,410,000	10,845,630,000	10,659,480,000	11,219,070,000
Net Income	6,311,010,000	6,129,398,000	9,501,702,000	7,063,564,000	13,954,600,000	3,125,993,000
Operating Cash Flow	10,307,600,000	11,643,590,000	11,947,790,000	11,943,250,000	8,419,977,000	8,757,094,000
Capital Expenditure	3,626,561,000	3,298,524,000	2,387,060,000	2,318,956,000	2,364,359,000	2,028,377,000
EBITDA	12,523,270,000	12,928,490,000	15,334,850,000	13,096,480,000	20,298,520,000	12,102,160,000
Return on Assets %	.04%	.04%	.07%	.05%	.11%	.02%
Return on Equity %	.07%	.07%	.12%	.09%	.19%	.05%
Debt to Equity	.17%	.22%	.22%	.28%	0.276	0.358

CONTACT INFORMATION:

Phone: 33-1-53-77-40-00   Fax:
Toll-Free:
Address: 54, rue La Boetie, Paris, 75008 France

STOCK TICKER/OTHER:

Stock Ticker: SNY   Exchange: NAS
Employees: 87,994   Fiscal Year Ends: 12/31
Parent Company:

SALARIES/BONUSES:

Top Exec. Salary: $1,475,596   Bonus: $4,795,687
Second Exec. Salary: $ Bonus: $

OTHER THOUGHTS:

Estimated Female Officers or Directors: 6
Hot Spot for Advancement for Women/Minorities: Y

SAP SE

NAIC Code: 511210H

TYPES OF BUSINESS:

Computer Software, Business Management & ERP
Consulting & Training Services
Hosting Services
Software Licensing
Software Development

BRANDS/DIVISIONS/AFFILIATES:

SAP HANA

GROWTH PLANS/SPECIAL FEATURES:

Founded in Germany in 1972 by former IBM employees, SAP is the world's largest provider of enterprise application software. Known as the leader in enterprise resource planning software, SAP's portfolio also includes software for supply chain management, procurement, travel and expense management, and customer relationship management, among others. The company operates in more than 180 countries and has more than 400,000 customers, approximately 80% of which are small to medium-size enterprises.

SAP offers medical, dental, vision and life insurance; a 401(k) and spending/saving accounts.

CONTACTS: Note: Officers with more than one job title may be intentionally listed here more than once.

Christian Klein, CEO
Julia White, Other Corporate Officer
Dominik Asam, CFO
Pekka Ala-Pietila, Chairman of the Board
Jurgen Muller, Chief Technology Officer
Hasso Plattner, Co-Founder
Lars Lamade, Deputy Chairman
Margret Klein-Magar, Director
Christine Regitz, Director
Thomas Saueressig, Other Corporate Officer
Scott Russell, Other Corporate Officer
Gina Vargiu-Breuer, Other Corporate Officer

FINANCIAL DATA: Note: Data for latest year may not have been available at press time.

In U.S. $	2024	2023	2022	2021	2020	2019
Revenue	38,792,281,540	35,422,247,557	33,506,242,433	30,593,644,709	31,030,647,461	31,274,687,234
R&D Expense	7,393,870,000	7,178,206,000	6,901,249,000	5,981,839,000	5,055,619,000	4,871,737,000
Operating Income	8,862,657,000	6,826,334,000	6,868,331,000	7,338,252,000	7,515,324,000	6,359,818,000
Operating Margin %	.23%	.19%	.20%	.24%	.24%	.20%
SGA Expense	11,946,650,000	11,568,670,000	10,482,410,000	9,129,398,000	9,604,994,000	10,581,160,000
Net Income	3,545,970,000	6,968,218,000	2,592,508,000	5,965,948,000	5,839,954,000	3,769,580,000
Operating Cash Flow	5,925,085,000	7,187,288,000	6,409,762,000	7,063,564,000	8,166,856,000	3,967,083,000
Capital Expenditure	904,653,800	891,032,900	995,042,700	795,686,700	926,220,200	927,355,300
EBITDA	7,345,062,000	8,121,453,000	7,175,937,000	11,728,720,000	10,676,500,000	7,838,819,000
Return on Assets %	.04%	.09%	.03%	.08%	.09%	.06%
Return on Equity %	.07%	.15%	.06%	.15%	.17%	.11%
Debt to Equity	.15%	.17%	.22%	.28%	0.458	0.362

CONTACT INFORMATION:

Phone: 49 6227747474   Fax: 49 6227757575
Toll-Free: 800-872-1727
Address: Dietmar-Hopp-Allee 16, Walldorf, 69190 Germany

STOCK TICKER/OTHER:

Stock Ticker: SAP   Exchange: NYS
Employees: 105,500   Fiscal Year Ends: 12/31
Parent Company:

SALARIES/BONUSES:

Top Exec. Salary: $1,248,581   Bonus: $2,482,293
Second Exec. Salary: Bonus: $2,155,732
$1,135,074

OTHER THOUGHTS:

Estimated Female Officers or Directors: 4
Hot Spot for Advancement for Women/Minorities: Y

Sargent & Lundy LLC

NAIC Code: 541330

www.sargentlundy.com

TYPES OF BUSINESS:

Engineering Consulting Services
Consulting
Engineering
Nuclear Power
Energy
Environmental Solutions
Electric Grid Infrastructure
Renewable Energy

BRANDS/DIVISIONS/AFFILIATES:

CONTACTS:
Note: Officers with more than one job title may be intentionally listed here more than once.

Victor Suchodolski, CEO
Michael Helminski, Exec. VP-Finance & Legal
Meghan Wilhelm, VP-Human Resources
Kuldip Mohanty, CTO
Victor Suchodolski, Chmn.

GROWTH PLANS/SPECIAL FEATURES:

Sargent & Lundy, LLC is a consulting, engineering, design, analysis and project provider for electric power generation and power delivery projects worldwide. The company's client base consists of investor-owned and government utilities, developers, industrial complexes, rural cooperatives, municipal and public power systems, regional transmission organizations, financial institutions and gas-line and oil companies. Sargent & Lundy operates through nine divisions. The nuclear power division has been Sargent & Lundy's core competency since 1954, with its services addressing emerging issues with solutions for both nuclear unit design and upgrades to operating units. The energy and industrial division provide related project development services through to completion. The environmental services division offers integrated environmental solutions such as compliance planning, permitting, civil/geotechnical, water optimization, modeling, siting and transmission routing, due diligence and decommissioning. The electric grid infrastructure division offers comprehensive services, from cross-country bulk power transmission lines to enclosed gas-insulated substations in urban locations to electronic fleet applications, as well as grid modernization. The renewable energy division provides solutions that tackle all aspects of renewable energy projects, from planning to commissioning, and from evaluating generation technology options to grid interconnection solutions. Projects include wind, solar, biomass, geothermal, hydroelectric, energy storage, hybrid power plants, microgrids and more. The energy business consulting division offers project development/planning, engineering site services, due diligence, asset transaction services, financial modeling, analysis, operational assessments and grid modernization consulting. The national security division provides a full range of security solutions for the U.S. government and its allies. The construction management and commissioning division provides services for both new and existing power stations, as well as for transmission and distribution systems. Last, the operations and maintenance support services division assist clients with continuous operational improvements in relation to nuclear and fossil power plants, new-generation nuclear and fossil power plants, and transmission and substation facilities.

FINANCIAL DATA:
Note: Data for latest year may not have been available at press time.

In U.S. $	2024	2023	2022	2021	2020	2019
Revenue						
R&D Expense						
Operating Income						
Operating Margin %						
SGA Expense						
Net Income						
Operating Cash Flow						
Capital Expenditure						
EBITDA						
Return on Assets %						
Return on Equity %						
Debt to Equity						

CONTACT INFORMATION:

Phone: 312-269-2000   Fax: 312-269-3680
Toll-Free:
Address: 55 E. Monroe St., Chicago, IL 60603 United States

STOCK TICKER/OTHER:

Stock Ticker: Private   Exchange:
Employees: 2,500   Fiscal Year Ends:
Parent Company:

SALARIES/BONUSES:

Top Exec. Salary: $ Bonus: $
Second Exec. Salary: $ Bonus: $

OTHER THOUGHTS:

Estimated Female Officers or Directors:
Hot Spot for Advancement for Women/Minorities:

Sales, profits and employees may be estimates. Financial information, benefits and other data can change quickly and may vary from those stated here.

SAS Institute Inc

www.sas.com

NAIC Code: 511210H

TYPES OF BUSINESS:

Computer Software, Statistical Analysis
Business Intelligence Software
Data Warehousing
Online Bookstore
Consulting
Artificial Intelligence
Internet of Things
Cloud Analytics

BRANDS/DIVISIONS/AFFILIATES:

Kamakura Corporation

CONTACTS: Note: Officers with more than one job title may be intentionally listed here more than once.

James Goodnight, CEO
Wm. David Davis, CFO
Jennifer Chase, CMO
Jenn Mann, Chief Human Resources Officer
Jay Upchurch, CIO
John Boswell, Chief Legal Officer
Carl Farrell, Exec. VP-SAS Americas
John Sall, Exec. VP
John Sall, Chmn.
Mikael Hagstrom, Exec. VP-EMEA & Asia Pacific

GROWTH PLANS/SPECIAL FEATURES:

SAS Institute, Inc. provides statistical analysis software. The company's products are designed to extract, manage and analyze large volumes of data, often assisting in financial reporting and credit analysis. Individual contracts can be tailored to specific global and local industries, such as banking, manufacturing and government. SAS' advanced analytics software is infused with cutting-edge, innovative algorithms that help clients solve intractable problems, make informed decisions and capture new opportunities. The software comprises data mining, statistical analysis, forecasting, text analysis, optimization and stimulation features. Other products that provide enterprise solutions include artificial intelligence, Internet of Things (IoT), business intelligence, cloud, data management, fraud and security, risk management and more. Industries that utilize SAS products and solutions include agriculture, banking, capital markets, education, health care, hospitality, insurance, life sciences, manufacturing, oil and gas, public sector, retail and consumer goods, small/medium business, sports analytics, telecommunications, media and technology, travel, transportation and utilities.

FINANCIAL DATA: Note: Data for latest year may not have been available at press time.

In U.S. $	2024	2023	2022	2021	2020	2019
Revenue	3,532,140,000	3,348,000,000	3,100,000,000	3,200,000,000	3,000,000,000	3,100,000,000
R&D Expense						
Operating Income						
Operating Margin %						
SGA Expense						
Net Income						
Operating Cash Flow						
Capital Expenditure						
EBITDA						
Return on Assets %						
Return on Equity %						
Debt to Equity						

CONTACT INFORMATION:

Phone: 919-677-8000   Fax: 919-677-4444
Toll-Free: 800-727-0025
Address: 100 SAS Campus Dr., Cary, NC 27513-2414 United States

STOCK TICKER/OTHER:

Stock Ticker: Private   Exchange:
Employees: 11,950   Fiscal Year Ends: 12/31
Parent Company:

SALARIES/BONUSES:

Top Exec. Salary: $ Bonus: $
Second Exec. Salary: $ Bonus: $

OTHER THOUGHTS:

Estimated Female Officers or Directors: 4
Hot Spot for Advancement for Women/Minorities: Y

Sasol Limited

NAIC Code: 325110

TYPES OF BUSINESS:

Synthetic Fuels Manufacturing
Crude Oil Refining
Natural Gas Production
Coal Mining
Polymers
Solvents

BRANDS/DIVISIONS/AFFILIATES:

GROWTH PLANS/SPECIAL FEATURES:

Sasol Ltd operates as a vertically integrated chemicals and energy company through its two main businesses: Southern Africa Energy & Chemicals business; and International Chemical business. It generates maximum revenue from the Southern Africa Energy & Chemicals business. The company operates coal mines and its upstream interests in oil and gas, both of which are used as feedstock in the company's energy and chemicals operations. Geographically the company generates the majority of its revenue from South Africa.

CONTACTS: Note: Officers with more than one job title may be intentionally listed here more than once.

Simon Baloyi, CEO
Walt Bruns, CFO
Vuyo Kahla, Director
Sarushen Pillay, Executive VP, Divisional
Hermann Wenhold, Executive VP, Divisional
Victor Bester, Executive VP, Divisional
Antje Gerber, Executive VP, Divisional
Charlotte Mokoena, Executive VP, Divisional
Christian Herrmann, Executive VP, Geographical

FINANCIAL DATA: Note: Data for latest year may not have been available at press time.

In U.S. $	2024	2023	2022	2021	2020	2019
Revenue	15,302,221,266	16,113,468,256	15,170,676,297	11,230,636,202	10,588,592,277	11,323,302,834
R&D Expense						
Operating Income	2,493,311,000	2,601,997,000	3,672,053,000	2,170,537,000	798,509,300	1,654,921,000
Operating Margin %	.16%	.16%	.24%	.19%	.08%	.15%
SGA Expense	2,666,240,000	2,584,698,000	2,394,416,000	2,273,493,000	2,517,452,000	2,524,516,000
Net Income	-2,462,441,000	489,417,900	2,166,810,000	502,377,800	-5,103,540,000	188,502,900
Operating Cash Flow	1,654,810,000	1,970,242,000	2,238,785,000	1,893,540,000	1,653,642,000	1,776,733,000
Capital Expenditure	1,677,504,000	1,716,161,000	1,263,342,000	887,059,600	1,955,892,000	3,103,707,000
EBITDA	-478,126,600	2,227,772,000	4,248,296,000	1,944,489,000	-4,939,900,000	1,463,415,000
Return on Assets %	-.11%	.02%	.10%	.02%	-.20%	.01%
Return on Equity %	-.26%	.05%	.23%	.06%	-.50%	.02%
Debt to Equity	.92%	.49%	.51%	.76%	1.082	0.621

CONTACT INFORMATION:

Phone: 27-11-441-3111   Fax: 27-11-788-5092
Toll-Free:
Address: 50 Katherine St., Sandton, 2196 South Africa

STOCK TICKER/OTHER:

Stock Ticker: SSL   Exchange: NYS
Employees: 28,141   Fiscal Year Ends: 06/30
Parent Company:

SALARIES/BONUSES:

Top Exec. Salary: $729,594   Bonus: $
Second Exec. Salary: Bonus: $
$613,121

OTHER THOUGHTS:

Estimated Female Officers or Directors: 2
Hot Spot for Advancement for Women/Minorities: Y

Saudi Aramco (Saudi Arabian Oil Company) www.saudiaramco.com

NAIC Code: 211100

TYPES OF BUSINESS:

Oil & Gas-Exploration & Production
Oil Refining
Gas Production
Chemicals and Petrochemicals
Refined Products
Retail Fuels
Power Systems
Hydrocarbon Reserves

BRANDS/DIVISIONS/AFFILIATES:

Rongsheng Petrochemical Co Ltd
Saudi Aramco Power Company

CONTACTS: *Note: Officers with more than one job title may be intentionally listed here more than once.*

Amin H. Nasser, CEO
Ziad T. Al-Murshed, CFO
Nabeel A. Al-Jama', Sr. VP-Human Resources & Corp. Svcs.
Khalid G. Al-Buainain, Sr. VP-Eng.
David B. Kultgen, General Counsel
Khalid G. Al-Buainain, Sr. VP-Oper. Support & Capital
Mohammad A. Al-Ali, Sr. VP-Finance
Salim S. Al-Aydh, Sr. VP
Amin H. Nasser, Sr. VP-Upstream Oper.
Abdulrahman F. Al-Wuhaib, Sr. VP-Oper. Svcs.
Abdulaziz F. Al-Khayyal, Sr. VP-Industrial Rel.
Yasir Othman al-Rumayyan, Chmn.

GROWTH PLANS/SPECIAL FEATURES:

Saudi Aramco (Saudi Arabian Oil Company) (Aramco) is a world-leading integrated energy and chemicals company, present in three major global energy markets of Asia, Europe and North America. Aramco's energy products include oil, gas production, chemicals, refined products and retail fuels. The company manages Saudi Arabia's hydrocarbon reserves base, and its downstream activities primarily consist of refining and petrochemical manufacturing. The firm's products are supplied, traded, distributed and retailed domestically and internationally, including transportation fuels, industrial feedstocks and base oils. Aramco is the sole supplier of natural gas to Saudi Arabia. The company's sustainable business division focuses on improving operational efficiency, efficient environmental performance of facilities, low carbon energy solutions and strategic sustainable investment. The technology development division invests in technology to enable the company's long-term viability, with an approach to uphold its global position in oil and gas via production efficiency and resilience. Therefore, this division focuses on innovative upstream and downstream technologies across Aramco's assets, including the development of innovative fuel formulations and internal combustion engine technologies. Aramco has a partnership with Aston Martin Racing, which competes in Formula One. Moreover, Saudi Aramco Power Company (SAPCO) is the firm's fully owned subsidiary that consolidates all conventional and renewable power investment under the entity.

FINANCIAL DATA: *Note: Data for latest year may not have been available at press time.*

In U.S. $	2024	2023	2022	2021	2020	2019
Revenue	479,398,426,000	494,721,548,000	552,250,000,000	359,460,000,000	229,891,000,000	329,809,000,000
R&D Expense						
Operating Income						
Operating Margin %						
SGA Expense						
Net Income	106,246,000,000	120,658,222,000	161,100,000,000	109,972,000,000	49,003,000,000	88,185,000,000
Operating Cash Flow						
Capital Expenditure						
EBITDA						
Return on Assets %						
Return on Equity %						
Debt to Equity						

CONTACT INFORMATION:

Phone: 966-3-872-0115   Fax: 966-3-873-8190
Toll-Free:
Address: North Park 3, Building 3302, Dhahran, 31311 Saudi Arabia

STOCK TICKER/OTHER:

Stock Ticker: 2222   Exchange: Riyadh
Employees: 79,000   Fiscal Year Ends: 12/31
Parent Company:

SALARIES/BONUSES:

Top Exec. Salary: $ Bonus: $
Second Exec. Salary: $ Bonus: $

OTHER THOUGHTS:

Estimated Female Officers or Directors:
Hot Spot for Advancement for Women/Minorities:

Schneider Electric SA

NAIC Code: 335311

www.se.com/ww/en

TYPES OF BUSINESS:

Electrical Distribution Products
Infrastructure Products
Building Automation & Control Products

BRANDS/DIVISIONS/AFFILIATES:

EcoStruxure
DC Systems BV

GROWTH PLANS/SPECIAL FEATURES:

Schneider Electric is a leading global supplier of electrical and industrial automation equipment. The group has four end markets: buildings, data centers, infrastructure, and industry, each of which, relies on Schneider's products and solutions to ensure their operations run safely and efficiently. Schneider sells its products via distributors (45% of revenue), direct to customers (40% of revenue), and the remainder through other channels such as panel builders or system integrators. The group's largest geographic markets are the US, China, and India.

CONTACTS:
Note: Officers with more than one job title may be intentionally listed here more than once.

Jean-Pascal Tricoire, Chairman of the Board
Fred Kindle, Director

FINANCIAL DATA:
Note: Data for latest year may not have been available at press time.

In U.S. $	2024	2023	2022	2021	2020	2019
Revenue	43,306,468,732	40,751,420,194	38,792,281,540	32,809,308,730	28,557,321,329	30,826,333,309
R&D Expense	1,484,676,000	1,325,766,000	1,180,477,000	970,488,100	814,983,000	745,743,500
Operating Income	7,457,435,000	6,769,581,000	6,311,010,000	5,173,666,000	4,194,098,000	4,587,968,000
Operating Margin %	.17%	.17%	.16%	.16%	.15%	.15%
SGA Expense	8,293,984,000	7,884,222,000	7,740,068,000	6,811,578,000	6,256,527,000	6,628,831,000
Net Income	4,845,630,000	4,543,700,000	3,946,651,000	3,636,776,000	2,413,167,000	2,738,933,000
Operating Cash Flow	6,333,712,000	6,704,881,000	4,942,111,000	4,104,427,000	5,034,052,000	4,860,386,000
Capital Expenditure	1,610,670,000	1,549,376,000	1,240,636,000	994,324,600	927,355,300	958,002,200
EBITDA	9,149,830,000	8,270,148,000	7,223,610,000	6,476,731,000	4,748,014,000	5,086,265,000
Return on Assets %	.07%	.07%	.06%	.06%	.05%	.06%
Return on Equity %	.15%	.15%	.14%	.14%	.10%	.11%
Debt to Equity	.36%	.44%	.29%	.31%	0.397	

CONTACT INFORMATION:

Phone: 33 141297000   Fax: 33 141297100
Toll-Free:
Address: 35 rue Joseph Monier, Rueil Malmaison, 92500 France

SALARIES/BONUSES:

Top Exec. Salary: $ Bonus: $
Second Exec. Salary: $ Bonus: $

STOCK TICKER/OTHER:

Stock Ticker: SBGSF   Exchange: PINX
Employees: 168,044   Fiscal Year Ends: 12/31
Parent Company:

OTHER THOUGHTS:

Estimated Female Officers or Directors: 2
Hot Spot for Advancement for Women/Minorities:

Science Applications International Corporation (SAIC)

www.saic.com
NAIC Code: 541512

TYPES OF BUSINESS:
IT Consulting
IT Infrastructure Management
Research & Development
Software Development
Engineering

BRANDS/DIVISIONS/AFFILIATES:

GROWTH PLANS/SPECIAL FEATURES:
Science Applications International Corp provides technical, engineering, and enterprise IT services mainly to the U.S. government. Specifically, it offers end-to-end solutions spanning the design, development, integration, deployment, management and operations, sustainment, and security of the customer's entire IT infrastructure. The company has two reportable segments which include Defense and Intelligence and the Civilian segment. Maximum revenue is generated from its Defense and Intelligence segment, which provides a diverse portfolio of national security solutions to the Department of Defense (DoD) and the Intelligence Community of the United States Government. The Civilian segment provides solutions to the civilian markets, encompassing federal, state, and local governments.

CONTACTS: Note: Officers with more than one job title may be intentionally listed here more than once.
Toni Townes-Whitley, CEO
Prabu Natarajan, CFO
Donna Morea, Chairman of the Board
David Ray, Executive VP, Divisional
Barbara Supplee, Executive VP, Divisional
Joshua Jackson, Executive VP, Divisional
Vincent DiFronzo, Executive VP, Divisional
Hilary Hageman, Executive VP

FINANCIAL DATA: Note: Data for latest year may not have been available at press time.

In U.S. $	2024	2023	2022	2021	2020	2019
Revenue	7,443,999,744	7,704,000,000	7,393,999,872	7,056,000,000	6,378,999,808	
R&D Expense						
Operating Income	500,000,000	514,000,000	516,000,000	444,000,000	418,000,000	
Operating Margin %	.07%	.07%	.07%	.06%	.07%	
SGA Expense	373,000,000	374,000,000	344,000,000	352,000,000	288,000,000	
Net Income	477,000,000	300,000,000	277,000,000	209,000,000	226,000,000	
Operating Cash Flow	396,000,000	532,000,000	518,000,000	755,000,000	458,000,000	
Capital Expenditure	27,000,000	25,000,000	36,000,000	46,000,000	21,000,000	
EBITDA	882,000,000	650,000,000	628,000,000	572,000,000	507,000,000	
Return on Assets %	.09%	.05%	.05%	.04%	.05%	
Return on Equity %	.27%	.18%	.18%	.14%	.16%	
Debt to Equity	1.22%	1.47%	1.58%	1.72%	1.428	

CONTACT INFORMATION:
Phone: 703 676-4300   Fax:
Toll-Free:
Address: 12010 Sunset Hills Road, Reston, VA 20190 United States

STOCK TICKER/OTHER:
Stock Ticker: SAIC   Exchange: NAS
Employees: 25,000   Fiscal Year Ends: 01/31
Parent Company:

SALARIES/BONUSES:
Top Exec. Salary: $1,200,000   Bonus: $6,384,074
Second Exec. Salary: Bonus: $1,000,000
$391,346

OTHER THOUGHTS:
Estimated Female Officers or Directors: 5
Hot Spot for Advancement for Women/Minorities: Y

Seagate Technology Public Limited Company www.seagate.com

NAIC Code: 334112

TYPES OF BUSINESS:

Computer Storage Equipment-Disk & Tape Drives
Driver Components
Business Intelligence Software

GROWTH PLANS/SPECIAL FEATURES:

Seagate is a leading supplier of hard disk drives for data storage to the enterprise and consumer markets. It forms a practical duopoly in the market with its chief rival, Western Digital; they are both vertically integrated.

BRANDS/DIVISIONS/AFFILIATES:

Seagate
LaCie
Backup Plus
Expansion
Maxtor

CONTACTS: Note: Officers with more than one job title may be intentionally listed here more than once.

William Mosley, CEO
Gianluca Romano, CFO
Michael Cannon, Chairman of the Board
James Lee, Chief Legal Officer
John Morris, Chief Technology Officer
Ban Seng Teh, Executive VP
Kian Fatt Chong, Senior VP, Divisional

FINANCIAL DATA: Note: Data for latest year may not have been available at press time.

In U.S. $	2024	2023	2022	2021	2020	2019
Revenue	6,551,000,064	7,384,000,000	11,660,999,680	10,680,999,936	10,508,999,680	10,389,999,616
R&D Expense	654,000,000	797,000,000	941,000,000	903,000,000	973,000,000	991,000,000
Operating Income	422,000,000	60,000,000	1,958,000,000	1,500,000,000	1,382,000,000	1,465,000,000
Operating Margin %	.06%	.01%	.17%	.14%	.13%	.14%
SGA Expense	460,000,000	491,000,000	559,000,000	502,000,000	473,000,000	453,000,000
Net Income	335,000,000	-529,000,000	1,649,000,000	1,314,000,000	1,004,000,000	2,012,000,000
Operating Cash Flow	918,000,000	942,000,000	1,657,000,000	1,626,000,000	1,714,000,000	1,761,000,000
Capital Expenditure	254,000,000	316,000,000	381,000,000	498,000,000	585,000,000	602,000,000
EBITDA	1,041,000,000	330,000,000	2,379,000,000	1,965,000,000	1,612,000,000	2,137,000,000
Return on Assets %	.04%	- .06%	.19%	.15%	.11%	.22%
Return on Equity %			4.46%	1.09%	.51%	1.05%
Debt to Equity			46.77%	7.82%	2.353	1.967

CONTACT INFORMATION:

Phone: 353 12343136   Fax:
Toll-Free: 800-732-4283
Address: 38/39 Fitzwilliam Square, Dublin, 2 Ireland

STOCK TICKER/OTHER:

Stock Ticker: STX   Exchange: NAS
Employees: 30,000   Fiscal Year Ends: 06/30
Parent Company:

SALARIES/BONUSES:

Top Exec. Salary: $676,928   Bonus: $
Second Exec. Salary: $442,391   Bonus: $

OTHER THOUGHTS:

Estimated Female Officers or Directors: 3
Hot Spot for Advancement for Women/Minorities: Y

Seatrium Limited

NAIC Code: 541330

www.seatrium.com

TYPES OF BUSINESS:

Marine & Offshore Engineering
Ship Construction & Conversion
Rigs
Floaters
Drill ships
Repair

BRANDS/DIVISIONS/AFFILIATES:

Estaleiro Jurong Aracruz
Gravifloat AS
LMG Marin AS
Sevan SSP AS
Sembmarine SLP Limited

GROWTH PLANS/SPECIAL FEATURES:

Singapore-based Seatrium (formerly known as Sembcorp Marine) is a leading global marine and offshore engineering group with a track record of more than 60 years. The company specializes in ship repair, shipbuilding, ship conversion, rig building, and offshore engineering and construction. The company's global network includes facilities in Singapore, Brazil, China, Indonesia, Japan, Norway, the United Kingdom and the United States. Its Singapore operations include one of the largest integrated yards globally, Sembcorp Marine Tuas Boulevard Yard.

CONTACTS:
Note: Officers with more than one job title may be intentionally listed here more than once.

Leng Yeow Ong, CEO
Mark Gainsborough, Chairman of the Board
How Chor, COO
Chee Keong Yap, Deputy Chairman

FINANCIAL DATA:
Note: Data for latest year may not have been available at press time.

In U.S. $	2024	2023	2022	2021	2020	2019
Revenue	7,148,378,499	5,646,625,827	1,507,933,804	1,442,124,182	1,169,580,941	2,232,292,938
R&D Expense						
Operating Income	164,525,700	-1,217,880,000	-159,873,000	-947,970,900	-450,356,200	-107,480,800
Operating Margin %	.02%	-.22%	-.11%	-.66%	-.39%	-.05%
SGA Expense	248,217,300	283,035,700	85,531,630	69,104,000	72,242,700	66,232,480
Net Income	121,457,400	-1,561,773,000	-202,231,100	-906,495,700	-451,103,500	-106,229,400
Operating Cash Flow	75,386,820	465,269,900	804,810,600	-456,225,500	-580,725,600	-229,357,200
Capital Expenditure	78,688,910	90,107,640	22,584,220	37,277,160	70,960,270	244,923,700
EBITDA	645,487,500	-996,024,100	62,327,110	-763,401,200	-261,847,700	147,357,700
Return on Assets %	.01%	-.16%	-.03%	-.13%	-.07%	-.02%
Return on Equity %	.02%	-.40%	-.07%	-.31%	-.20%	-.06%
Debt to Equity	.44%	.43%	.44%	.63%	0.463	1.488

CONTACT INFORMATION:

Phone: 65 6265-1766 Fax: 65 6710-3182
Toll-Free:
Address: 80 Tuas South Blvd., Singapore, 637051 Singapore

STOCK TICKER/OTHER:

Stock Ticker: SMBMY Exchange: PINX
Employees: 22,747 Fiscal Year Ends: 12/31
Parent Company:

SALARIES/BONUSES:

Top Exec. Salary: $ Bonus: $
Second Exec. Salary: $ Bonus: $

OTHER THOUGHTS:

Estimated Female Officers or Directors: 5
Hot Spot for Advancement for Women/Minorities: Y

Seiko Epson Corp

www.epson.jp

NAIC Code: 334118

TYPES OF BUSINESS:
Printers, Computer, Manufacturing
Printers
Office Machines
Smart Glasses
Manufacture
Robotics
Semiconductors
Alloy Powder

BRANDS/DIVISIONS/AFFILIATES:

GROWTH PLANS/SPECIAL FEATURES:
Seiko Epson Corp is a Japan-based electronics manufacturer of printers and imaging equipment. The firm's product portfolio includes inkjet, dot matrix, and laser printers, scanners, desktop computers, business, multimedia and home theatre projectors, large home theatre televisions, robots and industrial automation equipment, point of sale docket printers and cash registers, laptops, integrated circuits, and associated electronic components. The firm has operations in the Americas, Middle East and Africa, Australia, and Asia-Pacific regions.

CONTACTS: *Note: Officers with more than one job title may be intentionally listed here more than once.*
Yasunori Yoshino, COO, Divisional
Eiichi Abe, Director
Junkichi Yoshida, Director
Yasunori Ogawa, Director

FINANCIAL DATA: *Note: Data for latest year may not have been available at press time.*

In U.S. $	2024	2023	2022	2021	2020	2019
Revenue	9,122,452,251	9,235,844,458	7,837,503,454	6,914,329,405	7,245,209,778	7,565,093,170
R&D Expense						
Operating Income	399,423,800	673,743,400	655,922,000	330,838,700	274,090,500	495,390,200
Operating Margin %	.04%	.07%	.08%	.05%	.04%	.07%
SGA Expense	2,721,084,000	2,579,450,000	2,282,797,000	2,018,432,000	2,229,506,000	2,375,125,000
Net Income	365,287,400	520,987,200	640,710,900	214,676,500	53,686,480	372,882,600
Operating Cash Flow	1,149,472,000	425,652,600	769,237,800	924,895,900	710,386,000	534,303,000
Capital Expenditure	392,897,800	410,274,900	304,387,700	387,913,100	525,597,100	626,930,000
EBITDA	982,296,600	1,211,365,000	1,137,774,000	825,617,900	765,613,800	902,818,700
Return on Assets %	.04%	.06%	.08%	.03%	.01%	.05%
Return on Equity %	.07%	.11%	.15%	.06%	.01%	.10%
Debt to Equity	.22%	.27%	.33%	.43%	0.372	0.224

CONTACT INFORMATION:
Phone: 81 266-52-3131 Fax:
Toll-Free:
Address: 3-3-5 Owa, Suwa-shi, Nagano, 392-8502 Japan

STOCK TICKER/OTHER:
Stock Ticker: SEKEY Exchange: PINX
Employees: 76,647 Fiscal Year Ends: 03/31
Parent Company:

SALARIES/BONUSES:
Top Exec. Salary: $ Bonus: $
Second Exec. Salary: $ Bonus: $

OTHER THOUGHTS:
Estimated Female Officers or Directors:
Hot Spot for Advancement for Women/Minorities:

Sembcorp Industries Ltd

www.sembcorp.com.sg

NAIC Code: 221112

TYPES OF BUSINESS:

Electric Utility
Utilities
Water
Wastewater
Renewable Energy
Urban Development
Residential
Industrial

BRANDS/DIVISIONS/AFFILIATES:

GROWTH PLANS/SPECIAL FEATURES:

Sembcorp Industries Ltd is an investment holding company engaged in the production and supply of utility services, and handling and storage of petroleum products and chemicals. Its business is divided into five segments: Gas and Related Services, Renewables, Integrated Urban Solutions, Decarbonisation Solutions, Other Businesses and Corporate. The company's service portfolio includes power generation, process steam production, wastewater treatment, integrated solutions for offshore and marine industries such as specialized shipbuilding, and repairs & upgrades, and among others. A vast majority of the company's income is generated by the energy segment, and the majority of the company's revenue is earned in Singapore and India together.

Sembcorp Industries offers employees health and welfare benefits, term life insurance, personal accident insurance and a loan and interest subsidy.

CONTACTS: Note: Officers with more than one job title may be intentionally listed here more than once.

Heng Tan Tow, Chairman of the Board

FINANCIAL DATA: Note: Data for latest year may not have been available at press time.

In U.S. $	2024	2023	2022	2021	2020	2019
Revenue	4,969,410,400	5,453,418,692	6,059,784,393	4,962,440,729	4,218,229,552	5,215,673,943
R&D Expense						
Operating Income	799,194,600	888,252,200	568,419,400	345,388,400	440,641,200	631,146,900
Operating Margin %	.16%	.16%	.09%	.07%	.10%	.12%
SGA Expense	368,620,800	334,546,600	386,432,300	304,344,400	266,398,200	275,691,100
Net Income	782,931,900	729,497,300	656,702,500	216,061,300	-772,090,100	191,280,100
Operating Cash Flow	1,093,472,000	1,146,906,000	1,279,331,000	944,009,900	380,237,000	756,601,900
Capital Expenditure	1,245,257,000	647,409,500	476,264,200	224,579,900	257,879,600	723,302,100
EBITDA	1,599,164,000	1,611,554,000	1,253,001,000	781,383,000	971,114,400	1,228,994,000
Return on Assets %	.06%	.06%	.06%	.02%	- .05%	.01%
Return on Equity %	.20%	.22%	.22%	.08%	- .20%	.04%
Debt to Equity	1.62%	1.37%	1.57%	1.83%	2.201	1.256

CONTACT INFORMATION:

Phone: 65 6723-3113   Fax: 65 6822-3254
Toll-Free:
Address: 30 Hill St., #05-04, Singapore, 179360 Singapore

STOCK TICKER/OTHER:

Stock Ticker: SCRPF   Exchange: PINX
Employees: 5,063   Fiscal Year Ends: 12/31
Parent Company:

SALARIES/BONUSES:

Top Exec. Salary: $ Bonus: $
Second Exec. Salary: $ Bonus: $

OTHER THOUGHTS:

Estimated Female Officers or Directors: 1
Hot Spot for Advancement for Women/Minorities:

Sener Ingenieria Y Sistemas SA

www.group.sener

NAIC Code: 541330

TYPES OF BUSINESS:

Engineering Services
Engineering
Construction
Innovative Digital and Technology Solutions
Aerospace and Defense Solutions
Mobility Solutions
Renewable Energy Solutions
Product Development

BRANDS/DIVISIONS/AFFILIATES:

Sener Mobility
Sener Energy
Sener Diagnostics
Sener Renewables

CONTACTS: Note: Officers with more than one job title may be intentionally listed here more than once.

Jorge Sendagorta Cudos, CEO
Andres Sendagorta, Pres.

GROWTH PLANS/SPECIAL FEATURES:

Sener Ingenieria Y Sistemas SA (Sener) is an engineering and construction company in business since 1956, with current specialties across aerospace, mobility, energy, digital, naval, diagnosis, renewable markets and advanced installations. Sener develops innovative engineering and technology solutions across these market sectors to respond to the needs of its clients. Within the aerospace and defense market, the firm participates in space exploration, astronomy and defense technology, as well as in air traffic control and broadcasting. Sener Mobility provides sustainable and innovative solutions in infrastructure and transportation, with business lines including consulting, urban transport, railways, roads, architecture, airports, ports and coasts, water and environment. Sener Energy develops renewable solutions for sectors engaged in energy transition, including generation, manageability, decarbonization and related support. This division also offers services and solutions for conventional businesses, green hydrogen, offshore wind and the circular economy. For the digital sector, Sener provides engineering and technological solutions for solving day-to-day challenges, offering a completely digital approach toward operational efficiency. This division primarily serves the infrastructures, energy, naval, industry and health markets. The naval division engages in ship engineering projects worldwide, having more than 1,000 ships in shipyards that have been built with Sener's designs. Sener Diagnostics develops instruments for the automation of microbiology and molecular biology laboratory processes, in the clinical and industrial fields. Among all of them, AUTOPLAK is a flagship product that contributes to laboratory efficiency. Last, Sener Renewable Investments identifies opportunities in renewable energies to promote and invest the company's own capital in them and fully develop them until they operate commercially. Headquartered in Spain, Sener has offices worldwide, including the Americas, the U.K., Europe, the Middle East, Asia, Africa and Australia.

FINANCIAL DATA: Note: Data for latest year may not have been available at press time.

In U.S. $	2024	2023	2022	2021	2020	2019
Revenue	689,052,000	656,240,000	631,000,000	511,546,464	491,871,600	496,840,000
R&D Expense						
Operating Income						
Operating Margin %						
SGA Expense						
Net Income						
Operating Cash Flow						
Capital Expenditure						
EBITDA						
Return on Assets %						
Return on Equity %						
Debt to Equity						

CONTACT INFORMATION:

Phone: 34 944-817-500   Fax: 34 944-817-51
Toll-Free:
Address: Avda. de Zugazarte 56, Entrance Cervantes, 8, Getxo (Biscay), 48930 Spain

STOCK TICKER/OTHER:

Stock Ticker: Private   Exchange:
Employees: 3,700   Fiscal Year Ends: 12/31
Parent Company:

SALARIES/BONUSES:

Top Exec. Salary: $ Bonus: $
Second Exec. Salary: $ Bonus: $

OTHER THOUGHTS:

Estimated Female Officers or Directors:
Hot Spot for Advancement for Women/Minorities:

SEPCO Electric Power Construction Corporation en.sepco.net.cn/

NAIC Code: 541330

TYPES OF BUSINESS:
Engineering Services
Engineering
Power Construction
Electric Power Investments
Electric Power Infrastructure
Power Management

BRANDS/DIVISIONS/AFFILIATES:
Power Construction Corporation Group Co Ltd
Shandong Electric Power Construction

CONTACTS: *Note: Officers with more than one job title may be intentionally listed here more than once.*
Yuanhui Wang, Gen. Mgr.
Yulei Zhang, Chmn.

GROWTH PLANS/SPECIAL FEATURES:
SEPCO Electric Power Construction Corporation (SEPCO) is a comprehensive engineering company in project planning, investment, financing, survey, design, equipment supply, construction, installation, commissioning, operation and maintenance of electric power projects and infrastructures. SEPCO stands for Shandong Electric Power Construction and is a wholly owned subsidiary of Power Construction Corporation Group Co. Ltd. (also known as PowerChina), an engineering company. The firm has more than 20 qualifications in China, such as Level I general contracting for power, mechanical and electrical projects, architecture and petrochemical projects. SEPCO's main business is engineering, procurement and construction (EPC) of overseas power projects as well as project investment and financing. SEPCO operates primarily in the regions of Asia, Africa and South America, with additional projects in countries such as India, Indonesia and Saudi Arabia, among others. The firm provides customers with direct investment and China-sourced financing, planning, design, construction, manufacturing, operation, maintenance and other services.

FINANCIAL DATA: *Note: Data for latest year may not have been available at press time.*

In U.S. $	2024	2023	2022	2021	2020	2019
Revenue						
R&D Expense						
Operating Income						
Operating Margin %						
SGA Expense						
Net Income						
Operating Cash Flow						
Capital Expenditure						
EBITDA						
Return on Assets %						
Return on Equity %						
Debt to Equity						

CONTACT INFORMATION:
Phone: 86-531-5569-7751   Fax: 86-531-5596-7700
Toll-Free:
Address: A3-5 Bldg., No. 7000 Jingshi E. Rd., Ctr. Financial City, Jinan City, Shandong 250 014 China

STOCK TICKER/OTHER:
Stock Ticker: Government-Owned   Exchange:
Employees: 5,000   Fiscal Year Ends:
Parent Company: Power Construction Corporation Group Co Ltd

SALARIES/BONUSES:
Top Exec. Salary: $ Bonus: $
Second Exec. Salary: $ Bonus: $

OTHER THOUGHTS:
Estimated Female Officers or Directors:
Hot Spot for Advancement for Women/Minorities:

Shanghai Construction Group Co Ltd

www.scg.com.cn/scgen/scg_cu/List/list_0.htm

NAIC Code: 541330

TYPES OF BUSINESS:

Engineering Services
Construction
Engineering
Buildings
Urban Infrastructure
Facilities
Environmental Protection Projects

BRANDS/DIVISIONS/AFFILIATES:

Shanghai Construction (Group) General Corporation
Shanghai Construction No 1 (Group) Co Ltd
Shanghai Installation Engineering Group Co Ltd
Shanghai Foundation Engineering Group Co Ltd
Shanghai Building Decoration Engineering Group Co
SCG Real Estate Co Ltd
Shanghai Garden & Landscape (Group) Co Ltd
Shanghai Municipal Construction Co Ltd

CONTACTS: Note: Officers with more than one job title may be intentionally listed here more than once.

Zheng Xu, Chmn.

GROWTH PLANS/SPECIAL FEATURES:

Shanghai Construction Group Co., Ltd. (Shanghai Construction) is a Chinese construction and engineering company serving both domestic and international markets. The firm specializes in the construction of high-rise buildings, large bridges, light railways, public culture facilities, sport facilities, industrial plants, major environment protection projects and more. Shanghai Construction has completed more than 100 landmark projects in over 30 overseas countries and regions. The company not only engages in the construction of urban infrastructure but invests in and operates several of them as well. Shanghai Construction has more than 20 subsidiaries, including Shanghai Construction No. 1 (Group) Co., Ltd.; Shanghai Installation Engineering Group Co., Ltd.; Shanghai Foundation Engineering Group Co., Ltd.; Shanghai Building Decoration Engineering Group Co., Ltd.; S. C. G. Real Estate Co., Ltd.; Shanghai Garden & Landscape (Group) Co., Ltd.; and Shanghai Municipal Construction Co., Ltd. Shanghai Construction Group itself operates as a subsidiary of Shanghai Construction (Group) General Corporation.

FINANCIAL DATA: Note: Data for latest year may not have been available at press time.

In U.S. $	2024	2023	2022	2021	2020	2019
Revenue		42,967,121,000	40,161,672,500	36,149,208,000	35,440,400,000	23,861,496,750
R&D Expense						
Operating Income						
Operating Margin %						
SGA Expense						
Net Income		219,733,000	540,753,506	480,781,374	493,673,000	437,433,412
Operating Cash Flow						
Capital Expenditure						
EBITDA						
Return on Assets %						
Return on Equity %						
Debt to Equity						

CONTACT INFORMATION:

Phone: 86-21-55885959   Fax: 86-21-5588-6222
Toll-Free:
Address: No. 666, Daming Rd. E., Shanghai, Shanghai 200080 China

STOCK TICKER/OTHER:

Stock Ticker: 600170   Exchange: Shanghai
Employees: 51,353   Fiscal Year Ends: 12/31
Parent Company: Shanghai Construction (Group) General Corporation

SALARIES/BONUSES:

Top Exec. Salary: $ Bonus: $
Second Exec. Salary: $ Bonus: $

OTHER THOUGHTS:

Estimated Female Officers or Directors:
Hot Spot for Advancement for Women/Minorities:

Sharp Corp

NAIC Code: 334310

TYPES OF BUSINESS:

Audiovisual & Communications Equipment
Electronic Components
Solar Cells & Advanced Batteries
Home Appliances
Consumer Electronics
Manufacturing
Product Distribution
Communication Equipment

BRANDS/DIVISIONS/AFFILIATES:

Foxconn Technology Co Ltd
Smart Appliances & Solutions BU
Smart Business Solutions BU
Digital Imaging Solutions BU
Mobile Communication BU

GROWTH PLANS/SPECIAL FEATURES:

Sharp Corp is a Japan-based company that is principally engaged in producing and selling a broad range of consumer and industrial electronic products. The company's business segments consist of the consumer electronics segment, the energy solutions segment, the business solutions segment, the electronic components and devices segment, and the display devices segment. The company generates over half of its revenue from the consumer electronics segment and the display devices segment. It has a global business presence, with China, Japan, the Americas, and Europe its four largest markets.

CONTACTS: Note: Officers with more than one job title may be intentionally listed here more than once.

Masahiro Okitsu, Director
Po-Hsuan Wu, Director

FINANCIAL DATA: Note: Data for latest year may not have been available at press time.

In U.S. $	2024	2023	2022	2021	2020	2019
Revenue	16,119,974,706	17,690,343,620	17,325,660,611	16,841,919,014	15,705,944,051	16,662,538,550
R&D Expense						
Operating Income	-141,238,600	-178,554,600	588,149,200	577,006,400	357,296,600	584,150,300
Operating Margin %	- .01%	- .01%	.03%	.03%	.02%	.04%
SGA Expense						
Net Income	-1,041,239,000	-1,810,886,000	513,683,700	369,779,200	95,292,980	515,315,200
Operating Cash Flow	864,308,600	102,374,300	521,778,700	1,420,730,000	475,236,100	548,757,300
Capital Expenditure	364,988,900	395,820,600	437,885,300	356,720,400	653,332,400	991,724,500
EBITDA	-420,348,500	-971,591,200	1,156,950,000	998,993,400	761,302,400	1,102,555,000
Return on Assets %	- .09%	- .14%	.04%	.03%	.01%	.04%
Return on Equity %	- .85%	- .79%	.18%	.18%	.05%	.20%
Debt to Equity	3.20%	2.60%	1.26%	1.60%	2.10	1.534

CONTACT INFORMATION:

Phone: 81 666211221   Fax:
Toll-Free:
Address: 1 Takumi-cho. Sakai-Ku, Sakai City, Osaka, 590-8522 Japan

SALARIES/BONUSES:

Top Exec. Salary: $ Bonus: $
Second Exec. Salary: $ Bonus: $

STOCK TICKER/OTHER:

Stock Ticker: SHCAY   Exchange: PINX
Employees: 54,156   Fiscal Year Ends: 03/31
Parent Company: Foxconn Technology Co Ltd

OTHER THOUGHTS:

Estimated Female Officers or Directors:
Hot Spot for Advancement for Women/Minorities:

Sheladia Associates Inc

www.sheladia.com

NAIC Code: 541330

TYPES OF BUSINESS:

Engineering Consulting Services
Consulting
Project Development
Financial Analysis
Policy Design
Planning and Feasibility Studies
Engineering Design
Construction Management

BRANDS/DIVISIONS/AFFILIATES:

GROWTH PLANS/SPECIAL FEATURES:

Sheladia Associates, Inc. (Sheladia) has been in business since 1974 and is a multi-disciplinary international consulting firm serving the transportation, irrigation, agriculture, water supply, sanitation, monitoring and evaluation, facilities, vertical structures and energy industries. Sheladia provides project development services that include economic and financial analysis, policy design and institutional strengthening, planning and feasibility studies, detailed engineering design, environmental and social studies, procurement assistance and management, maintenance planning and management, construction supervision/management, as well as monitoring and evaluation. For international clients, the company also provides technical assistance to governments, their agencies and private sectors in order to strengthen and support institutional capabilities through organizational development, technology transfer and training. Sheladia is a minority-owned business enterprise, with offices in the U.S., Asia and Africa. The company has more than 1,000 projects via 300 clients across 80 countries.

CONTACTS: *Note: Officers with more than one job title may be intentionally listed here more than once.*

Manish D. Kothari, CEO

FINANCIAL DATA: *Note: Data for latest year may not have been available at press time.*

In U.S. $	2024	2023	2022	2021	2020	2019
Revenue						
R&D Expense						
Operating Income						
Operating Margin %						
SGA Expense						
Net Income						
Operating Cash Flow						
Capital Expenditure						
EBITDA						
Return on Assets %						
Return on Equity %						
Debt to Equity						

CONTACT INFORMATION:

Phone: 301-590-3939   Fax: 301-948-7174
Toll-Free:
Address: 2099 Gaither Rd., Rockville, MD 20850 United States

STOCK TICKER/OTHER:

Stock Ticker: Private   Exchange:
Employees: 400   Fiscal Year Ends:
Parent Company:

SALARIES/BONUSES:

Top Exec. Salary: $ Bonus: $
Second Exec. Salary: $ Bonus: $

OTHER THOUGHTS:

Estimated Female Officers or Directors:
Hot Spot for Advancement for Women/Minorities:

Shell plc

NAIC Code: 211100

TYPES OF BUSINESS:

Oil & Gas-Exploration & Production
Gas Stations
Refineries
Solar & Wind Power
Chemicals
Consulting & Technology Services
Hydrogen & Fuel Cell Technology

BRANDS/DIVISIONS/AFFILIATES:

Royal Dutch Shell plc

GROWTH PLANS/SPECIAL FEATURES:

Shell is an integrated oil and gas company that explores for, produces, and refines oil around the world. In 2023, it produced 1.5 million barrels of liquids and 7.3 billion cubic feet of natural gas per day. At end-2023, reserves stood at 9.6 billion barrels of oil equivalent, 49% of which, consisted of liquids. Its production and reserves are in Europe, Asia, Oceania, Africa, and North and South America. The company operates refineries with capacity of 1.6 mmb/d located in the Americas, Asia, Africa, and Europe and sells about 12 million tons per year of chemicals. Its largest chemical plants, often integrated with its local refineries, are in Central Europe, China, Singapore, and North America.

CONTACTS:
Note: Officers with more than one job title may be intentionally listed here more than once.

Wael Sawan, CEO
Sinead Gorman, CFO
Andrew Mackenzie, Chairman of the Board
Dick Boer, Deputy Chairman
Anthony Clarke, Secretary

FINANCIAL DATA:
Note: Data for latest year may not have been available at press time.

In U.S. $	2024	2023	2022	2021	2020	2019
Revenue	284,312,010,752	316,620,013,568	381,314,007,040	261,504,008,192	180,542,996,480	344,877,006,848
R&D Expense	1,099,000,000	1,287,000,000	1,075,000,000	815,000,000	907,000,000	962,000,000
Operating Income	29,992,000,000	30,737,000,000	63,109,000,000	22,283,000,000	-25,530,000,000	22,946,000,000
Operating Margin %	.11%	.10%	.17%	.09%	-.14%	.07%
SGA Expense	12,439,000,000	13,433,000,000	12,883,000,000	11,328,000,000	9,881,000,000	10,493,000,000
Net Income	16,094,000,000	19,359,000,000	42,309,000,000	20,101,000,000	-21,680,000,000	15,842,000,000
Operating Cash Flow	54,687,000,000	54,191,000,000	68,414,000,000	45,104,000,000	34,105,000,000	42,178,000,000
Capital Expenditure	19,601,000,000	22,993,000,000	22,600,000,000	19,000,000,000	16,585,000,000	22,971,000,000
EBITDA	57,483,000,000	60,361,000,000	88,690,000,000	56,506,000,000	2,224,000,000	55,151,000,000
Return on Assets %	.04%	.05%	.10%	.05%	-.06%	
Return on Equity %	.09%	.10%	.23%	.12%	-.14%	
Debt to Equity	.37%	.38%	.39%	.47%	0.587	0.436

CONTACT INFORMATION:

Phone: 31 703779111   Fax: 31 703773953
Toll-Free:
Address: Carel van Bylandtlaan 16, The Hague, 2596 HR Netherlands

STOCK TICKER/OTHER:

Stock Ticker: SHEL   Exchange: NYS
Employees: 103,000   Fiscal Year Ends: 12/31
Parent Company:

SALARIES/BONUSES:

Top Exec. Salary: $1,958,867   Bonus: $3,937,928
Second Exec. Salary: Bonus: $2,598,359
$1,293,794

OTHER THOUGHTS:

Estimated Female Officers or Directors: 1
Hot Spot for Advancement for Women/Minorities: Y

Shin-Etsu Chemical Co Ltd

www.shinetsu.co.jp

NAIC Code: 325211

TYPES OF BUSINESS:

Plastics Material and Resin Manufacturing
PVC
Silicones
Semiconductor Silicon
Rare Earth Magnets & Refined Rare Earth Elements
Synthetic Quartz
Construction & Plant Engineering
Importing & Exporting Goods

BRANDS/DIVISIONS/AFFILIATES:

GROWTH PLANS/SPECIAL FEATURES:

Shin-Etsu Chemical Co Ltd is a Japan-based company primarily engaged in chemical business. The company operates in six business segments namely Poly Vinyl Chloride, Specialty Chemicals, Silicon, Semiconductor Silicon, Electronic and Functional Materials and Diversified business. It derives majority of revenue through Poly Vinyl Chloride segment which manufactures and sells vinyl chloride, caustic soda products, chloromethane and methanol. The group is also involved in manufacturing and selling of various other chemical products such as Polyvinyl alcohol, Synthetic pheromones, Rare-earth magnets for electronics industry and general applications, Photoresists, Photomask blanks and others. Geographically, it operates from the market of Japan and its business is amplifying across the globe.

CONTACTS: Note: Officers with more than one job title may be intentionally listed here more than once.

Fumio Akiya, Chairman of the Board
Susumu Ueno, Director
Masahiko Todoroki, Director
Yasuhiko Saitoh, Director

FINANCIAL DATA: Note: Data for latest year may not have been available at press time.

In U.S. $	2024	2023	2022	2021	2020	2019
Revenue	16,765,740,009	19,500,305,680	14,401,750,310	10,392,293,734	10,715,947,130	11,066,621,160
R&D Expense						
Operating Income	4,866,968,000	6,930,034,000	4,695,376,000	2,722,945,000	2,818,946,000	2,802,728,000
Operating Margin %	.29%	.36%	.33%	.26%	.26%	.25%
SGA Expense						
Net Income	3,611,080,000	4,916,954,000	3,472,070,000	2,039,239,000	2,180,138,000	2,146,105,000
Operating Cash Flow	5,242,870,000	5,470,793,000	3,842,877,000	2,785,171,000	2,862,983,000	2,781,776,000
Capital Expenditure	2,620,647,000	2,078,360,000	1,371,536,000	1,647,959,000	1,870,508,000	1,583,602,000
EBITDA	7,114,642,000	8,576,319,000	6,011,580,000	3,721,327,000	3,873,494,000	3,843,565,000
Return on Assets %	.11%	.16%	.13%	.09%	.10%	.10%
Return on Equity %	.13%	.20%	.16%	.11%	.12%	.13%
Debt to Equity	.00%	.00%	.01%	.01%	0.006	0.003

CONTACT INFORMATION:

Phone: 81 332465091　　　　Fax:
Toll-Free:
Address: 6-1, Ohtemachi 2-chome, Tokyo, 100-0004 Japan

STOCK TICKER/OTHER:

Stock Ticker: SHECY　　　　Exchange: PINX
Employees: 24,380　　　　Fiscal Year Ends: 03/31
Parent Company:

SALARIES/BONUSES:

Top Exec. Salary: $　　　　Bonus: $
Second Exec. Salary: $　　　　Bonus: $

OTHER THOUGHTS:

Estimated Female Officers or Directors:
Hot Spot for Advancement for Women/Minorities:

Sales, profits and employees may be estimates. Financial information, benefits and other data can change quickly and may vary from those stated here.

Siemens AG

www.siemens.com

NAIC Code: 334513

TYPES OF BUSINESS:

Industrial Control Manufacturing
Digitalization
Smart Infrastructure
Mobility
Advanced Technologies
Artificial Intelligence
Internet of Things
Robotics

BRANDS/DIVISIONS/AFFILIATES:

Siemens Advanta
Siemens Healthineers AG
Siemens Financial Services
Siemens Real Estate
Next47

GROWTH PLANS/SPECIAL FEATURES:

Siemens is a multi-industry company focused on the areas of automation, electrification, mobility, and healthcare. Its top three geographic regions, the United States, Germany, and China, contribute over half of group revenue. Siemens has a 75% investment in separately listed Siemens Healthineers. Recent portfolio activity included the listing of Siemens Energy, spinning out its power and gas and Siemens Gamesa business divisions in 2020.

CONTACTS:
Note: Officers with more than one job title may be intentionally listed here more than once.

Jim Snabe, Chairman of the Board
Birgit Steinborn, Deputy Chairman
Werner Brandt, Deputy Chairman
Oliver Hartmann, Director

FINANCIAL DATA:
Note: Data for latest year may not have been available at press time.

In U.S. $	2024	2023	2022	2021	2020	2019
Revenue	86,186,153,791	84,996,593,562	81,699,206,626	70,675,368,902	62,717,366,260	66,382,519,136
R&D Expense	7,123,723,000	6,938,706,000	6,346,198,000	5,515,323,000	5,186,152,000	5,299,660,000
Operating Income	10,743,470,000	10,670,830,000	8,258,797,000	7,287,174,000	4,978,434,000	6,928,490,000
Operating Margin %	.12%	.13%	.10%	.10%	.08%	.10%
SGA Expense	15,872,870,000	15,383,660,000	14,593,640,000	12,702,610,000	12,124,860,000	12,131,670,000
Net Income	9,422,248,000	9,022,702,000	4,225,880,000	6,993,189,000	4,574,347,000	5,872,872,000
Operating Cash Flow	13,240,640,000	13,892,170,000	11,624,290,000	11,346,200,000	10,059,020,000	9,598,183,000
Capital Expenditure	2,370,034,000	2,435,868,000	2,365,494,000	1,963,678,000	1,700,340,000	2,020,431,000
EBITDA	18,354,140,000	18,205,450,000	12,944,380,000	12,729,850,000	10,685,580,000	11,552,780,000
Return on Assets %	.06%	.05%	.03%	.05%	.03%	.04%
Return on Equity %	.17%	.16%	.08%	.15%	.10%	.11%
Debt to Equity	.81%	.82%	.90%	.93%	1.044	0.632

CONTACT INFORMATION:

Phone: 49 8963633032   Fax: 49 8932825
Toll-Free:
Address: Werner-von-Siemens-Strabe 1, Munich, BY 80333 Germany

STOCK TICKER/OTHER:

Stock Ticker: SMAWF   Exchange: PINX
Employees: 327,000   Fiscal Year Ends: 09/30
Parent Company:

SALARIES/BONUSES:

Top Exec. Salary: $ Bonus: $
Second Exec. Salary: $ Bonus: $

OTHER THOUGHTS:

Estimated Female Officers or Directors: 5
Hot Spot for Advancement for Women/Minorities: Y

Siemens Digital Industries Software Inc

www.plm.automation.siemens.com
NAIC Code: 511210N

TYPES OF BUSINESS:

Software-Product Lifecycle Management
Digital Transformation Products and Solutions
Product Manufacturing Solutions
Mechanical Design Products
Electronic Products Solutions
Software Engineering
Internet of Things
Marine Vessel Solutions

BRANDS/DIVISIONS/AFFILIATES:

Siemens AG
Xcelerator

CONTACTS: Note: Officers with more than one job title may be intentionally listed here more than once.

Tony Hemmelgarn, CEO
Brenda Discher, Sr. VP-Bus. Strategy & Mktg.
Timo Nentwich, Exec. VP-Finance
Robert Jones, Exec. VP-Global Sales & Customer Svcs.
Paul Sicking, CTO
Steven Dietz, General Counsel
John Miller, VP-Strategy
Paul Vogel, Exec. VP-Global Sales & Svcs.
Kevin Eustace, Sr. VP-Prod. Driven Svcs.
Jim Rusk, Sr. VP-Prod. Eng. Software
Zvi Feuer, Sr. VP-Mfg. Eng. Software

GROWTH PLANS/SPECIAL FEATURES:

Siemens Digital Industries Software, Inc. (SDIS), a subsidiary of Siemens AG, offers digital transformation products and solutions to companies worldwide. The firm's Xcelerator platform enables businesses to design products faster, enhance manufacturing capabilities and continuously improve products and production. Products and software categories include electronic design, electrical systems, manufacturing, mechanical design, lifecycle management, simulation, software development, Internet of Things (IoT) and supply chain management. Solutions and service categories span product engineering, lifecycle management, manufacturing and services. Services include electronic design automation (EDA) services, cloud application services, digital transformation services, implementation services, engineering services, integration service practice and supply chain consulting. Industries solutions by SDIS include aerospace, airports, automotive manufacturing, battery manufacturing, cement, chemical industry, commercial buildings, cranes, data centers, distributors, electronic industry, food and beverage, glass and solar, healthcare, heavy equipment, higher education camps, intralogistics, machinery and plant construction, mining, oil and gas, panel building, pharmaceutical and life science, tires and more. SDIS also offers support services, training, online communities and blogs, podcasts and events. Headquartered in Texas, USA, Siemens Digital has global offices across the Americas, EMEA and Asia Pacific.

Siemens offers its employees health benefits, dental and prescription drug coverage, vision plan, life insurance, paid time off, a 401(k) and flexible spending account options.

FINANCIAL DATA: Note: Data for latest year may not have been available at press time.

In U.S. $	2024	2023	2022	2021	2020	2019
Revenue						
R&D Expense						
Operating Income						
Operating Margin %						
SGA Expense						
Net Income						
Operating Cash Flow						
Capital Expenditure						
EBITDA						
Return on Assets %						
Return on Equity %						
Debt to Equity						

CONTACT INFORMATION:

Phone: 972-987-3000   Fax: 972-987-3398
Toll-Free: 800-498-5351
Address: 5800 Granite Pkwy., Ste. 600, Plano, TX 75024 United States

STOCK TICKER/OTHER:

Stock Ticker: Subsidiary   Exchange:
Employees: Fiscal Year Ends: 12/31
Parent Company: Siemens AG

SALARIES/BONUSES:

Top Exec. Salary: $ Bonus: $
Second Exec. Salary: $ Bonus: $

OTHER THOUGHTS:

Estimated Female Officers or Directors:
Hot Spot for Advancement for Women/Minorities:

Siemens EDA

NAIC Code: 511210N

TYPES OF BUSINESS:

Software-Component Design, Simulation & Testing
Electronic Design Automation Software
Electronic Design Automation Hardware
Development Tools
Advanced Integrated Circuit Solutions
Performance Solutions
Software Training and Support Services

BRANDS/DIVISIONS/AFFILIATES:

Siemens AG

CONTACTS: Note: Officers with more than one job title may be intentionally listed here more than once.

Michael Ellow, Senior VP, Divisional
Brian Derrick, Vice President, Divisional
Dean Freed, Vice President
Jim Hagemann Snabe, Chmn.-Siemens

GROWTH PLANS/SPECIAL FEATURES:

Siemens EDA designs, develops and supplies electronic design automation (EDA) software and hardware and offers related services. The company's software and products enable customers worldwide to deliver innovative end-user solutions to their own customers. They can design, verify and manufacture advanced integrated circuits (ICs) for power, performance and functionality purposes. The IC solutions verify at all levels, from C++ prototype to silicon test to digital twin, and meet security, functional safety and silicon lifecycle requirements. EDA customers can scale seamlessly, from a single printed circuit board (PCB) to systems design, whether for individual or enterprise purposes. Electronic systems enable the nitration and optimization of entire digital processes, from specification to manufacturing. Siemens EDA's software and products are many and span several categories such as electronic design, electrical systems, manufacturing, mechanical design, lifecycle management, simulation, supply chain management, software development and Internet of Things (IoT). Industry solutions span electronics, semiconductors, energy/utilities, industrial machinery, consumer products, retail, medical devices, pharmaceuticals, small/medium businesses, heavy equipment, marine, aerospace, defense, automotive and transportation and more. Siemens EDA offers training and support services. Siemens EDA is wholly owned by German conglomerate Siemens AG.

FINANCIAL DATA: Note: Data for latest year may not have been available at press time.

In U.S. $	2024	2023	2022	2021	2020	2019
Revenue	1,947,429,225	1,854,694,500	1,750,000,000	1,509,048,139	1,423,630,320	1,271,098,500
R&D Expense						
Operating Income						
Operating Margin %						
SGA Expense						
Net Income						
Operating Cash Flow						
Capital Expenditure						
EBITDA						
Return on Assets %						
Return on Equity %						
Debt to Equity						

CONTACT INFORMATION:

Phone: 503 685-7000   Fax: 503 685-1202
Toll-Free: 800-547-3000
Address: 8005 SW Boeckman Rd., Wilsonville, OR 97070 United States

STOCK TICKER/OTHER:

Stock Ticker: Subsidiary   Exchange:
Employees: 6,000   Fiscal Year Ends: 01/31
Parent Company: Siemens AG

SALARIES/BONUSES:

Top Exec. Salary: $ Bonus: $
Second Exec. Salary: $ Bonus: $

OTHER THOUGHTS:

Estimated Female Officers or Directors:
Hot Spot for Advancement for Women/Minorities:

Siemens Gamesa Renewable Energy SA
www.siemensgamesa.com/en-int
NAIC Code: 333611

TYPES OF BUSINESS:
Wind Turbine Manufacturing
Wind Farms
Turbines
Product Development
Technology
Diagnostic Services
Hybrid Power Solutions
Energy Storage Solutions

BRANDS/DIVISIONS/AFFILIATES:
Siemens AG
Digital Ventures Lab

GROWTH PLANS/SPECIAL FEATURES:
Siemens Gamesa Renewable Energy SA (Siemens Gamesa), subsidiary to Siemens Energy AG, is a leading manufacturer of onshore and offshore wind turbines that produce clean energy for large cities, remote locations and everything in between. The firm operates in two business segments: onshore and offshore. Onshore operations are present in 90 countries throughout the world and offer an extensive range of onshore wind turbine technologies that are adapted to the unique climates and terrains of the projects' environment. Offshore operations have been conducted since 1991 and have been exponentially growing ever since. Siemens Gamesa also provides services in the forms of asset optimization, spares and repairs, storage and hydrogen and multi-brand.

CONTACTS:
Note: Officers with more than one job title may be intentionally listed here more than once.
Jochen Eickholt, CEO
Tim Dawidowsky, COO
Stefan Huppertz, CFO
Kirsten Schutz, Chief Human Resources Officer
Morten Pilgaard Rasmussen, Chief Technology Officer
Ricardo Chocarro, Manager-Oper.
Xabier Etxeberria, CEO-Business

FINANCIAL DATA:
Note: Data for latest year may not have been available at press time.

In U.S. $	2024	2023	2022	2021	2020	2019
Revenue	10,313,439,150	9,822,323,000	10,350,182,400	10,755,490,816	9,670,625,280	10,786,141,184
R&D Expense						
Operating Income						
Operating Margin %						
SGA Expense						
Net Income		-613,136,000	-991,888,448	-660,908,096	-936,323,904	147,658,080
Operating Cash Flow						
Capital Expenditure						
EBITDA						
Return on Assets %						
Return on Equity %						
Debt to Equity						

CONTACT INFORMATION:
Phone: 34-9144-037352 Fax:
Toll-Free:
Address: Parque Tecnologico de Bizkaia, Edificio 222, Zamudio, 48170 Spain

STOCK TICKER/OTHER:
Stock Ticker: Subsidiary Exchange:
Employees: 25,000 Fiscal Year Ends: 12/31
Parent Company: Siemens Energy AG

SALARIES/BONUSES:
Top Exec. Salary: $ Bonus: $
Second Exec. Salary: $ Bonus: $

OTHER THOUGHTS:
Estimated Female Officers or Directors:
Hot Spot for Advancement for Women/Minorities: Y

Sales, profits and employees may be estimates. Financial information, benefits and other data can change quickly and may vary from those stated here.

Siemens Healthineers AG

www.siemens-healthineers.com

NAIC Code: 334510

TYPES OF BUSINESS:

Electromedical and Electrotherapeutic Apparatus Manufacturing
Medical Technology
Imaging Systems
Diagnostic Tests & Products
Digital Services

BRANDS/DIVISIONS/AFFILIATES:

Siemens AG
Siemens Healthcare GmbH

GROWTH PLANS/SPECIAL FEATURES:

Siemens Healthineers is engaged in therapeutic imaging, radiotherapy, laboratory, and point-of-care diagnostics. The imaging segment (55% of sales in fiscal 2024) includes magnetic resonance imaging, computed tomography, X-ray systems, molecular imaging, and ultrasound. The Varian segment (17% of sales) offers radiotherapy and other oncology solutions. The portfolio of the diagnostics segment (20%) includes in vitro diagnostics products offered to providers and point-of-care diagnostics. The advanced therapies segment (9%) products are designed to support image-guided minimally invasive treatments in cardiology, interventional radiology, and surgery. Americas represents 42% of total sales, Europe, Middle East, and Africa 33%, and Asia-Pacific including China the remainder.

CONTACTS: Note: Officers with more than one job title may be intentionally listed here more than once.

Ralf Thomas, Chairman of the Board
Karl-Heinz Streibich, Deputy Chairman
Dorothea Simon, Deputy Chairman

FINANCIAL DATA: Note: Data for latest year may not have been available at press time.

In U.S. $	2024	2023	2022	2021	2020	2019
Revenue	25,383,655,909	24,608,400,735	24,646,991,936	20,427,923,636	16,413,167,164	16,479,000,717
R&D Expense	2,177,072,000	2,118,048,000	2,026,107,000	1,754,824,000	1,523,269,000	1,507,378,000
Operating Income	3,188,422,000	2,421,112,000	3,318,956,000	2,914,870,000	2,206,584,000	2,606,129,000
Operating Margin %	.13%	.10%	.13%	.14%	.13%	.16%
SGA Expense	4,178,206,000	4,094,211,000	3,868,332,000	3,197,503,000	2,586,833,000	2,513,053,000
Net Income	2,204,313,000	1,712,826,000	2,313,280,000	1,960,273,000	1,601,589,000	1,778,661,000
Operating Cash Flow	3,207,718,000	2,405,221,000	2,842,225,000	3,329,171,000	2,188,422,000	1,835,414,000
Capital Expenditure	790,011,300	951,191,800	967,082,900	765,039,700	632,236,100	657,207,700
EBITDA	4,792,282,000	4,291,714,000	4,836,549,000	4,002,270,000	3,229,285,000	3,332,577,000
Return on Assets %	.04%	.03%	.04%	.05%	.06%	.08%
Return on Equity %	.11%	.08%	.11%	.12%	.13%	.17%
Debt to Equity	.03%	.02%	.02%	.03%	0.025	0.006

CONTACT INFORMATION:

Phone: 49-69-797-6602   Fax:
Toll-Free:
Address: Henkestr. 127, Erlangen, D-91052 Germany

STOCK TICKER/OTHER:

Stock Ticker: SEMHF
Employees: 72,000
Parent Company: Siemens AG

Exchange: PINX
Fiscal Year Ends: 09/30

SALARIES/BONUSES:

Top Exec. Salary: $ Bonus: $
Second Exec. Salary: $ Bonus: $

OTHER THOUGHTS:

Estimated Female Officers or Directors: 3
Hot Spot for Advancement for Women/Minorities: Y

Siemens USA

NAIC Code: 541710

www.siemens.com/us/en.html

TYPES OF BUSINESS:

Research & Development
Innovative Technology
Hardware and Software Solutions
Smart Infrastructure
Digital Business Transformation
Automotive Drive Technology
Smart Power Distribution Systems
Medical Devices and Technologies

BRANDS/DIVISIONS/AFFILIATES:

Siemens AG
Siemens Healthineers
Siemens Mobility
Siemens Xcelerator

GROWTH PLANS/SPECIAL FEATURES:

Siemens USA is the American arm of Siemens AG, offering innovative technology, software, hardware and engineering services in all 50 states and Puerto Rico. The company's wide variety of products and services include smart infrastructure regarding building technologies, a digital business platform for accelerating digital transformation, automotive and motion control drive technology, energy applications regarding the smart grid and power distribution systems, financial solutions for businesses, medical solutions through the firm's subsidiary Siemens Healthineers and automation hardware and software regarding digitalized production. Mobility solutions are offered through the subsidiary Siemens Mobility with rail/highway/intermodal transport, related software and services. In addition, the Siemens Xcelerator marketplace offers solutions for sellers and developers with integrated hardware and software.

CONTACTS: Note: Officers with more than one job title may be intentionally listed here more than once.

Barbara Humpton, CEO
Marsha Smith, CFO
Joe Kaeser, Pres.

FINANCIAL DATA: Note: Data for latest year may not have been available at press time.

In U.S. $	2024	2023	2022	2021	2020	2019
Revenue	24,548,448,750	23,379,475,000	21,563,000,000	20,437,004,350	17,791,100,000	19,984,500,000
R&D Expense						
Operating Income						
Operating Margin %						
SGA Expense						
Net Income						
Operating Cash Flow						
Capital Expenditure						
EBITDA						
Return on Assets %						
Return on Equity %						
Debt to Equity						

CONTACT INFORMATION:

Phone: 609-734-6500 Fax:
Toll-Free:
Address: 200 Massachusetts Ave., NW Ste. 600, Washington, DC 20001
United States

STOCK TICKER/OTHER:

Stock Ticker: Subsidiary Exchange:
Employees: 7,400 Fiscal Year Ends: 09/30
Parent Company: Siemens AG

SALARIES/BONUSES:

Top Exec. Salary: $ Bonus: $
Second Exec. Salary: $ Bonus: $

OTHER THOUGHTS:

Estimated Female Officers or Directors:
Hot Spot for Advancement for Women/Minorities:

Singapore Technologies Engineering Limited　　www.stengg.com

NAIC Code: 336411

TYPES OF BUSINESS:

Aircraft Overhaul
Aerospace Engineering
Smart Technology
Shipbuilding
Defense Security Solutions
Public Security Solutions
Digital Technology Solutions

BRANDS/DIVISIONS/AFFILIATES:

Temasek Holdings Private Limited

GROWTH PLANS/SPECIAL FEATURES:

Singapore Technologies Engineering Limited is a Singaporean government-linked commercial and defense engineering group. Its key businesses include aircraft maintenance, repair and overhaul services, in which it is the world's largest independent third-party provider. The company's fastest-growing activities involve applications to smart city solutions where it provides tolling solutions, traffic control systems, command and control dashboards, cybersecurity tools, and other related components. Around two thirds of the company's revenue comes from commercial clients while the remainder is defense.

CONTACTS: Note: Officers with more than one job title may be intentionally listed here more than once.

Sy Chong, CEO
Ming Kian Teo, Chairman of the Board

FINANCIAL DATA: Note: Data for latest year may not have been available at press time.

In U.S. $	2024	2023	2022	2021	2020	2019
Revenue	8,732,021,033	7,822,365,229	6,996,904,537	5,957,457,353	5,543,472,085	6,093,298,128
R&D Expense						
Operating Income	778,703,600	650,592,400	470,738,000	472,773,900	434,339,800	521,241,300
Operating Margin %	.09%	.08%	.07%	.08%	.08%	.09%
SGA Expense	777,500,200	721,749,400	714,130,700	612,355,000	635,334,900	653,217,700
Net Income	543,836,400	454,167,900	414,320,400	441,833,800	404,119,900	447,568,400
Operating Cash Flow	1,330,486,000	912,690,300	521,253,700	862,907,100	1,187,033,000	456,874,400
Capital Expenditure	422,065,300	476,973,600	748,184,800	332,048,300	222,359,600	305,551,800
EBITDA	1,258,405,000	1,147,275,000	969,292,100	836,943,300	745,462,700	858,242,800
Return on Assets %	.04%	.04%	.04%	.06%	.05%	.07%
Return on Equity %	.27%	.24%	.22%	.24%	.23%	.26%
Debt to Equity	1.08%	1.44%	1.21%	.64%	0.676	0.211

CONTACT INFORMATION:

Phone: 65 6722-1818　　　　Fax: 65 6720-2293
Toll-Free:
Address: 1 Ang Mo Kio Electronics Park Road, #07-01, Singapore, 567710 Singapore

STOCK TICKER/OTHER:

Stock Ticker: SGGKF　　　　　　　　　Exchange: PINX
Employees: 25,734　　　　　　　　　　Fiscal Year Ends: 12/31
Parent Company: Temasek Holdings Private Limited

SALARIES/BONUSES:

Top Exec. Salary: $　　　　Bonus: $
Second Exec. Salary: $　　　Bonus: $

OTHER THOUGHTS:

Estimated Female Officers or Directors: 4
Hot Spot for Advancement for Women/Minorities: Y

Sino-Thai Engineering & Construction PCL

www.stecon.co.th

NAIC Code: 237310

TYPES OF BUSINESS:

Industrial Engineering Services
Construction
Engineering
Infrastructure
Industrial
Buildings
Energy Facilities
Wastewater Treatment Plants

BRANDS/DIVISIONS/AFFILIATES:

CONTACTS: *Note: Officers with more than one job title may be intentionally listed here more than once.*

Pakpoom Srichamni, Managing Dir.
Woraphant Chontong, Sr. Exec. VP-Admin.
Woraphant Chontong, Sr. Exec. VP-Finance
Rawat Chamchalerm, Chmn.

GROWTH PLANS/SPECIAL FEATURES:

Sino-Thai Engineering & Construction PCL (STECON) is a construction company serving the public and private sectors in Thailand. The company operates in five segments: infrastructure, industrial, buildings, energy and environmental works. The infrastructure segment constructs roads, elevated roads, highways, expressways, bridges and other facilities. In its Industrial works segment, the firm provides turnkey construction of refineries, petrochemical plants, steel structures and oil and gas pipelines. The building operations include the construction of office buildings, condominiums, aircraft maintenance centers, sports auditoriums, schools, hospitals, museums, convention buildings and airport terminals. The energy segment constructs power plants, sub-stations, oil refineries and natural gas facilities. The environmental works segment constructs wastewater treatment plants, water supply systems, solid waste management plants and irrigation systems. STECON's facilities include two fabrication plants; a pre-cast concrete plant; a construction equipment center (CEC); a construction assets center (CAC); an inventory control section (ICS); and a warehouse, all of which are in Chonburi, Thailand. The company has a second warehouse located in the Map-ta-put estate in Thailand.

FINANCIAL DATA: *Note: Data for latest year may not have been available at press time.*

In U.S. $	2024	2023	2022	2021	2020	2019
Revenue		861,524,000	898,595,500	838,824,787	1,205,450,000	1,110,460,000
R&D Expense						
Operating Income						
Operating Margin %						
SGA Expense						
Net Income			43,764,390	21,578,160	36,747,700	49,695,100
Operating Cash Flow						
Capital Expenditure						
EBITDA						
Return on Assets %						
Return on Equity %						
Debt to Equity						

CONTACT INFORMATION:

Phone: 66 26104900 Fax: 66 22601339
Toll-Free:
Address: 32/59-60, Fl. 29-30, Sukhumvit 21 Rd., Asoke Road, Klongtoey-Nua, Wattana, Bangkok, 10110 Thailand

STOCK TICKER/OTHER:

Stock Ticker: STEC Exchange: Bangkok
Employees: 1,040 Fiscal Year Ends: 12/31
Parent Company:

SALARIES/BONUSES:

Top Exec. Salary: $ Bonus: $
Second Exec. Salary: $ Bonus: $

OTHER THOUGHTS:

Estimated Female Officers or Directors: 2
Hot Spot for Advancement for Women/Minorities:

SK Ecoplant

NAIC Code: 541330

TYPES OF BUSINESS:

Engineering Services
Environmental Solutions
Eco-Friendly Technologies
Sustainable Research and Development
Carbon-Neutral Energy Innovation
ESG Space Development
Water Resource Facilities
LNG Power Plants

BRANDS/DIVISIONS/AFFILIATES:

SK Group

CONTACTS: Note: Officers with more than one job title may be intentionally listed here more than once.

Kyung-il Park, CEO

GROWTH PLANS/SPECIAL FEATURES:

SK Ecoplant (SK), part of the SK Group, is an environmental solutions provider based on the firm's innovative eco-friendly and sustainable technologies and strategies. SK primarily engages in business development and engineering/procurement/construction (EPC) projects, and its comprehensive environmental platform implements a 3R waste-to-resource focus: reducing incineration and landfill issues, reusing water via treatment solutions and recycling wasted materials. SK operates through six divisions. Green energy is a carbon-neutral innovative solution provider that utilizes eco-friendly energy technology to solve global warming problems. Sustainable space is an environmental/social/governance (ESG) space creation business that provides a new style of residential, office and commercial spaces for daily life. Solution for net-zero is a global civil infrastructure builder that constructs railways, roads, ports, underground spaces, housing and industrial complexes, water resource facilities and environmental facilities. ECO Hi-Tech is a technical solution provider with a diverse portfolio of industrial plant operations, such as semiconductor, electric vehicle battery and battery materials manufacturing facilities, power plants that generate electrical energy via liquefied natural gas (LNG), LNG storage terminals, and hydrogen service businesses. Eco R&D is a green ecosystem platform that links research and development strategies with business strategies to analyze the trends of eco-friendly technology policy and form a technology roadmap based on technology and market analysis. Last, the special technologies division develops specialty technologies and solutions across SK's entire operations, such as a bioreactor having a bio-ring to activate a microorganism, or a method for phosphorous removal from wastewater. SK operates through domestic and international subsidiaries throughout the U.S., Europe and Asia.

FINANCIAL DATA: Note: Data for latest year may not have been available at press time.

In U.S. $	2024	2023	2022	2021	2020	2019
Revenue	6,977,250,000	6,645,000,000	5,633,651,000	7,401,179,300	6,916,990,000	6,774,000,000
R&D Expense						
Operating Income						
Operating Margin %						
SGA Expense						
Net Income		24,807,000	4,760,054	1,574,996	110,798,000	65,231,670
Operating Cash Flow						
Capital Expenditure						
EBITDA						
Return on Assets %						
Return on Equity %						
Debt to Equity						

CONTACT INFORMATION:

Phone: 82-2-3700-7114   Fax: 82-23700-8200
Toll-Free:
Address: 32 Insadong 7-gil, Jongno-gu, Seoul, 135-798 South Korea

STOCK TICKER/OTHER:

Stock Ticker: Subsidiary   Exchange:
Employees: 3,488   Fiscal Year Ends:
Parent Company: SK Group

SALARIES/BONUSES:

Top Exec. Salary: $ Bonus: $
Second Exec. Salary: $ Bonus: $

OTHER THOUGHTS:

Estimated Female Officers or Directors:
Hot Spot for Advancement for Women/Minorities:

Skidmore Owings & Merrill LLP

www.som.com

NAIC Code: 541330

TYPES OF BUSINESS:

Architectural & Engineering Services
Architecture Planning and Design
Engineering and Construction
Graphics and Branding
Buildings and Facilities
Digital Design
Sustainable Engineering
Architecture and Engineering R&D

BRANDS/DIVISIONS/AFFILIATES:

CONTACTS: *Note: Officers with more than one job title may be intentionally listed here more than once.*

Candace Carroll, CFO
William F. Baker, Partner-Civil & Structural Eng.
Gene Schnair, Managing Partner-San Francisco
Thomas Behr, Managing Dir-New York
Rod Garrett, Managing Dir.-Washington, D.C.
Xuan Fu, Managing Partner-Chicago
Silas Chiow, Dir.-China

GROWTH PLANS/SPECIAL FEATURES:

Skidmore, Owings & Merrill, LLP (SOM) began in 1936 as an architecture and engineering firm and has become a global leader in these respective fields. SOM's specialties and expertise are vast, and include adaptive reuse, airports, civic and government, commercial, cultural, faÃ§ade design, graphics and branding, higher education, healthcare, hospitality, interiors, K-12 education, landscape and ecology, mixed-use, residential, science, structural and civil engineering, sustainable engineering, transportation, urban design and planning, and workplace. SOM considers itself as a laboratory that is constantly exploring new ways of practicing design and has invested in research that has transformed the architecture, engineering and construction industry, from collaborative computer-aided design (CAD) platforms to devising engineering solutions for tall buildings. Headquartered in Chicago, USA, SOM has additional domestic offices, as well as international offices in Dubai, Hong Kong, London, Melbourne and Shanghai.

FINANCIAL DATA: *Note: Data for latest year may not have been available at press time.*

In U.S. $	2024	2023	2022	2021	2020	2019
Revenue	367,500,000	350,000,000	347,000,000	333,768,094	370,853,438	380,362,500
R&D Expense						
Operating Income						
Operating Margin %						
SGA Expense						
Net Income						
Operating Cash Flow						
Capital Expenditure						
EBITDA						
Return on Assets %						
Return on Equity %						
Debt to Equity						

CONTACT INFORMATION:

Phone: 312-554-9090   Fax: 312-360-4545
Toll-Free: 866-269-2688
Address: 224 S. Michigan Ave., Ste. 1000, Chicago, IL 60604 United States

STOCK TICKER/OTHER:

Stock Ticker: Private   Exchange:
Employees: 1,700   Fiscal Year Ends: 09/30
Parent Company:

SALARIES/BONUSES:

Top Exec. Salary: $ Bonus: $
Second Exec. Salary: $ Bonus: $

OTHER THOUGHTS:

Estimated Female Officers or Directors: 2
Hot Spot for Advancement for Women/Minorities: Y

SLB

NAIC Code: 213112

TYPES OF BUSINESS:

Oil & Gas Field Services
Technology
Digital Solutions
Reservoir
Well Construction
Platform Manufacturing
Well Drilling
Components

BRANDS/DIVISIONS/AFFILIATES:

GROWTH PLANS/SPECIAL FEATURES:

SLB is the world's premier oilfield-services company as measured by market share. While the industry is mostly fragmented, SLB holds the first or second competitive position in many of the differentiated oligopolies it operates in. Also known as Schlumberger, the company was founded in 1926 by two brothers bearing the same last name. Today it's most known as a global industry leader in innovation, while it focuses its strategy on its three growth engines: its core, digital, and new energy businesses. Over three fourths of its revenue base is tied to international markets, while the company boasts roughly $3 billion in digital-related revenue.

CONTACTS: Note: Officers with more than one job title may be intentionally listed here more than once.

Olivier Le Peuch, CEO
Stephane Biguet, CFO
James Hackett, Chairman of the Board
Howard Guild, Chief Accounting Officer
Dianne Ralston, Chief Legal Officer
Demosthenis Pafitis, Chief Technology Officer
Ugo Prechner, Controller
Khaled Mogharbel, Executive VP, Divisional
Abdellah Merad, Executive VP, Divisional
Vijay Kasibhatla, Other Corporate Officer
Carmen Bejar, Other Executive Officer
Rakesh Jaggi, President, Divisional
Gavin Rennick, President, Divisional
Kevin Fyfe, Treasurer

FINANCIAL DATA: Note: Data for latest year may not have been available at press time.

In U.S. $	2024	2023	2022	2021	2020	2019
Revenue	36,288,999,424	33,134,999,552	28,091,000,832	22,929,000,448	23,601,000,448	32,917,000,192
R&D Expense	749,000,000	711,000,000	634,000,000	554,000,000	580,000,000	717,000,000
Operating Income	6,326,000,000	5,488,000,000	4,151,000,000	2,765,000,000	1,656,000,000	3,006,000,000
Operating Margin %	.17%	.17%	.15%	.12%	.07%	.09%
SGA Expense	385,000,000	364,000,000	376,000,000	339,000,000	365,000,000	474,000,000
Net Income	4,461,000,000	4,203,000,000	3,441,000,000	1,881,000,000	-10,518,000,000	-10,137,000,000
Operating Cash Flow	6,602,000,000	6,637,000,000	3,720,000,000	4,651,000,000	2,944,000,000	5,431,000,000
Capital Expenditure	2,129,000,000	2,092,000,000	1,715,000,000	1,180,000,000	1,217,000,000	1,955,000,000
EBITDA	8,069,000,000	7,544,000,000	6,430,000,000	4,617,000,000	-8,739,000,000	-6,220,000,000
Return on Assets %	.09%	.09%	.08%	.04%	-.21%	-.16%
Return on Equity %	.22%	.22%	.21%	.14%	-.59%	-.34%
Debt to Equity	.52%	.54%	.60%	.89%	1.328	0.622

CONTACT INFORMATION:

Phone: 713 375-3400   Fax:
Toll-Free:
Address: 5599 San Felipe St., 17/Fl, Houston, TX 77056 United States

STOCK TICKER/OTHER:

Stock Ticker: SLB   Exchange: NYS
Employees: 110,000   Fiscal Year Ends: 12/31
Parent Company:

SALARIES/BONUSES:

Top Exec. Salary: $1,650,000   Bonus: $
Second Exec. Salary: Bonus: $
$900,000

OTHER THOUGHTS:

Estimated Female Officers or Directors: 3
Hot Spot for Advancement for Women/Minorities: Y

SMEC Holdings Pty Ltd

www.smec.com

NAIC Code: 541330

TYPES OF BUSINESS:

Engineering Consulting Services
Engineering Consultancy
Infrastructure and Buildings
Project Management
Feasibility Studies
Planning and Design
Construction and Commissioning
Operation and Maintenance

BRANDS/DIVISIONS/AFFILIATES:

Temasek Holdings Pte Ltd
Surbana Jurong Private Limited

CONTACTS: *Note: Officers with more than one job title may be intentionally listed here more than once.*

Hari Poologasundram, CEO
Max Findlay, Chmn.

GROWTH PLANS/SPECIAL FEATURES:

SMEC Holdings Pty Ltd. (SMEC) is a global engineering, management and development consultancy, in business since 1970 with a presence in more than 40 countries worldwide. The company has engaged in building Australia's infrastructure and continues to provide technical expertise and advanced engineering services to resolve complex challenges across project lifecycles, from initial concept, feasibility, planning and design through to construction, commissioning, operation and maintenance. SMEC collaborates with its clients to deliver necessary solutions. Solutions include air quality, asset management, business and investor advisory, building services engineering, civil and structural engineering, communication and stakeholder engagement, construction phase services, development management, digital, energy efficiency, environment and social impact assessment, geospatial services, geotechnical investigations, geotechnics, independent verification, landscape architecture, master planning, operational readiness, operations and maintenance, pedestrian modeling, planning, project management, rail systems, survey, sustainability, tunnels, training and capacity building, urban design and water-sensitive urban design. SMEC serves several market sectors, including aviation, energy, renewables, environment, hydropower, dams, international development, ports and maritime, rail and metro, roads, bridges, highways, urban communities, water and wastewater. SMEC is privately-owned by Surbana Jurong Group, a global urban, infrastructure and managed services consulting firm based in Singapore. Surbana Jurong itself is a subsidiary of Temasek Holdings Pte., Ltd.

FINANCIAL DATA: *Note: Data for latest year may not have been available at press time.*

In U.S. $	2024	2023	2022	2021	2020	2019
Revenue	533,988,000	508,560,000	489,000,000	472,230,000	445,500,000	450,000,000
R&D Expense						
Operating Income						
Operating Margin %						
SGA Expense						
Net Income						
Operating Cash Flow						
Capital Expenditure						
EBITDA						
Return on Assets %						
Return on Equity %						
Debt to Equity						

CONTACT INFORMATION:

Phone: 61 2-9925 5555   Fax:
Toll-Free:
Address: Level 7, 40 Mount St., North Sydney, NSW 2060 Australia

STOCK TICKER/OTHER:

Stock Ticker: Private   Exchange:
Employees: 5,800   Fiscal Year Ends:
Parent Company: Temasek Holdings Pte Ltd

SALARIES/BONUSES:

Top Exec. Salary: $ Bonus: $
Second Exec. Salary: $ Bonus: $

OTHER THOUGHTS:

Estimated Female Officers or Directors:
Hot Spot for Advancement for Women/Minorities:

Smith & Nephew plc

www.smith-nephew.com

NAIC Code: 339113

TYPES OF BUSINESS:

Implants, Surgical, Manufacturing
Reconstructive Joint Implants
Arthroscopic Enabling Technologies
Wound Management Products

BRANDS/DIVISIONS/AFFILIATES:

GROWTH PLANS/SPECIAL FEATURES:

Smith & Nephew designs, manufactures, and markets orthopedic devices, sports medicine and arthroscopic technologies, and wound care solutions. Roughly 41% of the UK-based firm's revenue comes from orthopedic products, and another 30% is sports medicine and ENT. The remaining 29% of revenue is from the advanced wound therapy segment. Over half of Smith & Nephew's total revenue comes from the United States, just over 30% is from other developed markets, and emerging markets account for the remainder.

CONTACTS: Note: Officers with more than one job title may be intentionally listed here more than once.

Deepak Nath, CEO
John Rogers, CFO
Rupert Soames, Chairman of the Board
Helen Barraclough, General Counsel

FINANCIAL DATA: Note: Data for latest year may not have been available at press time.

In U.S. $	2024	2023	2022	2021	2020	2019
Revenue	5,809,999,872	5,549,000,192	5,215,000,064	5,212,000,256	4,560,000,000	5,137,999,872
R&D Expense	289,000,000	339,000,000	345,000,000	356,000,000	307,000,000	292,000,000
Operating Income	860,000,000	620,000,000	634,000,000	682,000,000	295,000,000	990,000,000
Operating Margin %	.15%	.11%	.12%	.13%	.06%	.19%
SGA Expense	2,652,000,000	2,602,000,000	2,435,000,000	2,394,000,000	2,562,000,000	2,314,000,000
Net Income	412,000,000	263,000,000	223,000,000	524,000,000	448,000,000	600,000,000
Operating Cash Flow	987,000,000	608,000,000	468,000,000	877,000,000	935,000,000	1,168,000,000
Capital Expenditure	381,000,000	427,000,000	358,000,000	408,000,000	443,000,000	408,000,000
EBITDA	1,221,000,000	956,000,000	874,000,000	1,242,000,000	866,000,000	1,320,000,000
Return on Assets %	.04%	.03%	.02%	.05%	.04%	.07%
Return on Equity %	.08%	.05%	.04%	.10%	.09%	.12%
Debt to Equity	.62%	.44%	.52%	.51%	0.635	0.384

CONTACT INFORMATION:

Phone: 44 2074017646   Fax: 44 2079303353
Toll-Free:
Address: Bldg. 5, Croxley Park, Hatters Ln., Watford, Herfordshire, WD18 8YE United Kingdom

STOCK TICKER/OTHER:

Stock Ticker: SNN   Exchange: NYS
Employees: 18,452   Fiscal Year Ends: 12/31
Parent Company:

SALARIES/BONUSES:

Top Exec. Salary: $1,560,000   Bonus: $2,034,000
Second Exec. Salary: $695,000   Bonus: $1,210,000

OTHER THOUGHTS:

Estimated Female Officers or Directors: 6
Hot Spot for Advancement for Women/Minorities: Y

Smiths Group plc

www.smiths.com

NAIC Code: 339991

TYPES OF BUSINESS:

Gasket, Packing, and Sealing Device Manufacturing
Medical Devices, Manufacturing
Security Equipment
Electronic Components

BRANDS/DIVISIONS/AFFILIATES:

Smiths Detection
Smiths Medical
Smiths Interconnect
John Crane
Flex-Tek

GROWTH PLANS/SPECIAL FEATURES:

Smiths Group operates four distinct industrial capital goods businesses, each with industry leadership positions that serve a diverse range of end markets, including oil and gas, aviation & defense, and the general industrial sector. Despite serving disparate markets, each of Smiths Group's constituent companies provide an advanced technology offering backed by the group's engineering expertise. John Crane, Smiths Group's largest business, is the global industry leader in the design and manufacture of highly engineered mechanical seals, boasting the largest installed base across its energy and general industrial end markets. Smiths Detection is a global leading supplier of security and detection scanning equipment to aviation, sea ports, and municipal customers.

CONTACTS: *Note: Officers with more than one job title may be intentionally listed here more than once.*

Roland Carter, CEO
Clare Scherrer, CFO
Steven Williams, Chairman of the Board
Matthew Whyte, Secretary

FINANCIAL DATA: *Note: Data for latest year may not have been available at press time.*

In U.S. $	2024	2023	2022	2021	2020	2019
Revenue	4,216,611,619	4,088,713,032	3,454,605,987	3,239,197,987	3,430,372,415	3,363,057,242
R&D Expense						
Operating Income	627,375,800	603,142,400	204,637,600	421,391,900	363,501,000	518,325,500
Operating Margin %	.15%	.15%	.06%	.13%	.11%	.15%
SGA Expense	868,363,500	844,130,100	741,811,300	731,040,900	838,744,900	864,324,600
Net Income	336,575,000	310,995,300	1,390,728,000	382,349,200	356,769,500	302,917,500
Operating Cash Flow	562,753,400	394,465,900	375,617,700	720,270,500	577,562,700	465,819,800
Capital Expenditure	115,781,800	109,050,300	118,474,400	157,517,100	148,093,000	158,863,400
EBITDA	780,854,000	780,854,000	386,388,100	578,909,000	453,703,100	687,959,300
Return on Assets %	.06%	.05%	.20%	.05%	.05%	.04%
Return on Equity %	.11%	.09%	.41%	.12%	.11%	.10%
Debt to Equity	.28%	.26%	.23%	.61%	0.641	0.636

CONTACT INFORMATION:

Phone: 44 2078085500   Fax: 44 2078085544
Toll-Free:
Address: 11-12 St James's Square, London, SW1Y 4LB United Kingdom

STOCK TICKER/OTHER:

Stock Ticker: SMGZY
Employees: 16,550
Parent Company:

Exchange: PINX
Fiscal Year Ends: 07/31

SALARIES/BONUSES:

Top Exec. Salary: $807,780   Bonus: $873,749
Second Exec. Salary: $430,816   Bonus: $538,520

OTHER THOUGHTS:

Estimated Female Officers or Directors:
Hot Spot for Advancement for Women/Minorities: Y

Solvay SA

NAIC Code: 325180

TYPES OF BUSINESS:

Chemicals & Plastics
Specialty Polymer Production
Composite Material Production
Technologies
Energy Efficiency Solutions
Chemical Intermediate Production
Surface Chemistry Solutions
Food and Crop Care Solutions

BRANDS/DIVISIONS/AFFILIATES:

Soda Ash Joint Venture

GROWTH PLANS/SPECIAL FEATURES:

Solvay SA is a Belgium-based producer of chemicals, plastics, and composites. Their five major businesses include soda ash, peroxides, silica, rare earths, and fluorine. The company has a top-three market position for nearly all of its products. Key business segments include Basic Chemicals, Performance Chemicals, and Corporate. High-value products include aerospace composites and specialty polymers while traditional chemical products include soda ash and hydrogen peroxide. Geographical exposure is relatively balanced, with Europe, North America, and Asia each contributing a third of sales.

CONTACTS: Note: Officers with more than one job title may be intentionally listed here more than once.

Philippe Kehren, CEO
Aude de Maisieres, Director

FINANCIAL DATA: Note: Data for latest year may not have been available at press time.

In U.S. $	2024	2023	2022	2021	2020	2019
Revenue	5,822,928,351	6,838,819,458	9,055,618,480	12,979,568,468	11,026,106,563	12,743,473,122
R&D Expense	38,592,510	53,348,470	52,213,390	368,899,000	340,522,100	366,628,800
Operating Income	738,933,100	929,625,400	910,329,200	1,374,574,000	958,002,200	1,347,333,000
Operating Margin %	.13%	.14%	.10%	.11%	.09%	.11%
SGA Expense	475,595,900	597,048,800	641,316,700	1,399,546,000	1,375,709,000	1,510,783,000
Net Income	253,121,500	2,375,709,000	2,162,316,000	1,076,050,000	-1,091,941,000	133,938,700
Operating Cash Flow	698,070,400	2,169,126,000	2,276,958,000	1,701,476,000	1,409,762,000	2,060,159,000
Capital Expenditure	323,496,000	1,207,719,000	1,031,782,000	721,906,900	623,155,500	972,758,200
EBITDA	913,734,400	1,483,542,000	2,393,871,000	2,326,901,000	1,990,919,000	1,538,025,000
Return on Assets %	.03%	.15%	.09%	.05%	-.05%	.01%
Return on Equity %	.17%	.35%	.20%	.12%	-.12%	.01%
Debt to Equity	1.29%	.19%	.23%	.29%	0.433	0.339

CONTACT INFORMATION:

Phone: 32 22642111   Fax: 32 22641484
Toll-Free:
Address: Rue De Ransbeek, 310, Brussels, B-1120 Belgium

STOCK TICKER/OTHER:

Stock Ticker: SLVYY   Exchange: PINX
Employees: 9,000   Fiscal Year Ends: 12/31
Parent Company:

SALARIES/BONUSES:

Top Exec. Salary: $ Bonus: $
Second Exec. Salary: $ Bonus: $

OTHER THOUGHTS:

Estimated Female Officers or Directors: 1
Hot Spot for Advancement for Women/Minorities: Y

Sony Corporation

NAIC Code: 334220

TYPES OF BUSINESS:

Smartphones
Entertainment and Technology Services
Televisions and Video Products
Sound Products
Product Development and Production
Cameras and Video Cameras
Entertainment Products and Digital Technology
Motion Pictures and Television Programming

BRANDS/DIVISIONS/AFFILIATES:

Sony Group Corporation
Playstation

CONTACTS: Note: Officers with more than one job title may be intentionally listed here more than once.

Bob Ishida, Deputy CEO
Yoshihiko Hatanaka, Chmn.-Corp.

GROWTH PLANS/SPECIAL FEATURES:

Sony Corporation is Sony Group's entertainment, technology and services business. The firm engages in product research, development, design, marketing, sales, production and distribution, as well as customer services for televisions, video and sound products. Sony Corporation does the same for interchangeable lens cameras, compact digital cameras, consumer and professional video cameras, as well as display products such as projectors and medical equipment. The company is responsible for Sony Group's broadcast and related professional business, the FeliCa contact integrated circuit (IC) card technology business, and the SOMED development of medical and imaging device solutions for operating rooms and other medical areas. Sony Corporation provides mobile phones and accessories, internet broadband network services, and the distribution of content through its portal services to various electronics product platforms such as personal computers and mobile phones. Sony Corporation also produces PlayStation hardware, software, content and network services, including digital software and add-on content. The firm distributes physical and digital recorded music; manages and licenses the words and music of songs; owns and acquires rights to musical compositions; and produces and distributes animation titles and game applications. Sony Corporation produces, acquires and distributes live-action and animation motion pictures and television programming. The company operates a network that delivers cable, satellite and other distribution platforms.

FINANCIAL DATA: Note: Data for latest year may not have been available at press time.

In U.S. $	2024	2023	2022	2021	2020	2019
Revenue	19,603,678,500	18,670,170,000	17,181,695,440	21,225,175,648	19,178,608,074	4,958,156,878
R&D Expense						
Operating Income						
Operating Margin %						
SGA Expense						
Net Income		1,353,204,135	15,640,931	1,931,789	1,186,085,766	787,064,568
Operating Cash Flow						
Capital Expenditure						
EBITDA						
Return on Assets %						
Return on Equity %						
Debt to Equity						

CONTACT INFORMATION:

Phone: 81-3-6748-2111   Fax:
Toll-Free:
Address: 1-7-1 Konan, Minato-ku, Tokyo, 108-0075 Japan

STOCK TICKER/OTHER:

Stock Ticker: Subsidiary   Exchange:
Employees: 9,000   Fiscal Year Ends: 03/31
Parent Company: Sony Group Corporation

SALARIES/BONUSES:

Top Exec. Salary: $ Bonus: $
Second Exec. Salary: $ Bonus: $

OTHER THOUGHTS:

Estimated Female Officers or Directors: 1
Hot Spot for Advancement for Women/Minorities:

Sony Group Corporation

www.sony.net

NAIC Code: 334310

TYPES OF BUSINESS:

Consumer Electronics Manufacturer
Film & Television Production
Music Production
Sensors and Cameras for use in Smartphones
Semiconductors
Technology Research
Video Games
Financial Services

BRANDS/DIVISIONS/AFFILIATES:

Sony Music Entertainment
Sony Pictures Entertainment
Sony Semiconductor Solutions Corporation
Sony Energy Devices Corporation
Sony Financial Holdings Inc
Sony Life Insurance Co Ltd
Sony Bank Inc
Sony Corporation

GROWTH PLANS/SPECIAL FEATURES:

Sony Group is a conglomerate with consumer electronics roots, which not only designs, develops, produces, and sells electronic equipment and devices, but also is engaged in content businesses, such as console and mobile games, music, and movies. Sony is a global top company of CMOS image sensors, game consoles, professional broadcasting cameras, and music publishing, and is one of the top players on digital cameras, wireless earphones, recorded music, movies, and so on. Sony's business portfolio is well diversified with six major business segments.

CONTACTS: Note: Officers with more than one job title may be intentionally listed here more than once.

Kenichiro Yoshida, CEO
Hiroki Totoki, CFO
Yoshihiko Hatanaka, Chairman of the Board
Toshimoto Mitomo, Chief Strategy Officer
Hiroaki Kitano, Chief Technology Officer
Wendy Becker, Director
Shiro Kambe, Other Corporate Officer
Kazushi Ambe, Other Corporate Officer

FINANCIAL DATA: Note: Data for latest year may not have been available at press time.

In U.S. $	2024	2023	2022	2021	2020	2019
Revenue	90,396,892,526	76,189,764,670	68,880,263,728	62,473,350,596	57,344,384,046	60,161,671,403
R&D Expense						
Operating Income	8,101,819,000	8,839,246,000	7,722,827,000	6,643,696,000	5,788,017,000	5,732,199,000
Operating Margin %	.09%	.12%	.11%	.11%	.10%	.10%
SGA Expense	14,969,150,000	13,670,990,000	11,028,000,000	10,227,400,000	10,432,000,000	10,947,130,000
Net Income	6,738,219,000	6,979,152,000	6,124,535,000	7,148,084,000	4,041,871,000	6,361,226,000
Operating Cash Flow	9,533,554,000	2,184,747,000	8,564,586,000	7,915,975,000	9,370,626,000	8,738,809,000
Capital Expenditure	4,331,755,000	4,260,171,000	3,062,316,000	3,318,044,000	3,053,048,000	2,170,536,000
EBITDA	17,041,370,000	16,005,860,000	13,658,260,000	11,799,130,000	10,809,440,000	12,126,030,000
Return on Assets %	.03%	.03%	.03%	.04%	.03%	.05%
Return on Equity %	.14%	.16%	.14%	.18%	.14%	.27%
Debt to Equity	.27%	.27%	.21%	.16%	0.193	0.152

CONTACT INFORMATION:

Phone: 81 367482111   Fax: 81 367482244
Toll-Free:
Address: 1-7-1 Konan, Minato-Ku, Tokyo, 108-0075 Japan

STOCK TICKER/OTHER:

Stock Ticker: SONY   Exchange: NYS
Employees: 113,200   Fiscal Year Ends: 03/31
Parent Company:

SALARIES/BONUSES:

Top Exec. Salary: $4,116,912   Bonus: $
Second Exec. Salary: $3,735,074   Bonus: $

OTHER THOUGHTS:

Estimated Female Officers or Directors:
Hot Spot for Advancement for Women/Minorities:

Sales, profits and employees may be estimates. Financial information, benefits and other data can change quickly and may vary from those stated here.

SpaceX (Space Exploration Technologies Corporation)

www.spacex.com
NAIC Code: 336414

TYPES OF BUSINESS:
Missile and Space Vehicle Manufacturing
Satellite Launch Services
Rockets, Reusable
Communications Satellites
Satellite Internet Access
Spaceships
Cargo and Passenger Spaceships
National Security Satellite Network

BRANDS/DIVISIONS/AFFILIATES:
Elon Musk Trust
SpaceX
Falcon
Dragon
Starlink
Starship
Smallsat
Starshield

CONTACTS: Note: Officers with more than one job title may be intentionally listed here more than once.
Elon Musk, CEO
Gwynne Shotwell, Pres.
Andy Lambert, VP-Prod.
Timothy Hughes, General Counsel
Barry Matsumori, VP-Bus. Dev.
Elon Musk, Chief Designer
Tim Buzza, VP-Launch & Test
James Henderson, VP-Quality Assurance
Hans Koenigsmann, VP-Mission Assurance

GROWTH PLANS/SPECIAL FEATURES:
Space Exploration Technologies Corporation (SpaceX) designs, manufactures and launches rockets and spacecraft. The private firm is majority-owned by the Elon Musk Trust. The firm has since flown many missions to the ISS under a cargo resupply contract. SpaceX's launch vehicles consist of the Falcon family of rockets, offering medium and heavy lift launch capabilities. Falcon 9, is a two-stage medium rocket powered by the SpaceX Merlin Engine, is used for International Space Station (ISS) resupply missions and capable of carrying other spacecraft. Falcon Heavy is a heavy lift rocket that carries spacecraft or satellites weighing approximately 64 metric tons (141,000 pounds). Falcon Heavy successfully lifted off from Launch Complex 39A at Kennedy Space Center in February 2018 and as of May 2025 had 11 launches, 19 landings and 16 re-flights. Dragon is a spacecraft that sends cargo, NASA astronauts and commercial astronauts to and from Earth orbit to the ISS and beyond. Starship is a reusable super heavy lift launch vehicle in development to carry both crew and cargo. Smallsat is a rideshare program in which individuals can experience orbit missions and can be booked online through the SpaceX website. Starshield is a satellite network for supporting national security, leveraging Starlink's technology and launch capabilities for three core purposes: observing Earth, providing global communication and hosting demanding payloads. Starlink is a satellite constellation that provides internet access to over 75 countries via over 7,500 small satellites in low Earth orbit.

FINANCIAL DATA: Note: Data for latest year may not have been available at press time.

In U.S. $	2024	2023	2022	2021	2020	2019
Revenue	9,135,000,000	8,700,000,000	4,600,000,000	2,300,000,000		
R&D Expense						
Operating Income						
Operating Margin %						
SGA Expense						
Net Income			-559,000,000	-968,000,000		
Operating Cash Flow						
Capital Expenditure						
EBITDA						
Return on Assets %						
Return on Equity %						
Debt to Equity						

CONTACT INFORMATION:
Phone: 310 363-6000   Fax:
Toll-Free:
Address: 1 Rocket Rd., Hawthorne, CA 90250 United States

STOCK TICKER/OTHER:
Stock Ticker: Private   Exchange:
Employees: 9,500   Fiscal Year Ends:
Parent Company:

SALARIES/BONUSES:
Top Exec. Salary: $ Bonus: $
Second Exec. Salary: $ Bonus: $

OTHER THOUGHTS:
Estimated Female Officers or Directors: 1
Hot Spot for Advancement for Women/Minorities: Y

Spirit AeroSystems Holdings Inc

www.spiritaero.com

NAIC Code: 336413

TYPES OF BUSINESS:

Aircraft Fuselage Wing Tail and Similar Assemblies Manufacturing
Aerostructures
Fuselages
Wings & Flight Control Components
Engineering, Design & Materials Testing
Custom Tool Fabrication
Spare Parts & Maintenance Services
Supply Chain Management

BRANDS/DIVISIONS/AFFILIATES:

Shorts and Bombardier Aerospace North Africa

GROWTH PLANS/SPECIAL FEATURES:

Spirit AeroSystems manufactures aerostructures, particularly fuselages, cockpits, wing sections, engine pylons, and nacelles for commercial and military aircraft. The company was spun out of Boeing in 2005 to become the largest independent supplier of aerostructures for commercial aircraft. Boeing and Airbus are the firm's primary customers, Boeing represented roughly 60% and Airbus roughly 20% of revenue in recent years. The company is highly exposed to Boeing's beleaguered 737 program, which accounts for nearly half the company's revenue. The company plans to be acquired by and reintegrated into Boeing in mid-2025.

Spirit offers comprehensive employee benefits.

CONTACTS: Note: Officers with more than one job title may be intentionally listed here more than once.

Patrick Shanahan, CEO
Irene Esteves, CFO
Robert Johnson, Chairman of the Board
Damon Ward, Chief Accounting Officer
Justin Welner, Chief Administrative Officer
Mindy McPheeters, General Counsel
Kailash Krishnaswamy, Senior VP, Divisional
Terry George, Senior VP, Divisional
Sean Black, Senior VP, Divisional
Mark Miklos, Senior VP, Divisional
William Brown, Senior VP, Divisional
Scott McLarty, Senior VP, Divisional

FINANCIAL DATA: Note: Data for latest year may not have been available at press time.

In U.S. $	2024	2023	2022	2021	2020	2019
Revenue	6,316,599,808	6,047,900,160	5,029,600,256	3,952,999,936	3,404,800,000	7,863,099,904
R&D Expense	47,500,000	45,400,000	50,400,000	53,300,000	38,800,000	54,500,000
Operating Income	-1,785,700,000	-164,700,000	-287,800,000	-451,000,000	-716,900,000	760,800,000
Operating Margin %	-.28%	-.03%	-.06%	-.11%	-.21%	.10%
SGA Expense	365,500,000	281,900,000	279,200,000	279,900,000	237,400,000	261,400,000
Net Income	-2,139,800,000	-616,200,000	-545,700,000	-540,800,000	-870,300,000	530,100,000
Operating Cash Flow	-1,120,900,000	-225,800,000	-394,600,000	-63,200,000	-744,900,000	922,700,000
Capital Expenditure	152,500,000	148,000,000	121,600,000	150,600,000	118,900,000	232,200,000
EBITDA	-1,482,700,000	41,000,000	41,800,000	15,000,000	-613,000,000	1,006,700,000
Return on Assets %	-.31%	-.09%	-.08%	-.07%	-.11%	.08%
Return on Equity %			-5.44%	-.83%	-.66%	.35%
Debt to Equity				8.52%	4.203	1.719

CONTACT INFORMATION:

Phone: 316 526-9000   Fax:
Toll-Free: 800-501-7597
Address: 3801 S. Oliver St., Wichita, KS 67210 United States

STOCK TICKER/OTHER:

Stock Ticker: SPR
Employees: 20,655
Parent Company:

Exchange: NYS
Fiscal Year Ends: 12/31

SALARIES/BONUSES:

Top Exec. Salary: $2,000,000   Bonus: $
Second Exec. Salary: $401,639   Bonus: $1,050,000

OTHER THOUGHTS:

Estimated Female Officers or Directors: 2
Hot Spot for Advancement for Women/Minorities: Y

SRI International

www.sri.com

NAIC Code: 541710

TYPES OF BUSINESS:

Research and Development (R&D) in Engineering, Materials, Aerospace, Health, Pharma and Medical

BRANDS/DIVISIONS/AFFILIATES:

GROWTH PLANS/SPECIAL FEATURES:

SRI International is an independent, nonprofit research organization with deep roots in Silicon Valley and a rich history of supporting government and industry. SRI has collaborated across technical and scientific disciplines to discover and develop groundbreaking products and technologies and bring innovations and ideas to the marketplace. Sectors of innovation include artificial intelligence (AI), climate and sustainability, education, health, quantum, security and space. The firm has over 13,000 patents filed, along with more than 500 research and development (R&D) projects each year. The firm is headquartered in California, with an additional office in Tokyo.

CONTACTS: Note: Officers with more than one job title may be intentionally listed here more than once.

David Parekh, CEO
Suresh Sunderrajan, CFO
Joann Lime, Chief Human Resources Officer
Michael Page, CIO

FINANCIAL DATA: Note: Data for latest year may not have been available at press time.

In U.S. $	2024	2023	2022	2021	2020	2019
Revenue						
R&D Expense						
Operating Income						
Operating Margin %						
SGA Expense						
Net Income						
Operating Cash Flow						
Capital Expenditure						
EBITDA						
Return on Assets %						
Return on Equity %						
Debt to Equity						

CONTACT INFORMATION:

Phone: 650 859-2000   Fax:
Toll-Free:
Address: 333 Ravenswood Ave., Menlo Park, CA 94025-3493 United States

STOCK TICKER/OTHER:

Stock Ticker: Private   Exchange:
Employees: Fiscal Year Ends:
Parent Company:

SALARIES/BONUSES:

Top Exec. Salary: $ Bonus: $
Second Exec. Salary: $ Bonus: $

OTHER THOUGHTS:

Estimated Female Officers or Directors:
Hot Spot for Advancement for Women/Minorities:

SSOE Group

www.ssoe.com

NAIC Code: 541330

TYPES OF BUSINESS:

Engineering Consulting Services
Engineering
Construction
Architecture
Project Management
Site Evaluation
Master Planning
Interior Design

BRANDS/DIVISIONS/AFFILIATES:

GROWTH PLANS/SPECIAL FEATURES:

SSOE Group is a privately-owned architecture and engineering firm. SSOE has offices throughout the U.S., as well as in India and Mexico, and specializes in delivering complicated, high-stakes projects via long-term program management and support. The company's services span across a range of industries and include architecture, program management, historic preservation, engineering, site evaluation, data/fire/security, master planning, project management, interior design and sustainable design. SSOE can execute projects in a number of delivery models so as to align with specific business needs and goals, including schedule, cost control, quality assurance or other conditions. Industries served by SSOE include automotive, battery manufacturing, chemical, consumer products, distribution centers, energy/power, food and beverage, glass, manufacturing/high-tech, pharmaceutical and semiconductor. The group also offers architectural solutions for industrial clients and in areas such as corporate workplace, healthcare, higher education, historic preservation/adaptive reuse, judicial/government, K-12 education, residential and hospitality.

SSOE offers its employees health and financial benefits, and a variety of perks.

CONTACTS: Note: Officers with more than one job title may be intentionally listed here more than once.

Vince Dipofi, CEO
Jim Jaros, CFO
Carrie Gonzalez, Dir.-Mktg.
Jennifer Wuertz, Dir.-Human Resources
Scott Thompson, VP-Tech.
Matthew Oberts, Chmn.

FINANCIAL DATA: Note: Data for latest year may not have been available at press time.

In U.S. $	2024	2023	2022	2021	2020	2019
Revenue	175,350,000	167,000,000	160,000,000	153,492,570	143,451,000	144,900,000
R&D Expense						
Operating Income						
Operating Margin %						
SGA Expense						
Net Income						
Operating Cash Flow						
Capital Expenditure						
EBITDA						
Return on Assets %						
Return on Equity %						
Debt to Equity						

CONTACT INFORMATION:

Phone: 419-255-3830   Fax: 419-255-6101
Toll-Free:
Address: 1001 Madison Ave., Toledo, OH 43604 United States

STOCK TICKER/OTHER:

Stock Ticker: Private   Exchange:
Employees: 1,500   Fiscal Year Ends:
Parent Company:

SALARIES/BONUSES:

Top Exec. Salary: $ Bonus: $
Second Exec. Salary: $ Bonus: $

OTHER THOUGHTS:

Estimated Female Officers or Directors:
Hot Spot for Advancement for Women/Minorities:

Stanley Black & Decker Inc

www.stanleyblackanddecker.com

NAIC Code: 333991

TYPES OF BUSINESS:

Power Tools & Accessories Manufacturer
Security Solutions
Household Appliances
Home Improvement Products
Fastening & Assembly Systems
Plumbing Products
Automotive Machinery

BRANDS/DIVISIONS/AFFILIATES:

DeWALT
Porter-Cable
Bostitch
Guaranteed Tough
Mac Tools
LaBounty
Dubuis
WanderGuard

GROWTH PLANS/SPECIAL FEATURES:

Stanley Black & Decker Inc is a manufacturer of hand and power tools. The company operates in two reportable segments namely Tools and Outdoor and Industrial. It generates maximum revenue from the Tools and Outdoor segment. The Tools and Outdoor segment is comprised of the Power Tools Group (PTG), Hand Tools, Accessories and Storage (HTAS), and Outdoor Power Equipment (Outdoor) businesses. Geographically, the company generates revenue from the United States, Canada, Other Americas, Europe, and Asia. It derives a majority of its revenue from the United States.

Stanley Black & Decker offers its employees medical, dental, life and disability insurance; and a 401(k).

CONTACTS: Note: Officers with more than one job title may be intentionally listed here more than once.

Donald Allan, CEO
Patrick Hallinan, CFO
Scot Greulach, Chief Accounting Officer
Christopher Nelson, COO
Janet Link, General Counsel
Deborah Wintner, Other Executive Officer
Tamer Abuaita, Other Executive Officer
Graham Robinson, President, Divisional

FINANCIAL DATA: Note: Data for latest year may not have been available at press time.

In U.S. $	2024	2023	2022	2021	2020	2019
Revenue	15,365,699,584	15,781,099,520	16,947,399,680	15,281,300,480	13,057,699,840	12,912,900,096
R&D Expense						
Operating Income	1,181,700,000	641,900,000	914,100,000	1,899,100,000	1,776,900,000	1,665,100,000
Operating Margin %	.08%	.04%	.05%	.12%	.14%	.13%
SGA Expense	3,310,500,000	3,282,000,000	3,355,700,000	3,193,100,000	2,599,500,000	2,542,000,000
Net Income	294,300,000	-310,500,000	1,062,500,000	1,689,200,000	1,233,800,000	955,800,000
Operating Cash Flow	1,106,900,000	1,191,300,000	-1,459,500,000	663,100,000	2,022,100,000	1,505,700,000
Capital Expenditure	353,900,000	338,700,000	530,400,000	519,100,000	348,100,000	424,700,000
EBITDA	1,329,200,000	808,800,000	948,600,000	2,349,400,000	2,020,500,000	1,936,800,000
Return on Assets %	.01%	- .01%	.04%	.07%	.06%	.05%
Return on Equity %	.03%	- .03%	.10%	.16%	.14%	.13%
Debt to Equity	.64%	.67%	.55%	.40%	0.438	0.402

CONTACT INFORMATION:

Phone: 860 225-5111   Fax: 860 827-3895
Toll-Free:
Address: 1000 Stanley Dr., New Britain, CT 06053 United States

STOCK TICKER/OTHER:

Stock Ticker: SWK   Exchange: NYS
Employees: 50,500   Fiscal Year Ends: 12/31
Parent Company:

SALARIES/BONUSES:

Top Exec. Salary: $1,350,000   Bonus: $
Second Exec. Salary: Bonus: $
$850,000

OTHER THOUGHTS:

Estimated Female Officers or Directors: 5
Hot Spot for Advancement for Women/Minorities: Y

Stanley Consultants Inc

www.stanleyconsultants.com

NAIC Code: 541330

TYPES OF BUSINESS:

Engineering Consulting Services
Engineering Consultancy
Project Management
Design-Build
Innovative Technologies
Data Analytics Consulting
Procurement
Energy and Environment, Infrastructure

BRANDS/DIVISIONS/AFFILIATES:

CONTACTS: Note: Officers with more than one job title may be intentionally listed here more than once.

Kate Harris, CEO
Greg Eldridge, COO
Jesse Herron, CFO
Keith Tucker, Chief Sales & Mktg. Officer
Dale Sweere, Chief Human Resources Officer
John Guilfoyle, CTO
Kate Harris, Chmn.

GROWTH PLANS/SPECIAL FEATURES:

Stanley Consultants, Inc. (Stanley) was founded in 1913 and is a member-owned consulting engineering firm with more than 20 offices worldwide. Through the development of its technologies and solutions, Stanley helps clients solve complex challenges via engineering, design, environmental, construction and consulting services. The company works with federal, state and local governments, offering master planning, whether it be business operations, communities or both. Stanley's augmented design technologies provide energy solutions for client projects, and its data analytics offer decision-making insight in areas such as climate, engineering and the economy. The firm works with clients to build, modernize and expand transportation and energy systems, as well as to maintain and enhance existing infrastructure. Stanley's multi-disciplinary, full lifecycle project services enable clients to plan, design, procure, manage, commission and permit capital projects. The company has served clients in more than 120 countries.

FINANCIAL DATA: Note: Data for latest year may not have been available at press time.

In U.S. $	2024	2023	2022	2021	2020	2019
Revenue						
R&D Expense						
Operating Income						
Operating Margin %						
SGA Expense						
Net Income						
Operating Cash Flow						
Capital Expenditure						
EBITDA						
Return on Assets %						
Return on Equity %						
Debt to Equity						

CONTACT INFORMATION:

Phone: 563-264-6600   Fax: 563-264-6658
Toll-Free: 800-553-9694
Address: 225 Iowa Ave., Muscatine, IA 52761 United States

STOCK TICKER/OTHER:

Stock Ticker: Private   Exchange:
Employees: 1,000   Fiscal Year Ends:
Parent Company:

SALARIES/BONUSES:

Top Exec. Salary: $ Bonus: $
Second Exec. Salary: $ Bonus: $

OTHER THOUGHTS:

Estimated Female Officers or Directors:
Hot Spot for Advancement for Women/Minorities: Y

Stellantis North America

NAIC Code: 336111

TYPES OF BUSINESS:

Automobile Manufacturing
Research & Development
Nanotechnology-Coatings
Light Truck Manufacturing
Financial Services
Electric Vehicles

BRANDS/DIVISIONS/AFFILIATES:

Stellantis NV
Chrysler
Jeep
Dodge
Mopar
Ram
Alfa Romeo
Fiat

GROWTH PLANS/SPECIAL FEATURES:

Stellantis North America (formerly FCA US LLC) is the U.S. automotive division of Stellantis NV. Based in Michigan, Stellantis North America designs engineers, manufactures and sells vehicles under the Abarth, Alfa Romeo, Chrysler, Citroen, Dodge, DS Automobiles, Fiat, Jeep, Lancia, Maserati, Opel, Peugeot, Ram Trucks, Vauxhall, Free2move and Leasys brands. Stellantis North America operates manufacturing plants throughout the U.S. Technologies include electrification, hydrogen fuel cell technology, intelligent vehicles and autonomous driving. Engineering breakthroughs made by the company include: Uconnect, which allows drivers to easily adjust seat or cabin temperature, select a new music station or make a call without taking their eyes from the road; various fuel efficiency features in relation to power, transmissions, engines and electrified propulsion systems; and design, development and vehicle integration of technologies in relation to customer safety and security.

CONTACTS: *Note: Officers with more than one job title may be intentionally listed here more than once.*

Antonio Filosa, COO
Ralph V. Gilles, Sr. VP-Prod. Design
Mark M. Chernoby, Sr. VP-Eng.
Mauro Pino, Sr. VP-Mfg. & World Class Mfg.
Peter Grady, VP-Network Dev. & Fleet
Marjorie Loeb, General Counsel
Barbara J. Pilarski, VP-Bus. Dev.
Gualberto Ranieri, Sr. VP-Comm.
Laurie A. Macaddino, VP-Audit
Doug D. Betts, Sr. VP-Quality
Alistair Gardner, Pres.
Reid Bigland, Head-U.S. Sales
Steven G. Beahm, Sr. VP-Supply Chain Mgmt.

FINANCIAL DATA: *Note: Data for latest year may not have been available at press time.*

In U.S. $	2024	2023	2022	2021	2020	2019
Revenue	100,238,103,000	95,464,860,000	92,950,643,500	78,969,046,400	74,090,200,000	82,149,600,000
R&D Expense						
Operating Income						
Operating Margin %						
SGA Expense						
Net Income						
Operating Cash Flow						
Capital Expenditure						
EBITDA						
Return on Assets %						
Return on Equity %						
Debt to Equity						

CONTACT INFORMATION:

Phone: 248-576-5741   Fax:
Toll-Free: 800-992-1997
Address: 1000 Chrysler Dr., Auburn Hills, MI 48326-2766 United States

STOCK TICKER/OTHER:

Stock Ticker: Subsidiary   Exchange:
Employees: 81,341   Fiscal Year Ends: 12/31
Parent Company: Stellantis NV

SALARIES/BONUSES:

Top Exec. Salary: $ Bonus: $
Second Exec. Salary: $ Bonus: $

OTHER THOUGHTS:

Estimated Female Officers or Directors: 3
Hot Spot for Advancement for Women/Minorities: Y

Stellantis NV

NAIC Code: 336111

TYPES OF BUSINESS:
Automobile Manufacturing
Mobility Solutions
Vehicles
Car Sharing
Vehicle Rental
Vehicle Leasing
Finance

GROWTH PLANS/SPECIAL FEATURES:
Stellantis was created out of the merger of US-based Fiat Chrysler Automobiles and French-based Peugeot in January 2021, resulting in the fourth-largest automotive original equipment manufacturer by vehicle sales. In 2024 it sold 5.5 million vehicles, 47%, 26% and 17% in Europe, North America, and South America, respectively. Its brands include Fiat, Jeep, Chrysler, Ram, Peugeot, CitroÃ«n, Opel, Alfa Romeo, and Maserati.

BRANDS/DIVISIONS/AFFILIATES:
PSA Groupe
Fiat Chrysler Automobiles
Chrysler
Fiat
Maserati
Vauxhall
Free2Move
Leasys SpA

CONTACTS: Note: Officers with more than one job title may be intentionally listed here more than once.
Carlos Tavares, CEO
Beatrice Foucher, Other Executive Officer
Natalie Knight, CFO
John Elkann, Chairman of the Board
Douglas Ostermann, COO, Geographical
Samir Cherfan, COO, Geographical
Uwe Hochgeschurtz, COO, Geographical
Carlos Zarlenga, COO, Geographical
Emanuele Cappellano, COO, Geographical
Ashwani Muppasani, COO, Geographical
Robert Peugeot, Director
Giorgio Fossati, General Counsel
Olivier Bourges, Other Corporate Officer
Philippe de Rovira, Other Executive Officer
Xavier Chereau, Other Executive Officer

FINANCIAL DATA: Note: Data for latest year may not have been available at press time.

In U.S. $	2024	2023	2022	2021	2020	2019
Revenue	178,068,100,114	215,146,431,141	203,850,174,548	169,601,589,067	54,093,077,851	66,961,408,072
R&D Expense	6,565,267,000	6,377,979,000	5,902,384,000	5,093,076,000	2,532,350,000	2,920,545,000
Operating Income	6,169,126,000	26,088,540,000	23,931,900,000	18,001,140,000	3,691,260,000	5,531,214,000
Operating Margin %	.03%	.12%	.12%	.11%	.07%	.08%
SGA Expense	10,555,050,000	10,829,740,000	10,194,100,000	10,363,220,000	4,452,895,000	5,586,833,000
Net Income	6,212,259,000	21,107,830,000	19,068,100,000	16,118,050,000	2,466,515,000	3,633,371,000
Operating Cash Flow	4,549,375,000	25,522,140,000	22,654,940,000	21,164,580,000	7,083,996,000	9,837,685,000
Capital Expenditure	12,553,920,000	11,569,810,000	10,231,560,000	11,479,000,000	3,348,468,000	4,162,316,000
EBITDA	14,507,380,000	35,524,400,000	31,203,180,000	24,710,560,000	6,223,609,000	6,674,234,000
Return on Assets %	.03%	.10%	.09%	.11%	.03%	.03%
Return on Equity %	.07%	.24%	.26%	.37%	.09%	.12%
Debt to Equity	.31%	.24%	.27%	.40%	0.52	0.281

CONTACT INFORMATION:
Phone: 3120-3421707   Fax:
Toll-Free:
Address: Singaporestraat 92-100, Lijnden, 1175 RA Netherlands

STOCK TICKER/OTHER:
Stock Ticker: STLA   Exchange: NYS
Employees: 258,275   Fiscal Year Ends: 12/31
Parent Company:

SALARIES/BONUSES:
Top Exec. Salary: $2,270,148   Bonus: $
Second Exec. Salary: $ Bonus: $

OTHER THOUGHTS:
Estimated Female Officers or Directors: 3
Hot Spot for Advancement for Women/Minorities: Y

Stellar Group Inc (The)

www.stellar.net

NAIC Code: 541330

TYPES OF BUSINESS:

Engineering Consulting Services
Engineering
Design Build
Construction
Project Management
Refrigerated Facilities
Industrial Solutions
Thermal Building Envelope

BRANDS/DIVISIONS/AFFILIATES:

GROWTH PLANS/SPECIAL FEATURES:

The Stellar Group, Inc. began in 1985, and is an architecture, engineering and construction company. Markets served by Stellar include food, logistics, distribution, commercial, federal, industrial solutions, refrigeration contracting and services, thermal/building, technical, mechanical and utility. Stellar's services are fully integrated, and encompass planning, design, pre-construction, construction, delivery methods, refrigeration, thermal/building envelope, mechanical and utility. The firm offers innovative solutions such as 4D, virtual reality, augmented reality and building information modeling (BIM). Projects by Stellar include JBS Prepared Foods-Principe Dried Meats Production Facility in Columbia, Missouri; Jacksonville University Botts Residence Hall in Jacksonville, Florida; and Borland Groover Clinic Ambulatory Surgical Center in Orange Park, Florida.

Stellar offers its employees comprehensive health benefits, telemedicine, counseling services, a 401(k), life and short/long-term disability coverage, a flexible spending account, a health savings account and other benefits, programs and perks.

CONTACTS: Note: Officers with more than one job title may be intentionally listed here more than once.

Brian Kappele, CEO
Scott Mark, COO
Clint Pyle, CFO
Stacey King, Chief Human Resources Officer

FINANCIAL DATA: Note: Data for latest year may not have been available at press time.

In U.S. $	2024	2023	2022	2021	2020	2019
Revenue	786,145,500	748,710,000	661,000,000	646,225,965	603,949,500	610,050,000
R&D Expense						
Operating Income						
Operating Margin %						
SGA Expense						
Net Income						
Operating Cash Flow						
Capital Expenditure						
EBITDA						
Return on Assets %						
Return on Equity %						
Debt to Equity						

CONTACT INFORMATION:

Phone: 904-260-2900   Fax:
Toll-Free: 800-488-2900
Address: 2900 Hartley Rd., Jacksonville, FL 32257 United States

STOCK TICKER/OTHER:

Stock Ticker: Private   Exchange:
Employees: 750   Fiscal Year Ends:
Parent Company:

SALARIES/BONUSES:

Top Exec. Salary: $ Bonus: $
Second Exec. Salary: $ Bonus: $

OTHER THOUGHTS:

Estimated Female Officers or Directors:
Hot Spot for Advancement for Women/Minorities:

STMicroelectronics NV

www.st.com

NAIC Code: 334413

TYPES OF BUSINESS:

Semiconductor Manufacturing
Integrated Circuits
Transistors & Diodes

GROWTH PLANS/SPECIAL FEATURES:

A merger between Italian firm SGS Microelettronica and the nonmilitary business of Thomson Semiconducteurs in France formed STMicroelectronics in 1987. STMicroelectronics is a leader in a variety of semiconductor products, including analog chips, discrete power semiconductors, microcontrollers, and sensors. It is an especially prominent chip supplier to the industrial and automotive industries.

BRANDS/DIVISIONS/AFFILIATES:

BeSpoon

CONTACTS: Note: Officers with more than one job title may be intentionally listed here more than once.

Jean-Marc Chery, CEO
Henry Cao, Exec. VP, Divisional
Lorenzo Grandi, CFO
Nicolas Dufourcq, Chairman of the Board
Maurizio Tamagnini, Director
Claudia Levo, Executive VP, Divisional
Giuseppe Notarnicola, Executive VP, Divisional
Christophe Ayela, Executive VP, Divisional
Rino Peruzzi, Executive VP, Divisional
Chouaib Rokbi, Executive VP, Divisional
Bertrand Stoltz, Executive VP, Divisional
Stefano Cantu, Executive VP, Divisional
Alberto Chiesa, Executive VP, Divisional
Nicolas Yackowlew, Executive VP, Divisional
Ricardo Earp, Executive VP, Divisional
Laurent Malier, Executive VP, Divisional
Edoardo Merli, Executive VP, Divisional
Matteo Presti, Executive VP, Divisional
Alexandre Balmefrezol, Executive VP, Divisional
Frederique Le Greves, Executive VP, Geographical

FINANCIAL DATA: Note: Data for latest year may not have been available at press time.

In U.S. $	2024	2023	2022	2021	2020	2019
Revenue	13,269,000,192	17,286,000,640	16,128,000,000	12,760,999,936	10,218,999,808	9,555,999,744
R&D Expense	2,077,000,000	2,100,000,000	1,901,000,000	1,723,000,000	1,548,000,000	1,498,000,000
Operating Income	1,494,000,000	4,556,000,000	4,280,000,000	2,280,000,000	1,363,000,000	1,237,000,000
Operating Margin %	.11%	.26%	.27%	.18%	.13%	.13%
SGA Expense	1,649,000,000	1,631,000,000	1,454,000,000	1,323,000,000	1,109,000,000	1,093,000,000
Net Income	1,557,000,000	4,211,000,000	3,960,000,000	2,000,000,000	1,106,000,000	1,032,000,000
Operating Cash Flow	2,965,000,000	5,992,000,000	5,202,000,000	3,060,000,000	2,093,000,000	1,869,000,000
Capital Expenditure	3,181,000,000	4,536,000,000	3,636,000,000	1,937,000,000	1,358,000,000	1,250,000,000
EBITDA	3,723,000,000	6,379,000,000	5,715,000,000	3,424,000,000	2,244,000,000	2,097,000,000
Return on Assets %	.06%	.19%	.22%	.13%	.08%	.09%
Return on Equity %	.09%	.29%	.36%	.23%	.14%	.15%
Debt to Equity	.12%	.17%	.21%	.28%	0.233	0.291

CONTACT INFORMATION:

Phone: 41 229292929　　Fax: 41 229292988
Toll-Free:
Address: 39, Chemin du Champ des FillesPlan-Les-Ouates, Geneva, CH1228 Switzerland

STOCK TICKER/OTHER:

Stock Ticker: STM　　Exchange: NYS
Employees: 51,323　　Fiscal Year Ends: 12/31
Parent Company:

SALARIES/BONUSES:

Top Exec. Salary: $936,357　　Bonus: $1,907,307
Second Exec. Salary: $　　Bonus: $

OTHER THOUGHTS:

Estimated Female Officers or Directors: 1
Hot Spot for Advancement for Women/Minorities: Y

Sales, profits and employees may be estimates. Financial information, benefits and other data can change quickly and may vary from those stated here.

Stryker Corporation

www.stryker.com

NAIC Code: 339100

TYPES OF BUSINESS:

Equipment-Orthopedic Implants
Powered Surgical Instruments
Endoscopic Systems
Patient Care & Handling Equipment
Imaging Software
Small Bone Innovations

BRANDS/DIVISIONS/AFFILIATES:

Wright Medical Group NV

GROWTH PLANS/SPECIAL FEATURES:

Stryker designs, manufactures, and markets an array of medical equipment, instruments, consumable supplies, and implantable devices. The product portfolio includes hip and knee replacements, extremities, endoscopy systems, operating room equipment, embolic coils, hospital beds and gurneys, and orthopedic robotics. Stryker remains one of the three largest competitors in reconstructive orthopedic implants and holds the leadership position in operating room equipment. Roughly one fourth of Stryker's total revenue currently comes from outside the United States.

Stryker offers employees health insurance, retirement programs, tuition reimbursement and wellness programs.

CONTACTS: *Note: Officers with more than one job title may be intentionally listed here more than once.*

Kevin Lobo, CEO
Glenn Boehnlein, CFO
William Berry, Chief Accounting Officer
Robert Fletcher, Chief Legal Officer
Yin Becker, Other Executive Officer
M. Fink, Other Executive Officer
Viju Menon, President, Divisional
Spencer Stiles, President, Divisional
J. Pierce, President, Divisional

FINANCIAL DATA: *Note: Data for latest year may not have been available at press time.*

In U.S. $	2024	2023	2022	2021	2020	2019
Revenue	22,595,000,320	20,497,999,872	18,449,000,448	17,107,999,744	14,350,999,552	14,883,999,744
R&D Expense	1,466,000,000	1,388,000,000	1,454,000,000	1,235,000,000	984,000,000	971,000,000
Operating Income	4,666,000,000	3,924,000,000	3,111,000,000	2,687,000,000	2,240,000,000	2,905,000,000
Operating Margin %	.21%	.19%	.17%	.16%	.16%	.20%
SGA Expense	7,685,000,000	7,111,000,000	6,386,000,000	6,427,000,000	5,361,000,000	5,356,000,000
Net Income	2,993,000,000	3,165,000,000	2,358,000,000	1,994,000,000	1,599,000,000	2,083,000,000
Operating Cash Flow	4,242,000,000	3,711,000,000	2,624,000,000	3,263,000,000	3,277,000,000	2,191,000,000
Capital Expenditure	755,000,000	575,000,000	588,000,000	525,000,000	487,000,000	649,000,000
EBITDA	5,716,000,000	4,952,000,000	4,109,000,000	3,677,000,000	3,052,000,000	3,683,000,000
Return on Assets %	.07%	.08%	.07%	.06%	.05%	.07%
Return on Equity %	.15%	.18%	.15%	.14%	.12%	.17%
Debt to Equity	.59%	.59%	.71%	.84%	1.011	0.799

CONTACT INFORMATION:

Phone: 269 385-2600   Fax: 269 385-1062
Toll-Free:
Address: 2825 Airview Blvd., Kalamazoo, MI 49002 United States

STOCK TICKER/OTHER:

Stock Ticker: SYK   Exchange: NYS
Employees: 52,000   Fiscal Year Ends: 12/31
Parent Company:

SALARIES/BONUSES:

Top Exec. Salary: $1,441,667   Bonus: $
Second Exec. Salary: Bonus: $
$793,334

OTHER THOUGHTS:

Estimated Female Officers or Directors: 7
Hot Spot for Advancement for Women/Minorities: Y

STV Incorporated

www.stvinc.com

NAIC Code: 541330

TYPES OF BUSINESS:

Architectural & Engineering Services
Construction Management
Infrastructure Design
Defense Systems Engineering
Industrial Process Engineering

BRANDS/DIVISIONS/AFFILIATES:

CONTACTS: *Note: Officers with more than one job title may be intentionally listed here more than once.*

Greg Kelly, CEO
Debra B. Trace, Dir.-Corp. Comm.
Michael D. Garz, Sr. VP-Buildings & Facilities Div.
William F. Matts, Exec. VP
Steve Pressler, Exec. VP
Gerald Donnelly, Exec. VP-STV Energy Svcs. Div.

GROWTH PLANS/SPECIAL FEATURES:

STV Incorporated is an architectural, engineering, planning, environmental and construction management firm. STV specializes in constructing airports, highways, bridges, ports, railroad systems and schools, almost all of which are in the U.S. The firm operates through four divisions: construction management, energy services, buildings/facilities and transportation/infrastructure. Construction management undertakes design and building contracts in nearly every field of industry; the company's personnel oversee construction programs through administrative, inspection and surveillance. STV's energy services division offers services related to engineering design, permitting and the environment, construction support and industry specialty support. The buildings/facilities division works directly with architects, to address the safety, practicality, cost and efficiency of its buildings. Transportation/infrastructure focuses on the management, planning and design of transportation systems and facilities. Markets STV serves include aviation, ports, corporate, industrial, energy, health, sciences, justice, institutional, rail transportation, resiliency, bus transportation, educational, cultural, environmental, highways/bridges/civil infrastructure, military, residential, retail and hospitality. Some of STV's representative projects include the MetroLink in St. Louis, Missouri; the Villanova University Center for Engineering Education and Research; Sprint PCS Environmental Site Assessments in seven states; the Metra Inner Circumferential Rail Study in Chicago, Illinois; Shea Stadium in Queens, New York; and engineering and technical services for the U.S. Naval Air Warfare Center in Patuxent River, Maryland. STV is headquartered in Pennsylvania and New York, with additional offices in throughout the U.S.

STV offers its employees comprehensive health benefits, life and disability coverage, a 401(k) and other benefits.

FINANCIAL DATA: *Note: Data for latest year may not have been available at press time.*

In U.S. $	2024	2023	2022	2021	2020	2019
Revenue	611,520,000	582,400,000	560,000,000	567,463,050	550,935,000	556,500,000
R&D Expense						
Operating Income						
Operating Margin %						
SGA Expense						
Net Income						
Operating Cash Flow						
Capital Expenditure						
EBITDA						
Return on Assets %						
Return on Equity %						
Debt to Equity						

CONTACT INFORMATION:

Phone: 610-385-8200   Fax: 610-385-8500
Toll-Free:
Address: 205 W. Welsh Dr., Douglassville, PA 19518-8713 United States

STOCK TICKER/OTHER:

Stock Ticker: Private   Exchange:
Employees: 2,200   Fiscal Year Ends: 09/30
Parent Company:

SALARIES/BONUSES:

Top Exec. Salary: $ Bonus: $
Second Exec. Salary: $ Bonus: $

OTHER THOUGHTS:

Estimated Female Officers or Directors: 2
Hot Spot for Advancement for Women/Minorities: Y

Subaru Corporation

NAIC Code: 336111

www.subaru.co.jp/en

TYPES OF BUSINESS:

Automobile Manufacturing
Aircraft Manufacturing & Components
Heavy-Duty Engines & Equipment
Sanitation Vehicles
Specialty Vehicles
Waste Treatment, Recycling & Alternative Energy Technologies
Industrial Robotics

BRANDS/DIVISIONS/AFFILIATES:

Legacy
Forester
Boxer Engine
Flying Forward Observation System
T-5
Subaru Bell 412EPX
AH-64D
Ascent

GROWTH PLANS/SPECIAL FEATURES:

Subaru Corp is a Japan-based company engaged in the automobile manufacturing business. The company is split into three segments: Automotive Business Unit, Aerospace Company, and Other Businesses. The Automotive Business, which constitutes the vast majority of the company's revenue, manufactures, repairs, and sells passenger cars and their components under the Subaru brand. The Aerospace Company includes airplanes and aerospace-related machinery and components. The Other Businesses segment consists of Industrial product, and real estate lease, among others. A vast majority of the sales is derived from North America.

CONTACTS: Note: Officers with more than one job title may be intentionally listed here more than once.

Atsushi Osaki, CEO
Katsuyuki Mizuma, CFO
Tomomi Nakamura, Chairman of the Board
Tetsuo Fujinuki, Chief Technology Officer
Fumiaki Hayata, Director

FINANCIAL DATA: Note: Data for latest year may not have been available at press time.

In U.S. $	2024	2023	2022	2021	2020	2019
Revenue	32,650,287,410	26,204,305,648	19,053,874,652	19,648,778,120	23,216,530,049	21,911,622,892
R&D Expense	788,031,100	794,223,900	719,154,400	723,111,700	641,905,000	753,665,700
Operating Income	3,256,713,000	1,856,026,000	637,059,200	712,218,800	1,461,691,000	1,259,004,000
Operating Margin %	.10%	.07%	.03%	.04%	.06%	.06%
SGA Expense	2,755,235,000	2,374,445,000	2,104,527,000	1,942,981,000	2,139,871,000	2,074,945,000
Net Income	2,673,452,000	1,391,495,000	486,024,700	531,171,900	1,059,338,000	981,796,800
Operating Cash Flow	5,329,527,000	3,497,355,000	1,358,310,000	2,008,998,000	1,458,859,000	1,740,711,000
Capital Expenditure	2,081,908,000	1,352,860,000	1,292,988,000	1,336,594,000	1,486,178,000	1,221,550,000
EBITDA	5,320,633,000	3,777,319,000	2,320,377,000	2,289,559,000	2,908,255,000	2,655,526,000
Return on Assets %	.09%	.05%	.02%	.02%	.05%	.05%
Return on Equity %	.17%	.10%	.04%	.04%	.09%	.09%
Debt to Equity	.13%	.12%	.15%	.17%	0.133	0.053

CONTACT INFORMATION:

Phone: 81-3 6447-8000   Fax: 81-3 6447-8184
Toll-Free:
Address: 1-20-8, Ebisu, Shibuya-ku, Tokyo, 150-8554 Japan

STOCK TICKER/OTHER:

Stock Ticker: FUJHF   Exchange: PINX
Employees: 43,057   Fiscal Year Ends: 03/31
Parent Company:

SALARIES/BONUSES:

Top Exec. Salary: $ Bonus: $
Second Exec. Salary: $ Bonus: $

OTHER THOUGHTS:

Estimated Female Officers or Directors:
Hot Spot for Advancement for Women/Minorities:

Sales, profits and employees may be estimates. Financial information, benefits and other data can change quickly and may vary from those stated here.

Suffolk Construction Company

NAIC Code: 236220

www.suffolk.com

TYPES OF BUSINESS:

Construction & Engineering Services
Construction
Real Estate Investment
Construction Management
Construction Technology
Design-Build Collaboration
Virtual Design and Construction
Project Lifecycle Management

BRANDS/DIVISIONS/AFFILIATES:

Suffolk Technologies
Suffolk Capital
Suffolk Design
CoLabs

CONTACTS: *Note: Officers with more than one job title may be intentionally listed here more than once.*

John Fish, CEO
Jeff Gouveia, Pres.
Puneet Mahajan, CFO
Katy O'Neil, CMO
Erin Lovering, Chief People Officer
Jit Kee Chin, CTO

GROWTH PLANS/SPECIAL FEATURES:

Suffolk Construction Company is a construction company founded in 1982 that offers end-to-end services throughout the entire project lifecycle, leveraging core construction management services with vertical service lines. These lines include real estate capital investment, design, self-perform construction, general contracting, construction management, technology and innovative research and development. Industries served by Suffolk Construction include healthcare, science, technology, education, gaming, transportation, aviation and commercial. Suffolk Technologies is a venture capital and innovation platform that invests in and partners with early- and growth-stage technology companies across the building lifecycle. Suffolk Capital is an investment vehicle that partners with real estate developers, investing in select projects throughout the U.S. Suffolk Capital primarily assists developers in their pre-construction raising of capital and pre-development process. Suffolk Design streamlines the workflow between design and construction by offering pre-construction design management strategies, including procurement and fabrication schedules, to ensure the construction process is in alignment from inception through completion. Headquartered in Boston, Massachusetts, Suffolk Construction has additional offices throughout the U.S., including New York, Texas, Florida and California. Several offices operate as CoLabs, which are dedicated spaces with full-time teams that leverage data, field ideas and problems, figure out solutions and help drive business decisions.

Suffolk offers its employees health and financial benefits.

FINANCIAL DATA: *Note: Data for latest year may not have been available at press time.*

In U.S. $	2024	2023	2022	2021	2020	2019
Revenue						
R&D Expense						
Operating Income						
Operating Margin %						
SGA Expense						
Net Income						
Operating Cash Flow						
Capital Expenditure						
EBITDA						
Return on Assets %						
Return on Equity %						
Debt to Equity						

CONTACT INFORMATION:

Phone: 617 445-3500   Fax: 617 541-2128
Toll-Free:
Address: 65 Allerton St., Boston, MA 02119 United States

STOCK TICKER/OTHER:

Stock Ticker: Private   Exchange:
Employees: Fiscal Year Ends:
Parent Company:

SALARIES/BONUSES:

Top Exec. Salary: $ Bonus: $
Second Exec. Salary: $ Bonus: $

OTHER THOUGHTS:

Estimated Female Officers or Directors:
Hot Spot for Advancement for Women/Minorities:

Sumitomo Chemical Co Ltd

www.sumitomo-chem.co.jp

NAIC Code: 325000

TYPES OF BUSINESS:

Chemicals Manufacturing, Incl Basic, Specialty, Petrochemicals,
Pharmaceuticals, Soaps, Paints
Basic Chemicals
Petrochemicals
Fine Chemicals
Agricultural Chemicals
IT-Related Chemicals
Pharmaceuticals
Sumitomo Group

BRANDS/DIVISIONS/AFFILIATES:

Sumitomo Corporation
Dainippon Sumitomo Pharma
Nihon Medi-Physics Co Ltd

GROWTH PLANS/SPECIAL FEATURES:

Sumitomo Chemical Co Ltd manufactures and sells chemicals
and chemical-based products. The firm is organized into six
segments by product type. The petrochemicals and plastics
segment, which generates more revenue than any other
segment, sells multiple products including propylene and
polypropylene used in automobile seat cushions and interior
panels. The pharmaceutical segment sells medicine to treat
diabetes, neurology, cancer, and infectious diseases. The IT-
related chemicals segment sells compound semiconductors
and polarizing films used in LCD displays for TVs and
smartphones. The other three segments are health and crop
sciences; energy and functional materials; and "others." The
majority of revenue comes from Japan and China.

CONTACTS: Note: Officers with more than one job title may be intentionally listed here more than once.

Masakazu Tokura, Chairman of the Board
Hiroshi Ueda, Director
Hiroshi Niinuma, Director
Noriaki Takeshita, Director
Keiichi Iwata, Director

FINANCIAL DATA: Note: Data for latest year may not have been available at press time.

In U.S. $	2024	2023	2022	2021	2020	2019
Revenue	16,987,594,208	20,100,548,849	19,198,284,989	15,877,382,301	15,452,679,525	16,096,723,165
R&D Expense						
Operating Income	-2,995,196,000	-167,918,600	1,199,827,000	1,038,420,000	890,613,800	1,012,018,000
Operating Margin %	-.18%	-.01%	.06%	.07%	.06%	.06%
SGA Expense	6,158,873,000	6,097,341,000	4,796,307,000	4,382,602,000	3,992,884,000	4,096,515,000
Net Income	-2,164,941,000	48,507,360	1,125,590,000	319,654,300	214,704,300	819,161,300
Operating Cash Flow	-356,269,100	774,930,600	1,192,134,000	2,599,722,000	735,990,000	1,445,036,000
Capital Expenditure	1,061,323,000	996,813,400				
EBITDA	-1,793,300,000	1,442,717,000	2,991,280,000	2,034,157,000	1,960,817,000	2,166,634,000
Return on Assets %	-.08%	.00%	.04%	.01%	.01%	.04%
Return on Equity %	-.29%	.01%	.14%	.05%	.03%	.12%
Debt to Equity	1.01%	.91%	.89%	1.08%	0.907	0.584

CONTACT INFORMATION:

Phone: 81 355435500   Fax: 81 355435901
Toll-Free:
Address: 27-1, Shinkawa 2-chome, Tokyo, 104-8260 Japan

STOCK TICKER/OTHER:

Stock Ticker: SOMMY   Exchange: PINX
Employees: 36,384   Fiscal Year Ends: 03/31
Parent Company: Sumitomo Corporation

SALARIES/BONUSES:

Top Exec. Salary: $ Bonus: $
Second Exec. Salary: $ Bonus: $

OTHER THOUGHTS:

Estimated Female Officers or Directors:
Hot Spot for Advancement for Women/Minorities:

Sales, profits and employees may be estimates. Financial information, benefits and other data can change quickly and may vary from those stated here.

Suzuki Motor Corp

www.globalsuzuki.com

NAIC Code: 336111

TYPES OF BUSINESS:

Automobile Manufacturing
Motorcycles
ATVs
Marine Products
Wheelchairs
Industrial Equipment

BRANDS/DIVISIONS/AFFILIATES:

Suzuki Auto Parts Mfg Co Ltd
Snic Co Ltd
Suzuki Akita Auto Parts Mfg Co Ltd
Celerio
Suzuki Toyama Auto Parts Mgf Co Ltd
Suzuki Transportation & Packing Co Ltd
Suzuki Engineering Co Ltd
Suzuki Finance Co Ltd

CONTACTS: *Note: Officers with more than one job title may be intentionally listed here more than once.*

Toshihiro Suzuki, Chairman of the Board
Katsuhiro Kato, Chief Technology Officer
Naomi Ishii, Director
Aritaka Okajima, Director
Shigetoshi Torii, Director

GROWTH PLANS/SPECIAL FEATURES:

Suzuki Motor Corp is an automobile manufacturing company. It organizes itself into three segments based on product type namely: automobile, motorcycle, and Marine business. The automotive business, which contributes the vast majority of revenue, largely focuses on passenger vehicles. The motorcycle business manufactures on- and off-road motorcycles and scooters, and contributes the next-largest portion of sales. The Marine business manufactures four-stroke motors for marine use. Nearly half of consolidated revenue is derived from Asian countries excluding Japan, with a third of sales made domestically.

FINANCIAL DATA: *Note: Data for latest year may not have been available at press time.*

In U.S. $	2024	2023	2022	2021	2020	2019
Revenue	37,310,852,629	32,224,687,403	24,773,535,152	22,064,767,116	24,218,502,906	26,877,923,297
R&D Expense						
Operating Income	3,232,179,000	2,433,706,000	1,329,221,000	1,349,854,000	1,493,120,000	2,251,916,000
Operating Margin %	.09%	.08%	.05%	.06%	.06%	.08%
SGA Expense						
Net Income	1,858,630,000	1,535,039,000	1,113,198,000	1,016,530,000	931,838,400	1,241,037,000
Operating Cash Flow	3,096,675,000	1,989,906,000	1,536,094,000	2,884,192,000	1,190,871,000	2,662,018,000
Capital Expenditure	2,122,258,000	1,793,113,000	1,322,355,000	1,192,072,000	1,706,644,000	1,746,091,000
EBITDA	4,835,796,000	3,922,931,000	3,066,766,000	2,655,818,000	2,886,282,000	3,134,942,000
Return on Assets %	.05%	.05%	.04%	.04%	.04%	.05%
Return on Equity %	.12%	.11%	.09%	.09%	.09%	.13%
Debt to Equity	.13%	.20%	.26%	.12%	0.138	0.156

CONTACT INFORMATION:

Phone: 81-53-440-2061   Fax:
Toll-Free:
Address: 300 Takatsuka-cho, Minami-ku, Hamamatsu, 432-8611 Japan

STOCK TICKER/OTHER:

Stock Ticker: SZKMF   Exchange: PINX
Employees: 68,739   Fiscal Year Ends: 03/31
Parent Company:

SALARIES/BONUSES:

Top Exec. Salary: $ Bonus: $
Second Exec. Salary: $ Bonus: $

OTHER THOUGHTS:

Estimated Female Officers or Directors:
Hot Spot for Advancement for Women/Minorities:

Syngenta Group Co Ltd

www.syngentagroup.com

NAIC Code: 325320

TYPES OF BUSINESS:

Pesticide and Other Agricultural Chemical Manufacturing
Crop Protection Products
Seed Production
Agrochemicals
Bioengineered Crop Protection Solutions
Bioengineered Seeds

BRANDS/DIVISIONS/AFFILIATES:

China National Chemical Corporation (ChemChina)
Syngenta Crop Protection
Syngenta Seeds
ADAMA
Syngenta Group China
ADEPIDYN
MIRAVIS
SOLATENOL

CONTACTS: Note: Officers with more than one job title may be intentionally listed here more than once.

Jeff Rowe, CEO
Hengde Qin, CFO
Caroline Barth, Chief Human Resources Officer
Robert Berendes, Interim Head-R&D
Christoph Mader, Head-Legal & Taxes
Mark Peacock, Head-Global Oper.
Davor Pisk, COO
Jonathan Seabrook, Head-Corp. Affairs

GROWTH PLANS/SPECIAL FEATURES:

Syngenta Group Co. Ltd., a product of the combination of Syngenta Crop Protection, Syngenta Seeds, ADAMA and Syngenta Group China, is an international science-based agrochemical company and a leading worldwide supplier of conventional and bioengineered crop protection and seeds. The firm's products designed for crop protection include seed treatments to control weeds, insects and diseases; herbicides; fungicides; and insecticides. Syngenta produces seeds for field crops, vegetables and flowers. Leading marketed products by Syngenta include: ADEPIDYN, the active ingredient in the MIRAVIS brand, is a next-generation fungicide based on a unique model that is potent, long-lasting and has a low application rate; and SOLATENOL, a succinate dehydrogenase inhibitor (SDHI) fungicide that shows very high potency and provides long-lasting control against major diseases and allows the preservation of green leaf area for higher yield capability. Syngenta has a seed portfolio of over 200 product lines and more than 5,000 varieties. The company markets seed for field crops, vegetables, fruits, garden plants and flowers. Syngenta spends more than $1 billion annually on research and development at its laboratories. Syngenta offers additional professional services such as pest control, ornamentals and turf and landscaping. Syngenta comprises production and supply sites, and research and development sites spread across more than 90 countries worldwide. Syngenta operates as a subsidiary of China National Chemical Corporation (ChemChina).

FINANCIAL DATA: Note: Data for latest year may not have been available at press time.

In U.S. $	2024	2023	2022	2021	2020	2019
Revenue	34,000,000,000	32,200,000,000	33,400,000,000	28,200,000,000	23,000,000,000	22,000,000,000
R&D Expense						
Operating Income						
Operating Margin %						
SGA Expense						
Net Income				4,600,000,000	4,000,000,000	3,900,000,000
Operating Cash Flow						
Capital Expenditure						
EBITDA						
Return on Assets %						
Return on Equity %						
Debt to Equity						

CONTACT INFORMATION:

Phone: 41 613231111   Fax: 41 613231212
Toll-Free:
Address: Schwarzwaldallee 215, Basel, 4058 Switzerland

STOCK TICKER/OTHER:

Stock Ticker: Subsidiary   Exchange:
Employees: 57,000   Fiscal Year Ends: 12/31
Parent Company: China National Chemical Corporation (ChemChina)

SALARIES/BONUSES:

Top Exec. Salary: $ Bonus: $
Second Exec. Salary: $ Bonus: $

OTHER THOUGHTS:

Estimated Female Officers or Directors: 3
Hot Spot for Advancement for Women/Minorities: Y

Synopsys Inc

NAIC Code: 511210N

TYPES OF BUSINESS:

Computer Software-Electronic Design Automation
Electronics Software
Integrated Circuit Testing
Semiconductor IP
Hardware
Software Security

BRANDS/DIVISIONS/AFFILIATES:

Light Tec

GROWTH PLANS/SPECIAL FEATURES:

Synopsys is a provider of electronic design automation software and intellectual property products. EDA software automates and aids in the chip design process, enhancing design accuracy, productivity, and complexity in a full-flow end-to-end solution. Synopsys' comprehensive portfolio is benefiting from a convergence of semiconductor companies moving up the stack of technologies toward systems-like companies, and systems companies moving down-stack toward in-house chip design. The resulting expansion in EDA customers alongside secular digitalization of various end markets benefits EDA vendors like Synopsys.

Synopsys offers its employees comprehensive health benefits, retirement accounts, stock purchase plans, among other assistance programs.

CONTACTS: Note: Officers with more than one job title may be intentionally listed here more than once.

Sassine Ghazi, CEO
Shelagh Glaser, CFO
Aart De Geus, Chairman of the Board
Sudhindra Kankanwadi, Chief Accounting Officer
John Runkel, General Counsel
Richard Mahoney, Other Executive Officer

FINANCIAL DATA: Note: Data for latest year may not have been available at press time.

In U.S. $	2024	2023	2022	2021	2020	2019
Revenue	6,127,435,776	5,318,013,952	4,615,713,792	4,204,193,024	3,685,281,024	3,360,694,016
R&D Expense	2,082,360,000	1,849,935,000	1,589,846,000	1,504,823,000	1,279,022,000	1,136,932,000
Operating Income	1,355,711,000	1,326,330,000	1,159,935,000	768,195,000	656,200,000	567,417,000
Operating Margin %	.22%	.25%	.25%	.18%	.18%	.17%
SGA Expense	1,427,838,000	1,101,611,000	956,283,000	1,035,479,000	916,540,000	862,108,000
Net Income	2,263,380,000	1,229,888,000	984,594,000	757,516,000	664,347,000	532,367,000
Operating Cash Flow	1,407,029,000	1,703,274,000	1,738,900,000	1,492,622,000	991,313,000	800,513,000
Capital Expenditure	123,161,000	191,822,000	139,082,000	95,740,000	158,762,000	202,388,000
EBITDA	1,844,084,000	1,553,768,000	1,333,555,000	1,012,555,000	853,285,000	758,841,000
Return on Assets %	.19%	.12%	.11%	.09%	.09%	.08%
Return on Equity %	.30%	.21%	.18%	.15%	.15%	.14%
Debt to Equity	.07%	.10%	.11%	.10%	0.115	0.029

CONTACT INFORMATION:

Phone: 650 584-5000   Fax: 650 965-8637
Toll-Free: 800-541-7737
Address: 690 E. Middlefield Rd., Mountain View, CA 94043 United States

STOCK TICKER/OTHER:

Stock Ticker: SNPS   Exchange: NAS
Employees: 20,000   Fiscal Year Ends: 10/31
Parent Company:

SALARIES/BONUSES:

Top Exec. Salary: $802,788   Bonus: $
Second Exec. Salary: $725,000   Bonus: $

OTHER THOUGHTS:

Estimated Female Officers or Directors: 3
Hot Spot for Advancement for Women/Minorities: Y

Taisei Corp

NAIC Code: 541330

www.taisei.co.jp

TYPES OF BUSINESS:

Civil Engineering Services

BRANDS/DIVISIONS/AFFILIATES:

GROWTH PLANS/SPECIAL FEATURES:

Taisei Corp provides civil engineering and building development services in many different areas. It enters contracts to develop and enhance urbanization in designated regions. The company has four operating segments: civil engineering (majority of total revenue), building construction, real estate development, and other. It participates in all phases of project development, including planning, design, construction, and aftermarket services. Multiple projects are conducted simultaneously as the company showcases its expansive network and technical know-how. Taisei's projects range from traffic infrastructure and tunnels to airport facilities and high-rise building offices. Customers in Japan account for majority of total sales.

CONTACTS: Note: Officers with more than one job title may be intentionally listed here more than once.

Yoshiro Aikawa, CEO
Shigeyoshi Tanaka, Chairman of the Board
Masahiko Okada, Director
Mayuki Yamaura, Director
Yuichiro Yoshino, Director
Junichi kasahara, Director
Kenji Shirakawa, Director

FINANCIAL DATA: Note: Data for latest year may not have been available at press time.

In U.S. $	2024	2023	2022	2021	2020	2019
Revenue	12,253,700,919	11,404,554,706	10,713,961,577	10,275,903,178	12,158,630,037	11,461,240,345
R&D Expense						
Operating Income	183,844,800	380,047,200	667,016,100	906,116,400	1,164,649,000	1,064,454,000
Operating Margin %	.02%	.03%	.06%	.09%	.10%	.09%
SGA Expense	700,631,800	645,869,200	636,344,100	612,892,300	631,220,500	611,878,700
Net Income	279,589,000	327,159,100	495,945,600	642,557,600	847,591,000	781,526,000
Operating Cash Flow	281,942,500	208,976,700	558,921,200	468,578,200	537,871,400	-493,113,000
Capital Expenditure	849,125,300	112,211,900	91,849,490	88,343,520	90,190,220	323,833,700
EBITDA	494,883,400	558,407,400	800,610,900	1,019,474,000	1,289,788,000	1,179,596,000
Return on Assets %	.02%	.02%	.04%	.05%	.07%	.06%
Return on Equity %	.05%	.06%	.08%	.12%	.17%	.16%
Debt to Equity	.29%	.15%	.12%	.16%	0.147	0.176

CONTACT INFORMATION:

Phone: 81 333481111   Fax: 81 333450481
Toll-Free:
Address: 1-25-1 Nishi-Shinjuku, Tokyo, 163-0606 Japan

STOCK TICKER/OTHER:

Stock Ticker: TISCY   Exchange: PINX
Employees: 18,082   Fiscal Year Ends: 03/31
Parent Company:

SALARIES/BONUSES:

Top Exec. Salary: $ Bonus: $
Second Exec. Salary: $ Bonus: $

OTHER THOUGHTS:

Estimated Female Officers or Directors:
Hot Spot for Advancement for Women/Minorities:

Taiwan Semiconductor Manufacturing Co Ltd (TSMC)

www.tsmc.com
NAIC Code: 334413

TYPES OF BUSINESS:
Contract Manufacturing-Semiconductors
Assembly & Testing Services
CAD Software Products

BRANDS/DIVISIONS/AFFILIATES:
WaferTech LLC
TSMC China Company Limited
TSMC Nanjing Company Limited
Global Unichip Corporation
Xintec Inc
Systems on Silicon Manufacturing Co Pty Ltd
Vanguard International Semiconductor Corp
VisEra Technologies Company Ltd

CONTACTS: Note: Officers with more than one job title may be intentionally listed here more than once.
Y. L. Wang, CEO, Subsidiary
J. Lin, Other Executive Officer
Y. Liaw, CEO, Subsidiary
Ray Chuang, CEO, Subsidiary
C.C. Wei, CEO
Wendell Huang, CFO
Rick Cassidy, Chairman of the Board, Subsidiary
Horng-Dar Lin, Chief Information Officer
Y. Chin, Co-COO
Y. J. Mii, Co-COO
Sylvia Fang, General Counsel
Kevin Zhang, Other Corporate Officer
T.S. Chang, Other Corporate Officer
L. Lu, Other Corporate Officer
Douglas Yu, Other Corporate Officer
Cliff Hou, Other Executive Officer
Sajiv Dalal, President, Geographical
Lora Ho, Senior VP, Divisional
Wei-Jen Lo, Senior VP, Divisional

GROWTH PLANS/SPECIAL FEATURES:
Taiwan Semiconductor Manufacturing Co. is the world's largest dedicated chip foundry, with mid-60s market share in 2024. TSMC was founded in 1987 as a joint venture of Philips, the government of Taiwan, and private investors. It went public in Taiwan in 1994 and as an ADR in the US in 1997. TSMC's scale and high-quality technology allow the firm to generate solid operating margins, even in the highly competitive foundry business. Furthermore, the shift to the fabless business model has created tailwinds for TSMC. The foundry leader has an illustrious customer base, including Apple, AMD, and Nvidia, that looks to apply cutting-edge process technologies to its semiconductor designs. TSMC employs more than 73,000 people.

TSMC offers employees health, fitness, incentive and employee assistance plans; and tuition reimbursement.

FINANCIAL DATA: Note: Data for latest year may not have been available at press time.

In U.S. $	2024	2023	2022	2021	2020	2019
Revenue	96,793,117,416	72,294,019,449	75,710,364,545	53,087,250,474	44,788,133,648	35,783,072,548
R&D Expense	6,828,366,000	6,098,930,000	5,459,909,000	4,171,453,000	3,661,494,000	3,057,277,000
Operating Income	44,211,190,000	30,814,990,000	37,496,710,000	21,737,130,000	18,954,580,000	12,464,030,000
Operating Margin %	.46%	.43%	.50%	.41%	.42%	.35%
SGA Expense	3,240,205,000	2,389,924,000	2,121,774,000	1,487,800,000	1,189,566,000	939,261,600
Net Income	38,739,220,000	28,484,380,000	33,205,920,000	19,810,020,000	17,080,600,000	11,836,930,000
Operating Cash Flow	61,072,070,000	41,534,590,000	53,862,590,000	37,193,520,000	27,512,080,000	20,571,830,000
Capital Expenditure	32,271,470,000	31,950,990,000	36,439,920,000	28,407,350,000	17,282,490,000	15,709,720,000
EBITDA	69,531,530,000	50,950,000,000	53,276,590,000	36,480,670,000	30,718,760,000	22,740,860,000
Return on Assets %	.19%	.16%	.23%	.18%	.20%	.16%
Return on Equity %	.30%	.27%	.39%	.30%	.30%	.22%
Debt to Equity	.23%	.28%	.30%	.30%	0.151	0.025

CONTACT INFORMATION:
Phone: 886 35636688   Fax: 866 35637000
Toll-Free:
Address: No. 8, Li-Hsin Rd. 6, Hsinchu Science Park, Hsinchu, 300 Taiwan

STOCK TICKER/OTHER:
Stock Ticker: TSM   Exchange: NYS
Employees: 66,336   Fiscal Year Ends: 12/31
Parent Company:

SALARIES/BONUSES:
Top Exec. Salary: $6,156,779   Bonus: $101,374,500
Second Exec. Salary: $535,081   Bonus: $21,262,790

OTHER THOUGHTS:
Estimated Female Officers or Directors: 4
Hot Spot for Advancement for Women/Minorities: Y

Sales, profits and employees may be estimates. Financial information, benefits and other data can change quickly and may vary from those stated here.

Takeda Pharmaceutical Company Limited

www.takeda.com

NAIC Code: 325412

TYPES OF BUSINESS:
Pharmaceuticals Discovery & Development
Over-the-Counter Drugs
Vitamins
Research and Development
Biopharmaceuticals
Plasma-based Therapies
Vaccines

BRANDS/DIVISIONS/AFFILIATES:
Adcetris
Cabozantinib
Ninlaro
Takhzyro
Vonvendi
Entyvio
Alofisel
Vonoprazan

GROWTH PLANS/SPECIAL FEATURES:
Takeda Pharmaceutical is Japan's largest pharmaceutical company, with revenue of JPY 4.6 trillion in fiscal 2024. The company's five core therapeutic areas are oncology, gastroenterology, neuroscience, rare diseases, and plasma-derived therapies, which account for more than 80% of revenue. Its geographic footprint is well diversified, with over 50% derived from the US, 20% from Japan, 20% from Europe and Canada.

CONTACTS:
Note: Officers with more than one job title may be intentionally listed here more than once.

Christophe Weber, CEO
Lauren Duprey, Other Executive Officer
Milano Furuta, CFO
Masami Iijima, Chairman of the Board
Mwana Lugogo, Chief Compliance Officer
Gabriele Ricci, Chief Technology Officer
Andrew Plump, Director
Yoshihiro Nakagawa, General Counsel
Thomas Wozniewski, Other Corporate Officer
Marcello Agosti, Other Corporate Officer
Elaine Shannon, Other Corporate Officer
Akiko Amakawa, Other Corporate Officer
Julie Kim, Other Corporate Officer
Takako Ohyabu, Other Executive Officer
Giles Platford, President, Divisional
Ramona Sequeira, President, Divisional
Teresa Bitetti, President, Divisional

FINANCIAL DATA:
Note: Data for latest year may not have been available at press time.

In U.S. $	2024	2023	2022	2021	2020	2019
Revenue	29,601,236,286	27,960,830,660	24,777,881,166	22,200,862,151	22,849,126,231	14,560,011,292
R&D Expense	5,067,509,000	4,396,869,000	3,652,368,000	3,164,628,000	3,418,363,000	2,556,915,000
Operating Income	2,228,221,000	3,852,312,000	3,790,913,000	2,898,868,000	1,990,669,000	1,334,921,000
Operating Margin %	.08%	.14%	.15%	.13%	.09%	.09%
SGA Expense	7,316,155,000	6,923,834,000	6,153,576,000	6,079,305,000	6,697,702,000	4,981,943,000
Net Income	1,000,188,000	2,200,896,000	1,597,188,000	2,610,421,000	307,143,800	938,572,700
Operating Cash Flow	4,973,230,000	6,783,921,000	7,797,174,000	7,018,405,000	4,649,764,000	2,280,471,000
Capital Expenditure	3,337,476,000	4,399,396,000	1,291,565,000	1,641,683,000	1,511,455,000	931,088,600
EBITDA	6,250,542,000	8,028,763,000	6,999,126,000	7,336,241,000	4,664,712,000	2,939,885,000
Return on Assets %	.01%	.02%	.02%	.03%	.00%	.02%
Return on Equity %	.02%	.05%	.04%	.08%	.01%	.04%
Debt to Equity	.62%	.64%	.73%	.89%	0.954	0.92

CONTACT INFORMATION:
Phone: 81 33278-2111   Fax: 81 33278-2000
Toll-Free:
Address: 1-1, Nihonbashi-Honcho 2-Chome, Chuo-ku, Osaka, 103-8668 Japan

STOCK TICKER/OTHER:
Stock Ticker: TAK   Exchange: NYS
Employees: 49,281   Fiscal Year Ends: 03/31
Parent Company:

SALARIES/BONUSES:
Top Exec. Salary: $1,673,146   Bonus: $1,784,227
Second Exec. Salary: $1,603,721 Bonus: $1,312,136

OTHER THOUGHTS:
Estimated Female Officers or Directors: 3
Hot Spot for Advancement for Women/Minorities: Y

Take-Two Interactive Software Inc   www.take2games.com

NAIC Code: 511210G

TYPES OF BUSINESS:

Computer Software, Electronic Games, Apps & Entertainment
Game Developer
Game Publisher
Game Distribution
Streaming Services
Online Platforms

BRANDS/DIVISIONS/AFFILIATES:

Rockstar Games
2K
T2 Mobile Games
Private Division
Grand Theft Auto
Max Payne
Socialpoint
Kerbal Space Program

CONTACTS: *Note: Officers with more than one job title may be intentionally listed here more than once.*

Strauss Zelnick, CEO
Lainie Goldstein, CFO
Daniel Emerson, Chief Legal Officer
Karl Slatoff, President

GROWTH PLANS/SPECIAL FEATURES:

Take-Two is one of the largest global developers and publishers of video games, with labels including Rockstar, 2K, and Zynga. Grand Theft Auto is the firm's biggest franchise, accounting for about 30% of total sales for the past decade. NBA 2K is the industry's dominant basketball video game, with Take-Two releasing a new version annually. Other notable franchises include Red Dead Redemption, Borderlands, and Civilization. Typically, more than three quarters of the firm's sales are from in-game spending, with the remainder coming from initial game sales. Since acquiring Zynga in 2022, mobile makes up about half of total sales.

FINANCIAL DATA: *Note: Data for latest year may not have been available at press time.*

In U.S. $	2024	2023	2022	2021	2020	2019
Revenue	5,349,600,256	5,349,899,776	3,504,800,000	3,372,800,000	3,088,969,984	
R&D Expense	948,200,000	887,600,000	406,600,000	317,300,000	296,398,000	
Operating Income	-1,143,900,000	-1,150,600,000	474,400,000	629,400,000	425,350,000	
Operating Margin %	-.21%	-.22%	.14%	.19%	.14%	
SGA Expense	2,266,300,000	2,426,000,000	1,027,300,000	835,400,000	776,659,000	
Net Income	-3,744,200,000	-1,124,700,000	418,000,000	588,900,000	404,459,000	
Operating Cash Flow	-16,100,000	1,100,000	258,000,000	912,300,000	685,678,000	
Capital Expenditure	141,700,000	204,200,000	158,600,000	68,900,000	53,384,000	
EBITDA	-1,800,600,000	582,500,000	747,000,000	890,800,000	700,229,000	
Return on Assets %	-.27%	-.10%	.07%	.11%	.09%	
Return on Equity %	-.51%	-.18%	.12%	.20%	.18%	
Debt to Equity	.61%	.23%	.06%	.05%	0.06	

CONTACT INFORMATION:

Phone: 646 536-2842   Fax: 646 536-2926
Toll-Free:
Address: 110 West 44th St., New York, NY 10036 United States

STOCK TICKER/OTHER:

Stock Ticker: TTWO   Exchange: NAS
Employees: 12,371   Fiscal Year Ends: 03/31
Parent Company:

SALARIES/BONUSES:

Top Exec. Salary: $1,000,000   Bonus: $
Second Exec. Salary: Bonus: $
$850,000

OTHER THOUGHTS:

Estimated Female Officers or Directors: 1
Hot Spot for Advancement for Women/Minorities:

Tata Consultancy Services Limited (TCS)

www.tcs.com

NAIC Code: 541512

TYPES OF BUSINESS:

IT Consulting
Software Consultancy
Analytics and Insight Services
Blockchain Services
Cybersecurity Services
Automation and Artificial Intelligence
Cloud Consulting
Internet of Things

BRANDS/DIVISIONS/AFFILIATES:

Tata Group
TCS BaNCS
TCS ADD
TCS BFSI Platforms
TCS CHROMA
ignio
TCS TAP
TCS MasterCraft

CONTACTS: Note: Officers with more than one job title may be intentionally listed here more than once.

K. Krithivasan, CEO
N.G. Subramaniam, COO
Samir Seksaria, CFO
Milind Lakkad, Chief Human Resources Officer
N. Chandrasekaran, Chmn.

GROWTH PLANS/SPECIAL FEATURES:

Tata Consultancy Services Limited (TCS) is one of India's largest consulting companies and one of Asia's largest independent software and services organizations, with a presence in 55 countries. The firm is part of the Tata Group, an Asian conglomerate with interests in banking, capital markets, consumer goods and distribution, communications, media and information services, education, energy, resources and utilities, healthcare, high tech, insurance life sciences, manufacturing, public services, retail and travel/logistics. TCS offers a range of services, including artificial intelligence (AI), cloud, cognitive business operations, consulting, cybersecurity, data and analytics, enterprise solutions, internet of things (IoT) and digital engineering, network solutions and services, TCS interactive and sustainability services. Some of the products TCS provides include TCS ADD, TCS BaNCS, TCS BFSI Platforms, TCS CHROMA, ignio, TCS TAP, TCS MasterCraft and many more. Industries served by TCS include banking, capital markets, consumer packaged goods and distribution, communication, media, technology, information services, education, energy, utilities, healthcare, high-tech, insurance, life sciences, manufacturing, public services, retail, travel and logistics. The firm has formed alliances with leading technology companies, academic institutions and consulting firms to provide customers with expertise in technology fields in which it does not specialize. Development of new strategies and technologies occurs in TCS' global centers of excellence, located in several nations. TCS has offices throughout North America (with a regional headquarters in New York City), some of which are development centers and centers of excellence.

FINANCIAL DATA: Note: Data for latest year may not have been available at press time.

In U.S. $	2024	2023	2022	2021	2020	2019
Revenue		27,441,170,000	25,700,000,000	22,803,318,123	21,470,898,933	23,219,300,000
R&D Expense						
Operating Income						
Operating Margin %						
SGA Expense						
Net Income		5,129,838,000	2,379,843,586	4,437,972,666	4,312,628,111	4,663,800,000
Operating Cash Flow						
Capital Expenditure						
EBITDA						
Return on Assets %						
Return on Equity %						
Debt to Equity						

CONTACT INFORMATION:

Phone: 91 22-6778-9999   Fax: 91-22-6630-3672
Toll-Free:
Address: TCS House, Raveline St., Mumbai, 400 001 India

STOCK TICKER/OTHER:

Stock Ticker: 532540   Exchange: Bombay
Employees: 607,350   Fiscal Year Ends: 03/31
Parent Company: Tata Group

SALARIES/BONUSES:

Top Exec. Salary: $ Bonus: $
Second Exec. Salary: $ Bonus: $

OTHER THOUGHTS:

Estimated Female Officers or Directors: 2
Hot Spot for Advancement for Women/Minorities:

Sales, profits and employees may be estimates. Financial information, benefits and other data can change quickly and may vary from those stated here.

Tata Group

www.tata.com

NAIC Code: 331110

TYPES OF BUSINESS:

Steel Production
Communication & Information Systems
Engineered Products
Energy Utilities
Solar Power
Automobiles
Hotels & Resorts
Pharmaceuticals & Chemicals

BRANDS/DIVISIONS/AFFILIATES:

Tata Sons Private Limited
Tata Consultancy Services
Tata Steel
Tata Motors
Tata Oil Mills Company (TOMCO)
Tata Capital
Tata Communications
Tata Investment Corporation

CONTACTS: Note: Officers with more than one job title may be intentionally listed here more than once.

Saurabh Agrawal, CFO
Nupur Mallick, Chief Human Resources Officer
Aarthi Subramanian, Chief Digital Officer
Madhu Kannan, Head-Bus. Dev.
Mukund G. Rajan, Chief Ethics Officer
Nirmalya Kumar, Head-Strategy
N. Chandrasekaran, Chmn.-Tata Sons

GROWTH PLANS/SPECIAL FEATURES:

Tata Group, owned by Tata Sons Private Limited, is an Indian conglomerate that oversees 30 companies across 10 verticals. Operating in more than 100 countries worldwide, the verticals include information technology, steel, automotive, consumer/retail, infrastructure, financial services, aerospace/defense, tourism/travel, telecommunications/media and trading/investments. Information technology is led by Tata Consultancy Services. Tata Steel has an annual crude steel capacity of 36.3 million tons per year. Tata Motors designs, manufactures and markets automobiles across all market segments. Its two iconic brands include Jaguar and Land Rover. The consumer/retail vertical is led by Tata Oil Mills Company (TOMCO), a producer of soaps, detergents, cooling oils, consumer durables, tea, packaged water and more. The infrastructure vertical is engaged in the energy sector, which supplies energy to residences, large cities and industries. Financial services are led by Tata Capital, which offers a range of financial services that cater to individuals and small businesses. This division's Tata Asset Management Company offers mutual funds, portfolio management services, alternative investment funds and offshore funds. The aerospace/defense vertical is a global, single-source supplier for fixed-wing and rotary-wing programs; and provides products and services for the Ministry of Defense, armed forces and Defense Research and Development Organization within India. Tourism/travel encompasses Tata's Taj Mahal hotel and its airline operations. Telecom/media includes Tata Communications, which owns and operates mobile and internet networks, and Tata Sky, a joint venture direct-to-home entertainment provider. Last, trading/investments offers private trading strategies through Tata International, Tata Industries and Tata Investment Corporation.

FINANCIAL DATA: Note: Data for latest year may not have been available at press time.

In U.S. $	2024	2023	2022	2021	2020	2019
Revenue	137,550,000,000	131,000,000,000	128,000,000,000	125,000,000,000	106,000,000,000	113,000,000,000
R&D Expense						
Operating Income						
Operating Margin %						
SGA Expense						
Net Income						
Operating Cash Flow						
Capital Expenditure						
EBITDA						
Return on Assets %						
Return on Equity %						
Debt to Equity						

CONTACT INFORMATION:

Phone: 91 22-6665-8282   Fax: 91-22-6665-8160
Toll-Free:
Address: 24 Homi Mody St., Mumbai, 400 001 India

STOCK TICKER/OTHER:

Stock Ticker: Private   Exchange:
Employees: 1,035,000   Fiscal Year Ends: 03/31
Parent Company: Tata Sons Private Limited

SALARIES/BONUSES:

Top Exec. Salary: $ Bonus: $
Second Exec. Salary: $ Bonus: $

OTHER THOUGHTS:

Estimated Female Officers or Directors:
Hot Spot for Advancement for Women/Minorities:

Tata Motors Limited

NAIC Code: 336111

www.tatamotors.com

TYPES OF BUSINESS:

Automobile Manufacturing
Light & Medium Commercial Vehicles Manufacturing
Heavy Commercial Vehicles Manufacturing
Passenger Vehicles Manufacturing

GROWTH PLANS/SPECIAL FEATURES:

Tata Motors Ltd. is an automobile manufacturing company that is part of Tata Group. Tata's main business segments include commercial vehicles, passenger vehicles, electric vehicles and luxury vehicles. The main operational hubs are the U.K., South Korea, Thailand, South Africa and Indonesia. The firm operates in approximately 125 countries and has seven total assembly facilities spread across the globe.

BRANDS/DIVISIONS/AFFILIATES:

Tata Group

CONTACTS: Note: Officers with more than one job title may be intentionally listed here more than once.

P.B. Balaji, CFO
Sitaram Kandi, Chief Human Resources Officer
Rajendra Petkar, CTO
Rajesh Bagga, VP-Legal
Ravindra Pisharody, Pres., Commercial Vehicles
S.B. Borwankar, Exec. Dir.
Ravi Kant, Vice Chmn.
Natarajan Chandrasekaran, Chmn.
Venkatram Mamillapalle, Sr. VP

FINANCIAL DATA: Note: Data for latest year may not have been available at press time.

In U.S. $	2024	2023	2022	2021	2020	2019
Revenue		42,108,678,000	33,408,751,616	29,976,573,952	32,590,317,568	36,161,589,248
R&D Expense						
Operating Income						
Operating Margin %						
SGA Expense						
Net Income		293,851,000	-1,373,417,216	-1,723,738,624	-1,431,376,640	-3,540,982,272
Operating Cash Flow						
Capital Expenditure						
EBITDA						
Return on Assets %						
Return on Equity %						
Debt to Equity						

CONTACT INFORMATION:

Phone: 91-22-66658282   Fax:
Toll-Free:
Address: Homi Mody St., Bombay House, 24, Mumbai, 400 001 India

STOCK TICKER/OTHER:

Stock Ticker: TAMO   Exchange: Mumbai
Employees: 81,811   Fiscal Year Ends: 03/31
Parent Company: Tata Group

SALARIES/BONUSES:

Top Exec. Salary: $ Bonus: $
Second Exec. Salary: $ Bonus: $

OTHER THOUGHTS:

Estimated Female Officers or Directors:
Hot Spot for Advancement for Women/Minorities:

Tate & Lyle plc

NAIC Code: 311942

www.tateandlyle.com

TYPES OF BUSINESS:

Synthetic Sweeteners (i.e., sweetening agents) Manufacturing
Animal Feed
Bulk Storage
Starches & Proteins
Sweeteners
Ethanol
Flavors & Ingredients
Cosmetic Ingredients

GROWTH PLANS/SPECIAL FEATURES:

Tate & Lyle is a global provider of food and beverage ingredients and solutions. Following the sale of its commodity ingredients business, as well as its exit from the sugar business a decade earlier, Tate & Lyle is now focused on specialty ingredients, sweeteners, starches, and soluble fiber. It has 3,300 employees and operates in over 120 countries, with most of its revenue generated in North America.

BRANDS/DIVISIONS/AFFILIATES:

CORNPRO
CLARIA
TASTEVA
ECLIPSE
PROMITOR
KRYSTAR
SPLENDA
TEXTURLUX

CONTACTS: *Note: Officers with more than one job title may be intentionally listed here more than once.*

Barry Zoumas,
Anthony Hampton, CEO
Sarah Kuijlaars, CFO
David Hearn, Chairman of the Board
Matthew Joy, General Counsel

FINANCIAL DATA: *Note: Data for latest year may not have been available at press time.*

In U.S. $	2024	2023	2022	2021	2020	2019
Revenue	2,217,356,196	2,357,371,397	1,851,162,594	1,630,369,393	3,880,036,445	3,709,056,602
R&D Expense						
Operating Income	315,034,200	306,956,400	223,485,800	207,330,200	433,508,600	398,504,800
Operating Margin %	.14%	.13%	.12%	.13%	.11%	.11%
SGA Expense						
Net Income	253,104,400	255,797,000	317,726,800	340,613,900	329,843,500	243,680,300
Operating Cash Flow	280,030,400	88,855,800	138,668,900	496,784,700	518,325,500	444,279,000
Capital Expenditure	148,093,000	105,011,400	199,252,400	204,637,600	224,832,100	175,019,000
EBITDA	464,473,500	375,617,700	226,178,400	393,119,600	674,496,300	569,484,900
Return on Assets %	.08%	.07%	.08%	.09%	.09%	.07%
Return on Equity %	.15%	.14%	.15%	.18%	.17%	.13%
Debt to Equity	.46%	.50%	.41%	.51%	0.486	0.249

CONTACT INFORMATION:

Phone: 44 2072572100   Fax: 44 2072572200
Toll-Free:
Address: 1 Kingsway, London, WC2B 6AT United Kingdom

STOCK TICKER/OTHER:

Stock Ticker: TATYF   Exchange: PINX
Employees: 3,318   Fiscal Year Ends: 03/31
Parent Company:

SALARIES/BONUSES:

Top Exec. Salary: $973,375   Bonus: $759,313
Second Exec. Salary: Bonus: $
$648,917

OTHER THOUGHTS:

Estimated Female Officers or Directors: 3
Hot Spot for Advancement for Women/Minorities: Y

TechnipFMC plc

www.technipfmc.com

NAIC Code: 333132

TYPES OF BUSINESS:

Oil & Gas Production & Processing Equipment
Subsea Engineering
Procurement
Manufacturing
Robotics
Surface Technologies

GROWTH PLANS/SPECIAL FEATURES:

TechnipFMC is the largest pure-play offshore oilfield service provider, offering integrated deep-water offshore oil and gas development solutions that span the full spectrum of subsea equipment and subsea engineering and construction services. The company also provides various surface equipment used with onshore oil and gas wells. TechnipFMC originated with the 2017 merger of predecessor companies Technip and FMC Technologies.

BRANDS/DIVISIONS/AFFILIATES:

iEPCI
iFEED
iComplete

CONTACTS: Note: Officers with more than one job title may be intentionally listed here more than once.

Douglas Pferdehirt, CEO
Alf Melin, CFO
David Light, Chief Accounting Officer
Cristina Aalders, Chief Legal Officer
Justin Rounce, Chief Technology Officer
Nisha Rai, Executive VP, Divisional
Luana Duffe, Executive VP, Divisional
Thierry Conti, President, Divisional
Jonathan Landes, President, Divisional

FINANCIAL DATA: Note: Data for latest year may not have been available at press time.

In U.S. $	2024	2023	2022	2021	2020	2019
Revenue	9,083,299,840	7,824,200,192	6,700,400,128	6,403,500,032	6,530,599,936	6,950,199,808
R&D Expense	73,400,000	69,000,000	67,000,000	78,400,000	75,300,000	149,500,000
Operating Income	982,600,000	529,200,000	212,500,000	100,600,000	-104,600,000	112,900,000
Operating Margin %	.11%	.07%	.03%	.02%	-.02%	.02%
SGA Expense	667,100,000	675,900,000	616,800,000	644,900,000	724,100,000	795,700,000
Net Income	842,900,000	56,200,000	-107,200,000	13,300,000	-3,287,600,000	-2,415,200,000
Operating Cash Flow	961,000,000	693,000,000	352,100,000	781,300,000	656,900,000	848,500,000
Capital Expenditure	281,600,000	225,200,000	157,900,000	191,700,000	256,100,000	412,700,000
EBITDA	1,430,500,000	706,600,000	584,800,000	740,800,000	-2,952,500,000	-1,968,500,000
Return on Assets %	.09%	.01%	-.01%	.00%	-.15%	-.10%
Return on Equity %	.27%	.02%	-.03%	.00%	-.56%	-.27%
Debt to Equity	.43%	.53%	.54%	.71%	0.835	0.609

CONTACT INFORMATION:

Phone: 440-203-4293950   Fax:
Toll-Free:
Address: One St. Paul's Churchyard, London,   EC4M 8AP United Kingdom

STOCK TICKER/OTHER:

Stock Ticker: FTI   Exchange: NYS
Employees: 25,027   Fiscal Year Ends: 12/31
Parent Company:

SALARIES/BONUSES:

Top Exec. Salary: $1,328,700   Bonus: $
Second Exec. Salary: Bonus: $
$750,000

OTHER THOUGHTS:

Estimated Female Officers or Directors: 3
Hot Spot for Advancement for Women/Minorities: Y

Tecnica Y Proyectos SA (TYPSA)

www.typsa.com/en

NAIC Code: 541330

TYPES OF BUSINESS:

Engineering Consulting Services
Civil Engineering
Architecture
Building Technology
Energy
Environment
Consulting
Development Programs

BRANDS/DIVISIONS/AFFILIATES:

CONTACTS: *Note: Officers with more than one job title may be intentionally listed here more than once.*

Pablo Bueno Tomas, CEO

GROWTH PLANS/SPECIAL FEATURES:

Tecnica Y Proyectos SA (TYPSA), along with its subsidiaries, provides consulting services in the fields of civil engineering, architecture, building technology, energy and environment worldwide. Since its 1966 inception, the firm has been involved in the development of all types of infrastructure and facilities across both Spanish and international markets. Over 70% of TYPSA are engineers, architects or other university graduates who work in highly skilled multidisciplinary teams. TYPSA is experienced in the fields of transport, water, urban development, renewable energy and the environment. Its professional services include master plans; technical, economic and environmental studies and reports, feasibility studies, preliminary and schematic designs, final designs, construction management and site supervision; construction project management; auditing and due diligence; operation and maintenance management; concession studies, expropriation management; identification, management and evaluation of projects and programs; health and safety; and environmental control laboratory. TYPSA has offices in Africa, Europe, Latin America, the Middle East, Asia and the U.S. Some of TYPSA's development program projects include a solar program in Sri Lanka, a non-revenue water reduction and optimization of energy efficiency in Costa Rica, a water supply canal in Pakistan, a road modernization program in Madagascar, a modern railway line in Senegal/Mali, and a freight traffic toll system in the UAE.

FINANCIAL DATA: *Note: Data for latest year may not have been available at press time.*

In U.S. $	2024	2023	2022	2021	2020	2019
Revenue	330,750,000	315,000,000	302,320,000	305,572,800	293,820,000	246,470,000
R&D Expense						
Operating Income						
Operating Margin %						
SGA Expense						
Net Income						
Operating Cash Flow						
Capital Expenditure						
EBITDA						
Return on Assets %						
Return on Equity %						
Debt to Equity						

CONTACT INFORMATION:

Phone: 34-917-227-300   Fax: 34-916-517-588
Toll-Free:
Address: C/ Gomera, 9, San Sebastian de los Reyes, Madrid, 28703 Spain

STOCK TICKER/OTHER:

Stock Ticker: Private   Exchange:
Employees: 3,126   Fiscal Year Ends: 12/31
Parent Company:

SALARIES/BONUSES:

Top Exec. Salary: $ Bonus: $
Second Exec. Salary: $ Bonus: $

OTHER THOUGHTS:

Estimated Female Officers or Directors:
Hot Spot for Advancement for Women/Minorities:

Teledyne FLIR LLC

www.flir.com

NAIC Code: 334511

TYPES OF BUSINESS:

Search, Detection, Navigation, Guidance, Aeronautical, and Nautical System and Instrument Manufacturing
Innovative Technologies
Sensing Products and Solutions
Imaging Products and Solutions
Measurement and Diagnostic Products
Threat Detection Systems
Product Design and Development
Product Manufacturing

BRANDS/DIVISIONS/AFFILIATES:

Teledyne Technologies Incorporated

CONTACTS: Note: Officers with more than one job title may be intentionally listed here more than once.

Earl Lewis, Chairman of the Board
Carol Lowe, Executive VP
Anthony Buffum, Other Executive Officer
Jeffrey Frank, Senior VP, Divisional
Charles Crocker, Chmn.-Corp.

GROWTH PLANS/SPECIAL FEATURES:

Teledyne FLIR, LLC designs, develops, manufactures, markets and distributes technologies that enhance perception and awareness. The firm is a subsidiary of Teledyne Technologies Incorporated, and produces innovative sensing solutions via thermal imaging, visible-light imaging, video analytics, measurement and diagnostic, artificial intelligent (AI) and advanced threat detection systems. Teledyne FLIR's solutions serve the automotive, defense, industrial, marine, outdoor, professional trades, public safety, research and development, security and smart city industries. Just a few of the company's products and solutions include advanced driver assistance systems, unmanned aerial and ground systems, thermal screening and resolution options, border security solutions, building diagnostics solutions, marine law enforcement, naval systems and coastal surveillance, farm management, parks and wildlife management, building inspection, facility management and maintenance, restoration and remediation, HAZMAT response, environment/health safety, NDT and materials testing, people flow intelligence, perimeter protection, and public transportation monitoring.

FLIR offers its employees comprehensive health and financial benefits.

FINANCIAL DATA: Note: Data for latest year may not have been available at press time.

In U.S. $	2024	2023	2022	2021	2020	2019
Revenue	1,830,192,000	1,743,040,000	1,676,000,000	2,041,007,374	1,962,507,090	1,887,026,048
R&D Expense						
Operating Income						
Operating Margin %						
SGA Expense						
Net Income						
Operating Cash Flow						
Capital Expenditure						
EBITDA						
Return on Assets %						
Return on Equity %						
Debt to Equity						

CONTACT INFORMATION:

Phone: 503 498-3547   Fax: 503 684-5452
Toll-Free:
Address: 27700 SW Parkway Ave., Wilsonville, OR 97070 United States

SALARIES/BONUSES:

Top Exec. Salary: $ Bonus: $
Second Exec. Salary: $ Bonus: $

STOCK TICKER/OTHER:

Stock Ticker: Subsidiary   Exchange:
Employees: 4,265   Fiscal Year Ends: 12/31
Parent Company: Teledyne Technologies Incorporated

OTHER THOUGHTS:

Estimated Female Officers or Directors:
Hot Spot for Advancement for Women/Minorities:

Teledyne Technologies Inc

www.teledyne.com

NAIC Code: 334511

TYPES OF BUSINESS:

Defense Electronics and Instrumentation
Systems Engineering Solutions
Aerospace Engines & Components
Energy Systems
Digital Imaging Equipment
Measuring Equipment
Instruments

BRANDS/DIVISIONS/AFFILIATES:

Teledyne Scientific Company
Teledyne Optech Inc
Teledyne Brown Engineering Inc
FLIR Systems Inc

GROWTH PLANS/SPECIAL FEATURES:

Teledyne Technologies Inc sells technologies for industrial markets. Roughly a fourth of Teledyne's revenue comes from contracts with the United States government. The firm operates in four segments: instrumentation, digital imaging, aerospace and defense electronics, and engineered systems. The instrumentation segment provides monitoring instruments primarily for marine and environmental applications. The digital imaging segment contributes majority of proportion of revenue and includes image sensors and cameras for industrial, government, and medical customers. The aerospace and defense electronics segment provides electronic components and communication products for aircraft. The engineered systems segment provides solutions for defense, space, environmental, and energy applications.

CONTACTS: Note: Officers with more than one job title may be intentionally listed here more than once.

Edwin Roks, CEO
Stephen Blackwood, CFO
Robert Mehrabian, Chairman of the Board
Cynthia Belak, Chief Accounting Officer
Melanie Cibik, Chief Compliance Officer
George Bobb, COO
Jason VanWees, Vice Chairman

FINANCIAL DATA: Note: Data for latest year may not have been available at press time.

In U.S. $	2024	2023	2022	2021	2020	2019
Revenue	5,670,000,128	5,635,500,032	5,458,599,936	4,614,300,160	3,086,200,064	3,163,599,872
R&D Expense	292,600,000	356,300,000	352,200,000			
Operating Income	1,041,600,000	1,034,400,000	972,400,000	624,300,000	480,100,000	491,700,000
Operating Margin %	.18%	.18%	.18%	.14%	.16%	.16%
SGA Expense	902,600,000	852,000,000	804,000,000	1,067,800,000	662,000,000	715,100,000
Net Income	819,200,000	885,700,000	788,600,000	445,300,000	401,900,000	402,300,000
Operating Cash Flow	1,191,900,000	836,100,000	486,800,000	824,600,000	618,900,000	482,100,000
Capital Expenditure	83,700,000	114,900,000	92,600,000	101,600,000	71,400,000	88,400,000
EBITDA	1,305,700,000	1,352,600,000	1,329,600,000	996,400,000	601,200,000	606,600,000
Return on Assets %	.06%	.06%	.05%	.05%	.08%	.10%
Return on Equity %	.09%	.10%	.10%	.08%	.14%	.16%
Debt to Equity	.28%	.29%	.44%	.54%	0.211	0.276

CONTACT INFORMATION:

Phone: 805 373-4545   Fax: 310 893-1669
Toll-Free:
Address: 1049 Camino Dos Rios, Thousand Oaks, CA 91360 United States

STOCK TICKER/OTHER:

Stock Ticker: TDY   Exchange: NYS
Employees: 14,900   Fiscal Year Ends: 12/31
Parent Company:

SALARIES/BONUSES:

Top Exec. Salary: $1,100,000   Bonus: $
Second Exec. Salary: $900,000   Bonus: $

OTHER THOUGHTS:

Estimated Female Officers or Directors: 6
Hot Spot for Advancement for Women/Minorities: Y

Tellabs Inc

www.tellabs.com

NAIC Code: 334210

TYPES OF BUSINESS:
Wireline & Wireless Products & Services
Fiber-Based Technology Innovation
Broadband Support
Passive Optical Local Area Network Solutions
Copper and Fiber Connectivity Solutions

BRANDS/DIVISIONS/AFFILIATES:
Marlin Equity Partners LLC

CONTACTS: Note: Officers with more than one job title may be intentionally listed here more than once.
Rich Schroder, CEO
Norm Burke, CFO
Karen Leos, VP-Global Sales
Tom Dobozy, VP-Engineering
James M. Sheehan, Chief Admin. Officer
James M. Sheehan, General Counsel
John M. Brots, Exec. VP-Global Oper.
Kenneth G. Craft, Exec. VP-Product Dev.

GROWTH PLANS/SPECIAL FEATURES:
Tellabs, Inc. innovates fiber-based technologies to offer products and solutions that support broadband access for service providers and passive optical local area networks (LANs) across all enterprise industries. Tellabs 1000 MSAP is a broadband digital loop carrier platform that converges legacy copper and modern fiber connectivity. Tellabs Optical LAN is an enterprise centric solution that offers a means of designing and operating networks inside buildings and across extended campuses. Solutions offered through these products include passive optical network, offering passive optical networking, passive optical LAN, operational efficiencies, sustainability, reliability, security, wireless, innovations; and network modernization, featuring 911 redundancy, broadband stimulus, broadband DSL, broadband ethernet, class-5 switch replace, narrowband services, broadband transport, 1/0 DCS and D4 replace for network optimization. Industries served include enterprise, education, government, healthcare, hospitality, transportation, manufacturing and service providers. Tellabs is a subsidiary of Marlin Equity Partners, LLC.

FINANCIAL DATA: Note: Data for latest year may not have been available at press time.

In U.S. $	2024	2023	2022	2021	2020	2019
Revenue	1,821,352,000	1,726,400,000	1,660,000,000	1,640,000,000	1,610,256,375	1,533,577,500
R&D Expense						
Operating Income						
Operating Margin %						
SGA Expense						
Net Income						
Operating Cash Flow						
Capital Expenditure						
EBITDA						
Return on Assets %						
Return on Equity %						
Debt to Equity						

CONTACT INFORMATION:
Phone: 972 588-7000   Fax:
Toll-Free:
Address: 4240 International Pkwy, St. 105, Carrollton, TX 75007 United States

STOCK TICKER/OTHER:
Stock Ticker: Private   Exchange:
Employees: 9,400   Fiscal Year Ends: 12/31
Parent Company: Marlin Equity Partners LLC

SALARIES/BONUSES:
Top Exec. Salary: $ Bonus: $
Second Exec. Salary: $ Bonus: $

OTHER THOUGHTS:
Estimated Female Officers or Directors: 1
Hot Spot for Advancement for Women/Minorities: Y

Tenneco Inc

NAIC Code: 336300

TYPES OF BUSINESS:

Automotive Parts Manufacturer
Emissions Systems
Manufacturing
Powertrain
Ride Performance Solutions
Suspension
Motor Parts
Engineering

BRANDS/DIVISIONS/AFFILIATES:

DRiV
Apollo Global Management Inc

CONTACTS: Note: Officers with more than one job title may be intentionally listed here more than once.

Jim Voss, CEO
Manavendra Sial, CFO
Tyler Best, CIO
Thomas Sabatino, Executive VP
Bradley Norton, Executive VP
Peng Guo, Executive VP
Scott Usitalo, Executive VP
Rainer Jueckstock, Executive VP
Kaled Awada, Other Executive Officer

GROWTH PLANS/SPECIAL FEATURES:

Tenneco Inc. was founded in 1940 and is a global automotive component and aftermarket parts manufacturing company. Tenneco primarily focuses on its business segments of clean air, powertrain, performance solutions and DRiV. Clean air solutions are designed to lower harmful emissions and enable improved vehicle performance. Markets served by this segment include light vehicles, commercial trucks off-highway, marine, rail and stationary power. Powertrain offers a variety of products that include piston rings, pistons, cylinder liners, bearings, valves, valve seats/guides, sealing/gaskets/heat shields, ignition and vehicle hybridization technologies. Performance solutions enhance performance on a variety of vehicles and include solutions such as advanced suspension technologies, ride control, NVH performance materials, braking and systems protection. Lastly, DRiV has a product portfolio of over 30 brands and, through those brands, develops auto parts that maintain optimum performance throughout a vehicle's life. Tenneco is owned by Apollo Global Management, Inc.

FINANCIAL DATA: Note: Data for latest year may not have been available at press time.

In U.S. $	2024	2023	2022	2021	2020	2019
Revenue	20,481,987,750	19,506,655,000	18,756,399,267	18,034,999,296	15,379,000,320	17,450,000,384
R&D Expense						
Operating Income						
Operating Margin %						
SGA Expense						
Net Income				35,000,000	-1,520,999,936	-334,000,000
Operating Cash Flow						
Capital Expenditure						
EBITDA						
Return on Assets %						
Return on Equity %						
Debt to Equity						

CONTACT INFORMATION:

Phone: 847 482-5000   Fax: 847 482-5940
Toll-Free:
Address: 27300 W. 11 Mile Rd., Southfield, MI 48034 United States

STOCK TICKER/OTHER:

Stock Ticker: Subsidiary   Exchange:
Employees: 71,000   Fiscal Year Ends: 12/31
Parent Company: Apollo Global Management Inc

SALARIES/BONUSES:

Top Exec. Salary: $ Bonus: $
Second Exec. Salary: $ Bonus: $

OTHER THOUGHTS:

Estimated Female Officers or Directors: 4
Hot Spot for Advancement for Women/Minorities: Y

Terex Corporation

www.terex.com

NAIC Code: 333120

TYPES OF BUSINESS:

Heavy Equipment
Cranes
Mining Equipment
Aerial Work Platforms
Road Building Equipment
Utility Products
Construction Equipment
Materials Handling Equipment

BRANDS/DIVISIONS/AFFILIATES:

Terex Financial Services
Murray Design & Engineering Ltd

GROWTH PLANS/SPECIAL FEATURES:

Terex Corp is a manufacturer of materials processing machinery, waste and recycling solutions, mobile elevating work platforms (MEWPs), and equipment for the electric utility industry. The company designs builds, and supports products used in maintenance, manufacturing, energy, waste and recycling, minerals and materials management, construction, and the entertainment industry. The products are manufactured in North America, Europe, and Asia Pacific and sold all over the world. The company reports business in the following segments: (i) Materials Processing, (ii) Aerial Work Platforms, and (iii) Environmental Solutions Group.

CONTACTS: *Note: Officers with more than one job title may be intentionally listed here more than once.*

Simon Meester, CEO
Julie Beck, CFO
David Sachs, Chairman of the Board
Stephen Johnston, Chief Accounting Officer
Scott Posner, General Counsel
Amy George, Other Executive Officer
Kieran Hegarty, President, Divisional
Joshua Gross, President, Subsidiary

FINANCIAL DATA: *Note: Data for latest year may not have been available at press time.*

In U.S. $	2024	2023	2022	2021	2020	2019
Revenue	5,127,000,064	5,152,000,000	4,417,999,872	3,886,799,872	3,076,400,128	4,353,099,776
R&D Expense						
Operating Income	526,000,000	637,000,000	420,000,000	328,000,000	68,400,000	335,000,000
Operating Margin %	.10%	.12%	.10%	.08%	.02%	.08%
SGA Expense	542,000,000	540,000,000	451,000,000	429,400,000	470,900,000	552,800,000
Net Income	335,000,000	518,000,000	300,000,000	220,900,000	-10,600,000	54,400,000
Operating Cash Flow	326,000,000	459,000,000	261,000,000	293,400,000	225,400,000	173,400,000
Capital Expenditure	137,000,000	127,000,000	110,000,000	59,700,000	64,500,000	108,900,000
EBITDA	579,000,000	699,000,000	463,000,000	365,500,000	126,600,000	385,000,000
Return on Assets %	.07%	.15%	.10%	.07%	.00%	.02%
Return on Equity %	.19%	.36%	.26%	.22%	-.01%	.06%
Debt to Equity	1.41%	.37%	.65%	.60%	1.266	1.254

CONTACT INFORMATION:

Phone: 203 222-7170   Fax: 203 222-7976
Toll-Free:
Address: 45 Glover Ave., Fl. 4, Norwalk, CT 06850 United States

STOCK TICKER/OTHER:

Stock Ticker: TEX   Exchange: NYS
Employees: 10,200   Fiscal Year Ends: 12/31
Parent Company:

SALARIES/BONUSES:

Top Exec. Salary: $917,847   Bonus: $
Second Exec. Salary: Bonus: $
$638,702

OTHER THOUGHTS:

Estimated Female Officers or Directors: 1
Hot Spot for Advancement for Women/Minorities:

Tesla Inc

www.teslamotors.com

NAIC Code: 336111

TYPES OF BUSINESS:

Automobile Manufacturing, All-Electric
Battery Manufacturing
Lithium Ion Battery Storage Technologies
Energy Storage Systems
Automobile Manufacturing
Electric Vehicles

GROWTH PLANS/SPECIAL FEATURES:

Tesla is a vertically integrated battery electric vehicle automaker and developer of autonomous driving software. The company has multiple vehicles in its fleet, which include luxury and midsize sedans, crossover SUVs, a light truck, and a semi truck. Tesla also plans to begin selling more affordable vehicles, a sports car, and offer a robotaxi service. Global deliveries in 2024 were a little below 1.8 million vehicles. The company sells batteries for stationary storage for residential and commercial properties including utilities and solar panels and solar roofs for energy generation. Tesla also owns a fast-charging network.

BRANDS/DIVISIONS/AFFILIATES:

Model S
Model X
Model 3
Model Y
Roadster
Tesla Semi
Tesla Cybertruck
Gigafactory

CONTACTS: Note: Officers with more than one job title may be intentionally listed here more than once.

Elon Musk, CEO
Vaibhav Taneja, CFO
Robyn Denholm, Chairman of the Board
Jeffrey Straubel, Co-Founder
Xiaotong Zhu, Senior VP, Divisional

FINANCIAL DATA: Note: Data for latest year may not have been available at press time.

In U.S. $	2024	2023	2022	2021	2020	2019
Revenue	97,690,001,408	96,772,997,120	81,462,001,664	53,823,000,576	31,536,001,024	24,578,000,896
R&D Expense	4,540,000,000	3,969,000,000	3,075,000,000	2,593,000,000	1,491,000,000	1,343,000,000
Operating Income	7,760,000,000	8,891,000,000	13,832,000,000	6,496,000,000	1,994,000,000	80,000,000
Operating Margin %	.08%	.09%	.17%	.12%	.06%	.00%
SGA Expense	5,150,000,000	4,800,000,000	3,946,000,000	4,517,000,000	3,145,000,000	2,646,000,000
Net Income	7,130,000,000	14,999,000,000	12,583,000,000	5,524,000,000	721,000,000	-862,000,000
Operating Cash Flow	14,923,000,000	13,256,000,000	14,724,000,000	11,497,000,000	5,943,000,000	2,405,000,000
Capital Expenditure	11,342,000,000	8,899,000,000	7,172,000,000	8,014,000,000	3,242,000,000	1,437,000,000
EBITDA	14,708,000,000	14,796,000,000	17,657,000,000	9,625,000,000	4,224,000,000	2,174,000,000
Return on Assets %	.06%	.16%	.17%	.10%	.02%	-.03%
Return on Equity %	.11%	.28%	.34%	.21%	.05%	-.15%
Debt to Equity	.14%	.10%	.08%	.23%	0.489	1.902

CONTACT INFORMATION:

Phone: 650 681-5000   Fax:
Toll-Free:
Address: 3500 Deer Creek Rd., Palo Alto, CA 94304 United States

STOCK TICKER/OTHER:

Stock Ticker: TSLA   Exchange: NAS
Employees: 140,473   Fiscal Year Ends: 12/31
Parent Company:

SALARIES/BONUSES:

Top Exec. Salary: $381,009   Bonus: $
Second Exec. Salary: Bonus: $
$300,000

OTHER THOUGHTS:

Estimated Female Officers or Directors: 1
Hot Spot for Advancement for Women/Minorities:

Texas Instruments Incorporated

www.ti.com

NAIC Code: 334413

TYPES OF BUSINESS:

Chips-Digital Signal Processors
Semiconductors
Calculators
Educational Software
Power Management Products
Broadband RF/IF & Digital Radio
MEMS
Microcontrollers (MCU)

BRANDS/DIVISIONS/AFFILIATES:

GROWTH PLANS/SPECIAL FEATURES:

Dallas-based Texas Instruments generates over 95% of its revenue from semiconductors and the remainder from its well-known calculators. Texas Instruments is the world's largest maker of analog chips, which are used to process real-world signals such as sound and power. Texas Instruments also has a leading market share position in processors and microcontrollers used in a wide variety of electronics applications.

CONTACTS: Note: Officers with more than one job title may be intentionally listed here more than once.

Haviv Ilan, CEO
Mark Gary, Senior VP
Rafael Lizardi, CFO
Richard Templeton, Chairman of the Board
Julie Knecht, Chief Accounting Officer
Cynthia Trochu, General Counsel
Ahmad Bahai, Senior VP
Mark Roberts, Senior VP
Christine Witzsche, Senior VP
Shanon Leonard, Senior VP
Mohammad Yunus, Senior VP
Hagop Kozanian, Senior VP
Amichai Ron, Senior VP

FINANCIAL DATA: Note: Data for latest year may not have been available at press time.

In U.S. $	2024	2023	2022	2021	2020	2019
Revenue	15,640,999,936	17,518,999,552	20,028,000,256	18,343,999,488	14,460,999,680	14,382,999,552
R&D Expense	1,959,000,000	1,863,000,000	1,670,000,000	1,554,000,000	1,530,000,000	1,544,000,000
Operating Income	5,341,000,000	7,331,000,000	10,397,000,000	9,156,000,000	6,116,000,000	5,975,000,000
Operating Margin %	.34%	.42%	.52%	.50%	.42%	.42%
SGA Expense	1,794,000,000	1,825,000,000	1,704,000,000	1,666,000,000	1,623,000,000	1,645,000,000
Net Income	4,799,000,000	6,510,000,000	8,749,000,000	7,769,000,000	5,595,000,000	5,017,000,000
Operating Cash Flow	6,318,000,000	6,420,000,000	8,720,000,000	8,756,000,000	6,139,000,000	6,649,000,000
Capital Expenditure	4,820,000,000	5,071,000,000	2,797,000,000	2,462,000,000	649,000,000	847,000,000
EBITDA	7,541,000,000	9,009,000,000	11,225,000,000	10,057,000,000	7,199,000,000	6,948,000,000
Return on Assets %	.14%	.22%	.34%	.35%	.30%	.28%
Return on Equity %	.28%	.41%	.62%	.69%	.62%	.56%
Debt to Equity	.76%	.63%	.56%	.57%	0.707	0.624

CONTACT INFORMATION:

Phone: 972 995-3773   Fax: 972 995-4360
Toll-Free: 800-336-5236
Address: 12500 TI Blvd., Dallas, TX 75266-0199 United States

STOCK TICKER/OTHER:

Stock Ticker: TXN   Exchange: NAS
Employees: 34,000   Fiscal Year Ends: 12/31
Parent Company:

SALARIES/BONUSES:

Top Exec. Salary: $1,241,667   Bonus: $2,380,000
Second Exec. Salary: $797,500   Bonus: $1,250,000

OTHER THOUGHTS:

Estimated Female Officers or Directors: 3
Hot Spot for Advancement for Women/Minorities: Y

Sales, profits and employees may be estimates. Financial information, benefits and other data can change quickly and may vary from those stated here.

Textron Inc

www.textron.com

NAIC Code: 336411

TYPES OF BUSINESS:

Helicopters & General Aviation Aircraft Manufacturing
Aerospace
Electrical Test & Measurement Equipment
Fiber Optic Equipment
Off-Road Vehicles
Financing

BRANDS/DIVISIONS/AFFILIATES:

Bell Helicopter Textron Inc
Textron Systems
Textron Aviation
TRU Simulation + Training Inc
Textron Specialized Vehicles Inc
Beechcraft
Cessna
Response Technologies LLC

CONTACTS: Note: Officers with more than one job title may be intentionally listed here more than once.

Scott Donnelly, CEO
Frank Connor, CFO
Mark Bamford, Chief Accounting Officer
E. Lupone, Chief Compliance Officer
Julie Duffy, Executive VP
David Rosenberg, Vice President, Divisional

GROWTH PLANS/SPECIAL FEATURES:

Textron is a conglomerate that designs, manufactures, and services a range of specialty aircraft including small jets, propeller-driven airplanes, helicopters, and tilt-rotor aircraft. Textron Aviation manufactures and services Cessna and Beechcraft planes. Bell is a helicopter and tilt-rotor manufacturer and servicer for both commercial and military customers. Textron Systems produces uncrewed aircraft and armored vehicles for the military market as well as aircraft simulators and training for the commercial and military markets. Textron Industrial contains the Kautex business, which manufactures plastic fuel tanks for conventional and hybrid motor vehicles, and other subsidiaries that produce specialized vehicles such as golf carts and all-terrain vehicles.

Textron offers its employees comprehensive benefits.

FINANCIAL DATA: Note: Data for latest year may not have been available at press time.

In U.S. $	2024	2023	2022	2021	2020	2019
Revenue	13,701,999,616	13,683,000,320	12,869,000,192	12,382,000,128	11,651,000,320	13,630,000,128
R&D Expense	491,000,000	570,000,000	601,000,000			
Operating Income	855,000,000	1,053,000,000	883,000,000	864,000,000	512,000,000	1,072,000,000
Operating Margin %	.06%	.08%	.07%	.07%	.04%	.08%
SGA Expense	1,156,000,000	1,225,000,000	1,186,000,000	1,221,000,000	1,045,000,000	1,152,000,000
Net Income	824,000,000	921,000,000	861,000,000	746,000,000	309,000,000	815,000,000
Operating Cash Flow	1,014,000,000	1,266,000,000	1,488,000,000	1,598,000,000	768,000,000	1,014,000,000
Capital Expenditure	364,000,000	402,000,000	354,000,000	375,000,000	317,000,000	339,000,000
EBITDA	1,422,000,000	1,559,000,000	1,520,000,000	1,405,000,000	839,000,000	1,529,000,000
Return on Assets %	.05%	.06%	.05%	.05%	.02%	.06%
Return on Equity %	.12%	.13%	.12%	.12%	.05%	.15%
Debt to Equity	.45%	.50%	.50%	.55%	0.66	0.589

CONTACT INFORMATION:

Phone: 401 421-2800   Fax: 401 421-2878
Toll-Free:
Address: 40 Westminster St., Providence, RI 02903 United States

STOCK TICKER/OTHER:

Stock Ticker: TXT   Exchange: NYS
Employees: 35,000   Fiscal Year Ends: 12/31
Parent Company:

SALARIES/BONUSES:

Top Exec. Salary: $1,413,461   Bonus: $
Second Exec. Salary: Bonus: $
$1,190,385

OTHER THOUGHTS:

Estimated Female Officers or Directors: 10
Hot Spot for Advancement for Women/Minorities: Y

Thales SA

NAIC Code: 334511

TYPES OF BUSINESS:

Aircraft Instruments Manufacturing
High Technology
Security
Digital Identity
Aerospace
Defense
Transportation

BRANDS/DIVISIONS/AFFILIATES:

Thales Alenia Space

GROWTH PLANS/SPECIAL FEATURES:

Thales is a French aerospace and defense industrial and one of Europe's largest defense contractors with EUR 18 billion in sales. The company has three segments: defense and security provides sensors, mission systems, communications, and control systems to European and export defense customers; aerospace sells avionics and satellites to the civil, defense, and governmental markets; and digital identity and security provides biometric, data, and identity security solutions, payments services, and the manufacturing of SIM cards.

CONTACTS: *Note: Officers with more than one job title may be intentionally listed here more than once.*

Patrice Caine, CEO

FINANCIAL DATA: *Note: Data for latest year may not have been available at press time.*

In U.S. $	2024	2023	2022	2021	2020	2019
Revenue	23,355,959,235	20,917,593,230	19,941,885,116	18,379,114,662	17,447,218,870	20,886,605,898
R&D Expense	1,445,743,000	1,257,321,000	1,207,265,000	1,165,607,000	1,070,261,000	1,246,878,000
Operating Income	2,062,429,000	1,877,071,000	1,637,798,000	1,402,157,000	1,020,772,000	1,595,573,000
Operating Margin %	.09%	.09%	.08%	.08%	.06%	.08%
SGA Expense	2,591,600,000	2,275,823,000	2,212,145,000	2,010,102,000	1,972,304,000	2,292,395,000
Net Income	1,611,237,000	1,161,635,000	1,271,964,000	1,235,868,000	548,694,700	1,273,439,000
Operating Cash Flow	3,117,367,000	1,715,550,000	3,434,052,000	3,072,304,000	1,311,464,000	2,009,308,000
Capital Expenditure	707,264,500	710,102,100	606,810,400	511,691,300	430,647,000	571,282,600
EBITDA	3,033,371,000	2,788,082,000	2,849,262,000	2,619,977,000	1,968,558,000	3,032,804,000
Return on Assets %	.04%	.03%	.03%	.03%	.02%	.04%
Return on Equity %	.20%	.15%	.16%	.19%	.09%	.20%
Debt to Equity	.61%	.84%	.56%	.71%	1.013	0.79

CONTACT INFORMATION:

Phone: 33 157778000   Fax: 33 157778300
Toll-Free:
Address: 45 rue de Villiers, Neuilly-sur-Seine, 92200 France

STOCK TICKER/OTHER:

Stock Ticker: THLEF   Exchange: PINX
Employees: 81,060   Fiscal Year Ends: 12/31
Parent Company:

SALARIES/BONUSES:

Top Exec. Salary: $ Bonus: $
Second Exec. Salary: $ Bonus: $

OTHER THOUGHTS:

Estimated Female Officers or Directors: 3
Hot Spot for Advancement for Women/Minorities: Y

Thinkpath Inc

www.thinkpath.com

NAIC Code: 541330

TYPES OF BUSINESS:

Engineering Services

GROWTH PLANS/SPECIAL FEATURES:

Thinkpath Inc provides customized engineering solutions with a wide range of support services guaranteeing timely, efficient and cost-effective completion of projects in numerous and varied industries. The company's customized solutions include Engineering & Design Services, Technical Publishing & Documentation and On-site Engineering Support.

BRANDS/DIVISIONS/AFFILIATES:

CONTACTS: *Note: Officers with more than one job title may be intentionally listed here more than once.*

Bob Trick, Pres.
Kelly Hankinson, CFO
Lisa Day, HR
Ken Stephenson, Dir.-IT

FINANCIAL DATA: *Note: Data for latest year may not have been available at press time.*

In U.S. $	2024	2023	2022	2021	2020	2019
Revenue						
R&D Expense						
Operating Income						
Operating Margin %						
SGA Expense						
Net Income						
Operating Cash Flow						
Capital Expenditure						
EBITDA						
Return on Assets %						
Return on Equity %						
Debt to Equity						

CONTACT INFORMATION:

Phone: 937 985-8079   Fax:
Toll-Free:
Address: 9080 Springboro Pike, Ste. 300, Miamisburg, OH 45342 United States

STOCK TICKER/OTHER:

Stock Ticker: THPHF   Exchange: PINX
Employees: 168   Fiscal Year Ends:
Parent Company:

SALARIES/BONUSES:

Top Exec. Salary: $ Bonus: $
Second Exec. Salary: $ Bonus: $

OTHER THOUGHTS:

Estimated Female Officers or Directors:
Hot Spot for Advancement for Women/Minorities:

Thornton Tomasetti Inc

www.thorntontomasetti.com

NAIC Code: 541330

TYPES OF BUSINESS:

Engineering Consulting Services
Engineering
Structural Design
Restoration/Renewal
Tall and Supertall Buildings
Infrastructure
Residential
R&D and Technology

BRANDS/DIVISIONS/AFFILIATES:

GROWTH PLANS/SPECIAL FEATURES:

Thornton Tomasetti, Inc. was founded in 1949 and is an independent engineering firm. The company's 130+ capabilities are categorized into client solutions that include acoustics/noise/vibration, aviation, commercial/residential, construction engineering, critical facilities, cultural/community, decarbonization, defense, education, energy, facades, forensics/investigations, government, healthcare/research, hospitality, gaming, insurance, life sciences, protective design and security, resilience, restoration/renewal, special structures, sports and public assembly, structural design, sustainability, tall and super-tall buildings, transportation and infrastructure. The company invests in research and development and technology, all of which play an essential role in Thornton Tomasetti in regard to learning, testing and innovating. Thornton Tomasetti has worked on projects of all scales and complexities in more than 50 countries. The company is headquartered in the U.S., and has offices throughout the Americas, Europe, the Middle East and the Pacific rim.

CONTACTS: *Note: Officers with more than one job title may be intentionally listed here more than once.*

Michael Squarzini, Co-CEO
Peter DiMaggio, Co-CEO

FINANCIAL DATA: *Note: Data for latest year may not have been available at press time.*

In U.S. $	2024	2023	2022	2021	2020	2019
Revenue						
R&D Expense						
Operating Income						
Operating Margin %						
SGA Expense						
Net Income						
Operating Cash Flow						
Capital Expenditure						
EBITDA						
Return on Assets %						
Return on Equity %						
Debt to Equity						

CONTACT INFORMATION:

Phone: 917-661-7800   Fax: 917-661-7801
Toll-Free:
Address: 120 Broadway, New York, NY 10271-0016 United States

STOCK TICKER/OTHER:

Stock Ticker: Private   Exchange:
Employees: 1,500   Fiscal Year Ends:
Parent Company:

SALARIES/BONUSES:

Top Exec. Salary: $ Bonus: $
Second Exec. Salary: $ Bonus: $

OTHER THOUGHTS:

Estimated Female Officers or Directors:
Hot Spot for Advancement for Women/Minorities:

Toshiba Corporate R&D Center

www.global.toshiba/ww/technology/corporate/rdc.html

NAIC Code: 541710

TYPES OF BUSINESS:

Research & Development
Semiconductor Processes
MEMS Applications
Biotechnology Tools
Electronic Devices
Software
Artificial Intelligence
Recognition Technologies

BRANDS/DIVISIONS/AFFILIATES:

Toshiba Corporation

CONTACTS: Note: Officers with more than one job title may be intentionally listed here more than once.

Taro Shimada, CEO
Hidemi Moue, Chmn.

GROWTH PLANS/SPECIAL FEATURES:

Toshiba Corporate R&D Center (CRDC) manages a global network of research laboratories, test facilities and planning groups that support the ongoing commercialization of products and technologies for Toshiba Corporation, its parent company. Toshiba is a global leader in the manufacture of consumer, industrial, medical and communications electronics. CRDC has focused the bulk of its short-term research and development initiatives on digital products and electronic devices, while its scientists and engineers continue to develop a range of platform technologies, including new nanometric semiconductor processes, innovative microelectromechanical systems (MEMS) applications and chip-based biotech tools. The firm has facilities in Japan, Europe, India and China. Its research and development areas include: information and communication, comprising the development of wireless real-time video transmission technology of whole-genome sequence data using quantum cryptography, and quantum encryption technology for large-capacity data transmission; intelligent systems, developing artificial intelligence (AI) with three-dimensional recognition that measures distance, utilizing AI solutions to enhance train time-tabling and to improve customer convenience, to develop machine learning algorithm for identifying failure factors from data, developing an algorithm that offers large-scale combinatorial optimization, developing an advanced service platform for rapid problem-solving in logistics, drug development and other social needs; nano materials, developing no-plug charging EV systems, photovoltaic modules, energy consumption reduction solutions, carbon recycling technology, magnetic material production, cancer detection test solutions, microRNA detection technology; and electronic devices, which develops a Gate dielectric process technology. Its insulation film process technology, and next-generation power device technology reduces power consumption and carbon dioxide emissions.

FINANCIAL DATA: Note: Data for latest year may not have been available at press time.

In U.S. $	2024	2023	2022	2021	2020	2019
Revenue						
R&D Expense						
Operating Income						
Operating Margin %						
SGA Expense						
Net Income						
Operating Cash Flow						
Capital Expenditure						
EBITDA						
Return on Assets %						
Return on Equity %						
Debt to Equity						

CONTACT INFORMATION:

Phone: 81-44-549-2056   Fax:
Toll-Free:
Address: 1, Komukai Toshiba-cho, Saiwai-ku, Kawasaki-shi, 212-8582 Japan

STOCK TICKER/OTHER:

Stock Ticker: Subsidiary   Exchange:
Employees: 50   Fiscal Year Ends: 03/31
Parent Company: Toshiba Corporation

SALARIES/BONUSES:

Top Exec. Salary: $ Bonus: $
Second Exec. Salary: $ Bonus: $

OTHER THOUGHTS:

Estimated Female Officers or Directors:
Hot Spot for Advancement for Women/Minorities:

Toshiba Corporation

www.toshiba.co.jp

NAIC Code: 334413

TYPES OF BUSINESS:

Memory Chip Manufacturing
Infrastructure Systems
Digital Products
Electronic Devices
Power Systems
Retail
Identification
Semiconductor

BRANDS/DIVISIONS/AFFILIATES:

Japan Industrial Partners Inc
SCiB

CONTACTS: Note: Officers with more than one job title may be intentionally listed here more than once.

Taro Shimada, CEO
Yasuhiro Matsunaga, CFO
Norio Sasaki, Vice Chmn.
Hidejiro Shimomitsu, Sr. Exec. VP
Hideo Kitamura, Sr. Exec. VP
Makoto Kubo, Sr. Exec. VP
Hidemi Moue, Chmn.

GROWTH PLANS/SPECIAL FEATURES:

Toshiba, founded in 1875, is a multinational electronics company that has operations in seven business segments. These segments include energy systems and solutions, embracing large-scale power generation systems for nuclear and thermal power, along with renewable energy generation systems for hydro, geothermal, solar and wind power; building solutions, covering elevators and escalators for buildings and facilities, as well as lighting, energy-saving, environmentally conscious products and services and building solutions that improve building security and reliability; electronic devices and storage solutions, focusing on semiconductors for automotive and industrial use, large-capacity hard disk drives (HDDs) for data centers, semiconductor manufacturing equipment, and parts and materials; battery business, developing, manufacturing and selling the SCiB product, which is a rechargeable lithium-ion battery that is highly safe, has a long lifetime, recharges fast and operates in low temperatures; infrastructure systems and solutions, providing products, systems and services to public-sector customers responsible for maintaining the infrastructure of essential utilities, as well as preparing to embrace Internet of Things (IoT) and artificial intelligence (AI) to establish safer, more secure and more convenient social infrastructure systems; retail and printing solutions, developing point of sale (POS) systems, multifunction peripherals (MFPs) and other products; and digital solutions, utilizing IoT, AI and other digital technologies, as well as groundbreaking work in quantum technologies to support global business development. Toshiba is headquartered in Tokyo, Japan, and has additional operations in the Americas, China, Asia-Pacific region, Europe, Africa and the Middle East. The firm is owned by Japan Industrial Partners, Inc.

FINANCIAL DATA: Note: Data for latest year may not have been available at press time.

In U.S. $	2024	2023	2022	2021	2020	2019
Revenue	23,000,000,000	21,119,710,000	25,225,779,200	23,271,782,400	25,139,951,616	28,141,676,544
R&D Expense						
Operating Income						
Operating Margin %						
SGA Expense						
Net Income		-480,782,000	1,471,462,912	868,439,872	-850,140,928	7,720,163,328
Operating Cash Flow						
Capital Expenditure						
EBITDA						
Return on Assets %						
Return on Equity %						
Debt to Equity						

CONTACT INFORMATION:

Phone: 81 334572096   Fax: 81 354449202
Toll-Free:
Address: 1-1, Shibaura 1-chome, Minato-ku, Tokyo, 105-8001 Japan

STOCK TICKER/OTHER:

Stock Ticker: Private   Exchange:
Employees: 128,697   Fiscal Year Ends: 03/31
Parent Company: Japan Industrial Partners Inc

SALARIES/BONUSES:

Top Exec. Salary: $ Bonus: $
Second Exec. Salary: $ Bonus: $

OTHER THOUGHTS:

Estimated Female Officers or Directors:
Hot Spot for Advancement for Women/Minorities:

Sales, profits and employees may be estimates. Financial information, benefits and other data can change quickly and may vary from those stated here.

TotalEnergies SE

NAIC Code: 211100

www.totalenergies.com

TYPES OF BUSINESS:

Oil & Gas Exploration & Production
Oil and Gas
Renewable Energy
Bioenergy
Exploration and Production
Electricity
Petrochemicals
Trading

BRANDS/DIVISIONS/AFFILIATES:

Hutchinson
Total SE

GROWTH PLANS/SPECIAL FEATURES:

TotalEnergies is an integrated oil and gas company that explores for, produces, and refines oil around the world. In 2024, it produced 1.5 million barrels of liquids and 5.2 billion cubic feet of natural gas per day. At the end of 2024, reserves stood at 11.1 billion barrels of oil equivalent, 54% of which are liquids. During 2024, it had LNG sales of 39.8 million metric tons. The company owns interests in refineries with a capacity of nearly 1.8 million barrels a day, primarily in Europe, distributes refined products in 65 countries, and manufactures commodity and specialty chemicals. At year-end, its gross installed renewable power generation capacity was 26 gigawatts.

CONTACTS:
Note: Officers with more than one job title may be intentionally listed here more than once.

Patrick Pouyanne, CEO
Charles de Bollardiere, Secretary

FINANCIAL DATA:
Note: Data for latest year may not have been available at press time.

In U.S. $	2024	2023	2022	2021	2020	2019
Revenue	195,610,001,408	218,944,995,328	263,310,000,128	184,633,999,360	119,704,002,560	176,248,995,840
R&D Expense						
Operating Income	24,105,000,000	30,857,000,000	49,693,000,000	23,925,000,000	-7,265,000,000	15,352,000,000
Operating Margin %	.12%	.14%	.19%	.13%	-.06%	.09%
SGA Expense						
Net Income	15,758,000,000	21,384,000,000	20,526,000,000	16,032,000,000	-7,242,000,000	11,267,000,000
Operating Cash Flow	30,854,000,000	40,679,000,000	47,367,000,000	30,410,000,000	14,803,000,000	24,685,000,000
Capital Expenditure	14,909,000,000	17,722,000,000	15,690,000,000	12,343,000,000	10,764,000,000	11,810,000,000
EBITDA	42,277,000,000	50,782,000,000	59,042,000,000	42,066,000,000	17,880,000,000	36,063,000,000
Return on Assets %	.06%	.07%	.07%	.06%	-.03%	.04%
Return on Equity %	.13%	.19%	.18%	.15%	-.07%	.10%
Debt to Equity	.35%	.33%	.37%	.43%	0.565	0.395

CONTACT INFORMATION:

Phone: 33 147444546   Fax: 33 147444944
Toll-Free:
Address: 2 Place Jean Millier, Courbevoie, 92400 France

STOCK TICKER/OTHER:

Stock Ticker: TTE   Exchange: NYS
Employees: 102,579   Fiscal Year Ends: 12/31
Parent Company:

SALARIES/BONUSES:

Top Exec. Salary: $ Bonus: $
Second Exec. Salary: $ Bonus: $

OTHER THOUGHTS:

Estimated Female Officers or Directors: 4
Hot Spot for Advancement for Women/Minorities: Y

Toyoda Gosei Co Ltd

www.toyoda-gosei.com

NAIC Code: 336390

TYPES OF BUSINESS:

Automobile (Car) and Truck Parts (Air Bags, Air-Conditioners, Mufflers & Radiators) Manufacturing
Automotive Parts
Manufacture
Safety Systems
Light Systems
Steering

BRANDS/DIVISIONS/AFFILIATES:

Toyota Motor Corporation

GROWTH PLANS/SPECIAL FEATURES:

Toyoda Gosei Co Ltd is a manufacturer of resins and rubber parts for automobiles. The company's products fall in three categories: automotive parts, LEDs, and general industry products. The automotive parts segment, making up the lion's share of Toyoda Gosei's generated revenue, produces weather strips, fuel tank and engine peripheral parts, chassis and drivetrain parts, interior and exterior parts, and safety systems such as airbags. In its other business segments, the company produces LEDs for crystal displays, LED light solutions and glass-encapsulated LEDs, air conditioning products, home construction components, and industrial and construction machinery parts.

CONTACTS: Note: Officers with more than one job title may be intentionally listed here more than once.

Naoki Miyazaki, Chairman of the Board
Hiroshi Yasuda, Director
Masaki Oka, Director
Mitsuhiro Nawashiro, Director
Katsumi Saito, Director

FINANCIAL DATA: Note: Data for latest year may not have been available at press time.

In U.S. $	2024	2023	2022	2021	2020	2019
Revenue	7,436,177,793	6,608,421,324	5,763,975,559	5,009,011,643	5,643,828,193	5,836,670,746
R&D Expense						
Operating Income	470,029,200	243,474,000	237,239,700	253,263,000	124,194,700	253,582,300
Operating Margin %	.06%	.04%	.04%	.05%	.02%	.04%
SGA Expense	587,566,000	531,234,400	444,668,200	391,717,600	427,124,400	433,122,800
Net Income	357,220,200	111,108,000	162,121,600	244,411,300	77,936,690	161,823,100
Operating Cash Flow	891,196,900	374,708,400	192,016,100	466,863,400	452,978,300	398,937,800
Capital Expenditure	324,278,000	320,251,300	359,122,500	344,314,100	322,028,600	343,508,800
EBITDA	898,326,800	601,548,200	571,306,600	543,106,000	410,594,300	512,614,600
Return on Assets %	.06%	.02%	.03%	.05%	.02%	.03%
Return on Equity %	.11%	.04%	.06%	.10%	.03%	.07%
Debt to Equity	.19%	.29%	.30%	.28%	0.30	0.263

CONTACT INFORMATION:

Phone: 81 524005131   Fax:
Toll-Free:
Address: 1 Haruhinagahata, Kiyosu, 452-8564 Japan

STOCK TICKER/OTHER:

Stock Ticker: TGOSF   Exchange: PINX
Employees: 46,243   Fiscal Year Ends: 03/31
Parent Company: Toyota Motor Corporation

SALARIES/BONUSES:

Top Exec. Salary: $ Bonus: $
Second Exec. Salary: $ Bonus: $

OTHER THOUGHTS:

Estimated Female Officers or Directors:
Hot Spot for Advancement for Women/Minorities:

Toyota Motor Corporation

NAIC Code: 336111

TYPES OF BUSINESS:

Automobile Manufacturing
Manufactured Housing
Advertising & e-Commerce Services
Financial Services
Telecommunications Services
Information Technology
Nanotechnology Research

BRANDS/DIVISIONS/AFFILIATES:

Daihatsu Motor Co Ltd
Hino Motors Ltd
Toyota Financial Services Corporation
Toyota Housing Corporation

GROWTH PLANS/SPECIAL FEATURES:

Founded in 1937, Toyota is one of the world's largest automakers, with 11.0 million units sold at retail in fiscal 2025, including 10.3 million across the Toyota and Lexus brands. Brands include Toyota, Lexus, Daihatsu, and truck maker Hino; market share in Japan is about 52% excluding mini-vehicles, while US share is around 15%. The firm also owns stakes in Denso, a parts supplier, about 20% of Subaru, and holds investments in many other firms, including shares of Uber Technologies, Joby Aviation, Aurora Innovation, Isuzu Motors, and about 5% in each of Mazda and Suzuki. Fiscal 2025 sales excluding financial services were JPY 43.8 trillion. Toyota also has a financing arm and manufactures homes and boats.

CONTACTS:
Note: Officers with more than one job title may be intentionally listed here more than once.

Koji Sato, CEO
Akio Toyoda, Chairman of the Board
Takeshi Uchiyamada, Chairman of the Board
Hiroki Nakajima, Director
Yoichi Miyazaki, Director
Kenta Kon, Director
Simon Humphries, Director
Shigeru Hayakawa, Director

FINANCIAL DATA:
Note: Data for latest year may not have been available at press time.

In U.S. $	2024	2023	2022	2021	2020	2019
Revenue	313,075,014,987	257,944,317,341	217,852,736,289	188,937,749,849	207,348,980,393	209,842,282,215
R&D Expense						
Operating Income	37,162,840,000	18,918,540,000	20,797,670,000	15,257,900,000	16,656,700,000	17,130,970,000
Operating Margin %	.12%	.07%	.10%	.08%	.08%	.08%
SGA Expense	27,876,860,000	24,909,680,000	20,660,770,000	18,290,930,000	20,702,340,000	20,663,370,000
Net Income	34,330,280,000	17,018,310,000	19,786,930,000	15,587,760,000	14,135,930,000	13,071,880,000
Operating Cash Flow	29,202,810,000	20,515,660,000	25,844,310,000	18,933,360,000	16,651,600,000	26,149,660,000
Capital Expenditure	35,048,550,000	25,727,800,000	26,591,530,000	26,159,020,000	26,010,660,000	25,957,280,000
EBITDA	63,294,120,000	39,961,070,000	40,578,110,000	32,067,930,000	30,772,030,000	28,505,400,000
Return on Assets %	.06%	.03%	.04%	.04%	.04%	.04%
Return on Equity %	.16%	.09%	.11%	.10%	.10%	.10%
Debt to Equity	.62%	.60%	.58%	.57%	0.555	0.57

CONTACT INFORMATION:

Phone: 81 565282121   Fax: 81 565235800
Toll-Free:
Address: 1 Toyota-Cho, Toyota City, Toyota, Aichi Prefecture 471-8571 Japan

STOCK TICKER/OTHER:

Stock Ticker: TM   Exchange: NYS
Employees: 380,793   Fiscal Year Ends: 03/31
Parent Company:

SALARIES/BONUSES:

Top Exec. Salary: $40,118,270   Bonus: $44,976,880
Second Exec. Salary: $12,077,130   Bonus: $25,958,880

OTHER THOUGHTS:

Estimated Female Officers or Directors:
Hot Spot for Advancement for Women/Minorities:

TPV Technology Co Ltd

NAIC Code: 334118

www.tpv-tech.com/en

TYPES OF BUSINESS:

Monitors, Computer Peripheral Equipment, Manufacturing
Television Manufacturing
Computer Monitor Manufacturing
Gaming Monitors
Professional Monitors
Sound Products
Manufacturing Facilities
Professional Bespoke Solutions

BRANDS/DIVISIONS/AFFILIATES:

China Electronics Corporation

CONTACTS: *Note: Officers with more than one job title may be intentionally listed here more than once.*

Jason Hsuan, CEO
Zhang Qiang, CFO
Lu Being-Chang, Sr. VP-R&D
Lee Neng-Sung, CTO
Houng Yu-Te, Sr. VP-Admin.
Houng Yu-Te, Sr. VP-Finance
Jason Hsuan, Chmn.
Hsieh Chi Tsung, Sr. VP-Procurement

GROWTH PLANS/SPECIAL FEATURES:

TPV Technology Co., Ltd. is a leading contract manufacturer of televisions and computer display monitors. The firm targets both the TV and personal computer (PC) markets on an original design manufacturer (ODM) basis. Products include 4K HDR monitors, QHD display monitors, gaming monitors, curved monitors, touch portable monitors, interactive display monitors and energy efficient monitors. TV products include 4K UHD LED televisions, OLED+ televisions and Ultra HD televisions. Professional display products include plug-and-play, multi-touch displays; 4K UHD displays; professional TVs powered by Android; and UHD picture quality displays. Sound products span wireless speakers, micro music systems, soundbars, headphones and hybrid active noise cancelling products. Product brands offered by TPV include AOC, Philips, AGON, Envision and Great Wall. TPV also tailors professional display solutions to businesses in various industries, including corporate, hospitality, education, transportation, retail, healthcare, public venues and many others. TPV has 12 manufacturing bases, eight innovation and development centers and more than 3,500 sales and service centers worldwide. TPV is a subsidiary of China Electronics Corporation.

FINANCIAL DATA: *Note: Data for latest year may not have been available at press time.*

In U.S. $	2024	2023	2022	2021	2020	2019
Revenue		7,700,789,000	10,130,699,140	11,078,535,207	10,503,045,503	9,605,016,422
R&D Expense						
Operating Income						
Operating Margin %						
SGA Expense						
Net Income		39,154,000	189,385,680	83,499,528	114,264,947	23,008,650
Operating Cash Flow						
Capital Expenditure						
EBITDA						
Return on Assets %						
Return on Equity %						
Debt to Equity						

CONTACT INFORMATION:

Phone: 86755 3635 8633   Fax:
Toll-Free:
Address: No. 77 Tianyou Rd., Qixia, Nanjing, Jiangsu 210033 China

STOCK TICKER/OTHER:

Stock Ticker: 727   Exchange: Shenzhen
Employees: 20,552   Fiscal Year Ends: 12/31
Parent Company: China Electronics Corporation

SALARIES/BONUSES:

Top Exec. Salary: $ Bonus: $
Second Exec. Salary: $ Bonus: $

OTHER THOUGHTS:

Estimated Female Officers or Directors: 1
Hot Spot for Advancement for Women/Minorities:

Tractebel Engineering GmbH

NAIC Code: 541330

TYPES OF BUSINESS:

Engineering Services
Engineering
Consulting
Energy
Water
Nuclear
Urban Infrastructure
Hydropower

BRANDS/DIVISIONS/AFFILIATES:

Engie SA
Tractebel Engie

CONTACTS: Note: *Officers with more than one job title may be intentionally listed here more than once.*

Anne Harvengt, CEO

GROWTH PLANS/SPECIAL FEATURES:

Tractebel Engineering GmbH (Tractebel Engie) is a subsidiary of Engie SA that offers engineering and consulting services for the energy, water, hydropower, nuclear and urban infrastructure sectors. Tractebel Engie operates in six business units: Global Power, Infrastructures, Global Nuclear, Complex and High-Tech Buildings (RED), Middle East and Asia and South America. Services include: strategy, with digital tools, master plans, roadmaps and technical/regulatory consultancy; pre-investment phase, with basic design, due diligence, environmental impact assessment and licensing, master plans, policy studies, power systems development and economics, and pre-feasibility/feasibility studies; decommissioning phase, with dismantling, site redevelopment studies and waste management; operation phase, with modification/renovation/lifetime extension, operation support solutions, simulators and training, and maintenance engineering; and implementation phase, with commissioning, detailed design, engineering procurement construction management, front-end engineering design, owner's or lender's engineer, project and contract management, and quality assurance. The company offers its multi-disciplinary solutions to customers on a global scale. Headquartered in Germany, Tractebel Engie has a presence in over 40 countries and has developed projects in over 80 countries.

FINANCIAL DATA: Note: *Data for latest year may not have been available at press time.*

In U.S. $	2024	2023	2022	2021	2020	2019
Revenue	757,870,050	721,781,000	629,639,340	655,659,600	713,610,000	770,000,000
R&D Expense						
Operating Income						
Operating Margin %						
SGA Expense						
Net Income						
Operating Cash Flow						
Capital Expenditure						
EBITDA						
Return on Assets %						
Return on Equity %						
Debt to Equity						

CONTACT INFORMATION:

Phone: 49-6101-55-0   Fax: 49-6101-55-2222
Toll-Free:
Address: Friedberger Strasse 173, Bad Vilbel, 61118 Germany

STOCK TICKER/OTHER:

Stock Ticker: Private   Exchange:
Employees: 5,600   Fiscal Year Ends:
Parent Company: Engie SA

SALARIES/BONUSES:

Top Exec. Salary: $ Bonus: $
Second Exec. Salary: $ Bonus: $

OTHER THOUGHTS:

Estimated Female Officers or Directors:
Hot Spot for Advancement for Women/Minorities:

Trane Technologies plc

NAIC Code: 333400

www.tranetechnologies.com/en

TYPES OF BUSINESS:

Refrigeration Systems & Controls
Heating Systems
Cooling Systems
Building Climate Controls
Energy Solutions
Transport Refrigeration Systems

GROWTH PLANS/SPECIAL FEATURES:

Trane Technologies manufactures and services commercial and residential HVAC systems and transportation refrigeration solutions under its prominent Trane, American Standard, and Thermo King brands. The $20 billion company generates approximately 70% of sales from equipment and 30% from parts and services. While the firm is domiciled in Ireland, North America accounts for over 80% of its revenue.

BRANDS/DIVISIONS/AFFILIATES:

Trane
Thermo King
Ingersoll Rand plc

CONTACTS: Note: Officers with more than one job title may be intentionally listed here more than once.

David Regnery, CEO
Christopher Kuehn, CFO
Elizabeth Elwell, Chief Accounting Officer
Raymond Pittard, Executive VP
Evan Turtz, General Counsel
Mairead Magner, Other Executive Officer
Donald Simmons, President, Geographical
Mark Majocha, President, Geographical
Keith Sultana, Senior VP, Divisional

FINANCIAL DATA: Note: Data for latest year may not have been available at press time.

In U.S. $	2024	2023	2022	2021	2020	2019
Revenue	19,838,199,808	17,677,600,768	15,991,700,480	14,136,399,872	12,454,700,032	13,075,900,416
R&D Expense						
Operating Income	3,500,100,000	2,894,000,000	2,418,900,000	2,023,300,000	1,532,800,000	1,670,100,000
Operating Margin %	.18%	.16%	.15%	.14%	.12%	.13%
SGA Expense	3,580,400,000	2,963,200,000	2,545,900,000	2,446,300,000	2,270,600,000	2,320,300,000
Net Income	2,567,900,000	2,023,900,000	1,756,500,000	1,423,400,000	854,900,000	1,410,900,000
Operating Cash Flow	3,145,600,000	2,389,600,000	1,504,000,000	1,588,300,000	1,435,000,000	1,919,500,000
Capital Expenditure	370,600,000	300,700,000	291,800,000	223,000,000	146,200,000	205,400,000
EBITDA	3,859,600,000	3,149,900,000	2,719,200,000	2,323,800,000	1,831,200,000	1,930,500,000
Return on Assets %	.13%	.11%	.10%	.08%	.04%	.07%
Return on Equity %	.36%	.31%	.28%	.22%	.13%	.20%
Debt to Equity	.58%	.57%	.62%	.72%	0.702	0.677

CONTACT INFORMATION:

Phone: 353 18707400   Fax:
Toll-Free:
Address: 170/175 Lakeview Dr., Airside Business Park, Dublin, 2 Ireland

STOCK TICKER/OTHER:

Stock Ticker: TT   Exchange: NYS
Employees: 40,000   Fiscal Year Ends: 12/31
Parent Company:

SALARIES/BONUSES:

Top Exec. Salary: $1,456,250   Bonus: $
Second Exec. Salary: $899,185   Bonus: $

OTHER THOUGHTS:

Estimated Female Officers or Directors: 3
Hot Spot for Advancement for Women/Minorities: Y

Sales, profits and employees may be estimates. Financial information, benefits and other data can change quickly and may vary from those stated here.

TRC Companies Inc

www.trccompanies.com

NAIC Code: 541330

TYPES OF BUSINESS:

Engineering Services
Digital Solutions
Management Services
Engineering
Environmental
Construction
Regulatory Compliance
Consultancy

BRANDS/DIVISIONS/AFFILIATES:

CONTACTS: Note: Officers with more than one job title may be intentionally listed here more than once.

Christopher P. Vincze, CEO
James Mayer, Exec. VP-Bus. Oper.
Jason S. Greenlaw, CFO
Mary Boucher, CMO
Laura Ramey, Chief People Officer
Rajeev Gollarahalli, CIO
James Mayer, Other Corporate Officer
John Cowdery, Other Corporate Officer
Martin Dodd, Senior VP
Christopher P. Vincze, Chmn.

GROWTH PLANS/SPECIAL FEATURES:

TRC Companies, Inc. offers professional services for public, private and government customers. The firm's services include digital solutions, emergency management and response, engineering, environmental management, health management, safety management, field services, inspection, operations support, planning, procurement, construction, regulatory and environmental compliance, remediation management, materials management and related consulting. Markets served by TRC include industrial, power, utilities, real estate, transportation, water and government. The company steers complex projects from concept to completion to help solve tough challenges. Projects include the renovation of public schools in the Salem district, lead contamination testing of drinking water for Portland's public schools, evaluating pilot testing for electric vehicle fleet and public charging programs with Xcel Energy in Minnesota and providing Arc Flash Studies for multiple wind farms being installed across the Midwestern U.S. TRC has employees in over 150 offices throughout the U.S., Canada, the U.K. and China.

FINANCIAL DATA: Note: Data for latest year may not have been available at press time.

In U.S. $	2024	2023	2022	2021	2020	2019
Revenue	829,920,000	790,400,000	760,000,000	732,823,740	684,882,000	691,800,000
R&D Expense						
Operating Income						
Operating Margin %						
SGA Expense						
Net Income						
Operating Cash Flow						
Capital Expenditure						
EBITDA						
Return on Assets %						
Return on Equity %						
Debt to Equity						

CONTACT INFORMATION:

Phone: 860-298-9692   Fax:
Toll-Free:
Address: 21 Griffin Rd. N., Windsor, CT 06095 United States

STOCK TICKER/OTHER:

Stock Ticker: Private   Exchange:
Employees: 5,228   Fiscal Year Ends: 06/30
Parent Company: Mountain Partners IV

SALARIES/BONUSES:

Top Exec. Salary: $ Bonus: $
Second Exec. Salary: $ Bonus: $

OTHER THOUGHTS:

Estimated Female Officers or Directors: 2
Hot Spot for Advancement for Women/Minorities:

Trevi-Finanziaria Industriale SpA (Trevi Group)

www.trevigroup.com
NAIC Code: 541330

TYPES OF BUSINESS:

Engineering & Construction Services
Underground Construction Services
Soil Consolidation
Machinery Manufacture
Engineering

BRANDS/DIVISIONS/AFFILIATES:

CDP Equity SpA
Polaris Capital Management LLC
Soilmec SpA

GROWTH PLANS/SPECIAL FEATURES:

Trevi-Finanziaria Industriale SpA (Trevi Group) is a global leader in subsoil engineering for special foundations, tunnel excavations, soil consolidation, production and marketing of machinery and specialized equipment. Founded in 1957, Trevi Group specializes in dams and levees, maritime works, ways of communication, industrial and civil construction, restorations, environment, automated parking and water research. Subsidiary Soilmec SpA designs, manufactures and markets machinery, systems and plant facilities used for underground engineering. Trevi Group itself is controlled by CDP Equity and Polaris Capital Management, LLC.

CONTACTS:
Note: Officers with more than one job title may be intentionally listed here more than once.

Giuseppe Caselli, CEO
Franco Cicognani, Head-Corp. Comm. Dept.
Stefano Trevisani, Managing Dir.
Cesare Trevisani, Managing Dir.

FINANCIAL DATA:
Note: Data for latest year may not have been available at press time.

In U.S. $	2024	2023	2022	2021	2020	2019
Revenue		649,790,000	599,172,000	549,724,000	578,329,000	671,607,250
R&D Expense						
Operating Income						
Operating Margin %						
SGA Expense						
Net Income		21,091,000	-20,421,000	-59,995,000	290,768,625	-172,253,550
Operating Cash Flow						
Capital Expenditure						
EBITDA						
Return on Assets %						
Return on Equity %						
Debt to Equity						

CONTACT INFORMATION:

Phone: 39 547319111   Fax: 39 547319594
Toll-Free:
Address: Via Larga, 201, Cesena, FO 47522 Italy

STOCK TICKER/OTHER:

Stock Ticker: TFI   Exchange: Milan
Employees: 3,274   Fiscal Year Ends: 12/31
Parent Company:

SALARIES/BONUSES:

Top Exec. Salary: $ Bonus: $
Second Exec. Salary: $ Bonus: $

OTHER THOUGHTS:

Estimated Female Officers or Directors: 1
Hot Spot for Advancement for Women/Minorities:

Tutor Perini Corporation

www.tutorperini.com

NAIC Code: 237310

TYPES OF BUSINESS:

Construction Services
HVAC
Construction Management
Contracting
Design-Build
Civil Works
Steel Erection
Concrete Forming

BRANDS/DIVISIONS/AFFILIATES:

Tutor-Saliba
Perini Corporation

CONTACTS: Note: Officers with more than one job title may be intentionally listed here more than once.

John Stankey, CEO
Gary Smalley, CEO
Pascal Desroches, CFO
Ryan Soroka, CFO
Ronald Tutor, Chairman of the Board
William Kennard, Chairman of the Board
Henry Dieu, Chief Accounting Officer
Sabrina Sanders, Chief Accounting Officer
Kellyn Smith Kenny, Chief Marketing Officer
F. Thaddeus Arroyo, Chief Strategy Officer
Jeffery McElfresh, COO

GROWTH PLANS/SPECIAL FEATURES:

Tutor Perini Corporation is a leading construction company offering diversified general contracting, construction management and design-build services to private customers and public agencies throughout the world. The company was formed through the 2008 merger between Tutor-Saliba Corporation and Perini Corporation, which was founded in 1894, when Perini's predecessor businesses began providing construction services. Tutor Perini offers general contracting, pre-construction planning and comprehensive project management services, and has strong expertise in planning and delivering design-bid-build, design-build, construction management and public-private partnership (P3) projects. The firm also offers earthwork, excavation, concrete forming and placement, steel erection, electrical, mechanical, plumbing, heating, ventilation and air conditioning (HVAC) and fire protection services.

Tutor Perini offers its employees comprehensive health benefits, a 401(k), life and disability insurance, and a variety of employee assistance programs.

FINANCIAL DATA: Note: Data for latest year may not have been available at press time.

In U.S. $	2024	2023	2022	2021	2020	2019
Revenue	4,326,922,240					
R&D Expense						
Operating Income	-103,753,000					
Operating Margin %	- .02%					
SGA Expense	300,791,000					
Net Income	-163,721,000					
Operating Cash Flow	38,771,000,000					
Capital Expenditure	20,263,000,000					
EBITDA	-34,746,000					
Return on Assets %	- .04%					
Return on Equity %	- .13%					
Debt to Equity	1.30%					

CONTACT INFORMATION:

Phone: 818 362-8391   Fax:
Toll-Free:
Address: 15901 Olden St., Sylmar, CA 91342 United States

STOCK TICKER/OTHER:

Stock Ticker: TPC   Exchange: NYS
Employees: 8,200   Fiscal Year Ends: 12/31
Parent Company:

SALARIES/BONUSES:

Top Exec. Salary: $2,400,000   Bonus: $
Second Exec. Salary: Bonus: $
$1,900,000

OTHER THOUGHTS:

Estimated Female Officers or Directors:
Hot Spot for Advancement for Women/Minorities:

UCB SA

www.ucb-group.com

NAIC Code: 325412

TYPES OF BUSINESS:

Pharmaceuticals Development
Industrial Chemical Products
Allergy & Respiratory Treatments
Central Nervous System Disorder Treatments

BRANDS/DIVISIONS/AFFILIATES:

Cimzia
Evenity
Briviact
Keppra
Vimpat
Neupro
Nayzilam

GROWTH PLANS/SPECIAL FEATURES:

UCB is a Belgium-based biopharma firm focused on the development of novel therapies for the treatment of central nervous system and immunologic diseases. Historically, revenue was derived from allergy medicine Zyrtec and epilepsy drug Keppra, which have both lost patent protection. The firm's key products are Cimzia (immunology), Vimpat (epilepsy), Neupro (Parkinson's disease and restless leg syndrome), Briviact (epilepsy), Bimzelx (psoriasis), Evenity (osteoporosis), Nayzilam (cluster seizures), and Fintepla (Dravet Syndrome and Lennox-Gastaut Syndrome).

CONTACTS: Note: Officers with more than one job title may be intentionally listed here more than once.

Jean-Christophe Tellier, CEO
Jonathan Peacock, Chairman of the Board
Fiona du Monceau, Director

FINANCIAL DATA: Note: Data for latest year may not have been available at press time.

In U.S. $	2024	2023	2022	2021	2020	2019
Revenue	6,982,973,901	5,961,407,207	6,262,202,268	6,557,321,160	6,069,239,289	5,576,617,413
R&D Expense	2,021,566,000	1,850,170,000	1,895,573,000	1,849,035,000	1,780,931,000	1,443,814,000
Operating Income	980,703,700	718,501,700	795,686,700	1,500,568,000	1,180,477,000	1,198,638,000
Operating Margin %	.14%	.12%	.13%	.23%	.19%	.21%
SGA Expense	2,664,018,000	2,070,375,000	1,945,516,000	1,763,905,000	1,608,399,000	1,479,001,000
Net Income	1,208,854,000	389,330,300	474,460,800	1,200,908,000	830,874,000	898,978,400
Operating Cash Flow	1,409,762,000	863,791,200	1,270,148,000	1,762,770,000	1,227,015,000	1,001,135,000
Capital Expenditure	365,493,800	358,683,300	421,112,400	559,591,400	396,140,700	333,711,700
EBITDA	2,228,150,000	1,448,354,000	1,329,171,000	1,809,308,000	1,477,866,000	1,513,053,000
Return on Assets %	.06%	.02%	.03%	.08%	.06%	.07%
Return on Equity %	.11%	.04%	.05%	.14%	.10%	.12%
Debt to Equity	.30%	.33%	.29%	.25%	0.319	0.139

CONTACT INFORMATION:

Phone: 32-2-559-99-99   Fax: 32-2-559-99-00
Toll-Free:
Address: 60, Allee de la Recherche, Brussels, B-1070 Belgium

STOCK TICKER/OTHER:

Stock Ticker: UCBJY
Employees: 9,083
Parent Company:

Exchange: PINX
Fiscal Year Ends: 12/31

SALARIES/BONUSES:

Top Exec. Salary: $ Bonus: $
Second Exec. Salary: $ Bonus: $

OTHER THOUGHTS:

Estimated Female Officers or Directors: 5
Hot Spot for Advancement for Women/Minorities: Y

Union Carbide Corporation

www.unioncarbide.com

NAIC Code: 325211

TYPES OF BUSINESS:

Basic Chemicals, Manufacturing
Chemicals
Polymers
Product Manufacturing

BRANDS/DIVISIONS/AFFILIATES:

Dow Chemical Company (The)

CONTACTS: Note: Officers with more than one job title may be intentionally listed here more than once.

James A. Varilek, Pres.
Bruce D. Fitzgerald, VP
Jim Fitterling, Chmn.-Dow

GROWTH PLANS/SPECIAL FEATURES:

Union Carbide Corporation, a wholly-owned subsidiary of The Dow Chemical Company (DOW), manufactures basic chemicals and polymers primarily for commercial manufacturers. Union Carbide's chemicals and polymers undergo one or more further conversions by customers before reaching consumers. Some of these materials are high-volume commodities, while others are specialty products that meet the needs of smaller market niches. End-uses served include paints, coatings, packaging, wire, cable, household products, personal care products, pharmaceuticals, automotive, textiles, agriculture and oil and gas. Union Carbide both produces and purchases ethylene, a basic building block chemical, which is converted to polyethylene or is reacted with oxygen to produce ethylene oxide. Ethylene oxide is the precursor to many of the products Union Carbide sells, including ethylene glycol and hundreds of solvents, alcohols, surfactants, amines and specialty products. Some of the chemicals the firm makes go directly into everyday products; for example, polyethylene and polypropylene are used in making food containers or toys; ethylene glycol is used in making automotive antifreeze; and isopropanol is used in making rubbing alcohol. Others are used in manufacturing processes to enhance quality and performance, including wet-strength in paper towels, biocides as bacteria-growth inhibitors in cosmetics and surfactants for soil removal in industrial cleaning. Union Carbide sells most of the products it manufactures to DOW.

Union Carbide offers a comprehensive medical plan, life insurance, long-term care insurance, personal lines insurance, a pension plan and a 401(k) plan.

FINANCIAL DATA: Note: Data for latest year may not have been available at press time.

In U.S. $	2024	2023	2022	2021	2020	2019
Revenue	5,678,400,000	5,408,000,000	5,200,000,000	5,105,000,000	3,703,000,000	4,377,000,000
R&D Expense						
Operating Income						
Operating Margin %						
SGA Expense						
Net Income				375,000,000	427,000,000	627,000,000
Operating Cash Flow						
Capital Expenditure						
EBITDA						
Return on Assets %						
Return on Equity %						
Debt to Equity						

CONTACT INFORMATION:

Phone: 361-553-2000   Fax: 361-553-3464
Toll-Free:
Address: 7501 State Highway 185 N., North Seadrift, TX 77983 United States

STOCK TICKER/OTHER:

Stock Ticker: Subsidiary   Exchange:
Employees: 2,300   Fiscal Year Ends: 12/31
Parent Company: Dow Chemical Company (The)

SALARIES/BONUSES:

Top Exec. Salary: $ Bonus: $
Second Exec. Salary: $ Bonus: $

OTHER THOUGHTS:

Estimated Female Officers or Directors:
Hot Spot for Advancement for Women/Minorities:

Sales, profits and employees may be estimates. Financial information, benefits and other data can change quickly and may vary from those stated here.

Unisys Corporation

www.unisys.com

NAIC Code: 541512

TYPES OF BUSINESS:

IT Consulting
Enterprise Systems & Servers
Outsourcing Services
Infrastructure Services
Security Technology
Server Software & Middleware

BRANDS/DIVISIONS/AFFILIATES:

ClearPath
Unisys Stealth

GROWTH PLANS/SPECIAL FEATURES:

Unisys Corp is engaged in the provision of technology solutions for clients across the government, financial services, and commercial markets. It operates through three business segments: Digital Workplace Solutions (DWS),Cloud, Applications & Infrastructure Solutions (CA&I), and Enterprise Computing Solutions (ECS). DWS provides workplace solutions featuring intelligent workplace services, proactive experience management and collaboration tools to support business growth. CA&I which provides digital transformation in the areas of cloud migration and management. ECS which provides solutions that harness secure, high-intensity enterprise computing and enable digital services through software-defined operating environments. Majority of revenue is from ECS segment.

The firm offers employees health services, recreational facilities and employee discounts.

CONTACTS: Note: Officers with more than one job title may be intentionally listed here more than once.

Peter Altabef, CEO
Debra McCann, CFO
David Brown, Chief Accounting Officer
Kristen Prohl, Chief Administrative Officer
Teresa Poggenpohl, Chief Marketing Officer
Dwayne Allen, Chief Technology Officer
Michael Thomson, COO
Shalabh Gupta, Treasurer

FINANCIAL DATA: Note: Data for latest year may not have been available at press time.

In U.S. $	2024	2023	2022	2021	2020	2019
Revenue	2,008,400,000	2,015,399,936	1,979,900,032	2,054,400,000	2,026,300,032	2,222,799,872
R&D Expense	25,200,000	24,100,000	24,200,000	28,500,000	26,600,000	31,300,000
Operating Income	191,000,000	70,300,000	19,800,000	124,800,000	58,000,000	125,300,000
Operating Margin %	.10%	.03%	.01%	.06%	.03%	.06%
SGA Expense	424,200,000	450,300,000	453,200,000	389,500,000	369,400,000	364,800,000
Net Income	-193,400,000	-430,700,000	-106,000,000	-448,500,000	750,700,000	-17,200,000
Operating Cash Flow	135,100,000	74,200,000	12,700,000	132,500,000	-681,200,000	123,900,000
Capital Expenditure	63,500,000	67,300,000	77,300,000	81,700,000	100,000,000	111,300,000
EBITDA	63,000,000	-178,200,000	153,300,000	-252,900,000	-81,600,000	148,900,000
Return on Assets %	-.10%	-.21%	-.05%	-.17%	.29%	-.01%
Return on Equity %						
Debt to Equity						

CONTACT INFORMATION:

Phone: 215 986-4011   Fax: 215 986-6850
Toll-Free: 800-874-8647
Address: 801 Lakeview Dr., Ste. 100, Blue Bell, PA 19422 United States

STOCK TICKER/OTHER:

Stock Ticker: UIS   Exchange: NYS
Employees: 16,500   Fiscal Year Ends: 12/31
Parent Company:

SALARIES/BONUSES:

Top Exec. Salary: $991,000   Bonus: $
Second Exec. Salary: $670,000   Bonus: $

OTHER THOUGHTS:

Estimated Female Officers or Directors: 2
Hot Spot for Advancement for Women/Minorities: Y

United Microelectronics Corporation

www.umc.com

NAIC Code: 334413

TYPES OF BUSINESS:

Chips/Semiconductors

BRANDS/DIVISIONS/AFFILIATES:

Mie Fujitsu Semiconductor Limited
United Semiconductor Japan Co Ltd

GROWTH PLANS/SPECIAL FEATURES:

Founded in 1980, United Microelectronics is the world's third-largest dedicated chip foundry, with 5% market share in 2024 after TSMC and SMIC. UMC's headquarters are in Hsinchu, Taiwan, and it operates 12 fabs in Taiwan, Mainland China, Japan and Singapore, with additional sales offices in Europe, the us, and South Korea. UMC features a diverse customer base that includes Texas Instruments, MediaTek, Qualcomm, Broadcom, Xilinx, and Realtek, supplying a wide range of products applied in communications, display, memory, automotive and more. UMC employs about 20,000 people.

UMC offers its employees counseling services and the use of a recreation center at its Hsinchu headquarters, which features sports facilities, an art gallery, a performance venue and meeting spaces.

CONTACTS:

Note: Officers with more than one job title may be intentionally listed here more than once.

Chi-Tung Liu, CFO
Stan Hung, Chairman of the Board
Jason Wang, Co-Pres.
Shan-Chieh Chien, Co-President

FINANCIAL DATA:

Note: Data for latest year may not have been available at press time.

In U.S. $	2024	2023	2022	2021	2020	2019
Revenue	7,768,797,834	7,442,077,246	9,320,623,231	7,123,637,970	5,913,347,360	4,956,244,946
R&D Expense	522,240,600	444,245,500	433,199,600	432,574,300	431,258,800	396,637,200
Operating Income	1,714,556,000	1,915,918,000	3,465,291,000	1,717,252,000	675,637,100	179,241,800
Operating Margin %	.22%	.26%	.37%	.24%	.11%	.04%
SGA Expense	328,369,300	357,908,900	463,365,100	423,431,800	361,728,600	305,203,200
Net Income	1,631,306,000	1,996,152,000	2,992,402,000	1,713,813,000	764,522,200	272,727,500
Operating Cash Flow	3,139,323,000	2,876,052,000	4,877,952,000	3,021,601,000	2,198,689,000	1,836,136,000
Capital Expenditure	3,054,746,000	3,144,278,000	2,771,847,000	1,670,776,000	948,242,000	634,140,700
EBITDA	3,574,717,000	3,692,334,000	5,203,019,000	3,593,040,000	2,456,533,000	1,910,573,000
Return on Assets %	.09%	.11%	.18%	.13%	.06%	.02%
Return on Equity %	.14%	.18%	.31%	.21%	.11%	.04%
Debt to Equity	.17%	.15%	.14%	.17%	0.134	0.263

CONTACT INFORMATION:

Phone: 886 35782258   Fax: 886 35779392
Toll-Free:
Address: No. 3 Li-Hsin 2nd Rd., Hsinchu Science Park, Hsinchu City, 30078 Taiwan

STOCK TICKER/OTHER:

Stock Ticker: UMC
Employees: 15,116
Parent Company:

Exchange: NYS
Fiscal Year Ends: 12/31

SALARIES/BONUSES:

Top Exec. Salary: $ Bonus: $
Second Exec. Salary: $ Bonus: $

OTHER THOUGHTS:

Estimated Female Officers or Directors:
Hot Spot for Advancement for Women/Minorities:

UniversalPegasus International Inc
www.universalpegasus.com
NAIC Code: 541330

TYPES OF BUSINESS:
Engineering Consulting Services
Engineering
Project Management
Construction Management
Survey
Inspection
Procurement
Energy Cybersecurity

BRANDS/DIVISIONS/AFFILIATES:
PMC Capital Partners LLC

CONTACTS: Note: Officers with more than one job title may be intentionally listed here more than once.
Kristy Stamper, CEO

GROWTH PLANS/SPECIAL FEATURES:
UniversalPegasus International, Inc. (UPI) is an engineering firm primarily serving the energy industry. UPI's services are divided into six categories: engineering and design, procurement, construction management, FEED/feasibility, survey and inspection. The engineering and design segment offers engineering and consulting services across a variety of upstream, midstream and power-related projects for both onshore and offshore purposes. Specialty areas include process engineering, mechanical, materials, pipeline, structural, civil, electrical, instrumentation, subsea and automation. The procurement category offers services for projects that require assurance for timeline, expenditure and risk management. This division collaborates with the client's engineering design team and ensures communication with vendors and alignment with purchases and delivery for the project's schedule. The construction management category operates to prevent delays, to handle scheduling challenges and order changes, and for addressing/handling execution errors during the construction phase. The front-end engineering design (FEED) and feasibility category performs preliminary feasibility studies, FEED analysis and cost estimates for oil and gas and power capital projects. The survey category offers a complete range of survey and mapping services, having surveyed and mapped more than 100,000 miles of pipeline, including well locations, preliminary, as-built surveys, operations and maintenance projects. This division's project experience ranges from simple upstream pipeline tasks to complex midstream projects. Its staff is nationally licensed. The inspection category provides related services to the oil and gas industry, including new construction, and the maintenance of pipelines, facilities, plants, tanks and terminals. UPI is owned by PMC Capital Partners LLC.

FINANCIAL DATA: Note: Data for latest year may not have been available at press time.

In U.S. $	2024	2023	2022	2021	2020	2019
Revenue						
R&D Expense						
Operating Income						
Operating Margin %						
SGA Expense						
Net Income						
Operating Cash Flow						
Capital Expenditure						
EBITDA						
Return on Assets %						
Return on Equity %						
Debt to Equity						

CONTACT INFORMATION:
Phone: 713-425-6000   Fax:
Toll-Free:
Address: 4848 Loop Central Dr., Ste. 137, Houston, TX 77081 United States

STOCK TICKER/OTHER:
Stock Ticker: Subsidiary   Exchange:
Employees: 900   Fiscal Year Ends:
Parent Company: PMC Capital Partners LLC

SALARIES/BONUSES:
Top Exec. Salary: $ Bonus: $
Second Exec. Salary: $ Bonus: $

OTHER THOUGHTS:
Estimated Female Officers or Directors:
Hot Spot for Advancement for Women/Minorities:

Valeo SA

www.valeo.com

NAIC Code: 336300

TYPES OF BUSINESS:

Automobile Parts Manufacturing
Driver Assistance Systems
Manufacturing
Technology
Artificial Intelligence
Research and Development
Electrification Systems
LIDAR

GROWTH PLANS/SPECIAL FEATURES:

Based in France, Valeo is an automotive parts supplier that operates through four business segments, including powertrain systems (PTS, 31% of 2022 revenue), thermal systems (THS, 22%), comfort and driving assistance systems (CDA, 22%), and visibility systems (VIS, 25%). As of 2022, Valeo generated 84% of its revenue through original equipment sales and 11% of revenue through aftermarket parts. The firm's five largest automaker customers accounted for 53% of 2022 revenue. Europe is Valeo's largest geographic market at 45% of 2022 revenue, followed by Asia at 33%, and Americas at 22%.

BRANDS/DIVISIONS/AFFILIATES:

Valeo SCALA

CONTACTS: Note: Officers with more than one job title may be intentionally listed here more than once.

Christophe Perillat-Piratoine, CEO
Gilles Michel, Chairman of the Board

FINANCIAL DATA: Note: Data for latest year may not have been available at press time.

In U.S. $	2024	2023	2022	2021	2020	2019
Revenue	24,395,006,573	25,021,566,719	22,743,472,406	19,593,643,753	18,656,072,374	22,107,832,251
R&D Expense	2,414,302,000	2,303,065,000	2,133,939,000	1,713,961,000	1,923,950,000	1,458,570,000
Operating Income	1,043,133,000	951,191,800	720,771,800	793,416,600	-422,247,500	1,173,666,000
Operating Margin %	.04%	.04%	.03%	.04%	-.02%	.05%
SGA Expense	1,174,801,000	1,230,420,000	1,057,889,000	943,246,300	944,381,400	987,514,200
Net Income	183,882,000	250,851,300	261,067,000	198,637,900	-1,236,095,000	355,278,100
Operating Cash Flow	3,049,943,000	2,794,552,000	2,165,721,000	1,846,765,000	2,088,536,000	2,796,822,000
Capital Expenditure	2,524,404,000	2,271,283,000	1,690,125,000	1,532,350,000	1,677,639,000	2,231,555,000
EBITDA	3,082,860,000	3,018,161,000	2,830,874,000	2,454,029,000	1,322,361,000	2,523,269,000
Return on Assets %	.01%	.01%	.01%	.01%	-.06%	.02%
Return on Equity %	.04%	.06%	.06%	.05%	-.28%	.07%
Debt to Equity	1.31%	1.41%	1.33%	1.18%	1.193	0.954

CONTACT INFORMATION:

Phone: 33 140552020   Fax: 33 140552171
Toll-Free:
Address: 43, Rue Bayen, Paris, 75017 France

STOCK TICKER/OTHER:

Stock Ticker: VLEEY   Exchange: PINX
Employees: 112,700   Fiscal Year Ends: 12/31
Parent Company:

SALARIES/BONUSES:

Top Exec. Salary: $ Bonus: $
Second Exec. Salary: $ Bonus: $

OTHER THOUGHTS:

Estimated Female Officers or Directors: 4
Hot Spot for Advancement for Women/Minorities: Y

Sales, profits and employees may be estimates. Financial information, benefits and other data can change quickly and may vary from those stated here.

Vatana Phaisal Engineering Co Ltd

www.vpe.co.th

NAIC Code: 332111

TYPES OF BUSINESS:

Steel Construction Materials Manufacturing
Steel Fabrication
Mechanical Services
Piping Services
Installation Services
Construction Materials
Boilers
Storage Tanks

BRANDS/DIVISIONS/AFFILIATES:

CONTACTS: Note: Officers with more than one job title may be intentionally listed here more than once.

Thomthong Tantikjrungruang, Pres.

GROWTH PLANS/SPECIAL FEATURES:

Vatana Phaisal Engineering Co., Ltd. (VPE) is a steel fabrication, mechanical and piping installation service company founded in 1961, and based in Thailand. VPE's business is operated through four divisions: steel fabrication, construction, modularization and service. The steel fabrication division manufactures standardized metal products for its client's needs, such as fired heaters and process furnaces, heat recovery steam generators, steam boilers, pollution control and environmental equipment, pressure vessels (code and non-code stamps), spherical tanks, storage tanks, silos, steel structures for buildings and plant facilities, pipe spoolers, material handling equipment and conveyors. The construction division provides mechanical installation of equipment and machineries for oil process plants, chemical plants, cement plants and chemical industrial plants, as well as piping installations and pipeline module assembly services for various plants. The modularization division manufactures steel and distributes steel framing products for project needs. Last, the service division supplies VPE products and provides related professional services that go along with them, including scaffolding material supply and installation, plant maintenance and shutdown service, manpower supply for plant facilities, power plant/cement plant services, steel milling, and tankage/silo installation.

FINANCIAL DATA: Note: Data for latest year may not have been available at press time.

In U.S. $	2024	2023	2022	2021	2020	2019
Revenue						
R&D Expense						
Operating Income						
Operating Margin %						
SGA Expense						
Net Income						
Operating Cash Flow						
Capital Expenditure						
EBITDA						
Return on Assets %						
Return on Equity %						
Debt to Equity						

CONTACT INFORMATION:

Phone: 66-2-398-0143   Fax: 66-2-398-2815
Toll-Free:
Address: 368 Moo 6, Sukhumvit Rd., Samrong Nua, Smutprakarn, 10270 Thailand

STOCK TICKER/OTHER:

Stock Ticker: Private   Exchange:
Employees: Fiscal Year Ends:
Parent Company:

SALARIES/BONUSES:

Top Exec. Salary: $ Bonus: $
Second Exec. Salary: $ Bonus: $

OTHER THOUGHTS:

Estimated Female Officers or Directors:
Hot Spot for Advancement for Women/Minorities: Y

VEPICA USA Inc

NAIC Code: 541330

www.vepica.com

TYPES OF BUSINESS:

Engineering Consulting Services
Engineering
Procurement
Construction
Project Management
Laser Scanning
Internet of Things
Project Integration

BRANDS/DIVISIONS/AFFILIATES:

CONTACTS: *Note: Officers with more than one job title may be intentionally listed here more than once.*

Migeul Bocco, CEO

GROWTH PLANS/SPECIAL FEATURES:

VEPICA USA, Inc. is a company that supports the industrial sector with related engineering, procurement and construction (EPC) management services. Founded in 1972, the firm operates worldwide, with services including studies and permitting, engineering and design, projects and EPCs, investments/financing, laser scanning and managing data, reverse engineering, 3D digital assets/data and vital signs (internet of things or IoT). VEPICA can integrate its services as a single provider, fully responsible from project conception to startup, or can offer single discipline support and linked teams. Markets primarily served by VEPICA include oil and gas, chemical, petrochemical, power generation, power transmission, renewable energy, mining, metallurgy, buildings and infrastructure. The firm's technologies include laser scanning and data management. Its 3D laser scanning services specialize in the collection of geometrical and dimensional data of existing assets using state-of-the-art laser scanners and robotic total stations. Bubble view files and Point Cloud data files can be delivered to the client through its web portal for access from field office or remote locations without compromising control of the data. The data can be accessed without the use of specialized software, and ideal for use in 3D intelligent modeling, 4D virtual facility and asset performance management systems. Based in the greater Houston, Texas area, the firm has international operations in Canada, China, Colombia and Venezuela.

FINANCIAL DATA: *Note: Data for latest year may not have been available at press time.*

In U.S. $	2024	2023	2022	2021	2020	2019
Revenue	122,850,000	117,000,000	112,000,000	112,000,000	100,000,000	110,000,000
R&D Expense						
Operating Income						
Operating Margin %						
SGA Expense						
Net Income						
Operating Cash Flow						
Capital Expenditure						
EBITDA						
Return on Assets %						
Return on Equity %						
Debt to Equity						

CONTACT INFORMATION:

Phone: 713 429-1246   Fax:
Toll-Free:
Address: 2002 W. Grand Pkwy N., Ste. 200, Katy, TX 77449 United States

STOCK TICKER/OTHER:

Stock Ticker: Private   Exchange:
Employees: 1,200   Fiscal Year Ends:
Parent Company:

SALARIES/BONUSES:

Top Exec. Salary: $ Bonus: $
Second Exec. Salary: $ Bonus: $

OTHER THOUGHTS:

Estimated Female Officers or Directors:
Hot Spot for Advancement for Women/Minorities:

VeriSign Inc

www.verisigninc.com

NAIC Code: 511210E

TYPES OF BUSINESS:

Computer Software: Network Security, Managed Access, Digital ID,
Cybersecurity & Anti-Virus
Domain Name Registration

BRANDS/DIVISIONS/AFFILIATES:

Registry Services
Security Services

GROWTH PLANS/SPECIAL FEATURES:

VeriSign is the sole authorized registry for several generic top-level domains, including the widely utilized .com and .net top-level domains. The company operates critical internet infrastructure to support the domain name system, including operating two of the world's 13 root servers that are used to route internet traffic. In 2018, the firm sold off its Security Services business, signaling a renewed focus on the core registry business.

Employees of VeriSign receive a flexible benefits package that includes health, dental, vision, disability and life insurance; flexible spending accounts; a 401(k); an employee assistance program; a group legal plan; domestic partner coverage; tuition ass

CONTACTS: *Note: Officers with more than one job title may be intentionally listed here more than once.*

D. Bidzos, CEO
George Kilguss, CFO
Danny McPherson, Executive VP, Divisional
Thomas Indelicarto, Executive VP

FINANCIAL DATA: *Note: Data for latest year may not have been available at press time.*

In U.S. $	2024	2023	2022	2021	2020	2019
Revenue	1,557,400,064	1,493,100,032	1,424,899,968	1,327,600,000	1,265,052,032	1,231,661,056
R&D Expense	96,700,000	91,000,000	85,700,000	80,500,000	74,671,000	60,805,000
Operating Income	1,058,200,000	1,000,600,000	943,100,000	866,800,000	824,201,000	806,127,000
Operating Margin %	.68%	.67%	.66%	.65%	.65%	.65%
SGA Expense	211,100,000	204,200,000	195,400,000	188,400,000	186,003,000	184,262,000
Net Income	785,700,000	817,600,000	673,800,000	784,800,000	814,888,000	612,299,000
Operating Cash Flow	902,600,000	853,800,000	831,100,000	807,200,000	730,183,000	753,892,000
Capital Expenditure	28,100,000	45,800,000	27,400,000	53,000,000	43,395,000	40,316,000
EBITDA	1,134,100,000	1,095,900,000	1,002,400,000	913,400,000	886,740,000	895,717,000
Return on Assets %	.50%	.47%	.36%	.42%	.45%	.32%
Return on Equity %						
Debt to Equity						

CONTACT INFORMATION:

Phone: 703 948-3200   Fax:
Toll-Free: 800-922-4917
Address: 12061 Bluemont Way, Reston, VA 20190 United States

STOCK TICKER/OTHER:

Stock Ticker: VRSN
Employees: 908
Parent Company:

Exchange: NAS
Fiscal Year Ends: 12/31

SALARIES/BONUSES:

Top Exec. Salary: $950,000   Bonus: $
Second Exec. Salary: Bonus: $
$555,000

OTHER THOUGHTS:

Estimated Female Officers or Directors:
Hot Spot for Advancement for Women/Minorities:

Versar Inc

www.versar.com

NAIC Code: 541330

TYPES OF BUSINESS:

Industrial Engineering Services
Project Management
Construction Management
Environmental Services
Security Systems
Engineering Services
Military Procedure Management

BRANDS/DIVISIONS/AFFILIATES:

Kingswood Capital Management LLC
BayFirst

CONTACTS: Note: Officers with more than one job title may be intentionally listed here more than once.

James M. Jaska, CEO
Christopher Phelps, CFO
James Villa, General Counsel
Wendell Newton, Senior VP, Divisional
Suzanne Bates, Senior VP, Divisional
Linda McKnight, Senior VP, Divisional
Rob Biedermann, Senior VP, Divisional

GROWTH PLANS/SPECIAL FEATURES:

Versar, Inc. is a global project management company based in Washington DC, with 21 locations worldwide. The firm offers three core solutions, environmental and sustainable infrastructure, national security and installation management and support services. The environmental and sustainable infrastructure unit is comprised of a team of engineers, biologists, scientists and archeologists who offer investigations and assessments of projects and suggest options for transformation, restoration, remediation and redevelopment, sustainment and compliance and resilience. The national security segment combats national threats such as man-made attacks and natural disasters. BayFirst solutions, under the national security segment, specializes in program management and engineering in national security and defense, helping government clients implement programs that protect public safety and enhance homeland security initiatives; and military programs, offering management concepts, principles and procedures. The installation and management support services segment offers program and construction management services including project and office engineering, quality assurance, facility condition assessments in 18 countries worldwide. Versar is privately-owned by Kingswood Capital Management LLC.

Versar offers its employees comprehensive health benefits, retirement savings, a 401(k), short-/long-term disability coverage, tuition reimbursement and other benefits.

FINANCIAL DATA: Note: Data for latest year may not have been available at press time.

In U.S. $	2024	2023	2022	2021	2020	2019
Revenue						
R&D Expense						
Operating Income						
Operating Margin %						
SGA Expense						
Net Income						
Operating Cash Flow						
Capital Expenditure						
EBITDA						
Return on Assets %						
Return on Equity %						
Debt to Equity						

CONTACT INFORMATION:

Phone: 703 750-3000   Fax: 703 642-6825
Toll-Free:
Address: 1025 Vermont Ave. NW, Ste. 500, Washington DC, VA 20005 United States

STOCK TICKER/OTHER:

Stock Ticker: Private   Exchange:
Employees: Fiscal Year Ends: 06/30
Parent Company: Kingswood Capital Management LLC

SALARIES/BONUSES:

Top Exec. Salary: $ Bonus: $
Second Exec. Salary: $ Bonus: $

OTHER THOUGHTS:

Estimated Female Officers or Directors:
Hot Spot for Advancement for Women/Minorities:

Vestas Wind Systems A/S

www.vestas.com

NAIC Code: 333611

TYPES OF BUSINESS:

Wind Turbine Manufacturing
Turbine Installation, Repair & Maintenance Services
Online Turbine Operating Systems
Turbine Technology
Plant Solutions and Services
Plant Design
Plant Integration
Performance Options

BRANDS/DIVISIONS/AFFILIATES:

EnVentus

GROWTH PLANS/SPECIAL FEATURES:

Vestas is a leading manufacturer of wind turbines with the highest installed capacity under service in the world. The firm operates two business segments: power solutions and services. The power solutions segment designs, manufactures, and installs onshore and offshore wind turbines. The services segment performs operating and maintenance service work on wind turbines.

CONTACTS:
Note: Officers with more than one job title may be intentionally listed here more than once.

Henrik Andersen, CEO
Hans Smith, CFO
Anders Runevad, Chairman of the Board
Karl-Henrik Sundstrom, Deputy Chairman

FINANCIAL DATA:
Note: Data for latest year may not have been available at press time.

In U.S. $	2024	2023	2022	2021	2020	2019
Revenue	19,631,100,534	17,459,704,464	16,442,678,356	17,692,395,388	16,820,658,724	13,787,741,581
R&D Expense	431,328,000	421,112,400	518,728,700	441,543,700	300,794,600	304,199,800
Operating Income	838,819,500	40,862,660	-1,307,605,000	485,811,600	851,305,300	1,139,614,000
Operating Margin %	.04%	.00%	-.08%	.03%	.05%	.08%
SGA Expense	1,064,699,000	994,324,600	922,815,000	838,819,500	593,643,600	555,051,100
Net Income	566,401,800	87,400,680	-1,784,336,000	152,099,900	868,331,500	799,092,000
Operating Cash Flow	2,646,992,000	1,165,721,000	-221,339,400	1,085,130,000	843,359,800	934,165,700
Capital Expenditure	1,311,010,000	1,012,486,000	929,625,400	948,921,700	780,930,800	880,817,300
EBITDA	2,001,135,000	1,278,093,000	-618,615,200	1,427,923,000	1,881,952,000	1,704,881,000
Return on Assets %	.02%	.00%	-.08%	.01%	.05%	.05%
Return on Equity %	.15%	.03%	-.41%	.03%	.19%	.22%
Debt to Equity	.87%	1.07%	.72%	.16%	0.186	0.201

CONTACT INFORMATION:

Phone: 45 97300000   Fax: 45 97300001
Toll-Free:
Address: Hedeager 42, Aarhus, 8200 Denmark

STOCK TICKER/OTHER:

Stock Ticker: VWSYF   Exchange: PINX
Employees: 30,586   Fiscal Year Ends: 12/31
Parent Company:

SALARIES/BONUSES:

Top Exec. Salary: $ Bonus: $
Second Exec. Salary: $ Bonus: $

OTHER THOUGHTS:

Estimated Female Officers or Directors: 3
Hot Spot for Advancement for Women/Minorities: Y

VINCI SA

NAIC Code: 237310

www.vinci.com

TYPES OF BUSINESS:

Highway, Street, and Bridge Construction
Infrastructure Management
Information & Energy Technologies
Commercial Construction
Engineering Services
Highway Construction
Airport Management & Support Services
Power Transmission Services

BRANDS/DIVISIONS/AFFILIATES:

VINCI Concessions SA
VINCI Contracting LLC
VINCI Autoroutes
VINCI Airports
VINCI Energies
Eurovia
VINCI Construction

GROWTH PLANS/SPECIAL FEATURES:

Vinci is one of the world's largest owners of transport infrastructure. Its concession assets include 4,400 kilometers of toll roads in France and 72 airports across 14 countries, making Vinci the world's largest airport operator in terms of managed passenger numbers. The concession's business contributes less than one fifth of group revenue but the majority of operating profit. Vinci's contracting business provides a broad variety of energy and construction services. France contributes 42% of group revenue.

CONTACTS: *Note: Officers with more than one job title may be intentionally listed here more than once.*

Xavier Huillard, CEO

FINANCIAL DATA: *Note: Data for latest year may not have been available at press time.*

In U.S. $	2024	2023	2022	2021	2020	2019
Revenue	82,597,044,248	79,324,633,148	70,958,002,201	57,014,757,909	50,077,184,635	55,561,863,469
R&D Expense						
Operating Income	9,736,663,000	9,121,453,000	7,269,012,000	4,997,730,000	2,959,138,000	6,162,316,000
Operating Margin %	.12%	.11%	.10%	.09%	.06%	.11%
SGA Expense						
Net Income	5,519,864,000	5,337,117,000	4,834,279,000	2,947,786,000	1,409,762,000	3,700,340,000
Operating Cash Flow	13,296,250,000	11,963,680,000	10,654,940,000	8,860,386,000	7,576,617,000	8,047,673,000
Capital Expenditure	4,599,319,000	3,782,066,000	3,973,893,000	2,341,657,000	2,451,759,000	2,719,637,000
EBITDA	14,510,780,000	13,614,070,000	12,006,810,000	8,841,090,000	6,561,862,000	9,805,902,000
Return on Assets %	.04%	.04%	.04%	.03%	.01%	.04%
Return on Equity %	.17%	.17%	.17%	.12%	.06%	.16%
Debt to Equity	1.04%	.98%	.97%	1.16%	1.337	1.357

CONTACT INFORMATION:

Phone: 33 157986100   Fax:
Toll-Free:
Address: 1973 bd de la Defense, CS 10268, Nanterre Cedex, 92757 France

STOCK TICKER/OTHER:

Stock Ticker: VCISF   Exchange: PINX
Employees: 279,426   Fiscal Year Ends: 12/31
Parent Company:

SALARIES/BONUSES:

Top Exec. Salary: $ Bonus: $
Second Exec. Salary: $ Bonus: $

OTHER THOUGHTS:

Estimated Female Officers or Directors: 2
Hot Spot for Advancement for Women/Minorities:

Visteon Corporation

NAIC Code: 336300

TYPES OF BUSINESS:
Automobile Parts
Climate Control Products
Fuel Storage & Delivery Products
Chassis & Power Train Components
Multimedia Systems

BRANDS/DIVISIONS/AFFILIATES:
SmartCore
DriveCore

GROWTH PLANS/SPECIAL FEATURES:
Visteon Corp is an automotive supplier. It manufactures electronics products for original equipment vehicle manufacturers including Ford, Nissan, Renault, Mazda, BMW, General Motors, and Honda, etc. The company offers information displays, instrument clusters, head-up displays, infotainment systems, telematics solutions, and Smartcore. The Company's reportable segment is Electronics. The Electronics segment provides vehicle cockpit electronics products to customers, including digital instrument clusters, domain controllers with integrated driver assistance systems, displays, Android-based infotainment systems, and battery management systems. Geographically, it operates in North America, Europe, China, Asia-Pacific, and South America and Others.

CONTACTS: *Note: Officers with more than one job title may be intentionally listed here more than once.*
Sachin Lawande, CEO
Jerome Rouquet, CFO
Francis Scricco, Chairman of the Board
Colleen Myers, Chief Accounting Officer
Brett Pynnonen, Chief Legal Officer
Qais Sharif, General Manager, Divisional
Robert Vallance, General Manager, Subsidiary
Kristin Trecker, Other Executive Officer
Joao Ribeiro, Senior VP, Divisional

FINANCIAL DATA: *Note: Data for latest year may not have been available at press time.*

In U.S. $	2024	2023	2022	2021	2020	2019
Revenue	3,865,999,872	3,953,999,872	3,756,000,000	2,772,999,936	2,548,000,000	2,944,999,936
R&D Expense						
Operating Income	324,000,000	280,000,000	180,000,000	79,000,000	52,000,000	103,000,000
Operating Margin %	.08%	.07%	.05%	.03%	.02%	.03%
SGA Expense	207,000,000	207,000,000	188,000,000	175,000,000	193,000,000	221,000,000
Net Income	274,000,000	486,000,000	124,000,000	41,000,000	-56,000,000	70,000,000
Operating Cash Flow	427,000,000	267,000,000	167,000,000	58,000,000	168,000,000	183,000,000
Capital Expenditure	137,000,000	125,000,000	81,000,000	70,000,000	104,000,000	142,000,000
EBITDA	409,000,000	378,000,000	297,000,000	199,000,000	100,000,000	219,000,000
Return on Assets %	.10%	.19%	.05%	.02%	-.02%	.03%
Return on Equity %	.24%	.57%	.21%	.09%	-.13%	.15%
Debt to Equity	.31%	.38%	.64%	.90%	1.279	1.015

CONTACT INFORMATION:
Phone: 734 710-5800   Fax:
Toll-Free: 800-847-8366
Address: 1 Village Center Dr., Van Buren Township, MI 48111 United States

STOCK TICKER/OTHER:
Stock Ticker: VC
Employees: 10,000
Parent Company:

Exchange: NAS
Fiscal Year Ends: 12/31

SALARIES/BONUSES:
Top Exec. Salary: $1,141,250   Bonus: $
Second Exec. Salary: $586,390   Bonus: $

OTHER THOUGHTS:
Estimated Female Officers or Directors:
Hot Spot for Advancement for Women/Minorities: Y

Volkswagen AG (VW)

NAIC Code: 336111

TYPES OF BUSINESS:

Automobile Manufacturing
Truck Manufacturing
Car Rental Services
Consumer Financing
Digital Services
Electric Cars

BRANDS/DIVISIONS/AFFILIATES:

Volkswagen
Audi
Bentley
Bugatti
Lamborghini
SEAT
Skoda
Ducati

GROWTH PLANS/SPECIAL FEATURES:

Volkswagen is the second-largest automotive original equipment manufacturer by vehicle sales globally, selling 9 million vehicles in 2024. 88% of group revenue is generated by its four vehicle segments, core (Volkswagen, SEAT, Skoda, and VW commercial), progressive (Audi, Lamborghini, and Bentley), sports luxury (Porsche), and Traton commercial vehicles (Traton, Scania, Navistar, MAN, and VW truck and bus). It also has a vehicle software business (Cariad), batteries, and power engineering production and financial services.

CONTACTS: Note: Officers with more than one job title may be intentionally listed here more than once.

Jorg Hofmann, Deputy Chairman

FINANCIAL DATA: Note: Data for latest year may not have been available at press time.

In U.S. $	2024	2023	2022	2021	2020	2019
Revenue	368,507,366,243	365,816,112,919	316,742,332,054	283,994,323,846	252,990,923,386	286,757,101,420
R&D Expense						
Operating Income	24,590,240,000	29,170,260,000	20,985,240,000	18,484,680,000	11,860,390,000	18,244,040,000
Operating Margin %	.07%	.08%	.07%	.07%	.05%	.06%
SGA Expense	39,811,580,000	38,676,500,000	35,749,150,000	33,652,670,000	31,561,860,000	34,897,840,000
Net Income	12,884,220,000	18,765,040,000	17,544,840,000	17,459,700,000	10,064,700,000	15,761,630,000
Operating Cash Flow	19,467,650,000	21,970,490,000	32,345,060,000	43,851,300,000	28,264,470,000	20,412,030,000
Capital Expenditure	31,153,230,000	29,279,230,000	25,733,260,000	20,996,600,000	20,143,020,000	22,021,570,000
EBITDA	58,567,540,000	61,640,180,000	59,249,710,000	56,140,750,000	46,054,490,000	51,099,890,000
Return on Assets %	.02%	.03%	.03%	.03%	.02%	.03%
Return on Equity %	.06%	.09%	.10%	.11%	.07%	.11%
Debt to Equity	.73%	.68%	.72%	.89%	0.885	0.913

CONTACT INFORMATION:

Phone: 49 536190   Fax: 49 5361-928282
Toll-Free:
Address: Berliner Ring 2, Wolfsburg, 38440 Germany

STOCK TICKER/OTHER:

Stock Ticker: VLKPF   Exchange: PINX
Employees: 678,825   Fiscal Year Ends: 12/31
Parent Company:

SALARIES/BONUSES:

Top Exec. Salary: $ Bonus: $
Second Exec. Salary: $ Bonus: $

OTHER THOUGHTS:

Estimated Female Officers or Directors:
Hot Spot for Advancement for Women/Minorities:

Volvo AB

NAIC Code: 336120

TYPES OF BUSINESS:

Truck Manufacturer
Engines
Buses
Aerospace Products
Construction Equipment
Financial Services
Intelligent Transport Systems
Overhaul & Repair Services

BRANDS/DIVISIONS/AFFILIATES:

Volvo Group
Volvo
Volvo Penta
Rokbak
Renault Trucks
Revost
Nova Bus
Mack

GROWTH PLANS/SPECIAL FEATURES:

Volvo AB drives prosperity through transport and infrastructure solutions, offering trucks, buses, construction equipment, power solutions for marine and industrial applications, financing, and services that increase the customers' uptime and productivity. Its segments are Trucks, Construction Equipment, Buses, Volvo Penta, Financial Services, and Group Functions & Other. A majority of its revenue is generated from the Trucks segment, which is engaged in the manufacturing and selling of trucks under several brands, including Volvo, Renault, and others. This segment also comprises the activities of Volvo Autonomous Solutions, Volvo Energy, VE Commercial Vehicles, Dongfeng Commercial Vehicles, Cellcentric, Milence, Flexis, and Cespira. Geographically, it derives maximum revenue from the USA.

CONTACTS: Note: Officers with more than one job title may be intentionally listed here more than once.

Martin Lundstedt, CEO
Mats Backman, CFO
Carl-Henric Svanberg, Chairman of the Board

FINANCIAL DATA: Note: Data for latest year may not have been available at press time.

In U.S. $	2024	2023	2022	2021	2020	2019
Revenue	54,951,652,613	57,604,859,546	49,388,123,299	38,825,482,026	35,302,965,520	45,059,403,709
R&D Expense	3,229,094,000	2,779,313,000	2,349,665,000	1,880,378,000	1,752,183,000	1,933,785,000
Operating Income	7,270,546,000	8,398,857,000	5,178,630,000	4,409,663,000	3,038,730,000	4,863,929,000
Operating Margin %	.13%	.15%	.10%	.11%	.09%	.11%
SGA Expense	4,431,986,000	4,279,903,000	3,642,888,000	3,007,124,000	3,247,244,000	4,196,351,000
Net Income	5,256,027,000	5,197,196,000	3,413,199,000	3,419,979,000	2,015,041,000	3,740,625,000
Operating Cash Flow	4,844,528,000	2,231,796,000	3,467,649,000	3,509,685,000	3,192,899,000	4,072,954,000
Capital Expenditure	1,917,721,000	1,919,077,000	2,695,971,000	2,278,004,000	1,806,632,000	2,295,737,000
EBITDA	9,528,628,000	9,349,946,000	6,989,851,000	6,579,499,000	4,992,751,000	7,206,918,000
Return on Assets %	.07%	.08%	.06%	.06%	.04%	.07%
Return on Equity %	.27%	.29%	.22%	.23%	.14%	.27%
Debt to Equity	.81%	.77%	.83%	.73%	0.652	0.722

CONTACT INFORMATION:

Phone: 46 31660000   Fax: 46 31665170
Toll-Free:
Address: Volvo Bergegardsvag 1, Torslanda, Gothenburg, SE-405 08 Sweden

STOCK TICKER/OTHER:

Stock Ticker: VOLAF   Exchange: PINX
Employees: 104,000   Fiscal Year Ends: 12/31
Parent Company:

SALARIES/BONUSES:

Top Exec. Salary: $ Bonus: $
Second Exec. Salary: $ Bonus: $

OTHER THOUGHTS:

Estimated Female Officers or Directors: 5
Hot Spot for Advancement for Women/Minorities: Y

Volvo Car AB

NAIC Code: 336111

TYPES OF BUSINESS:

Automobile Manufacturing
Rechargeable Vehicles
Vehicle Design and Production
Plug-in Hybrid Vehicles
Pure Electric Vehicles
Mild Hybrid Vehicles

GROWTH PLANS/SPECIAL FEATURES:

Volvo Car AB manufactures, designs, and supplies automobiles. The company offers a wide range of cars. Geographically, it has a presence in China, the USA; Sweden; Germany; the United Kingdom; Japan, and South Korea. It generates maximum revenue from the sale of new cars.

BRANDS/DIVISIONS/AFFILIATES:

Zhejiang Geely Holding Group Co Ltd
C40
XC60
XC90
V60
V90
S60
S90

CONTACTS: *Note: Officers with more than one job title may be intentionally listed here more than once.*

Jim Rowan, CEO
Shu fu Li, Chairman of the Board
Lone Schroder, Director

FINANCIAL DATA: *Note: Data for latest year may not have been available at press time.*

In U.S. $	2024	2023	2022	2021	2020	2019
Revenue	41,748,010,076	41,655,071,305	34,437,097,870	29,419,832,926	27,415,848,994	28,592,872,343
R&D Expense	1,771,480,000	1,343,917,000	1,201,014,000	1,326,185,000	1,185,159,000	1,193,921,000
Operating Income	2,785,989,000	2,809,980,000	1,782,537,000	2,047,482,000	1,030,364,000	1,453,442,000
Operating Margin %	.07%	.07%	.05%	.07%	.04%	.05%
SGA Expense	3,653,110,000	3,793,093,000	3,388,478,000	2,972,181,000	2,529,389,000	2,792,978,000
Net Income	1,606,463,000	1,361,545,000	1,624,821,000	1,308,661,000	608,538,800	742,158,600
Operating Cash Flow	4,941,326,000	4,471,414,000	3,504,678,000	3,113,832,000	3,576,234,000	3,376,900,000
Capital Expenditure	4,697,348,000	4,085,262,000	3,349,571,000	2,432,903,000	1,935,975,000	2,188,716,000
EBITDA	4,945,290,000	4,112,800,000	3,961,448,000	3,648,729,000	2,646,319,000	3,145,855,000
Return on Assets %	.04%	.04%	.05%	.04%	.02%	.03%
Return on Equity %	.12%	.11%	.15%	.16%	.10%	.13%
Debt to Equity	.22%	.22%	.27%	.29%	0.533	0.579

CONTACT INFORMATION:

Phone: 46-31-59-00-00   Fax:
Toll-Free:
Address: VAK Bldg., Assar Gabrielssons vag, Goteborg, 418 78 Sweden

STOCK TICKER/OTHER:

Stock Ticker: VLVOF   Exchange: PINX
Employees: 43,000   Fiscal Year Ends: 12/31
Parent Company: Zhejiang Geely Holding Group Co Ltd

SALARIES/BONUSES:

Top Exec. Salary: $ Bonus: $
Second Exec. Salary: $ Bonus: $

OTHER THOUGHTS:

Estimated Female Officers or Directors: 3
Hot Spot for Advancement for Women/Minorities: Y

VSE Corporation

NAIC Code: 541330

TYPES OF BUSINESS:

Engineering Consulting Services
Engineering Services
Logistics Services
Technology Research & Development
Equipment Maintenance, Refurbishment & Implementation
Information Technology Support

BRANDS/DIVISIONS/AFFILIATES:

GROWTH PLANS/SPECIAL FEATURES:

VSE Corp is a diversified aftermarket products and services company providing repair services, parts distribution, logistics, supply chain management, and consulting services for land, sea, and air transportation assets to commercial and government markets. Its operations include supply chain management solutions, parts supply and distribution, and maintenance, repair, and overhaul (MRO) services for vehicle fleet, aviation, maritime and other customers. Its reportable segments are; Aviation and Fleet. The majority of the revenue for the company is generated from the Aviation segment which is a provider of aftermarket parts distribution and MRO services for components and engine accessories supporting commercial, business, and general aviation operators.

CONTACTS: *Note: Officers with more than one job title may be intentionally listed here more than once.*

John Cuomo, CEO
Adam Cohn, CFO
Ralph Eberhart, Chairman of the Board
Tarang Sharma, Chief Accounting Officer
Farinaz Tehrani, Chief Legal Officer
Garry Snow, Other Executive Officer
Benjamin Thomas, President, Divisional

FINANCIAL DATA: *Note: Data for latest year may not have been available at press time.*

In U.S. $	2024	2023	2022	2021	2020	2019
Revenue	1,080,131,968	860,488,000	669,448,000	481,384,000	661,659,008	752,627,008
R&D Expense						
Operating Income	93,624,000	87,996,000	53,604,000	-2,705,000	54,763,000	60,257,000
Operating Margin %	.09%	.10%	.08%	-.01%	.08%	.08%
SGA Expense	14,576,000	7,619,000	3,635,000	3,454,000	3,120,000	4,192,000
Net Income	15,324,000	39,134,000	28,059,000	7,966,000	-5,171,000	37,024,000
Operating Cash Flow	-31,037,000	-21,829,000	8,051,000	-17,602,000	35,761,000	17,994,000
Capital Expenditure	20,704,000	18,666,000	11,212,000	10,520,000	4,427,000	9,630,000
EBITDA	110,181,000	111,412,000	78,206,000	21,884,000	38,058,000	87,184,000
Return on Assets %	.01%	.03%	.03%	.01%	-.01%	.05%
Return on Equity %	.02%	.07%	.06%	.02%	-.01%	.11%
Debt to Equity	.45%	.70%	.66%	.71%	0.712	0.764

CONTACT INFORMATION:

Phone: 703 960-4600   Fax: 703 960-2688
Toll-Free:
Address: 6348 Walker Ln., Alexandria, VA 22310 United States

STOCK TICKER/OTHER:

Stock Ticker: VSEC   Exchange: NAS
Employees: 1,200   Fiscal Year Ends: 12/31
Parent Company:

SALARIES/BONUSES:

Top Exec. Salary: $900,000   Bonus: $
Second Exec. Salary: Bonus: $
$450,000

OTHER THOUGHTS:

Estimated Female Officers or Directors: 6
Hot Spot for Advancement for Women/Minorities: Y

VTech Holdings Limited

NAIC Code: 334210

TYPES OF BUSINESS:

Cordless Telephone Sets
Electronic Learning Products
Contract Manufacturing Services
Data Networking Products
Cordless Phones
Telecommunications

BRANDS/DIVISIONS/AFFILIATES:

Vtech
Leap Frog

GROWTH PLANS/SPECIAL FEATURES:

VTech Holdings Ltd is engaged in designing, manufacturing, and distribution of consumer electronic products. It also provides contract manufacturing services. Its diverse collection of products includes Telephone Products, Business Phones, Electronic Learning Toys, Baby Monitors, and Hospitality Products. It offers turnkey services to customers in several product categories. The company operates through four geographical segments, North America including the United States and Canada, Europe, Asia Pacific, and Others, which covers sales of electronic products to the rest of the world. It generates a majority of its revenue from North America and Europe.

CONTACTS: Note: Officers with more than one job title may be intentionally listed here more than once.

Hon Kwong Leung, CEO, Divisional
Chi Yun Wong, CEO
King Fai Pang, Director

FINANCIAL DATA: Note: Data for latest year may not have been available at press time.

In U.S. $	2024	2023	2022	2021	2020	2019
Revenue	2,145,699,968	2,241,700,096	2,370,500,096	2,372,300,032	2,165,499,904	2,161,900,032
R&D Expense	81,700,000	83,300,000	84,300,000	86,400,000	81,700,000	77,200,000
Operating Income	196,900,000	180,800,000	204,300,000	262,000,000	213,800,000	187,300,000
Operating Margin %	.09%	.08%	.09%	.11%	.10%	.09%
SGA Expense	356,300,000	371,600,000	380,500,000	378,200,000	368,100,000	371,900,000
Net Income	166,600,000	149,200,000	172,700,000	230,900,000	190,700,000	171,300,000
Operating Cash Flow	355,200,000	238,800,000	139,600,000	280,300,000	237,000,000	249,300,000
Capital Expenditure	32,400,000	27,900,000	35,900,000	48,000,000	34,600,000	37,300,000
EBITDA	251,600,000	237,000,000	268,800,000	325,900,000	276,900,000	231,200,000
Return on Assets %	.13%	.11%	.12%	.17%	.17%	.16%
Return on Equity %	.26%	.23%	.24%	.35%	.32%	.27%
Debt to Equity	.22%	.26%	.26%	.26%	0.245	

CONTACT INFORMATION:

Phone: 852 26801000   Fax: 852 26801300
Toll-Free:
Address: 57 Ting Kok Rd., Tai Ping Ctr., Block 1, 23/Fl, Hong Kong, 999077 Hong Kong

STOCK TICKER/OTHER:

Stock Ticker: VTKLF
Employees: 20,000
Parent Company:

Exchange: PINX
Fiscal Year Ends: 03/31

SALARIES/BONUSES:

Top Exec. Salary: $ Bonus: $
Second Exec. Salary: $ Bonus: $

OTHER THOUGHTS:

Estimated Female Officers or Directors:
Hot Spot for Advancement for Women/Minorities:

Waldemar S Nelson and Company Inc

www.wsnelson.com

NAIC Code: 541330

TYPES OF BUSINESS:

Engineering Consulting Services
Engineering
Management
Architecture

BRANDS/DIVISIONS/AFFILIATES:

CONTACTS: *Note: Officers with more than one job title may be intentionally listed here more than once.*

Charles W. Nelson, Chmn.

GROWTH PLANS/SPECIAL FEATURES:

Waldemar S. Nelson and Company, Inc. (Nelson) provides engineering and architectural design, project management, procurement, environmental compliance and remediation consulting. The firm has offices in New Orleans, Louisiana and Houston, Texas, and has served multiple clients in a broad range of projects across the U.S., and at selective international sites since 1945. Nelson's services also comprise chemical and process engineering, civil and structural engineering, control systems engineering, electrical engineering, environmental engineering, LEED (leadership in energy and environmental design) consulting, energy audits, mechanical engineering, project and construction management and more. Industries the company has served include electrical utilities, marine, material handling, mining, oil and gas, petrochemical, public works and renewable energy, among others. Nelson is experienced in all aspects of design and construction management for industrial, manufacturing and power generation facilities such as offshore production platforms, floating production systems, refineries, petrochemical plants, gas processing plants, pipeline facilities, pumping stations, docks and marine terminals, water treating plants, pollution control and abatement systems, machine design for locks and bridges, drainage pump systems, steel manufacturing facilities and shipyard facilities.

FINANCIAL DATA: *Note: Data for latest year may not have been available at press time.*

In U.S. $	2024	2023	2022	2021	2020	2019
Revenue						
R&D Expense						
Operating Income						
Operating Margin %						
SGA Expense						
Net Income						
Operating Cash Flow						
Capital Expenditure						
EBITDA						
Return on Assets %						
Return on Equity %						
Debt to Equity						

CONTACT INFORMATION:

Phone: 504-523-5281   Fax: 504-523-4587
Toll-Free:
Address: 1200 St. Charles Ave., New Orleans, LA 70130 United States

STOCK TICKER/OTHER:

Stock Ticker: Private   Exchange:
Employees: 300   Fiscal Year Ends:
Parent Company:

SALARIES/BONUSES:

Top Exec. Salary: $ Bonus: $
Second Exec. Salary: $ Bonus: $

OTHER THOUGHTS:

Estimated Female Officers or Directors:
Hot Spot for Advancement for Women/Minorities:

Wanxiang Group Corporation

www.wanxiang.com.cn

NAIC Code: 336300

TYPES OF BUSINESS:

Automotive Parts Manufacturer
Agricultural Engineering
Aquaculture
Restaurant & Hotel Management
Road & Bridge Construction
Power Plant Construction
Leasing & Financial Services
Trade Consulting

BRANDS/DIVISIONS/AFFILIATES:

Wanxiang Innovative Energy Fusion City
Xanxiang Sannong
Zhejiang Ocean Family Co Ltd
Chengde Lolo Co Ltd
A123 Systems LLC
Beijing Doneed Seeds Industry Co Ltd

CONTACTS: Note: Officers with more than one job title may be intentionally listed here more than once.

Weiding Lu, CEO
Gary E. Wetzel, COO
Pin Ni, Pres., Wanxiang America Corp.

GROWTH PLANS/SPECIAL FEATURES:

Wanxiang Group Corporation is one of China's largest auto parts manufacturers, with strategically situated factories supplying automotive components throughout the world. Within China, the group's manufacturing facilities hold more than a 56% market share in the relevant industry. Internationally, the firm's overseas subsidiaries and factories are located in the U.S., Great Britain, Germany and other countries. Wanxiang Group's automotive parts and accessories include the development, production and selling of drive shafts, brakes, shock absorbers, rolling elements and related components. The company has/has had supporting partnerships with mainstream automotive manufacturers such as General Motors, Volkswagen, Ford and Chrysler. Wanxiang Group invested billions in new energy, innovation and transformation technologies and solutions for the purpose of becoming a clean energy company. Subsidiary Wanxiang Innovative Energy Fusion City is a hub focused on manufacturing new energy automobile components and batteries, as well as battery/electric passenger buses and vehicles. Other subsidiaries and investments include: Wanxiang Sannong, an agricultural industry group that provides services to agriculture, farmer and rural areas; Zhejiang Ocean Family Co. Ltd., which owns and operates ocean fisheries, and is engaged in seafood processing as well as the import/export of seafood products; Chengde Lolo Co Ltd., a provider of healthy, plant-based food and beverages; A123 Systems LLC, a lithium-ion powered battery researcher and manufacturer; and Beijing Doneed Seeds Industry Co. Ltd., a high-tech comprehensive seed enterprise, focusing on the research, production, management and service of seeds for the agricultural industry.

FINANCIAL DATA: Note: Data for latest year may not have been available at press time.

In U.S. $	2024	2023	2022	2021	2020	2019
Revenue	26,250,000,000	25,000,000,000	20,028,970,400	18,207,000,000	17,850,000,000	21,000,000,000
R&D Expense						
Operating Income						
Operating Margin %						
SGA Expense						
Net Income						
Operating Cash Flow						
Capital Expenditure						
EBITDA						
Return on Assets %						
Return on Equity %						
Debt to Equity						

CONTACT INFORMATION:

Phone: 86-571-8283-2999　　　Fax: 86-571-8283-3999
Toll-Free:
Address: Wang Xiang Rd., Xiao Shan Dist., Hangzhou, Zhejiang 311215 China

STOCK TICKER/OTHER:

Stock Ticker: Private
Employees: 20,000
Parent Company:

Exchange:
Fiscal Year Ends: 12/31

SALARIES/BONUSES:

Top Exec. Salary: $　　　　Bonus: $
Second Exec. Salary: $　　　Bonus: $

OTHER THOUGHTS:

Estimated Female Officers or Directors:
Hot Spot for Advancement for Women/Minorities:

Waymo LLC

NAIC Code: 561599

TYPES OF BUSINESS:

Robo-Taxi Service
Autonomous Vehicle Technologies
Self-Driving Software
Proprietary Sensors
Proprietary Technology
Autonomous Ride-Hailing Services

BRANDS/DIVISIONS/AFFILIATES:

Alphabet Inc
Google
Waymo Driver
Waymo One
Waymo Via

CONTACTS: Note: Officers with more than one job title may be intentionally listed here more than once.

Tekedra Mawakana, Co-CEO
Dmitri Dolgov, Co-CEO
Elisa de Martel, CFO
Becky Bucich, Chief People Officer

GROWTH PLANS/SPECIAL FEATURES:

Waymo, LLC is an autonomous car development company and subsidiary of Alphabet, Inc. Waymo was enabled as a separate entity to commercialize and distribute the self-driving vehicle technology that Google developed. Waymo is focused on competing in the autonomous robo-taxi, ride-on-demand market. Waymo offers both software and hardware for self-driving vehicles called the World's Most Experienced Driver (Waymo Driver), which is a combination of light detection and ranging (lidar) technology, cameras and radar. The Waymo One driverless system's vehicles have sensors and software designed to detect pedestrians, cyclists, vehicles, road work and more from up to three football fields away in all 360 degrees. The sensors and software detect and predict the behavior of all road users within the range. The sensors can even observe when a cyclist has extended his/her arm as a traffic signal. This signals the Waymo vehicle to slow down and make room for the cyclist to pass safely. Waymo Driver is a driverless system for large trucks which is under testing in various states. The Waymo app enables users to locate and hire a self-driving car. The vehicle comes to the confirmed rider, who is then able to follow the route through the app throughout the ride until the destination is reached. Waymo offers its autonomous ride-hailing service in San Francisco, Los Angeles and Phoenix.

FINANCIAL DATA: Note: Data for latest year may not have been available at press time.

In U.S. $	2024	2023	2022	2021	2020	2019
Revenue						
R&D Expense						
Operating Income						
Operating Margin %						
SGA Expense						
Net Income						
Operating Cash Flow						
Capital Expenditure						
EBITDA						
Return on Assets %						
Return on Equity %						
Debt to Equity						

CONTACT INFORMATION:

Phone: 650-253-0000   Fax:
Toll-Free:
Address: 1600 Amphitheatre Pkwy., Mountain View, CA 94043 United States

STOCK TICKER/OTHER:

Stock Ticker: Subsidiary   Exchange:
Employees: 1,500   Fiscal Year Ends: 12/31
Parent Company: Alphabet Inc

SALARIES/BONUSES:

Top Exec. Salary: $ Bonus: $
Second Exec. Salary: $ Bonus: $

OTHER THOUGHTS:

Estimated Female Officers or Directors:
Hot Spot for Advancement for Women/Minorities:

Webuild SpA

NAIC Code: 237000

www.webuildgroup.com

TYPES OF BUSINESS:

Heavy Construction
Civil Engineering
Construction
Railways
Roads
Bridges
Tunnels
Hydroelectric Plants

BRANDS/DIVISIONS/AFFILIATES:

Salini Impregilo SpA
Astaldi SpA

GROWTH PLANS/SPECIAL FEATURES:

WeBuild SpA is a construction company specializing in building large works and complex infrastructure for sustainable mobility, hydroelectric energy, water, green buildings, and the tunneling sectors.

CONTACTS: Note: Officers with more than one job title may be intentionally listed here more than once.

Pietro Salini, CEO
Donato Iacovone, Chairman of the Board
Nicola Greco, Deputy Chairman

FINANCIAL DATA: Note: Data for latest year may not have been available at press time.

In U.S. $	2024	2023	2022	2021	2020	2019
Revenue	12,516,721,630	10,544,969,528	8,690,131,841	6,785,268,094	4,820,847,878	5,415,021,845
R&D Expense						
Operating Income	-166,256,500	-129,250,800	-104,566,400	-472,289,400	-198,652,700	42,454,030
Operating Margin %	- .01%	- .01%	- .01%	- .07%	- .04%	.01%
SGA Expense	1,726,524,000	1,417,442,000	1,167,619,000	1,002,774,000	673,328,000	711,996,600
Net Income	220,745,700	140,752,600	11,229,290	-346,139,600	157,088,500	-25,116,910
Operating Cash Flow	1,266,757,000	2,148,632,000	30,080,590	1,377,721,000	222,507,400	98,519,860
Capital Expenditure	937,922,800	503,605,000	315,693,500	244,141,900	208,589,100	112,222,500
EBITDA	1,177,369,000	932,690,100	712,710,500	364,817,200	523,864,900	374,543,700
Return on Assets %	.01%	.01%	.00%	- .03%	.01%	.00%
Return on Equity %	.12%	.08%	.01%	- .20%	.10%	- .02%
Debt to Equity	1.25%	1.20%	1.41%	1.20%	1.517	1.392

CONTACT INFORMATION:

Phone: 39 244422111   Fax: 39 244422293
Toll-Free:
Address: Via Adige, 19, Milan, 20135 Italy

STOCK TICKER/OTHER:

Stock Ticker: IMPJY   Exchange: PINX
Employees: 79,499   Fiscal Year Ends: 12/31
Parent Company: Salini Costruttori SpA

SALARIES/BONUSES:

Top Exec. Salary: $ Bonus: $
Second Exec. Salary: $ Bonus: $

OTHER THOUGHTS:

Estimated Female Officers or Directors: 1
Hot Spot for Advancement for Women/Minorities:

Sales, profits and employees may be estimates. Financial information, benefits and other data can change quickly and may vary from those stated here.

Western Digital Corporation

NAIC Code: 334112

www.wdc.com

TYPES OF BUSINESS:

Data Storage Hardware
Data Storage
Cloud Storage

GROWTH PLANS/SPECIAL FEATURES:

Western Digital is a leading, vertically integrated supplier of hard disk drives. The HDD market is a practical duopoly with, Western Digital and Seagate being the two largest players. Western Digital designs and manufacturers its HDDs, with much of the manufacturing and workforce located in Asia. The primary consumers of HDDs are data centers.

BRANDS/DIVISIONS/AFFILIATES:

Western Digital Technologies Inc
Western Digital
WD
SanDisk
G-Technology

CONTACTS: Note: Officers with more than one job title may be intentionally listed here more than once.

David Goeckeler, CEO
Wissam Jabre, CFO
Matthew Massengill, Chairman of the Board
Cynthia Tregillis, Chief Legal Officer

FINANCIAL DATA: Note: Data for latest year may not have been available at press time.

In U.S. $	2024	2023	2022	2021	2020	2019
Revenue	13,002,999,808	12,318,000,128	18,793,000,960	16,922,000,384	16,736,000,000	16,568,999,936
R&D Expense	1,907,000,000	2,009,000,000	2,323,000,000	2,243,000,000	2,261,000,000	2,182,000,000
Operating Income	210,000,000	-1,092,000,000	2,434,000,000	1,173,000,000	367,000,000	253,000,000
Operating Margin %	.02%	- .09%	.13%	.07%	.02%	.02%
SGA Expense	828,000,000	970,000,000	1,117,000,000	1,105,000,000	1,153,000,000	1,317,000,000
Net Income	-798,000,000	-1,684,000,000	1,546,000,000	821,000,000	-250,000,000	-754,000,000
Operating Cash Flow	-294,000,000	-408,000,000	1,880,000,000	1,898,000,000	824,000,000	1,547,000,000
Capital Expenditure	487,000,000	821,000,000	1,122,000,000	1,146,000,000	647,000,000	876,000,000
EBITDA	324,000,000	-410,000,000	3,404,000,000	2,465,000,000	1,933,000,000	1,994,000,000
Return on Assets %	- .03%	- .07%	.06%	.03%	- .01%	- .03%
Return on Equity %	- .08%	- .15%	.13%	.08%	- .03%	- .07%
Debt to Equity	.53%	.53%	.57%	.79%	0.973	1.028

CONTACT INFORMATION:

Phone: 408-717-6000   Fax:
Toll-Free:
Address: 5601 Great Oaks Pkwy., San Jose, CA 95119 United States

STOCK TICKER/OTHER:

Stock Ticker: WDC
Employees: 51,000
Parent Company:

Exchange: NAS
Fiscal Year Ends: 06/30

SALARIES/BONUSES:

Top Exec. Salary: $1,245,192   Bonus: $
Second Exec. Salary: $707,269   Bonus: $

OTHER THOUGHTS:

Estimated Female Officers or Directors: 1
Hot Spot for Advancement for Women/Minorities:

Westinghouse Electric Company LLC   www.westinghousenuclear.com

NAIC Code: 332410

TYPES OF BUSINESS:

Nuclear Power Plant Equipment
Nuclear Power Plant Repair Services
Nuclear Fuel
Nuclear Power Plant Design & Engineering
Nuclear Reactor Development
Nuclear Component and Manufacturing
Boilers
Plant Decommissioning and Restoration

BRANDS/DIVISIONS/AFFILIATES:

Brookfield Corporation

CONTACTS: Note: Officers with more than one job title may be intentionally listed here more than once.

Dan Sumner, CEO
Ron Timperio, COO
Shravan Chopra, CFO
Jacques Besnainou, CCO
Ann Naqi, Chief Human Resources Officer
Lou Martinez Sancho, CTO
Yves Brachet, Pres., EMEA
Jack Allen, Pres., Asia

GROWTH PLANS/SPECIAL FEATURES:

Westinghouse Electric Company, LLC provides plant design, services, fuel, technology and equipment to utility, government and industrial clients in the international commercial nuclear electric power market. The company operates through four divisions, including energy systems, nuclear fuel, operating plants and environmental. The energy systems division plans, engineers and constructs nuclear reactors, instrumentation and control systems, automation systems, and large components complete with manufacturing and testing capabilities for reactor vessel internals, control rod drive mechanisms, reactor coolant pumps and related products. This division's large components include cranes and fuel-handling equipment. The nuclear fuel division supplies nuclear fuel products and services, including next-generation fuel products, pressurized water reactors, boiling water reactors and fuel fabrication. The operating plants division designs, builds and operates the company's nuclear power plants; and provides complete turn-key management services to any nuclear power plant in the world, from meeting operating/regulatory/manufacturing mandates to maximizing margins, increasing power output and extending plant life. The environmental division decommissions nuclear plant sites and restores the landscapes of those sites either by reviving, renewing or transforming them for other purposes. Services also include planning, licensing, spent fuel discharge, decontamination, dismantling, waste management, remediation and more. In addition, Westinghouse engages in power plant innovation across spectrums such as technology, microreactors, data analytics and fuel materials development. The company has operations across the Americas, Asia and EMEA (Europe, Middle East, Africa), and is owned by Brookfield Corporation.

FINANCIAL DATA: Note: Data for latest year may not have been available at press time.

In U.S. $	2024	2023	2022	2021	2020	2019
Revenue	4,695,600,000	4,472,000,000	4,300,000,000	4,334,575,000	3,995,000,000	4,250,000,000
R&D Expense						
Operating Income						
Operating Margin %						
SGA Expense						
Net Income						
Operating Cash Flow						
Capital Expenditure						
EBITDA						
Return on Assets %						
Return on Equity %						
Debt to Equity						

CONTACT INFORMATION:

Phone: 412-374-4111   Fax: 412-374-3272
Toll-Free: 888-943-8442
Address: 1000 Westinghouse Dr., Ste. 572A, Cranberry Township, PA 16066 United States

STOCK TICKER/OTHER:

Stock Ticker: Subsidiary   Exchange:
Employees: 9,000   Fiscal Year Ends: 03/31
Parent Company: Brookfield Corporation

SALARIES/BONUSES:

Top Exec. Salary: $ Bonus: $
Second Exec. Salary: $ Bonus: $

OTHER THOUGHTS:

Estimated Female Officers or Directors:
Hot Spot for Advancement for Women/Minorities:

Whirlpool Corporation

www.whirlpoolcorp.com

NAIC Code: 335220

TYPES OF BUSINESS:

Home Appliance Manufacturer
Laundry Appliances
Refrigerators & Freezers
Air Conditioning Equipment
Kitchen Appliances

BRANDS/DIVISIONS/AFFILIATES:

Whirlpool
Maytag
KitchenAid
Brastemp
Hotpoint
Diqua
Gladiator
JennAir

CONTACTS: Note: Officers with more than one job title may be intentionally listed here more than once.

Marc Bitzer, CEO
Christopher Conley, CFO, Divisional
James Peters, CFO
Roxanne Warner, Controller
Ludovic Beaufils, Executive VP
Carey Martin, Executive VP
Alessandro Perucchetti, Executive VP
Gilles Morel, Executive VP
Juan Puente, Executive VP

GROWTH PLANS/SPECIAL FEATURES:

Whirlpool Corp is a manufacturer and marketer of home appliances and related products. Its reportable segments consist of five operating segments, which consist of Domestic Appliances (MDA) North America; MDA Europe, MDA Latin America; MDA Asia; and Small Domestic Appliances (SDA). Product categories include refrigeration, laundry, cooking, and dishwashing. The company has also a portfolio of small domestic appliances, including the KitchenAid stand mixer. The company's international brands include Whirlpool, KitchenAid, Maytag, Consul, and Brastemp, among others.

Whirlpool offers its employees health and financial coverage, time off, discounts and other perks.

FINANCIAL DATA: Note: Data for latest year may not have been available at press time.

In U.S. $	2024	2023	2022	2021	2020	2019
Revenue	16,606,999,552	19,455,000,576	19,723,999,232	21,984,999,424	19,456,000,000	20,419,000,320
R&D Expense						
Operating Income	866,000,000	1,137,000,000	1,218,000,000	2,281,000,000	1,903,000,000	1,300,000,000
Operating Margin %	.05%	.06%	.06%	.10%	.10%	.06%
SGA Expense	1,684,000,000	1,993,000,000	1,820,000,000	2,081,000,000	1,877,000,000	2,142,000,000
Net Income	-323,000,000	481,000,000	-1,519,000,000	1,783,000,000	1,075,000,000	1,168,000,000
Operating Cash Flow	835,000,000	915,000,000	1,390,000,000	2,176,000,000	1,500,000,000	1,230,000,000
Capital Expenditure	451,000,000	549,000,000	570,000,000	525,000,000	410,000,000	532,000,000
EBITDA	503,000,000	1,376,000,000	-562,000,000	3,001,000,000	2,204,000,000	2,304,000,000
Return on Assets %	-.02%	.03%	-.08%	.09%	.05%	.06%
Return on Equity %	-.13%	.20%	-.42%	.41%	.30%	.43%
Debt to Equity	2.04%	2.97%	3.40%	1.18%	1.518	1.539

CONTACT INFORMATION:

Phone: 269 923-5000   Fax: 269 923-3978
Toll-Free:
Address: 2000 N. M-63, Benton Harbor, MI 49022-2692 United States

STOCK TICKER/OTHER:

Stock Ticker: WHR   Exchange: NYS
Employees: 59,000   Fiscal Year Ends: 12/31
Parent Company:

SALARIES/BONUSES:

Top Exec. Salary: $805,015   Bonus: $3,240,000
Second Exec. Salary: $1,348,333   Bonus: $

OTHER THOUGHTS:

Estimated Female Officers or Directors: 4
Hot Spot for Advancement for Women/Minorities: Y

Wipro Limited

NAIC Code: 541512

TYPES OF BUSINESS:

IT Consulting
Computer Hardware & Software Design
Hydraulic Equipment
Medical Electronics
Lighting Equipment
Soaps & Toiletries

BRANDS/DIVISIONS/AFFILIATES:

Cloud Studios
METRO-NOM GMBH
METRO Systems Romania SRL

GROWTH PLANS/SPECIAL FEATURES:

Wipro is a leading global IT services provider, with about 234,000 employees. Based in Bengaluru, this India IT services firm leverages its offshore outsourcing model to derive a significant portion of its revenue from North America. The company offers traditional IT services offerings: consulting, managed services, and cloud infrastructure services as well as business process outsourcing as a service.

CONTACTS: *Note: Officers with more than one job title may be intentionally listed here more than once.*

Srinivas Pallia, CEO
Aparna Iyer, CFO
Rishad Premji, Chairman of the Board
Azim Premji, Director

FINANCIAL DATA: *Note: Data for latest year may not have been available at press time.*

In U.S. $	2024	2023	2022	2021	2020	2019
Revenue	10,496,365,724	10,581,414,401	9,249,002,491	7,243,473,946	7,135,914,118	
R&D Expense						
Operating Income	1,563,808,000	1,580,226,000	1,589,546,000	1,403,931,000	1,199,325,000	
Operating Margin %	.15%	.15%	.17%	.19%	.17%	
SGA Expense	1,400,388,000	1,453,489,000	1,184,778,000	889,732,400	850,488,100	
Net Income	1,291,601,000	1,327,243,000	1,428,874,000	1,262,296,000	1,136,845,000	
Operating Cash Flow	2,060,630,000	1,527,218,000	1,295,635,000	1,725,416,000	1,176,896,000	
Capital Expenditure	122,901,600	173,465,400	235,664,600	228,929,000	274,768,600	
EBITDA	2,216,450,000	2,208,755,000	2,192,711,000	1,999,179,000	1,736,642,000	
Return on Assets %	.09%	.10%	.13%	.13%	.12%	
Return on Equity %	.14%	.16%	.20%	.19%	.17%	
Debt to Equity	.10%	.10%	.11%	.04%	0.031	

CONTACT INFORMATION:

Phone: 91 8028440055   Fax: 91 8028440256
Toll-Free:
Address: Doddakannelli, Sarjapur Rd., Bengaluru, Karnataka 560035 India

STOCK TICKER/OTHER:

Stock Ticker: WIT
Employees: 234,000
Parent Company:

Exchange: NYS
Fiscal Year Ends: 03/31

SALARIES/BONUSES:

Top Exec. Salary: $1,705,151   Bonus: $
Second Exec. Salary: $707,521   Bonus: $

OTHER THOUGHTS:

Estimated Female Officers or Directors: 3
Hot Spot for Advancement for Women/Minorities: Y

WL Meinhardt Group Pty Ltd

www.meinhardtgroup.com

NAIC Code: 541330

TYPES OF BUSINESS:

Engineering Consulting Services
Engineering
Urban Planning and Development
Infrastructure
Design
Environment and Sustainability
Project Management
Construction Management

BRANDS/DIVISIONS/AFFILIATES:

Meinhardt Group International Holdings Limited
MGi Capital

CONTACTS: Note: Officers with more than one job title may be intentionally listed here more than once.

Omar Shahzad, CEO
Eugene Seah, COO
Geok Hwee Tan, Dir.-Finance
Shahzad Nasim, Chmn.

GROWTH PLANS/SPECIAL FEATURES:

WL Meinhardt Group Pty. Ltd. (Meinhardt) is an Asian engineering company, with 55 offices across Asia, Australasia, Europe, Africa, the Middle East and the U.K. Meinhardt's services are grouped into four categories: plan, including urban planning, infrastructure planning, business planning and technical advisory; design, including civil, structural, mechanical, electrical and plumbing design; specialist, including facade, fire performance, environmentally sustainable, lighting and value engineering; and management, including engineering/procurement/construction management (EPCM), construction and project management, asset management, design management and lead consultancy. The company serves a myriad of sectors across the buildings, properties, transportation, utilities infrastructure, industrial manufacturing, information technology, research and communications industries. Subsidiary, MGi Capital, offers finance solutions as well as engineering consulting, leveraging the network and technical expertise of the Meinhardt group. Meinhardt operates as a subsidiary of Meinhardt Group International Holdings Limited.

FINANCIAL DATA: Note: Data for latest year may not have been available at press time.

In U.S. $	2024	2023	2022	2021	2020	2019
Revenue						
R&D Expense						
Operating Income						
Operating Margin %						
SGA Expense						
Net Income						
Operating Cash Flow						
Capital Expenditure						
EBITDA						
Return on Assets %						
Return on Equity %						
Debt to Equity						

CONTACT INFORMATION:

Phone: 65 6273-5255   Fax:
Toll-Free:
Address: 168 Jalan Bukit Merah, #09-01, Connection One, Singapore, 150168 Singapore

STOCK TICKER/OTHER:

Stock Ticker: Private   Exchange:
Employees: 5,000   Fiscal Year Ends:
Parent Company: Meinhardt Group International Holdings Limited

SALARIES/BONUSES:

Top Exec. Salary: $ Bonus: $
Second Exec. Salary: $ Bonus: $

OTHER THOUGHTS:

Estimated Female Officers or Directors:
Hot Spot for Advancement for Women/Minorities:

Wolfram Research Inc

www.wolfram.com

NAIC Code: 511210P

TYPES OF BUSINESS:

Mathematical Software
Software Development
Education Programs
Online Education
Engineering Education
Finance and Statistics Education
Web and App Development
Technology Development

BRANDS/DIVISIONS/AFFILIATES:

Wolfram-One
Mathematica
Wolfram-Alpha
Wolfram Player
Wolfram Engine
Wolfram Script

CONTACTS: Note: Officers with more than one job title may be intentionally listed here more than once.

Stephen Wolfram, CEO

GROWTH PLANS/SPECIAL FEATURES:

Wolfram Research, Inc. is a computer, web and software company that specializes in the development of programs for the disciplines of engineering, finance/statistics, business analysis, education, sciences, software and current technology trends. Engineering and research and development solutions span aerospace, chemical engineering, control systems, defense, electrical engineering, image processing, industrial engineering, mechanical engineering and many other like-kind fields. Finance, statistics and business analysis solutions span actuarial sciences, bioinformatics, data science, econometrics, financial risk management, statistics and more. Education solutions serve elementary through university levels, with products including math, programming, multi-domain systems engineering, mobile apps, web coding, technologies, postdoctoral research, continued education, computing and a variety of STEM-based disciplines (science, technology, engineering and mathematics). Software and web solutions cover software development, authoring and publishing, interface development and web development. Solutions for sciences include astronomy, biology, chemistry, environmental sciences, geosciences, mathematics, medical imaging and social/behavioral sciences. Technology and related trend solutions include computational notebooks, high-performance and parallel computing, multi-paradigm data science, Internet of Things (IoT) and machine learning. Products are primarily marketed under the Wolfram brand name, and include, but are not limited to: Wolfram-One, Mathematica, Wolfram-Alpha, Wolfram Player, Wolfram Engine and Wolfram Script. Headquartered in the U.S., Wolfram Research has global locations in the U.K., Japan, Peru, Sweden, India and France.

FINANCIAL DATA: Note: Data for latest year may not have been available at press time.

In U.S. $	2024	2023	2022	2021	2020	2019
Revenue						
R&D Expense						
Operating Income						
Operating Margin %						
SGA Expense						
Net Income						
Operating Cash Flow						
Capital Expenditure						
EBITDA						
Return on Assets %						
Return on Equity %						
Debt to Equity						

CONTACT INFORMATION:

Phone: 217-398-0700   Fax: 217-398-0747
Toll-Free: 800-965-3726
Address: 100 Trade Center Dr., Champaign, IL 61820-7237 United States

STOCK TICKER/OTHER:

Stock Ticker: Private   Exchange:
Employees: Fiscal Year Ends: 12/31
Parent Company:

SALARIES/BONUSES:

Top Exec. Salary: $ Bonus: $
Second Exec. Salary: $ Bonus: $

OTHER THOUGHTS:

Estimated Female Officers or Directors:
Hot Spot for Advancement for Women/Minorities:

WSP Global Inc

NAIC Code: 541330

www.wsp.com

TYPES OF BUSINESS:

Engineering Services
Engineering
Infrastructure
Consulting
Asset Management
Project Management
FaÃ§ade
Rail Design

BRANDS/DIVISIONS/AFFILIATES:

Golder Associates inc
b+p baurealisation

GROWTH PLANS/SPECIAL FEATURES:

WSP Global Inc provides a professional services consulting firm offering technical expertise and advice to clients in the Transportation & Infrastructure, Earth & Environment, Property & Buildings, and Power & Energy sectors. The Corporation also offers specialized services in project and program delivery and advisory services. The firm operates through four reportable segments namely, Canada, Americas (United States and Latin America), EMEIA (Europe, Middle East, India and Africa), and APAC (Asia Pacific, comprising Australia, New Zealand and Asia).

CONTACTS: Note: Officers with more than one job title may be intentionally listed here more than once.

Ivy Kong, CEO, Geographical
Tom Smith, Other Corporate Officer
Anna-Lena Oberg-Hogsta, CEO, Geographical
Dean Mcgrail, CEO, Geographical
Peter Myers, CEO, Geographical
Gregory Kane, CEO, Geographical
Mark Naysmith, CEO, Geographical
Lewis Cornell, CEO, Geographical
Marie-Claude Dumas, CEO, Geographical
Alexandre LHeureux, CEO
Alain Michaud, CFO
Christopher Cole, Chairman of the Board
Sandy Vassiadis, Chief Compliance Officer
Julianna Fox, Chief Compliance Officer
Gino Poulin, Chief Information Officer
Philippe Fortier, Chief Legal Officer
Chadi Habib, Chief Technology Officer
Ian Blair, Managing Director, Geographical
Andre-Martin Bouchard, Other Corporate Officer
Eric Peissel, Other Corporate Officer
Marc Chabot, Other Executive Officer

FINANCIAL DATA: Note: Data for latest year may not have been available at press time.

In U.S. $	2024	2023	2022	2021	2020	2019
Revenue	11,767,085,962	10,508,187,638	8,685,420,793	7,481,694,295	6,407,962,648	6,489,627,742
R&D Expense						
Operating Income	1,050,222,000	870,732,900	660,018,900	548,875,400	403,886,700	402,067,100
Operating Margin %	.09%	.08%	.08%	.07%	.06%	.06%
SGA Expense	6,469,102,000	5,857,122,000	4,861,999,000	4,258,825,000	3,800,713,000	3,768,251,000
Net Income	495,960,400	400,320,200	314,287,800	344,712,100	200,888,000	208,530,400
Operating Cash Flow	1,005,823,000	717,883,400	593,056,300	771,599,000	818,909,600	592,692,400
Capital Expenditure	119,222,600	131,305,000	121,187,900	88,216,020	67,763,300	108,450,400
EBITDA	1,397,118,000	1,213,917,000	934,129,000	905,597,100	695,902,100	703,399,000
Return on Assets %	.04%	.04%	.03%	.05%	.03%	.03%
Return on Equity %	.09%	.09%	.08%	.11%	.07%	.09%
Debt to Equity	.58%	.60%	.61%	.48%	0.26	0.58

CONTACT INFORMATION:

Phone: 514 340-0046   Fax: 514 340-1337
Toll-Free:
Address: 1600, Rene-Leveserd Bouleverd West, Montreal, QC H3H 1P9 Canada

STOCK TICKER/OTHER:

Stock Ticker: WSP   Exchange: TSE
Employees: 66,500   Fiscal Year Ends: 12/31
Parent Company:

SALARIES/BONUSES:

Top Exec. Salary: $ Bonus: $
Second Exec. Salary: $ Bonus: $

OTHER THOUGHTS:

Estimated Female Officers or Directors: 2
Hot Spot for Advancement for Women/Minorities:

Sales, profits and employees may be estimates. Financial information, benefits and other data can change quickly and may vary from those stated here.

WSP New Zealand Ltd

www.wsp.com/en-NZ

NAIC Code: 541330

TYPES OF BUSINESS:

Engineering Consulting Services
Engineering
Consulting
Infrastructure Development
Construction
Rail
Bridge
Buildings and Facilities

BRANDS/DIVISIONS/AFFILIATES:

WSP Global Inc

CONTACTS: Note: Officers with more than one job title may be intentionally listed here more than once.

Ian Blair, Managing Dir.
Ben Holland, CFO
David Fowler, Gen. Mgr.-People

GROWTH PLANS/SPECIAL FEATURES:

WSP New Zealand Ltd. is the New Zealand operational arm of engineering professional services firm, WSP Global Inc. The company specializes in infrastructure consultancy and plans, designs, manages and engineers solutions for its clients. Solutions include bridge design, bus rapid transit systems, civic and cultural spaces, commercial and mixed-use offices, defense facilities, digital solutions, educational institutions, energy solutions, environment solutions, healthcare facilities, hospitality projects, research and testing laboratories, light rail transit solutions, maritime engineering, metro and light metro engineering, oil and gas solutions, rail and transit infrastructure, rail terminal and station engineering and design, rapid transit systems and more. WSP New Zealand's work spans seven key sectors: property and buildings, transport, water, earth and environmental, digital, energy and research. The firm's technical experts and advisors include engineers, technicians, scientists, planners, surveyors, environmental specialists, as well as other design, program and construction management professionals. In New Zealand, WSP New Zealand operates from a network of 40+ main offices throughout the country, as well as regional offices and laboratories.

FINANCIAL DATA: Note: Data for latest year may not have been available at press time.

In U.S. $	2024	2023	2022	2021	2020	2019
Revenue	294,000,000	280,000,000	265,415,000	250,391,436	223,563,780	225,822,000
R&D Expense						
Operating Income						
Operating Margin %						
SGA Expense						
Net Income						
Operating Cash Flow						
Capital Expenditure						
EBITDA						
Return on Assets %						
Return on Equity %						
Debt to Equity						

CONTACT INFORMATION:

Phone: 64-4-471-7243   Fax: 64-4-473-3017
Toll-Free:
Address: 100 Willis St., Majestic Ctr., Level 9, Wellington, 6011 New Zealand

STOCK TICKER/OTHER:

Stock Ticker: Subsidiary
Employees: 2,200
Parent Company: WSP Global Inc

Exchange:
Fiscal Year Ends: 12/31

SALARIES/BONUSES:

Top Exec. Salary: $ Bonus: $
Second Exec. Salary: $ Bonus: $

OTHER THOUGHTS:

Estimated Female Officers or Directors:
Hot Spot for Advancement for Women/Minorities:

X Development LLC

x.company

NAIC Code: 541710

TYPES OF BUSINESS:

Research and Development in the Physical, Engineering, and Life Sciences (except Biotechnology)
Invention
Technologies
Research and Development
Laboratory Testing
Software and Hardware
Robotics
Artificial Intelligence

BRANDS/DIVISIONS/AFFILIATES:

Alphabet Inc
Bellweather
Chorus
Taara
Intrinsic
Brain
Glass Enterprise Edition
Malta

CONTACTS: *Note: Officers with more than one job title may be intentionally listed here more than once.*

Astro Teller, CEO

GROWTH PLANS/SPECIAL FEATURES:

X Development, LLC, a subsidiary of Alphabet, Inc., considers itself a moonshot factory with a mission to invent and launch moonshot technologies to solve global problems. Founded in 2010, current projects in development include: Chorus, which is developing sensor technology, software and machine learning tools to improve the handling of physical goods; Bellwether, a prediction intelligence platform to identify natural disasters and other catastrophic events early and effectively; Tapestry, for electric grid virtualization; Tidal, working with ocean farmers to develop an underwater camera system and a set of machine perception tools to protect the ocean and preserve its ability to support life and feed humanity; and Taara, which uses light to transmit high-speed date between two points to significantly accelerate the deployment of the extensive, high throughput networks necessary to support the future of the web. Graduated projects include Intrinsic industrial robotics software, Brain artificial intelligence (AI) and machine learning for products, Waymo self-driving cars, Wing autonomous delivery drones, Verily technologies, Glass Enterprise Edition wearable smart-glass, Malta grid-scale renewable energy storage technology, Dandelion geothermal energy, and Chronicle cybersecurity. Discontinued projects include Everyday Robot Project that operates autonomously in unstructured human environments, H2E atmospheric water harvesting, Loon internet connectivity air balloons, Makani energy kites, and Foghorn carbon-emission-reducing seawater fuel.

FINANCIAL DATA: *Note: Data for latest year may not have been available at press time.*

In U.S. $	2024	2023	2022	2021	2020	2019
Revenue						
R&D Expense						
Operating Income						
Operating Margin %						
SGA Expense						
Net Income						
Operating Cash Flow						
Capital Expenditure						
EBITDA						
Return on Assets %						
Return on Equity %						
Debt to Equity						

CONTACT INFORMATION:

Phone: Fax:
Toll-Free:
Address: 1600 Amphitheatre Pkwy., Mountain View, CA 94043 United States

STOCK TICKER/OTHER:

Stock Ticker: Subsidiary
Employees: 250
Parent Company: Alphabet Inc

Exchange:
Fiscal Year Ends:

SALARIES/BONUSES:

Top Exec. Salary: $ Bonus: $
Second Exec. Salary: $ Bonus: $

OTHER THOUGHTS:

Estimated Female Officers or Directors:
Hot Spot for Advancement for Women/Minorities:

Xerox Corporation

NAIC Code: 334118

TYPES OF BUSINESS:
Document Processing Technologies
Copiers
Software
Multipurpose Office Machines
Desktop Printers
Equipment Financing

BRANDS/DIVISIONS/AFFILIATES:

GROWTH PLANS/SPECIAL FEATURES:

Xerox Holdings Corp is an original equipment manufacturing and software company. Xerox operates in one segment-- design, development, and sale of printing technology and related solutions--while deriving 60% of its revenue from the U.S. and 40% from international markets. The company is an OEM of multifunction printers, or MFPs (printers that can print, copy, and scan), focusing on large enterprise markets. Apart from equipment, the company provides post-sales services like managed print services help to bring smart servicing and efficiencies to how employers use their print/copy equipment. Xerox is attempting to enter new markets like digital print packaging solutions and printed electronics.

Xerox employees receive health care, life insurance, employee assistance programs, retirement plans and child care/elder care resources.

CONTACTS: *Note: Officers with more than one job title may be intentionally listed here more than once.*
Steven Bandrowczak, CEO
Xavier Heiss, CFO
A. Letier, Chairman of the Board
Mirlanda Gecaj, Chief Accounting Officer
Louie Pastor, Chief Administrative Officer
Flor Colon, Chief Legal Officer
Chris Fisher, Chief Strategy Officer
John Bruno, COO
Suzan Morno-Wade, Executive VP
Deena Piquion, Other Executive Officer
Jacques-Edouard Gueden, Other Executive Officer

FINANCIAL DATA: *Note: Data for latest year may not have been available at press time.*

In U.S. $	2024	2023	2022	2021	2020	2019
Revenue	6,221,000,192	6,886,000,128	7,106,999,808	7,038,000,128	7,022,000,128	9,066,000,384
R&D Expense	191,000,000	229,000,000	304,000,000	310,000,000	311,000,000	373,000,000
Operating Income	159,000,000	353,000,000	212,000,000	320,000,000	417,000,000	1,147,000,000
Operating Margin %	.03%	.05%	.03%	.05%	.06%	.13%
SGA Expense	1,537,000,000	1,696,000,000	1,760,000,000	1,718,000,000	1,851,000,000	2,085,000,000
Net Income	-1,321,000,000	1,000,000	-322,000,000	-455,000,000	192,000,000	1,353,000,000
Operating Cash Flow	511,000,000	686,000,000	159,000,000	629,000,000	548,000,000	1,333,000,000
Capital Expenditure	44,000,000	37,000,000	57,000,000	68,000,000	74,000,000	65,000,000
EBITDA	-823,000,000	291,000,000	36,000,000	-49,000,000	714,000,000	1,357,000,000
Return on Assets %	-.15%	.00%	-.03%	-.03%	.01%	.09%
Return on Equity %	-.74%	.00%	-.09%	-.09%	.03%	.25%
Debt to Equity	2.75%	1.12%	.91%	.86%	0.77	0.626

CONTACT INFORMATION:
Phone: 203 968-3000   Fax:
Toll-Free: 800-275-9376
Address: 201 Merritt 7, Norwalk, CT 06851-1056 United States

STOCK TICKER/OTHER:
Stock Ticker: XRX   Exchange: NAS
Employees: 20,100   Fiscal Year Ends: 12/31
Parent Company:

SALARIES/BONUSES:
Top Exec. Salary: $1,066,667   Bonus: $
Second Exec. Salary: Bonus: $
$816,667

OTHER THOUGHTS:
Estimated Female Officers or Directors: 11
Hot Spot for Advancement for Women/Minorities: Y

ZF Friedrichshafen AG (ZF)

www.zf.com

NAIC Code: 336350

TYPES OF BUSINESS:
Automotive Components
Automotive Technology
Industrial Technology
Next Generation Mobility Solutions
Active Safety Systems
Autonomous Driving Technology
Electric Mobility
Integrated Safety Systems

BRANDS/DIVISIONS/AFFILIATES:
Zeppelin Foundation

CONTACTS: Note: Officers with more than one job title may be intentionally listed here more than once.
Holger Klein, CEO
Michael Frick, CFO
Lea Corzilius, Chief Human Resources Officer
Stefan Sommer, Dir.-Corp. Dev
Stefan Sommer, Dir.-Corp. Comm.
Konstantin Sauer, Exec. VP-Finance & Controlling
Wilhelm Rehm, Exec. VP-Industrial Tech.
Gerhard Wagner, Exec. VP-Powertrain Tech. Div.
Reinhard Buhl, Exec. VP-Car Chassis Tech. Div.
Rolf Lutz, Exec. VP-Commercial Vehicles, South America
Peter Ottenbruch, Exec. VP-Tech., Asia Pacific

GROWTH PLANS/SPECIAL FEATURES:
ZF Friedrichshafen AG is a global technology company that supplies systems for passenger cars, commercial vehicles and industrial technology, enabling next-gen mobility. Zeppelin Foundation, which is administered by the city of Friedrichshafen, holds a majority interest in the firm. Products and technologies of ZF are grouped into categories including technology domains, electric mobility, vehicle motion control, automated driving, digitalization and software and integrated safety. The company's products and technologies are vast and address areas such as automotives, offering passenger cars, commercial vehicles, trucks, trailers, buses, fleet solutions and more; industrial technology, consisting of products for construction machinery, agricultural machinery, marine, wind power, test systems, rail vehicles and more; aftermarket; and connectivity and mobility. ZF's products, technologies and solutions enable vehicles to see, think and act, and offers solutions for vehicle manufacturers and emerging transport and mobility service providers. The firm's products contribute to reducing emissions and enhancing safe mobility. ZF operates at more than 162 production locations in more than 30 countries.

FINANCIAL DATA: Note: Data for latest year may not have been available at press time.

In U.S. $	2024	2023	2022	2021	2020	2019
Revenue	54,032,393,100	51,459,422,000	47,630,748,000	43,385,641,200	40,054,134,640	39,627,840,000
R&D Expense						
Operating Income						
Operating Margin %						
SGA Expense						
Net Income		139,060,000	2,216,243,480	886,669,200	-910,125,840	434,045,624
Operating Cash Flow						
Capital Expenditure						
EBITDA						
Return on Assets %						
Return on Equity %						
Debt to Equity						

CONTACT INFORMATION:
Phone: 49-7541-77-0   Fax: 49-7541-77-908000
Toll-Free:
Address: Lowentaler Strasse 20, Friedrichshafen, 88046 Germany

STOCK TICKER/OTHER:
Stock Ticker: Private   Exchange:
Employees: 164,869   Fiscal Year Ends: 12/31
Parent Company: Zeppelin Foundation

SALARIES/BONUSES:
Top Exec. Salary: $ Bonus: $
Second Exec. Salary: $ Bonus: $

OTHER THOUGHTS:
Estimated Female Officers or Directors:
Hot Spot for Advancement for Women/Minorities:

ZTE Corporation

NAIC Code: 334210

www.zte.com.cn

TYPES OF BUSINESS:

Telecommunications Equipment Manufacturing
Optical Networking Equipment
Intelligent & Next-Generation Network Systems
Mobile Phones

BRANDS/DIVISIONS/AFFILIATES:

GROWTH PLANS/SPECIAL FEATURES:

ZTE Corp is a provider of integrated telecommunications and IT solutions with a full range of end-to-end ICT products and solutions integrating design, development, production, sales, and services with a special focus on carriers' networks, government and corporate business, and consumer business. It operates in three segments Carriers' network, Consumer Business, and Government and Corporate Business. It generates a majority of its revenue from equipment supporting carriers' networks. It has a presence in the PRC, Asia, Africa, Europe, and the Americas. It generates the majority of its revenue from the PRC region.

CONTACTS: *Note: Officers with more than one job title may be intentionally listed here more than once.*

Zixue Li, Chairman of the Board
Ziyang Xu, Director
Junying Gu, Director

FINANCIAL DATA: *Note: Data for latest year may not have been available at press time.*

In U.S. $	2024	2023	2022	2021	2020	2019
Revenue	16,838,395,917	17,248,202,876	17,068,230,655	15,897,614,046	14,083,133,340	12,595,829,986
R&D Expense	3,335,994,000	3,510,586,000	2,998,778,000	2,610,327,000	2,054,087,000	1,741,869,000
Operating Income	1,434,737,000	1,523,948,000	1,466,010,000	1,184,662,000	775,802,100	1,291,576,000
Operating Margin %	.09%	.09%	.09%	.07%	.06%	.10%
SGA Expense	704,309,200	903,636,900	887,418,000	891,543,500	727,672,000	767,388,900
Net Income	1,169,509,000	1,294,578,000	1,121,687,000	945,755,700	593,582,100	763,007,500
Operating Cash Flow	1,593,604,000	2,416,216,000	1,051,918,000	2,182,702,000	1,420,472,000	1,033,712,000
Capital Expenditure	557,314,900	555,920,300	687,412,900	789,367,700	898,378,800	909,341,100
EBITDA	2,449,473,000	2,536,275,000	2,093,900,000	2,022,297,000	1,461,905,000	1,730,595,000
Return on Assets %	.04%	.05%	.05%	.04%	.03%	.04%
Return on Equity %	.12%	.15%	.15%	.14%	.11%	.16%
Debt to Equity	.63%	.64%	.61%	.59%	0.539	0.305

CONTACT INFORMATION:

Phone: 86 75526770000   Fax: 86 75526770286
Toll-Free:
Address: Hi-tech Rd. S., No. 55, Shenzhen, Guangdong 518057 China

STOCK TICKER/OTHER:

Stock Ticker: ZTCOF   Exchange: PINX
Employees: 72,093   Fiscal Year Ends: 12/31
Parent Company:

SALARIES/BONUSES:

Top Exec. Salary: $ Bonus: $
Second Exec. Salary: $ Bonus: $

OTHER THOUGHTS:

Estimated Female Officers or Directors:
Hot Spot for Advancement for Women/Minorities:

ADDITIONAL INDEXES

CONTENTS:

INDEX OF FIRMS NOTED AS HOT SPOTS FOR ADVANCEMENT FOR WOMEN & MINORITIES

3M Company
ABB Ltd
Abbott Laboratories
Accenture plc
Adobe Inc
Advanced Micro Devices Inc (AMD)
AECOM
Agilent Technologies Inc
Air Products and Chemicals Inc
Allergan plc
Alphabet Inc (Google)
Alstom SA
Altana AG
Amdocs Limited
Amgen Inc
Analog Devices Inc
Applied Materials Inc
Arcadis NV
ASE Technology Holding Co Ltd
AstraZeneca plc
AtkinsRealis Group Inc
Atomic Energy of Canada Limited (AECL)
ATS Corp
Autodesk Inc
Babcock & Wilcox Enterprises Inc
BAE Systems plc
Baker Hughes Company
BASF SE
Bausch & Lomb Corp
Baxter International Inc
Bayerische Motoren Werke AG (BMW Group)
Bechtel Group Inc
Beckman Coulter Inc
Becton Dickinson and Company
Belden Inc
Biogen Inc
BIOS-BIOENERGYSYSTEME GmbH
Black & Veatch Holding Company
BMC Software Inc
Boeing Company (The)
Bombardier Inc
Boston Scientific Corporation
Bouygues SA
BP plc
Bristol-Myers Squibb Company
Broadcom Inc
Caterpillar Inc
Celanese Corporation
Celestica Inc
CGI Inc
Chevron Corporation
Cisco Systems Inc
ConocoPhillips Company
Corning Incorporated

CSL Limited
Cummins Inc
Curia Inc
Dana Incorporated
Dassault Systemes SA
Deere & Company (John Deere)
Dell Technologies Inc
Diebold Nixdorf Incorporated
DNV AS
Dow Inc
Downer EDI Limited
Eastman Chemical Company
Eaton Corp plc
Eli Lilly and Company
Emerson Electric Co
Empresas ICA SAB de CV
Eni SpA
Enviri Corporation
Equinor ASA
EssilorLuxottica SA
Exxon Mobil Corporation (ExxonMobil)
ExxonMobil Product Solutions Company
Flex Ltd
Fluor Corporation
Fomento de Construcciones y Contratas SA (FCC)
Ford Motor Company
GE Aerospace
GE HealthCare Technologies Inc
Gen Digital Inc
Genentech Inc
General Dynamics Corporation
General Motors Company (GM)
Georg Fischer AG
Gilead Sciences Inc
Globalvia Inversiones SAU
GSK PLC
Halliburton Company
Hewlett Packard Laboratories (HP Labs)
Hill-Rom Holdings Inc
Honeywell International Inc
HP Inc
Huawei Technologies Co Ltd
IBM Research
Illinois Tool Works Inc
IMI plc
Innolux Corporation
Intel Corporation
Intellectual Ventures Management LLC
International Business Machines Corporation (IBM)
Intertek Group plc
Intuit Inc
IQVIA Holdings Inc
ITT Inc
Jabil Inc
Jacobs Solutions Inc

Jaguar Land Rover Limited
Johnson & Johnson
Johnson Controls International plc
Juniper Networks Inc
KBR Inc
Koninklijke Philips NV (Royal Philips)
L3Harris Technologies Inc
Lanxess AG
Layne-A Granite Company
LM Ericsson Telephone Company (Ericsson)
Lockheed Martin Corporation
LyondellBasell Industries NV
McDermott International Ltd
Medtronic plc
Mercedes-Benz Group AG
Merck & Co Inc
Merck Serono SA
Meta Platforms Inc (Facebook)
Microsoft Corporation
NCR Voyix Corp
NetApp Inc
Nokia Corporation
Northrop Grumman Corporation
Novartis AG
Novo Nordisk AS
Novonesis AS
NVIDIA Corporation
Opel Automobile GmbH
Oracle Corporation
Orano SA
Page Southerland Page Inc
Palo Alto Research Center Inc (PARC)
Pfizer Inc
Pininfarina SpA
Qualcomm Incorporated
Renault SA
Robert Bosch GmbH
Roche Holding AG
Rolls-Royce Holdings plc
RTX Corp (Raytheon Technologies)
Saab AB
Safran SA
Sanofi SA
SAP SE
SAS Institute Inc
Sasol Limited
Science Applications International Corporation (SAIC)
Seagate Technology Public Limited Company
Seatrium Limited
Shell plc
Siemens AG
Siemens Gamesa Renewable Energy SA
Siemens Healthineers AG
Singapore Technologies Engineering Limited
Skidmore Owings & Merrill LLP
SLB
Smith & Nephew plc
Smiths Group plc

Solvay SA
SpaceX (Space Exploration Technologies Corporation)
Spirit AeroSystems Holdings Inc
Stanley Black & Decker Inc
Stanley Consultants Inc
Stellantis North America
Stellantis NV
STMicroelectronics NV
Stryker Corporation
STV Incorporated
Syngenta Group Co Ltd
Synopsys Inc
Taiwan Semiconductor Manufacturing Co Ltd (TSMC)
Takeda Pharmaceutical Company Limited
Tate & Lyle plc
TechnipFMC plc
Teledyne Technologies Inc
Tellabs Inc
Tenneco Inc
Texas Instruments Incorporated
Textron Inc
Thales SA
TotalEnergies SE
Trane Technologies plc
UCB SA
Unisys Corporation
Valeo SA
Vatana Phaisal Engineering Co Ltd
Vestas Wind Systems A/S
Visteon Corporation
Volvo AB
Volvo Car AB
VSE Corporation
Whirlpool Corporation
Wipro Limited
Xerox Corporation

INDEX OF SUBSIDIARIES, BRAND NAMES AND AFFILIATIONS, CONT.

INDEX OF SUBSIDIARIES, BRAND NAMES AND AFFILIATIONS, CONT.

INDEX OF SUBSIDIARIES, BRAND NAMES AND AFFILIATIONS, CONT.

INDEX OF SUBSIDIARIES, BRAND NAMES AND AFFILIATIONS, CONT.

INDEX OF SUBSIDIARIES, BRAND NAMES AND AFFILIATIONS, CONT.

INDEX OF SUBSIDIARIES, BRAND NAMES AND AFFILIATIONS, CONT.

INDEX OF SUBSIDIARIES, BRAND NAMES AND AFFILIATIONS, CONT.

INDEX OF SUBSIDIARIES, BRAND NAMES AND AFFILIATIONS, CONT.

INDEX OF SUBSIDIARIES, BRAND NAMES AND AFFILIATIONS, CONT.

INDEX OF SUBSIDIARIES, BRAND NAMES AND AFFILIATIONS, CONT.

NSX; **Honda Motor Co Ltd**
Numeta G13E; **Baxter International Inc**
NVIDIA RTX; **NVIDIA Corporation**
OC Latin America SA; **Oriental Consultants Global Co Ltd**
OCG East Africa Limited; **Oriental Consultants Global Co Ltd**
OCREVUS; **Biogen Inc**
Oculus; **Reality Labs**
Oculus; **Meta Platforms Inc (Facebook)**
Office 365; **Microsoft Corporation**
Olumiant; **Eli Lilly and Company**
OMTR; **Michael Baker International LLC**
One A Day; **Bayer Corporation**
One Equity Partners; **Amey Ltd**
OneDrive; **Microsoft Corporation**
ONEsolution; **CRB**
Onshape; **PTC Inc**
Opel Group GmbH; **Opel Automobile GmbH**
Openvia; **Globalvia Inversiones SAU**
Opseyes; **Ramboll Group A/S**
Optical Borehole Camera; **OYO Corporation**
Orano Med; **Orano SA**
Orano Projects; **Orano SA**
ORBIS; **Agfa-Gevaert NV**
Oriental Consultants Philippines Inc; **Oriental Consultants Global Co Ltd**
Otezla; **Amgen Inc**
Oticon; **Demant AS**
OTMRdata; **Michael Baker International LLC**
OTN Systems NV; **Belden Inc**
Outlander; **Mitsubishi Motors Corp**
Outlook.com; **Microsoft Corporation**
Overland Contracting Inc; **Black & Veatch Holding Company**
Overwatch; **Activision Blizzard**
OXIS Energy; **Safran SA**
OYO Corporation USA; **OYO Corporation**
Ozempic; **Novo Nordisk AS**
PA Consulting; **Jacobs Solutions Inc**
PACCAR Financial Services; **PACCAR Inc**
Pariet; **Eisai Co Ltd**
Parrot Automotive; **Forvia SE**
PB Consult; **Dorsch Holding GmbH**
Pemex Exploracion y Produccion; **Petroleos Mexicanos (Pemex)**
Pemex Logistica; **Petroleos Mexicanos (Pemex)**
Pemex Transformacion Industrial; **Petroleos Mexicanos (Pemex)**
Perodua Global Manufacturing Sdn Bhd; **Daihatsu Motor Co Ltd**
Perodua Manufacturing Sdn Bhd; **Daihatsu Motor Co Ltd**
PeroxyChem; **Evonik Industries AG**
Peterbilt Motors; **PACCAR Inc**
Petrobras; **Petrobras (Petroleo Brasileiro SA)**

Petrobras Distribuidora SA; **Petrobras (Petroleo Brasileiro SA)**
Petroleos Mexicanos; **Petroleos Mexicanos (Pemex)**
Phenom; **Embraer SA**
PIDGraph; **Bilfinger SE**
Pininfarina Deutschland GmbH; **Pininfarina SpA**
Pininfarina of America Corp; **Pininfarina SpA**
Pininfarina Shanghai Co Ltd; **Pininfarina SpA**
Pininfarina Wind Tunnel; **Pininfarina SpA**
Pioneer Green Mobility Program; **Pioneer Corporation**
PlantPAx; **Rockwell Automation Inc**
Plants vs Zombies; **Electronic Arts Inc (EA)**
Playstation; **Sony Corporation**
PLEGRIDY; **Biogen Inc**
PMC Capital Partners LLC; **UniversalPegasus International Inc**
PMI; **Petroleos Mexicanos (Pemex)**
Pokemon; **Nintendo Co Ltd**
Polaris Capital Management LLC; **Trevi-Finanziaria Industriale SpA (Trevi Group)**
PolyPacific Polymers Sdn Bhd; **LyondellBasell Industries NV**
Porocel Group; **Evonik Industries AG**
Porsche; **Porsche Automobil Holding SE**
Porter-Cable; **Stanley Black & Decker Inc**
Portofino; **Ferrari SpA**
Post-it; **3M Company**
Power Construction Corporation Group Co Ltd; **SEPCO Electric Power Construction Corporation**
PowerFlex; **Rockwell Automation Inc**
Praetor; **Embraer SA**
Pratt & Whitney; **RTX Corp (Raytheon Technologies)**
PrecisionBiotics Group Limited; **Novonesis AS**
Preclarus; **PPD Inc**
PreserVision; **Bausch & Lomb Corp**
Private Division; **Take-Two Interactive Software Inc**
ProArt; **ASUSTeK Computer Inc**
ProConnect; **Intuit Inc**
ProFile; **Intuit Inc**
Prolia; **Amgen Inc**
PROMITOR; **Tate & Lyle plc**
Promoter Technologies; **Eli Lilly and Company**
Proxion Plan Oy; **Golder Associates Corporation**
Proxion Pro Oy; **Golder Associates Corporation**
PSA Groupe; **Stellantis NV**
PT Astra Daihatsu Motor; **Daihatsu Motor Co Ltd**
PT JGC Indonesia; **JGC Holdings Corp**
PTX; **Juniper Networks Inc**
PureSinter Furnace; **Desktop Metal Inc**
PureVision; **Bausch & Lomb Corp**
Q2 Solutions; **IQVIA Holdings Inc**
Q3; **Audi AG**
Q50; **Nissan Motor Co Ltd**
Quadro; **NVIDIA Corporation**
Quantum for Business; **QuTech**
Qubit Research; **QuTech**

INDEX OF SUBSIDIARIES, BRAND NAMES AND AFFILIATIONS, CONT.

INDEX OF SUBSIDIARIES, BRAND NAMES AND AFFILIATIONS, CONT.

INDEX OF SUBSIDIARIES, BRAND NAMES AND AFFILIATIONS, CONT.

INDEX OF SUBSIDIARIES, BRAND NAMES AND AFFILIATIONS, CONT.

INDEX OF SUBSIDIARIES, BRAND NAMES AND AFFILIATIONS, CONT.

Zyprexa; **Eli Lilly and Company**

INDEX OF SUBSIDIARIES, BRAND NAMES AND AFFILIATIONS, CONT.

A Short Engineering & Research Industry Glossary

3-D Printer: See "Additive Manufacturing."

3-D Printing: See "Additive Manufacturing."

510(k): An application filed with the FDA for a new medical device to show that the apparatus is "substantially equivalent" to one that is already marketed.

5G: A wireless technology that can provide high download speeds of one gigabyte per second (Gbps) to 20 Gbps and more. The first specifications for 5G were agreed to by the global wireless industry from 2017 to 2019. While certain 5G features can be used to boost speeds of earlier 4G networks, a true rollout required major investment in new cellular infrastructure and systems.

802.15: See "Ultrawideband (UWB)." For 802.15.1, see "Bluetooth."

802.15.1: See "Bluetooth."

802.16: See "WiMAX."

Abbreviated New Drug Application (ANDA): An application filed with the FDA showing that a substance is the same as an existing, previously approved drug (i.e., an application for approval to market generic version of an existing drug).

Absorption, Distribution, Metabolism and Excretion (ADME): In clinical trials, the bodily processes studied to determine the extent and duration of systemic exposure to a drug.

Access Network: The network that connects a user's telephone equipment to the telephone exchange.

Active Server Page (ASP): A web page that includes one or more embedded programs, usually written in Java or Visual Basic code. See "Java."

Active X: A set of technologies developed by Microsoft Corporation for sharing information across different applications.

Additive Manufacturing: The use of 3-D "printers" that that build up layers of materials such as plastics, ceramic powders or metallic powders in order to create a finished product. Such printers follow instructions from computerized design files. Originally used mainly for creating prototypes of product concepts, this process is growing in popularity as a final manufacturing process.

ADME: See "Absorption, Distribution, Metabolism and Excretion (ADME)."

ADN: See "Advanced Digital Network (ADN)."

ADSL: See "Asymmetrical Digital Subscriber Line (ADSL)."

Advanced Digital Network (ADN): See "Integrated Digital Network (IDN)."

AE: See "Adverse Event (AE)."

AI: See "Artificial Intelligence (AI)."

Ambient: Refers to any unconfined portion of the air. Also refers to open air.

Analog: A form of transmitting information characterized by continuously variable quantities. Digital transmission, in contrast, is characterized by discrete bits of information in numerical steps. An analog signal responds to changes in light, sound, heat and pressure.

Analog IC (Integrated Circuit): A semiconductor that processes a continuous wave of electrical signals based on real-world analog quantities such as speed, pressure, temperature, light, sound and voltage.

Analytics: Generally refers to the deep examination of massive amounts of data, often on a continual or real-time basis. The goal is to discover deeper insights, make recommendations or generate predictions. Advanced analytics includes such techniques as big data, predictive analytics, text analytics, data mining, forecasting, optimization and simulation.

ANDA: See "Abbreviated New Drug Application (ANDA)."

ANSI: American National Standards Institute. Founded in 1918, ANSI is a private, non-profit organization that administers and coordinates the U.S. voluntary standardization and conformity assessment system. Its mission is to enhance both the global competitiveness of U.S. business and the quality of U.S. life by promoting and facilitating voluntary consensus standards and conformity assessment systems, and safeguarding their integrity. See www.ansi.org.

API: See "Application Programming Interface (API)."

Application Programming Interface (API): A set of protocols, routines and tools used by computer programmers as a way of setting common definitions regarding how one piece of software communicates with another.

Application Service Provider (ASP): A web site that enables utilization of software and databases that reside permanently on a service company's remote web server, rather than having to be downloaded to the user's computer. Advantages include the ability for multiple remote users to access the same tools over the Internet and the fact that the ASP provider is responsible for developing and maintaining the software. (ASP is also an acronym for "active server page," which is not related.) For the latest developments in ASP, see "Software as a Service (SaaS)."

Applied Research: The application of compounds, processes, materials or other items discovered during basic research to practical uses. The goal is to move discoveries along to the final development phase.

ARPANet: Advanced Research Projects Agency Network. The forefather of the Internet, ARPANet was developed during the latter part of the 1960s by the United States Department of Defense.

Artificial Intelligence (AI): The use of computer technology to perform functions somewhat like those normally associated with human intelligence, such as reasoning, learning and self-improvement.

ASCII: American Standard Code for Information Exchange. There are 128 standard ASCII codes that represent all Latin letters, numbers and punctuation. Each ASCII code is represented by a seven-digit binary number, such as 0000000 or 0000111. This code is accepted as a standard throughout the world.

ASEAN: Association of Southeast Asian Nations. A regional economic development association

established in 1967 by five original member countries: Indonesia, Malaysia, Philippines, Singapore, and Thailand. Brunei joined on 8 January 1984, Vietnam on 28 July 1995, Laos and Myanmar on 23 July 1997, and Cambodia on 30 April 1999.

Asia Pacific Advisory Committee (APAC): A multi-country committee representing the Asia and Pacific region.

ASP: See "Application Service Provider (ASP)."

Assay: A laboratory test to identify and/or measure the amount of a particular substance in a sample. Types of assays include endpoint assays, in which a single measurement is made at a fixed time: kinetic assays, in which increasing amounts of a product are formed with time and are monitored at multiple points: microbiological assays, which measure the concentration of antimicrobials in biological material: and immunological assays, in which analysis or measurement is based on antigen-antibody reactions.

Asymmetrical Digital Subscriber Line (ADSL): High-speed technology that enables the transfer of data over existing copper phone lines, allowing more bandwidth downstream than upstream.

Asynchronous Communications: A stream of data routed through a network as generated instead of in organized message blocks. Most personal computers use this format to send data.

Asynchronous Transfer Mode (ATM): A digital switching and transmission technology based on high speed. ATM allows voice, video and data signals to be sent over a single telephone line at speeds from 25 million to 1 billion bits per second (bps). This digital ATM speed is much faster than traditional analog phone lines, which allow no more than 2 million bps. See "Broadband."

Automation Bias: A user's overconfidence in output or data generated by artificial intelligence or machine learning--overlooking the risk that the output or data may be incorrect.

B2B: See "Business-to-Business."

B2C: See "Business-to-Consumer."

B2G: See "Business-to-Government."

Backbone: Traditionally the part of a communications network that carries the heaviest traffic: the high-speed line or series of connections that forms a large pathway within a network or within a region. The combined networks of AT&T, MCI and other large telecommunications companies make up the backbone of the Internet.

Baseline: A set of data used in clinical studies, or other types of research, for control or comparison.

Basic Research: Attempts to discover compounds, materials, processes or other items that may be largely or entirely new and/or unique. Basic research may start with a theoretical concept that has yet to be proven. The goal is to create discoveries that can be moved along to applied research. Basic research is sometimes referred to as "blue sky" research.

Baud: Refers to how many times the carrier signal in a modem switches value per second or how many bits a modem can send and receive in a second.

Beam: The coverage and geographic service area offered by a satellite transponder. A global beam effectively covers one-third of the earth's surface. A spot beam provides a very specific high-powered downlink pattern that is limited to a particular geographical area to which it may be steered or pointed.

Binhex: A means of changing non-ASCII (or non-text) files into text/ASCII files so that they can be used, for example, as e-mail.

Bioavailability: In pharmaceuticals, the rate and extent to which a drug is absorbed or is otherwise available to the treatment site in the body.

Biochemical Engineering: A sector of chemical engineering that deals with biological structures and processes. Biochemical engineers may be found in the pharmaceutical, biotechnology and environmental fields, among others.

Bioengineering: Engineering principles applied when working in biology and pharmaceuticals.

Bioequivalence: In pharmaceuticals, the demonstration that a drug's rate and extent of absorption are not significantly different from those of an existing drug that is already approved by the FDA.

This is the basis upon which generic and brand name drugs are compared.

Bioinformatics: Research, development or application of computational tools and approaches for expanding the use of biological, medical, behavioral or health data, including those to acquire, store, organize, archive, analyze or visualize such data. Bioinformatics is often applied to the study of genetic data. It applies principles of information sciences and technologies to make vast, diverse and complex life sciences data more understandable and useful.

Biologics: Drugs that are synthesized from living organisms. That is, drugs created using biotechnology, sometimes referred to as biopharmaceuticals. Specifically, biologics may be any virus, therapeutic serum, toxin, antitoxin, vaccine, blood, blood component or derivative, allergenic or analogous product, or arsphenamine or one of its derivatives used for the prevention, treatment or cure of disease. Also, see "Biologics License Application (BLA)," "Follow-on Biologics," and "Biopharmaceuticals."

Biologics License Application (BLA): An application to be submitted to the FDA when a firm wants to obtain permission to market a novel, new biological drug product. Specifically, these are drugs created through the use of biotechnology. It was formerly known as Product License Application (PLA). Also see "Biologics."

Biopharmaceuticals: That portion of the pharmaceutical industry focused on the use of biotechnology to create new drugs. A biopharmaceutical can be any biological compound that is intended to be used as a therapeutic drug, including recombinant proteins, monoclonal and polyclonal antibodies, antisense oligonucleotides, therapeutic genes, and recombinant and DNA vaccines. Also, see "Biologics."

Biotechnology: A set of powerful tools that employ living organisms (or parts of organisms) to make or modify products, improve plants or animals (including humans) or develop microorganisms for specific uses. Biotechnology is most commonly thought of to include the development of human medical therapies and processes using recombinant DNA, cell fusion, other genetic techniques and bioremediation.

Bit: A single digit number, either a one or a zero, which is the smallest unit of computerized data.

Bits Per Second (Bps): An indicator of the speed of data movement.

BLA: See "Biologics License Application (BLA)."

Bluetooth: An industry standard for a technology that enables wireless, short-distance infrared connections between devices such as cell phone headsets, Palm Pilots or PDAs, laptops, printers and Internet appliances.

BPO: See "Business Process Outsourcing (BPO)."

Bps: See "Bits Per Second (Bps)."

Brand Marketing: A marketing strategy that places a focus on the brand name of a product, service or firm in order to eventually enhance the brand's market share, increase sales, establish credibility, improve satisfaction, raise the profile of the firm and increase profits. Public relations and special events are common methods of brand marketing. In contrast, performance marketing is focused on getting the consumer of a message to take a specific action, such as a click on a link.

Branding: A marketing strategy that places a focus on the brand name of a product, service or firm in order to increase the brand's market share, increase sales, establish credibility, improve satisfaction, raise the profile of the firm and increase profits. Also, see "Brand."

Broadband: The high-speed transmission range for telecommunications and computer data. Broadband generally refers to any transmission at 2 million bps (bits per second) or higher (much higher than analog speed). A broadband network can carry voice, video and data all at the same time. Internet users enjoying broadband access typically connect to the Internet via DSL line, cable modem or T1 line. Several wireless methods offer broadband as well.

Buffer: A location for temporarily storing data being sent or received. It is usually located between two devices that have different data transmission rates.

Business Process Outsourcing (BPO): The process of hiring another company to handle business activities. BPO is one of the fastest-growing segments in the offshoring sector. Services include human resources management, billing and purchasing and call centers, as well as many types of customer service

or marketing activities, depending on the industry involved. Also, see "Knowledge Process Outsourcing (KPO)" and Business Transformation Outsourcing (BTO)."

Business Transformation Outsourcing (BTO): A segment within outsourcing in which the client company revamps its business processes with the goal of transforming its business by following a collaborative approach with its outsourced services provider.

Business-to-Business: An organization focused on selling products, services or data to commercial customers rather than individual consumers. Also known as B2B.

Business-to-Consumer: An organization focused on selling products, services or data to individual consumers rather than commercial customers. Also known as B2C.

Business-to-Government: An organization focused on selling products, services or data to government units rather than commercial businesses or consumers. Also known as B2G.

Byte: A set of eight bits that represent a single character.

Cable Modem: An interface between a cable television system and a computer or router. Most cable modems are external devices that connect to the PC through a standard 10Base-T Ethernet card and twisted-pair wiring. External Universal Serial Bus (USB) modems and internal PCI modem cards are also available.

Caching: A method of storing data in a temporary location closer to the user so that it can be retrieved quickly when requested.

CAD: See "Computer-Aided Design (CAD)."

CAE: See "Computer-Aided Engineering (CAE)."

CAM: See "Computer-Aided Manufacturing (CAM)."

CANDA: See "Computer-Assisted New Drug Application (CANDA)."

Capability Maturity Model (CMM): A global process management standard for software development established by the Software Engineering Institute at Carnegie Mellon University.

Capacitor: An electronic circuit device for temporary storage of electrical energy.

Carbon Capture and Storage: See "Carbon Sequestration."

Carbon Neutral: A goal for businesses who aim to balance the emissions of carbon dioxide with efforts to offset those emissions such as planting trees. See "Zero Energy Building."

Carbon Positive: A marketing term that implies that a building or business is removing more carbon dioxide from Earth's atmosphere than creating it. See "Zero Energy Building."

Carbon Sequestration: The absorption and storage of CO2 from the atmosphere by the roots and leaves of plants: the carbon builds up as organic matter in the soil. In the energy industry, carbon sequestration refers to the process of isolating and storing carbon dioxide (a so-called greenhouse gas). One use is to avoid releasing carbon dioxide into the air when burning coal at a coal-fired power plant. Instead, the carbon dioxide is stored in the ground or otherwise stored in a permanent or semi-permanent fashion. Other uses include the return to the ground of carbon dioxide that is produced at natural gas wells, and the introduction of carbon dioxide into oil wells in order to increase internal pressure and production. This process is also known as carbon capture and storage (CCS).

Cardiac Catheterization Laboratory: Facilities offering special diagnostic procedures for cardiac patients, including the introduction of a catheter into the interior of the heart by way of a vein or artery or by direct needle puncture. Procedures must be performed in a laboratory or a special procedure room.

Carrier: In communications, the basic radio, television or telephony center of transmit signal. The carrier in an analog signal is modulated by varying volume or shifting frequency up or down in relation to the incoming signal. Satellite carriers operating in the analog mode are usually frequency-modulated.

CASE: See "Computer-Assisted Software Engineering (CASE)."

CAT Scan: See "Computed Tomography (CT)."

Catheter: A tubular instrument used to add or withdraw fluids. Heart or cardiac catheterization involves the passage of flexible catheters into the great vessels and chambers of the heart. IV catheters add intravenous fluids to the veins. Foley catheters withdraw fluid from the bladder. Significant recent advances in technology allow administration of powerful drug and diagnostic therapies via catheters.

CATV: Cable television.

CBER: See "Center for Biologics Evaluation and Research (CBER)."

CCS: See "Carbon Sequestration."

CDER: See "Center for Drug Evaluation and Research (CDER)."

CDMA: See "Code Division Multiple Access (CDMA)."

CDRH: See "Center for Devices and Radiological Health (CDRH)."

CEM: Contract electronic manufacturing. See "Contract Manufacturing."

Center for Biologics Evaluation and Research (CBER): The branch of the FDA responsible for the regulation of biological products, including blood, vaccines, therapeutics and related drugs and devices, to ensure purity, potency, safety, availability and effectiveness. www.fda.gov/cber

Center for Devices and Radiological Health (CDRH): The branch of the FDA responsible for the regulation of medical devices. www.fda.gov/cdrh

Center for Drug Evaluation and Research (CDER): The branch of the FDA responsible for the regulation of drug products. www.fda.gov/cder

Central Processing Unit (CPU): The part of a computer that interprets and executes instructions. It is composed of an arithmetic logic unit, a control unit and a small amount of memory.

Ceramic: Ceramics are nonmetallic materials that have been created under intense heat. Ceramics tend to be extremely hard, heat-resistant and corrosion-resistant. They are generally poor conductors of temperature changes or electricity. Ceramics are used in low-tech and high-tech applications, ranging from the insulators in spark plugs to the heat shield on the Space Shuttle.

CGI: See "Common Gateway Interface (CGI)."

CGI-BIN: The frequently used name of a directory on a web server where CGI programs exist.

Channel Definition Format (CDF): Used in Internet-based broadcasting. With this format, a channel serves as a web site that also sends an information file about that specific site. Users subscribe to a channel by downloading the file.

Chemical Engineering: The sector that deals with technologies, safety issues, refining, production and delivery of chemicals and products that are manufactured partly or largely through the use of chemicals. Chemical engineers are also involved in the design and construction of major industrial plants, as well as the application of chemicals to scientific and industrial needs.

Class I Device: An FDA classification of medical devices for which general controls are sufficient to ensure safety and efficacy.

Class II Device: An FDA classification of medical devices for which performance standards and special controls are sufficient to ensure safety and efficacy.

Class III Device: An FDA classification of medical devices for which pre-market approval is required to ensure safety and efficacy, unless the device is substantially equivalent to a currently marketed device. See "510 K."

CLEC: See "Competitive Local Exchange Carrier (CLEC)."

Client/Server: In networking, a way of running a large computer setup. The server is the host computer that acts as the central holding ground for files, databases and application software. The clients are all of the PCs connected to the network that share data with the server. This represents a vast change from past networks, which were connected to expensive, complicated "mainframe" computers.

Climate Change (Greenhouse Effect): A theory that assumes an increasing mean global surface temperature of the Earth caused by gases (sometimes referred to as greenhouse gases) in the atmosphere (including carbon dioxide, methane, nitrous oxide, ozone and chlorofluorocarbons). The greenhouse effect allows solar radiation to penetrate the Earth's atmosphere but absorbs the infrared radiation returning to space.

Cloning (Reproductive): A method of reproducing an exact copy of an animal or, potentially, an exact copy of a human being. A scientist removes the nucleus from a donor's unfertilized egg, inserts a nucleus from the animal to be copied and then stimulates the nucleus to begin dividing to form an embryo. In the case of a mammal, such as a human, the embryo would then be implanted in the uterus of a host female. Also see "Cloning (Therapeutic)."

Cloning (Therapeutic): A method of reproducing exact copies of cells needed for research or for the development of replacement tissue or organs. A scientist removes the nucleus from a donor's unfertilized egg, inserts a nucleus from the animal whose cells are to be copied and then stimulates the nucleus to begin dividing to form an embryo. However, the embryo is never allowed to grow to any significant stage of development. Instead, it is allowed to grow for a few hours or days, and stem cells are then removed from it for use in regenerating tissue. Also see "Cloning (Reproductive)."

CMM: See "Capability Maturity Model (CMM)."

CMOS: Complementary Metal Oxide Semiconductor. The technology used in making modern silicon-based microchips.

Coaxial Cable: A type of cable widely used to transmit telephone and broadcast traffic. The distinguishing feature is an inner strand of wires surrounded by an insulator that is in turn surrounded by another conductor, which serves as the ground. Cable TV wiring is typically coaxial.

Code Division Multiple Access (CDMA): A cellular telephone multiple-access scheme whereby stations use spread-spectrum modulations and orthogonal codes to avoid interfering with one another. IS-95 (also known as CDMAOne) is the 2G CDMA standard. CDMA2000 is the 3G standard. CDMA in the 1xEV-DO standard offers data transfer speeds up to 2.4 Mbps. CDMA 1xRTT is a slower standard offering speeds of 144 kbps.

Code of Federal Regulations (CFR): A codification of the general and permanent rules published in the Federal Register by the executive departments and agencies of the Federal Government. The code is divided into 50 titles that represent broad areas subject to federal regulation. Title 21 of the CFR covers FDA regulations.

Codec: Hardware or software that converts analog to digital and digital to analog (in both audio and video formats). Codecs can be found in digital telephones, set-top boxes, computers and videoconferencing equipment. The term is also used to refer to the compression of digital information into a smaller format.

Co-Location: Refers to the hosting of computer servers at locations operated by service organizations. Co-location is offered by firms that operate specially designed co-location centers with high levels of security, extremely high-speed telecommunication lines for Internet connectivity and reliable backup electrical power systems in case of power failure, as well as a temperature-controlled environment for optimum operation of computer systems.

Commerce Chain Management (CCM): Refers to Internet-based tools to facilitate sales, distribution, inventory management and content personalization in the e-commerce industry. Also see "Supply Chain."

Commercial Off-The-Shelf (COTS): Generally refers to software purchased from a third party vendor, as opposed to developed in-house.

Committee for Veterinary Medicinal Products (CVMP): A committee that is a veterinary equivalent of the CPMP (see "Committee on Proprietary Medicinal Products (CPMP)") in the EU. See "European Union (EU)."

Committee on Proprietary Medicinal Products (CPMP): A committee, composed of two people from each EU Member State (see "European Union (EU)"), that is responsible for the scientific evaluation and assessment of marketing applications for medicinal products in the EU. The CPMP is the major body

involved in the harmonization of pharmaceutical regulations within the EU and receives administrative support from the European Medicines Evaluation Agency. See "European Medicines Evaluation Agency (EMEA)."

Common Gateway Interface (CGI): A set of guidelines that determines the manner in which a web server receives and sends information to and from software on the same machine.

Communications Satellite Corporation (COMSAT): Serves as the U.S. Signatory to INTELSAT and INMARSAT.

Competitive Local Exchange Carrier (CLEC): A newer company providing local telephone service that competes against larger, traditional firms known as ILECs (incumbent local exchange carriers).

Compression: A technology in which a communications signal is squeezed so that it uses less bandwidth (or capacity) than it normally would. This saves storage space and shortens transfer time. The original data is decompressed when read back into memory.

Computed Tomography (CT): An imaging method that uses x-rays to create cross-sectional pictures of the body. The technique is frequently referred to as a "CAT Scan." A patient lies on a narrow platform while the machine's x-ray beam rotates around him or her. Small detectors inside the scanner measure the amount of x-rays that make it through the part of the body being studied. A computer takes this information and uses it to create several individual images, called slices. These images can be stored, viewed on a monitor, or printed on film. Three-dimensional models of organs can be created by stacking the individual slices together. The newest machines are capable of operating at 256 slice levels, creating very high resolution images in a short period of time.

Computer-Aided Design (CAD): A tool used to provide three-dimensional, on-screen design for everything from buildings to automobiles to clothing. It generally runs on workstations.

Computer-Aided Engineering (CAE): The use of computers to assist with a broad spectrum of engineering design work, including conceptual and analytical design.

Computer-Aided Manufacturing (CAM): The use of computers to assist with manufacturing processes, thereby increasing efficiency and productivity.

Computer-Assisted New Drug Application (CANDA): An electronic submission of a new drug application (NDA) to the FDA.

Computer-Assisted Software Engineering (CASE): The application of computer technology to systems development activities, techniques and methodologies. Sometimes referred to as "computer-aided systems engineering."

COMSAT: See "Communications Satellite Corporation (COMSAT)."

Contract Manufacturing: A business arrangement whereby a company manufactures products that will be sold under the brand names of its client companies. For example, a large number of consumer electronics, such as laptop computers, are manufactured by contract manufacturers for leading brand-name computer companies such as Dell and Apple. Many other types of products, such as shoes and apparel, are made under contract manufacturing. Also see "Original Equipment Manufacturer (OEM)" and "Original Design Manufacturer (ODM)."

Contract Research Organization (CRO): An independent organization that contracts with a client to conduct part of the work on a study or research project. For example, drug and medical device makers frequently outsource clinical trials and other research work to CROs.

Coordinator: In clinical trials, the person at an investigative site who handles the administrative responsibilities of the trial, acts as a liaison between the investigative site and the sponsor, and reviews data and records during a monitoring visit.

Cost Plus Contract: A contract that sets the contractor's compensation as a percentage of the total cost of labor and materials.

COSTART: In medical and drug product development, a dictionary of adverse events and body systems used for coding and classifying adverse events.

COTS: See "Commercial Off-The-Shelf (COTS)."

CPMP: See "Committee on Proprietary Medicinal Products (CPMP)."

CPU: See "Central Processing Unit (CPU)."

CRO: See "Contract Research Organization (CRO)."

CT: See "Computed Tomography (CT)."

CVMP: See "Committee for Veterinary Medicinal Products (CVMP)."

Data Over Cable Service Interface Specification (DOCSIS): A set of standards for transferring data over cable television. DOCSIS 3.0 will enable very high-speed Internet access that may eventually reach 160 Mbps.

Decompression: See "Compression."

Defibrillator: In medicine, an instrument used externally (as electrodes on the chest) or implanted (as a small device similar in size to a pacemaker) that delivers an electric shock to return the heart to its normal rhythm.

Demand Chain: A similar concept to a supply chain, but with an emphasis on the end user.

Dendrimer: A type of molecule that can be used with small molecules to give them certain desirable characteristics. Dendrimers are utilized in technologies for electronic displays. See "Organic LED (OLED)."

Design Patent: A patent that may be granted by the U.S. Patent and Trademark Office to anyone who invents a new, original, and ornamental design for an article of manufacture.

Development: The phase of research and development (R&D) in which researchers attempt to create new products from the results of discoveries and applications created during basic and applied research.

Device: In medical products, an instrument, apparatus, implement, machine, contrivance, implant, in vitro reagent or other similar or related article, including any component, part or accessory, that 1) is recognized in the official National Formulary or United States Pharmacopoeia or any supplement to them, 2) is intended for use in the diagnosis of disease or other conditions, or in the cure, mitigation, treatment or prevention of disease, in man or animals or 3) is intended to affect the structure of the body of man or animals and does not achieve any of its principal intended purposes through chemical action within or on the body of man or animals and is not dependent upon being metabolized for the achievement of any of its principal intended purposes.

Diagnostic Radioisotope Facility: A medical facility in which radioactive isotopes (radiopharmaceuticals) are used as tracers or indicators to detect an abnormal condition or disease in the body.

Digital Local Telephone Switch: A computer that interprets signals (dialed numbers) from a telephone caller and routes calls to their proper destinations. A digital switch also provides a variety of calling features not available in older analog switches, such as call waiting.

Digital Rights Management (DRM): Restrictions placed on the use of digital content by copyright holders and hardware manufacturers. DRM for Apple, Inc.'s iTunes, for example, allows downloaded music to be played only on Apple's iPod player and iPhones, per agreement with music production companies Universal Music Group, SonyBMG, Warner Music and EMI.

Digital Signal Processing (DSP): Technology that enables instruments and computers to understand a stream of data coming from a sensor, such as an accelerometer, digital camera, heat probe or seismic monitor.

Digital Signal Processor: A chip that converts analog signals such as sound and light into digital signals.

Digital Subscriber Line (DSL): A broadband (high-speed) Internet connection provided via telecommunications systems. These lines are a cost-effective means of providing homes and small businesses with relatively fast Internet access. Common variations include ADSL and SDSL. DSL competes with cable modem access and wireless access.

Digital Transformation (DX): The implementation of digital technologies into as many areas of a business' operations as reasonably possible Goals may include: to fundamentally change how the enterprise operates: how data is gathered and tracked: how

innovation is launched: and how value is delivered to customers. The hoped-for result is to create new operating efficiencies and develop new revenue or profit opportunities, while better positioning the enterprise for the future. Also abbreviated as DX or DT.

Disaster Recovery: A set of rules and procedures that allow a computer site to be put back in operation after a disaster has occurred. Moving backups off-site constitutes the minimum basic precaution for disaster recovery. The remote copy is used to recover data if the local storage is inaccessible after a disaster.

Discrete Semiconductor: A chip with one diode or transistor.

Disk Mirroring: A data redundancy technique in which data is recorded identically on multiple separate disk drives at the same time. When the primary disk is off-line, the alternate takes over, providing continuous access to data. Disk mirroring is sometimes referred to as RAID.

Distributor: An individual or business involved in marketing, warehousing and/or shipping of products manufactured by others to a specific group of end users. Distributors do not sell to the general public. In order to develop a competitive advantage, distributors often focus on serving one industry or one set of niche clients. For example, within the medical industry, there are major distributors that focus on providing pharmaceuticals, surgical supplies or dental supplies to clinics and hospitals.

DNA Chip: A revolutionary tool used to identify mutations in genes like BRCA1 and BRCA2. The chip, which consists of a small glass plate encased in plastic, is manufactured using a process similar to the one used to make computer microchips. On the surface, each chip contains synthetic single-stranded DNA sequences identical to a normal gene.

Drug Utilization Review: A quantitative assessment of patient drug use and physicians' patterns of prescribing drugs in an effort to determine the usefulness of drug therapy.

DS-1: A digital transmission format that transmits and receives information at a rate of 1,544,000 bits per second.

DSL: See "Digital Subscriber Line (DSL)."

DSP: See "Digital Signal Processing (DSP)."

Duplicate Host: A single host name that maps to duplicate IP addresses.

DX: See "Digital Transformation (DX)."

Dynamic HTML: Web content that changes with each individual viewing. For example, the same site could appear differently depending on geographic location of the reader, time of day, previous pages viewed or the user's profile.

Ecology: The study of relationships among all living organisms and the environment, especially the totality or pattern of interactions: a view that includes all plant and animal species and their unique contributions to a particular habitat.

ELA: See "Establishment License Application (ELA)."

Electronic Data Interchange (EDI): An accepted standard format for the exchange of data between various companies' networks. EDI allows for the transfer of e-mail as well as orders, invoices and other files from one company to another.

Emission: The release or discharge of a substance into the environment. Generally refers to the release of gases or particulates into the air.

Endpoint: A clinical or laboratory measurement used to assess safety, efficacy or other trial objectives of a test article in a clinical trial.

Enterprise Resource Planning (ERP): An integrated information system that helps manage all aspects of a business, including accounting, ordering and human resources, typically across all locations of a major corporation or organization. ERP is considered to be a critical tool for management of large organizations. Suppliers of ERP tools include SAP and Oracle.

Environmental Audit: An independent assessment of a facility's compliance procedures, policies and controls. Many pollution prevention initiatives require an audit to determine where wastes may be reduced or eliminated or energy conserved.

EPC: Engineering, Procurement and Construction. Sometimes used as "EPCC," which means

Engineering, Procurement, Construction and Commissioning.

ERP: See "Enterprise Resource Planning (ERP)."

Establishment License Application (ELA): Required for the approval of a biologic (see "Biologics"). It permits a specific facility to manufacture a biological product for commercial purposes. Compare to "Product License Agreement (PLA)."

ESWL: See "Extracorporeal Shock Wave Lithotripter (ESWL)."

Ethernet: The standard format on which local area network equipment works. Abiding by Ethernet standards allows equipment from various manufacturers to work together.

EU: See "European Union (EU)."

EU Competence: The jurisdiction in which the European Union (EU) can take legal action.

European Community (EC): See "European Union (EU)."

European Medicines Evaluation Agency (EMEA): The European agency responsible for supervising and coordinating applications for marketing medicinal products in the European Union (see "European Union (EU)" and "Committee on Proprietary Medicinal Products (CPMP)"). The EMEA is headquartered in the U.K. www.eudraportal.eudra.org

European Union (EU): A consolidation of European countries (member states) functioning as one body to facilitate trade. Previously known as the European Community (EC). The EU has a unified currency, the Euro. See europa.eu.int.

Expert Systems: A practical development of AI that requires creation of a knowledge base of facts and rules furnished by human experts and uses a defined set of rules to access this information in order to suggest solutions to problems. See "Artificial Intelligence (AI)."

Extensible Markup Language (XML): A programming language that enables designers to add extra functionality to documents that could not otherwise be utilized with standard HTML coding.

XML was developed by the World Wide Web Consortium. It can communicate to various software programs the actual meanings contained in HTML documents. For example, it can enable the gathering and use of information from a large number of databases at once and place that information into one web site window. XML is an important protocol to web services. See "Web Services."

Extracorporeal Shock Wave Lithotripter (ESWL): A medical device used for treating stones in the kidney or urethra. The device disintegrates kidney stones noninvasively through the transmission of acoustic shock waves directed at the stones.

Extranet: A computer network that is accessible in part to authorized outside persons, as opposed to an intranet, which uses a firewall to limit accessibility.

Fab Lab: See "3-D Printing."

Fabless: A method of operation used by a product supplier that does not have its own fabrication or manufacturing facilities. This phrase is often used to describe certain semiconductor firms that design chips but rely on outside, contract manufacturers for their actual fabrication.

FASB: See "Financial Accounting Standards Board (FASB)."

FDA: See "Food and Drug Administration (FDA)."

FDDI: See "Fiber Distributed Data Interface (FDDI)."

Federal Communications Commission (FCC): The U.S. Government agency that regulates broadcast television and radio, as well as satellite transmission, telephony and all uses of radio spectrum.

Femtosecond: One a billionth of one millionth of a second.

Fiber Distributed Data Interface (FDDI): A token ring passing scheme that operates at 100 Mbps over fiber-optic lines with a built-in geographic limitation of 100 kilometers. This type of connection is faster than both Ethernet and T-3 connections. See "Token Ring."

Fiber Optics (Fibre Optics): A type of telephone and data transmission cable that can handle vast amounts of voice, data and video at once by carrying them along on beams of light via glass or plastic threads embedded in a cable. Fiber optics are rapidly replacing older copper wire technologies. Fiber optics offer much higher speeds and the ability to handle extremely large quantities of voice or data transmissions at once.

Field Emission Display (FED): A self-luminescent display that can be extremely thin, draw very low power, and be very bright from all angles and in all types of light. The latest FEDs are based on carbon nanotubes. Samsung is a leader in this field. Early applications include high-end television and computer monitors.

File Server: A computer that is modified to store and transfer large amounts of data to other computers. File servers often receive data from mainframes and store it for transfer to other, smaller computers, or from small computers to mainframes.

File Transfer Protocol (FTP): A widely used method of transferring data and files between two Internet sites.

Financial Accounting Standards Board (FASB): An independent organization that establishes the Generally Accepted Accounting Principles (GAAP).

Finite Element Analysis (FEA): Finite Element Analysis (FEA) is a tool in computerized design that can detect flaws in a computer-generated model. It analyzes how the model would react to extremes in heat, vibration and pressure by breaking it down into small pieces or cells in a three-dimensional grid. The computer applies simulated stimuli to one cell in the model and then tracks the response of that cell and those that surround it.

Firewall: Hardware or software that keeps unauthorized users from accessing a server or network. Firewalls are designed to prevent data theft and unauthorized web site manipulation by hackers.

Fissure: A long narrow crack or opening.

Follow-on Biologics: A term used to describe generic versions of drugs that have been created using biotechnology. Because biotech drugs ("biologics") are made from living cells, a generic version of a drug probably won't be biochemically identical to the original branded version of the drug. Consequently, they are described as "follow-on" biologics to set them apart. Since these drugs won't be exactly the same as the originals, there are concerns that they may not be as safe or effective unless they go through clinical trials for proof of quality. In Europe, these drugs are referred to as "biosimilars." See "Biologics."

Food and Drug Administration (FDA): The U.S. government agency responsible for the enforcement of the Federal Food, Drug and Cosmetic Act, ensuring industry compliance with laws regulating products in commerce. The FDA's mission is to protect the public from harm and encourage technological advances that hold the promise of benefiting society. www.fda.gov

Fracture: A break or rupture in the surface of a laminate due to external or internal forces.

Frame Relay: An accepted standard for sending large amounts of data over phone lines and private datanets. The term refers to the way data is broken down into standard-size "frames" prior to transmission.

Frequency: The number of times that an alternating current goes through its complete cycle in one second. One cycle per second is referred to as one hertz: 1,000 cycles per second, one kilohertz: 1 million cycles per second, one megahertz: and 1 billion cycles per second, one gigahertz.

Frequency Band: A term for designating a range of frequencies in the electromagnetic spectrum.

FTP: See "File Transfer Protocol (FTP)."

Fuel Cell: An environmentally friendly electrochemical engine that generates electricity using hydrogen and oxygen as fuel, emitting only heat and water as byproducts.

Fusion: See "Nuclear Fusion."

Fuzzy Logic: Recognizes that some statements are not just "true" or "false," but also "more or less certain" or "very unlikely." Fuzzy logic is used in artificial intelligence. See "Artificial Intelligence (AI)."

GAAP: See "Generally Accepted Accounting Principles (GAAP)."

Gateway: A device connecting two or more networks that may use different protocols and media. Gateways translate between the different networks and can connect locally or over wide area networks.

GCP: See "Good Clinical Practices (GCP)."

GDP: See "Gross Domestic Product (GDP)."

Gene Chip: See "DNA Chip."

Generally Accepted Accounting Principles (GAAP): A set of accounting standards administered by the Financial Accounting Standards Board (FASB) and enforced by the U.S. Security and Exchange Commission (SEC). GAAP is primarily used in the U.S.

Generative AI: Artificial intelligence (AI) and machine learning (ML)-driven tools that are capable of studying millions of digital groups of text, reference materials, photos/art and other items, and then generating new output or content, based on the user's statement about what the user is seeking. For example, a user could tell a system to "create a image of the Eiffel Tower in the style of Van Gogh" or "write a comparison of cancer therapies using radiation instead of surgery." The generative tools build the desired output in a matter of moments. Such platforms can be used to create music, write essays or magazine articles, complete homework assignments and generate computer software code. This also may create copyright, ownership and originality controversies. OpenAI is a pioneer in this technology.

Genetically Modified (GM) Foods: Food crops that are bioengineered to resist herbicides, diseases or insects: have higher nutritional value than non-engineered plants: produce a higher yield per acre: and/or last longer on the shelf. Additional traits may include resistance to temperature and moisture extremes. Agricultural animals also may be genetically modified organisms.

Geological Information System (GIS): A computer software system which captures, stores, updates, manipulates, analyzes, and displays all forms of geographically referenced information.

Geostationary: A geosynchronous satellite angle with zero inclination, making a satellite appear to hover over one spot on the earth's equator.

Geosynthetic: A synthetic material used for such construction purposes as strengthening a roadway base or embankment, erosion control and drainage liners, geosynthetics (sometimes referred to as geotextiles) are typically made of polymers. They may reduce costs, enhance the useful life of a project, save weight or increase strength.

Geotextile: See "Geosynthetic."

GERD: Gross domestic expenditure on R&D (research & development).

GHG: See "Greenhouse Gas (GHG)."

Gigabyte: 1,024 megabytes.

Gigahertz (GHz): One billion cycles per second. See "Frequency."

Global System for Mobile Communications (GSM): The standard cellular format used throughout Europe, making one type of cellular phone usable in every nation on the continent and in the U.K. In the U.S., Cingular and T-Mobile also run GSM networks. The original GSM, introduced in 1991, has transfer speeds of only 9.6 kbps. GSM EDGE offers 2.75G data transfer speeds of up to 473.6 kbps. GSM GPRS offers slower 2.5G theoretical speeds of 144 kbps.

Global Warming: An increase in the near-surface temperature of the Earth. Global warming has occurred in the distant past as the result of natural influences, but the term is most often used to refer to a theory that warming occurs as a result of increased use of hydrocarbon fuels by man. See "Climate Change (Greenhouse Effect)."

Globalization: The increased mobility of goods, services, labor, technology and capital throughout the world. Although globalization is not a new development, its pace has increased with the advent of new technologies.

GLP: See "Good Laboratory Practices (GLP)."

GMP: See "Good Manufacturing Practices (GMP)."

GNR: The convergence of three of the world's most promising technologies: genetics, nanotechnology and robotics. Some observers believe that synergies between these technologies will enable revolutionary breakthroughs in science, technology, manufacturing and medicine.

Good Clinical Practices (GCP): FDA regulations and guidelines that define the responsibilities of the key figures involved in a clinical trial, including the sponsor, the investigator, the monitor and the Institutional Review Board. See "Institutional Review Board (IRB)."

Good Laboratory Practices (GLP): A collection of regulations and guidelines to be used in laboratories where research is conducted on drugs, biologics or devices that are intended for submission to the FDA.

Good Manufacturing Practices (GMP): A collection of regulations and guidelines to be used in manufacturing drugs, biologics and medical devices.

Graphic Interchange Format (GIF): A widely used format for image files.

Greenhouse Gas (GHG): See "Climate Change (Greenhouse Effect)."

Gross Domestic Product (GDP): The total value of a nation's output, income and expenditures produced with a nation's physical borders.

Gross National Product (GNP): A country's total output of goods and services from all forms of economic activity measured at market prices for one calendar year. It differs from Gross Domestic Product (GDP) in that GNP includes income from investments made in foreign nations.

GSM: See "Global System for Mobile Communications (GSM)."

Handheld Devices Markup Language (HDML): A text-based markup language designed for display on a smaller screen (e.g., a cellular phone, PDA or pager). Enables the mobile user to send, receive and redirect e-mail as well as access the Internet (HDML-enabled web sites only).

HD Radio (High Definition Radio): A technology that enables station operators to slice existing radio spectrum into multiple, thin bands. Each band is capable of transmitting additional programming. One existing radio station's spectrum may be sliced into as many as eight channels.

HDML: See "Handheld Devices Markup Language (HDML)."

HDSL: See "High-Data-Rate Digital Subscriber Line (HDSL)."

Hertz: A measure of frequency equal to one cycle per second. Most radio signals operate in ranges of megahertz or gigahertz.

High-Data-Rate Digital Subscriber Line (HDSL): High-data-rate DSL, delivering up to T1 or E1 speeds.

High-Throughput Screening (HTP): Makes use of techniques that allow for a fast and simple test on the presence or absence of a desirable structure, such as a specific DNA sequence. HTP screening often uses DNA chips or microarrays and automated data processing for large-scale screening, for instance, to identify new targets for drug development.

HTML: See "Hypertext Markup Language (HTML)."

HTTP: See "Hypertext Transfer Protocol (HTTP)."

Hypertext Markup Language (HTML): A language for coding text for viewing on the World Wide Web. HTML is unique because it enables the use of hyperlinks from one site to another, creating a web.

Hypertext Transfer Protocol (HTTP): The protocol used most frequently on the World Wide Web to move hypertext files between clients and servers on the Internet.

ICANN: The Internet Corporation for Assigned Names and Numbers. ICANN acts as the central coordinator for the Internet's technical operations.

ICD9: International Classification of Diseases - Version 9. A government coding system used for classifying diseases and diagnoses.

IDE: See "Investigational New Device Exemption (IDE)."

IDN: See "Integrated Digital Network (IDN)."

IEEE: See "Institute of Electrical and Electronic Engineers (IEEE)."

IFRS: See "International Financials Reporting Standards (IFRS)."

ILEC: See "Incumbent Local Exchange Carrier (ILEC)."

Imaging: In medicine, the viewing of the body's organs through external, high-tech means. This reduces the need for broad exploratory surgery. These advances, along with new types of surgical instruments, have made minimally invasive surgery possible. Imaging includes MRI (magnetic resonance imaging), CT (computed tomography or CAT scan), MEG (magnetoencephalography), improved x-ray technology, mammography, ultrasound and angiography.

Immunoassay: An immunological assay. Types include agglutination, complement-fixation, precipitation, immunodiffusion and electrophoretic assays. Each type of assay utilizes either a particular type of antibody or a specific support medium (such as a gel) to determine the amount of antigen present.

In Vitro: Laboratory experiments conducted in the test tube, or otherwise, without using live animals and/or humans.

In Vivo: Laboratory experiments conducted with live animals and/or humans.

Incumbent Local Exchange Carrier (ILEC): A traditional telephone company that was providing local service prior to the establishment of the Telecommunications Act of 1996, when upstart companies (CLECs, or competitive local exchange carriers) were enabled to compete against the ILECS and were granted access to their system wiring.

IND: See "Investigational New Drug Application (IND)."

Industry Code: A descriptive code assigned to any company in order to group it with firms that operate in similar businesses. Common industry codes include the NAICS (North American Industrial Classification System) and the SIC (Standard Industrial Classification), both of which are standards widely used in America, as well as the International Standard Industrial Classification of all Economic Activities (ISIC), the Standard International Trade Classification established by the United Nations (SITC) and the General Industrial Classification of Economic Activities within the European Communities (NACE).

Inert Ingredients: Substances that are not active, such as water, petroleum distillates, talc, corn meal or soaps.

Information Technology (IT): The systems, including hardware and software, that move and store voice, video and data via computers and telecommunications.

Infrastructure: 1) The equipment that comprises a system. 2) Public-use assets such as roads, bridges, water systems, sewers and other assets necessary for public accommodation and utilities. 3) The underlying base of a system or network. 4) Transportation and shipping support systems such as ports, airports and railways.

Infrastructure (Telecommunications): The entity made up of all the cable and equipment installed in the worldwide telecommunications market. Most of today's telecommunications infrastructure is connected by copper and fiber-optic cable, which represents a huge capital investment that telephone companies would like to continue to utilize in as many ways as possible.

Initial Public Offering (IPO): A company's first effort to sell its stock to investors (the public). Investors in an up-trending market eagerly seek stocks offered in many IPOs because the stocks of newly public companies that seem to have great promise may appreciate very rapidly in price, reaping great profits for those who were able to get the stock at the first offering. In the United States, IPOs are regulated by the SEC (U.S. Securities Exchange Commission) and by the state-level regulatory agencies of the states in which the IPO shares are offered.

INMARSAT: The International Maritime Satellite Organization. INMARSAT operates a network of satellites used in transmissions for all types of international mobile services, including maritime, aeronautical and land mobile.

Institute of Electrical and Electronic Engineers (IEEE): An organization that sets global technical standards and acts as an authority in technical areas including computer engineering, biomedical technology, telecommunications, electric power, aerospace and consumer electronics, among others. www.ieee.org.

Institutional Review Board (IRB): A group of individuals usually found in medical institutions that is responsible for reviewing protocols for ethical consideration (to ensure the rights of the patients). An IRB also evaluates the benefit-to-risk ratio of a new

drug to see that the risk is acceptable for patient exposure. Responsibilities of an IRB are defined in FDA regulations.

Integrated Circuit (IC): Another name for a semiconductor, an IC is a piece of silicon on which thousands (or millions) of transistors have been combined.

Integrated Digital Network (IDN): A network that uses both digital transmission and digital switching.

Integrated Services Digital Networks (ISDN): Internet connection services offered at higher speeds than standard "dial-up" service. While ISDN was considered to be an advanced service at one time, it has been eclipsed by much faster DSL, cable modem and T1 line service.

Intellectual Property (IP): The exclusive ownership of original concepts, ideas, designs, engineering plans or other assets that are protected by law. Examples include items covered by trademarks, copyrights and patents. Items such as software, engineering plans, fashion designs and architectural designs, as well as games, books, songs and other entertainment items are among the many things that may be considered to be intellectual property. (Also, see "Patent.")

INTELSAT: The International Telecommunications Satellite Organization. INTELSAT operates a network of 20 satellites, primarily for international transmissions, and provides domestic services to some 40 countries.

Interactive TV (ITV): Allows two-way data flow between a viewer and the cable TV system. A user can exchange information with the cable system—for example, by ordering a product related to a show he/she is watching or by voting in an interactive survey.

Interexchange Carrier (IXC or IEC): Any company providing long-distance phone service between LECs and LATAs. See "Local Exchange Carrier (LEC)" and "Local Access and Transport Area (LATA)."

Interface: Refers to (1) a common boundary between two or more items of equipment or between a terminal and a communication channel, (2) the electronic device that interconnects two or more devices or items of equipment having similar or dissimilar characteristics or (3) the electronic device placed between a terminal and a communication channel to protect the network from the hazard of excess voltage levels.

International Financials Reporting Standards (IFRS): A set of accounting standards established by the International Accounting Standards Board (IASB) for the preparation of public financial statements. IFRS has been adopted by much of the world, including the European Union, Russia and Singapore.

International Telecommunications Union (ITU): The international body responsible for telephone and computer communications standards describing interface techniques and practices. These standards include those that define how a nation's telephone and data systems connect to the worldwide communications network.

Internet: A global computer network that provides an easily accessible way for hundreds of millions of users to send and receive data electronically when appropriately connected via computers or wireless devices. Access is generally through HTML-enabled sites on the World Wide Web. Also known as the Net.

Internet Appliance: A non-PC device that connects users to the Internet for specific or general purposes. A good example is an electronic game machine with a screen and Internet capabilities.

Internet Protocol (IP): A set of tools and/or systems used to communicate across the World Wide Web.

Internet Service Provider (ISP): A company that sells access to the Internet to individual subscribers. Leading examples are MSN and AOL.

Internet Telephony: See "Voice Over Internet Protocol (VOIP)."

Intranet: A network protected by a firewall for sharing data and e-mail within an organization or company. Usually, intranets are used by organizations for internal communication.

Investigational New Device Exemption (IDE): A document that must be filed with the FDA prior to initiating clinical trials of medical devices considered to pose a significant risk to human subjects.

Investigational New Drug Application (IND): A document that must be filed with the FDA prior to initiating clinical trials of drugs or biologics.

Investigator: In clinical trials, a clinician who agrees to supervise the use of an investigational drug, device or biologic in humans. Responsibilities of the investigator, as defined in FDA regulations, include administering the drug, observing and testing the patient, collecting data and monitoring the care and welfare of the patient.

IP: See "Intellectual Property (IP)."

IP Number/IP Address: A number or address with four parts that are separated by dots. Each machine on the Internet has its own IP (Internet protocol) number, which serves as an identifier.

IRB: See "Institutional Review Board (IRB)."

ISDN: See "Integrated Services Digital Networks (ISDN)."

ISO 9000, 9001, 9002, 9003: Standards set by the International Organization for Standardization. ISO 9000, 9001, 9002 and 9003 are the highest quality certifications awarded to organizations that meet exacting standards in their operating practices and procedures.

IT: See "Information Technology (IT)."

IT-Enabled Services (ITES): The portion of the Information Technology industry focused on providing business services, such as call centers, insurance claims processing and medical records transcription, by utilizing the power of IT, especially the Internet. Most ITES functions are considered to be back-office procedures. Also, see "Business Process Outsourcing (BPO)."

ITES: See "IT-Enabled Services (ITES)."

ITU: See "International Telecommunications Union (ITU)."

ITV: See "Interactive TV (ITV)."

Java: A programming language developed by Sun Microsystems that allows web pages to display interactive graphics. Any type of computer or operating systems can read Java.

Joint Photographic Experts Group (JPEG): A widely used format for digital image files.

Just-in-Time (JIT) Delivery: Refers to a supply chain practice whereby manufacturers receive components on or just before the time that they are needed on the assembly line, rather than bearing the cost of maintaining several days' or weeks' supply in a warehouse. This adds greatly to the cost-effectiveness of a manufacturing plant and puts the burden of warehousing and timely delivery on the supplier of the components.

Ka-Band: The frequency range from 18 to 31 GHz. The spectrum allocated for satellite communications is 30 GHz for the up-link and 20 GHz for the downlink.

Kavli Prize: A prize awarded in recognition of scientists for their seminal advances in three research areas: astrophysics, nanoscience and neuroscience. The Kavli Prize consists of 1,000,000 U.S. Dollars in each of the scientific fields. In addition to the prize money the laureates receive a scroll and a gold medal. The Kavli Prize is awarded every second year by The Norwegian Academy of Science and Letters at a ceremony in Oslo, Norway. The prizes are a partnership between The Norwegian Academy of Science and Letters, The Kavli Foundation (USA) and The Norwegian Ministry of Education and Research.

Kbps: One thousand bits per second.

Kilobyte: One thousand (or 1,024) bytes.

Kilohertz (kHz): A measure of frequency equal to 1,000 Hertz.

Knowledge Process Outsourcing (KPO): The use of outsourced and/or offshore workers to perform business tasks that require judgment and analysis. Examples include such professional tasks as patent research, legal research, architecture, design, engineering, market research, scientific research, accounting and tax return preparation. Also, see "Business Process Outsourcing (BPO)."

LAC: An acronym for Latin America and the Caribbean.

Large-Scale Integration (LSI): The placement of thousands of electronic gates on a single chip. This makes the manufacture of powerful computers possible.

LATA: See "Local Access and Transport Area (LATA)."

LDCs: See "Least Developed Countries (LDCs)."

Leased Line: A phone line that is rented for use in continuous, long-term data connections.

Least Developed Countries (LDCs): Nations determined by the U.N. Economic and Social Council to be the poorest and weakest members of the international community. There are currently 50 LDCs, of which 34 are in Africa, 15 are in Asia Pacific and the remaining one (Haiti) is in Latin America. The top 10 on the LDC list, in descending order from top to 10th, are Afghanistan, Angola, Bangladesh, Benin, Bhutan, Burkina Faso, Burundi, Cambodia, Cape Verde and the Central African Republic. Sixteen of the LDCs are also Landlocked Least Developed Countries (LLDCs) which present them with additional difficulties often due to the high cost of transporting trade goods. Eleven of the LDCs are Small Island Developing States (SIDS), which are often at risk of extreme weather phenomenon (hurricanes, typhoons, Tsunami): have fragile ecosystems: are often dependent on foreign energy sources: can have high disease rates for HIV/AIDS and malaria: and can have poor market access and trade terms.

LEC: See "Local Exchange Carrier (LEC)."

Light Emitting Diode (LED): A small tube containing material that emits light when exposed to electricity. The color of the light depends upon the type of material. The LED was first developed in 1962 at the University of Illinois at Urbana-Champaign. LEDs are important to a wide variety of industries, from wireless telephone handsets to signage to displays for medical equipment, because they provide a very high quality of light with very low power requirements. They also have a very long useful life and produce very low heat output when. All of these characteristics are great improvements over a conventional incandescent bulb. Several advancements have been made in LED technology. See "Organic LED (OLED)," "Polymer Light Emitting Diode (PLED)," "Small Molecule Organic Light Emitting Diode (SMOLED)" and "Dendrimer."

LINUX: An open, free operating system that is shared readily with millions of users worldwide. These users continuously improve and add to the software's code.

It can be used to operate computer networks and Internet appliances as well as servers and PCs.

Lithography: In the manufacture of semiconductors and MEMS (microelectromechanical systems), lithography refers to the transfer of a pattern of photosensitive material by exposing it to light or radiation. The photosensitive material changes physical properties when exposed to a source of radiation. Typically, a mask is employed that creates a desired pattern by blocking out light to some areas. Using this process to deposit materials on a substrate, integrated circuits can be manufactured.

Local Access and Transport Area (LATA): An operational service area established after the breakup of AT&T to distinguish local telephone service from long-distance service. The U.S. is divided into over 160 LATAs.

Local Area Network (LAN): A computer network that is generally within one office or one building. A LAN can be very inexpensive and efficient to set up when small numbers of computers are involved. It may require a network administrator and a serious investment if hundreds of computers are hooked up to the LAN. A LAN enables all computers within the office to share files and printers, to access common databases and to send e-mail to others on the network.

Local Exchange Carrier (LEC): Any local telephone company, i.e., a carrier, that provides ordinary phone service under regulation within a service area. Also see "Incumbent Local Exchange Carrier (ILEC)" and "Competitive Local Exchange Carrier (CLEC)."

LSI: See "Large-Scale Integration (LSI)."

M2M: See "Machine-to-Machine (M2M)."

M3 (Measurement): Cubic meters.

Machine-to-Machine (M2M): Refers to communications from one device to another (or to a collection of devices). It is typically through wireless means such as Wi-Fi or cellular. Wireless sensor networks (WSNs) will be a major growth factor in M2M communications, in everything from factory automation to agriculture and transportation. In logistics and retailing, M2M can refer to the advanced use of RFID tags. See "Radio Frequency Identification (RFID)." The Internet of Things is based on the principle of M2M communications. Also, see "Internet of Things (IoT)."

MAN: See "Metropolitan Area Network (MAN)."

Managed Service Provider (MSP): An outsourcer that deploys, manages and maintains the back-end software and hardware infrastructure for Internet businesses.

Manufacturing Resource Planning (MRP II): A methodology that supports effective planning with regard to all resources of a manufacturing company, linking MRP with sales and operations planning, production planning and master production scheduling.

Material Safety Data Sheet (MSDS): A document, required by OSHA (U.S. Occupational Safety and Health Administration) regulations, that provides a thorough profile of a potentially hazardous substance or product. The MSDS profile includes recommendations of how to handle the product, as well as how to treat a person who swallows the product, gets the product in the eyes or is otherwise overexposed. Manufacturers of such products, such as cleansers, solvents and coatings, provide these MSDS sheets at no cost to customers and end users. Employers using these substances in the workplace are required to have MSDS sheets on hand.

Materials Science: The study of the structure, properties and performance of such materials as metals, ceramics, polymers and composites.

Mbps (Megabits per second): One million bits transmitted per second.

M-Commerce: Mobile e-commerce over wireless devices.

Medical Device: See "Device."

Megabytes: One million bytes, or 1,024 kilobytes.

Megahertz (MHz): A measure of frequency equal to 1 million Hertz.

Metamaterials: Human-engineered materials that are not found in nature. Metamaterials are designed to offer unique advantages, and may have unique electromagnetic or light refracting abilities. The basic component of metamaterials is sometimes called a "superatom," which is a cluster of multiple atoms that behave as if they are a single atom.

Metrology: The science of measurement.

Metropolitan Area Network (MAN): A data and communications network that operates over metropolitan areas and recently has been expanded to nationwide and even worldwide connectivity of high-speed data networks. A MAN can carry video and data.

Microprocessor: A computer on a digital semiconductor chip. It performs math and logic operations and executes instructions from memory. (Also known as a central processing unit or CPU.)

Microwave: Line-of sight, point-to-point transmission of signals at high frequency. Microwaves are used in data, voice and all other types of information transmission. The growth of fiber-optic networks has tended to curtail the growth and use of microwave relays.

MIME: See "Multipurpose Internet Mail Extensions (MIME)."

MMS: See "Multimedia Messaging System (MMS)."

Modem: A device that allows a computer to be connected to a phone line, which in turn enables the computer to receive and exchange data with other machines via the Internet.

Modulator: A device that modulates a carrier. Modulators are found in broadcasting transmitters and satellite transponders. The devices are also used by cable TV companies to place a baseband video television signal onto a desired VHF or UHF channel. Home video tape recorders also have built-in modulators that enable the recorded video information to be played back using a television receiver tuned to VHF channel 3 or 4.

MPEG, MPEG-1, MPEG-2, MPEG-3, MPEG-4: Moving Picture Experts Group. It is a digital standard for the compression of motion or still video for transmission or storage. MPEGs are used in digital cameras and for Internet-based viewing.

MSDS: See "Material Safety Data Sheet (MSDS)."

MSP: See "Managed Service Provider (MSP)."

Multimedia Messaging System (MMS): See "Text Messaging."

Multipoint Distribution System (MDS): A common carrier licensed by the FCC to operate a broadcast-like omni-directional microwave transmission facility within a given city. MDS carriers often pick up satellite pay-TV programming and distribute it, via their local MDS transmitter, to specially installed antennas and receivers.

Multipurpose Internet Mail Extensions (MIME): A widely used method for attaching non-text files to e-mails.

NAICS: North American Industrial Classification System. See "Industry Code."

NAND: An advanced type of flash memory chip. It is popular for use in consumer electronics such as MP3 players and digital cameras.

Nanoparticle: A nanoscale spherical or capsule-shaped structure. Most, though not all, nanoparticles are hollow, which provides a central reservoir that can be filled with anticancer drugs, detection agents, or chemicals, known as reporters, that can signal if a drug is having a therapeutic effect. The surface of a nanoparticle can also be adorned with various targeting agents, such as antibodies, drugs, imaging agents, and reporters. Most nanoparticles are constructed to be small enough to pass through blood capillaries and enter cells.

Nanosecond (NS): A billionth of a second. A common unit of measure of computer operating speed.

Nanotechnology: The science of designing, building or utilizing unique structures that are smaller than 100 nanometers (a nanometer is one billionth of a meter). This involves microscopic structures that are no larger than the width of some cell membranes.

Nanowires: A nanometer-scale wire made of metal atoms, silicon, or other materials that conduct electricity. Nanowires are built atom by atom on a solid surface, often as part of a microfluidic device. They can be coated with molecules such as antibodies that will bind to proteins and other substances of interest to researchers and clinicians. By the very nature of their nanoscale size, nanowires are incredibly sensitive to such binding events and respond by altering the electrical current flowing through them, and thus can form the basis of ultra sensitive molecular detectors.

National Institutes of Health (NIH): A branch of the U.S. Public Health Service that conducts biomedical research. www.nih.gov

NDA: See "New Drug Application (NDA)."

Network: In computing, a network is created when two or more computers are connected. Computers may be connected by wireless methods, using such technologies as 802.11b, or by a system of cables, switches and routers.

Network Numbers: The first portion of an IP address, which identifies the network to which hosts in the rest of the address are connected.

New Drug Application (NDA): An application requesting FDA approval, after completion of the all-important Phase III Clinical Trials, to market a new drug for human use in the U.S. The drug may contain chemical compounds that were previously approved by the FDA as distinct molecular entities suitable for use in drug trials (NMEs). See "New Molecular Entity (NME)."

New Molecular Entity (NME): Defined by the FDA as a medication containing chemical compound that has never before been approved for marketing in any form in the U.S. An NME is sometimes referred to as a New Chemical Entity (NCE). Also, see "New Drug Application (NDA)."

New Urbanism: A relatively new term that refers to neighborhood developments that feature shorter blocks, more sidewalks and pedestrian ways, access to convenient mass transit, bicycle paths and conveniently placed open spaces. The intent is to promote walking and social interaction while decreasing automobile traffic. The concept may also include close proximity to stores and offices that may be reached by walking rather than driving.

NIH: See "National Institutes of Health (NIH)."

NME: See "New Molecular Entity (NME)."

Node: Any single computer connected to a network or a junction of communications paths in a network.

Nonclinical Studies: In vitro (laboratory) or in vivo (animal) pharmacology, toxicology and pharmacokinetic studies that support the testing of a product in humans. Usually at least two species are evaluated prior to Phase I clinical trials. Nonclinical studies continue throughout all phases of research to evaluate long-term safety issues.

NS: See "Nanosecond (NS)."

Nuclear Fusion: An atomic energy-releasing process in which light weight atomic nuclei, which might be hydrogen or deuterium, combine to form heavier nuclei, such as helium. The result is the release of a tremendous amount of energy in the form of heat. This is potentially an endless supply of energy for mankind, somewhat similar to the power of the Sun. Fusion is undergoing significant research efforts, including a multinational research consortium named ITER. In one approach, magnetic fusion, plasma heated to 100 million-degrees Celsius creates multiple fusion bursts controlled by powerful magnets. Under a different research approach, massive lasers bombard a frozen pellet of fuel creating a brief, intense fusion.

Object Technology: By merging data and software into "objects," a programming system becomes object-oriented. For example, an object called "weekly inventory sold" would have the data and programming needed to construct a flow chart. Some new programming systems–including Java–contain this feature. Object technology is also featured in many Microsoft products. See "Java."

OC3, up to OC768: Very high-speed data lines that run at speeds from 155 to 39,813.12 Mbps.

ODM: See "Original Design Manufacturer (ODM)."

OECD: See "Organisation for Economic Co-operation and Development (OECD)."

OEM: See "Original Equipment Manufacturer (OEM)."

OLED: See "Organic LED (OLED)."

Onshoring: The opposite of "offshoring." Providing or maintaining manufacturing or services within or nearby a company's domestic location. Sometimes referred to as reshoring.

Optical Character Recognition (OCR): An industry-wide classification system for coding information onto merchandise. It enables retailers to record information on each SKU when it is sold and to transmit that information to a computer. This is accomplished through computerized cash registers that include bar-code scanners (called point-of-sale terminals).

Optical Fiber (Fibre): See "Fiber Optics (Fibre Optics)."

Organic LED (OLED): A type of electronic display based on the use of organic materials that produce light when stimulated by electricity. Also see "Polymer," "Polymer Light Emitting Diode (PLED)," "Small Molecule Organic Light Emitting Diode (SMOLED)" and "Dendrimer."

Organic Polymer: See "Polymer."

Organisation for Economic Co-operation and Development (OECD): A group of more than 30 nations that are strongly committed to the market economy and democracy. Some of the OECD members include Japan, the U.S., Spain, Germany, Australia, Korea, the U.K., Canada and Mexico. Although not members, Estonia, Israel and Russia are invited to member talks: and Brazil, China, India, Indonesia and South Africa have enhanced engagement policies with the OECD. The Organisation provides statistics, as well as social and economic data: and researches social changes, including patterns in evolving fiscal policy, agriculture, technology, trade, the environment and other areas. It publishes over 250 titles annually, including a corporate magazine, the OECD Observer. It also has radio and TV studios, and has centers in Tokyo, Washington, D.C., Berlin and Mexico City that distribute the Organisation's work and organizes events.

Original Design Manufacturer (ODM): A contract manufacturer that offers complete, end-to-end design, engineering and manufacturing services. ODMs design and build products, such as consumer electronics, that client companies can then brand and sell as their own. For example, a large percentage of laptop computers, cell phones and PDAs are made by ODMs. Also see "Original Equipment Manufacturer (OEM)" and "Contract Manufacturing."

Original Equipment Manufacturer (OEM): 1) A company that manufactures a component (or a completed product) for sale to a customer that will integrate the component into a final product. The OEM's customer will put its own brand name on the end product and distribute or resell it to end users. 2) A firm that buys a component and then incorporates it into a final product, or buys a completed product and then resells it under the firm's own brand name. This usage is most often found in the computer industry, where OEM is sometimes used as a verb. Also see "Original Design Manufacturer (ODM)" and "Contract Manufacturing."

Orphan Drug: A drug or biologic designated by the FDA as providing therapeutic benefit for a rare disease affecting less than 200,000 people in the U.S. Companies that market orphan drugs are granted a period of market exclusivity in return for the limited commercial potential of the drug.

OS: See "Operating System (OS)."

OTC: See "Over-the-Counter Drugs (OTC)."

Over-the-Counter Drugs (OTC): FDA-regulated products that do not require a physician's prescription. Some examples are aspirin, sunscreen, nasal spray and sunglasses.

Packet Switching: A higher-speed way to move data through a network, in which files are broken down into smaller "packets" that are reassembled electronically after transmission.

Patent: An intellectual property right granted by a national government to an inventor to exclude others from making, using, offering for sale, or selling the invention throughout that nation or importing the invention into the nation for a limited time in exchange for public disclosure of the invention when the patent is granted. In addition to national patenting agencies, such as the United States Patent and Trademark Office, and regional organizations such as the European Patent Office, there is a cooperative international patent organization, the World Intellectual Property Organization, or WIPO, established by the United Nations.

PCMCIA: Personal Computer Memory Card International Association.

PDE Pulse Detonation Engine: Pulse detonation (PDE) is an advanced technology for jet engines. It does away with the intricate high-pressure compressor and the turbine found in today's jet engines, relying instead on the PDE Combustor. As a result, much higher output per engine may be possible, which may push aircraft to new levels of speed. Commercial models may be between 2015 and 2020.

Peer Review: The process used by the scientific community, whereby review of a paper, project or report is obtained through comments of independent colleagues in the same field.

Petabyte: 1,024 terabytes, or about 1 million gigabytes.

Pharmacodynamics (PD): The study of reactions between drugs and living systems. It can be thought of as the study of what a drug does to the body.

Pharmacoeconomics: The study of the costs and benefits associated with various drug treatments.

Pharmacogenetics: The investigation of the different reactions of human beings to drugs and the underlying genetic predispositions. The differences in reaction are mainly caused by mutations in certain enzymes responsible for drug metabolization. As a result, the degradation of the active substance can lead to harmful by-products, or the drug might have no effect at all.

Pharmacokinetics (PK): The study of the processes of bodily absorption, distribution, metabolism and excretion of compounds and medicines. It can be thought of as the study of what the body does to a drug. See "Absorption, Distribution, Metabolism and Excretion (ADME)."

Phase I Clinical Trials: Studies in this phase include initial introduction of an investigational drug into humans. These studies are closely monitored and are usually conducted in healthy volunteers. Phase I trials are conducted after the completion of extensive nonclinical or pre-clinical trials not involving humans. Phase I studies include the determination of clinical pharmacology, bioavailability, drug interactions and side effects associated with increasing doses of the drug.

Phase II Clinical Trials: Include randomized, masked, controlled clinical studies conducted to evaluate the effectiveness of a drug for a particular indication(s). During Phase II trials, the minimum effective dose and dosing intervals should be determined.

Phase III Clinical Trials: Consist of controlled and uncontrolled trials that are performed after preliminary evidence of effectiveness of a drug has been established. They are conducted to document the safety and efficacy of the drug, as well as to determine adequate directions (labeling) for use by the physician. A specific patient population needs to be clearly identified from the results of these studies. Trials during Phase III are conducted using a large number of patients to determine the frequency of adverse events and to obtain data regarding intolerance.

Phase IV Clinical Trials: Conducted after approval of a drug has been obtained to gather data supporting new or revised labeling, marketing or advertising claims.

Pivotal Studies: In clinical trials, a Phase III trial that is designed specifically to support approval of a product. These studies are well-controlled (usually by placebo) and are generally designed with input from the FDA so that they will provide data that is adequate to support approval of the product. Two pivotal studies are required for drug product approval, but usually only one study is required for biologics.

PLA: See "Product License Agreement (PLA)."

Plant Patent: A plant patent may be granted by the U.S. Patent and Trademark Office to anyone who invents or discovers and asexually reproduces any distinct and new variety of plant.

PLED: See "Polymer Light Emitting Diode (PLED)."

PLM: See "Product Lifecyle Management (PLM)."

Plug-In: Any small piece of software that adds extra functions to a larger piece of software.

PMA: See "Pre-Market Approval (PMA)."

Polymer: An organic or inorganic substance of many parts. Most common polymers, such as polyethylene and polypropylene, are organic. Organic polymers consist of molecules from organic sources (carbon compounds). Polymer means many parts. Generally, a polymer is constructed of many structural units (smaller, simpler molecules) that are joined together by a chemical bond. Some polymers are natural. For example, rubber is a natural polymer. Scientists have developed ways to manufacture synthetic polymers from organic materials. Plastic is a synthetic polymer.

Polymer Light Emitting Diode (PLED): An advanced technology that utilizes plastics (polymers) for the creation of electronic displays (screens). It is based on the use of organic polymers which emit light when stimulated with electricity. They are solution processable, which means they can be applied to substrates via ink jet printing. Also referred to as P-OLEDs.

Port: An interface (or connector) between the computer and the outside world. The number of ports on a communications controller or front-end processor determines the number of communications channels that can be connected to it. The number of ports on a computer determines the number of peripheral devices that can be attached to it.

Portal: A comprehensive web site for general or specific purposes.

Positron Emission Tomography (PET): Positron Emission Tomography (often referred to as a PET scan) is a nuclear medicine imaging technology that uses computers and radioactive (positron emitting) isotopes, which are created in a cyclotron or generator, to produce composite pictures of the brain and heart at work. PET scanning produces sectional images depicting metabolic activity or blood flow rather than anatomy.

Post-Marketing Surveillance: The FDA's ongoing safety monitoring of marketed drugs.

Powerline: A method of networking computers, peripherals and appliances together via the electrical wiring that is built in to a home or office. Powerline competes with 802.11b and other wireless networking methods.

Preclinical Studies: See "Nonclinical Studies."

Pre-Market Approval (PMA): Required for the approval of a new medical device or a device that is to be used for life-sustaining or life-supporting purposes, is implanted in the human body or presents potential risk of illness or injury.

Product License Agreement (PLA): See "Biologics License Application (BLA)."

Product Lifecycle (Product Life Cycle): The prediction of the life of a product or brand. Stages are described as Introduction, Growth, Maturity and finally Sales Decline. These stages track a product from its initial introduction to the market through to the end of its usefulness as a commercially viable product. The goal of Product Lifecycle Management is to maximize production efficiency, consumer acceptance and profits. Consequently, critical processes around the product need to be adjusted during its lifecycle, including pricing, advertising, promotion, distribution and packaging.

Product Lifecycle Management (PLM): See "Product Lifecycle (Product Life Cycle)."

Proteomics: The study of gene expression at the protein level, by the identification and characterization of proteins present in a biological sample.

Protocol: A set of rules for communicating between computers. The use of standard protocols allows products from different vendors to communicate on a common network.

PSTN: See "Public Switched Telephone Network (PSTN)."

Public Switched Telephone Network (PSTN): A term that refers to the traditional telephone system.

Public-Private Partnership (PPP, or P3): Partnerships that involve government agencies with private companies in the construction, operation and/or funding of publicly-needed buildings and infrastructure, such as toll roads, airports, waterworks, sewage plants or power plants.

Qdots: See "Quantum Dots (Qdots)."

QOL: See "Quality of Life (QOL)."

Quality of Life (QOL): In medicine, an endpoint of therapeutic assessment used to adjust measures of effectiveness for clinical decision-making. Typically, QOL endpoints measure the improvement of a patient's day-to-day living as a result of specific therapy.

Quantum Computing: A technology that uses the unique abilities of quantum systems, to be in multiple states at once. Such superpositions would allow the computer to perform many different computations simultaneously. This is a merger of physics (and its laws of quantum mechanics) with computer science. Quantum computing works with quantum bits, also known as qubits. The laws of quantum mechanics differ radically from the laws of traditional physics. Eventually, quantum computers incredible processing speeds may become feasible.

Quantum Dots (Qdots): Nanometer sized semiconductor particles, made of cadmium selenide (CdSe), cadmium sulfide (CdS) or cadmium telluride (CdTe) with an inert polymer coating. The semiconductor material used for the core is chosen based upon the emission wavelength range being targeted: CdS for UV-blue, CdSe for the bulk of the visible spectrum, CdTe for the far red and near-infrared, with the particle's size determining the exact color of a given quantum dot. The polymer coating safeguards cells from cadmium toxicity but also affords the opportunity to attach any variety targeting molecules, including monoclonal antibodies directed to tumor-specific biomarkers. Because of their small size, quantum dots can function as cell- and even molecule-specific markers that will not interfere with the normal workings of a cell. In addition, the availability of quantum dots of different colors provides a powerful tool for following the actions of multiple cells and molecules simultaneously.

Qubit: The basic unit of information in a quantum computer. A qubit can exist not only in a state corresponding to 0 or 1 as in a binary bit, but also in states corresponding to a blend or superposition of these states. See "Quantum Computing."

R&D: Research and development. Also see "Applied Research" and "Basic Research."

R&D-Flex Building: Industrial-type buildings that are designed to satisfy tenants that require an above-average amount of office space as well as an above-average level of finish that presents a more office-like environment, such as more windows and better landscape. From 30% to 100% of the space in such buildings may be devoted to office or laboratory space, with the balance devoted to light assembly or warehouse space.

Radiation Therapy: Radiation therapy is frequently used to destroy cancerous cells. This branch of medicine is concerned with radioactive substances and the usage of various techniques of imaging, for the diagnosis and treatment of disease. Services can include megavoltage radiation therapy, radioactive implants, stereotactic radiosurgery, therapeutic radioisotope services, or the use of x-rays, gamma rays and other radiation sources.

Radio Frequency Identification (RFID): A technology that applies a special microchip-enabled tag to an individual item or piece of merchandise or inventory. RFID technology enables wireless, computerized tracking of that inventory item as it moves through the supply chain from factory to transport to warehouse to retail store or end user. Also known as radio tags.

Radioisotope: An object that has varying properties that allows it to penetrate other objects at different rates. For example, a sheet of paper can stop an alpha particle, a beta particle can penetrate tissues in the body and a gamma ray can penetrate concrete. The varying penetration capabilities allow radioisotopes to be used in different ways. (Also called radioactive isotope or radionuclide.)

RAM: See "Random Access Memory (RAM)."

Random Access Memory (RAM): Computer memory used to hold programs and data temporarily.

Rapid Prototyping: See "3-D Printing."

RBOC: See "Regional Bell Operating Company (RBOC)."

Real Time: A system or software product specially designed to acquire, process, store and display large amounts of rapidly changing information almost instantaneously, with microsecond responses as changes occur.

Regional Bell Operating Company (RBOC): Former Bell system telephone companies (or their successors), created as a result of the breakup of AT&T by a Federal Court decree on December 31, 1983 (e.g., Bell Atlantic, now part of Verizon).

Reinforcement Learning with Human Feedback (RLHF): A strategy that uses human input as well as machine learning to help a system achieve the most accurate or reliable results.

Request for Bids (RFB): A request for pricing and supporting details, sent by a firm that requires products or services, outlining all the firm's requirements. Proposing companies are asked to place a bid based on the requested goods or services.

Request for Quotation (RFQ): A proposal that asks companies to submit pricing for goods or a described level of services. See "Request for Bids (RFB)."

Reshore: With regard to manufacturing, the return of some of the business to plants based in the country where sales are typically made. An example would be if Nike should shift some of its production from Asia to the U.S.

RFID: See "Radio Frequency Identification (RFID)."

RLHF: See "Reinforcement Learning with Human Feedback (RLHF)."

Router: An electronic device that enables networks to communicate with each other. For example, the local area network (LAN) in an office connects to a router to give the LAN access to an Internet connection such as a T1 or DSL. Routers can be bundled with several added features, such as firewalls.

S&R: Science and research.

SaaS: See "Software as a Service (SaaS)."

Safe Medical Devices Act (SMDA): An act that amends the Food, Drug and Cosmetic Act to impose additional regulations on medical devices. The act became law in 1990.

SAN: See "Storage Area Network (SAN)."

SBIR: See "Small Business Innovative Research (SBIR)."

Scalable: Refers to a network that can grow and adapt as the total customer count increases and as customer needs increase and change. Scalable websites (and the hardware and software behind them) are extremely vital to rapidly-growing online services. Scalable networks can easily manage increasing numbers of workstations, servers, user workloads and added functionality.

SCSI: See "Small Computer System Interface (SCSI)."

Selective Deposition Lamination (SDL): A paper-based 3D printing technology that lowers operating costs by using regular A4 size paper rather than polymers or metals.

Semiconductor: A generic term for a device that controls electrical signals. It specifically refers to a material (such as silicon, germanium or gallium arsenide) that can be altered either to conduct electrical current or to block its passage. Carbon nanotubes may eventually be used as semiconductors. Semiconductors are partly responsible for the miniaturization of modern electronic devices, as they are vital components in computer memory and processor chips. The manufacture of semiconductors is carried out by small firms, and by industry giants such as Intel and Advanced Micro Devices.

Serial Line Internet Protocol (SLIP): The connection of a traditional telephone line, or serial line, and modem to connect a computer to an Internet site.

Server: A computer that performs and manages specific duties for a central network such as a LAN. It may include storage devices and other peripherals. Competition within the server manufacturing industry is intense among leaders Dell, IBM, HP and others.

Short Messaging System (SMS): See "Text Messaging."

SIC: Standard Industrial Classification. See "Industry Code."

Simple Mail Transfer Protocol (SMTP): The primary form of protocol used in the transference of e-mail.

Simple Network Management Protocol (SNMP): A set of communication standards for use between computers connected to TCP/IP networks.

Six Sigma: A quality enhancement strategy designed to reduce the number of products coming from a manufacturing plant that do not conform to specifications. Six Sigma states that no more than 3.4 defects per million parts is the goal of high-quality output. Motorola invented the system in the 1980s in order to enhance its competitive position against Japanese electronics manufacturers.

SLIP: See "Serial Line Internet Protocol (SLIP)."

Small Business Innovative Research (SBIR): A three-phase program developed by the U.S. Department of Defense that allocates early-stage research and development funding to small technology companies.

Small Computer System Interface (SCSI): A dominant, international standard interface used by UNIX servers and many desktop computers to connect to storage devices: a physical connection between devices.

Small Molecule Organic Light Emitting Diode (SMOLED): A type of organic LED that relies on expensive manufacturing methods. Newer technologies are more promising. See "Polymer" and "Polymer Light Emitting Diode (PLED)."

Smart Buildings: Buildings or homes that have been designed with interconnected electronic sensors and electrical systems which can be controlled by computers. Advantages include the ability to turn appliances and systems on or off remotely or on a set schedule, leading to greatly enhanced energy efficiency.

SMDA: See "Safe Medical Devices Act (SMDA)."

SMDS: See "Switched Multimegabit Data Service (SMDS)."

SMOLED: See "Small Molecule Organic Light Emitting Diode (SMOLED)."

SMS: See "Short Messaging System (SMS)."

SMTP: See "Simple Mail Transfer Protocol (SMTP)."

SNMP: See "Simple Network Management Protocol (SNMP)."

Software as a Service (SaaS): Refers to the practice of providing users with software applications that are hosted on remote servers and accessed via the Internet. Excellent examples include the CRM (Customer Relationship Management) software provided in SaaS format by Salesforce. An earlier technology that operated in a similar, but less

sophisticated, manner was called ASP or Application Service Provider.

SONET: See "Synchronous Optical Network Technology (SONET)."

SPECT: Single Photon Emission Computerized Tomography. A nuclear medicine imaging technology that combines existing technology of gamma camera imaging with computed tomographic (CT) imaging technology to provide a more precise and clear image.

Sponsor: The individual or company that assumes responsibility for the investigation of a new drug, including compliance with the FD&C Act and regulations. The sponsor may be an individual, partnership, corporation or governmental agency and may be a manufacturer, scientific institution or investigator regularly and lawfully engaged in the investigation of new drugs. The sponsor assumes most of the legal and financial responsibility of the clinical trial.

SRDF: See "Symmetrix Remote Data Facility (SRDF)."

Stem Cells: Cells found in human bone marrow, the blood stream and the umbilical cord that can be replicated indefinitely and can turn into any type of mature blood cell, including platelets, white blood cells or red blood cells. Also referred to as pluripotent cells.

Storage Area Network (SAN): Links host computers to advanced data storage systems.

Study Coordinator: See "Coordinator."

Subsidiary, Wholly-Owned: A company that is wholly controlled by another company through stock ownership.

Superatom: See "Metamaterials."

Superconductivity: The ability of a material to act as a conductor for electricity without the gradual loss of electricity over distance (due to resistance) that is normally associated with electric transmission. There are two types of superconductivity. "Low-temperature" superconductivity (LTS) requires that transmission cable be cooled to -418 degrees Fahrenheit. Newer technologies are creating a so-called "high-temperature" superconductivity (HTS) that requires cooling to a much warmer -351 degrees Fahrenheit.

Supply Chain: The complete set of suppliers of goods and services required for a company to operate its business. For example, a manufacturer's supply chain may include providers of raw materials, components, custom-made parts and packaging materials.

Sustainable Development: Development that ensures that the use of resources and the environment today does not impair their availability to be used by future generations.

Switch: A network device that directs packets of data between multiple ports, often filtering the data so that it travels more quickly.

Switched Multimegabit Data Service (SMDS): A method of extremely high-speed transference of data.

Symmetrix Remote Data Facility (SRDF): A high-performance, host-independent business solution that enables users to maintain a duplicate copy of all or some of their data at a remote site.

Synchronous Optical Network Technology (SONET): A mode of high-speed transmission meant to take full advantage of the wide bandwidth in fiber-optic cables.

T1: A standard for broadband digital transmission over phone lines. Generally, it can transmit at least 24 voice channels at once over copper wires, at a high speed of 1.5 Mbps. Higher speed versions include T3 and OC3 lines.

T3: Transmission over phone lines that supports data rates of 45 Mbps. T3 lines consist of 672 channels, and such lines are generally used by Internet service providers. They are also referred to as DS3 lines.

Taste Masking: The creation of a barrier between a drug molecule and taste receptors so the drug is easier to take. It masks bitter or unpleasant tastes.

TCP/IP: Transmission Control Protocol/Internet Protocol. The combination of a network and transport protocol developed by ARPANet for internetworking IP-based networks.

TDMA: See "Time Division Multiple Access (TDMA)."

Technical Barriers to Trade (TBT): Instances when technical regulations and industrial standards differ from country to country, making free trade of goods difficult if not impossible.

Telecommunications: Systems and networks of hardware and software used to carry voice, video and/or data within buildings and between locations around the world. This includes telephone wires, satellite signals, wireless networks, fiber networks, Internet networks and related devices.

Telnet: A terminal emulation program for TCP/IP networks like the Internet, which runs on a computer and connects to a particular network. Directions entered on a computer that is connected using Telnet will be read and followed just as if they had been entered on the server itself. Through Telnet, users are able to control a server and communicate with other servers on the same network at the same time. Telnet is commonly used to control web servers remotely.

Terabyte: A measure of data equal to 1,024 gigabytes, or about 1 trillion bytes of data.

TESS: See "Adverse Event (AE)."

Text Messaging: The transmission of very short, text messages in a format similar to e-mail. Generally, text messaging is used as an additional service on cell phones. The format has typically been SMS (Short Messaging System), but a newer standard is evolving: MMS (Multimedia Messaging System). MMS can transmit pictures, sound and video as well as text.

Time Division Multiple Access (TDMA): A 2G digital service for relatively large users of international public-switched telephony, data, facsimile and telex. TDMA also refers to a method of multiplexing digital signals that combines a number of signals passing through a common point by transmitting them sequentially, with each signal sent in bursts at different times. TDMA is sometimes referred to as IS-136 or D-AMPS.

Tokamak: A reactor used in nuclear fusion in which a spiral magnetic field inside doughnut-shaped tube is used to confine high temperature plasma produced during fusion. See "Nuclear Fusion."

Token Ring: A local area network architecture in which a token, or continuously repeating frame, is passed sequentially from station to station. Only the station possessing the token can communicate on the network.

Transistor: A device used for amplification or switching of electrical current.

Trial Coordinator: See "Coordinator."

UDDI: See "Universal Description, Discovery and Integration (UDDI)."

Ultrashort Pulse Laser (USP): A technology that utilizes ultrafast lasers that pulse on and off at almost immeasurable speed. Scientists estimate that USP flashes once every femtosecond, which is a billionth of a millionth of a second. USP destroys atoms by knocking out electrons, which causes no rise in temperature in surrounding atoms as is associated with traditional lasers. Potential applications include vastly improved laser surgery, scanning for explosives, gemstone verification and processing donated human tissue for transplantation.

Ultrasound: The use of acoustic waves above the range of 20,000 cycles per second to visualize internal body structures. Frequently used to observe a fetus.

Ultrawideband (UWB): A means of low-power, limited-range wireless data transmission that takes advantage of bandwidth set aside by the FCC in 2002. UWB encodes signals in a dramatically different way, sending digital pulses in a relatively secure manner that will not interfere with other wireless systems that may be operating nearby. It has the potential to deliver very large amounts of data to a distance of about 230 feet, even through doors and other obstacles, and requires very little power. Speeds are scalable from approximately 100 Mbps to 2Gbps. UWB works on the 802.15.3 IEEE specification.

Uniform Resource Locator (URL): The address that allows an Internet browser to locate a homepage or web site.

Universal Description, Discovery and Integration (UDDI): A vital protocol used in web services. UDDI enables businesses to create a standard description of their activities so that they can be searched for appropriately by automatic software tools.

Universal Design: An approach to residential as well as commercial building design that attempts to accommodate as many people as possible, regardless of physical or mental limitations. For example, design elements may include wider doorways and stepless entries that are easy for the physically challenged to navigate.

Universal Memory: Future-generation digital memory storage systems that would be ultradense and run on extremely low power needs. Potentially, universal memory could replace today's flash memory, RAM and many other types of memory. The technology may be based on the use of vast numbers of tiny carbon nanotubes resulting in the storage of trillions of bits of data per square centimeter.

UNIX: A multi-user, multitasking operating system that runs on a wide variety of computer systems, from PCs to mainframes.

URL: See "Uniform Resource Locator (URL)."

Utility Patent: A utility patent may be granted by the U.S. Patent and Trademark Office to anyone who invents or discovers any new, useful, and non-obvious process, machine, article of manufacture, or composition of matter, or any new and useful improvement thereof.

UWB: See "Ultrawideband (UWB)."

Validation of Data: The procedure carried out to ensure that the data contained in a final clinical trial report match the original observations.

VDSL: Very high-data-rate digital subscriber line, operating at data rates from 55 to 100 Mbps.

Vertical Integration: A business model in which one company owns many (or all) of the means of production of the many goods that comprise its product line. For example, founder Henry Ford designed Ford Motor Company's early River Rogue plant so that coal, iron ore and other needed raw materials arrived at one end of the plant and were processed into steel, which was then converted on-site into finished components. At the final stage of the plant, completed automobiles were assembled.

Very Small Aperture Terminal (VSAT): A small Earth station terminal, generally 0.6 to 2.4 meters in size, that is often portable and primarily designed to handle data transmission and private-line voice and video communications.

Voice Over Internet Protocol (VOIP): The ability to make telephone calls and send faxes over IP-based data networks, i.e., real-time voice between computers via the Internet. Leading providers of VOIP service include independent firms Skype and Vonage. However, all major telecom companies, such as SBC are planning or offering VOIP service. VOIP can offer greatly reduced telephone bills to users, since toll charges, certain taxes and other fees can be bypassed. Long-distance calls can pass to anywhere in the world using VOIP. Over the mid-term, many telephone handsets, including cellular phones, will have the ability to detect wireless networks offering VOIP connections and will switch seamlessly between landline and VOIP or cellular and VOIP as needed.

VOIP: See "Voice Over Internet Protocol (VOIP)."

WAN: See "Wide Area Network (WAN)."

WAP: See "Wireless Access Protocol (WAP)."

Web Services: Self-contained modular applications that can be described, published, located and invoked over the World Wide Web or another network. Web services architecture evolved from object-oriented design and is geared toward e-business solutions. Microsoft Corporation is focusing on web services with its .NET initiative. Also see "Extensible Markup Language (XML)."

Web Services Description Language (WSDL): An important protocol to web services that describes the web service being offered.

WFH: Work from home.

Wide Area Network (WAN): A regional or global network that provides links between all local area networks within a company. For example, Ford Motor Company might use a WAN to enable its factory in Detroit to talk to its sales offices in New York and Chicago, its plants in England and its buying offices in Taiwan. Also see "Local Area Network (LAN)."

Wireless LAN (WLAN): A wireless local area network. WLANs frequently operate on 802.11-enabled equipment (Wi-Fi).

WLAN: See "Wireless LAN (WLAN)."

Workstation: A high-powered desktop computer, usually used by engineers.

World Health Organization (WHO): A United Nations agency that assists governments in strengthening health services, furnishing technical assistance and aid in emergencies, working on the prevention and control of epidemics and promoting cooperation among different countries to improve nutrition, housing, sanitation, recreation and other aspects of environmental hygiene. Any country that is a member of the United Nations may become a member of the WHO by accepting its constitution. The WHO currently has 191 member states.

World Trade Organization (WTO): One of the only globally active international organizations dealing with the trade rules between nations. Its goal is to assist the free flow of trade goods, ensuring a smooth, predictable supply of goods to help raise the quality of life of member citizens. Members form consensus decisions that are then ratified by their respective parliaments. The WTO's conflict resolution process generally emphasizes interpreting existing commitments and agreements, and discovers how to ensure trade policies to conform to those agreements, with the ultimate aim of avoiding military or political conflict.

World Wide Web: A system (the internet) that provides enhanced access to various sites on the Internet through the use of hyperlinks. Clicking on a link displayed in one document takes you to a related document. The World Wide Web is governed by the World Wide Web Consortium, located at www.w3.org. Also known as the web.

WSDL: See "Web Services Description Language (WSDL)."

WTO: See "World Trade Organization (WTO)."

XML: See "Extensible Markup Language (XML)."

Zettabyte: A unit of measure, used in describing data, a zettabyte is roughly 1,000 exabytes or 1 million terabytes.